The Duxbury Series in Statistics and Decision Sciences

Applications, Basics, and Computing of Exploratory Data Analysis, Velleman and Hoaglin

Applied Regression Analysis and Other Multivariate Methods, Second Edition, Kleinbaum, Kupper, and Muller

Classical and Modern Regression with Applications, Myers

A Course in Business Statistics, Second Edition, Mendenhall

Elementary Statistics for Business, Second Edition, Johnson and Siskin

Elementary Statistics, Fifth Edition, Johnson

Elementary Survey Sampling, Third Edition, Scheaffer, Mendenhall, and Ott

Essential Business Statistics: A Minitab Framework, Bond and Scott

Fundamental Statistics for the Behavioral Sciences, Second Edition, Howell

Fundamentals of Biostatistics, Second Edition, Rosner

Fundamentals of Statistics in the Biological, Medical, and Health Sciences, Runyon

Introduction to Contemporary Statistical Methods, Second Edition, Koopmans

Introduction to Probability and Mathematical Statistics, Bain and Englehardt

Introduction to Probability and Statistics, Seventh Edition, Mendenhall

An Introduction to Statistical Methods and Data Analysis, Third Edition, Ott

Introductory Statistical Methods: An Integrated Approach Using Minitab, Groeneveld

Introductory Statistics for Management and Economics, Third Edition, Kenkel

Linear Statistical Models: An Applied Approach, Bowerman, O'Connell, and Dickey

Mathematical Statistics with Applications, Third Edition, Mendenhall, Scheaffer, and Wackerly

Minitab Handbook, Second Edition, Ryan, Joiner, and Ryan

Minitab Handbook for Business and Economics, Miller

Operations Research: Applications and Algorithms, Winston

Probability Modeling and Computer Simulation, Matloff

Probability and Statistics for Engineers, Second Edition, Scheaffer and McClave

Probability and Statistics for Modern Engineering, Lapin

Quantitative Forecasting Methods, Farnum and Stanton

Quantitative Models for Management, Second Edition, Davis and McKeown

Statistical Experiments Using BASIC, Dowdy

Statistical Methods for Psychology, Second Edition, Howell

Statistical Thinking for Behavioral Scientists, Hildebrand

Statistical Thinking for Managers, Second Edition, Hildebrand and Ott

Statistics for Business and Economics, Bechtold and Johnson

Statistics for Management and Economics, Sixth Edition, Mendenhall, Reinmuth, and Beaver

Statistics: A Tool for the Social Sciences, Fourth Edition, Ott, Larson, and Mendenhall

Time Series Analysis, Cryer

Time Series Forecasting: Unified Concepts and Computer Implementation, Second Edition, Bowerman and O'Connell

Understanding Statistics, Fourth Edition, Ott and Mendenhall

Introductory Statistics for Management and Economics

Third Edition

James L. Kenkel
University of Pittsburgh

PWS-KENT PUBLISHING COMPANY ■ BOSTON

To Mom

PWS-KENT
Publishing Company

Acquisitions Editor: Michael Payne
Production Editor: Eve B. Mendelsohn
Text Designer: Nancy Blodget
Cover Designer: Lindgren Design Associates/Trisha Hanlon
Text Artist: Phil Carver & Friends and Deborah Schneck
Compositor: G&S Typesetters, Inc.
Cover Printer: New England Book Components, Inc.
Text Printer and Binder: Arcata Graphics/Halliday Lithograph

PWS-KENT Publishing Company is a division of Wadsworth, Inc.

Printed in the United States of America
3 4 5 6 7 8—92 91 90

Library of Congress Cataloging-in-Publication Data

Kenkel, James L.
Introductory statistics for management and economics/James L. Kenkel.—3rd ed.
p. cm.
Includes bibliographies and index.
ISBN 0-534-91693-7
1. Social sciences—Statistical methods. 2. Economics—Statistical methods. 3. Commercial statistics. 4. Statistics. I. Title.
HA29.K428 1989
519.5—dc19 88-25432
CIP

Preface

This text is written for students in business, economics, management, and related fields for use in an introductory statistics course. The entire book can be covered in two semesters or selected chapters can be used in a one-semester course. The book evolved from over nineteen years of teaching undergraduate and graduate students in statistics and econometrics courses at the University of Pittsburgh. The purpose of the book is to give students a strong background in probability and statistics that will enable them to apply statistical techniques when solving problems and making decisions. Whenever possible, I have explained statistical concepts in an applied, real-world setting, and I have made a special effort to use examples relevant and interesting to students pursuing careers in government or business. The text assumes a solid background in college algebra; calculus is not required.

Topical emphasis is placed on statistical inference and model building in a real-world context. There is a detailed discussion of probability theory to provide students with a solid background for the principles of statistical reasoning. Some of this material can be skimmed or omitted entirely by teachers who want to put more emphasis on estimation theory and hypothesis testing.

Changes in the Third Edition

Approximately 35 percent of the material in the third edition is new. All chapters contain new material, and many examples have been revised or updated using additional data that have become available since the second edition was published. The discussion of the multiple regression model and testing the assumptions of the multiple regression model has been greatly expanded.

The most important change in the third edition is the inclusion of a great deal of new material on computer applications. Nearly every chapter contains a new section discussing computer applications of the material covered in the chapter. The computer applications sections provide a detailed explanation of how to use the SPSSX statistical program and most of the examples utilize SPSSX computer output. Occasionally I have provided additional examples and computer output involving the Minitab and SAS statistical programs. SPSSX, Minitab, and SAS are the three most widely used statistical computer programs in the United States. Minitab is easier to use but is much less powerful than SPSSX or SAS. For teachers and students who prefer to use SAS or Minitab rather than SPSSX, Minitab and SAS user guides that were written expressly for use with this textbook are available from the publisher. Thus, teachers who want to emphasize the role of the computer in statistical analysis can use any of the three major statistical packages in conjunction with this text. The computer applications sections can be omitted by teachers who want to follow a more traditional approach and who do not want to use the computer in their course.

This edition contains a wealth of new examples and exercises, many of which are applicable to business situations. Most of my students learn primarily by studying the numerical examples and by solving numerical exercises. In my courses, I require students to hand in more than 200 homework problems, and they are required to do many more during in-class tests. Because I want students to learn by actually solving problems, I've included more than 400 examples and several thousand exercises in the text. Many of the exercises use real data obtained from various government and census publications. By working with real data, the students will see the practical uses of statistical analysis. My feeling is that to really learn probability and statistics it is important to solve lots of problems. Some of the exercises are relatively straightforward applications of the material in the corresponding chapter, but each chapter includes a few more difficult problems that will test the student's ingenuity. Answers to selected exercises are provided in an appendix at the end of the book.

Some students have difficulty in statistics courses because the language is new and there are so many mathematical formulas. I have tried to ease the burden a bit by enclosing all definitions and mathematical formulas in boxes for ease of reference. In addition, various important ideas and summaries appear in boxes.

Those who are familiar with the previous edition will notice numerous changes in both organization and content. The new arrangement of topics provides a logical and practical structure for the material. In the overview that follows, I have highlighted those features that are new to this edition.

Organization of the Book

The material in Chapters 1 through 12 is best covered in the order presented. Chapters 1 through 4 describe various types of problems that can be solved by using statistical methods and provide a comprehensive treatment of descriptive statistics. Because many students expect a statistics course to be boring, I have provided several real-world examples in the first few chapters that show interesting applications of statistical techniques. In addition to computer applications, new material in the first four chapters covers bivariate and multivariate data sets, box plots, and stem-and-leaf diagrams.

Chapters 5 and 6 cover elementary probability theory and discrete probability distributions. For teachers who do not have the inclination (or time) to cover probability theory in detail, some of the material in these two chapters can be omitted without interrupting the flow of ideas. Chapters 1 through 6 have been almost entirely rewritten to put more emphasis on business-world applications and to highlight how the computer can be used to analyze large data sets.

Chapter 7 covers the most important discrete probability distributions. The properties of the binomial, hypergeometric, geometric, and Poisson distributions are discussed and numerous examples are provided to show how these distributions can be used when analyzing business problems. These topics can be covered briefly or in detail depending on the course length. The discussions of the geometric distribution and acceptance sampling are new to this edition.

Chapter 8 provides an introduction to continuous probability distributions and covers the uniform, normal, and exponential distributions. The section on the exponential distribution is new to this edition.

Chapters 9 and 10 cover sampling distributions, estimation theory, and the construction of confidence intervals. The material in these chapters has been reorganized; the discussion of the *t* distribution has been moved to the middle of Chapter 10, which covers the construction of confidence intervals.

Chapter 11 provides a comprehensive discussion of hypothesis testing. It covers tests involving a single population mean, a single population proportion, or a single population variance. In this edition, greater emphasis has been placed on the construction and interpretation of null and alternative hypotheses in real-world situations. Also, the calculation and interpretation of prob-values has been given greater emphasis. My experience has been that many students have difficulty understanding the concept of the power of the test. Much of the material concerning the power of the test has been rewritten for this edition.

Chapter 12 covers tests of hypotheses involving two population means, two population proportions, or two population variances. The material concerning the *F* distribution and testing hypotheses about the equality of two population variances has been moved to Chapter 12 in order to keep all two sample tests in one chapter.

Chapter 13 covers chi-square goodness-of-fit tests and tests of independence. The chapter concludes with a new section showing how to use the computer to perform chi-square tests of independence.

Chapters 14 through 20 provide a detailed discussion of model building. In my opinion, these chapters cover some of the most important and most useful topics in statistics. Chapter 14 on analysis of variance has been expanded to include more material on two-way ANOVA and computer applications.

Chapters 15 through 18 follow a logical sequence in discussing correlation theory and regression analysis in progressively more detail. Chapter 15 provides a discussion of the simple linear regression model along with the classical assumptions. Chapter 16 treats the multiple regression model. Chapter 17 covers various special topics in regression analysis including polynomial regression and the use of dummy variables. A separate section has been added discussing stepwise regression. Due to the nature of this material, these chapters are heavily computer oriented. Chapter 18 is entirely new and covers techniques for testing the assumptions underlying the classical linear regression model. This material provides the student with an introduction to econometric theory. Chapters 19 and 20 treat model building using time series data. Once again this material is heavily computer oriented.

Chapters 21, 22, and 23 are relatively independent of one another and can be treated in any order once Chapter 12 has been covered. Chapter 21 covers nonparametric statistics and discusses an alternative nonparametric test corresponding to each of the tests discussed in Chapters 11 through 14. New material has been added showing how to use the computer to perform each of the nonparametric tests. Chapter 22 has been rewritten and condensed and covers index numbers. Chapter 23 on decision theory has been expanded to include additional material on utility theory.

Supplements

A complete set of supplementary materials is available to support the text.

For the student, there is the **student solutions manual** and the **Minitab** and **SAS primers**. The student solutions manual contains approximately 25 percent of the complete solutions to selected exercises in the text. The statistical software supplements give students instructions on how to use those Minitab and SAS capabilities that are relevant to the techniques covered in the text. The data sets in the text are available on a microcomputer IBM PC compatible disk that can be ordered, at the instructor's discretion, with the primers or the primers can be ordered without them.

For the instructor, there is a **complete solutions manual** and a set of **transparency masters** derived from important art in the text. In addition, the publisher offers to adopters of the text a **test bank file** available in either printed form or in a computer format for IBM and compatible microcomputers.

Acknowledgments

I am indebted to the thousands of students who class-tested my material in its earlier versions. I also want to thank the secretaries who typed various drafts of the document: Beth Wesoloski, Sharon Wetzel, Marilyn Newman, Jennifer Mayo, and Mary Gromiko. I especially want to thank Professor Terri Gollinger who read the entire document in its draft stages and made numerous useful suggestions. Finally, I want to thank Stacey Bardol, Rebecca Chapman, and Bob Truel, who helped prepare the solutions manual and some of the computer output.

I want to acknowledge and thank the artist, Deborah Schneck, the proofreader, Kathy Smith, and the manufacturing coordinator, Marcia Locke—all of whose fine work and expertise helped make the successful completion of this edition possible. I give special thanks to Paul Monsour who copyedited the entire manuscript and to the entire PWS-KENT staff, especially Eve Mendelsohn who did an excellent job as production editor. Finally, I want to thank Michael Payne who asked me to write the third edition and provided numerous helpful suggestions.

All or parts of earlier drafts were read by a number of reviewers including: Charlene Badeaux (Louisiana State University), Paul Baum (California State University–Northridge), S. Chakraborti (University of Alabama), Philip Cline (Washington & Lee University), Carolyn K. Cuff (University of Pittsburgh), Nancy Jo Delaney (Northeastern University), Peter B. Morgan (University of Western Ontario), Paul Nelson (Kansas State University), Elizabeth O'Bryant (Technical Texts, Inc.), R. Ramesh (State University of New York–Buffalo), Paul C. Rogers (University of Southern Maine), Stanley L. Sclove (University of Illinois at Chicago), Earl Weiner (University of Miami), and Roy H. Williams (Memphis State University).

James L. Kenkel

Contents

Twenty ▪ *Time Series Analysis II: Estimation of the Seasonal Component* 870

Twenty-One ▪ *Some Nonparametric Tests* 903

Twenty-Two ▪ *Index Numbers* 952

Twenty-Three ▪ *Introduction to Statistical Decision Theory* 975

Chapter One
What Statistics Is All About

1.1 ▪ The Role of Statistics

The word *statistics* has two different meanings. More commonly, *statistics* means a collection of numerical facts or data, such as stock prices, profits of firms, annual incomes of college graduates, and so forth. In its second meaning, *statistics* refers to an academic discipline, just as physics, biology, and computer science are academic disciplines.

Definition: Statistics

Statistics is a branch of mathematics that consists of a set of analytical techniques that can be applied to data to help in making judgments and decisions in problems involving uncertainty.

Statistics is a scientific discipline consisting of procedures for collecting, describing, analyzing, and interpreting numerical data. One of the main objectives of statistics is to provide a set of procedures that enables us to make inferences, predictions, and decisions about the characteristics of a population of data based on the information obtained from only a part of the population.

The field of statistics can be divided into two parts, descriptive statistics and inferential statistics. Years ago the study of statistics consisted mainly of the study of methods for summarizing and describing numerical data. This study has become known as *descriptive statistics* because it primarily describes the characteristics of large masses of data. In many such statistical studies, data are presented in a convenient, easy-to-interpret form, usually as a table or graph. Such studies usually describe certain characteristics of the data, such as the center and the spread of the data.

Definition: Descriptive Statistics

Descriptive statistics consists of procedures for (1) tabulating or graphing the general characteristics of a set of data and (2) describing some characteristics of this set, such as measures of central tendency or measures of dispersion.

The methods used to collect statistical data often require knowledge of sampling theory and experimental design; this topic is discussed in Chapter 2. Once the data have been collected, descriptive statistics is used to summarize the raw data in a simple, meaningful way. Often this is done by grouping the data into classes, thus forming what are called **frequency distributions.** When data are grouped into classes or categories, it becomes easy to see where most of the values are concentrated, but some information or detail may be lost due to the grouping. Methods of summarizing data by using tables and graphs are discussed in Chapter 3. In Chapter 4, we discuss ways of summarizing the characteristics of data sets by using measures of central tendency and measures of dispersion.

The second branch of statistics is called *inferential statistics*. While descriptive statistics describes characteristics of the observed data, inferential statistics provides methods for making generalizations about the population based on the sample of observed data.

Definition: Inferential Statistics

Inferential statistics consists of a set of procedures that helps in making inferences and predictions about a whole population based on information from a sample of the population.

For example, before building a large shopping center in a certain location, a real estate developer would want to know about the local community: the income and age distribution of residents in the area; their annual expenditures on items such as jewelry, clothing, sporting goods, and books; what proportion of them dine in expensive restaurants; and so forth.

To get this information, the developer would probably rely on a sample of data obtained by interviewing some residents. The developer would then organize the data so that general characteristics would become evident. Using the methods of descriptive statistics, the developer would construct frequency distributions, which show how many of the observations lie in a specific interval or category. Sample means could be calculated, which would show, for example, the average annual income in the community, the average age, the average annual expenditure on sporting goods, and so forth.

With this sample data, the developer could make inferences or predictions about the entire population of people in the community. However, the general characteristics of the sample of residents may not accurately reflect the general characteristics of all the residents in the community. It is always possible to make an error when ascribing properties to an entire population based on a sample of observations. The analysis of the types of errors that can be made involves inferential statistics, which depends on probability theory. Thus, some knowledge of probability theory is necessary to understand the methods of inferential statistics.

Example 1.1

A Study Using Descriptive Statistics: In the early 1980s, Sturgess Mechanical Supplies, a firm in Venango County, Pennsylvania, applied for a government patent on a newly designed pump jack. (A pump jack is the mechanical device that sits above an oil well and lifts the oil from the underground reservoir. When operating, the pump jack looks roughly like a playground seesaw.) This pump jack had a unique balance beam that greatly reduced the amount of electrical power required, thus decreasing the cost of operating the pump jack and increasing the profits derived from the oil well.

Sturgess intended to produce different models of pump jacks for wells of varying depths. In general, as the depth of the well increases, a larger (and more expensive) pump jack is required. Sturgess's jacks were designed primarily for use on wells under 5000 feet in depth. Before beginning to manufacture and advertise the pump jacks, Sturgess hired a consulting firm to gather data on the depths of oil wells in many counties in the Appalachian Basin where the pump jack was likely to be sold. (Venango County is located in northwestern Pennsylvania in the heart of the Appalachian Basin, a hotbed for oil-drilling activity. In fact, except for one county in California, more wells are drilled per year in Venango County than in any other county in the United States.)

Government records showed every drilling permit filed in the last few years, including the location and depth of each well. The consulting firm recorded the depth of every well drilled in Venango County. (This set of data is called a *population* because it includes *every* observation of interest in Venango County.) In addition, the consulting firm randomly selected some of the wells drilled in other counties adjacent to Venango County. (This set of data is called a *sample* because it includes only a portion of all possible observations.)

Eventually the consulting firm had a list showing the depths of several thousand oil wells in and around Venango County. These observations are called *raw data,* because no grouping techniques or statistical procedures have been applied to them. Because there were so many observations, it was necessary to summarize the data in some way. This is the purpose of descriptive statistics.

The consulting firm eventually produced a detailed report containing many tables and graphs. A table was created for each county. For example, one of the tables contained information only on the wells drilled in Venango County. The table showed how many wells were under 500 feet in depth, how many were between 500 and 1000 feet, how many were between 1000 and 1500 feet, and so forth. This table is an example of a frequency distribution. In addition, the consulting firm presented a table showing the *proportion* of wells in Venango County drilled at each depth category. (This table is called a *relative frequency distribution* because it shows the relative frequency, or proportion, of observations in each interval.) Similar frequency distributions and relative frequency distributions were created for each of the counties in the survey.

In order to compare the depths of wells in different counties, the consulting firm calculated the average depth of the wells drilled in each county. (These averages are called *sample means* when they are based on a sample of data and *population means* when they are based on a population of data. They provide a measurement of the middle or center of the data.) By examining the mean, or average, depth of wells in a county, it became possible to determine where Sturgess's pump jacks might sell best.

The consulting firm noticed that in some counties the depths of the wells varied considerably, while in other counties they varied only slightly. Because of this, the firm calculated estimates showing how spread out the observations were in each county. One measurement of the amount of variation, or dispersion, present in a set of data is called the *standard deviation.* If the standard deviation is large, then the observations tend to be widely dispersed; if it is small, the observations tend to be highly concentrated about a central value.

The mean and standard deviation are two examples of what are called summary statistics. A *summary statistic* describes some characteristic of the data as a single number. For example, there are various ways of measuring the center of a set of data and the amount of dispersion in the set. Methods of describing these and other general characteristics of a set of observations are part of the study of descriptive statistics, which is discussed in Chapters 3 and 4. ■

Deductive and Inductive Statistics

The field of statistics can also be divided into deductive statistics and inductive statistics. In **deductive statistics,** we deduce the properties of a sample of observations from the known characteristics of the population. In **inductive statistics,** we reverse the procedure—we start with a sample of observations and try to draw general conclusions about the properties of the population based on the characteristics of the sample.

Definitions: Deductive Statistics and Inductive Statistics

In **deductive statistics,** we try to deduce properties of a given sample based on known characteristics of the population. In **inductive statistics,** we infer properties of a population based on observations of a selected sample of the population.

The field of deductive statistics is often referred to as *probability theory.* As an example of a problem involving probability theory, suppose that an insurance agent has data which show that about 1% of the population will be involved in an accident this year. Thus, the agent knows something about the entire population. Now suppose that the agent insures a sample of 50 people. The agent might want to know the probability that no people in this particular sample will be involved in a serious accident. In this example, the agent is trying to use probability theory to deduce what is likely to be observed in a sample when given information about the characteristics of the entire population.

In Chapters 5 and 6, we will study probability theory or deductive statistics. In Chapters 7 and 8, we will study some discrete and continuous probability distributions and lay the foundation for the study of inferential statistics. In the remaining chapters of the book, we will reverse the direction of inquiry and study inductive statistics. In inductive statistics, inferences about populations are made based on information contained in a sample of data. In inductive statistics, only the sample is known, and we try to determine the characteristics of the population from the information contained in the sample.

Statistical Studies and Data Analysis

The first step in a statistical study is to determine what data are needed and how and from whom they should be obtained. If you are going to use a computer to analyze the data, you must make sure that the data are coded and recorded in a manner that makes it easy to enter the data into the computer. Methods of gathering, coding, and recording data are discussed in Chapter 2.

After you have prepared a data file, you are ready to begin analyzing the data. The first step in data analysis is to describe and summarize the data. You might count the number of people who have certain characteristics, such as how many are male or female, how many are employed, how many are married, and so forth. You might then examine how certain variables are distributed, such as the distribution of people's incomes or of SAT scores for high school seniors. Methods for describing how variables are distributed are discussed in Chapter 3.

Next you describe typical values by finding the average value of a variable, such as the average salary of lawyers or the average age of full professors at a university. In addition, you examine how much variation a variable has, such as the variation in the incomes of secretaries or the ages of truck drivers. In addition, you might look at several variables together. For example, how do SAT scores differ for males and females or how do salaries of adults differ for high school and college graduates? You can also look for values that appear to be unusual, such as ages in the 100s or incomes in the millions, and check the original data to make sure that these values are not due to errors in coding or entering the data. Methods for determining an average score and the amount of variation are discussed in Chapter 4. Chapter 4 also discusses how to study relationships between two or more variables.

Sometimes all you want to do is to describe your data. Chapters 2, 3, and 4 show how this is done. Sometimes, however, you want to test hypotheses about larger groups of persons or things than those included in your data set. For example, you may have data showing the salaries of a group of secretaries in your state and you want to make statements about the average salary of all secretaries in the state. To do so, you have to learn something about statistical inference. This requires a knowledge of probability theory and distribution theory, topics discussed in Chapters 5 through 9.

Chapters 10 through 14 show you how to draw conclusions about populations based on samples. You will learn how to test whether you have sufficient evidence to claim that the differences or relationships you find in your sample are true for the whole population.

Chapters 15 through 20 show you how to examine the relationships between two or more variables. For example, what is the relationship between dollars spent on advertising and sales revenue? What is the relationship between annual income and years of education? There are many different ways to study and model the relationship between sets of variables; you can build a model that lets you predict values of one variable based on the values of the other variables. That's what Chapters 15 through 20 are about.

Chapter 21 on nonparametric statistics discusses various statistical tests that can be performed when the assumptions underlying the tests in Chapters 11 through 14 fail to hold. Chapter 22 covers index numbers and Chapter 23 provides an introduction to decision theory.

1.2 ▪ Basic Sources of Data

Chapter 2 discusses some of the problems encountered in collecting original data. For example, suppose you need information on the sex, race, age, salary, and years of seniority of a set of employees at a certain corporation. To get such information you might need to obtain a sample of employees from the company. There are many different ways to obtain such a sample; some of these procedures are discussed in Chapter 2.

Before spending money to obtain a sample of data, the researcher should determine if the information needed is already available in some public or private publication. In this section we mention some of the most frequently used sources of business and economic data.

Federal Sources of Data

The federal government publishes more economic and business information than any other source, especially through the U.S. Department of Labor, the U.S. Department of Commerce, and the U.S. Department of Health and Human Services.

The Commerce Department publishes the monthly *Survey of Current Business,* which reports data on numerous sectors of the economy in tabular form. The data include information on output, employment, wages, prices, hours worked, and various financial statistics. The Commerce Department also publishes *Business Statistics,* a biennial publication containing all the data published in the monthly issues of the *Survey of Current Business* under one cover. The annual publication *National Income* presents a comprehensive description of the nation's economic accounts. All three sources contain information on the Gross National Product in both current and constant prices.

Other excellent public sources of business and economic data are *The Statistical Abstract of the United States,* published annually by the Bureau of the Census; the *Monthly Labor Review,* published by the Bureau of Labor Statistics; the *Economic Report of the President,* published annually by the U.S. Government Printing Office; and the *Handbook of Labor Statistics,* published annually by the Bureau of Labor Statistics.

Business Conditions Digest, published monthly by the Bureau of the Census, contains an enormous amount of data on the many economic time series (described in Chapter 20) that are used in constructing the indexes of leading, lagging, and coincident indicators. The Board of Governors of the Federal Reserve System publishes the monthly *Federal Reserve Bulletin.* This publication is the primary source for the Index of Industrial Production and is an excellent source of financial information.

Some other useful government publications are:

- *Census of Manufactures* (U.S. Bureau of the Census)
- *County Business Patterns* (U.S. Bureau of the Census)
- *Employment and Earnings* (U.S. Department of Labor)
- *Occupational Outlook Handbook* (U.S. Department of Labor)
- *Current Population Reports* (U.S. Bureau of the Census)
- *Vital Statistics of the United States* (National Center for Health Statistics)

Many state and city agencies gather regional and local data. Most states support a bureau of business and economic research, which can provide help in locating data.

Important sources of data are *United States Government Publications, Monthly Catalog, List of Available Publications of the Department of Commerce,* and *Census Publications, Catalog and Subject Guide.* In addition, most university libraries have employees who are trained in finding the data cited in these references.

Private Sources of Data

There are numerous nongovernmental sources of economic data. The *Wall Street Journal* is an excellent source for data about stocks, bonds, mutual funds, interest rates, exchange rates, and other financial topics. The *Dodge Report* of the F. W. Dodge Corporation is a leading source of data for the construction industry. The National Industrial Conference Board publishes the *Economic Almanac,* which contains data on production, inventory, and prices. Dun and Bradstreet, Inc., publishes *Dun's Statistical Review,* which contains data about business failures. Moody's Investors Service publishes three documents containing information on finance: *Moody's Dividend Record,* which is a semimonthly record of dividends and dates of payment; *Moody's Bond Record,* which provides semimonthly quotations on several thousand corporate, government, and municipal bonds; and *Moody's Manual of Investments,* which contains income and balance sheets for hundreds of companies. Standard and Poor's *Trade and Securities Statistics* and their *Bond Guide* are excellent sources of financial data on corporate and municipal bonds and stocks.

1.3 ▪ A Word About Computers

The widespread availability of computers has dramatically changed how statistics is taught in universities and how statistical methods are used in businesses. With the use of a statistical computer package, it is relatively easy to store and manipulate large data sets. Statistical calculations that were extremely tedious and time consuming a few years ago can now be performed in seconds by inserting a few lines into a computer program. Throughout this textbook, various applications of statistical methods will be illustrated by relying on three widely used statistical packages: SPSSX (Statistical Package for the Social Sciences), SAS (Statistical Analysis System), and Minitab (a statistical computer package designed specifically for students). At the end of nearly every chapter is a brief section on Computer Applications, which shows how these three computer packages can be used to perform many of the calculations discussed in the respective chapters.

Chapter 1 Summary

Statistics is a branch of mathematics and consists of a set of analytical techniques that are used to describe various characteristics of data sets and to help us make decisions in problems involving uncertainty. In *descriptive statistics,* we construct tables and graphs and calculate various summary statistics to describe characteristics of the data. In *inferential statistics,* we use the information obtained from the descriptive analysis of a sample of data and try to infer the properties of the population. Statistical procedures dealing with uncertainty can be deductive or inductive. In *deductive statistics,* or probability theory, we assume that the characteristics of the population are known and make statements about what we expect to observe in a sample taken from the population. In *inductive statistics,* we make statements about the unknown properties of the population based on a sample of data.

Federal, state, and local government agencies are useful sources of data used in many statistical studies. In addition to the many sources cited in this chapter, a detailed list of potential data sources is listed in the appendix of the government publication *Statistical Abstract of the United States, 1988.*

The use of the computer is becoming more and more prevalent in performing statistical analyses. In this text, the SPSSX statistical program is emphasized. Two other popular statistical packages, SAS and Minitab, are described in *User Guides* written for use with this text.

Every statistical study involves the analysis of data. The data can be obtained from reliable sources or by gathering it yourself. Chapter 2 discusses various methods of collecting your own data using different sampling techniques.

References

American Statistical Association and Institute of Mathematical Statistics. *Careers in Statistics.* Washington, D.C.: 1974.

Owen, Donald B. *Handbook of Statistical Tables.* Reading, Mass.: Addison-Wesley, 1962.

Tanur, Judith M., Frederick Mosteller, William H. Kruskal, Richard F. Link, Richard S. Pieters, and Gerald R. Rising, eds. *Statistics: A Guide to the Unknown.* 2d ed. San Francisco: Holden-Day, 1978. Prepared by a joint committee of the American Statistical Association and the National Council of Teachers of Mathematics.

U.S. Department of Labor, Bureau of Labor Statistics. *BLS Handbook of Methods,* 2 vols. Bulletins 2134-1 and 2134-2. Washington, D.C.: U.S. Government Printing Office, December 1982. Explains how the BLS obtains and prepares its economic data. Volume 1 contains this information for all BLS programs except the Consumer Price Index, which is described in volume 2.

Chapter Two
Data Collection and Sampling Theory

Before summarizing the characteristics of a set of data, we must collect the data. In this chapter, we will discuss different methods of collecting a sample of data as well as some of the purposes of collecting data.

2.1 ▪ Populations and Samples

Definition: Population and Sample

A statistical **population** is the set or collection of all possible observations of some specific characteristic. A **sample** is a portion of a population.

One of the main objectives of statistics is to make inferences about a population based on information contained in a sample of that population. The method used to select a sample from the population is called the *sampling design.* The main objective of the sampling design is to provide guidelines for selecting a sample that will provide a specific amount of information about the population at a minimum cost.

Definition: Sampling Design

The **sampling design** is the set of decisions that must be made before the data are collected.

If the elements in the population are relatively uniform, then almost any small sample will provide acceptable results. For example, doctors need to test only a few drops of blood to determine a person's hemoglobin count because, for a given individual, one drop of blood generally provides the same information as any other drop of blood.

When the elements in the population are not relatively uniform, care should be taken in determining how to obtain a sample of data. We want to obtain a sample that is representative of *all* the elements in the population, not just some subsector of the population. For example, when trying to determine people's attitudes about an issue such as drug use, it is important to represent the opinions of individuals of different sexes, ages, religious beliefs, ethnic backgrounds, incomes, and so forth.

One way of gathering information about a population is to examine every single element in the population. We conduct a **census** of a population when we record every element in the population. Because of time and cost constraints as well as other factors to be discussed later, it is often preferable to obtain a sample rather than to conduct a complete census.

Let us introduce some terms commonly used in survey sampling.

Definitions: Elementary Units and Frame

An **elementary unit** is a person or object on which a measurement is taken. A listing of all elementary units in a given problem is called the **frame.**

The statistical population is not the set of elementary units but the set of *observations* or *measurements* of some characteristic of interest associated with the elementary units. The frame is a listing of all the individuals or objects—that is, all the elementary units—on which a measurement is taken.

For example, suppose we want to study the incomes of the employees at a corporation with 500 employees. To do this, we decide to select a sample of the employees. Each employee is an *elementary unit*. The *frame* is a list containing the names of all 500 employees. The *sample observations* are the incomes of the selected employees, and the *population* is the set of incomes of all 500 employees.

Quantitative and Qualitative Variables

There are two basic kinds of populations, **quantitative populations** and **qualitative populations.** When the characteristic or variable being studied is nonnumerical, the variable is called a **qualitative variable** and the population of all observations is called a qualitative population. When the variable being studied can be expressed numerically, the variable is called a **quantitative variable,** and the population of all observations is called a quantitative population. Examples of qualitative variables are sex, marital status, race, religion, and occupation. The color of a person's eyes, the type of a car a person drives, one's ethnic background, one's state of residence, and one's academic major are other qualitative variables. Examples of quantitative variables are age, income, years of education, height, and weight. The diameter of a pipe, the lifetime of a test tube, the amount of money in a checking account, the number of cars owned by a family, the number of customers at a restaurant, and so forth are other quantitative variables.

Qualitative variables can be **dichotomous** or **multinomial.** Observations of a *dichotomous qualitative variable* have only two categories, such as male or female, correct or incorrect, defective or satisfactory, employed or unemployed. Observations about a *multinomial qualitative variable* can have more than two categories, such as a person's religion, occupation, or state of residence. Qualitative data can be stored in a computer by assigning a numerical code to each possible value of the variable. For example, for a dichotomous variable like sex we can record 0 for male and 1 for female. For a multinomial variable like the manufacturer of an automobile, we can record 1 for Ford, 2 for General Motors, 3 for Chrysler, and 4 for other. Assigning a numerical code to qualitative data is just a convenience, and the values assigned to the various categories carry no special significance. For example, for car manufacturer, we could just as easily have recorded 1 for General Motors, 2 for Chrysler, and so on.

For dichotomous data, it usually is best to assign the values 0 and 1 to the two categories rather than 1 and 2, because the average of a set of 0s and 1s represents the proportion of values that are 1. For example, suppose we have a sample of 20 people, 8 of whom are males, coded as 0, and 12 of whom are females, coded as 1. The sum of the 20 coded values is 12, and the average is 12/20, or .60. This indicates that 60% of the people in the sample are females. Note that no special meaning can be attached to the average of a multinomial variable. For example, if we code car manufacturers as described above, the average value for a set of observations might be 1.78. This value has no special meaning.

When the variable being studied is qualitative, we usually want to know how many observations and what proportion of the observations fall in each category. For example, we may be interested in what proportion of adults are married or what proportion of employees at a company have college degrees.

Quantitative variables can be classified as **continuous** or **discrete.** Observations of a *discrete quantitative variable* can assume values only at specific points on a scale of values, with gaps between them. Examples of discrete quantitative variables are number of children in a family, number of rooms in a house, number of cars owned by a family, number of students in a class, and so forth. Observations of a *continuous quantitative variable* can assume all values within an interval. Examples of continuous quantitative variables include the volume of fluid in a bottle, the weight of a shipment of cotton, and the length of time required to produce a product.

When the population is quantitative, we are usually interested in determining how the observations are distributed among all possible values and in determining the average value of the numerical observations. Often we also want to determine the amount of variability in the data.

Exercises for Section 2.1

1. Suppose that an auditor wants to obtain a sample of 50 checking account balances from the 1000 customers at a small bank.
   a. What is the frame?
   b. What is an elementary unit?
   c. What is the population?
   d. What is a sample observation?

2. An office manager wants to obtain a sample showing the length of phone calls for 50 randomly selected phone calls originating in her department last month.
   a. What is the frame?
   b. What is an elementary unit?
   c. What is the population?
   d. What is a sample observation?

3. Are multinomial data discrete or continuous?

4. Explain the difference between continuous and discrete data.
5. Explain the difference between qualitative and quantitative data.
6. Explain how to use a coded system to record a qualitative variable as a number.
7. Explain the difference between a dichotomous and a multinomial qualitative variable.
8. Explain why it is preferable to code a dichotomous qualitative variable as 0 and 1 rather than as 1 and 2.
9. Explain whether the following variables are discrete or continuous:
   a. The length of time for a long-distance phone call
   b. The volume of gasoline remaining in a car's tank
   c. The number of customers waiting in line at a cash register
   d. The number of courses taken by a college student

2.2 ▪ Reasons for Sampling

Since a sample is only a part of a population, any inferences we make about population characteristics based on the sample may be erroneous. Despite this possibility, there are various reasons for taking a sample rather than a census of the entire population. The most important reasons for sampling are as follows:

1. *Expense:* It is less expensive to obtain a sample than to survey the entire population.
2. *Speed of Response:* Information is often needed quickly because important decisions have to be made.
3. *Infinite Number of Observations:* Sometimes populations of observations are generated as a result of a continuing or recurring process. In these cases, it is not possible to observe every element because new observations are continually being made.
4. *Destructive Sampling:* Frequently testing a product, such as determining the life length of light bulbs or the range of ammunition, requires destruction of the product. Thus studying more than a sample is not practical.
5. *Accuracy:* At times a sample can be more accurate than a census of the entire population. This is especially true when the study involves large amounts of repetitive, tedious work, thus increasing the chance of making mistakes because of boredom, fatigue, or the use of unskilled people. A sample obtained by well-trained, skilled people can be more accurate than a census obtained by unskilled people.

A sample is expected to represent the population from which it was selected, but there is no guarantee that a sample will exactly reproduce the characteristics of the population. A sample may not be representative of the population for several reasons. The first reason is just chance or bad luck; we may just happen to obtain a sample containing a large number of atypical elements, thus leading to inaccurate estimates of the population parameters. The second reason is the existence of *sampling bias.*

Definition: Sampling Bias

A sample is **biased** if it is obtained by a method that favors the selection of elementary units having particular characteristics.

One form of sampling bias is called **selection bias.** Selection bias is a systematic exclusion of certain groups from the sample.

Example 2.1

A Biased Sample—The *Literary Digest* Poll: Public opinion polls are probably the most difficult random sample to construct. For example, in an election the statistical population consists of every person who votes. Unfortunately, when a sample is taken before an election, the set of people who will actually vote is unknown. In addition, many potential voters are very difficult to contact, and many people tell pollsters that they do not know who they will vote for. These problems make it difficult to predict the outcome of elections. Probably the most famous example of an inaccurate election prediction is the 1936 *Literary Digest* prediction of a 57% to 43% landslide victory for Alf Landon over Franklin Roosevelt. The *Digest* polled 2.4 million people, the largest political poll ever conducted, and claimed that its prediction would be "within a fraction of 1 percent" of the actual vote. The *Digest* mailed questionnaires to 10 million people, nearly a quarter of the voting population. In sampling, however, quality is much more important than quantity. Two thousand randomly sampled voters is much better than a sample of millions of unrepresentative voters. The *Literary Digest* got most of the 10 million names by selecting names from every single telephone book in the United States.

In 1936 telephone service was still a luxury item. There were only 11 million residential phones, and for the most part they were in the homes of the well-do-do, who tended to favor the Republican candidate Landon. Those without phones tended to have lower incomes and were overwhelmingly Democratic. Thus, the *Literary Digest* was soliciting information from a biased sample that was unrepresentative of the population. The magazine also got names from car registrations, club memberships, and its own subscription lists. These sources were even more biased than the telephone directories. ■

The best way to minimize errors due to chance or bad luck is to take a sufficiently large random sample. (By a random sample, we mean a sample in which every elementary unit in the population has an equal chance of being chosen for the sample.) Increasing the sample size increases the probability that the sample will be representative of the population. In fact, much of statistics is concerned with determining how large a random sample should be in order to minimize errors due to chance.

Errors caused by sampling bias are extremely important. Ensuring that we will not obtain a biased sample is very difficult, and it is frequently very difficult to detect if a sample is biased. The best way to minimize errors caused by sampling bias is to choose a proper sampling procedure.

In some cases, extreme accuracy is required; in other cases, rough estimates may be sufficient. Consequently, the nature of any sampling procedure and the amount of time and money spent on conducting the procedure should depend on the accuracy required as well as on the potential benefits derived from obtaining an accurate estimate of the characteristic being studied.

The conclusions drawn from a particular set of data depend on how and from whom the data were collected.

Example 2.2

Selecting the Source of the Data: Suppose you want to obtain a sample of observations in order to estimate the mean income of adult males. If you examine an individual's income tax records, you probably will get different information than if you conduct a personal interview and ask the person how much he or she earned last year. This demonstrates that how the data are obtained can affect the results of the study. ■

Example 2.3

Selection of the Sample: When estimating the average income of graduates from a certain college, it can make a big difference from whom the data are collected. Suppose the names of the subjects are obtained from a list of graduates from the college who have contributed to the alumni association. The people who contribute to the alumni association probably earn more income on the average than people who do not contribute. Because of this, an estimate of average income based on a sample selected from alumni association contributors is likely to be higher than the true average income of all graduates of the college. ■

Data Acquisition

There are various methods for gathering data in statistical studies. Two of the most frequently used methods are the personal interview and self-enumeration. These methods and their advantages and disadvantages are discussed below.

1. *Personal Interview:* In a personal interview, an interviewer asks questions that are printed on a questionnaire and records the respondents' answers on a prepared form.
   Advantages:
   (a) People tend to respond if they are approached directly; thus a personal interview survey has a high response rate.
   (b) Direct contact with the respondent enables the interviewer to clear up any problems the respondent might have in interpreting the questions.
   Disadvantages:
   (a) The interviewer may not follow the directions for selecting respondents. For example, the interviewer may be told to contact people living at certain addresses but may select other addresses that are more easily found.
   (b) The interviewer may influence the respondent by the manner or tone of voice with which the questions are asked.
   (c) The interviewer may record the respondents' answers incorrectly.
2. *Self-enumeration:* With self-enumeration, the respondent is given or mailed a questionnaire to complete along with a set of instructions, if necessary.
   Advantage:
   (a) Self-enumeration eliminates the errors introduced by the interviewer in a personal interview.
   Disadvantages:
   (a) When a questionnaire is mailed to a household, there is no control over which person answers the questions.
   (b) Typically response rates to a questionnaire mailed to a household are lower than response rates to a personal interview. This can cause a serious bias in survey results, because there is no guarantee that the people who do respond to the survey are representative of all the people who received the survey. When the nonresponse rate is high, it is useful to perform some sort of follow-up survey of the nonrespondents.
   (c) With a mailed questionnaire, it is difficult to clear up any problems that the respondents might have in interpreting questions.

The Stages of a Sample Study

A sample study has three major stages: (1) the *plan* or *sampling design,* (2) the actual *data collection,* and (3) the *analysis of the data* and the *statement of conclusions*. Each of these stages consists of several activities.

The following list describes some of the choices that must be made in creating the sampling design:

1. Identifying the target population and, if necessary, constructing a frame.
2. If necessary, designing a questionnaire that is simple to fill out and that elicits honest answers.
3. Choosing an appropriate sampling technique.
4. Deciding what estimates are needed, what tests are to be performed, or what forecasts have to be made. Selecting the appropriate statistical procedures to fulfill these goals.
5. Determining the sample size. In doing so, the gains in accuracy or reliability that a large sample provides must be balanced against the increased costs of getting more information.

The data collection phase of a sampling study usually requires the most time and cost. The major steps in data collection are as follows:

1. Selecting the sample of elementary units.
2. Obtaining the sample of observations from the sample of elementary units.

The statistical analysis phase of a sampling study consists of some of the following activities:

1. Describing the data using graphs or tables, and constructing frequency distributions.
2. Calculating various sample statistics, such as the sample mean, the sample variance, or the sample proportion.
3. Estimating the appropriate population parameters, and constructing point estimates and interval estimates.
4. Testing hypotheses and making forecasts.
5. Stating the conclusion.

Some Causes of Errors of Estimation

The planning stage of a sampling study is of the utmost importance. This is the stage when we should recognize the types of errors that can arise and take the necessary steps to avoid them. For example, suppose we wish to estimate some population parameter θ. We obtain a sample of data and calculate the sample estimate $\hat{\theta}$. In general, $\hat{\theta}$ will not be equal to θ.

Definition: Sampling Erroı, or Error of Estimation

Let $\hat{\theta}$ be a sample estimate of some population parameter θ. The **sampling error,** or **error of estimation,** is equal to $|\hat{\theta} - \theta|$.

Because of chance or bad luck, the possibility of obtaining a large error of estimation always exists. By choosing a sampling procedure wisely and selecting a large enough sample, we can control the probability of obtaining a sampling error of any given size. To reduce the probability of getting any given error of estimation, we have to increase the sample size. We should realize, however, that at some point the costs of gathering more data will eventually exceed the benefits obtained from a more reliable estimate.

Errors of estimation caused by a biased sample generally cannot be reduced by selecting a larger sample, and such errors will systematically lead to overestimates or underestimates of the population parameter θ.

Some of the conditions that contribute to bias are discussed below:

1. *Sensitive questions* may yield inaccurate or dishonest answers. For example, questions involving criminal activity, drinking habits, drug use, and sexual habits are likely to elicit dishonest, exaggerated, or incorrect answers.

2. The *bias of nonresponse* can occur when some individuals are systematically omitted from the sample. For example, daytime telephone surveys will tend to underrepresent adult males and overrepresent adult females because men are more likely than women to be working away from the home during the day.

3. The *bias of self-selection* can occur when the individuals being studied rather than the statistician determine which units shall be included in the sample. Self-selection bias is systematic refusal of some groups to respond to a poll. For example, radio talk shows frequently ask listeners to call and cast a vote on some controversial issue. The listener then decides whether to call and vote. In general, those people who call and vote may have different (and stronger) opinions than those who do not call. The same argument holds for conclusions based on mail received by members of Congress. People who write letters have selected themselves to be in the sample, and letter writers, in general, tend to be different (if only more opinionated) from nonwriters. Conclusions based on a sample of observations obtained by mail are likely to be subject to bias because not everyone will mail in a response. Often those people who do not respond to voluntary opinion polls are more willing to leave things as they are, whereas those who do respond tend to prefer a change.

4. *Interviewer bias* occurs when the interviewer has some effect on the answer. The personal characteristics of the interviewer, such as age, sex, race, or occupation, may influence the response. For example, when blacks in the army were asked about how they felt the army treated them, their responses were vastly different depending on whether the interviewer was black or white. The manner in which the interviewer poses the question may elicit an incorrect or skewed response. For example, "The federal deficit is too large, isn't it?" is more likely to elicit a positive response than "Do you think the federal deficit is too large?" or "What do you think about the size of the federal deficit?"

5. Bias can be caused by recording answers incorrectly or making errors in processing the data. For example, an inaccurate radar gun might be used to estimate the speed of a car, or an inaccurate watch might be used to clock the speed of an athlete. Probably the most common error in recording data occurs when an individual hits the wrong key while inputting data into a computer.

Unless a sample is selected randomly, it is reasonable to suspect that polls in general are biased toward people with more money, more education, more information and alertness, a better appearance, more conventional behavior, and more settled habits than the average individual of the population from which the sample is chosen.

After the 1936 *Literary Digest* fiasco, political pollsters turned from mailed questionnaires to quota sampling as an inexpensive way of obtaining a representative sample. In **quota sampling,** a sample is constructed by filling quotas of certain characteristics that are thought to reflect the population as a whole. For example, the interviewer is told to solicit responses from a certain number of males, females, whites, blacks, young people, old people, rich people, poor people, and so forth. The goal is to guarantee that the sample has certain characteristics that match characteristics believed to exist in the population.

However, for the reasons just discussed, quota sampling is biased, too. Whenever the interviewer is given freedom to choose who will or will not be included in the sample, there is the danger of selection bias. Quota sampling leaves too much discretion in the hands of the interviewer. In addition, most interviewers will tend to meet their quotas in the easiest possible way, which means that people in risky, unfamiliar, or inconvenient places will be ignored.

At the time of the *Literary Digest* poll, this selection bias tended to favor Republicans. This would lead one to suspect that if a poll used quota sampling to predict the outcomes of presidential elections, there would be a systematic tendency to overestimate the proportion of Republican votes.

The Gallup Poll, for example, was just starting at the time of the 1936 presidential election. Using quota sampling, the Gallup poll did better than the *Literary Digest,* but it still overestimated the vote for the Republican candidate in each of the first three elections it covered. Despite this selection bias, however, it was not large enough to cause an erroneous prediction of a Republican victory. In the 1948 election, though, the vote was close, and Gallup was one of several pollsters who incorrectly predicted that the Republican candidate Thomas Dewey would be elected over Harry Truman.

Pollsters sought a way to make their samples more random without incurring the extremely high expenses associated with a simple random sample. Eventually they settled upon a **sequential cluster sampling** procedure. First a random-number table is used to select the cities that will be sampled; the chance of a city being selected is proportional to its population. Random numbers are then used to select voting precincts within the city and to select voters from the voter registration lists in those precincts. The sequential nature of this process makes it unnecessary to list every single voter in the country, and every voter has an equal chance of being included in the sample. In addition, the clustering of observations at the precinct level makes it a much more economical sampling procedure. However, political polls still contain some selection bias. In general, pollsters do not consider very remote, difficult-to-reach households, and many interviewers still have some discretion over whom to interview.

At the present time, polling is a combination of random and quota sampling with a bit of interviewer discretion blended in. This is an economic compromise that greatly reduces the extreme expense of a simple random sample. Apparently this procedure works fairly well. The data on page 18 show the results of the Gallup Poll since 1936. Observe that since 1952, when the new sampling procedures were instituted, the size of the sampling error has been greatly reduced. In addition, the tendency to overestimate the Republican vote has largely been eliminated. Now the Republican proportion is underestimated about as often as it is overestimated. The amazing statistical fact is that the pre-1950 polls were based on samples of 50,000 registered voters, while current polls yield better predictions using samples of less than 4000 people.

Year	Predicted Republican Vote (percent)	Actual Republican Vote (percent)	Difference (percent)
1936	44	38	6
1940	48	45	3
1944	48	46	2
1948	50	45	5
1952	51	55.4	−4.4
1956	59.5	57.8	1.7
1960	49	49.9	−0.9
1964	36	38.7	−2.7
1968	43	43.4	−0.4
1972	62	61.7	0.3
1976	49	48.0	1.0
1980	47	50.7	−3.7
1984	59	58.8	0.2

Exercises for Section 2.2

1. List at least five different reasons why statisticians rely on samples.
2. List at least three examples where we rely on sample information rather than a census because the product is destroyed in the process of making an observation.
3. List at least three examples where we rely on sample information rather than a census because a census would be too expensive.
4. List at least three examples where we rely on sample information rather than a census because a census would be too time consuming.
5. List at least three examples where we rely on sample information rather than a census because the population is generated by a recurring process.
6. Explain why inferential statistics is not required if we have a census of data.
7. List some advantages of obtaining data from a personal interview. List some disadvantages.
8. List some advantages of obtaining data from a mailed questionnaire. List some disadvantages.
9. List at least five causes of errors of estimation due to bias.

2.3 ▪ Types of Samples

The two basic types of samples are **probability samples** and **nonprobability samples.** In a probability sample, the selected items are determined according to some randomization or chance procedure. For this reason probability samples are often called *random samples*. One of the objectives in taking a probability sample is to guarantee that each member of the population has an equal chance of being selected for the sample. We will cover some of the different ways of obtaining a probability sample after a brief discussion of nonprobability sampling.

The two primary types of nonprobability samples are *convenience* and *judgment samples*.

Definition: Convenience Sample

A **convenience sample** is obtained by selecting elementary units that can be acquired simply and conveniently.

If we stand on a street corner and select the next n people who pass by or if we obtain observations by interviewing our neighbors or our family members, we will produce a convenience sample. Letters received by a member of Congress or calls made to a radio talk show also form convenience samples.

Definition: Judgment Sample

A **judgment sample** is obtained by selecting elementary units according to the judgment, intuition, and discretion of an expert or someone familiar with the relevant characteristics of the population.

Both the convenience sample and the judgment sample are likely to yield biased results, although the adequacy of a judgment sample depends to a great extent upon the wisdom of the investigator.

Definition: Random Sample

A **random sample** (or **probability sample**) is obtained if every member of the population has an equal chance of being selected for the sample.

The great advantage of using a random sample is that there is no tendency to favor or select elementary units possessing certain characteristics. No particular item is systematically excluded from the study, and no particular item is more likely to be included than any other. Because each unit is selected independently, including one particular unit does not affect the chance of including another. Because of this property, the random sample is free from sampling bias. Furthermore, the theorems of probability and statistics can be used to assess the reliability of estimates obtained from random samples. Such is not the case with convenience and judgment samples.

Next we will briefly discuss the following six sampling procedures:

1. simple random samples,
2. systematic random samples,
3. stratified random samples,
4. cluster samples,
5. randomized response sampling, and
6. sequential sampling.

These types of samples and some of the reasons for using them will be explained briefly. Because a more detailed analysis of different sampling procedures is beyond the scope of this book, the interested reader should consult the references for other sources of information.

Simple Random Sampling

Definition: Simple Random Sample

A **simple random sample** is one in which (1) every possible set of n elementary units has the same probability of being selected and (2) the selection of any one elementary unit in no way affects the chance of selecting any other elementary unit.

Suppose that we have a frame containing a finite number of N elements. To select a simple random sample of size n, you could proceed as follows. Number each of the elementary units in the frame from 1 to N, and write the numbers 1 to N on small pieces of paper. Put the pieces of paper in a bowl, mix them thoroughly, and select a sample of size n of the papers. To obtain a simple random sample, select those elementary units whose numbers match the numbers pulled from the bowl. This procedure is tedious if the population is large, but it illustrates the idea that every member of the population has an equal chance of being selected and every combination of n observations is equally likely.

Another way of selecting a random sample is to number each elementary unit in the frame and then choose n numbers from a **random-number table.** A *random-number table* contains a set of digits generated by a process that gives each digit 0, 1, . . . , 9 an equal chance of being next anywhere in the series. Random numbers can be generated by physical processes, mathematical processes, or a combination of the two. Physical processes include the following: drawing a numbered capsule from a bowl, recording the number, replacing the drawn capsule, remixing the capsules in the bowl, and drawing again; and flashing a beam of light at irregular intervals onto a rotating disk and reading off numbers from the disk. Most mathematical processes entail programming a digital computer with a recurrence relation such that the next random number is always derived from one or more prior numbers.

The problem with generating random numbers with physical processes is that a specific sequence of numbers cannot be regenerated; therefore no procedure that made use of a particular sequence of numbers can be repeated unless the numbers are somehow stored. Tables of random numbers generated by using computers actually contain pseudo-random numbers, because if the same computer program is executed twice using the same start-up value, or "seed," the same set of random numbers will be generated. A set of random numbers was first published in tabular form in 1927. In 1955 the Rand Corporation published *A Million Random Digits,* a portion of which is reprinted in Table A.1 in the Appendix.

It does not matter how a random-number table is read (right to left, left to right, top to bottom, or bottom to top). If the numbers in the table are larger than required, then leading or trailing digits can be ignored. If a random number having no counterpart in the population is obtained, skip it and go on to the next random number. For example, if a population contains 8000 elementary units and the random-number table tells you to select the elementary unit numbered 9061, go on to the next random number. Example 2.4 illustrates the use of a random-number table.

Example 2.4

Using a Random-Number Table: Suppose a corporation has 600 employees, who are listed in alphabetical order and numbered sequentially from 1 to 600. To estimate the average number of days missed because of illness last year, an auditor wants to select a simple random sample of 40 of the employees. We have to determine which 40 of the 600 employees to examine.

Solution: We can use the random numbers given in Table A.1 in the Appendix. Because the table contains five-digit numbers, we delete the first two digits of each number to get numbers from 000 to 999, and we ignore any number greater than 600. We can start at any position in the table; let's choose row 6, column 1. If we decide to read the numbers across the rows, we will record the next 40 appropriate numbers from the table and contact the appropriate employees.

Row 6, column 1 contains the number 74146; we record 146. Row 6, column 2 contains the number 47887; we skip this number because 887 is greater than 600. Row 6, column 3 contains the number 62463; we record 463. Proceeding in this fashion, we would select the 40 employees having the following numbers for our simple random sample:

146	463	45	490	597	12	410	179	75	51
385	378	360	547	78	238	540	219	563	61
492	447	568	333	201	185	154	529	116	42
536	157	172	473	123	533	437	256	596	416

You should note that the numbers 540 and 201 each appeared twice in the random-number table, and so the second occurrence of each value was omitted. ■

Selecting a simple random sample can be a tedious, time-consuming, and costly procedure. The other random sampling methods can sometimes be simpler and reduce the time and cost of sampling.

Systematic Random Sampling

Definition: Systematic Random Sample

A **systematic random sample** is obtained in the following way: Number the elementary units in the frame from 1 to N. Calculate the ratio N/n, where N is the population size and n is the desired sample size. Let k be the largest integer less than or equal to N/n. Randomly select an elementary unit from the first k elements in the frame and then select every kth element thereafter.

When the frame consists of observations that are stored or recorded in an orderly form, then a systematic random sample can save a great deal of time. It is especially useful when sampling from the files of banks, corporations, credit agencies, and so forth.

Note that not all *combinations* of observations are equally likely to occur in a systematic random sample. For example, if $k = 10$, then the sampled observations are 10 units apart. Thus, units 6 and 8 would never appear together in the sample. Note, however, that every elementary unit would have a 1 in 10 chance of being in the sample because the starting value is picked randomly.

If the population size is unknown, we can still obtain a systematic random sample by selecting some reasonable value for k and proceeding as before. For example, a systematic sample of 50 shoppers at a store could be obtained by randomly selecting a customer entering the store and then selecting every 10th customer after that until a sample size of 50 was obtained.

A systematic sample may not adequately represent the population if hidden periodicities are present in the population. Suppose, for example, that a company uses 50 machines and that every 50th product coming off an assembly line is produced by the same machine. If we select every 10th product for our sample, then we will obtain products produced by only 5 of the 50 machines. If we select every 100th product, then our entire sample will be produced by the same machine.

Example 2.5

Systematic Random Sample: In Example 2.4, we used a random-number table to obtain a simple random sample of $n = 40$ items from a population containing $N = 600$ items. Let us obtain a systematic random sample of size 40 from that population.

Solution: We obtain $k = 600/40 = 15$. We need to pick a number randomly from 1 to 15. Let us enter the random-number table in, say, row 4, column 4. Let us go down this column until we find a number in which the last two digits are between 1 and 15 inclusive. The number obtained is 2, which is in row 20, column 4. Our starting point is employee number 2; we then select employees numbered 17, 32, 47, and so forth. All of these observations are $k = 15$ units apart. ■

Stratified Random Sampling

Definition: Stratified Random Sample

A **stratified random sample** is obtained by separating the population into a number of nonoverlapping subpopulations, called **strata,** and then selecting a simple random sample from each stratum.

In election polls it is customary to subdivide the population of voters into strata, such as white and nonwhite; urban and rural; Protestant, Catholic, Jewish, and other; and so forth. The sample size selected from each stratum is proportional to the stratum size, thus yielding a **proportional stratified sample.** This procedure is intended to increase the chances that the sample obtained is representative of the population. For example, if 22% of all voters are female, we may want to stipulate that 22% of the elementary units in our sample be female.

At times we may get better results by using a nonproportional method of stratified random sampling. For example, suppose that corporations are classified into strata (called "small," "medium," and "large") based on their total assets. The assets of the large corporations may be so much greater than the assets of the small corporations that the sample of large corporations should be proportionately greater than the sample of small corporations. Whether this is a good sampling procedure depends on the purpose of the study.

Stratified random sampling is most useful for an extremely heterogeneous population in which the various strata of the population are believed to behave differently. One advantage of stratified random sampling is that separate estimates are obtained for the parameters of each stratum, enabling us to analyze stratum differences.

Cluster Sampling

At times it may be too difficult or too expensive to obtain a simple or a stratified random sample. In these cases a cluster sample may be desirable. A *cluster* is defined as a group of elementary units located near one another, such as residents of the same neighborhood.

Definition: Cluster Sample

A **cluster sample** is obtained by separating the population into subpopulations called **clusters** and then selecting clusters by simple random sampling. After the clusters have been selected, a complete enumeration (or census) is taken of every elementary unit in each selected cluster.

Cluster sampling is cheaper and faster than other random sampling methods, but it is the least reliable. People who live in the same neighborhood, for example, tend to have similar characteristics, such as race, income level, ethnic background, educational background, and so forth. With cluster sampling certain types of people are more likely to be over- or underrepresented.

The goal of stratified sampling is to guarantee that all groups in a population are adequately represented, even if the costs of sampling are increased. The goal of cluster sampling is to gather data quickly and cheaply even if certain groups of people are not represented proportionately.

In **two-stage cluster sampling,** a random sample of clusters is selected and then a random sample of elementary units is selected from each cluster.

Randomized Response Sampling

A major source of bias in many studies occurs when the subject refuses to answer a sensitive question or does not give a truthful answer.

Definition: Randomized Response Sampling

The objective of **randomized response sampling** is to encourage subjects to provide truthful answers to sensitive questions.

In randomized response sampling, each subject is asked both the sensitive question and some other innocuous question regarding a topic about which we already have full information. The subject is given a randomization device, such as a bag containing black and white marbles. The subject selects a marble (without letting the interviewer see which color was selected) and answers the sensitive question if, say, the white marble is selected and the innocuous question otherwise.

The interviewer receives an answer (usually just a yes or no) but does not know which question was answered. This tends to keep the respondent from being embarrassed and encourages a truthful answer. There is no guarantee, of course, that the respondent will not lie when answering the sensitive question, but this procedure generally reduces the number of false answers. The following example shows how randomized sampling works.

Example 2.6

Randomized Response Sampling: Suppose we want to estimate the proportion of students at a university who have used illegal drugs. This is a sensitive topic and it is felt that, when questioned, many students will refuse to answer or will not answer truthfully out of fear of embarrassment. We select a random sample of 800 students. We hand each student a questionnaire containing two questions: The sensitive question is "Have you ever used illegal drugs?" The innocuous question is "Is your birthday between January 1 and July 1?" The student is given a bag containing, say, five black and five white marbles. The student is then told to select a ball randomly (without showing it to the interviewer) and to answer the first question if a black ball was selected and the second if a white ball was selected. The student gives the interviewer an answer of yes or no but does not tell the interviewer which question was being answered. The respondent has less reason to lie because a yes answer could be in answer to the birthday question.

At the completion of the study, suppose we have 240 yes answers and 560 no answers. How do we interpret the results? Because 50% of the balls were white, we assume that 50%, or 400, of the 800 respondents answered question 1 and that the remaining 400 answered question 2. Because 50% of all students should have birthdays between January 1 and July 1, the 400 replies to question 2 should yield about 200 yes answers and 200 no answers. Therefore, the remaining 40 yes answers and 360 no answers should be to question 1. Of the 400 people assumed to have answered question 1, we estimate that 40 (or 10%) answered yes, and thus we estimate that 10% of the student body has used illegal drugs. ■

Randomized response sampling is used along with or in addition to the other sampling procedures. We first have to select a sample of people who will be questioned; then we use the randomized response mechanism. The disadvantage of this method is that it is expensive. For instance, in Example 2.6 we assumed that 50% of the students were answering the innocuous question, which provided us with no information. Therefore, we had to interview 800 people in order to get about 400 answers to the sensitive question.

Sequential Sampling

Definition: Sequential Sampling

In **sequential sampling,** the sample size is not determined or fixed before the sample is taken. The final size of the sample depends on the results obtained.

Sequential sampling is frequently used in quality control inspections. Suppose an investigator wants to determine whether some production process is working properly. It might be decided that if 5 or more products are defective in a sample of 50 products, then the production process is not working properly. Rather than select a random sample of 50 products, the investigator would select the products one after another sequentially and then stop sampling when either 5 defective products or 46 good products were observed. Suppose, for example, that 5 of the first 10 products observed were defective. In this case, the sampling would stop after only 10 observations. In certain situations, sequential sampling can be less expensive and less time consuming than other forms of random sampling.

Exercises for Section 2.3

1. Explain why statisticians favor random samples to judgment samples or convenience samples.
2. Explain how to obtain a simple random sample of 50 observations from a population containing 250 observations. Describe how to use the random-number table to determine which elementary units to select.
3. Explain how to obtain a systematic random sample of 50 observations from a population containing 250 observations.
4. Describe some situations where it might be preferable to obtain a systematic random sample rather than a simple random sample.
5. Describe some situations where we might take a stratified random sample rather than a simple random sample.
6. Describe some situations where we might use sequential sampling rather than simple random sampling.
7. Suppose a sampling agency wants to obtain a random sample of a city's adult population. Discuss possible problems with using each of the following procedures:
   a. Random-digit dialing, where a computer places calls to randomly generated phone numbers
   b. Random selection of 10 places of employment and then random selection of employees within each location
   c. Selecting every fifth person entering a grocery store
   d. Randomly selecting children in all schools and then including their parents in the study

2.4 ▪ Computer Analysis of Multivariate Data Sets

When performing a statistical investigation, we gather samples or populations of data concerning the characteristics possessed by the elementary units. Suppose you want to examine the characteristics of a sample of employees at the Computech Corporation. A **data value** is a single measurement, such as an employee's income, an employee's age, or an employee's sex. The information about each employee—name, sex, age, income, and so forth—makes up one observation. An **observation** is a set of data values for the same experimental unit. Any characteristic being observed is called a **variable.** Thus, a variable is a set of data values regarding a particular characteristic. Possible variables include the age of all the employees at Computech, the incomes of all the employees at Computech, and so forth.

Each individual piece of information is a data value, and all data values for the same person or object are an observation. For each observation, you have one data value for each variable. Any collection of data values about one or more variables is called a **data set,** or **file.** A data set is said to be **univariate, bivariate,** or **multivariate** depending on whether it contains information on one variable only, two variables only, or more than two variables, respectively.

Many multivariate data sets for employees at a corporation contain hundreds or thousands of observations on numerous variables such as the employee's name, sex, race, age, monthly salary, education status, occupation, and so forth. When the number of observations is large, a computer is frequently used to analyze the data. The computer can perform calculations in a few seconds that might take hours or days to perform by hand. In the remainder of this section, we will show how to use the computer to analyze a multivariate data set for a sample of employees at the Computech Corporation.

Selected Characteristics of Employees at the Computech Corporation

Table 2.1 is a multivariate data set for a sample of 120 employees at Computech. Each row contains information on a particular employee, and each column shows the data values of a particular variable for all 120 employees.

- Column (1) of Table 2.1 shows the last names followed by the first names of the 120 employees.
- Column (2) of Table 2.1 shows the sex of each employee. Because SEX is a qualitative variable that can take only two values, it is a dichotomous qualitative variable. In Table 2.1, SEX is coded as {0 = female, 1 = male}. Be sure to include the code with any statistical output so that the reader will have no difficulty in decoding and understanding the data.
- Column (3) of Table 2.1 shows the race of each employee. In Table 2.1, RACE is a dichotomous variable that is coded {0 = black, 1 = white}. Sometimes a third value {2 = other} is included.
- Column (4) of Table 2.1 shows the variable DEGREE, which indicates the highest academic degree attained by each employee. DEGREE is a multinomial variable that is coded as follows: {1 = high school degree, 2 = college degree, 3 = postgraduate degree}.
- Column (5) of Table 2.1 shows the age of each employee. Theoretically AGE is a continuous variable, but in Table 2.1 it has been rounded down to the largest integer value.
- Column (6) shows the variable DIV (short for "division"), which indicates the division of the company where the employee works. DIV is a multinomial variable that is coded as follows: {1 = office, 2 = manufacturing, 3 = sales}.
- Column (7) shows the monthly salary of each employee. SALARY can be treated as a continuous variable.
- Column (8) indicates the years of seniority at Computech for each employee. SENIOR is a continuous variable that has been rounded down to the largest integer value.
- Column (9) indicates the number of tax exemptions claimed by each employee. Computech needs this information for deducting federal income taxes from each employee's paycheck. EXEMPT is a discrete quantitative variable that can take on whole-number values.

With this data set, we can determine general characteristics of the employees, such as the following:

1. the proportion of employees that are male,
2. the proportion of employees that are white,
3. the proportion of employees that have high school, college, or postgraduate degrees,
4. the proportion of employees that work in the office, in manufacturing, or in sales, and
5. the proportion of employees that have claimed one exemption, two exemptions, and so forth.

Using a computer, we can construct a frequency distribution. This topic will be discussed in more detail in the next chapter.

TABLE 2.1 **A multivariate data set**

Selected Characteristics of Computech Employees

(1) NAME	(2) SEX	(3) RACE	(4) DE-GREE	(5) AGE	(6) DIV	(7) SALARY	(8) SE-NIOR	(9) EX-EMPT
Abbott, Marie	0	1	1	35	1	1575	16	5
Allen, Joseph	1	1	1	31	2	1980	10	3
Anthony, Michael	1	1	1	51	2	2480	28	2
Ard, Debra	0	1	1	57	1	1925	30	2
Bardol, Stacey	0	1	2	28	3	1900	6	2
Bates, Robert	1	0	3	64	3	3050	40	2
Bollman, Phil	1	0	1	30	2	1920	7	3
Booth, James	1	1	1	35	2	1970	10	3
Brantly, Cynthia	0	1	1	26	2	1900	7	3
Brice, Derek	1	0	1	39	2	2250	18	4
Brown, Dave	1	1	2	25	3	2300	3	1
Brown, Gretchen	0	1	1	29	1	1425	10	2
Burns, Wesley	1	0	1	47	2	2200	20	1
Caste, Felix	1	1	1	22	2	1840	3	1
Cohen, Richard	1	1	1	24	2	1880	5	2
Coleman, Joyce	0	1	2	41	3	1840	12	3
Cooper, Jerry	1	1	1	58	2	2600	35	2
Cottrell, Bruce	1	1	3	45	3	5000	20	3
Cusick, Barb	0	1	1	52	1	1600	17	2
Dillon, Deborah	0	0	1	33	1	1300	6	1
Dixon, Katie	0	1	2	46	1	1850	25	5
Doane, David	1	0	1	49	2	2180	20	1
Doherty, Terry	1	1	1	21	2	1820	2	1
Donnelly, Mark	1	1	2	43	2	2580	24	5
Egan, Bryan	1	1	2	35	3	3000	14	4
Emerson, Michael	1	1	1	33	2	2080	15	3
Finnegan, John	1	1	1	64	2	2780	42	2
Folino, John	1	0	1	55	2	2680	36	2
Fowler, Eileen	0	1	1	33	1	1475	12	4
Gavett, Bob	1	0	1	55	2	2600	32	2
Ghent, Barb	0	1	1	42	1	1400	9	5
Grant, Linda	0	1	1	30	1	1275	4	3
Gray, Renee	0	1	3	44	3	2400	20	4
Green, Edward	1	1	1	23	2	1850	3	1
Gross, Bryan	1	1	2	35	3	3020	14	3

continued

TABLE 2.1 **continued**

Selected Characteristics of Computech Employees

(1) NAME	(2) SEX	(3) RACE	(4) DE-GREE	(5) AGE	(6) DIV	(7) SALARY	(8) SE-NIOR	(9) EX-EMPT
Hart, Julie	0	1	1	57	1	1725	22	2
Hicks, Mark	1	1	2	46	2	2580	23	5
Hill, Betsy	0	0	1	35	1	1450	11	3
Holtz, Al	1	1	2	36	2	2000	14	4
Horner, Susan	0	0	1	26	1	1860	4	1
Hunt, Penny	0	0	1	25	1	1880	5	1
Jackson, Tom	1	1	3	45	3	3200	21	5
Johnson, Sue	0	0	1	33	1	1450	11	4
Jones, Carol	0	0	1	33	1	1320	6	2
Katila, Ron	1	1	1	19	2	1800	1	1
Katz, Marie	0	1	1	55	1	1600	17	2
Kennedy, Sue	0	1	2	53	1	1975	32	2
Kesel, Laura	0	1	1	64	1	1925	30	2
King, Boyd	1	1	1	38	3	3400	18	5
Knight, Sharon	0	1	1	44	1	1275	4	6
Laird, William	1	1	1	21	2	1840	3	1
Lane, Katie	0	1	2	46	1	1850	25	5
Lerach, Dick	1	1	1	46	2	2340	22	4
Lerner, Kathryn	0	1	1	61	1	2050	35	2
Levering, Jeff	1	0	1	36	2	2010	11	2
Levine, Harvey	1	1	1	53	2	2560	33	2
Lewis, Carolyn	0	1	2	24	3	1980	1	1
Linn, Ron	1	1	1	23	2	1840	1	1
Lund, Dick	1	1	2	30	3	2200	9	1
Manke, Terry	1	1	1	37	2	2200	16	4
Martini, Gregory	1	1	1	20	2	1820	2	1
Masters, Bryan	1	1	1	54	2	2520	31	2
Meyer, Jane	0	1	1	41	1	1420	9	3
Miller, Wayne	1	1	1	30	2	1980	10	3
Moffitt, Brenda	0	1	1	31	1	1820	2	4
Molnar, Charles	1	1	3	55	3	4100	30	2
Morgan, Carl	1	0	2	52	3	2500	28	2
Morris, George	1	0	1	22	2	1800	4	1
Neufarth, Ray	1	1	1	41	2	2320	21	6
Nichols, William	1	1	2	23	3	2000	2	2
Nixon, Eileen	0	1	1	32	1	1465	12	2

continued

TABLE 2.1 **continued**

Selected Characteristics of Computech Employees

(1) NAME	(2) SEX	(3) RACE	(4) DE-GREE	(5) AGE	(6) DIV	(7) SALARY	(8) SE-NIOR	(9) EX-EMPT
Noll, Betty	0	1	1	40	1	1890	5	4
Nunn, Alex	1	1	2	49	3	3500	27	4
O'Connor, Tom	1	1	1	44	2	2400	25	5
Otto, Laura	0	1	1	54	1	1915	25	2
Park, Sandy	0	1	1	41	1	1375	8	3
Pasurka, Carl	1	1	1	32	2	2040	13	5
Peplin, Robert	1	1	1	26	2	1920	7	1
Perkins, Marcia	0	0	1	28	1	1425	10	2
Phillips, Laura	0	1	1	35	1	1200	1	4
Pollack, James	1	1	1	55	2	2560	33	2
Quinn, Denise	0	1	2	48	3	2800	17	3
Racine, Mary	0	1	1	30	2	1880	5	3
Ramsey, Henry	1	1	3	57	3	3300	22	2
Reed, Keith	1	1	1	48	2	2560	28	2
Reynolds, James	1	1	1	42	2	2330	22	6
Rosen, Donald	1	1	1	47	2	2420	23	4
Russell, Theresa	0	1	2	21	3	2000	1	1
Schmidt, Mildred	0	1	1	39	1	1425	10	3
Schmidt, Peter	1	1	1	20	2	1820	2	1
Scott, Donald	1	1	1	45	2	2400	25	4
Segal, Carol	0	1	1	55	1	1625	18	2
Seibert, Joan	0	0	1	32	1	1400	9	3
Shields, Terry	1	1	2	60	3	4800	38	2
Stacey, Leon	1	0	1	54	2	2580	34	3
Steen, Mark	1	1	1	28	2	1900	6	2
Stone, Janet	0	0	1	32	1	1410	9	3
Stockton, Matt	1	1	1	43	2	2360	23	3
Sullivan, Mark	1	0	1	26	2	1880	5	3
Sweeney, Tom	1	1	1	47	2	2500	30	4
Tinsley, Steven	1	1	2	32	2	1940	8	3
Tomlin, Shirley	0	1	3	34	3	2000	6	3
Troy, Guy	1	1	1	51	2	2480	29	2
Tunis, Kathie	0	0	1	28	1	1400	9	2
Volk, Sandy	0	1	1	28	1	1425	10	2
Voss, Jerry	1	1	2	64	3	5000	35	2
Walker, Bill	1	1	3	33	3	2400	5	3

continued

TABLE 2.1 **continued**

Selected Characteristics of Computech Employees

(1) NAME	(2) SEX	(3) RACE	(4) DE-GREE	(5) AGE	(6) DIV	(7) SALARY	(8) SE-NIOR	(9) EX-EMPT
Ward, Robert	1	1	1	41	2	2320	21	6
Warren, Jim	1	1	2	25	2	1860	4	1
West, Greg	1	1	1	20	2	1820	2	1
Wetzel, Sharon	0	1	1	44	1	1255	3	2
Wicks, Robert	1	0	1	27	2	1900	6	2
Williams, Stephen	1	1	1	46	2	2320	20	3
Wiltman, Robert	1	1	1	49	2	2400	25	4
Wollen, Fred	1	1	1	31	2	1960	9	5
Wood, Brenda	0	1	1	42	1	1350	7	5
Wooley, Jackie	0	0	2	29	3	2400	3	2
Yates, Michael	1	1	1	36	2	2000	11	3
Zielke, William	1	1	1	49	2	2460	28	4
Zimmer, Connie	1	1	1	55	1	1675	20	2

Codes: SEX: (0 = female, 1 = male)
RACE: (0 = black, 1 = white)
DEGREE: (1 = high school degree, 2 = college degree, 3 = postgraduate degree)
DIV: (1 = office, 2 = manufacturing, 3 = sales)

An SPSSX Computer Program

Figure 2.1 shows the SPSSX computer program that was used to construct the frequency distributions for the variables SEX, RACE, DEGREE, DIV, and EXEMPT. Each line in Figure 2.1 represents a specific command, which are explained as follows:

- The TITLE command gives a name to the SPSSX run.
- The DATA LIST command gives each variable a name and describes the data as being in FREE format. (In the SPSSX computer program, the employees' last and first names are denoted by the variable names LNAME and FNAME. The (A8) indicates that the data have been entered as letters rather than numbers. Each variable must be given a name, which cannot exceed eight characters in length. This feature is common to most statistical computer packages. Consequently the names of variables must often be abbreviated.)
- The VALUE LABELS command tells SPSSX to print out how the variables are coded.
- The BEGIN DATA command indicates to SPSSX that the data immediately follow.
- The next 120 lines contain the data.
- The END DATA command indicates the end of the data set.
- The FREQUENCIES command requests SPSSX to generate a frequency distribution for each of the variables listed.
- The FINISH command indicates the end of an SPSSX program.

FIGURE 2.1 **SPSSX program to obtain frequency distributions for data in Table 2.1.**

```
TITLE EMPLOYEE DATA'
DATA LIST FREE/ LNAME (A8), FNAME (A8), SEX, RACE, DEGREE, AGE,
    DIV, SALARY, SENIOR, EXEMPT
VALUE LABELS
    SEX 0 'FEMALE' 1 'MALE'
    RACE 0 'BLACK' 1 'WHITE'
    DEGREE 1 'HIGH SCHOOL' 2 'COLLEGE' 3 'POST-GRAD'
    DIV 1 'OFFICE' 2 'MANUFACTURING' 3 'SALES'
BEGIN DATA
ABBOTT, MARIE   0 1 1 35 1 1575 16 5
ALLEN, JOSEPH   1 1 1 31 2 1980 10 3
.
.
.

ZIM MER, CONNIE 1 1 1 55 1 1675 20 2
END DATA
FREQUENCIES VARIABLES = SEX, RACE, DEGREE, DIV, EXEMPT
FINISH
```

To generate additional output from other commands, just insert the additional commands anywhere between the END DATA command and the FINISH command. In the remaining chapters of this book, various computer techniques will be illustrated by issuing various commands to the computer through the SPSSX program. Any SPSSX command that is mentioned in the rest of the book can be inserted anywhere after the END DATA command and before the FINISH command. The SPSSX program executes the commands in the order in which they appear in the program.

Figure 2.2 shows the computer output generated by the SPSSX program in Figure 2.1. The computer output indicates that there are 45 female and 75 male employees. Thus, 37.5% of the employees are female and 62.5% are female. For the variable DEGREE, the value 1 occurs 89 times, 2 occurs 23 times, and 3 occurs 8 times. This means that 74.2% of the employees have high school degrees, 19.2% have college degrees, and 6.7% have postgraduate degrees. The other three variables can be similarly evaluated.

An SAS Computer Program

The SAS computer program is another widely used statistical program that can produce frequency distributions. The SAS listing in Figure 2.3 was used to request frequency distributions for the variables in Table 2.1. These distributions are shown in Figure 2.4. The program in Figure 2.3 also generates a vertical bar chart for the variable DEGREE,

FIGURE 2.2 SPSSX output for the program in Figure 2.1.

SEX

VALUE LABEL	VALUE	FREQUENCY	PERCENT	VALID PERCENT	CUM PERCENT
FEMALE	.00	45	37.5	37.5	37.5
MALE	1.00	75	62.5	62.5	100.0
	TOTAL	120	100.0	100.0	

VALID CASES 120 MISSING CASES 0

RACE

VALUE LABEL	VALUE	FREQUENCY	PERCENT	VALID PERCENT	CUM PERCENT
BLACK	.00	24	20.0	20.0	20.0
WHITE	1.00	96	80.0	80.0	100.0
	TOTAL	120	100.0	100.0	

VALID CASES 120 MISSING CASES 0

DEGREE

VALUE LABEL	VALUE	FREQUENCY	PERCENT	VALID PERCENT	CUM PERCENT
HIGH SCHOOL	1.00	89	74.2	74.2	74.2
COLLEGE	2.00	23	19.2	19.2	93.3
POST-GRAD	3.00	8	6.7	6.7	100.0
	TOTAL	120	100.0	100.0	

VALID CASES 120 MISSING CASES 0

DIV

VALUE LABEL	VALUE	FREQUENCY	PERCENT	VALID PERCENT	CUM PERCENT
OFFICE	1.00	38	31.7	31.7	31.7
MANUFACTURING	2.00	58	48.3	48.3	80.0
SALES	3.00	24	20.0	20.0	100.0
	TOTAL	120	100.0	100.0	

VALID CASES 120 MISSING CASES 0

EXEMPT

VALUE LABEL	VALUE	FREQUENCY	PERCENT	VALID PERCENT	CUM PERCENT
	1.00	21	17.5	17.5	17.5
	2.00	40	33.3	33.3	50.8
	3.00	26	21.7	21.7	72.5
	4.00	17	14.2	14.2	86.7
	5.00	12	10.0	10.0	96.7
	6.00	4	3.3	3.3	100.0
	TOTAL	120	100.0	100.0	

VALID CASES 120 MISSING CASES 0

FIGURE 2.3 SAS program to obtain frequency distributions for data in Table 2.1.

```
DATA;
INPUT LNAME$, FNAME$, SEX, RACE, DEGREE, AGE, DIV, SALARY,
SENIOR, EXEMPT;
CARDS;
ABBOTT, MARIE    0 1 1 35 1 1575 16 5
ALLEN, JOSEPH    1 1 1 31 2 1980 10 3
.
.
.
ZIM MER, CONNIE 1 1 1 55 1 1675 20 2
;
PROC FREQ;
 TABLES SEX RACE DEGREE DIV EXEMPT;
PROC CHART
 VBAR DEGREE;
```

which is shown in Figure 2.5. In SAS, every command ends with a semicolon. To generate additional results, new commands would be added at the end of the program. An explanation of the SAS program is as follows:

- The program starts with a DATA command.
- The INPUT command gives names to the variables. (A dollar sign following a variable name indicates that the data are letters rather than numbers.)
- The CARDS command indicates to SAS that the data follow.
- Next come the data.
- The semicolon (;) indicates the end of the data.
- The PROC FREQ command requests a frequency distribution.
- The TABLES command requests a frequency distribution for each of the variables specified.
- The PROC CHART command requests a bar chart.
- The VBAR command generates a vertical bar chart for the specified variable. The bar chart produced here shows how many employees have each type of academic degree.

Suppose the manager of Computech wanted to examine the variables AGE, SENIOR, and SALARY. For example, what is the average salary of the sample of 120 employees? Does salary vary with years of seniority? In later chapters, we will show how to use the SPSSX and SAS programs to answer these and other questions. Occasionally we will also show output from the Minitab statistical package. For information on Minitab, consult the study guide for this book. Figure 2.6 (page 36) shows a Minitab program and the corresponding output of frequency distributions for the variables SEX, RACE, DEGREE, DIV, and EXEMPT.

Throughout the book we will use the data in Table 2.1 to demonstrate new analyses and relationships.

FIGURE 2.4
SAS output for the program in Figure 2.3.

SAS

SEX	FREQUENCY	PERCENT	CUMULATIVE FREQUENCY	CUMULATIVE PERCENT
0	47	39.2	47	39.2
1	73	60.8	120	100.0

RACE	FREQUENCY	PERCENT	CUMULATIVE FREQUENCY	CUMULATIVE PERCENT
0	24	20.0	24	20.0
1	96	80.0	120	100.0

DEGREE	FREQUENCY	PERCENT	CUMULATIVE FREQUENCY	CUMULATIVE PERCENT
1	89	74.2	89	74.2
2	23	19.2	112	93.3
3	8	6.7	120	100.0

DIV	FREQUENCY	PERCENT	CUMULATIVE FREQUENCY	CUMULATIVE PERCENT
1	38	31.7	38	31.7
2	58	48.3	96	80.0
3	24	20.0	120	100.0

EXEMPT	FREQUENCY	PERCENT	CUMULATIVE FREQUENCY	CUMULATIVE PERCENT
1	21	17.5	21	17.5
2	40	33.3	61	50.8
3	26	21.7	87	72.5
4	17	14.2	104	86.7
5	12	10.0	116	96.7
6	4	3.3	120	100.0

FIGURE 2.5 SAS bar chart for the variable DEGREE in Table 2.1.

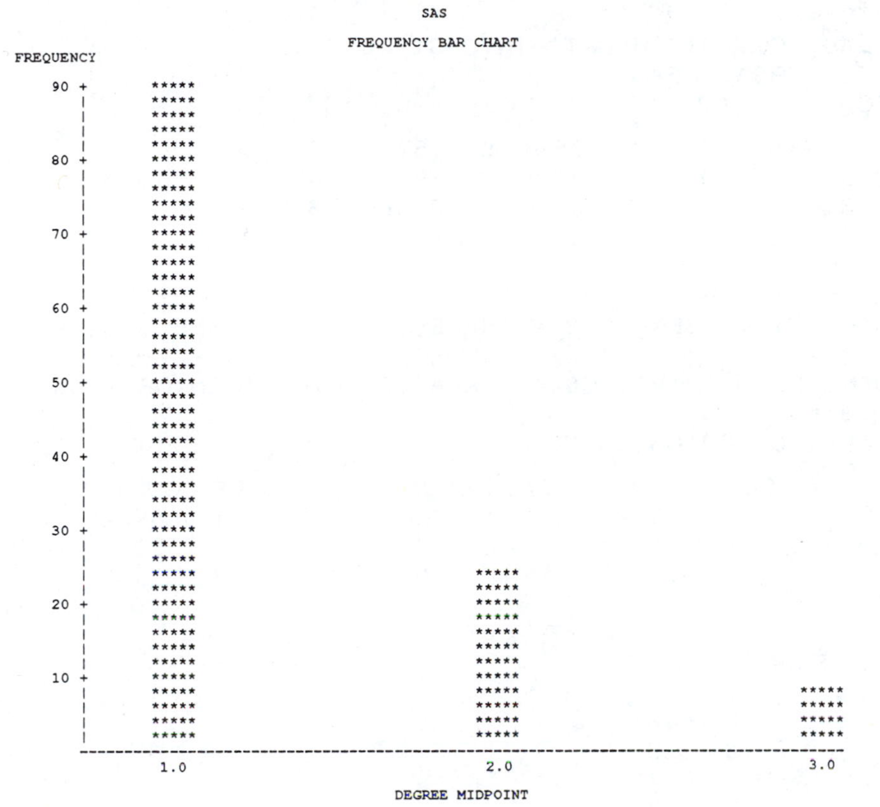

Exercises for Section 2.4

1. The data in Table 2.2 (pages 37–38) show selected characteristics of a sample of 50 students in a statistics class. The qualitative variables are coded at the end of the table. Use the computer to perform the following tasks and answer the following questions:

a. Generate a frequency distribution and determine what proportion of students are male and female.

b. What proportion of students are freshmen? Sophomores? Juniors? Seniors?

c. What proportion of students are in-state students? Out-of-state?

d. What proportion of students are economics majors? Math majors?

2. The data in Table 2.3 (pages 38–39) show information on the 50 states and the District of Columbia from *The Statistical Abstract of the United States, 1987*. The variables are coded at the end of the table; in your data set, name the six variables PCTUNION, SALARY, REVENUE, EXPEND, INCOME, and WAGE.

a. Create an SPSSX program to read these data. After the END DATA command, insert a LIST command, which tells the computer to print out the data.

b. Insert the following command into your program:

```
SCATTERGRAM SALARY WITH INCOME
```

FIGURE 2.6 Minitab program and output showing frequency distributions for data in Table 2.1.

```
MTB >
READ 'COMPUTECH.DAT' INTO C1-C8
  120 ROWS READ
ROW   C1   C2   C3   C4   C5     C6   C7   C8

  1    0    1    1   35    1   1575   16    5
  2    1    1    1   31    2   1980   10    3
  3    1    1    1   51    2   2480   28    2
  4    0    1    1   57    1   1925   30    2

MTB >
NAME C1 = 'SEX', C2 = 'RACE', C3 = 'DEGREE', C4 = 'AGE'
MTB >
NAME C5 = 'DIV', C6 = 'SALARY', C7 = 'SENIOR', C8 = 'EXEMPT'
MTB >
TALLY C1,C2,C3,C5,C8

        SEX COUNT      RACE COUNT      DEGREE COUNT      DIV COUNT
          0    47         0    24           1    89        1    38
          1    73         1    96           2    23        2    58
         N=   120        N=   120           3     8        3    24
                                           N=   120       N=   120

     EXEMPT COUNT
          1    21
          2    40
          3    26
          4    17
          5    12
          6     4
         N=   120

MTB >
STOP
```

This command will plot the salary and income data for each state. Examine this plot. Do states with the highest incomes per capita seem to pay the highest teacher salaries?

c. Are any of these variables discrete?

3. The data in Table 2.4 (page 40) show annual values from 1960 through 1986 for the following variables: the Gross National Product (GNP), federal government spending (TOTALGOV), federal government defense spending (DEFENSE), the national unemployment rate (URATE), the Consumer Price Index (CPI), the 6-month Treasury bill rate (TBILL), and the Dow Jones Industrial Index (DOWJONES). All data were taken from the *1987 Economic Report of the President*.

a. Create an SPSSX program that will read the data in Table 2.4. Use the variable names given in the table.

b. For each variable, create a time plot in which the values of the variable are plotted against time on a scatter diagram and connect the points. For example, to create a scatter diagram of GNP versus time, issue the command

```
SCATTERGRAM GNP WITH DATE
```

TABLE 2.2
Selected characteristics of statistics students

Name	Sex	Class	Residence	Major	SAT Score	GPA
Abel	0	2	1	1	1350	3.80
Barth	1	3	1	2	1240	3.25
Bell	0	3	0	0	1200	3.06
Bond	1	1	1	0	1200	3.32
Cohen	0	3	0	2	1230	3.23
Cross	0	4	1	3	1140	2.94
Cruz	1	4	1	2	900	2.43
Daley	1	2	1	1	1120	2.70
Davis	0	3	0	4	990	2.98
Dunne	1	4	0	3	1020	2.60
Ebel	0	4	1	1	990	2.65
Fong	0	3	1	1	1000	2.78
Ghent	1	4	0	4	910	2.37
Grant	0	4	1	3	970	2.59
Hale	0	1	1	0	1300	3.45
Hand	1	2	1	2	1000	2.55
Hart	1	2	1	4	1120	3.24
Hill	0	3	1	0	1140	3.02
James	1	4	0	1	1200	3.11
Jones	0	3	0	3	990	2.87
Kane	1	2	1	3	1040	2.69
Keim	0	2	1	1	1460	3.50
King	1	4	0	2	880	2.29
Klem	1	4	0	4	920	2.54
Land	0	3	1	3	1220	3.14
Lane	1	4	0	0	950	2.44
Levy	1	2	1	2	1140	3.12
Link	0	2	1	3	1230	3.22
Lott	0	3	0	3	1240	3.20
Luddy	0	4	0	4	930	2.45
Lyle	1	4	0	2	1000	2.61
Mann	1	3	1	3	1030	2.82
Mills	0	1	0	2	970	2.35
Mott	0	3	0	3	1140	2.94
Otis	0	3	0	1	1220	3.22
Ott	1	2	1	2	1130	2.69
Rand	1	1	1	1	1140	2.73
Reams	0	2	0	4	1330	3.72
Riley	0	1	0	1	1220	2.94
Rose	0	3	0	0	1310	3.51

continued

TABLE 2.2 continued

Name	Sex	Class	Residence	Major	SAT Score	GPA
Sand	1	2	1	4	1360	3.48
Smith	1	4	1	1	960	2.43
Thomas	0	3	1	3	1000	2.82
Tsiao	1	4	0	4	950	2.51
West	0	2	1	1	1490	3.68
Wiley	1	3	1	2	1300	3.00
Wolfe	0	3	0	3	1190	2.87
Wulf	0	3	0	2	1240	2.94
Yates	1	4	1	2	1160	2.71
Zorn	1	4	1	4	960	2.56

Codes:
Sex: (0 = male, 1 = female)
Class: (1 = freshman, 2 = sophomore, 3 = junior, 4 = senior)
Residence: (0 = in-state, 1 = out-of-state)
Major: (0 = undecided, 1 = economics, 2 = business, 3 = math, 4 = other)

TABLE 2.3 Selected characteristics of 50 states and Washington, D.C.

	X_1	X_2	X_3	X_4	X_5	X_6
Alabama	18.2	22,934	2729	1931	10,673	8.48
Alaska	30.4	41,480	8349	11,886	18,187	12.19
Arizona	12.8	24,680	2829	2082	12,795	9.47
Arkansas	13.2	19,538	2642	1619	10,476	7.57
California	25.4	29,132	3608	2524	16,065	10.12
Colorado	18.0	25,892	4042	2333	14,182	9.52
Connecticut	18.9	26,610	4888	2426	18,189	9.57
Delaware	20.3	24,624	4517	2735	14,272	9.84
D.C.	33.4	33,990	5020	4722	18,168	10.48
Florida	9.6	22,250	3731	1836	13,742	7.86
Georgia	12.7	22,080	2980	2010	12,543	8.02
Hawaii	31.5	25,845	3766	2535	13,814	8.65
Idaho	16.1	20,969	2509	1772	11,120	9.41
Illinois	27.5	27,190	3621	2232	14,738	10.37
Indiana	25.1	24,274	3159	1876	12,446	10.71
Iowa	20.5	21,690	3390	2141	12,594	10.32
Kansas	12.0	22,644	3476	2187	13,775	9.46

continued

TABLE 2.3 continued

	X_1	X_2	X_3	X_4	X_5	X_6
Kentucky	20.4	20,940	2853	1768	10,824	9.53
Louisiana	13.8	20,460	3124	2210	11,274	10.43
Maine	18.5	19,583	3346	2042	11,887	8.40
Maryland	18.6	27,186	4349	2414	15,864	9.73
Massachusetts	19.7	26,800	4642	2435	16,380	9.00
Michigan	33.7	30,168	3782	2630	13,608	12.64
Minnesota	24.5	27,360	3982	2926	14,087	10.05
Mississippi	9.3	18,443	2305	1761	9,187	7.22
Missouri	26.6	21,974	3155	1726	13,244	9.56
Montana	21.7	22,482	3947	2600	10,974	10.97
Nebraska	16.3	20,939	3285	2202	13,281	9.03
Nevada	22.1	25,610	2932	2351	14,488	9.15
New Hampshire	22.3	20,263	3114	1827	14,964	8.39
New Jersey	19.9	27,170	5536	2518	17,211	9.90
New Mexico	12.8	22,644	3402	3044	10,914	8.42
New York	35.8	30,678	5710	3296	16,050	9.67
North Carolina	8.9	22,795	3366	1750	11,617	7.29
North Dakota	14.2	20,816	3059	2694	12,052	8.06
Ohio	27.4	24,500	3547	2073	13,226	11.38
Oklahoma	12.9	21,419	2752	2021	12,232	9.86
Oregon	27.5	25,788	4123	2467	12,622	10.49
Pennsylvania	27.0	25,853	4168	2115	13,437	9.57
Rhode Island	19.4	29,470	4669	2470	13,906	7.59
South Carolina	5.8	21,570	2920	1743	10,586	7.61
South Dakota	10.3	18,095	2967	2221	11,161	7.44
Tennessee	17.3	21,800	2533	1666	11,243	8.29
Texas	12.5	25,160	3429	1923	13,483	9.41
Utah	16.8	22,341	2297	2275	10,493	9.40
Vermont	11.9	20,325	3554	2304	12,117	8.41
Virginia	10.9	23,382	3594	1952	14,542	8.52
Washington	32.9	26,015	3705	2369	13,876	11.70
West Virginia	28.9	20,627	2821	1930	10,193	10.42
Wisconsin	24.5	26,525	4247	2474	13,154	10.26
Wyoming	15.6	27,244	5440	4929	13,223	9.93

Code: X_1 = percentage of employees who are unionized
X_2 = average annual salary of teachers in the state
X_3 = average tax revenue per capita in the state
X_4 = average government expenditures per pupil in the state
X_5 = average personal income per capita
X_6 = average hourly earnings in manufacturing

TABLE 2.4 **Various economic variables**

DATE	GNP	TOTAL-GOV	DE-FENSE	URATE	CPI	TBILL	DOW-JONES
1960	515	54.5	45.3	5.4	88.7	3.247	618.04
1961	534	58.2	47.9	6.5	89.6	2.065	691.55
1962	575	64.6	52.1	5.4	90.6	2.908	639.76
1963	607	65.7	51.5	5.5	91.7	3.253	714.81
1964	650	66.4	50.4	5.0	92.9	3.686	834.05
1965	705	68.7	51.0	4.4	94.5	4.055	910.88
1966	772	80.4	62.0	3.7	97.2	5.082	873.60
1967	816	92.7	73.4	3.7	100.0	4.630	879.12
1968	873	100.1	79.1	3.5	104.2	5.470	906.00
1969	964	100.0	78.9	3.4	109.8	6.853	876.72
1970	1016	98.8	76.8	4.8	116.3	6.562	753.19
1971	1103	99.8	74.1	5.8	121.3	4.511	884.76
1972	1213	105.8	77.4	5.5	125.3	4.466	950.71
1973	1359	106.4	77.5	4.8	133.1	7.178	923.88
1974	1473	116.2	82.6	5.5	147.7	7.926	759.37
1975	1598	129.2	89.6	8.3	161.2	6.122	802.49
1976	1783	136.3	93.4	7.6	170.5	5.266	974.92
1977	1991	151.1	100.9	6.9	181.5	5.510	894.63
1978	2250	161.8	108.9	6.0	195.4	7.572	820.23
1979	2508	178.0	121.9	5.8	217.4	10.017	844.40
1980	2732	208.1	142.7	7.0	246.8	11.374	891.41
1981	3053	242.2	167.5	7.5	272.4	13.776	932.92
1982	3166	272.2	193.8	9.5	289.4	11.084	884.36
1983	3406	283.5	214.4	9.5	298.4	8.750	1190.34
1984	3765	311.3	235.0	7.4	311.1	9.800	1178.48
1985	3998	354.1	259.4	7.1	322.2	7.660	1328.23
1986	4209	367.2	278.4	6.9	328.4	6.032	1792.76

4. A survey was conducted to examine voter preferences. The following data were obtained from a sample of six people who were interviewed:

Name	Sex	Age	Voter Registration	Employment Status
Rogers	Male	38	Yes	Looking
Jones	Male	52	No	Employed
Kelly	Female	31	Yes	Housewife
Harmon	Female	21	Don't know	Student
Berry	Male	66	No	Retired

a. Discuss how to code the responses for each variable.
b. Using your coding scheme, code each case in the table.

Chapter 2 Summary

A *variable* is a quantity or quality that may take on more than one value. A *population* is the set of all observations on a given variable and a *sample* is a subset of a population. A *parameter* is a characteristic of a population and a *statistic* is a characteristic of a sample. Sample statistics are used to estimate population parameters.

Variables can be qualitative or quantitative and discrete or continuous. A *discrete variable* may assume only certain values in a range such as integers or categories. A *continuous variable* can assume any numerical value in a given interval.

In most statistical studies, we rely on samples of data to get information about the population. There are many different ways to obtain a sample of data. The problems with judgment or convenience samples are that they can be subject to *sampling bias* and we cannot use statistical techniques to determine the qualities of our estimators. With a biased sample, the accuracy of our estimators does not necessarily improve as the sample size increases. In a *simple random sample* from a finite population, every sample of size n has the same probability of being selected. When we examine a population in its entirety, we have taken a *census*.

There are many reasons for taking samples to estimate population characteristics, probably the two most important are speed and cost factors. Statisticians prefer random samples to judgment or convenience samples because random samples are not subject to sampling bias and because we can apply the laws of probability to random samples. *Sampling error* is the absolute value of the difference between the sample estimate and the true value of the population parameter being estimated. An estimator is biased if the average sampling error is not zero. Factors that can contribute to bias are sensitive questions, nonresponse of certain segments of the population, self-selection of individuals who will be included in the sample, and interviewer bias.

A *univariate analysis* is a study involving only one variable. A *multivariate analysis* involves studying two or more variables simultaneously. Chapter 3 discusses the most common ways of describing the characteristics of a population or sample of data involving a single variable and also includes a section showing how a multivariate analysis can be much more powerful and enlightening than a univariate analysis.

Chapter 2 ▪ Supplementary Exercises

1. Hotels often leave questionnaires concerning the quality of their service in the hotel rooms and ask the guests to fill them out. Do the results from such a procedure constitute a random sample? Why or why not?

2. Suppose that a firm wants to determine the mean income of the families in a particular city. The firm divides the city into six areas, each containing approximately the same number of families. The firm selects two of these areas randomly and then chooses a random sample of 100 families in each of these two areas.

a. What are the advantages of this sample design over a simple random sample of 200 families drawn from the entire suburb?

b. Is the result of this sample design likely to be as precise as the result of a random sample of 200 families drawn from the entire city?

3. Classify the following variables as qualitative or quantitative. Then classify the qualitative variables as dichotomous or multinomial and the quantitative variables as discrete or continuous.
a. The number of telephone calls received in a day by a secretary
b. The employment/unemployment status of an individual
c. The religion of an individual
d. The language spoken by an individual
e. The speed of a car on a racetrack

4. Classify the following variables as qualitative or quantitative. Then classify the qualitative variables as dichotomous or multinomial and the quantitative variables as discrete or continuous.
a. The sex of a randomly selected person in a restaurant
b. The number of individuals on a bus
c. The time required to drive from home to work
d. The age of a job applicant
e. The make of car owned by an individual

5. Classify the following variables as qualitative or quantitative. Then classify the qualitative variables as dichotomous or multinomial and the quantitative variables as discrete or continuous.
a. The number of female professors in the English department
b. The country of birth of a randomly selected graduate student
c. The favorite sport of a high school student
d. The color of an individual's hair
e. The brand of computer owned by a math professor
f. The volume of gasoline remaining in a storage tank

6. Consider the following situations and determine whether a census or sample would be more appropriate.
a. A doctor wants to study the side effects of a drug that appears to be effective against some types of cancer.
b. The Republican Party wants to determine what proportion of the electorate favors increased defense spending.
c. NASA wants to check all the components of a space shuttle fuel system.

7. Describe the type of sample that was taken in each of the following situations. Discuss whether you would expect to obtain biased results from each sample.
a. A newspaper reporter learns people's views on a presidential speech by interviewing people as they exit from a movie theater.
b. A reporter analyzes the stock market by examining the movements in the Dow Jones Industrial Index, which is a weighted average of 30 stock prices.
c. An inspector uses a random-number table to select a value from 1 to 20. Then the inspector examines that numbered item for defects and examines every 20th item thereafter. The goal is to find the proportion of defective items in a day's production run.
d. A congressman sends a questionnaire to all registered voters in the district. Replies are received from 20% of those receiving the questionnaire.
e. The dean's office wants to estimate the average annual income of the parents of students at a college. The dean tells an office worker to put the files in alphabetical order and to examine every 50th file.
f. The dean's office wants to estimate the average annual income of the parents of students at the college. The dean tells an office worker to sort the files according to the sex of the students. The dean tells the office worker to select every 50th file from the males and every 50th file from the females.

8. Describe how to obtain a systematic random sample of 200 bills at a department store from among 5000 bills.

9. Describe several ways of obtaining a sample of 10% of the employees of a firm containing 200 employees.

10. Describe what types of errors or biases (if any) are likely in the following situations:

a. A typist tends to hit the number 2 rather than the number 3 when recording the number of children in families.

b. An interviewer is told to contact 50 randomly selected families as part of a large survey to determine the average income in a community. The interviewer is unable to contact one of the families.

c. An interviewer is told to contact 50 randomly selected families as part of a large survey to determine the average income in a community. The interviewer contacts the families that live in the nice section of town and reports that the other families could not be contacted.

d. A radio announcer asks listeners to call the show to give their opinion about a controversial subject.

11. Which of the following methods is more likely to elicit correct information concerning the age of individuals, asking individuals to state their age or asking them to state their date of birth?

12. Describe a situation where it might be useful to use randomized response sampling.

13. Describe several situations where biased results are obtained because of self-selection bias.

14. Suppose a firm has 1000 employees. Describe how to take a simple random sample of 50 of the employees using the random-number table.

15. Suppose that a student's file contains information on the individual's sex, major, age, religion, grade point average, and monthly income of parents.

a. State whether each variable is qualitative or quantitative.

b. Describe how to code the qualitative variables numerically.

c. For each qualitative variable, describe whether it is dichotomous or multinomial.

d. State which variables are discrete and which are continuous.

16. Explain some problems in using the following procedures to obtain a random sample of a city's adult population.

a. Random-digit dialing, where a computer places calls to randomly generated phone numbers.

b. Random selection of ten places of employment and then random selection of employees within each place.

c. Selecting every tenth adult who enters a specific department store.

d. Randomly selecting children in the elementary schools in a city and then including their parents in the study.

17. You want to study the employees of the Vates Department Store. You have data like the following for the employees:

Name	Sex	Age	Education	Previous Employment	Religion
Jones	Male	45	High school	Accountant	Catholic
Smith	Female	22	College	None	Not reported
Clark	Male	?	High school	Clerk	Protestant
Hall	Female	35	No reply	Secretary	None

a. Discuss how to code the variable Sex so that it can be entered into a computer and analyzed.

b. For the variable Age, what will you do about Mr. Clark?

c. How will you code the variable Education so that it can be analyzed by the computer? What about Ms. Hall?

d. How will you code the variable Previous Employment so that it can be analyzed by the computer? What will you do about Ms. Smith?

e. How will you code the variable Religion so that it can be analyzed by the computer? What about Ms. Hall and Ms. Smith?

18. In the United States, about 10% of all women who divorce have a college degree, and about 5% have eight or fewer years of education. Do these data indicate that a woman with a grade school degree has a lower probability of getting a divorce than a woman with a college education? What is the correct way to interpret these data?

19. A researcher wants to estimate the average weight of all the students at the University of Tennessee. The researcher obtains a sample of data by asking the weights of the first 10 students in line when the dining hall opens for lunch at noon. What systematic biases might be introduced by this research procedure?

20. Obtain a sample of 50 students in order to estimate the proportion of students at your college who are left-handed. Tell how you selected these students and explain why you think this is a reasonable sampling procedure.

21. Estimate the proportion of students at your college who are out-of-state by obtaining a sample of 50 students. Tell how you selected these 25 students, and explain why you think this is a reasonable sampling procedure. Can you think of any reason why more care should be exercised in selecting this sample than in selecting a sample to estimate the proportion of left-handed people?

22. A television station includes a poll as part of its nightly news show. A provocative "question of the day" flashes on the screen and viewers are asked to call in their yes or no votes. Why might these poll results not be representative of community opinion?

23. A famous opinion poll asked blacks if the U.S. Army is unfair to blacks. Less than 15% said yes to white interviewers, but 35% said yes to black interviewers. What could account for this disparity?

24. A randomized response poll was given to 100 students in a statistics class. Each student was asked the following question:

> Is your birthdate an odd or even number? If it is even, please answer question (a); if it is odd, please answer question (b).
> (a) Are you a statistics student?
> (b) Have you ever cheated on a test?

Sixty yes answers and 40 no answers were obtained. If we assume that even and odd birthdates are equally likely, estimate the proportion of the class that has cheated on a test.

25. *Consumer Report*'s annual automobile issue includes frequency-of-repair records based on letters received from its readers. Is this a random sample? If not, what biases might appear?

26. The Census Bureau produces estimates of the lifetime earnings of people by age, sex, and education. Suppose that its analysis shows that, on the average, males with a high school degree can expect to earn just over $1.3 million from age 18 to age 64, while the average high school dropout can expect to earn about $601,000 for the same interval. Suppose John Smith is getting poor grades in high school and wants to quit high school and get a job. A teacher tells John that dropping out will cost him about $700,000. Is the teacher correct? Explain.

27. Health records show that males who have never smoked average 14.8 days of illness per year, while present smokers average 22.5 days and former smokers average 23.5 days. Do these data show that it is healthiest to never smoke, but once you start, it's better not to stop? Explain your answer.

28. Data show that people at bars consume more than twice as much beer if their beer comes in a pitcher than in a glass or bottle. A researcher therefore claims that banning pitchers in bars could help solve the drunk-driving problem. Suppose that, on average, bar patrons drink 44 ounces of beer per person when it comes from a pitcher but only 27 ounces from a bottle and 22 ounces from a glass. Is it reasonable to conclude that banning pitchers will reduce beer consumption? Explain.

29. The following question appeared on a randomized response poll of 100 people:

> Please flip a coin. If it is heads, write down yes. If it is tails, please answer this question truthfully: "Have you ever shoplifted?"

The answers turned out to be 58 yes and 42 no. Estimate the proportion of the population that has shoplifted.

30. A randomized response poll of 600 people included this question:

> Please flip this coin and then answer question (a) if a head appears and (b) if a tail appears.
> (a) Please roll this die and write down the number that comes up.
> (b) Please write down the number (from 1 to 6) that is closest to your annual income (in 10,000s of dollars).

The answers obtained were:

Number	1	2	3	4	5	6
Responses	110	160	120	90	70	50

Use these data and estimate the proportion of people with the following incomes:

a. From $25,000 to $35,000
b. From $35,000 to $45,000

References

COCHRAN, WILLIAM G. *Sampling Techniques*. 3d ed. New York: Wiley, 1977.

COCHRAN, WILLIAM G., and G. M. COX. *Experimental Designs*. 2d ed. New York: Wiley, 1957.

HUFF, DARRELL. *How to Take a Chance*. New York: Norton, 1959.

HUFF, DARRELL, and IRVING GEIS. *How to Lie with Statistics*. New York: Norton, 1954.

MORGENSTERN, OSKAR. *On the Accuracy of Economic Observations*. 2d ed. Princeton: Princeton University Press, 1963.

NIE, NORMAN, C. HADLAI HULL, JEAN G. JENKINS, KARIN STEINBRENNER, and DALE H. BENT. *SPSS Statistical Package for the Social Sciences*. 2d ed. New York: McGraw-Hill, 1975.

NORUSIS, MARIJA J. *SPSSX Introductory Statistics Guide*. New York: McGraw-Hill, 1983.

______. *SPSSX Advanced Statistics Guide*. Chicago: SPSS, 1985.

______. *The SPSS Guide to Data Analysis*. Chicago: SPSS, 1986.

RYAN, THOMAS A., BRIAN L. JOINER, and BARBARA F. RYAN. *Minitab Reference Manual*. University Park, Penn.: Minitab Project, 1985.

______. *Minitab Handbook*. 2d ed. Boston: PWS-Kent, 1985.

SAS Introductory Guide. 3d ed. Cary, N.C.: SAS Institute, 1985.

SAS Procedures Guide for Personal Computers. Version 6 ed. Cary, N.C.: SAS Institute, 1986.

SAS Statistics Guide for Personal Computers. Version 6 ed. Cary, N.C.: SAS Institute, 1986.

SAS User's Guide: Basics. Version 5 ed. Cary, N.C.: SAS Institute, 1985.

SAS User's Guide: Statistics. Version 5 ed. Cary, N.C.: SAS Institute, 1985.

SPSSX User's Guide. Chicago: SPSS, 1983.

TANUR, JUDITH M., FREDERICK MOSTELLER, WILLIAM H. KRUSKAL, RICHARD F. LINK, RICHARD S. PIETERS, and GERALD R. RISING., eds. *Statistics: A Guide to the Unknown*. 2d ed. San Francisco: Holden-Day, 1978.

WALD, ABRAHAM. *Sequential Analysis*. New York: Wiley, 1947.

——. *Statistical Decision Functions*. New York: Wiley, 1950.

Chapter Three
Summarizing Data in Tables and Graphs

As mentioned in Chapter 1, *descriptive statistics* is a branch of statistics consisting of procedures used to describe the general characteristics of a set of data. Basically, descriptive statistics entails grouping, graphing, and summarizing data so that an investigator can get insights or information that may not be apparent from the raw data.

Any set of data worth studying possesses one quite obvious characteristic: The observations are not all the same; that is, there is a spread, or *distribution,* of observations. The purpose of descriptive statistics is to describe this distribution in a concise manner.

For example, suppose we have a sample of observations showing the annual incomes of pilots for Delta Airlines. Suppose we draw a horizontal number line and place a mark on the line at the value of each annual income. It would be natural to observe how the observations are distributed over different portions of the line and where most of the observations are concentrated, to look for the center of the data, and to notice the amount of variation present. The center of the data would give us an estimate of the average income of the pilots. By observing the amount of variation, we could determine if the incomes of all the pilots are approximately equal to one another or if they differ substantially.

There are three commonly used methods of describing the characteristics of a set of data:

1. *Tables:* The data can be presented in **tables**, which show how the data are dispersed or distributed. We will discuss four types of tables in Section 3.1, *frequency distributions, relative frequency distributions, cumulative frequency distributions,* and *cumulative relative frequency distributions*.

2. *Graphs:* Each of the four types of frequency distributions can be presented as a **graph**. The graph of a frequency distribution is called a *histogram.* Histograms provide a visual display of how the data are distributed.

3. *Summary statistics:* The general characteristics of the data can be described by means of **summary statistics**, which describe the center of a data set, the amount of variation present, and other interesting characteristics of the data. The *mean,* the *median,* and the *mode* are different measures of the center of data. These summary statistics are called **measures of central tendency**. The *range,* the *standard deviation,* the *variance,* and the *mean absolute deviation* are different measures of the amount of variation present in data and are called **measures of dispersion**.

In this chapter, we will discuss tables and graphs. Chapter 4 discusses how to calculate and interpret summary statistics. All of the statistical procedures discussed in this chapter can be performed quite easily using computer programs that are readily available. Occasionally computer output generated by one of three popular computer programs—SPSSX (Statistical Package for the Social Sciences, Version X), SAS (Statistical Analysis System), or Minitab—will be used as illustrations. SPSSX and SAS are probably the best and most widely used computer programs for performing statistical analyses. There are numerous other statistical packages available, however, that generate essentially the same type of output. Minitab is a more user-friendly but less powerful program. Once the student learns how to read and understand the output from one statistical package, it is usually a simple task to learn how to read the output from other statistical packages.

3.1 ▪ *Frequency Distributions and Histograms*

As a first step in almost every statistical study, it is useful to describe the data in terms of a *frequency distribution*. The task of interpreting most data sets is usually made somewhat easier by reducing the amount of information that must be absorbed by grouping the observations in intervals and counting how many observations fall in each interval. The intervals are called **classes**, and the number of observations falling in any class is called the **frequency** of that class.

Definition: Frequency Distribution

A **frequency distribution** is a table that shows the number of observations falling in each class. The number of observations in the ith class is called the **class frequency** and is denoted by the symbol f_i.

Frequency distributions can be constructed both for populations and samples of data. Frequency distributions are especially useful when the number of observations is so large that it is difficult to get a good feel for the data by examining the observations individually.

Constructing a Frequency Distribution

The first step in constructing a frequency distribution is to define the class intervals. The second step is to count and record how many observations fall in each class.

Usually there are many different ways of choosing the classes. For example, the Bureau of the Census annually publishes a document called the *Current Population Report,* which contains frequency distributions of the annual incomes earned by full-time employees in the United States. One frequency distribution is a table that shows how many employees earn from \$0 to less than \$10,000 per year, how many earn from \$10,000 to less than \$20,000, and so forth. The bureau could have used different classes in the tables, such as \$0 to \$15,000, \$15,000 to \$30,000, and so forth. The person constructing the frequency distribution determines the number of classes and their location, but there are some general guidelines, which will be discussed later in this section.

Except for what are called *open-ended classes,* each class for a quantitative variable must have a **lower limit** and an **upper limit**, which together are called **class boundaries**. For example, the frequency distribution for incomes described above by the Bureau of the Census uses $0 and $10,000 for the lower and upper limits of the first class, respectively.

A class is **open-ended** if it has no lower limit or no upper limit. Open-ended intervals occur frequently when the data have a large amount of variation and most of the observations are concentrated in a fairly narrow range. This is common with income data, where an open-ended class might consist of all individuals who earn, say, $80,000 per year or more.

The **width** of any class is the upper limit minus the lower limit. For example, if a class consists of all individuals who earn from $20,000 to less than $30,000, then the width of the class is $10,000. (Note that an open-ended class does not have a width because one of the limits is not defined.)

The **class mark**, also called the **class midpoint**, is the arithmetic average of the two class limits. For example, if the class limits are $20,000 and $30,000, then the class mark is $25,000. (Note that an open-ended class does not have a class mark because one of the limits is not defined.)

Once the number of classes and the class limits have been chosen, the final step in constructing a frequency distribution is to count and record how many observations fall into each class.

Two Rules for Selecting Classes

Any system of classification used for a frequency distribution must satisfy the following two requirements: (1) The classes must be mutually exclusive, and (2) the classes must be exhaustive.

1. The classes in any frequency distribution must be *mutually exclusive*. The classes must be defined so that no observation can fall into more than one class. Frequently it is useful to choose classes so that the upper limit is excluded from that class. For example, when exact incomes are reported, the classes could be, say, $0 to less than $10,000, $10,000 to less than $20,000, and so forth. This notation makes it clear that an individual whose income is exactly $20,000 would be placed in the third class. Sometimes it can be useful to choose as class boundaries values that do not or cannot appear in the raw data. For example, suppose we wish to construct a frequency distribution showing the years of education of individuals. Here it might be useful to use as classes 5.5 to 7.5 years, 7.5 to 9.5 years, and so forth.

2. The classes should be *exhaustive;* that is, every observation must fall into some class. It may be necessary to construct an open-ended class to satisfy this requirement.

Helpful Guidelines

Frequently the construction of a satisfactory frequency distribution requires experimentation with the number of classes and the class boundaries. There are no rules available that apply to all situations. There are, however, some general guidelines that are helpful in constructing a frequency distribution.

1. *Number of classes:* Usually the number of classes should be between 5 and 20. As the number of observations increases, more classes are appropriate. If there are too many classes, the graph will be less effective because the frequency distribution will tend to have a choppy appearance. If there are too few classes, the distribution will give little insight into the underlying pattern of how the data are distributed, and much of the variation in the data will be obscured. A large number of classes provide more detail, but too many produce meaningless oscillations. It is common to construct several frequency distributions using different numbers of classes and different class limits to see if the shape of the distribution changes much when the classes are changed. Select the distribution that appears to give the most logical explanation of the underlying population pattern.

2. *Width of classes:* The choice of the class width depends on the range of the data (that is, the difference between the largest and the smallest observation), the number of observations, and the number of classes desired. For ease of interpretation, it is preferable that all classes have equal widths.

Occasionally class intervals must have unequal widths. This is often the case with income data and other data sets where the difference between the largest value and the smallest value is very large and where most of the observations are concentrated in a relatively narrow range. If most of the observations fall into a relatively narrow interval while others are widely dispersed, it may be desirable to have narrow classes where the bulk of the observations lie and wider classes elsewhere. In addition, it may be necessary to use open-ended classes.

3. *Choice of class limits:* Try to select class limits so that the class midpoint, or class mark, of each class is close to the average of the observations included in each class. The reason for this is that when calculating averages and other summary measures from frequency distributions, we assume that the class midpoint is representative of all the values in the class. (This will be discussed further in Chapter 4.) Often this can be accomplished without special concern about the class limits. Sometimes, however, the values tend to be bunched at regular intervals throughout the data. For example, many small items cost a few cents less than an even dollar, say, $1.99 or $2.99, while many large consumer items tend to be a few dollars less than $100, $200, $300, and so forth. In this latter case, it would probably be best to define class intervals as $50 to under $150, $150 to under $250, and so forth, rather than as $0 to under $100, $100 to under $200, and so forth. Another reason for requiring that class midpoints be representative of the observations falling in a class is that a graph of the distribution will present a more reliable picture of the true location of the data.

Relative Frequency Distributions

A frequency distribution shows the number of observations falling in each class. Usually it is more useful to indicate the *relative frequency,* or *proportion,* of observations that fall into each specific class.

Definitions: Relative Frequency and Relative Frequency Distribution

The **relative frequency** of the ith class is the proportion of observations falling in that class. If the ith class contains f_i observations, then the relative frequency of the ith class is f_i/n, where n denotes the total number of observations in the sample. If we are working with a population containing N observations, then the relative frequency of the ith class is f_i/N. A **relative frequency distribution** is a table that shows the proportion of observations that fall into each class.

Every relative frequency must be a nonnegative number greater than or equal to 0 and less than or equal to 1, and the sum of all the relative frequencies must equal 1.

Example 3.1 **A Frequency and Relative Frequency Distribution:** The raw data in Table 3.1 show the monthly salaries of all the employees at Lang's Trucking Company, a small trucking firm with 80 employees. To get a feel for the salary structure of the company, Mr. Lang needs to have the data simplified and condensed. Construct a frequency distribution and a relative frequency distribution to obtain information on the distribution of salaries.

TABLE 3.1 **Monthly salaries (in dollars) of employees at Lang's Trucking Company**

1550	1310	1575	1675	1585	1590	1580	1475	1300	1650
1380	1730	1640	2000	1400	1325	1900	1600	1600	1555
1565	1320	1750	1725	1650	1740	1650	1875	1620	1550
1590	1570	2015	1620	1860	1625	2000	1850	1640	1900
1700	1380	1620	1650	2000	1455	1625	1340	1530	1410
1450	1815	1440	1420	1550	1550	1660	1760	1550	1650
1500	1620	1600	1580	1705	1780	1400	1550	1390	1600
1775	2025	1450	1425	1820	1900	1700	1900	1475	1850

Solution: First, it is necessary to choose the number of classes and the class limits. The smallest observation is \$1300 and the largest is \$2025, so the range is \$2025 − \$1300, or \$725. Because it is convenient to use classes with a width of \$100, let's form 8 classes using the class limits \$1300, \$1400, . . . , \$2100. The first class contains all observations from \$1300 to under \$1400, the second class contains all observations from \$1400 to under \$1500, and so on up to the eighth class, which contains all observations from \$2000 to under \$2100.

After selecting the classes, the only task remaining is to count and record the number of observations belonging to each class. An easy way to do this is to prepare a *tally sheet* like the one shown in Table 3.2. On the tally sheet, each slash indicates one observation. The number of slashes for each class is the class frequency. In addition, the tally sheet provides a visual display of how the data are distributed.

The data in the column titled "Frequency" show the number of observations falling in each class. The sum of the frequencies must equal the total number of observations.

TABLE 3.2 **Tally sheet and frequency distribution of data in Table 3.1**

Monthly Salary (dollars)	Tally	Frequency	Relative Frequency
1300 to under 1400	///// ///	8	.1000
1400 to under 1500	///// ///// /	11	.1375
1500 to under 1600	///// ///// ///// //	17	.2125
1600 to under 1700	///// ///// ///// ////	19	.2375
1700 to under 1800	///// /////	10	.1250
1800 to under 1900	///// /	6	.0750
1900 to under 2000	////	4	.0500
2000 to under 2100	/////	5	.0625
Total		80	1.0000

The data in the column headed "Relative Frequency" show the proportion, or relative frequency, of observations falling in each class. The relative frequencies are obtained by dividing each class frequency by 80, the total number of observations. For example, the frequency of the first class is 8, so the relative frequency for the first class is 8/80, or .1000. The relative frequencies sum to 1.

The frequencies in Table 3.2 indicate that more monthly salaries fall in the $1600-to-$1700 interval than any other. The relative frequencies show that only 6.25% of the employees earn more than $2000 per month, and only 11.25% of the employees earn more than $1900 per month. On the other hand, 71.25% of the employees earn from $1400 to $1800. A glance at the distribution of tallies indicates that the center of the data appears to be between $1600 and $1700. The tally sheet also shows that the distribution of salaries is slightly bell shaped, with most salaries concentrated in a middle range and fewer salaries located in the tails of the distribution. ■

Graphing Frequency Distributions

Along with a frequency distribution, it usually is useful to prepare a graph showing how the values are distributed.

Definition: Frequency Histogram

A **frequency histogram** is a graphical presentation of a frequency distribution.

A histogram shows the general shape of the distribution and gives a quick visual impression of where most of the observations are concentrated. We can see if the distribution has long tails in either direction and whether there are any extreme or unusual values. We can also see where the data are centered and whether the center of the data is a good indicator of a typical observation. In addition, we can see how tightly the observations are clustered around a central value.

The histogram for the data in Table 3.2 is shown in Figure 3.1. In a histogram, the class boundaries are marked on the horizontal scale as in Figure 3.1, and the frequency of each class is measured on the vertical axis. Above each class interval, a rectangle is

FIGURE 3.1
Histogram for data in Table 3.2.

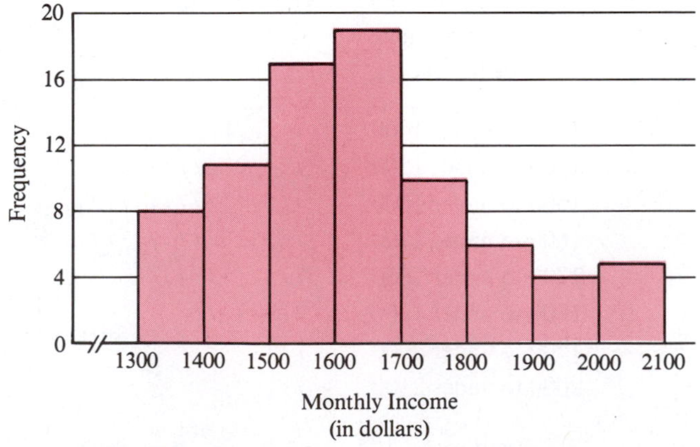

constructed whose area is proportional to the frequency of the class. If the classes all have equal widths, the height of each rectangle can be used to represent the frequency of the class.

Histograms with Classes of Unequal Widths

Remember that the frequency of a class is indicated on a histogram by the *area* of the rectangle above that class interval. When classes have unequal widths, the heights of the rectangles cannot be used to indicate class frequencies. For example, suppose that in a certain frequency distribution 500 observations fall between 1200 and 1400 and 500 observations fall between 1400 and 1500. The first class is twice as wide as the second class, but both classes contain the same number of observations. This indicates that, in a sense, the observations are twice as densely concentrated in the second class as in the first class. To represent this distribution on a histogram correctly, the height of the rectangle above the second class interval should be twice the height of the rectangle above the first. By making this adjustment, the areas of the two rectangles will be equal and thus correctly represent the class frequencies (which are equal).

A *relative frequency histogram* is similar to a frequency histogram except that the areas of the rectangles above each class interval indicate the relative frequency of the class rather than the actual frequency of the class, although the overall shapes of the frequency histogram and the relative frequency histogram are identical. The relative frequency distribution for the data in Table 3.2 is shown in Figure 3.2.

FIGURE 3.2
Relative frequency histogram for data in Table 3.2.

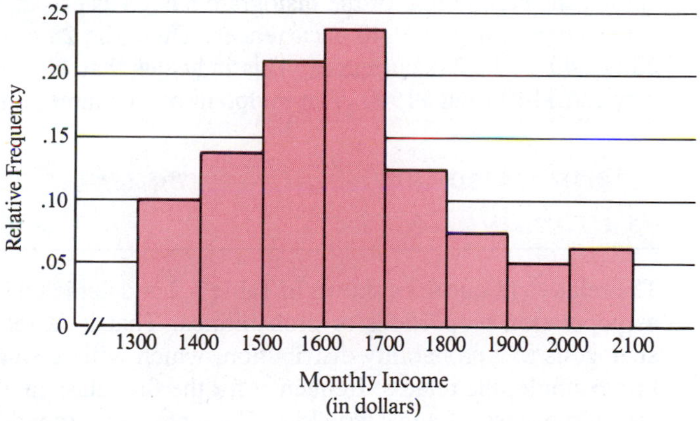

Computer Output

Figure 3.3 shows a histogram for the salary data in Table 3.1 generated by the SPSSX command FREQUENCIES. (Many other computer programs will generate output comparable to the SPSSX output.) The actual command that generated this output was the following:

```
FREQUENCIES VARIABLES = SALARY/
    HISTOGRAM MIN(1300) MAX(2100) INCREMENT(100)
```

FIGURE 3.3 **SPSSX-generated histogram of data in Table 3.1.**

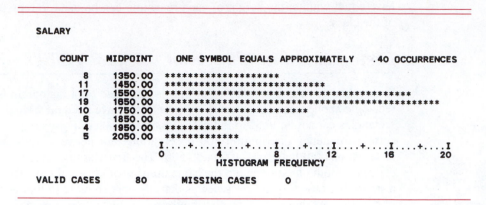

```
SALARY

    COUNT   MIDPOINT    ONE SYMBOL EQUALS APPROXIMATELY   .40 OCCURRENCES

       8     1350.00   ********************
      11     1450.00   ****************************
      17     1550.00   *******************************************
      19     1650.00   ************************************************
      10     1750.00   *************************
       6     1850.00   ***************
       4     1950.00   **********
       5     2050.00   *************
                      I....+....I....+....I....+....I....+....I....+....I
                      0         4         8        12        16        20
                                HISTOGRAM FREQUENCY

VALID CASES      80       MISSING CASES      0
```

This command tells the computer to use the procedure called FREQUENCIES to generate a frequency distribution and a histogram for the variable SALARY. The histogram should start at the minimum value 1300 and end at the maximum value 2100 with a class width of 100.

In Figure 3.3, the numbers in the first column titled "COUNT" show the class frequencies. The second column titled "MIDPOINT" gives the class mark, or midpoint, for each class. For example, the midpoint for the first class is $1350. Each row of asterisks represents the number of observations that falls in that class interval. For example, the second row of the histogram has 28 asterisks, and each asterisk in the graph equals approximately 0.40 occurrences. Thus, the 28 asterisks represent approximately $28 \times .40 = 11.2$ occurrences. This indicates that 11 employees have monthly salaries between $1400 and $1500. The midpoint of this interval is $1450.

Interpretation of Relative Frequencies as Probabilities

The relative frequencies shown in Table 3.2 and depicted in Figure 3.2 can be interpreted as population proportions or probabilities. That is, a relative frequency distribution is analogous to a probability distribution, which will be studied in detail in later chapters. For example, the relative frequency for the first class in Table 3.2 indicates that 10% of the employees at Lang's Trucking Company have monthly salaries from $1300 to less than $1400. If 1 of the 80 employees was selected randomly, the probability would be 10% that the employee had a monthly salary from $1300 to less than $1400.

Using Relative Frequencies to Compare Different Variables

Relative frequencies are more useful than absolute frequencies for comparing different samples of data, especially when the samples are of different sizes. For example, suppose that 20 women in a sample of 200 women have a college degree and that 40 men in a sample of 400 men have a college degree. A person who examined just the absolute frequencies might get the mistaken impression that men are more likely than women to have college degrees, although 10% of each group have college degrees.

Cumulative Frequency Distributions

Frequently we want to consider not only the number of observations in a particular class but also the total number of observations that fall in a particular class and all previous classes. This number is called the *cumulative frequency* of the class.

Definitions: Cumulative Frequency and Cumulative Frequency Distribution

Let f_i represent the class frequency of class i in a frequency distribution. The **cumulative frequency** of the ith class is the sum of the first i class frequencies. The cumulative frequency for the ith class can be obtained by using the formula

Cumulative frequency for class $i = f_1 + f_2 + \cdots + f_i$

The **cumulative frequency distribution** is a table that shows the cumulative frequency for each class in the frequency distribution.

Finally, we may want to consider the *proportion* of observations in a particular class and all previous classes. These proportions are called *cumulative relative frequencies.* A cumulative relative frequency shows the proportion of observations that are less than or equal to any specific value.

Definitions: Cumulative Relative Frequency and Cumulative Relative Frequency Distribution

The **cumulative relative frequency** of the ith class shows the proportion of observations falling in the ith class and all previous classes. It is the sum of the first i relative frequencies. A **cumulative relative frequency distribution** is a table that shows the cumulative relative frequency for each class in a frequency distribution.

Example 3.2

A Cumulative Frequency Distribution: Table 3.3 shows the cumulative frequency and cumulative relative frequency distributions obtained from the frequency distribution in Table 3.2. The first two columns of Table 3.3 repeat the class frequencies and class relative frequencies in Table 3.2. The last two columns of Table 3.3 show the cumulative frequency distribution and the cumulative relative frequency distribution.

For example, under the column headed "Cumulative Frequency," the third entry is the value 36. This indicates that 36 employees have a monthly income less than or equal to $1600. This cumulative frequency equals the sum of the first three class frequencies, 8 + 11 + 17.

The cumulative relative frequency for the third class is .4500, which indicates that 45% of the employees have monthly salaries less than or equal to $1600. The cumulative relative frequency for the third class is the sum of the class relative frequencies for the first three classes, .1000 + .1375 + .2125. Alternatively, the cumulative relative fre-

TABLE 3.3 Cumulative frequency distribution of data in Table 3.2

Monthly Salary (dollars)	Frequency	Relative Frequency	Cumulative Frequency	Cumulative Relative Frequency
1300 to under 1400	8	.1000	8	.1000
1400 to under 1500	11	.1375	19	.2375
1500 to under 1600	17	.2125	36	.4500
1600 to under 1700	19	.2375	55	.6875
1700 to under 1800	10	.1250	65	.8125
1800 to under 1900	6	.0750	71	.8875
1900 to under 2000	4	.0500	75	.9375
2000 to under 2100	5	.0625	80	1.0000
Total	80	1.0000		

quency for the third class is the class cumulative frequency divided by the number of observations; that is, 36/80 = .45. ■

The information in a cumulative frequency distribution and in a cumulative relative frequency distribution can also be presented graphically. Figure 3.4 shows the cumulative relative frequency histogram for the data in Table 3.3. In the figure, the area above each class interval is proportional to the cumulative relative frequency of the class.

FIGURE 3.4 Cumulative relative frequency distribution of data in Table 3.3

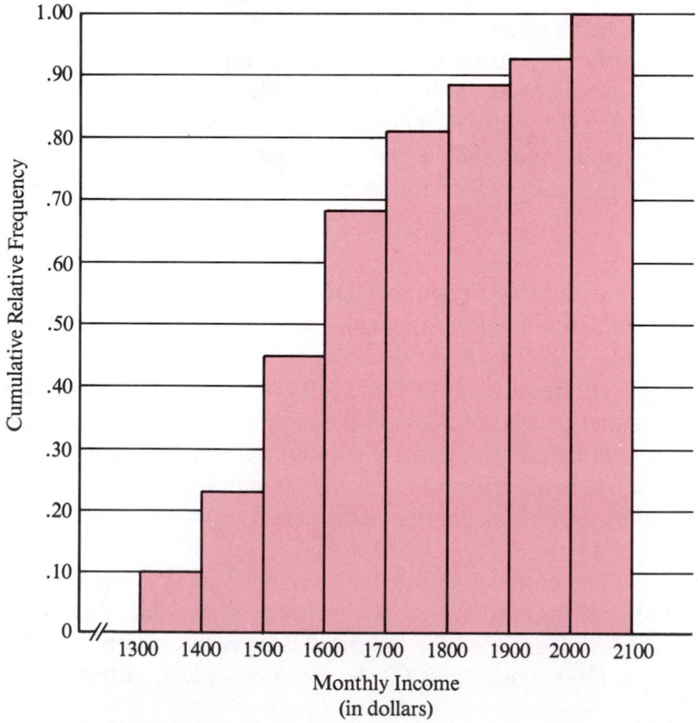

Frequency Distributions with Irregular Classes

Occasionally a frequency distribution will contain an open-ended class or classes with varying widths. Both of these characteristics are common when the data are very spread out, as is the case with adult incomes. Most observations will fall in the low- to medium-income range, whereas only a few will be in the high-income range. To avoid constructing a very large number of classes, it may be necessary to form open-ended classes or classes with unequal widths. The following example illustrates these points.

Example 3.3

Open-ended Classes and Classes with Varying Widths: A municipality is planning to initiate a local income tax to fund a program to improve its schools and recreational facilities. Before determining what tax rate to use, the municipality needs to know the distribution of incomes in the community. A survey of 300 randomly selected individuals is obtained. Table 3.4 shows the frequency distribution and relative frequency distribution for the sample of 300 annual incomes.

TABLE 3.4 **Distribution with open-ended classes and classes with varying widths**

Annual Income	Class Mark	Frequency	Relative Frequency
$0 to under $20,000	10,000	44	.147
$20,000 to under $30,000	25,000	105	.350
$30,000 to under $40,000	35,000	80	.267
$40,000 to under $50,000	45,000	36	.120
$50,000 to under $75,000	62,500	19	.063
$75,000 and higher	—	16	.053
Total		300	1.000

The last class is open-ended and does not have a class midpoint. Also, the classes have varying widths. The classes are narrower over the range covering most incomes; the first class and the last two classes are wider because fewer observations fall in these classes. ■

Frequency Distributions Using Integer Data

Frequently observations consist of a set of integers. In this case, class limits should be selected to insure that the class marks lie approximately in the middle of the class. Examples of variables that take only integer values are the number of children in a family and the number of rooms in a house. In these cases, we may want to form classes that contain both their upper and lower limits (such as 0 to 2, 3 to 5, etc.), that contain only a single point, or that have noninteger class limits (such as 3.5 to 5.5, 5.5 to 7.5, etc.).

As an example, suppose a real estate agent has a computer printout showing all houses for sale in a given community. The agent might classify houses as having 1 to 5 rooms, 6 to 10 rooms, and 11 to 15 rooms. In this case the classes could be 1 to 5, 6 to 10, and 11 to 15, and the class midpoints would be 3, 8, and 13, respectively. Each class would contain its class limits, and the width of each class would be 4.

In this example, it is not appropriate to denote the first class as 1 to under 6, since the class mark would be 3.5 and would not accurately represent the data contained in the class. As an alternative, the number of rooms in the house could be represented by the classes 0.5 to 5.5, 5.5 to 10.5, and 10.5 to 15.5; in this case, the class marks would again be 3, 8, and 13.

Example 3.4

A Frequency Distribution Based on Integer Data: The following data show the number of cars owned by a sample of 120 families who live in Detroit, Michigan:

2	1	3	1	2	1	2	3	4	2	2	0	5	2	1	1	2	2	0	2
2	3	1	1	0	3	2	4	2	1	2	3	1	1	2	2	1	2	4	3
2	0	1	1	2	3	1	2	0	1	2	3	2	5	2	1	1	2	3	0
0	2	1	1	3	1	2	1	3	0	1	2	2	1	1	2	3	2	1	2
2	3	0	2	2	1	1	2	2	3	2	1	2	2	1	4	2	2	1	2
2	1	2	1	2	1	4	5	2	1	1	2	1	1	2	3	1	2	1	4

Table 3.5 shows the frequency, relative frequency, cumulative frequency, and cumulative relative frequency distributions for these data. In the table, each class contains just a single point.

TABLE 3.5 **A frequency distribution based on integer data**

Number of Cars	Frequency	Relative Frequency	Cumulative Frequency	Cumulative Relative Frequency
0	9	.075	9	.075
1	39	.325	48	.400
2	48	.400	96	.800
3	15	.125	111	.925
4	6	.050	117	.975
5	3	.025	120	1.000
Total	120	1.000		

Observe that the relative frequency of the value 0 is .075, which means that 7.5% of the families in the sample do not own a car. Conversely, this means that 92.5% of the families in the sample own at least one car. The most frequent number of cars per family is two. In the sample, 40% of the families fall in this category.

Figure 3.5 shows the relative frequency histogram for the data in Table 3.5. In the histogram, the proportion of families with no car is represented by the area of the rectangle above the interval extending from -0.5 to 0.5; the proportion of families who own one car is represented by the area of the rectangle above the interval extending from 0.5 to 1.5; and so forth. Each class interval has a width of 1 unit and is centered at the appropriate integer. Because each rectangle has a width of 1 unit, the height of each rectangle represents the relative frequency of the class. ■

FIGURE 3.5
Relative frequency histogram for data in Table 3.5.

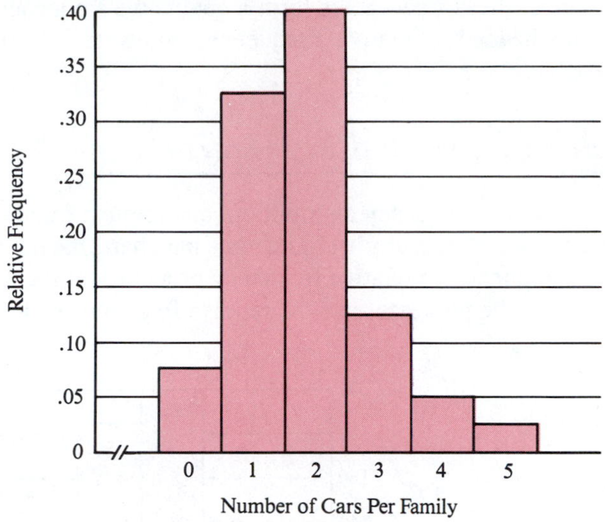

Analysis of Qualitative Variables

When the variable being studied is qualitative, we want to determine how many observations in a sample or population possess each specific value of the variable. Each value can be used to denote a class, or several values can be combined to form a single class. A table showing how many observations fall into each class is a frequency distribution of the qualitative variable.

Example 3.5

A Frequency Distribution Based on Qualitative Data: When studying the productivity of employees at a company, it is customary for economists to examine the educational background of the employees. The data in Table 3.6 show the highest academic degree earned by the 500 employees of the Cottrell Corporation. The data in the column headed "Frequency" show how many employees have the specified degree as their highest

TABLE 3.6
Frequency distribution based on qualitative data

Highest Degree	Frequency (number of employees)	Relative Frequency
Grade school	15	.03
High school	200	.40
Bachelor's	185	.37
Master's	55	.11
Doctorate	70	.14
Other	25	.05
Total	500	1.00

degree; these frequencies form a qualitative frequency distribution. The data in the column headed "Relative Frequency" show the proportion of employees falling into each class. ■

Bar Charts and Pie Charts

Qualitative frequency distributions and relative frequency distributions can be illustrated using **bar charts** or **pie charts**. In a bar chart, the height or length of each bar represents the frequency or relative frequency of a particular class. In a pie chart, the area of each slice of the pie represents the relative frequency of the particular class.

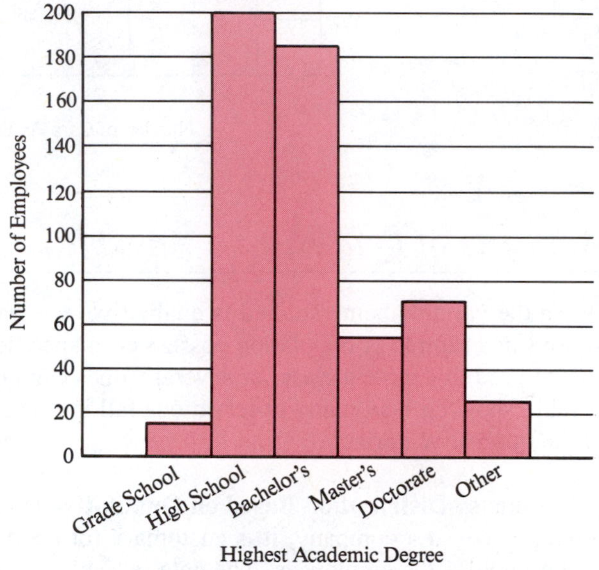

FIGURE 3.6
Bar chart for the data in Table 3.6.

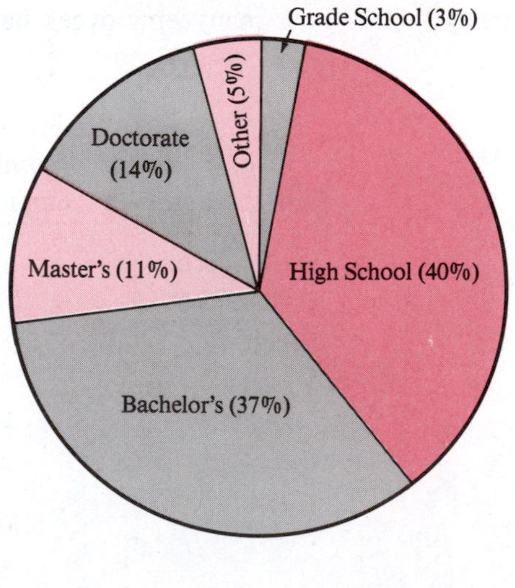

FIGURE 3.7
Pie chart for the data in Table 3.6.

Figure 3.6 is a bar chart that depicts the data presented in the frequency distribution in Table 3.6. For example, in Table 3.6, 200 of the employees listed high school as their highest degree. Thus, in the bar chart, the height of the bar above the title "High School" is 200 units. Figure 3.7 is a pie chart depicting the relative frequencies in Table 3.6. For example, in Table 3.6, 40% of the employees listed high school as their highest degree. Thus, in the pie chart, the area of the slice titled "High School" represents 40% of the entire pie.

Exercises for Section 3.1

1. The following data list the miles (in thousands) driven during the past four months by 50 sales representatives of a food distributor:

34	23	31	25	4	32	17	19	42	30
8	19	26	35	36	24	47	22	27	29
12	5	26	16	7	46	35	34	27	38
15	27	38	32	10	9	12	24	27	45
15	26	27	25	24	44	18	27	23	29

a. Construct a frequency distribution. As classes, use 0 to under 10, 10 to under 20, and so forth.
b. Construct the corresponding relative frequency distribution and cumulative frequency distribution.
c. Graph the histogram.

2. Repeat Exercise 1 but use the following classes: 0 to under 5, 5 to under 10, 10 to under 15, and so forth.
a. Comment on how the shape of the distribution changed and why.
b. Does the histogram in Exercise 1 or in this exercise better represent the data?

3. The following data show the number of cars owned by a sample of 50 households:

1	2	0	2	1	1	3	1	1	2
1	3	1	2	2	0	4	1	1	2
2	3	1	1	2	1	1	2	2	1
0	1	1	2	0	1	1	2	2	1
2	2	1	3	1	1	1	2	4	1

a. Construct a frequency distribution.
b. Construct the corresponding relative frequency distribution.
c. Construct the corresponding cumulative frequency distribution.
d. Construct the corresponding cumulative relative frequency distribution.
e. Graph each of the distributions above.

4. In the data that follow on page 62, 50 individuals are classified according to their highest academic degree.

Degree	Fre-quency
Grade school	5
High school	25
College	13
Postgraduate	7

a. Construct a relative frequency distribution.
b. Graph the relative frequency distribution as a bar chart.
c. Graph the relative frequency distribution as a pie chart.

5. Draw a pie chart to illustrate the following market shares by company in the U.S. soft drink industry: Coca-Cola, 36%; Pepsi-Cola, 25%; Dr. Pepper, 7%; Seven-Up, 6%; Royal Crown, 4%; others, 22%.

3.2 ▪ Common Shapes of Distributions

If we have the entire population of data, then we can construct histograms and relative frequency distributions for the population. Usually, however, only a sample of data is available, and our relative frequency graphs only approximate the curve for the population relative frequency. Frequency distributions and relative frequency distributions come in all shapes and sizes, but many special distributions and shapes of distributions occur regularly in statistical studies. Some of these distributions have been given special names, and a few will be described now.

Skewness and Symmetry

A distribution is said to be **symmetric** if the left half of the graph of the distribution is the mirror image of the right half. Figure 3.8 shows a symmetric distribution. A distribution is said to be **skewed** if it is not symmetric. A distribution is *skewed to the right* if the right-hand tail of the distribution is longer than the left tail and most of the observations are concentrated in the left side of the distribution. Figure 3.9 shows such a distribution.

FIGURE 3.8
A symmetric distribution.

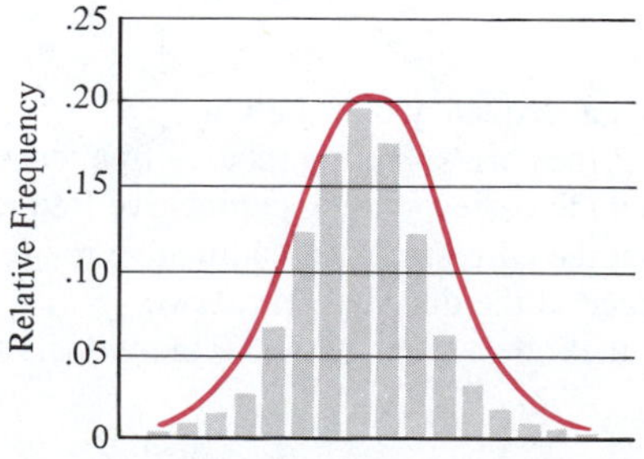

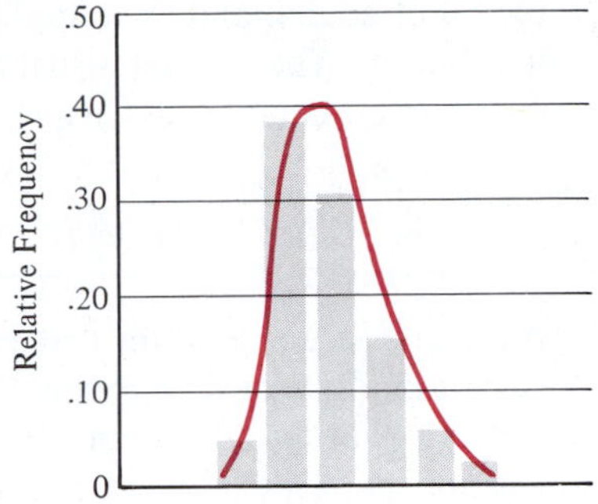

FIGURE 3.9
A distribution that is skewed to the right.

The distribution of annual incomes earned by adult males and the distribution of the wealth of individuals are probably the most obvious and important examples of distributions in economics that are skewed to the right. Most people have relatively modest incomes, but the incomes of the highest-income earners extend over a very wide range. Thus, most incomes are concentrated at the left side of the distribution, and the distribution has an extremely long right tail. The same pattern holds for the distribution of family wealth. Many other economic and demographic variables have distributions that are skewed to the right, including the annual sales of business firms in the United States, the population of cities and towns in the United States, and the number of cars owned by families.

A distribution is *skewed to the left* if the left-hand tail of the distribution is longer than the right-hand tail and most of the observations are concentrated in the right side of the distribution. Figure 3.10 shows a distribution that is skewed to the left. The age at death of U.S. citizens is an example of a variable whose distribution is skewed to the left. Most people die between the ages of 65 to 80, so most observations are concentrated toward the right side of the distribution. A long tail extends to the left, however, reflecting the frequencies of people who die between the ages of 0 and 60.

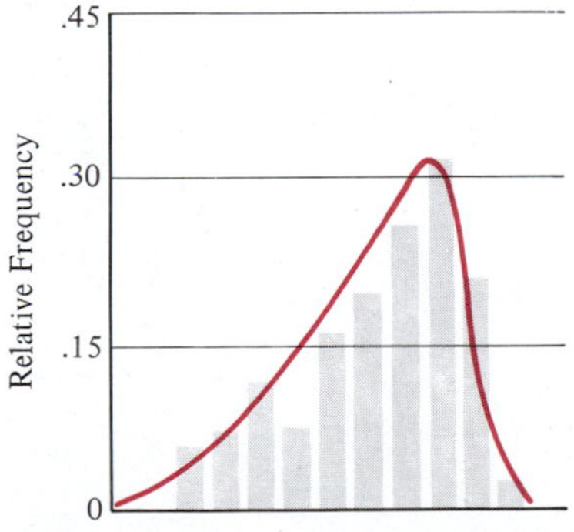

FIGURE 3.10
A distribution that is skewed to the left.

For many variables, most of the observations are concentrated near the middle of the distribution. As the distance from the middle increases, the frequencies and relative frequencies decrease. Such distributions are often described as "bell shaped." One example of such a distribution is called the **normal distribution**. A number of variables in nature and in society are approximately normally distributed, such as the height of adult males, the IQ of adults, and the blood pressure of adults. Figure 3.8 is an example of a normal distribution. The normal distribution, by far the most important distribution in statistics, is discussed in detail in Chapter 8.

Other Important Distributions

Figure 3.11 represents a distribution that peaks at the origin and then tails off to the right. This distribution, a type of **exponential distribution**, is skewed to the right and is useful in studying waiting-line or queuing problems. For example, the time between the arrivals of people entering a line at a grocery store or at a toll booth generally has an exponential distribution. The exponential distribution is studied in Chapter 8.

Figure 3.12 shows a graph of a **uniform distribution**. For variables with a uniform distribution, no particular interval of values has a higher relative frequency than any other interval of equal width. The uniform distribution is symmetric about its central value. Thus, if a variable takes some value between a lower limit a and an upper limit b and all values in this interval are equally likely, then the variable follows a uniform distribution. The uniform distribution is studied in Chapter 8.

FIGURE 3.11
An exponential distribution.

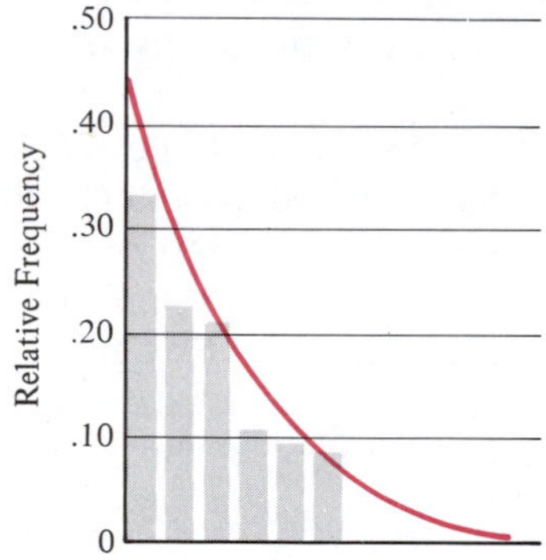

FIGURE 3.12
A uniform distribution.

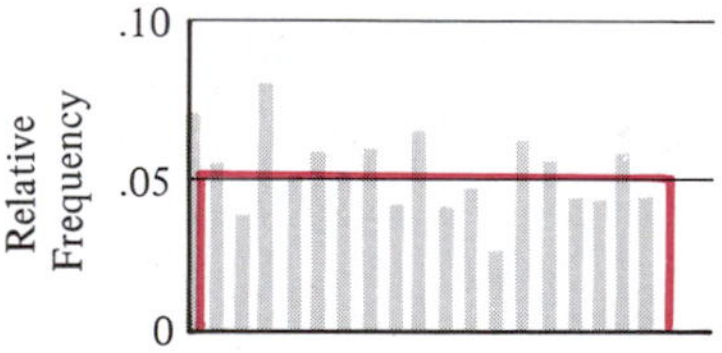

Unimodal and Bimodal Distributions

The location at which a population relative frequency distribution peaks is called the **mode** of the distribution. Distributions with only one peak are called *unimodal distributions;* distributions with two distinct peaks are called *bimodal distributions*. For example, the normal distribution shown in Figure 3.8 is a unimodal distribution, whereas Figure 3.13 is an example of a bimodal distribution.

A bimodal distribution is common in a population containing two nonhomogeneous sectors. For example, a relative frequency distribution of the heights of adults will have two distinct peaks, one at a value of about 64 inches and one at about 70 inches. The heights of males tend to cluster at about 70 inches, and those of females at 64 inches. If we separate the data into two subpopulations, one containing just males and one containing just females, we get two unimodal distributions. Similarly, a bimodal distribution results if we combine income data for college graduates with income data for high school graduates.

FIGURE 3.13
A bimodal distribution.

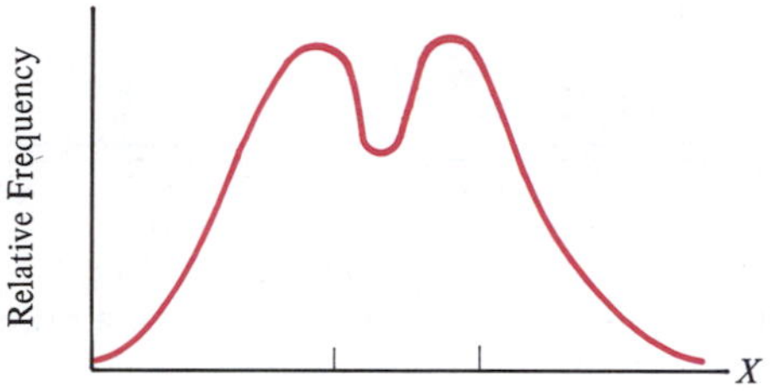

Populations Versus Samples

Keep in mind that the relative frequency distribution of a sample is different from the relative frequency distribution of the population from which the sample was drawn; although you may not have all the data needed to construct a population relative frequency distribution, such a distribution exists or can be imagined. Try to visualize this population relative frequency distribution, because the questions that statisticians try to answer concern this distribution.

Although we are interested in describing the characteristics of a sample of observations, we are more interested in describing the characteristics of the population from which the sample was selected. The most important feature of the graph of the sample relative frequency distribution is the information it provides about the population relative frequency distribution. The sample relative frequency distribution has approximately the same shape as the population relative frequency distribution, and the degree of similarity increases as the sample size increases.

Consider two relative frequency histograms, one based on a small sample of data and one based on a large sample. As the sample size increases, we obtain a better description of the data by decreasing the width of the class intervals. When the class intervals become small enough, a relative frequency histogram begins to look like a smooth curve. In the limit, this smooth curve represents the relative frequency histogram of the population. Figure 3.14 shows how the relative frequency distribution approaches a smooth curve as the number of observations increases and the width of the classes decreases.

FIGURE 3.14 **The relative frequency distribution approaches a smooth curve as sample size increases.**

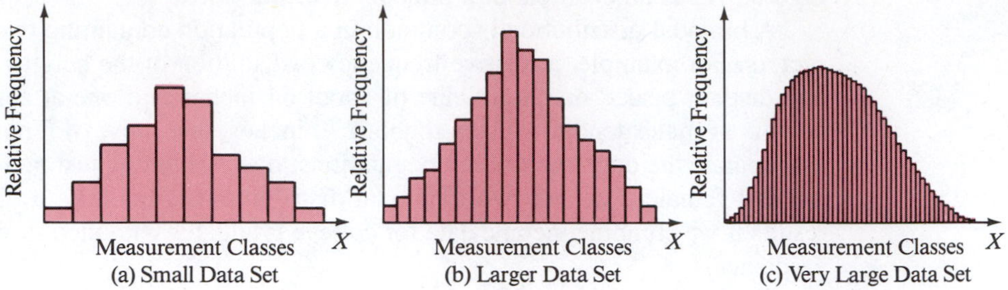

Exercises for Section 3.2

1. For each of the following variables, describe the likely shape of a histogram. Discuss if the distribution is likely to be symmetric, bell shaped, skewed to the right, skewed to the left, exponential, or uniform.
   a. Random numbers selected from the integers 0 to 9
   b. Ages of children at an elementary school
   c. Annual incomes of adult male college graduates in the United States
   d. Daily sales revenues at a small pizza shop
   e. Last digits of all telephone numbers in the Miami phone book

2. For each of the following variables, describe the likely shape of a histogram. Discuss if the distribution is likely to be symmetric, bell shaped, skewed to the right, skewed to the left, exponential, or uniform.
   a. The number of accidents incurred by a sample of 200 high school students last year
   b. The mileages traveled by all cars in the United States last year
   c. The amount deducted for charitable contributions when families file their income tax returns
   d. The age at which students receive their college degree
   e. The amount that households had in checking accounts on the last day of last year

3.3 ▪ *Lying with Statistics (Optional)*

In their famous book *How to Lie with Statistics,* D. Huff and I. Geis (New York: Norton, 1954) list numerous examples in which unscrupulous statisticians distorted data in order to mislead readers. At times it is possible to present a distorted picture of data even when one is trying one's best to be fair and honest. In this section we describe some common mistakes that people make when analyzing statistical data.

1. *Improper sizes of graphs:* Artists frequently draw a picture of some variable (such as a picture of a car to represent the annual dollar sales of cars) and indicate the magnitude of the variable by the size of the picture. For example, a person might be interested in describing the annual dollar sales of new cars between 1970 and 1985. Suppose that the dollar volume of car sales doubled during that time. To denote sales in 1970, the artist might draw a car 2 inches long and 1 inch high. To denote sales in 1985, the artist might then draw a car approximately 4 inches long and 2 inches high. The problem with this scale is that people usually compare areas of objects, not lengths. Because the area of the 4×2 inch car is 4 times larger than the area of the 2×1 inch drawing, the unwary reader might think that the dollar value of car sales had quadrupled between 1970 and 1985, rather than doubled.

2. *Emotional presentation of facts:* Occasionally a statistician can try to influence the opinion of the reader by using suggestive terms. For example, a statistician might report, "The monthly government income supplement given to permanently disabled war veterans is only $450 per month." By using the word *only* in this statement, the statistician would convey the impression that the monthly income supplement was too low. Whether or not the supplement was too low would be a subject for debate, but the statistician should not impose his or her views on the reader.

3. *Incomplete or inadequate numerical presentations:* Recently there was a legal case in Pennsylvania in which a woman claimed that her salary was too low and that she was the victim of sex discrimination. To support her claim, the woman produced a report comparing the salaries of males and females in five different departments of the company. The report stated that in three of the departments, every woman had a lower monthly salary than every man. On further analysis, it was found that there were only two women and three men in each of the three departments. In each department, each of the men had a master's degree in engineering, had been with the company for more than 10 years, and was responsible for doing complicated engineering analyses. In contrast, each of the females was a secretary without a college degree and with only a few years of experience. By hiding this information, the woman was trying to lead people to believe that women were underpaid. In the other two departments of the company, there were approximately 50 males and 50 females of varying educational backgrounds and with differing amounts of seniority, performing a myriad of different jobs. After taking into account their educational backgrounds, their seniority, and their duties, it was determined that neither men nor women were being paid inordinately high or low salaries.

Thus, before comparing incomes of individuals, we should take into account other factors, such as education, experience, length of service, and so forth. In the U.S. economy, males tend to earn more than females, and whites tend to earn more than nonwhites. At the same time, males tend to have more years of education than females and whites tend to have more years of education than nonwhites. Only after we have controlled for education (and other relevant variables) can we make conclusions concerning discrimination. A more detailed example of a problem similar to the one discussed here will be covered in the following section.

4. *Reading too much into a coincidence:* For 13 of the first 14 years in which the Super Bowl was played, the stock market went down when a team from the American Conference of the National Football League won, and went up when a team from the National Conference won. Suppose an American Conference team wins the next Super Bowl. Does this indicate that the stock market will drop during the following year? Even though the rule worked in 13 years out of 14, it is unreasonable to believe that the outcome of a football game could influence the stock market.

Given the large number of variables for which data have been collected, it should not be surprising that occasionally, just out of luck, some enterprising person will come across a few variables that are completely unrelated to one another but which tend to move together for a short period of time. Admittedly, the correlation between the behavior of the stock market and the outcome of the Super Bowl is unusual and surprising, but in this case, common sense should outweigh statistical evidence. Without a doubt, most statisticians would say that the correlation between the outcome of the Super Bowl and the behavior of the stock market is due to random chance. This is not unlike a person tossing a coin 14 times and calling heads or tails correctly on 13 of the tosses. If enough people try this feat, sooner or later someone will do it. This does not prove that the person can foretell the outcome of the next coin toss.

5. *Making general statements based on small samples:* It is very dangerous to make general statements about the properties of a population on the basis of a very small sample. Usually small samples contain too little information to make a conclusion with a high level of certainty. As we shall see when we discuss estimation and the construction of confidence intervals, generalization from a sample to a population becomes more reliable as the amount of sample evidence increases. When the sample is very small, one or two unusual observations can have a big effect on the outcome of the study. This is especially the case if the observations are selected from a population with a large amount of variation.

3.4 ▪ Bivariate Distributions

The distribution of a single variable is called a *univariate distribution*. However, some of the most interesting and most important problems in statistics involve the relationship between two or more variables. For example, we might want to examine how annual income is related to years of education or how the level of interest rates is related to the inflation rate. The branch of statistics devoted to the study of how different variables are related is called *multivariate statistical analysis*. A special case of multivariate analysis, the study of how two different variables are related, is called a *bivariate analysis*. We will spend a lot of time discussing bivariate and multivariate relationships later when we discuss correlation and regression techniques in Chapters 15 through 18. These are some of the most important and powerful of all statistical techniques. For now, we will restrict ourselves to the construction and interpretation of *bivariate frequency distributions*.

When we construct a bivariate frequency distribution, each observation is classified according to the values it takes for two different variables, and we record how many observations possess each possible combination of values. Each possible combination of values of the two variables is called a **cell**. In a bivariate distribution, a cell corresponds to the idea of a class in a univariate distribution. The number of observations that falls into a cell is called the **cell frequency**. As in a univariate distribution, the cells in any bivariate distribution must be mutually exclusive and exhaustive; each observation must fall into one and only one cell.

Definition: Bivariate Frequency Distribution

A **bivariate frequency distribution** is a table that shows all the cells and cell frequencies when observations are classified according to two different variables.

A bivariate frequency distribution of two variables can reveal much more information than two separate univariate frequency distributions for each variable.

Example 3.6

Two Univariate Distributions: Suppose that officials at a large state university in California are analyzing the characteristics of a sample of 2000 graduate students. Two of the variables being studied are sex and the place of home residence (Residence). It is observed that 1200, or 60%, of the students are male, and 800, or 40%, are female. This information yields the univariate frequency and relative frequency distribution for the variable Sex shown in Table 3.7.

TABLE 3.7
Univariate distribution of the variable Sex for 2000 students

Sex	Frequency	Relative Frequency
Male	1200	.600
Female	800	.400
Total	2000	1.000

TABLE 3.8
Univariate distribution of the variable Residence for 2000 students

Residence	Frequency	Relative Frequency
California	1400	.700
Out-of-state	240	.120
Foreign	360	.180
Total	2000	1.000

In addition, it is found that 1400, or 70%, of the students are from California; 240, or 12%, are from other states (out-of-state), and 360, or 18%, are from foreign countries. This information is shown in the univariate frequency distribution in Table 3.8. ■

Note that these two univariate distributions tell us absolutely nothing about any relationships between the two variables Sex and Residence. For example, there may be no foreign females or very few out-of-state males. To get this kind of information, we need to examine both variables simultaneously. Examine how much more information can be obtained by constructing a bivariate distribution, as shown in the following example.

Example 3.7

A Bivariate Frequency Distribution: Let's construct a bivariate distribution for the data in Example 3.6. The variable Sex has two possible values, "male" and "female." The variable Residence has three possible values, "California," "out-of-state," and "foreign." Each combination of a Sex value and a Residence value forms a cell, and each individual falls into one and only one cell. For example, all out-of-state males fall into one cell, all foreign females fall into another cell, and so forth. Because Sex has two possible values and Residence has three, there are $2 \times 3 = 6$ different cells.

Suppose that after placing each individual into a cell and counting the observations in each cell, we obtain the bivariate frequency distribution shown in Table 3.9. Note that Table 3.9 cannot be obtained from Tables 3.7 and 3.8, because two univariate tables tell us nothing about the relationship between the two variables.

In any bivariate frequency distribution, it is customary to present the data in rows and columns, where the rows identify the values of one variable and the columns identify the values of the other. Because Table 3.9 is a two-way classification table containing three rows and two columns, it is referred to as a 3×2 (read "3 by 2") table. In general, if one of the variables contains H possible values and the other contains K values, we obtain a table containing $H \times K$ cells.

TABLE 3.9
A bivariate frequency distribution

	Sex	
Residence	Male	Female
California	800	600
Out-of-state	100	140
Foreign	300	60

In Table 3.9, all students who are out-of-state and are male fall into one cell; all students who are foreign and are female fall into another cell; and so forth. This table shows only the six basic cell frequencies. Usually, however, the data are presented in a table like Table 3.10, which contains much more information. Table 3.10 is simply an expanded version of Table 3.9 that can be derived from the data in Table 3.9 alone.

TABLE 3.10
An expanded bivariate frequency distribution

	Sex		
Residence	Male	Female	Row Total
California			
Frequency	800	600	1400
Row proportion	.571	.429	
Column proportion	.667	.750	
Table proportion	.400	.300	.700
Out-of-state			
Frequency	100	140	240
Row proportion	.417	.587	
Column proportion	.083	.175	
Table proportion	.050	.070	.120
Foreign			
Frequency	300	60	360
Row proportion	.833	.167	
Column proportion	.250	.075	
Table proportion	.150	.030	.180
Column total	1200	800	2000
Column proportion	.600	.400	1.000

In Table 3.10, the top entry in each cell is the *cell frequency*. For example, there are 800 California males and 600 California females. The *row frequency* is the sum of all the frequencies in a particular row, and the *column frequency* is the sum of all frequencies in a particular column. For example, the row frequency for California is 1400, and the column frequency for males is 1200.

The second number shown in each cell, the cell's *row proportion* or *row relative frequency,* shows the proportion of all cases in a row that fall into a particular cell. For example, there are a total of 1400 California graduate students, of whom 800 are male. Thus of the 1400 California students, the proportion that is male is 800/1400, or .571.

To calculate any cell's row proportion, divide the individual cell frequency by the row frequency.

The third number in each cell is the cell's *column proportion,* or the *column relative frequency.* For example, there are 1200 male students, of whom 800 have a California residence. This implies that the proportion of males with a California residence is 800/1200, or .667. To calculate any cell's column proportion, divide the individual cell frequency by the column frequency.

The fourth number in each cell is the cell's *table proportion,* or *table relative frequency.* For example, there are 800 California males of the 2000 students in the sample. Thus, the table proportion for California males is 800/2000, or .400. To calculate any cell's table proportion, divide the individual cell frequency by the total number of observations in the entire sample.

The row and column frequencies, shown to the right of the cells and below the cells, respectively, are called **marginal frequencies.** The marginal frequencies show the total number of observations that falls in any row or any column of the table. These frequencies are called *marginal* because they are found in the margins of the table. For example, at the bottom of the table we see that there were a total of 1200 males and 800 females in the study. These values are the column marginal frequencies for the characteristics "male" and "female." Similarly, the marginal frequency in the first row for the residence characteristic "California" is 1400.

The numbers directly below the marginal frequencies are the *marginal relative frequencies* or *marginal proportions,* which show the proportion of observations falling in any specific row or column. For example, there are 1400 California students in the sample. Out of the 2000 students in the sample, this constitutes a marginal relative frequency for California students of 1400/2000, or .700. To calculate any marginal relative frequency, divide the marginal frequency by the total sample size. Note that the marginal frequencies and marginal relative frequencies are the same values that appear in the univariate distributions in Tables 3.7 and 3.8. It follows that these univariate distributions have condensed the information available in the bivariate distribution. The univariate distributions show only the sums of the row frequencies and the sums of the column frequencies.

In Table 3.10 the row, column, and table proportions convey different types of information, so it is important to choose carefully among them. In this example, the row proportions in the first row of cells indicate the distribution of males and females for California students, the row proportions in the second row of cells indicate the distribution of males and females for out-of-state students, and the row proportions in the third row of cells indicate the distribution of males and females for foreign students. Note that the row proportions for California show that 57.1% of the California students are male and 42.9% are female, while 41.7% of out-of-state students are male and 58.7% are female. An admissions officer or a recruiter might be interested in knowing why the row proportions are so different for California and out-of-state students.

The row proportions for foreign students indicate that 83.3% of foreign students are male and only 16.7% are female. The distribution of males and females among foreign students is totally different from the distribution of males and females for California or out-of-state students. The explanation is that the vast majority of foreign students in graduate school in the United States are male.

By examining the column proportions, you will note similar differences between the distribution of the variable Residence and the distribution of the variable Sex.

Because it is always possible to interchange the rows and columns of any table, there are no general rules about when to study row proportions and when to study column proportions. ■

Graphical Presentations of Bivariate Distributions

As with frequency distributions, visual representations of bivariate distributions are useful and can simplify the search for relationships between variables. Figure 3.15 is a bar chart showing the table relative frequencies in Table 3.10. The bar chart vividly shows that, among California students, males outnumber females; for out-of-state students, females outnumber males; and for foreign students, almost all students are male. Also, the chart shows that most males are from California and that there is a large proportion of foreign males. Of females, the vast majority are from California; there are very few foreign females.

FIGURE 3.15
A bivariate distribution for the data in Table 3.10.

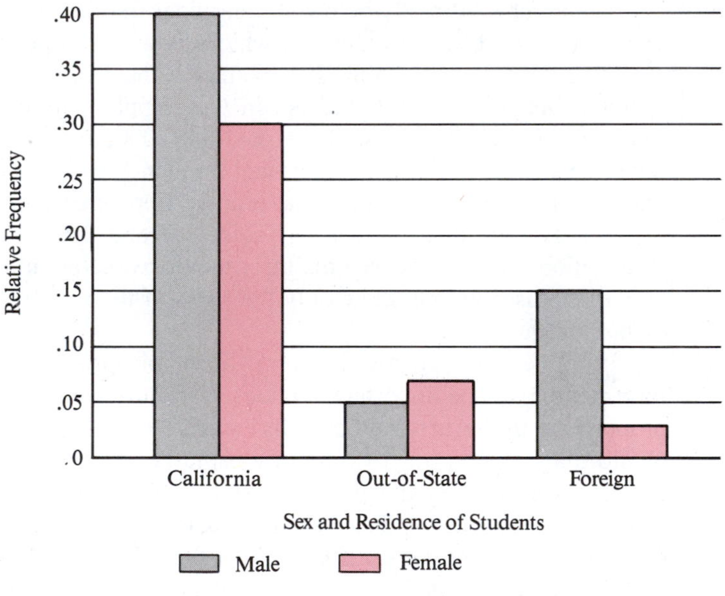

Computer Output

Figure 3.16 shows the SPSSX computer output obtained by analyzing the information for the 2000 graduate students in Table 3.10. In SPSSX, bivariate distributions are generated by a procedure called CROSSTABS. (This name is shorthand nota-

FIGURE 3.16
SPSSX-generated output for analysis of Table 3.10.

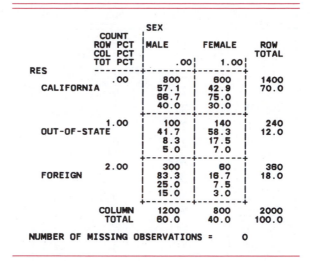

```
                          SEX
              COUNT     |
              ROW PCT   |MALE        FEMALE        ROW
              COL PCT   |                          TOTAL
              TOT PCT   |      .00|      1.00|
RES           ----------+---------+----------+
                    .00 |   800   |   600    |    1400
  CALIFORNIA            |   57.1  |   42.9   |    70.0
                        |   66.7  |   75.0   |
                        |   40.0  |   30.0   |
                        +---------+----------+
                   1.00 |   100   |   140    |     240
  OUT-OF-STATE          |   41.7  |   58.3   |    12.0
                        |    8.3  |   17.5   |
                        |    5.0  |    7.0   |
                        +---------+----------+
                   2.00 |   300   |    60    |     360
  FOREIGN               |   83.3  |   16.7   |    18.0
                        |   25.0  |    7.5   |
                        |   15.0  |    3.0   |
                        +---------+----------+
                 COLUMN     1200       800        2000
                  TOTAL     60.0      40.0       100.0

NUMBER OF MISSING OBSERVATIONS =          0
```

tion for "cross-tabulations".) The commands used to generate Figure 3.16 were the following:

```
CROSSTABS TABLES = RES BY SEX
OPTIONS 3,4,5
```

The CROSSTABS command tells the computer to create a bivariate frequency table based on the variables named RES and SEX. The OPTIONS command tells the computer to include the row percentages, the column percentages, and the table percentages in the printed output. The only difference between the data in Figure 3.16 and the data in Table 3.10 is that in SPSSX all the relative frequencies and marginal relative frequencies are indicated as percentages rather than proportions. Thus, the percentage of all students who are foreign females is shown as 3.0% in Figure 3.16, while Table 3.10 shows the proportion of all students who are foreign females as .030.

Exercises for Section 3.4

1. The data on page 74 show the sex of 60 applicants to medical school last year and whether the student was accepted. For the variable Sex, 0 denotes male and 1 denotes female; for the variable Status, 0 denotes not accepted and 1 denotes accepted.

a. Construct the bivariate frequency distribution.
b. Construct the bivariate relative frequency distribution.
c. Construct the marginal frequency distribution for sex.
d. Construct the marginal frequency distribution for application status.
e. What proportion of males were accepted?
f. What proportion of females were accepted?
g. Of the students who were accepted, what proportion were male?
h. Based on the information in parts (e) and (f), does it appear that the school might be discriminating against either males or females?

Student	Sex	Status	Student	Sex	Status	Student	Sex	Status
1	0	0	21	0	0	41	0	0
2	1	0	22	0	0	42	0	0
3	1	0	23	1	1	43	1	1
4	0	1	24	0	1	44	0	0
5	1	0	25	1	0	45	1	1
6	0	1	26	0	0	46	0	0
7	1	0	27	0	0	47	0	0
8	1	1	28	0	1	48	1	0
9	1	0	29	0	0	49	0	0
10	1	0	30	0	1	50	0	1
11	0	1	31	1	0	51	1	1
12	1	0	32	0	1	52	0	0
13	0	0	33	0	0	53	0	1
14	0	1	34	1	0	54	0	0
15	0	0	35	1	0	55	0	0
16	0	1	36	0	1	56	0	0
17	1	0	37	1	0	57	1	1
18	1	0	38	0	1	58	1	1
19	0	1	39	0	0	59	1	0
20	0	0	40	0	1	60	1	0

2. At the County Memorial Hospital, records classify each employee according to highest academic degree received {G = grade school, H = high school, C = college or higher} and department {A = administration, O = office, M = maintenance}. The data are as follows:

Degree	G	H	H	H	C	C	C	H	H	G	H	G	C	C	G	H	H	C	G	H
Job	M	O	O	O	A	O	A	O	A	M	A	O	A	O	O	O	M	A	O	O

Degree	H	G	H	C	C	C	G	H	G	H	H	C	C	G	H	H	C	G	H	C
Job	O	O	O	A	O	A	O	A	M	A	O	A	A	O	O	M	A	M	O	A

a. Construct the bivariate frequency distribution.
b. Construct the bivariate relative frequency distribution.
c. Construct the marginal frequency distribution for the variable Degree.
d. Construct the marginal frequency distribution for the variable Job.

3. Refer to the data in Exercise 2.

a. What proportion of employees with grade school degrees are employed in maintenance? In the office? In administration?
b. What proportion of employees with high school degrees are employed in maintenance? In the office? In administration?
c. What proportion of employees with college degrees are employed in maintenance? In the office? In administration?

4. Refer to the data in Exercise 2.
a. Of the employees in maintenance, what proportion have grade school degrees? High school degrees? College degrees?
b. Of the employees in the office, what proportion have grade school degrees? High school degrees? College degrees?
c. Of the employees in administration, what proportion have grade school degrees? High school degrees? College degrees?
d. Does there appear to be a relationship between academic degree and the type of job a person has at the hospital?

3.5 ▪ *A Case Study: Testing for Discrimination*

The outcomes of numerous legal cases have been influenced by statistical evidence presented during the trial. In this section we will provide an example that shows how important it is to take into account all the information relevant to a problem. In this example, we will show how to construct a *trivariate distribution,* where we take three variables into account simultaneously.

Suppose that a male has applied to graduate school at a prestigious university and has been rejected. The student files suit claiming that the university is discriminating against males in an effort to increase female enrollment. Suppose the university has data indicating the sex of each applicant, the field of study, and whether the applicant was admitted or rejected. After reviewing the data, the rejected student presents as evidence at the trial a bivariate frequency distribution, shown in Table 3.11, indicating the numbers of males and females who were accepted and rejected.

TABLE 3.11
Bivariate frequency distribution showing Sex Versus Admission Status

	Admission Status		
Sex	Admitted	Rejected	Total
Male	460	2740	3200
Female	830	470	1300
Total	1290	3210	4500

The student argues that an examination of the row relative frequencies shows that the university is discriminating against male students. Of the 3200 males who applied for admission, 2740, or 85.6%, were rejected. In contrast, only 470 of 1300 female applicants were rejected, or 36.1%. The rejected student claims that the difference between the two rejection rates of 85.6% and 36.1% is far too large to be due to chance.

In its defense, the university argues that the student has misrepresented the data because the influence of a third variable, Field of Study, has been ignored. The university presents a *trivariate frequency distribution,* shown in Table 3.12, that shows frequencies for all possible combinations of the three variables Sex, Admission Status, and Field of Study. The variable Field of Study assumes one of the values "engineering," "science," or "education." The university claims that by taking into account the applicant's proposed field of study, it is easy to show that there was no sexual discrimination during the admissions process.

TABLE 3.12
Trivariate frequency distribution showing Sex Versus Admission Status Versus Field of Study

School	Sex	Admission Status		
		Admitted	Rejected	Total
Science	Male	100	900	1000
	Female	10	90	100
Engineering	Male	200	1800	2000
	Female	20	180	200
Education	Male	160	40	200
	Female	800	200	1000
Total		1290	3210	4500

For example, in the School of Science, there were 1000 male applicants of whom 100 were admitted and 900 rejected, and 100 female applicants of whom 10 were admitted and 90 rejected. In the School of Engineering, of 2000 male applications, 200 were admitted and of 200 female applicants, 20 were admitted. In the School of Education, there were 200 male applicants, of whom 160 were admitted, and there were 1000 female applicants of whom 800 were admitted.

The university argues that the correct way to analyze the data is to compare row relative frequencies from the *trivariate table,* Table 3.12, rather than from the *bivariate table,* Table 3.11. In all three fields, the same percentages of male and female applicants were rejected (90% of the science applicants, 90% of the engineering applicants, and 20% of the education applicants).

The male student combined data from three heterogeneous sources, namely applicants to the three different schools, and did not take into account the information provided by the applicants' choice of school. The School of Science and the School of Engineering both have very high rejection rates, and both had many more male than female applicants. On the other hand, the School of Education has a very low rejection rate and many more female applicants. Because of this, the overall proportion of males rejected exceeds the overall proportion of females rejected.

Most people viewing Table 3.11 would probably conclude that the university was discriminating against male applicants, but Table 3.12 makes clear that there was no evidence of discrimination. Within each school, the male and female applicants had been treated exactly the same. Thus the university is not guilty of sex discrimination. This example shows how easy it is to get an incorrect impression of the relationships between variables if we do take into account all the variables pertinent to a study.

3.6 ▪ *The Stem-and-Leaf Diagram (Optional)*

Whenever we are presented with a set of numerical observations, it is natural for us to want to condense or simplify the data in some way so that we can recognize general characteristics of the data. For example, most people would like to know the following things:

1. How are the data distributed? What is the general shape of the distribution? Where are most of the observations concentrated?
2. Where is the center of the data?
3. How spread out, or dispersed, are the data about this central value?
4. Are there any very large or very small values that appear to be quite different from the other observations?

The most frequently used technique for answering these questions is to construct a frequency or relative frequency distribution and to calculate some summary statistics, which will be discussed in the next chapter. Another closely related way of answering these questions is to construct what is called a **stem-and-leaf diagram**, a technique proposed by John Tukey.[1] The stem-and-leaf diagram is partly tabular and partly graphical in nature. The purposes of the stem-and-leaf diagram are as follows:

1. to show the range of the data, that is, to make it easy to determine the difference between the largest observation and the smallest observation;
2. to show how the data are distributed;
3. to show in a general way where the center of the data is;
4. to show in a general way how spread out the data are; and
5. to show whether there are any extremely high or low values, called **outliers**.

Example 3.8

Construction of a Stem-and-Leaf Diagram: In 1984, a female employee who was laid off sued her employer alleging that she had been released because of age and sex discrimination. A statistician was asked to examine the plaintiff's allegations. In the course of the study, it became necessary to compare the ages of the employees who were laid off with the ages of the employees who were not. The data below show the ages of 60 employees who were laid off in 1984:

43	34	21	26	57	64	51	30	38	60
19	26	41	47	58	50	42	32	25	18
36	27	38	37	24	49	56	61	20	39
32	51	60	52	45	44	33	25	29	27
31	35	39	19	20	30	46	47	32	24
29	22	20	37	34	29	60	55	30	41

In a stem-and-leaf diagram, the first or leading digit serves as the **stem** and the trailing digit serves as the **leaf**. The leading digit determines the row in which an observation is placed; the trailing digit is written in this row to the right of a vertical bar that separates the stems from the leaves. In this example, the stems are the first digits for each person's age; thus the stems are the digits 1 through 6. For example, for a person aged 53, the stem is 5 and the leaf is 3. To improve the appearance of the diagram, it is useful to arrange the leaves in each row from lowest to highest. The stem-and-leaf diagram for the age data above is shown on the following page.

[1] J. Tukey, *Exploratory Data Analysis* (Reading, Mass.: Addison-Wesley, 1977).

1	8 9 9
2	0 0 0 1 2 4 4 5 5 6 6 7 7 9 9 9
3	0 0 0 1 2 2 2 3 4 4 5 6 7 7 8 8 9 9
4	1 1 2 3 4 5 6 7 7 9
5	0 1 1 2 5 6 7 8
6	0 0 0 1 4

The stem-and-leaf diagram allows us to pick out several important characteristics of the data. In this example, the smallest observation is 18 and the largest is 64. There are 18 leaves following the 3 stem and 16 leaves following the 2 stem, indicating that 18 people laid off were in their thirties and 16 employees were in their twenties. These are the biggest classes. Few people under 20 or over 60 were laid off.

Each stem in the diagram defines a class of ages, just as a class interval defines a class of ages in a frequency distribution. The number of leaves next to each stem represents the class frequency associated with that stem. If the stem-and-leaf diagram is rotated 90° counterclockwise, so that the leaves rise vertically rather than horizontally, the stem-and-leaf diagram looks very similar to a histogram, the height of the leaves in each column visually representing the frequency of that class. Two advantages of the stem-and-leaf diagram over the histogram are that it allows you to reconstruct the original data set and it lists the observations in order of magnitude.

There are several disadvantages of the stem-and-leaf diagram, however. It is suitable only for relatively small data sets. No one would want to list hundreds of observations in a stem-and-leaf diagram. Second, there is little flexibility in the choice of stems and thus in the number of classes.

With a bit of care, the stem-and-leaf diagram can be used with any data set. If the observations consist of numbers with, say, six digits, we might use the first digit as the stem and the second digit as the leaf and ignore the remaining digits. For the number 453,210, the stem could be 4 and the leaf 5, or the stem might be 45 and the leaf 3.

If narrower classes are desired, a stem can be used more than once. For example, each stem could be used twice in the example above. The first time the stem 3 is recorded it would be associated with the values 30, 31, 32, 33, and 34; the second time it would be associated with the values 35, 36, 37, 38, and 39. The same applies to the other stems.

The stem-and-leaf diagram has a few advantages over the frequency distribution. Unlike in the frequency distribution, no information on the value of each observation is lost. In addition, the stem-and-leaf diagram conveniently orders the data from lowest to highest, which makes it easy to pick out the middle value. ■

Exercises for Section 3.6

1. The following data show the number of customers at a General Motors service center on a sample of 30 days:

67	76	58	82	59	51	63	69	70	75
67	43	58	61	40	58	46	57	72	71
65	73	58	45	48	49	50	64	53	64

Construct a stem-and-leaf diagram. Based on the diagram, make an educated guess at the average number of customers per day.

2. The following data show the ages of 40 truck drivers employed by the Eastern Trucking Company:

26	34	22	45	37	30	19	26	34	20
32	43	51	50	40	44	45	36	35	42
49	38	26	28	37	42	40	38	32	43
41	23	18	19	26	52	43	37	47	50

Construct a stem-and-leaf diagram. Based on the diagram, make an educated guess at the average number of customers per day.

3. The following data show the number of years of seniority for the employees at the Hammermill Paper Company.

20	8	13	24	16	12	10	5	3	12	26	24	19	12	24
2	12	9	6	4	11	10	17	18	2	1	15	22	13	18
3	14	16	19	22	25	26	23	14	17	16	13	19	7	5

Construct a stem-and-leaf diagram. Make a guess at the average years of seniority of employees at the firm.

3.7 ▪ *Computer Applications*

You can use the SPSSX FREQUENCIES command to make a frequency table, bar chart, or histogram, or to calculate various descriptive statistics. For example, refer to the data in Table 2.1 in Chapter 2. To generate a frequency table showing how many employees at Computech work in each division, issue the following command:

```
FREQUENCIES VARIABLES = DIV
```

To generate a bar chart showing the same information, issue the command

```
FREQUENCIES VARIABLES = DIV/BARCHART
```

The bar chart showing the frequency distribution for the variable DIV is shown in Figure 3.17.

To generate a histogram showing the ages of employees at Computech, issue the following command:

```
FREQUENCIES VARIABLES = AGE
  /HISTOGRAM MINIMUM (18) MAXIMUM (68) INCREMENT (5)
```

The histogram will group employees into classes 5 units wide, beginning with age 18. The histogram generated by this FREQUENCIES command is shown in Figure 3.18.

In the histogram, the first line of stars represents employees from age 18 to 23, the second represents employees from age 23 to 28, and so forth. For each 5-year group of

FIGURE 3.17 SPSSX-generated bar chart for the variable DIV in Table 2.1.

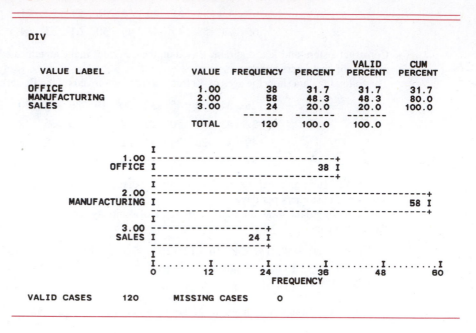

```
DIV

                                                               VALID     CUM
  VALUE LABEL                 VALUE  FREQUENCY  PERCENT  PERCENT  PERCENT

OFFICE                         1.00        38     31.7     31.7     31.7
MANUFACTURING                  2.00        58     48.3     48.3     80.0
SALES                          3.00        24     20.0     20.0    100.0
                                     -------  -------  -------
                              TOTAL      120    100.0    100.0

                 I
          1.00   --------------------------------+
        OFFICE   I                            38 I
                 --------------------------------+
                 I
          2.00   ------------------------------------------------+
 MANUFACTURING   I                                            58 I
                 ------------------------------------------------+
                 I
          3.00   --------------------+
         SALES   I                24 I
                 --------------------+
                 I
                 I.........I.........I.........I.........I.........I
                 0        12        24        36        48        60
                                      FREQUENCY

VALID CASES      120      MISSING CASES      0
```

FIGURE 3.18 SPSSX-generated histogram for the variable AGE in Table 2.1.

```
AGE

    COUNT    MIDPOINT    ONE SYMBOL EQUALS APPROXIMATELY    .40 OCCURRENCES

        9       20.50   ***********************
       13       25.50   *********************************
       20       30.50   **************************************************
       17       35.50   *******************************************
       12       40.50   ******************************
       17       45.50   *******************************************
       10       50.50   *************************
       15       55.50   **************************************
        3       60.50   ********
        4       65.50   **********
                        I....+....I....+....I....+....I....+....I....+....I
                        0         4         8        12        16        20
                                  HISTOGRAM FREQUENCY

VALID CASES      120      MISSING CASES      0
```

ages, the computer output shows a row of stars or asterisks (*) whose length indicates the number of observations in that group. The actual number of cases appears in the column labeled COUNT. The middle value of each interval is printed in the column labeled MIDPOINT. For example, the midpoint age for employees between age 18 and age 23 is 20.5.

The SAS program can be used to produce bar charts and pie charts for discrete variables and histograms for continuous variables. Suppose we wish to generate a bar chart showing the number of employees in each division at the Computech Corporation according to Table 2.1. We would insert the following commands at the end of the SAS program shown in Figure 2.3 in Chapter 2.

```
PROC CHART;
VBAR DIV;
```

The command PROC CHART tells SAS to draw a chart, and the command VBAR DIV tells SAS to construct a vertical bar chart for the variable DIV. The output is in Figure 3.19.

FIGURE 3.19 **SAS-generated bar chart for the variable DIV in Table 2.1.**

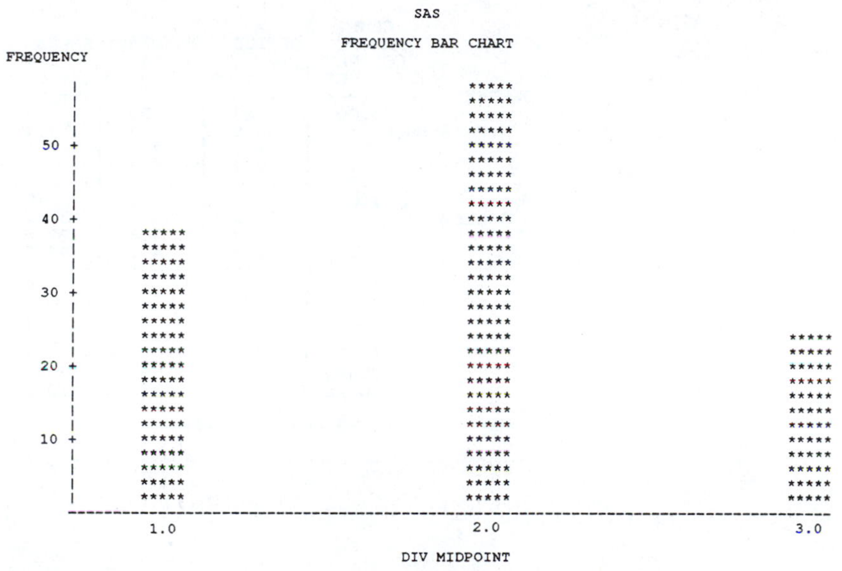

Generating a Bivariate Frequency Table

The SPSSX and SAS programs can be used to generate bivariate frequency tables. Suppose we wish to examine the data in Table 2.1 to see if there is any relationship between academic degree and division in which an individual is employed. In SPSSX, the command

```
CROSSTABS TABLES = DEGREE BY DIV
```

will generate a bivariate frequency distribution for the variables DEGREE and DIV. By inserting the additional command

```
OPTIONS 3, 4, 5
```

into the SPSSX program, the computer will also print out various relative frequencies along with the bivariate frequency distribution. The above two commands can be inserted anywhere between the END DATA command and the FINISH command. Figure 3.20 shows the output generated by these two commands using the data in Table 2.1.

In Figure 3.20, observe that of the 89 employees with a high school degree, only 1 is employed in sales, whereas only 3 of the 23 employees with college degrees are employed in the office. All 8 of the employees with postgraduate degrees are employed in sales. Of the 38 employees in the office, 35 have a high school degree and none have a postgraduate degree. Finally, of the 58 employees in manufacturing, 53 have high school degrees and 5 have college degrees. Thus, the data in Figure 3.20 show that there is a strong relationship between academic degree and division of employment.

FIGURE 3.20
SPSSX output obtained by using the CROSSTABS command on the variables DEGREE and DIV in Table 2.1.

DEGREE	COUNT / ROW PCT / COL PCT / TOT PCT	DIV: OFFICE 1.00	MANUFACTURING 2.00	SALES 3.00	ROW TOTAL
HIGH SCHOOL	1.00	35	53	1	89
		39.3	59.6	1.1	74.2
		92.1	91.4	4.2	
		29.2	44.2	.8	
COLLEGE	2.00	3	5	15	23
		13.0	21.7	65.2	19.2
		7.9	8.6	62.5	
		2.5	4.2	12.5	
POST-GRAD	3.00			8	8
				100.0	6.7
				33.3	
				6.7	
	COLUMN TOTAL	38	58	24	120
		31.7	48.3	20.0	100.0

NUMBER OF MISSING OBSERVATIONS = 0

Exercises for Section 3.7

1. Refer to the data in Table 2.1.
   a. Use the SPSSX program and a CROSSTABS command to generate a bivariate frequency table showing the relationship between SEX and DIV.
   b. Verify that your result in part (a) is correct by constructing the table by hand.
   c. Does there appear to be a relationship between these two variables?
2. Refer to the data in Table 2.1.
   a. Use the SPSSX program and a CROSSTABS command to generate a bivariate frequency table showing the relationship between SEX and DEGREE.
   b. Does there appear to be a relationship between these two variables?
3. Refer to the data in Table 2.1.
   a. Use the SPSSX program and a CROSSTABS command to generate a bivariate frequency table showing the relationship between race and division.
   b. Does it appear that there is a relationship between race and division of employment?

4. Refer to the data in Table 2.1.
   a. Use the SPSSX program and a CROSSTABS command to generate a bivariate frequency table showing the relationship between race and academic degree.
   b. Does it appear that there is a relationship between race and academic degree?
5. Refer to the data in Table 2.2 in Chapter 2.
   a. Generate a frequency distribution and determine what proportion of students are male and what proportion are female.
   b. What proportion of students are freshmen? Sophomores? Juniors? Seniors?
   c. What proportion of students are in-state students? Out-of-state?
   d. What proportion of students are economics majors? Math majors?
6. Refer to the data in Table 2.2.
   a. Generate a table showing Sex by Class.
   b. Generate a table showing Sex by Residence.
   c. Generate a table showing Sex by Major.
   d. Generate a table showing Class by Major.
   e. Generate a table showing Class by Residence.
   f. Generate a table showing Residence by Major.
7. Use the computer to generate frequency distributions for the data in Table 2.1.
   a. What proportion of the employees in the sample are male?
   b. What proportion of the employees in the sample are white?
   c. What proportion of the employees in the sample are office workers?
   d. What proportion of the employees in the sample are employed in sales?
   e. Construct a pie chart showing the distribution of employees by division.
   f. Construct a bar chart showing the distribution of employees by degree.
8. Refer to the data in Table 2.1.
   a. Construct a histogram showing the age of the employees. Start at age 18 and use increments of 5 years.
   b. Construct a histogram as in part (a) but use increments of 15 years. Compare this histogram with the histogram produced in the text and with the one produced in part (a).
   c. Construct a histogram showing the years of seniority of the employees. Start at 0 and use 5-year increments.
   d. Repeat part (c) using 10-year increments. Which histogram better represents the data?
9. Refer to the data in Table 2.1. Construct a bar chart showing the number of exemptions claimed by the employees. Examine this bar chart and make an educated guess concerning the average number of exemptions claimed.
10. Refer to the data in Table 2.2. Use the computer to generate various frequency distributions.
    a. Construct a histogram showing the SAT scores of the students. Based on this histogram, make an educated guess at the average SAT score in the sample.
    b. Construct a histogram showing the GPAs of the students. Make an educated guess at the average GPA in the sample.

Chapter 3 Summary

To summarize data, (1) arrange the data in numerical order, (2) construct a frequency distribution of the data, and (3) construct the appropriate graph.

Grouped frequency distributions are used to simplify the presentation of data by dividing the range of scores into intervals called *classes*. Grouping data makes certain features of the data clearer while obscuring others. To construct a *frequency distribution,* place the data values in order, from smallest to largest. The number of data values in each class is the *class frequency.* The proportion of values in each class is the *class relative frequency.*

A *histogram* is a graphical representation of a frequency distribution. When the data can assume only a few specific values, a *bar chart* provides a graphical summary showing the frequency or relative frequency of each value. Similarly, a pie chart can be used to illustrate the relative frequency distribution for a variable. A bar graph or pie chart is especially useful for graphing categorical or multinomial data.

A graph of a frequency distribution reveals the general shape, the approximate center, and amount of variation of the data. *Skewness* is a lack of symmetry in a frequency distribution. If the longer tail of the distribution is to the left (toward the lower numbers), it is skewed to the left and vice versa. Some frequently occurring distributions are the *uniform distribution,* which is symmetric and has a rectangular shape; the *normal distribution,* which is a symmetrical bell shaped curve; and the *exponential distribution,* which is skewed to the right and has a peak at the value 0.

A *bivariate frequency distribution* shows how the values of two variables are jointly distributed. A stem-and-leaf diagram is a useful way of displaying all the values in a small sample of data. It shows the distribution of the data and also shows each individual value in order, so no information is lost. It is inconvenient to use a stem-and-leaf diagram when working with a large data set.

Graphs of frequency distributions reveal the shape, center and spread of a distribution of data. In most statistical studies, some precise measure of the center of the set of data values and the amount of variation present in the data is required. Various ways of measuring the center and amount of spread present in a set of data are presented next in Chapter 4.

Chapter 3 ▪ Supplementary Exercises

1. Hospital records show the following number of days of hospitalization for 40 patients:

15	19	7	15	8	9	6	14
23	17	22	10	12	15	17	8
14	13	8	18	5	2	10	12
24	32	8	8	7	15	19	18
39	26	6	10	10	15	19	3

a. Put the data in order from lowest to highest.
b. Construct a frequency and relative frequency distribution for the data. As classes, use 0 to under 5, 5 to under 10, and so forth.
c. Construct a cumulative relative frequency distribution for the data.
d. Draw the histogram.

2. In October 1987, *USA Today* asked readers to answer the following question: "How much do you bet each year on sports of any kind?" The results are as follows:

Amount	\$0	\$1–\$20	\$21–\$100	\$101–\$500	\$501–\$1000	Over \$1000
Relative frequency	24	28	23	16	3	6

a. Plot this relative frequency distribution.

b. Is the distribution symmetric? If not, in which direction is it skewed?
c. Construct and plot the cumulative relative frequency distribution.

3. The duration of 40 long-distance telephone calls is shown below (time recorded in minutes).

13.5	6.0	18.3	26.8	4.2	12.1	11.0	2.0	14.2	2.2
10.2	17.5	8.5	14.2	18.2	3.2	14.6	8.8	14.5	12.6
16.6	13.4	2.1	3.4	5.6	14.5	14.0	5.5	15.5	8.9
23.3	21.0	3.7	7.6	2.3	3.4	0.9	23.3	2.7	8.6

a. Put the data in order from lowest to highest.
b. Construct a frequency distribution and a relative frequency distribution for the data. As classes, use 0 to under 5, 5 to under 10, and so forth.
c. Repeat part (b) but use as classes 0 to under 3, 3 to under 6, and so forth.
d. Draw the histograms in part (b) and part (c) and compare them to see how the shapes differ when the classes are changed.

4. Construct a stem-and-leaf diagram for the data in Exercise 3.

5. The Stop 'n' Go convenience store sold the following numbers of gallons of milk during a sample of 30 weeks:

36	39	49	45	27	26	34	41	61	53
28	46	54	50	31	40	48	42	35	39
44	52	41	47	35	55	60	30	46	38

a. Put the data in order from lowest to highest.
b. Construct a frequency distribution using class intervals 24.5 to 29.5, 29.5 to 34.5, and so forth.
c. Graph the histogram.
d. Construct the relative frequency distribution.
e. Construct the cumulative frequency distribution.
f. Construct the cumulative relative frequency distribution and graph it.

6. Construct a stem-and-leaf diagram for the data in Exercise 5.

7. A food distributor has 40 salespeople. The following data (in thousands of dollars) show their annual salaries:

16.8	19.2	24.5	23.6	19.0	23.2	17.7	24.3	25.4	29.3
15.4	18.9	26.5	24.7	23.4	22.1	26.5	18.6	19.3	20.0
17.6	16.8	26.9	25.4	24.7	20.2	25.3	18.2	16.8	22.3
25.1	24.0	28.2	28.6	24.6	24.3	22.1	27.4	26.8	21.9

a. Put the data in an ordered array.
b. Construct a frequency distribution using class intervals 15 to under 18, 18 to under 21, and so forth.
c. Graph the histogram.
d. Construct the relative frequency distribution.
e. Construct the cumulative frequency distribution.
f. Construct the cumulative relative frequency distribution and graph it.
g. Suppose someone asked you to guess the average salary of the salesman. By looking at the histogram, make an educated guess.

8. Construct a stem-and-leaf diagram for the data in Exercise 7.

9. The following data show the number of years of education for a sample of 25 taxicab drivers:

12	8	11	10	12	8	9	11	12	13	10	12	10
10	12	8	8	9	11	10	11	12	12	11	8	

a. Construct a bar chart.
b. Construct a relative frequency distribution.
c. Based on the bar chart, make an educated guess about the average number of years of education in the sample.
d. What number of years of education has the highest frequency?

10. Refer to the data in Table 2.1 of Chapter 2. Construct a stem-and-leaf diagram for the variable AGE. Based on this diagram, make an educated guess about the average age of the employees at Computech.

11. At a small college there are 40 assistant professors, 60 associate professors, and 20 full professors.
a. Construct a pie chart to represent the data.
b. Construct a bar chart to represent the data.

12. Suppose that in Problem 11 an artist drew a square having 1-inch sides to represent the full professors, a square having 2-inch sides to represent the assistant professors, and a square having 3-inch sides to represent the associate professors.
a. Explain what is wrong with this procedure.
b. Describe the dimensions of the square that accurately reflect the number of assistant professors given that the full professors are represented by a 1-inch square.

13. Suppose that we have data showing the annual salaries of all the players on the New York Yankees baseball team. Give an example where these data could be viewed as the following:
a. A population
b. A sample

14. Describe some of the biases that are likely to be involved in the following sampling situations:
a. A White House spokesperson reports that 85% of the phone calls received at the White House following a presidential speech were favorable.
b. A newspaper asks for readers' opinions about gun control laws. The paper reports that 400 readers voluntarily replied, and that 70% of the respondents were against gun control laws.

15. For which of the following variables would a frequency table be appropriate, where every value is shown along with its frequency? For which variables would it be more appropriate to group neighboring values?
a. Calories consumed per day by college students
b. Number of children in a family
c. Mileage on the family car
d. Preferred political party
e. Number of dentist visits during the last year
f. Religious affiliation

16. The following data show the number of income tax returns filed in 1983 and the number that were audited by the Internal Revenue Service. For each income class, find the proportion that were audited. Is a low- or high-income tax return more likely to be audited?

Total Income	Returns Filed	Returns Audited
Under $10,000	31,357,000	107,000
$10,000–$24,999	30,745,000	283,000
$25,000–$49,999	22,243,000	456,000
$50,000 and over	5,531,000	221,000

References

FISHER, RONALD A. *The Design of Experiments.* 9th ed. New York: Hafner, 1971.

NETER, JOHN, WILLIAM WASSERMAN, and G. A. WHITMORE. *Applied Statistics.* 3d ed. Boston: Allyn and Bacon, 1988.

NIE, NORMAN E., C. HADLAI HULL, JEAN G. JENKINS, KARIN STEINBRENNER, and DALE H. BENT. *SPSS Statistical Package for the Social Sciences.* 2d ed. New York: McGraw-Hill, 1975.

NORUSIS, MARIJA J. *SPSSX Introductory Statistics Guide.* New York: McGraw-Hill, 1983.

______. *SPSSX Advanced Statistics Guide.* Chicago: SPSS, 1985.

______. *The SPSS Guide to Data Analysis.* Chicago: SPSS, 1986.

RYAN, THOMAS A., BRIAN L. JOINER, and BARBARA F. RYAN. *Minitab Handbook.* 2d ed. Boston: PWS-KENT, 1985.

______. *Minitab Reference Manual.* University Park, Penn.: Minitab Project, 1985.

SAS Introductory Guide. 3d ed. Cary, N.C.: SAS Institute, 1985.

SAS Procedures Guide for Personal Computers. Version 6 ed. Cary, N.C.: SAS Institute, 1986.

SAS Statistics Guide for Personal Computers. Version 6 ed. Cary, N.C.: SAS Institute, 1986.

SAS User's Guide: Basics. Version 5 ed. Cary, N.C.: SAS Institute, 1985.

SAS User's Guide: Statistics. Version 5 ed. Cary, N.C.: SAS Institute, 1985.

SPSSX User's Guide. Chicago: SPSS, 1983.

WAINER, HOWARD. "How to Display Data Badly." *American Statistician* 38 (1984): 137–147.

Chapter Four
Summary Statistics: Measures of Location and Dispersion

In Chapter 3, we discussed how to use tables and graphs to describe and summarize a set of data. These tables and graphs enable us to visualize the shape of the distribution. In addition, we can visualize the amount of spread in the observations and the tendency of the data to cluster about a central value. In this chapter we discuss how to characterize the center and the amount of spread in the data by computing numerical measures.

When confronted with a large sample of data, the statistician typically wants to determine (1) the general shape or distribution of the data, (2) the average or typical value in the data set, and (3) the amount of dispersion or variation present in the data. For each of these three problems, several solutions are possible.

1. *What is the general shape or distribution of the data?* This problem can be solved by constructing frequency and relative frequency distributions, by drawing a histogram or stem-and-leaf diagram, or by constructing a box plot (discussed later in this chapter). The most popular solution is to construct a histogram.

2. *Where is the center of the data, or what is the average value of the data?* This problem can be solved in several ways. One solution is to calculate the mean, or arithmetic average. Another solution is to calculate the median. At times, a third possible solution is to calculate the mode of the data. The most popular solution to this problem is to calculate the mean, although for certain problems the median or mode is more appropriate.

3. *How dispersed, or spread out, are the data?* There are many ways of measuring the amount of variation in a set of data. Some of these measures are the range, the interquartile range, the mean absolute deviation, the variance, and the standard deviation. The most frequently used measure of variation is the standard deviation.

In Chapter 3, we discussed how to solve the first problem of determining the general shape or distribution of the data. In Chapter 4, we discuss how to locate the center of the data and how to measure the amount of dispersion. If we have all the observations in a population, then we can actually calculate the values for various population characteristics.

Definition: Parameters

Numbers that describe population characteristics are called **parameters**.

Examples of population parameters are the population mean, the population variance, the population standard deviation, and the population proportion. Much of the field of statistics is devoted to drawing inferences from a sample concerning the value of a population parameter. If we have only a sample of data, then we calculate *estimates* of the population parameters.

Definitions: Estimate and Estimator

Values calculated from a sample of data that are used to estimate population parameters are called **estimates**. The formula used to calculate an estimate is called an **estimator**.

An *estimator* is a function, while an *estimate* is a specific value. Examples of estimators are the formulas for determining the sample mean, the sample variance, and the sample standard deviation; the results of these operations are the estimates.

The mean, the median, and the mode are three different numerical measures used to describe the center of a data set. The range, the variance, the standard deviation, and the mean absolute deviation are four different measures used to measure the amount of spread, dispersion, or variability in a set of data. All of these numerical measures are population parameters if they refer to calculations made from a population of data and sample estimates if they are calculated from a sample of data.

In this text, variables will be denoted by uppercase letters and specific values of the variable by lowercase letters.

4.1 ▪ *Summation Notation*

Before describing these numerical measures, we introduce summation notation in order to simplify the formulas. The Greek letter Σ (uppercase sigma) is called the *summation sign* and indicates that we should find the sum of the values following the Σ.

Definition: Summation Sign

The expression $\sum_{i=1}^{n} x_i$ is used to represent the sum of the values $x_1, x_2, \ldots, x_n$ and is defined by the equation

$$\sum_{i=1}^{n} x_i = x_1 + x_2 + \cdots + x_n$$

The symbols above and below the summation sign Σ define the limits of the summation. The subscript $i = 1$ and the superscript n tell us to calculate the sum of all values from x_1 to x_n. When these subscripts and superscripts are omitted, as is usually the case, the symbol Σ means we should obtain the sum of all the available values of the variable.

For example, suppose we have seven observations concerning some variable X, denoted by $x_1, x_2, \ldots, x_7$. The sum of these seven numbers is represented by the symbol $\Sigma\, x_i$, or by the more detailed symbol

$$\sum_{i=1}^{7} x_i$$

Example 4.1

Sum of a Set of Values: On a sample of seven days, the numbers of customers at a small restaurant were

$$x_1 = 92, \quad x_2 = 84, \quad x_3 = 70, \quad x_4 = 76, \quad x_5 = 66, \quad x_6 = 80, \quad x_7 = 71$$

Calculate $\Sigma\, x_i$.

Solution: $\Sigma\, x_i$ represents the total number of customers during the week. The total number of customers is thus

$$\Sigma\, x_i = x_1 + x_2 + \cdots + x_7 = 539$$

■

Example 4.2

Salary Payroll at Lang's Trucking Company: Refer to the data in Table 3.1, the monthly salaries earned by the 80 employees at Lang's Trucking Company. Let x_i denote the monthly salary of the ith employee. Calculate $\Sigma\, x_i$.

Solution: $\Sigma\, x_i$ represents the sum of the monthly salaries for all 80 employees; that is, $\Sigma\, x_i$ represents the monthly payroll. From the data in Table 3.1, we obtain $\Sigma\, x_i =$ \$130,135. ■

Example 4.3

Total Number of Cars Owned: Refer to the data in Table 3.5, the number of cars owned by each family in a sample of 120 families. Let x_i denote the number of cars owned by the ith family. Calculate $\Sigma\, x_i$.

Solution: $\Sigma\, x_i$ denotes the total number of cars owned by all 120 families. From the data in Table 3.5, we obtain $\Sigma\, x_i = 219$. ■

Formulas Involving Summation Notation

There are several formulas involving summation signs that will be used throughout this book. They are summarized as follows:

1. $\Sigma\, cx_i = c\,\Sigma\, x_i$, where c is any constant.
2. $\Sigma(x_i - c) = \Sigma\, x_i - nc$
3. $\Sigma\, x_i^2 = x_1^2 + x_2^2 + \cdots + x_n^2$
4. $\Sigma\, cx_i^2 = c\,\Sigma\, x_i^2$
5. $\Sigma(x_i - c)^2 = \Sigma\, x_i^2 - 2c\,\Sigma\, x_i + nc^2$

The examples below illustrate the use of summation notation.

Example 4.4

Total Parking Revenue: Use the data in Example 4.1. Suppose that each customer at the restaurant pays \$3.00 for valet parking. Calculate the total parking revenue during the week.

Solution: We obtain

$$\Sigma\, 3x_i = 3x_1 + 3x_2 + \cdots + 3x_7$$
$$= 276 + 252 + \cdots + 213 = 1617$$

Alternatively, by using formula 1 above, we obtain

$$\Sigma\, 3x_i = 3\,\Sigma\, x_i = 3 \times 539 = 1617$$ ■

Example 4.5 **Sum of Squares:** Use the data in Example 4.1 and calculate $\Sigma\, x_i^2$.

Solution: We obtain

$$\Sigma\, x_i^2 = 92^2 + 84^2 + \cdots + 71^2 = 8464$$ ■

It is a tedious process to calculate sums by hand, and it is easy to make mistakes. When performing such calculations by hand, you should always do the work twice to check your result. Just as computer programs are useful for constructing frequency distributions, they are also useful for calculating sums of variables. For example, the FREQUENCIES procedure in the SPSSX computer program will calculate the sum of any set of numerical observations. For example, to get the sum of all values of the variable SALARY, issue the commands

```
FREQUENCIES VARIABLES = SALARY/
   STATISTICS SUM
```

Exercises for Section 4.1

1. Given the values for X of 5, 4, 2, 12, 12, 10, 6, 7, 9, and 4, calculate the following sums:
a. $\Sigma\, x_i$
b. $\Sigma\, 2x_i$
c. $\Sigma\, x_i^2$

2. In Exercise 1, let $y_i = 5x_i$. Calculate the following sums:
a. $\Sigma\, y_i$
b. $\Sigma\, 2y_i$
c. $\Sigma\, y_i^2$
Compare these sums to the corresponding sums in Exercise 1.

3. A man has five sons. Let x_i denote the weekly income of the ith son. During a given week, their incomes were as follows: \$542, \$433, \$289, \$400, and \$456. Each son had \$100 per week deducted for taxes.
a. Calculate the total weekly income of the five sons; that is, find the sum $\Sigma\, x_i$.
b. Calculate the sons' total take-home pay after taxes were deducted. That is, calculate $\Sigma(x_i - 100)$.

4. Write the following values in summation notation:
a. $x_1 + x_2 + \cdots + x_{15}$
b. $5x_1 + 5x_2 + \cdots + 5x_{22}$
c. $x_1 + y_1 + x_2 + y_2 + \cdots + x_9 + y_9$

5. Let $x_1 = 3$, $x_2 = 2$, $x_3 = 4$, and $x_4 = 1$. Calculate the following:
a. $\Sigma x_i - 3$
b. $\Sigma(x_i - 3)$
c. $\Sigma(x_i - 3)^2$
d. $(\Sigma x_i - 3)^2$

6. Are the following expressions true or false?
a. $(\Sigma x_i)(\Sigma y_i) = \Sigma x_i y_i$
b. $\Sigma x_i^2 = (\Sigma x_i)^2$
c. $\Sigma(x_i + y_i)^2 = \Sigma x_i^2 + \Sigma y_i^2$

4.2 ▪ The Mean, the Median, and the Mode

By far the most important and most frequently used measure of central tendency of a data set is the *arithmetic mean* or, simply, the *mean*. The mean is frequently called the *average* of a set of data.

If we calculate the mean from a population of N values, then we obtain the *population mean.*

Definition: Population Mean

The **population mean** is denoted by the symbol μ (Greek mu) and is calculated by using the following formula where N is the number of observations of the population

$$\mu = \frac{x_1 + x_2 + \cdots + x_N}{N} = \frac{\Sigma x_i}{N}$$

When the data set consists of a sample of n observations, we calculate the *sample mean* to estimate the population mean. The sample mean is denoted by the symbol $\bar{x}$ (called "x bar").

Definition: Sample Mean

Given the sample of n observations $x_1, x_2, \ldots, x_n$, the **sample mean** $\bar{x}$ is

$$\bar{x} = \frac{x_1 + x_2 + \cdots + x_n}{n} = \frac{\Sigma x_i}{n}$$

Example 4.6

Calculating the Sample Mean: The data in Example 4.1 showed that, on a sample of seven days, the numbers of customers at a small restaurant were

$$x_1 = 92, \quad x_2 = 84, \quad x_3 = 70, \quad x_4 = 76, \quad x_5 = 66, \quad x_6 = 80, \quad x_7 = 71$$

Calculate the sample mean.

Solution: The sample mean is

$$\bar{x} = \frac{\Sigma x_i}{7} = \frac{539}{7} = 77$$

■

Example 4.7

Mean Salary at Lang's Trucking Company: Table 3.1 shows the monthly salaries of all 80 employees at Lang's Trucking Company. Example 4.2 showed that the sum of all 80 salaries is \$130,135. Calculate the population mean salary.

Solution: The population mean is

$$\mu = 130{,}135/80 = 1{,}626.6875$$

This means that the average monthly salary for the 80 employees is approximately \$1,626.69. ■

Example 4.8

Average Number of Cars Owned: Table 3.5 shows the number of cars owned by 120 different families. Example 4.3 showed that the total number of cars owned is 219. Calculate the sample mean.

Solution: The sample mean is

$$\bar{x} = 219/120 = 1.825$$ ■

The Median

Another important measure of the center or middle of a set of data is called the *median*.

Definition: Median

The **median** is the middle value of data ordered from lowest to highest. If the sequence contains an odd number of observations, the median is the *middle value* in the ordered sequence. If the sequence contains an even number of observations, the median is the *arithmetic average* of the two central values.

When a population of data is available, we calculate the *population median*. The median calculated from a sample of data is called the *sample median* and is an estimate of the population median. Only rarely will the sample median be exactly equal to the population median, but as the sample size becomes larger, the chances increase that the sample median will be close to the population median.

Example 4.9

Median for an Odd Number of Observations: Calculate the median for the data on restaurant customers in Example 4.1.

Solution: To calculate the median, the observations must be ordered from lowest to highest. The ordered sequence is

$$66 \quad 70 \quad 71 \quad 76 \quad 80 \quad 84 \quad 92$$

The number of observations is odd, so the median is the middle, or fourth, value in the ordered sequence.

$$\text{Sample median} = 76$$

Recall from Example 4.6 that the sample mean was 77. In this example, the median is slightly less than the mean. This shows that the mean and median are not necessarily equal to one another. ■

Example 4.10

Median for an Even Number of Observations: Calculate the median salary for the monthly salary data presented in Table 3.1.

Solution: To calculate the median salary, the 80 values must be placed in order from lowest to highest. The ordered values are shown in Table 4.1. Because the number of observations is even, the median is the average of the 40th and 41st values. The 40th value is 1600; the 41st value is 1620. The median monthly salary is the arithmetic average of these two values.

$$\text{Population median} = (1600 + 1620)/2 = 1610$$

TABLE 4.1 Ordered monthly salaries from Table 3.1

1300	1310	1320	1325	1340	1380	1380	1390	1400	1400
1410	1420	1425	1440	1450	1450	1455	1475	1475	1500
1530	1550	1550	1550	1550	1550	1550	1555	1565	1570
1575	1580	1580	1585	1590	1590	1600	1600	1600	1600
1620	1620	1620	1620	1625	1625	1640	1640	1650	1650
1650	1650	1650	1660	1675	1700	1700	1705	1725	1730
1740	1750	1760	1775	1780	1815	1820	1850	1850	1860
1875	1900	1900	1900	1900	2000	2000	2000	2015	2025

Recall from Example 4.7 that the mean monthly salary for the 80 employees is approximately \$1626.69. In this example, the median is slightly less than the mean. ■

Example 4.11

Median Number of Cars Owned: Calculate the median number of cars owned per family for the car ownership data in Table 3.5.

Solution: In Table 3.5, the 120 values have already been put in order from lowest to highest. The number of observations (120) is even, so the median is the average of the 60th and 61st values. After ordering the data, the first 9 families own no cars, the next 39 families each own one car, the next 48 families own two cars each, and so forth. Thus, the 60th family owns two cars and the 61st family also owns two cars. The median number of cars owned is

$$\text{Median} = \frac{2 + 2}{2} = 2$$

Recall from Example 4.8 that the mean number of cars owned is 1.825. In this example, the median is slightly greater than the mean. ■

The Mode

A third measure of central tendency for a population or sample of observations is called the *mode*.

Definition: Mode

The **mode** of a set of observations is the value that occurs with the greatest frequency. The mode is not necessarily unique.

Example 4.12

Mode of Number of Restaurant Customers: Calculate the mode for the number of customers at the restaurant in Example 4.1.

Solution: Each of the seven values occurs exactly once. Because each value has the same frequency, each value could be called a mode. In this problem, the mode conveys no useful information. ■

Example 4.13

Mode of Monthly Salaries: Calculate the mode for the data in Table 3.1.

Solution: The salary $1550 occurs six times. Because no other value occurs this often, the mode is $1550.

This value is not necessarily a good measure of the center of the salary data. For example, the value $1650 occurs five times; the value $1600 occurs four times; $1620, four times; and $1900, four times. Thus there is no reason to expect the most frequently occurring salary to be located near the center of the data. With just a few minor changes in salaries, the mode could easily be $1900, and this value certainly does not fall near the center of the data. For the data in Table 3.1, the mode is not a useful measure of central tendency, varying considerably from the mean salary of $1626.69 and the median salary of $1610. ■

Example 4.14

Mode of Number of Cars Owned: Calculate the mode for the data in Table 3.4.

Solution: The most common value in Table 3.4 is the value 2, which has a frequency of 48. The value 1 is the second most common, with a frequency of 39. In this case, the mode is a useful measure of location. In some studies, it could be useful to know that more families have two cars than any other number. Note from Example 4.11 that the median for this data set equals the mode. ■

Example 4.15

Mode for Highest Academic Degree: Calculate the mode for the highest academic degree earned by employees at the Cottrell Corporation. Use the data in Table 3.6.

Solution: The modal class is the class having the highest frequency. For this set of data, it is the group having a high school education, which has a frequency of 200. In this case, the mode conveys useful information about the distribution of degrees. Note that since the data are qualitative, there is no mean or median. ■

Example 4.16

Mode for Residence of Students: Calculate the mode for residence for the data in Table 3.8.

Solution: Of the 2000 students, 1400 were from California, 240 were from out of state, and 360 were foreign. The modal class is California. As in Example 4.15, it is meaningless to talk about the mean or median of the distribution because the variable is qualitative. ■

Comparison of the Mean, Median, and Mode

To get a visual interpretation of the mean, examine the histogram in Figure 4.1. Suppose we cut a piece of plywood in the exact shape of the histogram. Now stand the piece of plywood upright on its lower edge and try to balance the piece of plywood on a fulcrum. There will be exactly one point on the lower edge where we can place the fulcrum so that the plywood histogram will just balance. That point is the mean of the distribution. The mean can be thought of as the *center of gravity* of the distribution.

FIGURE 4.1
The mean of a distribution can be interpreted as the distribution's center of gravity.

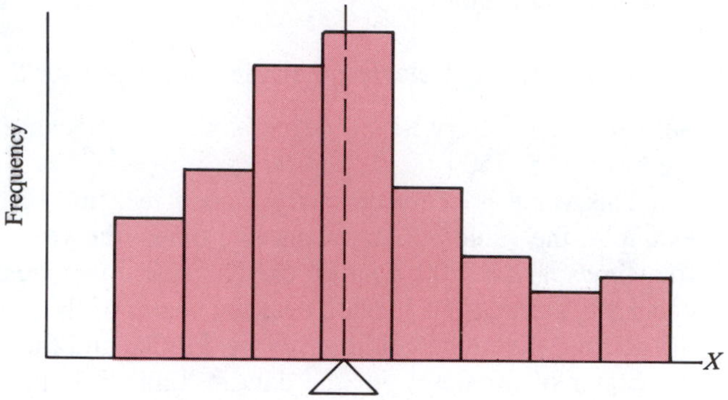

If we think of the mean in this way, it is easy to see how a few extreme values can have a big influence on the value of the mean. If the extreme values are much larger than the rest of the data, then the fulcrum will have to be shifted far to the right to keep the plywood histogram in balance.

When the relative frequency distribution is represented by a smooth curve or histogram, the median is the value such that 50% of the area under the curve lies to its left and 50% of the area lies to its right. When the relative frequency distribution is represented by a smooth curve, the mode is the value lying beneath the highest point on the curve. When the relative frequency distribution is represented by a histogram, the *modal class* is the class with the greatest frequency.

The mean is affected by the value of every observation; if there are a few extreme values, then the mean may not be the best way to describe the center of the set of data. This is often the case with data such as the incomes of individuals, the profits or sales of corporations, and so forth. In these cases the median may be a better measure of the typical value, because it is not so strongly affected by extreme values. In general, the mean does not equal the median, nor do they have to be close to one another. The mean and the median are quite different ways of measuring the center of a set of data.

Both the mean and the median are sometimes called the *average* of a set of data, but most people use the term *average* to indicate the mean. Some serious problems can arise when it is not clear which average is being used.

Example 4.17 **Comparing the Mean and the Median:** Consider a sample of eight individuals whose incomes are as follows:

$x_1 = \$15{,}000, \quad x_2 = \$16{,}000, \quad x_3 = \$19{,}000, \quad x_4 = \$21{,}000$
$x_5 = \$24{,}000, \quad x_6 = \$25{,}000, \quad x_7 = \$26{,}000, \quad x_8 = \$210{,}000$

Calculate the mean and median.

Solution: The mean income for these eight individuals is \$44,500, and the median income is (\$21,000 + \$24,000)/2 = \$22,500. In this example, the mean income is almost twice as large as the median income, because it is strongly influenced by the extreme value \$210,000. ■

A Graphical Comparison of the Mean, Median, and Mode

When a distribution is unimodal and symmetric like the bell-shaped normal distribution, the mean, median, and mode all coincide. If the distribution is skewed to the right, the mean is larger than the mode because it is affected by the large values in the tail, whereas the mode is influenced only by the most frequently occurring values, which are small. The median is less influenced by the values in the right-hand tail than is the mean, so the median will be less than the mean. Furthermore, the peak of a right-skewed distribution will be to the left of the value that divides the area under the curve into two equal parts, and so the median will exceed the mode.

Relationships Between the Mean, Median, and Mode

If a distribution is skewed to the right, the following relationships hold among the mean, median, and mode:

Skewed to the right: mode < median < mean

If a distribution is skewed to the left, then the relationships are reversed:

Skewed to the left: mean < median < mode

The relationship between the mean, median, and mode is illustrated in Figure 4.2.

When the Median Is Useful

There are two situations in which the median is preferable to the mean as a measure of central tendency.

1. *Open-ended class intervals*: If you want to calculate an average from a frequency distribution with an open-ended class, there may be no alternative but to use the median, because calculating the mean requires knowledge of the midpoint of the open-ended class or of the sum of the measurements in the open-ended class.

2. *Outliers*: The mean is far more influenced by extreme values than is the median. Consequently, the median provides a better measure of central tendency than the mean when there are some extremely large or small values.

FIGURE 4.2
Relationships among the mean, median, and mode.

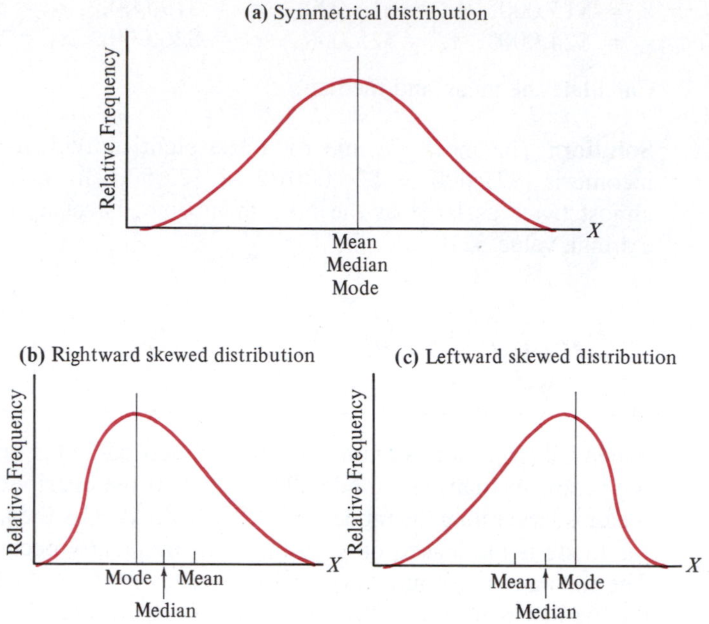

When the Mode Is Useful

There are three situations in which the mode is preferable as a measure of central tendency.

1. *Qualitative data*: Frequently the mode is a useful measure of the typical value of a qualitative variable.

2. *Sizes of products*: The mode can be useful for data on the sizes of products. For example, managers of clothing stores are interested in the most frequently purchased sizes of dresses and shirts, and managers of supermarkets are interested in the most frequently purchased size of a box of laundry detergent.

3. *Grouped data*: The mode is usually a more meaningful measure of central tendency of numerical data if it is calculated from a frequency distribution or a relative frequency distribution. When data are grouped into classes, as in a frequency distribution or a relative frequency distribution, the *modal class* is the class having the greatest frequency or relative frequency.

Exercises for Section 4.2

1. Most people have a basic understanding of the mean and the median. In this exercise you are asked to guess the value of the mean or median for different variables. The answers should be obvious. If you make any mistakes, then you should reread this chapter carefully to make sure that you understand the concept of the mean.

In each of the following circumstances, select the value that you think best represents the mean.

a. The mean price of a gallon of gasoline at a sample of 10 service stations in a certain neighborhood: \$0.10, \$1.00, or \$10.00.
b. The mean price of a can of three tennis balls at a sample of 10 sporting goods stores: \$0.40, \$4.00, or \$40.00.
c. The mean weight of a sample of 100 male college seniors: 120 lbs.; 170 lbs.; 250 lbs.
d. The mean height of a sample of 100 female college seniors: 40 inches; 66 inches; 86 inches.

2. The data that follow show the monthly rental payments (in dollars) for a random sample of 50 apartment dwellers in a certain city:

200	310	150	225	140	135	110	190	130	240
145	95	165	185	150	310	100	175	165	130
165	110	160	150	130	210	210	315	125	245
220	140	210	165	90	190	200	185	150	220
290	125	220	370	75	185	215	160	180	170

a. Calculate the sample mean.
b. Calculate the sample median.
c. Form a frequency distribution using as classes 0 to under 50, 50 to under 100, and so forth.
d. Find the modal class in part (c).

3. The annual salary of a salesperson during five years was \$10,000, \$13,000, \$21,000, \$14,000, and \$16,000. Find the mean and median salaries.

4. A company has 80 male employees, who have a mean salary of \$12,000, and 40 female employees, who have a mean salary of \$9,000. Find the mean salary of all 120 employees.

5. A department store manager is interested in the number of complaints received by the customer service department about the quality of electrical products sold by the store. Records over a 10-month period yield the following data:

Month	1	2	3	4	5	6	7	8	9	10
Complaints	18	12	10	16	8	3	13	11	3	13

a. Find the mean number of weekly complaints for this population.
b. Find the median number of weekly complaints for this population.

6. Let $x_1, x_2, \ldots, x_N$ denote the N observations in a population with mean μ. Let K be any number. Show that

$$\Sigma(x_i - K)^2 = \Sigma(x_i - \mu)^2 + N(K - \mu)^2$$

Hence, deduce that the value of K for which $\Sigma(x_i - K)^2$ is smallest is $K = \mu$.
(*Hint:* $\Sigma(x_i - K)^2 = \Sigma[(x_i - \mu) + (\mu - K)]^2$.)

7. For each of the following populations, discuss the shape of the distribution and indicate whether the mean, median, or mode would be the best measure of central tendency:

a. Annual incomes of adult males
b. Ages of cars in the United States
c. Collar sizes of men's shirts sold at a department store
d. Amounts in savings accounts at a large bank
e. Number of bus passengers on weekdays during a given year on a particular bus route at 8 A.M.

8. The data on the following page show a sample of home mortgage loan amounts (in dollars) handled by a particular loan officer at a savings and loan association.

20,000	38,500	33,000	27,500	34,000
12,500	25,900	43,200	37,500	36,200
25,200	30,900	23,800	28,400	13,000
31,000	35,500	25,400	33,500	20,200
39,000	38,100	30,500	45,500	30,500
52,000	40,500	51,600	42,500	44,800

Find the sample mean, median, and mode.

4.3 ▪ Calculating the Mean, Median, and Mode of Grouped Data

When individual data values are available for a frequency distribution, they should be used to compute summary statistics, such as the mean and the median. Calculations based on grouped data will generally not yield the same values as calculations based on individual observations, because some information is lost when data are grouped. Thus, summary statistics based on grouped data are only approximations or estimates of what they would have been if they had been calculated from the individual values.

When using grouped data, the class midpoint for each class is used to represent the typical observation in that class. Thus if most of the values in a class are bunched near one of the class limits, the class midpoint will not provide a good approximation for the values in the class.

Calculating the Mean of Grouped Data

To calculate the mean using grouped data, we must approximate the sum of the observations in each class. To do this, we assume that all of the observations in class i fall at the class midpoint M_i, and we multiply this class midpoint by the class frequency f_i. The product, f_iM_i, approximates the sum of the observations in class i. Then we use the procedure described in the accompanying box to estimate the mean.

Formula for Calculating Sample Mean of Grouped Data

Let k denote the number of groups or classes, and let $M_1, M_2, \ldots, M_k$ denote the midpoints of the k classes. Let $f_1, f_2, \ldots, f_k$ denote the frequencies of the k classes. The mean is estimated using the formula

$$\bar{x} = \frac{\Sigma f_iM_i}{n} = \frac{f_1M_1 + f_2M_2 + \cdots + f_kM_k}{n}$$

Example 4.18 **Mean of Grouped Data for Salaries:** Estimate the mean for the grouped data in Table 3.2, which shows the frequency distribution for salaries of employees at Lang's Trucking Company.

Solution: There are $k = 8$ classes. The eight class midpoints are $M_1 = \$1350$, $M_2 = 1450, \ldots, M_8 = 2050$. The eight class frequencies and the eight class midpoints are shown in Table 4.2 along with the eight products $f_1M_1, f_2M_2, \ldots, f_8M_8$.

TABLE 4.2
Calculation of the mean of grouped data

Monthly Salary (dollars)	Frequency (f_i)	Relative Frequency	Midpoint (M_i)	Product (f_iM_i)
1300 to under 1400	8	.1000	1350	10,800
1400 to under 1500	11	.1375	1450	15,950
1500 to under 1600	17	.2125	1550	26,350
1600 to under 1700	19	.2375	1650	31,350
1700 to under 1800	10	.1250	1750	17,500
1800 to under 1900	6	.0750	1850	11,100
1900 to under 2000	4	.0500	1950	7,800
2000 to under 2100	5	.0625	2050	10,250
Total	80	1.0000		131,100

We obtain the sum

$$\Sigma f_iM_i = 131{,}100$$

The estimated mean is

$$\bar{x} = \Sigma f_iM_i/n = 131{,}100/80 = 1{,}638.75$$

Recall from Example 4.7 that the mean using the raw data was \$1,626.69. In this case, using grouped data changes the estimate of the mean by \$12.06. Whether this difference is significant depends on the reason for performing the analysis. ■

We also could have obtained the grouped mean by making use of the relative frequency distribution. The formula for $\bar{x}$ for grouped data is

$$\bar{x} = \frac{f_1M_1 + f_2M_2 + \cdots + f_kM_k}{n}$$

or equivalently,

$$\bar{x} = M_1\left(\frac{f_1}{n}\right) + M_2\left(\frac{f_2}{n}\right) + \cdots + M_k\left(\frac{f_k}{n}\right)$$

But note that f_i/n is the relative frequency of the ith class. Thus, using the relative frequencies, we can obtain $\bar{x}$ by multiplying each class midpoint by the class relative frequency and summing these products. Using the preceding data, we obtain

$$\bar{x} = 1350(.1000) + 1450(.1375) + \cdots + 2050(.0625) = 1638.75$$

This is the same value calculated previously.

If one of the classes is open-ended, the mean cannot be calculated from the grouped data unless an estimate of the midpoint of the open-ended class is available. At times, it is better to avoid calculating the sample mean for open-ended distributions.

Calculating the Median of Grouped Data

When sample data have been grouped and presented as a frequency or relative frequency distribution, the median cannot be calculated by ordering the individual observations. To estimate the median in this case, we can use either the frequency distribution or the relative frequency distribution. First the class containing the median must be determined, and then the median is located inside this class by interpolation. The steps are as follows:

1. Determine which class contains the median.
2. Denote the lower boundary of this class by A and the upper boundary by B.
3. If a relative frequency distribution is being used, let C denote the percentage (not the proportion) of observations less than A, and let D denote the percentage of observations between A and B.
4. If a frequency distribution is being used, let c denote the number of observations less than A, and let d denote the number of observations between A and B.
5. Let n denote the sample size.

If the data are in a frequency distribution, estimate the median using the following formula:

Estimating the Median from a Frequency Distribution

$$\text{Median} = A + \frac{n/2 - c}{d}(B - A)$$

If the data are given in a relative frequency distribution, use the following formula:

Estimating the Median from a Relative Frequency Distribution

$$\text{Median} = A + \frac{50 - C}{D}(B - A)$$

These formulas for estimating the median from grouped data result from interpolating between points A and B.

Example 4.19 **Calculating the median for grouped data:** Calculate the median for the grouped data in Table 4.2, which shows the frequency and relative frequency distribution of monthly salaries of the 80 employees at Lang's Trucking Company.

Solution: The median must fall in the 1600-to-1700 interval because 45% of the observations are less than 1600 and 31.25% of the observations are greater than 1700. Thus the value that evenly splits the data must lie between 1600 and 1700.

The lower limit of the class containing the median is $A = 1600$ and the upper limit is $B = 1700$. The percentage of observations falling below A is $C = 45$, and the percentage of observations falling between A and B is $D = 23.75$. Finally, the number of observations less than A is denoted by $c = 36$, and the number of observations between 1600 and 1700 is $d = 19$.

From the frequency distribution, we obtain

$$\text{Median} = 1600 + \frac{80/2 - 36}{19}(1700 - 1600)$$
$$= 1600 + 0.2105(100) = 1621.05$$

Using the relative frequency distribution, we have

$$\text{Median} = 1600 + \frac{50 - 45}{23.75}(1700 - 1600)$$
$$= 1600 + 0.2105(100) = 1621.05$$

Recall from Example 4.10 that the true population median was \$1610. Estimating the median from the grouped data causes us to overestimate the true median by approximately \$11. ■

Calculating the Mode for Grouped Data

When individual observations are not available, the mode cannot be calculated exactly. The *modal class* is the class with the greatest frequency.

Exercises for Section 4.3

1. The accompanying frequency distribution shows the monthly starting salaries of a sample of recent college graduates.

Monthly Starting Salary (dollars)	Frequency
1300 to under 1400	6
1400 to under 1500	13
1500 to under 1600	17
1600 to under 1700	20
1700 to under 1800	9
1800 to under 1900	6
1900 to under 2000	5
2000 to under 2100	4
Total	80

Compute the sample mean, median, and mode, using as midpoints \$1350, \$1450, and so forth.

2. Consider the accompanying frequency distribution for automobile repair costs in an insurance company's minor claims category.

Repair Costs (dollars)	Frequency
0 to under 100	10
100 to under 200	18
200 to under 300	60
300 to under 400	70
400 to under 500	42
Total	200

Compute the mean, median, and mode for this sample of data, using as midpoints \$50, \$150, and so forth.

3. A sample of automobiles traveling on the Ohio Turnpike are checked for speed by a state police radar system. The accompanying frequency distribution shows the clocked speeds.

Speed (miles per hour)	Frequency
40 to under 45	10
45 to under 50	40
50 to under 55	150
55 to under 60	175
60 to under 65	75
65 to under 70	15
70 to under 75	7
75 to under 80	3
Total	475

a. What is the sample mean speed of the automobiles traveling on the Ohio Turnpike?
b. What are the median and modal speeds?

4. Examine the accompanying frequency distribution of monthly telephone bills for a sample of households.

a. Calculate the sample mean.
b. Calculate the sample median.
c. Find the modal class.

Amount of Bill (dollars)	Number of Households
\$0 to under \$10	15
\$10 to under \$30	63
\$30 to under \$50	162
\$50 to under \$75	237
\$75 to under \$100	103
\$100 to under \$150	13

5. Examine the accompanying frequency distribution of ages of cars owned by a car rental agency.
a. Calculate the sample mean.
b. Calculate the sample median.
c. Find the modal class.

Age of Car (months)	Number of Cars
0 to under 2	15
2 to under 4	36
4 to under 6	47
6 to under 8	105
8 to under 10	86
10 to under 12	33

4.4 ▪ *Quartiles and Percentiles*

The mean, median, and mode are three different measures of the center or the most representative value of a set of data. There are other summary statistics that can be used to locate specific values in a distribution. Sometimes we want to know the position of a particular observation relative to the others. For example, if you received a score of 1100 on the SAT, you might want to know the percentage of participants who scored lower than 1100. Such a *measure of relative standing* of an observation within a data set is called a *percentile*.

Definition: Percentiles

Suppose the observations $x_1, x_2, \ldots, x_n$ have been arranged in ascending order. The pth **percentile** is the value x_p such that p percent of the observations are less than or equal to x_p and $(1 - p)$ percent of the observations are greater than or equal to x_p.

Consider the eight observations 4, 6, 8, 10, 12, 14, 16, and 18. Twenty-five percent of the observations are less than 6.5 and 75% are greater. Similarly, 25% are less than 7 and 75% are greater. Thus, both 6.5 and 7.0 could be called the 25th percentile; in fact, any value between 6 and 8 could be called the 25th percentile. Some statisticians recommend interpolating to find percentiles. In most problems of practical interest, however, there are a large number of observations, and interpolation changes the value obtained only slightly. We shall adopt the rules in the accompanying box for calculating a percentile.

Procedure for Calculating Percentiles

1. Arrange the n observations in ascending order. The smallest observation is given rank 1, the second smallest observation is given rank 2, and so forth.
2. Calculate the index $i = (p \times n)/100$, where p is the percentile of interest and n is the sample size.
3. If i is an integer, the pth percentile is the arithmetic average of the values having ranks i and $(i + 1)$.
4. If i is not an integer, the next integer value greater than i denotes the rank of the value which is the pth percentile.

Example 4.20

Calculating Percentiles: Calculate the 70th and 80th percentiles for the following set of 15 values:

18, 14, 45, 32, 65, 43, 25, 41, 83, 51, 26, 36, 40, 55, 20

Solution: First, arrange the 15 values in ascending order:

14, 18, 20, 25, 26, 32, 36, 40, 41, 43, 45, 51, 55, 65, 83

For the 70th percentile, the index is

$$i = (70 \times 15)/100 = 10.5$$

Because i is not an integer, the position of the 70th percentile is the next integer greater than 10.5, that is, the 11th position. The 70th percentile corresponds to the 11th data value, 45.

For the 80th percentile, the index is

$$i = (80 \times 15)/100 = 12.0$$

Because i is an integer, the 80th percentile is the average of the data values in positions 12 and 13. Thus the 80th percentile is

$$(51 + 55)/2 = 53$$

■

For a continuous distribution, the pth percentile is the value such that the area to its right is p and the area to its left is $(1 - p)$. Figure 4.3 shows the 30th percentile for a continuous distribution. The median is the 50th percentile.

Other than the median, the most commonly used percentiles are *quartiles*. Quartiles divide the set of observations into four groups, each containing 25% of the data.

Definition: Quartiles

The **lower quartile** of a set of observations, also called the **first quartile**, is the 25th percentile of the data. That is, 25% of the data lie below the first quartile and thus 75% lie above it. The first quartile is denoted Q_1. The **upper quartile**, also called the **third quartile**, is denoted by the symbol Q_3 and is the 75th percentile of the data. That is, 75% of the observations lie below the third quartile and 25% lie above it. The median is the 50th percentile (or second quartile), because 50% of the data lie below the median and 50% lie above it.

FIGURE 4.3
The 30th percentile for a continuous distribution.

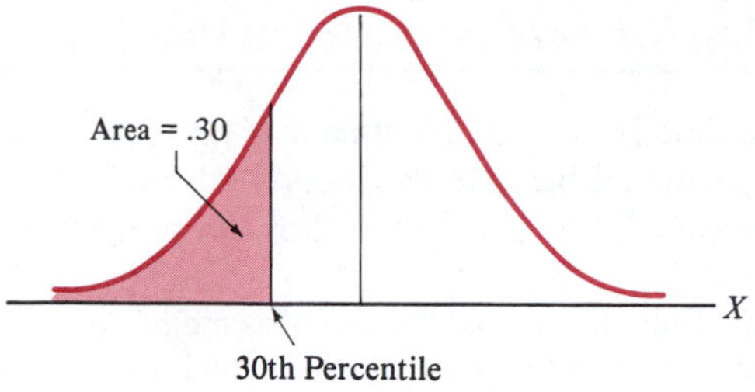

Example 4.21

Calculation of Quartiles: The following 24 observations have been ordered from lowest to highest:

6	8	12	17	20	22	25	26	26	28	30	32
34	37	40	50	61	63	65	67	69	80	82	86

Find the first and third quartiles.

Solution: For the lower quartile, calculate the index with $p = 25$ and $n = 24$. Using the formula $i = (p \times n)/100$, we get $i = 6.0$. Because i is an integer, Q_1 is the average of observations having ranks 6 and 7. Because the 6th observation is 22 and the 7th observation is 25, the lower quartile is $Q_1 = (22 + 25)/2 = 23.5$.

For the upper quartile, calculate the index $i = (p \times n)/100$, where $p = 75$ and $n = 24$. The index is $i = 18.0$. Because i is an integer, Q_3 is the average of observations having ranks 18 and 19. The 18th observation is 65 and the 19th observation is 65. The upper quartile Q_3 is $(63 + 65)/2 = 64.0$. ■

Example 4.22

Quartiles for Salaries at Lang's Trucking Company: Calculate Q_1 and Q_3 for the data in Table 4.1.

Solution: To find the lower quartile, we first calculate the index, $i = (25 \times 80)/100 = 20$. Because this is an integer, the lower quartile is the average of the values whose ranks are 20 and 21. These values are 1500 and 1530, and so the lower quartile is $(1500 + 1530)/2 = 1515$. This tells us that 25% of the employees at the company earn less than or equal to \$1515 per month.

To find the upper quartile, we calculate the index $i = (75 \times 80)/100 = 60$. Because this is an integer, the upper quartile is the average of the values whose ranks are 60 and 61. Because these values are 1730 and 1740, the upper quartile is $(1730 + 1740)/2 = 1735$. ■

Figure 4.4 shows the lower and upper quartiles for a continuous distribution. The area to the left of Q_1 is .25, and the area to the right of Q_3 is .25.

FIGURE 4.4
The lower and upper quartiles for a continuous distribution.

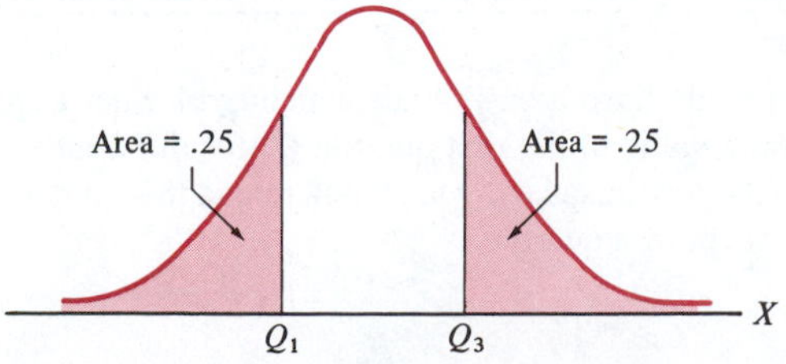

Calculations of Percentiles for Grouped Data

If the data have been grouped as a frequency distribution, the pth percentile can only be approximated because the individual observations are not known. The pth percentile is approximated by using the following procedure:

1. Find the interval that contains the pth percentile.
2. Let A and B denote the lower and upper boundaries of this interval.
3. Let c denote the number of observations less than A.
4. Let d denote the number of observations between A and B.
5. Let n denote the sample size and let p denote the percentile desired. Let $m = np/100$.
6. The pth percentile can be approximated as the value

$$p\text{th percentile} = A + \frac{m - c}{d}(B - A)$$

This formula is the result of interpolating between points A and B.

Example 4.23 **Percentiles for Salaries at Lang's Trucking Company:** Refer to the data in Table 3.3, which shows the distribution of salaries at Lang's Trucking Company. Estimate the lower quartile. That is, find the 25th percentile.

Solution: To find the class containing the lower quartile, examine the cumulative relative frequencies in Table 3.3. The lower quartile must fall in the 1500-to-1600 interval, because 23.75% of the observations are less than 1500 and 45% of the observations are less than 1600. Thus, we have $A = 1500$, $B = 1600$, $p = 25$, $m = 20$, $c = 19$, and $d = 17$. The lower quartile is then estimated as

$$\text{Lower quartile} = A + \frac{m - c}{d}(B - A)$$

$$= 1500 + \frac{20 - 19}{17}(1600 - 1500) = 1505.88$$

Recall from Example 4.22 that the lower quartile calculated from the raw data was \$1515. The estimate of the lower quartile obtained from the grouped data differs from the value calculated from the raw data by approximately \$9. ■

Exercises for Section 4.4

1. Most people have a basic understanding of what a quartile is. In this exercise you are asked to guess the value of the first quartile Q_1 for different variables. The answers should be obvious. If you make any mistakes, you should reread this chapter carefully to make sure that you understand the concept of a quartile.

In each of the following circumstances, select the value that you think best represents Q_1:

a. The mean price of a gallon of gasoline at a sample of 10 service stations in a certain neighborhood is \$1.00. Is the first quartile \$0.10, \$0.98, or \$10.00?
b. The mean price of a can of three tennis balls at a sample of 10 sporting goods stores is \$4.00. Is the first quartile \$1.40, \$3.35, or \$40.00?
c. The mean weight of a sample of 100 male college seniors is 170 pounds. Is the first quartile 120, 158, or 250 pounds?
d. The mean height of a sample of 100 female college seniors is 66 inches. Is the first quartile 40, 62, or 86 inches?

2. The data given below show the number of automobiles arriving at a toll booth during 24 four-minute intervals.

18	33	27	36	19	27	21	28
26	26	38	24	16	20	33	24
32	22	15	33	27	30	31	34

a. Calculate the mean.
b. Calculate the median.
c. Calculate the mode.
d. Calculate the first and third quartiles.

3. The following data show the number of tennis players who used a racquet club's facilities during a random sample of 40 weekdays:

46	87	69	50	64	35	37	76	84	46
53	66	90	43	27	47	86	74	45	65
36	48	76	78	79	63	47	60	50	52
49	69	82	58	46	58	67	64	35	58

a. Calculate the sample mean.
b. Calculate the sample median.
c. Calculate the first and third quartiles.
d. Calculate the 30th percentile.
e. Construct a frequency distribution and plot it.

4. The following data show the number of personal computers in use at 8 P.M. on a sample of 50 weekday evenings at a university computer center:

27	34	36	38	46	52	35	46	12	25
46	37	62	52	53	36	42	28	56	43
37	39	40	50	52	42	47	49	51	36
39	28	30	38	45	47	48	45	36	48
49	45	43	42	46	48	49	52	36	45

a. Calculate the sample mean.
b. Calculate the sample median.
c. Calculate the first and third quartiles.
d. Calculate the 30th percentile.
e. Construct a frequency distribution and plot it.

4.5 ▪ Measures of Dispersion

A measure of central tendency does not completely characterize a set of observations because it tells us nothing about variability in the data. Summary statistics that measure the amount of variation in a data set are called **measures of dispersion**.

For example, the notion of variability in statistical analysis is important in production management, where a major concern is to reduce variations in the quality of manufactured products or in some important characteristics of a product, such as the diameter of a bearing or the hardness of steel. In many financial problems, risk is measured by the amount of variability in the potential returns from an investment.

In addition to a measure of central tendency, some measure of dispersion is needed to tell whether a particular observation ranks near the top or bottom of a set of observations. Suppose you receive a grade of 70 on a mathematics test and a grade of 70 on a chemistry test. To guess what letter grade you will receive on the tests, you would probably want some information concerning the typical score of all the students who took the test and the amount of variation in the grades for the two tests. Suppose the math scores have a mean of 60 and are highly concentrated about the mean so that all the scores fall between 50 and 72. In this case a score of 70 would place you near the top of the class, and you could expect an A. Assume that the average score on the chemistry test is also 60 but that the scores are much more widely dispersed than the math scores. Some scores are in the 30s and 40s, and some are in the 80s and 90s. A score of 70 would put you closer to the middle of the class than to the top, and you might expect a B or a C.

We discuss five different summary measures of dispersion: the range, the interquartile range, the mean absolute deviation, the variance, and the standard deviation. Of these, the standard deviation is the measure used most frequently by statisticians.

The Range

Definition: Range

The **range** of a set of observations is the difference between the largest value and the smallest value.

Example 4.24

Calculating a Range: A sporting goods store has seven employees whose ages are 22, 33, 26, 21, 44, 63, and 58. A paint store has eight employees whose ages are 32, 30, 27, 30, 27, 34, 40, and 35. Calculate the ranges of the ages of employees at these stores.

Solution: At the sporting goods store, the oldest employee is 63 and the youngest is 21. The range is thus $63 - 21 = 42$ years. At the paint store, where the oldest employee is 40 and the youngest is 27, the range is $40 - 27 = 13$ years. The range at the sporting goods store is more than 3 times as large as that at the paint store. ■

Example 4.25

Range of Salaries at Lang's Trucking Company: Calculate the range for the data in Table 4.1.

Solution: The smallest salary is $1300 per month and the largest salary is $2025. Therefore the range of salaries is $2025 − $1300, or $725. ■

The range is very easy to calculate and interpret. Because of this, it is frequently used by the general public to describe the amount of variation in a set of data. It is less frequently used in scientific circles, however, because its value is easily influenced by the number of observations. In general, the range of a large sample of observations taken from a population is likely to be larger than the range of a small sample taken from the same population.

Another problem with the range is that two data sets with the same range can have vastly different dispersions. As an example, suppose we have data on the daily number of customers at two grocery stores. During a given year, the lowest number of customers at each store during the day was 100 and the highest number was 500. However, in one store the number of customers per day was almost always between 275 and 325, while at the other store the number of customers was frequently between 100 and 125 and between 475 and 500. At both stores, the range was 400, but the number of customers at the second store exhibited much more variation than the number of customers at the first. Here the range is an inadequate measure of the amount of variation in the two sets of data.

Finally, the range can be an unsatisfactory measure of dispersion because it is influenced too much by a single very high or very low observation. Because it depends only on the largest and smallest observations, the range is susceptible to considerable distortion if there are any extreme values. One way around this difficulty is to arrange the observations in ascending order, discard a few of the highest and lowest observations, and find the range of the remaining observations. Such a measurement is called a *trimmed range*. If we discard the lowest and the highest 25% of the observations, the trimmed range will measure the range of the middle 50% of the data. This measure is called the *interquartile range*.

Definition: Interquartile Range

For any population or sample of values, the **interquartile range** is $(Q_3 - Q_1)$, where Q_3 represents the upper quartile (or 75th percentile) and Q_1 represents the lower quartile (or 25th percentile).

The **semiinterquartile range** (half the interquartile range) can be thought of as an average distance from the center of the distribution. If the distribution is symmetric, the semiinterquartile range is the distance between Q_1 and the median (or Q_3 and the median).

One advantage of the interquartile range over the range is that the interquartile range can usually be calculated from a frequency distribution having open-ended classes, while the range cannot.

Deviations from the Mean

To measure the amount of variation in a set of data, we could calculate how far each observation is from the mean and then calculate the average (or mean) of these deviations. If the population mean is known, then we calculate deviations from the population mean; otherwise, we calculate deviations from the sample mean.

Definition: Deviation from the Mean

For any value x, the **deviation from the mean** is the difference $(x - \mu)$ if the population mean is known or $(x - \bar{x})$ if the sample mean is used.

If x exceeds the mean, the deviation is positive; if x is less than the mean, the deviation is negative. Deviations from the mean convey important information about the amount of variation in a set of data. If they tend to be large in absolute value, then the data are very spread out and are highly variable. If the deviations are small in absolute value, then the data are tightly clustered about the mean and do not exhibit much variability.

Averaging all the deviations from the mean might seem a useful way to measure dispersion. However, the average of all the deviations from the mean is 0 for any set of data, as shown in the following:

$$\begin{aligned} \Sigma (x_i - \bar{x}) &= (x_1 - \bar{x}) + (x_2 - \bar{x}) + \cdots + (x_n - \bar{x}) \\ &= (x_1 + x_2 + \cdots + x_n) - n\bar{x} \\ &= \Sigma x_i - n\frac{\Sigma x_i}{n} = 0 \end{aligned}$$

Example 4.26

Deviations from the Mean: Calculate the sum of the deviations from the mean for the data in Example 4.1.

Solution: In Example 4.6, the mean was shown to be 77. The seven deviations from the mean are as follows:

$92 - 77 = 15$ $\quad 84 - 77 = 7$ $\quad 70 - 77 = -7$ $\quad 76 - 77 = -1$

$66 - 77 = -11$ $\quad 80 - 77 = 3$ $\quad 71 - 77 = -6$

The sum of the seven deviations is:

$$\Sigma (x_i - \bar{x}) = 15 + 7 - 7 - 1 - 11 + 3 - 6 = 0$$

■

To avoid the problem of deviations from the mean summing to 0, we have two alternatives. We can take the absolute values of the deviations before we average them, or we can square the deviations before we average them.

The Mean Absolute Deviation

The *mean absolute deviation* is the arithmetic average of the absolute deviations from the mean; hence, the name *mean* absolute deviation.

Definition: Mean Absolute Deviation

The **mean absolute deviation** (M.A.D.) is calculated using the formula

$$\text{M.A.D.} = \frac{|x_1 - \bar{x}| + |x_2 - \bar{x}| + \cdots + |x_n - \bar{x}|}{n} = \frac{\Sigma |x_i - \bar{x}|}{n}$$

Example 4.27

Calculating the Mean Absolute Deviation: Refer to the data in Example 4.26, which showed the numbers of customers at a restaurant on a sample of seven days. Calculate the mean absolute deviation.

Solution: Example 4.26 showed the deviations from the mean for the number of customers at a restaurant on seven days. The absolute values of the deviations are:

$$|92 - 77| = 15 \quad |84 - 77| = 7 \quad |70 - 77| = 7 \quad |76 - 77| = 1$$
$$|66 - 77| = 11 \quad |80 - 77| = 3 \quad |71 - 77| = 6$$

The mean absolute deviation is

$$\text{M.A.D.} = (15 + 7 + 7 + 1 + 11 + 3 + 6)/7 = 7.143$$

The M.A.D. is 7.143, which indicates that on any given day the number of customers deviates from the mean by about 7. This deviation is relatively small and indicates that the number of customers at the restaurant does not vary very much. ■

Example 4.28

Calculating Another Mean Absolute Deviation: The following data show the adjusted gross incomes reported on a sample of five income tax returns:

$6,800 $10,000 $33,000 $14,500 $27,700

Calculate the mean absolute deviation.

Solution: The sample mean is $\bar{x} = \$18{,}400$. The absolute deviations from the mean are as follows:

$$|\$6{,}800 - \$18{,}400| = \$11{,}600 \quad |\$10{,}000 - \$18{,}400| = \$8{,}400$$
$$|\$33{,}000 - \$18{,}400| = \$14{,}600 \quad |\$14{,}500 - \$18{,}400| = \$3{,}900$$
$$|\$27{,}700 - \$18{,}400| = \$11{,}300$$

The mean absolute deviation is

$$\text{M.A.D.} = (\$11{,}600 + \$8{,}400 + \$14{,}600 + \$3{,}900 + \$11{,}300)/5 = \$9{,}960$$

Note that in this example the data are much more spread out than in Example 4.27, and consequently the mean absolute deviation is much larger. ■

The mean absolute deviation is not used very frequently because absolute values are difficult to work with mathematically.

The Variance and Standard Deviation

By far the most important and most frequently used summary statistics for measuring variation in a set of data are the *variance* and the *standard deviation*. Because the standard deviation is the square root of the variance, the two statistics convey exactly the same amount of information. Like the mean absolute deviation, these statistics are based on the deviations from the mean. To calculate the variance, we square the deviations and average the results; to get the standard deviation, we then take the square root.

How we calculate the variance depends on whether we have a population or sample of data. If we are using the entire population of data, then we can calculate the *population variance*, denoted by the symbol σ^2 (read "sigma squared").

Definition: Population Variance

The **population variance** is calculated using the formula

$$\sigma^2 = \frac{\Sigma(x_i - \mu)^2}{N}$$

where N is the population size.

To calculate the population variance, we square each deviation from the population mean, sum these squared values, and divide the sum by N. Thus the population variance measures the average of the squared deviations from the population mean.

The variance is an inconvenient measure of spread because it measures the average of the *squared* deviations from the mean. Thus, the variance is not expressed in the same units as the original observations. For example, if the original data are in dollars, then the deviations from the mean are measured in dollars and the variance is measured in squared dollars. In addition, the variance is frequently an extremely large number relative to the original observations. For example, if an individual's annual income is $5,000 above the mean, then the squared deviation is 25,000,000 squared dollars. When calculating the variance of income data where the deviations from the mean exceed $1,000, the variance will usually exceed 1,000,000. To overcome these difficulties, we work with the square root of the variance rather than the variance itself. This leads us to the concept of the *standard deviation,* the most important and most frequently used measure of variation present in a data set.

Definition: Population Standard Deviation

The **population standard deviation** is the positive square root of the population variance and is denoted by the symbol σ.

If we have a sample of data, we calculate the *sample variance* and the *sample standard deviation*. The sample variance is denoted by the symbol s^2, and the sample standard deviation by the symbol s.

Definition: Sample Variance and Sample Standard Deviation

To calculate the **sample variance**, we use the formula

$$s^2 = \frac{\Sigma\,(x_i - \bar{x})^2}{n - 1}$$

where n is the sample size. The **sample standard deviation** is the positive square root of the sample variance and is denoted by the symbol s.

The formula for calculating the sample variance differs from the formula for calculating the population variance in two important ways:

1. The denominator of the population variance is N, while the denominator of the sample variance is $(n - 1)$, and
2. the population variance is based on deviations from the population mean μ, while the sample variance is based on deviations from the sample mean $\bar{x}$.

The use of $(n - 1)$ rather than n in the denominator of s^2 should be explained. Recall that $\bar{x}$ and s^2 are calculated from sample data and are estimates of the population parameters μ and σ^2. In general, the sample will not exactly reproduce the characteristics of the population, and it is unlikely that $\bar{x}$ will be exactly equal to μ.

When estimating a population parameter, we want to use a procedure that has no tendency to over- or underestimate the population value on the average. If an estimator equals the population value on the average (i.e., overestimates and underestimates balance out), then we have an unbiased estimator.

s^2 has $(n - 1)$ rather than n as its denominator so that it will be an unbiased estimator of σ^2. If n were used as the denominator, on the average s^2 would be smaller than σ^2 and thus be a biased estimator. The reason for this bias is that, on the average, the sample squared deviations $(x_i - \bar{x})^2$ are slightly smaller than the population squared deviations $(x_i - \mu)^2$. The use of $(n - 1)$ in the denominator corrects this bias.

The number $(n - 1)$ is sometimes called the *degrees of freedom*. The phrase "degree of freedom" arises from the fact that to calculate the variance, we need to find the n deviations from the mean; if $(n - 1)$ of these deviations are known, the last deviation can be calculated. That is, if we know the first $(n - 1)$ deviations from the mean, the last deviation can be deduced from the fact that $\Sigma(x_i - \bar{x}) = 0$.

Example 4.29

Sample Standard Deviation for Number of Customers: Calculate the sample standard deviation for the data in Example 4.1.

Solution: From Example 4.6, we know the mean is $\bar{x} = 77$. The subsequent calculations are shown in Table 4.3. The second column of the table shows the deviations from the mean, and the third column shows the squares of these deviations. The sum of these squared deviations is $\Sigma(x_i - \bar{x})^2 = 490$. We divide this sum by $n - 1 = 6$ to obtain the sample variance

$$s^2 = 490/6 = 81.667$$

The sample standard deviation is simply

$$s = \sqrt{81.667} = 9.037$$

In Example 4.27, we showed that the mean absolute deviation for the same sample of data is M.A.D. = 7.143. In this example, the standard deviation is slightly larger than the mean absolute deviation. ■

TABLE 4.3
Calculating the sample standard deviation

	x	$x - \bar{x}$	$(x - \bar{x})^2$
	92	$92 - 77 = 15$	225
	84	$84 - 77 = 7$	49
	70	$70 - 77 = -7$	49
	76	$76 - 77 = -1$	1
	66	$66 - 77 = -11$	121
	80	$80 - 77 = 3$	9
	71	$71 - 77 = -6$	36
Total	539	0	490

Alternative Formula for Calculating the Variance

The following formula provides another way of calculating the sample variance, which is frequently more convenient when performing the calculations by hand.

Alternative Formula for Sample Variance

$$s^2 = \frac{\Sigma x_i^2 - n\bar{x}^2}{n - 1}$$

Example 4.30

Calculating the Sample Standard Deviation with the Alternative Formula: Calculate the sample standard deviation for the data in Example 4.1 using the alternative formula.

Solution: The squared values of the data are

8464 7056 4900 5776 4356 6400 5041

We sum these values to obtain $\Sigma x_i^2 = 41{,}993$. Since we know the sample mean is $\bar{x} = 77$, the alternative formula for the sample variance yields

$$s^2 = \frac{41{,}993 - 7(77)^2}{7 - 1} = \frac{490}{6} = 81.667$$

The sample standard deviation, $s = \sqrt{81.667} = 9.037$, is identical to the value calculated in Example 4.29. ■

Example 4.31

Sample Standard Deviation for Data in Example 4.28: Calculate the sample standard deviation for the data in Example 4.28, the adjusted gross incomes for a sample of five individuals.

Solution: From Example 4.28, we know that the sample mean is $\bar{x} = \$18{,}400$. Because the mean is an integer, it is convenient to use the deviations from the mean to calculate the variance and standard deviation. The deviations from the mean are

−11,600, −8,400, 14,600, −3,900, 11,300

Squaring these deviations, we get

134,560,000, 70,560,000, 213,160,000, 15,210,000, 127,690,000

Finally, the sum of these squared deviations is $\Sigma(x_i - \bar{x})^2 = 561{,}180{,}000$. Dividing by $(n - 1)$, we get the sample variance of:

$$s^2 = 561{,}180{,}000/4 = 140{,}295{,}000$$

The sample standard deviation is thus

$$s = \sqrt{140{,}295{,}000} = 11{,}844.62$$

Recall from Example 4.28 that the mean absolute deviation is 9,960 for these data. ■

Example 4.31 shows that calculating the variance and standard deviation when the observations consist of large values can be a very tedious chore. Fortunately, there are numerous computer programs, such as SPSSX, SAS, and Minitab, that can perform the calculations for us.

Example 4.32

Standard Deviation of Data in Table 3.1: Calculate the population standard deviation for the data in Table 3.1.

Solution: The 80 observations represent the entire population of data, so we calculate the variance and standard deviation by using $N = 80$ in the denominator. It is left to the reader to show that the variance is $\sigma^2 = 33{,}267.71$ and the standard deviation is $\sigma = 182.39$. Examine the histogram plotted in Figure 3.1. The center of gravity of the histogram is the mean value of \$1,626.69, and the standard deviation shows that the typical deviation from this central value is approximately \$182.

If the data are widely scattered about the mean, deviations from the mean will be large, and the variance and the standard deviation will also be large. If the observations are concentrated near the mean, then the variance and standard deviation will be small. This idea is illustrated in Figure 4.5.

FIGURE 4.5
Comparing the variances for two distributions.

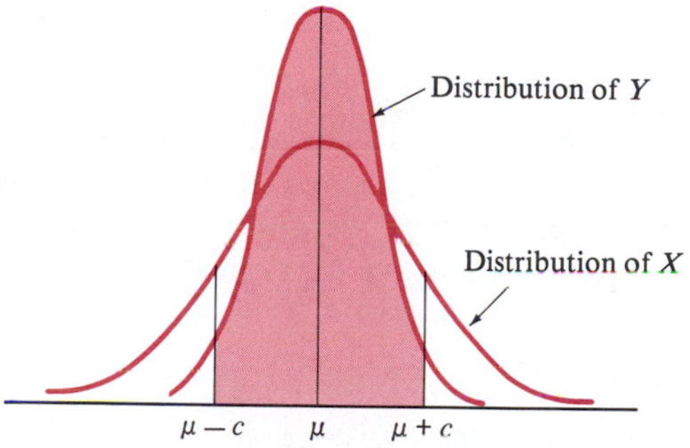

Figure 4.5 shows the distributions of two different hypothetical variables, X and Y. Because the distributions are centered at the same value, both X and Y have the same mean μ. However, the distribution of X is more spread out than the distribution of Y, so the variance of X (denoted σ_x^2) is larger than the variance of Y (σ_y^2). In Figure 4.5, consider any interval of values centered about the mean μ, such as the interval $(\mu - c, \mu + c)$ for any positive value c. A larger proportion of the Y values will fall in the interval than of the X values. In Figure 4.5, about 95% of the Y values fall between $(\mu - c)$ and $(\mu + c)$, whereas only about 75% of the X values fall in this interval.

Example 4.33

Comparing Two Standard Deviations: To see how the sample standard deviation measures the spread in a set of data, calculate the sample standard deviation for the following two samples of data. The first data set shows the weights of a random sample of 50 seven-year-old boys, and the second the weights of a random sample of 50 adult men.

Weights of boys (in pounds)

53	48	45	47	52	61	44	52	48	51
68	57	53	56	55	46	47	47	41	53
63	48	59	57	54	44	66	64	66	67
51	52	59	62	51	65	48	46	49	52
52	53	47	49	56	63	67	71	61	73

Weights of men (in pounds)

126	154	171	204	165	174	178	184	167	172
139	146	128	147	159	157	163	174	181	188
162	154	203	148	171	198	186	162	171	184
142	138	166	159	178	196	174	183	188	191
172	177	196	212	168	171	229	217	187	166

Solution: The sample means, sample variances, and sample standard deviations for the boys' weights and the men's weights are as follows:

$$\bar{x}_{\text{boys}} = 54.78 \qquad \bar{x}_{\text{men}} = 172.52$$
$$s^2_{\text{boys}} = 62.91 \qquad s^2_{\text{men}} = 475.48$$
$$s_{\text{boys}} = 7.93 \qquad s_{\text{men}} = 21.81$$

The sample standard deviation for the men is much larger than that for the boys, indicating that the distribution of the men's weights is much more spread out than the distribution of the boys' weights. For the boys, the sample standard deviation is only 7.93, which indicates that the typical deviation from the mean is only 7.93 pounds. For

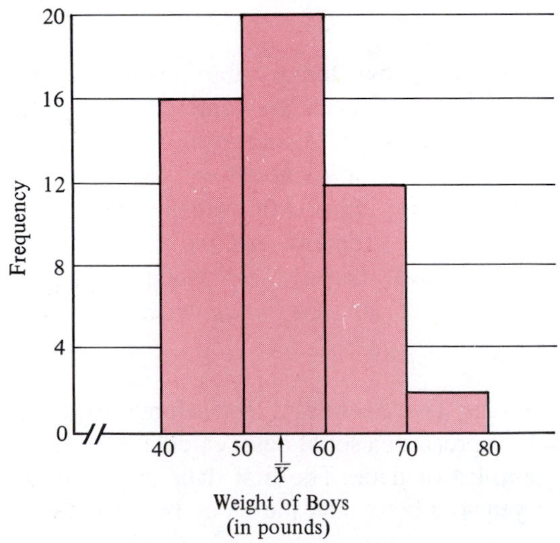

FIGURE 4.6
Distribution of weights for a sample of boys.

FIGURE 4.7 **Distribution of weights for a sample of men.**

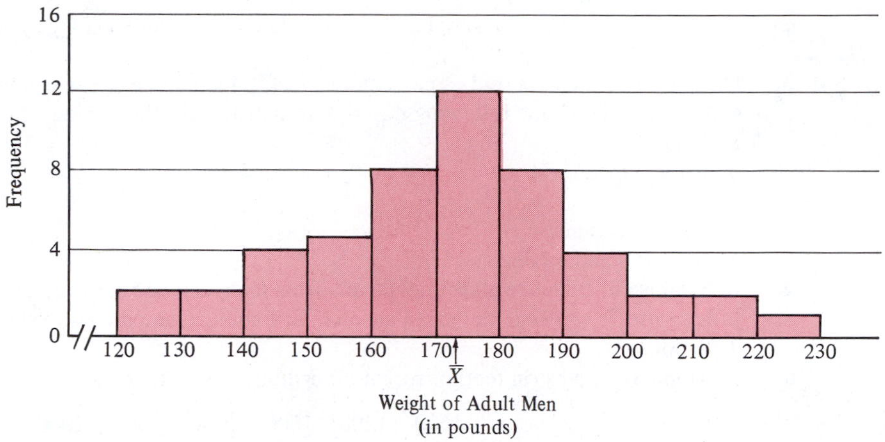

the men, the typical deviation from the mean is 21.81 pounds, or nearly 3 times as large. The histograms in Figures 4.6 and 4.7 show the differences in the spread of the two distributions. ■

Exercises for Section 4.5

1. Many people do not have a basic understanding of the standard deviation. In this exercise you are asked to guess the value of the standard deviation for different variables. The answers should be obvious. If you make any mistakes, you should reread this chapter carefully to make sure that you understand the concept of standard deviation.

   In each of the following circumstances, select the value that you think best represents the standard deviation.

   a. We obtain data showing the price of a gallon of gasoline at a sample of 10 service stations in a certain neighborhood. The mean price is \$1.00. Is a reasonable guess for the standard deviation of prices \$0.01, \$1.00, or \$10.00?
   b. The mean starting salary is \$21,000 for 100 recent college graduates. Is a reasonable guess at the standard deviation \$1.00, \$10.00, or \$1000?
   c. The mean weight of a sample of 100 male college seniors is 170 pounds. Is the standard deviation 12, 120, or 250 pounds?
   d. The mean height of a sample of 100 female college seniors is 66 inches. Is the standard deviation 2, 12, or 86 inches?

2. In this exercise you are asked to guess the value of the variance for different variables. The answers should be obvious. Select the value that you think best represents the variance.

   a. The mean price of a gallon of gasoline at a sample of 10 service stations in a certain neighborhood is \$1.00. Is a reasonable guess concerning the variance of prices 0.0001, 1.04, or 10.00?
   b. The mean starting salary is \$21,000 for 100 recent college graduates. Is a reasonable guess at the variance \$1.00, \$100.00, or \$1,000,000?

c. The mean weight of a sample of 100 male college seniors is 170 pounds. Is the variance 12, 144, or 1250?
d. The mean height of a sample of 100 female college seniors is 66 inches. Is the variance 0.04, 4, or 400?

3. During a five-week period, a carpenter's weekly incomes were as follows: 180, 165, 190, 170, and 200. Compute the following descriptive statistics for these data:
a. Range
b. Sample mean
c. Median
d. Sample variance
e. Sample standard deviation

4. In Exercise 3, calculate all the deviations from the mean and show that these deviations sum to 0.

5. In Exercise 3, calculate the mean absolute deviation. Compare this value to the sample standard deviation.

6. A sample of depths (in feet) of recent oil drilling was as follows:

1500 1200 1600 1700 1500 2000

a. Compute the sample mean, median, and mode.
b. Calculate the range, the sample variance, and sample standard deviation.
c. Calculate the deviations from the mean and verify that they sum to 0.
d. Calculate the mean absolute deviation and compare it to the sample standard deviation.

7. Refer to the data in Exercise 6. Multiply each depth by 10.
a. Compute the sample mean, median, and mode.
b. Calculate the range, the sample variance, and sample standard deviation.
c. Calculate the deviations from the mean and verify that they sum to 0.
d. Calculate the mean absolute deviation and compare it to the standard deviation.
e. Calculate the range.

8. The Walker Printing Company has 12 employees. Last year those employees missed the following number of days of work due to illness:

8 6 1 13 20 9 8 6 7 14 2 3

a. Calculate the population mean and median.
b. Calculate the variance. Note that these observations represent the entire population, so the denominator in calculating σ^2 is 12, not 11.
c. Calculate the standard deviation.
d. Calculate the mean absolute deviation and compare it to the standard deviation.
e. Calculate the range.

9. The following data represent the population of test scores received by 50 applicants on a civil service exam:

69	45	78	98	87	73	46	68	69	91
83	87	78	89	84	56	78	92	47	62
74	81	80	76	59	62	93	88	77	65
56	67	78	79	81	80	64	67	78	83
68	69	80	94	93	76	79	89	92	59

a. Find the range of the data.
b. Find the mean.
c. Find the population variance.
d. Find the population standard deviation.
e. Find the median.

f. Find the first and third quartiles.
g. Find the interquartile range.
h. Find the mean absolute deviation.
i. Plot the data on a histogram and locate the mean, the first quartile, and the third quartile.

4.6 ▪ Calculating the Standard Deviation Using Grouped Data

When the individual observations are not known, the sample standard deviation cannot be calculated using the formulas presented earlier. When the data are presented in a frequency distribution, it is necessary to use formulas for grouped data. As with the sample mean, the formula is based on the assumption that the midpoint of a class represents the typical observation in the class.

To calculate the sample variance and the sample standard deviation for grouped data, use one of the following two formulas. Both produce identical answers, but the second formula is usually easier when performing calculations by hand. The first formula may be easier to use when the mean is an integer.

Formulas for Calculating the Variance for Grouped Data

Let k denote the number of classes in the frequency distribution; let $M_1, M_2, \ldots, M_k$ denote the k class midpoints; and let $f_1, f_2, \ldots, f_k$ denote the k class frequencies. The sample variance is

$$s^2 = \frac{\Sigma f_i(M_i - \bar{x})^2}{n - 1}$$

At times, especially when the mean is not an integer, it is computationally easier to use the following method to calculate s^2:

$$s^2 = \frac{\Sigma f_i M_i^2 - n\bar{x}^2}{n - 1}$$

To calculate the population variance σ^2 for grouped data, use the following formula:

$$\sigma^2 = \frac{\Sigma f_i M_i^2 - N\mu^2}{N}$$

The standard deviation is simply the square root of the variance.

When we use grouped data to calculate the mean, variance, or standard deviation, the answer obtained will not be exactly the same as the answer obtained if the raw data had been used. We lose some information when we do not have the raw data and approximate the raw data values by using the midpoints of the classes.

Example 4.34 **Standard Deviation of Grouped Data in Table 3.2:** Calculate the population variance and standard deviation for the grouped data in Table 4.2.

TABLE 4.4 **Calculation of the standard deviation for Example 4.34**

Monthly Salary (dollars)	Frequency (f_i)	Midpoint (M_i)	f_iM_i	$f_iM_i^2$
1300 to under 1400	8	1350	10,800	14,580,000
1400 to under 1500	11	1450	15,950	23,127,500
1500 to under 1600	17	1550	26,350	40,842,500
1600 to under 1700	19	1650	31,350	51,727,500
1700 to under 1800	10	1750	17,500	30,625,000
1800 to under 1900	6	1850	11,100	20,535,000
1900 to under 2000	4	1950	7,800	15,210,000
2000 to under 2100	5	2050	10,250	21,012,500
Total	80		131,100	217,660,000

Solution: Recall from Example 4.18 that the mean using the grouped data was estimated to be 1,638.75. To approximate the population variance using the grouped data, refer to the calculations shown in Table 4.4. Based on the grouped data, the approximate value of the population variance is

$$\sigma^2 = \frac{\Sigma f_i M_i^2 - N\mu^2}{N} = \frac{217{,}660{,}000 - 80(1{,}638.75)^2}{80} = 35{,}248.44$$

The denominator is $N = 80$ because we have the entire population of data. The population standard deviation is approximately

$$\Sigma = \sqrt{35{,}248.44} = 187.75$$

Recall from Example 4.32 that the population standard deviation based on the individual observations was $\sigma = 182.39$. ■

Example 4.35

Standard Deviation of Grouped Data in Table 3.5: Calculate the sample variance and sample standard deviation for the grouped data in Table 3.5.

Solution: In this situation, the number of cars owned is analogous to the midpoint of a class. Thus, the formulas for calculating the mean and standard deviation for grouped data are applicable. The sample mean is

$$\bar{x} = 219/120 = 1.825$$

Table 4.5 shows the calculations needed to determine the sample variance. The sample variance is

$$s^2 = \frac{\Sigma f_i M_i^2 - n\bar{x}^2}{n - 1} = \frac{537 - 120(1.825)^2}{119} = 1.154$$

The sample standard deviation is

$$s = \sqrt{1.154} = 1.074$$

TABLE 4.5
Calculation of the standard deviation for Example 4.35

Number of Cars (M_i)	Frequency (f_i)	f_iM_i	$f_iM_i^2$
0	9	0	0
1	39	39	39
2	48	96	192
3	15	45	135
4	6	24	96
5	3	15	75
Total	120	219	537

■

Exercises for Section 4.6

1. Look at the accompanying frequency distribution for the duration of 20 long-distance telephone calls.

Call Duration (minutes)	Frequency
4 to under 8	4
8 to under 12	5
12 to under 16	7
16 to under 20	2
20 to under 24	1
24 to under 28	1
Total	20

a. Compute the sample mean, median, and mode.
b. Calculate the sample variance and sample standard deviation.

2. A service station has recorded the accompanying frequency distribution for the number of gallons of gasoline purchased by a sample of its customers.

Gasoline (gallons)	Frequency
0 to under 5	74
5 to under 10	192
10 to under 15	280
15 to under 20	105
20 to under 25	23
25 to under 30	6
Total	680

a. Compute the sample mean, median, and mode.
b. Calculate the sample variance and sample standard deviation.
c. If the service station expects to service about 100 cars on a given day, what is an estimate of the total number of gallons of gasoline that will be sold?

3. In a survey of 400 spectators at a professional football game, each individual was asked to indicate the one-way mileage from his or her home to the stadium. A partial relative frequency distribution is given.

Miles	Relative Frequency
0 to under 5	.12
5 to under 10	.20
10 to under 15	
15 to under 20	.17
20 to under 25	.15

a. Complete the relative frequency distribution.
b. How many spectators live more than 10 but less than 15 miles from the stadium?
c. Show the frequency distribution for the data.
d. Calculate the sample mean.
e. Calculate the sample variance and sample standard deviation.

4. Based on a sample of 200 customers, a computer salesman calculated the number of returns per customer for the correction of defects during the warranty period. The proportions for this variable are as follows:

Number of Returns	0	1	2	3	4
Proportion	.23	.38	.32	.06	.01

a. Calculate the sample mean number of times a computer was returned.
b. Calculate the sample variance and sample standard deviation.
c. In the sample, how many computers were returned more than twice?
d. In the sample, what proportion of computers were returned fewer than three times?

5. The following data show the number of weeks between sending an item and receipt of payment at a mail order store for a sample of 500 items:

Weeks	0	1	2	3	4
Proportion	.15	.48	.20	.12	.05

a. Calculate the sample mean number of weeks until payment was received.
b. Calculate the sample variance and sample standard deviation.
c. What proportion of items were paid for in three weeks or less?

6. The following data on a sample of 500 cars show the numbers of occupants on an interstate highway:

Number of Occupants	1	2	3	4	5	6
Proportion	.42	.38	.10	.07	.02	.01

a. Calculate the sample mean number of occupants in a car.

b. Calculate the sample variance and sample standard deviation.
c. In the sample, how many cars contained four or more occupants?

7. The Matthews Transmission Company specializes in repairing automobile transmissions. The data in the accompanying table show the repair bills of customers whose transmissions were repaired in the last six months.

Cost of Repairs (dollars)	Number of Customers
0.00– 49.99	80
50.00– 99.99	160
100.00–149.99	70
150.00–199.99	60
200.00–250.00	40

a. Calculate the sample mean and median. For midpoints use 25, 75, and so forth. For the median use $A = 50$ and $B = 100$.
b. Calculate the sample variance.
c. Construct a relative frequency distribution.

4.7 ▪ *The Empirical Rule and Standardized Scores*

The standard deviation is an important characteristic of any distribution. The proportion of observations expected to fall between any two specific values depends, at least partly, on the standard deviation of the distribution.

An important theorem, called Chebyshëv's Theorem after the Russian mathematician Pafnuti Lvovich Chebyshëv (1821–1894) who proved it, illustrates the importance of the role of the standard deviation in statistical theory.

Definition: Chebyshëv's Theorem

Let c be any number greater than 1. For any sample or population of data, the proportion of observations that lie *fewer than c* standard deviations from the mean is at least $1 - 1/c^2$.

Chebyshëv's Theorem applies to both populations and samples. For a population, the interval $(\mu - c\sigma, \mu + c\sigma)$ contains all values fewer than c standard deviations from the mean. When $c = 2$, we have $(1 - 1/c^2) = (1 - 1/2^2) = .75$. This implies that at least 75% of the observations in any population or sample will lie within 2 standard deviations of the mean. When $c = 3$, we obtain $(1 - 1/c^2) = (1 - 1/3^2) = .89$. Thus Chebyshëv's Theorem tells us that at least 89% of the observations in any population fall in the interval $(\mu - 3\sigma, \mu + 3\sigma)$, and at least 89% of the observations in any sample fall in the interval $(\bar{x} - 3s, \bar{x} + 3s)$.

Example 4.36 **Application of Chebyshëv's Theorem:** Use Chebyshëv's Theorem to find an interval that covers at least 75% of the data in Table 4.1.

Solution: In Example 4.7, we found that the mean monthly salary is

$$\mu = \$1626.69$$

In Example 4.32, we found that the standard deviation is

$$\sigma = 182.39$$

From Chebyshëv's Theorem we can deduce, using $c = 2$, that at least 75% of the employees have monthly incomes between $(1626.69 - 2 \times 182.39)$ and $(1626.69 + 2 \times 182.39)$. That is, at least 75% of the monthly salaries must fall in the interval (1261.91, 1991.47). By actually counting the number of salaries, we find that 75 of the 80 salaries, or 93.75%, fall in this interval. ■

Example 4.36 shows that Chebyshëv's Theorem gives a conservative estimate of the proportion of observations in an interval about the mean. When the exact form of the distribution is known, the proportion of values falling in any interval can be determined more precisely. Chebyshëv's Theorem is useful because it highlights the importance of the standard deviation in statistical theory and because it places a lower limit on the proportion of values falling in any interval around the mean and an upper limit on the proportion of values falling in the tails of the distribution. Figure 4.8 illustrates Chebyshëv's Theorem.

FIGURE 4.8
Illustration of Chebyshëv's Theorem.

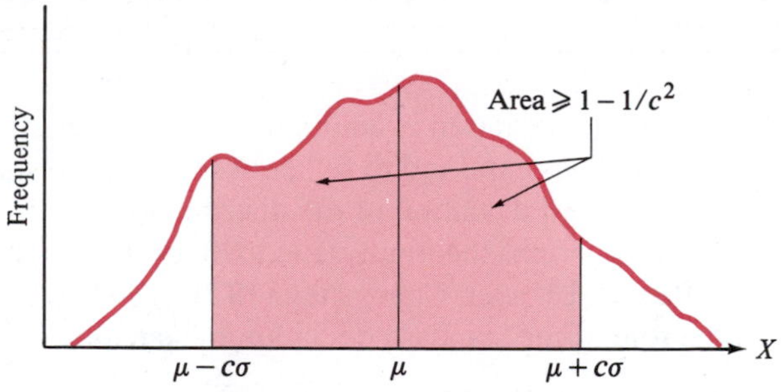

Application of Chebyshëv's Theorem

For any sample or population of data,

1. at least 75% of the observations lie within 2 standard deviations of the mean,
2. at least 89% of the observations lie within 3 standard deviations of the mean, and
3. at least 93% of the observations lie within 4 standard deviations of the mean.

The Empirical Rule

When a distribution is bell shaped, then the proportion of values that fall in the interval $(\mu - c\sigma, \mu + c\sigma)$ will exceed the values given by Chebyshëv's Theorem. When the distribution is approximately bell shaped, the following rule, called the *Empirical Rule*, holds at least approximately.

Definition: Empirical Rule

When the distribution of a population or sample of data is approximately bell shaped, then approximately 68% of the values will fall within 1 standard deviation of the mean, approximately 95% of the values will fall within 2 standard deviations of the mean, and approximately 99% of the values will fall within 3 standard deviations of the mean.

Example 4.37

Application of the Empirical Rule: The distribution of IQs of adults in the United States is known to have a mean of 100, a standard deviation of 15, and a bell-shaped distribution. Suppose that a job applicant has an IQ of 150. Is it reasonable to say that this job applicant is very intelligent?

Solution: An IQ of 150 is 50 units, or 3.33 standard deviations, above the mean of 100. The Empirical Rule tells us that approximately 99% of all IQs should be between 55 and 145, that is, within 3 standard deviations of the mean. The job applicant's IQ lies outside the interval (55, 145); thus the applicant ranks in the upper 1% of the population. ■

Standardized Scores

Often it is desirable to describe the *relative* position of an observation within a distribution. For example, knowing that an individual finished a downhill ski race in 125 seconds conveys little information about performance. Judgment of the performance would depend on whether 125 seconds is a slow, medium, or fast time.

One way of describing the location of an observation in a distribution is to calculate its *standardized score*. This score, sometimes called the Z score, indicates how many standard deviations an observation lies above or below the mean.

Definition: Standardized Score

If the population mean and the population standard deviation are known, the **standardized score** for an observation x is

$$z = \frac{x - \mu}{\sigma}$$

When the sample mean and sample standard deviation are used, the standardized score is

$$z = \frac{x - \bar{x}}{s}$$

The standardized score is sometimes called the **Z score**.

The Z score is the signed distance from the mean measured in units of standard deviation. For any population or sample of data, the mean of all the Z scores is 0 and the standard deviation of all the Z scores is 1.

If an observation is above the mean, then the Z score will be positive. For example, if $z = 1$, then an observation falls exactly 1 standard deviation above the mean. If $z = -2$, then the observation is exactly 2 standard deviations below the mean.

Chebyshëv's Theorem shows how the standardized scores can be of use. The theorem tells us, for example, that at least 75% of the data lie within 2 standard deviations of the mean. Any value within 2 standard deviations of the mean has a standardized score between -2 and 2. Thus, at least 75% of the standardized scores must be between -2 and 2. The Empirical Rule tells us that for a bell-shaped distribution approximately 95% of the observations have Z scores between -2 and 2.

Example 4.38

Calculation of Standardized Scores: Suppose three students' scores on a test were 675, 600, and 625. The mean score was $\mu = 625$ and the standard deviation was $\sigma = 25$. Calculate the standardized scores for these students.

Solution: The first student's standardized score is

$$z = \frac{675 - 625}{25} = 2$$

The second student's standardized score is

$$z = \frac{600 - 625}{25} = -1$$

The third student's standardized score is

$$z = \frac{625 - 625}{25} = 0$$

■

Use of standardized scores can help us compare observations from different distributions. For example, suppose that in a ski race a competitor records a time of 125 seconds on his first run and 135 seconds on his second run. To judge the competitor, we have to compare his time to the times of all other competitors. The competitor's time on the first run could translate to a standardized score of 2, while the time on the second run could translate to a standardized score of -2. By examining the standardized scores, we could determine that the competitor was one of the slowest racers on the first run and one of the fastest racers on the second.

Detecting Outliers

An **outlier** is an observation that falls far out in the tail of a distribution. Sometimes an outlier can be an indication of a faulty or incorrectly recorded observation. Because of this possibility, outliers should be examined carefully. A Z score can be helpful in detecting an outlier. From Chebyshëv's Theorem, we know that for any distribution of data, fewer than 11% of the observations lie more than 3 standard deviations from the mean. If the data are approximately normally distributed, then fewer than 1% of the observations have Z scores less than -3 or greater than $+3$.

Suppose we observe a measurement that has a Z score of 4.5. This means that the observation lies 4.5 standard deviations above the mean. The Empirical Rule tells us that a Z score this large is very improbable and could indicate a faulty observation.

Coefficient of Variation

In some situations, we may be more interested in a *relative* measure of the amount of variation present in a data set than in the absolute measure provided by the standard deviation or the variance. For example, the price of a share of stock in Company A varies over time in such a way that the mean price during a given year is \$100 with a standard deviation of \$5. Suppose that the stock of Company B has a mean price of \$10 per share with a standard deviation of \$4. Comparing the variability of the prices of the two stocks is difficult because when the means of the variables differ greatly, we do not get an accurate picture of the relative variability in the two data sets by comparing the standard deviations. A measure of variability that overcomes these difficulties is the *coefficient of variation,* denoted as CV. The coefficient of variation, also called the *relative standard deviation,* expresses the standard deviation as a percentage of the mean.

Definition: Coefficient of Variation

The coefficient of variation is calculated as follows:

$$\text{Coefficient of variation} = (\text{standard deviation/mean}) \times 100\%$$

For a population of data, the coefficient of variation is

$$CV = (\sigma/\mu) \times 100\%$$

For a sample of data, the coefficient of variation is

$$CV = (s/\bar{x}) \times 100\%$$

The coefficient of variation is useful for comparing the relative variation in data sets that have different means and different standard deviations or that are measured in different units, such as incomes in different countries with different currencies. For example, for the high-priced stock of Company A, the coefficient of variation is \$5/\$100 × 100% = 5%. For the low-priced stock of Company B, the coefficient of variation is \$4/\$10 × 100% = 40%. In relative terms, the price of the Company B stock is much more variable than the price of the Company A stock.

Graphical Methods Versus Summary Measures

Frequently the important features of a set of data can be described quite concisely by a few summary statistics. In general, however, summary measures provide much less information than the entire frequency distribution. Actually, it is quite surprising that data analysts do not emphasize tables and graphs of frequency distributions more. Whenever possible, you should present the entire frequency distribution in either tabular or graphical form when analyzing a set of data.

One reason that summary measures of central tendency and dispersion are so popular in statistics is that they are the primary tools used by statisticians for testing hypotheses. Just as we use the sample histogram to make inferences about the shape and location of the population frequency distribution, we use the sample mean, the sample standard deviation, and the sample proportion to test inferences about the comparable population measures.

Exercises for Section 4.7

1. Suppose that on a statistics test the mean grade in a class is 75 and the population standard deviation is 8.
   a. Find the standardized score for a student whose grade was 83.
   b. Find the standardized score for a student whose grade was 59.
   c. Find the standardized score for a student whose grade was 75.
   d. Based on Chebyshëv's theorem, at least what proportion of students received grades between 59 and 91?
   e. Assume that the distribution of grades is approximately bell shaped. Approximately what proportion of students received grades between 59 and 91?

2. The following data represent a sample of test scores:

88 76 67 90 98 68 75 86 82 90

   a. Calculate the sample mean.
   b. Calculate the sample standard deviation.
   c. Calculate the standardized score for a student whose grade was 90.
   d. Find the interval that contains all values within 2 standard deviations of the mean. What proportion of the sample values fall within this interval?
   e. Calculate the coefficient of variation.

3. On a placement exam, an applicant was told that his score was 660 and that his standardized score was 2.5. Another applicant was told that her score was 690 and her standardized score was 3.0.
   a. Find the mean and standard deviation for the population.
   b. Find the standardized score for an applicant whose score was 600.
   c. Find the coefficient of variation.

4. Eight values of a variable X are 1, 4, 0, 0, 1, 2, 5, and 3. Find the range, mean absolute deviation, variance, and standard deviation. What is the standardized score for an X-value of 3?

5. In Exercise 4 multiply each X-value by 10. Find the range, mean absolute deviation, variance, and standard deviation. If $x = 30$, find the standardized score.

6. On a certain test the mean score was 70 and the standard deviation was 12.
   a. Ann's score was 1 standard deviation above the mean. What was Ann's score and what was her standardized score?
   b. Jim's score was 2 standard deviations below the mean. What was Jim's score and what was his standardized score?
   c. Al's score was A standard deviations from the mean. Calculate Al's standardized score.

7. The data below show the monthly salaries (in dollars) of a population of 480 high school students who worked part-time at 20 Acme Supermarkets during the last month. The data were grouped at the centers of the classes.

Salary	74	82	90	98	106	114	122
Frequency	13	44	110	157	92	45	19

   a. Find the population mean salary.
   b. Find the population variance.
   c. If an individual's salary is \$120, find the standardized score.

8. Using the data in Exercise 7, standardize each of the 480 salaries.
   a. List the frequency distribution of these standardized scores.
   b. Find the mean of these standardized scores.
   c. Find the variance of these standardized scores.

9. Prove that the mean and standard deviation of a set of standardized scores are equal to 0 and 1, respectively. See Exercise 8 for an illustration.

10. A public utility claims that at a large manufacturing plant daily demand for electricity has averaged 25 kilowatts with a standard deviation of 4 kilowatts. Assume that daily energy usage can be described by a bell-shaped distribution. Use the Empirical Rule to find the following:
a. The proportion of days that demand exceeds 17.5 kilowatts
b. The proportion of days that demand is less than 20.0 kilowatts

11. For distribution A, the mean is 20 and the standard deviation is 7. Distribution B has a mean of 23 and a standard deviation of 2. In which distribution will a raw score of 27 have a higher standing?

4.8 ▪ Construction of Box Plots (Optional)

We have presented several graphical techniques, including histograms and stem-and-leaf diagrams, for displaying frequency distributions. The **box plot** is another such technique. The box plot is designed to indicate the median of the data and to highlight the behavior of the data at the ends of the distribution. The box plot also highlights outliers, the observations that lie very far from the center of the distribution. By graphing two box plots on a single page, it is easy to visualize differences in the center and spread of two data sets and to detect outliers.

A Z score identifies outliers by computing their distance from the mean in standard deviation units. In a box plot, we measure the distance between the outlier and the upper or lower quartile, using the interquartile range (abbreviated IQR) as the unit of measurement. The advantage of this method is that the sample quartiles, unlike the sample mean and sample standard deviation, do not depend on the values of the extreme observations.

To construct a box plot, first locate the median of the data and the lower and upper quartiles Q_1 and Q_3. Draw a horizontal line and mark the positions of the median, Q_1, and Q_3. Draw a rectangle, or *box,* which extends from Q_1 to Q_3. Approximately half the observations should fall within the box.

The next step is to decide how far away from the median a measurement must lie before it is classified as an outlier. The decision is made by constructing two sets of *fences*. The *inner fences* are located 1.5 IQR below Q_1 and 1.5 IQR above Q_3. The inner fences are defined as follows:

$$\text{Lower inner fence} = Q_1 - 1.5(\text{IQR})$$
$$\text{Upper inner fence} = Q_3 + 1.5(\text{IQR})$$

The second set of fences, the *outer fences,* are located 3 IQR below Q_1 and 3 IQR above Q_3:

$$\text{Lower outer fence} = Q_1 - 3(\text{IQR})$$
$$\text{Upper outer fence} = Q_3 + 3(\text{IQR})$$

Values lying between an inner fence and the corresponding outer fence are considered to be "mild" outliers; values outside the outer fences are considered to be "extreme" outliers. An example of a box plot is given in Figure 4.10 on page 133.

Example 4.39

Constructing a Box Plot: In the early 1980s, a large corporation confronted with financial losses laid off a substantial portion of its work force. One of the male employees who was laid off sued the corporation alleging that he was the victim of age discrimination. To see if the employee had been discriminated against, the characteristics of all the employees who were laid off were compared with the characteristics of the employees who were not laid off. Every year the corporation rated every employee from 0 to 5 in each of 13 job categories. Thus, in a given year, an employee received a total rating between 0 and 65. The corporation's employment manual indicated that promotions, raises, and layoffs would be determined mainly by these ratings. The data in Table 4.6 show the employee ratings for a sample of 50 employees.

The stem-and-leaf diagram for the data in Table 4.6 is shown in Figure 4.9. In the stem-and-leaf diagram, each stem is used twice. The first time it is associated with the trailing digits 0, 1, 2, 3, and 4; the second time, with the trailing digits 5, 6, 7, 8, and 9.

TABLE 4.6
Employee ratings

39	37	32	40	40	37	39	35	42	43
40	41	31	38	38	37	24	34	42	47
40	51	33	37	36	29	39	44	49	37
34	37	39	38	35	36	43	45	38	42
41	41	56	40	42	48	37	42	39	41

FIGURE 4.9
Stem-and-leaf diagram for data in Table 4.6.

Stem	Leaves
2	4
2	9
3	1 2 3 4 4
3	5 5 6 6 7 7 7 7 7 7 7 8 8 8 8 9 9 9 9 9
4	0 0 0 0 0 1 1 1 1 2 2 2 2 2 3 3 4 5
4	7 8 9
5	1
5	9

For the data in Table 4.6, the median is the average of the 25th and 26th observations, after the observations have been arranged in ascending order. The median is thus 39. The lower quartile is the 13th observation, which is 37, and the upper quartile is the 37th observation, which is 42. The interquartile range is

$$\text{IQR} = 42 - 37 = 5$$

The inner and outer fences are calculated as follows:

$$\begin{aligned}
\text{Lower inner fence} &= Q_1 - 1.5(\text{IQR}) = 37 - 7.5 = 29.5 \\
\text{Upper inner fence} &= Q_3 + 1.5(\text{IQR}) = 42 + 7.5 = 49.5 \\
\text{Lower outer fence} &= Q_1 - 3.0(\text{IQR}) = 37 - 15 = 22.0 \\
\text{Upper outer fence} &= Q_3 + 3.0(\text{IQR}) = 42 + 15 = 57.0
\end{aligned}$$

The box plot for these data is shown in Figure 4.10. In the box plot, a rectangle is drawn whose ends correspond to the values of the lower and upper quartiles, 37 and 42. Next, a line is drawn through the rectangle at the value of the median, which is 39. Mild

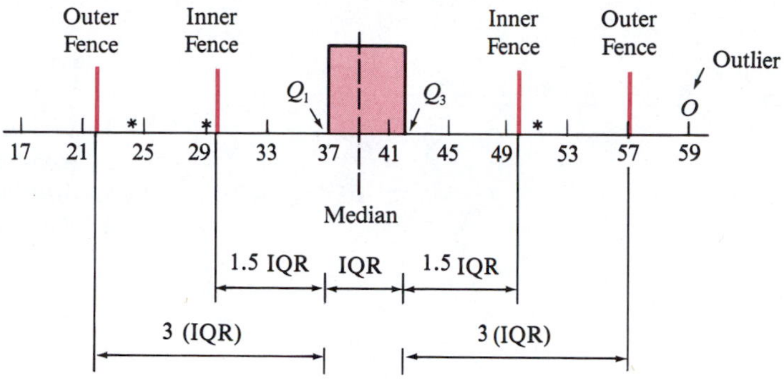

FIGURE 4.10
Box plot for data in Table 4.6.

outliers are values between the inner and outer fences. The mild outliers are 24, 29, and 51, which are denoted on the plot by asterisks. Extreme outliers lie outside the outer fences. In this example, the value 59 is the only extreme outlier and is denoted by an uppercase O on the box plot.

It turns out that the employee who filed the suit was the employee with a rating of 59. He claimed that, based on his job performance, he should not have been terminated. He won in court and was awarded more than $200,000 in back pay and other damages. ■

Both Z scores and box plots can be used to detect outliers. A disadvantage of the Z score is that it is based on the mean and standard deviation, both of which are sensitive to extreme values. The box plot is less sensitive to extreme values, since it is based on the interquartile range that uses only the middle 50% of the data and ignores the largest and smallest values.

Table 4.7 on page 134 provides a summary of many important measures of centrality and dispersion mentioned in this chapter.

Exercises for Section 4.8

1. The following data show the yields in 1987 of a sample of mutual funds:

10.61	11.42	12.28	14.45	13.32
12.42	13.34	12.75	14.18	13.44
12.92	12.78	13.05	11.31	13.24
11.47	10.24	13.63	11.48	13.26
12.10	12.70	13.64	12.39	13.30
11.41	13.31	13.15	13.57	13.58
10.51	12.59	12.34	13.26	13.37
11.04	13.34	13.57	13.59	13.60
12.31	14.06	13.34	13.73	13.54
14.23	13.33	13.09	13.40	13.36

TABLE 4.7

Name	Formula	Comments
Sample mean	$\bar{x} = \dfrac{\sum_{i=1}^{n} x_i}{n}$	1. $\bar{x}$ is the most frequently used measure of the center of a distribution. 2. We have a sample of n observations $x_1, x_2, \ldots, x_n$. 3. $\bar{x}$ represents the center of gravity of the data. 4. $\bar{x}$ can be adversely affected by outliers.
Sample mean of grouped data	$\bar{x} = \dfrac{\sum_{i=1}^{k} f_i M_i}{n}$	1. $M_1, M_2, \ldots, M_k$ represent the midpoints of the k classes. 2. $f_1, f_2, \ldots, f_k$ represent the class frequencies. 3. n is the total sample size; $n = \sum f_i$.
Sample median	Middle observation after putting the data in order from lowest to highest	1. Half the observations are larger than the median, and half are smaller. 2. The median is not affected much by outliers.
Range	Range = largest value − smallest value	
Sample variance	$s^2 = \dfrac{\sum_{i=1}^{n} (x_i - \bar{x})^2}{n - 1}$ or $s^2 = \dfrac{\sum_{i=1}^{n} x_i^2 - n\bar{x}^2}{n - 1}$	1. s^2 is the most frequently used measure of the spread of a distribution. 2. $n - 1$ is called the degrees of freedom of s^2. 3. s^2 is an unbiased estimator of the population variance σ^2. 4. $s^2 \geq 0$. $s^2 = 0$ if and only if all observations are identical.
Sample standard deviation	$s = +\sqrt{s^2}$	
Mean absolute deviation	$\text{M.A.D.} = \dfrac{\sum_{i=1}^{n} \lvert x_i - \bar{x} \rvert}{n}$	1. Another measure of the spread of a distribution.
Standardized score	$z = \dfrac{s - \bar{x}}{s}$	1. Average value of Z is 0. 2. Variance of Z is 1. 3. Standardized score adjusts data for mean and variance so that different data sets can be meaningfully compared.

a. Put the data in order.
b. Represent these data with a histogram.
c. Find the mean and median for these data.
d. Draw a box plot for these data.

2. Refer to the civil service exam scores in Exercise 9 of Section 4.5.
a. Represent these data with a histogram.
b. Draw a box plot for these data.

4.9 ▪ Computer Applications

The SPSSX, SAS, and Minitab computer programs can be used to find means, standard deviations, and other descriptive statistics. For example, to request descriptive statistics in SPSSX, we use the CONDESCRIPTIVE command. The command

```
CONDESCRIPTIVE AGE, SALARY, SENIOR
```

tells SPSSX to find the mean and standard deviation for each of the variables AGE, SALARY, and SENIOR. The computer output using the data in Table 2.1 for the sample of 120 employees at the Computech Corporation is shown in Figure 4.11. In addition to the mean and standard deviation, the CONDESCRIPTIVE command also gives the lowest and highest values, as well as the number of observations used in the calculation.

FIGURE 4.11 **SPSSX-generated descriptive statistics for data in Table 2.1.**

NUMBER OF VALID OBSERVATIONS (LISTWISE) = 120.00

VARIABLE	MEAN	STD DEV	MINIMUM	MAXIMUM	VALID N	LABEL
AGE	39.242	12.022	19.00	64.00	120	
SALARY	2133.000	687.433	1200.00	5000.00	120	
SENIOR	15.358	10.871	1.00	42.00	120	

To get summary statistics for all the numerical variables in the data set in SAS, issue the command

```
PROC MEANS;
```

Place this command anywhere after the semicolon that ends the data set in the SAS program. If you want the summary statistics for just a specific set of variables, say, AGE, SALARY, SENIOR, and EXEMPT, issue the following two commands

```
PROC MEANS;
     VAR AGE SALARY SENIOR EXEMPT;
```

Figure 4.12 shows the SAS computer output generated by these two commands using the data in Table 2.1.

FIGURE 4.12 SAS-generated descriptive statistics for data in Table 2.1

SAS

VARIABLE	N	MEAN	STANDARD DEVIATION	MINIMUM VALUE	MAXIMUM VALUE	STD ERROR OF MEAN	SUM	VARIANCE	C.V.
AGE	120	39.24166667	12.02168617	19.0000000	64.0000000	1.09742478	4709.00000	144.52094	30.635
SALARY	120	2133.00000000	687.43323587	1200.0000000	5000.0000000	62.75378168	255960.00000	472564.45378	32.228
SENIOR	120	15.35833333	10.87112885	1.0000000	42.0000000	0.99239375	1843.00000	118.18144	70.783
EXEMPT	120	2.75833333	1.35346324	1.0000000	6.0000000	0.12355372	331.00000	1.83186	49.068

FIGURE 4.13 Minitab-generated descriptive statistics for data in Table 2.1.

```
MTB >
READ 'COMPUTEC.DAT'  INTO C1-C8
     120 ROWS READ
ROW   C1   C2   C3   C4   C5    C6   C7   C8
  1    0    1    1   35    1  1575   16    5
  2    1    1    1   31    2  1980   10    3
  3    1    1    1   51    2  2480   28    2
  4    0    1    1   57    1  1925   30    2

MTB >
NAME C1 = 'SEX', C2 = 'RACE', C3 = 'DEGREE', C4 = 'AGE'
MTB >
NAME C5 = 'DIV', C6 = 'SALARY', C7 = 'SENIOR', C8 = 'EXEMPT'
MTB >
DESCRIBE C4 C6 C7 C8

                 N      MEAN    MEDIAN    TRMEAN     STDEV    SEMEAN
AGE            120     39.24     38.50     38.99     12.02      1.10
SALARY         120    2133.0    1972.5    2060.5     687.4      62.8
SENIOR         120    15.358    12.000    14.907    10.871     0.992
EXEMPT         120     2.758     2.000     2.694     1.353     0.124

               MIN       MAX        Q1        Q3
AGE          19.00     64.00     30.00     48.75
SALARY      1200.0    5000.0    1820.0    2400.0
SENIOR       1.000    42.000     6.000    23.750
EXEMPT       1.000     6.000     2.000     4.000

MTB >
STOP
```

Figure 4.13 shows Minitab output for the data in Table 2.1. The Minitab output shows the number of observations (N), the sample mean, median, standard deviation, minimum value, maximum value, lower quartile, and upper quartile for each variable. (The notation TRMEAN denotes the *trimmed mean,* which is the sample mean after deleting the lowest 5% and the highest 5% of the values. The notation SEMEAN denotes the standard deviation of the sample mean and equals STDEV/$\sqrt{N}$).

Exercises for Section 4.9

1. Refer to the data in Table 2.1 of Chapter 2. Use the SPSSX program and a CONDESCRIPTIVE command to calculate the mean number of exemptions for the employees in the table. Verify that this sample mean is correct by actually calculating the mean using the output from the FREQUENCIES command.
2. Refer to the data in Table 2.1. Use the SAS program and a PROC MEANS; command to find the mean number of exemptions.
3. Refer to the data in Table 2.2. Use the SPSSX program and a CONDESCRIPTIVE command to find the mean GPA and the mean SAT score for the students in the sample. Find the sample standard deviation for GPA and for SAT scores.
4. Refer to the data in Table 2.2. Use the SAS program and a PROC MEANS; command to find the mean GPA and the mean SAT score for the students. What are the sample standard deviations?
5. Refer to the data in Table 2.3.
   a. Use the SPSSX program and a CONDESCRIPTIVE command to find the mean of teachers' salaries in the United States.
   b. Find the mean and standard deviation of tax revenue per capita.
   c. Find the mean expenditure per pupil.
   d. Find the mean income per capita.
   e. Find the mean wage of employees in manufacturing.
6. Repeat Exercise 5 using the SAS program.
7. A sample of 50 individuals at a medical clinic consists of 25 patients with a mild case of a disease (coded 1), 10 patients with a moderately severe case (coded 2), and 15 patients with an extremely severe case (coded 3). Does it make sense to determine the following statistics? If so, compute them.
   a. Modal severity
   b. Median severity
   c. Mean severity
8. A sample consists of 12 blacks (coded 1), 10 Asians (coded 2), and 15 whites (coded 3). Does it make sense to determine the following statistics? If so, compute them.
   a. Modal race
   b. Median race
   c. Mean race
9. The "average" sex for a sample where sex is coded {female = 1, male = 0} is .72. What, if anything, does this average mean?
10. Given the Z scores shown, calculate the original scores if the mean is 10, and the standard deviation is 2.

Case	Standard Score	Original Score
1	1	
2	0	
3	−2	

11. The sample mean and standard deviation on a history test are 70 and 12. Calculate the standardized scores for the following students:

Student	Standard Score	Test Score
1		70
2		58
3		94

Chapter 4 Summary

Chapter 4 discusses the most important measures of central tendency, dispersion, and location that are used to describe important characteristics of a set of data values. The most important measures of central tendency are the mean, median, and mode.

The *mean* is the sum of all values divided by the number of values. Since the mean takes into account the exact magnitude of each observation, it is sensitive to extreme values.

The *median* is the middle value of data ordered from highest to lowest. To find the median for ungrouped data, first arrange the values in order of magnitude. The median is the value such that 50% of the data fall to its right and 50% fall to its left. If the number of values is odd, the median is the middle value. If the number is even, the median is the average of the two middle values. The median is sensitive to the number of values above or below it, but not to the specific magnitude of the values. Thus, the median is especially useful when there are extreme values in a distribution (when the distribution is skewed).

The *mode* is the simplest measure of central tendency. It refers to the most common value in a distribution. The mode is a *value* or *category,* not a frequency. Distributions can have one or more modes. If two values occur with the same frequency and more than any other value, the distribution is bimodal (has two modes). The mode is the only measure of central tendency appropriate for categorical data.

For symmetrical unimodal distributions, the mean, median, and mode are identical. For unimodal distributions that are skewed to the right, the relationship between the three measures of central tendency is: mean > median > mode. For unimodal distributions that are skewed to the left, the relationship is: mode > median > mean.

To measure the variation within a set of data, we use measures of dispersion: the range, mean absolute deviation, variance, standard deviation, and interquartile range. These measures are summarized as follows:

1. *Range*: (highest value) − (lowest value)
   - Advantage: easy to compute
   - Disadvantages: relies on two most extreme values, thus sensitive to outliers; does not utilize a measure of central tendency
2. *Mean absolute deviation*: $\Sigma |x_i - \mu|/n$
   - Advantages: sensitive to every value; utilizes a measure of central tendency
   - Disadvantage: difficult to use in more advanced statistics
3. *Sample variance*: $\Sigma(x_i - \overline{x})^2/(n - 1)$
   - Advantages: sensitive to every value; utilizes a measure of central tendency
   - Disadvantages: affected by outliers; value is in square units
4. *Standard deviation*: square root of variance
   - Advantages: sensitive to every value; expressed in the same units as the original data; can be interpreted as the average distance that values lie from the mean
   - Disadvantage: affected by skew and outliers
5. *Interquartile range*: $Q_3 - Q_1$
   - Advantage: not sensitive to outliers
   - Disadvantage: ignores 50% of values; does not utilize a measure of central tendency

Percentiles, quartiles, and standardized scores are used to indicate the relative position of a data value in the distribution and are measures of position or location. A *percentile* is a value in a distribution at or below which a given percentage of values are located. The *lower* and *upper quartiles* are the 25th and 75th percentiles, respectively. The *standardized score* $z = (x - \mu)/\sigma$ represents the difference from the mean in standard deviation units. Z has a mean of 0 and a standard deviation of 1 for *any* distribution.

The two most commonly used summary statistics are the sample mean and standard deviation. The mean can be interpreted as the center of gravity of the distribution. The mean and standard deviation can be used together to describe the sample data by applying Chebyshëv's Theorem or the Empirical Rule. The Empirical Rule draws a stronger conclusion about the concentration of the data values about the mean value and assumes that the population being studied is at least approximately bell-shaped.

For a bell-shaped distribution, approximately 68% of the values will fall within 1 standard deviation of the mean, approximately 95% will fall within 2 standard deviations, and approximately 99% fall within 3 standard deviations.

A *box plot* is a diagram that is useful for identifying *outliers* or extreme values. The box plot shows the median, the upper and lower quartiles, and the interquartile range. Values falling more than a specified distance from the median are easily identified on the box plot.

This concludes our discussion of descriptive statistics. In Chapter 5, we begin our discussion of deductive statistics and introduce the basic rules of probability theory.

Chapter 4 ▪ Supplementary Exercises

1. At a grocery store, customers purchased 90 bags of grapes. Each bag was weighed to the closest half pound. The data are shown in the accompanying table.

Weight of Bag (pounds)	Frequency (number sold)
0.5	25
1.0	15
1.5	20
2.0	12
2.5	8
3.0	6
3.5	4

a. Plot the histogram.
b. Calculate the sample mean.
c. Calculate the sample variance.
d. Calculate the median.

2. The accompanying data show the percentages of cars of various ages in use during selected years.

Age of Car (years)	1977	1982	1987
Under 4	40	36	42
4 to under 8	40	36	32
8 to under 12	16	20	22
12 to 15	4	8	4
Total	100	100	100

a. Present these distributions graphically.
b. Estimate the median age in 1977, 1982, and 1987.
c. Estimate the mean age in 1977, 1982, and 1987.

3. The computer center at Miami University classifies computer jobs according to time required to complete them. Data are shown for a random sample of 200 jobs.

Time Elapsed (minutes)	Frequency
0 to under 2	40
2 to under 4	80
4 to under 6	50
6 to under 8	27
8 and over	3
Total	200

a. Plot the histogram using 10 as the class mark for the highest class.
b. Explain why the sample mean cannot be calculated.

c. Find the median.
d. Suppose the "8 and over" jobs took 10, 16, and 42 minutes. Now calculate the sample mean.

4. At a jewelry store, a sample of sales were classified as follows:

Value of Sale (dollars)	Number of Sales
15 to under 25	9
25 to under 35	21
35 to under 45	42
45 to under 55	17
55 to under 65	6
65 to 75	5

a. Plot the histogram.
b. Calculate the sample mean.
c. Calculate the sample variance and sample standard deviation.

5. A random sample of 100 students yielded the following information on the number of hours per week that they work:

Hours Worked	Number of Students
0 to under 5	20
5 to under 10	11
10 to under 15	23
15 to under 20	24
20 to under 30	16
30 to 40	6
Total	100

a. Plot the histogram.
b. Calculate the sample mean and sample variance. Note that the class intervals vary in width.

6. The following data show the weekly sales of a certain machine tool corporation in Houston, Texas:

Weekly Sales (dollars)	Number of Weeks
0– 4,999	4
5,000– 9,999	6
10,000–14,999	10
15,000–19,999	16
20,000–24,999	12
25,000–29,999	4
Total	52

a. Plot the relative frequency distribution.
b. Calculate mean weekly sales. Use midpoints 2,500, 7,500, 12,500, and so on.
c. Calculate the sample variance.
d. Calculate the standardized score if weekly sales were $20,000.

7. A TV producer shows a new TV program to a random sample of viewers, asks for their comments, and obtains the following results, arranged by age groups:

Reaction	Under 20	20 to under 30	30 to under 40	40 to 50
Liked the show	160	80	75	25
Disliked the show	40	60	95	75

a. Plot histograms showing the age distributions of those who liked and disliked the show.
b. Find the sample mean for each class.
c. Find the median and mode for each class.
d. At what age groups should an advertising campaign be aimed?

8. The following data represent a sample of weekly wages (in dollars) earned by part-time employees at a department store:

80	98	75	69	81	88	78	96
70	88	85	88	75	58	97	67
61	52	76	81	83	70	98	83
85	90	64	95	63	82	108	109
100	96	92	100	73	94	105	78

a. Put the data in order.
b. Construct a frequency distribution using the classes $50 to under $60, $60 to under $70, and so forth.
c. Graph the histogram.
d. Construct and graph the relative frequency distribution.
e. Explain the difference between the height and area of a bar in the histogram.
f. Construct the cumulative frequency distribution.
g. Calculate the sample mean, sample variance, and sample standard deviation.
h. What is the median?
i. Find the first and third quartiles.

9. The following data represent a sample of test scores for a group of 50 students:

44	13	47	27	55	41	58	35	58	48
37	45	55	32	45	48	54	78	66	58
66	57	30	72	57	81	33	63	54	79
45	82	36	45	51	24	79	26	33	60
53	35	22	18	58	47	35	64	68	42

a. Put the data in order.
b. Construct a frequency distribution using the classes 10 to under 20, 20 to under 30, and so forth.
c. Graph the histogram.
d. Construct and graph the relative frequency distribution.
e. Construct the cumulative frequency distribution.

f. Calculate the sample mean, sample variance, and sample standard deviation.
g. Find the median and the first and third quartiles.

10. Can the mean absolute deviation ever be negative? Why or why not?

11. Consider the sample of observations, $x_1, x_2, \ldots, x_n$, which has sample mean $\overline{x}$ and sample variance s^2. Suppose that each observation is multiplied by a constant k so that the new observations are $kx_1, kx_2, \ldots, kx_n$. Find the mean and variance of the new observations.

12. Suppose a sample consists of n observations that are all identical and equal to C.
a. Calculate the sample mean, median, and mode.
b. Calculate the range, absolute mean deviation, variance, and standard deviation.

13. Is it possible for a sample variance to be 0 or negative? Why or why not?

14. A random sample of 100 adult males was taken to determine their annual incomes. The data were grouped as follows:

Income (dollars)	Frequency
0 to under 5,000	0
5,000 to under 10,000	9
10,000 to under 15,000	23
15,000 to under 20,000	32
20,000 to under 25,000	22
25,000 to under 30,000	10
30,000 to under 35,000	4

a. Define the class marks as $M_1 = \$2,500$, $M_2 = \$7,500$, and so forth. Let f_i denote the class frequency of the ith class. Calculate $\Sigma M_i f_i$.
b. Calculate the sample mean.
c. Calculate the median. Use $A = 15,000$ and $B = 19,999$.
d. Calculate $\Sigma f_i M_i^2$.
e. Calculate the sample variance.
f. Graph the frequency distribution and the cumulative frequency distribution.

15. A random sample of 50 scraps of wood lying in a lumber yard were measured, and the following frequency distribution was obtained:

Length (inches)	Frequency
0 to under 10	10
10 to under 20	10
20 to under 30	20
30 to 40	10

a. Calculate the sample mean.
b. Calculate the sample variance.

16. A transportation agency is interested in how far people travel to see pro football games. At a certain football game, a random sample of 10 people were asked how many miles each person traveled to get to the game. The data were as follows:

16 5 7 42 10 6 10 3 4 7

Find the standardized score for a person who traveled 5 miles.

17. The following data show the income distribution of residents of Greenville. The Greenville City Commission has decided to raise the income taxes of those residents whose incomes were above the 75th percentile. Estimate the income level that determines if a resident's taxes will be increased.

Income (dollars)	Number of Residents
0 to under 10,000	1,216
10,000 to under 20,000	4,812
20,000 to under 30,000	9,644
30,000 to under 40,000	2,610
40,000 or more	808

18. An efficiency expert for a large metropolitan bank claims that an efficient bank teller should spend more than 3 minutes per customer with only 25% of the customers. The data that follow show the lengths of time a new teller spent with customers. Does this teller satisfy the expert's efficiency requirement?

Time (minutes)	Number of Customers
0 to under 1	216
1 to under 2	484
2 to under 3	366
3 to under 4	154
4 or more	90

19. The accompanying frequency distribution shows the ages of new car buyers at the Gollinger Automobile Agency. Find the mean, variance, and standard deviation. Assume this is a population.

Age of Buyers (years)	Frequency
20 to under 30	116
30 to under 40	248
40 to under 50	234
50 to 60	112

20. To plan for the educational, recreational, and medical needs of the community, the city commissioners need to know the age distribution of the residents of the city. The accompanying relative frequency distribution was constructed from a random sample of 500 residents. Find the following:

a. Average age of the residents
b. Sample variance
c. Median age
d. 75th percentile

Age of Residents (years)	Relative Frequency
0 to under 10	.15
10 to under 20	.20
20 to under 30	.18
30 to under 40	.10
40 to under 50	.15
50 to under 60	.12
60 to 70	.10

21. Given a sample of observations $x_1, x_2, \ldots, x_n$, prove that $\Sigma(x_i - \bar{x}) = 0$.

22. Given a sample of observations $x_1, x_2, \ldots, x_n$, prove that $\Sigma(x_i - \bar{x})^2 = \Sigma x_i^2 - n\bar{x}^2$.

23. The Internal Revenue Service has examined a random sample of 100 income tax returns. The accompanying cumulative frequency distribution shows the distribution of deductions for charitable contributions. Find the indicated quantities.

a. Sample mean
b. Sample variance
c. Median
d. 25th percentile

Charitable Contribution (dollars)	Cumulative Frequency
0 to under 100	20
100 to under 200	40
200 to under 500	70
500 to under 1000	95
1000 to 5000	100

24. Consider a sample of data $x_1, x_2, \ldots, x_n$ having sample mean $\bar{x}$ and sample variance s^2. Suppose that a constant d is subtracted from each observation. Show that the sample mean and sample variance of the new data are $\bar{x} - d$ and s^2, respectively.

25. Suppose that last year 250 new homes were constructed and sold in Washington County. The accompanying frequency distribution shows the prices paid for these homes.

Price (thousands of dollars)	Number of Homes
25 to under 35	35
35 to under 45	45
45 to under 55	45
55 to under 65	50
65 to under 75	40
75 to under 85	35

a. Calculate the mean price of new homes in Washington County.
b. What proportion of homes sold for $55,000 or more?

26. The credit manager of the Wilson Department Store compiled information on a sample of 100 of the accounts receivable that were delinquent. The manager recorded the number of days that each account was past due.
a. Use midpoints 25, 35, and so on, and calculate the sample mean.
b. Calculate the sample variance.
c. What is the modal class?
d. What is the coefficient of variation?

Days Past Due	Number of Accounts
20 to under 30	35
30 to under 40	20
40 to under 50	20
50 to under 60	10
60 to under 70	10
70 to 80	5

27. The accompanying data show the number of employees in five different divisions of the Conroy Engineering Company. The data also show the mean income of individuals in those departments. What is the mean income of the entire set of individuals?

Department	Number of Em- ployees	Mean Income (dollars)
Accounting	22	21,000
Finance	14	24,000
Marketing	28	25,000
Manufacturing	106	19,000
Purchasing	23	27,000

28. During a 5-week period, a salesperson's weekly income was $400, $250, $175, $300, and $375.
a. Calculate the sample mean.
b. Calculate the deviations from the mean and verify that they sum to 0.
c. Calculate the mean absolute deviation.
d. Calculate the sample variance and sample standard deviation.

29. The athletic department at the University of Nebraska is interested in the amount of money donated to it by season ticket holders of the preferred seats for football games. The table shows donations by a sample of these ticket holders.

Donation (dollars)	Number of Ticket Holders
0 to under 400	13
400 to under 800	25
800 to under 1200	34
1200 to under 1600	16
1600 to under 2000	8

a. Draw the histogram.
b. Find the sample relative frequencies.
c. Find the sample cumulative relative frequencies.
d. Find the sample mean donation.
e. Find the sample standard deviation for those donations.
f. What is the modal class for this sample?

30. For a sample of new full-size cars, miles per gallon figures were obtained, which are summarized below.

Miles per gallon	14–16	16–18	18–20	20–22	22–24
Number of Cars	14	16	33	20	7

a. Draw the histogram.
b. Find the sample relative frequencies.
c. Find the sample cumulative relative frequencies.
d. Find the sample mean miles per gallon.
e. Find the sample standard deviation of miles per gallon.
f. What is the modal class for this sample?

31. The accompanying data show household incomes for a sample of families in Oklahoma City.

Household Income (dollars)	Relative Frequency
10,000 to under 15,000	.06
15,000 to under 20,000	.11
20,000 to under 25,000	.24
25,000 to under 30,000	.22
30,000 to under 40,000	.17
40,000 to under 50,000	.12
50,000 to under 60,000	

a. Find the relative frequency of the last class.
b. Suppose there were 400 households in the sample. Find the frequency distribution.
c. Find the sample mean.
d. Find the sample standard deviation.

32. The following data show the accumulated years of service before voluntary resignation of a sample of employees at a large oil company.

Years of Service	Number of Employees
0– 2	14
2– 4	41
4– 6	67
6–10	82
10–14	28

a. Draw the histogram.
b. Find the relative frequency distribution.

c. Find the sample mean.
d. Find the sample standard deviation.
e. Find the standardized score for an employee who has 10 years of service.

33. A sample consists of 50 patients at a hospital. In the sample, 28 patients have a mild case of the flu (coded 1), 10 have a moderate case of the flu (coded 2), and 12 have a severe case of the flu (coded 3). Does it make sense to determine the following statistics? If so, compute them.
a. Modal severity
b. Median severity
c. Mean severity

34. If a sample has 155 observations ranked so that the first observation is the largest, the second is next largest, and so on, which observation is the median?

35. A researcher transformed data into standardized scores and obtained a mean standardized score of 1.247. Does this constitute grounds for rechecking the calculations? Why or why not?

36. Which of the following statements are true?
a. Unlike the variance, the range is not greatly affected by extreme values.
b. Distributions with similar means, medians, and modes also tend to have similar variances.
c. The variance measures how spread out observations are, a larger variance indicating greater spread.

37. In a certain corporation, a very small group of employees have extremely high salaries, while the majority of employees receive much lower salaries. If you were the bargaining agent for the union, what statistic would you calculate to illustrate the low pay level and why? If you were the employer, what statistic would you use to demonstrate a higher pay level and why?

38. A sample contains 12 students who graduated from Michigan State (coded 1), 15 students who graduated from Boston College (coded 2), 8 students who graduated from the University of Michigan (coded 3), and 24 students who graduated from Northwestern (coded 4). Calculate the listed statistic if you think it is meaningful.
a. Modal college
b. Median college
c. Mean college
d. Range

39. In a sample of 60 families, 10 own no car, 25 own one car, 15 own two cars, and 10 own three cars. Calculate the listed statistic if you think it is meaningful.
a. Mode
b. Median
c. Mean

40. A sample contains 321 observations ranked from highest to lowest.
a. Which observation is the median?
b. Suppose the observations are ranked from lowest to highest. Which observation is the median?

41. Suppose a variable has two categories, such as "acceptable" and "defective." Suppose you have coded the variable so that acceptable products are coded as 0 and defectives are coded as 1.
a. What, if anything, does the mean of the 0s and 1s tell you?
b. Suppose the sample mean is .20. What does this mean?

42. At a university, a small group of faculty members have extremely high salaries, while the majority of faculty members receive much lower salaries.
a. If you were the bargaining agent for the faculty, which statistic would you use to illustrate the low pay level, the mean or the median?
b. If you were the bargaining agent for the university, which statistic would you use to illustrate the high pay level, the mean or the median? Explain.

43. The accompanying data show the distribution of income for U.S. households for whites and blacks in 1985:

Income (dollars)	Relative Frequency White	Relative Frequency Black
0– 4,999	.0641	.1762
5,000– 9,999	.1166	.1879
10,000–14,999	.1115	.1405
15,000–19,999	.1080	.1242
20,000–24,999	.1014	.0852
25,000–29,999	.0933	.0738
30,000–34,999	.0819	.0553
35,000–39,999	.0673	.0452
40,000–49,999	.0975	.0539
50,000–74,999	.1101	.0467
75,000 and over	.0482	.0110
Total	1.0000	1.0000

a. Draw histograms for the two distributions. For the highest class, use $75,000 to $225,000.
b. Calculate the mean income for blacks and for whites. For the $75,000 and over class, use a midpoint of $150,000.

44. The following data show the age distribution of the cars in use in the United States in 1984:

Age (years)	0–3	3–6	6–9	9–12	12 and up
Number (millions)	22.0	26.8	26.8	17.4	19.0

a. Construct a histogram. For the last interval use 12 to 20 years.
b. Estimate the mean age.

45. The following data show the age distribution of U.S. residents who were below the poverty level in 1984:

Age	0–16	16–22	22–45	45–65	65–80
Number	12,132,000	3,132,000	9,886,000	4,398,000	3,330,000

a. Draw a histogram.
b. Estimate the mean and median age of people living in poverty in 1984.

46. The National Bureau of Economic Research identifies the beginning of a recession (when economic activity peaks) and its end (when the economy hits its trough and begins to recover). The accompanying table shows the beginning and end of each recession since 1920:

Peak to Trough	Length of Recession (months)	Length of Preceding Expansion (months)
Jan 1920–Jul 1921	18	10
May 1923–Jul 1924	14	22

Oct 1926–Nov 1927	13	27
Aug 1929–Mar 1933	43	21
May 1937–Jun 1938	13	50
Feb 1945–Oct 1945	8	80
Nov 1948–Oct 1949	11	37
Jul 1953–May 1954	10	45
Aug 1957–Apr 1958	8	39
Apr 1960–Feb 1961	10	24
Dec 1969–Nov 1970	11	106
Nov 1973–Mar 1975	16	36
Jan 1980–Jul 1980	6	58
Jul 1981–Dec 1982	18	12

a. Calculate the mean length of these 14 recessions and 14 expansions.
b. Calculate the median length of these 14 recessions and 14 expansions.
c. Compare the answers in parts (a) and (b) and explain why they are different.

47. The U.S. Census Bureau reported that in 1985 the mean household income was approximately $29,000 and the median income was approximately $23,600. Why do you think that the mean and the median are not the same? Explain why the mean exceeds the median.

References

NETER, JOHN, WILLIAM WASSERMAN, and G. A. WHITMORE. *Applied Statistics*. 3d ed. Boston: Allyn and Bacon, 1988.

NIE, NORMAN E., C. HADLAI HULL, JEAN G. JENKINS, KARIN STEINBRENNER, and DALE H. BENT. *SPSS Statistical Package for the Social Sciences*. 2d ed. New York: McGraw-Hill, 1975.

NORUSIS, MARIJA J. *SPSSX Introductory Statistics Guide*. New York: McGraw-Hill, 1983.

———. *SPSSX Advanced Statistics Guide*. Chicago: SPSS, 1985.

———. *The SPSS Guide to Data Analysis*. Chicago: SPSS, 1986.

RYAN, THOMAS A., BRIAN L. JOINER, and BARBARA F. RYAN. *Minitab Reference Manual*. University Park, Penn.: Minitab Project, 1985.

———. *Minitab Handbook*. 2d ed. Boston: PWS-KENT, 1985.

SAS Introductory Guide. 3d ed. Cary, N.C.: SAS Institute, 1985.

SAS Procedures Guide for Personal Computers. Version 6 ed. Cary, N.C.: SAS Institute, 1986.

SAS Statistics Guide for Personal Computers. Version 6 ed. Cary, N.C.: SAS Institute, 1986.

SAS User's Guide: Basics. Version 5 ed. Cary, N.C.: SAS Institute, 1985.

SAS User's Guide: Statistics. Version 5 ed. Cary, N.C.: SAS Institute, 1985.

SPSSX User's Guide. Chicago: SPSS, 1983.

Chapter Five
Introduction to Probability

The previous chapters showed how to use raw data to describe the general characteristics of any population or sample. In this chapter we assume that the characteristics of the population are known, and, using probability theory, we describe what we can expect to observe if we select an observation from the population.

5.1 ▪ Experiments, Outcomes, Events, and Sample Spaces

In general, when some activity is performed, several different outcomes are possible. In this chapter, we are interested in determining the probability or likelihood that any particular outcome occurs. The probability of an outcome is a numerical measure of the chance of an outcome's occurrence. Probability is measured on a scale from 0 to 1. A probability near 0 indicates that the outcome is very unlikely to occur, while a probability near 1 indicates that the event is almost certain to occur.

In order to analyze a probability problem, we need to develop a *model* that describes the problem. The model consists of a listing (perhaps theoretical) of all the possible basic outcomes of the activity being studied and the probability associated with each outcome. In statistics the activities being studied are given the formal name *experiments*. Do not confuse the statistical meaning of the word *experiment* with the notion of mixing chemicals in a laboratory.

Definition: Experiment

An **experiment** is any activity from which an outcome, measurement, or result is obtained. When the outcomes cannot be predicted with certainty, then the experiment is a **random experiment**.

Some examples of experiments are as follows:

1. Measuring the lifetime (time to failure) of a given product
2. Inspecting an item to determine if it is defective
3. Recording the income of a bank employee
4. Recording the balance in an individual's checking account

Before an experiment is performed, several different outcomes are possible. The set of all these possible outcomes is called the *sample space* of the experiment. At the conclusion of an experiment, there will be exactly one outcome.

Definition: Basic Outcomes and Sample Space

Each possible outcome of a random experiment is called a **basic outcome**. The set of all possible basic outcomes for a given experiment is called the **sample space** of the experiment.

It is customary to denote each basic outcome by the letter o followed by a subscript. Thus, if an experiment has n possible outcomes, then the basic outcomes will be denoted $o_1, o_2, \ldots, o_n$, where o_i denotes the ith possible outcome and $i = 1, 2, \ldots, n$. The sample space will be denoted by the symbol S and will be represented as $S = \{o_1, o_2, \ldots, o_n\}$.

Example 5.1

Sample Space and Basic Outcomes: Suppose that a corporation has offices in six cities, San Diego, Los Angeles, San Francisco, Denver, Paris, and London. Suppose a new employee will be assigned to work in one of these six offices. Determine the sample space for this experiment.

Solution: The possible assignments are as follows:

o_1 = San Diego $\quad o_2$ = Los Angeles $\quad o_3$ = San Francisco

o_4 = Denver $\quad o_5$ = Paris $\quad o_6$ = London

The sample space is denoted $S = \{o_1, o_2, o_3, o_4, o_5, o_6\}$. If the employee is assigned to work in Denver, then we say that the basic outcome o_4 has occurred. ■

Venn Diagrams

In many cases, it is useful to represent the sample space graphically. This can be done by using a diagram called a **Venn diagram**, named after the English logician John Venn (1834–1923), who popularized their use. In a Venn diagram, the basic outcomes of the experiment are represented as points on a graph. The basic outcomes in Example 5.1 are represented by a Venn diagram in Figure 5.1.

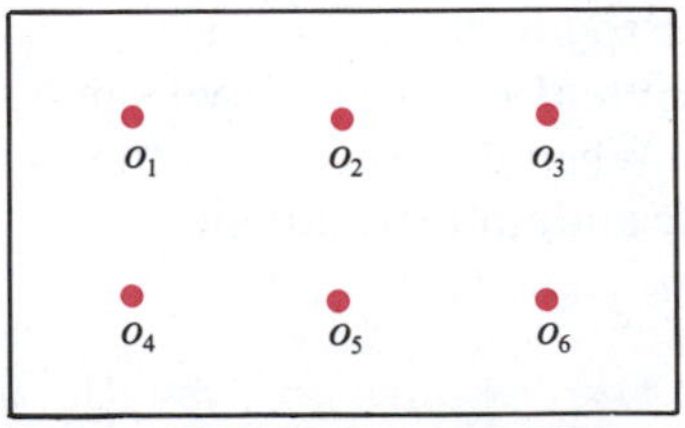

FIGURE 5.1
A Venn diagram showing possible outcomes in Example 5.1.

At times, we form sets or collections of basic outcomes, which are called *events*.

Definition: Event

An **event** is a specific collection of basic outcomes, that is, a set containing one or more of the basic outcomes from the sample space. We say that an event occurs if any one of the basic outcomes in the event occurs.

An event can be thought of as any collection of basic outcomes or as any subset of the sample space. Usually events are denoted by an uppercase letter.

Example 5.2

Events: Refer to Example 5.1, in which an employee was assigned to work in one of six different cities. Suppose we want to know whether the employee was assigned to work in California. Describe this event.

Solution: Let symbol A denote the event {employee assigned to work in California}. We obtain

$$A = \{o_1, o_2, o_3\}$$

Thus we say that event A has occurred if the employee is assigned to work in San Diego, Los Angeles, or San Francisco.

Let event B denote the event that the employee was assigned to work in Europe. We obtain

$$B = \{o_5, o_6\}$$

Event B occurs if the employee is assigned to work in Paris or London. ■

Keep in mind that an experiment will have one and only one basic outcome, and a particular event occurs if any basic outcome in that event occurs. An event can be represented on a Venn diagram by encircling its basic outcomes in that event. Events A and B in Example 5.2 are shown in Figure 5.2.

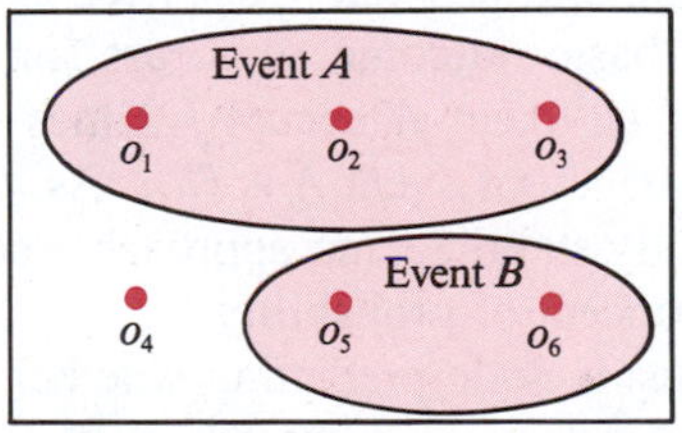

FIGURE 5.2
A Venn diagram showing events A and B in Example 5.2.

Exercises for Section 5.1

1. Suppose a fair die is tossed and we record the value that appears. Construct the sample space and represent it by a Venn diagram.
2. Suppose a pair of dice are tossed and we record the sum of the values that appear. Construct the sample space and represent it using a Venn diagram.

5.2 ▪ Assigning Probabilities to Events

There are two types of random experiments, those that can be repeated over and over again under essentially identical conditions and those that are unique and cannot be repeated. Corresponding to these two types of experiments are two types of probability numbers. A numerical measure that indicates the likelihood of a specific outcome in a repeatable random experiment is called an **objective probability**, whereas the probability associated with a specific outcome of a unique and nonrepeatable random experiment is called a **subjective probability**. Objective probabilities can be determined in one of two ways: empirically, by actually conducting the experiment a large number of times, and theoretically, by studying the basic underlying symmetry in the problem. Objective probabilities that can be found theoretically involve experiments where certain outcomes can be considered equally likely.

This section discusses three different approaches to assigning probabilities to basic outcomes. These three approaches are

1. the relative frequency approach,
2. the equally likely approach, and
3. the subjective approach.

The Relative Frequency Approach

Consider an experiment that can be repeated many times. Assume that after each experiment, it is possible to return to the initial state and repeat the same experiment so that the resulting outcome is unaffected by the previous outcomes. When the experiment is repeated many times, a certain proportion of experiments will result in basic outcome o_1, a certain proportion will result in basic outcome o_2, and so forth. In practical applications, it is customary to think of the proportion of experiments resulting in basic outcome o_i as the *probability of* o_i.

If an experiment has been repeated n times and the basic outcome o_i occurs f_i times, the proportion of times that o_i occurred is f_i/n. The fraction f_i/n is the relative frequency with which basic outcome o_i occurs (or, more simply, the relative frequency of o_i). Similarly, if an event A occurs f_A times in n replications of the experiment, then the relative frequency of event A is f_A/n. As n increases, the proportion of occurrences of A will eventually stabilize and approach a constant value. This idea underlies the *relative frequency* concept of probability.

Examples include predicting whether a fair coin that is tossed will come up heads, whether oil exists at a site based on existing geological conditions, and whether it will rain based on existing meteorological conditions. In assessing the probability of finding oil, a geologist would cite the frequency with which oil had been found at sites in the past with essentially the same conditions.

Relative Frequency Concept of Probability

Let f_A be the number of occurrences, or frequency of occurrence, of event A in n repeated identical trials. The probability that A occurs is the limit of the ratio f_A/n as the number of trials n becomes infinitely large.

Under the relative frequency approach, the probability of an event A can be thought of as the relative frequency of event A in an infinite number of repeated trials of the experiment. The probability of a basic outcome o_i is denoted $P(o_i)$, and the probability of event A is denoted $P(A)$.

The relative frequency approach has several difficulties. Because we can never replicate an experiment an infinite number of times, it is impossible to determine the limit of the ratio f_A/n as n approaches infinity. Furthermore, we can never be sure that we have repeated an experiment under identical conditions. When we use the relative frequency approach, we use the observed ratio f_A/n to approximate the theoretical probability that event A occurs. That is, we assume that $P(A) \approx f_A/n$ when n is "large."

Example 5.3

Relative Frequency Approach to Probability: A marketing research agency surveyed 1000 randomly selected residents in a community. Each resident was asked whether he or she favored expansion of the local shopping mall. Of those questioned, 300 favored the expansion. Let's use the relative frequency approach to estimate the probability that a randomly selected individual will favor expansion.

Solution: The relative frequency of favoring expansion is 300/1000 = .3. Thus we approximate the population proportion of all residents who favor expansion by the proportion .3 and estimate that the probability is .3 that a randomly selected resident will favor expansion. ■

The Equally Likely Approach

In many cases the relative frequency with which some event occurs in a large number of replications of an experiment can be determined theoretically by relying on a basic underlying symmetry in the problem. This situation occurs when all basic outcomes are considered to be equally likely. In this case, the idea of repeated experimentation is a purely conceptual notion, and we do not have to carry out the experiments repeatedly.

Definition: Probability of Equally Likely Outcomes

Suppose that an experiment must result in one of n equally likely outcomes. Then each possible basic outcome is considered to have probability $1/n$ of occurring on any replication of the experiment.

That the basic outcomes of some experiment are equally likely cannot be proved; it is an assumption based on some underlying symmetry in the experiment. In Example 5.3, randomly selected residents were asked whether they favored expanding a shopping mall. Although there are only two possible answers (basic outcomes), yes or no, these outcomes are *not* equally likely.

Example 5.4

The Draft Lottery: In the 1960s men were selected to be drafted into the armed services according to the day of the year on which they were born. The 366 dates of the year (including February 29) were written on balls placed in a box, mixed thoroughly, and withdrawn one at a time. Each ball had an equal chance of being selected first. Thus, the probability that your birthday would have been the first one selected was 1/366. ■

Example 5.5

Criticism of the Draft Lottery: Some people criticized the results of the draft lottery described in Example 5.4, claiming that all birthdays did not have an equal chance of being selected first. They argued that the balls were dropped into the box in such a way that balls representing dates early in the year tended to be near the bottom of the box and the balls representing dates late in the year tended to be near the top. The critics further argued that the balls were not mixed thoroughly and that the person selecting the balls tended to choose balls from the top of the pile. If these critics were correct, then dates in November and December were more likely to be selected first than dates in January and February, and thus all dates were not equally likely to be selected first. ■

Example 5.6

Some Common Equally Likely Models: Some of the most frequently used examples of equally likely events involve coin tossing, dice tossing, drawing cards, and lotteries.

(a) *Coin tossing:* Toss a fair coin. The sample space S consists of two possible basic outcomes, {heads, tails}. If the coin being tossed is fair, we can assume that these two outcomes are equally likely. Thus, based on the equally likely approach, the probability of each basic outcome is 1/2.

(b) *Die tossing:* Toss a symmetrically balanced fair die. It is reasonable to assume that each of the numbers 1 through 6 is equally likely. The sample space S is thus $\{1, 2, 3, 4, 5, 6\}$. Based on the equally likely model, it is assumed that each basic outcome has probability 1/6.

(c) *Card selection:* Select a card randomly from a 52-card poker deck that has been thoroughly shuffled. Based on the assumption that each basic outcome is equally likely, each card has a probability of 1/52 of being selected.

(d) *Lottery gambling:* Many states conduct a lottery called something like the "Daily Number Game." To play the game, you buy a ticket that is imprinted with a number from 000 to 999. Then a number from 000 to 999 is selected randomly. You win a prize if the number selected matches the number on your ticket. It is reasonable to assume that each of the 1000 numbers from 000 to 999 has an equal chance of being selected. Thus, the probability that the number selected matches the number on your ticket is 1/1000, or .001. ■

In many problems of interest, there is no reason a priori to believe that all possible outcomes of an experiment are equally likely. In many of these instances, we use the relative frequency method to estimate the probability of any particular occurrence.

Example 5.7

Inapplicability of Equally Likely Model: In a marketing study, a woman is chosen randomly and asked which of three brands of iced tea she prefers. What is the probability that the woman selects Brand A?

Solution: There is no reason to assume that all brands are equally likely to be selected, so we need to know the relative frequency with which Brand A is selected. Suppose that in a random sample of $n = 1000$ women, Brand A was selected with frequency $f_A = 200$. Thus, the relative frequency of selecting Brand A is $f_A/n = 200/1000 = .2$. We thus estimate that the probability is about .2 that a randomly selected woman prefers Brand A. ■

Definition: Objective Probability

A probability obtained by using a relative frequency approach or an equally likely approach is called an **objective probability**.

The probabilities discussed so far are termed *objective* because they are based on actual sample data or on theoretical considerations concerning the underlying symmetry in a problem. If several independent researchers were given the same information and asked to calculate the probabilities of different outcomes, each researcher should obtain exactly the same answer. That is, these probabilities are not based on personal beliefs or individual opinions.

The Subjective Approach

In many problems the equally likely model does not apply because it is unreasonable to assume that the basic outcomes are all equally likely. In addition, at times the relative frequency approach may be difficult or impossible to apply because we may not be able to perform an experiment a large number of times. In these cases we may have to use our *subjective judgment* to assign a probability to some specific event.

For example, suppose a company is planning to produce an entirely new and untested product. An executive asks, "What is the probability that the company will earn a profit from marketing this product?" How can such a probability be assigned? There are two possible outcomes, earning a profit or not earning a profit, but there is no reason to believe that these outcomes are equally likely. Thus, the equally likely model cannot be applied. In addition, the relative frequency approach is not applicable because the experiment cannot be replicated.

As another example, suppose a stockbroker states that there is a 40% chance that two companies will merge. This is a one-time event that will not be replicated. In situations like this, the probability is the stockbroker's own subjective assessment of the likelihood of a merger. There is no objective way of testing this assessment, and there is no well-defined technique for enabling us to duplicate the stockbroker's thought processes in arriving at her assessment.

Economists speculate about the likelihood of a recession next year; lawyers speculate about the likelihood of winning a particular case; executives speculate about the likelihood of a new product's success. All of these situations involve subjective probabilities.

Definition: Subjective Probability

A **subjective probability** is a number in the interval [0, 1] that reflects a person's degree of belief that an event will occur.

Subjective probabilities are usually applied to experiments that occur only once. It may be useful to think of a subjective probability as representing the opinion of a so-called expert. If you do not think that the person is an expert, then it is reasonable to ignore the subjective opinion when formulating your own opinion about the event's probability.

Assigning Probabilities to Basic Outcomes

We have seen that there are three different ways to assign probabilities to basic outcomes of an experiment: the relative frequency approach, the equally likely approach, and the subjective approach. The nature of the problem determines which approach is best.

Problems with an underlying symmetry, such as coin, dice, and card problems, are especially suited to the equally likely approach. Problems for which we have large samples of data based on many replications of an experiment are especially suited to the relative frequency approach. Problems that occur only once, such as a sporting event, are especially suited to the subjective approach. The major criticism of the subjective approach is that the conclusions depend on the subjectively assigned probabilities, and these, in turn, depend on the insight and wisdom of the analyst. Note, however, that in many problems the subjective approach is the only way of assigning probabilities.

Odds

Occasionally people express their opinions about the probability of some event occurring in terms of **odds** rather than probabilities. Suppose, for example, that a person claims that the odds in favor of some event occurring are 4 to 1. This means that the person thinks the probability that the event will occur is .8.

Converting Odds to a Probability

If the odds in favor of event A occurring are a to b, then

$$P(A) = a/(a + b)$$

Example 5.8

Converting Odds to Probabilities: A meteorologist states that the odds are 5 to 2 that it will rain tomorrow. Convert this statement to a probability statement.

Solution: We have $a = 5$ and $b = 2$. We obtain

$$P(\text{rain}) = 5/(5 + 2) = .714$$

Thus, the meteorologist thinks the probability is .714 that it will rain tomorrow. ■

Exercises for Section 5.2

1. Each purchaser of a yearly subscription to *Reader's Digest* has his or her name placed in a hopper. One of these names is selected and the person is given a new car. Are all of the magazine subscribers equally likely to win?

2. A family has three children. There are four possible outcomes: no boys, one boy, two boys, or three boys. Are each of these outcomes equally likely?

3. In a certain gambling game at a carnival, a box contains six red and six blue envelopes. The six red envelopes contain \$1, \$2, . . . , \$6 each, and similarly for the six blue envelopes. A contestant randomly selects one red and one blue envelope and keeps the contents. For example, if the contestant selects the red envelope containing \$5 and the blue envelope containing \$4, then the contestant gets to keep \$9. The contestant will win from \$2 to \$12.

a. Are all these sums equally likely?
b. In how many ways can the contestant win \$7?
c. What is the probability of winning \$8?

4. A certain town has 500 voters. A poll is taken by choosing a random sample of 50 voters. All 500 names are placed in a box and thoroughly mixed; then the sample of 50 names is selected. Are all samples equally likely?

5. The credit department at a department store had the following history for 850 receivables: 120 were paid early, 340 were settled on time, 220 were paid late, and 170 were uncollectible. Assuming that this experience is representative of the future, estimate the probabilities that a particular account receivable will fall into each of the four categories.
6. Suppose there are four roads (A, B, C, and D) from Town X to Town Y, and three roads (E, F, and G) from Town Y to Town Z. Suppose a criminal travels from Town X to Town Y to Town Z, and a detective is asked which route the criminal took from Town X to Town Z. The detective does not know which route was taken and considers each possible route equally likely. Eventually the detective is forced to guess and hypothesizes that the criminal went via road A between Town X and Town Y and via road F from Town Y to Town Z. What is the probability that the detective is correct?
7. At the racetrack, a spectator hears a gambler claim that the odds are 2 to 5 that a particular horse will win. What is the gambler's subjective assessment of the probability that the horse will win?
8. An executive states that the odds are 10 to 1 against a recession next year. Does this mean that the executive thinks there is a 10% chance of a recession?

5.3 ▪ *Some Basic Rules of Probability*

This section covers some basic rules that must be satisfied by any logical system of assigning probabilities to basic outcomes. The probability of any basic outcome o_i can be thought of as the relative frequency with which the basic outcome o_i occurs in a large number of trials. Every relative frequency is a number in the interval [0, 1], so the probability of any basic outcome o_i must be a value from 0 to 1.

Probability of a Basic Outcome

For each basic outcome o_i, $0 \leq P(o_i) \leq 1$.

Suppose that event A contains the k basic outcomes $o_1, o_2, \ldots, o_k$. The probability of event A is the relative frequency of occurrence of the basic outcomes $o_1, o_2, \ldots, o_k$. We obtain the following rule:

Probability of an Event

Let event $A = \{o_1, o_2, \ldots, o_k\}$, where $o_1, o_2, \ldots, o_k$ are k different basic outcomes. The probability of any event A is the sum of the probabilities of the basic outcomes in A. That is,

$$P(A) = P(o_1) + P(o_2) + \cdots + P(o_k) = \Sigma_A P(o_i)$$

where Σ_A means to obtain the sum over all basic outcomes in event A.

The probability of any event represents the relative frequency of occurrence of all the basic outcomes in A. Thus, the probability of any event must fall in the interval [0, 1]; no event can have a probability that is negative or that exceeds 1.

Probability of an Event

For any event A, $0 \leq P(A) \leq 1$.

The sample space S contains all possible outcomes of an experiment, one of which must occur. It follows that exactly one of the basic outcomes in S must occur and the probability that event S occurs must be 1. The probabilities assigned to all the basic outcomes in an experiment must sum to 1.

Probability of a Sample Space

Let $S = \{o_1, o_2, \ldots, o_n\}$ represent the sample space of an experiment. The probability of S is

$$P(S) = \Sigma_S P(o_i) = 1$$

Example 5.9

Probability of a Sample Space: The quality control division of an electronics firm tests a product for defects. The basic outcomes are $o_1 = \{\text{good}\}$ and $o_2 = \{\text{defective}\}$, and so the sample space is $S = \{o_1, o_2\} = \{\text{good, defective}\}$. Suppose that past experience indicates that about 90% of the products produced are good. Show that the sample space has a probability equal to 1.

Solution: Based on the relative frequency approach, we assign the probabilities $P(o_1) = .9$ and $P(o_2) = .1$. Then we obtain $P(S) = P(o_1) + P(o_2) = 1$. Thus, the probabilities assigned to o_1 and o_2 satisfy all of the rules. That is, $0 \leqslant P(o_i) \leqslant 1$ for $i = 1$ or 2, and $P(S) = \Sigma P(o_i) = 1$. ■

Probabilities for Infinite Sample Spaces

At times we want to consider problems in which the sample space contains an infinite number of equally likely outcomes. For example, suppose a tiny leak has developed in a pipe that is 12 feet long. Let us assume that all points on the pipe are equally likely to be the source of the leak. How can we assign probabilities to the infinite number of points on the pipe and still satisfy the basic rules of probability? We cannot assign positive probabilities to the infinite number of individual points, because the sum of all the probabilities would exceed unity. In this case, the probability assigned to each individual point is 0. Some point on the pipe has to be the source of the leak, but chances are that any particular point is not the source.

Now consider a slightly different problem. What is the probability that the source of the leak occurs within 3 feet from the left end of the pipe? That is, what is the probability that the source of the leak falls in the interval (0, 3)? By assumption, the source of the leak must fall in the interval (0, 12), and all points in the interval are equally likely. A reasonable way to assign a probability to the event that the source of the leak falls in the interval (0, 3) is to assume that the probability of the interval (0, 3) is the ratio of the length of the interval of interest (0, 3) to the length of the entire interval (0, 12). That is, the probability that the point falls in the interval (0, 3) is $3/12 = .25$. Similarly, the probability that the source of the leak falls in the interval (3, 9) is $6/12 = .50$.

In problems in which all points on a line interval are assumed to be equally likely, the probability that a randomly selected point falls in a specific subinterval is equal to the ratio of the length of the subinterval of interest to the length of the entire interval. Thus, in equally likely problems involving all points in an interval, we measure probabilities by the ratios of lengths of lines. In other equally likely problems involving an infinite number of points, we measure probabilities by ratios of areas or of volumes rather than of lengths.

Example 5.10 **Probabilities of Infinite Sample Spaces:** Suppose that an airplane crashed in a rectangular wilderness area A, which is 10 miles wide and 20 miles long. Assume that all points in area A are equally likely to represent the location of the plane. Searchers will thoroughly cover a rectangular area B, which is 4 miles wide and 5 miles long inside A. Find the probability that the plane is found.

Solution: Since the area of A is 200 square miles and that of B is 20 square miles, we calculate the ratio of the areas:

$$P(\text{plane is in area } B) = \frac{\text{area of } B}{\text{area of } A} = \frac{20}{200} = .1$$

■

Exercises for Section 5.3

1. The research department of the Karscig Chemical Company has four chemists and three engineers. The vice-president of the firm randomly selects two of these individuals and gets their opinions about the chances of developing a certain product. Suppose that none of the engineers thinks that the product can be developed and that all the chemists think that it can.
   a. List all possible ways of selecting two individuals to be questioned.
   b. How many outcomes are possible?
   c. Are all possible outcomes equally likely?
   d. How many of the possible outcomes contain two chemists?
   e. What is the probability that both individuals being questioned are chemists?
2. In Exercise 1 what is the probability that at least one person being questioned is a chemist?
3. In Exercise 1 what is the probability that neither person being questioned is a chemist?
4. An oil company that has purchased a square tract of land in Alaska 20 miles on a side is going to pick a site on the tract at random and drill a well. Assume that oil exists in two rectangular pools, each having dimensions 2 miles by 3 miles. If one well is drilled, what is the probability of striking oil?
5. The army shoots a long-range missile to destroy an enemy target. The army can guarantee that the missile will hit within a 6-mile radius of the target. The missile destroys everything within 1 mile of its point of impact. If all points in the 6-mile circle are equally likely to be the point of impact, what is the probability that the missile will destroy the target?
6. A gas line has burst under a major highway running east to west in New York somewhere in a 200-foot length of pipe. Assume that all points on the 200-foot section of pipe are equally likely to be the location of the break. Find the probability that the break occurred more than 40 feet from the eastern end of the pipe.
7. The public works department must repair a section of sewer pipe that is cracked. The pipe starts under the center of the street and connects to another pipe under the front wall of a warehouse. The wall is 150 feet from the center of the street. The plumbers think that the crack could be at any point on the pipe with equal probability. Find the probability that the crack is located as follows:
   a. Within 30 feet of the wall
   b. More than 40 feet from the wall
   c. Between 80 and 100 feet from the wall

8. The U.S. Coast Guard begins searching for a fishing vessel that sank in a lake during a fierce storm. The lake has a circular shape with a radius of 10 miles. The commanding officer wants to concentrate the search efforts in the areas where the vessel most likely sank.

a. Suppose that all points are considered equally likely. Find the probability that the vessel sank less than 2 miles from shore.

b. Suppose we know that the vessel sank in the eastern half of the lake. Find the probability that the vessel sank more than 1 mile from shore.

c. Suppose we know that the vessel sank in the northeast quarter of the lake. Find the probability that the ship sank between 3 and 4 miles from shore.

9. Suppose that 65% of the students in a class are male and 40% are seniors. The teacher picks one of the students randomly. Indicate whether the following statements are true, false, or indeterminate.

a. The probability that the student is a male or a senior (or both) is 1.05.

b. The probability that the student is a male or a senior (or both) is .7.

c. The probability that the student is a male or a senior (or both) is .6.

d. The probability that the student is both a male and a senior is .6.

e. The probability that the student is both a male and a senior is .7.

f. The probability that the student is a male or a senior (or both) is 1.00.

g. The probability that the student is a female is .35.

10. In the daily lottery, a number from 000 to 999 is picked randomly. Yesterday the number 463 won the lottery.

a. What is the probability that 463 wins today?

b. What is the probability that 463 does not win today?

c. Pick any integer from 000 to 999. What is the probability that your number will win the lottery today?

11. During the last 200 days, the number 463 won the lottery twice. What is the probability that 463 will be the winning number tomorrow?

5.4 ▪ Probabilities of Compound Events

In many probability problems it is necessary to combine events to define new events. In this section, we will discuss some rules that are helpful in determining the probabilities of these new events.

Definition: Complement of an Event

Let A denote some event in the sample space S. The **complement** of A, denoted by $\overline{A}$, represents the event composed of all basic outcomes in S that do not belong to A.

Exactly one of the basic outcomes in the sample space S must occur. If the basic outcome that occurs is not in A, then one of the basic outcomes of $\overline{A}$ must occur. It follows that the probability of $\overline{A}$ is 1 minus the probability of A.

Probability of Complement of an Event

Let $\overline{A}$ denote the complement of A. Then $P(\overline{A}) = 1 - P(A)$.

For a sample space containing n basic outcomes, it is easy to prove this rule. Consider the sample space $S = \{o_1, o_2, \ldots, o_n\}$. Let $A = \{o_1, o_2, \ldots, o_k\}$. Then $\bar{A} = \{o_{k+1}, o_{k+2}, \ldots, o_n\}$.

We have

$$P(S) = \sum_{i=1}^{k} P(o_i) + \sum_{i=k+1}^{n} P(o_i) = 1$$

Thus

$$P(S) = P(A) + P(\bar{A}) = 1$$

or

$$P(\bar{A}) = 1 - P(A)$$

Although this proof is based on the assumption that the sample space contains a finite number of basic outcomes, the basic theorem holds for all sample spaces.

The complement of an event can be represented graphically in a Venn diagram. In Figure 5.3 the rectangle represents all basic outcomes in the sample space, the unshaded area in the circle represents all basic outcomes in event A, and the shaded area represents $\bar{A}$.

FIGURE 5.3
Venn diagram showing the complement of an event.

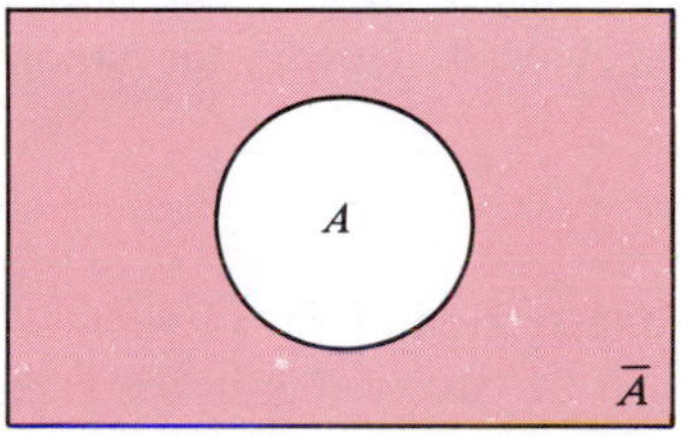

Example 5.11

Probability of the Complement of an Event: Suppose that the computer center has 10 personal computers. Seven of the computers are in perfect condition and 3 have keyboards with a key that sticks occasionally. A student randomly selects 1 computer. What is the probability that the student gets a defective computer?

Solution: By using the equally likely approach, we obtain

$$P(A) = P(\text{perfect computer}) = 7/10 = .7$$

For the complement, we obtain

$$P(\bar{A}) = P(\text{defective computer}) = 1 - P(A) = 1 - .7 = .3$$ ■

Example 5.12

Probability of the Complement of Another Event: An underground pipe 12 miles long connecting two storage facilities for fuel has a tiny hole that is leaking. Suppose that all points on the pipe are equally likely to be the source of the leak. Investigators begin by examining the 5-mile stretch of pipe that is above ground. Find the probability that the leak is not found above ground.

Solution: By using the equally likely model for events containing an infinite number of possible outcomes, we obtain

$$P(A) = P(\text{leak is above ground}) = \frac{\text{length of pipe examined}}{\text{total length of pipe}} = \frac{5}{12}$$

$$P(\bar{A}) = P(\text{leak is not above ground}) = 1 - P(A) = \frac{7}{12}$$

■

Unions and Intersections of Two Events

Let S denote the sample space for an experiment, and let A and B be two events in S. At times we may wish to determine the probability that the basic outcome of an experiment is a member of A or B or both. All the basic outcomes that belong to at least one of the events A or B belong to an event called the *union* of A and B. At other times we may wish to determine the probability that the basic outcome is a member of *both* events A and B. All basic outcomes that belong to both A and B belong to an event called the *intersection* of A and B.

Definition: Union of Two Events

Let A and B be two events in the sample space S. Their **union,** denoted $A \cup B$, is the event composed of all basic outcomes in S that belong to *at least one* of the two events A or B. Hence, the union $A \cup B$ occurs if either A or B (or both) occurs.

Definition: Intersection of Two Events

Let A and B be two events in the sample space S. The **intersection** of A and B, denoted $(A \cap B)$, is the event composed of all basic outcomes in S that belong to both A and B. Hence, the intersection $A \cap B$ occurs if *both* A and B occur.

The notions of union and intersection can be illustrated by Venn diagrams. In Figures 5.4 and 5.5, the rectangle represents the sample space, and the circles inside the rectangle represent events A and B. In Figure 5.4 the shaded area represents the union of A and B, and in Figure 5.5 the shaded area represents the intersection of A and B. The intersection of two events appears in a Venn diagram as the overlapping area between A and B.

FIGURE 5.4
Venn diagram showing the union of two sets.

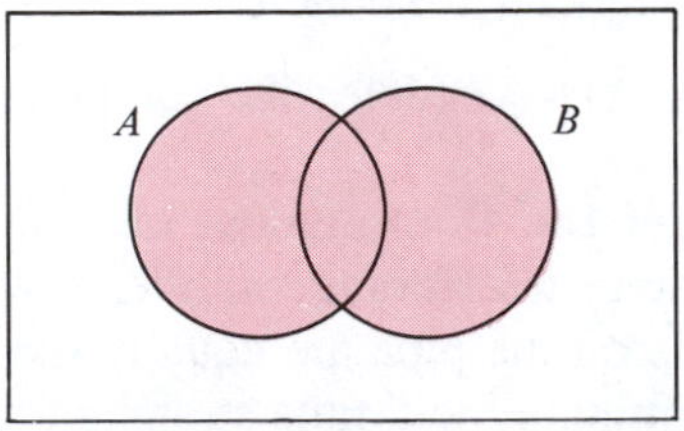

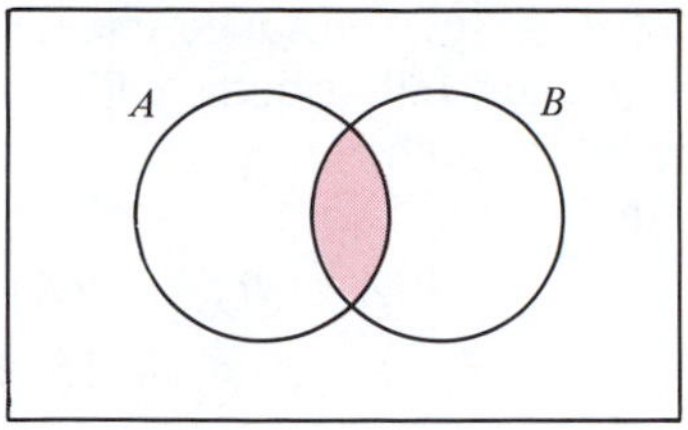

FIGURE 5.5
Venn diagram showing the intersection of two sets.

Additive Law of Probability

The probability that the union of events A and B occurs is the sum of the probabilities of all the basic outcomes in A and B. If A and B have several basic outcomes in common, then the sum of $P(A)$ and $P(B)$ counts the probabilities of the common basic outcomes twice. Thus to obtain the probability of their union, we must subtract from the sum of $P(A)$ and $P(B)$ the probability of all the basic outcomes common to both events, which is the probability of their intersection. This leads to the theorem called the **additive law of probability**.

Additive Law of Probability

Let A and B be events in the sample space S. The probability of the union of A and B is

$$P(A \cup B) = P(A) + P(B) - P(A \cap B)$$

This theorem is illustrated by the Venn diagram in Figure 5.6. The rectangle S contains all the basic outcomes o_i of the sample space. Portion A contains all the basic outcomes in A, and portion B contains all the basic outcomes in B. The shaded area contains all the basic outcomes common to both A and B. From Figure 5.6, we see that $P(A) + P(B)$ includes the probability of the shaded portion twice.

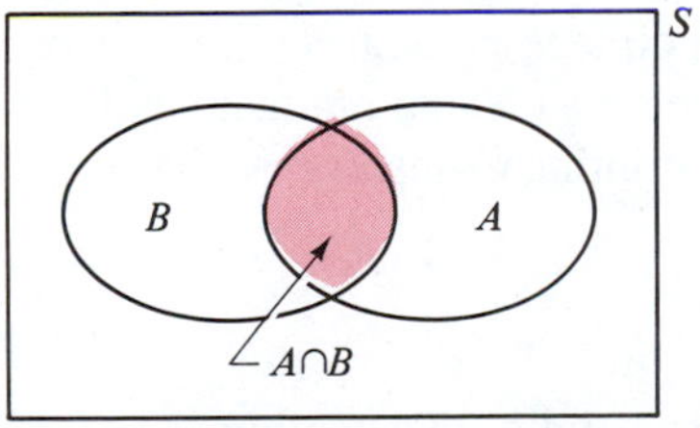

FIGURE 5.6
Venn diagram illustrating the additive law of probability, $P(A \cup B) = P(A) + P(B) - P(A \cap B)$.

Example 5.13 **Additive Law of Probability:** At a certain university, all first-year students must take a chemistry course and a math course. Suppose that 15% of the freshmen fail chemistry, 12% fail math, and 5% fail both. Suppose a first-year student is picked at random. Find the probability that the student failed at least one of the courses.

Solution: Let A = {person failed chemistry}, and let B = {person failed math}. Then $(A \cap B)$ = {person failed both math and chemistry} and $(A \cup B)$ = {person failed math, chemistry, or both}.

We obtain

$$P(A \cup B) = P(A) + P(B) - P(A \cap B)$$
$$= .15 + .12 - .05 = .22$$

This result is illustrated in the Venn diagram in Figure 5.7. ■

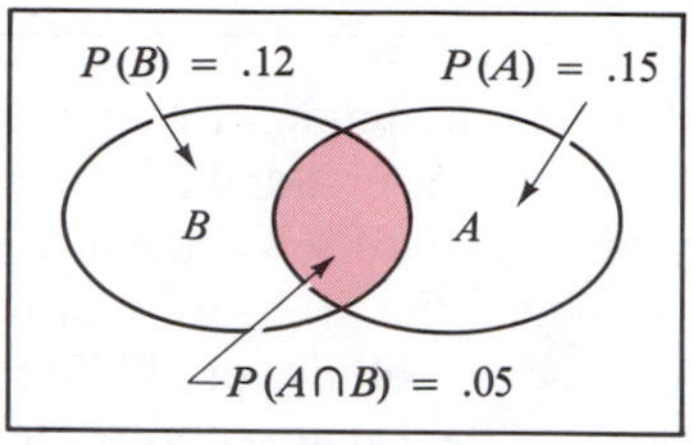

FIGURE 5.7
Venn diagram for Example 5.13.

Definition: Mutually Exclusive Events

Let A and B be two events in a sample space S. If A and B have no basic outcomes in common, then they are said to be **mutually exclusive**. If A and B are mutually exclusive events, we write $(A \cap B) = \varnothing$, where $\varnothing$ denotes the empty set.

Two events are mutually exclusive if they cannot both occur in a single trial of an experiment. If events A and B are mutually exclusive, then $P(A \cap B) = 0$. In a Venn diagram, mutually exclusive events have no overlapping area.

Example 5.14

Mutually Exclusive Events: At the Gromyko Printing Company, 10% of the employees have college degrees. Suppose that 50% of the employees are male, 50% are female, and all of the college graduates are male. Find the probability that a randomly selected person is either a college graduate or a female or both.

Solution: Let A = {person is a college graduate} and B = {person is female}. There are no female college graduates. Thus, events A and B have no common basic outcomes. Because being a college graduate and being female are mutually exclusive events at the Gromyko Printing Company, we have $(A \cap B) = \varnothing$ and $P(A \cap B) = 0$. We thus obtain

$$P(A \cup B) = P(A) + P(B) - P(A \cap B)$$
$$= .10 + .50 - .00 = .60$$ ■

The probability that neither A nor B occurs is denoted $P(\overline{A} \cap \overline{B})$. You should be able to prove the following statement:

$$P(\overline{A} \cap \overline{B}) = 1 - P(A \cup B)$$

By drawing a Venn diagram, you should be able to show that this statement is true. In addition, you should be able to show that the following statement is true by drawing a Venn diagram:

$$P(\overline{A} \cup \overline{B}) = 1 - P(A \cap B)$$

Exercises for Section 5.4

1. The energy commission of a state consists of four people, two of whom are in favor of nuclear power and two of whom are opposed. The governor must select at random two members from the commission to represent the state at a conference.

a. List the sample points contained in the following events:

S = {sample space}

A = {exactly one pronuclear member chosen}

B = {exactly two pronuclear members chosen}

C = {both antinuclear members chosen}

b. Find the probabilities of events A, B, $(A \cap B)$, $(A \cap C)$, and $(A \cup B)$.

2. A large department store claims that 60% of shoplifters in the store will be detected by the store's closed-circuit TV system, 40% by the store's security officers, and 20% by both. Assuming the claims to be true, what is the probability that a shoplifter will be detected?

3. At the University of Texas, 60% of the students are male, and exactly 10% of the men and 5% of the women are married. Find the probability that a randomly chosen student is the following:

a. Male and married

b. Male and unmarried

c. Female and married

d. Female and unmarried

4. A personnel manager constructed the table shown here to define nine combinations of talent and motivation. The numbers in the table are the manager's estimates of the probabilities that a managerial prospect will be classified in the respective categories.

		Talent		
		High	Medium	Low
Motivation	High	.05	.16	.05
	Medium	.19	.32	.05
	Low	.11	.05	.02

Suppose the personnel manager has decided to hire a new manager. Define the following events:

A = {prospect places high in motivation}

B = {prospect places high in talent}

C = {prospect places medium or better in both categories}

D = {prospect places low in at least one category}

E = {prospect places high in both categories}

a. Does the sum of the probabilities in the table equal 1?

b. Find the probability of each event defined above.

c. Find $P(A \cup B)$, $P(A \cap B)$, and $P(A \cup C)$.

5. The following data show the percentages of employees at a company based on sex and level of education.

	Highest Degree Obtained			
	High School	Bachelor's	Master's	Doctorate
Males	5	20	12	11
Females	18	15	14	5

Suppose an employee is selected at random from the firm's 5000 employees and the following events are defined:

$$A = \{\text{employee is male}\}$$
$$B = \{\text{employee is female}\}$$
$$C = \{\text{employee has doctorate}\}$$
$$D = \{\text{employee has master's}\}$$
$$E = \{\text{employee has bachelor's}\}$$
$$F = \{\text{employee has high school diploma}\}$$

Find the probabilities of the following events:

a. A, B, C, D, E, F b. $A \cup B$ c. $B \cap C$ d. $A \cap F$ e. $A \cap B$ f. $C \cap D$

6. A small bank has 1000 customers having both checking and savings accounts. The customers are categorized according to their average monthly account balances as follows:

	Savings Account	
Checking Account	Under \$1000	Over \$1000
Under \$500	300	400
\$500 or more	200	100

Let A denote the set of people with savings of \$1000 or more and B denote the set of people with checking accounts of \$500 or more. If a person is selected at random, find the following:

a. $P(A)$ b. $P(B)$ c. $P(A \cup B)$ d. $P(\bar{A} \cup \bar{B})$ e. $P(A \cap B)$

7. Twenty percent of the population watched a TV football game on Saturday, 30% watched a football game on Sunday, and 15% watched both games. A automobile firm purchased advertising on both telecasts and wants to know the probability that a person saw at least one of the games.

a. What proportion of the population saw at least one of the games?
b. What proportion of the population saw neither of the games?

8. Of the employees for a supermarket chain, 60% are women, 50% work part-time, and 35% of the women work part-time.

a. What proportion of employees are females who work part-time?
b. What proportion of employees are males who work full-time?

9. A campus restaurant features two luncheon meals. Meal A features meat and potatoes, and meal B consists of fish and a salad. Ninety percent of the male customers order meal A, 20% of the female customers order meal A, and 60% of all customers are male.

a. What proportion of customers will order meal A?
b. If you were planning to prepare 1000 meals, how many would you prepare of meal A?

10. In the Department of Labor, 70% of the employees are male, 30% are female, and 35% of the employees have business degrees. Of those having business degrees, 40% are female. Calculate the following probabilities:

a. A randomly selected employee is a female with a business degree.
b. A randomly selected male has a business degree.

11. At the Middletown Appliance Company, 10% of the employees are in accounting, 40% are in sales, 20% are in manufacturing, and the rest are in other departments. On any given day, the absentee rates for each of these departments are 2%, 6%, 3% and 5%, respectively.
a. What proportion of absentees are from the accounting department?
b. What proportion of absentees are from the sales department?

12. A roulette wheel has 38 numbered slots; 18 are black, 18 are red, and 2 are green. Half of the black slots are even numbers and half are odd, and similarly for the red slots. The green slots are numbered 0 and 00.
a. You bet $1 that a black slot will occur. Find the probability that you win the bet.
b. On a single trial, you bet $1 that a black value will occur and $1 that an odd value will occur. Find the probability that you will lose both bets.
c. On a single trial, you bet $1 that a black value will occur and another $1 that an odd value will occur. Find the probability that you will win both bets.
d. On a single trial, you bet $1 that a black value will occur and another $1 that an odd value will occur. Find the probability that you will win one bet and lose the other.

13. State the complement of the following events:
a. The inflation rate will be less than 4% next year.
b. A family with two children has two boys.
c. A basketball player who shoots two free throws will make at least one of the two shots.

14. Are the following occurrences unions or intersections of basic events?
a. Selecting the ace of clubs from a poker deck
b. Selecting a female senior from a statistics class
c. Selecting a voter who is a Democrat or a college student
d. Selecting a magazine subscriber who is married and employed
e. Selecting a magazine subscriber who is male or over age 40

15. Let A denote the set of people who are employed, B the set of people who are over age 50, and C the set of people who are male. Describe the following sets:
a. Union of A and B
b. Intersection of A and C
c. Intersection of A, B, and C
d. Intersection of $\overline{B}$ and $\overline{C}$

5.5 ▪ Conditional Probability

In many applications we may be interested in determining the probability that some event A occurs given that some other event B has already occurred. This probability is called a **conditional probability**. If the probability of one event varies depending on whether a second event has occurred, the two events are said to be **dependent**. Let A denote the event that a person has a college degree and B the event that a person earns more than $50,000 per year. Events A and B are related because the probability that a randomly selected person earns more than $50,000 per year, $P(B)$, is not the same as the probability that the person earns more than $50,000 per year given that the person is a college graduate. For example, across the United States, less than 20% of all adults earn more than $50,000 per year, but among college graduates more than 20% of adults earn more than $50,000 per year.

The probability $P(B)$ is an unconditional probability. It shows the proportion of all adults who earn more than \$50,000 per year. Now examine just the group of adults who are college graduates. Of this subpopulation, what proportion earns more than \$50,000 per year? This latter proportion is the *conditional probability of event B given A,* and is denoted $P(B|A)$.

Joint Probability Tables

Before discussing conditional probability, it will be helpful to introduce the concepts of *joint probability* and *marginal probability.* Suppose that a male student who was rejected for admission into graduate school presented the data in Table 5.1 in support of his claim that the university was discriminating against male applicants. The student argued that of the 12,500 applicants, 4700 (or 37.6%) were males who were rejected. On the other hand, only 2400 of the students (or 19.2%) were females who were rejected. Should we accept the student's claim that the university seems to be discriminating against males?

TABLE 5.1
Joint frequency table for applicants to graduate school

	Admission Status		
Sex	Admitted	Rejected	Total
Male	3,800	4,700	8,500
Female	1,600	2,400	4,000
Total	5,400	7,100	12,500

Table 5.1 shows how all students who applied for admission to the graduate school were distributed according to the two variables Sex and Admission Status. Table 5.1 is an example of a *joint frequency table,* or a *joint frequency distribution.* It is a *bivariate* table because only two variables are being considered. If three variables (such as Race, Sex, and Admission Status) had been considered, we would have had a *trivariate* table. Joint frequency tables show the frequency, or number, of observations possessing several characteristics simultaneously.

If we divide each entry in Table 5.1 by the total number of applicants (12,500), we obtain a set of relative frequencies, which can be used to represent probabilities. The data in Table 5.2 show these relative frequencies or probabilities. Table 5.2 is an example of a *joint probability distribution,* or a *joint relative frequency distribution.*

Definition: Joint Probability

A **joint probability** shows the probability that an observation will possess two (or more) characteristics simultaneously. Every joint probability must be a number in the closed interval [0, 1], and the sum of all joint probabilities must be 1.

TABLE 5.2
Joint probability table for applicants to graduate school

Sex	Admission Status: Admitted	Admission Status: Rejected	Marginal Probability
Male	.304	.376	.680
Female	.128	.192	.320
Marginal Probability	.432	.568	1.000

Example 5.15

Calculating Joint Probabilities: Use the frequency data in Table 5.1 to find the probability that an individual was both male and rejected. Also find the probability that a student was female and was rejected.

Solution: Table 5.1 indicates that there were 12,500 applicants to graduate school, of whom 4700 were males who were rejected. The relative frequency 4,700/12,500 = .376 is the joint probability that an individual possesses both characteristics, namely, being male and being rejected. This probability is shown at the intersection of the row "Male" and the column "Rejected" in Table 5.2. We obtain

$$P(\text{male} \cap \text{rejected}) = 4{,}700/12{,}500 = .376$$

Similarly, the probability that a student was female and rejected is

$$P(\text{female} \cap \text{rejected}) = .192$$

■

Marginal Probability

Whereas a joint probability shows the proportion of observations possessing two characteristics simultaneously, a *marginal probability* shows the proportion of observations that possess any single specific characteristic. The numbers at the bottom and on the right side of Table 5.2 (bottom and right margins) are *marginal probabilities*.

Rule for Marginal Probabilities

To obtain the marginal probability of any particular value of a variable, sum the appropriate joint probabilities over all values of the other variable. Every marginal probability must be a number in the closed interval [0, 1]. For any variable, the sum of all marginal probabilities must be 1.

Example 5.16

Marginal Probability: In Table 5.2, the variable Admission Status has two categories, "admitted" and "rejected." Find the marginal probabilities for these categories.

Solution: The marginal probability that a randomly selected applicant was admitted is the sum of the appropriate joint probabilities summed over the variable Sex. We obtain:

$$\begin{aligned} P(\text{admitted}) &= P(\text{male} \cap \text{admitted}) + P(\text{female} \cap \text{admitted}) \\ &= .304 + .128 = .432 \end{aligned}$$

This result can also be obtained from Table 5.1, which indicates that 5,400 of the 12,500 applicants were admitted. Thus, $P(\text{admitted}) = 5{,}400/12{,}500 = .432$.

The marginal probability that an applicant was rejected (.568) can be obtained as follows:

$$P(\text{rejected}) = P(\text{male} \cap \text{rejected}) + P(\text{female} \cap \text{rejected})$$
$$= .376 + .192 = .568$$

We have $P(\text{admitted}) = .432$ and $P(\text{rejected}) = .568$. These two marginal probabilities sum to 1. ■

Now suppose that we want to compare the rejection rate for males with the rejection rate for females. To do this, we have to calculate the conditional probabilities.

To calculate $P(A|B)$, we restrict ourselves to the subpopulation of experiments that resulted in event B. The conditional probability $P(A|B)$ measures the fraction of those occurrences of B that also resulted in event A. Figure 5.8 helps explain the notion of conditional probability. The rectangle S denotes the sample space. The two portions labeled A and B represent the basic outcomes in the events A and B, respectively. The shaded portion represents the basic outcomes common to both A and B, that is, the intersection of A and B. Let us use the areas of A, B, and their intersection to represent their probabilities. For any sample space S, $P(S) = 1$, so the area of the rectangle is 1.

FIGURE 5.8
Conditional probability (see text discussion).

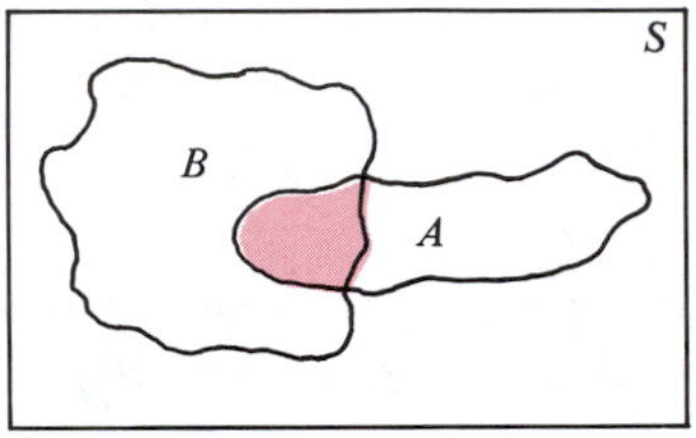

We want to know the probability that a basic outcome in A has occurred given that a basic outcome in B has occurred. This requires that the basic outcome be in the intersection $(A \cap B)$. The conditional probability $P(A|B)$ equals the ratio of the area of the intersection of A and B divided by the area of B, where these areas measure the probabilities of the events.

We obtain the following rule for calculating conditional probabilities:

Formula for Conditional Probability

The conditional probability that event A occurs given that event B has occurred is

$$P(A|B) = \frac{P(A \cap B)}{P(B)} \quad \text{provided } P(B) \neq 0$$

Note that if A and B have no basic outcomes in common, then $(A \cap B) = \varnothing$ and $P(A \cap B) = 0$. Thus, it follows that if A and B have no outcomes in common, then

$P(A|B) = 0$. That is, if we know B has occurred and A has no basic outcomes in common with B, then it follows that A has not occurred.

Example 5.17 **Conditional Probability:** Refer again to Tables 5.1 and 5.2. To determine if the university has been discriminating against male applicants, we need to compare the two conditional probabilities P(applicant was rejected given that applicant was male) and P(applicant was rejected given that applicant was female). We will denote these two probabilities by $P(\text{rejected}|\text{male})$ and $P(\text{rejected}|\text{female})$, respectively. Calculate these two conditional probabilities.

Solution: From the joint and marginal probabilities in Table 5.2, we obtain

$$P(\text{rejected}|\text{male}) = P(\text{rejected} \cap \text{male})/P(\text{male}) = .376/.680 = .553$$

We can obtain this same result by using the data in Table 5.1. Table 5.1 indicates that there were 8500 male applicants, of whom 4700 were rejected. The proportion of males who were rejected is given by

$$P(\text{rejected}|\text{male}) = 4700/8500 = .553$$

Similarly, by using the data in Table 5.2, we obtain the conditional probability

$$P(\text{rejected}|\text{female}) = P(\text{rejected} \cap \text{female})/P(\text{female}) = .192/.320 = .600$$

By using the data in Table 5.1, we obtain the same result

$$P(\text{rejected}|\text{female}) = 2400/4000 = .600$$

■

Does the evidence in Tables 5.1 and 5.2 support the claim that the university is discriminating against male applicants? The joint probabilities in Table 5.2 show that 37.6% of all applicants were rejected males, whereas only 19.2% of the applicants were rejected females. This shows that the proportion of applicants who were both male and rejected is approximately twice as high as the proportion of applicants who were both female and rejected. Does this indicate that the university is discriminating against male applicants? Not necessarily. You have to examine conditional probabilities, not joint probabilities, to determine if there has been discrimination.

The appropriate conditional probabilities are $P(\text{rejected}|\text{male}) = .553$ and $P(\text{rejected}|\text{female}) = .600$. These probabilities indicate that 60% of the female applicants and 55.3% of the male applicants were rejected. Therefore, the data indicate that the rejection rate for females was actually slightly higher than that for males. These values are close enough, however, to support the argument that the university was not discriminating against either sex.

Can you find the flaw in the original claim that males were being discriminated against? The reason the joint probabilities are larger for males than for females is because there were far more male applicants than female. If males and females are treated exactly alike and there are far more male applicants than female applicants, the majority of the applicants who are rejected will be male. (It also follows that the majority of applicants who will be accepted will be male.)

An Application of Conditional Probability

Most companies that provide automobile insurance charge lower premiums to teenage females than to teenage males. In Pennsylvania some state legislators argued that this was an example of sex discrimination. After a lengthy debate, the state legislature passed a bill making it illegal for insurance companies to charge different premiums based on the sex of the applicant. Later the bill was declared unconstitutional by the state supreme court. Do you think that there should be a law requiring insurance premiums to be equal for males and females? Do you think that charging males and females different premiums is evidence of sex discrimination?

The insurance companies have data showing that teenage females are involved in fewer accidents per driver than teenage males. There are two reasons for this: Females tend to drive fewer miles than males, and females tend to have fewer accidents per mile driven. It follows that the conditional probability that an insured individual will be involved in an accident given that the insured individual is a female is lower than the conditional probability that an insured individual will be involved in an accident given that the insured individual is a male.

Do you think this information is relevant to determining what premiums insurance companies should charge? Who would gain and who would lose if the Pennsylvania bill had been declared legal? How do you think the insurance companies would react if the bill had been declared legal?

Multiplicative Law of Probability

The joint probability $P(A \cap B)$ shows the probability that *both* events A and B occur. By manipulating the rule for conditional probability,

$$P(A|B) = P(A \cap B)/P(B)$$

we can obtain a useful formula for calculating $P(A \cap B)$, called the *multiplicative law of probability*.

Multiplicative Law of Probability

The probability that the two events A and B both occur is given by

$$P(A \cap B) = P(B)\ P(A|B)$$

and by

$$P(A \cap B) = P(A)\ P(B|A)$$

Example 5.18 **Multiplicative Law of Probability:** Suppose that Valencia's Discount Store has received a shipment of 60 television sets, 5 of which are defective. On the following day, 2 televisions are sold. Find the probability that both of the televisions are defective.

Solution: Let A denote the event {first television is defective} and B the event {second television is defective}. Then the intersection of A and B denotes the event {both televisions are defective}. By using the equally likely model, the probability that the first television is defective is $P(A) = 5/60$. Also, we know that $P(B|A) = 4/59$, because after the first defective television is sold, 59 televisions remain, of which 4 are defective. Now we use the multiplicative law of probability to obtain

$$\begin{aligned} P(A \cap B) &= P(A)\ P(B|A) \\ &= (5/60)(4/59) = 1/177 = .0056 \end{aligned}$$

■

Example 5.19 **Multiplicative Law of Probability:** Find the probability that the first television sold is defective and that the second is not defective.

Solution: Let C denote the event that the second television is not defective. We obtain $P(C|A) = 55/59$, because if the first television is defective, then 59 televisions remain, 55 of which are not defective. We obtain

$$P(A \cap C) = P(A)\ P(C|A) = (5/60)(55/59) = .0777$$

■

Exercises for Section 5.5

1. A quality control engineer has been asked to examine a complex electronic system that is out of control. The examination will involve testing five mechanisms within the system to identify the one that is faulty. Assume that one and only one mechanism is faulty. If the mechanisms are randomly chosen for examination by the engineer but excluded from further consideration if found satisfactory, what is the probability that the faulty switching mechanism will be discovered at the following times:
a. During the second examination
b. During the third examination
c. Before the third examination

2. An inspector for a food processing firm has accepted 98% of all good shipments and has incorrectly rejected 2% of good shipments. In addition, the inspector accepts 94% of all shipments, and it is known that 5% of all shipments are of inferior quality.
a. Find the probability that a shipment is rejected.
b. Find the probability that a shipment is good.
c. Find the probability that a shipment is good and that it is accepted.
d. Find the probability that a shipment is of inferior quality and that it is accepted.
e. Find the probability that a shipment is accepted given that it is of inferior quality.
f. Find the probability that a shipment is rejected given that it is good.

3. By mistake, a quality control inspector accepts 5% of all bad items and rejects 1% of all good items. Overall, 90% of the items are good. Find the following:
a. $P(\text{accept}|\text{bad})$
b. $P(\text{reject}|\text{good})$
c. $P(\text{good})$
d. What is the probability that the inspector will accept or reject the next item incorrectly?

4. A national credit card company is interested in getting more young female customers. In a recent survey, the company gathered data on the marital and employment status of 25-year-old women. Suppose that 60% of all 25-year-old women are married, 50% have full-time jobs, and 20% are both married and have full-time jobs. Given that a 25-year-old woman has a full-time job, what is the probability that she is married?

5. In Exercise 4, what is the probability that a 25-year-old woman has a full-time job given that she is married?

6. To see whether a trainee is doing an acceptable job as a product inspector, the trainee is told to inspect a shipment of 1000 products. It is known that 800 of the products are good (G) and 200 are defective (D). The trainee rejects 40 of the good products and accepts 6 of the defective products. Let R denote the set of rejected products and A the set of accepted products. Find the following probabilities:

a. $P(G)$ b. $P(D)$ c. $P(R|G)$ d. $P(R|D)$
e. $P(G|R)$ f. $P(G|A)$ g. $P(A)$ h. $P(R)$

7. For a nationwide oil company, 15% of its credit card customers have annual incomes of $10,000 or less, 55% have annual incomes between $10,000 and $30,000, and the rest have annual incomes of $30,000 or more. In the lowest income category, 20% of the accounts are delinquent; in the middle category, 10% are delinquent; in the highest category, 5% are delinquent.

a. If an account is selected at random, what is the probability that it is delinquent?
b. An account is selected and found to be delinquent. What is the probability that it is in the lowest income category?
c. If the company has 10,000 accounts, how many would you expect to be delinquent and in the middle category?

8. A research study found that 60% of the employees at a financial institution read the *Wall Street Journal*, 45% read *Time*, and 30% read both.

a. What is the probability that an employee selected at random does not read either publication?
b. What is the probability that a person selected at random reads at least one of the publications?
c. Given that a person reads *Time*, what is the probability that the person also reads the *Wall Street Journal*?

9. The dean of the college of arts and sciences is undertaking a study to see if grades are being inflated in various academic departments. The dean obtains the following data on the grades of 200 students in three courses:

Grade	History	Economics	Math	Total
A	25	25	30	80
B	10	60	20	90
C or less	5	15	10	30
Total	40	100	60	200

Suppose one of the 200 students is chosen randomly. Find the following probabilities:

a. P(student got an A) d. $P(\text{A}|\text{economics})$
b. P(student got B or less) e. $P(\text{math}|\text{B})$
c. P(student is in economics) f. $P(\text{history}|\text{B or less})$

10. Three different production lines produce valves for the O'Toole Corporation. They make large and small valves, and their output (in thousands) for a given week was as follows:

Type of Valve	Line 1	Line 2	Line 3	Total
Large	300	200	100	600
Small	200	100	100	400
Total	500	300	200	1000

A customer comes to Mr. O'Toole with a large defective valve. Mr. O'Toole wants to determine which line made this defective valve. Find the following probabilities:

a. $P(\text{line } 1|\text{large})$
b. $P(\text{line } 2|\text{large})$
c. $P(\text{line } 3|\text{large})$

11. A recent census of a small town in Minnesota showed that 60% of the residents are male, 20% have college degrees, and 15% are both male and college graduates.

a. If a randomly selected person is a male, what is the probability that he has a college degree?
b. What is the probability that the person selected is either male or a college graduate?
c. What is the probability that the person selected is neither male nor a college graduate?
d. Given that a female is selected, what is the probability that she is not a college graduate?

12. Mr. Wilson, the owner of a used car agency, meets about 45% of the agency's potential customers and makes a sale to about 60% of those he meets. The other salespeople meet the other 55% of the potential customers and make a sale to about 50% of these individuals.

a. What proportion of potential customers eventually buy a car?
b. What proportion of sales can be attributed to Mr. Wilson?

5.6 ▪ *Independence*

If the conditional probability $P(A|B)$ differs from the unconditional probability $P(A)$, then the probability that A occurs depends on whether B has occurred. If $P(A|B)$ equals $P(A)$, then the probability of occurrence of A does not depend on the occurrence of B and we say that A and B are independent. If A and B are **independent**, then events A and B have no influence on one another; the probability of A occurring is unaffected by whether or not B has occurred.

If A is independent of B, then the probability that A occurs given that B has occurred should be the same as the probability of A given no information about B. Recall that it is always the case that

$$P(A|B) = \frac{P(A \cap B)}{P(B)}$$

If A is independent of B, we also have

$$P(A|B) = P(A)$$

If A and B are independent, we can equate the two expressions for $P(A|B)$ and obtain the following rule: If A and B are independent then

$$\frac{P(A \cap B)}{P(B)} = P(A)$$

After multiplying both sides by $P(B)$, we obtain the important *formula for independent events.*

Formula for Independent Events

Events A and B are **independent** if and only if

$$P(A \cap B) = P(A)\,P(B)$$

Thus, when two events are independent, the probability that they both occur is obtained by multiplying their respective individual probabilities. This rule can be generalized to apply to any number of independent events. Thus, if events A, B, and C are independent of one another, then the probability that all three events will occur is equal to the product of their individual probabilities.

Note that this theorem works in two directions. That is, if we know a priori that events A and B are independent, then we also know that $P(A \cap B) = P(A)\,P(B)$. On the other hand, if we can show that $P(A \cap B) = P(A)\,P(B)$, then we know that events A and B are independent.

The definition of statistical independence can be explained intuitively as follows. Suppose that the probability that event A will occur is $P(A)$. Suppose now that additional information is provided that event B has occurred. If this information does not change my opinion about the likelihood of the occurrence of event A, then my conditional probability assessment $P(A|B)$ will be the same as $P(A)$. I will have concluded that knowing the occurrence of event B is of no use in determining whether A will occur.

In some circumstances, independence can be deduced, or at least reasonably inferred, from the nature of the random experiment. In these cases, the probability of the joint occurrence of events A and B can be calculated as the product of their individual probabilities. This idea is particularly useful for evaluating experiments repeated many times under identical conditions. Because successive outcomes are independent of one another, the probability of any specific set of basic outcomes equals the product of the individual probabilities.

Consider the relationship between mutually exclusive events and independent events. If events A and B are mutually exclusive, then A and B cannot occur together. Are they independent? That is, does the assumption that B has occurred alter our assessment of the probability that A will occur? It certainly does, because if we assume that B has occurred, then we know that A will not or has not occurred. Thus, mutually exclusive events are *dependent* events.

Example 5.20

Probability of Independent Events: Approximately 30% of the sales representatives hired by a firm quit in less than one year. Suppose that two independent sales representatives are hired and assume that the first sales representative's behavior is independent of the second sales representative's behavior.
(a) What is the probability that both quit within a year?
(b) Find the probability that exactly one representative quits.

Solution: (a) Use the theorem for independent events. Let A = {first sales representative quits} and B = {second sales representative quits}.

$$\begin{aligned} P(\text{both quit}) &= P(A \cap B) \\ &= P(A)\,P(B) \\ &= (.3)(.3) = .09 \end{aligned}$$

(b) Let $\overline{A}$ = {first sales representative stays} and $\overline{B}$ = {second sales representative stays}. Applying the rule about complementary events yields the probabilities $P(\overline{A}) = 1 - P(A) = .7$, and similarly $P(\overline{B}) = .7$.

We obtain

$$
\begin{aligned}
P(\text{exactly one quits}) &= P(\text{first quits and second stays}) \\
&\quad + P(\text{first stays and second quits}) \\
&= P(A \cap \overline{B}) + P(\overline{A} \cap B) \\
&= P(A)\,P(\overline{B}) + P(\overline{A})\,P(B) \\
&= (.3)(.7) + (.7)(.3) = .42
\end{aligned}
$$

■

Tree Diagrams

When events are independent, a **tree diagram** can be a useful device for calculating probabilities. In a tree diagram, each branch represents a possible outcome. We find the joint probability of a sequence of outcomes by multiplying the corresponding probabilities. This is illustrated in Figure 5.9, which shows the tree diagram for Example 5.20.

FIGURE 5.9
Tree diagram for Example 5.20.

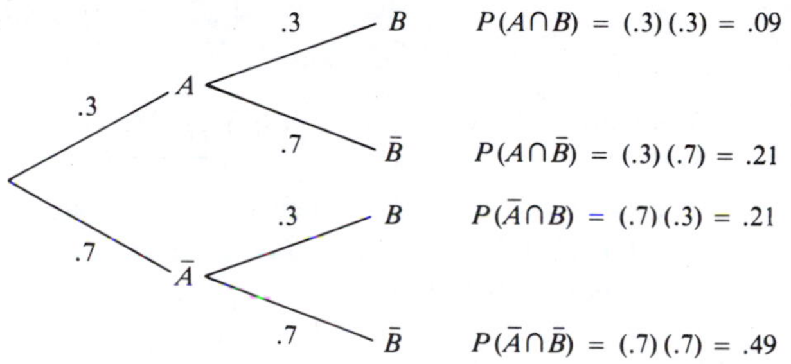

Example 5.21

Probability of Independent Events: A husband and wife, each 20 years old, are debating whether to set up a retirement program for themselves. Benefits are paid to the man or the woman at the age of 70. If both have died before reaching age 70, no benefits are paid. Assume that the probability that a man aged 20 lives to age 70 is approximately .6 and the probability that a woman aged 20 lives to age 70 is approximately .7. If the husband and wife join the program, what is the probability that either the man or the woman will collect benefits? Assume that the chances of the man or woman dying are independent of each other.

Solution: Benefits are paid if either the man or the woman or both live to age 70. The appropriate probabilities can be found by applying the rule for probability of independent events. Let M = {man lives to age 70}; $\overline{M}$ = {man dies before age 70}; W = {woman lives to age 70}; and $\overline{W}$ = {woman dies before age 70}. The probability of collecting benefits is the probability that both live to age 70 plus the probability that just the woman lives to age 70 plus the probability that just the man lives to age 70. The possible outcomes and their probabilities are as follows:

$$
\begin{aligned}
P(M \cap W) &= (.6)(.7) = .42 \\
P(\overline{M} \cap W) &= (.4)(.7) = .28 \\
P(M \cap \overline{W}) &= (.6)(.3) = .18 \\
P(\overline{M} \cap \overline{W}) &= (.4)(.3) = .12 \\
P(\text{at least one lives}) &= P(M \cap W) + P(\overline{M} \cap W) + P(M \cap \overline{W}) \\
&= .42 + .28 + .18 = .88
\end{aligned}
$$

Alternatively, by using the rule for complementary events, we have

$$P(\text{at least one lives}) = 1 - P(\text{both die}) = 1 - (.4)(.3) = .88$$

Figure 5.10 shows the tree diagram for Example 5.21.

FIGURE 5.10
Tree diagram for Example 5.21.

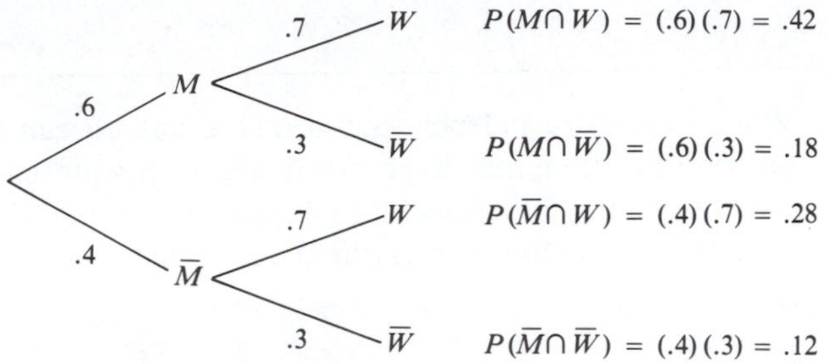

Sampling with and without Replacement

There is a broad class of problems in which successive outcomes can be considered independent that involve *sampling with replacement.* In contrast, when we *sample without replacement* from a finite population, the successive outcomes will not be independent.

Selecting a random sample can be viewed as a process in which we sequentially obtain one observation after another. At each step of the process, we select one observation from the remaining population of observations. When we sample with replacement, we put each unit back into the original population before selecting the next observation. When we sample without replacement, we do not put a unit back before the next observation.

When we sample with replacement, successive outcomes are independent because the probability of obtaining any particular observation on any selection does not depend on which units were previously selected. When we sample without replacement, successive outcomes are not independent because the composition of the remaining population changes after each selection. Therefore, at each selection the probability of a specific outcome depends on the previous outcomes. When we sample without replacement, we find the joint probability $P(A \cap B)$ by using the general multiplicative law of probability

$$P(A \cap B) = P(A)\,P(B|A) \quad \text{or} \quad P(A \cap B) = P(B)\,P(A|B)$$

When we sample with replacement, we can use the law for independent events, which is a special case of the multiplicative law:

$$P(A \cap B) = P(A)\,P(B)$$

Example 5.22

Sampling without Replacement: Suppose that a car rental agency has 10 seemingly identical cars. Unknown to anyone, 2 of these cars contain defective brakes because of abuse by former drivers. Two customers arrive and rent cars. Find the probability that the first customer gets a good car and the second gets a car with defective brakes.

Solution: Define A = {first customer gets a good car} and B = {second customer gets a defective car}. This problem involves sampling without replacement, so we use the multiplicative law $P(A \cap B) = P(A)\,P(B|A)$. Initially 10 cars are available, of which 8 are good. By using the equally likely model, we obtain $P(A) = 8/10$. After renting out a good car to the first customer, 9 cars are available for the second customer, of which 2 are defective. We have $P(B|A) = 2/9$. We obtain the desired probability

$$P(A \cap B) = P(A)\,P(B|A) = (8/10)(2/9) = .178$$

■

Example 5.23 **Sampling with Replacement:** The Internal Revenue Service (IRS) wants to investigate whether gambling casinos have been making illegal deductions on their income tax returns. The IRS makes a list with the names of 10 potential offenders, 3 of which have reported no illegal deductions. The IRS selects 1 of the 10 casinos randomly and conducts a full-scale audit. During the following year, to keep all the casinos honest, the IRS again selects 1 of the 10 casinos randomly and conducts a full-scale audit. In this problem, the casino audited in the first year could be audited again in the second; thus, the sampling is done with replacement. Find the probability that the casino audited first reported illegal deductions and that the casino audited second reported illegal deductions.

Solution: Because this problem involves sampling with replacement, successive events are independent. Define A = {first casino made no illegal deductions} and B = {second casino made illegal deductions}. We apply the equally likely model and obtain $P(A) =$ .7 and $P(B) = .3$. We obtain the joint probability by using the law for independent events:

$$P(A \cap B) = P(A)\,P(B) = (.7)(.3) = .21$$

■

Exercises for Section 5.6

1. A real estate agent is showing houses to two potential buyers, Mr. Smith and Mr. Jones. The agent assigns .5 as the subjective probability that Smith will buy a house and .5 as the subjective probability that Jones will buy a house. Let S indicate that Smith buys a house, and let J denote that Jones buys a house. Assume that the decisions of Smith and Jones are independent of one another.

a. Construct a tree diagram showing all possible outcomes denoting whether Smith and/or Jones bought a house. List the sample space.

b. Find the probability of each element in the sample space.

c. Let A denote the event {agent has at least one sale}. List the elements of A and find $P(A)$.

d. List $\bar{A}$ and find $P(\bar{A})$.

2. Two teams A and B are of equal ability, so each has a probability of .5 of defeating the other. Assume that the outcome of any game is independent of the outcome of any other game. What is the probability that team A wins four games in a row?

3. When you purchase candy from a candy machine, the probability of a failure is .01 on any try. Assume that each result is independent of all other results. If you use the candy machine four times, what is the probability that the machine works properly all four times?

4. Approximately 60% of all applicants passed a managerial trainee test. Five applicants have just taken the exam. Based on past experience, what is the probability for each of the following:

a. All five pass?

b. All five fail?
c. At least one passes?

5. The CPA examination has four parts, one each on accounting problems, auditing, business law, and the theory of accounting. To be certified, an applicant must pass all four parts. Past history shows that on the first attempt 30% pass the accounting part, 35% pass auditing, 30% pass law, and 20% pass theory.
a. If success on one part of the examination is independent of success on any other part, what is the probability that an applicant becomes certified on the first attempt to pass the CPA examination?
b. Do you believe that this probability is a reasonable approximation if you know that more than 10% of applicants pass all parts of the examination on their first attempt? Comment on the assumption of independence among parts of the test.

6. A secret government document stated that one missile had a probability of .12 of destroying an enemy missile silo and two such missiles had a probability of .2 of destroying the silo. Are the outcomes of the two firings statistically independent? Explain.

7. In handling a customer's order, the order department will fill it incorrectly with probability .03. Also, the order will be delivered to the wrong address with probability .01. Assume that the two variables Filling of Order and Delivery of Order are statistically independent.
a. What is the probability that a customer's order is filled incorrectly and delivered to the wrong address?
b. What is the probability that an order is filled correctly and delivered to the right address?

8. At the McVay Advertising Agency, 80% of newly hired employees quit within one year. A man and a woman are hired on the same day. Assume that their decisions to stay or leave are independent of one another. What is the probability of the following:
a. Both will work there more than a year.
b. At least one will work there more than a year.
c. Neither works there for a year.

9. The Gavett Management Company wants to purchase stock in the Wiltman Manufacturing Company. Mr. Gavett feels that if inflation decreases, the probability is .9 that the investment will be profitable. If inflation remains constant or increases, the probability is .6 that the investment will be profitable. Assume that the probability that the inflation rate declines is .3. What is the probability that the investment will be profitable?

10. A bank has two emergency sources of power for its computers. There is a 95% chance that source 1 will operate during a total power failure, and an 80% chance that source 2 will operate. Find the probability that in a total power failure, neither emergency power source will operate. Assume the energy sources are independent.

11. A doctor claims that the probability of a patient surviving a particular type of open heart surgery is .7. If the doctor performs three such operations, find the probability for each of the following:
a. All three patients survive.
b. None of the patients survives.
c. At least one patient survives.

12. About 5% of the population becomes ill during whitewater raft tours. Suppose a raft contains five randomly selected tourists, and assume that all illnesses are independent of one another. What is the probability of each of the following:
a. None of the five tourists becomes ill.
b. At least one becomes ill.

13. At Williamson's Appliance Store, 20% of the customers pay cash and the remainder use a credit card. Six independent customers make purchases. Find the probability of the following:
a. All six pay cash.
b. All six charge their purchases.

14. A group of individuals concerned about environmental problems claims that 30% of the adults in a certain town have been adversely affected by a new nuclear power plant that pollutes the air and causes lung damage. To test their claim, you randomly select four adult residents of the town.

a. If the environmental group is correct, what is the probability that all four people have been adversely affected?

b. What is the probability that at least one of the four individuals has been adversely affected?

15. An insurance company has data indicating that the probability that Mr. Jones will be alive in 25 years is .6, and the probability that his wife will be alive in 25 years is .7. Assume their probabilities of living are independent of one another.

a. What is the probability that in 25 years at least one of them is alive?

b. What is the probability that in 25 years only Mr. Jones is alive?

c. What is the probability that in 25 years both are alive?

16. A homeowner in Greenville is considering flood insurance for a riverfront property. One flood occurs every four years in Greenville on the average. If the probability of a flood in any year is assumed to be .25, what is the probability that no flood occurs in Greenville during the next four years?

17. In a southern California county, the probability of a forest fire in any year is .2. An investor has just bought a home near the edge of the forest and intends to keep the home for four years before selling it. The investor decides not to buy fire insurance.

a. If events are independent of one another, what is the probability that no fire occurs during the next four years?

b. What is the probability that at least one fire occurs during the next four years?

5.7 ▪ Bayes' Theorem (Optional)

An interesting application of probability theory involves estimating or revising probabilities when new information on a random experiment is obtained. An English philosopher, the Reverend Thomas Bayes (1702–1761), was one of the first to work with rules for revising probabilities in light of sample information. Bayes' contribution, published in 1763, consists of a method for calculating conditional probabilities.

To see how Bayes' Theorem works, suppose the sample space of an experiment is partitioned into k mutually exclusive and exhaustive events $E_1, E_2, \ldots, E_k$. Assume the probabilities of these events are equal to $P(E_1), P(E_2), \ldots, P(E_k)$, respectively. These probabilities are called **prior probabilities**, because they are determined before any new information is taken into account.

A probability that has been revised based on new information is called a **posterior probability**, because it represents a probability calculated after new information is taken into account. By using Bayes' Theorem, a prior (unconditional) probability that an event E_i will occur or has occurred is revised to a new probability, a posterior (conditional) probability.

Let E_i represent some event whose prior probability is $P(E_i)$. Let A represent the new information. For any conditional probability, we have the rule

$$P(E_i|A) = P(E_i \cap A)/P(A)$$

In addition, from the multiplicative rule of probability, we have,

$$P(A \cap E_i) = P(E_i)\ P(A|E_i)$$

If we substitute this result into the preceding equation, we obtain the formula for calculating the posterior probability that E_i occurred given that A occurred:

$$P(E_i|A) = P(E_i)\,\frac{P(A|E_i)}{P(A)}$$

Bayes' Theorem

Let E_i be an event having a prior probability $P(E_i)$. Let A be some new event or information. Then the posterior probability of E_i is given by

$$P(E_i|A) = \frac{P(E_i)\,P(A|E_i)}{P(A)}$$

Let $E_1, E_2, \ldots, E_n$ be a set of mutually exclusive and exhaustive events so that $E_i \cap E_j = \varnothing$ and $[E_1 \cup E_2 \cup \cdots \cup E_n]$ is the entire sample space. Frequently, when applying Bayes' Theorem, $P(A)$ will not be directly given, but it can be calculated by using the formula

$$P(A) = P(A \cap E_1) + P(A \cap E_2) + \cdots + P(A \cap E_n)$$

Recall that $P(A \cap E_i) = P(E_i)\,P(A/E_i)$. Therefore, to calculate $P(A)$, we can use the equivalent formula

$$P(A) = P(E_1)\,P(A|E_1) + P(E_2)\,P(A|E_2) + \cdots + P(E_n)\,P(A|E_n)$$

In this case Bayes' Theorem becomes

$$P(E_i|A) = \frac{P(E_i)\,P(A|E_i)}{\Sigma\,P(E_i)\,P(A|E_i)}$$

When $n = 2$, we obtain

$$P(E_i|A) = \frac{P(E_i)\,P(A|E_i)}{P(E_1)\,P(A|E_1) + P(E_2)\,P(A|E_2)}$$

The following examples illustrate applications of Bayes' theorem.

Example 5.24

An Application of Bayes' Theorem: A hospital has developed a test to discover if newborn babies have a certain type of mental disorder. From past records, the doctors know that the probability that a baby has this disorder is .003. If the baby does have the disorder, the test will be positive 98% of the time and negative 2% of the time. If the baby does not have the disorder, the test will be negative 99% of the time and positive 1% of the time. A test administered on a newborn baby is positive. What is the probability that the baby actually has the disorder?

Solution 1: Before applying Bayes' Theorem, let us solve the problem intuitively. Suppose the test was administered to 100,000 randomly selected babies. Based on the prior information, we would expect 300 of the 100,000 babies (or 0.3%) to have the disorder and 99,700 to be healthy. Of the 300 who have the disorder, we would expect 294 (or 98%) to test positively and 6 to test negatively. Of the 99,700 who do not have the disorder, we would expect 98,703 (or 99%) to test negatively and 997 to test positively.

Thus, of 100,000 babies we would expect

$$294 + 997 = 1291$$

to test positively and

$$6 + 98{,}703 = 98{,}709$$

to test negatively. All of these expected frequencies are shown in Table 5.3.

TABLE 5.3
Joint frequency table for testing 100,000 babies

Health Status	Test Result: Positive	Test Result: Negative	Total
Healthy	997	98,703	99,700
Mental Disorder	294	6	300
Total	1,291	98,709	100,000

Of the 1291 babies who yield a positive test result, we would expect 294 to actually have the disorder. Thus, $P(\text{disorder}|\text{positive test}) = 294/1291 = .2277$.

Solution 2: Now let us apply Bayes' Theorem to solve this problem. Define the following events: $P_1 = \{\text{test is positive}\}$, $P_2 = \{\text{test is negative}\}$, $D_1 = \{\text{baby has mental disorder}\}$, and $D_2 = \{\text{baby is healthy}\}$. The following information is known:

$$P(D_1) = .003, \qquad P(P_1|D_1) = .98, \qquad P(P_2|D_2) = .99$$

We want to find $P(D_1|P_1)$. From Bayes' Theorem we have

$$P(D_1|P_1) = \frac{P(D_1)\, P(P_1|D_1)}{P(P_1)}$$

To solve the problem, we must find $P(P_1)$. We obtain

$$\begin{aligned} P(P_1) &= P(P_1 \cap D_1) + P(P_1 \cap D_2) \\ &= P(D_1)\, P(P_1|D_1) + P(D_2)\, P(P_1|D_2) \\ &= (.003)(.98) + (.997)(.01) = .01291 \end{aligned}$$

Thus,

$$P(D_1|P_1) = \frac{(.003)(.98)}{.01291} = \frac{.00294}{.01291} = .2277$$

This is the same answer we obtained in solution 1. This result can be illustrated by the tree diagram in Figure 5.11. When applying Bayes' Theorem, you should first construct a tree diagram like that in Figure 5.11 or a table like Table 5.3 to help you visualize the necessary calculations.

What did we learn by applying Bayes' Theorem in Example 5.24? Without testing, the probability that a baby has the disorder is .003. Given a positive test result, many people mistakenly think that the probability is .98 that the baby has the mental disorder. This is not correct. The probability .98 represents $P(P_1|D_1)$, that is, the probability that the test is positive, given that the disorder is present. What we are seeking is

FIGURE 5.11
Tree diagram for Example 5.24.

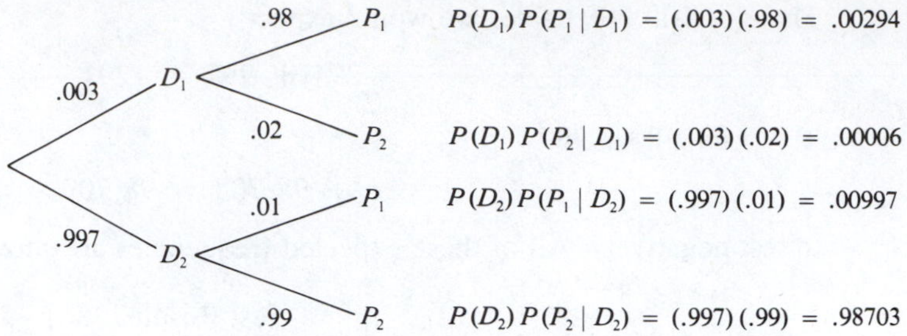

$P(D_1|P_1)$—the probability that the disorder is present, given that the test is positive. After learning that the test is positive, the probability that the baby has the disorder is only .2277.

Example 5.25

Another Application of Bayes' Theorem: A corporation operates two factories that make engines for automobiles. Let E_1 denote an engine made at plant 1 and E_2 an engine made at plant 2. Let A denote the event that an engine is defective. From past records, it is known that 2% of the engines at plant 1 are defective, and 3% of the engines at plant 2 are defective. That is, $P(A|E_1) = .02$ and $P(A|E_2) = .03$. Assume that plant 1 makes 40% of the engines and plant 2 makes the rest. That is, $P(E_1) = .4$ and $P(E_2) = .6$. An engine selected at random is defective. Find the probability that it was made at plant 1.

Solution: We want to find $P(E_1|A)$. We first find $P(A)$ as

$$\begin{aligned} P(A) &= P(A \cap E_1) + P(A \cap E_2) \\ &= P(E_1)\, P(A|E_1) + P(E_2)\, P(A|E_2) \\ &= (.4)(.02) + (.6)(.03) = .026 \end{aligned}$$

From Bayes' Theorem we have

$$\begin{aligned} P(E_1|A) &= \frac{P(E_1)\, P(A|E_1)}{P(A)} \\ &= \frac{(.4)(.02)}{.026} = \frac{.008}{.026} = .308 \end{aligned}$$

This result is illustrated in Figure 5.12.

FIGURE 5.12
Tree diagram for Example 5.25.

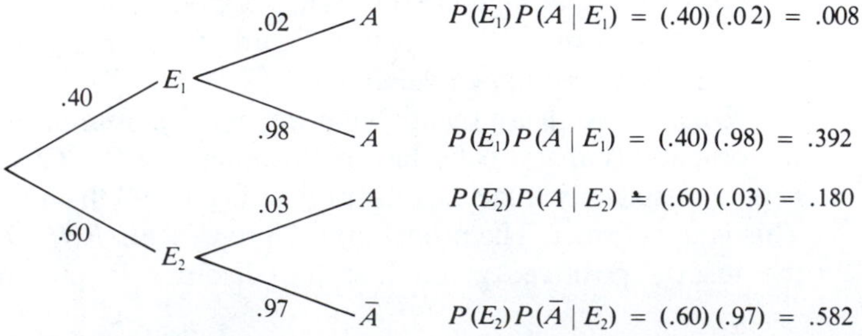

Exercises for Section 5.7

1. At a particular factory, every product is inspected by two men. The first inspector catches 80% of the defectives and sends them back for repairs. All remaining items are sent to a second inspector, who misses about 40% of the defectives that get past the first inspector.
   a. What proportion of the defectives will get by both inspectors?
   b. Given that a product was found to be defective, what is the probability that it was found by the first inspector?
2. Mr. Smith processes 55% of the loans at a particular bank, and Ms. Jones processes 45%. About 10% of Mr. Smith's loans eventually default, whereas about 6% of Ms. Jones's loans do. What is the probability of the following?
   a. A defaulted loan was processed by Ms. Jones.
   b. A good loan was processed by Mr. Smith.
3. A trucking firm receives a message that one of its trucks has broken down on the highway. The firm has three types of trucks and does not know which type has broken down. Because the firm wants to send a replacement truck of the same type, it wants to calculate which type is most likely. Of the firm's trucks, 20% are type T_1, 30% are type T_2, and 50% are type T_3. Let B denote that a truck broke down. From past experience, the firm has the following data:

$$P(B|T_1) = .1, \qquad P(B|T_2) = .1, \qquad P(B|T_3) = .05$$

   Calculate the following probabilities:

   a. $P(T_1|B)$ b. $P(T_2|B)$ c. $P(T_3|B)$ d. $P(B)$
4. In the general population, the proportion of individuals who have a particular disease is .03. A test for the disease is positive in 90% of the people who have the disease and in 8% of the people who do not.
   a. If you just received a positive reaction from this test, what is the probability that you have the disease?
   b. If you received a negative reaction from the test, what is the probability that you have the disease?
5. The producers of a new movie think that the movie has a prior probability for success of .3. An influential film critic, who has liked 70% of all successful films and disliked 80% of all unsuccessful films that she has reviewed, is going to review the film. Find the posterior probability that the movie will be a success given the following:
   a. The critic likes it.
   b. The critic dislikes it.
6. An oil wildcatter has assigned a probability of .5 to striking oil on a certain plot of property. The wildcatter orders a seismic survey that has proven to be 90% reliable in the past. That is, when oil is present, it predicts favorably 90% of the time, and when no oil is present, it predicts no oil 90% of the time.
   a. Given a favorable seismic result, what is the probability for oil?
   b. Given an unfavorable seismic result, what is the probability for oil?

5.8 ▪ Counting Techniques

In many probability problems, it is necessary to determine the number of ways in which some sequence of events can occur. If a sequence of activities must be performed, the total number of possible outcomes can be determined by using the **fundamental rule of counting**.

Fundamental Rule of Counting

If event A can occur in n_1 different ways and event B can occur in n_2 different ways, then A and B can occur in sequence in $(n_1 \times n_2)$ different ways. Similarly, if A can occur n_1 ways, B can occur n_2 ways, and C can occur n_3 ways, then A, B, and C can occur together in $n_1 \times n_2 \times n_3$ different ways.

Example 5.26

The Fundamental Rule of Counting: Let event A consist of choosing a car from the set {Ford, Chevrolet, Buick}. Thus, $n_1 = 3$. Let event B consist of selecting an automatic or manual transmission, so $n_2 = 2$. Let event C consist of purchasing tires, either blackwalls or whitewalls; thus, $n_3 = 2$. Let event D consist of getting a red, brown, or blue car; thus $n_4 = 3$.

There are

$$n_1 \times n_2 \times n_3 \times n_4 = 3 \times 2 \times 2 \times 3 = 36$$

different ways to choose A, B, C, and D together. These 36 possibilities are listed in the tree diagram of Figure 5.13. ■

Factorial Notation

At times, it is necessary to calculate the product of all the positive integers from 1 to N. A shorthand way to denote this product is by the symbol $N!$, which is read "N factorial."

Definition: Factorial

Let N be a positive integer. The product of all integers from 1 to N is called **N factorial** and is denoted $N!$.

$$N! = N(N-1)(N-2)\cdots(3)(2)(1)$$

We define $0!$ to be equal to 1.

Example 5.27

Factorial Notation:

(a) $5! = 5 \times 4 \times 3 \times 2 \times 1 = 120$
(b) $8! = 8 \times 7 \times 6 \times 5 \times 4 \times 3 \times 2 \times 1 = 40{,}320$
(c) $1! = 1$ ■

Factorial notation is very useful when we try to count the number of ways that N things can be arranged. Suppose we want to rank four students. How many possible rankings are there? We have four choices for the first student, three choices for the next, and so forth. Thus, there are $4 \times 3 \times 2 \times 1 = 4!$ ways of arranging the four students.

Permutations

At times we are interested in determining how many different ways we can select R items from N items and then arrange them in some specific order. For example, suppose there are $N = 8$ planes requesting clearance to land at the Buffalo airport. Because of a

FIGURE 5.13
Tree diagram for Example 5.26.

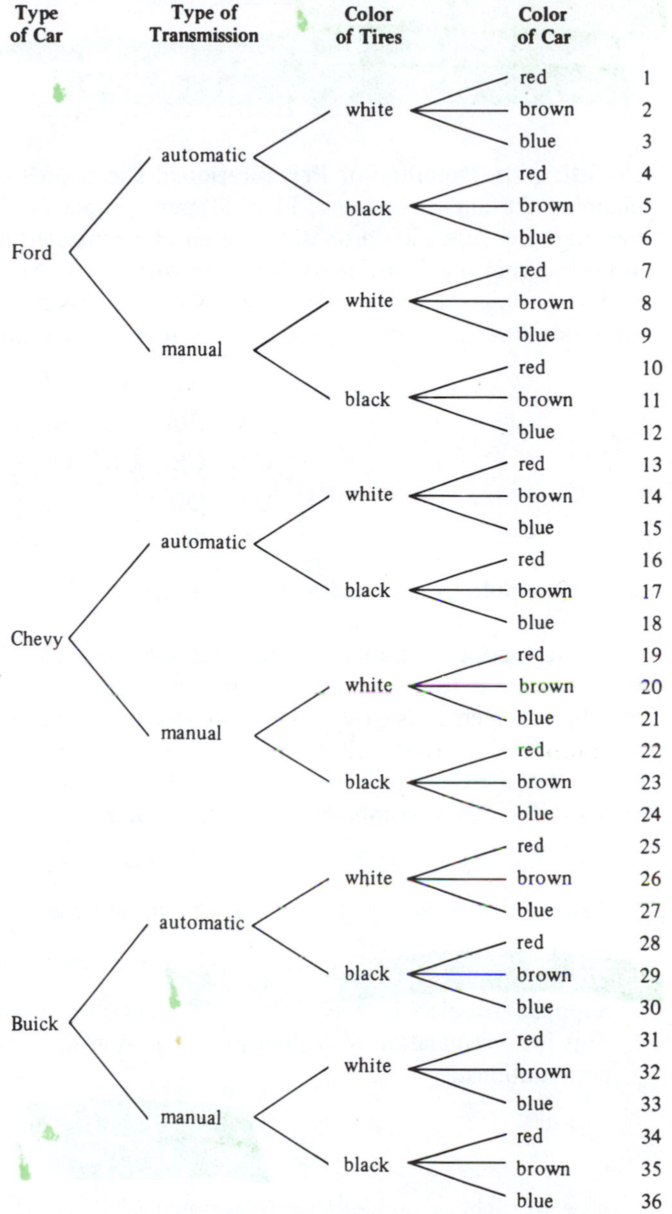

snowstorm, only $R = 5$ of the planes can land, and the remaining 3 planes must be rerouted to Cleveland. The flight control attendant must select 5 of the 8 planes for landing in Buffalo and then put them in order (i.e., the pilots must be told who will land first, second, and so on). This arrangement of the 5 planes in a specific order is an example of a *permutation* of 8 things taken 5 at a time.

Definition: Permutation

A **permutation** of N different things taken R at a time, denoted ${}_NP_R$, is an arrangement in a specific order of any R of the N things.

Example 5.28

Counting the Number of Permutations: The board of directors of a corporation is planning the annual meeting. Five different proposals are under consideration for the meeting. Because each proposal is sure to be subjected to a long and emotional debate at the meeting, the board feels that there will only be enough time to discuss two of the proposals; thus it must decide which two to discuss and in which order. The listing of all possibilities is as follows (each listing represents a different permutation):

AB	AC	AD	AE
BA	BC	BD	BE
CA	CB	CD	CE
DA	DB	DC	DE
EA	EB	EC	ED

In this example, $N = 5$ and $R = 2$, and there are 20 different possible permutations. ■

Determining the number of possible permutations of N things taken R at a time can be quite time consuming if we actually list all the possibilities. We have N choices for the object selected first, $(N - 1)$ choices for the object selected second, and so on down to $(N - R + 1)$ choices for the object selected on the Rth choice. The discussion above shows that the number of permutations of N things taken R at a time, denoted by the symbol ${}_NP_R$, can be computed using the formula

$${}_NP_R = N(N - 1)(N - 2) \cdots (N - R + 1)$$

This formula can be simplified as shown in the accompanying box.

Formula for Number of Permutations

Suppose we select R objects from N distinct objects and put the R objects in order. This is a permutation of N things taken R at a time. The total number of different permutations is

$${}_NP_R = \frac{N!}{(N - R)!}$$

As a special case, when $R = N$, we obtain ${}_NP_N = N!$.

When thinking of a permutation, it might be useful to think of a batting lineup in a baseball game. There are $N = 24$ players on a professional team. The manager must select $R = 9$ to play the game and then set up the batting order for these 9 players. Each different lineup is a different permutation.

Example 5.29

Calculating the Number of Permutations: The personnel manager at a corporation has interviewed 10 job applicants for 3 jobs at 3 different salaries. The manager must select the 3 best applicants and rank them. In how many ways can 3 applicants be selected and ranked?

Solution: We need to calculate ${}_{10}P_3$. We obtain

$$ {}_{10}P_3 = \frac{10!}{(10-3)!} = \frac{10!}{7!} = 10 \times 9 \times 8 = 720 $$

Example 5.30

Calculating the Number of Permutations: Every year the American Economic Association holds an annual meeting. The directors want to choose the sites for the next four meetings. If the four sites will be New York, Chicago, Miami, and Dallas, in how many ways can the locations be ordered?

Solution: There are four choices for the first location, three choices for the second location, two for the third, and one for the fourth. From the fundamental rule of counting, we obtain

$$ {}_4P_4 = 4 \times 3 \times 2 \times 1 = 24 $$

Alternatively, if we use the formula for permutations, we have $N = 4$, $R = 4$, and

$$ {}_4P_4 = \frac{4!}{(4-4)!} = \frac{4!}{0!} = 24 $$

Combinations

Definition: Combinations

A **combination** of N things taken R at a time, denoted ${}_NC_R$, is an arrangement of any R of these things without regard to order.

As an example of a combination, think of the starting lineup for a basketball team. The team contains a total of, say, $N = 12$ players, and the coach selects $R = 5$ of the players to play the game. Each group of 5 players represents a different combination. Unlike a permutation, however, the order in which the objects are picked does not matter.

The notion of a combination is important in statistical theory because a combination can be thought of as a particular sample of R items selected from a population containing N items. When we obtain a sample, the order in which the observations appear usually does not matter. In this case, the sample $\{A, B, C\}$ is the same as the samples $\{B, A, C\}$, $\{C, B, A\}$, and so forth.

Example 5.31

Calculating the Number of Combinations: A brewing company produces four different brands of beer, denoted by A, B, C, and D. The company has purchased two blocks of commercial time during a television special and wants to promote a different product during each of the two commercials. List all possible combinations.

Solution: There are six combinations of four things taken two at a time, namely AB, AC, AD, BC, BD, and CD.

The combination AB is identical to BA, but these are different permutations. That is, the combination AB can form the permutations AB and BA; the combination AC yields the permutations AC and CA. Thus, there are $6 \times 2! = 12$ permutations of four things taken two at a time, and we have ${}_4C_2 = 6$ and ${}_4P_2 = 6 \times 2! = 12$. ■

Example 5.32 **Calculating the Number of Combinations:** In Example 5.31, suppose that the brewery has purchased three commercial slots rather than two. List all possible combinations if the brewery wants to advertise three brands.

Solution: There are four combinations of the four products taken three at a time, namely ABC, ACD, ABD, and BCD.

For every combination containing three items, there are 3! permutations of those same items. That is, the combination ABC yields the $3! = 6$ permutations ABC, ACB, BAC, BCA, CAB, and CBA. Similarly, the combination BCD yields the six permutations BCD, BDC, CBD, CDB, DBC, and DCB. ■

We want to derive a formula to determine how many combinations exist of N things taken R at a time. To do this, we start with the formula for the number of permutations of N things taken R at a time. Consider a listing of all the possible permutations of N things taken R at a time. Many of these permutations are just rearrangements of the same R objects. In fact, because R objects can be ordered in $R!$ ways, each combination of R objects will yield $R!$ different permutations. Thus if we divide the number of permutations by $R!$, we will obtain the number of combinations. That is,

$${}_NC_R = {}_NP_R/R!$$

Now recall that

$${}_NP_R = N!/(N - R)!$$

After substitution, we obtain the important formula for the number of combinations of N things taken R at a time.

Formula for Number of Combinations

Suppose we select R objects from N distinct objects. The number of different combinations of these R objects is

$${}_NC_R = \frac{N!}{(N - R)!R!}$$

Note that ${}_NC_R = {}_NC_{N-R}$.

Example 5.33 **Calculating the Number of Combinations:** Refer to Example 5.31. Use the formula to calculate the number of combinations of four things taken two at a time.

Solution:

$${}_4C_2 = \frac{4!}{(4 - 2)!\,2!} = \frac{4 \times 3 \times 2 \times 1}{2 \times 1 \times 2 \times 1} = 6$$

which agrees with the answer calculated in Example 5.31.

Example 5.34 **Calculating the Number of Combinations:** Refer to Example 5.32. Calculate the number of combinations of four things taken three at a time.

Solution:

$$_4C_3 = \frac{4!}{(4-3)!\,3!} = \frac{4 \times 3 \times 2 \times 1}{1 \times 3 \times 2 \times 1} = 4$$

which agrees with the answer calculated in Example 5.32. ■

Example 5.35 **Calculating the Number of Combinations:** A hospital laboratory employs 11 technicians. A sample of 3 must be selected for training on a new computer. How many different samples are possible?

Solution:

$$_{11}C_3 = \frac{11!}{(11-3)!\,3!} = \frac{11!}{8!\,3!} = \frac{11 \times 10 \times 9}{3 \times 2 \times 1} = 165$$ ■

Exercises for Section 5.8

1. Calculate 6!, 5!, 7!/5!, and 10!/8!.
2. Calculate 15!/15!, 5!/0!, and 4!/6!.
3. Evaluate $_5P_4$, $_6P_4$, $_8P_8$, $_7P_2$, and $_NP_N$.
4. Evaluate $_8C_3$, $_9C_1$, $_{11}C_1$, and $_NC_{N-2}$.
5. Evaluate $_5C_2$, $_5C_3$, $_9C_2$, and $_9C_7$.
6. A restaurant gives a customer a choice of three meat dishes (steak, beef, or chicken) and four drinks (coffee, tea, milk, or cola). If a meal consists of meat and a drink, how many different meals are possible? Make a tree diagram showing all possibilities.
7. A clothing manufacturer has a line of coordinated children's wear consisting of six different pairs of pants, five shirts, and three vests. How many different three-piece ensembles are available to the consumer?
8. A TV station has four programs scheduled for Monday night but has not yet decided in which order to air them. How many different orders are possible?
9. A ballot contains the names of five candidates. Because it is supposedly an advantage to have your name near the top of the ballot, different ballots are printed listing the candidates' names in all possible ways. How many different ballots are possible?
10. A publishing company publishes five different how-to books for the handy person, and it has a special offer of three books for $10. A woman has decided to buy three books and give them to her husband one at a time to entice him to make three desired home repairs. In how many ways can three books be selected and ordered from the list of five books?
11. A bride has eight close friends and wants five of them to be her bridesmaids. Thus, she must select five friends and decide in what order to place them. How many different ways are possible?
12. A swimming race contains six contestants. In how many different ways can the race finish?
13. A construction firm builds homes using four basic floor plans. The purchaser has to choose one of these. In addition, the purchaser must select one of four colors of carpet, one of three colors of wallpaper, and one of five types of kitchen cabinet. How many variations of the firm's homes are there?

14. The menu on an airplane offers a choice of four drinks, three salads, five entrees, four vegetables, two kinds of potatoes, and five desserts. If a meal consists of one of each item, how many different meals are possible?

5.9 ▪ Computer Applications

As discussed in Section 5.2, the probabilities of many events are estimated by calculating the relative frequency of occurrence of the event in a large number of repeated trials. When we have a large data set, it is convenient to calculate relative frequencies with a computer. In the SPSSX program, the FREQUENCIES command requests the computer to construct frequency distributions and relative frequency distributions for discrete and for qualitative variables.

Refer to the data in Table 2.1 of Chapter 2. To obtain a relative frequency distribution to estimate the proportions of employees at the Computech Corporation who are employed in the various divisions, insert the command

```
FREQUENCIES VARIABLES = DIV
```

into the SPSSX program.

Figure 5.14 shows the computer output obtained by executing the FREQUENCIES command. The output shows that 38 of the 120 employees (or 31.7%) are employed in the office. The value 31.7% is shown in the "PERCENT" column on the computer output. Similarly, we see that 48.3% of the employees are in manufacturing and 20.0% are in sales.

FIGURE 5.14 **SPSSX output from executing FREQUENCIES command on data in Table 2.1.**

```
DIV

                                                        VALID     CUM
 VALUE LABEL              VALUE  FREQUENCY  PERCENT   PERCENT  PERCENT

OFFICE                     1.00         38     31.7      31.7     31.7
MANUFACTURING              2.00         58     48.3      48.3     80.0
SALES                      3.00         24     20.0      20.0    100.0
                                   -------  -------   -------
                          TOTAL        120    100.0     100.0

VALID CASES      120     MISSING CASES      0
```

The SPSSX program also can be used to generate bivariate frequency and relative frequency distributions. For example, suppose we wish to determine what proportion of employees have a specific academic degree and are employed in a particular division. By inserting the commands

```
CROSSTABS TABLES = DEGREE BY DIV
OPTIONS 3, 4, 5
```

into the SPSSX program, we can generate a bivariate table that shows how many employees have a particular degree and are employed in a particular division. In addition, the output will show the relative frequency for each pair of values along with the row and column relative frequencies. Figure 5.15 shows the computer output generated by the CROSSTABS statement above.

FIGURE 5.15
SPSSX output from executing CROSSTABS command on data in Table 2.1 to show relationship between DEGREE and DIV.

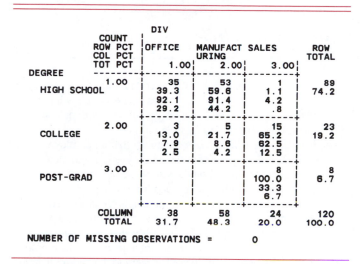

```
                             DIV
                    COUNT  |
                   ROW PCT |OFFICE     MANUFACT  SALES           ROW
                   COL PCT |           URING                    TOTAL
                   TOT PCT |     1.00|     2.00|     3.00|
  DEGREE           --------+---------+---------+---------+
                      1.00 |     35  |     53  |      1  |        89
    HIGH SCHOOL            |   39.3  |   59.6  |    1.1  |      74.2
                           |   92.1  |   91.4  |    4.2  |
                           |   29.2  |   44.2  |     .8  |
                           +---------+---------+---------+
                      2.00 |      3  |      5  |     15  |        23
    COLLEGE                |   13.0  |   21.7  |   65.2  |      19.2
                           |    7.9  |    8.6  |   62.5  |
                           |    2.5  |    4.2  |   12.5  |
                           +---------+---------+---------+
                      3.00 |         |         |      8  |         8
    POST-GRAD              |         |         |  100.0  |       6.7
                           |         |         |   33.3  |
                           |         |         |    6.7  |
                           +---------+---------+---------+
                    COLUMN       38        58        24          120
                     TOTAL     31.7      48.3      20.0        100.0

  NUMBER OF MISSING OBSERVATIONS =         0
```

The computer output shows that 35 of the 120 employees, or 29.2%, have a high school degree and are employed in the office. The value 29.2% is located in the row labeled "TOT PCT" in Figure 5.15 (indicated in the upper left-hand corner of the table). Similarly, 53 of the 120 employees, or 44.2%, have a high school degree and are employed in the manufacturing division.

The computer output also shows that 89 of the 120 employees, or 74.2%, have a high school degree. Similarly, 19.2% of the employees have a college degree and 6.7% have a postgraduate degree. The data also show that 31.7% of the employees work in the office, 48.3% work in manufacturing, and 20% work in sales. These percentages, when divided by 100, represent marginal relative frequencies and are located in the margins of the table.

The output in Figure 5.15 can be used to find conditional relative frequencies, which are used to estimate conditional probabilities. For example, we see that of the 89 employees who have a high school degree, 35 are employed in the sales division. This means that the conditional relative frequency of being in the office, given that the employee has a high school degree, is 35/89, or 39.3%. This conditional probability is shown in the row titled "ROW PCT" in Figure 5.15. Similarly, we see that 59.6% of the employees with a high school degree are employed in the manufacturing division, and so forth. Observe that 100% of the employees having a postgraduate degree are employed in the sales division.

In Figure 5.15, the values in the row titled "COL PCT" show the conditional probabilities of having any specific academic degree, given that the employee is employed in any specific division. For example, of the 58 employees in the manufacturing division,

53 have a high school degree and 5 have a college degree. This indicates that the conditional probability of having a high school degree, given that the person is employed in the manufacturing division, is 53/58 or 91.4%. The value 91.4% is reported in Figure 5.15 in the "COL PCT" row of the cell for manufacturing and high school. When the percentages labeled "ROW PCT" or "COL PCT" are divided by 100, we obtain conditional relative frequencies.

Exercises for Section 5.9

1. Refer to the data in Table 2.1. Generate a joint frequency distribution for DIV and SEX.
   a. Find the proportion of employees in the sample who are male and work in the office, who are male and work in manufacturing, and who are male and work in sales.
   b. Repeat part (a) for females.
   c. Estimate the conditional probability that an employee is in sales given that the employee is a male and then given that the employee is a female. Does the probability that a person is in sales seem to depend on the sex of the individual?
   d. Estimate the conditional probability that an employee is in the office given that the employee is a male and then given that the employee is a female. Does the probability that a person is in the office seem to depend on the sex of the individual?
   e. Estimate the conditional probability that an employee is in the manufacturing division given that the employee is a male and then given that the employee is a female. Does the probability that an employee is in the office seem to depend on the sex of the individual?

2. Refer to the data in Table 2.2. Generate a joint frequency distribution for the variables SEX and MAJOR.
   a. Find the proportion of students in the sample who are male and are undecided about their major, who are male and are economics majors, who are male and are math majors, who are male and are business majors, and who are male and have other majors.
   b. Repeat part (a) for females.
   c. Estimate the conditional probability that a student is majoring in economics given that the student is a male and then given that the student is a female. Does the probability that a student is majoring in economics seem to depend on the sex of the individual?
   d. Estimate the conditional probability that a student is majoring in an unspecified major ("Other") given that the student is a male and then given that the student is a female. Does the probability that a person has an "Other" major seem to depend on the sex of the individual?
   e. Estimate the conditional probability that a student is majoring in math given that the student is a male and then given that the student is a female. Does the probability that a student is majoring in math seem to depend on the sex of the individual?

3. Refer to the data in Table 2.1.
   a. Use the SPSSX program and a CROSSTABS command to determine the relative frequency of employees who are male and are employed in the office.
   b. Find the proportions of all employees who are male and are employed in manufacturing and of those who are male and employed in sales.
   c. Find the proportions of all employees who are female and are employed in manufacturing and of those who are female and employed in sales.
   d. Given that an employee is male, find the conditional probabilities that the employee is in the office, in manufacturing, and in sales.
   e. Given that an employee is in manufacturing, find the conditional probabilities that the employee is male and that the employee is female.

f. Based on the conditional probabilities in (d) and (e), do SEX and DIV seem to be independent of one another?

4. Refer to the data in Table 2.1.

a. Use the SPSSX program and a CROSSTABS command to determine the relative frequency of employees who are male and have a high school degree.

b. Find the proportions of all employees who are male and have a college degree and who are male and have a postgraduate degree.

c. Find the proportions of all employees who are female and have a high school degree, a college degree, and a postgraduate degree.

d. Find the proportion of all employees with a high school degree who are male and the proportion with a high school degree who are female.

e. Find the proportion of all employees with a college degree who are male and the proportion with a college degree who are female.

f. Find the proportion of all employees with a postgraduate degree who are male and the proportion with a postgraduate degree who are female.

g. Given that an employee is male, find the conditional probabilities that the employee has a high school degree, a college degree, and a postgraduate degree.

h. Given that an employee has a college degree, find the conditional probabilities that the employee is male or is female.

i. Based on the conditional probabilities in (g) and (h), does it appear that SEX and DEGREE are independent of one another?

Chapter 5 Summary

Chapter 5 discusses the concept of probability. Any activity that results in an uncertain outcome is called an *experiment,* and the possible outcomes of an experiment are called *events.* A *probability* is a number from 0 to 1 that measures the chance or likelihood that a particular event occurs. There are several different approaches that can be used to assign a probability to a particular event. The *relative frequency approach* assigns a probability to an event based on the relative frequency of occurrence of the event in a large number of past experiments. In the *equally likely approach,* it is assumed that all possible outcomes are equally likely. If there are n equally likely possible outcomes, then each basic outcome has probability $1/n$. In the *subjective approach,* probabilities are assigned based on subjective opinions or feelings.

The *sample space* is a listing of all possible outcomes of an experiment, and a *Venn diagram* is a graphical representation of the sample space. There are several important probability rules:

1. For any event A, $0 \leq P(A) \leq 1$
2. If $\overline{A}$ is the complement of A, then $P(\overline{A}) = 1 - P(A)$
3. To calculate the probability of the *joint* occurrence of events A and B, use the *multiplicative law of probability:*

$$P(A \cap B) = P(A)\ P(B|A)$$

4. To calculate the probability that event A or B (or both) occurs, use the *additive law of probability:*

$$P(A \cup B) = P(A) + P(B) - P(A \cap B)$$

5. To calculate the *conditional probability* that A occurs given that B has occurred, use the rule

$$P(A|B) = P(A \cap B)/P(B)$$

6. Events A and B are *independent* if and only if

$$P(A \cap B) = P(A)\ P(B)$$

Two events are independent if the occurrence of the one event has no effect on the probability that the other event occurs.

7. *Bayes' theorem* provides a method for calculating a posterior probability by taking into account prior information. The rule is

$$P(E_i|A) = P(E_i)\ P(A|E_i)/P(A)$$

In many probability problems we need to count the number of possible ways of performing different acts in sequence. The *fundamental rule of counting* states that if an activity can be performed in n_1 ways and a second activity can be performed in n_2 ways then the two acts can be performed in sequence in $n_1 \times n_2$ ways. A *permutation* is an arrangement in a specific order of R objects selected from N objects; the number of permutations of N things taken R at a time is given by

$${}_NP_R = N!/(N - R)!$$

A *combination* is a set containing R objects selected from N objects; the number of combinations of N things taken R at a time is

$${}_NC_R = N!/[R!\ (N - R)!]$$

Chapter 5 introduces the fundamental rules of probability theory. In Chapter 6, we will build on this foundation by discussing various probability models where the sample space consists of a countable set of real numbers. In such a model, the variable being analyzed is called a *discrete random variable*.

Chapter 5 ▪ Supplementary Exercises

1. The following data pertain to U.S. federal tax returns filed with the Internal Revenue Service (IRS) in 1982:

Income	Number of Filers (millions)	Percentage Audited
Under $10,000	35.0	1.33
$10,000–$24,999	32.4	3.02
$25,000–$49,999	17.7	2.90
$50,000 or more	3.3	5.68

a. If a tax filer was randomly selected from this population (i.e., if each tax filer had an equal probability of being selected), what is the probability that the tax filer would have been audited?

b. If a tax filer was randomly selected from this population, what is the probability that the tax filer had an income between \$10,000 and \$24,999 and was audited?
c. What is the probability that a tax filer had an income of \$50,000 or more in 1982 or was not audited?
d. If it were known that a randomly selected tax filer had been audited, what is the probability that the person had an income of \$50,000 or more?
e. What is the probability that a tax filer with an income of \$50,000 or more was audited?

2. A company found that only 20% of its products introduced over the last few years have become profitable. When two new products were introduced during the same year, both products became profitable only 5% of the time. Suppose the company plans to introduce two new products, A and B, next year. What is the probability of the following?
a. Product A will become profitable.
b. Product B will not become profitable.
c. At least one of the two products will become profitable.
d. Neither of the two products will become profitable.
e. Either product A or product B (but not both) will become profitable.
f. Product A becomes profitable, given that product B is profitable.
g. Given that at least one of the products is profitable, product A is profitable.

3. Two reviewers for a publishing house independently screen unsolicited manuscripts, giving a grade of "good," "fair," or "poor" to each manuscript.
a. Show the sample space describing the possible outcomes of the joint review of a manuscript. Is this sample space univariate or bivariate?
b. Let E_1 denote the event that at least one reviewer assigns a grade of "good." What basic outcomes constitute E_1?
c. Let E_2 denote the event that the reviewers give different grades. What basic outcomes constitute E_2?
d. Are E_1 and E_2 mutually exclusive here?

4. Suppose we define the following events: A_1 = {family owns a home}, A_2 = {family does not own a home}, B_1 = {family income is under \$20,000}, B_2 = {family income is \$20,000 to \$50,000}, and B_3 = {family income is \$50,000 or more}. Suppose we also know the following probabilities:

$$P(A_2) = .52 \qquad P(A_1|B_1) = .20$$
$$P(B_1) = .50 \qquad P(A_1|B_3) = .80$$
$$P(B_3) = .10$$

a. Find $P(A_1 \cap B_3)$.
b. Find $P(A_1 \cup B_3)$.
c. Find $P(B_3|A_1)$.

5. For each of the following probability statements, state whether it is always true, always false, or neither for any pairs of events E and F of a sample space. Justify each answer.
a. $P(E) < P(E \cap F)$
b. $P(E) > P(E \cup F)$
c. $P(E \cup F) \leq P(E) + P(F)$
d. $P(E) + P(F) = 1$

6. For each of the following probability statements, state whether it is always true, always false, or neither for any pairs of events E and F of a sample space. Justify each answer.
a. Both $P(E|F) < P(E)$ and $P(E|\bar{F}) < P(E)$
b. $P(\bar{E}|F) = 1 - P(E|F)$

7. A defense department report stated that the probability is .1 of downing an attacking airplane at any defense station. A news reporter then stated that if a plane had to pass through five independent stations before arriving at a target, the probability that the plane would be downed before reaching the target was .5.

a. Do you agree with this reasoning?
b. If not, what is the correct answer?

8. A woman is selling her house. She believes there is a .3 chance that each person who inspects the house will purchase it. What is the probability that more than two people will have to inspect the house before the woman finds a buyer? (Assume that the decisions of the people inspecting the house are independent.)

9. The probability that a launch of a particular spacecraft will occur on time is .4. Whether a launch occurs on time is independent of whether previous launches occurred on time. If three such launches take place, compute the probability that the first two will occur on time but the third will not.

10. The Kenmont Carbide Company has two machines that produce a certain product. Machine 1 produces 40% of the product, and machine 2 produces 60%. Machine 1 produces 3% defective products, and machine 2 produces 5% defective products. What is the probability of the following:
a. A randomly selected product is defective.
b. A product that is found to be defective was made on machine 1.
c. A product that is found to be good was made on machine 2.

11. The probability that a candidate passes the bar exam on the first try is .8. Of those who fail on the first try, 70% pass on the second try, and of those who fail on the second try, 88% pass on the third. Calculate the following probabilities:
a. A candidate does not pass the bar exam after two tries.
b. A candidate takes three tries to pass the bar exam.

12. A company has the following data on the age and marital status of 140 employees:

		Single	Married
Age	Under 30	77	14
	30 or over	28	21

a. What proportion of employees are single and under the age of 30?
b. If an employee is under 30, what is the probability that he or she is single?

13. Shown below are data from a sample of 80 families in a midwestern city on the record of college attendance by fathers and their oldest sons.

	Son	
Father	College	No college
College	18	7
No College	22	33

a. What is the probability that a son attended college given that his father did not attend college?
b. Is attending college by the son independent of whether his father attended college? Explain using probability values.

14. Assume that we have two mutually exclusive events A and B. Assume further that it is known that $P(A) = .3$ and $P(B) = .4$.
a. What is $P(A \cap B)$?
b. What is $P(A|B)$?
c. A student argues that the concepts of mutually exclusive events and independent events are really the same and that if events are mutually exclusive they must be independent. Do you

agree with this statement? Use the probability information in this problem to justify your answer.

d. What general conclusion would you make about mutually exclusive and independent events given the results of this problem?

15. In the past, approximately 5% of credit card holders have defaulted, and a bank has been unable to collect the outstanding balance. Thus the bank has established a prior probability of .05 that any particular cardholder will default. The bank has further found that the probability that customers who do not default will miss one or more monthly payments is .2. Of course, the probability that those who default will miss one or more payments is 1.

a. Given that a customer has missed a monthly payment, compute the posterior probability that the customer will default.

b. The bank would like to recall its card if the probability that a customer will default is greater than .2. Should the bank recall its card if the customer misses a monthly payment? Why or why not?

16. A market survey of 800 people found the following facts about the ability to recall a television commercial for a product and the actual purchase of the product:

	Recalled	Did Not Recall	Total
Purchased	150	90	240
Did Not Purchase	250	310	560
Total	400	400	800

Let *R* denote the event that a person could recall the television commercial, and let *P* denote the event that a person purchased the product.

a. Find $P(R)$, $P(P)$, and $P(R \cap P)$.

b. What is the probability that a person who recalled seeing the television commercial actually purchased the product?

c. Are *R* and *P* independent events? Use probability values to explain.

d. Does the commercial seem to help sell the product?

17. A research study investigating the relationship between smoking and heart disease in a sample of 1000 men over 50 years of age provided the following data:

	Smoker	Non-smoker	Total
Heart disease	100	80	180
No heart disease	200	620	820
Total	300	700	1000

a. For the entire population, estimate the probability that a man over 50 years of age is a smoker and has a record of heart disease.

b. Given that a man over 50 years of age is a smoker, what is the estimated probability that he has heart disease?

c. Given that a man over 50 years of age is a nonsmoker, what is the estimated probability that he has heart disease?

d. Does the research indicate that heart disease and smoking are independent events? Explain.

18. In the setup of a manufacturing process, the probability that a machine is correctly adjusted is .98. When correctly adjusted, the machine operates with a 4% defective rate. However, if it is incorrectly adjusted, the defective rate is 75%.

a. After the machine starts a production run, what is the probability that a defect is observed when one part is tested?

b. Suppose that the part selected by an inspector is found to be defective. What is the probability that the machine is incorrectly adjusted?

19. Sixty percent of the graduates of a driver training school pass their driver's license test on the first attempt and the other 40% fail. The school gives a pretest to graduates before they take the official test. Of the graduates who pass the official test on the first attempt, 85% passed the pretest. Of the graduates who fail the official test on the first attempt, 10% pass the pretest. Let A_1 denote that a graduate passed the official test on the first attempt and A_2 that the graduate failed, and let B denote that the graduate passed the pretest.

a. Find the following probabilities: $P(A_1)$, $P(A_2)$, $P(B|A_1)$, and $P(B|A_2)$.

b. Suppose that a student has passed the pretest. Obtain the posterior probabilities $P(A_1|B)$ and $P(A_2|B)$ and interpret them. Does the information provided by the pretest lead to a substantial modification of the prior probabilities? Discuss.

20. In Johnstown, 10% of the people leave their keys in their cars. Nationwide surveys indicate that 15% of the cars with keys left in the ignition are stolen. On the other hand, only 0.1% of the cars without keys left in the ignition are stolen.

a. A car in Johnstown is stolen. What is the probability that the keys were left in the ignition?

b. If Johnstown contains 100,000 cars, how many would you expect to be stolen?

21. A mail order firm can make three possible errors in filling an order, defined as the following events: $A = \{\text{wrong item sent}\}$, $B = \{\text{item lost in transit}\}$, and $C = \{\text{item damaged in transit}\}$. Assume that the events A, B, and C are independent of one another with $P(A) = .03$, $P(B) = .01$, and $P(C) = .04$. What is the probability that none of these errors will occur for a randomly selected order?

22. The probability of an accident on any day at a large manufacturing plant is .05.

a. What is the probability that on 5 successive days no accidents occur?

b. What is the probability that an accident occurs on at least 1 of 3 days?

23. An investment broker has provided all clients with a list of several possible independent investments, each having a probability of .7 of yielding a substantial profit. A client, Mr. McManus, decides to purchase four of the investments. What is the probability that all four yield a profit?

24. In Exercise 23, what is the probability that Mr. McManus's first four investments are not profitable?

25. A car manufacturer wants to determine how many different cars can be produced if all options are considered. The possible choices a customer can make are as follows:

Choice	Number
Body type	3
Engine size	4
Exterior color	8
Interior color	4
Tire type	3
Accessories	10

How many different cars can be made?

26. A bank vault has a computerized lock that opens when three numbers are selected in sequence.

The same number can be repeated three times as a possible solution, and each of the three numbers is an integer from 1 to 25. The bank manager has forgotten the correct sequence and decides to try all the possible combinations (actually, they are permutations!) until the vault opens. How many possibilities are there?

27. The Bollman Brewing Company has a new brand of beer and wishes to begin an intense advertising campaign. It has produced eight different commercials and purchased four advertising spots during a televised football game. The company must now decide which four commercials to use and in which order. How many arrangements of four commercials are possible?

28. The secretaries at the Metro Life Insurance Company file insurance policies by classifying a person according to age, sex, and marital status. Age is classified as under 25 years, 25 to 50 years, and over 50. Marital status is single or married. What is the total number of classifications?

29. In a particular city, 45% of all households have a color television and 22% have a microwave oven. If 15% of all households have both items, what is the probability that a randomly chosen household will have at least one of them?

30. Candidates for employment at a large corporation must pass through two initial screening procedures, a written aptitude test and an oral interview. Fifty percent of the candidates are unsuccessful on the written test, 30% are unsuccessful in the interview, and 11% are unsuccessful in both. The corporation gives further consideration only to candidates who are successful in both procedures.

a. What is the probability that a randomly chosen candidate will receive further consideration for employment?

b. What is the probability that a candidate who is unsuccessful in the written test will be successful in the interview?

c. What is the probability that a candidate who is successful in the interview will also be successful on the written test?

d. Are successes in the two screening procedures independent of one another?

31. Suppose that 45% of all bachelor's degrees are obtained by women, 27% of bachelor's degrees in business are obtained by women, and 17.5% of all bachelor's degrees are in business.

a. What is the probability that a randomly selected new bachelor's degree holder will be a woman with a degree in business?

b. What is the probability that a randomly selected woman bachelor's degree holder will have a degree in business?

32. A bank classifies borrowers as "high risk" or "low risk," and 15% of its loans are made to those in the "high risk" category. Of all its loans, 5% are in default, and 40% of those in default are to high-risk borrowers. What is the probability that a high-risk borrower will default?

33. Households in a certain city were surveyed to determine whether they would or would not subscribe to a cable television service. The households were classified as "low," "middle," or "high" income. The table gives the proportions of households in each of the six joint classifications.

Income	Will Subscribe	Will Not Subscribe
Low	.03	.17
Middle	.14	.46
High	.10	.10

a. Find the probability that a randomly chosen household would subscribe.

b. Are income and willingness to subscribe independent?

c. Given that a high-income family has been contacted, find the probability that the household will subscribe.

34. There are many consulting organizations that predict whether increases in stock prices will be unusually low, unusually high, or normal. Before deciding whether to continue purchasing these forecasts, a stockbroker compares past predictions with actual outcomes. The accompanying table shows the past performance of a certain consultant.

	Prediction		
Outcome	Unusually High	Normal	Unusually Low
Unusually high	.20	.14	.04
Normal	.07	.22	.06
Unusually low	.02	.05	.20

a. What proportion of predictions were for unusually high increases?
b. What proportion of outcomes were for unusually high increases?
c. When the consultant predicted unusually high increases in stock prices, what was the probability that he was correct?
d. Given that there were unusually high increases, what was the probability that the consultant had predicted unusually low increases?

35. A publisher sends advertising material for an economics text to 75% of all professors teaching the appropriate economics course. Thirty percent of the professors who received this material adopted the book, and 8% of the professors who did not receive the advertising material adopted the book.
a. What proportion of all professors adopted the book?
b. What is the probability that a professor who adopts the book has received the advertising material?

36. State whether each of the following statements is true or false, and explain your answer:
a. The probability of the union of two events cannot be less than the probability of their intersection.
b. The probability of the union of two events cannot exceed the sum of their individual probabilities.
c. The probability of the intersection of two events cannot exceed either of their individual probabilities.
d. The individual probabilities of a pair of events cannot sum to more than 1.

37. State whether each of the following claims is true or false and explain:
a. The conditional probability of A given B must be at least as large as the probability of A.
b. The probability of A given B must be at least as large as the probability of the intersection of A and B.
c. The probability of the intersection of two events cannot exceed the product of their individual probabilities.

38. A professor finds that she awards a final grade of A to 22% of her students, and of these students, 72% got an A on the midterm examination. Also, 12% of students who did not get a final grade of A earned an A on the midterm exam. What is the probability that a student with an A on the midterm examination will obtain a final grade of A?

39. Assume that the probability that a target is destroyed by any single plane is .4. If two planes are sent, what is the probability that the target will be destroyed? That is, what is the probability that the target is hit at least once? Assume that the outcomes are independent.

40. A company based in Alaska has found that 30% of the employees who come to Alaska from California have difficulty adjusting to the Alaskan climate and quit within two years of moving. Four California residents have recently been hired.

a. Find the probability that all four quit within two years. Assume that all decisions to stay or quit are independent of one another.

b. What is the probability that none of the four employees quits within two years?

c. What is the probability that at least one of the four employees quits within two years?

41. Four machines are used to produce golf balls, labeled A, B, C, and D. Of the total output, machine A produces 10%, B produces 20%, C produces 30%, and D produces 40%. Of the golf balls produced by machine A, 1% are defective; by machine B, 2%; machine C, 3%; and machine D, 4%.

a. What proportion of golf balls are defective?

b. Given that a ball is defective, what is the probability that machine D made it?

c. Given that a ball is defective, what is the probability that machine A did not make it?

42. The quality control department in a factory has found that 10% of the products manufactured by a given machine are defective. If four of the products made by this machine are selected randomly, what is the probability that at least one is defective?

43. Suppose that when certain geological conditions exist, there is a 20% chance of striking oil. A drilling company finds five independent locations where these geological conditions exist and drills one well at each location. If five wells are drilled, what is the probability that at least one of them will strike oil?

44. On an assembly line, an inspector checks every article and destroys those that are defective, passing the remaining articles to a second inspector. The first inspector catches 70% of the defectives and destroys them. The second inspector catches and destroys 80% of the defectives that he or she inspects. What percentage of the defectives will get by both inspectors?

45. Suppose I own an outdoor construction company. During any week, the probability that I make a profit is .9 if the weather is good and .2 if the weather is bad. Next week the probability is .7 that the weather will be good.

a. What is the probability that I will make a profit next week?

b. If I made a profit last week, what is the probability that the weather was good?

46. A sales representative has a 30% probability of making a sale to any customer. Assume all customers are independent of one another.

a. What is the probability that the first sale is made to the third customer?

b. What is the probability that the first four customers do not purchase the product?

47. The sales representative at a garden center claims that about 40% of all newly planted apple trees eventually bear fruit. How many trees should I plant so that there is at least a 90% probability of having at least one apple tree that bears fruit?

48. A basketball promoter has decided to hold a holiday tournament at the University of Kentucky involving eight highly ranked college teams. The promoter hopes that Kentucky and Louisville eventually play each other in the final game so that television rights can be sold for a handsome profit. Because Louisville and Kentucky are in opposite halves of the draw, they cannot play each other before the final game. To reach the finals, a team must win its two preceding games. The probability that Louisville will win its opening game is .7; given that it wins its first game, the probability that Louisville wins it second game is .4. The probability that Kentucky wins its opening game is .8; given that it wins its first game, the probability that Kentucky wins its second game is .5. What is the probability of the following:

a. Louisville reaches the finals.

b. Kentucky reaches the finals.

c. Kentucky plays Louisville in the finals.

d. Neither Kentucky nor Louisville plays in the finals.

49. The Cooper Construction Company is bidding on two contracts, one in New York and one in Boston. The probabilities are .6 of winning the New York contract and .3 of winning the Boston contract. The contracts are independent of one another. Find the probability that the company gets the following:
a. Both contracts
b. At least one contract

50. The chemistry building at a certain university has two elevators. One is waiting at the first floor 20% of the time, and the other is waiting there 15% of the time. Assume that both elevators operate independently. Find the following probabilities.
a. Both are waiting at the first floor.
b. At least one is waiting at the first floor.

51. The Peterson Lumber Company specializes in the production of wood paneling for game rooms. Mr. Peterson knows from past experience that about 10% of the panels contain minor flaws, 5% contain major flaws, and 2% contain both types of flaws. A customer orders three panels selected randomly. Find the probability of the following:
a. The first panel is nondefective.
b. None of the panels contain a defect.
c. At least one of the panels contains a major defect.

52. The Gruver Glass Company produces thermal pane glass windows in three states. The Ohio plant produces 50% of the output, the Kentucky plant produces 30%, and the Missouri plant produces 20%. Of the windows produced in Ohio, 1% are defective; in Kentucky, 3%; and in Missouri, 2%.
a. What proportion of all windows are defective?
b. Given that a window is defective, find the probability that it was produced at the Kentucky plant.

53. A market survey shows that 60% of the population like Brand A, 45% like Brand B, and 20% like both. What proportion of the population likes Brand A or Brand B?

54. Approximately 80% of all new cars sold in the United States have air conditioning and 40% have power windows.
a. Determine the maximum possible percentage of these cars that have both air conditioning and power windows.
b. Determine the minimum possible percentage of these cars that have both air conditioning and power windows.
c. Determine the maximum possible percentage of these cars that have neither air conditioning nor power windows.

55. Last year an investment advisor picked four stocks as good investments. As it turned out, although 75% of the stocks on the New York Stock Exchange increased in price that year, all four of this advisor's stocks went down. If a monkey had thrown four darts at the financial pages at the beginning of the year, what is the probability that all four picks would have gone down in price?

56. A team of experts is examining the reliability of lie detector tests. To determine the probability that a lie detector test is correct, a lie detector test is given to a group of students. Unknown to the experts, 80% of the students are told to be truthful and 20% are told to lie occasionally. At the conclusion of the test, the experts judged 85% of the truthful students as truthful and 60% of the liars as liars.
a. If the lie detector test tells the expert that the person is truthful, what is the probability that the person is a liar?
b. If the test indicates that the person is a liar, what is the probability that the person is truthful?

57. In a laboratory experiment, pigeons were trained to push one of two buttons in order to receive food. The experiment was set up so that button A would give a reward 70% of the time and no reward 30% of the time. Button B was constructed to give a reward 30% and no reward 70% of the time. The pigeons eventually began choosing button A 70% of the time and button B 30% of the time. When a group of rats was offered the same sort of options, the rats soon began choosing button A every time. Did the pigeons or rats act more intelligently? Prove your answer.

References

FELLER, WILLIAM. *An Introduction to Probability Theory and Its Applications.* Vol. 1. 3d ed. New York: Wiley, 1968.

HERON HOUSE, editors. *The Odds on Virtually Everything.* New York: Putnam's, 1980.

HUFF, DARRELL. *How to Take a Chance.* New York: Norton, 1959.

HUFF, DARRELL, and IRVING GEIS. *How to Lie with Statistics.* New York: Norton, 1954.

Chapter Six
Discrete Probability Distributions

In this chapter we discuss the properties of discrete random variables, including how to construct a discrete probability distribution and how to calculate the mean, variance, and standard deviation of a discrete random variable. A probability distribution is the theoretical or analytical counterpart of the relative frequency distribution discussed in Chapter 3. As described in Chapter 4, the mean is a measure of the center of a distribution, and the variance and standard deviation are measures of a distribution's spread.

6.1 ▪ Random Variables

As we saw in Chapter 5, the sample space of an experiment may or may not consist of a set of real numbers. When the variable studied is a qualitative variable, the sample space consists of the possible values or attributes that the variable can have. In this chapter, however, we are especially interested in problems in which the variable studied is a quantitative variable, which takes on values that are real numbers.

Sometimes a qualitative variable is converted into a quantitative variable by assigning a numerical value or code to each qualitative category. For example, suppose that an adult male is selected randomly and classified as "employed" or "unemployed"; the employment status of the individual male is thus a qualitative variable. This variable can be transformed to a quantitative variable by using 0 to represent "unemployed" and 1 to represent "employed." Thus, even when the outcomes of an experiment are not real numbers, we can think of a process (or function) that associates some real number with each possible outcome.

Definition: Random Variable

A variable X is a **random variable** if the value that X assumes at the conclusion of an experiment is a chance or random occurrence that cannot be predicted with certainty.

Suppose we select a random sample of 30 adults and ask each individual whether he or she is employed. The number of individuals in the sample who are employed is a random variable X that can take any of the values from 0 to 30. Each of these values corresponds to a particular experimental outcome, where the experiment consists of selecting a sample of 30 adults and noting how many are employed. The variable X is a random variable because the value that X assumes cannot be predicted with certainty before performing the experiment.

The set of possible values $\{x_1, x_2, \ldots, x_k\}$ assumed by the random variable X is called the *sample space of the random variable* X. In the definition, it has been assumed that the sample space contains a finite number of elements, but this is not always the case. The sample space may contain an infinite but countable number of outcomes, or the sample space may contain all values in some interval.

Definition: Discrete and Continuous Random Variables

A random variable X is **discrete** if X can assume only a finite or countably infinite number of different values. A random variable X is **continuous** if it can assume all the values in some interval.

By "countably infinite" we mean that the possible values of X can be put in one-to-one correspondence with the positive integers. *Countable* means that you can count the possible values that the variable can take. The total number can be infinite because we can conceive of the count as proceeding forever without end.

Example 6.1

Discrete Random Variables:

(a) X = number of days of rainfall in New York City in May (possible values of X are 0, 1, 2, . . . , 31)
(b) X = number of defective parts in a sample of 1000 parts (possible values of X are 0, 1, 2, . . . , 1000)
(c) X = number of highway deaths on the Fourth of July (possible values of X are 0, 1, 2, . . .) ■

Example 6.2

Continuous Random Variables:

(a) X = height of an individual
(b) X = time required for an airplane to travel from Chicago to New York
(c) X = distance traveled by a truck driver in a given month
(d) X = diameter of a ball bearing
(e) X = volume of gasoline in a storage tank

Measuring a continuous random variable is always problematic because, at least conceptually, a continuous variable can take all values in an interval. Thus we cannot measure, say, the diameter of a ball bearing exactly; similarly, we cannot exactly measure heights, weights, times, distances, volumes, and so forth. Consequently, there is always a certain amount of approximation and round-off error in measuring a continuous variable.

In this chapter, we will discuss discrete random variables and their properties. In Chapter 7 we will discuss some special discrete probability distributions, and in Chapter 8 we will discuss continuous random variables.

It is common to use uppercase letters (e.g., X, Y, and Z) to denote random variables and lowercase letters (e.g., x, y, and z) or lowercase subscripted letters (e.g., x_1, x_2, and x_3) to denote particular values assumed by random variables. The expression $P(X = x_i)$ denotes the probability that a random variable X assumes the value x_i. Similarly, the expression $P(X = x)$ denotes the probability that the random variable X assumes the specific value x. Frequently the notation $P(X = x)$ will be abbreviated to $P(x)$, where it is understood that x is a specific value of the random variable X.

Exercises for Section 6.1

1. Which of the following describe continuous random variables, and which describe discrete random variables?
   a. Number of houses sold by a real estate developer during a given week
   b. Quantity of natural gas used per month for heating an apartment building
   c. Volume of milk in a quart container
   d. Number of accidents per week at a manufacturing plant
   e. Number of people per day who report for work at a manufacturing plant
   f. Number of errors found in an audit of a company's financial records
   g. Length of time a customer waits for service at a supermarket checkout counter
   h. Number of automobiles recalled by General Motors next year
2. Which of the following random variables are discrete and which are continuous?
   a. $X =$ income of a secretary
   b. $X =$ number of heads obtained in 10 tosses of a coin
   c. $X =$ weight of a child at birth
   d. $X =$ time required to run 100 yards
   e. $X =$ weight of fluid in a bottle
   f. $X =$ number of Democrats in a certain precinct
3. For each of the cases in Exercise 2, describe the sample space.
4. A company drills three oil wells at an expense of \$10,000 each. Any well that strikes oil will produce \$25,000 in revenue, resulting in a profit of \$15,000. Let X denote the total profit or loss achieved by the company drilling the wells. Describe the sample space and list all possible values of X.
5. A student commutes to college every weekday. The student rides a motorcycle on sunny days and takes the bus on rainy days, and he leaves home at either 8 A.M. or 10 A.M. The bus ride takes 20 minutes more than the motorcycle ride, and the 10 A.M. ride takes 10 minutes less than the 8 A.M. ride by bus or motorcycle. The 8 A.M. motorcycle ride takes 15 minutes. Let X denote the time it takes for the student to get to school. Describe the sample space and list all possible values of X.
6. A student is registered for courses in economics and in math. A new math book costs \$18 and a used one costs \$10; a new economics book costs \$20, a good used one costs \$15, and a worn one costs \$8. The student will buy the cheapest math and economics texts that are still available at the bookstore. Let X denote the total cost of the two books. Describe the sample space and list all possible values of X.

6.2 ▪ *Properties of Discrete Probability Distributions*

When we discuss any discrete random variable X, we usually want to know all possible values of X and the probability with which each possible value will occur. This set of facts is called a *discrete probability distribution,* or a *probability function*.

Definition: Discrete Probability Distribution

A **discrete probability distribution** is a table, graph, or rule that associates a probability $P(X = x_i)$ with each possible value x_i that the discrete random variable X can assume.

Every discrete probability distribution must satisfy the following rules:

1. No probability can be negative. That is, for any value x,

$$P(X = x) \geq 0$$

2. The sum of the probabilities of all the possible values of the random variable X must sum to 1. That is,

$$\Sigma\, P(X = x) = 1$$

where the summation is over all possible values of X.

Example 6.3

A Discrete Probability Distribution: Suppose that a car salesman is trying to sell a new car to a customer who is interested in buying one of three different cars. The selling prices of the cars are \$10,000, \$15,000 and \$20,000, and the salesman gets a 5% commission on every sale. Suppose the salesman believes that there is a 30% chance that the customer will purchase the \$10,000 car, a 20% chance that the customer will purchase the \$15,000 car, a 10% chance that the customer will purchase the \$20,000 car, and a 40% chance that the customer will not buy a car. Let the random variable X denote the salesman's potential commission. Construct the discrete probability distribution of the random variable X.

Solution: Based on a 5% commission, the salesman will receive \$0 if the customer does not buy a car, \$500 if the \$10,000 car is sold, \$750 if the \$15,000 car is sold, and \$1000 if the \$20,000 car is sold. If it is assumed that the customer will not buy two cars, the possible outcomes are $x_1 = \$0$, $x_2 = \$500$, $x_3 = \$750$, and $x_4 = \$1000$. The sample space of the random variable X is $S = \{\$0, \$500, \$750, \$1000\}$. The corresponding probabilities are .4, .3, .2, and .1. The probability distribution of the discrete random variable X is shown in Table 6.1 (on page 212). This probability distribution can also be drawn as a graph, as illustrated in Figure 6.1.

FIGURE 6.1
Graph of the discrete probability distribution for Example 6.3.

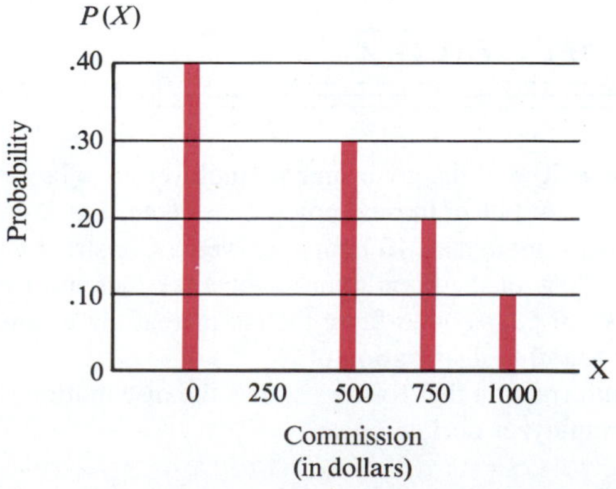

TABLE 6.1
Discrete probability distribution for Example 6.3

x	$P(x)$
\$ 0	.4
500	.3
750	.2
1000	.1
	1.0

■

A discrete probability distribution shows the relative frequency distribution of the population. For a discrete random variable, a relative frequency distribution shows the proportion of times each value occurred in a large number of random experiments. When we assign various probabilities to the basic outcomes of an experiment, we are trying to approximate population relative frequencies.

The data in Table 6.1 indicate that 10% of the time the salesman can expect to earn a \$1000 commission, 20% of the time he can expect to earn \$750, and so forth. That is, the probabilities in Table 6.1 can be interpreted as predictions of the relative frequencies of occurrence of each value of X in a large number of repeated trials of the experiment, provided all potential customers have the same tendencies.

A discrete probability function like that in Table 6.1 is similar to the relative frequency distributions presented in Chapter 3. The probability function tells us the limiting relative frequency of occurrence of each possible value of X when the random experiment is repeated many times.

Suppose that a random experiment can be repeated a large number of times and that each occurrence of the experiment generates a value of the random variable X. If the discrete random variable X is observed a very large number of times and the values that occur are arranged in a relative frequency distribution, then this relative frequency distribution will be indistinguishable from the probability distribution of the random variable X. Thus, the probability distribution of a random variable is a theoretical model for the relative frequency distribution of a population.

The probability distribution contains all the information about the probability properties of the random variable, and a graph of the probability distribution will also reveal the general characteristics of the probability distribution.

Exercises for Section 6.2

1. Suppose 50% of the government employees at a large agency work more than 40 hours per week. A sample of two of these employees is taken. Let X denote the number of employees in the sample who work more than 40 hours per week. Construct and graph the probability distribution of X.
2. About 30% of the population favor a tax increase to improve school services. Let X denote the number of people who favor the tax increase in a sample of two individuals. Construct and graph the probability distribution of X.
3. The information that follows shows the distribution of the number of days of sick leave taken by 200 employees during a year:

Days	0	1	2	3	4	5	6	7
Number of employees	20	40	40	30	20	10	10	30

Let X denote the number of days of sick leave taken by an employee.
a. Construct and graph the probability distribution of X.
b. Find $P(X \geq 4)$.
c. Find $P(X \leq 3)$.
d. Find $P(X \geq 3)$.
e. Find $P(3 \leq X \leq 6)$.

4. A lawn and garden center has 80 cherry trees to sell. The following information shows their heights to the nearest foot:

Height	8	9	10	11	12	13	14
Number of trees	10	14	20	25	6	4	1

Let X denote the height of a tree that is randomly selected.
a. Construct and graph the probability distribution of X.
b. Find $P(X \leq 10)$.
c. Find $P(X > 9)$.
d. Find $P(10 \leq X < 13)$.

5. A new math book costs \$20 and a used one costs \$10. A new chemistry book costs \$18, a good used one costs \$14, and a worn one costs \$9. A student wants to buy the cheapest math book and chemistry book available in the bookstore. The probability of getting a used math book is .4, of getting a worn chemistry book is .3, and of getting a good used chemistry book is .2. Let X denote the cost of the two books the student purchases. Assume that the purchases are independent of one another.
a. Construct and graph the probability distribution of X.
b. Find $P(X > \$15)$.
c. Find $P(X > \$25)$.
d. Find $P(\$27 \leq X \leq \$35)$.

6. An investor makes two independent investments and believes the following: Investment 1 will yield a profit of \$1000 with probability .6 or a loss of \$400 with probability .4; investment 2 will yield a profit of \$2000 with probability .1, a profit of \$700 with probability .4, and a loss of \$500 with probability .5.
a. Construct and graph the probability distribution of X where X represents the total profit or loss yielded on the two investments.
b. Find $P(X < \$1600)$.

7. In Tampa the distribution of incomes is as shown in the accompanying table. If a resident is randomly selected, find the probability that the person's income is the following:
a. At least \$20,000
b. \$20,000 to \$59,999
c. Less than \$40,000

Income (dollars)	Relative Frequency
0– 9,999	.15
10,000–19,999	.25
20,000–39,999	.45
40,000–59,999	.10
60,000 or more	.05

8. In Exercise 7, suppose that three Tampa residents are randomly selected and asked whether wealthy people should pay higher taxes. What is the probability of the following?
a. All three residents earn less than $10,000.
b. At least one resident earns $60,000 or more.

9. The Chesler Car Rental Agency claims that 70% of its customers rent compact cars. Suppose four customers rent cars (assume the rentals are independent of one another.) What is the probability of the following?
a. All four cars are compacts.
b. At least one car is a compact.

10. The manager of a retail television outlet thinks that it is equally likely that it will sell zero, one, two, or three televisions in a day. (Suppose that the store has never sold more than three televisions on any day.) Let X denote the number of televisions sold on any given day.
a. Construct a table showing the probability distribution of X.
b. Plot the probability distribution of X.
c. What is the probability that the number of televisions sold on a given day will be less than two?
d. Suppose the outlet has only one salesman, whose income depends on the number of televisions he sells per day. Suppose he receives $10 on the first television sold per day, a $20 commission on the second, and a $45 commission on the third. (Thus, if he sells three televisions in a given day, his commissions will total $75.) Let Y denote the salesman's daily commission. Construct a table showing the probability distribution of Y.
e. What is the probability that the salesman's commission in part (d) on a particular day will exceed $10?

11. Suppose that a random variable X has the following discrete probability distribution:

x	-2	-1	0	1	2
$P(x)$	.10	.15	.40	.20	.15

a. Find $P(X \leq 0)$.
b. Find $P(X > 0)$.
c. Find $P(-1 \leq X \leq 1)$.
d. Find $P(X < 2)$.
e. Find $P(-1 < X < 2)$.
f. Find $P(X < 1)$.

6.3 ▪ Cumulative Distribution Function

For a discrete random variable X, the cumulative distribution function shows the probability that X assumes a value less than or equal to any specific value. The cumulative distribution function of X is denoted by $F(x)$, where x is any specified value.

Definition: Cumulative Distribution Function

Let X be a discrete or continuous random variable and let x be any real number. The **cumulative distribution function** (CDF) of X is the function

$$F(x) = P(X \leq x)$$

Every cumulative distribution function must satisfy the following rules:

1. For any value x, $0 \leq F(x) \leq 1$.
2. If $x_1 < x_2$, then $F(x_1) \leq F(x_2)$.
3. $F(-\infty) = 0$ and $F(\infty) = 1$.

Let X be a discrete random variable that can assume the values $x_1, x_2, \ldots, x_n$, where $x_1 < x_2 < \cdots < x_n$. Then $F(x_r)$ denotes the probability that X assumes a value that is less than or equal to x_r and is given by

$$F(x_r) = P(X \leq x_r) = \sum_{i=1}^{r} P(X = x_i)$$
$$= P(X = x_1) + P(X = x_2) + \cdots + P(X = x_r)$$

The CDF for a discrete random variable is a step function. A step (or jump) occurs at each point x_i where $P(X = x_i)$ is positive, and the height of the step is $P(X = x_i)$. If X can assume only the n values $x_1, x_2, \ldots, x_n$, then there are n steps in the CDF. The cumulative distribution function will change values only at those points x_i that can occur with positive probability. For any values a and b such that $b \geq a$, we have

$$P(a < X \leq b) = F(b) - F(a)$$

Example 6.4 **A Cumulative Distribution Function:** The cumulative distribution function for Example 6.3 is as follows:

$$F(0) = P(X \leq 0) = .4$$
$$F(500) = P(X \leq 500) = .4 + .3 = .7$$
$$F(750) = P(X \leq 750) = .4 + .3 + .2 = .9$$
$$F(1000) = P(X \leq 1000) = .4 + .3 + .2 + .1 = 1.0$$

■

Exercises for Section 6.3

1. A computer salesman calculates the proportion of new computers sold that have been returned during the warranty period to correct defects. The results are as follows:

Number of Returns	0	1	2	3	4
Proportion	.30	.33	.18	.16	

a. Find the missing proportion.
b. Graph the probability distribution.
c. Calculate and graph the cumulative distribution function.

2. A credit card company examines its records to determine the length of time (in weeks) between the time a bill is sent and payment is received. The following table shows the results:

Number of Weeks	1	2	3	4	5
Proportion	.35	.20	.20		.05

a. Find the missing proportion.
b. Graph the probability distribution.
c. Calculate and graph the cumulative distribution function.
d. For a randomly chosen bill, what is the probability that payment will be received within three weeks or less from the time the bill is sent out?

3. In a study to investigate traffic patterns, the numbers of occupants in cars on an interstate highway were counted. The following table shows the proportions for all cars:

Number of Occupants	1	2	3	4	5	6
Proportion	.40	.36	.10		.02	.01

a. Find the missing proportion.
b. Graph the probability distribution.
c. Calculate and graph the cumulative distribution function.
d. What is the probability that a randomly chosen car will have at least four occupants?

6.4 ▪ Expected Value of a Discrete Random Variable

In Chapter 4 we saw that the population mean and the population variance are useful population parameters that help us describe and compare different quantitative populations. In the same manner, the mean and variance of a random variable X help us describe the characteristics of its distribution and compare it with other random variables.

The *expected value,* or *mean,* of a random variable is used as a measure of the center of the probability distribution. The expected value of a discrete random variable is the weighted average of the possible values of the random variable where the weight assigned to x_i is the probability $P(X = x_i)$.

Definition: Expected Value, or Mean, of a Discrete Random Variable

The **expected value**, or **mean**, of a discrete random variable X is denoted by the symbol $E(X)$ or the symbol μ_X. The expected value of X is

$$E(X) = \mu_X = \Sigma\, xP(x)$$

where the sum is taken over all possible values of X.

When there is no danger of confusion, we will occasionally use the symbol μ instead of μ_X to denote the expected value of X. The mean is called the "expected value" because it denotes the average value that we would expect to occur if the experiment were repeated a large number of times.

Example 6.5

Expected Value of a Random Variable: Find the expected value for the salesman's commission in Example 6.3.

Solution: Suppose the situation described for the salesman occurred day after day. Thus, on 40% of the days the salesman would receive no commission, on 30% of the days the salesman would receive \$500, on 20% of the days the salesman would receive \$750, and on 10% of the days the salesman would receive \$1000. The calculations to determine the salesman's expected commission are shown in Table 6.2. In the third column, we calculate the weighted value $xP(x)$ for each value of X. The sum of these values is the mean, or the expected value, of X. We obtain

$$\begin{aligned} E(X) &= \Sigma\, xP(x) \\ &= (0)(.4) + (500)(.3) + (750)(.2) + (1000)(.1) \\ &= \$400 \end{aligned}$$

TABLE 6.2
Calculation of expected commission in Example 6.3

x	$P(x)$	$xP(x)$
$ 0	.4	$ 0
500	.3	150
750	.2	150
1000	.1	100
	1.0	$400

■

Some Applications of Expected Value

In many problems in business and economics, the random variable X measures the possible profit or loss of an investment or gamble. Then $E(X)$ measures the amount that we can expect to win or lose by undertaking the investment or gamble. A negative $E(X)$ implies that, in the long run, we can expect to lose money by participating in the particular investment or gamble.

Example 6.6

Expected Profit from an Investment: The L. M. Corporation purchases old, run-down buildings, remodels them, and then sells them. The corporation has the opportunity to purchase a building for $100,000, which will cost $60,000 to remodel. The manager thinks that there is a 50% chance that the remodeled building will sell for $120,000, yielding a $40,000 loss. (We are ignoring interest costs to keep the problem simple.) However, there is a 20% chance that the building will sell for $180,000, yielding a $20,000 profit, and a 30% chance that the building will sell for $230,000, yielding a $70,000 profit. Calculate the expected profit or loss from buying, remodeling, and selling the building.

Solution: The data are shown in Table 6.3, where the random variable X denotes the profit (loss is shown as negative profit). The expected profit is $E(X) = \$5000$. Because the expected profit is positive, the corporation could expect to earn about $5000 per project on the average by undertaking a large number of similar projects.

TABLE 6.3
Calculation of expected return on investment in Example 6.6

x	$P(x)$	$xP(x)$
−$40,000	.5	−$20,000
20,000	.2	4,000
70,000	.3	21,000
	1.0	$ 5,000

■

In almost all gambling situations, the gambler's expected profit is negative. This means that the gambler will lose money if he or she plays the game long enough. If the gambler's expected profit is $0, then the game is a fair game and the gambler can expect to break even in the long run. Generally, there are no gambling situations at casinos where the gambler's expected profit is positive. If such a gamble existed, the casino would be subsidizing the gambler!

Example 6.7

Expected Gain or Loss from Playing Roulette: Roulette is a gambling game that is popular in Las Vegas and Atlantic City. A roulette wheel contains 38 slots, numbered 00, 0, 1, 2, . . . , 36. Eighteen of the slots are red, 18 are black, and 2 (0 and 00) are green. A ball is dropped onto the wheel while it is spinning. Suppose you bet $1 that the ball will stop in a red slot. If it does, you win $1; if it stops in a black slot, you lose $1; if it stops in a green slot, you lose $0.50. Calculate the expected gain or loss from betting $1 on red in roulette.

Solution: Let X denote the payoff from betting $1 on red. There are 38 equally likely possibilities for the slot where the ball will stop. Thus, each slot has probability 1/38. There are 18 red slots, so the probability that the ball stops in a red slot is 18/38. The probability that the ball stops in a black slot is 18/38, and the probability that the ball stops in a green slot is 2/38. The calculation of the expected gain is shown in Table 6.4. The expected gain is

$$E(X) = -0.026$$

This means that, in the long run, playing roulette will result in a loss of 2.6 cents per $1 bet. If you play the game 1000 times and bet $1 on red each time, you can expect to be $26.00 behind.

TABLE 6.4
Calculation of expected return for roulette problem in Example 6.7

x	$P(x)$	$xP(x)$
$1.00	18/38	$0.474
−0.50	2/38	−0.026
−1.00	18/38	−0.474
	1.00	−$0.026

■

Expected Values of Functions of X

Let X be a random variable and let $g(X)$ denote some function of X, such as X^2, $5X$, $(X - 5)^2$, and so on. At times we may be interested in finding the expected value of $g(X)$. We do this by using the rule on the expected value of a function of X.

Definition: Expected Value of a Function of X

Let X be a discrete random variable, and let Y be any function of X such that $Y = g(X)$. Then the expected value of Y, or the expected value of $g(X)$, is

$$E(Y) = E[g(X)] = \Sigma\, g(x)P(x)$$

where the sum is over all values of X.

Example 6.8

Expected Value of a Function of *X*: Suppose a wealthy gambler bets $100 on the red in roulette. Find the gambler's expected gain or loss. Refer to Example 6.7.

Solution: Define the random variable $Y = g(X) = 100X$, where X is the random variable described in Example 6.7. To calculate the expected value of Y, we weight each possible value of Y by its probability of occurrence. The expected value of Y, calculated in Table 6.5, is $E(Y) = -\$2.63$. The expected gain is negative, which means the gambler can expect to lose \$2.63 per \$100 bet.

TABLE 6.5
Calculation of expected return from roulette problem in Example 6.8

x	$y = g(x)$ $= 100x$	$P(x)$	$g(x)P(x)$
\$ 1.00	\$ 100	18/38	\$ 47.37
−0.50	−50	2/38	−2.63
−1.00	−100	18/38	−47.37
		1.00	−\$2.63

Tips on Problem Solving
To find the expected value of a discrete random variable X, construct a table containing three columns. The first column shows all the values of X, the second shows all the probabilities $P(X = x)$, and the third shows the cross products $xP(X = x)$. The sum of the values in column 3 is the expected value of X.

Exercises for Section 6.4

1. Consider the following probability distribution for the random variable X:

x	−2	−1	0	1	2
$P(x)$	.08	.12	.40	.30	.10

a. Find $E(X)$.
b. Graph $P(x)$ and locate $E(X)$ on the graph.

2. A roulette wheel at a Las Vegas casino has 18 red numbers, 18 black numbers, and 2 green numbers. Assume that a \$5 bet is placed on the black numbers. If a black number comes up, the player wins \$5; if a green number comes up, the player loses \$2.50; otherwise, the player loses \$5.
a. Let X be a random variable indicating the player's net winnings on one bet. Find the probability distribution for X.
b. What are the expected winnings? What is your interpretation of this value?
c. If a player makes 100 bets of \$5 each, what is the expected profit or loss? Can you explain why casinos like a high volume of betting?

3. A grocer has shelf space for three units of a highly perishable item that must be disposed of at the end of the day if it is not sold. Each unit costs \$2.80 and sells for \$5.50. Demand probabilities are as follows: $P(\text{demand} = 0) = .35$, $P(\text{demand} = 1) = .40$, and $P(\text{demand} = 2) = .25$. Let X be a random variable indicating daily profit if a retailer stocks two units each day. Let Y be a random variable indicating daily profit if a retailer stocks one unit each day.
a. Show the probability distribution for X and Y.
b. Using the expected values of X and Y, determine whether the retailer would be better off stocking one or two units per day.

4. At a carnival, a prize bag contains 15 packages worth \$25 each, 8 packages worth \$50 each, and 1 package worth \$100.
   a. If one package is chosen at random, what is the expected value of its worth?
   b. If you want to take the action that maximizes expected gain, should you pay \$35 for the opportunity to pick a package at random from this bag?
5. A rock concert producer has scheduled an outdoor concert. If it does not rain, the producer expects to make a \$55,000 profit from the concert. If it does rain, the producer will be forced to cancel the concert and will lose \$15,000 (due to the rock star's fee, advertising costs, stadium rental, administrative costs, etc.). The producer has learned from the U.S. Weather Bureau that the probability of rain next Saturday is .3.
   a. Find the producer's expected profit from the concert.
   b. For a fee of \$3000, an insurance company has offered to insure the producer against all losses resulting from a rained-out concert. If the producer buys the insurance, what is the producer's expected profit from the concert?
   c. Assuming the weather bureau's forecast is accurate, do you believe the insurance company has charged too little for the insurance policy? Explain.
6. A manufacturing representative is considering the purchase of an insurance policy to cover possible losses from marketing a new product. If the product is a complete failure, the company will lose \$88,000; if it is only moderately successful, the company will lose \$23,000. The probabilities that the product will be a failure or only moderately successful are .04 and .16, respectively. Assuming that the manufacturing representative would be willing to ignore all other possible losses, what premium should the insurance company charge for the policy in order to break even?
7. A basketball player who makes 75% of his free throws comes to the line to shoot a one-and-one. (That is, if the first shot is successful, the player is given a second shot; if not, he gets no second shot. One point is scored for each successful shot.) Assume that the outcome of the second shot, if any, is independent of that of the first.
   a. Find the expected number of points resulting from the one-and-one.
   b. Compare this with the expected number of points from a two-shot foul, where a second shot is always given.
8. You pay \$2 to bet at a racetrack. The probability is 1/10 that you will be paid \$6 (i.e., that you win \$4), and the probability is 1/20 that you will be paid \$10 (i.e., that you win \$8). What is the expected gain or loss from betting?
9. A customer for a home insurance policy owns a \$40,000 home. The probability is .001 that the home will be totally destroyed by fire, and the probability is .005 that the home will suffer a 50% loss due to fire. If we ignore all other partial losses, what premium should the insurance company charge for a policy just to break even?
10. A person owns a new car valued at \$5000. Past records indicate that the probability is .005 that a car like this will be totally destroyed in an accident in any year. The car may also suffer damages of \$1000 or \$3000 with probabilities .1 and .01, respectively. If we ignore all other partial losses, what premium should the insurance company charge for a yearly policy in order to break even?
11. A student admitted to graduate school is told that the probability is .2 of receiving a full-tuition scholarship, .5 of receiving a half-tuition scholarship, and .3 of no scholarship and thus paying the full \$900 tuition. Let X denote the student's tuition expenses.
    a. Construct and graph the probability distribution of X.
    b. Find the student's expected tuition expenses.
12. An individual makes three independent investments. The possible profits or losses from each investment are listed in the accompanying table along with their probabilities. Let X denote the total profit or loss yielded by the three investments.
    a. Construct and graph the probability distribution of X.
    b. Find the mean value of X.

Investment 1		Investment 2		Investment 3	
Profit	Probability	Profit	Probability	Profit	Probability
\$ 700	.6	\$2000	.3	\$900	.5
−300	.4	1000	.5	400	.5
		−600	.2		

6.5 ▪ Variance of a Discrete Random Variable

Suppose that the discrete random variable X can take only the values $x_1, x_2, \ldots, x_k$ with probabilities $P(X = x_1), P(X = x_2), \ldots, P(X = x_k)$. Thus, we would observe the squared deviation from the mean $(x_1 - \mu)^2$ with probability $P(X = x_1)$, the squared deviation from the mean $(x_2 - \mu)^2$ with probability $P(X = x_2)$, and so forth.

The squared deviations $(x_i - \mu)^2$ can be used to provide a measure of how spread out a probability distribution is. To obtain the *variance* of a discrete probability distribution, we calculate the expected value of all possible squared deviations from the mean $(x_1 - \mu)^2, (x_2 - \mu)^2, \ldots, (x_k - \mu)^2$. To obtain the expected value of these squared deviations, we weight each squared deviation by its probability of occurrence.

The variance of the random variable X, denoted as Var (X) or by the symbol σ^2 (Greek sigma and read "sigma squared"), is defined in the accompanying box.

Definition: Variance and Standard Deviation of a Discrete Random Variable

The **variance** of a discrete random variable X is given by the formula

$$\sigma^2 = (x_1 - \mu)^2\, P(X = x_1) + (x_2 - \mu)^2\, P(X = x_2) + \cdots + (x_k - \mu)^2\, P(X = x_k)$$

Using summation notation, we obtain

$$\sigma^2 = \Sigma(x - \mu)^2 P(X = x)$$

where the summation is over all values of X.

The **standard deviation**, denoted by the symbol σ, is the square root of the variance.

The variance represents the average or expected value of the squared deviations from the mean and is often denoted by $E[(X - \mu)^2]$. By using the rule $E[g(X)] = \Sigma\, g(x)P(x)$ and letting $g(x) = (x - \mu)^2$, we obtain

$$\sigma^2 = E[(X - \mu)^2] = \Sigma(x - \mu)^2\, P(x)$$

The formula for calculating the variance of a random variable X can be expressed in a different but equivalent way, as indicated in the accompanying box. In some cases, especially when the mean is not an integer, it may be easier to calculate the variance by using the alternative formula rather than the original definition.

Alternative Formula for the Variance

$$\text{Var}(X) = \Sigma\, x^2\, P(x) - \mu^2$$

That is, $\text{Var}(X) = E(X^2) - [E(X)]^2$.

Because $(x - \mu)^2$ is always nonnegative and $P(x)$ is always nonnegative, it follows that $\Sigma(x - \mu)^2\, P(x)$ is always nonnegative. Thus, every variance is nonnegative, and $\text{Var}(X) \geqslant 0$. If $\text{Var}(X) = 0$, then it must be that $(x - \mu)^2 = 0$ for all possible values of X; that is, X must take the value μ with probability 1. Thus if $\text{Var}(X) = 0$, then X is a constant.

Application: Portfolio Selection

Large investors such as corporations, banks, and insurance companies do not hold just a single financial asset; rather, they hold *portfolios* of financial assets. These investors are less concerned with the rate of return achieved by any single particular asset than with the overall rate of return earned by the entire portfolio. Because the future rate of return of the portfolio is uncertain, a probability distribution is used to characterize the portfolio's possible rates of return.

Investors frequently use the mean and variance of a portfolio's future rate of return to judge its quality. The standard deviation of a portfolio's rate of return is frequently used as a measure of the *risk* associated with the portfolio. The greater the standard deviation, the greater the risk associated with the portfolio; that is, the greater the uncertainty of the portfolio's rate of return.

In forming a portfolio, an investor can select from many individual assets. Because of this, the investor has numerous different portfolios to choose from. Which portfolio should the investor select? This problem was addressed by Harry M. Markowitz in his famous book *Portfolio Selection* (New Haven: Yale University Press, 1959). He argued that the mean return and the standard deviation of the possible return should be used to characterize all portfolios.

Markowitz argued that any portfolio that is not an "efficient portfolio" should not be considered for investment. He defined an efficient portfolio as any portfolio that provides the highest possible mean rate of return for any *given* degree of risk (i.e., any given standard deviation) or that provides the lowest possible degree of risk for any given mean rate of return. From the set of efficient portfolios, the investor should choose the portfolio that best suits his or her needs.

Example 6.9

Portfolio Selection: Suppose that an investor is contemplating investing \$10,000 in one of two different portfolios of stocks, portfolio A or portfolio B. The potential profits from investing in the portfolios are assumed to be random variables whose probability distributions are shown in Table 6.6. The random variables X and Y are used to denote the potential profits from portfolios A and B, respectively. Determine which of the portfolios is an efficient portfolio.

Solution: We need to calculate the mean return and variance for each portfolio; these calculations are shown in Table 6.7. For portfolio A, the expected return is $E(X) =$ \$780, the variance is $\sigma_X^2 = 27{,}600$, and the standard deviation is $\sigma_X = \sqrt{27{,}600} =$

TABLE 6.6
Probability distributions for portfolio returns in Example 6.9

Portfolio A		Portfolio B	
Profit	Probability	Profit	Probability
x	$P(x)$	y	$P(y)$
$ 600	.40	$600	.10
800	.30	700	.40
1000	.30	880	.50

TABLE 6.7 **Calculation of mean and variance of portfolio returns in Example 6.9**

Portfolio A

x	$P(x)$	$xP(x)$	$x - \mu$	$(x - \mu)^2$	$(x - \mu)^2P(x)$
$ 600	.40	240	−180	32,400	12,960
800	.30	240	20	400	120
1000	.30	300	220	48,400	14,520
	1.00	780		Variance =	27,600

Portfolio B

y	$P(y)$	$yP(y)$	$y - \mu$	$(y - \mu)^2$	$(y - \mu)^2 P(y)$
$600	.10	60	−180	32,400	3,240
700	.40	280	−80	6,400	2,560
880	.50	440	100	10,000	5,000
	1.00	780		Variance =	10,800

$166.13. For portfolio B, the expected return is $E(Y) = \$780$, the variance is $\sigma_Y^2 = 10{,}800$, and the standard deviation is $\sigma_Y = \sqrt{10{,}800} = \$103.92$.

Because both portfolios have the same expected return of $780 but the variance for portfolio B is less than that for portfolio A, portfolio A is not an efficient portfolio. ■

Tips on Problem Solving

To find the mean and variance of a discrete random variable X, construct a table like Table 6.7 containing six columns. The first column shows all the values of the random variable X, the second shows all the probabilities $P(X = x)$, and the third shows the cross products $xP(x)$. The sum of the values in column 3 is the mean or expected value of X. Column 4 shows the deviations from the mean $(x - \mu)$, column 5 shows the squared deviations from the mean $(x - \mu)^2$, and column 6 shows the cross products $(x - \mu)^2P(x)$. The sum of the values in column 6 is the variance σ^2.

Exercises for Section 6.5

1. You have been given a ticket for a sweepstakes with five possible mutually exclusive outcomes. You could win a grand prize valued at $8000 with probability .00005, a major prize of value $4000 with probability .00005, a prize valued at $150 with probability .0002, and a prize of value $3 with probability .003. Finally, you could win nothing (valued at $0). Find the mean and standard deviation of the value of your ticket.
2. A publisher finds that the probability distribution for the number of errors per page of text depends on whether the material is mathematical or nonmathematical. The two probability distributions are shown in the accompanying table. Suppose that a mathematics book contains 300 pages and a nonmathematics book 200 pages. Assume that the number of errors on any one page is independent of the number on any other. Find the mean and standard deviation of the number of errors per page in each book.

Number of errors per page: x	0	1	2	3	4	5	6
Mathematical Text: $P(x)$	.45	.15	.10	.10	.10	.05	.05
Nonmathematical Text: $P(x)$	.75	.13	.10	.01	.01	0.00	0.00

3. In Wildwood, N.J., the police give tickets to individuals who park in designated no-parking zones. The amount of the fine depends on the time of day the ticket is given. Past data indicate that 50% of the tickets are for $2, 20% are for $4, 20% are for $6, and 10% are for $8. Let X denote the amount of the fine.
   a. List the probability distribution of X.
   b. Find the mean value of X.
   c. Find the variance of X.
4. In New York City the fines described in Exercise 3 cost 10 times as much as in Wildwood. That is, the fines are $20, $40, $60 and $80.
   a. List the probability distribution of X.
   b. Find the mean value of X.
   c. Find the variance of X.
5. Let X be a discrete random variable with the following probability distribution:

x	2	6	10	14	20
$P(x)$	.1	.2	.3	.3	.1

   Find the mean and variance of X.

6. Let X be a discrete random variable with the following probability distribution:

x	1	2	3	4	5
$P(x)$	.2	.2	.3	.1	.2

   Find the mean and variance of X.

6.6 ▪ Functions of Random Variables (Optional)

Occasionally we need to find the expected value of a linear function of a random variable. The next example shows how to do this.

Theorem: Expected Value of a Linear Function of X

Let X be a random variable and let $Y = a + bX$, where a and b are known constants. The expected value of Y is given by

$$E(Y) = a + bE(X)$$

Example 6.10

Expected Value of a Function of *X*: Suppose a sporting goods store plans to sell football jerseys for \$30 each. Let the random variable X denote the number of jerseys that will be sold. Assume that $E(X) = 100$; that is, we expect to sell 100 jerseys. Let R denote the total revenue from selling the jerseys. We have $R = f(X) = 30X$. The expected revenue is

$$\begin{aligned} E(R) &= E(30X) \\ &= 30E(X) = 30(100) \\ &= \$3000 \end{aligned}$$

The store can expect to receive \$3000 from sales of football jerseys. ■

Occasionally we need to determine the variance or standard deviation of a linear function of a random variable X. For example, suppose that $Y = f(X) = a + bX$, where a and b are known constants. When the variance of X is known, we can obtain the variance of Y by using the theorem for the variance and standard deviation of a linear function of a random variable.

Theorem: Variance and Standard Deviation of a Linear Function of X

Let X be a random variable and let $Y = a + bX$, where a and b are known constants. The **variance** of Y is given by

$$\text{Var}(Y) = \text{Var}(a + bX) = b^2\text{Var}(X)$$

or more simply,

$$\sigma_Y^2 = b^2\sigma_X^2$$

The **standard deviation** of Y is the square root of the variance; that is,

$$\sigma_Y = b\sigma_X$$

Example 6.11

Variance of a Linear Function of *X*: Let the random variable X represent the number of patients that a doctor sees on a given day. Assume the variance of variable X is 9. If each patient pays a fee of \$15, the doctor's daily revenue is $Y = 15X$. According to the theorem, the variance of Y is

$$\sigma^2 = (15)^2(9) = 2025$$

The standard deviation of Y is

$$\sigma = 45$$

■

Exercises for Section 6.6

1. The following data show the probability distribution of the number of customers who enter the Summerhill Florist Shop during a five-minute period. Let X denote the number of customers who arrive during the next five minutes.

Number of customers	0	1	2	3	4
Probability	.70	.20	.05	.03	.02

   a. Find the expected number of customers arriving in the next five-minute period.
   b. Find the variance of X.
   c. Suppose that the typical customer spends \$15. If Y denotes the total revenue during the next five minutes, find the expected value of Y.
   d. Find the variance of Y.
   e. Find $P(Y > \$30)$.

2. Suppose a consultant who charges \$75 per hour is hired to examine some financial records. The consultant claims that the amount of time required to examine the records X has the following distribution:

Time (in hours)	4	6	8	10
Probability	.2	.3	.4	.1

   a. Find the expected time required to examine the records.
   b. Find the expected fee for the consultant.
   c. Find the standard deviation for the consultant's fee.

6.7 ▪ Bivariate Probability Distributions (Optional)

Frequently we are interested in how two or more random variables vary together. In this section we restrict ourselves to problems involving only two discrete random variables and the resulting bivariate probability distribution. However, analogous relationships also hold for continuous random variables.

Definition: Discrete Bivariate Probability Function

Let X and Y be two discrete random variables. The **bivariate probability function**, denoted $P(X = x, Y = y)$, shows the joint probability that the random variable X assumes the specific value x and that the random variable Y assumes the specific value y.

Example 6.12 **A Bivariate Probability Distribution:** The Hawaiian Bureau of Tourism has conducted a survey to determine the characteristics of individuals who are likely to vacation in Hawaii. The bureau, which wants to send tour literature to these people, thinks that a good predictor of individuals who will vacation in Hawaii is the number of credit cards held by the family.

Table 6.8 is a bivariate frequency distribution in which the variable X represents the number of credit cards held by the family and the variable Y represents the number of vacations taken by the family during the last two years. The numbers in the table show how many families had any specific values of X and Y based on a random sample of 400 families.

TABLE 6.8
Bivariate frequency distribution for Example 6.12

Number of Credit Cards (X)	Number of Vacations (Y)				Total
	0	1	2	3	
0	80	36	12	4	132
1	60	40	16	8	124
2	28	32	20	16	96
3	4	8	16	20	48
Total	172	116	64	48	400

For example, Table 6.8 shows there are 32 families who own two credit cards and took one vacation. If we use the relative frequency approach to assign probabilities, we get $32/400 = .08$ as the probability that a family owns two credit cards and takes one vacation. This is denoted as $P(X = 2, Y = 1) = .08$. Table 6.9 shows the bivariate relative frequencies for the data in Table 6.8. If we assume that the relative frequencies based on the sample of 400 families accurately reflect the population relative frequencies, then Table 6.9 can be considered as an approximation to the population bivariate probability distribution. In Table 6.9, no probability is negative or exceeds 1. That is, for all x and y, $0 \leq P(X = x, Y = y) \leq 1$. Also observe that the sum of all the bivariate probabilities is 1.

TABLE 6.9
Bivariate probability distribution for Example 6.12

Number of Credit Cards (X)	Number of Vacations (Y)				Total
	0	1	2	3	
0	.20	.09	.03	.01	.33
1	.15	.10	.04	.02	.31
2	.07	.08	.05	.04	.24
3	.01	.02	.04	.05	.12
Total	.43	.29	.16	.12	1.00

■

Marginal Probabilities

The values in the margins of Table 6.9 show the individual probability distributions for the random variables X and Y, called the *marginal probability distributions* of X and Y. For example, by summing the probabilities down the first column of Table 6.9, we see that 43% of the families took no vacations. Thus, we obtain the marginal probability $P(Y = 0) = .43$. In general, the marginal probabilities are obtained by using the following formulas:

$$P(X = x) = \sum_{\text{all } y} P(X = x, Y = y)$$

$$P(Y = y) = \sum_{\text{all } x} P(X = x, Y = y)$$

Definition: Marginal Probability Function

Let X and Y be discrete random variables having the bivariate probability function $P(X = x, Y = y)$. The **marginal probability functions** of X and Y show the individual probabilities $P(X = x)$ and $P(Y = y)$, where x and y are specific values of the random variables X and Y, respectively.

Example 6.13

A Marginal Probability Distribution: Find the marginal probability functions for X and Y in Table 6.9.

Solution: We obtain

$$\begin{aligned} P(X = 0) &= P(X = 0, Y = 0) + P(X = 0, Y = 1) + P(X = 0, Y = 2) \\ &\quad + P(X = 0, Y = 3) \\ &= .20 + .09 + .03 + .01 = .33 \\ P(X = 1) &= P(X = 1, Y = 0) + P(X = 1, Y = 1) + P(X = 1, Y = 2) \\ &\quad + P(X = 1, Y = 3) \\ &= .15 + .10 + .04 + .02 = .31 \end{aligned}$$

Similarly, we obtain $P(X = 2) = .24$ and $P(X = 3) = .12$.

In a similar fashion, we obtain the marginal probabilities for Y:

$$\begin{aligned} P(Y = 0) &= P(X = 0, Y = 0) + P(X = 1, Y = 0) \\ &\quad + P(X = 2, Y = 0) + P(X = 3, Y = 0) \\ &= .20 + .15 + .07 + .01 = .43 \end{aligned}$$

Similarly, we obtain $P(Y = 1) = .29$, $P(Y = 2) = .16$, and $P(Y = 3) = .12$. These marginal probabilities are shown in the margins of Table 6.9. ■

Conditional Probabilities

Recall from Chapter 5 that the conditional probability that event A occurs given that event B has occurred is

$$P(A|B) = P(A \cap B)/P(B)$$

This same idea can be used to find the conditional probability that a random variable X will take the value x given that the random variable Y has taken the value y.

Definition: Conditional Probability

The **conditional probability** that a random variable X will assume a value x given that a random variable Y has assumed a value y, denoted $P(X = x|Y = y)$, is calculated using the formula

$$P(X = x|Y = y) = \frac{P(X = x, Y = y)}{P(Y = y)}$$

Similarly, we obtain

$$P(Y = y|X = x) = \frac{P(X = x, Y = y)}{P(X = x)}$$

Example 6.14 **A Conditional Probability Distribution:** Using Table 6.9, find the conditional probability that a family took $Y = 2$ vacations given that the family owns $X = 3$ credit cards.

Solution: We obtain the conditional probability

$$P(Y = 2|X = 3) = \frac{P(X = 3, Y = 2)}{P(X = 3)} = \frac{.04}{.12} = .33$$

Compare this conditional probability with the marginal probability

$$P(Y = 2) = .03 + .04 + .05 + .04 = .16$$

These results show that if we have no information about the number of credit cards owned, then the probability is .16 that a family took $Y = 2$ vacations. However, if we know that the family owns $X = 3$ credit cards, then the probability that the family took $Y = 2$ vacations increases to .33. This result indicates that the number of vacations taken by a family is not independent of the number of credit cards the family owns. Thus, knowing that 3 credit cards are owned is useful information that influences the probability that 2 vacations were taken. Knowing the number of credit cards owned apparently helps us predict the number of vacations that will be taken. ■

Independence of Discrete Random Variables

The discrete random variables X and Y are independent if knowledge about the occurrence of Y does not affect the probability that $X = x$ will occur. Thus, X and Y are independent if the conditional probability $P(Y = y|X = x)$ equals the marginal probability $P(Y = y)$ for all x and y and if the conditional probability $P(X = x|Y = y)$ equals the marginal probability $P(X = x)$ for all x and y.

If X and Y are independent, we obtain

$$P(X = x|Y = y) = \frac{P(X = x, Y = y)}{P(Y = y)}$$
$$= P(X = x)$$

After manipulating, we see that if X and Y are independent, then

$$P(X = x, Y = y) = P(X = x)\, P(Y = y)$$

Definition: Independence of Two Discrete Random Variables

The discrete random variables X and Y are independent if and only if

$$P(X = x, Y = y) = P(X = x)\, P(y = y)$$

for all possible values of X and Y.

Example 6.15

Checking for Independence: Looking at the data in Table 6.9, is the number of vacations taken independent of the number of credit cards owned?

Solution: Let us examine the case where $X = 3$ and $Y = 2$. We have the marginal probabilities $P(X = 3) = .12$ and $P(Y = 2) = .16$. We also have the joint probability $P(X = 3, Y = 2) = .04$. The product of the marginal probabilities is $P(X = 3)$ $P(Y = 2) = (.12)(.16) = .0192$. Because $P(X = 3, Y = 2)$ does not equal $P(X = 3)$ $P(Y = 2)$, X and Y are *not* independent. This implies that knowledge of the value of X is helpful in predicting the value of Y, and vice versa. ■

Exercises for Section 6.7

1. The Vastola Motor Company has data showing the number of new cars sold (X) and the number of salespersons working (Y) on 200 days. The data are shown in the accompanying table.

Number of Cars Sold (X)	Number of Salespersons Working (Y)		
	1	2	3
0	18	16	12
1	10	14	16
2	16	12	26
3	20	24	16

a. Construct the bivariate probability distribution for X and Y using the relative frequency approach.
b. Find the marginal distribution of X.
c. Find the marginal distribution of Y.
d. Find the conditional probability $P(X = 2|Y = 2)$.
e. Find the conditional probability $P(Y = 2|X = 1)$.
f. Are the random variables X and Y independent?
g. Find the cumulative probability $P(X \leq 2)$.
h. Use the marginal distribution of X and find $E(X)$.

2. The Biringer Marketing Agency has data showing the number of cars (X) and the number of televisions (Y) owned by a sample of 500 families. The data are shown in the accompanying table.

Number of Cars (X)	Number of Televisions (Y) 0	1	2
0	25	30	15
1	50	100	60
2	25	70	45
3	10	40	30

a. Construct the bivariate probability distribution of X and Y using the relative frequency approach.
b. Construct the marginal distribution of X.
c. Construct the marginal distribution of Y.
d. Find $E(X)$.
e. Find $E(Y)$.
f. Find $P(X = 3|Y = 2)$.
g. Find $P(Y = 2|X = 3)$.
h. Find $P(Y \leq 1)$.

3. In a survey taken of 1000 adult males, each person was asked to record his income (X) to the nearest $10,000 and his years of education (Y) to the nearest value of 8, 12, or 16. If income and education are positively correlated, then we should find that low values of income (X) tend to occur with low values of education (Y), and vice versa. The data are shown in the accompanying table.

Income in $10,000s ($X$)	Years of Education (Y) 8	12	16
$10	90	40	10
20	80	170	20
30	70	140	130
40	20	40	80
50	10	20	80

a. Construct the bivariate probability distribution of X and Y.
b. Find the marginal probability of X.
c. Find the marginal distribution of Y.
d. Find $P(X = 10|Y = 8)$ and $P(X = 10|Y = 16)$.
e. Find $P(X = 50|Y = 8)$ and $P(X = 50|Y = 16)$.

4. Suppose that an advertiser wants to determine whether a new product advertised during a noon news program has achieved more name recognition among those who regularly watch that show than among those who do not. Let the random variable X equal 1 if a person watched the noon news and 0 otherwise, and let Y equal 1 if a person correctly identifies the product and 0 otherwise. From a survey, the joint probability distribution for this pair of random variables is estimated as follows:

	X	
Y	0	1
0	.38	.14
1	.30	.18

a. Find the marginal probability distributions of X and Y.
b. Find the conditional probability function of Y given $X = 1$.
c. Are watching the noon news and identification of the product independent of one another?

5. The accompanying data show the joint probability function for the number of repairs in a year and the age in years of copying machines in the mathematics department at a major university.

	Breakdowns			
Age	0	1	2	3
0	.16	.04	.02	.01
1	.15	.06	.04	.01
2	.10	.09	.05	.05
3	.08	.10	.04	.00

a. Find the marginal distribution for the number of breakdowns in a year.
b. Find the marginal distribution for the machine ages.
c. Find the expected number of breakdowns in a year.
d. For machines that are two years old, find the expected number of breakdowns in a year.
e. Find the mean age of the machines.
f. Find the standard deviation of the machine ages.
g. What is the probability that a two-year-old machine will break down at least once a year?

6. A company introduced a new product and classified the responses of customers as favorable or unfavorable in four different cities. The proportions of responses were as follows:

	City			
Response	New York	Boston	Chicago	Detroit
Favorable	.15	.09	.17	.13
Unfavorable	.09	.13	.08	.16

a. What is the probability that a randomly chosen respondent is both favorable to the product and from New York?
b. Find the probability that a respondent from Boston reacts favorably to the product.
c. Is reaction to the product independent of city?
d. Given that a respondent is from Chicago, find the probability that the response is favorable.

6.8 ▪ Computer Applications

The SPSSX computer program can be used to find relative frequencies on a discrete random variable based on a sample of observations, as well as the mean and standard deviation of the variable. For example, suppose we use the sample of data in Table 2.1

to estimate the discrete probability distribution for the number of exemptions claimed by all employees at the Computech Corporation. We make this estimate by determining the relative frequency distribution for the sample of employees. To obtain the frequency, relative frequency, and cumulative relative frequency distributions for the variable EXEMPT, issue the command

```
FREQUENCIES VARIABLES = EXEMPT
```

To obtain the sample mean and sample standard deviation of the variable EXEMPT, insert the command

```
STATISTICS = ALL
```

on the line following the FREQUENCIES command. Thus to get the estimated discrete probability distribution as well as the estimated sample mean and sample standard deviation, issue the commands

```
FREQUENCIES VARIABLES = EXEMPT
STATISTICS = ALL
```

Figure 6.2 shows the computer output generated by these two commands. For example, 17.5% of the 120 employees claimed one exemption, 33.3% of the employees claimed two exemptions, and so forth. The data in the column titled "CUM PERCENT" show cumulative relative frequencies expressed as percentages. For example, 72.5% of the employees claimed three or fewer exemptions; 86.7% of the employees claimed four or fewer exemptions.

FIGURE 6.2 **SPSSX-generated output showing the discrete probability distribution, mean, and standard deviation for the variable EXEMPT in Table 2.1.**

```
EXEMPT

                                                          VALID     CUM
 VALUE LABEL                  VALUE  FREQUENCY  PERCENT  PERCENT  PERCENT

                               1.00        21     17.5     17.5     17.5
                               2.00        40     33.3     33.3     50.8
                               3.00        26     21.7     21.7     72.5
                               4.00        17     14.2     14.2     86.7
                               5.00        12     10.0     10.0     96.7
                               6.00         4      3.3      3.3    100.0
                                      -------  -------  -------
                              TOTAL       120    100.0    100.0

MEAN          2.758    STD ERR       .124     MEDIAN        2.000
MODE          2.000    STD DEV      1.353     VARIANCE      1.832
KURTOSIS     -0.446    S E KURT      .438     SKEWNESS       .595
S E SKEW       .221    RANGE        5.000     MINIMUM       1.000
MAXIMUM       6.000    SUM        331.000

VALID CASES     120    MISSING CASES     0
```

The computer output shows that the mean of the variable EXEMPT is 2.758. This indicates that, on the average, an employee has 2.758 exemptions. The sample standard deviation is 1.353.

Exercises for Section 6.8

1. Refer to the sample of data in Table 2.2 in Chapter 2. The variable Class indicates whether the student is a freshman, sophomore, junior, or senior.
   a. Use the computer to estimate the discrete probability distribution for the variable Class.
   b. Find the mean of the variable Class by using the computer. What does this mean indicate?
   c. Verify the answer in part (b) by using a hand calculator.
2. Refer again to Table 2.2. The variable Major indicates the academic major of each student.
   a. Use the computer to estimate the discrete probability distribution for the variable Major.
   b. Does it make sense to find the mean of the variable Major?

Chapter 6 Summary

When the outcome of an experiment must be one of a countable set of real numbers, the variable being studied is a *discrete random variable* and a table showing the possible values and their corresponding probabilities is a *discrete probability distribution*. Two other ways of representing such a distribution are to graph a bar chart or to find a formula or rule that assigns the appropriate probability to each value of the random variable.

Important characteristics of a random variable are its mean and variance. The *mean*, or expected value, of a discrete random variable represents the average value of the variable if the variable could be observed repeatedly over an indefinite period. The mean, or expected value, of a discrete random variable is found by using the rule

$$E(X) = \Sigma xP(x)$$

The *variance* of a discrete random variable is a measure of the amount of variation in the distribution and is calculated using the rule

$$\sigma^2 = \Sigma(x - \mu)^2P(x)$$

The *standard deviation* is an alternative measure of the amount of variation present in a distribution and is the square root of the variance.

Chapter 6 shows how to analyze the general characteristics of any discrete probability distribution. In Chapter 7, we will discuss the characteristics of several of the most important discrete probability distributions.

Chapter 6 ▪ Supplementary Exercises

1. The Watson Construction Company is bidding on two contracts, one in New York and one in Boston. The probability is .6 of winning the New York contract and .3 of winning the Boston contract. Suppose the contracts are independent of one another. If Watson gets the New York contract, the net profit will be \$20,000; if it does not get the contract, the loss will be \$4000 in costs for preparing the bids. If they get the Boston contract, the net profit will be \$54,000; if they do not get the Boston contract, the loss will be \$9000 in costs. Let X denote the net profit or loss for the Watson Construction Company after making the two bids.

a. Determine the probability distribution of X.
b. Find the mean value of X.

2. An investor is considering three potential investment strategies. Strategy 1 will yield a profit of \$2000 with probability .15 and a loss of \$1000 with probability .85. Strategy 2 will yield a profit of \$1300 with probability .5, a profit of \$600 with probability .3, and a loss of \$500 with probability .2. Strategy 3 will yield a certain profit of \$400.
a. Which strategy has the highest expected profit?
b. Would you advise the investor to adopt the strategy in part (a)?

3. A personnel officer suspects that job applicants who have had many previous jobs are more likely to leave the company relatively quickly after employment than those with few previous jobs. A review of the records for all employees who stayed four years or less yielded the joint probability distribution shown in the table.

Years Before Leaving (Y)	Number of Previous Jobs (X) 1	2	3	4
1	.03	.06	.08	.12
2	.05	.07	.08	.07
3	.05	.08	.06	.02
4	.07	.09	.05	.02

a. Find the marginal probability distribution of X.
b. Find the mean number of previous jobs.
c. Find the marginal probability distribution of Y.
d. Find the mean number of years before leaving.
e. Find the conditional probability distribution of Y given $X = 4$.
f. Are the number of previous jobs and the years before leaving independent of one another?

4. Let X denote the number of times a housewife visits a grocery store in a one-week period. Assume that the table below is the probability distribution of X. Find the expected value of X.

x	0	1	2	3
$P(x)$	.1	.4	.3	.2

5. A potential customer for a \$60,000 fire insurance policy has a home that may sustain a total loss in a given year with a probability of .0005 and a 50% loss with a probability of .001. Ignoring all other partial losses, what premium should the insurance company charge for a yearly policy in order to break even?

6. Many farmers insure their crops each year against possible losses due to bad weather. Determine the annual premium for an insurance policy to cover a farmer's \$500,000 wheat crop. Insurance actuaries suggest that chances are 1 in 50 that the crop will be destroyed by adverse weather conditions.

7. The probability distribution of X, the number of passengers on a daily helicopter shuttle run from Airport A to Airport B, follows:

x	0	1	2	3	4
$P(x)$	.1	.4	.3	.1	.1

a. Find the probability that fewer than three customers will appear on a given day.
b. Find the expected number of customers on a given day.

8. The probability distribution of X, the length of a long distance telephone call in minutes, follows:

x	5	10	15	20
$P(x)$	.3	.5	.1	.1

a. Find the probability that a call will last more than 10 minutes.
b. Find the expected length of a call.
c. Let Y denote the cost of a long distance telephone call in dollars. Suppose the cost per minute is \$0.70 and the initial connection charge is \$0.55. Calculate the expected value of Y.
d. Which would increase the expected cost of the telephone call by more, an increase in the initial connection charge to \$1.00 or an increase in the cost per minute to \$0.85?

9. Suppose the probability that a \$50 million oil drilling platform will be totally lost at sea next year is .006. How much should the platform's owners expect to pay for complete insurance against this contingency in the next year (excluding administrative and other costs and profits of the insurance company)?

10. A farmer's crop will receive a grade of A, B, or C. If the crop is graded A, the farmer will receive \$5.20 per bushel. For grades B and C, the prices per bushel will be \$4.00 and \$3.20, respectively. The probabilities for the grade of the harvest when done at the normal time are $P(\text{A}) = .35$, $P(\text{B}) = .55$, and $P(\text{C}) = .10$. The yield of the harvest at the normal time is expected to be 66,000 bushels. If the harvest is early, the probabilities are $P(\text{A}) = .50$, $P(\text{B}) = .50$, and $P(\text{C}) = 0$, but the yield is reduced to 58,000 bushels. Should the farmer harvest early or at the normal time if he wishes to maximize expected revenue?

11. Consider the following probability distribution for the random variable X:

x	10	20	30	40	50	60
$P(x)$	.05	.25	.35	.20	.10	.05

a. Find the expected value and the variance of X.
b. Graph the distribution.
c. Locate μ and the interval $(\mu - 2\sigma, \mu + 2\sigma)$ on your graph. What is the probability that X will fall within this interval? Does this probability satisfy Chebyshëv's Theorem?

12. A company sells packages of chocolate chip cookies. The numbers of cookies per package vary as follows:

Number of cookies	20	21	22	23
Proportion of packages	.10	.40	.30	

a. Find the missing proportion.
b. Find the mean number of cookies per package.
c. Find the standard deviation of the number of cookies per package.
d. What proportion of packages contain at least 21 cookies?
e. What proportion of packages contain fewer than 22 cookies?
f. The cost (in cents) of producing a package of cookies is $3 + 2.2X$, where X is the number of cookies in the package. That is, packaging costs \$0.03 and cookies cost \$0.022 each. The revenue from selling a package, regardless of how many cookies it contains, is \$0.70. If profit is defined as the difference between revenue and cost, find the expected profit per package.

13. Millions of people are believed to gamble on the outcomes of college and professional football games. In one version of betting, the gamblers pay \$1.00 and select the winners of any four games after one of the teams in each game has been "spotted" enough points so that each team has a 50% chance of winning. If the gambler correctly picks all four winners after taking into account the point spread, then the gambler receives \$10 (i.e., he wins \$9). Otherwise, the gambler loses \$1.00. Let X denote the amount of money that the gambler wins or loses.

a. Find the probability distribution of X.
b. Find the mean value of X. That is, find the expected gain or loss from betting \$1.00.
c. When the gambler wins, he is given \$10. How much should the gambler be given so that the bet is fair? That is, how much should the gambler be given when he wins so that the expected loss is \$0?

14. A company is drilling for oil. When it strikes oil, it expects a profit of \$100,000. The cost of drilling is \$5000. If the probability of striking oil is .1, what is the expected profit for the company from this project?

15. The following information shows the amount of time in minutes by which a mechanic on an assembly line misses the design completion time when working on a certain job. Negative values indicate early completion.

Minutes (x)	-2	-1	0	1	2
$P(x)$	.1	.1	.2	.35	.25

a. Graph the probability distribution of X.
b. Find the mean and variance of X.
c. Find $P(X < 0)$.

16. An individual has \$10,000 to invest. If he or she invests in project A, the estimated profit is \$40,000, \$20,000, or $-$\$10,000 with probabilities .2, .5, and .3, respectively. If he or she invests in project B, the profit is estimated to be \$20,000, \$15,000, or \$0 with probabilities .3, .4, and .3, respectively. Let the random variables X and Y denote the return from projects A and B, respectively. Assume that the investments are independent of one another.

a. Graph the probability distributions of X and Y.
b. Find $E(X)$ and $E(Y)$.
c. In your opinion, which project is the better investment? Note that $E(X)$ exceeds $E(Y)$, but in project A it is possible to lose \$10,000, whereas in project B it is not possible to lose money.

17. A soap manufacturing company is planning to introduce two new laundry detergents. The potential profits or losses are partly dependent on whether the leading competitor is already planning to market similar products. The first product will yield a profit of \$100,000 if the competitor has not developed a competing product but a loss of \$50,000 otherwise. The second product will yield a profit of \$80,000 without competition but a loss of \$30,000 otherwise. The probability that the competitor has developed a rival is .6 for the first product and .7 for the second. Let X denote the total profit or loss from developing the two products. Assume the probabilities are independent of one another.

a. Find the probability distribution of X and graph it.
b. Find the mean value of X.

18. A computer sales representative for T.L.G. Industries gets a certain commission on all sales made. Several months were spent trying to get two large banks to purchase equipment from T.L.G. The sales representative thinks there is a 70% chance that Bank 1 will purchase a small computer, a 20% chance that Bank 1 will purchase a large computer, and a 10% chance that Bank 1 will purchase nothing. Bank 2 will see what Bank 1 does before making its decision. If Bank 1 buys a small computer, there is a 60% chance that Bank 2 will buy a small computer, a 25% chance that it will buy a large computer, and a 15% chance that it will buy nothing. If Bank 1 buys a large computer, there is a 10% chance that Bank 2 will buy a small computer, an 85% chance that it will buy a large computer, and a 5% chance that it will buy nothing. If Bank 1 buys nothing there is a 5% chance that Bank 2 will buy a small computer and a 95% chance that it will buy nothing. The sales representative's commission is \$14,000 on a small computer and \$32,000 on a large computer. Let X denote the total commission earned.

a. Find the probability distribution of X.
b. Find the sales representative's expected commission.

19. Suppose that a race car driver will drive in four races and always has a $\frac{1}{3}$ probability of winning any specific race. The driver signs a contract with an advertiser. The driver's bonus is based on how many races he or she wins. For one win and three losses, the bonus is \$5000; for two wins and two losses, the bonus is \$10,000; for three wins and one loss, the bonus is \$20,000. If the driver wins all four races, the bonus is \$50,000, and if the driver loses all four races, \$5000 must be paid back from his or her salary; that is, the bonus is − \$5000. Let X denote the driver's bonus.
a. Find the probability distribution of X.
b. Find the mean value of X.

20. When it is sunny, a man walks to work at a cost of \$0.00. When it is cloudy, he takes the bus, which costs \$1.00. When it is raining, he drives his car, which costs \$2.00. It is sunny 50% of the time, cloudy 30% of the time, and raining 20% of the time. Find the average or expected cost of a trip to work.

21. Julie is shopping for an automobile insurance policy. During the following year, there is a .01 probability that her car will be totally destroyed in an accident and she will lose \$5000. There is a .05 probability that she will have an accident in which she will lose \$2500. There is a .20 probability that an accident will cause \$300 in damage. Suppose she pays \$300 for her insurance policy. What is the insurance company's expected profit on her policy? That is, find the difference between the price of the policy and the company's expected payment to Julie.

22. Suppose you buy an insurance policy that pays you \$1000 if a certain event occurs. Suppose the probability that this event occurs is .04. You pay a premium P to purchase the insurance. What premium should you pay to make your expected gains or losses equal to \$0?

23. Ed Conner contacts people and tries to convince them to purchase a one-, two-, or three-year subscription to *Sports Illustrated* magazine. Of those people contacted, 10% buy a one-year subscription, 5% buy a two-year subscription, and 4% buy a three-year subscription. The remaining 81% do not buy anything. Ed's commission is \$2 for each one-year subscription, \$5 for each two-year subscription, and \$10 for each three-year subscription.
a. On his next contact, what is Ed's expected commission?
b. If Ed contacts 100 people, how much money can he expect to earn?

24. A store owner stocks an out-of-town newspaper that a small number of customers sometimes request. Each copy of this newspaper costs the owner 22¢ and is sold for 35¢. Any copies left over at the end of the day have no value and are destroyed. The probability distribution of the number of requests for the newspaper in a day is as follows:

Number of requests	0	1	2	3	4	5
Probability	.10	.15	.20	.30	.15	.10

If the store owner defines total daily profit as total revenue from newspaper sales less total cost of newspapers ordered, how many copies per day should he order to maximize expected profit?

25. A promoter is bidding for the rights to a rock concert. After paying all expenses, the promoter thinks there is a 20% chance of losing \$50,000, a 45% chance of earning a net profit of \$20,000, and a 35% chance of earning a net profit of \$50,000. Find the expected profit from promoting the concert.

26. You have two friends who want to bet you on an upcoming basketball game. One wants to bet you that the Boston Celtics will beat the Los Angeles Lakers, while the second wants to bet you that the Lakers will beat the Celtics. The first will put up \$1 for every \$1 that you bet. The second will put up \$1.30 for every \$0.70 that you wager.
a. If you bet \$50 with each friend, find your net profit if the Celtics win. If the Lakers win.
b. If you bet \$40 with the first friend and \$60 with the second, find your net profit if the Celtics win. If the Lakers win.
c. Assume the probability that the Celtics win is .5. If you have \$100 available, how should you divide your wagers between these two gamblers to maximize your expected net profit?

References

FELLER, WILLIAM. *An Introduction to Probability Theory and Its Applications*. 2 vols. New York: Wiley, 1950–1966.

FREUND, JOHN E., and R. E. WALPOLE. *Mathematical Statistics*. 4th ed. Englewood Cliffs, N.J.: Prentice-Hall, 1987.

MOOD, ALEXANDER M., and FRANKLIN A. GRAYBILL. *Introduction to the Theory of Statistics*. 3d ed. New York: McGraw-Hill, 1973.

Chapter Seven
Some Important Discrete Distributions

In Chapter 6 we discussed how to construct a discrete probability distribution as well as how to calculate the expected value and variance of any discrete random variable. Recall that for any probability distribution we are interested in several important characteristics:

1. *Formula:* Is there a general mathematical formula that we can use to determine the probability that certain events will occur?
2. *Shape:* What is the general shape of the distribution? Is it symmetric? Is it skewed to the right or left? Over what interval is most of the probability concentrated? Are there long tails in either direction?
3. *Mean:* Where is the center of gravity of the distribution? That is, what is the expected value, or mean, of the random variable?
4. *Standard deviation and variance:* How spread out is the distribution? What is the variance or standard deviation of the distribution?

Several different discrete probability distributions occur over and over again in business, economics, and numerous other fields. In this chapter, we discuss the characteristics of the most important discrete probability distributions: the Bernoulli, the binomial, the hypergeometric, the geometric, and the Poisson distributions.

7.1 ▪ The Bernoulli Distribution

The **Bernoulli distribution,** named after Jakob Bernoulli (1654–1705), is the simplest of all discrete probability distributions. Consider an experiment that must result in one of two possible mutually exclusive basic outcomes. For convenience, we will label these outcomes as "success" (denoted by the letter s) and "failure" (denoted by the letter f). The sample space of the experiment is thus $S = \{\text{success, failure}\}$, or more simply $S = \{s, f\}$. Let p denote the probability of a success and $q = (1 - p)$ denote the probability of a failure. Now define a discrete random variable X such that X takes the value 1 if the outcome of the experiment is a success and the value 0 otherwise. This random variable X is called a **Bernoulli random variable** and follows the Bernoulli distribution.

Example 7.1

Some Examples of Bernoulli Experiments: In each experiment, let X equal 1 if a success occurs and 0 if a failure occurs.

(a) Toss a coin. Determine if it lands heads up (s) or tails up (f).
(b) Select a product randomly. Determine if it is good (s) or defective (f).
(c) Select a person randomly. Determine if the person is employed (s) or unemployed (f).
(d) Select a shopper randomly. Determine if the shopper did (s) or did not (f) purchase a particular product.
(e) Select an investment. Determine if the investment did (s) or did not (f) yield a profit. ■

The mean and variance of the Bernoulli distribution can be found by applying the definitions for the mean and variance of any discrete random variable. The mean is

$$\begin{aligned} E(X) &= \Sigma\, xP(X = x) \\ &= 0P(0) + 1P(1) \\ &= 0(1 - p) + 1p = p \end{aligned}$$

and the variance is

$$\begin{aligned} \sigma^2 &= \Sigma(x - \mu)^2 P(X = x) \\ &= (0 - p)^2(1 - p) + (1 - p)^2 p \\ &= p(1 - p) = pq \end{aligned}$$

Characteristics of the Bernoulli Distribution

Probability Function, Mean, Variance, and Standard Deviation of the Bernoulli Distribution

Let X be a discrete random variable that has the Bernoulli distribution, where the probability of a success is p and the probability of a failure is $(1 - p)$. The sample space of X is $S = \{0, 1\}$, and the probability function of X is

$$P(X = 0) = 1 - p, \quad P(X = 1) = p$$

The mean, variance, and standard deviation of X are as follows:

$$\begin{aligned} \mu &= E(X) = p \\ \sigma^2 &= \text{Var}(X) = p(1 - p) = pq \\ \sigma &= \sqrt{pq} \end{aligned}$$

Example 7.2

A Bernoulli Random Variable: An individual has just had a new solar room added to the rear of his house. The customer is told that, within five years, approximately 30% of all solar rooms develop leaks around the windows because the rubber seals harden. Let the random variable X take the value 1 if leaks develop within five years and the value 0 if no leaks develop in that time. Then X is a Bernoulli random variable where the probability of a leak is $p = .3$. The probability distribution of X is

$$P(0) = .7, \quad P(1) = .3$$

The expected value of X is

$$E(X) = p = .3$$

The variance of X is

$$\sigma_X^2 = p(1 - p) = .3(.7) = .21$$

The standard deviation is

$$\sigma = \sqrt{.21} = .458$$

Figure 7.1 shows a graph of the probability distribution of X.

FIGURE 7.1
The Bernoulli distribution for Example 7.2.

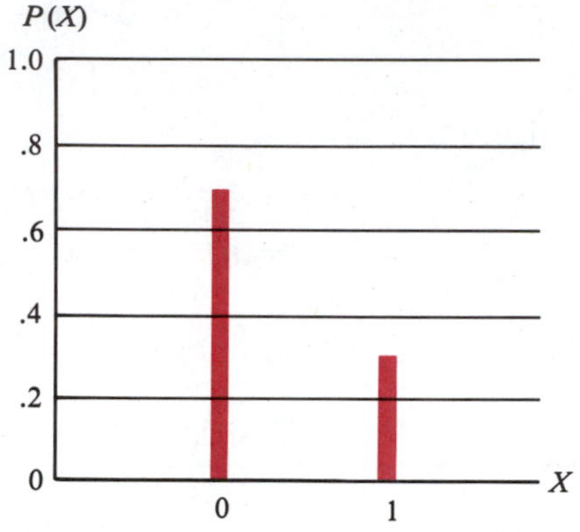

For any Bernoulli random variable, the graph of the probability distribution consists of two spikes, one above the value $X = 0$ and another above $X = 1$. In Figure 7.1, the lengths of the spikes above $X = 0$ and $X = 1$ represent $P(X = 0)$ and $P(X = 1)$, respectively.

Exercises for Section 7.1

1. A class contains 60 males and 20 females. One student is selected randomly. Let X be 0 if the student is female and 1 if the student is male.
a. Find the probability distribution of X.
b. Derive the mean and variance of X.

2. In Detroit, 15% of the residents are unemployed. A resident of Detroit is selected randomly. Let the random variable X be 0 if the person selected is employed and 1 if the person is unemployed.
a. Find the probability distribution of X.
b. Derive the mean and variance of X.

7.2 ▪ The Binomial Distribution

The Bernoulli distribution applies to an experiment that is performed just once and has only two possible outcomes, "success" and "failure." An important generalization of the Bernoulli distribution occurs when a random experiment with two possible outcomes is repeated several times. This generalization leads to the concept of the **binomial distribution**.

In a binomial experiment, the random variable X denotes the number of successes obtained in n repeated independent trials of a Bernoulli experiment. The probability of obtaining a success on any trial is denoted by the letter p. Because the trials are independent of one another, this probability remains constant for all trials. If p denotes the probability of a success, then $q = (1 - p)$ is the probability of a failure on any trial. Numerous problems fit this model, at least approximately.

Example 7.3 **Examples of Binomial Experiments:**

(a) A manufacturing firm claims that about 2% of its products are defective. Suppose we randomly select 10 products and test them. If the products are randomly selected, the outcome of any test is independent of any other test. Thus, we have performed the experiment 10 independent times. Let X denote the number of defective products obtained in the sample of size $n = 10$. The random variable X is a binomial random variable where $p = .02$.

(b) In Alabama 10% of the labor force is unemployed. Select a random sample of $n = 100$ individuals. Let X denote the number of individuals in the sample who are unemployed. Then X is a binomial random variable with $p = .1$.

(c) A brokerage firm sends an application form to a random sample of $n = 300$ individuals asking them to invest in the firm's new mutual fund. Industry data indicate that approximately 5% of the people who receive such an application eventually reply. Let X denote the number of replies received in this sample of $n = 300$ individuals. Then X is a binomial random variable with $p = .05$.

(d) Industry data show that 25% of the people who purchase contact lenses experience difficulty and stop wearing the lenses within one year. We take a random sample of $n = 60$ individuals who have just purchased contact lenses. Let X denote the number of these individuals who stop wearing the lenses within one year. Then X is a binomial random variable with $p = .25$. ■

If a Bernoulli experiment has been performed n independent times, the possible number of successes in n trials must be one of the values $0, 1, 2, \ldots, n$. Thus, the sample space for the binomial random variable X is $S = \{0, 1, 2, \ldots, n\}$. Now we want to derive a general mathematical formula, or probability function, that will enable us to calculate the probability of obtaining a specific number of successes in independent trials of an experiment.

Example 7.4 **Derivation of the Binomial Probability Function:** Based on past data, approximately 30% of the oil wells drilled in areas having a certain favorable geological formation have struck oil. A company has identified $n = 5$ locations that possess this formation. Because the locations are widely separated, it is safe to assume that the chance of striking oil on any location is independent of the chance of striking oil on any of the others. The company decides to drill a well on each of the 5 sites. Calculate the probability that exactly 2 of the 5 wells strike oil.

Solution: The number of independent trials is $n = 5$. The probability of a success on any trial is $p = .3$. Thus, the probability of a failure is $q = (1 - p) = .7$. Let the random variable X denote the number of successes in five attempts. We want to know the probability that $X = 2$. Let A denote the event A = {exactly 2 successes in 5 attempts}. We obtain the basic outcomes A = {*ssfff, sfsff, sffsf, sfffs, fssff, fsfsf, fsffs, ffssf, ffsfs, fffss*}. Since we obtain 2 successes in 5 attempts if any 1 of the 10 basic outcomes of A occurs, we have

$$\begin{aligned} P(A) &= P(X = 2) = P(ssfff) + P(sfsff) + \cdots + P(fffss) \\ &= (.3)^2(.7)^3 + (.3)^2(.7)^3 + \cdots + (.3)^2(.7)^3 \\ &= 10(.3)^2(.7)^3 = .3087 \end{aligned}$$

In this equation, the number 10 represents the number of basic outcomes in event A; that is, it represents the number of ways of arranging 2 successes and 3 failures among 5 attempts. The number of ways of arranging 2 successes and 3 failures is given by the combination formula

$$_5C_2 = \frac{5!}{2!\,(5 - 2)!} = 10$$

The number $(.3)^2(.7)^3$ represents the probability of any single basic outcome in event A, such as {*sfsff*}. ■

The method used in Example 7.4 can be used to determine any binomial probability.

General Formula for the Binomial Distribution

Formula for the Binomial Distribution

Let the random variable X denote the number of successes obtained in n independent trials of an experiment where the probability of a success on any trial is p. Let $q = (1 - p)$. Let x denote a certain value of the random variable X. The probability of x successes in n trials is given by the formula

$$P(X = x) = {}_nC_x\, p^x q^{n-x} \qquad x = 0, 1, 2, \ldots, n$$

where the symbol $_nC_x$ denotes the combination formula

$$_nC_x = \frac{n!}{x!(n - x)!}$$

Example 7.5

Using the Binomial Formula: In Example 7.4, find the complete probability distribution of X where X denotes the number of successes when 5 independent wells are drilled.

Solution: The complete probability distribution of X is shown in Table 7.1 and illustrated in Figure 7.2. The probability $P(X = 0)$ is represented by the area of the rectangle

TABLE 7.1
Distribution of oil strikes in Example 7.5

x	Probability	$P(X = x)$
0	${}_5C_0(.3)^0(.7)^5$	.16807
1	${}_5C_1(.3)^1(.7)^4$	.36015
2	${}_5C_2(.3)^2(.7)^3$	.30870
3	${}_5C_3(.3)^3(.7)^2$	.13230
4	${}_5C_4(.3)^4(.7)^1$	.02835
5	${}_5C_5(.3)^5(.7)^0$	.00243
		1.00000

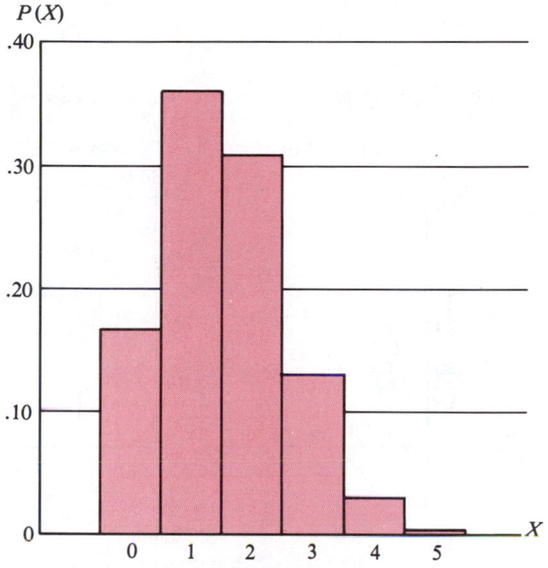

FIGURE 7.2
Binomial distribution for Example 7.5 where $n = 5$ and $p = .3$.

extending from -0.5 to 0.5 that is centered at $X = 0$; the probability $P(X = 1)$ is represented by the area of the rectangle extending from 0.5 to 1.5 that is centered at $X = 1$; and so forth. The areas of all the rectangles sum to 1. Because the width of each rectangle is one unit, the height of each rectangle is the same as the area of the rectangle.

Shape of the Binomial Distribution

Actually, the binomial distribution is a family of distributions. There is a different binomial distribution for each set of values of the parameters n and p, and the shape of the binomial distribution varies with these values. For $p = .5$, the graph of the binomial distribution is symmetric. That is, the probability of obtaining 0 successes and n failures in n trials will be the same as the probability of obtaining n successes and 0 failures in n trials; the probability of 1 success and $(n - 1)$ failures will be the same as the probability of 1 failure and $(n - 1)$ successes; and so forth.

If p is greater than .5, successes are more likely than failures, and the graph of the binomial distribution is not symmetric. The probabilities on the right-hand side of the graph will be larger than those on the left-hand side. If p is less than .5, the argument is just reversed, as is evident in Example 7.5.

An interesting characteristic of the graph of the binomial distribution for p close to .5 is its bell shape. It can be shown that when the number of trials n becomes larger and larger, the graph of the binomial distribution always becomes bell shaped. If p is very close to .5, this bell-shaped appearance is evident even when n is fairly small. In general, a bell-shaped curve can be used to approximate the probabilities of the binomial distribution provided n and p are such that $np \geqslant 5$ and $nq \geqslant 5$. This will be discussed in more detail in Chapter 8.

FIGURE 7.3 **Graphs of binomial distributions for various values of *n* and *p*.**

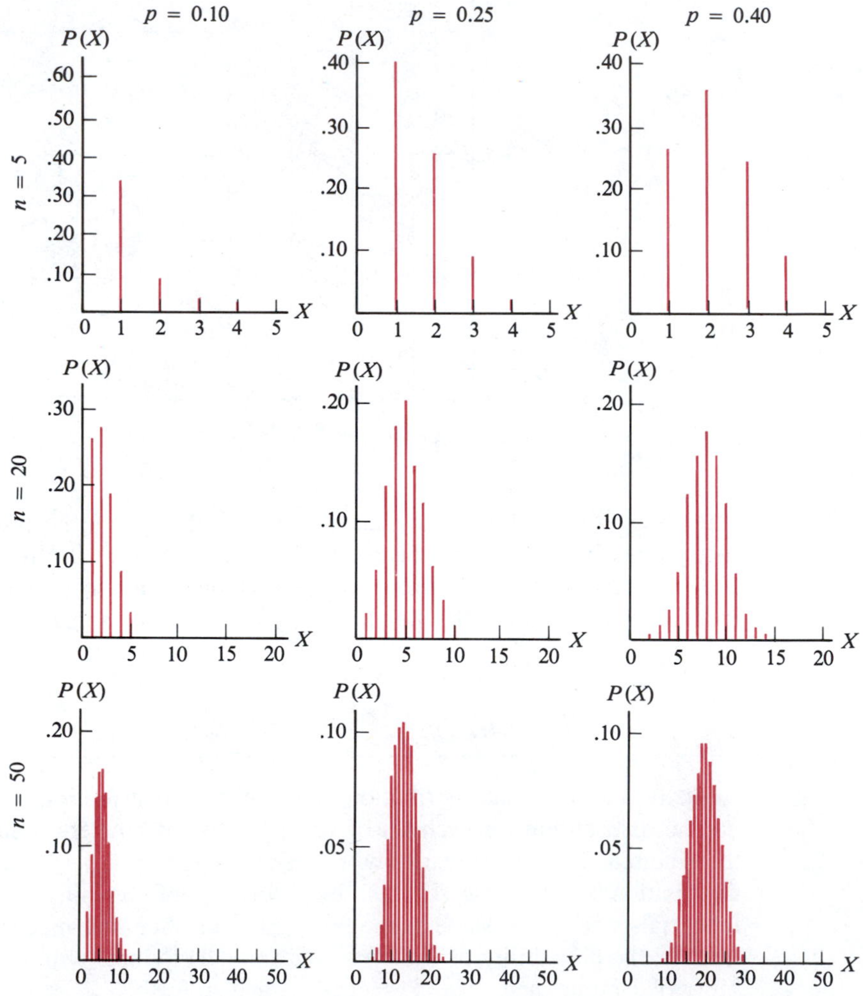

Figure 7.3 shows the graphs of several binomial distributions for various values of n and p. Observe how the probability shifts to the right as p increases. Also, observe that the distribution becomes more symmetric as p approaches .5.

Mean and Variance of the Binomial Distribution

Mean, Variance, and Standard Deviation for the Binomial Distribution

Let X denote the number of successes obtained in n independent trials of an experiment where the probability of success on any trial is p. Let $q = 1 - p$. The mean, variance, and standard deviation of X are as follows:

$$\mu = E(X) = np$$
$$\sigma^2 = \text{Var}(X) = npq$$
$$\sigma = \sqrt{npq}$$

The mean value of X represents the average number of successes that would be obtained in n independent trials.

Example 7.6 **Mean and Variance of the Binomial Distribution:**

(a) Find the mean, variance, and standard deviation of the random variable X in Example 7.5, where $n = 5$ and $p = .3$.

Solution: We obtain

$$E(X) = np = 5(.3) = 1.5$$
$$\text{Var}(X) = npq = 5(.3)(.7) = 1.05$$
$$\sigma = \sqrt{npq} = \sqrt{1.05} = 1.025$$

(b) Verify that the mean is 1.5 by actual computation.

Solution: For any discrete random variable, the mean is obtained by using the formula

$$E(X) = \Sigma\, xP(X = x)$$

By using the probabilities given in Example 7.5, we obtain

$$\begin{aligned} E(X) &= 0P(0) + 1P(1) + \cdots + 5P(5) \\ &= 0(.16807) + 1(.36015) + 2(.30870) \\ &\quad + 3(.13230) + 4(.02835) + 5(.00243) \\ &= 1.5 \end{aligned}$$

■

Using the Binomial Table

In many practical applications, we want to calculate the probability that a binomial variable X assumes any one of the values 0, 1, 2, . . . , c, where c is some integer between 0 and n. That is, we want to determine the *cumulative probability* $P(X \leq c)$. The cumulative binomial distribution function is given in Table A.2 of the Appendix, which shows $P(X \leq c)$ for selected values of n, p, and c. More extensive tables are available, but the tables rarely go beyond $n = 50$. As will be shown in Chapter 8, the normal distribution often provides an excellent approximation to the binomial distribution, thus reducing the need for tables for $n > 50$.

Example 7.7

Use of the Binomial Table: According to the Internal Revenue Service, approximately 20% of all income tax returns contain mathematical errors. Find the probability that 3 or fewer returns out of a random sample of 10 contain mathematical errors.

Solution: Let X denote the number of returns containing a mathematical error. Then X follows the binomial distribution with $n = 10$ and $p = .20$. We seek

$$P(X \leq 3) = P(X = 0) + P(X = 1) + P(X = 2) + P(X = 3)$$

From Table A.2, using $n = 10$, $p = .20$, and $c = 3$, we obtain

$$P(X \leq 3) = .8791$$

■

Sampling with and without Replacement

Suppose that a proportion p of the items in a certain population possess a certain characteristic. There are two ways to obtain a random sample of size n from the population—with or without replacement. If we sample with replacement, then the probability is always p that the next item chosen will possess the characteristic. If we sample without replacement from a finite population, then the probability that the second item selected has the characteristic will be greater than or less than p, depending upon whether or not the first item possessed the characteristic. If sampling is done without replacement from a finite population, then successive selections are not independent; the probabilities change after each selection. If the population is large relative to the sample size, however, then the probabilities change very little on successive drawings, and we can proceed as if successive drawings were independent of one another. For this reason, the binomial distribution is often used despite the fact that a sample has been selected without replacement.

Sample Proportion of Successes

Frequently statisticians are more interested in the proportion of successes in a sample than in the number of successes. If we obtain X successes in n trials, then the sample proportion $\hat{p}$ is calculated using the formula $\hat{p} = X/n$.

The random variable X must take one of the discrete values $0, 1, 2, \ldots, n$; similarly, the random variable $\hat{p}$ must take one of the values $0/n, 1/n, 2/n, \ldots, 1$. For example, when $X = 3$, $\hat{p} = 3/n$. Also, the probability that $X = 3$ is the same as the probability that $\hat{p} = 3/n$. For any specific value x, we obtain

$$P(X = x) = P(\hat{p} = x/n)$$

This shows that the probability distribution for the random variable $\hat{p}$ can be derived from the probability distribution of X.

Example 7.8

Probabilities for the Sample Proportion: An experiment is tried 10 independent times, and the probability of a success on any trial is $p = .3$. Find the probability of obtaining a success on 40% of the trials.

Solution: Let X denote the number of successes in 10 trials. Then X follows the binomial distribution with $n = 10$ and $p = .3$. We have

$$P(\hat{p} = .4) = P(\hat{p} = 4/10) = P(X = 4)$$
$$= {}_{10}C_4(.3)^4(.7)^6 = .2001$$

■

Mean and Variance of $\hat{p}$

Let $\hat{p}$ denote the sample proportion of successes obtained in n independent trials of an experiment. The expected value of $\hat{p}$ is

$$E(\hat{p}) = p$$

This result means that the sample proportion $\hat{p}$ is an unbiased estimator of the population proportion p.

In addition, it is possible to show that the variance of $\hat{p}$ is

$$\text{Var}(\hat{p}) = pq/n$$

Of course, the standard deviation of the random variable $\hat{p}$ is then $\sqrt{pq/n}$.

Knowledge of the mean and variance of $\hat{p}$ can help us test hypotheses about the population parameter p.

Example 7.9

Testing a Claim about the Population Proportion: A councilman claims that at least 30% of the voters of a large city are in favor of increasing taxes on alcoholic beverages. To test this claim, a polling agent obtains a random sample of 500 voters. Suppose that $X = 100$ voters in the sample say they favor the tax. Thus, the sample proportion is $\hat{p} = 100/500 = .2$. Is it reasonable to reject the claim that in the population p is at least .3?

Solution: If the claim is true, then the sample proportion $\hat{p}$ has expected value $E(\hat{p}) = p = .3$. The variance of $\hat{p}$ is given by

$$\text{Var}(\hat{p}) = pq/n = (.3)(.7)/500 = .00042$$

and the standard deviation of $\hat{p}$ is $\sqrt{.00042} \approx .02$.

Because the distribution of X is bell shaped, so is the distribution of $\hat{p}$. By applying the Empirical Rule, we can state that in repeated sampling more than 99% of the values of $\hat{p}$ should fall within 3 standard deviations of the mean. This interval is

$$(.3 - .06, .3 + .06) = (.24, .36)$$

Since our observed value $\hat{p} = .2$ lies outside this interval, we have strong evidence that in the population $\hat{p}$ does not equal .3. If p were .3, it would be quite unusual to observe a value as extreme as $\hat{p} = .2$ in a sample size of $n = 500$. ■

Tips on Problem Solving
You can recognize a binomial distribution problem by the fact that the same experiment is performed over and over again n times. To solve the problem, you need to know the probability p of a success on any single trial. Thus, this probability has to be stated somewhere in the problem. Record the values of n and p. Next record the value of X, the desired number of successes. If n is small, you can do the calculations on a hand calculator or use the tables in the Appendix. If n is large, you will want to approximate binomial probabilities by using the Poisson distribution, discussed in Section 7.5, or the normal distribution, discussed in Section 8.5.

Exercises for Section 7.2

1. About 30% of the adult population are smokers. Use the binomial distribution and find the probability that 2 out of 5 randomly selected adults are smokers.

2. An advertising agency seeks comments on an advertisement that appeared during television coverage of the Super Bowl. About 40% of the adult population saw the Super Bowl on TV. If the agency takes a random sample of 4 adults, find the probability that exactly 2 of them saw the Super Bowl.

3. On any given day, about 45% of the stocks on the American Stock Exchange increase in value.
a. If I randomly select 4 independent stocks, what is the probability that exactly 3 of them increase in value?
b. What is the probability that at least 3 stocks increase in value?

4. In a very large class, 40% of the students favor a take-home test over an in-class test. A random sample of 6 students is taken. What is the probability that a majority in the sample favor the following:
a. Take-home tests
b. In-class tests
(If we sample without replacement, the probabilities change slightly on every selection. To avoid this problem, assume the sampling is done with replacement, or assume that the class is so large that the changes in the probabilities are insignificant.)

5. Approximately 20% of the cars produced by a certain manufacturer have a defect. A sales representative receives a shipment of 5 randomly selected cars.
a. What is the probability that 1 car has a defect?
b. What is the probability that at least 1 car has a defect?
c. Let X denote the number of defective cars. List the possible values of X and their probabilities.
d. Calculate the mean value of X using part (c).

6. A book publisher thinks that about 25% of the books it decides to publish are ultimately profitable. Four independent books are accepted for publication. What is the probability of the following:
a. None are profitable.
b. All 4 are profitable.

7. About 20% of all pro football players are injured during a given season. A team has 4 star players. What is the probability that at least 1 of the star players gets injured?

8. A manufacturer of digital watches claims that the probability of its watch running more than one minute fast or slow after a year of use is .05. A consumer protection agency has purchased 3 of the manufacturer's watches with the intention of testing the claim.

a. If the manufacturer's claim is correct, what is the probability that all 3 of the watches are accurate within a minute?
b. If the manufacturer's claim is correct, what is the probability that exactly 2 of the 3 watches fail to meet the claim?

9. A plumber installs 6 hot water heaters in a particular housing development. The probability that any individual heater will last more than ten years is .7, and their lives are independent. Let X denote the number of water heaters that last more than 10 years.
a. Construct the probability distribution of X.
b. Find the probability that more than 3 of the water heaters will last more than 10 years.
c. Find the mean and variance of the random variable X.

10. An accountant believes that 10% of the company's invoices contain arithmetic errors. To check this, the accountant randomly samples 10 invoices and finds that 3 contain errors. If the accountant's theory is correct, what is the probability that 3 or more invoices contain errors in a random sample of 10?

11. A critical component of a machine operates successfully only 75% of the time. To increase the reliability of the system, 4 of the components will be installed so that the system will operate successfully if at least one of the components is functioning correctly. What is the probability that the system will fail? Assume that the components operate independently.

12. A doctor estimates that 5% of her patients have no real physical ailment. We randomly sample the records of the doctor and find that 3 of 15 patients had no ailment.
a. What is the probability of observing 3 or more patients who have no ailment in a sample of 15 patients if the population proportion is actually .05?
b. Why might your answer to part (a) make you believe that p is larger than .05?

13. Approximately 10% of all computers are returned for repair while their guarantee is still in effect. If a firm purchased 9 computers, what is the probability that 3 or more will need repair while their guarantees are still in effect?

14. About 5% of the finished products coming off an assembly line are defective. What is the probability that at least 1 of the next 4 products coming off the line is defective? What assumption do you have to make to solve this problem?

15. An apartment manager knows that 15% of new washing machines purchased require maintenance during the first year of operation. The manager purchases 4 new machines. Assume the performances of the machines are independent of one another.
a. What is the probability that all 4 machines will require maintenance during the first year of operation?
b. What is the probability that none of them will require maintenance during the first year of operation?
c. What is the probability that at least 2 of them will require maintenance during the first year of operation?

16. Approximately 50% of a bank's customers would be willing to pay a fee to have pay-by-phone privileges. A sample is taken of 6 of the bank's customers. Let X denote the number who would pay for pay-by-phone privileges.
a. Construct the probability distribution of X.
b. Graph the probability distribution of X.
c. Calculate $E(X)$.

17. A doctor knows that about 20% of the population will have a bad reaction to a certain type of medicine. The doctor prescribes the medicine for 20 patients. Find the probability that the number of patients who suffer a bad reaction is the following:
a. Less than 5
b. More than 2
c. Exactly 3

18. Suppose that X is a random variable having the binomial distribution. Given the following data, graph the distribution of X using rectangles.

a. $n = 5, p = .1$
b. $n = 5, p = .9$
c. $n = 5, p = .5$

19. Let X be a binomial variable with $p = .5$. Let $n = 10$. Which of the following statements are true? Can you prove your answers?
a. $P(X = 0) = P(X = 1)$
b. $P(X = 0) = P(X = n)$
c. $P(X = 1) = P(X = n)$
d. $P(X = 1) = P(X = n - 1)$
e. $P(X = 2) = P(X = n - 2)$

20. A survey indicates that the probability of any student purchasing the school yearbook is .7. The school has 1000 students and the yearbook costs $12.
a. What is the expected number of sales?
b. What is the expected revenue from yearbook sales?

21. The airline industry thinks that about 1 commercial flight in 100,000 results in a crash. On the average, a crash of a commercial jet results in $1 million damages. Suppose that Southeast Airlines expects to have 40,000 commercial flights this year.
a. What is the expected number of crashes for Southeast Airlines?
b. What are the expected damages?

22. The National Record Store has taken surveys which indicate that 25% of the people who enter the store make a purchase. A survey of the cash register tapes indicates that the average revenue from a sale is $5.50. Next year the store expects to have 100,000 people entering its store.
a. What is the expected number of people who will make a purchase?
b. What is the expected revenue for the year?

23. Surveys indicate that 85% of the people who go to a racetrack bet on the first race. The surveys also indicate that the average bet is $3.20. The attendance at a race track is 10,000.
a. How many of these people would you expect to make a bet on the first race?
b. How much money would you expect to be bet on the first race?

7.3 ▪ Binomial Distribution Application: Acceptance Sampling

An important application of the binomial distribution is in *acceptance sampling*. When a firm receives a very large shipment of goods from a manufacturer, it has to decide whether to accept the delivery based on information about the quality of the goods received. Typically an inspection of every item in the shipment is prohibitively expensive and time consuming, so a small random sample of items is selected. Based on the results of an examination of this sample, the firm decides whether to accept the shipment.

For example, the firm might decide to examine $n = 10$ items. As a decision rule, the firm might decide to reject the shipment if the number of defective items in the sample is 2 or more. With a decision rule of this kind, it is possible to calculate the probability of accepting or rejecting a shipment with any given proportion of defectives. This is true because if p is the proportion of defectives in the shipment and n is the number of items sampled, the number of defectives in the sample follows the binomial distribution. In this analysis, it is assumed that the number of items in the sample is a very small proportion of the total number of items in the shipment; thus successive examinations of goods can be considered to be approximately independent of one another.

Example 7.10

Acceptance Sampling: A company receives a very large shipment of goods. Unknown to the company, 10% of the items in the shipment are defective. The firm decides to accept the shipment if fewer than 2 of 20 randomly selected items are found to be defective. Thus, the shipment will be accepted if the number X of defectives in the sample is 0 or 1. We have

$$P(\text{shipment is accepted}) = P(0) + P(1)$$

For the binomial distribution with $n = 20$ and $p = .1$, we have $P(0) = .1216$ and $P(1) = .2701$. Thus, the probability that the shipment will be accepted is

$$P(\text{shipment is accepted}) = .1216 + .2701 = .3917$$

Now suppose that 20% of the items in the shipment are defective. For the binomial distribution with $n = 20$ and $p = .2$, we obtain $P(0) = .0115$ and $P(1) = .0577$. If in fact 20% of the items are defective, the probability of accepting the shipment is

$$P(\text{shipment is accepted}) = .0115 + .0577 = .0692$$

By following a similar procedure for $p = .3$, we obtain

$$P(\text{shipment is accepted}) = .0008 + .0068 = .0076$$

■

The higher the proportion of defectives in a shipment, the lower the probability of accepting the shipment. For any proportion of defectives and any decision rule, the probability of accepting the delivery can be calculated. For a given decision rule, we can graph the probability of accepting the delivery against p, the proportion of defective items in the shipment. Such a graph, shown in Figure 7.4, gives the acceptance probabilities for any proportion p of defective items.

FIGURE 7.4
Probability of accepting a shipment as a function of the proportion of defectives in the entire shipment; in this figure, the shipment is accepted if there are fewer than 2 defectives in a random sample of 20 items.

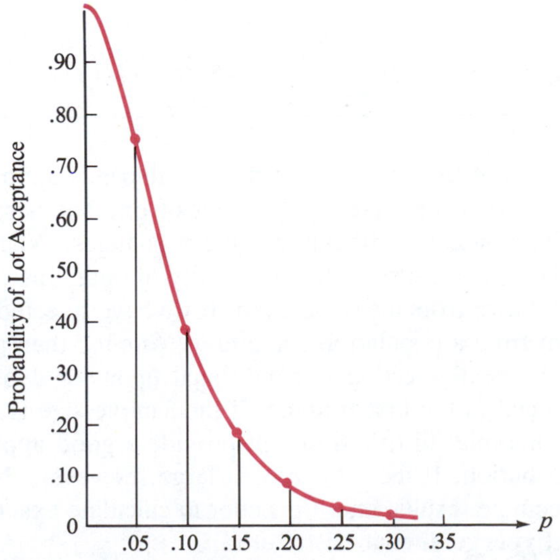

Different curves relating acceptance probabilities to the proportion of defectives in the shipment can be constructed by choosing different sample sizes n and different decision rules. In this way, a company can choose a procedure that balances the costs of accepting a shipment with a particular proportion of defectives against the costs of inspecting the n items.

Exercises for Section 7.3

1. A large university receives a shipment of 500 electronic typewriters. It chooses a sample of 10 typewriters and will reject the shipment if 1 or more of the typewriters are defective. What is the probability that this agency will accept the shipment if the proportion that is defective is .05?
2. An automobile manufacturer inspects each shipment of new tires. Each shipment (which contains 500 tires) is subjected to the following acceptance sampling procedure: Each of a sample of 8 tires taken from the shipment is tested for defects. If more than 1 of the tires are found to be defective, the shipment is rejected.
   a. If a shipment contains 10% defectives, what is the probability that it will be accepted?
   b. If a shipment contains 5% defectives, what is the probability that it will be accepted?
   c. If a shipment contains 1% defectives, what is the probability that it will be accepted?
3. A company receives a very large shipment of parts. A random sample of 12 is checked. If fewer than 2 are defective, the shipment will be accepted. What is the probability of accepting a shipment containing the following proportion of defectives?
   a. 5% b. 10% c. 20%
4. The following two acceptance rules are being considered for the delivery of a large shipment of components:
   a. A random sample of 8 components is checked, and the shipment is rejected if 1 or more are defective.
   b. A random sample of 16 components is checked, and the shipment is rejected if 2 or more are defective.

   Which of these rules has the smaller probability of accepting a shipment containing 20% defectives?

7.4 ▪ The Hypergeometric Distribution (Optional)

The use of the binomial distribution depends upon the assumption that successive trials of an experiment are independent of one another; thus, the probability of obtaining a success on any particular trial never changes. When we sample from a finite population without replacement, the probability of obtaining a success changes as sample units are withdrawn from the population. If we have selected a sample of n items without replacement from a population containing N items, then the probability of obtaining a success on the next selection is conditional upon, or depends upon, the number of successes obtained in the first n items. If the sample size is small relative to the population size, the binomial distribution will provide a good approximation to the correct probability distribution. If the ratio n/N is large, however, the binomial distribution may provide inaccurate results, and it is better to calculate exact probabilities by using what is called the **hypergeometric distribution**.

In general, the binomial distribution is used when sampling without replacement from a finite population provided the sample size n is less than 5% of the population size. If n/N exceeds 5%, then it is preferable to calculate the exact probabilities by using the hypergeometric distribution.

Let the random variable X denote the number of successes obtained when a random sample of n items is selected without replacement from a finite population containing N elements, of which N_1 are successes and $N_2 = (N - N_1)$ are failures. This random variable X is said to be a **hypergeometric random variable**.

Example 7.11

Calculating a Hypergeometric Probability: A population contains 12 items, of which 4 are known to be defective. If we take a random sample of 5 of these items, what is the probability that we will obtain exactly 2 defective items and 3 good items?

Solution: We use the following notation:

$$\begin{aligned}
&\text{Population size} = N = 12\\
&\text{Sample size} = n = 5\\
&\text{Number of successes in population (good items)} = N_1 = 8\\
&\text{Number of failures in population (defective items)} = N_2 = 4\\
&\text{Number of successes obtained in sample} = X = 3
\end{aligned}$$

There are ${}_{12}C_5 = 792$ different samples of size 5, all of which are equally likely. We must determine how many of these samples contain 3 good and 2 defective items. Because we must select 3 items from the 8 good ones and 2 items from the 4 bad ones, the number of ways of doing this is $({}_8C_3)({}_4C_2) = 336$. Thus we obtain

$$P(X = 3) = 336/792 = .42$$

■

Example 7.12

Calculating a Hypergeometric Probability: The Senate contains 70 liberals and 30 conservatives. If 5 senators are randomly selected without replacement, find the probability of getting $X = 3$ liberals.

Solution: We obtain

$$\begin{aligned}
N &= 100\\
n &= 5\\
N_1 &= 70\\
N_2 &= 30\\
X &= 3
\end{aligned}$$

There are ${}_{100}C_5$ different samples of size 5, all of which are equally likely. There are $({}_{70}C_3)({}_{30}C_2)$ ways of selecting 3 liberals and 2 conservatives. We obtain

$$P(X = 3) = \frac{({}_{70}C_3)({}_{30}C_2)}{{}_{100}C_5} = .316$$

Because the ratio $n/N = 5/100 = .05$ is quite small in this example, we might want to use the binomial distribution with $p = .7$. The probability of obtaining a success on the first selection would be .7, but it is 69/99 or 70/99 on the second selection, depending on whether a liberal or a conservative was obtained on the first. If we use the binomial distribution to obtain the (approximate) probability of getting 3 successes, we obtain

$$P(X = 3) = {}_5C_3\,(.7)^3(.3)^2 = .3087$$

In this case the binomial approximation is very good, and the approximation improves as N increases and the ratio n/N decreases. ■

General Formula for the Hypergeometric Distribution

The preceding examples indicate how to express the probability of getting x successes in a random selection of n items without replacement from a population containing N items. The general formula is given in the accompanying box.

Formula for the Hypergeometric Distribution

Let X be a random variable having the hypergeometric distribution, and let x denote a specific value of X. The probability distribution of X is determined by the formula

$$P(X = x) = \frac{({}_{N_1}C_x)\,({}_{N_2}C_{n-x})}{{}_NC_n} \quad \text{for } x = 0, 1, 2, \ldots, \min(n, N_1)$$

where

$$\begin{aligned} N &= \text{population size} \\ N_1 &= \text{number of successes in the population} \\ N_2 = N - N_1 &= \text{number of failures in the population} \\ n &= \text{sample size (selected without replacement)} \\ x &= \text{number of successes in the sample} \\ n - x &= \text{number of failures in the sample} \\ \min(n, N_1) &= \text{minimum of } n \text{ and } N_1 \end{aligned}$$

Like the binomial distribution, the hypergeometric distribution is really a family of distributions. Each member of the family is determined by the three parameters N, N_1, and n.

Mean and Variance of the Hypergeometric Distribution

The mean of the hypergeometric distribution represents the expected number of successes we would obtain when selecting n items without replacement from a population containing N items, N_1 of which are successes. The expressions for the mean and variance of the hypergeometric variable X are given in the accompanying box.

Mean and Variance of a Hypergeometric Random Variable

Let X be a hypergeometric random variable. The mean $E(X)$ and the variance $\text{Var}(X)$ of X are given by

$$E(X) = n(N_1/N)$$

$$\text{Var}(X) = \left(\frac{N - n}{N - 1}\right) n \left(\frac{N_1}{N}\right)\left(1 - \frac{N_1}{N}\right)$$

For the binomial distribution, the mean number of successes is given by $\mu = np$, the product of the sample size multiplied by the proportion of successes in the population. The same idea holds true for the hypergeometric distribution. The variances of the binomial and hypergeometric distributions are similar except for the term $[(N - n)/(N - 1)]$, which is called the *finite population correction factor.*

Example 7.13

Mean and Variance of the Hypergeometric Distribution: A company has 1000 employees, 800 of whom are college graduates. The Internal Revenue Service randomly audits 100 of the employees. Let X denote the number of employees selected for an audit who are college graduates. Find $E(X)$ and $\text{Var}(X)$.

Solution: We have $N = 1000$, $N_1 = 800$, and $n = 100$. We obtain

$$E(X) = 100(800/1000) = 80$$

$$\text{Var}(X) = \frac{1000 - 100}{1000 - 1}(100)\left(\frac{800}{1000}\right)\left(1 - \frac{800}{1000}\right) = 14.41$$

Exercises for Section 7.4

1. A population contains 8 items, of which 3 are defective. Two of the items are selected randomly and without replacement.
a. Find the probability that the sample contains 1 good item.
b. Find the probability that the sample contains at least 1 bad item.
c. Find the expected number of good items in the sample and find the variance.

2. A car rental agency has 6 compact cars and 8 luxury cars. Five customers come to the agency to rent cars. Suppose the cars are randomly picked. Let X denote the number of luxury cars rented. Find the following:
a. $P(X = 5)$
b. $P(X = 2)$
c. $P(X > 2)$
d. $P(X \leqslant 2)$

3. Suppose that on Halloween 6 children come to a house to get treats. A bag contains 8 plain chocolate bars and 7 nut bars. Each child reaches into the bag and randomly selects 1 candy bar. Let X denote the number of nut bars selected. Find the following:
a. $P(X = 0)$
b. $P(X = 1)$
c. $P(X \leqslant 2)$

4. At a grocery store, 15 loaves of bread are on the shelf. Ten loaves are fresh and 5 are stale. Customers randomly select 6 loaves of bread to purchase. Let X denote the number of stale loaves selected. Find the following:
   a. $P(X = 5)$
   b. $P(X = 0)$
   c. $P(X = 1)$
5. In an office raffle, 20 tickets are sold and 3 prizes will be awarded. You buy 5 of the tickets.
   a. Find the probability that you do not win a prize.
   b. Find the probability that you win exactly 1 prize.
   c. Find the probability that you win exactly 2 prizes.
   d. Each ticket costs \$5 and each prize is worth \$20. What is your expected gain or loss from buying 5 tickets?
6. A small town contains 30 registered voters, 10 Democrats and 20 Republicans. A pollster from the Roper Polling Agency has been instructed to interview a random sample of 6 voters from this town. What is the probability that exactly 4 of the voters in the sample are Democrats?
7. Ten watches are in the window of a jewelry store. Seven of the watches are worth more than \$200 each, while the other 3 watches are worth approximately \$20 each. A thief steals 3 watches. Find the probability that the thief stole the following:
   a. Three expensive watches
   b. Three inexpensive watches
   c. Exactly 1 expensive watch and 2 inexpensive watches
8. A personnel manager has a list of 10 job applicants; 6 are male and 4 are female. Three applicants are selected randomly to be interviewed for a job. Find the probability of the following:
   a. All 3 selected are female.
   b. All 3 selected are male.
   c. At least 1 of the selected applicants is a male.

7.5 ▪ The Poisson Distribution

The Poisson distribution is named after the French mathematician Simeon Denis Poisson (1781–1840), who published an article in 1837 discussing the distribution. The Poisson distribution has many applications in problems concerning the number of occurrences of some event during some continuous time interval or in some continuous region of space, including many applications in waiting-time problems and in queuing theories. The Poisson random variable X is a discrete random variable and indicates the number of occurrences of some event in a certain amount of time or space. The set of possible values of X is the set containing all the nonnegative integers $S = \{0, 1, 2, \ldots\}$.

Example 7.14 **Examples of Poisson Random Variables:** In waiting-time problems, some variables that may have the Poisson distribution are the following:

(a) Number of telephone calls to a switchboard in a given minute (This assumes that incoming calls are independent of one another, an assumption that could be violated if there has been some type of emergency that leads to a rush of phone calls.)
(b) Number of customers entering a checkout line at a supermarket in a given minute
(c) Number of airplanes arriving at an airport in an hour

(d) Number of accidents at a factory in a day
(e) Number of customers purchasing a product during a day
(f) Number of cars crossing a bridge during a five-second interval

The Poisson distribution also relates to the problems concerning the number of occurrences of an event in a certain interval of space, such as the following:

(g) Number of misprints on a page of newsprint
(h) Number of flaws in a sheet of glass
(i) Number of paint scratches on a new car
(j) Number of bacteria in an ounce of fluid
(k) Number of flaws in a bolt of fabric ■

Characteristics of the Poisson Process

Variables that follow the Poisson distribution are said to be generated by a **Poisson process**, which has the following characteristics:

1. The occurrences of events are independent; that is, they have no effect on the probability of another occurrence of the event in the same or any other interval of time or space.
2. The probability of occurrence is approximately proportional to the length of the time or space interval.
3. The probability of more than one occurrence in any infinitesimally small interval is negligible.

In addition, the Poisson distribution can be used to approximate the binomial distribution in cases where the number of trials of the binomial experiment is large (say, $n \geqslant 50$) and where p is close to 0 so that $np < 5$. When p is close to 0 in a binomial experiment, then we are studying what is called a *rare event*. The Poisson distribution is frequently used to determine probabilities in situations involving rare events.

The following formula gives the probability function for a Poisson random variable:

Formula for Poisson Distribution

$$P(X = x) = \frac{\mu^x e^{-\mu}}{x!} \quad \text{for } x = 0, 1, 2, \ldots$$

In the formula, e is the number 2.71828 . . . , and μ is a nonnegative number representing the mean of the Poisson distribution. The value μ represents the average number of occurrences of some rare event over a given interval of time or space. The values of $P(X = x)$ can be computed with a hand calculator that can calculate powers of e. If the mean has only one decimal place, Poisson probabilities can be obtained directly from Table A.4 in the Appendix.

Example 7.15

Calculating Poisson Probabilities: From noon to 4 P.M., the number of airplanes taking off from a certain runway during any one-minute interval has the Poisson distribution with mean $\mu = 1.5$.

(a) Find the probability that during a specific one-minute interval, no planes take off.

Solution: We obtain

$$P(X = 0) = \frac{e^{-1.5}(1.5)^0}{0!} = .223$$

(b) Find the probability that exactly 2 planes take off during a specific one-minute interval.

Solution: We obtain

$$P(X = 2) = \frac{e^{-1.5}(1.5)^2}{2!} = .251$$

(c) Find the probability that during a one-minute interval at least 1 plane takes off.

Solution: We obtain

$$P(X \geq 1) = 1 - P(X = 0) = 1 - .223 = .777$$

■

Example 7.16

Calculating Poisson Probabilities: Suppose the number of misprints on a newspaper page has a Poisson distribution with mean $\mu = 2.2$. Construct the probability distribution of X.

$$P(X = 0) = \frac{(2.2)^0 e^{-2.2}}{0!} = e^{-2.2} \approx .111$$

$$P(X = 1) = \frac{(2.2)^1 e^{-2.2}}{1!} \approx .244$$

Similarly, we obtain the results shown in Table 7.2. Figure 7.5 shows the Poisson distribution for the case when $\mu = 2.2$.

TABLE 7.2
Poisson distribution for $\mu = 2.2$ (Example 7.16)

x	Probability
0	.111
1	.244
2	.268
3	.196
4	.109
5	.047
6	.018
7	.005
8	.002
9 and above	.000
	1.000

■

Example 7.17

Mean of the Poisson Random Variable: Use the formula for the mean of a discrete random variable and verify that the mean of the Poisson random variable in Example 7.16 is $\mu = 2.2$.

Solution: For any discrete random variable, the mean is given by

$$E(X) = \Sigma\, xP(X = x)$$

We obtain

$$\mu = 0(.111) + 1(2.44) + 2(.268) + 3(.196) + 4(.109) + 5(.047) + 6(.018) + 7(.005) + 8(.002) + 9(.000) = 2.2$$

■

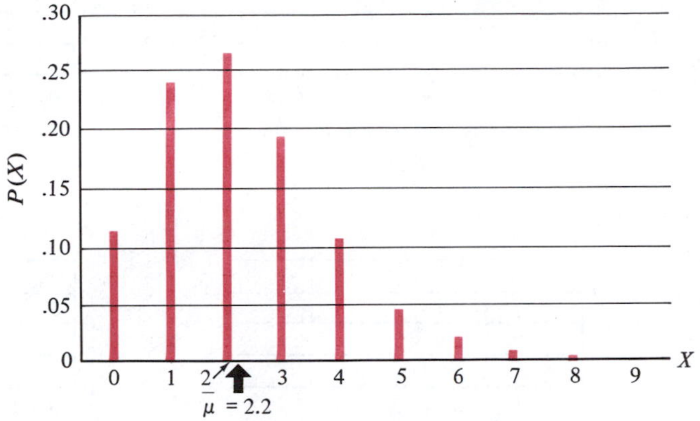

FIGURE 7.5
Poisson distribution for $\mu = 2.2$ (Example 7.16).

Use of the Poisson Probability Table

The Poisson distribution depends on the single parameter μ, and both the mean and variance of the Poisson random variable are equal to μ. Each value of μ determines a different distribution. Thus, like the binomial distribution, the Poisson distribution is really a family of distributions, where each member is determined by the specific value of μ.

If the distribution is going to be used extensively, it is convenient to use a table of Poisson probabilities. Extensive Poisson distribution tables are available at most libraries. Poisson probabilities for selected values of μ are given in Table A.4 of the Appendix.

Example 7.18 **Using a Table to Calculate Poisson Probabilities:** Assume that X has a Poisson distribution with mean $\mu = 1.7$. Calculate $P(X \leq 4)$.

Solution: From Table A.4, we obtain for $\mu = 1.7$

$$P(X \leq 4) = P(X = 0) + P(X = 1) + P(X = 2) + P(X = 3) + P(X = 4) = .1827 + .3106 + .2640 + .1496 + .0636 = .9705$$

■

Shape of the Poisson Distribution

The shape of the Poisson distribution varies with the value of the mean μ. Figure 7.6 shows Poisson probability distributions for different values of μ. As μ increases, the probability shifts to the right and the distribution becomes more bell shaped. When μ is no more than 1, the distribution is extremely skewed to the right with almost all of the probability located at $P(0)$ and $P(1)$.

FIGURE 7.6 **Poisson distributions for various values of μ.**

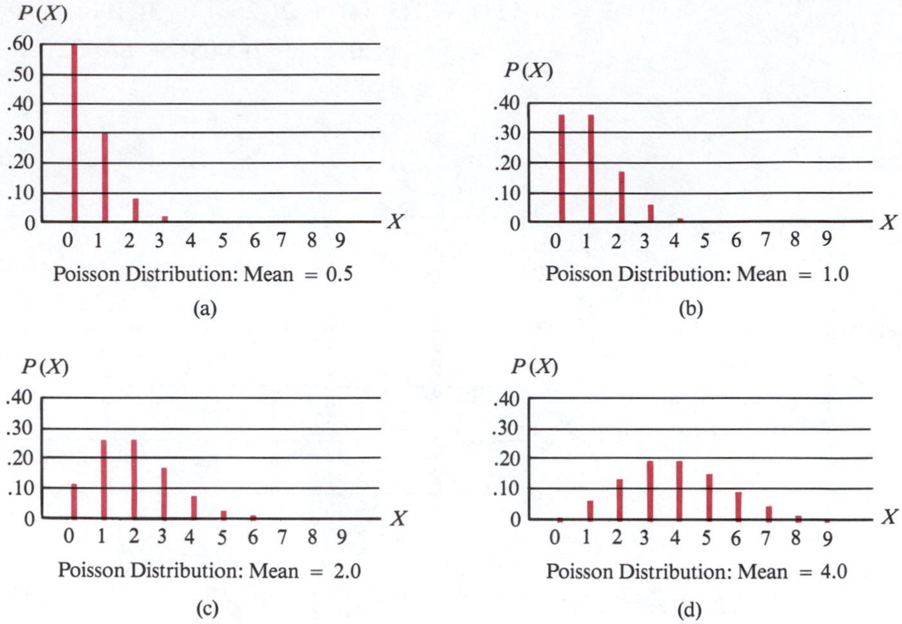

Poisson Distribution as Approximation to the Binomial Distribution

The Poisson distribution is used to approximate the binomial distribution when the number of trials n is large and the probability of a success on any trial p is small. The rule for this application of the Poisson distribution is given in the accompanying box.

Poisson Approximation to the Binomial Distribution

The Poisson distribution provides a good approximation to the binomial distribution provided $n \geqslant 50$ and $np < 5$. Recall that the mean of the binomial distribution is given by $\mu = np$. When using the Poisson distribution to approximate the binomial distribution, set the mean of the Poisson distribution equal to np.

Example 7.19

Poisson Approximation to the Binomial: A company sells insurance policies to a random sample of $n = 1000$ men who are 35 years of age. The probability that a 35-year-old man dies within a year is approximately .002 (from *Vital Statistics of the United States, Life Tables*). What is the probability that the insurance company will have to pay claims on 2 or more policies in the next year?

Solution: Let X denote the number of men in the sample who die within one year. Then X is a binomial random variable with $n = 1000$ and $p = .002$. Because $n > 50$ and $np < 5$, we use the Poisson distribution to approximate the binomial where $\mu = np = (1000)(.002) = 2$. We obtain

$$\begin{aligned} P(X \geqslant 2) &= 1 - P(X = 0) - P(X = 1) \\ &= 1 - \frac{e^{-2}2^0}{0!} - \frac{e^{-2}2^1}{1!} \\ &= 1 - .1353 - .2707 \\ &= .5940 \end{aligned}$$

The exact binomial probability is

$$P(X \geqslant 2) = 1 - .13506 - .27067 = .59427$$

The Poisson approximation to the binomial is extremely accurate in this case. ■

Example 7.20 **Another Poisson Approximation to the Binomial:** About 1 person in 1000 suffers a bad reaction to a certain medicine. If a doctor gives this medicine to a random sample of 2600 patients, what is the probability that exactly 1 person will suffer a bad reaction?

Solution: We have $n = 2600$, $p = .001$, and $np = 2.6$. We use the Poisson distribution with $\mu = 2.6$ and obtain

$$\begin{aligned} P(X = 1) &= \frac{2.6^1 e^{-2.6}}{1!} \\ &\approx .1931 \end{aligned}$$

The exact binomial probability is $P(X = 1) = .19305$, which is virtually identical to the Poisson approximation. ■

Example 7.21 **Comparing Poisson and Binomial Probabilities:** To show that the Poisson distribution provides a good approximation to the binomial distribution, let us calculate some exact binomial probabilities when $n = 100$ and $p = .02$ and the corresponding Poisson probabilities using $\mu = 2$.

Solution: Table 7.3 shows corresponding binomial and Poisson probabilities. The Poisson probabilities were obtained from Table A.4. Note the similarities in the probabilities and in the graphs of the probability distributions, shown in Figures 7.7 and 7.8. Figure 7.8 shows the typical shape of a Poisson random variable, with most of the probability concentrated near 0 and a long tail extending to the right.

TABLE 7.3 **Comparison of Probabilities for Binomial ($n = 100$, $p = .02$) and Poisson ($\mu = 2$) Distributions, $P(X = x)$**

	Value of x							
	0	1	2	3	4	5	6	7
Binomial $P(X = x)$	.1326	.2707	.2734	.1823	.0902	.0353	.0114	.0037
Poisson $P(X = x)$	.1353	.2707	.2707	.1804	.0902	.0361	.0120	.0034

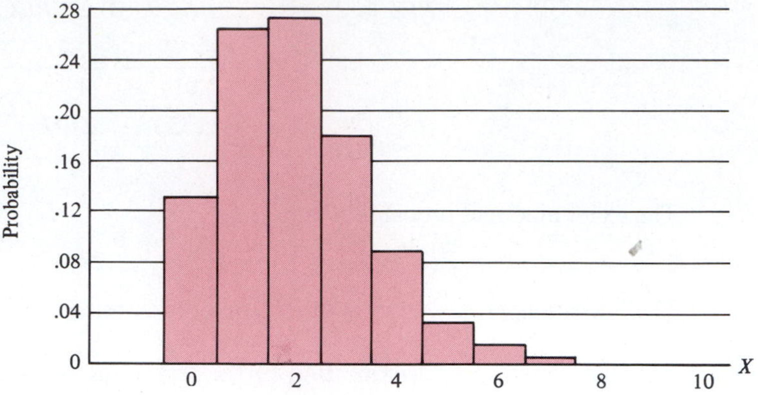

FIGURE 7.7 **Binomial probability distribution for $n = 100$ and $p = .02$.**

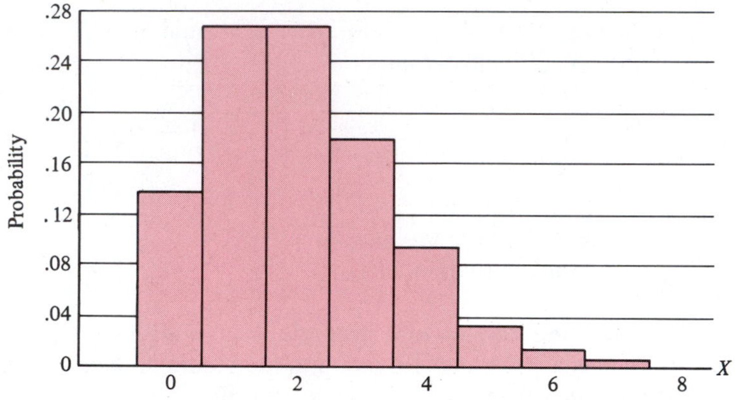

FIGURE 7.8 **Poisson probability distribution for $\mu = 2$.**

Tips on Problem Solving

Probably the most frequent use of the Poisson distribution is as an approximation to the binomial distribution. This approximation works for rare events, where n is large (say 50 or more) and np is less than 5. Whenever you have a problem where the same experiment is repeated n times and the probability of success on any trial is very small, you should consider using the Poisson distribution to determine the probability of any specific number of successes. As when solving binomial problems, always write down the values of n and p. Also record the value of X, the desired number of successes.

Exercises for Section 7.5

1. Let X have the Poisson distribution with $\mu = 3$. Find the following:
a. $P(X = 0)$ b. $P(X = 1)$ c. $P(X = 2)$ d. $P(X \geqslant 3)$

2. Let X have the Poisson distribution with $\mu = 2$. Find the following:
a. $P(X \leq 2)$ b. $P(X > 2)$

3. Let X have the Poisson distribution with $\mu = 1.6$. Find the following:
a. $P(X = 0)$ b. $P(X = 1)$ c. $P(X = 2)$ d. $P(X = 3)$

4. Let X have the Poisson distribution with $\mu = 0.5$.
a. Calculate the probability distribution of X and graph it.
b. Calculate the mean and verify that the mean is 0.5.

5. Let X have the Poisson distribution with $\mu = 0.5$.
a. Calculate $P(X = 2)$ by performing the computations.
b. Find $P(X = 2)$ by using the Poisson distribution table (Table A.4) in the Appendix.
c. Verify that the answers in parts (a) and (b) are the same.
d. Repeat parts (a) through (c) for $P(X = 3)$ and $P(X = 4)$.

6. The number of flaws in a sheet of glass follows the Poisson distribution. The average number of flaws in a sheet of glass measuring 10 square feet is 1. Find the probability of the following:
a. A 2×5 foot sheet contains no flaws.
b. A 2×5 foot sheet contains 2 flaws.
c. A 3×10 foot sheet contains no flaws.

7. During any one-minute interval, the number of cars arriving at a toll booth has a Poisson distribution. The average number of arrivals in any one-minute period is 3. Find the probability of the following:
a. Two cars arrive between 3 P.M. and 3:01 P.M.
b. More than 2 cars arrive between 3 P.M. and 3:01 P.M.

8. On Saturday nights, the number of crimes reported to police headquarters follows the Poisson process. During any 10-minute interval, the average number of reports is 2. Find the probability that no crimes are reported during intervals of the following lengths:
a. 10 minutes b. 30 minutes

9. Assume that the number of mufflers purchased at a service station in a week follows the Poisson distribution with $\mu = 2$. Deliveries are made every Monday, so every Monday the mechanic has to decide how many mufflers to stock. How large a stock should the mechanic have on hand on Monday to be 95% certain that the week's demand can be satisfied?

10. The number of people entering a bank during any two-minute interval follows the Poisson distribution with mean $\mu = 2$. Find the probability of the following during a five-minute interval:
a. No one enters the bank.
b. At least 2 people enter the bank.

11. The Simmons Muffler Repair Shop can handle at most 5 customers per hour. Suppose that the number of arrivals per hour, denoted by X, has the Poisson distribution with mean $\mu = 3$. Find the probability that, during a given hour, the service facility is overloaded.

12. Suppose that the number of accidents per week over a certain stretch of highway has a Poisson distribution with mean $\mu = 2$. Find the probability that on that stretch there will be the following:
a. No accidents next week
b. Two accidents next week
c. More than 3 accidents next week

13. At a certain university, computer breakdowns occur randomly at the rate of 1 every 10 days. Assume that the number of breakdowns in any 10-day period has a Poisson distribution with mean $\mu = 1$. Find the probability of the following:
a. No breakdowns during the next 10 days
b. More than 1 breakdown during the next 20 days

14. Customers arrive at a busy checkout counter at an average rate of 2.5 per minute. If the distribution of arrivals is Poisson, find the probability that in any given minute there will be 3 or fewer arrivals.

15. An insurance office has 400 typewriters. The probability that any one of them will require repair on a given day is .01. Find the probability that fewer than 4 of the typewriters require repair on a particular day. Use the Poisson approximation to the binomial distribution.

16. The Internal Revenue Service reports that 2.5% of all taxpayers make arithmetic mistakes on their income tax returns. A random sample of 100 returns will be checked.
a. What is the probability that none of them will contain errors?
b. What is the probability that at least 3 of them will contain errors?

7.6 ▪ The Geometric Distribution

Another important discrete random variable that has many business applications is the **geometric random variable**. Like the binomial random variable, the geometric random variable arises from an experiment that can have only one of two possible outcomes, denoted "success" and "failure." In the binomial experiment, we fix n, the number of trials, and determine the number of successes obtained in n trials. In the geometric distribution, we let the random variable X denote the number of trials needed to obtain the first success. As with the binomial experiment, we assume that successive trials of the experiment are independent of one another. The geometric random variable is obtained from an experiment that has the characteristics described in the accompanying box.

Characteristics of the Geometric Experiment

1. The experiment consists of a sequence of independent trials.
2. Each trial results in one of two possible outcomes, denoted "success" (s) and "failure" (f).
3. On every trial, the probability of a success is p, and the probability of a failure is $q = (1 - p)$.
4. The geometric random variable X denotes the number of trials required until the first success is obtained.

Example 7.22 **Calculating a Geometric Probability:** A recruiter is interviewing job candidates. From past data, the recruiter thinks that about 20% of the potential job candidates have the qualifications necessary to be hired for a certain middle management position.

(a) Find the probability that the first suitable job prospect is the fourth candidate interviewed.

Solution: If the fourth candidate is the first suitable prospect, then the first three prospects must all be classified as failures (f). Thus, we seek the probability of the sequence $\{fffs\}$. Because successive trials are independent, the probability of obtaining 3 failures and then a success is

$$P(X = 4) = P(fffs) = (.8)^3(.2) = .1024$$

(b) Find the probability that the first suitable job candidate is the sixth candidate interviewed.

Solution: The sixth candidate will be the first suitable prospect if we obtain the sequence $\{fffffs\}$. The probability of obtaining 5 failures and then a success is

$$P(X = 6) = P(fffffs) = (.8)^5(.2) = .0655$$

(c) Find the probability that more than 2 candidates will have to be interviewed before the first suitable prospect is obtained.

Solution: The probability that more than 2 job candidates must be interviewed before observing a suitable prospect is denoted $P(X > 2)$. We obtain

$$P(X > 2) = 1 - [P(X = 1) + P(X = 2)]$$

We have $P(X = 1) = P(s) = .20$ and $P(X = 2) = P(fs) = (.8)(.2) = .16$. We obtain

$$P(X > 2) = 1 - [.20 + .16] = .64$$

■

Formula for the Geometric Distribution

Let the random variable X denote the number of independent trials required until the first success is obtained and let x denote a specific value of X. The probability function for the random variable X is

$$P(X = x) = q^{x-1}p \qquad x = 1, 2, \ldots$$

where

p = probability of a success on each trial

$q = 1 - p$

x = number of trials until the first success is obtained

The mean, variance, and standard deviation of the geometric random variable are specified in the accompanying box.

Mean, Variance, and Standard Deviation for the Geometric Distribution

$$\text{Mean} = 1/p$$

$$\text{Variance} = q/p^2$$

$$\text{Standard deviation} = \sqrt{q}/p$$

Example 7.23 **Calculating a Geometric Probability:** Suppose the probability is .2 that a job candidate will be suitable for a certain job position. What is the expected number of candidates who will be interviewed before the first suitable prospect is obtained and what is the standard deviation of X?

Solution: The mean of the geometric random variable is

$$\mu = 1/.2 = 5$$

This means that, on the average, it will take 5 interviews to locate the first suitable prospect. Sometimes more than 5 interviews will be required, sometimes less, but the average will be 5.

The variance of X is

$$\sigma^2 = .8/(.2)^2 = 20$$

The standard deviation of X is

$$\sigma = \sqrt{20} = 4.472$$ ■

Figure 7.9 shows the graphs of the probability distribution of a geometric random variable for different values of p.

FIGURE 7.9 **Geometric probability distributions for various values of *p*.**

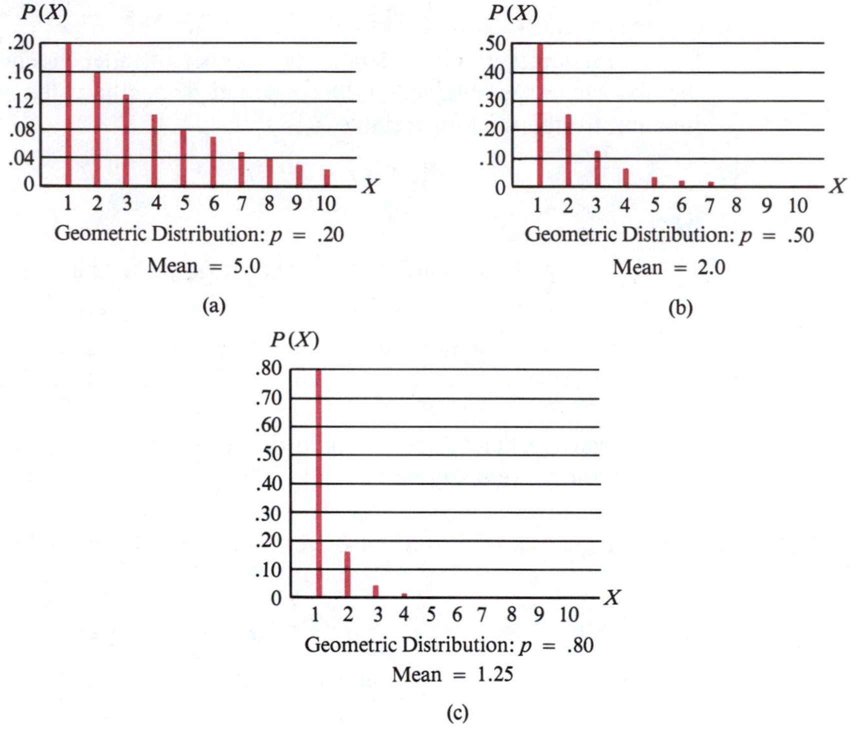

Exercises for Section 7.6

1. The manufacturer of a price-reading scanner claims that the probability that the scanner will misread a price is .004. Shortly after one of the scanners was installed in a supermarket, the store manager tested the performance of the scanner.

a. If the manufacturer's claim is true, what is the probability that the scanner did not misread any of the first 6 prices?

b. What is the probability that the first 5 prices were read correctly and the sixth price was read incorrectly?

c. If, in fact, the sixth price was misread, what inference can be made about the manufacturer's claim? Explain.

2. Of the 38 numbers on the roulette wheel, 18 are colored black, 18 are red, and 2 are green. A gambler decides to place money on a black number. If the gambler loses on both of the first two spins of the wheel, he will leave the casino; otherwise, he will continue playing. Let X denote the number of spins until the gambler achieves the first win.
   a. Find the probability that the gambler loses at the roulette wheel and hence leaves the casino (i.e., the probability that $X > 2$).
   b. Find the probability that the gambler stays at the roulette table after two spins of the wheel.
   c. If the gambler always plays black, what is the expected number of spins before he achieves the first win [i.e., find $E(X)$]?
   d. Is X likely to exceed 5? Explain. (Assume the gambler will play the game until he achieves the first win.)
3. The probability that a newborn child will be a boy is .51. A husband and wife have decided to continue to have children until they have a boy. What is the probability that their first boy is the fourth child?
4. A slot machine at a casino randomly rewards 20% of the attempts. What is the probability that your first reward occurs on your fifth trial?
5. A woman has opened a small dress shop. She thinks that the probability of making a profit in any year is .6. She has enough money to support the store for a few years, but she will need to earn a profit in one of the first few years. What is the probability that the first profit is earned during the fourth year?
6. A sales representative makes 10 house calls a day. The probability of making a sale at a randomly selected house is .1. Find the probability that the first sale is made at the seventh household.
7. A major oil company has decided to drill independent test wells in the Alaskan wilderness. The probability of any well producing oil is .4. Find the probability that the fifth well is the first to produce oil.

Chapter 7 Summary

The most commonly used discrete probability distributions are the binomial, the hypergeometric, the Poisson, and the geometric. The *binomial distribution* is used to find the probability of finding X successes in n independent trials of some experiment, while the *geometric distribution* is used to find the probability that the first success will occur on the Xth trial when successive trials are independent.

The *hypergeometric distribution* is used to find the probability of obtaining X successes when selecting n items without replacement from a finite population containing N_1 successes and N_2 failures. If the sample size is small relative to the population size, hypergeometric probabilities can be approximated by binomial probabilities.

The *Poisson distribution* is used to find the probability of X occurrences of some event in a specific amount of time or space. The Poisson distribution provides a good approximation to the binomial distribution when n is large and np is less than 5.

To find binomial probabilities when n is 20 or less, use the binomial probability table in the Appendix (Table A.2). To find Poisson probabilities when the mean is an integer multiple of .1, use the Poisson table in the Appendix (Table A.4). When n is large, the binomial probabilities can be approximated by the Poisson distribution when np is less than 5 and by the normal distribution when np is 5 or more.

The following is an itemized summary of the binomial, hypergeometric, Poisson, and geometric distributions:

Binomial Distribution

1. X denotes the number of successes in n independent trials. On every trial the probability of success is p. We set $q = 1 - p$.
2. *Formula:* $P(X = x) = {}_nC_x\, p^x q^{n-x}$; $x = 0, 1, 2, \ldots, n$.
3. *Mean:* $\mu = E(X) = np$.
4. *Variance:* $\sigma^2 = npq$; *standard deviation:* $\sigma = \sqrt{npq}$.
5. Use the Poisson distribution to approximate the binomial distribution when $n \geqslant 50$ and $np < 5$.
6. Use the normal distribution to approximate the binomial distribution when $np \geqslant 5$ and $nq \geqslant 5$ (see Chapter 8).

Hypergeometric Distribution

1. X denotes the number of successes obtained when selecting a sample of size n without replacement from a finite population containing N elements.
2. *Formula:*

$$P(X = x) = \frac{({}_{N_1}C_x)\,({}_{N-N_1}C_{n-x})}{{}_NC_n}$$

where the random variable X can take the value of any whole number through the minimum of n and N_1. In the formula, N_1 is the number of successes in the population.

3. *Mean:*

$$\mu = E(X) = n\left(\frac{N_1}{N}\right)$$

4. *Variance:*

$$\sigma^2 = \left(\frac{N-n}{N-1}\right)n\left(\frac{N_1}{N}\right)\left(1 - \frac{N_1}{N}\right)$$

Poisson Distribution

1. X denotes the number of occurrences of some rare event.
2. *Formula:* $P(X = x) = e^{-\mu}\mu^x/x!$, where $x = 0, 1, 2, \ldots$
3. *Mean:* $E(X) = \mu$
4. *Variance:* $\sigma^2 = \mu$
5. The Poisson distribution provides a good approximation to the binomial distribution provided $n \geqslant 50$ and $np < 5$.

Geometric Distribution

1. X denotes the number of independent trials needed to obtain the first success.
2. *Formula:* $P(X = x) = q^{x-1}p$, where $x = 1, 2, \ldots$
3. *Mean:* $\mu = E(X) = 1/p$
4. *Variance:* $\sigma^2 = q/p^2$
5. p denotes the probability of a success on any trial; $q = 1 - p$.

Chapter 8 discusses the most important *discrete* probability distributions. In Chapter 9, we discuss some important *continuous* probability distributions.

Chapter 7 ▪ Supplementary Exercises

1. The probability that a sales representative makes a sale to any customer is .5.
   a. Find the probability of making exactly 2 sales to 6 customers. Assume that events are independent.
   b. Find the probability of getting more than 1 sale in 6 tries.
2. A stockbroker has suggested 3 industrial stocks to a client. The broker claims that each of these stocks has a probability of .6 of increasing in price within a week. The client decides to buy the stocks. Assume that movements in the prices of these 3 stocks are independent of one another. What is the probability of the following?
   a. At least 1 of these stocks does not increase in value within a week.
   b. All 3 increase in price.
3. In the past about 30% of the new toys manufactured by the Martel Toy Company have yielded a profit. The profits from the successful products have been large enough to cover the losses from marketing the unsuccessful ones. For the next Christmas season, the company is planning to introduce 4 independent new toys. What is the probability of the following?
   a. At least 1 of the toys yields a profit.
   b. None of the toys yields a profit.
   c. All 4 toys yield a profit.
4. It is known that about 0.3% of the population have an allergic reaction to the chemicals used at the Moore Chemical Company. Suppose that the company hires 500 new employees. What is the probability of the following:
   a. None of the new employees has an allergic reaction.
   b. More than one have an allergic reaction.
5. The profits earned by the owner of an orange grove in Florida depend on the weather. If a severe frost hits during the growing season, a loss will be incurred; otherwise, a large profit will be made. Past weather records indicate that the probability of a severe frost during the growing season in any year is .3.
   a. What is the probability that the orange grower suffers a loss at least once in 5 years?
   b. What is the probability that the first loss occurs during the fourth year?
6. A sales representative sells life insurance policies to 5 men, each 30 years of age. Suppose that the probability is .8 that any 30-year-old man will live for 20 more years. Let X denote the number of these men alive after 20 years.
   a. Construct and graph the probability distribution of X.
   b. Calculate the mean and variance of X. Use the general formulas for mean and variance and check your results using the formulas $\mu = np$ and $\sigma^2 = npq$.
7. A certain doctor has a great reputation for performing successful heart transplants. She has performed 4 heart transplants, and 2 of the patients survived for more than five years. The doctor thinks that she is not better than other doctors in the field and that she has been very lucky. She thinks that the probability of a heart transplant patient surviving for five years or more is .2. What is the probability of having 2 patients out of 4 survive for five years if the probability of survival is .2?
8. Suppose that the weather bureau claims that a tornado will hit a certain area in a given year with a probability of .03. Find the probability of one tornado during the next 60 years.
9. Suppose that 20% of all income tax returns contain mathematical errors. An auditor for the Internal Revenue Service randomly selects 10 returns.

a. Find the probability that 1 or more of these returns contain a mathematical error.
b. Find the probability that the first error is found on the sixth return.

10. Approximately 80% of the people in a community would pay to have cable TV. A salesperson visits a random sample of 9 homes. Find the probability that fewer than 7 of the homes want cable TV.

11. A copying machine has an average rate of 1 defective copy per 100 pages. Suppose you need to copy 200 pages.
a. Find the probability of 0 defective pages.
b. Find the probability of exactly 1 defective page.
c. Find the probability of at least 2 defective pages.

12. About 70% of the driving population would use self-service gas stations if the price of gas were lower than at full-service gas stations. What is the probability that in a random sample of 8 drivers, from 4 to 6 inclusive will say that they would use self-service gas stations?

13. A grocery store has 10 loaves of bread on its shelves, of which 7 are fresh and 3 are stale. You buy 4 loaves. Find the probability that 2 are fresh and 2 are stale.

14. The actuary of a life insurance company has found that the probability of a person having a certain type of fatal accident in a given year is .0002. If the company holds 8000 life insurance policies, what is the probability that the company will have to pay 3 or more claims next year?

15. In a baseball pool, the names of the 24 major league baseball teams are written on slips of paper and placed in a hat. It costs $5 to select one team randomly from the hat. You pay $25 and select 5 teams randomly. At the end of the season, 4 of the teams participate in the league playoffs. For every one of your selected teams that is in the playoffs, you receive $20.
a. What is the probability that none of your teams make the playoffs?
b. What is the probability that exactly 2 of your teams make the playoffs?
c. What is your expected gain or loss from playing this game?

16. A gasoline station sells gas at a 5¢-per-gallon discount if the customer uses self-service. Past data indicate that 70% of all customers choose the self-service system. During a given time period, 10 customers enter the station. What is the probability of the following?
a. More than 5 customers use self-service.
b. Fewer than 8 customers use self-service.

17. Surveys show that 10% of the population is left-handed. A classroom contains 10 students and 10 chairs, all of which are designed for right-handed people.
a. What is the expected number of left-handed students in the class?
b. What is the probability that all of the students are right-handed?

18. A sales representative for the Zavos Air Conditioning Company makes 10 house calls a day. The probability of making a sale at a randomly selected house is .1. Find the probability that the sales representative makes the following:
a. No sales in a day
b. One or more sales in a day
c. Exactly 2 sales in a day

19. The Walker Motor Company sells new cars, 15% of which use diesel fuel. On a given day, 8 new cars are sold. Find the probability that the following number of cars that use diesel fuel are sold in a day:
a. 0
b. More than 2
c. Fewer than 3

20. Data show that 30% of all college students smoke. A freshman, Bill Johnston, lives in a campus dormitory and is given 4 roommates. What is the probability of the following:
a. None of Bill's roommates smokes.
b. At least 2 of Bill's roommates smoke.

21. An assistant professor, Dr. Jones, has been denied tenure by a major eastern university. Dr. Jones has filed a protest with Dean Burnside in hopes of having the tenure decision reversed. The dean decides to select 5 people randomly from Jones's department to review the case. Jones's department contains 18 faculty members, 11 of whom support him and 7 of whom are against him. Find the probability that the committee contains at least 3 people who favor Jones.

22. A major oil company has drilled 6 independent test wells in Alaska. If the probability of any well producing oil is .4, find the probability of the following:
a. Two of the wells are productive.
b. Five of the wells are productive.
c. None of the wells is productive.

23. On the average, 1% of the items made by a machine are defective. Assume independence. Find the probability that 3 defective items are found in a sample of 100 items.

24. At an urban medical clinic, 80% of the incoming patients are covered by some sort of medical insurance. Find the probability of the following among the next 10 incoming patients:
a. More than 4 are covered.
b. Fewer than 8 are covered.

25. Thirty percent of the employees at the Conroy Insurance Company travel to work on the bus and will be hours late whenever the bus system fails. A sudden snowstorm has shut down all bus service in the city. Suppose that the accounting department contains 10 people. Assume independence. Find the probability of the following in the accounting department:
a. At least 2 people are late.
b. Fewer than 5 people are late.

26. A salesman knows from past experience that 15% of all calls he makes eventually result in a sale. Assume the salesman makes 5 calls in a day and that the results of the calls are independent.
a. What is the probability that exactly 3 sales will result?
b. What is the probability that no sales will result?
c. What is the probability that at least 2 sales will result?
d. What is the probability that the first sale will be made on the fourth call?

27. On the average an airline loses about 1 piece of luggage out of 1000. Suppose that the airline handles 3000 pieces of luggage per day. If the airline promises its employees a bonus for every day on which no luggage is lost, what is the probability that the employees get a bonus on any given day?

28. In a suburban area, it is thought that 20% of the households will purchase an automatic garage door opener. If a salesperson randomly contacts 6 different families, what is the probability that the salesperson makes the following:
a. 0 sales
b. 1 sale
c. More than 2 sales

29. A columnist claims that 50% of all cars on the state highways have something wrong with the brake system. If the claim is correct, what is the probability that in a random sample of 6 cars, none is defective?

30. Let $\mu = .7$. Construct the probability distribution of X, where X has the Poisson distribution.

31. Construct and graph the probability distribution of the Poisson variable X having mean $\mu = 1$.

32. The probability is .005 that a person will buy a product that is brought to his or her attention through a phone call by a sales representative. If a salesman makes 500 independent phone calls, what is the probability that he will sell at least 2 products? That is, find $P(X \geq 2)$.

33. The number of customers who enter a service station to buy gas in any five-minute period has the Poisson distribution with mean .3. Find the probability that during a five-minute period, 4 customers enter the station.

34. At a large metropolitan university, on the average 1 college student in 10,000 commits suicide. If the university contains 30,000 students, what is the probability that exactly 1 of these students commits suicide?

35. A car manufacturer places a one-year guarantee on the steering mechanism of its cars, and about 1 car in 5000 has a faulty steering mechanism on the average. If 20,000 cars are sold, what is the probability that more than 3 cars will have faulty steering mechanisms? Assume independence.

36. On the average, 1 person in 1000 is allergic to a certain type of food. If the food is served to 500 schoolchildren, what is the probability that no one is allergic to the food? Assume independence.

37. The number of telephone calls passing through a switchboard has a Poisson distribution with mean equal to $3t$, where t is the time in minutes. Find the probability of the following:

a. 2 calls in any one minute
b. 4 calls in two minutes
c. At least 2 calls in two minutes
d. At least 1 call in one minute

38. At a particular computer center, a keypunch operator must have an error rate of 0.1% or less. That is, on the average there can be no more than 1 incorrect keystroke for every 1000. A job applicant punches 2000 keystrokes and makes 5 errors.

a. If the applicant really has a 0.1% error rate, what is the probability that more than 4 errors will be made on 2000 keystrokes?
b. What is the probability that fewer than 3 errors will be made on 2000 keystrokes?
c. What is the probability that no errors will be made on 2000 keystrokes?

39. Assume that on the average 1 person out of 25 who make plane reservations fails to show. An airline takes 100 independent reservations and has 96 seats. What is the probability that every passenger will have a seat?

40. On the average 1 child in 100 is born with some serious physical or mental disability. Assume that a researcher is interested in testing the hypothesis that the children born from intrafamily marriages are more likely to have these disabilities than other children are. Using the Poisson distribution, determine the probability that in a random sample of 200 children, more than 6 will have a disability.

41. On the average about 1 person out of 100 dies between the age of 20 and 30. An insurance company insures 350 twenty-year-old people. What is the probability that fewer than 3 of these people die before they are 30?

42. Assume that about 1 prospective homeowner in 1000 defaults on a home mortgage. A local savings and loan has issued 500 mortgages, and 3 have defaulted. The Federal Home Loan Bank Board is accusing the savings and loan of shoddy lending practices. If 1 person in 1000 defaults, what is the probability of getting 2 or fewer defaults from 500 customers?

43. About 1 person in 20 withdraws from a class before the first test. Sixty students register for the course, but there are only 58 seats in the classroom. What is the probability that everyone will have a seat at the first test?

44. A company claims that, on the average, a certain rocket motor will fail to start only 2 times out of 1000 tries. In a test, the motor failed to start 3 times out of 500 tries. What is the probability of this occurring if the company's claim is true?

45. A car manufacturer knows that, on the average, 1 car in 500 has a defective windshield. The company wants to know if an employee is causing more than the typical number of defectives. The employee has produced 800 cars, and 4 of them have defective windshields. What is the probability of producing 4 or more defective windshields in 800 cars?

46. The probability that an individual suffers a serious industrial accident in a given year is .00025. If a company insures 5000 industrial employees, what is the probability that more than 2 of these employees will lose a limb during a given year?

47. A political science professor has argued that the probability of a nuclear war occurring during any given year is .02. Assume that annual events are independent of one another. Using the binomial distribution, find the probability of the following:

a. There is no nuclear war in the next 10 years.
b. There is no nuclear war in the next 50 years.

48. The Koch Electric Company makes electric shavers. If the probability that an electric shaver is defective is .01, what is the probability of the following in a shipment of 500 electric shavers?
a. None is defective.
b. One is defective.
c. More than 3 are defective.

49. Assume that at the college library, books can be checked out for one month. Assume that the number of requests per month for *The General Theory* by John Maynard Keynes follows a Poisson distribution with mean $\mu = 2$. How many copies should the library have in order that in a given month it can fulfill all requests with a probability of .95?

50. A company has determined that the probability that a newly appointed apprentice will remain with them for at least one year is .7. Four apprentices are appointed.
a. Find the probability distribution for the number of apprentices who remain with the company after a year's employment if their decisions to remain are made independently.
b. Find the probability that at least 3 of these apprentices will remain with the company for a year or more.

51. The St. Petersburg paradox is a famous problem in statistics. The problem involves a gamble between player A and player B. Player A tosses a coin repeatedly until the first tails appears. If the first tails appears on the first toss, player B is paid \$1; if the first tails appears on the second toss, player B is paid \$2; if the first tails appears on the third toss, player B is paid \$4; and so forth. Thus, if the first tails appears on the kth toss, player B is paid $\$2^{k-1}$. Let X denote the amount that is paid to player B.
a. Find the probability distribution of X.
b. Find the mean value of X. (Note that few people would pay more than \$20 or \$30 to play this game, although the expected payoff is infinitely large!)

52. A delivery service claims that 90% of its parcels are delivered within 48 hours. If the claim is true, find the probability of the following in a random sample of 10 parcels:
a. Exactly 7 are delivered in less than 48 hours.
b. Fewer than 6 are delivered in less than 48 hours.
c. Assume that fewer than 6 of the parcels were delivered in less than 48 hours. Would this make you doubt the shipper's claim? Explain.

53. If boys and girls are equally likely, find the probability that a family's fifth child is their first daughter.

54. When the mailroom clerk of a publishing house is in a hurry to go home, the probability that he or she will make a mistake in an address is .25. If 5 shipments have to be sent out just before closing time, find the probability that a mistake will be made in addressing at least 2 of these shipments. Assume errors are independent of one another.

55. The Sleep Cheap Motel has 40 rooms. Its experience has been that 20% of the people who make reservations never show up.
a. How many no-shows can be expected if this motel accepts reservations for 45 rooms?
b. If the motel accepts reservations from 45 people, what is the probability that 5 or more of these people fail to show?

56. A store sells an average of 3 jars of pizza sauce a week and brings its inventory up to 5 jars every Saturday when the delivery truck stops by. Assume that the Poisson distribution applies. What is the probability that more than 5 jars will be sold in a week's time?

57. A bookie offers gamblers the following bet. The gambler must guess the sex of the next 10 babies born at the city hospital. There is a \$2 fee, but the gambler wins \$1000 if the sex of each child is guessed correctly. Assume that boys and girls are equally likely.
a. What is a gambler's probability of winning the bet?
b. What is the gambler's expected return?

58. In major league baseball, the World Series is won by the first team to win 4 games. Assume that all games are independent and that the teams are evenly matched (each with a .5 probability of winning any game).

a. What is the probability that Team A wins the series in 4 games?
b. What is the probability that Team B wins the series in 4 games?
c. What is the probability that the series will end after 4 games?
d. What is the probability that the series will take exactly 5 games? 6 games? 7 games?

59. There are 40,000 people and one hospital in a town. On any given day, there is a .0001 probability that a person will require a hospital bed. How many beds must the hospital have to be 99% sure that there will be enough beds for everyone that requires one on any given day?

60. A con artist mails gambling advice concerning an evenly matched football game to 320 wealthy gamblers. Half of the letters predict Team A will win and half predict Team A will lose. Suppose Team A wins. The con artist crosses out the 160 gamblers who were given bad advice and mails another prediction concerning another evenly matched football game to the 160 who were given correct advice. Half of these 160 people are told that Team A will win the game and half are told that it will lose. At the end of this game, 80 gamblers have been given two correct predictions in a row. These people are given a third prediction; again, half are told that one team will win and the other half are told that the team will lose. By the end of five games, there are 10 gamblers who have received five correct predictions in a row, and they should be eager to subscribe to the con artist's expensive advice.

a. What is the probability of 5 correct predictions in a row?
b. If you had received these 5 correct predictions, would you be impressed?
c. If you knew how these predictions were made, would you be impressed by 5 correct predictions?

61. A computer magazine claims that about 1 out of 100 floppy disks is defective. Suppose an academic department buys a random sample of 300 floppy disks. Find the probability that fewer than 2 are defective.

62. The economics department has mailed fellowship offers to 5 prospects for graduate school. In the past, 32% of all offers have been accepted. Find the probability that exactly 3 of the 5 offers will be accepted.

63. The probability that a college female will live to age 60 or more is .99. In a random sample of 200 college women, what is the probability that more than 3 of these women die before reaching age 60?

64. An office has 5 computer terminals, and each terminal is broken 10% of the time.

a. Find the probability that at least 2 terminals are working.
b. Find the probability that at least 1 terminal is broken.

References

Feller, William. *An Introduction to Probability Theory and its Applications.* 2 vols. New York: Wiley, 1950–1966.

Freund, John E., and R. E. Walpole. *Mathematical Statistics.* 4th ed. Englewood Cliffs, N.J.: Prentice-Hall, 1987.

Handbook of Tables for Probability and Statistics. 2d ed. Cleveland: Chemical Rubber Co., 1968.

Hoel, Paul G. *Elementary Statistics.* 4th ed. New York: Wiley, 1976.

National Bureau of Standards. *Tables of the Binomial Probability Distribution.* Washington, D.C.: Government Printing Office, 1949.

Neter, John, William Wasserman, and G. A. Whitmore. *Fundamental Statistics for Business and Economics.* 4th ed. Boston: Allyn and Bacon, 1973.

Chapter Eight
Some Useful Continuous Probability Distributions

8.1 ▪ Properties of Continuous Probability Distributions

As we discussed in Chapter 6, a *continuous random variable X* is a random variable that can take all values in an interval. In this chapter we study some of the most important continuous probability distributions. The simplest one, the *uniform distribution,* is discussed first. Next, the normal distribution is treated in detail. The normal curve is a smooth, bell-shaped curve that can be used to approximate many different probability distributions, and it is by far the most important distribution in statistics. Finally, we discuss the exponential distribution, which has many applications in problems involving the time required to complete a task or the amount of time that passes before the next occurrence of some event.

Strictly speaking, every measured variable is discrete because no continuous variable can be measured exactly. Any measurement has to be rounded off after a finite number of significant digits. Nevertheless, it is conceptually advantageous to view many variables as strictly continuous, In fact, some discrete variables are treated as though they were continuous, either because it would be too tedious to list all the values of X and their associated probabilities or because the differences between successive values of the random variable X are insignificant. It is convenient to regard as continuous those essentially discrete random variables that are measured on such a fine grid that the probability of occurrence of any specific value is extremely small. Examples of discrete variables that usually are treated as continuous variables are family income, college grade point average, taxes paid by a corporation, and the sales revenue of a company. Any monetary figure can be expressed only to the nearest unit of currency, so every monetary amount is inherently discrete, but in most cases we treat monetary amounts as continuous variables.

Representing Probabilities by Areas

Because the number of points in an interval is infinite, we cannot assign a positive probability to every point and still have the probabilities sum to one. Thus we need to use a different approach when constructing and interpreting a continuous probability distribution. The approach relies on the relative frequency histogram and the notion that the probability of some event can be approximated by the relative frequency of occurrence of that event in a large number of repeated experiments.

Example 8.1

Approximating a Continuous Distribution: We select a random sample of 100 individuals and record the time required for each individual to perform a certain task. Table 8.1 shows a hypothetical frequency distribution and relative frequency distribution for 100 observations, where each class interval has a width of 4 seconds. Figure 8.1 shows the relative frequency histogram for the data in Table 8.1.

TABLE 8.1
Hypothetical frequency distribution for a continuous random variable (Example 8.1)

Time (seconds)	Frequency	Relative Frequency
16 to under 20	6	.06
20 to under 24	9	.09
24 to under 28	22	.22
28 to under 32	27	.27
32 to under 36	21	.21
36 to under 40	12	.12
40 to under 44	3	.03
Total	100	1.00

FIGURE 8.1
Relative frequency distribution for data in Table 8.1.

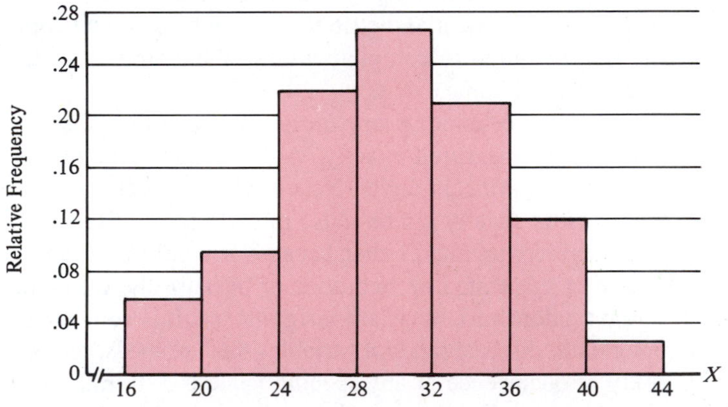

Now suppose we repeat the experiment using a sample of 100,000 individuals and then construct a relative frequency distribution with a very large number of very narrow classes, say, 0.01 or 0.001 unit wide. The graph of the resulting relative frequency distribution will contain a large number of very narrow rectangles.

As the number of observations becomes very large and the class intervals become very narrow, the shape of the relative frequency histogram approaches a smooth curve, as shown in Figure 8.2. This smooth curve, which is approximately the same as the population probability distribution or population relative frequency distribution, is called a *density function*.

FIGURE 8.2
Relative frequency distribution approaching a continuous distribution.

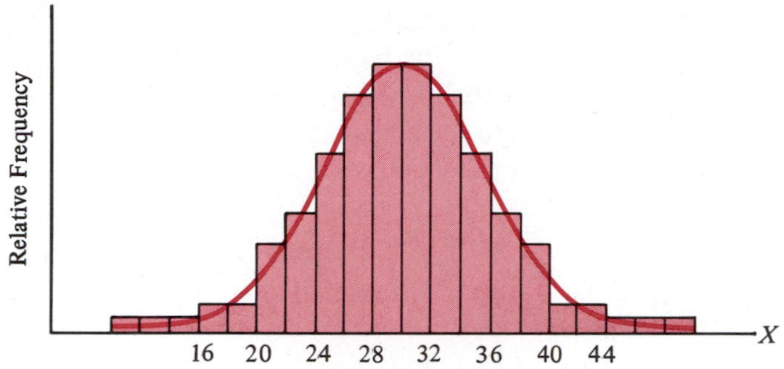

For continuous variables, probabilities are measured by areas under the density function. The probability that the random variable X falls in any particular interval (a, b) is the area under the curve between the points a and b.

Definition: Density Function

Let a smooth curve represent the probability distribution of a continuous random variable X, and let the smooth curve be represented in mathematical notation by the function $f(x)$. The function $f(x)$ is called the **density function** of the continuous random variable X, where x represents a specific value of the random variable X.

Numerous different smooth curves have been used to represent the probability distributions of different continuous random variables. Whether or not we obtain good results by selecting a certain density function to approximate a population relative frequency distribution depends on how well the density function reflects reality. For a density function to provide useful results, it should closely approximate the true underlying population relative frequency histogram.

Characteristics of Density Functions

All density functions must satisfy the following two requirements:

1. The curve must never fall below the horizontal axis. That is,

$$f(x) \geq 0 \quad \text{for all } x$$

2. The total area between the curve and the horizontal axis must be 1. In calculus this is expressed as

$$\int f(x)\, dx = 1$$

A density function must be nonnegative. If $f(x)$ could be negative, it would be possible to obtain negative areas between the curve and the horizontal axis, and negative probabilities are meaningless. The total area under the curve must equal 1 to guarantee that the probability is 1 that X takes some value between $-\infty$ and $+\infty$. If the area exceeded 1, we could find some interval having a probability greater than 1.

Because the area above any single point is 0, every specific single value of X has a probability of 0. That is, if X is a continuous random variable, then for any specific value x, $P(X = x)$ is equal to 0.

Figure 8.3 shows the hypothetical probability distribution of a continuous random variable X. The probability that X falls between two values a and b is denoted $P(a < X < b)$ and is equal to the area under the curve between the points $X = a$ and $X = b$. The shaded portion of the graph represents this area.

FIGURE 8.3
For a continuous distribution, the area between *a* and *b* represents *P*(*a* < *X* < *b*).

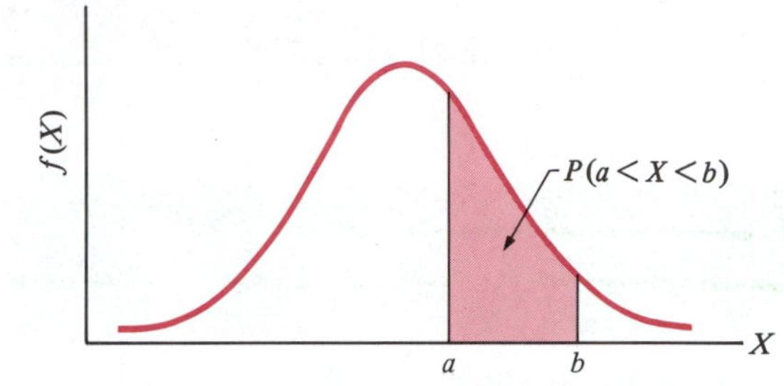

For the specific points $X = a$ and $X = b$, we have $P(X = a) = 0$ and $P(X = b) = 0$. Thus we have

$$P(a \leq X \leq b) = P(a < X < b)$$

That is, if X is a continuous random variable, including or excluding the end points of the interval will not change the probability that X falls within the interval.

A particular density function $f(x)$ provides a mathematical model that approximates the population relative frequency distribution that exists in reality. Presented graphically, the density function represents an approximation to the population relative frequency histogram. In actual practice, however, there will almost always be some disparity between the theoretical model $f(x)$ and the actual relative frequency distribution generated when an experiment is repeated an extremely large number of times.

Just as with discrete probability distributions, we are interested in several characteristics of the probability distribution of any random variable. First, we would like to know the *general shape* of the graph representing the relative frequency distribution—whether it is symmetric or skewed, whether it has long tails in either direction, whether it is relatively flat or bell shaped, and so forth. Second, we would like to determine the *center of gravity* of the distribution. This is the *mean,* or *expected value,* of the random variable X. Third, we would like some measure of the *amount of spread,* or dispersion, present in the distribution. As before, this is measured by the *variance* of the random variable X and is denoted by the symbol σ_X^2. Again, the square root of the variance is the *standard deviation,* denoted by the symbol σ_X. When there is no danger of confusion, the subscript X can be deleted.

Mean and Variance of a Continuous Distribution

Just as with discrete probability distributions, the mean μ and the variance σ^2 are important summary statistics that reveal characteristics of a continuous probability distribution. Except in simple cases, integral calculus is required to calculate the mean and variance of a continuous random variable. Because this is beyond the scope of this book, in most cases we will state the mean and variance of various continuous distributions without providing an analytical proof.

Just as with discrete variables, the mean μ measures the center of gravity of the distribution. If we cut a piece of plywood in the exact shape of the density function, it would just balance if we placed a fulcrum at one particular point perpendicular to its horizontal axis. This point is the mean μ of the variable X (see Figure 8.4). As with discrete random variables, the standard deviation σ and the variance σ^2 measure the spread of the distribution.

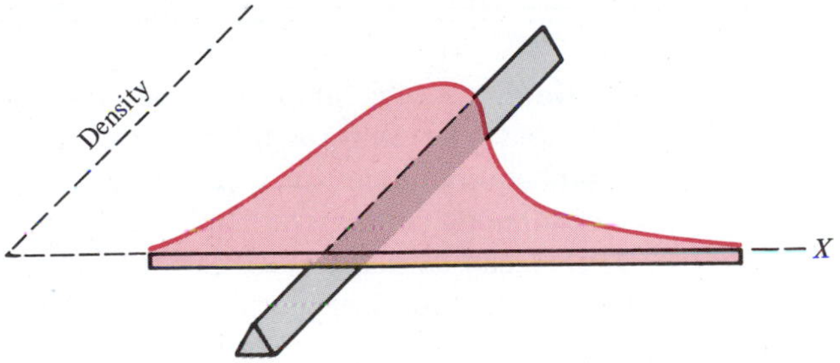

FIGURE 8.4
Mean as the center of gravity of a continuous probability distribution.

Exercises for Section 8.1

1. Which of the following variables are continuous and which are discrete?
   a. Number of heads in 10 tosses of a coin
   b. Length of a telephone call
   c. Temperature of liquid in a test tube
   d. Number of books on a library shelf
   e. Miles per gallon averaged by a car
2. A distribution is symmetric about its mean. What can we say about the median of the distribution?
3. Let X be a continuous random variable having a symmetric distribution. Find the following:
   a. $P(X \leq \mu)$ b. $P(X \geq \mu)$
4. Is $P(X \leq \mu - 1)$ equal to $P(X \geq \mu + 1)$ if X is symmetric about μ?
5. For a certain random variable, $P(X \geq \mu + 2)$ equals $P(X \leq \mu - 2)$. Does this imply that the distribution of X is symmetric about μ?
6. The time of death is equally likely to be any moment during the week. What proportion of people can be expected to die on Mondays?
7. At a certain airport, the amount of time people must wait to get their luggage is a random variable that is evenly distributed between 10 minutes and 20 minutes. (This is an example of a uniform distribution, which will be discussed in the next section.)
   a. Find the probability that the luggage will arrive in less than 13 minutes.
   b. Can you determine the expected waiting time?

8. A certain random variable X has the following density function:

$$f(x) = 2 - 2x \qquad 0 \leq x \leq 1$$
$$f(x) = 0 \qquad \text{otherwise}$$

Graph this density function and determine the following probabilities:
a. $P(0 \leq X \leq 1)$ b. $P(X \geq 0.5)$ c. $P(X \leq 0.25)$

9. A certain random variable X has the following density function:

$$f(x) = 1 + x \qquad -1 \leq x \leq 0$$
$$f(x) = 1 - x \qquad 0 \leq x \leq 1$$
$$f(x) = 0 \qquad \text{otherwise}$$

Graph this probability distribution and determine the following probabilities:
a. $P(-1 \leq X \leq 1)$ b. $P(-1 \leq X \leq 0)$ c. $P(0 \leq X \leq 0.5)$

8.2 ▪ The Uniform Distribution

In this section, we discuss the simplest of all continuous probability distributions, the *uniform distribution*. The uniform distribution is the continuous counterpart of the equally likely probability model for discrete random variables, which we discussed in Chapter 6. A continuous random variable X follows the uniform distribution over the interval $[a, b]$ if X can take any value in the closed interval $[a, b]$ and if the density function of X is constant (or flat) over this interval. Figure 8.5 shows a uniform density function.

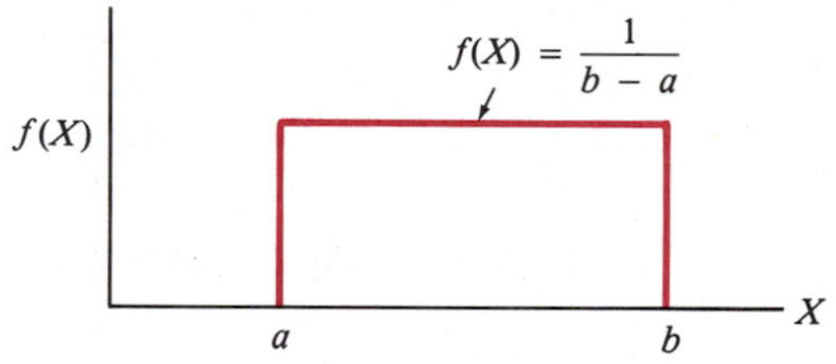

FIGURE 8.5
A uniform distribution.

Definition: Uniform Density Function

Let the continuous random variable X follow the uniform distribution over the interval $[a, b]$. The **uniform density function** of X is

$$f(x) = 1/(b - a) \quad \text{for } a \leq x \leq b$$

Characteristics of the Uniform Distribution

The uniform distribution has the simplest shape of all probability distributions—a rectangle that extends from a to b that has a height of $1/(b - a)$. The distribution is symmetric about its mean value, which is $(b + a)/2$. The characteristics of the uniform distribution are described in the accompanying box.

Characteristics of the Uniform Distribution

Let X be a uniform random variable defined over the interval $[a, b]$.

1. The mean value of X, or the expected value of X, is

$$\mu = E(X) = (a + b)/2$$

2. The median is

$$\text{Median} = (a + b)/2$$

3. The variance is

$$\sigma^2 = \text{Var}(X) = (b - a)^2/12$$

4. The standard deviation is

$$\sigma = (b - a)/\sqrt{12}$$

Calculating Uniform Probabilities

Let c and d be any two numbers such that $a \leq c \leq d \leq b$. The probability $P(c \leq X \leq d)$ is the area under the density function between c and d. The width of this rectangle is $(d - c)$, and the height is $1/(b - a)$; therefore the area of the rectangle is $(d - c)/(b - a)$.

Calculating Probabilities with the Uniform Distribution

Let X follow the uniform distribution over the interval $[a, b]$. The probability that X takes a value between c and d is

$$P(c \leq X \leq d) = (d - c)/(b - a) \quad \text{where } a \leq c \leq d \leq b$$

Example 8.2

The Uniform Distribution: An investor in a bank's trust department thinks that in 100 days the price of gold will be between \$420 and \$460 an ounce and that all prices in the interval [\$420, \$460] are equally likely. Let X denote the price of gold in 100 days. Find the probability that X is between \$425 and \$435.

Solution: X can be treated as a continuous random variable having a uniform distribution. The value of X varies from $a = 420$ to $b = 460$. The probability that X takes a value between $c = 425$ and $d = 435$ is given by

$$P(425 \leq X \leq 435) = \frac{435 - 425}{460 - 420} = .25$$

This probability is represented by the shaded area in Figure 8.6.

FIGURE 8.6
Uniform distribution associated with Example 8.2.

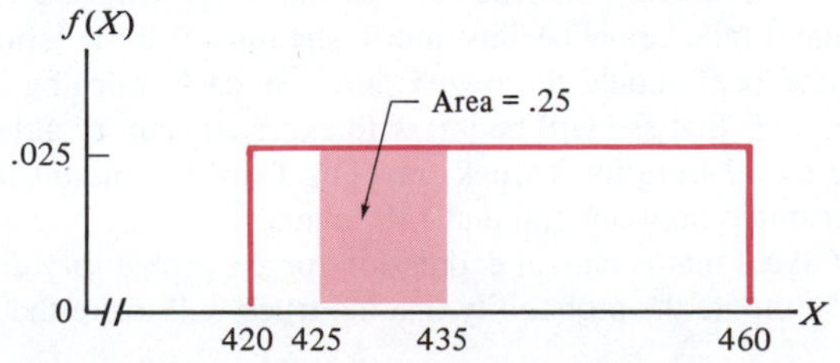

Exercises for Section 8.2

1. If X is uniformly distributed between 0 and 1, find the following:
a. $P(X \leq .5)$ b. $P(0 \leq X \leq .4)$ c. $P(0 < X < .4)$ d. $P(X > .8)$

2. An investor thinks that the price of a stock will increase tomorrow, and the increase (denoted by X) will be some value between \$0 and \$3. Thus, the change in price is uniformly distributed between \$0.00 and \$3.00. Find the following:
a. $P(0.50 \leq X \leq 1.00)$ b. $P(X \leq 1.20)$ c. $P(X \leq 1.00)$
d. $P(0.25 \leq X \leq 0.75)$ e. Mean of X

3. The annual report of the Jones Metal Company claims that next year's stock dividend will increase by an amount in the interval [\$0, \$2]. Let the random variable X denote the increase in the dividend. If X has the uniform distribution, find the following:
a. $P(X > 1.00)$ b. $P(X \leq 1.00)$ c. $P(X \leq 2.00)$
d. $P(0.50 \leq X \leq 2.00)$ e. $P(0.50 \leq X \leq 1.50)$ f. Mean of X

4. An economist claims that next year the rate of change of sales at a corporation will fall in the interval [−5%, 5%]. If the rate of change is a random variable X having the uniform distribution, find the following:
a. $P(X < 0)$ b. $P(X < 2)$ c. $P(X < -2)$
d. $P(-2 \leq X \leq 2)$ e. Mean of X

5. A bus is supposed to arrive at a certain bus stop every half hour. At the end of the day, buses are equally likely to arrive at any time during any given half hour because of delays earlier in the day. If you arrive at a bus stop at the end of the day, what is the probability that you will have to wait more than 10 minutes for the bus (no matter when you show up)? How long can you expect to wait for the bus?

6. A car breaks down on an interstate highway. The driver has noticed the frequency of police patrols along the highway and believes that the time before a patrol car arrives on the scene is a uniformly distributed random variable between 0 and 30 minutes.
a. Graph the probability density function.
b. Find the probability that a patrol car arrives within 20 minutes of the breakdown.
c. Find the probability that a patrol car does not arrive within 10 minutes of the breakdown.
d. Find the probability that a patrol car arrives between 15 and 20 minutes after the breakdown.

7. In St. Louis, the rescue team of the city fire department is responsible for approximately a 7-mile stretch of river. The distance between the northernmost point and the location of an emergency is a uniformly distributed random variable over the interval [0, 7].
a. Graph the probability density function.
b. Find the probability that a given emergency arises within 1 mile of the northernmost point of this stretch of river.
c. Find the probability that a given emergency arises between 2 and 4 miles from the northernmost point of the stretch.
d. Suppose that the rescue team has its headquarters at the midpoint of this stretch of river. Find the probability that a given emergency arises more than 2 miles from the team's headquarters.

8. The owner of a delicatessen knows from past experience that the daily demand for fresh ground beef is uniformly distributed over the range from 35 to 55 pounds. The owner realizes that if demand falls below her inventory, she must sell the leftover meat at a loss. How many pounds of ground beef should the owner purchase each morning if she wishes the chances to be no more than 25% that she will be left with excess inventory at the day's end?

9. The travel time for a truck traveling from Fairmount to Wheeling, West Virginia is uniformly distributed between 100 and 140 minutes.
a. Give a mathematical expression for the probability density function.
b. Compute the probability that the truck will make the trip in 125 minutes or less.

c. Compute the probability that the trip will take longer than 125 minutes.
d. Find the expected travel time and its standard deviation.
e. What is the probability that the trip will take exactly 115 minutes?

8.3 ▪ The Normal Distribution

The normal distribution, first used in 1733 by Antoine de Moivre (1667–1745), is the most important statistical distribution. It is sometimes called the *Gaussian distribution* in honor of Carl F. Gauss (1777–1855), a famous German mathematician who did extensive work with it.

The normal curve is represented by the density function

$$f(x) = \frac{1}{\sqrt{2\pi\sigma^2}} e^{-(x-\mu)^2/2\sigma^2}$$

where $\pi = 3.14159\ldots$ and $e = 2.71828\ldots$ and where x is a specified value of the random variable X. The numbers μ and σ^2 in the formula represent the mean and variance, respectively, of the distribution. Consequently, different values of μ and σ^2 give us different members of the family of normal distributions.

Characteristics of the Normal Distribution

Some of the most important characteristics of the density function of the normal distribution are as follows:

1. The curve is bell shaped and symmetric about the value $X = \mu$.
2. The curve extends from $-\infty$ to $+\infty$.
3. The total area under the curve is 1. (This is required of all density functions.)
4. The curve is always above the X-axis. (Thus, $f(x) \geq 0$ for all x.)
5. The mean, median, and mode are all equal to the parameter μ.

The three normal distributions graphed in Figure 8.7 all have the same variance σ^2 (and thus the same standard deviation σ), but they have different means. Increasing the mean shifts the curve to the right, but each curve remains symmetric about its mean. In contrast to Figure 8.7, the three normal curves in Figure 8.8 all have the same mean but different variances. Curve 1 has the smallest variance and thus is least spread out; curve 3 has the largest variance and is most spread out.

FIGURE 8.7 **Three normal distributions with different means but equal variances.**

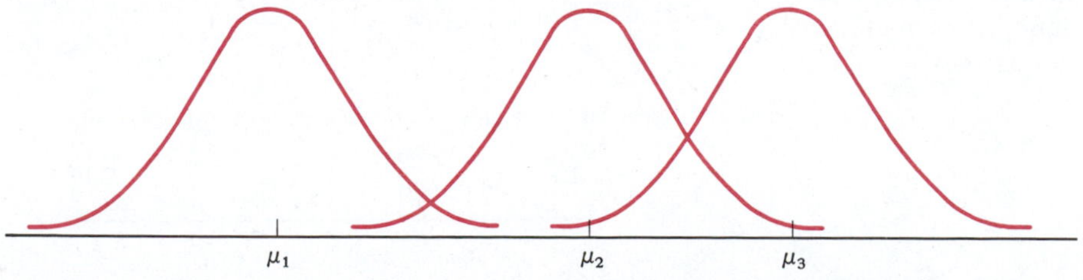

FIGURE 8.8
Three normal distributions with equal means but different variances.

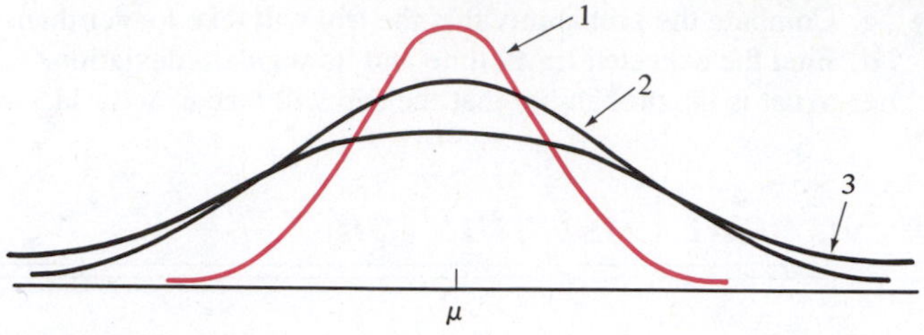

The value of μ determines the center of the normal curve, and the value of σ^2 determines the spread. Together μ and σ^2 completely determine the shape of the curve. It is customary to denote the normal distribution that has mean μ and variance σ^2 by the notation $N(\mu, \sigma^2)$. Thus, if we write that X is distributed as $N(8, 68)$, we mean that the random variable X is distributed normally with a mean of 8 and a variance of 68.

The Standard Normal Distribution

The normal distribution is actually a family of distributions comprised of a different normal distribution for every unique combination of mean and variance. A special case of the normal distribution, called the *standard normal distribution,* exists when the mean is 0 and the variance is 1.

Definition: Standard Normal Distribution

A random variable is said to have the **standard normal distribution** if it has the normal distribution with mean $\mu = 0$ and variance $\sigma^2 = 1$, denoted as $N(0, 1)$. It is common to denote the standard normal random variable by the letter Z rather than the letter X.

Figure 8.9 shows the standard normal distribution. In it the area between $z = 0$ and $z = 1$ is .341, which indicates that the probability is 34.1% that the standard normal variable Z is between 0 and 1. By symmetry, the probability is 34.1% that Z falls between 0 and -1. By adding these two probabilities we determine that the probability is .682 that Z falls between -1 and $+1$. Note that more than 95% of the area under the curve lies between -2 and $+2$, and more than 99% of the area lies between -3 and $+3$. This is the reasoning behind the Empirical Rule, discussed in Chapter 4.

FIGURE 8.9
The standard normal distribution and its area.

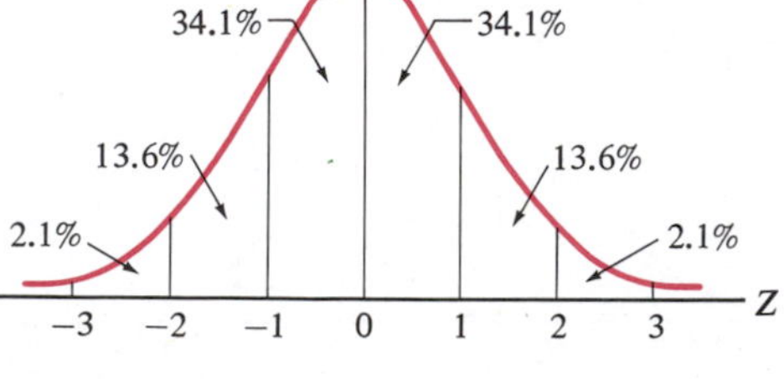

In order to calculate probabilities in problems involving the normal distribution, we need to know how to calculate areas under the normal curve $N(\mu, \sigma^2)$ between any two points a and b. The standard normal distribution is so important because any area under any normal curve can be found by calculating an appropriate related area under the standard normal curve $N(0, 1)$. To determine any area under any normal curve, simply convert the $N(\mu, \sigma^2)$ curve of interest to the $N(0, 1)$ curve and then calculate the area under the standard normal, or $N(0, 1)$, curve.

Calculating Areas Under the Standard Normal Curve

To calculate areas under the standard normal curve, we use Table A.5 in the Appendix. For ease of reference, this table has been duplicated on the inside front cover of the book. The numbers in the body of the table show the area under the standard normal curve between 0 and a positive value of Z, say z_0. That is, the values in the table show $P(0 \leq Z \leq z_0)$. Values of z_0 correct to the nearest tenth are shown in the left-hand column of the table, and the second decimal place, corresponding to hundredths, is listed across the top row of the table.

Example 8.3

Area Between the Mean and a Positive Value Under the Standard Normal Curve: Find the area under the standard normal curve between 0 and 2.34. That is, find $P(0 \leq Z \leq 2.34)$.

Solution: To find the shaded area in Figure 8.10, first move down the left-hand side of Table A.5 to the row value 2.3. Now move across to the hundredths column headed by the digit 4. The number found at the intersection of this row and column is .4904, which represents the area between 0 and 2.34. Thus we write

$$P(0 \leq Z \leq 2.34) = .4904$$

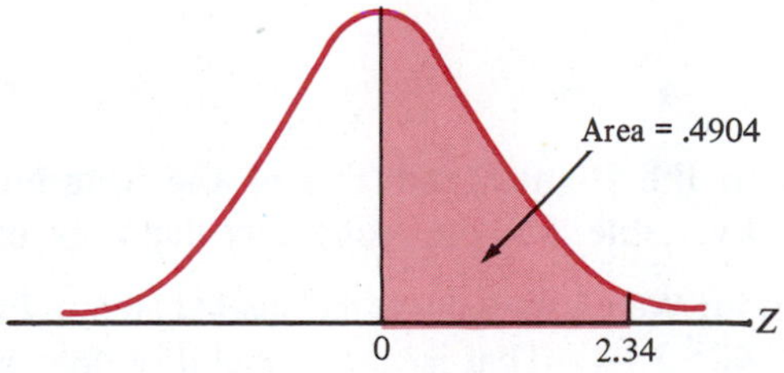

FIGURE 8.10
Area between 0 and 2.34 under the standard normal curve.

■

Example 8.4

Area Between the Mean and a Negative Value Under the Standard Normal Curve: Find the area under the standard normal curve between 0 and -1.67.

Solution: We want to find the shaded area in Figure 8.11. Because the normal distribution is symmetric, the area between -1.67 and 0 is the same as the area between 0 and 1.67. From Table A.5, we see that the area between 0 and 1.67 is .4525. We thus obtain

$$P(-1.67 \leq Z \leq 0) = .4525$$

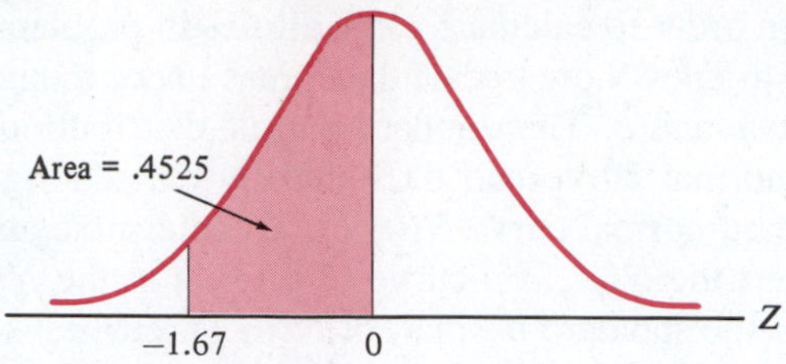

FIGURE 8.11
Area between − 1.67 and 0 under the standard normal curve.

To find areas under the standard normal distribution that are to the left of 0, calculate the corresponding area to the right of 0. ■

Example 8.5

Area Between a Negative and a Positive Value Under the Standard Normal Curve: Let Z be distributed as $N(0, 1)$. Calculate the probability that Z is between -1.21 and 2.15; that is, evaluate $P(-1.21 \leq Z \leq 2.15)$.

Solution: We want to find the area under the curve between -1.21 and 2.15 in Figure 8.12. To calculate this area requires two steps. From Table A.5, the area between 0 and 2.15 is .4842, and the area between 0 and -1.21 is .3869. The area between -1.21 and 2.15 is simply the sum of these two areas. We obtain

$$P(-1.21 \leq Z \leq 2.15) = .4842 + .3869 = .8711$$

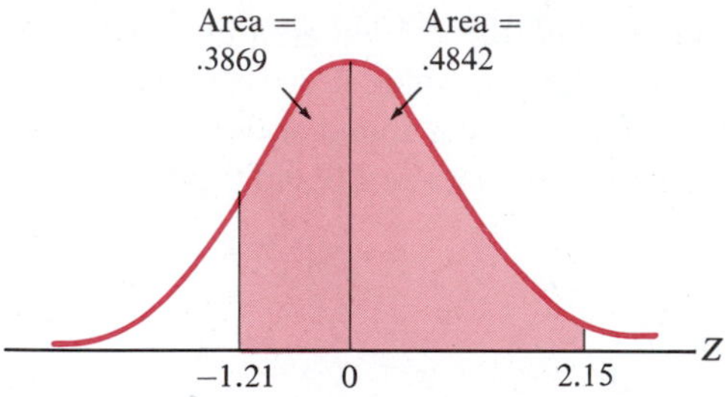

FIGURE 8.12
Area between − 1.21 and 2.15 under the standard normal curve.

■

Example 8.6

Area in the Right-Hand Tail of the Standard Normal Curve: If Z is a standard normal variable, find the probability that Z exceeds 1.64; that is, find $P(Z > 1.64)$.

Solution: We must evaluate the shaded area in Figure 8.13. First, note that $P(Z > 1.64) = P(Z \geq 1.64)$. That is, the probability does not change if we include or exclude the single point $z = 1.64$, because $P(Z = 1.64) = 0$. By symmetry, the total area under the curve to the right of $z = 0$ is .5000. Since from Table A.5 we know that the area between 0 and 1.64 is .4495, the area to the right of 1.64 must be .5000 − .4495. We thus obtain

$$P(Z > .164) = .5000 - .4495 = .0505$$

To calculate the area in a tail of the distribution beyond some value z_0, first calculate the area between 0 and z_0 and subtract this amount from .5000.

FIGURE 8.13
Area to the right of 1.64 under the standard normal curve.

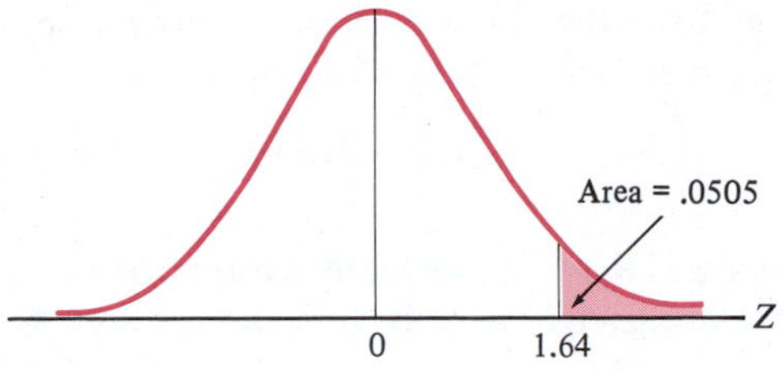

Whenever you are required to use the normal distribution to calculate a probability, it is a good practice to draw a graph and shade the appropriate area. Students sometimes report a probability as 45%, say, when the correct answer is 5% because they record the area between 0 and some positive value z_0 rather than the area in the tail of the distribution to the right of z_0.

Example 8.7 **Area in the Left-Hand Tail of the Standard Normal Curve:** Find $P(Z \leqslant -2.02)$.

Solution: We want to evaluate the shaded area in Figure 8.14. From Table A.5, the area between 0 and 2.02, and thus between −2.02 and 0, is .4783. Because the area to the left of 0 is .5000, we obtain

$$P(Z \leqslant -2.02) = .5000 - .4783 = .0217$$

FIGURE 8.14
Area to the left of −2.02 under the standard normal curve.

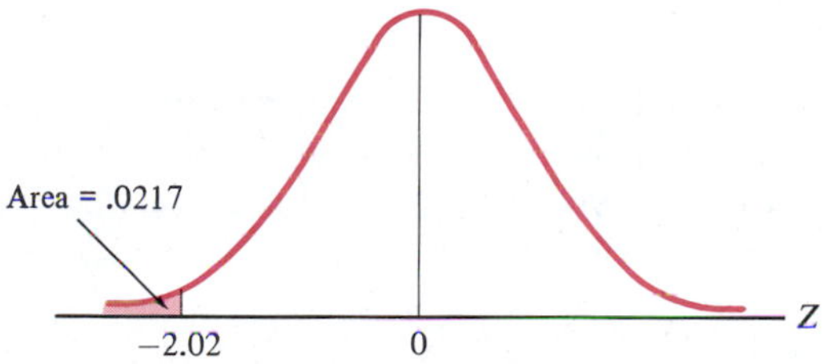

Example 8.8 **Areas in the Extreme Tail of the Standard Normal Curve:** Find $P(Z > 4.63)$.

Solution: Note that Table A.5 does not contain Z values above 4. To four decimal places, the area between 0 and 4 is .5000, so the area to the right of $z = 4$ is 0. Refer to Figure 8.15. Because the normal curve extends from $-\infty$ to $+\infty$, there is always some area between any two values of Z. In this case, however, the area is so small that

FIGURE 8.15
Area to the right of z = 4.00 under the standard normal curve.

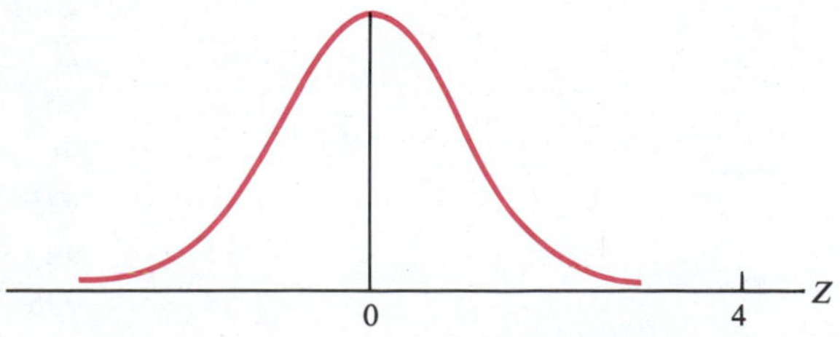

we would say that the area is 0 if we only measure it to four decimal places. Thus, to four-decimal-place accuracy, we have

$$P(Z \leqslant 4.63) = 1 \quad \text{and} \quad P(Z \geqslant 4.63) = 0$$

Example 8.9

Finding a Z Score Associated with a Specific Area: Find the values z_1 and z_2 such that the area to the right of z_2 is .025 and the area to the left of z_1 is .025.

Solution: Refer to Figure 8.16. If the area to the right of z_2 is .025, then the area between 0 and z_2 is .475. From Table A.5 we see that when $z_2 = 1.96$, the area between 0 and z_2 is .475. Similarly, the area between 0 and -1.96 is also .475. Thus, we obtain

$$P(-1.96 \leqslant Z \leqslant 1.96) = .95$$

FIGURE 8.16
Area between − 1.96 and 1.96 under the standard normal curve.

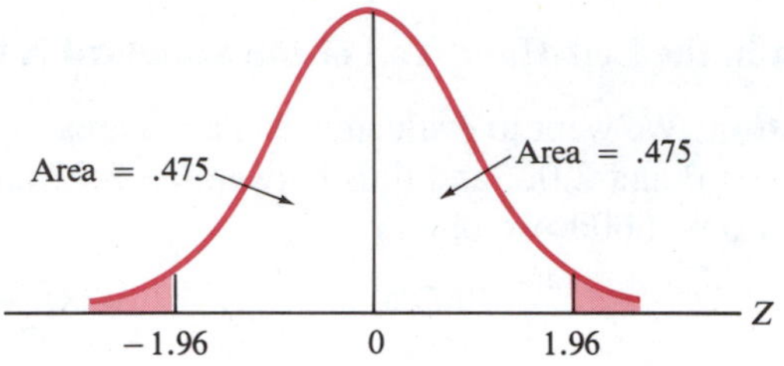

In Example 8.9, we showed that the area under the standard normal distribution between $z = 0$ and $z = 1.96$ is .475. Because the area to the left of $z = 0$ is .5000, we obtain $P(Z < 1.96) = .975$. This is a *cumulative probability.* Some other points on the cumulative distribution are shown in Table 8.2.

TABLE 8.2
Some cumulative probabilities for the standard normal distribution

z	$P(Z < z)$
−2.58	.005
−2.33	.01
−1.96	.025
−1.645	.05
−1.28	.10
−0.67	.25
0.00	.50
0.67	.25
1.28	.90
1.645	.95
1.96	.975
2.33	.99
2.58	.995

Exercises for Section 8.3

In these exercises let Z be distributed as $N(0, 1)$:

1. Find $P(0 \leq Z \leq 1.5)$.
2. Find $P(Z \leq 1.82)$.
3. Find $P(Z \geq -1.64)$.
4. Find $P(Z \leq -1.54)$.
5. Find $P(-1.61 \leq Z \leq 2.34)$.
6. Find $P(Z \leq 4.20)$.
7. Find $P(Z \leq -4.20)$.
8. Find $P(-2 \leq Z \leq 2)$.
9. Find $P(Z > 5.10)$.
10. Find $P(Z < 4.20)$.
11. Find $P(1.26 \leq Z \leq 2.45)$.
12. Find $P(-2.12 \leq Z \leq -.74)$.
13. Find z_1 such that $P(Z > z_1) = .2296$.
14. Find z_1 such that $P(Z < z_1) = .9495$.
15. Find $P(|Z| < 2.222)$.
16. Find z_1 such that $P(|Z| < z_1) = .9544$.

8.4 ▪ Calculating Areas Under Any Normal Curve

Now that we know how to find areas under the standard normal curve, we can proceed to the problem of finding areas under any normal curve $N(\mu, \sigma^2)$. By using Table A.5, we can find any area under the normal curve $N(\mu, \sigma^2)$ by exploiting the fact that any normal variable X having mean μ and variance σ^2 can be transformed into the standard normal variable Z by using what is called the *standardizing transformation*.

Definition: Standardizing Transformation

Suppose X is distributed as $N(\mu, \sigma^2)$; that is, X has a normal distribution with mean μ and variance σ^2. The transformation to the standard normal distribution is accomplished by means of the formula

$$Z = \frac{X - \mu}{\sigma}$$

This formula is called the **standardizing transformation**, and the random variable Z is called the **standardized score**, or the **Z-score**.

The formula

$$Z = \frac{X - \mu}{\sigma}$$

transforms each value of X from the $N(\mu, \sigma^2)$ distribution into a value of Z from the standard normal distribution $N(0, 1)$.

Example 8.10

Area Under the Normal Curve $N(\mu, \sigma^2)$: Suppose the random variable X has a normal distribution with mean 10 and variance 25, as shown in Figure 8.17. Find the area under the curve between $x_1 = 12$ and $x_2 = 16$.

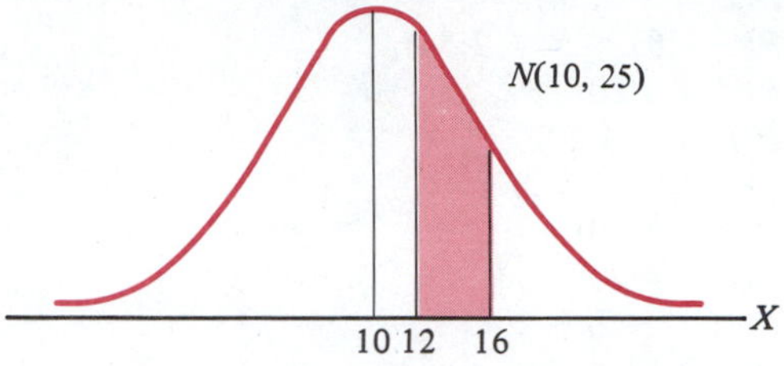

FIGURE 8.17
Area under the normal distribution $N(10, 25)$ between $x_1 = 12$ and $x_2 = 16$.

Solution: In Figure 8.17, the variable X is distributed as $N(10, 25)$; that is, $\mu = 10$ and $\sigma = 5$. To find the area under the curve between the values $x_1 = 12$ and $x_2 = 16$, we first have to find the standardized scores associated with 12 and 16. Using the formula $Z = (X - \mu)/\sigma$, we obtain

$$z_1 = \frac{x_1 - \mu}{\sigma} = \frac{12 - 10}{5} = 0.4$$

and

$$z_2 = \frac{x_2 - \mu}{\sigma} = \frac{16 - 10}{5} = 1.2$$

The area between $x_1 = 12$ and $x_2 = 16$ under the curve $N(10, 25)$ is thus equal to the area under the curve $N(0, 1)$ between $z_1 = 0.4$ and $z_2 = 1.2$. This is illustrated in Figure 8.18.

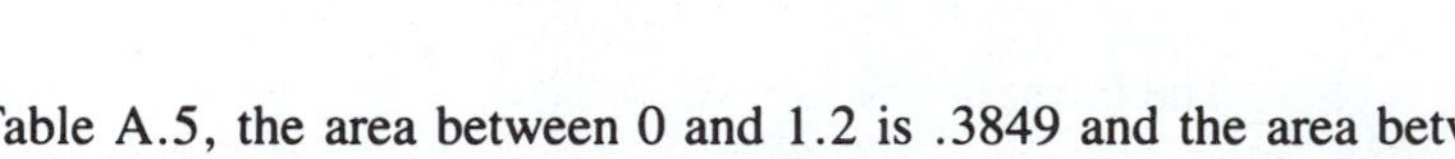

FIGURE 8.18
Area under the standard normal distribution between $z_1 = 0.4$ and $z_2 = 1.2$.

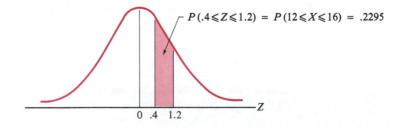

From Table A.5, the area between 0 and 1.2 is .3849 and the area between 0 and 0.4 is .1554. Therefore the area between 0.4 and 1.2 under the standard normal curve is

$$P(0.4 \leq Z \leq 1.2) = .3849 - .1554 = .2295$$

Because this area is the same as the area between 12 and 16 under the $N(10, 25)$ curve, we obtain $P(12 \leq X \leq 16) = .2295$. ■

Example 8.11

Application of the Standardizing Transformation: A company has been hired to dig a tunnel as part of a new subway system. The amount of tunnel that can be constructed during any week is a random variable that depends mainly on geological conditions. Let the random variable X denote the number of feet of tunnel completed during any week and assume that X is approximately normally distributed with mean 100 and variance 400. Find the probability that during the next week the length of tunnel completed is between $x_1 = 80$ feet and $x_2 = 120$ feet. That is, find $P(80 \leq X \leq 120)$.

Solution: The problem as stated and as transformed to standardized form is shown in Figures 8.19 and 8.20, respectively. We use the standardizing transformation and obtain

$$z_1 = \frac{x_1 - \mu}{\sigma} = \frac{80 - 100}{20} = -1$$

and

$$z_2 = \frac{x_2 - \mu}{\sigma} = \frac{120 - 100}{20} = 1$$

From Table A.5, we obtain

$$P(80 \leq X \leq 120) = P(-1 \leq Z \leq 1) = .3413 + .3413 = .6826$$

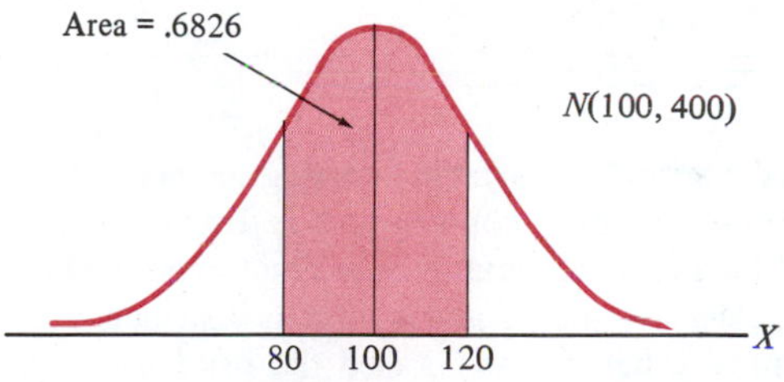

FIGURE 8.19
Area under the normal distribution $N(100, 400)$ between $x_1 = 80$ and $x_2 = 120$.

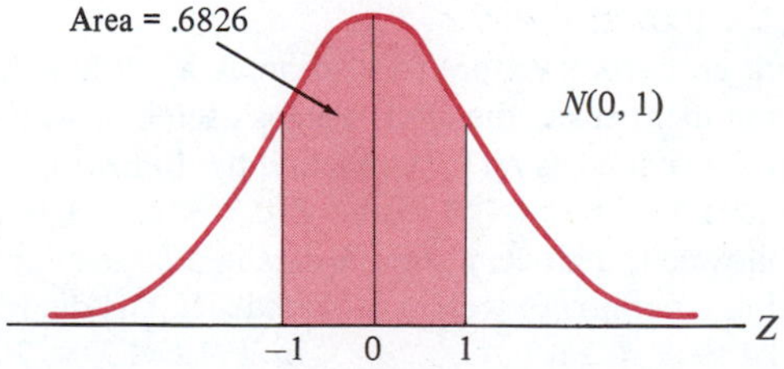

FIGURE 8.20
Area under the standard normal distribution between $z_1 = -1.0$ and $z_2 = 1.0$.

■

Example 8.12

Verification of the Empirical Rule: In Chapter 4 we introduced the Empirical Rule, which stated that if a variable has an approximately bell-shaped distribution, about 95% of the values fall within 2 standard deviations of the mean and approximately 99% of the observations fall within 3 standard deviations. The Empirical Rule is nothing more than a statement about areas under the normal distribution. For example, suppose that a random variable X is distributed as $N(\mu, \sigma^2)$. Let us find the probability that X is within 2 standard deviations of the mean. According to the Empirical Rule, this probability should be approximately .95.

Solution: If X is within 2 standard deviations of the mean, then X falls between $(\mu - 2\sigma)$ and $(\mu + 2\sigma)$. Let x_1 equal $(\mu - 2\sigma)$ and x_2 equal $(\mu + 2\sigma)$.

After making the standardizing transformation, we obtain the Z scores as follows:

$$z_1 = \frac{x_1 - \mu}{\sigma} = \frac{(\mu - 2\sigma) - \mu}{\sigma} = -2$$

and

$$z_2 = \frac{x_2 - \mu}{\sigma} = \frac{(\mu + 2\sigma) - \mu}{\sigma} = +2$$

Thus,

$$\begin{aligned} P(\mu - 2\sigma \leq X \leq \mu + 2\sigma) &= P(-2 \leq Z \leq 2) \\ &= .4772 + .4772 \\ &= .9544 \end{aligned}$$

If a variable follows the normal distribution exactly, then approximately 95% of the values fall within 2 standard deviations of the mean. ■

Exercises for Section 8.4

1. Let X be a random variable denoting the percentage change in the cost of living in the next year in a South American country. If X is distributed as $N(8, 36)$, find $P(6 \leq X \leq 12)$.
2. Let X be a random variable denoting the amount of weight that an underweight child gains after being placed on a special diet. If X is distributed as $N(6, 25)$, find $P(X > 1)$.
3. A company has recently raised the price of its product and simultaneously instituted a large advertising campaign. In the past the company had about 70 customers per day. Let X denote the increase in customers per day after the price increase and advertising campaign. If X is distributed as $N(10, 100)$, find $P(X \leq 22)$.
4. A clerk at a grocery store tries to break apart bunches of grapes into one-pound bunches. After breaking them apart, the clerk weighs each bunch. Let X denote the weight of a bunch of grapes. If X is distributed as $N(1, 0.09)$, find the following:
   a. $P(1.01 \leq X \leq 1.04)$ b. $P(0.7 \leq X \leq 1.06)$
5. At Halloween, a grocery store brings in a large supply of pumpkins. Let X be a random variable denoting a pumpkin's weight in pounds. If X is distributed as $N(22, 16)$, find the following:
   a. $P(21 \leq X \leq 25)$ b. $P(18 \leq X \leq 20)$ c. $P(X \leq 18)$
   d. $P(X \geq 17)$ e. $P(X > 30)$
6. If X is distributed as $N(50, 25)$, find the following:
   a. c such that $P(X \leq c) = .95$
   b. d such that $P(X \leq d) = .05$
   c. e such that $P(X \leq e) = .99$
   d. f such that $P(X \leq f) = .50$
   e. a and b, which are equidistant from 50 such that $P(a \leq X \leq b) = .95$

7. The IQs of college students are normally distributed with variance 400 and unknown mean. Find the mean if it is known that 2.5% of college students have IQs exceeding 150.
8. The lives of light bulbs follow a normal distribution. If 90% of the bulbs have lives exceeding 2000 hours and 3% have lives exceeding 6000 hours, what are the mean and variance of the lives of light bulbs?
9. A flashlight battery is guaranteed to last for 40 hours. Tests indicate that the length of life of these batteries is normally distributed with mean 50 and variance 16. What percentage of the batteries will fail to meet the guarantee?
10. The length of life of a certain type of television tube is normally distributed with mean $\mu = 3.8$ years and variance $\sigma^2 = 1.2$. All TV components are guaranteed for two years. What proportion of TVs will require a new tube before the guarantee expires?
11. Scores on a personnel examination at the Anderson Electronics Company are normally distributed with mean $\mu = 73$ and standard deviation $\sigma = 5$. Mary Jonathon scored 80 on the test. What proportion of people taking the test got a score higher than Mary's?
12. The number of patients entering the St. Joseph Hospital emergency room during any given weekday is approximately normally distributed with mean $\mu = 46$ and standard deviation $\sigma = 10$. Find the probability that during a given weekday, the number of patients entering the emergency room is the following:
    a. At least 30 b. More than 50 c. Less than 60 d. Between 40 and 50
13. At the Metropolitan Insurance Company, the salaries of secretaries are approximately normally distributed with mean $\mu = \$10,000$ and standard deviation $\sigma = \$1000$.
    a. Mrs. Jones claims that her salary is high enough to just put her among the highest paid 10% of all secretaries. Find her salary.
    b. Ms. Black claims that her salary is so low that 75% of the secretaries make more than she does. Find her salary.
14. The heights of adult males are normally distributed with $\mu = 68$ inches and $\sigma = 5$ inches. How tall must a male be to be among the tallest 5% of the population?
15. On a civil service exam, the grades are distributed as $N(70, 100)$. The police department will hire the applicants whose grades are among the top 10% of the population. What is the minimum grade required to be hired?
16. X is a normal random variable with mean $\mu = 500$. Find the probability $P(490 \leqslant X \leqslant 510)$ for $\sigma = 10, 16$, and 25.
17. A review of a plumber's records indicates that the time taken for a service call can be represented by a normal distribution with mean 50 minutes and standard deviation 10 minutes.
    a. What proportion of the service calls take more than 30 minutes?
    b. What proportion of the service calls take less than an hour?
    c. A plumber is scheduled to make three calls in a morning. The times taken for each of these calls are independent of one another. What is the probability that at least one of them will take more than an hour?
18. Seniors at a public school who take a placement test have scores that are normally distributed with a mean of 280 and a standard deviation of 40. Seniors at a private school who take the same test have scores that are normally distributed with a mean of 310 and a standard deviation of 60. A student qualifies for a state scholarship if his or her score exceeds 380.
    a. For a randomly chosen senior from the public school, what is the probability his or her score on the test will qualify the student for the scholarship?
    b. For a randomly selected senior from the private school, what is the probability his or her score will qualify the student for the scholarship?
19. I have two possibilities for investment. In both cases I am unsure about the percentage return but believe my uncertainty can be represented by normal distributions with a mean of 10.4 and standard deviation of 1.2 for investment A and 11.0 and 4.0 for investment B. I want to make the investment that is more likely to produce a return of at least 10%. Which should I choose? Which

should I choose if I want to choose the investment that is more likely to produce a return of at least 12%?

20. The length of time required for a crew of mechanics to complete a routine pit stop during an automobile race can be represented by a normal random variable with mean 15 seconds and standard deviation 2.0 seconds.
a. The probability is .95 that a pit stop will take at least how many seconds?
b. The probability is .70 that a pit stop will take at most how many seconds?

21. Tom drives to work every day and has meticulously recorded his driving time, which has a mean of 10 minutes and is normally distributed with standard deviation 10 minutes. If he leaves home at 9:05 A.M., what is the probability that he will be late for work if he has to punch in by 9:30 A.M.?

22. The scores for a statistics test have a normal distribution $N(80, 8)$. Tom's score was 84. Mary's score was at the 60th percentile, and John's score corresponded to a Z score of $+0.75$. If these students were listed from highest score to lowest score, what would be the correct ordering?

8.5 ▪ *The Normal Distribution as an Approximation to the Binomial Distribution*

The normal distribution can be used to solve problems involving the binomial distribution when the number of trials n is relatively large and the binomial distribution has a bell-shaped appearance closely resembling the normal curve. Solving these problems is very difficult and time consuming when we must calculate a large number of binomial probabilities. However, these probabilities can be approximated by an area under the appropriate normal curve. In Chapter 7 we indicated that the binomial distribution is approximately bell shaped (i.e., it resembles a normal distribution) when $np \geq 5$ and $nq \geq 5$, where $q = (1 - p)$.

Normal Approximation to the Binomial

Use of the normal curve to approximate binomial probabilities is appropriate provided $np \geq 5$ and $nq \geq 5$. When approximating the binomial distribution, use the normal distribution having mean $\mu = np$ and variance $\sigma^2 = npq$.

Recall from Chapter 7 that the mean of the binomial distribution is $\mu = np$ and the variance is $\sigma^2 = npq$. To use the normal curve to approximate the binomial distribution, use the normal curve having the same mean and variance as the binomial distribution it is to approximate. After verifying that the two conditions $np \geq 5$ and $nq \geq 5$ both hold, draw a graph of a normal distribution and shade the appropriate area.

A *continuity correction* is needed when we use the normal distribution to approximate the binomial distribution. When we graph the relative frequency histogram of a binomial variable X, we represent the probability that $X = x_0$ by the area of a rectangle extending from $(x_0 - 0.5)$ to $(x_0 + 0.5)$. When we use the normal distribution to approximate the binomial distribution, we approximate the area of this rectangle in the binomial histogram by the area under the normal curve between $(x_0 - 0.5)$ and $(x_0 + 0.5)$.

For example, if X follows the binomial distribution, the probability that X is, say, 6, 7, 8, or 9 is represented by the areas of the four rectangles that extend from 5.5 to 9.5. The areas of these rectangles can be approximated by the area under the normal curve between $X = 5.5$ and $X = 9.5$.

Definition: Continuity Correction

The **continuity correction** is made when we approximate a discrete probability $P(X = x)$ by the continuous probability $P(x - 0.5 \leq X \leq x + 0.5)$.

Example 8.13

Normal Approximation to the Binomial Distribution: The discrete random variable X follows the binomial distribution with $n = 10$ and $p = .5$. Let us find the probability that X takes one of the values 3, 4, 5, or 6. We will calculate the exact binomial probability and then use the normal distribution to approximate it.

Solution: For the exact binomial probabilities, we obtain $P(X = 3) = .1172$, $P(X = 4) = .2051$, $P(X = 5) = .2461$, and $P(X = 6) = .2051$. The exact binomial probability of getting 3, 4, 5, or 6 successes in 10 trials, when $p = .5$, is thus

$$P(3 \leq X \leq 6) = .1172 + .2051 + .2461 + .2051 = .7735$$

Figure 8.21 shows the relative frequency histogram of the binomial distribution for the case when $n = 10$ and $p = .5$. The probability that X is 3, 4, 5, or 6 is represented by the area of the shaded rectangles extending from 2.5 to 6.5.

FIGURE 8.21
$P(3 \leq X \leq 6)$ using the binomial distribution.

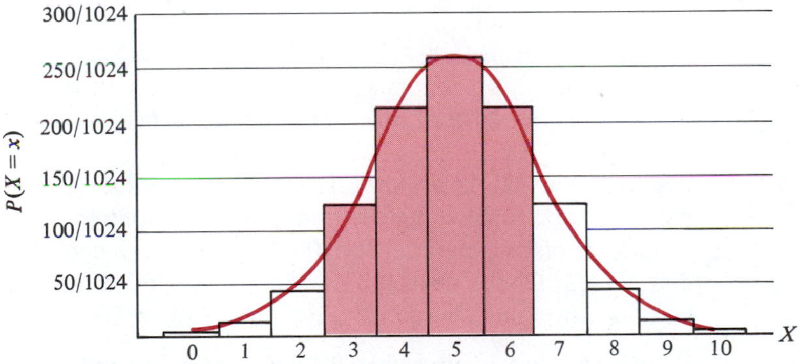

Our rule indicates that areas under the normal curve should yield good approximations to binomial probabilities provided $np \geq 5$ and $nq \geq 5$. In this case, $np = 5$ and $nq = 5$, so our rule is just satisfied.

To approximate the binomial distribution, we use the normal distribution having mean $\mu = np = 5$ and variance $\sigma^2 = npq = 2.5$. Figure 8.22 shows the normal curve with mean $\mu = np = 5$ and variance $\sigma^2 = npq = 2.5$ (the standard deviation is $\sigma = 1.58$). The shaded area in Figure 8.22 is used to approximate the shaded area in Figure 8.21.

If we use the normal curve to approximate the binomial, we should make the continuity correction. To approximate the binomial probability $P(3 \leq X \leq 6)$, we find the area under the normal curve between $x_1 = 2.5$ and $x_2 = 6.5$.

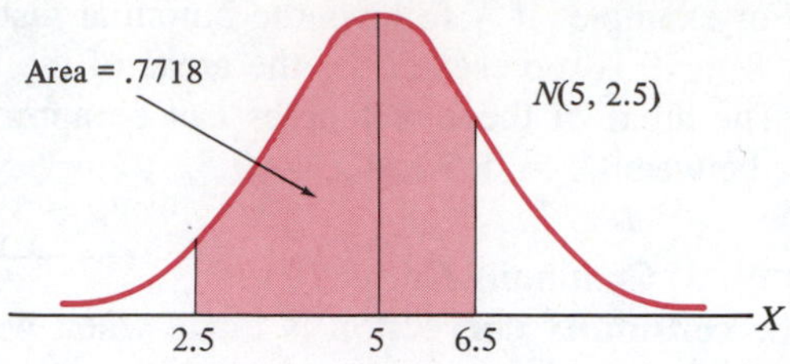

FIGURE 8.22
Area between 2.5 and 6.5 using the normal distribution *N*(5, 2.5).

To find the area under the normal distribution, make the standardizing transformation and obtain the Z scores associated with the values $x_1 = 2.5$ and $x_2 = 6.5$. We obtain

$$z_1 = \frac{x_1 - \mu}{\sigma} = \frac{2.5 - 5}{1.58} = \frac{-2.5}{1.58} = -1.58$$

and

$$z_2 = \frac{x_2 - \mu}{\sigma} = \frac{6.5 - 5}{1.58} = \frac{1.5}{1.58} = 0.95$$

From Table A.5, we obtain

$$\begin{aligned} P(-1.58 \leqslant Z \leqslant 0.95) &= (\text{area between 0 and 0.95}) \\ &\quad + (\text{area between } -1.58 \text{ and } 0) \\ &= .3289 + .4429 = .7718 \end{aligned}$$

The approximate answer .7718 obtained from the normal distribution agrees quite well with the exact binomial value .7735. The normal approximation to the binomial improves as the value of n gets larger and p gets closer to .5. ■

Example 8.14

Another Normal Approximation to the Binomial: About 50% of the individuals who purchase a personal computer from a certain supplier also order a hard disk drive. The supplier is placing an order for 100 PCs and has to decide how many to order with hard disk drives. Of the next 100 purchasers of a PC from this supplier, let X denote the number who want a hard disk drive. Find $P(X > 60)$.

Solution: If we assume that the purchasers are independent of one another, then X follows the binomial distribution with $n = 100$ and $p = .5$. To see if the normal approximation to the binomial is appropriate, we evaluate np and nq. We obtain $np = 50$ and $nq = 50$. Since both exceed 5, our rule indicates that the normal distribution should give a good approximation to the correct answer. Thus we use the normal distribution having mean $\mu = np = 50$ and variance $\sigma^2 = npq = 100(.5)(.5) = 25$.

The binomial probability that X exceeds 60 is the probability that X is 61, 62, 63, and so on, which is represented by the area under the normal curve to the right of $x_1 = 60.5$. Refer to Figure 8.23.

Using the standardizing transformation, we obtain the Z score as follows:

$$z_1 = \frac{x_1 - \mu}{\sigma} = \frac{60.5 - 50}{5} = 2.10$$

FIGURE 8.23
Area to the right of $X = 60.5$ under the normal distribution $N(50, 25)$.

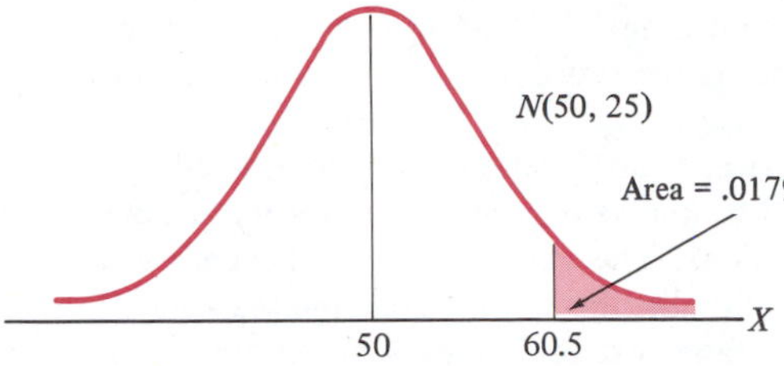

FIGURE 8.24
Area to the right of 2.10 under the standard normal distribution.

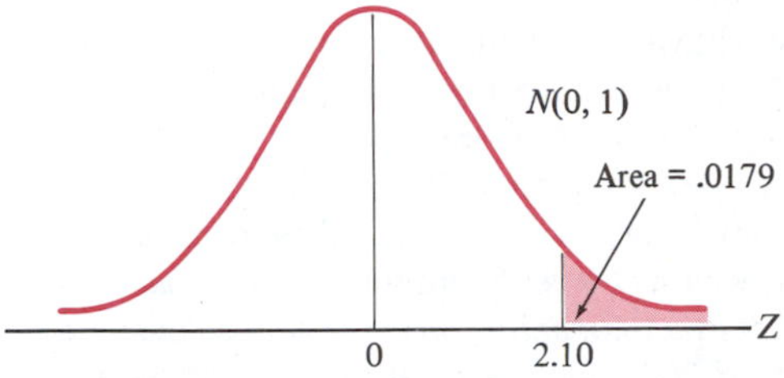

The desired probability is the area to the right of $z = 2.10$. (Refer to Figure 8.24.) The area between $z = 0$ and $z = 2.10$ is .4821, so the required area in the right-hand tail is $(.5000 - .4821) = .0179$. This answer shows that the probability is very small that more than 60 of the next 100 customers will order a PC with a hard disk drive. ■

> **Tips on Problem Solving**
> Whenever you need to find an area under the normal curve, always draw a graph and shade the appropriate area. If you are using the normal distribution to approximate the binomial, draw the normal curve and sketch a few rectangles so that you can see how to make the appropriate continuity correction. No continuity correction is needed for a continuous variable. The continuity correction is used when we approximate the distribution of a discrete binomial variable by areas under the normal curve. The continuity correction is needed when we *count* the number of successes obtained in n trials.

Exercises for Section 8.5

1. Approximately 50% of all new Ph.D.'s in economics accept government-related jobs. In a random sample of 100 new Ph.D.'s in economics, find the probability of getting from 45 to 55 government employees.
2. In Exercise 1, find the probability of getting fewer than 40 government employees.
3. If a coin is tossed 100 times, find the probability of getting 40 heads or fewer.
4. Of the students who enter law school, 80% eventually graduate. If we take a sample of 100 new law students, what is the probability that fewer than 75 eventually graduate?
5. A doctor claims that a certain drug will cure 20% of the patients suffering from a certain illness within one week. The drug is given to a random sample of 100 patients.

a. If the doctor's claim is correct, what is the probability that fewer than 15 patients are cured?
b. What is the probability of fewer than 12 of the patients being cured if the doctor's claim is correct?
c. If fewer than 12 patients are cured, would you doubt the doctor's claim? Explain.

6. An airline knows that about 20% of the people who buy tickets for a certain flight cancel their reservations. The airline sells 100 tickets for a flight that contains only 90 seats. What is the probability that there will be enough seats for all the passengers?

7. A true–false test containing 100 questions is given to a student who is totally ignorant of the subject matter. What is the probability that the student gets 65 or more correct? Use the continuity correction.

8. To test whether a person has extra sensory perception (ESP), you pick cards randomly from a 52-card deck and ask the person to guess the suit. What is the probability that the person guesses correctly 20 times or more in 48 tries? Use the continuity correction.

9. On any given day, about 30% of the stocks listed on the New York Stock Exchange increase in value, 40% stay the same, and 30% decrease in value. If you select a random sample of 100 stocks, what is the probability that more than 40 of them increase in value?

10. In a certain community, 60% of the residents are in favor of building a new library. A random sample of 200 residents is taken. What is the probability that fewer than 100 of these residents favor the construction of the library?

11. A civil service exam consists of 100 multiple choice problems. Each problem has 5 possible answers, only 1 of which is correct. What is the probability that a person with no knowledge of the test material could guess more than 35 correct answers on the exam?

12. A large shipment of a product is received at a manufacturing plant in boxes containing 100 items. Suppose that 5% of all products are defective. We randomly select 10 items from a box. If 2 or more of the items are defective, the entire box is sent back. What is the probability of the following?
a. A box will be sent back.
b. All 10 items will be good.
c. Exactly 1 of the 10 items is defective.

13. National data indicate that 80% of those who purchase a certain brand of color television will make no claims covered by the guarantee. A dealer sells 30 of these color TVs to different customers. What is the probability of the following?
a. At least 3 of these customers will have claims against the guarantee.
b. Fewer than 5 customers will have claims.

14. In many cities, downtown parking lots operate on an honor system after 9 P.M. A survey indicates that the probability is 25% that a person will not pay for his or her parking under the system. On a given night, a parking lot has 40 cars parked in it. What is the probability of the following?
a. More than 10 of the drivers do not pay.
b. More than 35 of the drivers do pay.

15. A census report states that 15% of the country's households have incomes below the poverty line. Suppose that 1000 households are randomly selected. Find the probability that fewer than 200 of these households are below the poverty line.

16. A credit card company claims that 80% of all clothing purchases in excess of $60 are made with credit cards. A random sample of 90 clothing purchases in excess of $60 is obtained. If, in fact, 80% of all clothing purchases in excess of $60 are made with credit cards and if X is the number in a sample of 90 that make credit card purchases, find values for the following:
a. $P(X \leq 75)$ b. $P(75 \leq X \leq 85)$

17. In the last election, 60% of all voters in a certain county voted for a tax increase to pay for a better school system. Suppose we select a random sample of 400 of all those who voted.
a. What is the probability that more than 260 of the sample members voted for the tax increase?
b. What is the probability that at least 200 of the sample members voted for the tax increase?

18. A car rental company has determined that the probability that a car will need service work in any given month is .1. The company has 500 cars.
a. What is the probability that more than 80 will require service work in a particular month?
b. What is the probability that fewer than 60 will need service work in a given month?

19. A survey research organization has found that answers are received from 25% of people sent a particular mail questionnaire. If this questionnaire is sent to 1000 people, what is the probability that at least 300 answers will be received?

8.6 ▪ The Exponential Distribution (Optional)

The exponential probability distribution is a family of continuous probability distributions that is useful in describing the time it takes to complete a task. The exponential random variable can be used to describe such phenomena as the time between arrivals at a checkout line in a supermarket, the time required to respond to a fire alarm, and the time required for a machine to paint a car door. The exponential distribution is represented by the following density function:

$$f(x) = (1/\mu)e^{-x/\mu} \quad \text{for } x \geqslant 0$$

The parameter μ, which is always positive for the exponential distribution, is the mean of the probability distribution and $e = 2.71828$. . . . Figure 8.25 shows the exponential distribution when $\mu = 15$. Each different value of μ yields a different member of the exponential family.

FIGURE 8.25
Exponential distribution with $\mu = 15$.

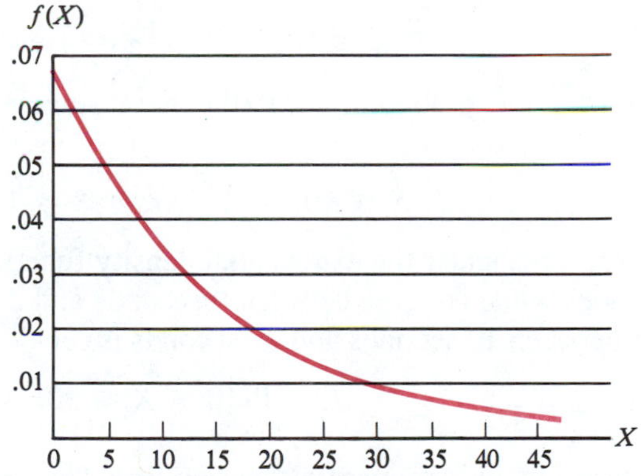

Characteristics of the Exponential Distribution

1. The random variable X can take any value from 0 to ∞.
2. The exponential distribution is skewed to the right.
3. The mode of the distribution is 0. That is, regardless of the value of μ, the peak of the density function occurs at $X = 0$ and the function decreases as X increases.
4. Because the distribution is skewed to the right, we have

$$\text{Mode} < \text{median} < \text{mean}$$

Computing Probabilities for the Exponential Distribution

To calculate areas under the exponential density function, we use the accompanying formula, which shows the area under the exponential density function between 0 and any specific value $X = x$.

Computing Exponential Probabilities

Let the random variable X follow the exponential distribution with mean μ. The probability that X takes a value between $X = 0$ and $X = x$ is given by

$$P(X \leq x) = 1 - e^{-x/\mu}$$

Example 8.15

Computing an Exponential Probability: The number of seconds X between vehicle arrivals at a toll booth follows the exponential distribution with mean $\mu = 15$ seconds. Find the probability that the next vehicle arrives in less than 30 seconds.

Solution: The corresponding exponential density function is

$$f(x) = (1/15)e^{-x/15} = .067e^{-0.067x}$$

This density function is shown in Figure 8.25. The probability that the next vehicle arrives in less than 30 seconds is given by

$$P(X \leq 30) = 1 - e^{-30/15} = 1 - e^{-2} = .8647$$

Similarly, the probability that the next vehicle arrives in less than 10 seconds is given by

$$P(X \leq 10) = 1 - e^{-10/15} = 1 - e^{-0.667} = .4868$$

The area under the exponential density function between 0 seconds and 10 seconds is .4868, while the area between 0 seconds and 30 seconds is .8647. It follows that the area between 10 seconds and 30 seconds is .8647 − .4868 = .3779, and so

$$P(10 \leq X \leq 30) = .3779$$

■

Example 8.16

Calculating an Exponential Probability: The time required for a police car to respond to a call follows the exponential distribution with mean $\mu = 4$ minutes. Find the probability that a car will respond to a call in less than 2 minutes and in less than 6 minutes.

Solution: The probability that a car will respond in less than 2 minutes is given by

$$P(X \leq 2) = 1 - e^{-2/4} = 1 - e^{-0.5} = .3935$$

Similarly, the probability that a car will respond in less than 6 minutes is given by

$$P(X \leq 6) = 1 - e^{-6/4} = 1 - e^{-1.5} = .7769$$

■

Relationship Between Poisson and Exponential Distributions

The Poisson and exponential probability distributions are closely related to one another. The Poisson distribution is a discrete distribution that is frequently used in problems concerning the number of occurrences of some event in a specified interval of time or space, whereas the exponential distribution is a continuous distribution that is used for problems concerning the amount of time between occurrences of some event. If the Poisson distribution describes the number of occurrences per interval, then the exponential distribution describes the length of the interval between occurrences. Statistical theory gives us the accompanying theorem on the relationship between the Poisson and exponential distributions.

Relationship Between Poisson and Exponential Distributions

If occurrences of some event are generated by a process that follows the Poisson distribution where the mean number of occurrences in a certain interval is μ, then the length of time between successive occurrences of the event follows the exponential distribution with mean $1/\mu$.

Example 8.17 **Relationship Between Poisson and Exponential Distributions:** The number of accidents at a manufacturing plant follows a Poisson distribution with a mean of 4 per year. Find the average length of time between accidents.

Solution: If the average number of accidents per year is 4, then the length of time between successive accidents at the plant follows an exponential distribution with mean $\frac{1}{4}$, or 0.25 year. ■

Exercises for Section 8.6

1. Machines are used to mix sand and cement at a large construction site. The time between breakdowns for each of the machines is best represented by an exponential distribution with mean equal to 200 hours of operation. Suppose a particular machine was just put into service.
   a. What is the probability that it will not break down for at least 50 hours?
   b. What is the probability that it will break down within the next 100 hours?

2. The shelf life of bread is approximated by an exponential distribution with mean equal to 2.8 days. What proportion of the loaves stocked today would you expect to be sellable (i.e., not stale) 3 days from now?

3. The time an individual has to wait in line at a fast-food hamburger franchise has an exponential distribution with mean equal to 1.5 minutes.
   a. What is the probability that an individual will have to wait more than 2 minutes before being served?
   b. What is the probability that an individual will have to wait less than 30 seconds?

4. The time needed to service a car at a service station is an exponential random variable with a mean of 2 minutes. Determine the probability that a newly arriving car will be serviced as follows:
   a. Within 1 minute b. Within 2 minutes

5. The length of life of a critical computer component is an exponential random variable with a mean of 5 years. Suppose the warranty period is 3 years. What proportion of components can be expected to fail in less than 3 years?

Chapter 8 Summary

A continuous random variable can assume any value in a specific interval. The probability distribution of a continuous random variable is represented by a *density function,* denoted $f(x)$. For any density function, $f(x)$ must be nonnegative for all values of x and the total area under any density function must equal 1. The probability that a continuous random variable falls between the values a and b is represented by the area under the appropriate density function between a and b. The mean, or expected value, of a continuous random variable is the center of gravity of the probability distribution. The variance σ^2 and its square root, the standard deviation σ, measure the amount of dispersion in the population of values.

Three important continuous distributions were discussed in this chapter: the *uniform distribution,* the *normal distribution,* and the *exponential distribution.* The formula for the uniform density function is

$$f(x) = 1/(b - a) \quad \text{where } a \leqslant x \leqslant b$$

The graph of the uniform density function is a level curve extending from a lower bound a to an upper bound b. The mean of the uniform distribution is $(a + b)/2$ and the variance is $(b - a)^2/12$.

The normal curves are a family of bell-shaped, unimodal, symmetric distributions. The normal distribution having mean μ and variance σ^2 is denoted $N(\mu, \sigma^2)$. The *standard normal curve* has mean of 0 and standard deviation of 1. Any normal random variable X can be transformed to a standard normal random variable Z by using the *standardizing transformation* $Z = (X - \mu)/\sigma$.

Table A-5 in the Appendix shows areas under the standard normal distribution. To determine areas under any normal distribution, find the appropriate area under the standard normal curve after you first standardize the variable by using the transformation $Z = (X - \mu)/\sigma$.

The normal distribution can be used to approximate binomial probabilities when the number of trials is large enough so that $np \geqslant 5$ and $nq \geqslant 5$. Because the normal distribution is continuous and the binomial is discrete, a continuity correction is applied when approximating the binomial distribution by the appropriate normal distribution.

The exponential distribution has applications in queueing theory and in waiting-time problems. The exponential density function is

$$f(x) = (1/\mu)e^{-x/\mu} \quad \text{for } x \geqslant 0$$

and is a monotonically decreasing function of x. Areas under the exponential density function are obtained by using the formula

$$P(0 \leqslant X \leqslant x) = 1 - e^{-x/\mu}$$

In the next chapter, we will discuss the Central Limit Theorem and show why the normal distribution is the most important of all continuous probability distributions.

Chapter 8 ▪ Supplementary Exercises

1. Let Z be distributed as $N(0, 1)$. Find the following probabilities:
   a. $P(0 \leqslant Z \leqslant 1.53)$ b. $P(-1.67 \leqslant Z \leqslant 0)$ c. $P(-2.25 < Z < 1.96)$
   d. $P(Z < -2.44)$ e. $P(Z > -2.57)$ f. $P(Z > 2.72)$
   g. $P(Z \leqslant 1.90)$ h. $P(Z < 4.61)$ i. $P(Z \leqslant -4.44)$
   j. $P(Z > -6.21)$ k. $P(Z \geqslant 6.24)$ l. $P(1.31 \leqslant Z \leqslant 2.42)$
   m. $P(-2.61 \leqslant Z \leqslant -1.44)$
2. Let X be distributed as $N(7, 100)$. Find the following probabilities:
   a. $P(0 < X < 8)$ b. $P(-2 < X < 5)$ c. $P(8.5 < X < 10.7)$
   d. $P(2.7 < X < 6.6)$ e. $P(X < 11.8)$ f. $P(X \geqslant 18)$
   g. $P(X < 0)$ h. $P(1.4 < X < 27.2)$
3. Let X be distributed as $N(\mu, \sigma^2)$. Find the following probabilities:
   a. $P(X < \mu)$ b. $P(X \geqslant \mu)$ c. $P(\mu - \sigma < X < \mu + \sigma)$
   d. $P(\mu - 2\sigma \leqslant X \leqslant \mu + 2\sigma)$ e. $P(\mu - 3\sigma \leqslant X \leqslant \mu + 3\sigma)$
   f. $P(\mu - 1.96\sigma \leqslant X \leqslant \mu + 1.96\sigma)$
4. Find the probability that a student can guess more than 65 answers correctly on a true–false test with 100 questions.
5. Candidate A is favored by 64% of the registered voters. You select a random sample of 100 registered voters. What is the probability that fewer than 50 of these people favor Candidate A?
6. Students' grade point averages at a school are normally distributed with mean 2.9 and variance 0.16. What average must a student attain to be in the upper 10% of the school?
7. To test whether a person has extra sensory perception, you select a card from a deck and ask the person to guess the suit. What is the probability that he or she will be correct 70 times or more in 192 tries by just guessing?
8. On the average, 20% of the individuals who reserve a table at a restaurant will not appear. If the restaurant has 90 tables and takes 100 reservations, what is the probability that it will have enough tables to accommodate everyone? Assume all reservations are independent of one another.
9. Scores on a typing exam are normally distributed with mean 245 and variance 100. To be hired, an individual must score in the top 30% of the population. What is the minimum score required to get hired?
10. A doctor claims to have found a drug that will cure 80% of the people who use it. If the drug is given to 10,000 people, what is the probability that 7000 or fewer will be cured?
11. On a civil service exam, the scores are normally distributed with a mean of 70 and a standard deviation of 10. The highest 10% get A's, the next 20% get B's, the next 40% get C's, the next 20% get D's, and the lowest 10% get F's. Determine the scores that separate A from B, B from C, C from D, and D from F.
12. IQs are normally distributed with mean 100 and variance 225. What proportion of the population have IQs between 120 and 135?
13. The weight of cereal in a box is normally distributed with mean 16.5 ounces and standard deviation 0.1 ounce. What percentage of the boxes contain less than 16 ounces of cereal?
14. The diameters of steel rods manufactured by a company are normally distributed with mean 2 inches and standard deviation 0.02 inch. A rod is defective if its diameter is less than 1.95 inches. What percentage of the rods are defective?

15. The amount of liquid placed in a soft drink cup is normally distributed with mean 10.5 ounces and standard deviation 0.5 ounce. If we purchase two drinks, what is the probability that each cup contains less than 10 ounces of liquid?
16. A college basketball coach is seeking tall recruits who are smart enough to be eligible for college. The recruit must be at least 74 inches tall and have an IQ of 115 or above. Height and IQ are independent of one another. IQ is normally distributed with mean 100 and standard deviation 12, and height is normally distributed with mean 70 and standard deviation 2 inches. What percentage of the population satisfies the coach's requirements?
17. At a shoe store, the time between customer arrivals follows the exponential distribution with mean $\mu = 2$ minutes. Find the probability that the next customer arrives in less than 3 minutes.
18. According to actuarial tables, the probability is .03 that a person aged 70 will die within one year. A company insures 6400 people of age 70. What is the probability that 200 or more of these people will die within one year?
19. The loan department of the Bank of Austin has determined that the home loans they have issued during the last three years are normally distributed with a mean of \$35,000 and a standard deviation of \$6000. What proportion of loans are of the following amounts?
    a. \$25,000 or less
    b. Between \$25,000 and \$30,000
    c. Between \$25,000 and \$35,000
    d. At least \$41,000
    e. More than \$38,000
20. During the last year at Sandy's Hamburger Shop, the amount of time customers took to complete lunch after being seated and served was normally distributed with mean 24 minutes and standard deviation 4. A customer is randomly selected. When eating lunch, what proportion of customers require the following amounts of time?
    a. Less than 20 minutes
    b. More than 29 minutes
    c. Less than 32 minutes
    d. More than 14 minutes
    e. Between 16 and 18 minutes
21. The Acme Computer Company has two sales representatives, Mr. Smith and Ms. Brown, who sell computer equipment. Smith sells to banks and Brown to the insurance companies. Sales to banks are normally distributed with mean $\mu = \$200,000$ per month and standard deviation $\sigma = \$30,000$, and sales to insurance companies are normally distributed with mean $\mu = \$260,000$ per month and standard deviation $\sigma = \$40,000$.
    a. During a given month, Smith sells \$260,000 worth of computer equipment. To do an equally good job, how much equipment must Brown sell to insurance companies?
    b. If Smith sold \$160,000 worth of computer equipment, how much equipment must Brown sell to do an equally good job?
22. The mayor of Oakmont wants to know what proportion of the population favor raising taxes to build a new community swimming pool. Suppose 40% of the population favor a new pool. The mayor's office contacts a random sample of 100 Oakmont citizens. Find the probability of the following:
    a. More than 50 citizens favor raising taxes.
    b. Fewer than 35 favor raising taxes.
23. In Asheville, about 20% of all phone calls coming through a certain telephone operator are long distance calls. If the operator takes 280 calls, find the probability of the following number of long distance calls:
    a. Fewer than 50
    b. More than 70

c. Between 60 and 72
d. Fewer than 66

24. In a recent survey, it was found that 15% of the residents of Bedford listened to radio station WAMX between 5 P.M. and 6 P.M. To see if the ratings have changed, a random sample of 400 residents are contacted. If p is still .15, find the probability that the number of residents in the sample who listen to WAMX during the prescribed hour is as follows:
a. Fewer than 40
b. More than 50
c. More than 100
d. If more than 100 people in the sample listen to WAMX, would this convince you that the population proportion exceeds .15? Explain.

25. The Polychrome Camera Company produces flashbulbs for inexpensive cameras, and about 5% of the flashbulbs are defective. If a random sample of 2000 flashbulbs is shipped to a certain retail outlet, find the probability that the number of defective bulbs is as follows:
a. More than 120
b. Fewer than 75
c. Between 80 and 90

26. The Cuneo Cosmetics Company has decided to sponsor a daytime television program because an industry report stated that 70% of the program's viewers are female. If this assumption is correct, find the probability that in a random sample of 150 viewers, the number of females is as follows:
a. Fewer than 100
b. Fewer than 90
c. Suppose Cuneo took a random sample of 150 viewers and fewer than 90 were female. Would this convince you that the population proportion is less than .75? Explain.

27. Household incomes in the town of Wilkinsburg are normally distributed with mean μ = \$26,000 and standard deviation σ = \$6000. What proportion of households have incomes exceeding \$20,000?

28. Gavett's Appliance Store has a rule that any credit purchase exceeding \$200 has to be approved by a department supervisor. It is known that credit purchases are normally distributed with mean μ = \$130 and standard deviation σ = \$50.
a. What proportion of credit purchases must be approved by department supervisors?
b. Three credit sales are made. What is the probability that approval is needed at least once?

29. At the Kennedy Construction Company, the average wage is \$8.60 per hour and the standard deviation is \$0.50. If wages follow a normal distribution, what proportion of the workers earn the following amounts?
a. More than \$10 per hour
b. Less than \$8 per hour
c. What is the probability that two randomly selected workers both earn more than \$9 per hour?

30. Past experience indicates that 30% of the spectators at major league baseball games buy a hot dog. The attendance at a baseball game is 25,000, and the team has a supply of 15,000 hot dogs.
a. How many spectators do you expect to buy a hot dog?
b. Assume that no one buys more than one hot dog. What is the probability that the supply will run out?

31. The manager of Walton's Discount Shoe Store knows that daily revenue from shoe sales is normally distributed with mean \$4000 and standard deviation \$700. Find the probability of the following:
a. On 3 successive days, revenue never exceeds \$3000.
b. On 2 consecutive days, revenue exceeds \$5000.

32. The weight of luggage on international flights averages 22.6 pounds with a standard deviation of 5.4 pounds.

a. If the weights are normally distributed, what proportion of the luggage weighs more than 30 pounds?
b. In a shipment of 200 pieces of luggage, how many can be expected to weigh less than 20 pounds?

33. The probability that a critical component in a space shuttle will fail in its first 100 hours of use is .06. Suppose that 1400 of these components are randomly selected. Find the probability of the following:
a. More than 100 of these components fail in their first 100 hours of use.
b. Fewer than 60 of these components fail in their first 100 hours of use.
c. How many of the 1400 components would you expect to fail in their first 100 hours of use?

34. An accountant helps people prepare their income tax returns. The accountant is paid $40 per hour, and the time required to complete a tax form is normally distributed with mean $\mu = 45$ minutes and standard deviation $\sigma = 10$ minutes.
a. What proportion of the customers will have to pay more than $25?
b. What is the probability that a tax form will require less than 30 minutes to complete?

35. Traffic studies indicate that the number of cars using a certain bridge on weekday afternoons between 4 P.M. and 5 P.M. is normally distributed with mean $\mu = 2000$ and standard deviation $\sigma = 200$. Severe traffic jams occur if more than 2500 cars try to use the bridge in any one-hour period.
a. Find the probability that on any given weekday, a severe traffic jam occurs between 4 P.M. and 5 P.M.
b. During a period covering 200 weekdays, how many traffic jams would you expect to occur?

36. In a midwestern state, the age of members of the state legislature is normally distributed with mean $\mu = 50$ years and standard deviation $\sigma = 5$. What proportion of the legislators have the following ages?
a. Over 60 years of age
b. 55 or younger

37. The time between arrivals at a service station follows the exponential distribution with mean $\mu = 50$ seconds. Find the probability that the next customer arrives in less than 20 seconds.

38. The Cooper Auto Repair Center has just received a shipment of 1000 spark plugs from a supplier. In past shipments, the gap in 6% of the spark plugs obtained from the supplier has been set incorrectly.
a. In the new supply, what is the expected number of misgapped plugs?
b. What is the probability that there will be 50 or fewer misgapped plugs?
c. What is the probability that there will be 74 or more misgapped plugs?

39. The Montgomery Employment Agency claims that it finds jobs for 75% of its clients.
a. What is the probability that in a sample of 160 job applicants the agency finds employment for fewer than 100?
b. If fewer than 100 applicants find jobs, would this convince you that Montgomery's claim is false? Explain.

40. An airline analyst predicts an average monthly demand of 3900 passengers with a standard deviation of 400 passengers on a particular plane route. Assume the monthly demand is approximately normally distributed.
a. Find the probability that in a given month the demand for the flight is between 3500 and 4300.
b. Next month the actual demand is 2500. Find the probability that the demand for this route would be 2500 or less if the analyst's predictions are correct.
c. If the actual demand next month turns out to be 2500 passengers, would you be convinced that the analyst's predictions are wrong? Explain.

41. At a fast-food restaurant, the daily demand for ground beef is normally distributed with a mean of 680 pounds and a standard deviation of 80 pounds. The manager would like to ensure that sufficient ground beef is available in the restaurant each day so that the probability is no greater than 2% that the day's supply is exhausted. How many pounds of ground beef should the manager have available for use each day?

42. GMAT (Graduate Management Admissions Test) scores are normally distributed with a mean of 500 and a standard deviation of 100.

a. What proportion of scores fall in the interval from 350 to 450?

b. What proportion of scores fall in the interval from 550 to 650?

c. A certain graduate business school automatically accepts all applicants whose GMAT scores exceed 620. Approximately what proportion of all those taking the GMAT would qualify for admission to this school?

43. At Domino's Pizza Shop, the time between calls for pizza follows the exponential distribution with mean $\mu = 80$ seconds. Find the probability that the next call occurs in less than 2 minutes.

44. The duration of a flight between two cities is normally distributed with mean $\mu = 4.6$ hours and standard deviation $\sigma = 0.30$ hour. Let X denote the duration of a randomly selected flight.

a. Find $P(X \leq 4.0)$.

b. Find $P(4.2 \leq X \leq 5.0)$.

c. Find the 80th percentile of the probability distribution.

d. During 90% of the flights, within what interval centered about μ will the flight duration fall?

45. In restoring an office building, the required number of carpentry man-hours (X) is assumed to be a random variable that is distributed $N(100, 144)$. The required number of painting man-hours (Y) is assessed to be $N(25, 25)$. Both X and Y are assumed to be independent random variables.

a. Let $T = X + Y$. What does T represent?

b. If X and Y are normally distributed, then the probability distribution of T is normal. What is the expected value of T?

c. The variance of T is the sum of the variances of X and Y. What is the variance of T?

d. Find the probability that T exceeds 150.

e. The labor cost of either type of work is $10 per hour. A sum of $1600 has been budgeted for all labor. What is the probability that the total labor cost will not exceed the budget?

46. The proportion of fat in the bodies of adult American men is an approximately normal random variable with mean $\mu = .15$ and standard deviation $\sigma = .04$. Suppose that 22% or more body fat is considered obese. What proportion of men are obese?

47. If $p = .20$ and $n = 100$, should you use the normal distribution or the Poisson distribution to approximate the binomial distribution?

48. Given $p = .01$ and $n = 300$, should you use the normal distribution or the Poisson distribution to approximate the binomial distribution?

49. The sulfur content of a shipment of coal can be assumed to be uniformly distributed between 1% and 3%. Let X denote the sulfur content of a particular shipment of coal.

a. Draw the probability density function for the random variable X.

b. Find the probability that a randomly chosen shipment has sulfur content over 1.6%.

50. The time of arrival of the early bus is uniformly distributed between 7:00 A.M. and 7:15 A.M.

a. Determine the probability that the bus will arrive before 7:05 A.M.

b. If I get to the bus stop at exactly 7:00 A.M., determine the expected waiting time.

51. Records show that the time required to treat patients in the emergency room of a hospital is an exponential random variable with a mean of 30 minutes.

a. Find the probability that the next treatment takes more than 45 minutes.

b. Find the probability that the next treatment takes less than 30 minutes.

52. Use the table for the standard normal distribution and find the values of Z such that the area in the right-hand tail of the standard normal distribution is as follows:

a. 10% b. 5% c. 2.5% d. 1% e. 0.5%

53. A certain college has found that 40% of the applicants accepted eventually decide to attend school elsewhere. How many students should be admitted if the admissions committee wants the expected size of the freshman class to be 500?

54. Suppose the school in Exercise 53 can accommodate a maximum of 550 new students. How many students should be accepted if the committee wants the probability of more than 550 new students to be less than .10?

55. If too few students show up at the school in Exercise 53, then a severe financial strain is put on the college. How many students should be accepted if the committee wants the probability of fewer than 450 students coming in to be less than .10?

56. The *University of California, Berkeley Wellness Letter* of May 1988 states that the average American man is 5 feet 9 inches tall and the average woman is 5 feet 4 inches tall. It states that about 10% of men are over 6 feet and 10% are under 5 feet 6 inches; about 10% of all women are under 5 feet and 10% are over 5 feet 8 inches. If heights are normally distributed, find the standard deviations for men's and women's heights.

References

FREUND, JOHN E., and R. E. WALPOLE. *Mathematical Statistics*. 4th ed. Englewood Cliffs, N.J.: Prentice-Hall, 1987.

Handbook of Tables for Probability and Statistics. 2d ed. Cleveland: Chemical Rubber Co., 1968.

HOEL, PAUL G. *Elementary Statistics*. 4th ed. New York: Wiley, 1976.

National Bureau of Standards. *Tables of the Binomial Probability Distribution*. Washington, D.C.: Government Printing Office, 1949.

NETER, JOHN, WILLIAM WASSERMAN, and G. A. WHITMORE. *Fundamental Statistics for Business and Economics*. 4th ed. Boston: Allyn and Bacon, 1973.

Chapter Nine
Sampling Theory and Some Important Sampling Distributions

Many important statistical problems involve estimating or testing hypotheses about population parameters. For example, we may be interested in estimating the average starting salary of college graduates, the average number of miles traveled per year by rental cars, the proportion of the population that watched a certain television program, or the proportion of the labor force that is unemployed.

In each of these problems, we are interested in finding the mean of some population or the proportion of individuals in a population that possess some characteristic. In each case, it is unreasonable to examine the entire population. To estimate the population parameters or to test hypotheses about these parameters, we use sample data. In general, estimates based on a sample of data will not equal the true values of the population parameters and will vary from sample to sample. For this reason, the estimates themselves are random variables and have probability distributions. We discuss these distributions in detail in this chapter.

9.1 ▪ *Estimators and Estimates*

There is a fine distinction between an *estimator* and an *estimate*. These terms are defined in the accompanying box.

Definition: Estimator and Estimate

Suppose we have a random sample $x_1, x_2, \ldots, x_n$ of observations from some population. An **estimator** of a population parameter is a rule that tells us how to use the values $x_1, x_2, \ldots, x_n$ to estimate the parameter. An **estimate** is the *value* obtained after the observations $x_1, x_2, \ldots, x_n$ have been substituted into the formula.

For a given population, numerous different samples of size n can be selected. Given the n observations $x_1, x_2, \ldots, x_n$, we can calculate an estimate $\hat{\theta}$, whose value varies from sample to sample and depends on chance. The estimator $\hat{\theta}$ is a random variable because *before* the sample is selected, we do not know what the value of $\hat{\theta}$ will be. The *sampling distribution* of an estimator $\hat{\theta}$ shows how the different possible values of $\hat{\theta}$ are distributed when different samples of size n are selected.

Definition: Sampling Distribution

For a given population, an estimator $\hat{\theta}$ will assume various values with probabilities that depend on the characteristics of the population. Because the value that the estimator $\hat{\theta}$ assumes varies from sample to sample, $\hat{\theta}$ is a random variable that has a probability distribution. This probability distribution is called the **sampling distribution** of the random variable $\hat{\theta}$.

Desirable Properties of Estimators

Because different estimators can be used to estimate any population parameter, we need some criteria for evaluating estimators. What properties does a good estimator have? In general, a good estimator produces estimates that are close to the unknown population parameter being estimated. The distance between the estimate and the value being estimated is called the *sampling error.*

Definition: Sampling Error

Let $\hat{\theta}$ be an estimator of some unknown population parameter θ. The distance

$$D = |\hat{\theta} - \theta|$$

is called the **sampling error**, or the **error of estimation**.

The sampling error will vary from sample to sample, of course. For some samples, $\hat{\theta}$ will be close to θ and the sampling error D will be small; for other samples, D might be quite large. A good estimator is one in which the "typical" sampling error is small. The typical sampling error will be small if most of the possible values of $\hat{\theta}$ are close to θ. In other words, the typical sampling error will be small if the probability distribution of $\hat{\theta}$ is highly concentrated about θ. Consequently, a good estimator is one whose sampling distribution is highly concentrated about θ.

An estimator is *biased* if there is a systematic tendency to either overestimate or underestimate the population parameter being estimated. If the sampling distribution of $\hat{\theta}$ is centered at the value θ that we are trying to estimate, $\hat{\theta}$ is said to be an *unbiased* estimator of θ. If $E(\hat{\theta}) \neq \theta$, then $\hat{\theta}$ is a biased estimator of θ and the *bias* is

$$\text{Bias}(\hat{\theta}) = E(\hat{\theta}) - \theta$$

Definition: Unbiased Estimator

Let $\hat{\theta}$ be an estimator of an unknown population parameter θ. $\hat{\theta}$ is an **unbiased estimator** of θ if

$$E(\hat{\theta}) = \theta$$

An estimator $\hat{\theta}$ is an unbiased estimator of θ if, in many repeated samples, the average value of $\hat{\theta}$ is equal to the population parameter being estimated so there is no tendency to overestimate or underestimate the population parameter. An unbiased estimator is correct "on the average."

The sample mean, the sample proportion, and the sample variance are unbiased estimators of the corresponding population parameters. In general, however, the sample standard deviation is *not* an unbiased estimator of the population standard deviation.

Figure 9.1 shows the sampling distributions of two hypothetical estimators θ_1 and θ_2 used to estimate some population parameter θ. Because the sampling distribution of θ_1 is centered at θ, it follows that $E(\theta_1) = \theta$ and that θ_1 is an unbiased estimator of θ. In contrast, the sampling distribution of θ_2 is centered at some value higher than θ, which means that θ_2 is a biased estimator of θ. As a result, if we use θ_2 to estimate θ, our estimate will usually be too high. Other things being equal, we prefer an unbiased estimator to a biased estimator.

FIGURE 9.1
Biased and unbiased estimators.

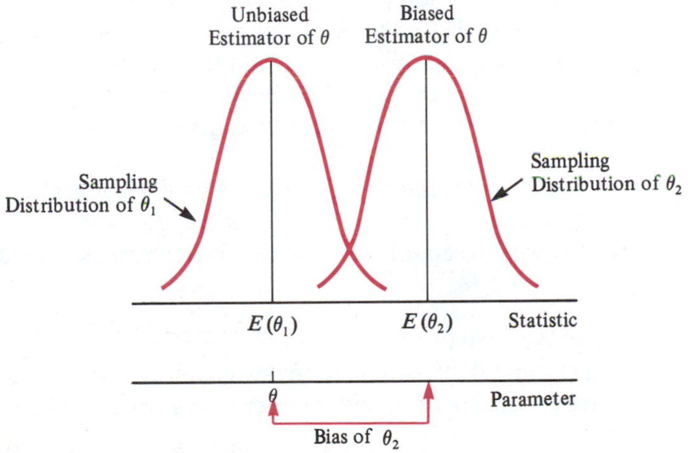

Now suppose we have an estimator $\hat{\theta}$ that is an unbiased estimator of θ. The fact that the sampling distribution of $\hat{\theta}$ is centered at θ does not imply that any one value of $\hat{\theta}$ will be close to θ. Even though the sampling distribution of $\hat{\theta}$ is centered at θ, it may not be highly concentrated about θ. A desirable estimator would be one whose sampling distribution is centered at θ *and* whose sampling distribution has a small variance. If the sampling distribution of $\hat{\theta}$ is centered at θ and has a small variance, then the sampling distribution of $\hat{\theta}$ will be highly concentrated about θ.

For any population parameter θ, several different unbiased estimators can usually be obtained. For example, if a random variable has a symmetric probability distribution, the sample mean and the sample median are both unbiased estimators of the population mean. Naturally, we prefer the estimator whose distribution is more highly concentrated about the population parameter being estimated.

Example 9.1

Comparing Two Unbiased Estimators, the Mean and Median: Let the random variable X follow the normal distribution with unknown mean μ and known variance σ^2. To estimate the mean, take a random sample of size n from the population. To estimate μ, we can use either the sample mean $\bar{X}$ or the sample median M. Which estimator is preferable?

Solution: For any specific sample, either $\bar{x}$ or M could be closer to μ. That is, for any specific sample, we cannot tell which sampling error will be smaller, $|\bar{x} - \mu|$ or $|M - \mu|$.

In deciding which estimator to use, we should consider which estimator would yield smaller sampling errors if we could repeat the sampling procedure many times. That is, we want to use the estimator whose sampling distribution is most highly concentrated about μ. In this example, because the population is symmetric, both $\bar{X}$ and M are unbiased estimators of μ. Consequently, we want to use the estimator whose sampling distribution has the smaller standard deviation.

The standard deviation of the population is σ. It can be shown that the standard deviation of the sampling distribution of $\bar{X}$ is $(\sigma/\sqrt{n})$, where n is the sample size, while the sampling distribution of M has a standard deviation approximately equal to $1.25(\sigma/\sqrt{n})$. Thus, the typical sampling error $|\bar{X} - \mu|$ is smaller than the typical sampling error $|M - \mu|$. For this reason we use the sample mean $\bar{X}$ rather than the sample median M to estimate the mean of a symmetric distribution. ■

When comparing two unbiased estimators, it is natural to select the estimator whose sampling distribution has the smaller variance (or the smaller standard deviation). This leads to the concept of the *relative efficiency* of an estimator.

Definition: Relative Efficiency

Let θ_1 and θ_2 be two unbiased estimators of some population parameter. The **relative efficiency** of θ_1 with respect to θ_2 is the ratio of their variances; that is,

$$\text{Relative efficiency} = \text{Var}(\theta_2)/\text{Var}(\theta_1)$$

The estimator θ_1 is said to be *more efficient* than θ_2 if

$$\text{Var}(\theta_1) < \text{Var}(\theta_2)$$

Example 9.2

Relative Efficiency of the Sample Mean to the Sample Median: In Example 9.1, we showed that the sample mean is a more efficient estimator of the population mean than is the sample median. (Refer to Figure 9.2.) Let us find the relative efficiency of the sample mean to the sample median.

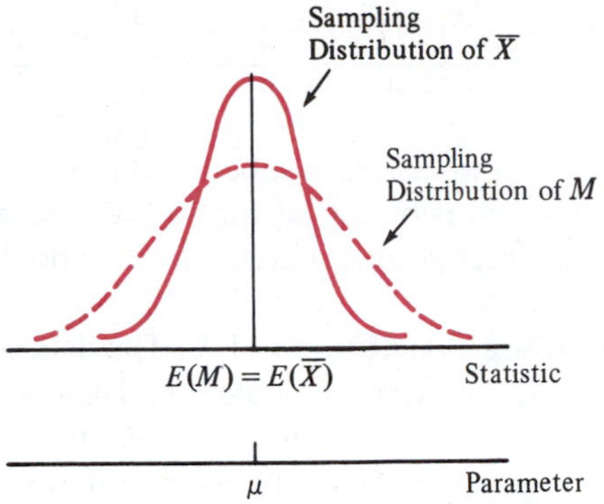

FIGURE 9.2
Sampling distributions of the sample mean and the sample median.

Solution: The variance of the sample mean is σ^2/n, and the variance of the sample median is approximately $1.57(\sigma^2/n)$. The relative efficiency of $\overline{X}$ to M is

$$\text{Relative efficiency} = \text{Var}(M)/\text{Var}(\overline{X}) = 1.57$$

This equation shows that the variance of the sample median is 57% larger than the variance of the sample mean. Figure 9.2 shows that $\overline{X}$ has a higher probability than M of falling within any specific interval about the population mean. ■

In a few cases, it is possible to find the most efficient of all unbiased estimators of a population parameter. This leads to the concept of the *minimum variance unbiased estimator,* also called the *most efficient unbiased estimator.*

Definition: Minimum Variance Unbiased Estimator

An estimator $\hat{\theta}$ is a **minimum variance unbiased estimator** of θ if $\hat{\theta}$ is an unbiased estimator of θ and if no other unbiased estimator has a smaller variance.

It is not always possible to find minimum variance unbiased estimators; however, some do exist. The sample mean when sampling from a normal distribution, the sample variance when sampling from a normal distribution, and the sample proportion are minimum variance unbiased estimators.

Exercises for Section 9.1

1. Rotor bearings are produced with mean weight $\mu = 1.64$ grams and standard deviation $\sigma = 0.03$ gram. What is the mean of the sampling distribution of $\overline{X}$ when $n = 10$? When $n = 50$?
2. In Exercise 1, what is the standard deviation of the sampling distribution of $\overline{X}$ when $n = 10$? When $n = 50$?
3. In Exercise 1, for which sample size ($n = 10$ or $n = 50$) is it more likely that the sample mean will be within 0.02 gram of μ? Why?
4. In Exercise 1, if a random sample of 10 bearings was selected from the process and another random sample of 50 chips was selected independently, would the sample mean based on the larger sample necessarily be closer to the population mean? Discuss.

9.2 ▪ Sampling Distribution of the Sample Mean

It is important to distinguish between the distribution of the population of values X and the sampling distribution of the sample mean $\bar{X}$. The following example utilizes sampling without replacement and illustrates how to obtain the sampling distribution of $\bar{X}$.

Example 9.3

The Sampling Distribution of $\bar{X}$: The data in Table 9.1 show 200 random digits. Consider these values to be a population. The population mean for these values is $\mu = 4.62$. Table 9.2 shows the frequency and relative frequency distributions for the data in Table 9.1, and Figure 9.3 shows the relative frequency histogram.

TABLE 9.1
200 random digits

1	2	6	5	1	6	1	6	4	6	1	1	7	6	9	7	5	1	0	9
8	6	9	9	6	9	7	6	6	9	2	5	7	5	7	3	2	5	3	5
0	7	1	2	2	7	6	7	6	3	8	1	7	6	9	7	4	4	3	6
0	2	6	3	0	7	2	3	1	0	4	5	0	4	9	1	8	0	2	9
0	7	4	6	9	4	2	3	4	1	9	8	1	7	3	7	9	2	6	0
3	6	7	3	7	9	8	8	6	3	7	7	2	4	0	7	6	2	5	1
0	0	6	5	4	6	4	6	8	8	0	9	3	4	3	7	0	2	7	8
6	7	3	3	1	9	8	7	2	9	8	2	8	6	1	5	4	3	7	1
7	6	6	1	0	9	4	9	3	4	7	2	7	4	8	4	4	1	2	4
0	5	6	1	0	5	3	7	5	0	9	5	9	3	8	0	1	4	8	5

TABLE 9.2 **Distribution of data in Table 9.1**

X	0	1	2	3	4	5	6	7	8	9
Frequency	19	20	17	19	20	15	27	28	15	20
Relative frequency	.095	.100	.085	.085	.100	.075	.135	.140	.075	.100

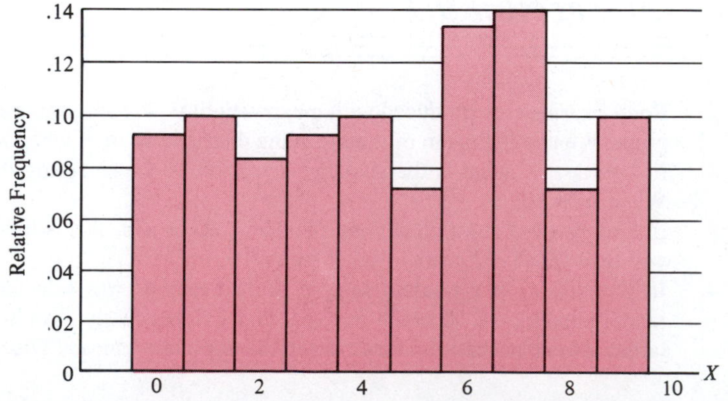

FIGURE 9.3
Relative frequency histogram of data in Table 9.1.

In Table 9.1 the values $x_1, x_2, \ldots, x_{20}$ are in the first row; $x_{21}, x_{22}, \ldots, x_{40}$ are in the second row; and so forth. To get information about the sampling distribution of the sample mean, we took 80 different samples of size $n = 10$ and calculated the sample mean $\bar{x}$ for each sample. The first sample, which contained the first 10 observations in the first row of Table 9.1, had a sample mean of 3.8. The second sample contained the last 10 observations in the first row of Table 9.1 and had a sample mean of 4.6. An additional 78 samples of size 10 were obtained, and the sample mean was calculated for each sample. The 80 values of $\bar{X}$ obtained in this fashion are shown in Table 9.3. Note that if we sample without replacement, ${}_{200}C_{10}$ different samples of size 10 can be selected from Table 9.1. We have chosen 80 of these possible samples to illustrate that $\bar{X}$ is a random variable with a value that varies from sample to sample. Table 9.4 shows the relative frequency distribution of the 80 sample means, and Figure 9.4 shows the relative frequency histogram of these 80 sample means.

TABLE 9.3
Eighty sample means using samples of size 10 for data in Table 9.1

3.8	4.6	7.5	4.4	4.1	5.5	2.4	4.2	4.0	5.2
6.0	4.1	4.7	4.3	5.5	4.5	4.9	4.3	3.2	5.2
2.5	4.8	5.4	3.8	3.0	7.1	4.5	6.2	4.5	4.3
5.5	4.5	5.1	4.9	5.7	4.8	4.3	2.4	4.3	4.8
3.3	5.1	5.1	4.3	4.0	4.4	5.0	6.2	4.0	4.3
4.2	4.1	5.0	6.4	4.8	5.6	5.0	4.3	2.7	4.8
3.5	5.7	4.6	3.2	4.7	5.1	3.5	4.8	4.8	4.9
4.9	6.2	5.0	3.4	4.5	5.0	5.5	5.2	4.4	3.5

TABLE 9.4
Distribution of 80 sample means in Table 9.3

$\bar{X}$	Frequency	Relative Frequency
2.0 to under 2.5	2	.0250
2.5 to under 3.0	2	.0250
3.0 to under 3.5	5	.0650
3.5 to under 4.0	5	.0650
4.0 to under 4.5	19	.2375
4.5 to under 5.0	20	.2500
5.0 to under 5.5	13	.1625
5.5 to under 6.0	7	.0875
6.0 to under 6.5	5	.0625
6.5 to under 7.0	0	.0000
7.0 to under 7.5	2	.0250
Total	80	1.0000

Figure 9.3 shows that the relative frequency distribution of the population of data is approximately a uniform distribution. This result is reasonable because if the digits are truly random, each digit should be equally likely with a relative frequency of .1.

FIGURE 9.4
Relative frequency histogram of 80 sample means in Table 9.3.

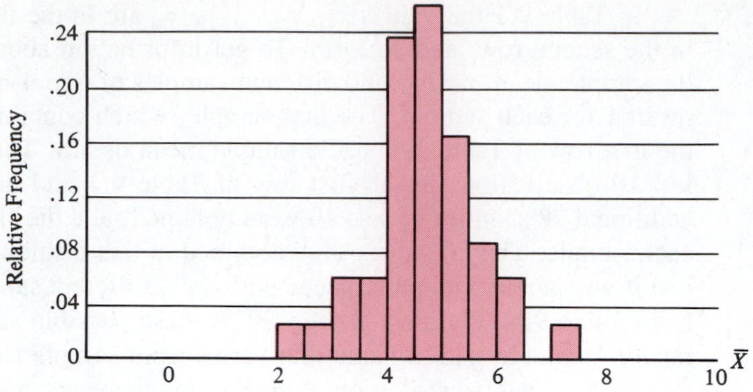

Figure 9.4 shows the distribution of $\bar{X}$ values. This distribution is approximately bell shaped, and most of the values of $\bar{X}$ are clustered around 4.62, which is the mean of the original population of data. Even though the population is approximately uniformly distributed, the sampling distribution of $\bar{X}$ is approximately normal. It can be shown that this approximation to the normal distribution improves as the sample size increases. For example, if we had taken samples of size $n = 30$ rather than $n = 10$, the approximation to normality would have been more exact. ■

Mean and Variance of the Random Variable $\bar{X}$

The mean and variance of the sampling distribution of $\bar{X}$ depend on the mean and variance of the population and on the sample size n. The formulas for the mean and variance of the sampling distribution of $\bar{X}$ are given in the accompanying box.

Formulas for the Mean and Variance of $\bar{X}$

Let $x_1, x_2, \ldots, x_n$ denote a random sample of size n selected from a population having mean μ_X (or μ) and variance σ_X^2 (or σ^2). Let $\bar{X}$ denote the sample mean.

1. The mean value, or expected value, of $\bar{X}$ is

$$E(\bar{X}) = \mu_X = \mu$$

2. If the population is infinitely large or if sampling is done with replacement, then the variance of $\bar{X}$ is

$$\mathrm{Var}(\bar{X}) = \sigma_X^2/n$$

and the standard deviation of $\bar{X}$ is given by $\sigma_X/\sqrt{n}$.

3. If sampling is done *without replacement from a finite population* containing N elements, then the variance of $\bar{X}$ is

$$\mathrm{Var}(\bar{X}) = \frac{\sigma^2}{n}\left(\frac{N-n}{N-1}\right)$$

The value $[(N - n)/(N - 1)]$ in the formula for calculating the variance when sampling is done without replacement is called the *finite population correction factor,* where N is the population size and n is the sample size. If the population size N is much larger than the sample size n, this correction factor is close to 1; in such cases it makes little difference whether we sample with or without replacement. Unless explicitly noted, we will assume henceforth that sampling is done from an extremely large population so that this correction factor can be ignored.

According to the theorem, the standard deviation of the $\bar{X}$ values is $\sigma_{\bar{X}} = \sigma/\sqrt{n}$. This shows that $\sigma_{\bar{X}}$ will be small if σ is small or if n is large. If the population standard deviation σ is small, there is little variation in the population and we would expect sample means obtained from different samples to be highly concentrated. If the sample size is large, we would expect the different estimates $\bar{X}$ obtained from different samples to be highly concentrated about the mean μ.

Example 9.4

Effect of a Small Population Standard Deviation: An employment agency wants to estimate the mean hourly wage earned by high school students who work as cashiers at supermarkets. The agency hires several pollsters and asks each one to obtain a random sample of $n = 25$ students. Because most students earn between \$3.35 and \$5.00 per hour, the population standard deviation is relatively small, say, $\sigma = \$1.00$. Because the students' wages are highly concentrated and do not exhibit much variation, the estimates obtained by the different pollsters should not exhibit much variation either. That is, we would expect the values of $\bar{X}$ obtained by each pollster to be quite close to one another. Thus, if the population has a small standard deviation, the sampling distribution of sample means will also be highly concentrated. ■

Example 9.5

Effect of a Large Population Standard Deviation: The employment agency in Example 9.4 is also interested in estimating the mean annual income earned by lawyers. Again pollsters are hired, and each is told to obtain a random sample of $n = 25$ lawyers. The population mean is, say, \$70,000 per year. However, the standard deviation of this population is very large, say $\sigma = \$20{,}000$, because the annual incomes are widely dispersed about the mean. As a result, the sample mean obtained by one pollster could be quite different from the sample mean obtained by another. We would not necessarily expect the values of $\bar{X}$ obtained by the pollsters to be quite so close to one another. If the population has a large standard deviation, the sampling distribution of the sample mean can also have a large amount of dispersion. ■

The following example illustrates the point that the variance of the sampling distribution of $\bar{X}$ depends on the sample size n. If the sample size is large, then the sampling distribution of $\bar{X}$ will be highly concentrated about the population mean.

Example 9.6

Effect of Sample Size on the Variance of $\bar{X}$: Several economists are interested in estimating the mean annual income of accountants. Suppose the unknown population mean is $\mu = \$50{,}000$ and the population standard deviation is $\sigma = \$10{,}000$. Now suppose one economist takes a random sample of $n = 4$ employees. Because this sample size is very small, the estimate obtained by the economist could be quite different from the true population mean. For example, the standard deviation of the sampling distribution of $\bar{X}$ is $\sigma/\sqrt{n} = 10{,}000/\sqrt{4} = \$5000$. From the Empirical Rule, approximately 68% of the data lie within 1 standard deviation of the mean if the distribution is approximately bell shaped, so only about 68% of the potential estimates of the population mean will be within \$5000 of the true mean. Since the remaining 32% of the estimates will be more than \$5000 from the mean, the probability is approximately .32 that the sampling error will be more than \$5000. An estimate of the mean income that is in error by more than \$5000 could be useless in many economic studies. Because the sample size is very small, the sampling distribution of $\bar{X}$ is widely dispersed about the population mean.

Now suppose another economist takes a random sample of $n = 1600$ employees. Because this sample size is quite large, we would expect to obtain a very good estimate of the population mean. In this case, the standard deviation of the sampling distribution of $\bar{X}$ is $\sigma/\sqrt{n} = \$10{,}000/\sqrt{1600} = \$250$. From the Empirical Rule, the probability is approximately .95 that the sampling error $|\bar{X} - \mu|$ will be less than 2 standard deviations, namely \$500, if the distribution is approximately bell shaped. Thus, in approximately 95% of the potential samples of size 1600, the estimated sample mean will be within \$500 of the true population mean. An estimate of the mean income that is in error by less than \$500 would probably be quite useful in most economic studies. When the sample size is large, the sampling distribution of the sample mean is highly concentrated about the population mean. ■

Graphical Representation of the Distribution of $\bar{X}$

The graphs in Figure 9.5 show that the sampling distribution of $\bar{X}$ is centered at the population mean and becomes more concentrated as the sample size increases. Also note that as the sample size gets larger, the distribution of $\bar{X}$ begins to approach normality regardless of the shape of the original distribution.

Exercises for Section 9.2

1. Suppose the average IQ of all college seniors is 125 and the variance is 144. You take a random sample of 100 students and calculate the sample mean IQ ($\bar{X}$). The sample mean $\bar{X}$ is a random variable having a probability distribution. What is the mean, variance, and standard deviation of this distribution?
2. A city council is studying the tourist trade. During a certain year, the mean expenditure per tourist was $\mu = \$500$ with variance 8100. The city takes a random sample of 10 tourists and calculates their average expenditure $\bar{X}$. What is the mean, variance, and standard deviation of this distribution?
3. In Exercise 2 the city takes a random sample of 1000 tourists and calculates the mean expenditure. Now what is the mean, variance, and standard deviation of the distribution of $\bar{X}$? In this case would you be very confident that your value of $\bar{X}$ is very close to μ?
4. You take a random sample of size $n = 10$ and obtain $x_1 = 8$, $x_2 = 6$, $x_3 = 5$, $x_4 = 5$, $x_5 = 8$, $x_6 = 7$, $x_7 = 6$, $x_8 = 2$, $x_9 = 4$, and $x_{10} = 6$. Calculate the sample mean and sample standard deviation.
5. A person takes a random sample of 10 college seniors to obtain their IQs and gets the values $x_1 = 110$, $x_2 = 145$, $x_3 = 150$, $x_4 = 130$, $x_5 = 120$, $x_6 = 105$, $x_7 = 130$, $x_8 = 105$, $x_9 = 125$, and $x_{10} = 120$. Use the formulas in Chapter 4 to calculate the sample mean and sample variance. Use the formula S^2/n to estimate the variance of $\bar{X}$.

FIGURE 9.5 **Sampling distribution of $\bar{X}$ for n = 2, 5, and 30.**

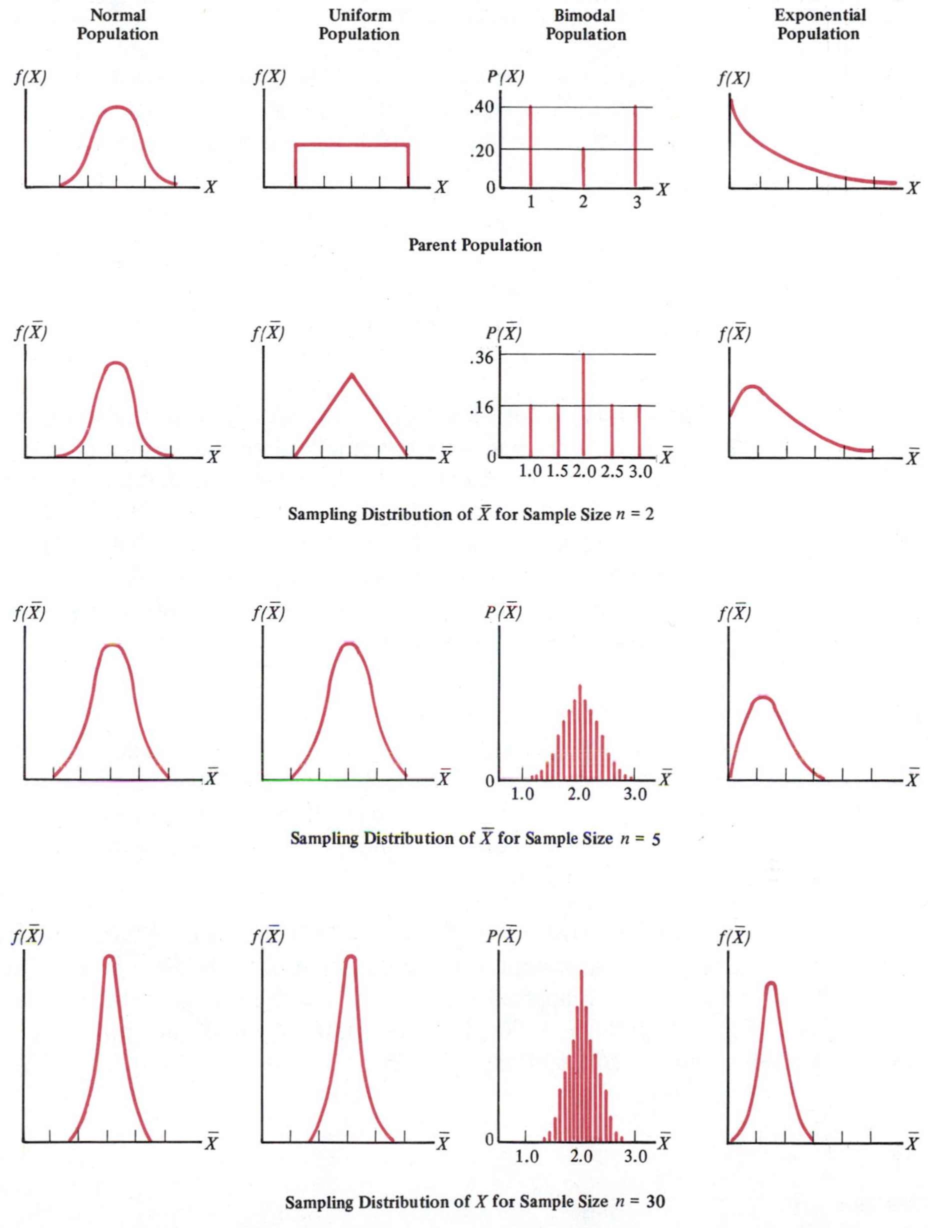

6. Five randomly selected tourists are asked how much they spent on their vacation. We obtain x_1 = \$600, x_2 = \$800, x_3 = \$400, x_4 = \$1000, and x_5 = \$500. Calculate the sample mean and sample variance. Estimate the variance of $\bar{X}$ using the estimator S^2/n.
7. If the population is approximately normal, the variance of the sample median equals $(\pi/2)(\sigma^2/n)$. If a sample median is to have a standard deviation equal to that of a sample mean (from the same population), how much bigger must the sample size be?

9.3 ▪ *The Central Limit Theorem*

The Central Limit Theorem, one of the most important theorems in statistics, is the reason that the normal distribution is the most important of all probability distributions. One version of the Central Limit Theorem is given in the accompanying box.

The Central Limit Theorem

Let $x_1, x_2, \ldots, x_n$ denote a random sample selected from a population having mean μ and variance σ^2. Let $\bar{X}$ denote the sample mean. If n is large, then $\bar{X}$ has approximately a normal distribution with mean μ and variance σ^2/n.

The Central Limit Theorem would be of little practical value if the approximation was applicable only if n were extremely large, but in fact it works in most cases, even when n is fairly small. A common rule of thumb is that the theorem applies as n gets up to 20 or 30. We shall assume that the theorem applies whenever n is at least 30.

If the original population follows the normal distribution, then the distribution of $\bar{X}$ is *exactly* a normal distribution, regardless of the sample size. The Central Limit Theorem is important because it states that *even if the original population is not normal,* the distribution of $\bar{X}$ will be approximately normal (provided $n \geq 30$).

Example 9.7

Application of the Central Limit Theorem: Suppose the Bureau of Labor Statistics wants to estimate the mean starting salary of newly graduated chemical engineers. Suppose the population mean is actually $\mu = \$25{,}000$ and the population standard deviation is $\sigma = \$2000$. In order to estimate μ, the bureau takes a random sample of 100 recently graduated chemical engineers. Find the probability that the sample mean will be within \$400 of the true mean.

Solution: We have $n = 100$, $\mu = \$25{,}000$, and $\sigma = \$2000$. Because the sample size exceeds 30, we assume that the Central Limit Theorem holds. Thus, the sampling distribution of $\bar{X}$ is approximately normal with mean $\mu = \$25{,}000$ and standard deviation $\$2000/\sqrt{100} = \$200$. If $\bar{X}$ is within \$400 of the population mean, then $\bar{X}$ will be between \$24,600 and \$25,400. Thus we seek $P(24{,}600 \leq \bar{X} \leq 25{,}400)$. Refer to Figure 9.6.

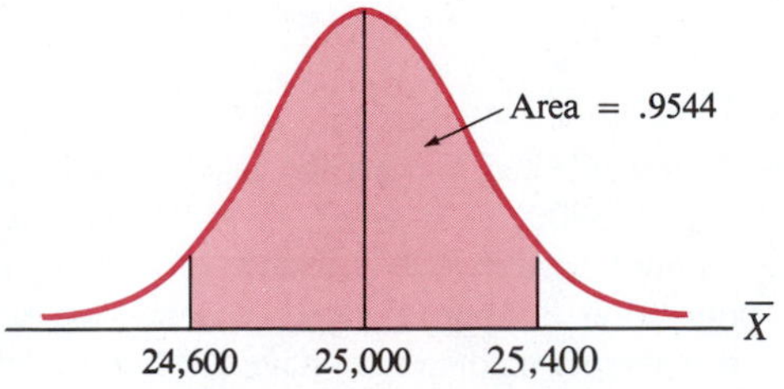

FIGURE 9.6
Normal distribution for Example 9.7.

We obtain the standardized Z scores

$$z_1 = (24{,}600 - 25{,}000)/200 = -2.00$$

$$z_2 = (25{,}400 - 25{,}000)/200 = 2.00$$

From Table A.5, we obtain

$$P(24{,}600 \leq \overline{X} \leq 25{,}400) = P(-2.00 \leq Z \leq 2.00)$$
$$= .4772 + .4772 = .9544$$

Thus, if the Bureau of Labor Statistics takes a random sample of 100 chemical engineers, the probability is .9544 that the sample mean will be within \$400 of the true population mean. ■

Tips on Problem Solving
To calculate the probability that the random variable $\overline{X}$ falls in some interval, follow these steps:

1. List the sample size n, the population mean μ, and the population variance σ^2.
2. The sampling distribution of $\overline{X}$ is (approximately) normal if the sample size is large ($n \geq 30$) or if the population is normal.
3. List the variance of the random variable $\overline{X}$. This variance is σ^2/n, *not* σ^2.
4. List the standard deviation of $\overline{X}$. This standard deviation is $\sigma/\sqrt{n}$, *not* σ.
5. Sketch the appropriate normal distribution and shade the appropriate area.
6. Calculate the Z scores corresponding to the values of interest in the problem. Sketch a standard normal curve and find the appropriate area.
7. Examine your sketch and verify that the calculated answer agrees with the shaded area.

Exercises for Section 9.3

1. A consumer research agency takes a random sample of 100 people in order to estimate the average number of hours per month that adults watch TV. Suppose the population mean is $\mu = 100$ hours with standard deviation $\sigma = 20$. Find the probability that the sample mean $\overline{X}$ is between 100 and 105.

2. If the variance of some population is 100 and we obtain a random sample of size 64, what is the probability that $\overline{X}$ will be within 1 unit of μ?

3. A certain random variable X has mean 50 and variance 144.

a. We obtain a random sample of size 81. What is the distribution of the sample mean $\overline{X}$, at least approximately?

b. If X is normally distributed and the sample size is 10, what is the distribution of the sample mean $\overline{X}$?

4. On weekdays at noon, the number of people in a downtown cafeteria has mean $\mu = 140$ and standard deviation $\sigma = 50$. The manager counts the number of noontime customers on 100 randomly selected days and calculates the sample mean $\overline{X}$. What is the probability that $\overline{X}$ is between 130 and 150?

5. In Exercise 4, what is the probability that $\bar{X}$ is between 135 and 145? Do the results from Exercise 4 and this exercise convince you that it is possible to get a fairly good estimate of a population mean by taking a relatively small sample?
6. At a certain bank, the mean checking account balance is $\mu = \$150$ and the population standard deviation is $\sigma = \$60$. What is the probability that the sample mean of 400 randomly chosen checking account balances is as follows:
   a. Between \$135 and \$165
   b. Between \$144 and \$156
7. In a certain state, the mean income of full-time high school teachers is \$20,500 and the standard deviation is \$4000. What is the probability that in a random sample of 400 full-time high school teachers, the sample mean income is between \$20,000 and \$21,000?
8. The IRS wants to determine the mean amount of money that married couples contribute to charity. Assume the standard deviation of contributions is \$360. What is the probability that in a random sample of 100 married couples, the sample mean contribution is within \$10 of the population mean?
9. A study is being undertaken to determine if the new cash registers installed at Foodland Supermarkets have sped up the checkout process. In the past the mean time spent in a checkout line was $\mu = 11$ minutes with standard deviation $\sigma = 3$. A random sample of 100 customers is observed. If μ is in fact still 11, find the probability of the following results in the sample:
   a. $\bar{X}$ exceeds 13.
   b. $\bar{X}$ exceeds 15.
   c. $\bar{X}$ is less than 9.
10. The mean expenditure on food and candy by movie patrons is $\mu = \$1.40$, and the population standard deviation is $\sigma = 0.36$. The owner of the cinema takes a random sample of 144 customers to estimate μ. Find the probability of the following:
   a. $\bar{X}$ exceeds \$1.60.
   b. $\bar{X}$ is between \$1.30 and \$1.50.
11. A teacher gives a test to a class containing several hundred students. It is known that the standard deviation of the scores is about 12 points. A random sample of 36 scores is obtained. What is the probability that the sample mean will differ from the population mean by more than 6 points?
12. A local bank reported to the federal government that its savings accounts have a mean balance of \$1890 and a standard deviation of \$264. Government auditors randomly sample 144 of the bank's accounts to assess the reliability of the mean balance reported by the bank. The auditors will certify the bank's report only if the sample mean balance is within \$50 of the reported mean balance. What is the probability that the auditors will not certify the bank's report, even if the mean balance really is \$1890? (Assume the standard deviation reported by the bank is accurate.)

9.4 ▪ *Sampling Distribution of the Difference Between Two Sample Means*

Frequently we are interested in determining if the mean of one population is equal to the mean of another. For example, we might want to answer questions of the following type:

1. Is the mean credit card balance for single males the same as the mean credit card balance for females?
2. Is the mean starting salary for college graduates who majored in economics the same as the mean starting salary for college graduates who majored in English?

3. Is the mean number of cavities for children who use Brand A toothpaste the same as the mean number of cavities for children who use Brand B?

In each case we have two different populations, which we shall call Population 1 and Population 2. Population 1 has mean μ_1 and variance σ_1^2, and Population 2 has mean μ_2 and variance σ_2^2.

To make such comparisons, we take independent random samples of n_1 observations from Population 1 and n_2 observations from Population 2 and then calculate the respective sample means, which are denoted $\bar{x}_1$ and $\bar{x}_2$. Frequently, the two sample sizes are equal ($n_1 = n_2$), but this does not have to be the case. To obtain information about the difference between two population means ($\mu_1 - \mu_2$), we rely on the sample estimate ($\bar{x}_1 - \bar{x}_2$).

Recall that $\bar{X}_1$ and $\bar{X}_2$ are random variables with values that vary from sample to sample. Similarly, ($\bar{X}_1 - \bar{X}_2$) is a random variable whose value varies from sample to sample. Before examining the distribution of ($\bar{X}_1 - \bar{X}_2$), we should note that at this point we are actually concerned with five different probability distributions. First, we have the two distributions of the two populations, which have means μ_1 and μ_2 and variances σ_1^2 and σ_2^2. Second, we have the two sampling distributions of $\bar{X}_1$ and of $\bar{X}_2$. According to the Central Limit Theorem, if n_1 is sufficiently large, then $\bar{X}_1$ has approximately a normal distribution with mean μ_1 and variance σ_1^2/n_1, and similarly for $\bar{X}_2$. Finally, we have the sampling distribution of ($\bar{X}_1 - \bar{X}_2$). If both samples are sufficiently large (say, $n_1 \geqslant 30$ and $n_2 \geqslant 30$), then the distribution of ($\bar{X}_1 - \bar{X}_2$) will be approximately normal no matter how the original populations are distributed. If the original populations are normally distributed, then ($\bar{X}_1 - \bar{X}_2$) is exactly normally distributed for any values of n_1 and n_2.

Figures 9.7 and 9.8 show the five distributions described above for two different cases, where both populations are approximately normal and where both populations are not normal. In Figure 9.7 the distributions of $\bar{X}_1$ and $\bar{X}_2$ are normal because the populations are normal (i.e., we do not need the Central Limit Theorem). In Figure 9.8 the distributions of $\bar{X}_1$ and $\bar{X}_2$ are approximately normal because the sample sizes are assumed to be large (i.e., we *do* need the Central Limit Theorem here). Once again, the sampling distribution of ($\bar{X}_1 - \bar{X}_2$) will be approximately normal.

Mean and Variance of ($\bar{X}_1 - \bar{X}_2$)

The expected value of the random variable ($\bar{X}_1 - \bar{X}_2$) is

$$E(\bar{X}_1 - \bar{X}_2) = \mu_1 - \mu_2$$

This implies that the random variable ($\bar{X}_1 - \bar{X}_2$) is an unbiased estimator of ($\mu_1 - \mu_2$).

The variance of ($\bar{X}_1 - \bar{X}_2$) depends on the four numbers σ_1^2, σ_2^2, n_1, and n_2. If the two random samples are independent of one another, then the variance of ($\bar{X}_1 - \bar{X}_2$) is given by the formula

$$\text{Var}(\bar{X}_1 - \bar{X}_2) = \frac{\sigma_1^2}{n_1} + \frac{\sigma_2^2}{n_2}$$

where σ_1^2 and σ_2^2 represent the variances of the two populations and n_1 and n_2 are the sample sizes.

FIGURE 9.7 **Population and sampling distributions of two normal populations.**

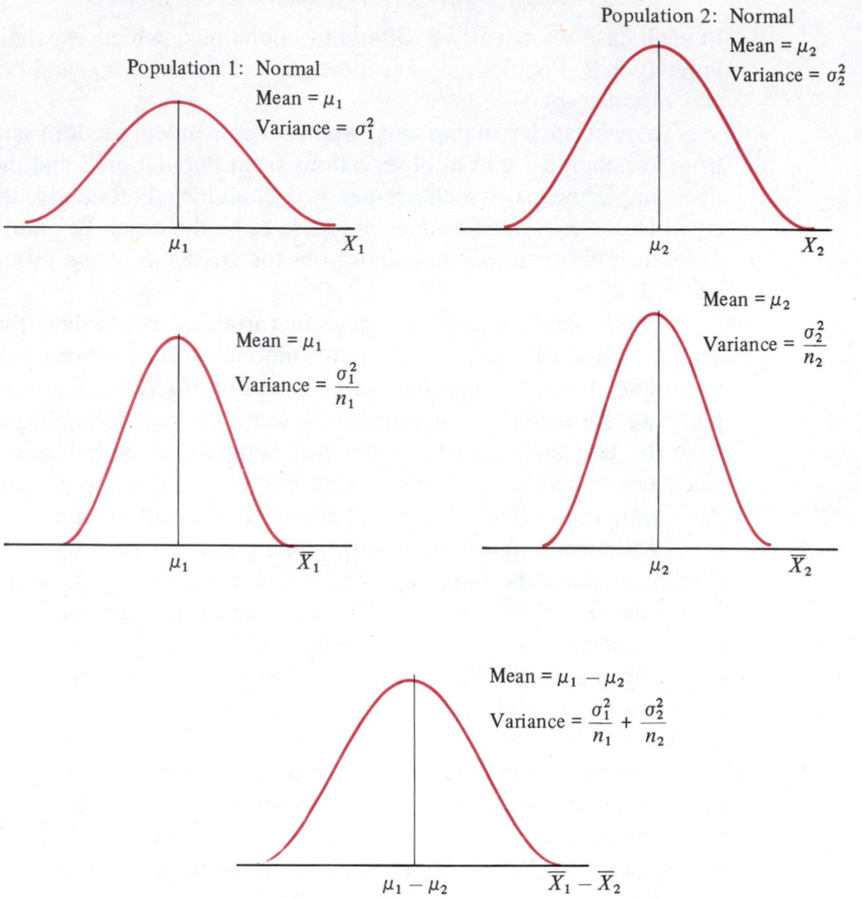

Example 9.8

Distribution of $(\bar{X}_1 - \bar{X}_2)$: A financial loan officer claims that the mean monthly payment for credit cards is \$80 with a variance of 1400 for single females and \$80 with a variance of 1320 for single males. You take a random sample of 100 females (Population 1) and an independent random sample of 120 males (Population 2). What is the probability that the sample mean for females will be at least \$5 higher than the sample mean for males?

Solution: We have

$$\mu_1 = 80, \quad \sigma_1^2 = 1400, \quad n_1 = 100$$
$$\mu_2 = 80, \quad \sigma_2^2 = 1320, \quad n_2 = 120$$

The random variable $(\bar{X}_1 - \bar{X}_2)$ is approximately normally distributed with mean $(\mu_1 - \mu_2) = 0$ and variance

$$(\sigma_1^2/n_1) + (\sigma_2^2/n_2) = (1400/100) + (1320/120) = 14 + 11 = 25$$

FIGURE 9.8 Population and sampling distributions of two nonnormal populations.

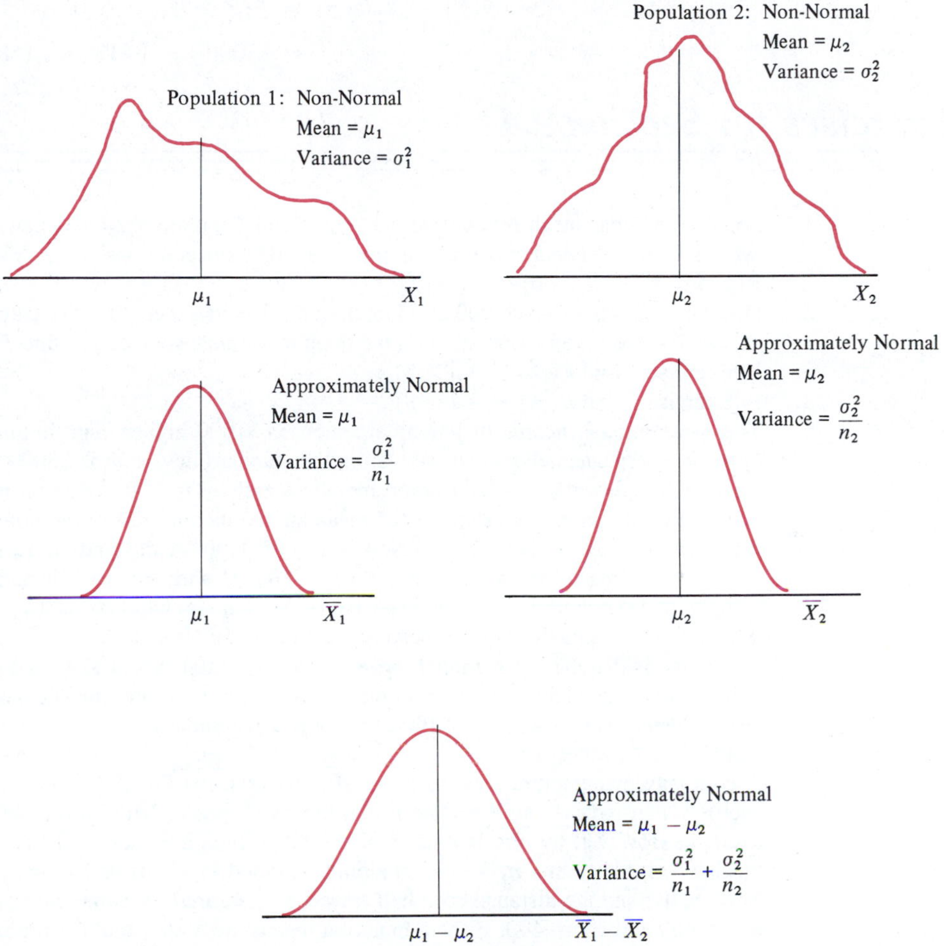

We seek the probability that $\bar{X}_1$ is at least \$5 more than $\bar{X}_2$. That is, we seek $P(\bar{X}_1 - \bar{X}_2 \geq 5)$. (See Figure 9.9.) We obtain the Z score

$$Z = \frac{5 - 0}{\sqrt{25}} = 1$$

FIGURE 9.9
Area under the normal distribution for Example 9.8.

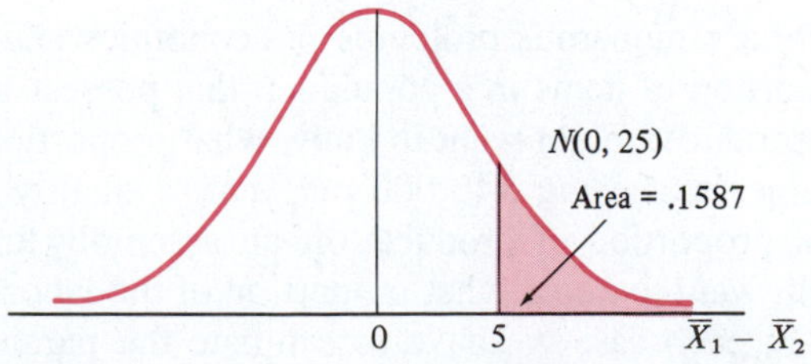

Thus,

$$P(\bar{X}_1 - \bar{X}_2 \geq 5) = P(Z \geq 1)$$
$$= .5000 - .3413 = .1587$$

■

Exercises for Section 9.4

1. Population 1 has mean 60 and variance 125, and Population 2 has mean 60 and variance 125. We take independent random samples of 100 observations from each population. Find $P(-6 < \bar{X}_1 - \bar{X}_2 < 6)$.
2. Population 1 has variance 900 and Population 2 has variance 700. We take independent samples of size 100 from each population. If the population means are equal, find $P(\bar{X}_1 - \bar{X}_2 > 5)$.
3. In Exercise 2 find $P(|\bar{X}_1 - \bar{X}_2| > 5)$.
4. In Exercise 2 find $P(|\bar{X}_1 - \bar{X}_2| > 9)$.
5. The mean annual income of union carpenters is \$1000 higher than the mean annual income of nonunion carpenters. For each population the standard deviation is \$3000. We take independent random samples of $n_1 = 100$ union members and $n_2 = 200$ nonunion members. What is the probability that in the two samples the mean annual incomes differ by more than \$1500?
6. The mean income of secretaries in New York is \$21,000 with standard deviation \$2000, whereas in Dallas the mean income of secretaries is \$18,000 with standard deviation \$1500. A random sample of 100 secretaries is taken in each city. Find the probability that $(\bar{X}_1 - \bar{X}_2)$ exceeds \$2000, where $\bar{X}_1$ represents the sample mean for secretaries in New York.
7. Hertz claims that the mean annual repair bill for its rental cars is \$290 and the standard deviation is \$50. Avis also claims its mean annual repair bill is \$290 and the standard deviation is \$50. If independent random samples of 100 cars from each company are obtained, what is the probability that $|\bar{X}_1 - \bar{X}_2|$ exceeds \$5?
8. A company manufactures two varieties of golf balls, the Pro (\$2.25 each) and the Maxi (\$2.00 each). When struck with the same force, the two types of balls travel the same distance on the average. However, the Pro ball has a better cover, which is more difficult to cut. Suppose that a mechanical device hits $n_1 = 100$ randomly selected Pro balls and $n_2 = 100$ randomly selected Maxi balls, and the distance each ball travels is measured. Assume the population variances are $\sigma_1^2 = 400$ and $\sigma_2^2 = 400$. If the population means are equal, find the probability that $(\bar{X}_1 - \bar{X}_2)$ is as follows:
   a. Between -5 and $+5$ yards
   b. Between -3 and $+3$ yards

9.5 ▪ Sampling Distribution of the Sample Proportion

There are numerous problems in economics and business where we want to know the proportion of items in a population that possess a certain characteristic. For example, a TV producer might want to know what proportion of viewers of a certain program have incomes exceeding \$40,000 per year, a quality control engineer might want to know what proportion of products off an assembly line are defective, or a labor economist might want to know what proportion of the labor force is unemployed.

In each case we have to estimate the parameter p, the proportion of the population having the characteristic of interest. Let $q = (1 - p)$. To estimate the population proportion p, we take a random sample on n observations from the population. Let X denote the number of observations in the sample that possess the characteristic of interest. We use the sample proportion $\hat{p} = X/n$ to estimate the population proportion p. In Chapter 8, we showed that, when $np \geqslant 5$ and $nq \geqslant 5$, the distribution of X is approximately normal with mean np and variance npq; under the same constraints, the sampling distribution of $\hat{p}$ is approximately normal.

Sampling Distribution of the Sample Proportion

Let p denote the proportion of a population possessing some characteristic of interest. Take a random sample of n observations from the population. Let X denote the number of items in the sample possessing the characteristic. We estimate the population proportion p by the sample proportion $\hat{p} = X/n$. If $np \geqslant 5$ and $nq \geqslant 5$, the random variable $\hat{p}$ has approximately a normal distribution with mean

$$E(\hat{p}) = p$$

and variance

$$\text{Var}(\hat{p}) = pq/n$$

The standard deviation of $\hat{p}$ is

$$\sigma_{\hat{p}} = \sqrt{pq/n}$$

The standard deviation of $\hat{p}$ is called the **standard error of $\hat{p}$**.

Notice that for fixed p, the standard error of the sample proportion decreases as the sample size increases. This implies that as sample size increases, the distribution of $\hat{p}$ becomes more concentrated about its mean, as illustrated in Figure 9.10.

If the distribution of $\hat{p}$ is approximately normal, then the random variable

$$Z = \frac{(\hat{p} - p)}{\sqrt{pq/n}}$$

is approximately distributed as standard normal.

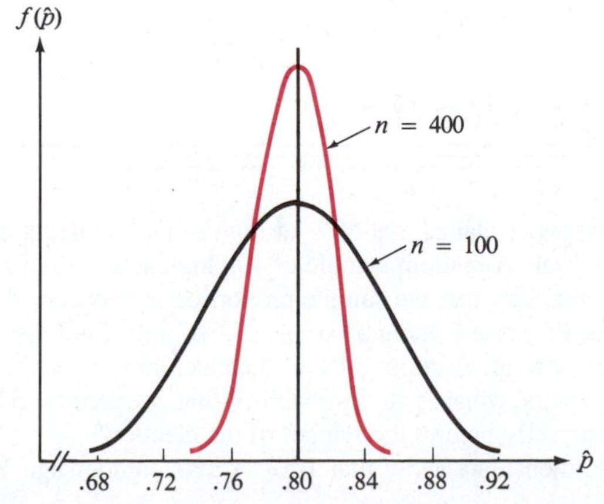

FIGURE 9.10
Sampling distribution of the sample proportion when $p = .8$.

Example 9.9

Distribution of the Sample Proportion: In an election, 55% of the registered voters favor a certain candidate. If we take a random sample of 400 voters, what is the probability that, based on the sample proportion, we will predict the wrong winner? That is, what is the probability that $\hat{p}$ will be less than .5?

Solution: We have $n = 400$, $p = .55$, and $q = (1 - p) = .45$. First, we check to see if $np \geqslant 5$ and $nq \geqslant 5$, so that we can use the normal distribution. We have $np = 400(.55) = 220 \geqslant 5$ and $nq = 400(.45) = 180 \geqslant 5$. Thus, $\hat{p}$ is approximately normally distributed with mean $p = .55$ and variance $pq/n = (.55)(.45)/(400) = .00062$. We seek $P(\hat{p} < .50)$.

We obtain the Z score

$$Z = \frac{.50 - .55}{\sqrt{.00062}} \approx \frac{-.05}{.025} = -2$$

Thus,

$$\begin{aligned} P(\hat{p} \leqslant .5) &= P(Z < -2) \\ &= .5000 - .4772 = .0228 \end{aligned}$$

Therefore, the probability is only .0228 that we will predict the wrong winner if we take a sample of size 400. ■

Tips on Problem Solving

To calculate the probability that the random variable $\hat{p}$ falls in some interval, follow these steps:

1. List the sample size n, the population proportion p, and $q = (1 - p)$.
2. The sampling distribution of $\hat{p}$ is (approximately) normal if $np \geqslant 5$ and $nq \geqslant 5$. Verify that these conditions hold.
3. List the variance of the random variable $\hat{p}$, which is pq/n.
4. List the standard deviation of $\hat{p}$, which is $\sqrt{pq/n}$.
5. Sketch the appropriate normal distribution and shade the appropriate area. The mean of the distribution is p.
6. Calculate the Z scores corresponding to the values of interest in the problem. Sketch a standard normal curve and find the appropriate areas.
7. Examine your sketch and verify that the calculated answer agrees with the shaded area.

Exercises for Section 9.5

1. A newspaper claims that 50% of high school students have used drugs at some time during their senior year. A random sample of 400 high school seniors is obtained. If the claim is correct, find the probability that the sample proportion is between .47 and .53.
2. Repeat Exercise 1 using a sample size of 900. Find the probability that $\hat{p}$ is between .47 and .53.
3. Just prior to an election, 54% of the electorate favor Candidate A. If we take a random sample of 1500 voters, what is the probability that $\hat{p}$ exceeds .5? That is, what is the probability that we will correctly predict the winner of the election?
4. Government data show that 10% of males under age 25 are unemployed. A random sample is

taken of 400 males who are in the labor force and under age 25. Find the probability that the sample unemployment rate is .12 or more.

5. Solve Exercise 4 if the sample size is 900.

6. In a certain community, 60% of the population would pay for cable TV. A random sample of 400 residents is obtained. Find the probability that the sample proportion is between .5 and .7.

7. The commissioners of Lane County are trying to decide whether to pass a law that will loosen restrictions on environmental pollution in an effort to attract manufacturing firms to the county. To learn how the county's residents feel about the law, a random sample of 100 residents are questioned. Suppose that 70% of the county's residents favor the new law. Find the probability that in the sample the proportion who favor the law is as follows:
a. Between .60 and .70 b. Between .60 and .65 c. Less than .50

8. The Chrysler Corporation claims that 80% of its cars meet the tough new standards of the Environmental Protection Agency (EPA). The EPA tests a random sample of 400 Chrysler cars. Find the probability that the percentage of cars that pass the test is as follows:
a. Less than .75 b. Between .70 and .78 c. More than .82

9. On a tropical island that is a major tourist attraction, the weather is so variable that the occurrence of rain on any day is independent of whether rain has fallen on previous days. Suppose it rains on 25% of the days. Determine the probability that during a sample of 100 days when the tourist trade is at its peak, the proportion of days on which rain falls is as follows:
a. Less than .20 b. More than .30 c. More than .35

10. A medical journal states that the probability of surviving open heart surgery is .9. To check this claim, you examine the records of a sample of 200 patients who had open heart surgery. In the sample, 77% survived.
a. If the journal's claim is correct, find the probability that the proportion of survivors is 77% or less.
b. Does the result in part (a) make you doubt the journal's claim? Explain.

11. The Internal Revenue Service claims that 65% of all tax returns lead to a refund. A random sample of 100 tax returns is taken. What is the probability that the sample proportion exceeds .72?

12. A record store owner claims that 25% of customers entering the store make a purchase. One morning 120 people, who can be regarded as a random sample of all customers, enter the store. What is the probability that the sample proportion is less than .2?

13. A TV producer claims that 30% of all homes in a city have cable TV. To test this claim, a random sample of 400 homes is examined.
a. What is the probability that the sample proportion is less than .25?
b. What is the probability that the sample proportion is more than .20?
c. Suppose the sample proportion was .18. Would this make you doubt the producer's claim? Explain.

14. The Nielsen Company takes random samples of viewers in order to estimate the proportion of the public that watches particular TV shows. Suppose a particular program was watched by 30% of all adults and that Nielsen takes a random sample of 1500 adults.
a. What is the probability that the sample proportion is between .27 and .33?
b. What is the probability that the sample proportion is between .25 and .35?

9.6 ▪ *Sampling Distribution of the Difference Between Sample Proportions*

Frequently we are interested in determining if the proportion of items in one population that possess a certain characteristic is the same as the proportion possessing the characteristic in another population. For example, a doctor who gives one type of medicine to some patients and another type of medicine to others may want to determine if the percentage of people cured by the first medicine is the same as the percentage of people cured by the second.

This and many other types of problems concern the difference between two proportions. Let p_1 and p_2, respectively, denote the proportions of Populations 1 and 2 possessing a certain characteristic. If we don't know these proportions, we can take independent random samples of size n_1 and n_2 from the two populations to obtain estimates of p_1 and p_2. Let X_1 and X_2 denote the number of items in each sample possessing the characteristic of interest. The two sample proportions are then

$$\hat{p}_1 = X_1/n_1 \quad \text{and} \quad \hat{p}_2 = X_2/n_2$$

Because inferences about the difference between two population proportions is based on the random variable $(\hat{p}_1 - \hat{p}_2)$, it is necessary to study the sampling distribution of the random variable $(\hat{p}_1 - \hat{p}_2)$.

Sampling Distribution of $(\hat{p}_1 - \hat{p}_2)$

Suppose we take independent samples of size n_1 and n_2 from two populations. Let p_1 and p_2 be the proportion of items in each population that possess a certain characteristic, and let $q_1 = (1 - p_1)$ and $q_2 = (1 - p_2)$. If $n_1p_1 \geq 5$, $n_1q_1 \geq 5$, $n_2p_2 \geq 5$, and $n_2q_2 \geq 5$, then the random variable $(\hat{p}_1 - \hat{p}_2)$ is approximately normally distributed with mean

$$E(\hat{p}_1 - \hat{p}_2) = p_1 - p_2$$

and variance

$$\text{Var}(\hat{p}_1 - \hat{p}_2) = (p_1q_1/n_1) + (p_2q_2/n_2)$$

Example 9.10

Distribution of the Difference of Sample Proportions: A marketing agency is interested in determining if a certain TV program appeals equally to upper-income and lower-income people. Suppose that 40% of the upper-income people and 50% of the lower-income people in the population like the show. The agency takes a random sample of 100 upper-income people (Population 1) and an independent sample of 200 lower-income people (Population 2). Let $\hat{p}_1$ and $\hat{p}_2$ denote the proportions in each sample that like the program. Find the probability that the two sample proportions differ by less than .05.

Solution: We need to calculate the probability

$$P(-.05 \leq \hat{p}_1 - \hat{p}_2 \leq .05)$$

We have $p_1 = .4$, $q_1 = .6$, $n_1 = 100$, $p_2 = .5$, $q_2 = .5$, and $n_2 = 200$. The two samples are independent. The distribution of $(\hat{p}_1 - \hat{p}_2)$ is approximately normal because $n_1p_1 \geq 5$, $n_1q_1 \geq 5$, $n_2p_2 \geq 5$, and $n_2q_2 \geq 5$. The mean is $(p_1 - p_2) = .40 - .50 = -.10$ and the variance is

$$\frac{p_1q_1}{n_1} + \frac{p_2q_2}{n_2} = \frac{(.4)(.6)}{100} + \frac{(.5)(.5)}{200} = .00365$$

We obtain the Z scores

$$z_1 = \frac{-.05 - (-.1)}{\sqrt{.00365}} = \frac{.05}{.06} = .83$$

$$z_2 = \frac{.05 - (-.1)}{\sqrt{.00365}} = \frac{.15}{.06} = 2.50$$

Thus,

$$P(-.05 \geqslant \hat{p}_1 - \hat{p}_2 \leqslant .05) = P(.83 \leqslant Z \leqslant 2.50)$$
$$= .4938 - .2967 = .1971$$

■

Exercises for Section 9.6

1. A company is interested in determining if a new product appeals equally to men and women. Independent random samples are taken of 200 men and 400 women. In the populations $p_m = .7$ and $p_w = .6$. Find

$$P(-.04 \leqslant \hat{p}_m - \hat{p}_w \leqslant .04)$$

2. On a Sunday afternoon, a random sample of 400 people is taken to estimate p_1, the proportion of the population that watched a hockey game on TV. On the following Sunday, an independent random sample of 400 people is taken to estimate p_2, the proportion of the population who watched a basketball game on TV. If $p_1 = .3$ and $p_2 = .4$, find the probability that $\hat{p}_2 < \hat{p}_1$ in our samples. That is, find $P(\hat{p}_1 - \hat{p}_2 > 0)$. If this event actually occurred, the producer would mistakenly think that more people watched hockey than basketball.
3. At a certain university, there is a movement to form a faculty union. Approximately 40% of the entire faculty favor unionizing. A prounion professor takes a random sample of 100 faculty members. Let $\hat{p}_1$ denote the proportion in this sample who favor a union. An antiunion professor takes an independent random sample of 100 professors. Let $\hat{p}_2$ denote the proportion in this sample who favor a union. Calculate the probability that $\hat{p}_1$ exceeds $\hat{p}_2$ by .1 or more.

9.7 ▪ Effects of Different Sampling Procedures (Optional)

The sampling distribution of $\bar{X}$ discussed previously in this chapter is based on the assumption that we have taken a simple random sample from the population. We have shown that if the population is infinitely large or if we sample with replacement, then the variance of the sample mean is given by $\text{Var}(\bar{X}) = \sigma^2/n$, where σ^2 is the population variance. If the population size is finite and we sample *without replacement*, then the variance of the sample mean $\bar{X}$ is

$$\sigma_{\bar{X}}^2 = \frac{\sigma^2}{n}\left(\frac{N-n}{N-1}\right)$$

where N is the population size and n is the sample size.

The same type of argument holds for the variance of the sample proportion $\hat{p}$. If we take a simple random sample from an infinite population or if we sample with replacement, the variance of $\hat{p}$ is $\sigma_{\hat{p}}^2 = pq/n$. If we sample without replacement, the variance of $\hat{p}$ is $(pq/n)(N - n)/(N - 1)$. The number $(N - n)/(N - 1)$, the finite population correction factor, measures the extent to which the variances of $\bar{X}$ and $\hat{p}$ are reduced when sampling is done without replacement from a finite population. In practice, the correction factor can usually be ignored provided the ratio n/N is small, say, .05 or less.

These results depend upon the assumption that we have selected a *simple random sample* with or without replacement. The formulas change if we take a *stratified random sample* as described in Chapter 2. The changes in the various formulas are discussed in the following section.

Estimating a Mean Using a Stratified Random Sample

Suppose we have a finite population containing N elements and K strata. Let N_i denote the number of elements in stratum i, so that $N_1 + N_2 + \cdots + N_K = N$. Let n_i denote the size of the simple random sample selected from stratum i, and let n denote the total size of the sample so that $n_1 + n_2 + \cdots + n_K = n$. Let σ_i^2 denote the variance of the elements in stratum i, and let $\bar{X}_i$ denote the sample mean of the n_i sample observations from sample i.

Formula for the Sample Mean and Sample Mean Variance

The population mean μ is estimated by the sample mean $\bar{X}$ by using the formula

$$\bar{X} = \frac{\sum_{i=1}^{K} N_i \bar{X}_i}{N}$$

Let S_i^2 denote the sample variance for the observations selected from stratum i. The variance of $\bar{X}$ is estimated using the formula

$$S_{\bar{X}}^2 = \frac{1}{N^2}\sum_{i=1}^{K} N_i^2 \left(\frac{N_i - n_i}{N_i - 1}\right)\left(\frac{S_i^2}{n_i}\right)$$

As usual, the sample standard deviation of $\bar{X}$ is the square root of the sample variance.

Example 9.11 **Estimating the Mean Using a Stratified Random Sample:** A town contains 4 high schools. Mr. Doherty, the superintendent of schools, wants to estimate the mean annual income of the parents of the high school students. The data in the following table show the total number of students at each school (N_i), the size of the sample taken at each school (n_i), the sample mean income for parents of students at each school ($\bar{X}_i$), and the sample standard deviation at each school (S_i):

School	N_i	n_i	$\bar{X}_i$	S_i
1	2000	200	\$18,000	\$2000
2	1000	100	25,000	4000
3	1500	150	20,000	3000
4	1500	150	22,000	3000
	6000	600		

Within what bounds can the population mean income be expected to lie?

Solution: The population size is $N = 6000$, and the total sample size is $n = 600$. The sample mean is calculated using the formula

$$\bar{X} = \frac{2000(\$18{,}000) + 1000(\$25{,}000) + 1500(\$20{,}000) + 1500(\$22{,}000)}{6000}$$

$$= \$20{,}666.67$$

The estimated variance of $\bar{X}$ is

$$S_{\bar{X}}^2 = \left(\frac{1}{6000^2}\right)\left[2000^2\left(\frac{2000 - 200}{2000 - 1}\right)\left(\frac{2000^2}{200}\right) + 1000^2\left(\frac{1000 - 100}{1000 - 1}\right)\left(\frac{4000^2}{100}\right)\right.$$
$$\left. + 1500^2\left(\frac{1500 - 150}{1500 - 1}\right)\left(\frac{3000^2}{150}\right) + 1500^2\left(\frac{1500 - 150}{1500 - 1}\right)\left(\frac{3000^2}{150}\right)\right]$$
$$= 12{,}759.508$$

The standard deviation is $S_{\bar{X}} = \$112.96$.

By using the Empirical Rule, we can say that the population mean should be within 2 standard deviations of $\bar{X}$ about 95% of the time. Approximately 95% of the possible intervals $(\bar{X} - 2S_{\bar{X}}, \bar{X} + 2S_{\bar{X}})$ will contain the population mean. Thus, we should feel very confident that the population mean lies in the interval [20,666.67 − 2(122.96), 20,666.67 + 2(112.96)], or (20,440.75, 20,892.59). ■

Estimating Proportions Using a Stratified Random Sample

Suppose we obtain a stratified random sample with K strata in order to estimate a population proportion p. Let n_i denote the size of the sample taken from stratum i, and let $\hat{p}_i$ denote the proportion of observations from the sample from stratum i that have the characteristic of interest. Let N_i denote the total number of observations in stratum i.

Formula for the Sample Proportion and Sample Proportion Variance

The population proportion p is estimated by the sample proportion $\hat{p}$ by using the following formula:

$$\hat{p} = \frac{\sum_{i=1}^{K} N_i \hat{p}_i}{N}$$

The variance of the sampling distribution of $\hat{p}$ depends on the unknown parameters p_i, $i = 1, 2, \ldots, K$, so the variance is unknown. To estimate the variance of $\hat{p}$, we use the following formula:

$$S_{\hat{p}}^2 = \frac{1}{N^2} \sum_{i=1}^{K} N_i^2 \left(\frac{N_i - n_i}{N_i - 1}\right)\left(\frac{\hat{p}_i \hat{q}_i}{n_i}\right)$$

Example 9.12

Estimating a Mean Using a Stratified Sample: A guidance counselor wants to estimate the proportion of students in the four high schools in the community who have two parents who graduated from college. The counselor takes random samples of size n_i from each of the four high schools. The data are as follows:

School	N_i	n_i	$\hat{p}_i$
1	2000	200	.10
2	1000	150	.30
3	1500	100	.20
4	1500	50	.25
	6000	500	

Within what bounds can the population proportion be expected to lie?

Solution: We obtain $N = 6000$ and

$$\hat{p} = \frac{2000(.10) + 1000(.30) + 1500(.20) + 1500(.25)}{6000} = .1958$$

The estimated variance of $\hat{p}$ is

$$S_{\hat{p}}^2 = \frac{1}{6000^2}\left[2000\left(\frac{2000 - 200}{2000 - 1}\right)\frac{(.1)(.9)}{200} + 1000^2\left(\frac{1000 - 150}{1000 - 1}\right)\frac{(.3)(.7)}{150} + 1500^2\left(\frac{1500 - 100}{1500 - 1}\right)\frac{(.2)(.8)}{100} + 1500^2\left(\frac{1500 - 50}{1500 - 1}\right)\frac{(.25)(.75)}{50}\right]$$

$$= .0003793$$

The standard deviation is

$$S_{\hat{p}} = .0194751 \approx .02$$

From the Empirical Rule, approximately 95% of the time the interval ($\hat{p} - 2S_{\hat{p}}$, $\hat{p} + 2S_{\hat{p}}$) should contain the population proportion p. The desired interval is thus (.1558, .2358). ■

9.8 ▪ Computer Applications

The SPSSX computer program can be used to find the sample mean and sample standard deviation for any sample of data. To find the mean and standard deviation, use the CONDESCRIPTIVE command followed by the names of the variables to be analyzed. For example, to find the mean and standard deviation for the variables AGE, SALARY, and SENIOR in Table 2.1 of Chapter 2, use the command

```
CONDESCRIPTIVE AGE, SALARY, SENIOR
```

Figure 9.11 shows the resulting computer output. The mean age of the sample of employees is 39.242 and the standard deviation is 12.022. The respective values for SALARY are $2133.00 and 687.433; for SENIOR, 15.358 and 10.871.

FIGURE 9.11 **SPSSX-generated output showing descriptive statistics for variables AGE, SALARY, and SENIOR for data in Table 2.1.**

NUMBER OF VALID OBSERVATIONS (LISTWISE) = 120.00

VARIABLE	MEAN	STD DEV	MINIMUM	MAXIMUM	VALID N	LABEL
AGE	39.242	12.022	19.00	64.00	120	
SALARY	2133.000	687.433	1200.00	5000.00	120	
SENIOR	15.358	10.871	1.00	42.00	120	

By issuing a BREAKDOWN command, we can request the SPSSX program to split the data into subsamples and compute statistics for each subsample. Procedure BREAKDOWN prints means and standard deviations of a variable within subgroups defined by another variable. For example, it will provide descriptive statistics on the variable SALARY broken down by SEX, or RACE, or academic DEGREE, and so forth. For example, the command

```
BREAKDOWN TABLES = SALARY BY SEX
```

tells SPSSX to calculate the mean and standard deviation of the variable SALARY for all individuals whose sex is classified as 0 (female) and as 1 (male). The output from the BREAKDOWN command is shown in Figure 9.12. Observe that the mean salary for females is $1676.89 and the standard deviation is $347.372; for males, the comparable figures are $2406.67 and $696.973.

FIGURE 9.12 **SPSSX-generated output showing descriptive statistics for variable SALARY broken down according to SEX for data in Table 2.1.**

```
CRITERION VARIABLE    SALARY
   BROKEN DOWN BY     SEX

- - - - - - - - - - - - - - - - - - - - - - - - - - - - - - - - - - - - - - - -

VARIABLE          VALUE  LABEL                    MEAN      STD DEV     CASES

FOR ENTIRE POPULATION                        2133.0000     687.4332       120

SEX                 .00  FEMALE              1676.8889     347.3721        45
SEX                1.00  MALE                2406.6667     696.9733        75

  TOTAL CASES =          120
```

Exercises for Section 9.8

In Exercises 1–4, use the SPSSX program and the BREAKDOWN command on the data in Table 2.1 of Chapter 2:

1. Find the sample mean and sample standard deviation for the variables AGE and SENIOR broken down according to the variable SEX.
2. Find the sample mean and sample standard deviation for the variables AGE, SALARY, and SENIOR broken down according to the variable RACE.
3. Find the sample mean and sample standard deviation for the variables AGE, SALARY, and SENIOR broken down according to the variable DEGREE.
4. Find the sample mean and sample standard deviation for the variables AGE, SALARY, and SENIOR broken down according to the variable DIV.
5. Use the SPSSX program and the CONDESCRIPTIVE command on the data in Table 2.2 of Chapter 2 to find the sample mean and sample standard deviation for SAT scores and GPAs.

In Exercises 6–9, use the SPSSX program and the BREAKDOWN command on the data in Table 2.2 of Chapter 2:

6. Find the sample mean and sample standard deviation for SAT scores and GPAs broken down according to the variable SEX.
7. Find the sample mean and sample standard deviation for SAT scores and GPAs broken down according to the variable CLASS.
8. Find the sample mean and sample standard deviation for SAT scores and GPAs broken down according to the student's residence.
9. Find the sample mean and sample standard deviation for SAT scores and GPAs broken down according to the student's major.

Chapter 9 Summary

In inferential statistics we take samples of data and calculate sample statistics to estimate unknown population parameters, such as the population mean μ, the population variance σ^2, and the population proportion p.

A *sample statistic* is a random variable whose value depends on the sample observations. Important examples of sample statistics are the sample mean, the sample variance, and the sample proportion. Every sample statistic has a *sampling distribution* that shows how the possible values of the sample estimate would be distributed if we could take repeated samples from the population. The *Central Limit Theorem* states that, for large samples, the sample mean $\bar{X}$ follows approximately the normal distribution with mean μ and variance σ^2/n. If the population is normally distributed, then $\bar{X}$ will follow an exact normal distribution regardless of the sample size. The Central Limit Theorem establishes the normal distribution as the most important of all continuous distributions. The strength of the Central Limit Theorem is that no assumptions are required concerning the shape of the population, provided the sample is large (say, $n > 30$).

The random variable $(\bar{X}_1 - \bar{X}_2)$ is used to estimate the difference between two population means. If the populations are normal or if the sample sizes are large, the sampling distribution of the difference between two sample means is normal with mean $(\mu_1 - \mu_2)$ and variance $(\sigma_1^2/n_1 + \sigma_2^2/n_2)$.

The *sample proportion* $\hat{p}$ is used to estimate the population proportion p. If $np \geqslant 5$ and $nq \geqslant 5$, then the sampling distribution of $\hat{p}$ is approximately normal with mean p and variance pq/n.

The random variable $(\hat{p}_1 - \hat{p}_2)$ is used to estimate the difference between two population proportions. If $n_1p_1 \geqslant 5$, $n_1q_1 \geqslant 5$, $n_2p_2 \geqslant 5$, and $n_2q_2 \geqslant 5$, the sampling distribution of the difference between two sample proportions is approximately normal with mean $(p_1 - p_2)$ and variance $(p_1q_1/n_1 + p_2q_2/n_2)$.

In the next chapter we will show how to use these sampling distributions to construct confidence intervals for population means and population proportions.

Chapter 9 ▪ Supplementary Exercises

1. Suppose light bulbs last 4000 hours on the average with a variance of 40,000. If we take a sample of 100 light bulbs and calculate $\bar{X}$, what is the probability that $\bar{X}$ will be between 3950 and 4050?
2. We want to determine the mean income of college professors. We take a random sample of 144 professors, and the population standard deviation is assumed to be \$12,000. What is the probability that the value of $\bar{X}$ is within \$2000 of the population mean μ?
3. A government agency wants to determine if a meat packing company is short-weighting the public. The company claims it puts 32 ounces of meat in each package on the average with a variance of 0.04. The government takes a random sample of 64 meat packages and calculates the mean weight. If the mean of the population is 32 ounces, then what is the probability that the value of $\bar{X}$ will be less than 31.95 ounces?
4. Four hundred ball bearings are selected from a population having a mean weight of 5 ounces and a variance of 0.09. What is the probability that the mean weight of bearings in our sample is between 4.95 and 5.05 ounces?
5. The probability is approximately .1 that a person aged 80 will die within one year. An insurance company insures 900 eighty-year-olds. What is the probability that more than 12% of these people will die in the following year?
6. A government agency wants to estimate the mean amount of money spent per week for gasoline by truck drivers. A sample of 400 drivers is taken. If the population standard deviation is \$40, what is the probability that $\bar{X}$ will be within \$6 of the true mean μ?

7. A student commission wants to know the mean amount of money spent by college students for textbooks in the senior year. Assume the variance of the population is 400. If a sample of 625 students is taken, what is the probability that $\bar{X}$ will be within \$3 of the population mean?
8. In a certain district, 55% of the voters want Congress to decrease expenditures on defense. A member of Congress takes a random sample of 2475 voters. What is the probability that the sample proportion who want defense expenditures cut is less than .5?
9. We want to estimate the mean grade point average of college seniors. We take a random sample of 9 seniors and obtain the following values:

$$x_1 = 3.0 \quad x_2 = 3.3 \quad x_3 = 2.4$$

$$x_4 = 2.7 \quad x_5 = 2.4 \quad x_6 = 3.6$$

$$x_7 = 3.3 \quad x_8 = 2.4 \quad x_9 = 2.7$$

   a. Calculate $\bar{X}$ in order to estimate μ.
   b. Calculate s^2 in order to estimate σ^2.
   c. Calculate s^2/n in order to estimate the variance of $\bar{X}$.
10. In a small town, 30% of the residents use the library regularly. The city council is debating a bill that would increase the library's budget. Before increasing the budget, the council wants to estimate the proportion of residents who use the library regularly. Suppose a sample of 400 residents is taken. What is the probability that the sample proportion will be within .03 of the population proportion?
11. A company claims that Method 2 of making TV tubes is superior to the old Method 1. In a random sample of 1000 tubes produced by Method 1, the mean lifetime was $\bar{x}_1 = 4000$ hours. Assume that the variance in Population 1 is 40,000. In a random sample of 1000 tubes made by Method 2, the mean lifetime was 4025 hours with a variance of 41,000. If, in fact, $(\mu_1 - \mu_2)$ is 0, find the probability that $(\bar{X}_1 - \bar{X}_2)$ will be between -25 and $+25$.
12. The United States Golf Association wants to determine if golf balls of Type 1 are livelier than balls of Type 2. A mechanical device hits a sample of 400 balls of Type 1 and 300 balls of Type 2. The distance (in yards) traveled by each ball is measured and the sample means are obtained. If $\sigma_1^2 = 2000$ and $\sigma_2^2 = 1200$, and if $(\mu_1 - \mu_2) = 0$, find $P(-10 \leq \bar{X}_1 - \bar{X}_2 \leq 10)$.
13. In a small town, 40% of the population watched a certain television program. If we take a random sample of 2400 people, what is the probability that the sample proportion is between .38 and .42?
14. In Exercise 13 suppose the sample size is 9600. What is the probability that $\hat{p}$ is between .38 and .42?
15. I want the probability to be .9544 that the proportion of heads obtained in n tosses of a fair coin is between .46 and .54. How large does the sample size have to be?
16. In a congressional election, 55% of the electorate prefers Candidate A. If I take a random sample of 900 voters, what is the probability that Candidate A will get less than half the vote? That is, what is the probability that I will project the wrong candidate as the winner?
17. The Internal Revenue Service (IRS) wants to know the mean amount of money deducted for contributions to charity by people earning \$15,000 to \$20,000. The IRS takes a sample of 400 income tax reports of people in this income bracket. If the variance of contributions is 10,000, what is the probability that $\bar{X}$ will be within \$15 of the population mean?
18. The police department wants to estimate the number of unreported crimes. Suppose that during the last year, 10% of the adults in a city have been victims of some unreported crime. The police contact a random sample of 900 adults in order to estimate the proportion of people who were victims of an unreported crime. What is the probability that the sample proportion will be between .07 and .13?
19. In Exercise 18, let the sample size be 2500. What is the probability that $\hat{p}$ will be between .09 and .11?
20. At a restaurant, the mean expenditure per customer is \$12 and the variance is 9. If we take a

random sample of 81 customers, what is the probability that the sample mean will be between \$11 and \$13?

21. A rehabilitation counselor wants to estimate the proportion of high school dropouts who have used drugs. Assume that 80% of all dropouts have used drugs. If the counselor obtains a random sample of 240 dropouts, what is the probability that fewer than 70% have used drugs?

22. Suppose that about 5% of the population has a serious accident or illness during any given year. If an insurance company insures 47,500 people, what is the probability that more than 6% of these people will have a serious accident or illness next year?

23. A random variable X has mean μ and variance σ^2. We take a random sample of size n and calculate $\bar{X}$. Find the number z such that

$$P[\mu - z(\sigma/\sqrt{n}) \leq \bar{X} \leq \mu + z(\sigma/\sqrt{n})] = .90$$

24. In Exercise 23, find z such that

$$P[\mu - z(\sigma/\sqrt{n}) \leq \bar{X} \leq \mu + z(\sigma/\sqrt{n})] = .99$$

25. In Exercise 23, find z such that

$$P[\bar{X} \geq \mu + z(\sigma/\sqrt{n})] = .05$$

26. Ball bearings have a mean weight of 0.5 ounce with a variance of 0.01. The bearings are sold in boxes of 400. If we randomly choose two boxes of bearings, what is the probability that the mean weights of the two boxes of bearings differ by more than 0.0125 ounce?

27. A fair coin is tossed 200 times. The percentage of heads obtained is denoted $\hat{p}_1$. Again the coin is tossed 200 times. The percentage of heads obtained is denoted $\hat{p}_2$. Calculate $P(|\hat{p}_1 - \hat{p}_2| > .02)$.

28. In a random sample of 100 children who used Toothpaste A, the mean number of cavities was $\bar{X}_A = 3.1$ with population variance $\sigma_A^2 = 1$. In a random sample of 100 children who used Toothpaste B, the mean number of cavities was $\bar{X}_B = 3.4$ with population variance $\sigma_B^2 = 1.25$. If the toothpastes are actually identical, what is the probability that $\bar{X}_B$ will exceed $\bar{X}_A$ by 0.3 unit or more?

29. In 1973, a federal judge ruled that the selection of juries in Montgomery County, Alabama, was discriminatory. The judge observed that blacks made up 30% of the jury age population but only 12% of the jury rolls, and that women made up 54% of the jury age population but only 16% of the jury rolls. If there are 100 people on a jury roll, what are the probabilities that random selection yields the following:

a. No more than 12% blacks

b. No more than 16% females

c. Do these data lend evidence for or against the hypothesis that jury rolls are chosen without regard to race or sex?

30. I take a random sample of size n from a population that is normally distributed with mean μ and variance σ^2. The sample variance S^2 is a random variable having mean σ^2 and variance $2\sigma^4/(n - 1)$. As the sample size increases, the distribution of S^2 approaches a normal distribution. I take a sample of size 50 from a normal population having $\sigma^2 = 196$.

a. What is the approximate probability that S^2 will exceed 202?

b. Find $P(190 \leq S^2 \leq 202)$.

c. Find $P(S^2 \leq 180)$.

31. An environmental agency wants to estimate the number of fish in a lake. They catch 10,000 fish, tag them, and put them back in the lake, distributing them evenly. A short while later they catch another 10,000 fish and find that 500 have been tagged.

a. Based on this sample, what is your estimate of the proportion of fish in the lake that are tagged?

b. What is your estimate of the total number of fish in the lake?

32. The Kelly Advertising Agency is doing a marketing study to determine if adult males watch more or less television than adult females. They obtain a random sample of $n_1 = 40$ males and $n_2 = 30$ females and ask each person how much TV he or she watches per month. Assume that the population variances are $\sigma_1^2 = 160$ and $\sigma_2^2 = 150$. If $\mu_1 = \mu_2$, what is the probability that the difference between the sample means will be less than 4 units?

33. The mean daily output at a small West Virginia coal mine is 38 tons of coal. The log book showing the tonnage mined each day indicates that the standard deviation of the daily output is $\sigma = 5$ tons. What is the probability of the following?

a. During a random sample of 40 days, the sample mean output exceeds 42 tons.

b. During a random sample of 60 days, the mean output is less than 35 tons.

34. The mean tread life of all Jensen radial tires is $\mu = 44{,}500$ miles with standard deviation $\sigma = 1900$ miles. If the population is normally distributed, what is the probability of the following?

a. The mean life of 6 randomly selected tires exceeds 43,000 miles.

b. The mean life of 100 randomly selected tires exceeds 43,000 miles.

35. A dentist tells an Internal Revenue Service auditor that his mean fee is \$25 per patient with standard deviation $\sigma = \$5$. The auditor selects a random sample of 70 patients and calculates the sample mean $\bar{X}$. Find the probability of the following in the auditor's sample:

a. $\bar{X}$ exceeds \$30.

b. $\bar{X}$ exceeds \$27.

36. At the Caste Automobile Company, the mean profit from selling new cars was \$400 per car with standard deviation $\sigma = \$80$. If Mr. Levine is a typical salesperson, find the probability that in a random sample of 60 sales, Mr. Levine shows a mean profit $\bar{X}$ of less than \$320.

37. The customers who rent compact cars from the Rankin Car Rental Agency travel 400 miles on the average. The population standard deviation is $\sigma = 70$. A random sample of 64 customers is checked during a certain time period. Find the probability of the following:

a. $\bar{X}$ exceeds 420 miles.

b. $\bar{X}$ is less than 390 miles.

38. The light bulbs used in the U.S. space shuttle have an average life expectancy of $\mu = 100$ hours. The distribution of life expectancies is normal with $\sigma = 10$ hours. For a trip that is expected to last 380 hours, the crew takes along 4 new bulbs (1 in place and 3 spares). If each bulb is replaced immediately when it burns out, what is the probability that the 4 bulbs will be sufficient for the entire 380-hour trip? (*Note:* For the 4 bulbs to total 380 hours, they must average 95 hours per bulb.)

39. Probability theory tells us that if the probability of some event is .5, then in a very large number of independent trials, the relative frequency with which this event occurs is almost certain to be very close to .5. To check this claim, suppose a fair coin is tossed n times, where n is some large number. Calculate the probability that the proportion of heads will be between .499 and .501 if the number of tosses is as follows:

a. $n = 10{,}000$ b. $n = 100{,}000$ c. $n = 1{,}000{,}000$

40. Suppose the life of a tire is normally distributed with a mean of 30,000 miles and a standard deviation of 6000 miles. What is the probability of the following:

a. A tire will last more than 40,000 miles.

b. The average life of 4 tires will be more than 40,000 miles.

41. The gasoline mileage for a brand of compact car is normally distributed with a mean of 31 miles per gallon (mpg) and a standard deviation of 4 mpg. If an impartial group measures the mileages for a sample of these cars, what is the probability that their average will be greater than 30 mpg if only 1 car is tested? If 25 cars are tested? If 100 cars are tested?

References

COCHRAN, WILLIAM G. *Sampling Techniques*. 3d ed. New York: Wiley, 1977.

COCHRAN, WILLIAM G., and G. M. COX. *Experimental Designs*. 2d ed. New York: Wiley, 1957.

FREUND, JOHN E., and R. E. WALPOLE. *Mathematical Statistics*. 4th ed. Englewood Cliffs, N.J.: Prentice-Hall, 1987.

Handbook of Tables for Probability and Statistics. 2d ed. Cleveland: Chemical Rubber Co., 1968.

HOEL, PAUL G. *Elementary Statistics*. 4th ed. New York: Wiley, 1976.

NATIONAL BUREAU OF STANDARDS. *Tables of the Binomial Probability Distribution*. Washington, D.C.: Government Printing Office, 1949.

NETER, JOHN, WILLIAM WASSERMAN, and G. A. WHITMORE. *Fundamental Statistics for Business and Economics*. 4th ed. Boston: Allyn and Bacon, 1973.

Chapter Ten
Estimating and Constructing Confidence Intervals

10.1 ▪ Interval Estimation

In this chapter we discuss how to construct an interval estimate for the population mean μ, the population proportion p, the difference of means $(\mu_1 - \mu_2)$, and the difference between proportions $(p_1 - p_2)$. For most problems of interest, a point estimate is inadequate without some additional information concerning its reliability. A sample estimate is a random variable and will not exactly equal the population parameter being estimated. After obtaining a point estimate, it is reasonable to ask, "How close is the estimate to the true value of the population parameter being estimated?"

When we try to evaluate the goodness, or reliability, of an estimator $\hat{\theta}$, we are trying, in general, to put some bound on the possible error of estimation $|\hat{\theta} - \theta|$, where θ represents the true value of the parameter being estimated. The error of estimation $|\hat{\theta} - \theta|$, called the *sampling error,* measures the distance between the estimated value and the true value of the population parameter.

A systematic method of indicating the precision of an estimator $\hat{\theta}$ exists, provided we know the form of the sampling distribution of θ. We indicate the precision of our estimator by constructing **confidence intervals** for θ, where we use the estimate $\hat{\theta}$ to determine two values $\hat{\theta}_1$ and $\hat{\theta}_2$ such that the interval $(\hat{\theta}_1, \hat{\theta}_2)$ contains the value θ with a specified probability. The probability is usually denoted as $(1 - \alpha)$, and the percentage $100(1 - \alpha)\%$ is called the **confidence coefficient** or **level of confidence** of the confidence interval $(\hat{\theta}_1, \hat{\theta}_2)$.

In any estimation problem, we would like our estimators to have two important properties:

1. We want an *unbiased* estimator, so there is no systematic tendency to overestimate or underestimate the true value of the population parameter.
2. We want an estimator with a sampling distribution that is highly concentrated about the value of the population parameter θ. That is, we want the variance of the random variable $\hat{\theta}$ to be small.

Now consider $\bar{X}$ and $\hat{p}$ as estimates of μ and p, respectively. Recall that the variance of the sample mean $\bar{X}$ is given by $\text{Var}(\bar{X}) = \sigma_X^2/n$. Thus, the variance of the sampling distribution of $\bar{X}$ depends on n and is controllable. That is, we can make $\text{Var}(\bar{X})$ as small as we desire by increasing the sample size. Similarly, the variance of the sample proportion $\hat{p}$, given by $\text{Var}(\hat{p}) = pq/n$, can also be controlled. Since the sampling distributions of $\bar{X}$ and $\hat{p}$ are centered at μ and p, respectively, we can virtually guarantee that our estimate $\bar{x}$ or $\hat{p}$ will be close to the desired value μ or p by choosing a sufficiently large sample.

Before discussing the idea of a confidence interval, it is useful to introduce some new notation that will help us identify areas in the tail of the standard normal distribution. The value z_α is the value of the standard normal variable such that the area to its right is α. The following examples explain this notation.

Value of z_α

Let Z be a standard normal random variable and let α be any number such that $0 < \alpha < 1$. Then z_α denotes the number for which

$$P(Z \geqslant z_\alpha) = \alpha$$

Example 10.1

Finding a Value of z_α: Suppose we select $\alpha = .025$. Find the value z_α.

Solution: If 2.5% of the area falls in the right tail of the distribution beyond z_α, then the area between 0 and z_α is .475. From Table A.5 in the Appendix, the area between 0 and 1.96 is .475. Thus, $P(Z > 1.96) = .025$ and $z_{.025} = 1.96$. This value is found by locating .475 in the body of Table A.5 and finding the corresponding value of Z. By symmetry, we know that 2.5% of the area lies to the left of the value $-z_{.025} = -1.96$. Thus we have

$$P(Z > 1.96) = .025 \quad \text{and} \quad P(Z < -1.96) = .025$$

This idea is illustrated in Figure 10.1.

FIGURE 10.1
z_α for $\alpha = .025$.

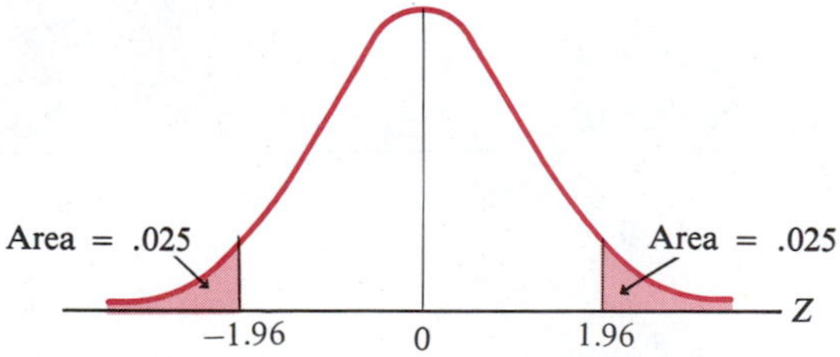

■

Example 10.2

Finding More Values of z_α: Find the values $z_{.05}$ and $z_{.005}$ such that $P(Z > z_{.05}) = .05$ and $P(Z > z_{.005}) = .005$.

Solution: If 5% of the area falls in the right tail of the distribution, then $P(Z > z_{.05}) = .05$ and $P(0 \leqslant Z \leqslant z_{.05}) = .45$. From Table A.5 in the Appendix, we obtain $z_{.05} \approx 1.645$. This is illustrated in Figure 10.2. Similarly, if 0.5% of the area under the standard normal distribution falls to the right of $z_{.005}$, then 49.5% of the area falls between 0 and $z_{.005}$. We obtain $P(Z > z_{.005}) = .005$ and $P(0 \leq Z \leq z_{.005}) = .495$. From Table A.5, we obtain $z_{.005} \approx 2.58$.

FIGURE 10.2
z_α for $\alpha = .05$.

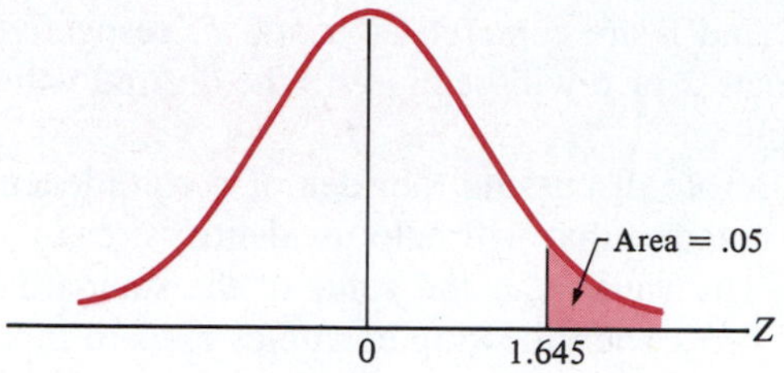

The symbol $z_{\alpha/2}$ denotes the value of the standard normal variate Z such that the area in the right tail of the distribution is $\alpha/2$. We have

$$P(Z > z_{\alpha/2}) = \alpha/2$$

and

$$P(Z < -z_{\alpha/2}) = \alpha/2$$

We obtain

$$P(-z_{\alpha/2} \leq Z \leq z_{\alpha/2}) = 1 - \alpha$$

Thus, the area under the standard normal distribution between $-z_{\alpha/2}$ and $z_{\alpha/2}$ is $(1 - \alpha)$. The area in each tail of the distribution is $\alpha/2$, and the total area in the two tails of the distribution is α. (See Figure 10.3.)

FIGURE 10.3
$P(-z_{\alpha/2} \leq Z \leq z_{\alpha/2}) = 1 - \alpha$.

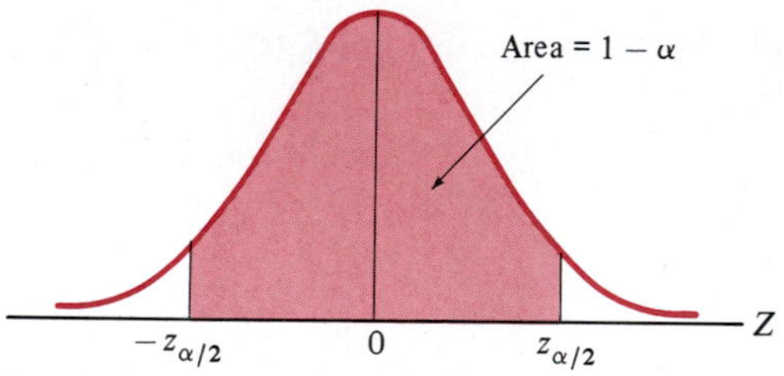

Exercises for Section 10.1

1. Find z_α for the following values of α: .005, .01, .025, .05, .10.
2. Find $z_{\alpha/2}$ for the following values of α: .005, .01, .025, .05, .10.
3. Find the value $z_{\alpha/2}$ such that $P(-z_{\alpha/2} \leq Z \leq z_{\alpha/2}) = K$ for the following values of K: .80, .90, .95, .99.

4. Find the value z_α such that $P(Z > z_\alpha) = K$ for the following values of K: .10, .05, .025, .01, .005.

10.2 ▪ Confidence Intervals for the Mean with Known Population Variance

Suppose that we take a random sample of size n from a normal population having mean μ and variance σ^2. The random variable $\overline{X}$ will have exactly a normal distribution with mean μ and variance $\text{Var}(\overline{X}) = \sigma^2/n$. In addition, the standardized random variable

$$Z = \frac{\overline{X} - \mu}{\sigma/\sqrt{n}}$$

will follow the standard normal distribution.

Our previous discussion showed that, for the standard normal distribution, the area to the right of $z_{\alpha/2}$ is $\alpha/2$ and the area to the left of $-z_{\alpha/2}$ is $\alpha/2$. Thus the area between $-z_{\alpha/2}$ and $z_{\alpha/2}$ is $1 - \alpha$. We obtain

$$1 - \alpha = P(-z_{\alpha/2} < Z < z_{\alpha/2})$$

After substituting for Z, we obtain

$$\begin{aligned} 1 - \alpha &= P\left(-z_{\alpha/2} < \frac{\overline{X} - \mu}{\sigma/\sqrt{n}} < z_{\alpha/2}\right) \\ &= P(-z_{\alpha/2}\sigma/\sqrt{n} < \overline{X} - \mu < z_{\alpha/2}\sigma/\sqrt{n}) \\ &= P(\overline{X} - z_{\alpha/2}\sigma/\sqrt{n} < \mu < \overline{X} + z_{\alpha/2}\sigma/\sqrt{n}) \end{aligned}$$

This last probability statement tells us that the probability is $(1 - \alpha)$ that the random interval $(\overline{X} - z_{\alpha/2}\sigma/\sqrt{n}, \overline{X} + z_{\alpha/2}\sigma/\sqrt{n})$ will contain the true population mean μ.

Definition: Level of Confidence

The **level of confidence** of a confidence interval measures the probability that a population parameter will be contained in an interval calculated after a random sample has been selected from a population. The level of confidence is denoted by the symbol $(1 - \alpha)$.

The value α indicates the proportion of times that we will be incorrect in assuming that an interval contains the population parameter. If $\alpha = .05$, then the level of confidence of the interval is $(1 - \alpha) = .95$, or 95%; if $\alpha = 10$, then the level of confidence of the interval is $(1 - \alpha) = .90$, or 90%; and so forth. Thus, it is possible to construct a confidence interval having any desired level of confidence. To do this, we must find the Z scores from Table A.5 such that the combined areas in the two tails of the distribution total α.

Definition: Confidence Interval for the Mean of a Normal Population with Known Population Variance

Suppose we take a random sample of n observations from a normal population with mean μ and variance σ^2. If σ^2 is known and the observed sample mean is $\bar{x}$, then the **confidence interval** for the mean with a level of confidence $100(1 - \alpha)\%$ is given by

$$(\bar{x} - z_{\alpha/2}\sigma/\sqrt{n},\ \bar{x} + z_{\alpha/2}\sigma/\sqrt{n})$$

where $z_{\alpha/2}$ is the number for which

$$P(Z > z_{\alpha/2}) = \alpha/2$$

and where the random variable Z has a standard normal distribution.

Example 10.3

Constructing a 95% Confidence Interval for the Mean: A student advisor wants to estimate the mean annual income of all college students who graduated last year. The population standard deviation is believed to be \$2000. Based on a random sample of 25 college graduates, the advisor obtains $\bar{x} = \$19{,}500$. Let us construct a 95% confidence interval for the unknown population mean μ.

Solution: We have $\sigma = \$2000$, $n = 25$, $\bar{x} = \$19{,}500$, and $(1 - \alpha) = .95$. Thus, we have $\alpha = .05$ and $\alpha/2 = .025$. From Table A.5 we see that 2.5% of the area under the standard normal curve lies to the right of 1.96. We obtain $z_{\alpha/2} = 1.96$. The desired confidence interval is

$$(\bar{x} - z_{\alpha/2}\sigma/\sqrt{n},\ \bar{x} + z_{\alpha/2}\sigma/\sqrt{n})$$

or

$$(19{,}500 - 1.96(2000)/\sqrt{25},\ 19{,}500 + 1.96(2000)/\sqrt{25})$$

or

$$(18{,}716,\ 20{,}284)$$

Thus, we are 95% confident that the population mean is between \$18,716 and \$20,284. We cannot be sure that this interval contains the population mean, but if we repeated this process a large number of times, 95% of the confidence intervals obtained would contain the population mean. ■

The confidence interval obtained in Example 10.3 depends on the specific value $\bar{x} = \$19{,}500$ obtained from the sample of n observations. Suppose we take another random sample of n observations, calculate a new value of $\bar{x}$, and obtain the 95% confidence interval $(\bar{x} - 1.96\sigma/\sqrt{n},\ \bar{x} + 1.96\sigma/\sqrt{n})$. Like the first confidence interval, this one may or may not contain the population mean μ.

If we repeated this process, say, 1000 times, we would have 1000 different sample means and 1000 different confidence intervals. A 95% level of confidence means that approximately 95% (or 950) of these confidence intervals would contain μ and 5% (or 50) would not.

The idea that 95% of the samples of size n produce intervals $(\bar{x} - 1.96\sigma/\sqrt{n}, \bar{x} + 1.96\sigma/\sqrt{n})$ containing μ is illustrated in Figure 10.4. This figure shows 10 confidence intervals that could be obtained by repeated sampling. In the figure, 9 of the 10 intervals contain μ. If many repeated samples were taken from the same population, the proportion of intervals containing μ would be approximately .95.

FIGURE 10.4 **Ten possible confidence intervals for the mean.**

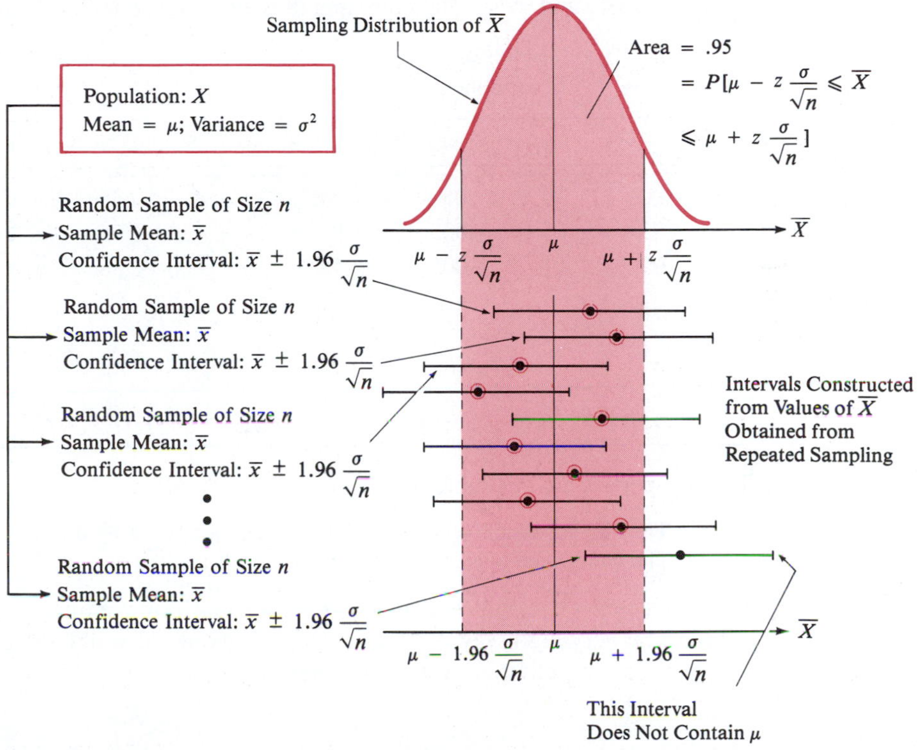

It is important that the probability statement

$$P(\bar{X} - z_{\alpha/2}\sigma/\sqrt{n} < \mu < \bar{X} + z_{\alpha/2}\,\sigma/\sqrt{n}) = 1 - \alpha$$

be interpreted correctly. In this statement, the parameter μ *is not* a random variable and does not vary from sample to sample; rather the mean μ is an unknown population parameter. On the other hand, $\bar{X}$ is a random variable and varies from sample to sample. If we take many samples of size n from the population, we get a different value of $\bar{X}$ for each sample. For a particular estimate $\bar{x}$, we can calculate the endpoints of the interval $(\bar{x} - z_{\alpha/2}\sigma/\sqrt{n}, \bar{x} + z_{\alpha/2}\sigma/\sqrt{n})$; these endpoints vary from sample to sample. The probability statement says that $100(1 - \alpha)\%$ of these random intervals contain the value μ. We say that we are $100(1 - \alpha)\%$ confident that our interval contains μ because, essentially, our interval is just one of many possible intervals.

Before selecting the random sample, the probability is $(1 - \alpha)$ that the confidence interval will contain the population mean. After we have taken the sample, we say that we are $100(1 - \alpha)\%$ confident that our interval contains the mean, because if we performed the same experiment a large number of times, then in $100(1 - \alpha)\%$ of the cases the interval would contain the mean.

Formulas for Commonly Constructed Confidence Intervals

The most frequently constructed confidence intervals use levels of confidence 90%, 95%, and 99%. The corresponding confidence intervals are as follows:

Level of Confidence				Confidence Interval
$(1 - \alpha)$	α	$\alpha/2$	$z_{\alpha/2}$	$(\bar{x} - z_{\alpha/2}\sigma/\sqrt{n}, \bar{x} + z_{\alpha/2}\sigma/\sqrt{n})$
.90	.10	.05	1.645	$(\bar{x} - 1.645\sigma/\sqrt{n}, \bar{x} + 1.645\sigma/\sqrt{n})$
.95	.05	.025	1.96	$(\bar{x} - 1.96\sigma/\sqrt{n}, \bar{x} + 1.96\sigma/\sqrt{n})$
.99	.01	.005	2.58	$(\bar{x} - 2.58\sigma/\sqrt{n}, \bar{x} + 2.58\sigma/\sqrt{n})$

Desirable Properties of Confidence Intervals

Two properties are desirable in a confidence interval:

1. The interval should have a high level of confidence $(1 - \alpha)$.
2. The confidence interval should have a narrow width.

In most cases we would like the probability that our confidence interval contains the mean to be very high, say, 90% or more. We would also like the confidence interval to be very narrow so that our estimate is very precise.

Definition: Width of a Confidence Interval for μ

The **width** W of a confidence interval for the population mean is

$$W = 2z_{\alpha/2}\sigma/\sqrt{n}$$

The width of a confidence interval for the mean depends on three factors:

1. the level of confidence of the confidence interval $(1 - \alpha)$,
2. the standard deviation of the population σ, and
3. the sample size n.

The following properties hold for all confidence intervals:

1. The larger the level of confidence $(1 - \alpha)$, the larger will be $z_{\alpha/2}$ and the wider will be the confidence interval. That is, if we hold σ and n constant, an increase in $(1 - \alpha)$ causes an increase in W. This means that if we want to increase the probability that our interval will contain the true mean, we have to make the confidence interval wider. For example, all other things being equal, a 99% confidence interval will be wider than a 95% confidence interval.

2. The smaller the population standard deviation σ, the narrower the confidence interval. If the population is highly concentrated, our estimate of the mean is very reliable. Because the estimate is very reliable, only a narrow confidence interval is required.

3. As the sample size increases, the width of the confidence interval decreases. As we obtain more information, our estimate should become better, as reflected by a narrower confidence interval. Note that in order to cut the width of a confidence interval in half, it is necessary to multiply the sample size by a factor of 4.

Example 10.4

Comparing Widths of Confidence Intervals: Suppose we take a random sample of size n from a population having known variance σ^2. Construct 99%, 95%, and 90% confidence intervals for the population mean and compare their widths.

Solution: For 99%, 95%, and 90% confidence intervals, the respective Z scores are $z_{.005} = 2.58$, $z_{.025} = 1.96$, and $z_{.05} = 1.645$. The widths of these three confidence intervals are $W_1 = 2(2.58)\sigma/\sqrt{n}$, $W_2 = 2(1.96)\sigma/\sqrt{n}$, and $W_3 = 2(1.645)\sigma/\sqrt{n}$. The fact that $W_1/W_2 = 1.32$ means that a 99% confidence interval is 32% wider than a 95% confidence interval. We obtain $W_2/W_3 = 1.19$, which indicates that a 95% confidence interval is 19% wider than a 90% confidence interval. This idea is illustrated in Figure 10.5. In the figure, note how rapidly the width of the confidence interval increases as the level of confidence gets near 100%. ■

FIGURE 10.5
Width of several confidence intervals.

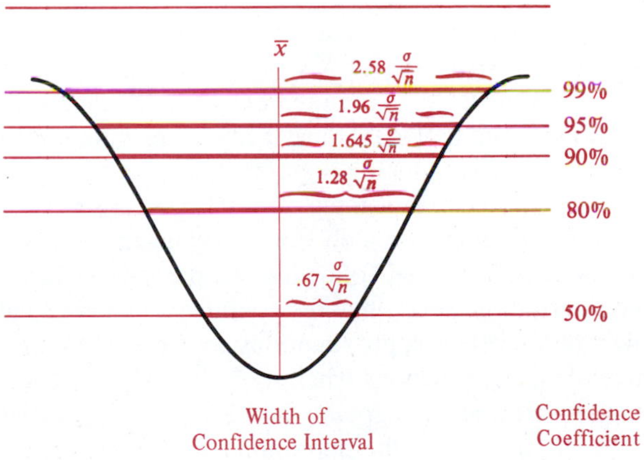

To decrease the width of the confidence interval, we must either use a smaller level of confidence $(1 - \alpha)$, which decreases $z_{\alpha/2}$, or increase the sample size n. By making the sample size larger and larger, one can make the confidence interval (for any value of α) as narrow as desired, but at an increased cost of sampling.

Example 10.5

99% Confidence Interval for the Mean: Construct a 99% confidence interval for the mean in Example 10.3 and compare with the 95% confidence interval calculated there.

Solution: We have $\sigma = 2000$, $n = 25$, $\bar{x} = \$19{,}500$, and $(1 - \alpha) = .99$. Thus, $\alpha = .01$ and $\alpha/2 = .005$. From Table A.5, we obtain $z_{\alpha/2} = 2.58$. The desired confidence interval is thus

$$(\bar{x} - z_{\alpha/2}\sigma/\sqrt{n},\ \bar{x} + z_{\alpha/2}\sigma/\sqrt{n})$$

or

$$(19{,}500 - 2.58(2000)/\sqrt{25},\ 19{,}500 + 2.58(2000)/\sqrt{25})$$

or

$$(18{,}468,\ 20{,}532)$$

The width of this confidence interval is $W_1 = \$2064$. The 95% confidence interval is (18,716, 20,284) with a width of \$1568. We obtain $W_1/W_2 = 2064/1568 = 1.32$, which shows that the 99% confidence interval is 32% wider than the 95% confidence interval. This coincides with the result obtained in Example 10.4. ■

Confidence Intervals for Large Samples

The development of confidence intervals for the mean presented here is limited by two requirements:

1. The population distribution must be normal.
2. The population variance or standard deviation must be known.

When the sample size is large, neither requirement is too important. Because the sampling distribution of $\bar{X}$ will be approximately normal because of the Central Limit Theorem for large n, requirement 1 is eliminated. In addition, the sample standard deviation should provide a fairly accurate estimate of the population standard deviation for large n, thus eliminating requirement 2.

Thus, when the sample size is large, say 30 or more, we can find confidence intervals that are approximately correct by using the observed sample standard deviation s as an estimate of σ and following the procedures developed in this section. It should not be inferred, however, that the confidence intervals calculated as described in this section will be excellent approximations to the exact confidence intervals when $n \geqslant 30$ and terrible approximations when $n < 30$. The use of $n = 30$ as the breaking point at which the approximation is good is just a rule of thumb that most statisticians recommend.

The quality of the approximation gradually improves as n increases because the sampling distribution of $\bar{X}$ gradually approaches the normal distribution, thus as n increases, our estimate of σ gradually improves.

Tips for Problem Solving

When constructing a confidence interval for the population mean, it is important to use the standard deviation of the sampling distribution of $\bar{X}$, namely $\sigma/\sqrt{n}$, rather than σ, which is the standard deviation of the population. Students frequently make the mistake of forgetting the $\sqrt{n}$ term when constructing a confidence interval for the mean.

Exercises for Section 10.2

1. Construct a 95% confidence interval for the mean if $\bar{x} = 400$, $\sigma^2 = 25$, and $n = 100$.
2. Construct a 90% confidence interval for the mean if $\bar{x} = 400$, $\sigma^2 = 25$, and $n = 100$.
3. Construct a 99% confidence interval for the mean if $\bar{x} = 400$, $\sigma^2 = 25$, and $n = 100$.
4. To estimate the mean age of subscribers to *Sports Illustrated* magazine, a random sample of 100 subscribers is taken. The sample mean is $\bar{x} = 31$, and the sample variance is 144. Calculate the following confidence intervals for μ:
   a. 95% b. 99%
5. To estimate the mean monthly costs of room and board, a random sample of 100 students is taken. Suppose that $s^2 = 4900$ and $\bar{x} = \$300$. Calculate the following confidence intervals for μ:
   a. 95% b. 95% assuming the sample size is $n = 900$
6. The Summerhill Trucking Company owns a large fleet of rental trucks. Many of the trucks need substantial repairs from time to time. The company president takes a random sample of 64 trucks and finds that the sample mean annual repair bill is \$1245 with sample standard deviation $s =$ \$288. Construct the following confidence intervals for μ:
   a. 95% b. 99%
7. A statistical report states that a 95% confidence interval for the mean salary of new Ph.D.'s in economics is (\$24,000, \$26,000) with a population standard deviation σ of \$2000. How large was the sample used to find the confidence interval?
8. The president of the Thomas Cookie Company wanted to estimate the mean amount of money that households spend per week on cookies and crackers. The company took a random sample of 200 households and determined how much each household spent on cookies and crackers last week. The sample standard deviation was $s =$ \$1.45 and the sample mean was $\bar{x} =$ \$4.16. Construct a 95% confidence interval for μ.
9. An executive for the Rankin Car Rental Agency wants to know the average mileage driven by customers who rent cars from Rankin. A random sample of 200 customers is obtained. The sample mean mileage is $\bar{x} = 325$ miles, and the sample standard deviation is $s = 60$. Construct the following confidence intervals for μ:
   a. 90% b. 95%
10. For winter months the standard deviation for monthly heating bills for residential homes in a certain area is believed to be \$100. A random sample of 16 homes in a particular subdivision will be used to estimate the mean monthly heating bills for all homes in this type of subdivision.
    a. What is the standard error of the mean?
    b. Find the sampling distribution for the sample mean heating bill.
    c. Find the 95% confidence interval for the mean monthly heating bill if the sample mean is \$195.00.
11. A research report stated that the mean return on invested capital in 1988 was between 6.1% and 10.8% per year with a confidence coefficient of 95%. One person interpreted this as meaning that 95% of investors had investment returns between 6.1% and 10.8%. Another person interpreted the statement to mean that if many random samples were taken, 95% would have sample means between 6.1% and 10.8%. Why are these interpretations incorrect?

10.3 ▪ Student's t Distribution

In Section 10.2 we showed how to use the Z score to construct confidence intervals for the population mean in the following cases:

- *Case 1:* The population is normal and the population variance is known.
- *Case 2:* The sample size is large, say $n \geqslant 30$. In this case, the population may or may not be normal, and the variance may or may not be known.

How do we construct a confidence interval for the mean when the sample size is small and the population variance is unknown? There are two different cases to consider:

- *Case 3:* The population is approximately normal, the variance is unknown, and the sample is small.
- *Case 4:* The population is nonnormal and the sample size is small.

In Section 10.4, we will discuss how to construct confidence intervals for the population mean μ for case 3. Under these circumstances, confidence intervals can be obtained by using a t score and the t distribution, which we will describe in this section.

In case 4 above, where the population is nonnormal and the sample is small, the Z score is not appropriate because the population is nonnormal, the variance is unknown, and the Central Limit Theorem does not apply. In addition, the use of the t distribution is not theoretically correct because the population is nonnormal. Nevertheless, many people use the t distribution in this situation and then qualify their confidence intervals by stating that they are only approximate.

The use of the t distribution is based on the following argument. If the population is normally distributed with mean μ and variance σ^2, the sample mean $\overline{X}$ is distributed as $N(\mu, \sigma^2/n)$ and the standardized Z score

$$Z = \frac{\overline{X} - \mu}{\sigma/\sqrt{n}}$$

is a standard normal variable. If σ is unknown and replaced by the sample standard deviation S in the Z score formula, the Z score no longer follows the standard normal distribution (although the approximation is good when $n \geqslant 30$). If we replace the true standard deviation σ by its estimate S, we obtain what is called the *t score,* where

$$t = \frac{\overline{X} - \mu}{S/\sqrt{n}}$$

It can be shown that when the population is normally distributed, then the t score follows what is called the *Student t distribution,* or more simply the *t distribution*. The t distribution was first studied and used by William Sealy Gosset (1876–1937) in a 1908 paper, "The Probable Error of the Mean." Because Gosset was employed by Arthur Guinness and Son, a Dublin brewery, and not permitted to publish company research, he published under the pseudonym "Student." Thus the t distribution is frequently referred to as Student's t distribution; the distribution is also called the t distribution because Gosset used the letter t to denote the random variable whose distribution was being studied.

Gosset showed that the random variable t

$$t = \frac{\overline{X} - \mu}{S/\sqrt{n}}$$

follows the t distribution provided the population is normal, where S is the sample standard deviation and n is the sample size.

The statistic t might be thought of as an estimated standardized normal variable because the estimated standard deviation S, rather than the true standard deviation σ, is used in its calculation. As the sample size gets large, the estimated standard deviation S approaches the true standard deviation σ. Thus, as the sample size becomes large, the statistic $t = (\bar{X} - \mu)/(S/\sqrt{n})$ approaches $Z = (\bar{X} - \mu)/(\sigma/\sqrt{n})$. Because the random variable Z is a standard normal variable, the t distribution approaches the standard normal distribution as n gets large.

Characteristics of the t Distribution

1. The t distribution is symmetric about 0 and ranges from $-\infty$ to ∞.
2. The t distribution is bell shaped and has approximately the same appearance as the standard normal distribution.
3. The mean of the t distribution is 0.
4. The t distribution depends on a paramater ν (Greek nu), called the **degrees of freedom** of the distribution. When constructing confidence intervals for the population mean, the appropriate degrees of freedom is $\nu = (n - 1)$, where n is the sample size.
5. The variance of the t distribution is $\nu/(\nu - 2)$ for $\nu > 2$.
6. The variance of the t distribution always exceeds 1.
7. As ν increases, the variance of the t distribution approaches 1 and the shape approaches that of the standard normal distribution.
8. Because the variance of t exceeds 1 while the variance of the standard normal variable Z equals 1, the t distribution is slightly flatter in the middle than the standard normal distribution and has thicker tails.
9. The t distribution is actually a family of distributions with a different density function corresponding to each different value of the parameter ν.

Figure 10.6 compares the shapes of the t distribution and the standard normal distribution.

FIGURE 10.6
Student's *t* distribution and the standard normal distribution.

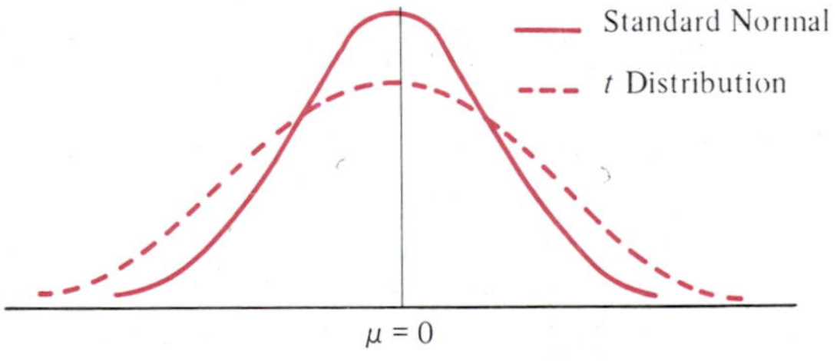

Because each value of ν yields a different density function, it is not feasible to present tables showing areas under each possible t distribution. However, Table A.6 in the Appendix shows the values of t such that the area in one tail of the distribution is 10%, 5%, 2.5%, 1%, and 0.5% for various values of ν. To use the table, we must know the degrees of freedom of the distribution and how much area we want in the right-hand tail of the curve.

Value of $t_{\alpha,\nu}$

The symbol $t_{\alpha,\nu}$ denotes the value of t such that the area to its right is α and t has ν degrees of freedom. The value $t_{\alpha,\nu}$ satisfies the equation

$$P(t > t_{\alpha,\nu}) = \alpha$$

where the random variable t has the t distribution with ν degrees of freedom.

Example 10.6

Area Under the Right Tail of the t Distribution: Consider the t distribution having $\nu = 9$ degrees of freedom. Find the value $t_{.05,9}$, such that the area in the right tail of the t distribution is .05.

Solution: To find $t_{.05,9}$ in Table A.6, we search down the "Degrees of Freedom" column until we reach the row $\nu = 9$. Move across this row to the column headed by the value .05. The number at the intersection of this row and column is $t_{.05,9} = 1.83$. Thus, if the random variable t follows the t distribution with 9 degrees of freedom, then $P(t > 1.83) = .05$. This is illustrated in Figure 10.7.

FIGURE 10.7
t distribution having 9 degrees of freedom and right-tail area of 5%.

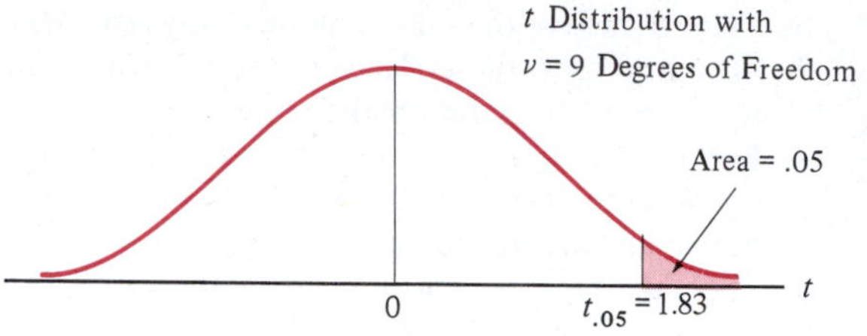

■

Example 10.7

Area under the Left Tail of the t Distribution: Consider the t distribution having $\nu = 9$ degrees of freedom. Find the value of t such that the area in the left tail of the distribution is 5%. Refer to Figure 10.8.

FIGURE 10.8
t distribution having 9 degrees of freedom and left-tail area of 5%.

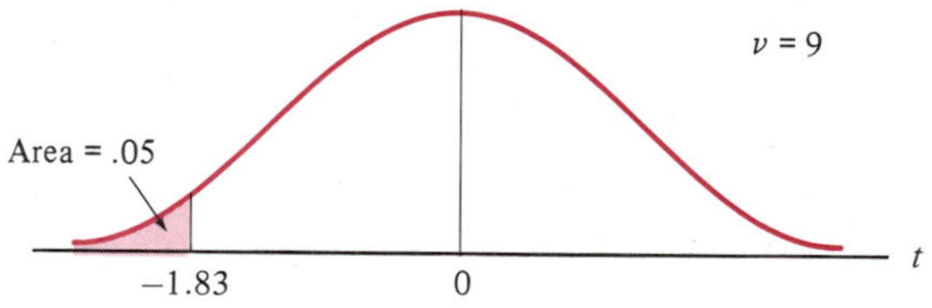

Solution: In Example 10.6, we showed that 5% of the area under the distribution lies to the right of $t_{.05,9} = 1.83$. Because the t distribution is symmetric, 5% of the area under the distribution lies to the left of -1.83. We obtain $P(t < -1.83) = .05$. ■

Example 10.8

Area under the t distribution: Consider the t distribution with 9 degrees of freedom. Find the values $t_{.025,9}$ and $-t_{.025,9}$ such that each tail of the distribution contains area .025.

Solution: From Table A.6, we obtain $t_{.025,9} = 2.26$. By symmetry, the value of t such that the left-hand tail contains an area of .025 is -2.26. We have $P(t > 2.26) = .025$ and $P(t < -2.26) = .025$. It follows that $P(-2.26 \leq t \leq 2.26) = .95$. Refer to Figure 10.9.

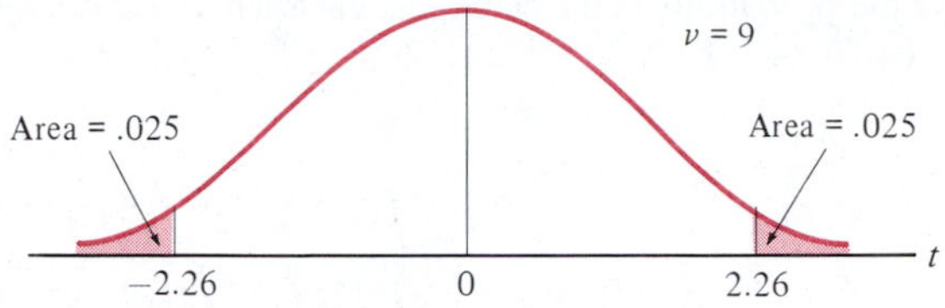

FIGURE 10.9
t distribution having 9 degrees of freedom and area of .025 in each tail.

Example 10.8 shows that for $\nu = 9$ degrees of freedom, 95% of the area under the t distribution lies between -2.26 and 2.26. For the standard normal distribution, 95% of the area under the curve lies between -1.96 and 1.96. This shows that the tails of the t distribution are fatter than the tails of the standard normal distribution.

Example 10.9

Determining $t_{.025,20}$: Consider the t distribution with 20 degrees of freedom. Find the value of $t_{.025,20}$ such that the right tail of the distribution contains area .025.

Solution: From Table A.6, the desired value of t associated with $\nu = 20$ and $\alpha = .025$ is $t_{.025,20} = 2.09$. Thus, $P(t \leq 2.09) = .975$ and $P(t > 2.09) = .025$. See Figure 10.10.

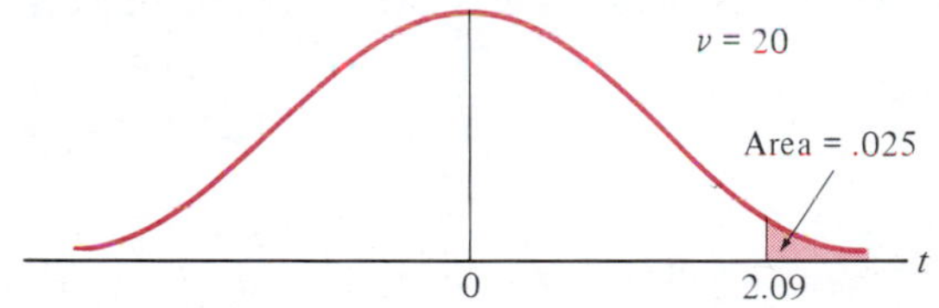

FIGURE 10.10
t distribution having 20 degrees of freedom and right-tail area of .025.

Exercises for Section 10.3

1. Find the value of t such that the area in the right-hand tail of the t distribution is .05 (that is, find $t_{.05}$) if the number of degrees of freedom is as follows:
a. 2 b. 5 c. 10 d. 20 e. 25

2. Recall that for the standard normal distribution, 95% of the area lies between $-z_{.025} = -1.96$ and $z_{.025} = 1.96$. Find the corresponding values of t (that is, find $t_{.025}$ and $-t_{.025}$) if the number of degrees of freedom is as follows:
a. 2 b. 5 c. 10 d. 20 e. 25

3. Find the critical value of the t distribution such that 0.5% of the area is in each tail of the distribution (that is, find the values $t_{.005}$ and $-t_{.005}$) when the number of degrees of freedom is as follows:
a. 2 b. 5 c. 10 d. 25

4. We want 1% of the area to lie in the left tail of the t distribution. Find the critical value of t if the number of degrees of freedom is as follows:
a. 2 b. 5 c. 10 d. 20 e. 25
f. What is the corresponding critical value for a standard normal variable?

5. Compare the t distribution to the standard normal distribution when the degrees of freedom of the t distribution is infinity. For example, for the random variable t and the random variable Z, show that the probability is the same that each will exceed the following values:
a. 1.645 b. 1.96 c. 2.58

10.4 ▪ Confidence Intervals for the Mean with Unknown Population Variance

We know that if a population is normal with mean μ and variance σ^2, then the statistic

$$Z = \frac{\overline{X} - \mu}{\sigma/\sqrt{n}}$$

has exactly a normal distribution with mean 0 and variance 1. The statement also holds, at least approximately, when the population is not normal provided the sample size is large, even when the sample standard deviation has been used to estimate the population standard deviation.

Usually, however, the population variance σ^2 is unknown and must be estimated from the sample data. When the population standard deviation σ is replaced by the sample standard deviation S, we obtain the t score

$$t = \frac{\overline{X} - \mu}{S/\sqrt{n}}$$

Definition: t statistic or t score

Suppose we take a random sample of size n from some population having mean μ and calculate the sample mean $\overline{X}$ and the sample variance S^2. If the population is normal, then the ***t* statistic**

$$t = \frac{\overline{X} - \mu}{S/\sqrt{n}}$$

has the t distribution with $\nu = (n - 1)$ degrees of freedom. The t statistic is also called the ***t* score.**

Constructing Confidence Intervals Using the t Distribution

The area to the right of $t_{\alpha/2,\nu}$ is $\alpha/2$ for the t distribution having ν degrees of freedom. Similarly, the area to the left of $-t_{\alpha/2,\nu}$ is $\alpha/2$. Thus, we obtain

$$P(-t_{\alpha/2,\nu} < t < t_{\alpha/2,\nu}) = 1 - \alpha$$

If we replace t by

$$t = \frac{\overline{X} - \mu}{S/\sqrt{n}}$$

we obtain

$$P\left(-t_{\alpha/2,\nu} \leq \frac{\overline{X} - \mu}{S/\sqrt{n}} \leq t_{\alpha/2,\nu} \right) = 1 - \alpha$$

Thus, the probability is $(1 - \alpha)$ that the t score will fall between the values $-t_{\alpha/2,\nu}$ and $t_{\alpha/2,\nu}$. Multiplying through by the denominator of the t score yields the following:

$$P(-t_{\alpha/2,\nu}S/\sqrt{n} \leq \overline{X} - \mu \leq t_{\alpha/2,\nu}S/\sqrt{n}) = 1 - \alpha$$

A bit of algebra yields

$$P(\overline{X} - t_{\alpha/2,\nu}S/\sqrt{n} \leq \mu \leq \overline{X} + t_{\alpha/2,\nu}S/\sqrt{n}) = 1 - \alpha$$

This expression indicates that when sampling from a normal population, the probability is $(1 - \alpha)$ that the interval

$$(\overline{X} - t_{\alpha/2,\nu}S/\sqrt{n},\ \overline{X} + t_{\alpha/2,\nu}S/\sqrt{n})$$

will contain the population mean.

Definition: Confidence Interval for the Mean of a Normal Population with Unknown Population Variance

Suppose we take a random sample of n observations from a normal population with mean μ and unknown variance σ^2. If the observed sample mean is $\overline{x}$ and the observed sample standard deviation is s then the **confidence interval** for the mean having level of confidence $100(1 - \alpha)\%$ is given by

$$(\overline{x} - t_{\alpha/2,\nu}s/\sqrt{n},\ \overline{x} + t_{\alpha/2,\nu}s/\sqrt{n})$$

where $t_{\alpha/2,\nu}$ is the number such that

$$P(t > t_{\alpha/2,\nu}) = \alpha/2$$

and the random variable t has a t distribution with $\nu = (n - 1)$ degrees of freedom.

Example 10.10 **Constructing a 95% Confidence Interval for the Mean:** A newly hired employee of the U.S. Postal Service wants to estimate the mean annual income of first-year mail carriers. Assume the population of incomes is approximately normal and the population variance is unknown. The employee takes a random sample of 25 first-year carriers and obtains $\overline{x}$ = \$19,500 and s = \$2000. Construct a 95% confidence interval for the unknown population mean μ.

Solution: We have $n = 25$, $\overline{x}$ = \$19,500, s = \$2000, and $(1 - \alpha) = .95$. Thus, we have $\alpha = .05$ and $\alpha/2 = .025$. The appropriate degrees of freedom is $\nu = (n - 1) = 24$. From Table A.6, we find $t_{.025,24} = 2.064$. The desired confidence interval is

$$(\overline{x} - t_{\alpha/2,\nu}s/\sqrt{n},\ \overline{x} + t_{\alpha/2,\nu}s/\sqrt{n})$$

or

$$(19{,}500 - 2.064(2000)/\sqrt{25},\ 19{,}500 + 2.064(2000)/\sqrt{25})$$

or

$$(18{,}674.40,\ 20{,}325.60)$$

Thus, we are 95% confident that the mean income of the population is between \$18,674.40 and \$20,325.60. ■

The confidence interval based on the t score is always wider than the corresponding confidence interval based on the Z score because the latter confidence interval uses more information (the population variance is known). One way of gauging the greater dispersion of the t distribution is to see how wide an interval must be to encompass 95% of the observations. The probability is .95 that Z will be between -1.96 and $+1.96$, while with degrees of freedom $\nu = 9$, for example, there is a .95 probability that t will be between -2.26 and $+2.26$.

As the sample size increases, the width of the confidence interval decreases for two reasons: First, the square root of n is in the denominator, and second, the t value decreases as the degrees of freedom increases. The following confidence intervals show how the width of the confidence interval decreases as the sample size increases:

Sample Size n	Degrees of Freedom $n - 1$	95% Confidence Interval
5	4	$\bar{x} \pm 2.78(s/\sqrt{n})$
10	9	$\bar{x} \pm 2.26(s/\sqrt{n})$
20	19	$\bar{x} \pm 2.09(s/\sqrt{n})$
30	29	$\bar{x} \pm 2.05(s/\sqrt{n})$
∞	∞	$\bar{x} \pm 1.96(s/\sqrt{n})$

Note that when the degrees of freedom parameter exceeds 30, the confidence interval computed using the t distribution is approximately the same as the confidence interval obtained using the standard normal distribution. That is, for $\nu = 29$, we have $t_{.025} = 2.05$, while the corresponding Z score is $z_{.025} = 1.96$. Thus, if you have the 30 or more observations recommended for invoking the Central Limit Theorem, you also have a large enough sample to ignore the distinction between the normal distribution and Student's t distribution. As a rule of thumb, the t distribution rather than the standard normal distribution should be used when the sample size is small, say 29 or less.

Example 10.11 **99% Confidence Interval for the Mean:** As part of a traffic control program, the city planner needs to know the number of cars that pass through a certain intersection on weekday mornings. On a sample of 8 Monday mornings, the number of cars passing through the intersection between 7 A.M. and 9 A.M. are counted. Assume the population is normal. Construct a 99% confidence interval for the population mean if the sample mean is $\bar{x} = 1500$ and the sample standard deviation is 300.

Solution: There are $\nu = (n - 1) = 7$ degrees of freedom. For a 99% confidence interval, we have $(1 - \alpha) = .99$. Thus we obtain $\alpha = .01$ and $\alpha/2 = .005$. We obtain $t_{\alpha/2,\nu} = t_{.005,7} = 3.499$. The 99% confidence interval is given by

$$(\bar{x} - t_{\alpha/2,\nu}s/\sqrt{n},\ \bar{x} + t_{\alpha/2,\nu}s/\sqrt{n})$$

or

$$[1500 - 3.499(300/\sqrt{8}),\ 1500 + 3.499(300/\sqrt{8})]$$

or

$$(1500 - 371.12\ ,\ 1500 + 396.75)$$

The 99% confidence interval is

$$(1128.88,\ 1871.12)$$

■

Example 10.12 **Confidence Intervals Using Large Samples:** The purpose of this example is to show that when the sample size is large, confidence intervals calculated using the standard normal distribution will be approximately the same as those obtained using the t distribution. Suppose we have taken a random sample of $n = 121$ observations and obtain the estimates $\bar{x} = \$20{,}000$ and $s = \$4000$; also, assume that the population is normal so that the use of the t distribution is theoretically correct. In addition, because the sample size is large, the use of the standard normal distribution is justified even though the population variance is unknown. Let us construct two 95% confidence intervals for the mean, one using the t distribution and one using the standard normal distribution.

Solution: There are $\nu = (n - 1) = 120$ degrees of freedom. For a 95% confidence interval, we have $\alpha = .05$ and $\alpha/2 = .025$. We obtain $t_{.025,120} = 1.984$ and $z_{.025} = 1.96$.

If we use the t distribution, a 95% confidence interval for the mean is given by

$$(\bar{x} - t_{\alpha/2,\nu}s/\sqrt{n},\ \bar{x} + t_{\alpha/2,\nu}s/\sqrt{n})$$

or

$$[20{,}000 - 1.984(4000/\sqrt{121}),\ 20{,}000 + 1.984(4000/\sqrt{121})]$$

Thus, the 95% confidence interval for the mean based on the t distribution is

$$(\$19{,}278.55,\ \$20{,}721.45)$$

If we use the standard normal distribution, a 95% confidence interval for the mean is given by

$$(\bar{x} - z_{\alpha/2}s/\sqrt{n},\ \bar{x} + z_{\alpha/2}s/\sqrt{n})$$

or

$$[20{,}000 - 1.96(4000/\sqrt{121}),\ 20{,}000 + 1.96(4000/\sqrt{121})]$$

The 95% confidence interval for the mean based on the standard normal distribution is

$$(\$19{,}287.27,\ \$20{,}712.73)$$

This is very similar to the interval obtained using the t distribution. The confidence interval based on the standard normal distribution is centered at \$20,000 and has width \$1425.46, whereas that based on the t distribution is centered at \$20,000 and has width \$1442.90. Thus the confidence interval based on the t distribution is approximately 1.2% wider than the confidence interval based on the standard normal distribution. ■

Consider the difference between a confidence interval based on the standard normal value $z_{\alpha/2}$ and a confidence interval based on the value $t_{\alpha/2,\nu}$. As the degrees of freedom increases, the t distribution approaches the standard normal distribution. If the sample size is large, then $t_{\alpha/2,\nu} \approx z_{\alpha/2}$, so it will make little practical difference whether the t score or the z score is used in constructing the confidence interval. For this reason, statisticians emphasize that the use of the t distribution is especially important when the sample size is small. When the sample size is large, the difference between using $t_{\alpha/2,\nu}$ and $z_{\alpha/2}$ is relatively minor.

Example 10.13 **Comparing Confidence Intervals:** Suppose a sample of size $n = 10$ is obtained and we want to construct a confidence interval for μ having level of confidence $(1 - \alpha) = .95$. If the population is normal with known variance, then we should use $z_{\alpha/2} = 1.96$ to construct the interval. If the variance is unknown and has to be estimated, we use $t_{\alpha/2,9} = 2.262$. In this case there is a substantial difference of 14% between the Z value and the t statistic. Thus the confidence interval based on the t value will be 14% wider than that based on the Z value. ■

The use of the t distribution is based on the assumption that the sample of observations has been selected from a normal population. In practical situations, it may be difficult to determine the exact distribution of the population, especially if the sample size is small. Fortunately, the t distribution is relatively "robust"; that is, the confidence intervals obtained by using the t distribution are still approximately correct provided the population does not differ significantly from a normal distribution and provided the population distribution is approximately symmetric.

Tips for Problem Solving

To construct a confidence interval for the population mean, follow these steps:

1. Record the sample size n, the level of confidence $100(1 - \alpha)$, and the sample mean $\bar{x}$.
2. Record the population standard deviation σ (if it is known). Otherwise, record the sample standard deviation s.
3. If σ is known, find the Z scores $\pm z_{\alpha/2}$. If the population is approximately normal or if the sample size is at least 30, calculate the confidence interval
$$(\bar{x} \pm z_{\alpha/2}\sigma/\sqrt{n})$$
4. If σ is unknown, estimate it using the sample standard deviation s. If the population is approximately normal, calculate the confidence interval
$$(\bar{x} \pm t_{\alpha/2}s/\sqrt{n})$$

5. If the sample size is large and σ is unknown, the two confidence intervals

$$(\bar{x} \pm t_{\alpha/2}s/\sqrt{n})$$

and

$$(\bar{x} \pm z_{\alpha/2}s/\sqrt{n})$$

yield approximately the same result, so either can be used.

Exercises for Section 10.4

1. During a water shortage, a water company randomly sampled residential water meters in order to monitor daily water consumption. On one particular day, a sample of 30 meters showed a sample mean of $\bar{x} = 240$ gallons and a sample standard deviation of $s = 45$ gallons. Find a 90% confidence interval for the mean water consumption for the population.

2. A management firm would like to estimate the mean cost of repairing damage to apartments that are vacated by tenants. A sample of 26 vacated apartments resulted in a sample mean repair cost of \$116.00 with a sample standard deviation of \$12.00. Develop a 95% confidence interval to estimate the mean repair cost for the population of apartments.

3. To test a drug to be marketed for the treatment of an exotic virus, each patient was first given injections of the live virus until he or she was infected, and then treated with the drug. Due to obvious dangers, only 15 volunteers could be obtained. One parameter of interest is the mean recovery time. The following recovery times (in days) were recorded:

10	11	12	17	22
9	14	12	6	8
12	9	14	11	18

Find a 95% confidence interval for the mean recovery time.

4. An examination of the records for a random sample of 10 motor vehicles in a large fleet reveals the following operating costs (in cents per mile): 25.3, 27.3, 26.5, 27.0, 22.5, 23.5, 29.1, 26.8, 26.7, and 30.9. Construct a 90% confidence interval for μ. Assume that operating costs are normally distributed.

5. A political scientist is interested in the amount of time voters spend in the voting booth. A random sample of 64 voters showed an average of 7.20 minutes in the booth and a sample standard deviation of 2.10 minutes. Find a 99% confidence interval for the mean amount of time spent by all voters in the voting booth.

6. A chief of police is concerned about the speed of cars traveling over a stretch of highway on which there have been many accidents. A random sample of 36 automobiles showed an average speed of 59.4 miles per hour on this stretch and a sample standard deviation of 4.8 miles per hour. Find 90% and 99% confidence intervals for the mean speed of all cars traveling on this stretch of the highway.

7. A car rental company is interested in the amount of time its vehicles are out of operation for repair work. A random sample of 12 cars showed that, over the past year, the numbers of days each had been inoperative were as follows:

15, 11, 19, 24, 6, 18, 20, 15, 18, 12, 14, 19

Assuming that the population distribution is normal, find a 95% confidence interval for the mean number of days that vehicles in the company's fleet are out of operation.

8. A manufacturer of video games wants to install some machines in shopping malls. In a pilot study on the potential profitability of this enterprise, games were placed for one week in 10 randomly chosen shopping malls. The weekly profits in dollars were as follows:

110.80	67.90	141.20	93.60	75.80
131.30	106.40	87.80	94.10	98.00

Assume the population distribution is normal. Find a 99% confidence interval for the mean weekly profit for these games in all shopping malls.

9. An economist wants to determine the average annual income of full-time truck drivers. A random sample of 25 truck drivers is taken. We obtain $\bar{x} = \$20{,}000$ and $s = \$6000$. Calculate the following confidence intervals for μ:

a. 95% b. 90%

10. A random sample of 16 college teachers was taken to determine how much time they spent each week preparing lectures. The average number of hours was $\bar{x} = 10$ with $s^2 = 9$. Calculate the following confidence intervals for μ:

a. 95% b. 95% assuming $n = 25$

11. During the past 20 years, the average number of days of rainfall annually in a northwestern city was $\bar{x} = 147$ with $s = 10$. Calculate the following confidence intervals for μ:

a. 95% b. 99%

12. A random sample of 25 families with 8-year-old daughters was taken to determine the average annual expenditure on clothes for the child. The sample results are $\bar{x} = \$107$ and $s = \$40$. Calculate a 95% confidence interval for μ.

10.5 ▪ *Confidence Intervals for Proportions (Large Samples)*

In many problems in economics and business, we want to estimate the proportion of population members possessing some characteristic. For example, we may want to estimate the proportion of households with gross incomes below the poverty level or the proportion of individuals who are unemployed. Let p denote the proportion of items in a population that possess a certain characteristic. To estimate p, we take a random sample of n observations from the population and count the number X of items in the sample that possess the characteristic. The sample proportion $\hat{p} = X/n$ is used to estimate the population proportion p.

From Chapter 9, we know that $\hat{p}$ is a random variable having approximately a normal distribution (provided $np \geqslant 5$ and $nq \geqslant 5$) with mean p and variance pq/n where $q = (1 - p)$. In addition, the standardized random variable

$$Z = \frac{\hat{p} - p}{\sqrt{pq/n}}$$

follows the standard normal distribution. In Section 10.2 we showed that for the standard normal variable Z

$$P(-z_{\alpha/2} < Z < z_{\alpha/2}) = 1 - \alpha$$

After substituting for Z, we obtain

$$P\left(-z_{\alpha/2} < \frac{\hat{p} - p}{\sqrt{pq/n}} < z_{\alpha/2}\right) = 1 - \alpha$$

After multiplying through by the denominator we obtain

$$P(-z_{\alpha/2}\sqrt{pq/n} < \hat{p} - p < z_{\alpha/2}\sqrt{pq/n}) = 1 - \alpha$$

Finally, a bit of algebra yields

$$P(\hat{p} - z_{\alpha/2}\sqrt{pq/n} < p < \hat{p} + z_{\alpha/2}\sqrt{pq/n}) = 1 - \alpha$$

This last probability statement tells us that the probability is $(1 - \alpha)$ that the random interval

$$(\hat{p} - z_{\alpha/2}\sqrt{pq/n},\ \hat{p} + z_{\alpha/2}\sqrt{pq/n})$$

contains the true population proportion p. Because p and q are unknown, we replace their values by their sample estimates $\hat{p}$ and $\hat{q}$. Thus we can say that the probability is approximately $(1 - \alpha)$ that the random interval

$$(\hat{p} - z_{\alpha/2}\sqrt{\hat{p}\hat{q}/n},\ \hat{p} + z_{\alpha/2}\sqrt{\hat{p}\hat{q}/n})$$

contains the true population proportion p.

Definition: Confidence Interval for the Population Proportion p

Let p denote the population proportion. Suppose we take a random sample of n observations and obtain the sample proportion $\hat{p}$. A **confidence interval** for the population proportion having level of confidence $100(1 - \alpha)\%$ is given by

$$(\hat{p} - z_{\alpha/2}\sqrt{\hat{p}\hat{q}/n},\ \hat{p} + z_{\alpha/2}\sqrt{\hat{p}\hat{q}/n})$$

where $z_{\alpha/2}$ is the standard normal variate such that

$$P(Z > z_{\alpha/2}) = \alpha/2$$

Example 10.14 **Confidence Interval for a Proportion:** A government study is designed to estimate the proportion of families having annual incomes below \$25,000 per year. A random sample of 500 families is contacted. In the sample, 200 families had annual incomes below \$25,000. Construct a 95% confidence interval for the population proportion p.

Solution: The sample proportion is $\hat{p} = x/n = 200/500 = .4$ and $\hat{q} = (1 - \hat{p}) = .6$. For a 95% confidence interval, we have $\alpha = .05$ and $\alpha/2 = .025$. We obtain $z_{\alpha/2} = 1.96$. The 95% confidence interval for p is given by

$$(\hat{p} - z_{\alpha/2}\sqrt{\hat{p}\hat{q}/n},\ \hat{p} + z_{\alpha/2}\sqrt{\hat{p}\hat{q}/n})$$

or

$$(.4 - 1.96\sqrt{(.4)(.6)/500},\ .4 + 1.96\sqrt{(.4)(.6)/500})$$

or

$$(.357,\ .443)$$

This means that we can be 95% confident that the true population proportion is between .357 and .443. ■

Tips for Problem Solving
To construct a confidence interval for the population proportion, follow these steps:

1. Record the sample size n, the level of confidence $100(1 - \alpha)$, and the sample proportion $\hat{p}$. Record $\hat{q} = (1 - \hat{p})$.
2. Find the Z scores $\pm z_{\alpha/2}$.
3. Calculate the confidence interval

$$(\hat{p} \pm z_{\alpha/2}\sqrt{\hat{p}\hat{q}/n})$$

Exercises for Section 10.5

1. In a sample of 900 voters, 400 prefer Candidate A. Find a 90% confidence interval for p.
2. Suppose that 55% of the people in a random sample of n people favor a law requiring stricter enforcement of traffic laws. Find a 95% confidence interval for p for the following sample sizes:
   a. $n = 100$
   b. $n = 400$
   c. $n = 1600$
   d. Discuss how the width of the confidence interval changes when the sample size is multiplied by 4.
3. A nationwide television polling agency randomly selects 600 people, of whom 100 watched a particular TV show. Calculate a 90% confidence interval for the proportion of the population who watched the program.
4. A random sample of 100 charge accounts at Koch's Clothing Store indicated that 25 of the accounts owed \$100 or more.
   a. Find an 80% confidence interval for the proportion of charge accounts owing \$100 or more.
   b. Find a 95% confidence interval for p.
5. A private consulting firm is given a governmental grant to study underreporting of income on federal income tax returns. The firm takes a random sample of 160 taxpayers and determines that 64 of them underreported their income on their tax return.
   a. Construct a 90% confidence interval for the proportion of all taxpayers who underreport their income.
   b. Construct a 99% confidence interval.
6. An AM radio station, WROK, wants to know what proportion of the radio-listening population prefers listening to rock and roll music over any other type of music. The station takes a random sample of 144 radio listeners. In the sample 80 say that their favorite music is rock and roll.
   a. Construct a 90% confidence interval for the proportion of the population that prefers rock and roll music.
   b. Construct a 95% confidence interval for p.
7. One hundred economists were randomly selected to get information about their reading habits. In the sample 75 said that they read the *Wall Street Journal* regularly.
   a. Construct a 90% confidence interval for the proportion of all economists who read the *Wall Street Journal*.
   b. Construct a 98% confidence interval for p.
8. In a random sample of 100 students at a particular college, 60 indicated that they favored having the option of receiving pass–fail grades for elective courses. Obtain a 95% confidence interval

for the proportion of the population of students who favor pass–fail grades for elective courses. Does this confidence interval contain the value $p = .5$? Explain why this particular value might be of interest.

9. An airline wants to determine the proportion of passengers that bring only carry-on luggage. In a random sample of 200 passengers, 44 passengers have only carry-on luggage. Find a 95% confidence interval for the proportion of passengers who have only carry-on luggage.

10. A fast-food restaurant took a random sample of 400 customers to determine the proportion of customers who are female. A confidence interval of .73 to .87 was reported.
  a. Find the sample proportion.
  b. Find the level of confidence of this interval.

11. A random sample of 400 faculty members at a certain university contained 120 people who believed that the university should curtail its investments in South Africa. On the basis of this sample information, an analyst calculated the confidence interval (.25, .35) for the population proportion of faculty members favoring curtailment. What is the level of confidence of this interval?

10.6 ▪ Determining the Sample Size

So far we have developed techniques for finding confidence intervals for a population mean or a population proportion based on a sample of information. At the conclusion of such a process, the researcher may feel that the resulting confidence interval is too wide—that there is too much uncertainty about the parameter being estimated. For a fixed level of confidence, the only way to obtain a narrower confidence interval is to increase the sample size.

Sometimes the researcher will fix in advance the desired width of the confidence interval and then choose a sample size big enough to obtain it. In this section, we show how this is done. First, we discuss confidence intervals for the mean, and then for the population proportion.

Confidence Intervals for the Mean

Suppose an individual is interested in estimating the mean of a population having a known variance σ^2. How large a sample must be taken if the investigator wants the probability to be $(1 - \alpha)$ that the sampling error $|\overline{X} - \mu|$ is less than some amount D?

Recall that a $100(1 - \alpha)\%$ confidence interval for μ is given by

$$(\bar{x} - z_{\alpha/2}\sigma/\sqrt{n},\ \bar{x} + z_{\alpha/2}\sigma/\sqrt{n})$$

This confidence interval is centered at the sample mean $\bar{x}$ and extends a distance

$$D = \frac{z_{\alpha/2}\sigma}{\sqrt{n}}$$

on each side of the sample mean, so D is half the width of the confidence interval. The investigator wants to fix D in advance and use a large enough sample size to guarantee that the confidence interval does not extend more than D units from the sample mean. If we solve this equation for n, we obtain

$$\sqrt{n} = \frac{z_{\alpha/2}\sigma}{D}$$

By squaring both sides of this equation, we obtain

$$n = \frac{z_{\alpha/2}^2 \sigma^2}{D^2}$$

Therefore choosing a sample of this size guarantees that the confidence interval extends a distance D on each side of the sample mean.

Sample Size for a Specific Confidence Interval for the Mean

Suppose we take a random sample from a normal population with known variance σ^2. Then a $100(1 - \alpha)\%$ confidence interval for the population mean extends a distance D on each side of the sample mean if the number of observations is

$$n = \frac{z_{\alpha/2}^2 \sigma^2}{D^2}$$

The number of observations in a sample must be an integer, of course, so if the value of n in the preceding formula is not an integer, we round up to the next whole number to guarantee that our confidence interval does not exceed the required width. Note that specifying a smaller D requires a larger sample.

When σ^2 is unknown, as will usually be the case, it may be necessary to estimate its value by taking a small sample called a *pilot sample*. Otherwise, it may be necessary to make an educated guess.

Example 10.15 **Sample Size Required to Estimate a Mean:** An economist wants to estimate the mean annual income of households in a particular congressional district. It is assumed that the population standard deviation is $\sigma = \$4000$. The economist wants the probability to be .95 that the sample mean will be within $D = \$500$ of the true mean μ. How large a sample is required?

Solution: We have $(1 - \alpha) = .95$, $z_{\alpha/2} = 1.96$, $D = 500$, and $\sigma = \$4000$. We obtain

$$n = \frac{z_{\alpha/2}^2 \sigma^2}{D^2}$$

$$= \frac{1.96^2(4000^2)}{500^2} = 245.86$$

To satisfy the requirement, a sample of at least 246 observations is needed. ■

Confidence Intervals for Proportions

We proceed in exactly the same way if we want to determine the sample size needed to estimate a proportion p with a specified precision D at a certain level of confidence. At the level of confidence $(1 - \alpha)$, a confidence interval for p is given by

$$(\hat{p} - z_{\alpha/2}\sqrt{\hat{p}\hat{q}/n},\ \hat{p} + z_{\alpha/2}\sqrt{\hat{p}\hat{q}/n})$$

This confidence interval is centered at the sample proportion $\hat{p}$ and extends a distance

$$D = z_{\alpha/2}\sqrt{\hat{p}\hat{q}/n}$$

on each side of the sample proportion. The distance D is half the width of the confidence interval. Now suppose that the investigator wants to fix D in advance. If we solve this equation for n, we obtain

$$\sqrt{n} = z_{\alpha/2}\sqrt{\hat{p}\hat{q}}/D$$

After squaring both sides, we obtain

$$n = \frac{z^2_{\alpha/2}\hat{p}\hat{q}}{D^2}$$

This equation cannot be used directly because it involves the sample proportion $\hat{p}$, which will not be known at the outset of the investigation. If we have an initial estimate of p, substitute this value for $\hat{p}$ in the equation. If there is no such estimate available, substitute .5 for $\hat{p}$ in the formula. The product $\hat{p}\hat{q}$ cannot exceed .25 (the value when $\hat{p} = .5$), so the largest possible value for n is

$$n = \frac{.25z^2_{\alpha/2}}{D^2}$$

This equation shows the largest sample needed so that the probability is $(1 - \alpha)$ that the sampling error will be less than or equal to some amount D.

Sample Size for a Specific Confidence Interval for the Proportion

Suppose we take a random sample from some population. Then a $100(1 - \alpha)\%$ confidence interval for the population proportion extends at most a distance D on each side of the sample proportion if the number of observations is

$$n = \frac{.25z^2_{\alpha/2}}{D^2}$$

If an estimate of p exists, use the formula

$$n = \frac{z^2_{\alpha/2}\hat{p}\hat{q}}{D^2}$$

Example 10.16

Sample Size Required to Estimate a Proportion: A polling agency is interested in predicting what proportion of votes a certain presidential candidate will receive. How large a sample must be taken if the agency wants to be 95% confident that its estimate is within .03 of the correct value?

Solution: We have $(1 - \alpha) = .95$, $z_{\alpha/2} = 1.96$, and $D = .03$. We use $\hat{p} = \hat{q} = .5$ for lack of a better estimate. We obtain

$$n = \frac{.25z^2_{\alpha/2}}{D^2}$$

$$= \frac{.25(1.96^2)}{.03^2} = 1067.1$$

If an estimate $\hat{p}$ of the population proportion had been available, we would have used it in the formula for D. ■

The sample size formula contains no information about the cost of obtaining additional sample information. Eventually a point is reached where the cost of obtaining additional information outweighs the benefits obtained from that information.

Exercises for Section 10.6

1. Starting annual salaries for college graduates with business administration degrees are believed to have a standard deviation of approximately \$1800. A 95% confidence interval estimate of the mean annual starting salary is desired. How large a sample should be taken if we want to be 95% confident that the maximum sampling error is to be as follows?
a. \$500 b. \$200

2. The percentage of defective products produced by a certain method is thought to be about 5%. How large a sample is required if we want to be
a. 99% confident that p is within .01 of $\hat{p}$?
b. 99% confident that p is within .02 of $\hat{p}$?
c. 90% confident that p is within .02 of $\hat{p}$?

3. A polling agency wants to determine what percentage of the population watched a particular TV show. How large a sample is required if they want to be
a. 95% confident that p is within .05 of $\hat{p}$?
b. 95% confident that p is within .01 of $\hat{p}$?
c. 90% confident that p is within .01 of $\hat{p}$?

4. A survey is to be taken to determine the average age of purchasers of *Newsweek* magazine. A preliminary study yielded an estimated variance of $\sigma^2 = 64$. How large a sample is required if we want to be
a. 95% confident that μ is within 4 units of $\bar{x}$?
b. 95% confident that μ is within 2 units of $\bar{x}$?
c. 99% confident that μ is within 2 units of $\bar{x}$?

5. A supermarket manager wishes to make an estimate of the average time in minutes a customer spends at the checkout counter. Assume the variance is $\sigma^2 = 9$. How large a sample is required if we want to be
a. 90% confident that μ is within 1 unit of $\bar{x}$?
b. 90% confident that μ is within 0.5 unit of $\bar{x}$?

6. Radio station WRKC has an evening sports talk show that gets a lot of publicity because the host of the show is very popular. The host wants a raise because the show is so popular. Before granting a raise, WRKC executives want to know what proportion of the public listens to the show. How large a sample is required if they want to be 95% confident that their estimate is within .02 of the true proportion? Assume that p is approximately .2.

7. The State Unemployment Commission wants to estimate the proportion of the labor force that was unemployed during any part of last year. How large a sample is required if the commission wants to be 90% confident that the estimate is within .01 of the true proportion? Assume that p is approximately .1.

8. Every year *Sports Illustrated* publishes a "bathing suit issue," in which a feature article shows pictures of models in skimpy bathing suits. In succeeding weeks the magazine is swamped with letters praising or denouncing this practice. Suppose that the editors want to know what proportion of their subscribers dislike this issue within .03 with a level of confidence of .95. How large a sample is required?

9. A school system wants to order 1000 new desks, some of which will be designed for left-handed people. The purchasing agent needs to know what proportion of the population is left-handed. How large a sample is required to be 90% confident that the estimate is within .02 of the true value? Assume that p is approximately .2.

10. A firm conducts surveys and provides interval estimates of population proportions at the 95% confidence level. How large a sample size would you recommend if the firm desired the sampling error to be as follows?
a. 3% or less b. 2% or less c. 1% or less

11. A well-known bank credit card firm is interested in estimating the proportion of credit card holders that carry a nonzero balance at the end of the month and thus incur an interest charge. The desired precision for the proportion estimate is ± 3% at a 99% confidence level.
a. How large a sample should be recommended if it is anticipated that roughly 70% of the firm's cardholders carry a nonzero balance at the end of the month?
b. How large a sample would be recommended if no planning value for the population proportion could be specified?

12. A sample of 300 people were asked to identify their major source of news; 180 stated that their major source was television.
a. Construct a 95% confidence interval for the proportion of the people in the population for whom television is the major source of news.
b. How large a sample would be necessary to estimate the population proportion with a sampling error of .05 or less at a 95% confidence level?

13. How many accounts of a manufacturing company should be audited to estimate p, the proportion of accounts in error, to within ±.04 with a level of confidence of 95%? Assume it is believed that p is approximately .1.

14. A television station claims that its evening news reaches 50% of the viewing audience in its area. A firm considering the purchase of advertising time during this news program wishes to test the validity of the station's claim. How large a sample should the firm select if it wants to be 95% confident that the bound on the error of estimation is 5%?

15. A nationwide survey of practicing physicians is to be undertaken to estimate the mean number of prescriptions written per day. The desired margin of sampling error is ±.5 with a 99% confidence coefficient. A pilot study revealed that a reasonable planning value for the population standard deviation is 7.
a. How many physicians should be contacted in the survey to estimate μ?
b. If the desired confidence coefficient were lowered to 95%, would the required sample size be substantially reduced?

10.7 ▪ *Confidence Intervals for the Difference of Two Means*

At times we may be interested in constructing confidence intervals for the difference between two population means $(\mu_1 - \mu_2)$. The techniques discussed here are based on the assumption that we have two independent random samples from two normal populations with known variances.

Confidence Intervals for $(\mu_1 - \mu_2)$ When the Variances Are Known or the Sample Sizes Are Large

Alternatively, the results hold at least approximately if the sample sizes are large even though the populations are not normal and the variances have been estimated. How large n_1 and n_2 have to be to make the results approximately correct varies from problem to problem. The approximation is fairly good provided n_1 and n_2 are both at least 30.

Confidence Interval for $(\mu_1 - \mu_2)$ When Variances Are Known or Sample Sizes Are Large—Independent Samples

Suppose we have independent random samples of size n_1 and n_2 from two normal populations having unknown means μ_1 and μ_2 and known variances σ_1^2 and σ_2^2. If the observed sample means are $\bar{x}_1$ and $\bar{x}_2$, a $100(1 - \alpha)\%$ confidence interval for $(\mu_1 - \mu_2)$ is given by

$$\left((\bar{x}_1 - \bar{x}_2) - z_{\alpha/2}\sqrt{\frac{\sigma_1^2}{n_1} + \frac{\sigma_2^2}{n_2}},\ (\bar{x}_1 - \bar{x}_2) + z_{\alpha/2}\sqrt{\frac{\sigma_1^2}{n_1} + \frac{\sigma_2^2}{n_2}}\right)$$

If the sample sizes are large, say 30 or more, and the population variances are unknown, then to a good approximation, a $100(1 - \alpha)\%$ confidence interval for $(\mu_1 - \mu_2)$ is obtained by replacing the population variances in the previous confidence interval by the corresponding sample variances s_1^2 and s_2^2. For large sample sizes, this approximation will usually be adequate even if the population distributions are not normal.

Example 10.17 **Confidence Interval for $(\mu_1 - \mu_2)$ with Large Sample Sizes:** In a sex discrimination case, an employee alleged that a large corporation paid men more than women for comparable work. Let Population 1 represent all male employees performing certain jobs and Population 2 all females performing comparable jobs at the corporation. Independent samples are taken of $n_1 = 100$ males and $n_2 = 100$ females; the sample means are $\bar{x}_1 = \$20{,}600$ and $\bar{x}_2 = \$19{,}700$, and the sample standard deviations are $s_1 = \$3000$ and $s_2 = \$2500$. Construct a 95% confidence interval for $(\mu_1 - \mu_2)$.

Solution: Because the sample sizes are large, we can use the sample variances in place of the population variances and obtain the confidence interval by using the formula

$$\left((\bar{x}_1 - \bar{x}_2) - z_{\alpha/2}\sqrt{\frac{s_1^2}{n_1} + \frac{s_2^2}{n_2}},\ (\bar{x}_1 - \bar{x}_2) + z_{\alpha/2}\sqrt{\frac{s_1^2}{n_1} + \frac{s_2^2}{n_2}}\right)$$

We have $z_{\alpha/2} = 1.96$. We obtain $(\bar{x}_1 - \bar{x}_2) = (20{,}600 - 19{,}700) = 900$. The confidence interval is

$$\left(900 - 1.96\sqrt{\frac{3000^2}{100} + \frac{2500^2}{100}},\ 900 + 1.96\sqrt{\frac{3000^2}{100} + \frac{2500^2}{100}}\right)$$

or

$$(\$134.60, \$1665.40)$$

Because this interval contains only positive values, we can be quite confident that $(\mu_1 - \mu_2) > 0$. Thus, it is reasonable to assume that the mean salary for males exceeds the mean salary for females. ■

Confidence Intervals for $(\mu_1 - \mu_2)$ When Variances Are Unknown and Sample Sizes Are Small

We now consider the case when the sample sizes are small, the population variances are unknown, and the populations are normal. The problem of finding a confidence interval has been solved for the special case when the unknown variances are equal. A general solution has not been found for the case where the unknown variances are unequal.

If we assume that the population variances are equal, then it is useful to pool the data from the two random samples to obtain one estimate of the common population variance σ^2. Let $\bar{x}_1$ and $\bar{x}_2$ denote the observed sample means, and s_1^2 and s_2^2 the observed sample variances. Let s_p^2 denote the pooled estimate of the common population variance. The pooled variance s_p^2 is given by

$$s_p^2 = \frac{(n_1 - 1)s_1^2 + (n_2 - 1)s_2^2}{(n_1 + n_2 - 2)}$$

Since the population variances are unknown, we estimate them by the pooled estimate s_p^2.

Confidence Interval for $(\mu_1 - \mu_2)$ When Variances Are Unknown but Equal—Independent Samples

Suppose we have independent random samples of n_1 and n_2 observations from normal populations with means μ_1 and μ_2 and a common variance σ^2. If the observed sample means are $\bar{x}_1$ and $\bar{x}_2$, then a $100(1 - \alpha)\%$ confidence interval for $(\mu_1 - \mu_2)$ is based on the t distribution and is given by

$$\left((\bar{x}_1 - \bar{x}_2) - t_{\alpha/2,\nu}\sqrt{\frac{s_p^2}{n_1} + \frac{s_p^2}{n_2}},\ (\bar{x}_1 - \bar{x}_2) + t_{\alpha/2,\nu}\sqrt{\frac{s_p^2}{n_1} + \frac{s_p^2}{n_2}}\right)$$

where the degrees of freedom is $\nu = (n_1 + n_2 - 2)$ and s_p^2 is the pooled estimate of the common variance.

Example 10.18 **Confidence Interval for $(\mu_1 - \mu_2)$ with Small Sample Sizes:** Two manufacturing companies produce carbide drill tips that are used to cut holes in steel sheets. A customer wishing to know which drill tips have the longer life purchases independent samples of $n_1 = 20$ drill tips from Company 1 and $n_2 = 15$ drill tips from Company 2. The mean lives of the drill tips are $\bar{x}_1 = 78$ minutes and $\bar{x}_2 = 84$ minutes. The population variances are unknown but assumed to be equal. The sample variances are $s_1^2 = 41$ and $s_2^2 = 36$. Construct a 95% confidence interval for $(\mu_1 - \mu_2)$.

Solution: We obtain the pooled variance estimate s_p^2 as follows:

$$s_p^2 = \frac{(20 - 1)(41) + (15 - 1)(36)}{(20 + 15 - 2)} = \frac{1283}{33} = 38.88$$

For a 95% confidence interval, we have $\alpha = .05$ and $\alpha/2 = .025$. The degrees of freedom parameter is $\nu = (n_1 + n_2 - 2) = (20 + 15 - 2) = 33$. For 33 degrees of freedom, we obtain approximately $t_{\alpha/2,\nu} \approx 2.04$. The 95% confidence interval for $(\mu_1 - \mu_2)$ is

$$\left((\bar{x}_1 - \bar{x}_2) - t_{\alpha/2,\nu}\sqrt{\frac{s_p^2}{n_1} + \frac{s_p^2}{n_2}},\ (\bar{x}_1 - \bar{x}_2) + t_{\alpha/2,\nu}\sqrt{\frac{s_p^2}{n_1} + \frac{s_p^2}{n_2}}\right)$$

The left end of the interval is

$$(78 - 84) - 2.04\sqrt{38.88/20 + 38.88/15} = -10.34$$

The right end is

$$(78 - 84) + 2.04\sqrt{38.88/20 + 38.88/15} = -1.66$$

The 95% confidence interval is $(-10.34, -1.66)$. This interval contains only negative values, indicating that the drill tips made by Company 1 do not last as long, on the average, as those made by Company 2. ■

Exercises for Section 10.7

1. A school board wants to determine how the mean IQ of the students at inner city schools compares with the mean IQ of students at suburban schools. Independent random samples of 80 students are obtained from each school location. At inner city schools, the sample mean IQ is 105 and the sample standard deviation is 11. At suburban schools, the sample mean IQ is 101 and the standard deviation is 9.

a. Compute a 90% confidence interval for the difference between the mean IQs.

b. Compute a 99% confidence interval for this difference.

2. A department store sends out monthly statements to its credit customers. In the past it has not enclosed a preaddressed envelope for returning payments with these statements. In a random sample of 100 of these accounts, the mean time to payment was 11.4 days and the sample standard deviation was 3.3 days. As an experiment, the company sent preaddressed envelopes with the accounts of 100 randomly and independently selected customers. For this sample, the mean time to payment was 8.2 days and the standard deviation was 3.3 days. Find a 95% confidence interval for the difference between the two population means.

3. A farmer wants to determine if different types of feed can influence the mean number of eggs that hens lay per month. In a random sample of 100 hens that ate Feed 1, the average number of eggs per month was $\bar{x} = 15.2$ with variance 4. In a random sample of 100 hens that ate Feed 2, the average number of eggs per month was $\bar{x}_2 = 14$ with variance 4. Construct a 95% confidence interval for $(\mu_1 - \mu_2)$.

4. Five-year-old children were being studied to determine whether children whose parents are college graduates watched more or less TV than children whose parents are not college graduates. Independent random samples of 21 children were selected from each population. The sample means and variances were $\bar{x}_1 = 22$ hours, $s_1^2 = 16$, $\bar{x}_2 = 26$ hours, and $s_2^2 = 14$. The population variances are assumed to be equal and the populations are assumed to be normal. Calculate the following confidence intervals for the difference between the population means:

a. 95% b. 90% c. 99%

5. A national restaurant franchise buys bakery goods from two suppliers who specialize in making cherry pies. The manager of a franchise wants to know if the two bakers are filling the pies with the same quantity of cherries on the average. It is assumed that the unknown population variances are equal and that the populations are normal. The manager takes a random sample of 40 cherry pies, 25 from the first baker and 15 from the second. The quantity of cherries in each pie is weighed. The results are: $\bar{x}_1 = 11.6$ ounces, $s_1 = 1.8$, $\bar{x}_2 = 12.2$ ounces, and $s_2 = 2.0$. Construct a 95% confidence interval for $(\mu_1 - \mu_2)$.

6. In a sex discrimination case, a female employee alleged that a certain corporation paid females lower average salaries than males. The corporation argued that females had lower salaries because the mean years of seniority for females was lower than the mean years of seniority for males. To test this claim, independent random samples of 25 males and 25 females were obtained. It is assumed that the populations are normal and the population variances are equal. The sample means and sample standard deviations were: $\bar{x}_m = 12.4$ years, $s_m = 5.1$, $\bar{x}_f = 9.4$, and $s_f = 4.8$.

a. Construct a 99% confidence interval for the difference between the population means.

b. Does the result in part (a) provide strong support for the hypothesis that males have greater seniority than females? Explain.

10.8 ▪ Confidence Intervals for the Difference of Two Population Proportions

In Section 10.5 we showed how to construct a confidence interval for a single population proportion, but sometimes we are interested in comparing two population proportions. For example, in a large corporation we might be interested in comparing the proportion of male college students who eventually graduate to the proportion of female students who eventually graduate. In this section we show how to obtain confidence intervals for the difference between two population proportions when independent large samples are taken from each population.

To construct a confidence interval for $(p_1 - p_2)$, the difference between two population proportions, follow the procedure in the box.

Confidence Interval for $(p_1 - p_2)$

Let $\hat{p}_1$ denote the observed proportion of successes in a random sample of n_1 observations from a population with proportion p_1 successes, and let $\hat{p}_2$ denote the observed proportion of successes in an independent random sample of n_2 observations from a population with proportion p_2 successes. A $100(1 - \alpha)\%$ confidence interval for $(p_1 - p_2)$ is given by the interval

$$\left((\hat{p}_1 - \hat{p}_2) - z_{\alpha/2}\sqrt{\frac{\hat{p}_1\hat{q}_1}{n_1} + \frac{\hat{p}_2\hat{q}_2}{n_2}},\ (\hat{p}_1 - \hat{p}_2) + z_{\alpha/2}\sqrt{\frac{\hat{p}_1\hat{q}_1}{n_1} + \frac{\hat{p}_2\hat{q}_2}{n_2}}\right)$$

This result holds provided $n_1p_1 \geqslant 5$, $n_1q_1 \geqslant 5$, $n_2p_2 \geqslant 5$, and $n_2q_2 \geqslant 5$.

Example 10.19 **Confidence Interval for $(p_1 - p_2)$:** An employee alleged that a large corporation was discriminating against older employees by illegally terminating their employment. The company replied that, due to a decline in sales, it was necessary to cut the labor force by terminating employees. The company agreed that many older employees were terminated but argued that many younger employees were also terminated. In court, the opposing attorneys argued about whether the proportions of young and old employees who were terminated were equal. In a random sample of 100 young employees, 35 were terminated. In an independent sample of 100 old employees, 30 were terminated. Thus, we have $\hat{p}_1 = .35$ and $\hat{p}_2 = .30$. Find a 99% confidence interval for $(p_1 - p_2)$, the difference between the two population proportions.

Solution: We have $(1 - \alpha) = .99$, so $\alpha = .01$ and $\alpha/2 = .005$. We obtain $z_{\alpha/2} = 2.58$. The confidence interval is

$$\left((.35 - .30) - 2.58\sqrt{\frac{(.35)(.65)}{100} + \frac{(.30)(.70)}{100}},\right.$$

$$\left.(.35 - .30) + 2.58\sqrt{\frac{(.35)(.65)}{100} + \frac{(.30)(.70)}{100}}\right)$$

or

$$(-.12, .22)$$

Thus, we are 99% confident that the true difference between p_1 and p_2 is between $-.12$ and .22. Since this interval contains the value 0, we cannot conclude that the two population proportions are different. ■

Exercises for Section 10.8

1. A TV executive is interested in determining if the proportion of people who watch a late-night talk show is higher with the regular host or a guest host. In a random sample of 400 people, 175 watch the show when the regular host is on. In a random sample of 500 people, 185 watch the show when a guest host is on. Calculate a 95% confidence interval for $(p_1 - p_2)$.
2. In a random sample of 100 graduates from a university's business school, 42 received starting salaries exceeding $18,000. In an independent random sample of 100 graduates from the school of engineering, 50 received starting salaries exceeding $18,000. Let p_1 and p_2 denote the proportion of all business majors and engineering majors who received starting salaries exceeding $18,000. Calculate a 95% confidence interval for $(p_1 - p_2)$.
3. In a random sample of 200 city residents, 150 thought that the condition of local roads was very poor. In a random sample of 160 tourists, 90 thought the condition of local roads was very poor. Find a 90% confidence interval for the difference between the two population proportions.
4. A city planner claims that homeowners tend to have closer ties to their community than do renters. Thus, homeowners are more willing to pay for good schools and recreational facilities than are renters. In a random sample of 120 homeowners, 50 stated that the local tax rates were too high and 70 stated that tax rates were "about right." In an independent random sample of 200 renters, 70 thought that the local tax rates were too high and 130 thought they were "about right."
   a. Find a 99% confidence interval for the difference in the population proportions who think taxes are too high.
   b. Do the data support the city planner's claim?

10.9 ▪ Computer Applications

When we construct a confidence interval for a population mean, we typically have a random sample of n observations from a population with an unknown variance. To construct a confidence interval, we need to calculate both the sample mean $\overline{X}$ and the sample standard deviation S. In Chapter 4, we showed that to obtain the sample mean and sample variance using the SPSSX program, we issue the CONDESCRIPTIVE command followed by the names of the variables whose means and standard deviations are desired.

For example, refer to the data in Table 2.2 of Chapter 2, which shows selected characteristics of a sample of 50 students in a statistics class. Suppose we wish to construct a 95% confidence interval for the mean SAT score and the mean GPA for the population of all statistics students. To obtain the sample mean and sample standard deviation, issue the command

```
CONDESCRIPTIVE SAT, GPA
```

Figure 10.11 shows the appropriate computer output. Here we see that the sample mean for the SAT score is $\overline{x} = 1122.40$, and the sample standard deviation is $s = 152.925$. For GPA, the sample mean is 2.921 and the sample standard deviation is 0.387.

FIGURE 10.11 **SPSSX-generated output showing the sample mean and sample standard deviation for SAT scores and GPA in Table 2.2.**

```
NUMBER OF VALID OBSERVATIONS (LISTWISE) =        50.00

VARIABLE        MEAN     STD DEV    MINIMUM    MAXIMUM VALID N   LABEL

SAT         1122.400     152.925     880.00    1490.00      50
GPA            2.921        .387       2.29       3.80      50
```

Because the sample size is $n = 50$, there are $\nu = 49$ degrees of freedom. The appropriate value of the t statistic is $t_{\alpha/2,\nu} \approx 2.02$. (We have used 40 degrees of freedom to find the critical value because t values for $\nu = 49$ are not in Table A.6.) The appropriate confidence interval is

$$(\overline{x} - t_{\alpha/2}s/\sqrt{n},\ \overline{x} + t_{\alpha/2}s/\sqrt{n})$$

or

$$[1122.40 \pm 2.02(152.925/\sqrt{50})]$$

or

$$(1122.40 \pm 43.686)$$

The desired confidence interval is thus (1078.714, 1166.086).

Exercises for Section 10.9

1. Construct a 95% confidence interval for the mean GPA for all students in the population using the data in Table 2.2 of Chapter 2.
2. Construct a 95% confidence interval for the mean age for all employees at Computech using the data in Table 2.1 of Chapter 2.
3. Construct a 95% confidence interval for the mean monthly salary for all employees at Computech using the data in Table 2.1 of Chapter 2.
4. Construct a 95% confidence interval for the mean number of years of seniority for all employees at Computech using the data in Table 2.1 of Chapter 2.

Chapter 10 Summary

The sample mean and sample proportion are used to estimate the corresponding population parameters. A *confidence interval* provides information concerning the precision or quality of the point estimate. When the population is normal and the population variance σ^2 is known, a confidence interval for μ having *level of confidence* $(1 - \alpha)$ is given by

$$(\bar{x} - z_{\alpha/2}\sigma/\sqrt{n},\ \bar{x} + z_{\alpha/2}\sigma/\sqrt{n})$$

If the sample size is large and the population variance is unknown, we can replace σ in the formula by the observed sample standard deviation s. If the population is normal with unknown variance and the sample size is small, the t distribution is used to construct a confidence interval for μ. The confidence interval is

$$(\bar{x} - t_{\alpha/2,\nu}s/\sqrt{n},\ \bar{x} + t_{\alpha/2,\nu}s/\sqrt{n})$$

where the appropriate number of degrees of freedom is $\nu = (n - 1)$. When the sample size is large, it makes little difference whether the standard normal distribution or the t distribution is used to construct the confidence interval for the mean.

A confidence interval for the population proportion having level of confidence $100(1 - \alpha)\%$ is given by

$$(\hat{p} - z_{\alpha/2}\sqrt{\hat{p}\hat{q}/n},\ \hat{p} + z_{\alpha/2}\sqrt{\hat{p}\hat{q}/n})$$

In a similar fashion, confidence intervals can be constructed for the difference between two population means or the difference between two population proportions. If we have independent samples from normal populations with known variances, a $100(1 - \alpha)\%$ confidence interval for $(\mu_1 - \mu_2)$ is given by

$$(\bar{x}_1 - \bar{x}_2) - z_{\alpha/2}\sqrt{\frac{\sigma_1^2}{n_1} + \frac{\sigma_2^2}{n_2}},\ (\bar{x}_1 - \bar{x}_2) + z_{\alpha/2}\sqrt{\frac{\sigma_1^2}{n_1} + \frac{\sigma_2^2}{n_2}}$$

where $\bar{x}_1$ and $\bar{x}_2$ are the observed sample means. If the sample sizes are large, the observed sample variances s_1^2 and s_2^2 can be used in place of the values σ_1^2 and σ_2^2. When the sample sizes are small and the population variances are unknown but assumed to be equal, the t distribution is used. A $100(1 - \alpha)\%$ confidence interval for $(\mu_1 - \mu_2)$ is

$$(\bar{x}_1 - \bar{x}_2) - t_{\alpha/2,\nu}\sqrt{\frac{s_p^2}{n_1} + \frac{s_p^2}{n_2}},\ (\bar{x}_1 - \bar{x}_2) + t_{\alpha/2,\nu}\sqrt{\frac{s_p^2}{n_1} + \frac{s_p^2}{n_2}}$$

where s_p^2 is a pooled estimate of the population variances

$$s_p^2 = \frac{(n_1 - 1)s_1^2 + (n_2 - 1)s_2^2}{(n_1 + n_2 - 2)}$$

and where the degrees of freedom is $\nu = (n_1 + n_2 - 2)$.

A $100(1 - \alpha)\%$ confidence interval for the difference between two population proportions $(p_1 - p_2)$ is

$$(\hat{p}_1 - \hat{p}_2) - z_{\alpha/2}\sqrt{\frac{\hat{p}_1\hat{q}_1}{n_1} + \frac{\hat{p}_2\hat{q}_2}{n_2}},\ (\hat{p}_1 - \hat{p}_2) + z_{\alpha/2}\sqrt{\frac{\hat{p}_1\hat{q}_1}{n_1} + \frac{\hat{p}_2\hat{q}_2}{n_2}}$$

For many applications, the required precision of the point estimate is specified in advance by stating a maximum permissible error and a required level of confidence. When estimating the mean, the sample size needed to achieve a desired accuracy at a specified level of confidence requires knowledge of the population variance σ^2. The sample size required to estimate the mean within a distance D at level of confidence $(1 - \alpha)$ is given by

$$n = \frac{z_{\alpha/2}^2\sigma^2}{D^2}$$

The sample size required to estimate the population proportion within a distance D at level of confidence $(1 - \alpha)$ is

$$n = \frac{z_{\alpha/2}^2 pq}{D^2}$$

In this formula, some preliminary estimate of p is required. When no preliminary estimate of p is available, replace pq by .25.

A confidence interval provides information about the likely value of some population parameter. Another way of obtaining this information is to state some hypothesis about the potential value of the parameter and then test this hypothesis by examining whether the sample data support this hypothesis. The topic of hypothesis testing is discussed in the following chapter.

Chapter 10 ▪ Supplementary Exercises

1. In order to determine how many hours per day first grade pupils watch TV, a random sample of 100 children was taken. The sample variance was $s^2 = 16$ and $\bar{x} = 4$. Calculate a 95% confidence interval for the mean.

2. The Cincinnati Reds took a random sample of 400 spectators at several baseball games to estimate the mean distance that spectators traveled to attend the game. The results were $\bar{x} = 20.4$ miles and $s = 7$. Find a 99% confidence interval for the mean.
3. The highway department wants to estimate the mean number of cars that cross a certain bridge into town between 8 A.M. and 9 A.M. on weekdays. Traffic was counted on 16 different days. The sample variance was $s^2 = 25{,}000$ and $\bar{x} = 1200$. Calculate a 90% confidence interval for the mean. Assume the population is normal.
4. A market researcher wants to select one sample to estimate both μ, the average age of people living within five miles of a proposed shopping mall site, and p, the proportion of people within that five-mile radius who are between 21 and 45 years of age. The researcher wants to estimate μ with a 95% confidence interval that is no more than 6 years wide and p with a 90% confidence interval of width no greater than .1. It is known from previous studies that the standard deviation of age in the population is 15 years, and it is believed that p is near .3. How large a sample is required to construct confidence intervals for both μ and p that satisfy the above specifications?
5. After nominating a presidential candidate, the Democratic party set itself to the task of nominating a vice-presidential candidate. In a random sample of 400 voters, 240 preferred a certain midwestern politician. Find a 90% confidence interval for the proportion p of all voters who preferred this individual.
6. In a random sample of 900 new cars, 10% had defective parts. Construct a 95% confidence interval for the proportion of all new cars having defective parts.
7. In California, the presidential election is expected to be very close (p is approximately .5). The outcome in this state is crucial because the winning candidate gets the state's entire block of electoral votes. How large a sample is needed if we want the sample proportion $\hat{p}$ to be within .02 of p with probability .95?
8. In a random sample of 100 people who watched a certain TV program, 20 people could remember the name of the commercial sponsor a day later. Construct a 95% confidence interval for the population proportion.
9. On election day, an exit poll is taken of a random sample of 2400 voters. Candidate A gets 60% of the votes in this sample.
   a. Construct a 95% confidence interval for the percentage of votes the candidate will receive in the election.
   b. Is this sufficient evidence to convince you that Candidate A will win the election?
   c. If you were the producer of an election night news program, would you be willing to announce that Candidate A has won the election (before the votes were counted)? Explain.
10. For many years beer has been sold in aluminum cans. Recently a wine producer has proposed selling wine in cans, but the producer fears that many wine drinkers will refuse to buy wine unless it comes in a bottle. The producer hires a marketing agency to sample customers' opinions. The producer wants an estimate of the proportion of wine drinkers who would refuse to buy wine in a can within 3% of the population proportion with probability .95. Tentatively, the true percentage is estimated to be near 80%. How large a sample will be required?
11. A random sample of 1000 adults was taken in Phoenix to estimate the unemployment rate in that city. In the sample 8% of the labor force was unemployed.
    a. Find a 95% confidence interval for the unemployment rate in Phoenix.
    b. How large a sample must be taken if we want the estimated unemployment rate to be within .01 of the true unemployment rate with probability .95? Assume p is about .08.
12. The basic source of labor market information is the monthly survey data collected by the Bureau of the Census for the Bureau of Labor Statistics. Approximately 50,000 randomly selected households are surveyed monthly to represent the civilian noninstitutional population. The results are subject to some sampling error, which should be taken into account when analyzing the data.
    a. If a sample of 50,000 yields an estimated unemployment rate of 8%, find a 95% confidence interval for the true unemployment rate.

b. How large a sample is required if we want to be 95% confident that p is within .02 of $\hat{p}$? Use $\hat{p}$ = .08.

13. The American Cancer Society wants to estimate what proportion of high school seniors smoke regularly. In a random sample of 1000 seniors, 200 smoke regularly. Construct the following confidence intervals for the population proportion:

a. 90% b. 99%

14. The Wilson Company is doing tests to determine if yellow, white, or orange tennis balls are easiest to see. During testing, it became necessary to estimate what proportion of the male population is color-blind, because color-blind males have difficulty seeing the orange ball. In a random sample of 1600 males, 240 were color-blind.

a. Construct a 95% confidence interval for the proportion of the population that is color-blind.

b. Construct a 99% confidence interval for p.

15. In a nationwide survey, individuals were asked to describe their religious preferences. In a random sample of 400 teenage males, 300 said that they attended church regularly. In an independent random sample of 400 males over age 30, 220 said that they attended church regularly. For the difference between the two population proportions, construct the following:

a. A 95% confidence interval

b. A 99% confidence interval

16. A physical education teacher claims that left-handed people have an advantage in sports such as tennis, baseball, and basketball because most people are right-handed and thus right-handed people do not get to practice enough against left-handed opponents. The instructor obtains independent random samples of 400 professional athletes and 400 nonathletes and finds that 95 of the athletes and 50 of the nonathletes are left-handed.

a. Construct a 95% confidence interval for the difference between the population proportions.

b. Is this sample evidence strong enough to make you agree with the instructor? Explain.

17. To prevent erosion along the sides of many highways, the highway department has spent a large sum of money planting grass. Because the cost of labor and equipment is a substantial part of the department's budget, the department wants to make sure that the grass seed being planted will help prevent erosion. Before purchasing a certain brand of seed, the department examined a random sample of 600 seeds. In the sample, 500 seeds germinated.

a. Construct a 95% confidence interval for p.

b. The seed company has claimed that the probability of germination is at least .9. Do you agree? Explain.

18. A Department of Agriculture publication claims that more than 70% of all farms in the United States are operated and managed by the farm owner. A random sample of 200 farms is obtained, of which 110 are operated by the owner and 90 are managed by a hired contractor. Construct a 95% confidence interval for the proportion of farms that are owner operated.

19. Congress is debating an antipollution proposal that will increase the cost of manufacturing steel and ultimately reduce the level of employment in certain steel-producing states. A politician claims that people's opinions about the proposed bill differ depending on whether they live in steel-producing states. In a random sample of 200 people from steel-producing states, 80 favor the bill. In an independent sample of 200 people from non-steel-producing states, 120 favor the bill.

a. Calculate a 95% confidence interval for the difference between the population proportions.

b. Does this confidence interval contain the value 0? Explain the significance of this result.

20. Executives of Foodfair Supermarkets want to compare the amounts that households spend each week on groceries at the inner city store, Store 1, and at the suburban store, Store 2. Independent random samples of size 100 are taken at each store. The sample means are $\bar{x}_1$ = \$93.82 and $\bar{x}_2$ = \$116.27. The standard deviations are σ_1 = \$14 and σ_2 = \$19. Construct a 95% confidence interval for the difference between the population means.

21. The county commissioners are contemplating instituting a \$0.50 tax on all hotel customers. The commissioners want to estimate the proportion of citizens who favor the tax. (Obviously the hotel owners oppose it.) The commissioners want their estimate to be within .05 of the population proportion with a level of confidence of .95. Determine the maximum sample size that is needed to meet the commissioners' requirements.

22. A quality control engineer would like to estimate the proportion of defects being produced on an assembly line to within .04 with 99% confidence. How large a sample is required if it is believed that p is approximately .1?

23. A company supervisor wants to estimate the mean length of time it takes employees to install mufflers on new cars. It is believed from previous studies that the population standard deviation is $\sigma = 4$ minutes. How large a sample is required to be 95% confident that $\bar{X}$ is within 1.5 minutes of the true value of μ?

24. The Newberry Toy Store has received a shipment of several thousand dolls from a foreign supplier. In a random sample of 100 dolls, 18 are found to be of such poor quality that they cannot be sold.

a. Find a 95% confidence interval for the proportion of defectives in the entire shipment.

b. Find a 99% confidence interval for the proportion of defectives in the entire shipment.

25. Two different manufacturing methods, casting and die forging, can be used to make parts for a newly developed supersonic airplane. One hundred parts were made by each method, and each part was subjected to a severe stress test. In the test, 40 of the castings failed and 30 of the forged parts failed. Find a 95% confidence interval for the difference between the population proportions of the cast and the forged parts that would fail the same test.

26. A national corporation is debating hiring a certain controversial sports star as its spokesman for a particular product. A polling agency is hired to estimate what percentage of the public has a favorable opinion of the proposed spokesman. The agency wants its estimate to be accurate to within .03 with 95% confidence. How large a sample is required if it is believed that about 60% of the public have a favorable opinion of the individual?

27. The Coca-Cola Company is debating whether to launch an intensive advertising campaign to increase the consumption of diet drinks by teenagers. A random sample of 500 high school students are questioned concerning whether they prefer regular or diet cola. In the sample, 225 say that they prefer regular cola. Find a 95% confidence interval for the proportion of high school students who prefer regular cola to diet cola.

28. The federal government requires states to certify that they are enforcing the 55-mile-per-hour speed limit and that motorists are driving at that speed. A state is in jeopardy of losing millions of dollars in federal road funds if more than 50% of the vehicles on interstate highways are exceeding the 55-mile-per-hour speed limit. Suppose the state police conduct a radar survey to estimate the proportion of vehicles exceeding the limit.

a. How large a sample should be selected to estimate p to within 3% with 95% confidence? Suppose that last year approximately 60% of all vehicles exceeded 55 miles per hour.

b. The highway patrol also estimates μ, the average speed of vehicles on state highways. It wants to estimate μ to within .3 mile per hour with 95% confidence. Assume that the standard deviation of vehicle speeds is approximately 2.5 miles per hour. How large a sample should be taken to estimate μ with the desired reliability?

29. A congressman would like to know how voters feel about a particular issue. Approximately how many voters should the congressman survey in order to estimate the true proportion favoring this bill to within .05 with probability .99? Since you do not have prior knowledge about p, substitute $p = .5$ into the formula to find the sample size.

30. A police department wants to estimate the proportion of customers at a large inner city department store who are shoplifters. Plainclothes detectives select a random sample of shoppers and check closely to determine whether they steal any merchandise while in the store. Assume past police records suggest that the percentage of shoplifters is near 10%. How many customers should be included in the sample if the police want to estimate the proportion of shoplifters correct to within .02 with probability .95?

31. Find the value $t_{.05}$ such that $P(t > t_{.05}) = .05$, where t follows the t distribution having the following degrees of freedom:

a. 10 b. 20 c. 30 d. 40

e. Compare these values with the standard normal variable Z; that is, find $z_{.05}$ such that $P(Z > z_{.05}) = .05$.

32. Find the mean and variance of the t distribution having the following degrees of freedom:

a. 10 b. 15 c. 30

33. What is the probability that a t score with 14 degrees of freedom will exceed 1.761?

34. Approximately what is the 90th percentile of a t distribution having 500 degrees of freedom?

35. Will a 95% confidence interval based on the t distribution be larger or smaller than a 95% confidence interval based on the standard normal distribution? Explain.

36. A random sample of 100 households is obtained to estimate the average number of hours per week that televisions are in use. The sample results are $\bar{x} = 35$ and $s^2 = 64$.

a. Calculate a 95% confidence interval for the population mean using the t distribution.

b. What is the appropriate degrees of freedom for the t distribution in part (a)?

c. Repeat part (a) using the normal distribution.

d. Do you agree that when the sample size is large it makes little difference whether we use the t distribution or the standard normal distribution when constructing confidence intervals for the mean?

37. A random sample of 200 households is taken to estimate the average annual expenditures on magazines. The results are: $\bar{x} = \$52$ and $s^2 = 400$.

a. Construct a 99% confidence interval for the population mean.

b. Construct a 95% confidence interval for the population mean.

c. What is the appropriate degrees of freedom?

38. A large university is considering giving each faculty member a telephone answering machine rather than having calls be forwarded to a secretary when the professor is not in his or her office. A budget committee wants to estimate the average amount of time that secretaries spend handling phone calls for absent faculty members. Because getting the information is relatively expensive, the sample size must be kept small. A random sample of 16 secretaries is observed. The results are $\bar{x} = 36$ minutes per day with $s^2 = 320$.

a. Construct a 90% confidence interval for the population mean.

b. Construct a 95% confidence interval for the population mean.

39. A manufacturer of ski equipment is interested in estimating the average annual expenditures on ski clothes by visitors at a ski resort. A random sample is taken of 25 visitors at the resort. The results are $\bar{x} = \$116$ with $s^2 = 1000$. Construct the following confidence intervals for the population mean:

a. 99% b. 90%

40. In a certain city, baseball fans complain that they do not like to attend games because of huge traffic jams after the game. The fans claim that it takes about 35 minutes to get out of the stadium parking lots following a game when the attendance exceeds 30,000. To determine if the complaints of the fans are justified, a random sample of 150 fans are observed during various games when the attendance exceeds 30,000. The average time it takes these 150 fans to exit from the parking lot is $\bar{x} = 27$ minutes with $s^2 = 49$. Construct a 95% confidence interval for the mean departure time.

41. An executive for Tri-State Coal Incorporated wants to determine the average amount of coal mined per day by miners in a certain mine. A random sample of 10 miners produces the following tonnages of coal on a certain day:

8, 11, 9, 6, 12, 10, 13, 9, 11, 9

a. Find the sample mean and sample variance.
b. Find a 90% confidence interval for the mean tonnage.
c. Find a 95% confidence interval for the mean tonnage.

42. A college student wants to be a radio disc jockey but does not know if the salaries of disc jockeys are high enough to satisfy him. A random sample of 16 disc jockeys is obtained. In the sample, the average salary is $\bar{x} = \$40{,}000$ per year and the sample standard deviation is $s = \$7000$. Assume the population is approximately normal. Find the following confidence intervals for the mean:
a. 99% b. 95%

43. In a random sample of 20 homeowners in Meadville, the average monthly electric bill during October was $64. The sample standard deviation was $s = \$11$. For the mean monthly electric bill in October, find the following:
a. A 90% confidence interval
b. A 95% confidence interval

44. Professor Johnson has published an article in a psychology journal claiming that flight control operators (FCOs) and stockbrokers suffer the most stress during their jobs. Dr. Johnson selected a random sample of 15 FCOs and 10 stockbrokers and performed a series of tests to measure the stress of each individual. For the FCOs, the average score was $\bar{x}_1 = 216$ with standard deviation $s_1 = 22$; for the stockbrokers the sample mean was $\bar{x}_2 = 198$ with standard deviation $s_2 = 36$. Assume the populations are approximately normal and that the population variances are equal. Construct the following confidence intervals for $(\mu_1 - \mu_2)$:
a. 90% b. 95%

45. The U.S. Department of Agriculture wants to determine the average number of eggs that children under 14 years of age consume each year. A random sample of 900 such children is obtained. In this sample the average number of eggs consumed was $\bar{x} = 86$, and the sample standard deviation was $s = 16$. Find the following confidence intervals for the population mean:
a. 70% b. 95%

46. Random samples of weights were taken from two package-filling processes at the Adams Feed Corporation. The first sample consisted of $n_1 = 150$ packages, and the second consisted of $n_2 = 175$ packages. The sample means were $\bar{x}_1 = 100.8$ pounds and $\bar{x}_2 = 101.4$ pounds, and the sample standard deviations were $s_1 = 0.9$ pound and $s_2 = 1.1$ pounds. Construct the following confidence intervals for $(\mu_1 - \mu_2)$:
a. 90% b. 99%

47. The Nevada Highway Commission wants to know the mean weight of commercial vehicles traveling on a particular section of interstate highway. An inspector takes a sample of 100 randomly selected trucks and weighs them. The mean gross weight is $\bar{x} = 14.7$ tons with sample standard deviation of $s = 4.8$ tons.
a. Construct a 90% confidence interval for the mean gross weight of commercial vehicles traveling on that section of the highway.
b. Construct a 99% confidence interval for μ.

48. The Maine Transportation Department wants to compare the durabilities of two different types of paint used to paint center lines on highways. On a heavily traveled road, 40 lines were painted, 20 with each type of paint. After three weeks, reflectometer readings were obtained. The higher the readings, the better is the durability of the paint. From the two independent samples of data, the following information was obtained: $\bar{x}_1, = 12.3$, $s_1^2 = 3$, $\bar{x}_2 = 11.6$, and $s_2^2 = 3$. Assume that the populations are normal and that the population variances are equal. Construct the following confidence intervals for $(\mu_1 - \mu_2)$:
a. 95% b. 99%

49. A computer manufacturer wants to estimate the speed of its new printer. Assume the population is approximately normal. A random sample yielded the following measured speeds (in characters per second):

116	130	112	105	115	136	111	127	118	124	111	126
117	119	107	110	134	123	122	114	122	103	115	130

a. Construct a 95% confidence interval for the population mean.
b. Construct a 99% confidence interval for the population mean.

50. The Nielsen television ratings are based on a sample of 2000 homes out of a population of 80,000,000 homes. Suppose Nielsen estimates that 30% of these homes were watching a certain program.
a. Construct a 99% confidence interval for the population proportion.
b. Estimate the number of households that watched the program.
c. Find a 99% confidence interval for the number of households that watched the program.

51. I want to estimate the number of households in Allegheny County that own a personal computer (PC). Suppose Allegheny County has 400,000 households. I take a random sample of 200 households, in which 60 own a PC.
a. Estimate the proportion of households that own a PC.
b. Estimate the number of households that own a PC.
c. Construct a 99% confidence interval for the population proportion.
d. Construct a 99% confidence interval for the number of households that own a PC.

52. The *University of California, Berkeley Wellness Letter* of May 1988 states that 12 million blood donors were tested for AIDS between April 1985 and May 1987. In this sample, 0.02% tested positive.
a. Construct a 99% confidence interval for the population proportion.
b. The population of the United States is approximately 244 million. Estimate the number of individuals in the United States that would test positive.
c. Do you think that blood donors represent a random sample of the entire population? If not, do you think the sample proportion is biased downward or upward?

References

FISHER, RONALD A. *Statistical Methods for Research Workers.* 14th ed. New York: Hafner Press, 1970.

FREUND, JOHN E., and R. E. WALPOLE. *Mathematical Statistics.* 4th ed. Englewood Cliffs, N.J.: Prentice-Hall, 1987.

Handbook of Tables for Probability and Statistics. 2d ed. Cleveland, Ohio: Chemical Rubber Co., 1968.

HOEL, PAUL G. *Elementary Statistics.* 4th ed. New York: Wiley, 1976.

NIE, NORMAN E., C. HADLAI HULL, JEAN G. JENKINS, KAREN STEINBRENNER, and DALE H. BENT. *SPSS Statistical Package for the Social Sciences.* 2d ed. New York: McGraw-Hill, 1975.

NORUSIS, MARIJA J. *SPSSX Introductory Statistics Guide.* New York: McGraw-Hill, 1983.

———. *SPSSX Advanced Statistics Guide.* Chicago: SPSS, 1985.

———. *The SPSS Guide to Data Analysis.* Chicago: SPSS, 1986.

RYAN, THOMAS A., BRIAN L. JOINER, and BARBARA F. RYAN. *Minitab Handbook.* 2d ed. Boston: PWS-KENT, 1985.

———. *Minitab Reference Manual.* University Park, Penn.: Minitab Project, 1985.

SAS Introductory Guide. 3d ed. Cary, N.C.: SAS Institute, 1985.

SAS Procedures Guide for Personal Computers. Version 6 ed. Cary, N.C.: SAS Institute, 1986.

SAS Statistics Guide for Personal Computers. Version 6 ed. Cary, N.C.: SAS Institute, 1986.
SAS User's Guide: Basics. Version 5 ed. Cary, N.C.: SAS Institute, 1985.
SAS User's Guide: Statistics. Version 5 ed. Cary, N.C.: SAS Institute, 1985.
SPSSX User's Guide. Chicago: SPSS, 1983.
STUDENT. "The Probable Error of a Mean." *Biometrica* 6 (1908): 1–25. The crucial article on the *t* distribution.

Chapter Eleven
Hypothesis Testing

Inferences about population parameters can be made in two ways: We can estimate the parameters and construct confidence intervals around the estimates, or we can make decisions about the parameters by testing hypotheses.

For example, suppose a traffic engineer wants to know the mean number of cars that pass through a particular intersection on weekday mornings between 8 A.M. and 9 A.M. The engineer would probably obtain data for a sample of days and calculate the sample mean to estimate the population mean μ. Finally, he or she could construct a confidence interval to place bounds on the possible sampling error.

In contrast, suppose the engineer knows from years of experience that the average number of cars passing through the intersection between 8 A.M. and 9 A.M. is 2500. New traffic lights have been installed and the engineer wants to determine if the new system increases the traffic flow. Thus, the engineer wants to test the hypothesis that the mean is still 2500 cars per day against the alternative hypothesis that the mean is greater than 2500. This is a typical example of hypothesis testing.

To determine if the mean is 2500 or greater than 2500, the engineer observes the traffic flow on a random sample of, say, 25 days and computes the sample mean and sample standard deviation. Suppose the sample mean is $\bar{x} = 2800$ cars and the sample standard deviation is $s = 250$. What should the engineer conclude? It is not impossible to observe a sample mean of 2800 if the true mean is 2500, but it is very unlikely if the sample standard deviation is only 250. If the mean was 2500 or lower, the probability of observing a sample mean as high as 2800 would be very small. Thus, the engineer concludes that the population mean exceeds 2500.

The hypothesis being tested, that the mean is 2500, is called the *null hypothesis*. The decision to reject this hypothesis is based on the value of the sample mean, which serves as a *test statistic*. The entire set of values that the test statistic can assume is divided into two subsets, one corresponding to the *rejection region* and the other to the *acceptance region*. For the engineer, the rejection region would contain values of $\overline{X}$ that are far above the hypothesized value $\mu = 2500$. If the test statistic computed from a sample assumes a value in the rejection region, the null hypothesis is rejected in favor of the alternative hypothesis. If the test statistic falls in the acceptance region, then the null hypothesis is not rejected.

A problem in testing any hypothesis is deciding which values of the test statistic to assign to the rejection region and which to the acceptance region. For example, should the value $\bar{x} = 2600$ be assigned to the acceptance or rejection region? The answer to this question depends on the risks you are willing to take and the costs of making a mistake.

For example, since the new traffic light system in the example described above is very expensive, the engineer definitely wants to avoid the mistake of concluding that the mean is greater than 2500 if, in fact, it is not. This mistake, called a *Type I error,* occurs when we incorrectly reject a null hypothesis that is true. To avoid this mistake, the engineer would decide to reject the null hypothesis only if $\bar{X}$ far exceeds 2500. Suppose the engineer uses the *decision rule* "Reject the null hypothesis if $\bar{X} \geq 2600$." The value 2600 is then the *critical value* of the test statistic that separates the rejection region from the acceptance region.

Even if the true value of μ were 2500, it would still be possible (though unlikely) to obtain a sample mean exceeding 2600. If this happened, the engineer would incorrectly reject the null hypothesis and commit a Type I error. The probability of such an error is called the *level of significance* of the test. By increasing the critical value to, say, 2650, the engineer would decrease the probability of committing a Type I error but make it easier to commit a *Type II error,* which occurs when we accept the null hypothesis when it is false.

For example, suppose the new traffic light system actually increases the hourly traffic flow to 2650 cars. If the true mean is 2650, the probability is .5 that the sample mean will be less than 2650. Thus, if the engineer used the critical value 2650, the probability would be .5 that the null hypothesis would not be rejected. Thus, the probability of a Type II error would be .5.

To decrease this probability, the engineer could decrease the critical value to, say, 2600. However, by doing so he or she would then raise the probability of a Type I error. Thus, the choice of an appropriate critical value plays a crucial role in hypothesis testing. We will now discuss the elements of a hypothesis test in more detail and provide examples of various types of tests.

11.1 ▪ *Concepts of Hypothesis Testing*

A population parameter is a number that describes some characteristic of a population, and a hypothesis is a statement about the value or set of values that a parameter or group of parameters can take. Many types of hypotheses can be tested by statistical methods.

Frequently we are concerned about the value of a single parameter such as a population mean, a population variance, or a population proportion. At other times we may wish to test a hypothesis that the means of two different populations are equal or that the proportions of two different populations possessing a certain characteristic are equal. In these cases we are testing hypotheses that involve parameters of two populations. We can generalize this concept to the problem of testing a hypothesis about k population means or proportions.

In this chapter we discuss how to test hypotheses about a single population mean, a single population proportion, and a single population variance. In Chapter 12 we discuss how to test hypotheses about the difference between two population means and two population proportions. In Chapters 13 and 14, we extend this theory to cover tests of hypotheses concerning three or more means or proportions. Also in Chapter 14, we discuss how to test hypotheses about the equality of two population variances.

The Null Hypothesis H_0 and the Alternative Hypothesis H_1

The purpose of hypothesis testing is to choose between two conflicting hypotheses about the possible value of a population parameter. The two conflicting hypotheses are called the *null hypothesis,* denoted H_0, and the *alternative hypothesis,* denoted H_1. These two hypotheses are mutually exclusive; that is, when one is true, the other must be false.

Definition: Null Hypothesis and Alternative Hypothesis

The **null hypothesis** is an assumption concerning the value of the population parameter being studied. The **alternative hypothesis** specifies all possible values of the population parameter that are not specified in the null hypothesis.

In some hypotheses, only one particular value of the population parameter is specified; in other hypotheses, a range of values is specified. Conclusions about the validity of these hypotheses are based on information obtained from random samples of observations collected from the populations of interest.

Suppose some hypothesis has been formed about the parameter being studied. We will not reject this hypothesis, which is the null hypothesis, unless the sample data provide strong evidence that the hypothesis is false.

Example 11.1

Null Hypothesis About a Population Proportion: In 1987 the Environmental Protection Agency reported that the emissions equipment had been tampered with on 20% of the cars and trucks in the United States. Suppose you want to test this claim because you think this proportion is too high. In this example, the null hypothesis would be written

$$H_0\colon p = .20$$

where p represents the proportion of emissions systems that have been tampered with. ■

In Example 11.1, the null hypothesis is a statement about a population proportion p that may be true or false. We will not reject the hypothesis unless we obtain strong evidence indicating that it is false. Before performing the test, we must formulate an alternative hypothesis, denoted H_1, against which the null hypothesis is tested. For example, we could test the null hypothesis against the alternative hypothesis that the true population proportion is less than .20. In this case, the alternative hypothesis would be denoted

$$H_1\colon p < .20$$

Definition: Simple Hypothesis and Composite Hypothesis

If a hypothesis states that a certain population parameter θ equals a single specific value, such as $\theta = \theta_0$, then the hypothesis is said to be a **simple hypothesis.** This simple null hypothesis can be expressed as follows:

$$H_0: \theta = \theta_0$$

When the hypothesis contains a range of possible values for the parameter of interest, then the hypothesis is said to be a **composite hypothesis**. Examples of composite null hypotheses and their respective alternative hypotheses about a parameter θ are as follows:

$$H_0: \theta \geq \theta_0$$
$$H_1: \theta < \theta_0$$

and

$$H_0: \theta \leq \theta_0$$
$$H_1: \theta > \theta_0$$

In Example 11.1, the null hypothesis, H_0: $p = .20$, is a simple null hypothesis, and the alternative hypothesis, H_1: $p < .20$, is a composite alternative hypothesis. This alternative hypothesis is called a *one-sided alternative hypothesis* because all possible values of p in H_1 fall below $p = .20$, the value specified in H_0.

Example 11.2

One-Sided Alternative Hypothesis: Suppose that a government inspector is concerned about whether a particular cereal producer is putting an average of at least 32 ounces of cereal into each box as claimed. In this case, it would be natural for the null hypothesis to be that the average amount of cereal in the boxes is at least 32 ounces and for the alternative hypothesis to be that the company is putting less than 32 ounces of cereal into the boxes. The null hypothesis is thus

$$H_0: \mu \geq 32$$

and the alternative hypothesis is

$$H_1: \mu < 32$$

Because this alternative hypothesis lies entirely on one side of the null hypothesis, it is a one-sided alternative hypothesis. ■

On some occasions, we might want to test a simple null hypothesis against a two-sided alternative hypothesis.

Example 11.3

Two-Sided Alternative Hypothesis: The Kemco Company has purchased several new and less expensive pumps to remove water from flooded mines and construction sites. Kemco wants to compare them to the standard model pumps that the company has been using. Kemco may or may not switch exclusively to the new model depending on how well it performs compared to the standard model. Kemco knows that the standard models remove 5000 gallons of water per hour on the average, and wants to test whether the new model is better or worse than the standard model. The null hypothesis is

$$H_0: \mu = 5000$$

where μ represents the mean amount of water pumped in an hour by the new machines. The alternative hypothesis is the *two-sided alternative*

$$H_1: \mu \neq 5000$$

■

In Example 11.3, H_1 is a two-sided alternative hypothesis because it contains values of μ on both sides of the point specified in H_0.

The following formats show three common sets of the null hypothesis H_0 and the alternative hypothesis H_1:

1. Test $H_0: \theta = \theta_0$ against $H_1: \theta \neq \theta_0$ (two-sided test)
2. Test $H_0: \theta \geqslant \theta_0$ against $H_1: \theta < \theta_0$ (one-sided test)
3. Test $H_0: \theta \leqslant \theta_0$ against $H_1: \theta > \theta_0$ (one-sided test)

Sometimes we are not interested in the inequalities stated in the null hypotheses in formats 2 and 3; instead these hypotheses might be expressed as follows:

4. Test $H_0: \theta = \theta_0$ against $H_1: \theta < \theta_0$.
5. Test $H_0: \theta = \theta_0$ against $H_1: \theta > \theta_0$.

Students frequently confuse which hypothesis to call the null hypothesis and which to call the alternative hypothesis. In many statistical applications, the null hypothesis should correspond to the assumption that no change occurs when some new process or technique is tried, as was the case in Example 11.3 where the null hypothesis claims that the new pumps remove exactly the same amount of water as the old pumps. This explains the origin of the name "null" hypothesis, indicating no change between an old and a new situation.

Some statisticians argue that the null hypothesis should be the hypothesis that the decision maker wants to disprove. That is, the null hypothesis should specify the value(s) of the population parameter that the researcher thinks does not represent the true value(s) of the parameter; the alternative hypothesis then specifies those values of the parameter that the researcher believes do hold. The researcher then tests whether the sample data lead to rejection of H_0 and acceptance of H_1. Another common practice is to assign no special meaning to either the null or the alternative hypothesis, but to let these hypotheses merely represent two different assumptions about the population parameter.

How do we decide whether the null hypothesis should be simple or composite? In some cases, the choice arises quite naturally from the statement of the problem, as illustrated in the following examples.

Example 11.4

Choosing a Null and Alternative Hypothesis I: The Better Business Bureau is investigating a meat company that sells ground beef in 5-pound packages. There have been many complaints that the company is short-weighting its customers. The null hypothesis would be

$$H_0: \mu \geqslant 5$$

The Better Business Bureau (and a jury) will accept the null hypothesis unless the data strongly suggest that the null hypothesis is false. We have no interest in whether the mean is actually greater than 5. Thus, the null hypothesis could also be

$$H_0\colon \mu = 5$$

As far as we are concerned, either the mean is 5 or the mean is less than 5. The alternative hypothesis would thus be

$$H_1\colon \mu < 5$$

■

Example 11.5

Choosing a Null and Alternative Hypothesis II: A company produces light bulbs for use in traffic signals in New York City. The average life of these light bulbs is 2000 hours. Because it is very expensive to replace bulbs, the city wants to purchase the lights having the longest expected life for a given price. A second company claims that it produces better bulbs at the same cost. The city wants to examine a sample of the new bulbs to test if, on the average, they last more than 2000 hours. Because the new bulbs cost the same as the old bulbs, the city would not switch to the new bulbs unless the evidence was strong that the new bulbs outlast the old. When testing the new bulbs, the null hypothesis would be

$$H_0\colon \mu \leqslant 2000$$

The alternative hypothesis would then be

$$H_1\colon \mu > 2000$$

■

Example 11.6

Choosing a Null and Alternative Hypothesis III: A company produces a product that is used regularly by 30% of the people in a country; that is, $p = .30$, where p represents the proportion of people who use the product. The company has used a standard advertising approach for many years and is reluctant to change its ads unless strong evidence exists that a new advertising campaign would increase the proportion of people who use the product. New ads are used in a sample of cities to determine if they are more effective than the old. The company would test the null hypothesis

$$H_0\colon p \leqslant .30$$

against the alternative hypothesis

$$H_1\colon p > .30$$

In this example we are comparing the effects of a new advertising format with the effects of the old. The null hypothesis represents the status quo, or the state of affairs without the proposed change. The alternative hypothesis represents the state of affairs if the change has the effect claimed by its proponents. ■

Example 11.7

Choosing a Null and Alternative Hypothesis IV: Under controlled laboratory conditions, a car door painted with standard paint will rust in 5 years on the average when subjected to a certain amount of dampness. A scientist claims that by using a new type of paint on the door, the rust can be retarded. The car company will not accept the scientist's claim unless the evidence strongly supports it. Thus, the null hypothesis would be

$$H_0\colon \mu \leqslant 5$$

and the alternative hypothesis would be

$$H_1\colon \mu > 5$$

where μ is the average number of years before rust develops on treated car doors. ■

How the null and alternative hypotheses are formulated can have important consequences, because, in classical hypothesis testing, we do not reject the null hypothesis unless we have strong evidence against it. Thus, the null hypothesis is in a favored position relative to the alternative hypothesis. The null hypothesis has the status of a maintained hypothesis that will not be rejected because it is assumed to be true *unless the sample data provide strong contrary evidence*.

Example 11.8 **Consequences of Choosing H_0 and H_1:** Consider the problem faced by the officials of the Food and Drug Administration (FDA) when they are asked to approve a new medicine for sale to the public. There are two possibilities:

1. The medicine is beneficial.
2. The medicine is not beneficial.

Either of these possibilities could be chosen as the null, or maintained, hypothesis. The FDA uses the null hypothesis

H_0: The medicine is not beneficial and should not be marketed.

The alternative hypothesis is thus

H_1: The medicine is beneficial and should be marketed.

Thus, the FDA will not approve a new medicine unless the drug manufacturer can produce strong evidence that the null hypothesis is false. Because of this method of choosing H_0 and H_1, getting a new medicine approved in the United States is quite difficult.

There are various costs and benefits from choosing H_0 and H_1 in this way. The potential benefit is that it is very difficult to get harmful medicines onto the market, but the potential cost is that beneficial drugs can be delayed or even prohibited from being marketed. This cost can be enormous in terms of the pain (or death) suffered by individuals who could have been cured by a drug if it had been approved.

Now consider what would happen if the FDA used the following null and alternative hypotheses:

H_0: The medicine is beneficial and should be marketed.

H_1: The medicine is not beneficial and should not be marketed.

In this case, it would be assumed that a drug was beneficial and would not be prohibited unless there were strong evidence that it was ineffective or harmful. There would be a benefit and a cost involved in this choice of H_0, as well. The benefit of this procedure would be that if a drug was beneficial, it would not be delayed from reaching the market and patients would be cured more quickly; the cost would be that harmful drugs could reach the market relatively easily. ■

Example 11.8 shows that when performing a test, we should keep in mind the potential costs and benefits associated with a decision. In the United States, officials for the FDA feel that the potential costs of approving a harmful drug are so high that they make it very difficult to get a new drug approved. This viewpoint is an important factor in determining which drugs get approval and how long it takes to get approval.

When testing a hypothesis, we would like to be able to calculate a probability such as

$$P(\text{theory is true} \mid \text{observed data})$$

This notation represents the probability that a theory is true given the available data. Instead, we actually calculate the conditional probability,

$$P(\text{observed data} \mid \text{theory is true})$$

That is, what we actually determine is the probability that the data would look as they do if the theory were true.

These are two very different probabilities, and recognizing the difference is crucial to understanding the meaning and limitations of classical hypothesis tests. A hypothesis test is an attempted proof by statistical contradiction. For any particular theory, statisticians can deduce that if the theory is true, a sample of data is likely to look a certain way and unlikely to look some other way. If the observed sample data are of the likely kind, then they are consistent with the theory and tend to confirm it. If, on the other hand, the data are of the unlikely kind, then the data are not consistent with the theory, and the theory is rejected.

Of course, we cannot be certain that we are correct in rejecting a theory because the unlikely may well happen. Note also that not rejecting the null hypothesis is a relatively weak conclusion, because there can often be many other theories that would be consistent with the data.

Decision Rules

Based on the information provided by the sample, we must make a decision concerning the null hypothesis. There are two possibilities, namely, rejecting the null hypothesis H_0 in favor of the alternative H_1 or not rejecting H_0. Occasionally statisticians say that the null hypothesis is "accepted," but it is more common to say that the null hypothesis is "not rejected."

In a sense, a statistical test is like a trial by jury. Like the defendant in a criminal case, the null hypothesis is on trial. Also like the defendant, the null hypothesis is given the benefit of the doubt and assumed to be true unless the sample data provide strong evidence indicating that it is false. Note that in a jury trial, two types of mistakes can be made: Innocent people can be convicted, and criminals can be acquitted. Similarly, in hypothesis testing, two types of mistakes are possible: We can reject a null hypothesis that is correct (Type I error), or we can accept a null hypothesis that is incorrect (Type II error).

Before arriving at a conclusion, we need some *decision rule* for when to reject H_0. The decision to reject the null hypothesis is based on a *test statistic* such as a sample mean $\overline{X}$, a sample proportion $\hat{p}$, a Z score, or a t score. We will show how to use these statistics to test hypotheses as we proceed through this chapter.

Definition: Test Statistic

A **test statistic** is a random variable whose value is used to determine whether we reject the null hypothesis.

Definition: Decision Rule

The **decision rule** specifies the set of values of the test statistic for which the null hypothesis H_0 is rejected in favor of H_1 and the set of values for which H_0 is accepted (i.e., not rejected).

The decision rule separates the set of possible values of the test statistic into two exhaustive and mutually exclusive regions, the *acceptance region* and the *rejection region* (or *critical region*).

Definition: Rejection Region and Acceptance Region

The **rejection region** of a test, also called the **critical region**, consists of all values of the test statistic for which H_0 is rejected. The **acceptance region** consists of all values of the test statistic for which H_0 is accepted (not rejected).

When the alternative hypothesis is one-sided, the entire rejection region falls on one side of the acceptance region. When the alternative hypothesis is two-sided, part of the rejection region lies on either side of the acceptance region.

Definition: Critical Value

A **critical value** of the test statistic is the value that separates the critical region from the acceptance region.

A one-sided alternative hypothesis has one critical value, while a two-sided alternative hypothesis has two. These ideas will be developed in more detail in Section 11.2.

Type I and Type II Errors

There are four possible outcomes of any hypothesis test, two of which are correct and two of which are incorrect (see Table 11.1):

1. H_0 is true and we do not reject H_0 (correct decision).
2. H_0 is false and we reject H_0 (correct decision).
3. H_0 is true and we reject H_0 (incorrect decision—Type I error).
4. H_0 is false and we do not reject H_0 (incorrect decision—Type II error).

The two types of error are given special names, and it is very important to identify them correctly. If we reject the null hypothesis when in fact it is true (outcome 3), we commit a *Type I error.* If we accept the null hypothesis (or fail to reject it) when it is actually false and some other hypothesis is true (outcome 4), we commit a *Type II error.* Table 11.1 shows the four possible situations in hypothesis testing. A Type I error occurs if the test statistic falls in the rejection region even though the null hypothesis is true. The probability of making a Type I error is called the *level of significance* of the test and is denoted by the symbol α (Greek alpha).

TABLE 11.1
Four possible outcomes of a hypothesis test

Decision	Actual Situation: H_0 True	Actual Situation: H_0 False
H_0 not rejected	Correct decision	Type II error
H_0 rejected	Type I error	Correct decision

Definition: Type I and Type II Errors

A **Type I error** occurs if we reject H_0 when H_0 is true. A **Type II error** occurs if we accept (do not reject) H_0 when H_0 is false.

Definition: Level of Significance

The **level of significance** of a test is the probability that the test statistic falls in the critical region given that H_0 is true. The level of significance is denoted by the symbol α where

$$\begin{aligned} \alpha &= P(\text{Type I error}) \\ &= P(H_0 \text{ reject} | H_0 \text{ true}) \\ &= P(\text{test statistic in rejection region} | H_0 \text{ true}) \end{aligned}$$

The notation "$P(H_0 \text{ reject}|H_0 \text{ true})$" denotes the probability that we reject the null hypothesis H_0 *given that* the null hypothesis H_0 is true. That is, the vertical line is read "given that."

Definition: Probability of a Type II Error

The probability of making a Type II error is denoted by the symbol β (Greek beta). The probability β of making a Type II error is the probability that the test statistic falls in the acceptance region when the null hypothesis is false. In symbols, we have

$$\beta = P(\text{test statistic in acceptance region} | H_0 \text{ false})$$

Example 11.9

Example of a Type I Error: In 1987 *USA Today* reported that a secret government survey found that illegal gambling amounts to at least \$200 per year per adult in the United States. Suppose you feel that this figure is too high. You take a random sample of n individuals to estimate the mean amount of illegal gambling per person. You want to test the null hypothesis

$$H_0: \mu \geqslant \$200$$

against the alternative hypothesis

$$H_1: \mu < \$200$$

Suppose that H_0 is in fact true but you obtain a sample mean $\bar{x}$ that is much lower than \$200. Based on this sample information, you reject H_0 in favor of H_1. In this case, you would be making a Type I error because you rejected H_0 when H_0 was true.

Note that this Type I error occurred because of bad luck. Although H_0 is true, you were unlucky because you obtained a sample that led you to believe that H_0 was false. ■

Example 11.10

Example of a Type II Error: In Example 11.9, suppose that the amount of illegal gambling is actually much less than \$200 per person per year. Thus, H_0 is false and H_1 is true. However, suppose you obtain a sample mean $\bar{x}$ that is close to \$200 and thus decide that the evidence is not strong enough to make you reject H_0. You would then be making a Type II error, because you would not reject H_0 when it was false.

Note that like the Type I error in Example 11.9, this Type II error occurred because of bad luck. Although H_0 was false, you were unlucky in that you obtained a sample that led you to believe that H_0 was true. ■

Implications of Rejecting or Accepting the Null Hypothesis

When the test statistic falls in the rejection region, this does not *prove* that the null hypothesis is false. Rather, it indicates that we should have strong doubts concerning the truth of the null hypothesis. Either the null hypothesis is false, or we have observed a very unlikely event that should occur with a small probability (less than α). Similarly, when the test statistic falls in the acceptance region, this does not *prove* that the null hypothesis is true, but merely indicates that the evidence is not strong enough to make us reject the null hypothesis.

Because the null hypothesis is assumed to be true before the test, it is not rejected unless the data provide strong contrary evidence. Usually we choose some small number, such as .05 or .01, as the level of significance of the test, thereby guaranteeing that the probability is low that we will reject a true null hypothesis.

If we have only a small sample of data, it is not likely that we will be able to reject an incorrect null hypothesis unless the hypothesis is wildly in error. Thus, accepting a null hypothesis on the basis of a small sample of information does not necessarily say a great deal in favor of the hypothesis. As the number of sample observations increases, however, it becomes more likely that we will detect a false null hypothesis.

Cost Analysis and Practical Significance

Statistical significance is not at all the same as practical importance. A statistically significant result is one that cannot be reasonably explained by sampling error. Such a result may well be of little or no practical importance. Conversely, a very important result may not appear to be statistically significant because the sample size is too small to allow us to reject the null hypothesis.

Whenever the test statistic falls in the rejection region, we say that the test statistic is *statistically significant* and reject the null hypothesis. Note that the word *significant* here is used in a technical sense and does not imply that the finding is of any practical importance. For example, the manufacturer of a water pump used to drain flooded construction sites may perform a test and conclude that a new model pump produces a statistically significant increase in the average amount of water pumped per hour. In such a case we can feel quite confident that the new pump actually does pump more water than the old. However, the increase might be so small compared with the increased cost of the new pump that switching to the new pump is not economically justified.

Exercises for Section 11.1

1. If we were to compare a one-tailed test and a two-tailed test for a particular population parameter, what difference would we find in the form of the null and alternative hypotheses?

2. In each of the following hypothesis-testing situations, suggest whether a one-tailed test or a two-tailed test is more appropriate. In each case justify your answer and then write a null and alternative hypothesis.

a. A marketing research study is conducted to determine whether the proportion of buyers who favor a particular product is greater than the proportion who favor the product of a competing manufacturer.

b. A study is conducted to determine whether unionized employees in the electronics industry receive benefits different from those who do not belong to a union.

3. When evaluating a loan applicant, a financial officer is faced with the problem of granting loans to people who are good risks and denying loans to people who appear to be poor risks. In effect, the financial officer is testing the null hypothesis

$$H_0\text{: The applicant is a good risk.}$$

against the alternative hypothesis

$$H_1\text{: The applicant is a poor risk.}$$

The officer commits a Type I error when she rejects an applicant who is actually a good risk; she commits a Type II error when she grants a loan to an applicant who is a poor risk. Discuss the selection of a significance level α in the following instances:

a. Lending money is tight, interest rates are high, and loan applicants are numerous.

b. Lending money is plentiful, interest rates are moderate, and there is intense competition for loan applicants.

4. The manager of an exclusive resort hotel believes that the mean guest bill is at least \$250. A sample of billing statements is used to test the manager's claim. Which of the following pairs of hypotheses should be used to test whether the manager's claim is correct? Explain.

$$H_0\text{: } \mu = 250 \qquad H_0\text{: } \mu \leq 250 \qquad H_0\text{: } \mu \geq 250$$

$$H_1\text{: } \mu \neq 250 \qquad H_1\text{: } \mu > 250 \qquad H_1\text{: } \mu < 250$$

5. A quality control inspector tests the dimensions of parts used in a machining operation. Specifications require that the mean diameter of the parts be 2 inches. If a sample leads the quality control inspector to believe that the diameters are too large or too small, the machine is shut down and readjusted. State the appropriate null and alternative hypotheses for determining whether the machine should be shut down.

6. For each of the following situations, indicate whether a correct decision has been made or if a Type I or Type II error has occurred.

a. The null and alternative hypotheses are as follows:

H_0: New system is no better than the old one.

H_1: New system is better.

(1) Adopt new system when new one is better.
(2) Retain old system when new one is better.
(3) Retain old system when new one is not better.
(4) Adopt new system when new one is not better.

b. The null and alternative hypotheses are as follows:

H_0: New product is satisfactory.

H_1: New product is unsatisfactory.

(1) Introduce new product when unsatisfactory.
(2) Do not introduce new product when unsatisfactory.
(3) Do not introduce new product when satisfactory.
(4) Introduce new product when satisfactory.

c. The null and alternative hypotheses are as follows:

H_0: Batch of transistors is of good quality.

H_1: Batch of transistors is of poor quality.

(1) Reject good-quality batch.
(2) Accept good-quality batch.
(3) Reject poor-quality batch.
(4) Accept poor-quality batch.

7. An experiment is carried out to determine whether a new anesthetic results in lower death rates than other anesthetics.

a. What should the null hypothesis be? The alternative hypothesis?
b. What are the consequences of a Type I error? A Type II error?

8. Indicate whether the following statements are true or false. If false, explain why.

a. Committing a Type II error is the same as accepting the alternative hypothesis when it is false.
b. Either a Type I or a Type II error must occur.
c. The significance level is the probability of accepting the null hypothesis when it is true.

9. For the following situation, describe the implications of a Type I or Type II error in nonstatistical terms: The null hypothesis is that a new manufacturing process is no improvement over the existing one. If sample evidence indicates that it is better, the new process will be adopted.

10. For each of the following test situations, specify the null and alternative hypotheses and describe the possible Type I and Type II errors:

a. The mean donation per contributor to a certain charity was \$11.65 before a new public relations program was initiated. A random sample of donations received after the new program went into effect is used to determine whether the mean contribution is now larger.
b. Last year the mean duration of marriages that ended in divorce or annulment in a certain state was 4.7 years. A sociologist wishes to test whether new divorce legislation has changed the mean duration, based on a random sample of divorce records filed since the legislation was enacted.

c. A chemist has developed a process for reducing the amount of sulfur emissions at nuclear power plants. Random samples of emissions treated by this process are obtained to test if the mean sulfur content of the emissions has decreased.

11. Some chemists have invented a cola sweetener that is slightly less expensive than the sweetener now in use. Fearful of bad publicity and expensive lawsuits, the company's president orders some tests to determine whether this new sweetener is carcinogenic.
a. Should the null hypothesis be that it does or does not cause cancer?
b. Should the level of significance be fairly big or very small?

12. A computer software company has devised a new type of spreadsheet unlike any now on the market. The company's president thinks it is equally likely that this idea will be a sensation or a flop. If it does flop, there will be small losses, but if it is a sensation, the gains will be substantial. The president orders a marketing survey to test consumer interest.
a. Should the null hypothesis be that the idea will be a sensation or a flop?
b. What value of α would you recommend?

11.2 ▪ *Testing Hypotheses About a Population Mean When Variance Is Known*

In this section, we use the methodology of Section 11.1 to test hypotheses about the mean of a normal population with a known population variance σ^2. In Section 11.3 we shall see that these assumptions can be relaxed when the sample size is large.

We begin by testing the simple null hypothesis that the population mean is equal to some specified value μ_0. The null hypothesis is denoted

$$H_0: \mu = \mu_0$$

Suppose the alternative hypothesis is the one-sided alternative that the population mean is less than μ_0. Thus, the alternative hypothesis is

$$H_1: \mu < \mu_0$$

Once we have solved this problem, the solutions to other problems with different hypotheses will follow as natural extensions.

It is natural to base a test concerning the population mean on the sample mean $\overline{X}$. If the population is normal (or if the sample size is large), then *when the null hypothesis is true,* the random variable $\overline{X}$ has a normal distribution with mean μ_0 and variance σ^2/n, as shown in Figure 11.1. We would reject H_0 in favor of H_1 only if the observed sample mean $\bar{x}$ was substantially less than μ_0. In Figure 11.1, we would reject H_0 in favor of H_1 when the observed sample mean fell in the left-hand tail of the distribution to the left of a critical value, denoted $\bar{x}^*$. For this test, the rejection region is the set of

FIGURE 11.1
Critical value $\bar{x}^*$ for a one-tailed test.

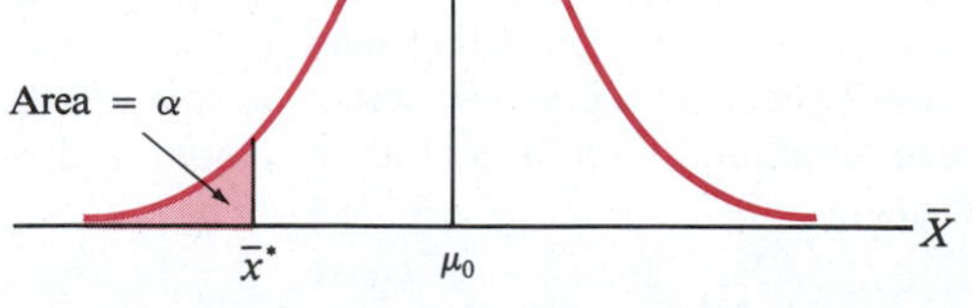

all values of the sample mean less than $\bar{x}^*$, and the acceptance region is the set of all values of the sample mean greater than or equal to $\bar{x}^*$. In Figure 11.1, we need to find the value $\bar{x}^*$ such that the area to its left is α, the level of significance of the test.

When we test H_0: $\mu = \mu_0$ against H_1: $\mu < \mu_0$, we use the decision rule:

> Reject H_0 in favor of H_1 if and only if the observed sample mean $\bar{x}$ is less than the critical value $\bar{x}^*$.

When H_0 is true, the probability of observing a sample mean less than $\bar{x}^*$ is $P(\bar{X} < \bar{x}^*)$. We select $\bar{x}^*$ so that this probability is α, the level of significance of the test. That is, when H_0 is true, the probability of observing a sample mean less than $\bar{x}^*$ is α. If this event occurs, we will reject H_0 even though it is true. Thus, we have designed the test so that the probability of committing a Type I error equals the preassigned value α.

The Critical Value $\bar{x}^*$

If the population is normal with mean μ_0 and variance σ^2, then the random variable $\bar{X}$ follows a normal distribution with mean μ_0 and variance σ^2/n. Thus the random variable

$$Z = \frac{\bar{X} - \mu_0}{\sigma/\sqrt{n}}$$

follows the standard normal distribution $N(0, 1)$. If the area in the left tail of the distribution is α, we have

$$P(Z < -z_\alpha) = \alpha$$

When H_0 is true, we obtain

$$P\left(\frac{\bar{X} - \mu_0}{\sigma/\sqrt{n}} < -z_\alpha\right) = \alpha$$

After multiplying by $\sigma/\sqrt{n}$, we obtain

$$P(\bar{X} - \mu_0 < -z_\alpha\sigma/\sqrt{n}) = \alpha$$

or

$$P(\bar{X} < \mu_0 - z_\alpha\sigma/\sqrt{n}) = \alpha$$

Thus we find that the critical value $\bar{x}^*$ is the value

$$\bar{x}^* = \mu_0 - z_\alpha\sigma/\sqrt{n}$$

Critical Value $\bar{x}^*$

When testing the null hypothesis

$$H_0\text{: } \mu = \mu_0$$

against the one-sided alternative hypothesis

$$H_1\text{: } \mu < \mu_0$$

the critical value $\bar{x}^*$ is

$$\bar{x}^* = \mu_0 - z_\alpha\sigma/\sqrt{n}$$

Whenever the observed sample mean $\bar{x}$ is less than $\bar{x}^*$, the observed Z score

$$z = \frac{\bar{x} - \mu_0}{\sigma/\sqrt{n}}$$

is less than $-z_\alpha$, and vice versa. Thus, the rule that we should reject H_0 if and only if the observed sample mean $\bar{x}$ is less than the critical value $\bar{x}^*$ is equivalent to the decision rule that we should reject H_0 if and only if the observed Z score is less than $-z_\alpha$. This situation is illustrated in Figure 11.2.

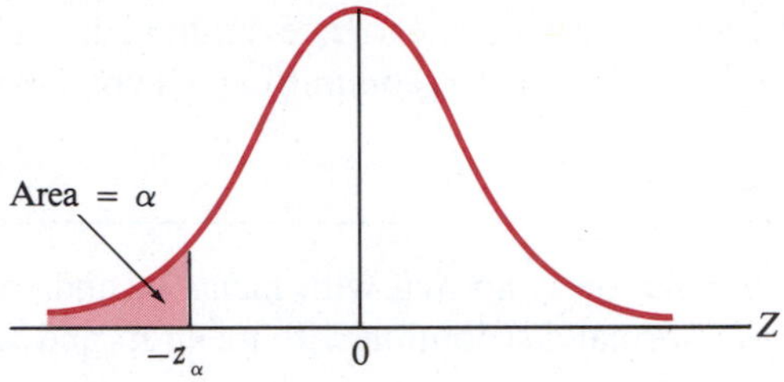

FIGURE 11.2
Critical value $-z_\alpha$ for a one-tailed test.

Procedure for Testing a Hypothesis About a Population Mean

The six-step procedure in the accompanying box summarizes how to test the null hypothesis H_0: $\mu = \mu_0$ against the alternative hypothesis H_1: $\mu < \mu_0$ when the population is normal and the variance is known.

Testing the Mean of a Normal Population with Population Variance Known

Step 1: State H_0 and H_1.

Step 2: Select a level of significance α.

Step 3: Determine the critical value $-z_\alpha$ using Table A.5 in the Appendix.

Step 4: Obtain the sample of n observations and calculate the observed sample mean $\bar{x}$.

Step 5: Calculate the observed Z score

$$z = \frac{\bar{x} - \mu_0}{\sigma/\sqrt{n}}$$

Step 6: Reject H_0 in favor of H_1 if $z < -z_\alpha$. An equivalent decision rule is:

Reject H_0 in favor of H_1 if $\bar{x} < \bar{x}^*$

where $\bar{x}$ is the observed value of the sample mean and where

$$\bar{x}^* = \mu_0 - z_\alpha\sigma/\sqrt{n}.$$

Example 11.11 **Testing a Hypothesis About a Mean of a Normal Population with Known Variance I:** Metaltech Industries manufactures carbide drill tips used in drilling oil wells. The life of a carbide drill tip is measured by how many feet can be drilled before the tip wears out. Metaltech claims that under typical drilling conditions, the life of a carbide tip follows a normal distribution with mean 32 feet and population variance 16. Suppose some customers disagree with Metaltech's claims and argue that Metaltech is overstating the mean. Metaltech agrees to examine a random sample of $n = 25$ carbide tips to test the null hypothesis

$$H_0: \mu = 32$$

against the alternative hypothesis

$$H_1: \mu < 32$$

If the null hypothesis is rejected, Metaltech has agreed to give customers a price rebate on past purchases. Suppose Metaltech decides to use a 5% level of significance and the observed sample mean is $\bar{x} = 29.5$. Test H_0 against H_1.

Solution: To perform the test, we follow the six-step testing procedure.

Step 1: State the null and alternative hypothesis. We have

$$H_0: \mu = 32 \quad \text{and} \quad H_1: \mu < 32$$

Step 2: The level of significance is $\alpha = .05$.
Step 3: From Table A.5, we obtain $-z_\alpha = -z_{.05} = -1.645$.
Step 4: Based on a sample of 25 observations, the sample mean is $\bar{x} = 29.5$ feet.
Step 5: Calculate the observed Z score:

$$z = \frac{\bar{x} - \mu_0}{\sigma/\sqrt{n}} = \frac{29.5 - 32}{4/\sqrt{25}} = -3.125$$

Step 6: Compare the observed Z score $z = -3.125$ with the critical value $-z_\alpha = -1.645$. We reject H_0 in favor of H_1 because the observed Z score is less than the critical value and falls in the rejection region. This situation is illustrated in Figure 11.3.

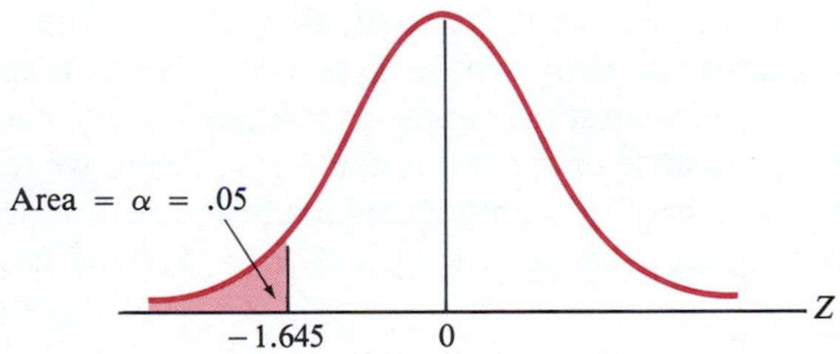

FIGURE 11.3
Critical value $-z_{.05} = -1.645$ associated with the test in Example 11.11.

■

Example 11.12 **Calculation of the Critical Value $\bar{x}^*$:** In Example 11.11, we showed that the critical value of Z was -1.645, so the rejection region consisted of all Z scores less than -1.645. Suppose we decide to use the sample mean as the test statistic rather than the Z score. Let us find the critical value $\bar{x}^*$.

Solution: We have

$$\begin{aligned} \bar{x}^* &= \mu_0 - z_\alpha \sigma/\sqrt{n} \\ &= 32 - 1.645(4/\sqrt{25}) \\ &= 30.684 \end{aligned}$$

This means that rejecting H_0 when $z < -1.645$ is equivalent to rejecting H_0 when the observed sample mean is less than 30.684. Because the observed sample mean is $\bar{x} = 29.5$, we reject H_0 in favor of H_1. ■

In Example 11.11, the fact that we rejected H_0 in favor of H_1 does not mean that we have *proved* that the true population mean is less than 32. Of course, the observed sample mean $\bar{x} = 29.5$ does cast doubt on the truth of the null hypothesis. In the sample of 25 observations, Metaltech obtained a Z score that was substantially less than the critical value -1.645. Metaltech now has two options: (1) It can continue to assume that the null hypothesis H_0: $\mu = 32$ is true, or (2) it can reject H_0 in favor of the alternative hypothesis that $\mu < 32$. Which course of action seems more reasonable? If Metaltech continues to support the null hypothesis, then it must admit that it has obtained a very unlikely sample of observations. That is, if H_0 was true, we would be very unlikely to obtain a sample of observations yielding a Z score less than -1.645. When H_0 is true, we should get a Z score less than -1.645 only 5% of the time. In other words, only 5% of all possible samples from the population would yield a Z score less than the critical value -1.645 if $\mu = 32$. However, if H_0 was *false* (so $\mu < 32$), it would not be so unusual to get a Z score less than -1.645. Thus, if we choose $\alpha = .05$, it is reasonable to reject the null hypothesis H_0: $\mu = 32$ in favor of H_1: $\mu < 32$ in Example 11.11.

Testing a Composite Null Hypothesis

Now consider the difference between testing the simple null hypothesis H_0: $\mu = \mu_0$ against H_1: $\mu < \mu_0$ and testing the composite null hypothesis H_0: $\mu \geqslant \mu_0$ against H_1: $\mu < \mu_0$ at a significance level α. If the population mean is exactly μ_0, the level of significance of each test will be exactly α. That is, if $\mu = \mu_0$, then the probability that the test statistic will fall in the rejection region is exactly α. On the other hand, if in fact $\mu > \mu_0$, then we are even less likely to incorrectly reject H_0. That is, if $\mu > \mu_0$, then the probability that the test statistic will fall in the rejection region is *less* than α and the probability of committing a Type I error is less than α.

When we test the simple hypothesis H_0: $\mu = \mu_0$ against H_1: $\mu < \mu_0$, then the level of significance of the test is exactly α. When we test H_0: $\mu \geqslant \mu_0$ against H_1: $\mu < \mu_0$, then the level of significance of the test is less than or equal to α. Specifically, the significance level is exactly α if $\mu = \mu_0$, and the significance level is less than α if $\mu > \mu_0$.

Testing a Composite Null Hypothesis

To test the composite null hypothesis

$$H_0\colon \mu \geqslant \mu_0$$

against the one-sided alternative hypothesis

$$H_1\colon \mu < \mu_0$$

follow the same six steps as when testing the simple null hypothesis H_0: $\mu = \mu_0$ against H_1: $\mu < \mu_0$.

Now consider the problem of testing the simple null hypothesis

$$H_0: \mu = \mu_0$$

against the one-sided alternative hypothesis

$$H_1: \mu > \mu_0$$

In this case, we would doubt the validity of the null hypothesis if the sample mean was substantially *greater than* the hypothesized value μ_0. Once again, if the population is normal and the variance is known, the random variable

$$Z = \frac{\overline{X} - \mu_0}{\sigma/\sqrt{n}}$$

follows the standard normal distribution. Because Z is a standard normal variable, we have

$$P(Z > z_\alpha) = \alpha$$

After substituting for Z we obtain the decision rules given in the accompanying box. For this test, the rejection region consists of all observed Z scores greater than z_α. Equivalently, the rejection region consists of all values of the sample mean greater than the critical value $\bar{x}^*$.

Testing a Simple Null Hypothesis: Normal Population with Known Variance

To test the null hypothesis

$$H_0: \mu = \mu_0$$

against the alternative hypothesis

$$H_1: \mu > \mu_0$$

use the decision rule

$$\text{Reject } H_0 \text{ in favor of } H_1 \text{ if } z > z_\alpha.$$

An equivalent decision rule is

$$\text{Reject } H_0 \text{ in favor of } H_1 \text{ if } \bar{x} > \bar{x}^*,$$

where the critical value is $\bar{x}^* = \mu_0 + z_\alpha \sigma/\sqrt{n}$.

When the alternative hypothesis is one-sided, the entire rejection region is placed under one tail of the distribution of the test statistic. When the alternative hypothesis is

$$H_1: \mu > \mu_0$$

the entire rejection region is placed under the right tail of the distribution. When the alternative hypothesis is

$$H_1: \mu < \mu_0$$

the entire critical region is placed under the left tail of the distribution.

The most frequently used levels of significance are 10%, 5%, and 1%. The following table shows the most common critical values z_α and $-z_\alpha$ used in one-tailed tests:

Level of Significance α	Critical Z Score $H_1: \mu < \mu_0$	$H_1: \mu > \mu_0$
10%	$-z_{.10} = -1.28$	$z_{.10} = 1.28$
5%	$-z_{.05} = -1.645$	$z_{.05} = 1.645$
1%	$-z_{.01} = -2.33$	$z_{.01} = 2.33$

Example 11.13 **Testing a Hypothesis About a Mean of a Normal Population with Known Variance II:** A teachers' union is on strike for higher wages. The union claims that the mean salary for teachers is at most \$25,000 per year, but a state legislator thinks that it is higher than \$25,000 per year. The legislator does not want to reject the union's claim, however, unless the evidence is very strong against it. Because of this, a 1% level of significance is chosen. The legislator wants to test the null hypothesis

$$H_0: \mu \leq \$25{,}000$$

against the one-sided alternative hypothesis

$$H_1: \mu > \$25{,}000$$

Assume that salaries follow a normal distribution and that the population standard deviation is known to be $\sigma = \$4000$. A random sample of $n = 100$ teachers is obtained, and the sample mean is $\bar{x} = \$27{,}000$. Perform the test.

Solution: To perform the test, follow the six-step testing procedure. For level of significance $\alpha = .01$, the critical value is $z_\alpha = z_{.01} = 2.33$. Because the observed sample mean is $\bar{x} = \$27{,}000$, the Z score is

$$z = \frac{\bar{x} - \mu_0}{\sigma/\sqrt{n}} = \frac{27{,}000 - 25{,}000}{4000/\sqrt{100}} = 5.0$$

Because $z = 5.0$ exceeds the critical value $z_\alpha = 2.33$ and falls in the rejection region, we reject H_0 in favor of H_1. This situation is illustrated in Figure 11.4.

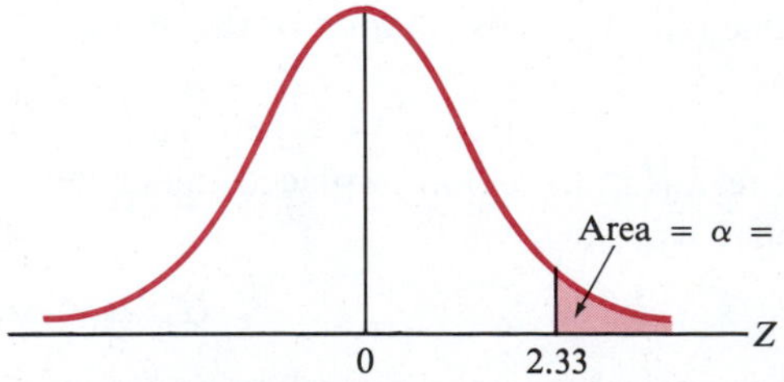

FIGURE 11.4
One-tailed test for Example 11.13.

■

A Two-Tailed Test of the Population Mean

Now consider the test of the simple null hypothesis

$$H_0: \mu = \mu_0$$

against the two-sided alternative hypothesis

$$H_1: \mu \neq \mu_0$$

In performing this test, it is assumed that we have no reason to suspect that the population mean is on one side or the other of the hypothesized value μ_0. Thus we would reject H_0 if the observed sample mean was much greater than μ_0 or much less. Once again, if the population is normal with variance σ^2, then the Z score

$$Z = \frac{\overline{X} - \mu_0}{\sigma/\sqrt{n}}$$

follows the standard normal distribution. For a level of significance α, we have

$$P(Z < -z_{\alpha/2}) = \alpha/2 \quad \text{and} \quad P(Z > z_{\alpha/2}) = \alpha/2$$

Thus, the probability that Z exceeds $z_{\alpha/2}$ or is less than $-z_{\alpha/2}$ is α. We reject the null hypothesis if the observed Z score is less than $-z_{\alpha/2}$ or greater than $z_{\alpha/2}$.

Performing a Two-Tailed Test of a Mean of a Normal Population

Assume the population is normal and the variance is known. To test the null hypothesis

$$H_0: \mu = \mu_0$$

against the two-sided alternative hypothesis

$$H_1: \mu \neq \mu_0$$

select a level of significance α and find the critical values $-z_{\alpha/2}$ and $z_{\alpha/2}$ using Table A.5 in the Appendix. Obtain the sample of n observations and calculate the observed sample mean $\bar{x}$. Then calculate the observed Z score

$$z = \frac{\bar{x} - \mu_0}{\sigma/\sqrt{n}}$$

and use the decision rule:

Reject H_0 in favor of H_1 if $z < -z_{\alpha/2}$ or if $z > z_{\alpha/2}$.

An equivalent decision rule is

Reject H_0 if $\bar{x} < \bar{x}_1^*$ or if $\bar{x} > \bar{x}_2^*$,

where the critical values that separate the acceptance region from the rejection region are

$$\bar{x}_1^* = \mu_0 - z_{\alpha/2}\sigma/\sqrt{n} \quad \text{and} \quad \bar{x}_2^* = \mu_0 + z_{\alpha/2}\sigma/\sqrt{n}$$

Thus, if the alternative hypothesis is two-sided, we perform a *two-tailed test* because part of the rejection region is placed in each tail of the distribution of the test statistic. This is illustrated in Figure 11.5.

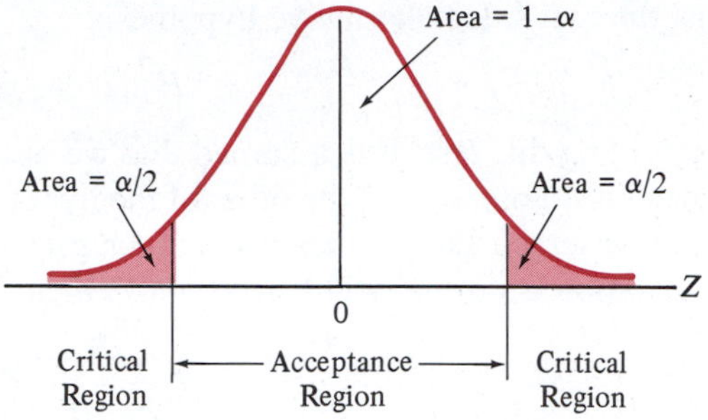

FIGURE 11.5
Critical values $-z_{\alpha/2}$ and $z_{\alpha/2}$ for a two-tailed test.

As with one-tailed tests, the most commonly used values for the level of significance α are 10%, 5%, and 1%. The following table shows the most commonly used critical values $z_{\alpha/2}$ and $-z_{\alpha/2}$ when performing a two-tailed test:

Level of Signifi-cance α	Critical Z Score $H_1: \mu \neq \mu_0$
10%	$-z_{.05} = -1.645$ and $z_{.05} = 1.645$
5%	$-z_{.025} = -1.96$ and $z_{.025} = 1.96$
1%	$-z_{.005} = -2.58$ and $z_{.005} = 2.58$

Example 11.14 **A Two-Tailed Test of a Mean of a Normal Population with Known Variance:** Members of Congress regularly tour foreign countries on fact-finding missions. A newspaper claims that daily expenditures of individuals on such junkets are normally distributed with mean \$300 and standard deviation $\sigma = \$50$. To test this claim, a random sample of 25 people is obtained. Because we have no reason to suspect that the true mean is greater than \$300 rather than less than \$300, it is natural to test the simple null hypothesis

$$H_0: \mu = 300$$

against the composite two-sided alternative hypothesis

$$H_1: \mu \neq 300$$

Suppose the sample mean is $\bar{x} = \$260$. Test the null hypothesis using a 5% level of significance.

Solution: For level of significance $\alpha = .05$, the two critical values are $z_1 = -z_{\alpha/2} = -1.96$ and $z_2 = z_{\alpha/2} = 1.96$. Thus the rejection region contains all Z scores less than -1.96 or greater than 1.96. The observed Z score is

$$z = \frac{\bar{x} - \mu_0}{\sigma/\sqrt{n}} = \frac{260 - 300}{50/\sqrt{25}} = -4$$

The test statistic falls in the rejection region because the observed Z score $z = -4$ is less than the critical value $z_1 = -1.96$, and so we reject H_0 in favor of H_1. See Figure 11.6. It appears that the population mean is less than the \$300 claimed in the newspaper.

FIGURE 11.6
Two-tailed test for Example 11.14.

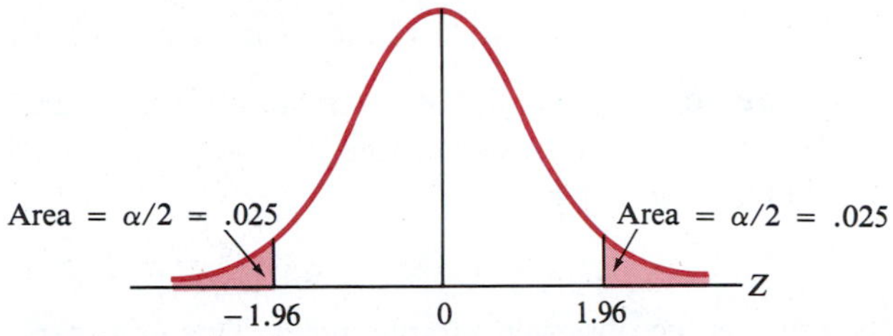

Example 11.15 **Finding the Critical Values of $\overline{X}$ for a Two-Tailed Test:** For Example 11.14, find the critical values of $\overline{X}$ that separate the critical region from the acceptance region.

Solution: Because we have used a two-tailed test, there are two critical values of $\overline{X}$. We obtain

$$\bar{x}_1^* = \mu_0 - z_{\alpha/2}\sigma/\sqrt{n} = 300 - 1.96(50/\sqrt{25}) = 280.40$$

and

$$\bar{x}_2^* = \mu_0 + z_{\alpha/2}\sigma/\sqrt{n} = 300 + 1.96(50/\sqrt{25}) = 319.60$$

See Figure 11.7.

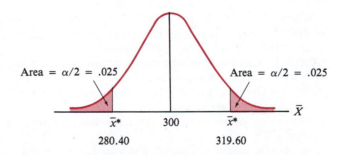

FIGURE 11.7
Critical values for the two-tailed test in Example 11.15.

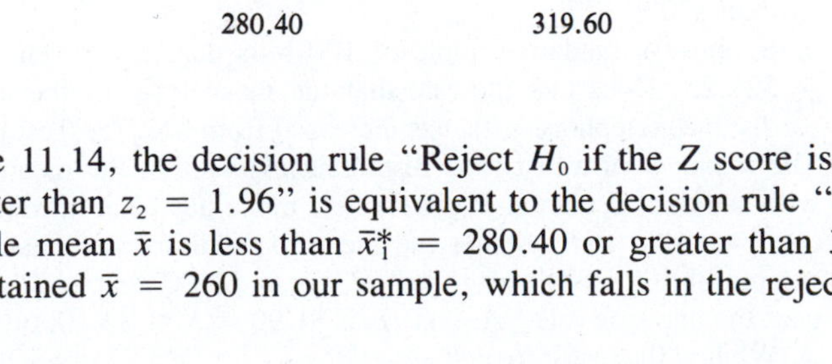

In Example 11.14, the decision rule "Reject H_0 if the Z score is less than $z_1 = -1.96$ or greater than $z_2 = 1.96$" is equivalent to the decision rule "Reject H_0 if the observed sample mean $\bar{x}$ is less than $\bar{x}_1^* = 280.40$ or greater than $\bar{x}_2^* = 319.60$." Because we obtained $\bar{x} = 260$ in our sample, which falls in the rejection region, we reject H_0.

Two-Sided Hypothesis Tests and Confidence Intervals

There is a close connection between performing a two-tailed test with a level of significance α and calculating a confidence interval having level of significance $(1 - \alpha)$. As already stated, for a two-tailed test using level of significance α, the acceptance region consists of all values of the sample mean between

$$\bar{x}_1^* = \mu_0 - z_{\alpha/2}\sigma/\sqrt{n} \quad \text{and} \quad \bar{x}_2^* = \mu_0 + z_{\alpha/2}\sigma/\sqrt{n}$$

Thus we accept H_0 if and only if the observed sample mean $\bar{x}$ is less than $z_{\alpha/2}\sigma/\sqrt{n}$ units from the hypothesized value μ_0. A $100(1 - \alpha)\%$ confidence interval for the population takes the form

$$(\bar{x} - z_{\alpha/2}\sigma/\sqrt{n}, \bar{x} + z_{\alpha/2}\sigma/\sqrt{n})$$

where $\bar{x}$ is the observed sample mean. This confidence interval contains all values of μ that are less than $(z_{\alpha/2}\sigma/\sqrt{n})$ units from $\bar{x}$. Thus, the $100(1 - \alpha)\%$ confidence interval for μ contains all possible values of μ_0 that would not be rejected if we performed a two-tailed test to test H_0: $\mu = \mu_0$ against H_1: $\mu \neq \mu_0$ using level of significance α.

Exercises for Section 11.2

1. Suppose we test the null hypothesis

$$H_0: \mu = \mu_0$$

against the one-sided alternative hypothesis

$$H_1: \mu > \mu_0$$

using $\alpha = .05$. Suppose we accept the null hypothesis.

a. Does this necessarily imply that μ_0 is contained in the 95% confidence interval for μ?

b. Does this necessarily imply that μ_0 is contained in the 90% confidence interval for μ, if the observed sample mean is bigger than μ_0?

2. Records indicate that customers pay an average of \$18.75 per month for long-distance telephone calls with a standard deviation of \$7.80.

a. If a random sample of 50 long-distance phone bills is taken, what is the probability that the sample mean is greater than \$20?

b. If a random sample of 100 bills is taken, what is the probability that the sample mean is greater than \$20?

c. Suppose a random sample of 100 bills during a given month produced a sample mean of \$21.25. Does this indicate that the mean level of the amounts billed per month for long-distance telephone calls has increased from \$18.75? Test using $\alpha = .05$.

3. The manager of a fast-food restaurant claims that the mean expenditure per customer is \$2.00 with standard deviation \$0.60. A new menu has been introduced at the restaurant, and the manager wants to test whether the mean expenditure has changed. The manager takes a random sample of 100 customers to test H_0: $\mu = \$2.00$ against H_1: $\mu \neq \$2.00$. Suppose the manager uses the decision rule "Accept H_0 if $\$1.90 \leq \bar{X} \leq \$2.10$; otherwise, reject H_0."

a. What is the test statistic?

b. What is the acceptance region?

c. What is the critical region?
d. What are the critical values of the test statistic?
e. Calculate α, the level of significance of the test.

4. Repeat Exercise 3 using the decision rule "Accept H_0 if $\$1.95 \leq \bar{X} \leq \$2.05$."
a. What is the test statistic?
b. What is the acceptance region?
c. What is the critical region?
d. What are the critical values of the test statistic?
e. Calculate α, the level of significance of the test.
f. How did the change in the decision rule affect the level of significance of the test?

5. Repeat Exercise 3 assuming that the sample size is 200 rather than 100.
a. What is the test statistic?
b. What is the acceptance region?
c. What is the critical region?
d. What are the critical values of the test statistic?
e. Calculate α, the level of significance of the test.
f. How did the change in the sample size affect the level of significance of the test?

6. The job placement center at a university claims that the mean starting salary of college graduates is \$21,000 with standard deviation \$2500. A random sample of 100 college graduates is taken to test this claim. Use the decision rule "Accept H_0 if $\$20{,}500 \leq \bar{X} \leq \$21{,}500$; otherwise, reject H_0."
a. Is this a one-tailed or two-tailed test?
b. What is the test statistic?
c. What is the null hypothesis?
d. Given the decision rule, what do you think is the alternative hypothesis?
e. State the critical region, the acceptance region, and the critical values of the test statistic.
f. What is the distribution of the test statistic if H_0 is true?
g. Calculate α, the level of significance of this test.

7. A tire manufacturer claims that its tires have a mean life of at least 35,000 miles. A random sample of 16 of these tires is tested and the sample mean is 33,000 miles. Assume the population standard deviation is 3000 miles and the lives of tires are approximately normally distributed. Test the manufacturer's claim using a 5% level of significance. Did you perform a one-tailed test? Why?

8. In past years the mean IQ of enlisted men in the U.S. Army was $\mu = 103$ with standard deviation $\sigma = 8$. A general claims that, due to low pay, the average IQ of new enlisted men is lower than in the past. A random sample of 25 enlisted men is tested. In the sample, the average IQ is $\bar{x} = 98$. Use a 5% level of significance and test H_0: $\mu \geq 103$ against H_1: $\mu < 103$. Assume the population of IQs is approximately normal.

9. A small accounting firm prepares income tax returns for individuals. In its advertising, the firm claims that the average bill for its services is at most \$22. A consumer agency obtains a random sample of 36 tax returns prepared by the company and finds that the average preparation bill was $\bar{x} = \$27$. Assume that the population of bills is approximately normal and that the standard deviation is $\sigma = \$5$. Use a 5% level of significance and test the firm's claim. State the null and alternative hypotheses. Did you perform a one-tailed test? Why or why not?

10. In Pennsylvania automobiles must be inspected every 12 months. Many consumers want the state legislature to repeal this law, claiming that the law gives auto mechanics an opportunity to collect unnecessary inspection fees from the public. A lobbyist for the auto mechanics claims that the average inspection bill is at most $\mu = \$25$. A coalition of consumers claims the average is larger than \$25. A random sample of 30 inspection bills is obtained, and the sample mean is $\bar{x} = \$31.86$. Assume the population is approximately normal with variance $\sigma^2 = 64$. Use a 5% level of significance and test the lobbyist's claim. State H_0 and H_1. Did you perform a one-tailed test? Why or why not?

11.3 ▪ Prob-Values: Interpretation and Use

As described in this chapter, classical hypothesis testing involves choosing a test statistic and a level of significance α and then finding the associated rejection and acceptance regions. A difficulty arises, however, because in many problems the choice of α is completely arbitrary, particularly when it is difficult or impossible to determine the costs associated with Type I or Type II errors. In another approach to hypothesis testing, the smallest level at which the observed test statistic would be significant in a particular direction is reported.

Consider testing any one-tailed hypothesis. The observed value of the test statistic can be used to compute a tail probability called the *prob-value, p value,* or *observed level of significance*.

Definition: Prob-Value

The **prob-value**, or **p value**, of a test is the probability of obtaining a value of the test statistic as extreme or more extreme than the observed sample value when the null hypothesis H_0 is true.

A prob-value answers the question, "If the null hypothesis is true, what is the probability that a random sample will yield the observed test statistic or one whose value is further from the expected value?" If this probability is very small, then we reject the null hypothesis by concluding that the discrepancy is too large to be explained by chance alone. The observed difference is then said to be statistically significant. If the prob-value is not small, then we do not reject the null hypothesis, because the observed discrepancy may well be due to chance, that is, sampling error.

The prob-value is the smallest level of significance α at which a null hypothesis can be rejected. The smaller the prob-value, the more doubt is cast on the validity of the null hypothesis.

Calculating a Prob-Value

To calculate a prob-value:

Step 1: Record the observed sample mean $\bar{x}$, the hypothesized value of the mean μ_0, the sample size n, and the population standard deviation σ.

Step 2: Record the standard deviation of the sampling distribution of $\bar{X}$. This standard deviation is $\sigma/\sqrt{n}$, *not* σ.

Step 3: Sketch a normal distribution showing the sampling distribution of the random variable $\bar{X}$. On the graph, denote the mean as μ_0. Locate the value $\bar{x}$ and shade the area under the curve beyond $\bar{x}$. This area is the one-tailed prob-value.

Step 4: To determine this area, calculate the Z score associated with the value $\bar{x}$.

Step 5: Sketch a standard normal distribution and find the area under the curve beyond this Z score. This area is the one-tailed prob-value.

Step 6: If the test is a two-tailed test, double the prob-value in step 5.

Step 7: Examine your sketch and check that the prob-value you have calculated is reasonable.

Example 11.16 **Calculation of a Prob-Value:** In Example 11.11, we performed a one-tailed test to test H_0: $\mu = 32$ against the alternative hypothesis H_1: $\mu < 32$. The observed Z score was $z = -3.125$. Calculate the prob-value of the test.

Solution: The prob-value of the test is the probability of obtaining a Z score more extreme than the observed Z score of -3.125. From Table A.5, we obtain

$$\text{Prob-value} = P(Z < -3.125) = .5 - .4991 = .0009$$

This situation is illustrated in Figure 11.8. This prob-value indicates that if H_0 is true, then in repeated samples we should obtain a Z score as small or smaller than the one actually observed only 9 times out of 10,000, that is, with probability .0009. Because this value is extremely small, we have serious doubts about the validity of the null hypothesis.

FIGURE 11.8
Prob-value of the test described in Example 11.16.

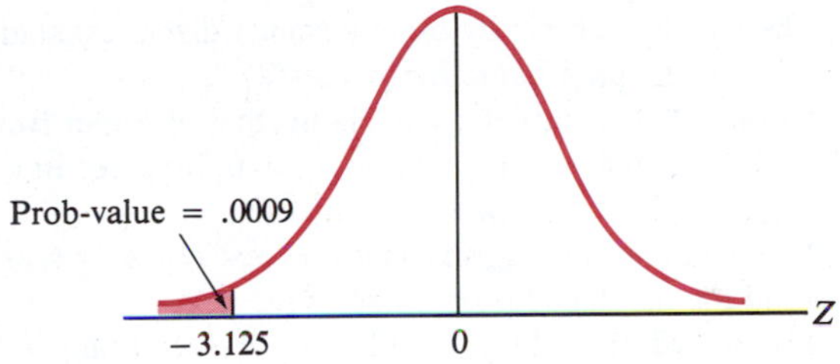

In Example 11.11, we used a 5% level of significance and rejected H_0. Similarly, if we had used a 1% level of significance, the critical value of Z would have been -2.33, and the observed Z score would still have fallen in the rejection region. In fact, if we had used any level of significance greater than .0009, the observed Z score of -3.125 would have fallen in the rejection region. It follows that the prob-value .0009 is the smallest level of significance at which the null hypothesis would have been rejected. ■

In statistical decision making, a prob-value conveys more information than a report of whether the observed test statistic is statistically significant at some preselected level of significance α. For example, a prob-value of, say, .002 is considerably more informative than the report that the test statistic is "significant at the .05 level." If we know that the prob-value is .002, we know that we would have rejected H_0 not only at the .05 level of significance but also at the .005 level of significance. In fact, a prob-value of .002 tells us that we would have rejected H_0 at all levels of significance exceeding .002.

When the prob-value of a test is reported, the decision of whether to reject the null hypothesis is left up to the reader. Suppose a reported prob-value is .04. A researcher who wants to use a 1% level of significance will not reject the null hypothesis, while a researcher who wants to use a 5% level of significance will.

It is especially useful to report a prob-value when we do not have any specific reason for choosing a particular level of significance or when we have little or no information concerning the costs and consequences of committing a Type I or Type II error.

There is no general agreement on how to define prob-values when the alternative hypothesis is two-sided. One approach is to report the one-tailed prob-value and mention that the two-tailed prob-value is presumably nearly twice as large as the one-tailed prob-value. This is reasonable when the sampling distribution of the test statistic under H_0 is symmetric, because this corresponds to the idea that the standard two-sided test is a combination of two one-sided tests, each at level of significance $\alpha/2$. When the sampling distribution of the test statistic is not symmetric, then doubling the prob-value to obtain a two-sided prob-value is less reasonable.

Exercises for Section 11.3

1. At a state university, the mean SAT score of entering students has been 1000 with a standard deviation of 180. Each year a sample of applications is taken to see if the examination scores are at the same level as in previous years. Test the null hypothesis H_0: $\mu = 1000$ against a two-sided alternative hypothesis. A sample of 200 students in this year's class had a sample mean score of 980. Use a .05 level of significance.
   a. Test this hypothesis by estimating the confidence interval.
   b. Test this hypothesis by using a standardized test statistic.
   c. What is the prob-value for this test?

2. A nationwide hamburger chain claims that its Super Burgers contain an average of $\mu = 6$ ounces of beef. The standard deviation is $\sigma = 0.7$ ounce. In a random sample of 50 Super Burgers, the average weight of beef was 5.7 ounces.
   a. Use a 1% level of significance and test H_0: $\mu \geqslant 6$ against H_1: $\mu < 6$.
   b. Find the one-tailed prob-value of the test.

3. Just before Mother's Day, the Florists' Association places some commercials on television claiming that the average cost of a dozen roses is at most \$18. A television station checks a random sample of 16 florists and finds that the average cost of a dozen roses is \$23. Suppose the population standard deviation is \$3 and assume that the population of prices is approximately normal.
   a. Use a 1% level of significance and test H_0: $\mu \leqslant \$18$ against H_1: $\mu > \$18$.
   b. Find the one-tailed prob-value of the test.

4. The TLG Insurance Company wants to decrease the average length of long-distance phone calls made by its employees. Last year the mean was $\mu = 5.6$ minutes with standard deviation $\sigma = 1.6$ minutes. Last week the sample mean was 5.4 minutes for a random sample of 50 long-distance calls.
   a. Use a 5% level of significance and test H_0: $\mu = 5.6$ against H_1: $\mu < 5.6$.
   b. Find the one-tailed prob-value of the test.

5. A firm claims that its flashlight batteries will operate continuously for 100 hours on the average. You select a random sample of 200 of those batteries to test H_0: $\mu = 100$ against H_1: $\mu \neq 100$ using a 5% level of significance. In your sample you obtain $\bar{x} = 92$. Assume that the population is normal with variance $\sigma^2 = 600$.
   a. Do you reject H_0?
   b. Find the two-tailed prob-value of the test.

11.4 ▪ Testing Hypotheses About a Population Mean with Large Sample Sizes

In Section 11.2 we showed how to test a null hypothesis about a mean of a normal population with a known variance σ^2. Often, however, we need such a test when the population is not normal or the variance is not known. Fortunately, if the sample size is large, say 30 or more, then we can use all the methods described in Section 11.2, with only slight modifications, to test hypotheses under these less rigorous circumstances.

The tests in Section 11.2 rely on the fact that when the population distribution is normal with mean μ_0 and variance σ^2, then the sample mean $\overline{X}$ follows a normal distribution with mean μ_0 and variance σ^2/n. According to the Central Limit Theorem, the sampling distribution of $\overline{X}$ for large samples is approximately normal even though the population is not normal. In addition, when the sample size is large, we can replace the unknown standard deviation σ in the formula for the Z score by the sample standard deviation S and still obtain an approximately standard normal variable.

A Large-Sample Test of the Population Mean

Suppose it is desired to test a simple or composite null hypothesis about the population mean against some appropriate alternative hypothesis. *If the sample size is large,* the test procedures developed in Section 11.2 can be employed even when the population is not normal and the population variance is unknown, provided we replace σ in all the formulas by the observed sample standard deviation s.

Example 11.17 **Two-Tailed Test of a Population Mean Using a Large Sample:** The Knight Metalworking Company produces metal ducts that are used in heating and air-conditioning systems in skyscrapers. Several holes have to be drilled in each duct so that they can be connected together with small screws. When a drill press machine is working properly, the holes have a mean of 10 millimeters; the population standard deviation is unknown. When the drilling machine is not operating properly (mainly because of human error and incorrect gauge settings), the holes are either too big or too small. In either case, the metal sheets are defective and cannot be used. The owner of the company wishes to test whether a particular machine is working properly. In this case, it would be natural to test the simple null hypothesis

$$H_0\colon \mu = 10$$

against the composite two-sided alternative hypothesis

$$H_1\colon \mu \neq 10$$

A two-sided alternative hypothesis is appropriate because the machine would be operating improperly and need to be adjusted if the sample mean was either much greater than or much less than $\mu = 10$. A random sample of $n = 100$ holes is examined. The observed sample mean is $\bar{x} = 9.6$ millimeters, and the observed sample standard deviation is $s = 1$ millimeter. Test whether the machine is operating properly using a 5% level of significance.

Solution: Because the sample size is large, the procedure described in Section 11.2 can be used if we substitute the sample standard deviation for the population standard deviation when calculating the Z score. There are two critical values of Z, denoted z_1 and z_2. For $\alpha = .05$, the two critical values are $z_1 = -z_{\alpha/2} = -1.96$ and $z_2 = z_{\alpha/2} = 1.96$. Thus the rejection region contains all Z scores less than -1.96 or greater than 1.96. The observed Z score is

$$z = \frac{\bar{x} - \mu_0}{s/\sqrt{n}} = \frac{9.6 - 10}{1/\sqrt{100}} = -4$$

Since the observed Z score falls in the rejection region (it is less than the critical value $z_1 = -1.96$), we reject H_0 in favor of H_1. See Figure 11.9.

FIGURE 11.9
Two-tailed test described in Example 11.17.

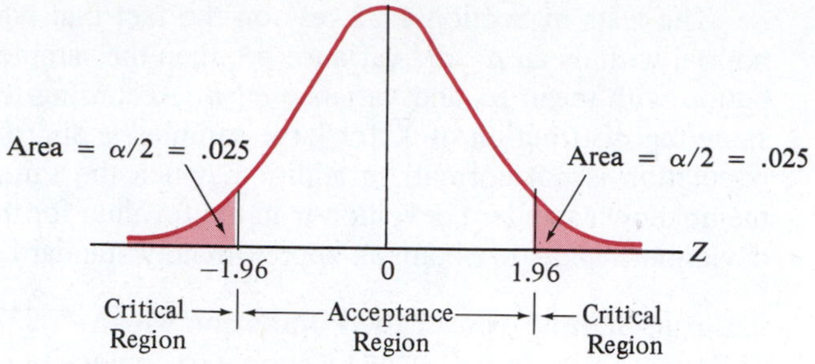

Example 11.18 **Finding the Critical Values of $\overline{X}$ When Variance Is Unknown:** In Example 11.17, find the critical values of $\overline{X}$ that separate the critical region from the acceptance region.

Solution: Because we have used a two-tailed test, there are two critical values of $\overline{X}$. We obtain

$$\bar{x}_1^* = \mu_0 - z_{\alpha/2}s/\sqrt{n} = 10 - 1.96(1/\sqrt{100}) = 9.804$$

and

$$\bar{x}_2^* = \mu_0 + z_{\alpha/2}s/\sqrt{n} = 10 + 1.96(1/\sqrt{100}) = 10.196$$

The decision rule "Reject H_0 if Z is less than $z_1 = -1.96$ or greater than $z_2 = 1.96$" is equivalent to the decision rule "Reject H_0 if $\overline{X}$ is less than $\bar{x}_1^* = 9.804$ or greater than $\bar{x}_2^* = 10.196$." In our sample we obtained $\bar{x} = 9.6$, which falls in the rejection region, and thus we reject H_0. See Figure 11.10.

FIGURE 11.10
Critical values for the two-tailed test described in Example 11.18.

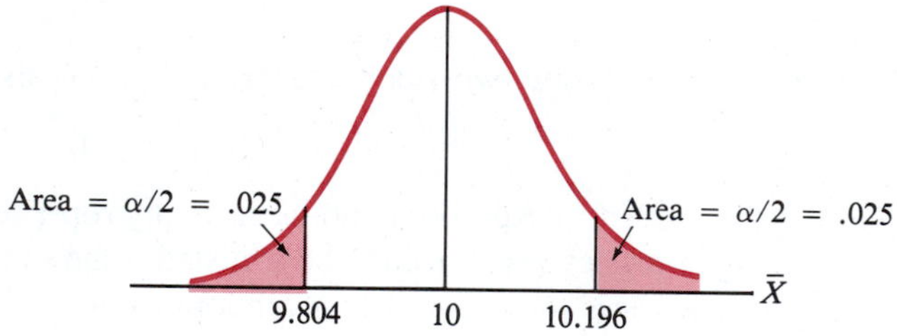

Exercises for Section 11.4

1. For each of the following situations, find the level of significance α that corresponds to the stated decision rule. In all cases, use a sample of $n = 100$ and assume that the population is large.
   a. Accept H_0 if $\overline{X} \geq 12$ and reject H_0 if $\overline{X} < 12$ where $\mu_0 = 14$ and $\sigma = 16$.
   b. Accept H_0 if $\overline{X} \leq 100$ and reject H_0 if $\overline{X} > 100$ where $\mu_0 = 97$ and $\sigma = 20$.
2. For each of the following situations, $n = 100$ and $\alpha = .05$. In each case, state whether H_0 should be accepted or rejected.
   a. H_0: $\mu \geq 24$; H_1: $\mu < 24$; $\bar{x} = 23.0$; $s = 4.7$
   b. H_0: $\mu \leq 14.9$; H_1: $\mu > 14.9$; $\bar{x} = 15.3$; $s = 1.5$
   c. H_0: $\mu = 167$; H_1: $\mu \neq 167$; $\bar{x} = 169$; $s = .92$

3. Suppose you wish to test the null hypothesis H_0: $\mu = 200$ against the one-sided alternative hypothesis H_1: $\mu > 200$. Use the decision rule: "Reject H_0 if the sample mean of a random sample of 100 items is more than 208." Assume the population standard deviation is 80.
   a. Express the decision rule in terms of Z.
   b. For this decision rule, find α.
4. A small company that produces a sweetened cereal for children claims that its cereal boxes contain 16 ounces of cereal on the average. One of the company's filling machines has been readjusted recently, and the company wishes to test H_0: $\mu \geqslant 16$ against H_1: $\mu < 16$ using a 1% level of significance. The plant manager randomly selects 100 boxes of this cereal and obtains $\bar{x} = 15.8$ ounces with $s = 0.3$ ounce. Should we reject H_0?
5. Last year, the mean number of books borrowed per cardholder at a major university was 18.5 books per semester. A random sample of 100 cardholders showed the following results for this semester: $\bar{x} = 19.54$ books with $s = 6.31$ books. The library administration would like to know whether this semester's mean usage has changed from last semester's. Perform the appropriate two-tailed test using $\alpha = .05$.

11.5 ▪ *Testing Hypotheses About a Mean of a Normal Population with Unknown Variance*

In this section we consider the problem of how to test hypotheses about a population mean μ when the population is normal, the population variance is unknown, and the sample size is small ($n < 30$). Because the variance σ^2 is unknown and the sample size is small, the procedures discussed in Sections 11.2 and 11.3 are not appropriate. Instead, we use a test based on the Student t distribution rather than the standard normal distribution.

In Chapter 10 we showed that if the population is normal with mean μ_0, then the random variable

$$t = \frac{\overline{X} - \mu_0}{S/\sqrt{n}}$$

follows a Student t distribution with $\nu = (n - 1)$ degrees of freedom, where $\overline{X}$ is the sample mean and S is the sample standard deviation based on a random sample of n observations.

Suppose we want to test the null hypothesis

$$H_0\colon \mu = \mu_0 \quad \text{or} \quad H_0\colon \mu \leqslant \mu_0$$

against the one-sided alternative hypothesis

$$H_1\colon \mu > \mu_0$$

As before, a sample mean that greatly exceeds μ_0 would cast doubt on the validity of the null hypothesis. Let $t_{\alpha,\nu}$ denote the critical value of the t distribution such that

$$P(t > t_{\alpha,\nu}) = \alpha$$

If the null hypothesis is true, the t score

$$t = \frac{\overline{X} - \mu_0}{S/\sqrt{n}}$$

follows the Student t distribution with $\nu = (n - 1)$ degrees of freedom, and the t score should exceed the critical value $t_{\alpha,\nu}$ with probability α. If the level of significance of the test is α, we reject H_0 in favor of H_1 whenever the observed t score exceeds $t_{\alpha,\nu}$, where the observed t score is the value

$$t = \frac{\bar{x} - \mu_0}{s/\sqrt{n}}$$

where $\bar{x}$ is the observed sample mean and s is the observed sample variance.

The above discussion pertains to a one-tailed test where the rejection region falls in the right tail of the distribution. Alternatively, we can perform a one-tailed test where the rejection region is in the left tail, or a two-tailed test. Thus, there are three different cases, depending on the form of H_0 and H_1. The summary in the accompanying box describes how to test a hypothesis about the population mean when the population is normal and when the population variance is unknown.

Testing the Mean of a Normal Population with Unknown Variance and a Small Sample

Case 1: To test the null hypothesis

$$H_0\colon \mu = \mu_0 \quad \text{or} \quad H_0\colon \mu \leqslant \mu_0$$

against the one-sided alternative hypothesis

$$H_1\colon \mu > \mu_0$$

calculate the observed t score

$$t = \frac{\bar{x} - \mu_0}{s/\sqrt{n}}$$

and use the decision rule

Reject H_0 in favor of H_1 if $t > t_{\alpha,n-1}$.

Case 2: To test the null hypothesis

$$H_0\colon \mu = \mu_0 \quad \text{or} \quad H_0\colon \mu \geqslant \mu_0$$

against the one-sided alternative hypothesis

$$H_1\colon \mu < \mu_0$$

use the decision rule

Reject H_0 in favor of H_1 if $t < -t_{\alpha,n-1}$.

Case 3: To test the null hypothesis

$$H_0\colon \mu = \mu_0$$

against the two-sided alternative hypothesis

$$H_1\colon \mu \neq \mu_0$$

use the decision rule

Reject H_0 in favor of H_1 if $t < -t_{\alpha/2,n-1}$ or if $t > t_{\alpha/2,n-1}$.

Example 11.19 **Small-Sample Test of the Mean of a Normal Population with Unknown Variance:** The manufacturer of a popular low-priced car claims that total repair costs resulting from low-speed car crashes follow a normal distribution with mean at most \$200. A consumer agency thinks that this claim might be false and decides to test it. The null hypothesis is the manufacturer's claim

$$H_0: \mu \leq \$200$$

and the alternative hypothesis is

$$H_1: \mu > \$200$$

The consumer agency does not want to reject the manufacturer's claim unless the evidence against H_0 is very strong. Thus, the agency decides to use a 1% level of significance. Because it is very costly to test-crash a sample of cars, the agency test-crashes a random sample of only $n = 9$ cars. Use the following sample data to determine whether the null hypothesis should be rejected:

$$x_1 = \$245 \quad x_2 = \$305 \quad x_3 = \$175 \quad x_4 = \$250 \quad x_5 = \$280$$
$$x_6 = \$160 \quad x_7 = \$250 \quad x_8 = \$195 \quad x_9 = \$210$$

Solution: The observed sample mean is

$$\bar{x} = \frac{\Sigma x_i}{n} = \frac{2070}{9} = 230$$

The observed sample variance is

$$s^2 = \frac{\Sigma(x_i - \bar{x})^2}{n - 1} = \frac{18{,}700}{8} = 2337.5$$

The observed standard deviation is $s \approx \$48.35$. We use a one-tailed test and a 1% level of significance. The appropriate number of degrees of freedom is $(n - 1) = 8$, and the critical value is $t_{.01,8} = 2.90$. The rejection region therefore consists of all t scores exceeding 2.90. We obtain the observed t score

$$t = \frac{\bar{x} - \mu_0}{s/\sqrt{n}} = \frac{230 - 200}{48.35/\sqrt{9}} \approx 1.86$$

We do not reject H_0 because $t = 1.86$ falls in the acceptance region. See Figure 11.11.

FIGURE 11.11
Critical value for the test described in Example 11.19.

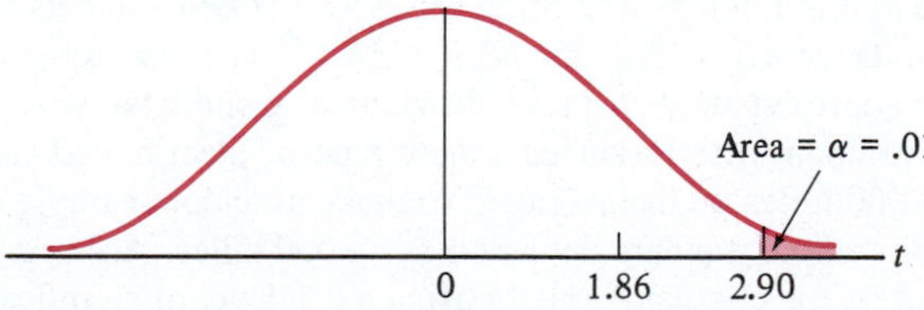

Exercises for Section 11.5

1. A trucking firm believes that its mean weekly loss due to damaged shipments is \$1800 or less. A sample of 15 weeks of operation shows a sample mean weekly loss of \$2000 with a sample standard deviation of \$500. Use a .05 level of significance to test the trucking firm's claim.

2. Glo-Dry paint is labeled as having a mean coverage of 380 square feet per gallon. Mean coverage more or less than 380 square feet indicates that the paint is not covering satisfactorily. Use a 5% level of significance and test H_0: $\mu = 380$. Sample results show $\bar{x} = 365$ square feet and $s = 25$ square feet for a sample of 16 gallons. What is your conclusion about the paint coverage?

3. A contractor assumes that construction workers are idle 75 minutes per day or less. A sample of 25 construction workers had a mean idle time of 84 minutes per day. The sample standard deviation was 20 minutes. Assume the population is approximately normal.
a. What is the two-tailed prob-value associated with the sample result?
b. Using a .05 level of significance, test the hypothesis H_0: $\mu \leq 75$.

4. For each of the following situations, state whether the test is right- or left-tailed and find the critical value z_α. For each sample result, calculate the normal deviate value Z and indicate whether the null hypothesis should be accepted or rejected. Finally, for each outcome, determine the approximate probability of obtaining a value of the test statistic as rare as or rarer than the one you obtained by finding the tail area under the normal curve corresponding to the computed Z.
a. H_0: $\mu \leq 100$; H_1: $\mu > 100$; $\alpha = .05$; $n = 100$; $\bar{x} = 103$; $s = 15$
b. H_0: $\mu \geq 15$; H_1: $\mu < 15$; $\alpha = .01$; $n = 100$; $\bar{x} = 13.8$; $s = 2$
c. H_0: $\mu \geq .8$; H_1: $\mu < .8$; $\alpha = .10$; $n = 36$; $\bar{x} = 0.6$; $s = 0.6$

5. Suppose 16 tax returns are randomly sampled by the Internal Revenue Service from the population of 1987 tax returns with adjusted gross incomes between \$25,000 and \$30,000. The interest deductions claimed on the returns are as follows:

\$2984	\$3050	\$3101	\$3415
2416	2910	3333	3002
1897	3872	3102	3222
2134	2806	2851	2999

a. Find the sample mean.
b. Find the sample standard deviation.
c. Assume the population of interest deductions from which the sample was drawn is approximately normally distributed. In 1980 the average interest deduction for individuals in this tax bracket was \$3011. Do the sample data provide sufficient evidence to conclude that in 1987 the average interest deduction claimed by taxpayers in this income bracket was different from 1980? Use $\alpha = .05$.
d. Find the prob-value for the test.

6. In a study of risk-taking behavior, a researcher gave each subject a lottery ticket whereby the subject could win \$500 with probability .1 and \$0 with probability .9. By subsequent questioning, the researcher determined the minimum price at which the subject would sell the lottery ticket. Since the expected value of the lottery ticket was \$50, the researcher wanted to test whether the mean minimum selling price was \$50. Sixteen subjects participated in the study, and the sample results were $\bar{x} = \$41.25$ and $s = \$4.52$. The researcher believes that the minimum selling prices are approximately normally distributed. Conduct a two-sided test using $\alpha = .05$.

7. A company has produced a new type of steel-belted radial tire that it claims will last at least 40,000 miles on the average. You take a random sample of 16 tires and obtain $\bar{x} = 35{,}000$ miles with sample standard deviation $s = 3000$ miles. Assume the population is approximately normal.
a. Test the company's claim using a 5% level of significance.
b. Did you perform a one-tailed test? Why or why not?

8. The director of a secretarial school claims that its graduates can type at least 50 words per minute on the average. You hire 18 of these graduates and test their typing speed. On your test the average typing speed was $\bar{x} = 38$ words per minute with $s^2 = 720$. Test H_0: $\mu \geq 50$ against H_1: $\mu < 50$ using a 5% level of significance.

11.6 ▪ Tests of the Population Proportion

Frequently we want to test hypotheses concerning the proportion of members of a population possessing some particular attribute. Such tests are based on the sample proportion $\hat{p}$. In Chapter 9 it was shown that if the population proportion is p, the sample proportion $\hat{p}$ follows approximately a normal distribution with mean p and variance pq/n, where $q = (1 - p)$, provided $np \geqslant 5$ and $nq \geqslant 5$. Throughout the remainder of this section, it is always assumed that $np \geqslant 5$ and $nq \geqslant 5$, so that the distribution of $\hat{p}$ is approximately normal.

Suppose we want to test the null hypothesis

$$H_0\colon p = p_0 \quad \text{or} \quad H_0\colon p \geqslant p_0$$

against the alternative hypothesis

$$H_1\colon p < p_0$$

where p_0 is some hypothesized value for the population proportion. If H_0 is true, then the sample proportion is approximately normal with mean p_0 and variance p_0q_0/n, and the Z score

$$Z = \frac{\hat{p} - p_0}{\sqrt{p_0q_0/n}}$$

approximately follows the standard normal distribution. Naturally, values of $\hat{p}$ far less than p_0 would cast doubt on the validity of the null hypothesis. If $\hat{p}$ is far less than p_0, the observed Z score will be far less than 0. This implies that the rejection region should be placed under the left tail of the standard normal distribution. This is precisely the same argument used in developing a test for the population mean.

Suppose the level of significance of the test is selected to be α. Then we reject H_0 if $Z < -z_\alpha$ where $-z_\alpha$ is the value such that

$$P(Z < -z_\alpha) = \alpha$$

The three possible cases—when the alternative hypothesis H_1 specifies values of p less than p_0, when H_1 specifies values greater than p_0, and when H_1 is two-sided—are discussed in the accompanying box.

Testing Hypotheses About the Population Proportion

Suppose we want to test the null hypothesis that the population proportion is p_0 using a level of significance α. To perform the test, we take a sample of size n from the population and calculate the sample proportion $\hat{p}$. The tests are based on the assumption that $np_0 \geqslant 5$ and $nq_0 \geqslant 5$. If these conditions hold, then the random variable

$$Z = \frac{\hat{p} - p_0}{\sqrt{p_0q_0/n}}$$

approximately follows the standard normal distribution. Let z denote the observed value of the random variable Z after substituting the observed sample proportion $\hat{p}$ into the formula above.

Case 1: To test the null hypothesis

$$H_0: p = p_0 \quad \text{or} \quad H_0: p \geq p_0$$

against the one-sided alternative hypothesis

$$H_1: p < p_0$$

use the decision rule

$$\text{Reject } H_0 \text{ in favor of } H_1 \text{ if } z < -z_\alpha.$$

This is equivalent to the rule

$$\text{Reject } H_0 \text{ in favor of } H_1 \text{ if } \hat{p} < \hat{p}^*,$$

where the critical value is $\hat{p}^* = p_0 - z_\alpha\sqrt{p_0 q_0/n}$.

Case 2: To test the null hypothesis

$$H_0: p = p_0 \quad \text{or} \quad H_0: p \leq p_0$$

against the alternative hypothesis

$$H_1: p > p_0$$

use the decision rule

$$\text{Reject } H_0 \text{ in favor of } H_1 \text{ if } z > z_\alpha.$$

This is equivalent to the rule

$$\text{Reject } H_0 \text{ in favor of } H_1 \text{ if } \hat{p} > \hat{p}^*,$$

where the critical value is $\hat{p}^* = p_0 + z_\alpha\sqrt{p_0 q_0/n}$.

Case 3: To test the null hypothesis

$$H_0: p = p_0$$

against the two-sided alternative hypothesis

$$H_1: p \neq p_0$$

use the decision rule

$$\text{Reject } H_0 \text{ in favor of } H_1 \text{ if } z < -z_{\alpha/2} \text{ or if } z > z_{\alpha/2}.$$

This is equivalent to the rule

$$\text{Reject } H_0 \text{ if } \hat{p} < \hat{p}_1^* \text{ or if } \hat{p} > \hat{p}_2^*,$$

where the critical values are $\hat{p}_1^* = p_0 - z_{\alpha/2}\sqrt{p_0 q_0/n}$ and $\hat{p}_2^* = p_0 + z_{\alpha/2}\sqrt{p_0 q_0/n}$.

Example 11.20 **Testing a Population Proportion:** A politician claims that at least 60% of the population favors a strict gun control proposal that would severely restrict ownership of guns.

A local hunting club claims that p is much less than 60%. You take a sample of size 100 to test the null hypothesis

$$H_0: p = .6$$

against the one-sided alternative hypothesis

$$H_1: p < .6$$

Suppose that 55 people in the sample favor the legislation. If we use a 5% level of significance, what decision should be made?

Solution: If H_0 is true, then $\hat{p}$ has a normal distribution with mean $p = .6$ and variance $pq/n = (.6)(.4)/100 = .0024$. If we use a one-tailed test at the 5% level of significance, the critical region consists of all values of Z less than $-z_\alpha = -z_{.05} = -1.645$. In our sample, we obtained $\hat{p} = x/n = 55/100 = .55$. The observed Z score is

$$z = \frac{\hat{p} - p_0}{\sqrt{p_0 q_0/n}} = \frac{.55 - .60}{\sqrt{(.60)(.40)/100}} = -1.02$$

We do not reject H_0 because the Z score -1.02 exceeds the critical value $-z_\alpha = -1.645$ and falls in the acceptance region. See Figure 11.12.

FIGURE 11.12
Critical value for the test described in Example 11.20.

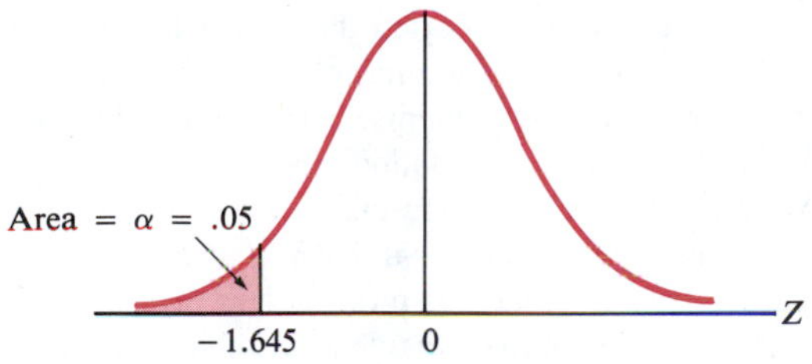

Alternatively, we can calculate the critical value

$$\hat{p}^* = p_0 + z_\alpha\sqrt{p_0 q_0/n} = .6 - 1.645\sqrt{(.6)(.4)/100} \approx .519$$

We do not reject H_0 because the observed sample proportion $\hat{p} = .55$ exceeds the critical value .519.

For this test the prob-value is

$$\text{Prob-value} = P(Z < -1.02) = .1539$$

■

Exercises for Section 11.6

1. A magazine claims that at least 25% of its subscribers are college graduates. In a random sample of 200 subscribers, 41 are college graduates.

a. Use a 5% level of significance to test the validity of the magazine's claim.

b. Using the sample results, develop a 90% confidence interval for the proportion of the population that are college graduates.

c. Use the interval estimate of part (b) to test the magazine's claim about its subscribers. What is your conclusion?

2. An employment placement officer claims that at least 40% of all engineers switch jobs within three years of being hired. The alternative hypothesis is that the rate of job changing is below 40%. At a significance level of .01, should the claim be accepted or rejected if the sample results show that 25 out of 100 engineers changed jobs?
3. A producer of a certain brand of coffee claims that at least 20% of all coffee drinkers prefer its product over the major competing brand. To test the validity of this claim, an individual samples 200 coffee drinkers and finds that 43 prefer the producer's brand. Test the producer's claim using $\alpha = .05$.
4. In checking the reliability of a bank's records, auditing firms sometimes ask a sample of the bank's customers to confirm the accuracy of their savings account balances as reported by the bank. An auditing firm is interested in estimating the proportion of a bank's savings accounts where the bank and the customer disagree. Of 400 savings account customers questioned by the auditors, 30 said their balance disagreed with that reported by the bank.
   a. Estimate the actual proportion of the bank's savings accounts on whose balances the bank and customer disagree using a 95% confidence level.
   b. The bank claims that the true fraction of accounts on which there is disagreement is no more than .05. You, as an auditor, doubt this claim. Does the sample provide evidence that the true fraction of accounts subject to disagreement exceeds .05? Use $\alpha = .05$ to perform the test.
5. A manufacturer of videodiscs believes that, under adequate quality control, no more than 6% of the discs should be returned as faulty. For a random sample of 250 sales of these discs, it was found that 22 were returned as faulty. Test at the 10% significance level the null hypothesis that the population percentage of discs returned as faulty is at most 10%.
6. A national newspaper reported that at least 70% of all high school seniors at inner-city schools drink alcohol at least once a month. Test the paper's claim using a 5% level of significance. In a random sample of 500 students, 280 said that they drink alcohol at least once a month.
   a. What decision would you make?
   b. Why would you use a one-tailed test in this problem?
7. A psychology text states that 10% of the population is left-handed. You do not know if the proportion of left-handers is more or less than .10. You obtain a random sample of 200 people to test the book's claim using a 5% level of significance.
   a. What decision would you make if, in your sample, 38 people were left-handed?
   b. Why would it be appropriate to use a two-tailed test in this problem?
8. Toss a coin 900 times to test H_0: $p = .5$ against H_1: $p \neq .5$ using a 1% level of significance. If you observe 460 heads in 900 tosses, would you reject H_0?
9. An economist states that 10% of a city's labor force is unemployed. You do not know if the economist's estimate is too high or too low. Thus, you want to test H_0: $p = .10$ against H_1: $p \neq .10$ using a 5% level of significance. You obtain a random sample of 400 people in the labor force, of whom 27 are unemployed. Would you reject H_0?
10. A state legislature says that it is going to decrease its funding of the state university because, according to its sources, 36% of the graduates move out of the state within three years of graduation. As a faculty member at the university, you want to show that the proportion of graduates who move out of state is less than .36. You decide to test H_0: $p = .36$ against H_1: $p < .36$ using a 5% level of significance. You obtain a random sample of 160 graduates and find that 40 moved out of state within three years of graduation. Would you reject H_0? Use $\alpha = .05$.

11.7 ▪ Measuring the Power of a Test

As discussed in Section 11.1, when testing any null hypothesis H_0 against an alternative hypothesis H_1, two types of errors can be committed. A Type I error occurs when we reject H_0 when it is true. The probability of a Type I error, denoted α and called the level of significance of the test, measures the probability that the test statistic falls in the critical region given that H_0 is true. A Type II error occurs when H_0 is false but we do not reject it. The probability of a Type II error, denoted by β, is the probability that the test statistic falls in the acceptance region when H_0 is false. This probability depends on the actual situation and varies with the value of the population parameter being tested.

For example, suppose the null hypothesis states that a population parameter θ equals some specific value θ_0. That is, the null hypothesis is

$$H_0: \theta = \theta_0$$

If the true value of the population parameter θ was different from, but close to, θ_0, then it would not be unusual to obtain a test statistic that falls in the acceptance region; in such a case it would be relatively easy to accept the null hypothesis incorrectly. Thus, the probability of making a Type II error would be large. On the other hand, if the true value of θ was extremely different from θ_0, it would be very unlikely that the test statistic would fall in the acceptance region, and the probability of making a Type II error would be small.

It is important to know the probability of making a Type II error, so that if we accept the null hypothesis, we have some idea how likely such a decision would be if the null hypothesis is false. If the probability of making a Type II error is large, accepting the null hypothesis does not necessarily provide much evidence that the null hypothesis is true. Thus, when β is large, we cannot distinguish very well between the null hypothesis and various alternative hypotheses.

The probability β of making a Type II error is a conditional probability. We have

$$\begin{aligned}\beta &= P(\text{Type II error})\\ &= P(H_0 \text{ not rejected} \mid H_0 \text{ false})\\ &= P(\text{test statistic in acceptance region} \mid H_0 \text{ false})\end{aligned}$$

The probability $(1 - \beta)$ measures the probability that the test statistic falls in the rejection region when H_0 is false. Thus $(1 - \beta)$ measures the probability that the test correctly leads us to reject H_0 when H_0 is false. This probability $(1 - \beta)$ is called the *power of the test*. The reason for this name is that one way of measuring how good, or powerful, a test is is to determine how frequently the test will reject H_0 when H_0 is actually false.

Definition: Power of a Test

Let β denote the probability of making a Type II error. The probability $(1 - \beta)$ is called the **power of the test.** Thus,

$$\begin{aligned}1 - \beta &= P(H_0 \text{ reject} \mid H_0 \text{ false})\\ &= P(\text{test statistic falls in rejection region} \mid H_0 \text{ false})\end{aligned}$$

The power of the test measures the probability that the test correctly leads us to reject H_0 when H_0 is false.

Suppose we want to calculate the power of a test of the null hypothesis

$$H_0: \mu = \mu_0$$

against the one-sided alternative hypothesis

$$H_1\colon \mu > \mu_0$$

where the level of significance is α. This is a one-sided test where the rejection region lies entirely in the right-hand tail of the distribution. We obtain a random sample of n observations from a normal population with a known variance σ^2. To find the power of the test, we first need to determine the critical value $\bar{x}^*$ that separates the acceptance region from the rejection region. In Section 11.2, we showed that the critical value is

$$\bar{x}^* = \mu_0 + z_\alpha \sigma/\sqrt{n}$$

Suppose the value of the population mean is actually μ_1 rather than the hypothesized value μ_0. We will correctly reject H_0 in favor of H_1 if the observed sample mean exceeds the critical value $\bar{x}^*$. Thus, the power of the test is the probability that the sample mean $\bar{X}$ exceeds $\bar{x}^*$, *given that* $\mu = \mu_1$. We obtain the rule described in the accompanying box.

Calculating the Power of a Test with Rejection Region in Right-Hand Tail

Suppose we have a random sample of n observations from a normal population with a known variance σ^2. Suppose we want to test the null hypothesis

$$H_0\colon \mu = \mu_0$$

against the one-sided alternative hypothesis

$$H_1\colon \mu > \mu_0$$

where the level of significance is α. Suppose the mean is μ_1 rather than the hypothesized value μ_0. The *power of the test* is

$$\begin{aligned} \text{Power} = 1 - \beta &= P(\bar{X} > \bar{x}^*) \\ &= P(\bar{X} > \mu_0 + z_\alpha \sigma/\sqrt{n}) \end{aligned}$$

where $\bar{X}$ follows the normal distribution with mean μ_1 and variance σ^2/n. We obtain

$$\text{Power} = P\left(Z > \frac{(\bar{x}^* - \mu_1)}{\sigma/\sqrt{n}}\right)$$

where $\bar{x}^* = \mu_0 + z_\alpha \sigma/\sqrt{n}$.

Example 11.21 **Calculating the Power of a Right-Tailed Test:** In Example 11.13 we tested the null hypothesis that the mean salary of teachers was \$25,000. We tested

$$H_0\colon \mu \leqslant \$25{,}000$$

against the one-sided alternative hypothesis

$$H_1\colon \mu > \$25{,}000$$

It was assumed that the population was normal with standard deviation $\sigma = \$4000$. The sample size was $n = 100$, and the level of significance was .01. Find the power of the test if, in fact, the true population mean was \$26,000.

Solution: For $\alpha = .01$, the critical value of Z is $z_\alpha = 2.33$. Thus the critical value $\bar{x}^*$ is

$$\begin{aligned}\bar{x}^* &= \mu_0 + z_\alpha \sigma/\sqrt{n} \\ &= 25{,}000 + 2.33(4000/\sqrt{100}) = 25{,}932\end{aligned}$$

The power of the test is calculated as follows:

$$\begin{aligned}\text{Power} &= P(\bar{X} > \bar{x}^*) \\ &= P(\bar{X} > 25{,}932) \\ &= P\left(Z > \frac{\bar{x}^* - \mu_1}{\sigma/\sqrt{n}}\right) \\ &= P\left(Z > \frac{(25{,}932 - 26{,}000)}{4000/\sqrt{100}}\right) \\ &= P(Z > -.17) = .5675\end{aligned}$$

The rejection region consists of all values of $\bar{X}$ exceeding \$25,932, so the power of the test is the probability that $\bar{X}$ exceeds \$25,932 when $\mu = \$26{,}000$. The shaded area in Figure 11.13, which shows the power of the test, represents the probability that we will correctly reject H_0 when, in fact, $\mu = \$26{,}000$.

FIGURE 11.13
Power of test described in Example 11.21.

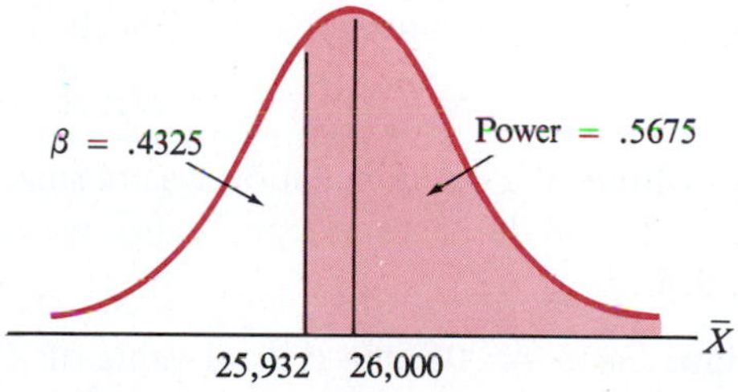

Since the power of the test is $(1 - \beta) = .5675$, it follows that $\beta = .4325$. Thus, for $\mu = \$26{,}000$, the probability is .5675 that we will reject H_0 in favor of H_1; consequently, the probability is .4325 that we will incorrectly accept H_0. ■

In Example 11.21, the rejection region fell in the right-hand tail of the distribution. Now consider the case when the rejection region falls in the left-hand tail. We obtain the rule described in the accompanying box.

Calculating the Power of a Test with Rejection Region in Left-Hand Tail

Suppose we have a random sample of n observations from a normal population with a known variance σ^2. Suppose we want to test the null hypothesis

$$H_0: \mu = \mu_0$$

against the one-sided alternative hypothesis

$$H_1: \mu < \mu_0$$

where the level of significance is α. Suppose the mean is μ_1 rather than the hypothesized value μ_0. The power of the test is the probability that the sample mean $\overline{X}$ is less than the critical value $\bar{x}^*$ where

$$\bar{x}^* = \mu_0 - z_\alpha \sigma/\sqrt{n}$$

We have

$$\begin{aligned} \text{Power} &= P(\overline{X} < \bar{x}^*) \\ &= P(\overline{X} < \mu_0 - z_\alpha \sigma/\sqrt{n}) \end{aligned}$$

where $\overline{X}$ follows a normal distribution with mean μ_1 and variance σ^2/n. Equivalently, we obtain

$$\begin{aligned} \text{Power} &= P(\overline{X} < \bar{x}^*) \\ &= P\left(Z < \frac{\bar{x}^* - \mu_1}{\sigma/\sqrt{n}}\right) \end{aligned}$$

where $\bar{x}^* = \mu_0 - z_\alpha \sigma/\sqrt{n}$.

Example 11.22 **Calculating the Power of a Right-Tailed Test:** In Example 11.11 we tested the null hypothesis

$$H_0: \mu = 32$$

against the one-sided alternative hypothesis

$$H_1: \mu < 32$$

It was assumed that the population was normal with variance $\sigma^2 = 16$. The sample size was $n = 25$ and the level of significance was .05. Find the power of the test if, in fact, $\mu = 29.5$.

Solution: For $\alpha = .05$, the critical value of Z is $z_\alpha = 1.645$. For the critical value $\bar{x}^*$, we obtain

$$\begin{aligned} \bar{x}^* &= \mu_0 - z_\alpha \sigma/\sqrt{n} \\ &= 32 - 1.645(4/\sqrt{25}) = 30.684 \end{aligned}$$

This is the same critical value calculated in Example 11.12.

The power of the test is

$$\begin{aligned} \text{Power} &= P(\overline{X} < \bar{x}^*) \\ &= P(\overline{X} < 30.684) \\ &= P\left(Z < \frac{\bar{x}^* - \mu_1}{\sigma/\sqrt{n}}\right) \\ &= P\left(Z < \frac{30.684 - 29.5}{4/\sqrt{25}}\right) \\ &= P(Z < 1.48) = .9306 \end{aligned}$$

The shaded area in Figure 11.14 represents the power of the test when $\mu = 29.5$. Under these conditions, the probability is .9306 that we will correctly reject H_0 in favor of H_1, and so the probability of making a Type II error is $\beta = .0694$.

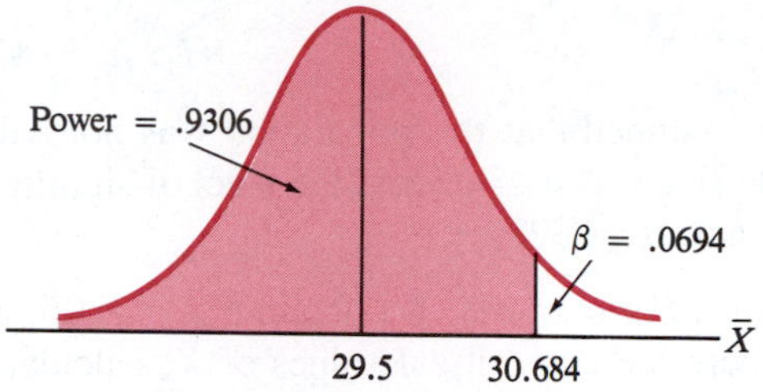

FIGURE 11.14
Power of test described in Example 11.22.

■

In the accompanying box, we consider the power of the test of a null hypothesis

$$H_0: \mu = \mu_0$$

against the two-sided alternative hypothesis

$$H_1: \mu \neq \mu_0$$

Calculating the Power of a Test with Rejection Regions in Both Tails

Suppose we have a random sample of n observations from a normal population with a known variance σ^2. Suppose we want to test the null hypothesis

$$H_0: \mu = \mu_0$$

against the two-sided alternative hypothesis

$$H_1: \mu \neq \mu_0$$

where the level of significance is α. The power of the test is the probability that the sample mean $\bar{X}$ is less than $\bar{x}_1^*$ or greater than $\bar{x}_2^*$ when $\mu = \mu_1$, where $\bar{x}_1^*$ and $\bar{x}_2^*$ are the critical values given by

$$\bar{x}_1^* = \mu_0 - z_{\alpha/2}\sigma/\sqrt{n}$$

and

$$\bar{x}_2^* = \mu_0 + z_{\alpha/2}\sigma/\sqrt{n}$$

That is,

$$\begin{aligned}\text{Power} &= P(\bar{X} < \bar{x}_1^*) + P(\bar{X} > \bar{x}_2^*) \\ &= P(\bar{X} < \mu_0 - z_{\alpha/2}\sigma/\sqrt{n}) + P(\bar{X} > \mu_0 + z_{\alpha/2}\sigma/\sqrt{n})\end{aligned}$$

where $\bar{X}$ follows a normal distribution with mean μ_1 and variance σ^2/n. Equivalently, we obtain

$$\begin{aligned}\text{Power} &= P(\bar{X} < \bar{x}_1^*) + P(\bar{X} > \bar{x}_2^*) \\ &= P\left(Z < \frac{(\bar{x}_1^* - \mu_1)}{\sigma/\sqrt{n}}\right) + P\left(Z > \frac{\bar{x}_2^* - \mu_1}{\sigma/\sqrt{n}}\right)\end{aligned}$$

Example 11.23 **Calculating the Power of a Two-Tailed Test:** In Example 11.14 we tested the null hypothesis

$$H_0: \mu = \$300$$

against the two-sided alternative hypothesis

$$H_1: \mu \neq \$300$$

It was assumed that the population was normal with standard deviation $\sigma = 50$. The sample size was $n = 25$ and the level of significance was .05. Find the power of the test if, in fact, $\mu = \$270$.

Solution: For $\alpha = .05$, we obtain $z_{\alpha/2} = 1.96$. Because we have performed a two-tailed test, there are two critical values of $\bar{X}$, calculated in Example 11.15 as $\bar{x}_1^* = \$280.40$ and $\bar{x}_2^* = \$319.60$.

The power of the test is

$$\begin{aligned}
\text{Power} &= P(\bar{X} < \bar{x}_1^*) + P(\bar{X} > \bar{x}_2^*) \\
&= P(\bar{X} < 280.40) + P(\bar{X} > 319.60) \\
&= P\left(Z < \frac{\bar{x}_1^* - \mu_1}{\sigma/\sqrt{n}}\right) + P\left(Z > \frac{\bar{x}_2^* - \mu_1}{\sigma/\sqrt{n}}\right) \\
&= P\left(Z < \frac{280.40 - 270}{50/\sqrt{25}}\right) + P\left(Z > \frac{319.60 - 270}{50/\sqrt{25}}\right) \\
&= P(Z < 1.04) + P(Z > 5.96) \\
&= .8508 + .0000 = .8508
\end{aligned}$$

The shaded area in Figure 11.15 represents the power of the test when, in fact, $\mu = \$270$. Under these circumstances the probability is .8508 that we will correctly reject H_0 in favor of H_1, and so the probability of making a Type II error is $\beta = .1492$.

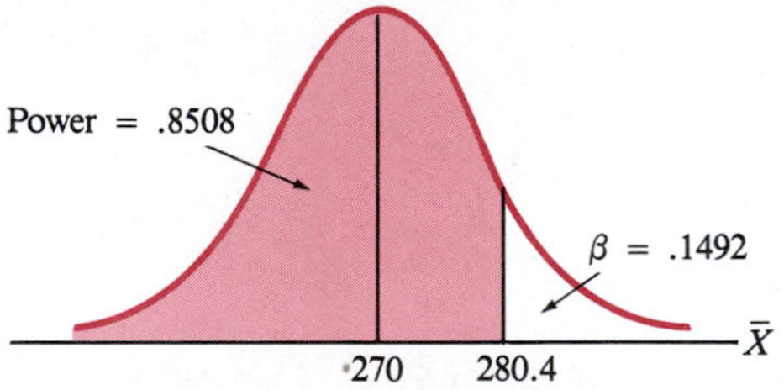

FIGURE 11.15
Power of test described in Example 11.23.

The Power Curve

Suppose we are testing the null hypothesis $H_0: \mu = \mu_0$ and the true value of the mean is μ_1 rather than the hypothesized value μ_0. Other things being equal, we will be more likely to correctly reject H_0 when μ_1 is far from μ_0 than when μ_1 is relatively close to μ_0. The next example illustrates this point.

Example 11.24 **Calculating the Power of a Test for Different Values of μ:** Suppose a car manufacturer claims that, when driven at a speed of 50 miles per hour on a test track, the mileage of a certain model follows a normal distribution with mean 30 miles per gallon and standard deviation 4 miles per gallon. A consumer advocate thinks that the manufacturer is overestimating average mileage. The advocate decides to test the null hypothesis H_0: $\mu = 30$ against the one-sided alternative hypothesis H_1: $\mu < 30$. Suppose the consumer advocate tests a sample of $n = 25$ cars and uses a 5% level of significance. Find the power of the test if the true mean is $\mu_1 = 28.5$.

Solution: For $\alpha = .05$, we obtain $z_\alpha = 1.645$. We calculate the critical value

$$\begin{aligned}\bar{x}^* &= \mu_0 - z_\alpha \sigma/\sqrt{n} \\ &= 30 - 1.645(4/\sqrt{25}) = 28.684\end{aligned}$$

The power of the test is

$$\text{Power} = P(\bar{X} < \bar{x}^*) = P(\bar{X} < 28.684)$$

when $\mu = 28.5$. To calculate this probability, we calculate the Z score

$$z = \frac{\bar{x}^* - \mu_1}{\sigma/\sqrt{n}} = \frac{28.684 - 28.5}{4/\sqrt{25}} = .23$$

We obtain

$$\text{Power} = P(Z < .23) = .5910$$

Thus, the probability is only .5910 that the null hypothesis will be rejected if the true mean is 28.5 miles per gallon, and the probability is .4090 that the null hypothesis will be incorrectly accepted. This shows that the test is not very powerful in testing the null hypothesis H_0: $\mu = 30$ against the alternative hypothesis H_1: $\mu < 30$ when $\mu = \mu_1 = 28.5$. The power of the test is illustrated in Figure 11.16.

FIGURE 11.16
Power of test for Example 11.24 when $\mu_1 = 28.5$.

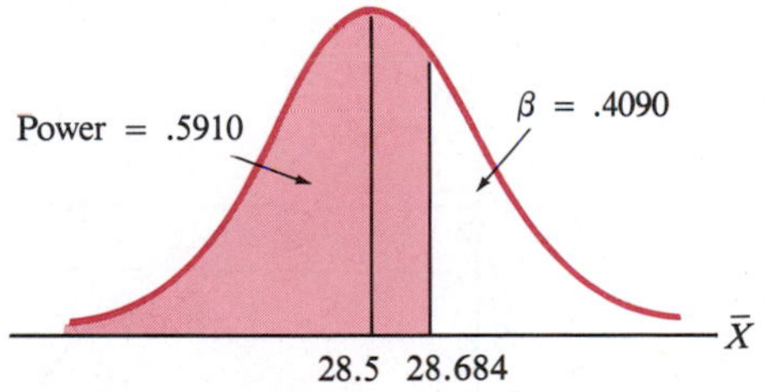

Now let us repeat the entire procedure for the case when the true value of the mean is $\mu = 28.0$. The power of the test is now

$$\text{Power} = P(\bar{X} < \bar{x}^*) = P(\bar{X} < 28.684)$$

given that $\mu = 28.0$. We obtain the Z score

$$z = \frac{\bar{x}^* - \mu_1}{\sigma/\sqrt{n}} = \frac{28.684 - 28.0}{4/\sqrt{25}} \approx .86$$

and

$$\text{Power} = P(Z < .86) = .8051$$

This probability is the shaded area in Figure 11.17. A comparison of Figures 11.16 and 11.17 shows that the power of the test increases as the true mean μ_1 moves away from $\mu_0 = .30$.

FIGURE 11.17
Power of test for Example 11.24 when $\mu = 28.0$.

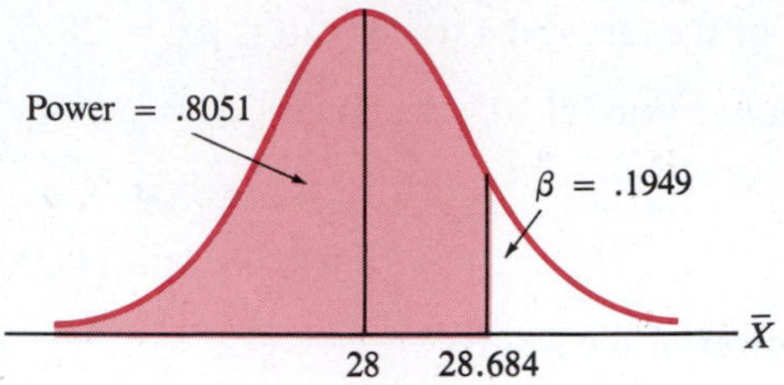

The power of the test in Example 11.24 can be calculated for any specific value of μ. The following table shows the power of the test associated with different values of μ when the sample size is $n = 25$:

μ	29.5	29.0	28.5	28.0	27.5	27.0	26.5
Power	.1539	.3446	.5910	.8051	.9306	.9846	.9968

Definition: Power Curve

A **power curve** is a graph showing the power of the test associated with different values of the parameter of interest.

These data are graphed in Figure 11.18. The height of the curve above any value μ shows the probability that we will reject H_0 if the true mean is that particular value.

FIGURE 11.18
Power curve for Example 11.24.

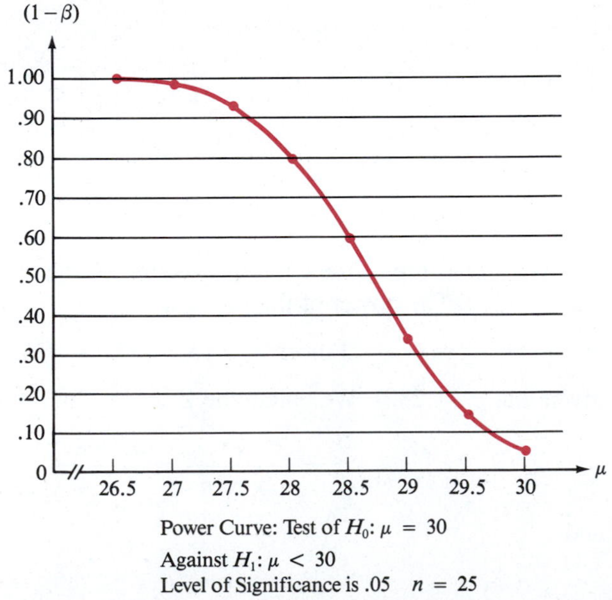

Note how the curve rises as μ moves away from the hypothesized value $\mu_0 = 30$. The higher the power curve, the more powerful the test and the more likely it is that we will correctly reject a false null hypothesis.

Other things equal, the more powerful the test, the better. We can increase the power of a test by increasing the sample size. The following example illustrates this point.

Example 11.25 **Effect of Increased Sample Size on the Power of a Test:** Let us repeat Example 11.24 using a larger sample size of $n = 64$.

Solution: As in Example 11.24, for $\alpha = .05$, the critical value of Z is $z_\alpha = 1.645$, but the critical value for $\bar{x}^*$ now becomes

$$\begin{aligned}\bar{x}^* &= \mu_0 - z_\alpha \sigma/\sqrt{n} \\ &= 30 - 1.645(4/\sqrt{64}) = 29.1775\end{aligned}$$

This change is due to the increase in the sample size, which decreases the value $\sigma/\sqrt{n}$. The power of the test is

$$\text{Power} = P(\bar{X} < \bar{x}^*) = P(\bar{X} < 29.1775)$$

when the true value of μ is 28.5. To calculate this probability, we calculate the Z score as follows:

$$Z = \frac{\bar{x}^* - \mu_1}{\sigma/\sqrt{n}} = \frac{29.1775 - 28.5}{4/\sqrt{64}} \approx 1.36$$

We then obtain

$$\text{Power} = P(Z < 1.36) = .9131$$

Thus, the probability is .9131 that the null hypothesis will be rejected if the true mean is 28.5 miles per gallon, as illustrated in Figure 11.19. This shows that the test is fairly powerful in detecting that the null hypothesis is false when, in fact, $\mu = 28.5$. Recall from Example 11.24 that when $\mu = 28.5$ and the sample size is $n = 25$, the power of the test is .5910. Increasing the sample size increases the probability of detecting a false null hypothesis.

FIGURE 11.19
Power of test for Example 11.25.

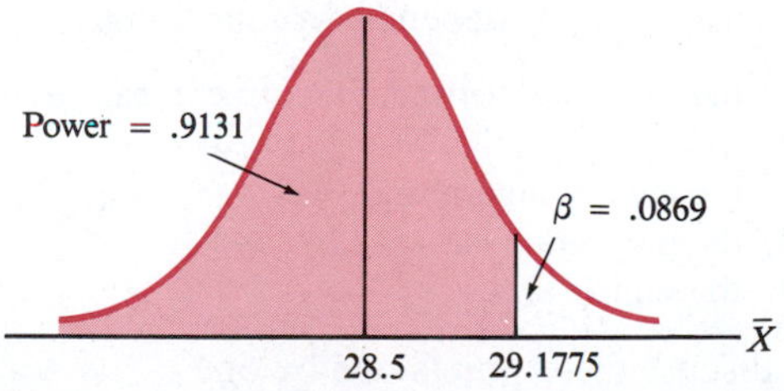

As in Example 11.24, the power of a test can be calculated for different values of μ_1 based on a sample size of $n = 64$ rather than $n = 25$. Table 11.2 shows the power of the test associated with different values of μ and n. For any specific value $\mu = \mu_1$, the power of the test when $n = 64$ exceeds the power of the test when $n = 25$. Table 11.2 also shows that the power is greater when $n = 100$ than when $n = 64$. The power curves for these three values of n are shown in Figure 11.20.

TABLE 11.2
Power of test in Example 11.25 for different values of μ and n:

	n		
μ	25	64	100
29.5	.1539	.2578	.3446
29.0	.3446	.6406	.8051
28.5	.5910	.9131	.9826
28.0	.8051	.9909	.9996
27.5	.9306	.9996	1.0000
27.0	.9846	1.0000	1.0000
26.5	.9968	1.0000	1.0000

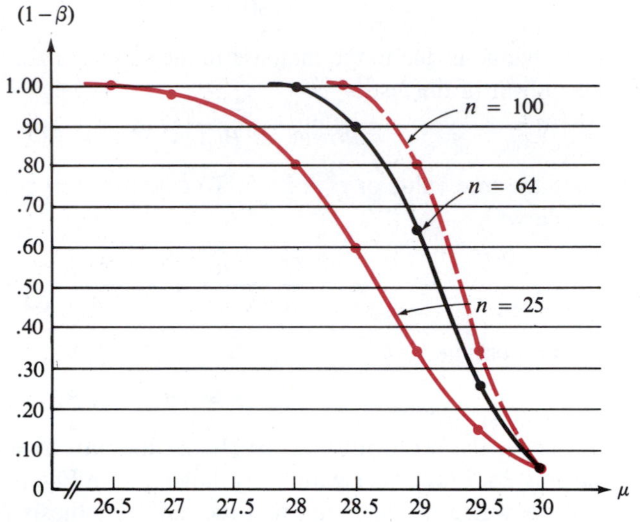

FIGURE 11.20
Power curves for Example 11.25 for different sample sizes.

Properties of the Power Curve

The power of a test depends on four things:

1. the distance between the true mean μ_1 and the hypothesized mean μ_0, which is $|\mu_1 - \mu_0|$,
2. the level of significance α,
3. the population variance σ^2, and
4. the sample size n.

Let's discuss these points one by one.

For given n, α, and σ^2, the further the true mean μ_1 is from the hypothesized mean μ_0, the greater the power of the test. Thus, as $|\mu_1 - \mu_0|$ increases, we are more likely to detect that the true mean is not μ_0.

For given n, σ^2, and μ_1, the smaller the significance level α, the smaller the power of the test. This is true because reducing α reduces the size of the rejection region, thus making it more difficult to reject the null hypothesis.

For given n, α, and μ_1, the larger the population variance σ^2, the lower the power of the test. It is more difficult to detect that the null hypothesis is false when there is greater variability in the population because increasing σ moves the critical value $\bar{x}^*$ farther out into the tail of the distribution and reduces the size of the rejection region. Consequently, this reduces the power of the test.

For given α, σ^2, and μ_1, the greater the sample size n, the higher the power of the test. The more information we have, the easier it becomes to detect any deviation from the null hypothesis.

Because the level of significance is usually set at some low value such as .05 or .01, it is relatively unlikely that a *true* null hypothesis will be rejected. In fact, a low level of significance makes it unlikely that we will reject the null hypothesis *even when it is false*. This is especially the case when the sample size is small or when the true value of the population parameter is close to that specified in the null hypothesis. Thus, the fact that we do not reject the null hypothesis does not necessarily mean that the null hypothesis is true, nor does it necessarily provide strong support for the null hypothesis.

Choosing a small value for α means that the power of the test will be small in many situations. Occasionally this is a reasonable procedure to follow. For example, in some manufacturing situations, we may not want to make costly alterations to a production process, retool a plant, or change a chemical formula unless we have very strong evidence that the change will be beneficial. On the other hand, there are many situations where the null hypothesis should not be accorded special status. In some circumstances, treating the null and alternative hypotheses more equally may be more appropriate. For example, if the costs of Type I and Type II errors are approximately equal, then the optimal strategy is to balance the probabilities of making these two types of errors. When the costs of errors are not known, however, there is no optimal procedure for balancing the costs of Type I and Type II errors.

A potential problem arises when we have a very large sample of data. As the sample size increases, the power of the test increases. By constantly increasing the sample size, we can make the power of the test approach 1 and virtually guarantee that a false null hypothesis will be rejected. Of course, we want to reject H_0 when H_0 is false, but occasionally people *misinterpret* the results of the statistical decision. It is customary for researchers to report that the results of a test are "statistically significant" and that the null hypothesis has been rejected. If the statistical results are "significant," we are led to conclude that the true situation differs from that stated in the null hypothesis.

When n is large and the power of the test approaches 1, it becomes relatively easy to detect even small deviations from the null hypothesis. In this situation, we must avoid the assumption that, just because we have rejected the null hypothesis, the difference between the null hypothesis and the true situation is of practical significance. This may or may not be the case. For instance, the null hypothesis may indeed be false, but the true situation may be so close to the null hypothesis that the difference is of no practical significance. In this situation, a statistical result that is "statistically significant" is not "practically significant." This issue is illustrated in the next example.

Example 11.26 **Statistical Versus Practical Significance:** The newspaper *USA Today* stated that, in the United States, the mean annual salary of male lawyers is $47,635 per year. A law firm in Texas wants to test whether the average salary of male lawyers in Texas is the same as the national average. Thus, the law firm will reject the *USA Today* claim if it obtains a sample mean that is either much higher or much lower than \$47,635. Thus a two-tailed test is appropriate, and the law firm wants to test

$$H_0: \mu = \$47{,}635$$

against the two-sided alternative hypothesis

$$H_1: \mu \neq \$47{,}635$$

Assume the population is normal with standard deviation $\sigma = \$10{,}000$, and use a 5% level of significance. Now consider two extreme cases: (1) The sample size is very small, $n = 9$; and (2) the sample size is very large, $n = 2500$. Find the acceptance region of the test statistic $\overline{X}$ in both cases.

Solution: Because the test is two-sided, the critical values of the test are

$$\bar{x}_1^* = \mu_0 - z_{\alpha/2}\sigma/\sqrt{n}$$

and

$$\bar{x}_2^* = \mu_0 + z_{\alpha/2}\sigma/\sqrt{n}$$

where $\mu_0 = \$47{,}635$, $z_{\alpha/2} = 1.96$, and $\sigma = \$10{,}000$. When $n = 9$, the acceptance region is any value of $\overline{X}$ between \$41,101.67 and \$54,168.33. When $n = 2500$, the acceptance region is any value of $\overline{X}$ between \$47,243 and \$48,027. Thus when $n = 9$, we would not reject H_0 even if we obtained $\bar{x} = \$54{,}000$, an amount almost \$7000 higher than the hypothesized mean. Here the true mean could be quite different from the hypothesized mean and it still might be very difficult to detect this difference.

When $n = 2500$, we would reject the null hypothesis if we obtained a sample mean such as $\bar{x} = \$48{,}028$. This sample mean is only \$393 from the hypothesized mean of \$47,635, which to most people is of little practical significance. Although the difference would be *statistically* significant, it would not be *practically* significant. ■

Power Curve for Two-Sided Tests

When the alternative hypothesis is two-sided, part of the rejection region falls in each tail of the distribution. To calculate the power of the test, we have to calculate the probability that the test statistic falls in either rejection region given that H_0 is false, as illustrated in the next example.

Example 11.27 **Calculating the Power of the Test When the Alternative Hypothesis Is Two-Sided:** A marketing report states that the annual per capita expenditures on cereal follow a normal distribution with mean $\mu = \$60$ and standard deviation $\sigma = \$15$. We want to test

$$H_0: \mu = 60$$

against the two-sided alternative hypothesis

$$H_1: \mu \neq 60$$

using a 5% level of significance and a random sample of $n = 100$ customers. Find the power curve associated with this test.

Solution: For $\alpha = .05$, we obtain $z_{\alpha/2} = 1.96$. The critical values of the test are

$$\bar{x}_1^* = \mu_0 - z_{\alpha/2}\sigma/\sqrt{n} = 57.06$$

and

$$\bar{x}_2^* = \mu_0 + z_{\alpha/2}\sigma/\sqrt{n} = 62.94$$

We accept H_0 if $(57.06 \leqslant \bar{X} \leqslant 62.94)$, as shown in Figure 11.21. The power of the test is the probability that $\bar{X}$ falls in the rejection region when H_0 is indeed false. Suppose that the true value of the mean is $\mu = 58$. We then obtain

$$\begin{aligned} \text{Power} &= P(\bar{X} < \bar{x}_1^*) + P(\bar{X} > \bar{x}_2^*) \\ &= P(\bar{X} < 57.06) + P(\bar{X} > 62.94) \end{aligned}$$

FIGURE 11.21
Acceptance region for Example 11.27.

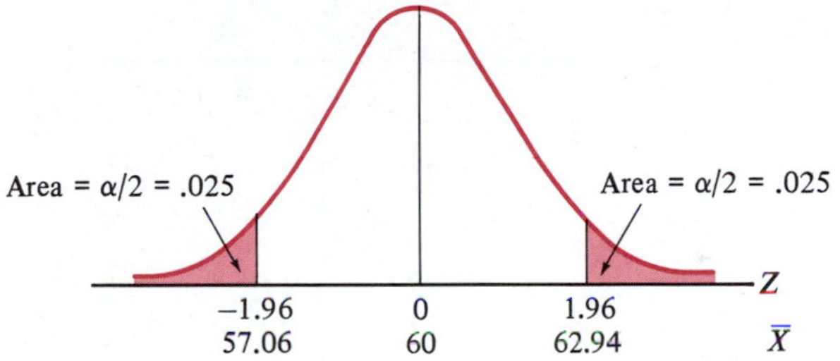

This probability is shown as the shaded area in Figure 11.22. To calculate the shaded area, we obtain the Z scores using $\mu = 58$ as follows:

$$z_1 = \frac{57.06 - 58}{15/\sqrt{100}} = -.63 \quad \text{and} \quad z_2 = \frac{62.94 - 58}{15/\sqrt{100}} = 3.29$$

FIGURE 11.22
Power of test for Example 11.27.

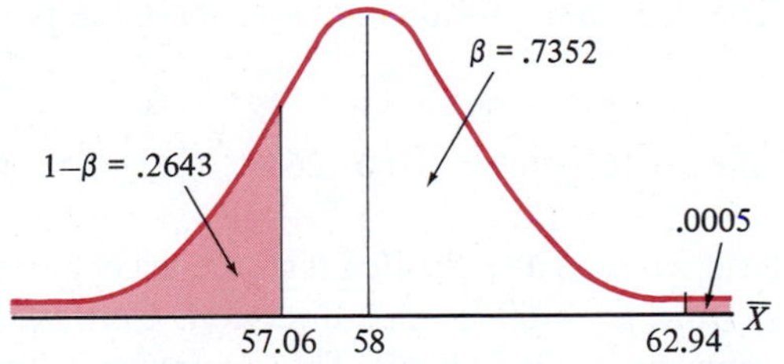

We then obtain

$$\begin{aligned} \text{Power} &= P(\bar{X} < 57.06) + P(\bar{X} > 62.94) \\ &= P(Z < -.63) + P(Z > 3.29) \\ &= .2643 + .0005 = .2648 \end{aligned}$$

To get other points on the power curve, assign μ other values and repeat the process. The shaded areas in Figure 11.23 show the power of the test for several values of μ.

FIGURE 11.23
Power of test for different values of μ in Example 11.27.

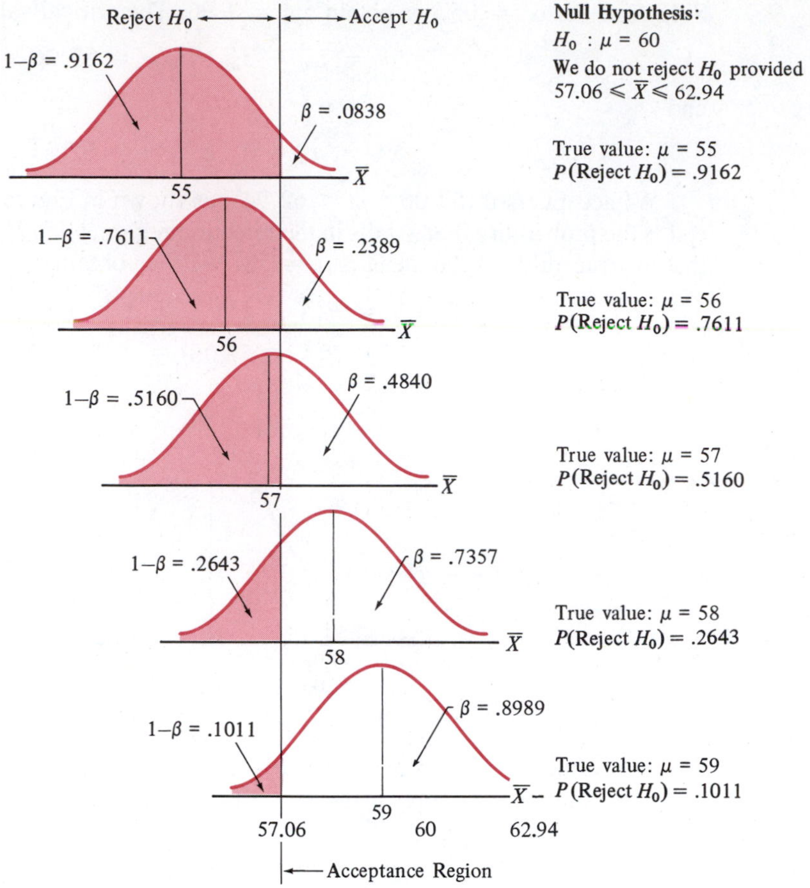

The data in the following table show the power of the test for various values of μ:

μ	55	56	57	58	59		60	61	62	63	64	65
Power	.9162	.7611	.5160	.2648	.1011	α =	.0500	.1011	.2648	.5160	.7611	.9162

Because we used a two-tailed test, the acceptance region extends an equal distance (2.94 units) from $\mu = 60$ in each direction. Consequently, the power curve for this problem is symmetric about $\mu = 60$. This symmetry is present in any two-tailed test of the mean. Because the null hypothesis H_0 is true when $\mu = 60$, it is not possible to commit a Type II error when $\mu = 60$. When H_0 is true, the probability that the test statistic falls in the rejection region is not the power of the test but rather it is α, the level of significance of the test. When the true value of μ is extremely close to 60, the probability that the test statistic falls in the rejection region is approximately equal to α, the level of significance. Thus, the power of the test always exceeds α and approaches α as μ approaches 60. Figure 11.24, the power curve associated with the preceding data, illustrates that the power curve is symmetric about $\mu = 60$. ■

FIGURE 11.24
Power curve for Example 11.27.

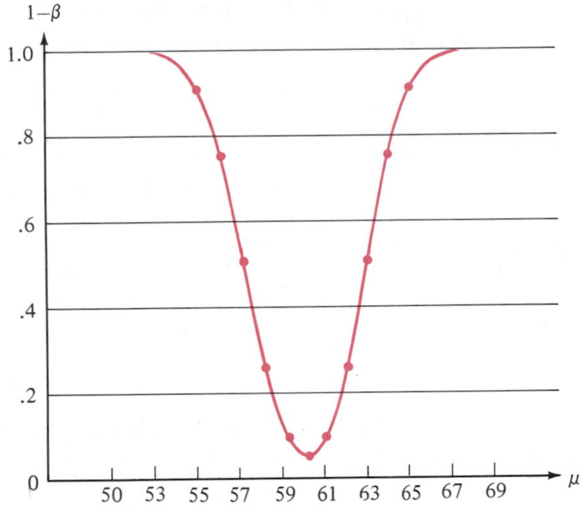

Tips for Problem Solving

Suppose you are testing the null hypothesis

$$H_0\colon \mu = \mu_0$$

To calculate the power of a test, follow these steps:

1. Record the sample size n, the level of significance α, the hypothesized mean μ_0, and the population standard deviation σ.
2. Record the standard deviation of $\overline{X}$. This standard deviation is $\sigma/\sqrt{n}$, *not* σ.
3. Sketch the normal distribution showing the sampling distribution of $\overline{X}$. This distribution has mean μ_0 and standard deviation $\sigma/\sqrt{n}$. For a one-tailed test, shade an area equal to α in the appropriate tail. For a two-tailed test, shade an area of $\alpha/2$ in each tail.
4. Sketch a standard normal distribution and shade the tail area as in step 3. Find the critical values of the Z scores associated with the shaded tail area(s).
5. Find the critical value(s) of $\overline{X}$ associated with the critical value(s) of Z.
6. State the critical region and the acceptance region in terms of the critical values of $\overline{X}$.
7. Record the new hypothesized value of the population mean, denoted μ_1.
8. Sketch the new normal distribution showing the hypothesized sampling distribution of $\overline{X}$. This distribution has mean μ_1 and standard deviation $\sigma/\sqrt{n}$. Shade the areas corresponding to the critical region found in step 5.
9. Evaluate the shaded area(s) obtained in step 8. This is the power of the test.

Calculating the Power of the Test of a Population Proportion

The following procedures summarize how to calculate the power of the test of a hypothesis about a population proportion p using a one-sided or two-sided test:

Case 1: Suppose we take a random sample of n observations and calculate the sample proportion $\hat{p}$ to test the null hypothesis

$$H_0\colon p = p_0$$

against the one-sided alternative hypothesis

$$H_1\colon p > p_0$$

where the significance level is α. If $np_0 \geqslant 5$ and $nq_0 \geqslant 5$, then $\hat{p}$ has an approximately normal distribution. Because the alternative hypothesis lies entirely to the right of $p = p_0$, the entire rejection region is placed in the right tail of the sampling distribution of $\hat{p}$ and consists of all values of the sample proportion exceeding the critical value $\hat{p}^*$ where

$$\hat{p}^* = p_0 + z_\alpha \sqrt{p_0 q_0 / n}$$

The power of the test equals the probability that the test statistic falls in the rejection region when H_0 is false, so we obtain

$$\begin{aligned} \text{Power} &= P(\hat{p} > \hat{p}^*) \\ &= P(\hat{p} > p_0 + z_\alpha \sqrt{p_0 q_0 / n}) \end{aligned}$$

when $p = p_1$. Equivalently, we obtain

$$\text{Power} = P\left(Z > \frac{(\hat{p}^* - p_1)}{\sqrt{p_1 q_1 / n}} \right)$$

Case 2: Suppose we are testing the null hypothesis

$$H_0\colon p = p_0$$

against the alternative hypothesis

$$H_1\colon p < p_0$$

where the significance level is α and n is the sample size. If we use $\hat{p}$ as a test statistic, then the rejection region consists of all values of the sample proportion less than the critical value $\hat{p}^*$, where

$$\hat{p}^* = p_0 - z_\alpha \sqrt{p_0 q_0 / n}$$

In this case, the entire rejection region is placed in the left tail of the sampling distribution of $\hat{p}$ because the alternative hypothesis $H_1\colon p < p_0$ lies entirely to the left of $p = p_0$. In this case, we obtain

$$\begin{aligned} \text{Power} &= P(\hat{p} < \hat{p}^*) \\ &= P(\hat{p} < p_0 - z_\alpha \sqrt{p_0 q_0 / n}) \end{aligned}$$

when $p = p_1$. Equivalently, we obtain

$$\text{Power} = P\left(Z < \frac{\hat{p}^* - p_1}{\sqrt{p_1 q_1 / n}} \right)$$

Case 3: Suppose we are testing the null hypothesis

$$H_0\colon p = p_0$$

against the two-sided alternative hypothesis

$$H_1: p \neq p_0$$

where the significance level is α and n is the sample size. If we use $\hat{p}$ as a test statistic, then the two critical values are

$$\hat{p}_1^* = p_0 - z_{\alpha/2}\sqrt{p_0 q_0/n}$$

and

$$\hat{p}_2^* = p_0 + z_{\alpha/2}\sqrt{p_0 q_0/n}$$

We obtain

$$\text{Power} = P(\hat{p} < \hat{p}_1^*) + P(\hat{p} > \hat{p}_2^*)$$

when $p = p_1$. Equivalently, we obtain

$$\text{Power} = P\left(Z < \frac{\hat{p}_1^* - p_1}{\sqrt{p_1 q_1/n}}\right) + P\left(Z > \frac{\hat{p}_2^* - p_1}{\sqrt{p_1 q_1/n}}\right)$$

Example 11.28 **Power Curve for a One-Tailed Test of a Proportion:** Last year 40% of the TV audience watched the late night news on Channel 2. Hoping to increase its audience share, the station expands its sports coverage. If the new format does not increase the station's share of the audience during a trial period, the station will return to its old format. Because the station will not retain the expanded sports format unless $p > .4$, the station wants to test the null hypothesis

$$H_0: p \leqslant .4$$

against the one-sided alternative hypothesis

$$H_1: p > .4$$

Suppose we take a random sample of $n = 100$ viewers and perform a one-tailed test using 5% level of significance. Find the power curve associated with this test.

Solution: We have $z_\alpha = 1.645$, $n = 100$, and $p_0 = .4$. The rejection region consists of all values of the sample proportion $\hat{p}$ exceeding the critical value $\hat{p}^*$ where

$$\begin{aligned}\hat{p}^* &= p_0 + z_\alpha\sqrt{p_0 q_0/n} \\ &= .4 + 1.645\sqrt{(.4)(.6)/100} \approx .48\end{aligned}$$

The rejection region consists of all values of $\hat{p}$ such that $\hat{p} > .48$.

Now assume that the new news format actually increases the station's market share to .5. Then the sample proportion $\hat{p}$ is approximately normally distributed with mean .5 and variance $(.5)(.5)/100$. (Note that the variance is different when $p = .5$ than when $p = .4$.) The power of the test is given by

$$\text{Power} = P(\hat{p} > .48 | p = .5)$$

This situation is shown in Figure 11.25.

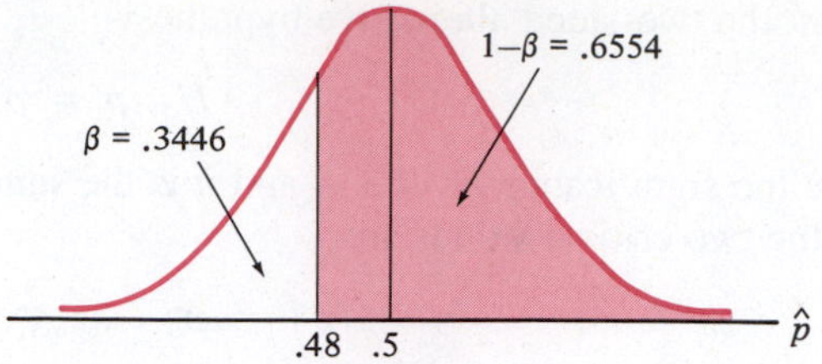

FIGURE 11.25
Power of test in Example 11.28.

We obtain the Z score

$$z = \frac{.48 - .5}{\sqrt{(.5)(.5)/100}} = -.40$$

Finally, we get

$$P(\hat{p} > .48) = P(Z > -.40) = .6554$$

To find other points on the power curve, we assume other values for p, as calculated in the following table:

p	.40	.42	.45	.48	.50	.55	.60
Power	(α = .0500)	.1093	.2709	.5000	.6554	.9207	.9929

Using these data we obtain the power curve shown in Figure 11.26. The power curve shows that this test is relatively powerful when p exceeds .5 but not when p is less than .5.

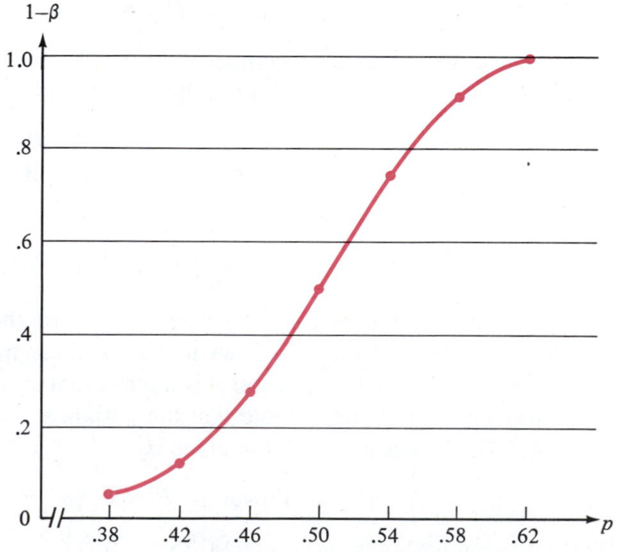

FIGURE 11.26
Power curve for Example 11.28.

Example 11.29 **Effect of Increasing Sample Size in Example 11.28:** In Example 11.28, we showed that when $p = .50$, the power of the test is .6554. This value depends upon the fact that $\alpha = .05$ and $n = 100$. Suppose we increase the sample size to $n = 400$ and keep $\alpha = .05$. Show that the power will increase.

Solution: To show this relationship, we must find a new rejection region based on a sample of 400. We have $z_\alpha = 1.645$, $n = 400$, and $p_0 = .4$. The rejection region consists of all values of the sample proportion $\hat{p}$ exceeding the critical value $\hat{p}^*$ where

$$\begin{aligned}\hat{p}^* &= p_0 + z_\alpha\sqrt{p_0q_0/n}\\ &= .4 + 1.645\sqrt{(.4)(.6)/400} \approx .44\end{aligned}$$

When $n = 100$, the rejection region is $\hat{p} > .48$. In the present case, when $n = 400$, the rejection region is $\hat{p} > .44$. The power of the test is

$$\text{Power} = P(\hat{p} > .44|p = .5)$$

We obtain the Z score

$$z = \frac{.44 - .5}{\sqrt{(.5)(.5)/400}} = -2.46$$

which gives us

$$P(\hat{p} > .44) = P(Z > -2.46) = .9931$$

Increasing the sample size from 100 to 400 increases the power of the test from .6554 to .9931. For a fixed value of α, we can always increase the power of the test by increasing n. ■

Exercises for Section 11.7

1. An inspector takes a random sample of 100 components to test the null hypothesis that the population proportion of defectives is at most 10% against the alternative hypothesis that more than 10% are defective. The decision rule is to reject the null hypothesis if the sample proportion of defectives exceeds .13.
   a. What is the significance level of this test?
   b. What is the power of the test if the population proportion of defectives is .15?
2. At a supermarket, the average number of register mistakes per day per clerk was 18 with standard deviation 5. The owner of the supermarket purchased new cash registers in an effort to decrease the number of errors. The manager then took a random sample of 100 clerks on randomly selected days using the new registers to test H_0: $\mu = 18$ against H_1: $\mu \neq 18$.
   a. Find the critical values of the sample mean $\bar{X}$ such that the level of significance is 5%.
   b. Find the critical values of the sample mean $\bar{X}$ such that the level of significance is 1%.
   c. Suppose the sample size is 36 rather than 100. Find the critical values of the sample mean $\bar{X}$ such that the level of significance is 5%.
   d. In part (c), suppose the population mean is $\mu = 16$. Find the power of the test.
   e. In part (a), suppose that $\mu = 16$. Find the power of the test.
   f. Compare and explain the differences between answers to parts (d) and (e).

3. With traditional advertising by mail, magazine sales in a community have averaged 26 per day with standard deviation 5. A new sales technique is devised in which customers are given samples of the magazines and a certificate entitling them to a reduced price on a meal at a local restaurant. The technique is tried for 100 days. We want to test H_0: $\mu = 26$ against H_1: $\mu > 26$.

a. Design a one-tailed test having a 5% level of significance. Find the critical value $\bar{x}^*$ that separates the acceptance region from the critical region.

b. If $\bar{x} = 27$, what decision would you make in part (a)?

c. Suppose the population mean is $\mu = 27$. Find the power of the test.

4. A psychologist claims that male juvenile delinquents tend to be shorter than average and attributes some of their behavior problems to the fact that they are self-conscious about their height. Suppose the average height of 16-year-old boys is 62 inches with standard deviation 5. In a random sample of 100 male 16-year-old juvenile delinquents, the average height was $\bar{x} = 60.4$ inches.

a. Design a one-tailed test having a 5% level of significance to test H_0: $\mu = 62$ against H_1: $\mu < 62$.

b. Using part (a), find the power of the test if, in fact, the average height of juvenile delinquents is $\mu = 60$.

c. Using part (a), what decision would you make if $\bar{x} = 60.4$?

5. The quality control department of a food processing firm wants to test whether the average weight per package of a certain food is at least 25 ounces. Past experience indicates that the standard deviation of weight is 0.3 ounce. A random sample of 144 packages is obtained.

a. Design a decision rule to test H_0: $\mu = 25$ against H_1: $\mu \neq 25$ such that $\alpha = 5\%$.

b. If the true population mean is $\mu = 24.8$, find the power of the test.

c. Repeat part (a) assuming the sample size is 36.

d. In part (c), assume the population mean is 24.8. Find the power of the test.

6. A college administrator claims that at most 60% of the people who take evening courses while working part-time finish the course. The college introduces a new program of monitoring the progress of students in order to help them complete their courses. A random sample of 100 students is taken to determine if the new program reduces the number of dropouts.

a. Design a rule to test H_0: $p = .6$ against H_1: $p > .6$ using a 5% level of significance.

b. In part (a), find the power of the test if $p = .65$.

7. A business executive thinks that opening a Japanese restaurant would be profitable if at least 5% of the people in the community are interested in dining there. A random sample of 500 people in the community is obtained.

a. Design a rule to test H_0: $p \geqslant .05$ against H_1: $p < .05$ using a 5% level of significance.

b. If $\hat{p} = .04$, what decision would you make?

c. Find the power of the test if the actual proportion is $p = .035$.

8. The McCormick Food Company sells 10-ounce cans of peas. The cans always contain several ounces of water. The quality control department wants to test whether the average weight of peas in the cans is at least 7 ounces. It is assumed that the standard deviation is $\sigma = 0.2$ ounce. A random sample of 100 cans of peas is tested.

a. Design a decision rule to test H_0: $\mu \geqslant 7$ against H_1: $\mu < 7$ using a 1% level of significance.

b. If in the sample $\bar{x} = 6.7$, what decision should be made?

c. Find the power of the test if $\mu = 6.9, 6.8, 6.7$, and 6.6 ounces.

11.8 • The Chi-Square Distribution

So far we have discussed how to test hypotheses about a population mean or a population proportion, but in many situations we are interested in testing a hypothesis about the population variance. To test such a hypothesis, we must compute a test statistic that depends on the sample variance S^2. If the null hypothesis is true and the population follows a normal distribution, then the test statistic used has a sampling distribution that follows the **chi-square distribution.** Thus, to test a hypothesis about a population variance, we need to know how to find the critical region of a chi-square distribution. In this section, we discuss the properties of the chi-square distribution and show how to calculate areas under the chi-square density function.

Like the t distribution, the chi-square distribution is a continuous probability distribution that depends on only one parameter, the degrees of freedom (ν) and consists of a family of distributions, one for each value of ν. Just as random variables that follow the t distribution are denoted by the letter t, random variables that follow the chi-square distribution are denoted by the symbol χ^2 (Greek chi squared).

Characteristics of the Chi-Square Distribution

1. The random variable χ^2 varies from 0 to ∞ and is never negative.
2. As with all probability density functions, the density function of χ^2 is always nonnegative and the area beneath the curve is 1.
3. For small values of ν, the chi-square distribution is skewed to the right, but as ν increases the curve becomes approximately symmetric. For $\nu = 1$ and $\nu = 2$, the curve is decreasing.
4. For large values of ν, say, 20 or more, the distribution is closely approximated by a normal curve.
5. The mean of the chi-square distribution is ν.
6. The variance of the chi-square distribution is 2ν. Thus, the mean and variance depend on the degrees of freedom.

Figure 11.27 shows some chi-square distributions for different degrees of freedom. Note that as the degrees of freedom increases, the curve becomes more symmetric. Because each value of ν yields a separate distribution, as with the t distribution, presenting detailed tables showing the areas under all the curves is not feasible. Instead, we have a table (Table A.7 in the Appendix) showing the critical values of χ^2 for different degrees of freedom, as we had for the t distribution. To test hypotheses with the chi-square distribution, we need to find the critical values of the chi-square distribution

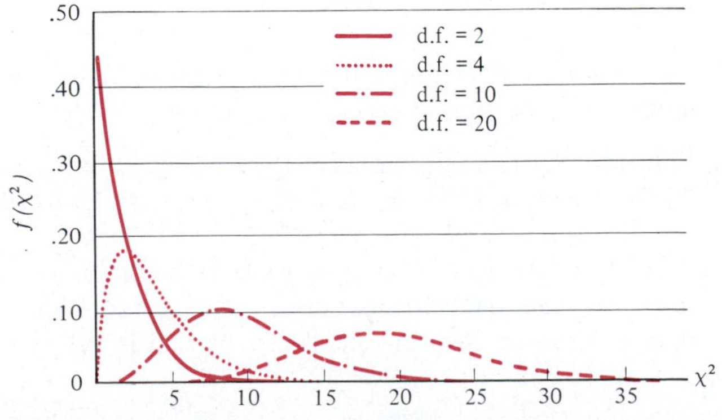

FIGURE 11.27
Some chi-square distributions with different degrees of freedom.

having a right-hand tail area of α, where α is the level of significance of the test. The critical value depends on the degrees of freedom. The examples below indicate how to calculate the critical value for a chi-square distribution having ν degrees of freedom.

Critical Value $\chi^2_{\alpha,\nu}$

Let the random variable χ^2 follow the chi-square distribution having ν degrees of freedom. The expression $\chi^2_{\alpha,\nu}$ denotes the value such that

$$P(\chi^2 > \chi^2_{\alpha,\nu}) = \alpha$$

That is, if χ^2 follows a chi-square distribution with ν degrees of freedom, then the area under the density function to the right of $\chi^2_{\alpha,\nu}$ is α and the probability that χ^2 exceeds $\chi^2_{\alpha,\nu}$ is α.

Example 11.30 **Finding a Critical Value for a Chi-Square Distribution I:** Figure 11.28 shows the graph of the chi-square distribution with $\nu = 6$ degrees of freedom. Find the critical value of χ^2 such that the shaded area is .05.

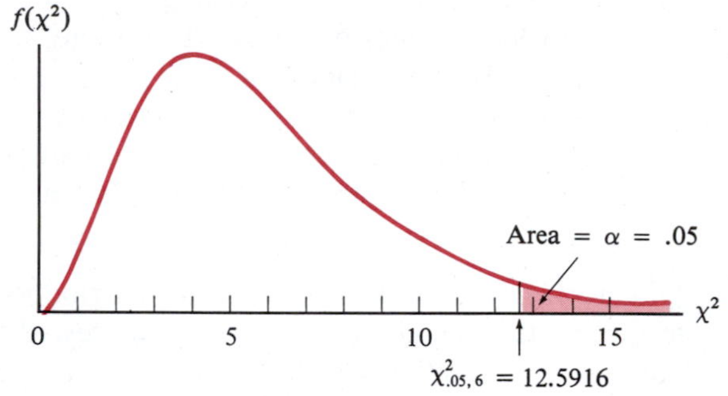

FIGURE 11.28
Chi-square distribution having 6 degrees of freedom.

Solution: Turn to Table A.7. Proceed down the "Degrees of Freedom" column to $\nu = 6$. Now move to the right until you reach the column ".05." The result is $\chi^2_{.05,6} =$ 12.5916. Thus, we know

$$P(\chi^2 > 12.5916) = .05$$

if χ^2 has 6 degrees of freedom. ■

Example 11.31 **Finding a Critical Value for a Chi-Square Distribution II:** Find the value of χ^2 such that the shaded area in Figure 11.28 is .01.

Solution: Once again we have $\nu = 6$ degrees of freedom. We seek the value $\chi^2_{.01,6}$ in Table A.7. When $\nu = 6$, we find that $\chi^2_{.01,6} = 16.8119$. ■

To construct confidence intervals for a population variance and to perform two-tailed tests, we need to find critical values of χ^2 such that the area in *each* tail of the distribution is $\alpha/2$. Because the chi-square distribution is not symmetric, the critical value for the left tail must be calculated independently of that for the right tail. The critical value such that the area in the left tail is $\alpha/2$ is denoted $\chi^2_{(1-\alpha/2),\nu}$ because the area to its right is $(1 - \alpha/2)$.

Exercises for Section 11.8

1. Suppose that χ^2 has $\nu = 8$ degrees of freedom. Find the values of χ^2 such that the right-hand tail has the following areas:
   a. .05 b. .01 c. .10
2. Suppose that χ^2 has $\nu = 4$ degrees of freedom. Find the values of χ^2 such that the right-hand tail has the following areas:
   a. .05 b. .01 c. .10
3. Let the random variable χ^2 have a chi-square distribution with ν degrees of freedom. Find the value $\chi^2_{\alpha,\nu}$ such that $P(\chi^2 > \chi^2_{\alpha,\nu}) = \alpha$ where the values of α and ν are as follows:
   a. $\alpha = .01$; $\nu = 4$ b. $\alpha = .05$; $\nu = 7$
4. Suppose that χ^2 has $\nu = 6$ degrees of freedom. Find the values of χ^2 such that the left-hand tail has the following areas:
   a. .01 b. .05 c. .10

11.9 ▪ Testing Hypotheses and Constructing Confidence Intervals About a Population Variance

To estimate a population variance σ^2, we take a random sample of size n and calculate the sample variance S^2 using the formula

$$S^2 = \sum_{i=1}^{n} \frac{(X_i - \overline{X})^2}{n - 1}$$

Because S^2 varies from sample to sample, S^2 is a random variable and has a sampling distribution. A variance can never be negative, so the probability distribution of S^2 begins at $S^2 = 0$. Since the mean of this probability distribution is the true value σ^2, the sample variance S^2 is an unbiased estimator of σ^2. The exact form of the sampling distribution of S^2 depends upon the probability distribution of the population.

In this discussion, we assume that a random sample is selected from a normal population. The results will still hold approximately when the parent population is nonnormal, provided the deviations from normality are not too severe.

It can be shown that if the population is normal, the random variable

$$\chi^2 = \frac{(n - 1)S^2}{\sigma^2}$$

follows the chi-square distribution with $\nu = (n - 1)$ degrees of freedom. We use this result when testing hypotheses about σ^2 and constructing confidence intervals for σ^2.

Testing Hypotheses About σ^2

Let X be a random variable that follows a normal distribution with mean μ and variance σ^2. Suppose we want to test the hypothesis that the variance σ^2 equals some specific value σ_0^2 using level of significance α. The test is based on the sample variance S^2 and the test statistic $(n - 1)S^2/\sigma_0^2$, where σ_0^2 is the hypothesized variance. Let $\chi^2_{\alpha/2,\nu}$ be the value of the chi-square variable such that the area to its right is $\alpha/2$. It follows that $\chi^2_{(1-\alpha/2),\nu}$ is the value of the chi-square variable such that the area to its right is $(1 - \alpha/2)$ and the area to its left is $\alpha/2$. This idea is illustrated in Figure 11.29. Given the value of α, we can find $\chi^2_{1-\alpha/2,\nu}$ and $\chi^2_{\alpha/2,\nu}$ for the chi-square distribution having ν degrees of freedom by using Table A.7.

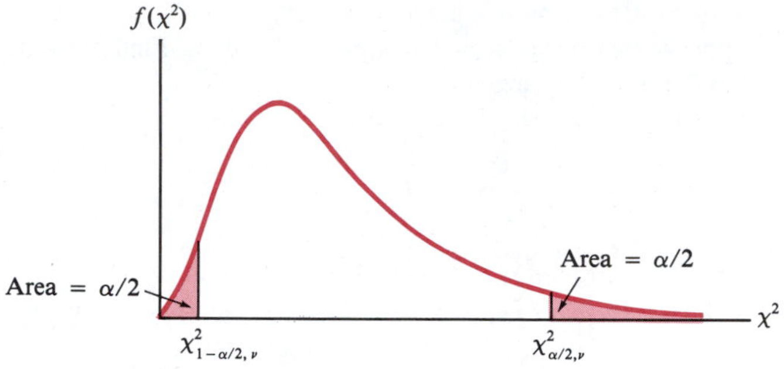

FIGURE 11.29
Critical region for the chi-square statistic when performing a two-tailed test about a population variance.

Suppose we want to test the null hypothesis

$$H_0: \sigma^2 = \sigma_0^2$$

against the two-sided alternative hypothesis

$$H_1: \sigma^2 \neq \sigma_0^2$$

If H_0 is true, then the following probability statement holds:

$$P\left(\chi^2_{1-\alpha/2,\nu} \leqslant \frac{(n - 1)S^2}{\sigma_0^2} \leqslant \chi^2_{\alpha/2,\nu}\right) = \alpha$$

Using level of significance α, we would accept the null hypothesis if $(n - 1)S^2/\sigma_0^2$ was between $\chi^2_{1-\alpha/2,\nu}$ and $\chi^2_{\alpha/2,\nu}$, as shown in Figure 11.29. If $(n - 1)S^2/\sigma_0^2$ was less than $\chi^2_{1-\alpha/2,\nu}$ or greater than $\chi^2_{\alpha/2,\nu}$, then we would reject H_0 in favor of H_1.

For a one-tailed test, the entire rejection region is placed in one tail of the chi-square distribution, and we reject H_0 in favor of H_1 if the test statistic $\chi^2 = (n - 1)S^2/\sigma_0^2$ falls in the rejection region. The procedure for testing an hypothesis about the population variance is summarized in the accompanying box.

Testing Hypotheses About the Variance of a Normal Population

Suppose we have a random sample of n observations from a normal population with variance σ_0^2. Let s^2 denote the observed sample variance. The following tests have level of significance α:

Case 1: To test the null hypothesis

$$H_0: \sigma^2 = \sigma_0^2 \quad \text{or} \quad H_0: \sigma^2 \leqslant \sigma_0^2$$

against the one-sided alternative hypothesis

$$H_1: \sigma^2 > \sigma_0^2$$

calculate the test statistic

$$\chi^2 = (n - 1)s^2/\sigma_0^2$$

and use the decision rule

$$\text{Reject } H_0 \text{ in favor of } H_1 \text{ if } \chi^2 > \chi^2_{\alpha,n-1}.$$

Case 2: To test the null hypothesis

$$H_0: \sigma^2 = \sigma_0^2 \quad \text{or} \quad H_0: \sigma^2 \geqslant \sigma_0^2$$

against the one-sided alternative hypothesis

$$H_1: \sigma^2 < \sigma_0^2$$

use the decision rule

$$\text{Reject } H_0 \text{ in favor of } H_1 \text{ if } \chi^2 > \chi^2_{1-\alpha,n-1}$$

Case 3: To test the null hypothesis

$$H_0: \sigma^2 = \sigma_0^2$$

against the two-sided alternative hypothesis

$$H_1: \sigma^2 \neq \sigma_0^2$$

use the decision rule

$$\text{Reject } H_0 \text{ in favor of } H_1 \text{ if } \chi^2 > \chi^2_{\alpha/2,n-1} \text{ or if } \chi^2 < \chi^2_{1-\alpha/2,n-1}$$

Example 11.32 **Testing a Hypothesis About a Population Variance:** Suppose we take a random sample of $n = 26$ observations from a normal population in order to test the null hypothesis

$$H_0: \sigma^2 = 150$$

against the two-sided alternative hypothesis

$$H_1: \sigma^2 \neq 150$$

using a 10% level of significance. Suppose the observed sample variance is $s^2 = 175$. Perform the test.

Solution: The test statistic is

$$\frac{(n-1)s^2}{\sigma_0^2} = \frac{(25)(175)}{150} = 29.167$$

For a two-tailed test with $\alpha = .10$, we place an area of .05 in each tail of the distribution. From Table A.7 using $(n - 1) = 25$ degrees of freedom, we obtain the critical values $\chi^2_{.95,25} = 14.61$ and $\chi^2_{.05,25} = 37.65$. Because 29.167 lies between 14.61 and 37.65, we do not reject the null hypothesis. See Figure 11.30.

FIGURE 11.30
Chi-square distribution for Example 11.32.

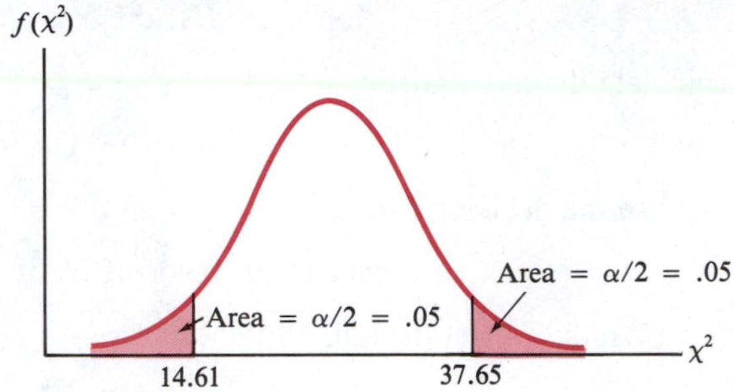

■

Confidence Intervals for the Population Variance

To construct confidence intervals for a population variance, we again make use of the test statistic $(n - 1)S^2/\sigma^2$ and the chi-square probability distribution. To construct a confidence interval having level of confidence $(1 - \alpha)$, we utilize the probability statement

$$P\left(\chi^2_{1-\alpha/2,\nu} \leq \frac{(n-1)S^2}{\sigma^2} \leq \chi^2_{\alpha/2,\nu}\right) = 1 - \alpha$$

This is equivalent to the statement

$$P\left(\frac{\chi^2_{1-\alpha/2,\nu}}{(n-1)S^2} \leq \frac{1}{\sigma^2} \leq \frac{\chi^2_{\alpha/2,\nu}}{(n-1)S^2}\right) = 1 - \alpha$$

Finally, we obtain

$$P\left(\frac{(n-1)S^2}{\chi^2_{\alpha/2,\nu}} \leq \sigma^2 \leq \frac{(n-1)S^2}{\chi^2_{1-\alpha/2,\nu}}\right) = 1 - \alpha$$

Formula for a Confidence Interval for σ^2

Suppose we have a random sample of n observations from a normal population with unknown variance σ^2. Let the observed sample variance be s^2. A confidence interval for σ^2 having level of confidence $(1 - \alpha)$ is given by

$$\left(\frac{(n-1)s^2}{\chi^2_{\alpha/2,\nu}}, \frac{(n-1)s^2}{\chi^2_{1-\alpha/2,\nu}}\right)$$

Example 11.33 **Establishing a Confidence Interval for the Population Variance:** A new radar device is intended to enable police officers to measure the speed of passing cars instantaneously. To determine the reliability of the device, 61 cars were driven past an inspection point at precisely 50 miles per hour, and each car's speed was estimated by using the radar device. It is assumed that the population of readings is normal. Suppose the observed sample variance was $s^2 = 5$. Construct a 95% confidence interval for σ^2.

Solution: The desired level of confidence is $(1 - \alpha) = .95$. Thus, each tail of the chi-square distribution should contain an area equal to 0.025. By using Table A.7 and 60 degrees of freedom, we obtain $\chi^2_{.975,60} = 40.48$ and $\chi^2_{.025,60} = 83.30$. This yields a 95% confidence interval of

$$\left(\frac{(60)(5)}{83.30}, \frac{(60)(5)}{40.48}\right)$$

or

$$(3.60, 7.41)$$

Thus, we are 95% confident that the true value of σ^2 lies between 3.60 and 7.41.

If the variance is 3.60, then the standard deviation is $\sqrt{3.60} = 1.90$. Similarly, if the variance is 7.41, then the standard deviation is 2.72. Thus, a 95% confidence interval for the standard deviation is (1.90, 2.72). If the radar gun readings are approximately normally distributed, then about 95% of the observations should lie within 1.96σ units of the mean. If the population standard deviation is as large as 2.72, then approximately 95% of the radar readings should be within $(1.96)(2.72) = 5.33$ units of the true value. However, a radar measurement that is in error by as much as 5.33 miles per hour would be unsatisfactory for highway patrols, so a better measuring device is needed. On the other hand, knowing that the device measures the speed correctly within about 5.33 miles per hour indicates that the police should feel safe in giving tickets to anyone who is clocked going more than 5.33 miles per hour above the speed limit. ■

Exercises for Section 11.9

1. A certain population of individuals has a mean IQ of 100, but the variance is unknown. In a random sample of 21 individuals, the sample variance was $s^2 = 214$. Calculate the following confidence intervals for σ^2:
   a. 95% b. 99%
2. A machine at the Romano Drill Bit Company makes $\frac{1}{4}$-inch ball bearings. When the machine is operating properly, the variance of the diameter of the bearings is at most 0.0004 inch. In a random sample of 41 bearings, the sample variance was $s^2 = .0007$. Use a 1% level of significance and test H_0: $\sigma^2 \leq 0.0004$ against H_1: $\sigma^2 > 0.0004$.
3. To be accepted in professional tournaments, tennis balls must pass rigorous tests proving that there is a minimum variance in liveliness from one ball to another. When the balls are dropped from a specified height, they must rebound to a height of 4 feet on the average. The brand of ball satisfying this requirement with the least variance will be selected for use on the pro tour. A new brand of ball, the Australian Gold, is produced. In a random sample of 91 balls, the height of each bounce had a sample mean of 4 feet with a sample variance of 0.36.

a. Find a 90% confidence interval for the population variance.
b. Find a 95% confidence interval for the population variance.
c. The ball currently used on the tour has a population variance $\sigma^2 = 0.46$. The Australian Gold ball will be used if its variance is smaller. For the Australian Gold ball, test the null hypothesis H_0: $\sigma^2 \geqslant 0.46$ against H_1: $\sigma^2 < 0.46$ with a 5% level of significance.

11.10 ▪ Computer Applications

When we test a null hypothesis about a population mean, we typically obtain a random sample of n observations from a population having an unknown variance. As described earlier, to test the null hypothesis H_0: $\mu = \mu_0$ where μ_0 is some specified value of μ, we use the test statistic

$$t = \frac{\overline{X} - \mu_0}{S/\sqrt{n}}$$

To perform the test we need to calculate both the sample mean $\overline{X}$ and the sample standard deviation S. When the sample size is large, these tasks can be tedious. In Chapter 4, we showed that to obtain the sample mean and sample variance using the SPSSX program, we issue the CONDESCRIPTIVE command followed by the names of the variables whose means and standard deviations are desired.

For example, refer to the data in Table 2.2 of Chapter 2, showing the selected characteristics of a sample of 50 students in a statistics class. Suppose we wish to test the null hypothesis that in the population the mean SAT score is 1000 using a two-tailed test and a 5% level of significance. To obtain the sample mean and sample standard deviation for the variables SAT and GPA, issue the command

```
CONDESCRIPTIVE SAT, GPA
```

The computer output in Figure 11.31 shows that the sample mean for SAT scores in the Table 2.2 data is $\bar{x} = 1122.400$ and the sample standard deviation is $s = 152.925$.

FIGURE 11.31 **SPSSX-generated output showing the descriptive statistics for variable SAT in Table 2.2.**

NUMBER OF VALID OBSERVATIONS (LISTWISE) = 50.00

VARIABLE	MEAN	STD DEV	MINIMUM	MAXIMUM	VALID N	LABEL
SAT	1122.400	152.925	880.00	1490.00	50	
GPA	2.921	.387	2.29	3.80	50	

We then obtain the t statistic

$$t = \frac{1122.400 - 1000}{152.925/\sqrt{50}} = 5.66$$

Since there are $\nu = 49$ degrees of freedom, the critical value of the t statistic is $t_{\alpha/2,\nu} \approx 2.02$. We have used 40 degrees of freedom to find the critical value because values for

$\nu = 49$ are not in the table. Alternatively, because the sample size is large, we can use the critical value $z_{.025} = 1.96$ from the standard normal distribution. The observed value of the test statistic, 5.66, exceeds the critical value and falls in the critical region. Thus, based on the sample of 50 observations, we reject the null hypothesis.

Exercises for Section 11.10

1. For the data in Table 2.2 of Chapter 2, test the hypothesis H_0: $\mu = 3.0$ for the GPA against H_1: $\mu \neq 3.0$ for all students in the population. Let $\alpha = .05$.
2. For the data in Table 2.1 of Chapter 2 on the sample of 120 employees at Computech, test the hypothesis H_0: $\mu = 33.0$ for the mean age for all employees against H_1: $\mu \neq 33.0$. Let $\alpha = .05$.
3. For the data in Table 2.1 of Chapter 2, test the hypothesis that H_0: $\mu = 2000$ for the monthly salary against H_1: $\mu \neq 2000$ for all employees at Computech.
4. For the data in Table 2.1 of Chapter 2, test the hypothesis that H_0: $\mu = 12$ for the number of years of seniority for all employees at Computech against H_1: $\mu \neq 12$. Let $\alpha = .05$.

Chapter 11 Summary

In Chapter 9 we introduced the concept of statistical inference by discussing the concept of estimating a population parameter (such as μ or p) by using a corresponding sample estimate. In Chapter 10 the quality of the estimator was determined by constructing a confidence interval for the corresponding population parameter. Chapter 11 presents an alternative view of statistical inference—testing hypotheses about a population parameter.

To test a hypothesis concerning a population parameter, we must first state the *null hypothesis* H_0 and an *alternative hypothesis* H_1. The *acceptance region* contains all values of the test statistic for which the null hypothesis will be accepted (or not rejected). The *rejection region,* or *critical region,* contains all values of the test statistic for which the null hypothesis will be rejected. The *critical value* of the test statistic is the value that separates the acceptance region from the rejection region. In a *one-tailed test,* the entire rejection region is placed in one tail of the distribution of the test statistic. In a *two-tailed test,* part of the rejection region is placed in each tail of the distribution.

A *Type I error* occurs when a true null hypothesis is rejected. The probability of committing a Type I error is called the *level of significance of the test* and is denoted by α. The probability of committing a Type I error is the probability that the test statistic falls in the rejection region when the null hypothesis is true. In classical hypothesis testing, the value of α is specified before performing the test. A *Type II error* occurs when a false null hypothesis is not rejected. The probability of committing a Type II error, denoted by β, is the probability that the test statistic falls in the acceptance region when the null hypothesis is false.

To test a hypothesis about a population mean when the population is normal and the population variance is known or when the sample size is large, we use the test statistic

$$z = \frac{\bar{x} - \mu_0}{\sigma/\sqrt{n}}$$

and compare z with critical values obtained from the standard normal distribution.

If the population is approximately normal and the population variance has been estimated, we use the test statistic

$$t = \frac{\bar{x} - \mu_0}{s/\sqrt{n}}$$

and compare t with critical values obtained from the t distribution having $(n - 1)$ degrees of freedom.

To test a hypothesis about a population proportion, we use the test statistic

$$z = \frac{\hat{p} - p_0}{\sqrt{p_0 q_0/n}}$$

and compare z with critical values obtained from the standard normal distribution.

The *prob-value* of a test is the probability of obtaining a sample estimate more extreme than the value that was actually obtained. Small prob-values provide evidence against the null hypothesis. When using a predetermined level of significance α, we reject H_0 whenever the prob-value is less than α.

The *power of a test* is the probability that we correctly reject H_0 when H_0 is false. The power of a test is $(1 - \beta)$ and is the probability that the test statistic falls in the rejection region when H_0 is false. The power of a test depends on the actual value of the parameter under investigation. A graph showing the power of a test for each value of the parameter being tested is called a *power curve*.

To test a hypothesis about a population variance, we use the test statistic

$$\chi^2 = (n - 1)s^2/\sigma_0^2$$

and compare χ^2 with critical values obtained from the *chi-square distribution* having $(n - 1)$ degrees of freedom.

Chapter 11 discusses how to test hypotheses concerning a single population mean, proportion, or variance. Chapter 12 shows how to test hypotheses about the difference between two population means or proportions and about the equality of two population variances.

Summary of Which Distribution to Use When Testing

Students sometimes become confused about whether to use the normal distribution or the t distribution when constructing confidence intervals and testing hypotheses about a population mean μ. The distribution to use depends on whether the population is normal, whether the sample size is large (say, $n \geqslant 30$), and whether the population variance σ^2 is known or must be estimated. There are eight possible cases in all. The accompanying table shows when to use the normal (Z) distribution and when to use the t distribution for constructing confidence intervals and testing hypotheses about μ.

Distribution for testing populations means

	Population Distribution	Population Variance	Sample Size	Distribution for Testing
1.	Normal	Known	Small	Z
2.	Normal	Known	Large	Z
3.	Normal	Unknown	Small	t
4.	Normal	Unknown	Large	Z or t
5.	Nonnormal	Known	Small	Unknown
6.	Nonnormal	Known	Large	Z
7.	Nonnormal	Unknown	Small	Unknown
8.	Nonnormal	Unknown	Large	Z

When n is large, the t distribution is approximately the same as the standard normal distribution; thus it does not make much difference whether we use the t distribution or the normal distribution in Case 4 in the table. Cases 6 and 8 are only approximately correct and are based on the Central Limit Theorem. Approximations under these circumstances improve as the sample size increases. To test hypotheses in Cases 5 or 7, it may be necessary to use the nonparametric procedures discussed in Chapter 19. When n is large, we obtain approximately the same critical values when we use the standard normal distribution as when we use the t distribution. That is, when n is large, $z_\alpha \approx t_{\alpha,n-1}$.

Chapter 11 ▪ *Supplementary Exercises*

1. A company sells breakfast cereal in 16-ounce boxes. In a sample of 100 boxes of this cereal, the average weight was 15.89 ounces with a sample standard deviation $s = 0.2$ ounce. Test H_0: $\mu = 16$ against H_1: $\mu < 16$ using a 5% level of significance.

2. To make a reasonable profit, an airline must average at least 58 passengers per flight on a certain route. In a sample of 100 flights, the average number of passengers was 57 with sample variance 36. Test H_0: $\mu \geqslant 58$ against H_1: $\mu < 58$ using a 1% level of significance.

3. The advertising rates of many magazines are partly determined by the average incomes of the readers of the magazine. A magazine claims that the mean income of its readers is at least \$20,000. In a random sample of 64 readers, the average income was \$17,500 with sample standard deviation \$3000.

a. Test H_0: $\mu = \$20{,}000$ against H_1: $\mu < \$20{,}000$ using a 5% level of significance.

b. Find the one-tailed prob-value of the test.

4. A university publication claims that students spend an average of at most \$110 per semester for textbooks. Suppose you take a random sample of 100 students and obtain $\bar{x} = \$130$. Assume the sample standard deviation is \$40. Test H_0: $\mu \leqslant \$110$ against H_1: $\mu > \$110$ using a 5% level of significance.

5. In Exercise 4, find the power of the test if $\mu = \$120$.

6. In Exercise 4, find the power of the test if $\mu = \$115$.

7. A state legislator claims that at least 20% of the population would buy tickets in a state lottery if the lottery were made legal. In a random sample of 200 people, 35 say they would purchase lottery tickets.

a. Test the claim using a 5% level of significance.
b. Did you use a one-tailed test? Why or why not?

8. A self-proclaimed psychic claims that he has the ability to read other people's minds. To test the psychic's claims, we randomly select a card from a standard poker deck and have the psychic guess whether the card is a heart, diamond, club, or spade. In 400 attempts, the psychic guessed correctly 105 times. Test the psychic's claim using a 1% level of significance.
a. State H_0 and H_1.
b. Did you use a one-tailed test? Why or why not?

9. A newspaper advertisement claims that at least 80% of the people who wear contact lenses experience no difficulty. You take a random sample of 400 people who have purchased contact lenses and find that 280 of them have experienced no difficulty. Test H_0: $p = .80$ against H_1: $p < .80$ using a 1% level of significance. Explain why we are using a one-tailed test.

10. In Exercise 9, find the one-tailed prob-value of the test.

11. In Exercise 9, find the power of the test if $p = .75$. If $p = .70$.

12. One hundred students are polled to determine if a certain controversial politician should be invited to lecture on campus. In the poll, 63 students favored inviting the speaker. Test H_0: $p = .5$ against H_1: $p > .5$ using a 5% level of significance.

13. An instructor gives a quiz consisting of 6 true–false questions. The null hypothesis is that the student is guessing at each answer. If the student gets 5 or 6 answers correct, the instructor will assume that the student really knows the material and deserves a passing grade. If the student gets fewer than 5 correct, the instructor will fail the student. Thus, the decision is: Reject H_0 (the student is guessing) if 5 or 6 answers are correct; otherwise, do not reject it.
a. Find the probability of making a Type I error in this problem.
b. Suppose the probability is .7 that the student knows any specific answer. Find the power of the test.

14. We toss a coin 400 times to determine if it is a fair coin. We use a two-tailed test and a 5% level of significance. Suppose the coin is not balanced and that the probability of a head on any toss is $p = .53$. What is the power of the test?

15. In a random sample of 400 record albums produced by the Royal Record Company, 22 were defective. Is this sufficient evidence for concluding that the percentage of albums having flaws exceeds 4%? Use a 1% level of significance.

16. In a random sample of 200 walnut panels, 32 had major flaws. Is this sufficient evidence for concluding that the proportion of walnut panels that contain major flaws is greater than 10%? Use a 5% level of significance.

17. Last year 60% of the patients at a hospital rented a television. For a trial period, the rental agency raised the fee for a random sample of 200 patients. In the sample, 90 patients decided to rent the TV. Is this sufficient evidence to convince the rental agency that the proportion of renters will be less than .6 if the price is raised for everyone? Use a 5% level of significance.

18. A sample of 1600 voters is polled to estimate the percentage of votes a candidate will receive. We wish to test H_0: $p \leq .5$ against H_1: $p > .5$ using a 5% level of significance.
a. Find the critical value of $\hat{p}$ associated with this test.
b. Find the power of the test if $p = .55, .54, .53, .52$, and $.51$.
c. Plot the power curve.
d. Repeat parts (a), (b), and (c) using a sample size $n = 2500$.

19. A company claims that it puts at least 12 ounces of potato chips into its packages on the average. Assume the weights follow a normal distribution. You randomly select 10 bags of potato chips and obtain a sample mean of 11.8 ounces with a sample standard deviation of .30. Test H_0: $\mu \geq 12$ against H_1: $\mu < 12$ using a 5% level of significance.

20. A campus coffee machine is supposed to put 8 ounces of coffee into a cup on the average. A random sample of 10 cups of coffee is taken. Test H_0: $\mu = 8$ against H_1: $\mu < 8$ using the t test and a 5% level of significance. The sample data are as follows:

6.8 7.6 8.1 8.3 7.7 8.2 7.9 7.5 7.7 7.9

a. Find the sample mean.
b. Find the sample standard deviation.
c. Perform the test.

21. A union bricklayer is supposed to be able to lay 100 bricks per hour on the average. An apprentice is suspected of working significantly slower than average. The apprentice is checked during 10 randomly selected hours, and the number of bricks laid each hour recorded is as follows:

92 88 104 97 78 89 106 89 92 101

a. Find the sample mean.
b. Find the sample standard deviation.
c. Use a one-tailed t test and a 5% level of significance to test if the bricklayer is working significantly slower than average.

22. The Douglas Drug Company claims that its medication takes effect within 12 minutes. The following data show the times that 10 patients required before feeling the effects of the medication:

8.1 11.6 9.4 13.3 16.2 10.3 14.6 15.3 13.6 15.2

It is assumed that the population is normally distributed.
a. Find the sample mean.
b. Find the sample standard deviation.
c. Use a 5% level of significance and test H_0: $\mu \leqslant 12$ minutes against H_1: $\mu > 12$ minutes.

23. A sales representative for the Kaminski Fish Company claims that at least 50% of the American population eat fish regularly. In a random sample of 240 people, 106 said that they eat fish regularly.
a. Calculate the sample proportion who eat fish regularly.
b. Use a 5% level of significance to test the sales claim. Did you use a one-tailed test? Why or why not?

24. A newswoman on the 6 o'clock news has a clause in her contract that grants her a $10,000 bonus if the show is watched by at least 40% of the viewing audience. In a random sample of 400 individuals watching TV at 6 o'clock, 180 are watching the newswoman's show.
a. Calculate the sample proportion.
b. Is this conclusive evidence that the broadcaster has earned her bonus? Use a 1% level of significance.
c. In part (b) did you use a one-tailed test? Why or why not?

25. An economist claims that the unemployment rate for non-English-speaking individuals in New York City is at least 30%. In a random sample of 400 non-English-speaking residents of New York City, 90 are unemployed.
a. Calculate the sample proportion who are unemployed.
b. Test H_0: $p \geqslant .30$ against H_1: $p < .30$ using a 5% level of significance.

26. The economist in Exercise 25 claims that the mean age of the unemployed people in New York City is 23 years or less. In a random sample of 100 individuals who were unemployed in New York City, the sample mean age was $\bar{x} = 22.6$ with sample standard deviation $s = 2$. Use a 5% level of significance and test H_0: $\mu \leqslant 23$ years against H_1: $\mu > 23$ years. (*Hint:* The answer to this problem should be obvious.)

27. In a best-selling book, the author states that the average cost of a funeral is \$800 or more. To test this claim, an investigator examines a random sample of 20 funerals. In the sample, the sample mean funeral cost was $\bar{x} = \$600$ with sample standard deviation $s = \$108$. Assume that the population is approximately normal. Use a 1% level of significance and test H_0: $\mu \geqslant \$800$ against H_1: $\mu < \$800$.

28. In the past, 30% of the viewing audience watched the 11 o'clock news on Channel 7. To increase its share of the audience, Channel 7 hired some new newscasters. After one month, a random sample of 500 viewers were questioned. The executives will claim that their share has increased if at least 175 of the viewers in the sample were watching Channel 7.

a. What is the level of significance of this test?

b. If $p = .35$, what is the probability of incorrectly concluding that the proportion watching Channel 7 has not increased?

29. An executive for the Midwest Barge Line claims that barges that pass through lock 16 on the Mississippi River carry on the average at least 800 tons of coal. In a random sample of 8 barges, the following tonnages were measured:

780 760 775 805 780 770 790 810

a. Find the sample mean.

b. Find the sample standard deviation.

c. Use a 5% level of significance and test H_0: $\mu \geq 800$ against H_1: $\mu < 800$.

30. Last year an airline found that the number of no-shows on the 10:00 A.M. flights to Chicago averaged 3.1. On a random sample of 20 of these flights during the last three months, the average number of no-shows was $\bar{x} = 2.4$ with standard deviation $s = 0.7$. Let $\alpha = .01$. Can we conclude the average number of no-shows per flight has declined?

31. The Cottrell Soap Company has produced a new dishwashing liquid that it thinks is better than competitive products on the market. The company's market research department has distributed the new product to 400 randomly selected households. The board of directors has indicated that the product will be marketed if more than 25% of the public prefer the product over its competitors. Design the decision rule so that the probability of incorrectly concluding that the product should be marketed is no greater than 5%. The decision rule will be based on the proportion of individuals in the random sample who prefer the product.

32. Last year Alston County received \$180,000 in federal grants because the census showed that 6% of the county's families were below the poverty level. The county will receive \$200,000 in federal aid this year provided the proportion below the poverty level this year is at least 6%. A research firm takes a random sample of 1000 families in the county and determines that 52 were below the poverty level. Use a 5% level of significance. Should we conclude that the proportion of families below the poverty level is less than 6%?

33. Suppose that in Exercise 32 the true proportion of families in Alston County who are below the poverty level is .063. What is the probability that in a sample of 1000 families we would get 52 or fewer impoverished families?

34. In Exercise 32, what is the probability of incorrectly concluding that $p = .06$ if, in fact, $p = .04$? That is, find the probability of making a Type II error if $p = .04$.

35. It is claimed that at most 25% of Americans are financially independent at age 65 and do not have to continue to work or become dependent on friends, relatives, or charity. Suppose you wish to test the validity of this claim by conducting a survey among 400 senior citizens. How many people in the sample would have to indicate financial independence in order to reject the claim? Use a 5% level of significance.

36. A doctor claims that a new serum is effective in preventing the common cold. A sample of 144 people were injected with the serum and observed over the winter. Suppose that 90 survived the winter without a cold. From prior information, it is known that the probability of surviving the winter without a cold is .5 when the serum is not used. Given the results of this experiment, what conclusions would you make regarding the effectiveness of the serum?

37. A market study for a new industrial product indicates that the firm should launch the product if the mean number of units sold per customer in the first solicitation of the firm's customers is more than 3.0. It is believed that the standard deviation of the number of units purchased in initial orders will be $\sigma = 1.8$ units. It is desired to test the null hypothesis that the mean number of orders in the population is less than or equal to 3.0 per customer against the alternative hypothesis that the mean number is greater than 3.0. In a random sample of 100 customers included in the first solicitation, the following decision rule is adopted: "Accept H_0 if $\overline{X} \leq 3.10$ and reject H_0 if $\overline{X} > 3.10$." Calculate the power of the test for μ values of 3.05, 3.10, 3.15, 3.20, 3.25, 3.30, 3.35, and 3.40. Sketch the power curve for this decision rule.

38. Last year 4% of the customers at a restaurant indicated that they were dissatisfied with their food or service. Management initiates a training program for waiters and gives pay incentives to improve service. A random sample of 1600 customers were then asked to rate the quality of the food and service. In the sample, 36 people were dissatisfied. Use this information to test whether the proportion of dissatisfied customers has declined. Use a 1% level of significance.

39. Several gamblers examined the performance of professional football teams that were big underdogs (given more than 15 points by bookmakers). After taking into account the point spreads, these underdogs won 32 of 50 games. Is this winning proportion significantly different from .5? Use a two-tailed test with a 5% level of significance.

40. "As the sample size increases, the width of a confidence interval for the population mean shrinks to 0. Furthermore, if the sample is the entire population, the sample mean will exactly equal the population mean and there will be no sampling error at all. Thus, if the sample size is extremely large, every null hypothesis would be rejected except for the one that has the correct value for the population mean. However, the probability of picking the precise value of μ is minimal. Consequently, whatever null hypothesis we use, we are sure to reject it if we gather enough data. Thus, a critical way of viewing the theory of hypothesis testing is that accepted hypotheses are those that we do not have enough data to reject." Discuss the above argument.

41. "Tests of hypotheses focus on the probability of incorrectly rejecting a particular hypothesis, the null hypothesis. By setting up the test to have a low probability of a Type I error, the researcher insures that the test is unlikely to lead to the incorrect rejection of this particular hypothesis when it is true." Do you agree or disagree with this argument?

42. "Statistical significance is closely related to practical importance." Do you agree or disagree with this argument?

43. Suppose there are serious consequences of incorrectly rejecting a particular hypothesis.
a. Should this hypothesis be the null hypothesis or the alternative hypothesis?
b. Should α be large or small?
c. Give an example of such a situation.

44. It is known that the random variable X has the continuous density function

$$f(x) = 1/\theta \quad \text{for } 0 \leq X \leq \theta$$
$$f(x) = 0 \quad \text{otherwise}$$

but it is not known whether the value of θ is 1 or 2. You will have just a single observation of X on which to base your choice between H_0: $\theta = 1$ and H_1: $\theta = 2$.
a. You decide to accept $\theta = 1$ if $X \leq 0.8$ and to accept $\theta = 2$ if $X > 0.8$. What are the probabilities of Type I and Type II errors?
b. What are the probabilities of Type I and Type II errors if you decide to accept $\theta = 1$ if $X \leq 0.6$ and to accept $\theta = 2$ if $X > 0.6$?
c. Which of these two rules is more appropriate if the consequences of a Type II error are more serious than those of a Type I error?

45. The Nutritious Foods Company claims that there are on average at least 4 ounces of raisins in a box of its cereal. A consumer group wants to test the null hypothesis H_0: $\mu \geq 4$. The group needs to choose a sample size and a level of significance. The following three possibilities are considered:

$$n = 25; \quad \alpha = .05$$
$$n = 25; \quad \alpha = .01$$
$$n = 100; \quad \alpha = .05$$

a. Which design has the smallest probability of falsely rejecting the company's claim?
b. Does the first or second design have the smaller probability of incorrectly accepting the company's claim? Why?
c. Does the first or third design have the smaller probability of incorrectly accepting the company's claim? Why?

References

Fisher, Ronald A. *Statistical Methods for Research Workers.* 14th ed. New York: Hafner Press, 1970.

McClosky, Donald N. "The Loss Function Has Been Mislaid: The Rhetoric of Significance Tests." *American Economic Review.* May 1985, pp. 201–205.

Morrison, Donald, and Ramon E. Henkel. *The Significance Test Controversy.* Chicago: Aldine, 1970.

Neyman, Jerzy, and Egon S. Pearson. "On the Use and Interpretation of Certain Test Criteria for Purposes of Statistical Hypotheses." *Biometrika,* 1928, pp. 175–294.

______. "On the Problem of the Most Efficient Tests of Statistical Hypotheses." *Philosophical Transactions of the Royal Society,* 1933, pp. 289–337.

Norusis, Marija J. *SPSSX Introductory Statistics Guide.* New York: McGraw-Hill, 1983.

______. *SPSSX Advanced Statistics Guide.* Chicago: SPSS, 1985.

______. *The SPSS Guide to Data Analysis.* Chicago: SPSS, 1986.

Popper, Karl R. *The Logic of Scientific Discovery.* New York: Harper, 1965.

Ryan, Thomas A., Brian L. Joiner, and Barbara F. Ryan. *Minitab Handbook.* 2d ed. Boston: PWS-KENT, 1985.

______. *Minitab Reference Manual.* University Park, Penn.: Minitab Project, 1985.

SAS Introductory Guide. 3d ed. Cary, N.C.: SAS Institute, 1985.

SAS Procedures Guide for Personal Computers. Version 6 ed. Cary, N.C.: SAS Institute, 1986.

SAS Statistics Guide for Personal Computers. Version 6 ed. Cary, N.C.: SAS Institute, 1986.

SAS User's Guide: Basics. Version 5 ed. Cary, N.C.: SAS Institute, 1985.

SAS User's Guide: Statistics. Version 5 ed. Cary, N.C.: SAS Institute, 1985.

SPSSX User's Guide. Chicago: SPSS, 1983.

Chapter Twelve
Tests of Hypotheses Involving Two Populations

In this chapter we discuss how to test hypotheses concerning the means μ_1 and μ_2, proportions p_1 and p_2, or the variances σ_1^2 and σ_2^2 of two populations.

Let θ_1 and θ_2 denote unknown population parameters from two populations. To test hypotheses about θ_1 and θ_2, we take random samples of size n_1 and n_2 from the two populations and calculate sample estimates $\hat{\theta}_1$ and $\hat{\theta}_2$. We then use these estimates to help us decide whether to reject some null hypothesis about the respective population parameters.

The hypotheses that will be considered in this chapter are as follows:

1. Test H_0: $\theta_1 - \theta_2 = D_0$ against H_1: $\theta_1 - \theta_2 \neq D_0$
2. Test H_0: $\theta_1 - \theta_2 \leq D_0$ against H_1: $\theta_1 - \theta_2 > D_0$
3. Test H_0: $\theta_1 - \theta_2 \geq D_0$ against H_1: $\theta_1 - \theta_2 < D_0$

In most cases the value of D_0 is hypothesized to be 0, but this does not have to be the case. From the last chapter, you will recognize test 1 as a two-sided test and tests 2 and 3 as one-sided tests.

When $D_0 = 0$ is the hypothesized value of the difference $\theta_1 - \theta_2$, testing the null hypothesis H_0: $\theta_1 = \theta_2$ against the two-sided alternative hypothesis H_1: $\theta_1 \neq \theta_2$ is equivalent to testing H_0: $\theta_1 - \theta_2 = 0$ against H_1: $\theta_1 - \theta_2 \neq 0$.

12.1 ▪ Tests for the Differences of Means

In order to test H_0: $\mu_1 - \mu_2 = D_0$, take random samples of n_1 observations from Population 1 and n_2 observations from Population 2. (It is not necessary that n_1 and n_2 be equal, but that is frequently the case.) The samples should be independent of one another. This means, for example, that the samples should not contain the same experimental units. (Examples of observations in two samples that are dependent on one another would be the before-diet and after-diet weight of a sample of individuals and the car mileage achieved with gasoline A and with gasoline B using the same cars. Testing the difference between two population means when the samples are dependent is discussed in Section 12.3.) When the samples are independent, the test statistic used to test H_0 will be either a Z score or a t score, depending upon whether the population variances are known or must be estimated.

To determine a critical region for the test statistic, we must know the sampling distribution of the test statistic. The test statistic will depend on the random variable $(\overline{X}_1 - \overline{X}_2)$. Values of $(\overline{X}_1 - \overline{X}_2)$ that are not close to D_0 would support the alternative hypothesis that D_0 is not the correct value for the difference $(\mu_1 - \mu_2)$.

If the two populations are both normally distributed or if the sample sizes are large (i.e., $n_1 \geq 30$ and $n_2 \geq 30$), then the random variable $(\overline{X}_1 - \overline{X}_2)$ has an approximately normal distribution with mean $(\mu_1 - \mu_2)$ and variance $[\sigma_1^2/n_1 + \sigma_2^2/n_2]$. Thus, if D_0 is the correct value for the difference between the two means, then the random variable

$$Z = \frac{(\overline{X}_1 - \overline{X}_2) - D_0}{\sqrt{\sigma_1^2/n_1 + \sigma_2^2/n_2}}$$

has a standard normal distribution.

The accompanying box describes how to perform a test concerning the difference between two population means when the population variances are known and the samples are independent.

Testing the Difference Between Population Means

Using Large Independent Samples

Suppose we have independent random samples of n_1 and n_2 observations from two normal distributions with means μ_1 and μ_2 and variances σ_1^2 and σ_2^2, respectively. If the observed sample means are $\bar{x}_1$ and $\bar{x}_2$, then the following tests have significance level α:

Case 1: To test the null hypothesis

$$H_0\colon \mu_1 - \mu_2 = D_0 \quad \text{or} \quad H_0\colon \mu_1 - \mu_2 \leq D_0$$

against the one-sided alternative hypothesis

$$H_1\colon \mu_1 - \mu_2 > D_0$$

calculate the test statistic

$$z = \frac{(\bar{x}_1 - \bar{x}_2) - D_0}{\sqrt{\sigma_1^2/n_1 + \sigma_2^2/n_2}}$$

and use the decision rule

$$\text{Reject } H_0 \text{ in favor of } H_1 \text{ if } z > z_\alpha.$$

Case 2: To test the null hypothesis

$$H_0\colon \mu_1 - \mu_2 = D_0 \quad \text{or} \quad H_0\colon \mu_1 - \mu_2 \geq D_0$$

against the one-sided alternative hypothesis

$$H_1\colon \mu_1 - \mu_2 < D_0$$

use the decision rule

$$\text{Reject } H_0 \text{ in favor of } H_1 \text{ if } z < -z_\alpha.$$

Case 3: To test the null hypothesis

$$H_0\colon \mu_1 - \mu_2 = D_0$$

against the two-sided alternative

$$H_1\colon \mu_1 - \mu_2 \neq D_0$$

use the decision rule

$$\text{Reject } H_0 \text{ in favor of } H_1 \text{ if } z > z_{\alpha/2} \text{ or if } z < -z_{\alpha/2}.$$

If the population variances are unknown but the sample sizes n_1 and n_2 are large (say, 30 or more), then, to a good approximation, tests for the difference between population means can be performed by replacing the population variances by the observed sample variances s_1^2 and s_2^2. For large sample sizes, these approximations are good even when the population distributions are not normal.

In most tests the value of D_0 is chosen to be 0. In this case, the null hypothesis states that the means of the two populations are equal.

Example 12.1

Testing the Difference Between Two Means (Large Samples): Procter & Gamble (P&G) has made huge profits by selling Crest Toothpaste. P&G showed that brushing your teeth with toothpaste that contained fluoride helped prevent tooth decay, and Crest was the first toothpaste to contain fluoride. Now, of course, almost all toothpastes contain fluoride. Suppose you want to test the claim that the use of fluoride toothpaste helps prevent tooth decay by testing a group of 10-year-old children, all of whom have identical dental records at the start of the test. Let Population 1 denote children who are told to use nonfluoridated toothpaste for a year, and let Population 2 denote children who use fluoridated toothpaste for a year. Let μ_1 and μ_2 denote the mean number of cavities at the end of the year for children in each of the two populations. We want to test the null hypothesis

$$H_0\colon \mu_1 - \mu_2 = 0$$

against

$$H_1\colon \mu_1 - \mu_2 > 0$$

Because the population variances are unknown, we will estimate them by using the sample variances.

Suppose that in a random sample of 100 children who used the nonfluoridated toothpaste, the sample mean was $\bar{x}_1 = 4.8$ cavities with sample variance $s_1^2 = 1.1$, and in an independent random sample of 120 children who used fluoridated toothpaste, we obtained $\bar{x}_2 = 3.6$ cavities and $s_2^2 = 0.9$. Because the sample sizes are large, we can use the Z score when performing the test, replacing the population variances in the test statistic by the sample variances. We will use a 5% level of significance.

Solution: For a one-tailed test using a level of significance $\alpha = .05$, the critical value of the test statistic is $z_\alpha = 1.645$. The observed value of the test statistic is

$$z = \frac{(\bar{x}_1 - \bar{x}_2) - D_0}{\sqrt{s_1^2/n_1 + s_2^2/n_2}}$$

where

$$s_1^2/n_1 + s_2^2/n_2 = 1.1/100 + 0.9/120 = 0.0189$$

We obtain the Z score

$$z = \frac{(\bar{x}_1 - \bar{x}_2) - 0}{\sqrt{0.0189}} = \frac{4.8 - 3.6}{0.136} \approx 8.82$$

We reject H_0 because $z = 8.82$ falls in the critical region. ■

In Example 12.1, we found a statistically significant difference between the two sample means. Children who used the fluoridated toothpaste got fewer cavities than children who did not. Is this result of any practical significance? That is, are the results strong enough to make you switch from nonfluoridated to fluoridated toothpaste? Most parents and children would probably say that the results are of practical significance. Children and parents both seem to abhor visits to the dentist to have cavities filled, and a 25% reduction in the expected number of cavities is probably sufficient enticement to get people to switch to fluoridated toothpaste (provided the price difference is not too great). The fact that nearly all toothpastes now contain fluoride shows that people do feel that this result is of both statistical and practical significance.

Exercises for Section 12.1

1. A superintendent of schools wants to determine if children in public schools and in private schools read equally well. A reading test is given to 100 public school children at age 8 and 100 private school children at age 8. The sample statistics are $\bar{x}_1 = 206$, $s_1^2 = 450$; $\bar{x}_2 = 191$, $s_2^2 = 450$. Test H_0: $\mu_1 - \mu_2 = 0$ against H_1: $\mu_1 - \mu_2 \neq 0$ using a 5% level of significance.
2. A major producer of ice cream wants to increase its sales and its share of the market. It wants to spend most of its advertising expenditures on the segment of the market that consumes the most ice cream. To determine if males or females eat more ice cream on the average, we take a random sample of 100 men (sample 1) and 100 women (sample 2) and determine how much ice cream each person eats during a year. We obtain $\bar{x}_1 = 12$ quarts, $s_1^2 = 8$; $\bar{x}_2 = 14$ quarts, $s_2^2 = 8$. Test H_0: $\mu_1 - \mu_2 = 0$ against H_1: $\mu_1 - \mu_2 \neq 0$ using a 1% level of significance.
3. The National Highway Safety Association wants to determine if drinking alcohol affects a person's reaction time and coordination. We randomly select 100 people and calculate how long each person takes to perform a certain task. We obtain $\bar{x}_1 = 47$ seconds, $s_1^2 = 24$. We select 50 other people, each of whom are given three glasses of beer to drink. Then we calculate how long each of these people takes to perform the task. We obtain $\bar{x}_2 = 44$ seconds and $s_2^2 = 20$. Test H_0: $\mu_1 - \mu_2 = 0$ against H_1: $\mu_1 - \mu_2 > 0$ using a 5% level of significance.
4. The public transportation agency wants to determine if the average income of people who ride the bus to work every day is the same as the average income of people who use the bus only occasionally or never. Random samples of size 100 are taken from each population. Assume that each

population has a standard deviation of \$1,800. We obtain $\bar{x}_1 = \$23,800$ and $\bar{x}_2 = \$25,000$. Test $H_0: \mu_1 - \mu_2 = 0$ against $H_1: \mu_1 - \mu_2 \neq 0$ using a 1% level of significance.

5. The Jones Oil Company has undertaken a nationwide drive to obtain new credit card holders, because it believes that credit card holders (Population 1) spend more money per month on gasoline than do non-credit-card holders (Population 2). The firm decides to test $H_0: \mu_1 - \mu_2 = 0$ against $H_1: \mu_1 - \mu_2 > 0$ using a 5% level of significance. Assume that each population has variance 400. Random samples of size 200 are taken from each population. The sample means are $\bar{x}_1 = \$41$ and $\bar{x}_2 = \$37$. Should the firm reject H_0?

6. Suppose that the National Association of Truck Drivers is interested in improving the public image of truck drivers. They decide to test whether the average speed of trucks traveling on an interstate highway is significantly greater than the average speed of cars. In random samples of 100 cars and 200 trucks checked at one point on the highway, the average speed of the cars is $\bar{x}_1 = 52$ miles per hour and the average speed of the trucks is $\bar{x}_2 = 54$ miles per hour. Assume that the population variances are $\sigma_1^2 = 25$ and $\sigma_2^2 = 16$. Test $H_0: \mu_1 - \mu_2 = 0$ against $H_1: \mu_1 - \mu_2 < 0$ using a 5% level of significance.

7. The superintendent of schools thinks that good students in the school system tend to have fewer days of absence than poor students. In a random sample of 400 good students, the average number of days absent per year was $\bar{x}_1 = 14.3$; in a random sample of 300 poor students, the average was $\bar{x}_2 = 18.9$. Assume the sample variances are $s_1^2 = 27$ and $s_2^2 = 36$. Use a 1% level of significance and test $H_0: \mu_1 - \mu_2 = 0$ against $H_1: \mu_1 - \mu_2 < 0$.

8. A psychologist thinks that, other things being equal, people who wear glasses tend to have fewer automobile accidents than people who do not. She reasons that people who wear glasses are conscious of their vision problem and drive more carefully and conservatively. Random samples of 400 people who wear glasses and 400 people who do not wear glasses are obtained. The people are of approximately the same age and drive approximately the same number of miles per year. During a 12-month period, people wearing glasses had an average of $\bar{x}_1 = 0.72$ accident with sample standard deviation $s_1 = 0.3$. People not wearing glasses had an average of $\bar{x}_2 = 0.82$ accident with standard deviation $s_2 = 0.3$. Does this evidence support the psychologist's claim? Use a 5% level of significance.

12.2 ▪ *Tests of Differences of Means Using Small Samples from Normal Populations When the Population Variances Are Equal but Unknown*

Suppose we want to test a hypothesis about the difference between the means of two normal populations when the population variances σ_1^2 and σ_2^2 are equal but unknown. If the sample sizes are large, we can replace the unknown population variances by their sample estimates and follow the procedures developed in Section 12.1. However, when the sample sizes are small, we use a t statistic as the test statistic to obtain critical values from the t distribution. The populations are assumed to be normally distributed and the samples must be independent of one another. Because the t test is relatively robust, the test results are approximately correct when the population distributions are not exactly normal provided they do not deviate too far from normal.

The procedure in the accompanying box describes how to test a null hypothesis about the difference between two populations means when the sample sizes are small. The test is based on the following assumptions:

1. The two populations are normal (or approximately normal).
2. The population variances are unknown but are assumed to be equal.
3. The samples are independent of one another.

Testing the Difference Between the Means of Two Normal Populations Using Small Independent Samples When the Population Variances Are Equal but Unknown

Suppose we have independent random samples of n_1 and n_2 observations from normal distributions with means μ_1 and μ_2 and a common variance. Suppose the observed sample variances are s_1^2 and s_2^2. Let the observed sample means be $\bar{x}_1$ and $\bar{x}_2$, and let s_p^2 denote the observed pooled sample variance. The pooled estimate of the common population variance is calculated as follows:

$$s_p^2 = \frac{\Sigma(x_{i1} - \bar{x}_1)^2 + \Sigma(x_{i2} - \bar{x}_2)^2}{n_1 + n_2 - 2}$$

where x_{i1} is the ith observation from Sample 1 and x_{i2} is the ith observation from Sample 2. This is equivalent to the estimator

$$s_p^2 = \frac{(n_1 - 1)s_1^2 + (n_2 - 1)s_2^2}{n_1 + n_2 - 2}$$

The following tests have significance level α:

Case 1: To test the null hypothesis

$$H_0: \mu_1 - \mu_2 = D_0 \quad \text{or} \quad H_0: \mu_1 - \mu_2 \leqslant D_0$$

against the one-sided alternative hypothesis

$$H_1: \mu_1 - \mu_2 > D_0$$

calculate the test statistic

$$t = \frac{(\bar{x}_1 - \bar{x}_2) - D_0}{\sqrt{s_p^2/n_1 + s_p^2/n_2}}$$

and use the decision rule

Reject H_0 in favor of H_1 if $t > t_{\alpha,\nu}$.

The random variable t follows the t distribution with $\nu = (n_1 + n_2 - 2)$ degrees of freedom.

Case 2: To test the null hypothesis

$$H_0: \mu_1 - \mu_2 = D_0 \quad \text{or} \quad H_0: \mu_1 - \mu_2 \geqslant D_0$$

against the one-sided alternative hypothesis

$$H_1: \mu_1 - \mu_2 < D_0$$

use the decision rule

$$\text{Reject } H_0 \text{ in favor of } H_1 \text{ if } t < -t_{\alpha,\nu}$$

where the number of degrees of freedom is $\nu = (n_1 + n_2 - 2)$.

Case 3: To test the null hypothesis

$$H_0\colon \mu_1 - \mu_2 = D_0$$

against the two-sided alternative hypothesis

$$H_1\colon \mu_1 - \mu_2 \neq D_0$$

use the decision rule

$$\text{Reject } H_0 \text{ in favor of } H_1 \text{ if } t > t_{\alpha/2,\nu} \text{ or if } t < -t_{\alpha/2,\nu},$$

where the number of degrees of freedom is $\nu = (n_1 + n_2 - 2)$.

Example 12.2

Testing the Difference Between Two Means (Small Samples): A market research firm wishes to know if the mean number of hours of TV viewing per week is the same for teenage boys (Population 1) as for teenage girls (Population 2). They want to test H_0: $\mu_1 - \mu_2 = 0$ against H_1: $\mu_1 - \mu_2 \neq 0$ using a 5% level of significance. The unknown population variances are assumed to be equal. The following data were obtained: $n_1 = 20$, $\bar{x}_1 = 24.5$, $s_1^2 = 64$; $n_2 = 12$, $\bar{x}_2 = 28.7$, $s_2^2 = 71$.

Solution: Because the sample sizes are small, we use the t score as our test statistic. Because the level of significance is $\alpha = .05$, there are $\nu = (n_1 + n_2 - 2) = 30$ degrees of freedom, and we are performing a two-tailed test, the critical values of the test statistic are $\pm t_{.025} = \pm 2.04$. Using the observed sample means 24.5 and 28.7 and the pooled estimate of the variance

$$s_p^2 = \frac{(19)(64) + (11)(71)}{20 + 12 - 2} = 66.57$$

we calculate the observed t statistic

$$t = \frac{(24.5 - 28.7) - 0}{\sqrt{(66.57/20) + (66.57/12)}} = \frac{-4.20}{\sqrt{8.88}} = -1.41$$

Thus, we do not reject H_0 because the test statistic falls in the acceptance region. See Figure 12.1.

FIGURE 12.1
The *t* distribution for Example 12.2.

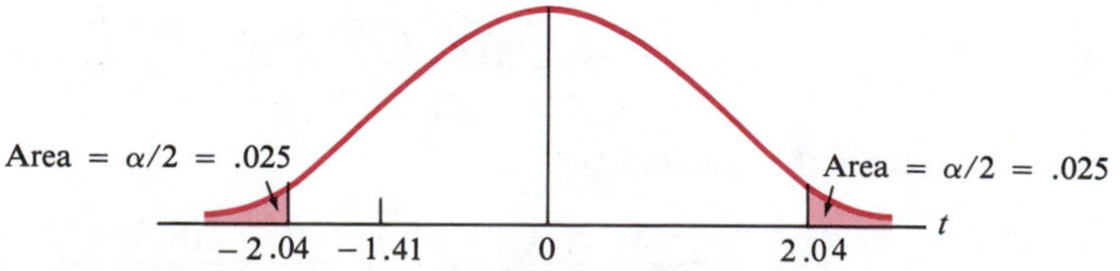

Does this result seem reasonable? In the samples, the boys watched TV an average of 24.5 hours per week, while the girls averaged 28.7 hours. Because the sample sizes are relatively small and the pooled estimate of the variance is fairly large, our estimates of the population means are not very precise. Consequently, the observed difference of 4.2 hours in the sample means is not sufficient evidence to convince us that the two population means are different.

When the population variances are unknown and unequal, we cannot pool the data to obtain a single estimate of the variance. If the sample sizes are large, the appropriate test statistic is the Z score described in Section 12.1.

Formula for Testing Difference of Means (Unequal Variances and Large Samples)

$$z = \frac{(\bar{x}_1 - \bar{x}_2) - (\mu_1 - \mu_2)}{\sqrt{(s_1^2/n_1) + (s_2^2/n_2)}}$$

When the sample sizes are small and the population variances are unknown and unequal, neither the t test nor the z test is theoretically appropriate. Nevertheless, many people still resort to one of these two tests for lack of a better alternative. However, an alternative test based on the ranks of the observations will be described in Chapter 21.

The results in this section are based on the assumption that the two samples used to calculate $\bar{x}_1$ and $\bar{x}_2$ are independent of one another. When the samples are not independent, we should use the methods discussed in Section 12.3 on paired difference tests.

As an example, observe how the t test leads to the wrong conclusion in the following problem.

Example 12.3

Inappropriate Use of the *t* Test: Suppose 10 automobiles are randomly selected. One gallon of Gasoline 1 is placed into each car, and each car is driven around a racetrack at a constant speed until all the gas is used. The process is then repeated using Gasoline 2. The data in Table 12.1 show the distances (in miles) traveled by each car using Gasoline 1 and Gasoline 2. A researcher would be interested in testing whether, in a large population of cars, the mean mileages are equal when using the two brands of gasoline. We obtain $\bar{x}_1 = 18.3$ miles, $s_1^2 = 89.79$; $\bar{x}_2 = 20.4$ miles, $s_2^2 = 86.27$.

Suppose we incorrectly used the t test to test

$$H_0: \mu_1 - \mu_2 = 0$$

against the alternative hypothesis

$$H_1: \mu_1 - \mu_2 \neq 0$$

using $\alpha = .05$. The pooled estimate of the variance is

$$s_p^2 = \frac{(9)(89.79) + (9)(86.27)}{10 + 10 - 2} = 88.03$$

We obtain the test statistic

$$t = \frac{\bar{x}_1 - \bar{x}_2}{\sqrt{(s_p^2/n_1) + (s_p^2/n_2)}} = \frac{18.3 - 20.4}{\sqrt{(88.03/10) + (88.03/10)}} = -.50$$

TABLE 12.1
Car distances for Example 12.3

Car	Gasoline 1	Gasoline 2	Difference D_0
1	14	16	−2
2	21	24	−3
3	19	20	−1
4	11	15	−4
5	15	17	−2
6	16	19	−3
7	8	10	−2
8	32	33	−1
9	37	39	−2
10	10	11	−1
Total	183	204	−21
$\bar{x}$	18.3	20.4	−2.1
s^2	89.79	86.27	.9888

For $\nu = 18$ degrees of freedom and $\alpha = .05$, the critical values of t are $\pm t_{.025,18} = \pm 2.101$. Because the observed value $t = -.50$ falls in the acceptance region for this test, we would not reject H_0.

However, if we compare the mileages car by car, we see that every car traveled farther using Gasoline 2 than using Gasoline 1. This provides very strong evidence that H_0 is false. Using the t test here leads to the wrong conclusion because the assumption of independent random samples has been violated. In Section 12.3, we will explain the appropriate procedure for performing this test.

Exercises for Section 12.2

1. A time-and-motion study is conducted to test whether the mean length of time required to perform a certain task is the same for the employees on the day shift (Population 1) and employees on the night shift (Population 2). The data are as follows: $n_1 = 10$, $\bar{x}_1 = 26$, $s_1^2 = 64$; $n_2 = 8$, $\bar{x}_2 = 29$, $s_2^2 = 50$. Use a 5% level of significance and a two-tailed test. Assume the populations are approximately normal, the population variances are equal, and the samples are independent.

2. To test the effectiveness of a new fertilizer, a farm was divided into 50 plots of equal area. The soil quality of all plots was approximately the same. The new fertilizer was applied to 25 plots, and the old fertilizer was applied to the remaining 25. We obtain the following data: $\bar{x}_1 = 22$ bushels of wheat per plot; $s_1^2 = 4$; $\bar{x}_2 = 24$ bushels of wheat per plot, $s_2^2 = 6$. Test H_0: $\mu_1 - \mu_2 = 0$ against H_1: $\mu_1 - \mu_2 < 0$ using 5% level of significance. Assume the population variances are equal, the populations are approximately normal, and the samples are independent.

3. A business school wants to test the hypothesis that male (Population 1) and female (Population 2) college graduates have the same mean starting salaries against H_1: $\mu_1 - \mu_2 \neq 0$. Use a 5% level of significance and the following data: $n_1 = 20$, $\bar{x}_1 = \$16{,}500$, $s_1 = \$1000$; $n_2 = 20$,

$\bar{x}_2 = \$15{,}000$, $s_2 = \$2000$. Assume the population variances are equal, the populations are approximately normal, and the samples are independent.

12.3 ▪ Tests for Differences of Means of Paired Samples

When the observations from two populations occur in pairs or are related, then the samples are not independent and the tests described in Sections 12.1 and 12.2 are inappropriate.

Examples of observations that occur in pairs are sales at stores before and after an advertising campaign and reading rates of individuals before and after taking a speed reading course. In these cases, rather than having two independent random samples, we have one random sample of n pairs of observations. Hypotheses concerning the differences between the means μ_1 and μ_2 are tested by treating the differences of the n pairs as a random sample from a population of such differences.

Let x_{i1} be the ith observation from Population 1, and let x_{i2} denote the ith observation from Population 2. Because the observations x_{i1} and x_{i2} occur in pairs, we have a random sample of n pairs of observations: $(x_{11}, x_{12}), (x_{21}, x_{22}), \ldots, (x_{n1}, x_{n2})$. For each pair we calculate the difference d_i as follows:

$$d_i = x_{i1} - x_{i2} \qquad i = 1, 2, \ldots, n$$

Let $\mu_d = \mu_1 - \mu_2$ denote the mean of the population of differences, and let μ_0 denote some hypothesized value. The null hypothesis is

$$H_0\colon \mu_d = \mu_0$$

and the alternative hypothesis takes one of the forms

$$H_1\colon \mu_d \neq \mu_0, \quad H_1\colon \mu_d < \mu_0, \quad \text{or} \quad H_1\colon \mu_d > \mu_0$$

To test H_0 against H_1, we first calculate the sample mean and sample variance of the observed differences $d_1, d_2, \ldots, d_n$. We obtain the sample mean

$$\bar{d} = \frac{\sum_{i=1}^{n} d_i}{n}$$

and the sample variance is

$$s_d^2 = \frac{\sum_{i=1}^{n} (d_i - \bar{d})^2}{n - 1}$$

$$= \frac{\sum_{i=1}^{n} d_i^2 - n\bar{d}^2}{n - 1}$$

Suppose we have obtained a random sample of differences $d_1, d_2, \ldots, d_n$ from a population of differences that has a normal distribution with mean μ_0 and variance σ_d^2. Then the t statistic

$$t = \frac{\bar{d} - \mu_0}{s_d/\sqrt{n}}$$

follows the t distribution with $\nu = (n - 1)$ degrees of freedom. Values of t close to 0 support the null hypothesis, and values of t far from 0 support the alternative hypothesis.

The sample variance s_d^2 is an estimate of the population variance σ_d^2. If σ_d^2 is known, then we use σ_d^2 rather than s_d^2 and the Z score rather than the t score as the test statistic. In addition, we use the Z score when the sample size is large, even if the population variance is estimated. The procedure described in the accompanying box shows how to test the difference of two means when we have matched pairs of observations.

Testing the Difference Between Population Means of Matched Pairs

Suppose we have a random sample of n matched pairs of observations from populations with means μ_1 and μ_2. Let d_i be the ith difference where

$$d_i = x_{i1} - x_{i2}$$

where x_{i1} is the ith observation from Population 1 and x_{i2} is the ith observation from Population 2. Let $\bar{d}$ and s_d denote the observed sample mean and standard deviation respectively, for the n differences $d_1, d_2, \ldots, d_n$. If the population of differences is normal, then the following tests have significance level α:

Case 1: To test the null hypothesis

$$H_0: \mu_1 - \mu_2 = \mu_0 \quad \text{or} \quad H_0: \mu_1 - \mu_2 \leq \mu_0$$

against the one-sided alternative hypothesis

$$H_1: \mu_1 - \mu_2 > \mu_0$$

calculate the test statistic

$$t = \frac{\bar{d} - \mu_0}{s_d/\sqrt{n}}$$

and use the decision rule

Reject H_0 in favor of H_1 if $t > t_{\alpha,\nu}$,

where the random variable t follows the t distribution with $\nu = (n - 1)$ degrees of freedom.

Case 2: To test the null hypothesis

$$H_0: \mu_1 - \mu_2 = \mu_0 \quad \text{or} \quad H_0: \mu_1 - \mu_2 \geq \mu_0$$

against the one-sided alternative hypothesis

$$H_1: \mu_1 - \mu_2 < \mu_0$$

use the decision rule

Reject H_0 in favor of H_1 if $t < -t_{\alpha,\nu}$.

Case 3: To test the null hypothesis

$$H_0: \mu_1 - \mu_2 = \mu_0$$

against the two-sided alternative hypothesis

$$H_1: \mu_1 - \mu_2 \neq \mu_0$$

use the decision rule

Reject H_0 in favor of H_1 if $t > t_{\alpha/2,\nu}$ or if $t < -t_{\alpha/2,\nu}$.

When we want to test the null hypothesis that the two population means are equal, we set μ_0 equal to 0 in the formulas.

Example 12.4 **Testing a Difference Between Means of Matched Pairs:** Use the data in Table 12.1 to test the null hypothesis $H_0: \mu_1 - \mu_2 = 0$ against the two-sided alternative hypothesis $H_1: \mu_1 - \mu_2 \neq 0$ described in Example 12.3. That is, test $H_0: \mu_d = 0$ against $H_1: \mu_d \neq 0$. Use $\alpha = .05$.

Solution: Because each car was driven twice, once with Gasoline 1 and once with Gasoline 2, the observations are paired and are not independent. Thus we should use a paired difference test. We will use a two-tailed test with the level of significance set at $\alpha = .05$. For $\nu = (n - 1) = 9$ degrees of freedom and $\alpha = .05$, the critical values of t are $\pm t_{.025,9} = \pm 2.262$. From Table 12.1, we obtain $\bar{d} = -2.1$, $s_{\bar{d}}^2 = 0.9888$, and $s_d = 0.9944$.

The appropriate test statistic is

$$t = \frac{-2.1 - 0}{0.9944/\sqrt{10}} = -6.68$$

The observed value $t = -6.68$ falls in the rejection region, so we reject H_0.

Exercises for Section 12.3

1. The manager of a car rental agency wants to determine if the cars supplied by the agency get higher gasoline mileage using premium gasoline (Gasoline 1) or regular gasoline (Gasoline 2). Ten cars are randomly selected for the test. One gallon of Gasoline 1 is put in each car, which is driven under identical conditions until the tank is empty and the mileage is recorded. The same procedure is repeated with Gasoline 2. Use a 5% level of significance and test $H_0: \mu_1 - \mu_2 = 0$ against $H_1: \mu_1 - \mu_2 \neq 0$. Use the following data on gasoline mileage and a paired difference test:

Car	1	2	3	4	5	6	7	8	9	10
Gasoline 1	23.2	22.6	21.9	22.4	23.2	24.0	23.5	22.4	20.8	20.7
Gasoline 2	22.1	21.4	22.0	21.9	21.7	23.4	22.8	22.6	21.0	20.2

2. A publishing company wants to test whether secretaries type faster using word processor Brand 1 or Brand 2. Twelve secretaries are tested on each word processor, and their speeds in words per minute are recorded. Use a paired difference test and a 5% level of significance to test $H_0: \mu_1 - \mu_2 = 0$ against $H_1: \mu_1 - \mu_2 \neq 0$ using the following data on typing speed in words per minute:

Secretary	1	2	3	4	5	6	7	8	9	10	11	12
Brand 1	66	73	55	50	60	66	78	45	52	65	57	48
Brand 2	60	70	53	56	60	62	71	41	50	61	55	44

3. A tire manufacturer claims that its tires last at least as long as those of a competitor. Fifteen tires of each brand are randomly chosen. One tire of each type is placed on the rear of 15 different cars, which are driven until no tire tread remains. Use a 5% level of significance and a paired difference test to test H_0: $\mu_1 - \mu_2 \geqslant 0$ against H_1: $\mu_1 - \mu_2 < 0$ given the following results of tire mileage in thousands of miles:

Car	1	2	3	4	5	6	7	8	9	10	11	12	13	14	15
Brand 1	42	36	54	50	40	33	44	50	41	31	37	34	33	33	30
Brand 2	40	35	55	45	37	31	42	45	43	30	33	35	29	28	27

4. Suppose that a psychologist thinks that age influences IQ. Suppose that a random sample of 100 middle-aged persons whose IQs had been tested at age 16 were tested again. Subtracting their earlier scores from their new scores resulted in a mean difference of $\bar{x} = 6$ points with a standard deviation of the sample of differences of $s = 7$ points. Using $\alpha = .01$ as the significance level, the psychologist wishes to test the null hypothesis H_0: $\mu_d \leqslant 0$ against H_1: $\mu_d > 0$. Perform the appropriate test. Does it appear that IQ improves with age?

12.4 ▪ *Tests Concerning Differences of Proportions*

Frequently we are interested in testing the hypothesis that the proportion of individuals who possess a certain characteristic in Population 1 is the same as that in Population 2. Let p_1 and p_2 denote such proportions of Populations 1 and 2, respectively. Suppose we want to test the null hypothesis that the difference between p_1 and p_2 is some value D_0 (i.e., H_0: $p_1 - p_2 = D_0$).

To test this hypothesis, we take a sample of size n_1 from Population 1 and calculate $\hat{p}_1$, the proportion in this sample possessing the characteristic. Then we do likewise for Population 2 and calculate $\hat{p}_2$. If H_0 is true and if $n_1p_1 \geqslant 5$, $n_1q_1 \geqslant 5$, $n_2p_2 \geqslant 5$, and $n_2q_2 \geqslant 5$, then the random variable $(\hat{p}_1 - \hat{p}_2)$ is approximately normally distributed with mean D_0 and variance

$$p_1q_1/n_1 + p_2q_2/n_2$$

The null hypothesis typically is H_0: $p_1 - p_2 = 0$. Because p_1 and p_2 are unknown (only their difference D_0 is specified), we cannot find the variance of $(p_1 - p_2)$ without first obtaining estimates of p_1 and p_2. When the null hypothesis assumes that $p_1 = p_2$, a reasonable way to estimate the variance is to pool the two samples together to obtain one estimate of $p = p_1 = p_2$. To estimate p, we pool the data from the two samples and use the following formula:

$$\hat{p} = \frac{x_1 + x_2}{n_1 + n_2}$$

where x_1 and x_2 are the numbers of observations in the first and second sample, respectively, that possess the characteristic of interest. To test the null hypothesis H_0: $p_1 - p_2 = 0$ follow the procedure described in the accompanying box.

Testing the Equality of Two Population Proportions

Let $\hat{p}_1$ denote the sample proportion of successes in a random sample of n_1 observations from Population 1, and let $\hat{p}_2$ denote the sample proportion of successes observed in an independent random sample of n_2 observations from Population 2. If it is hypothesized that the population proportions are equal, an estimate of the common proportion is given by

$$\hat{p} = \frac{n_1\hat{p}_1 + n_2\hat{p}_2}{n_1 + n_2} = \frac{x_1 + x_2}{n_1 + n_2}$$

If the sample sizes are large, the following tests have significance level α:

Case 1: To test the null hypothesis

$$H_0: p_1 - p_2 = 0 \quad \text{or} \quad H_0: p_1 - p_2 \leq 0$$

against the one-sided alternative hypothesis

$$H_1: p_1 - p_2 > 0$$

calculate the test statistic

$$z = \frac{\hat{p}_1 - \hat{p}_2}{\sqrt{\hat{p}\hat{q}/n_1 + \hat{p}\hat{q}/n_2}} = \frac{\hat{p}_1 - \hat{p}_2}{\sqrt{\hat{p}\hat{q}\left(\dfrac{n_1 + n_2}{n_1 n_2}\right)}}$$

where $\hat{p}$ is the pooled estimate of p. Use the decision rule

Reject H_0 in favor of H_1 if $z > z_\alpha$.

Case 2: To test the null hypothesis

$$H_0: p_1 - p_2 = 0 \quad \text{or} \quad H_0: p_1 - p_2 \geq 0$$

against the one-sided alternative hypothesis

$$H_1: p_1 - p_2 < 0$$

use the decision rule

Reject H_0 in favor of H_1 if $z < -z_\alpha$.

Case 3: To test the null hypothesis

$$H_0: p_1 - p_2 = 0$$

against the two-sided alternative hypothesis

$$H_1: p_1 - p_2 \neq 0$$

use the decision rule

Reject H_0 in favor of H_1 if $z > z_{\alpha/2}$ or if $z < -z_{\alpha/2}$.

Example 12.6 **Testing the Equality of Two Population Proportions:** In a sample of 400 products produced by Machine 1, 23 were defective, and in a sample of 400 products produced by Machine 2, 17 were defective. Test $H_0: p_1 - p_2 = 0$ against $H_1: p_1 - p_2 \neq 0$ using a 5% level of significance.

Solution: We use a two-tailed test. For $\alpha = .05$, the critical values are $\pm z_{.025} = \pm 1.96$. To calculate the estimated variance, we obtain the pooled proportion

$$\hat{p} = \frac{x_1 + x_2}{n_1 + n_2} = \frac{23 + 17}{400 + 400} = \frac{40}{800} = .05$$

Thus, we estimate the variance of $(\hat{p}_1 - \hat{p}_2)$ as

$$\frac{\hat{p}\hat{q}}{n_1} + \frac{\hat{p}\hat{q}}{n_2} = \frac{(.05)(.95)}{400} + \frac{(.05)(.95)}{400} = .0002375$$

We have $\hat{p}_1 = 23/400 = .0575$ and $\hat{p}_2 = 17/400 = .0425$, and so we obtain the test statistic

$$z = \frac{.0575 - .0425}{\sqrt{.0002375}} \approx \frac{.015}{.015} = 1$$

Because the observed value $z = 1$ falls in the acceptance region, we do not reject H_0. See Figure 12.2.

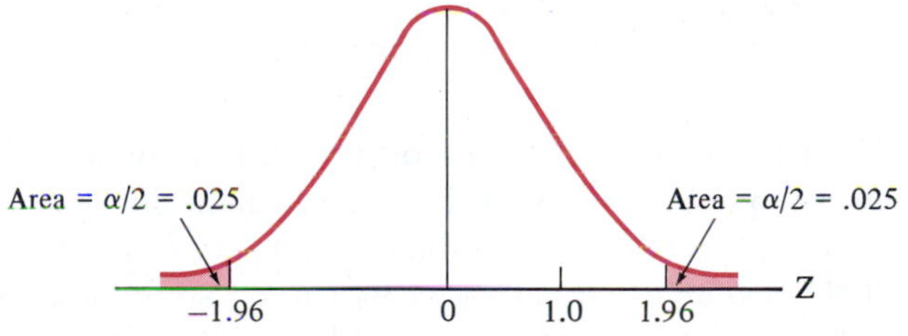

FIGURE 12.2
The Z distribution for Example 12.6.

Exercises for Section 12.4

1. A pharmaceutical company wants to test whether Aspirin 1 is as effective as Aspirin 2. A random sample of 400 people with headaches are given Aspirin 1, and 260 report that they feel better within one hour. Another independent random sample of 400 people with headaches are given Aspirin 2, and 252 report that they feel better within one hour. Test $H_0: p_1 - p_2 = 0$ against $H_1: p_1 - p_2 \neq 0$ using a 5% level of significance.
2. In a sample poll of 100 voters from District 1, 60 favored a certain political candidate. In a sample poll of 100 voters from District 2, 40 favored the candidate. Test $H_0: p_1 - p_2 = 0$ against $H_1: p_1 - p_2 > 0$ using a 1% level of significance.
3. In a random sample of 200 males, 60 reported that they preferred to watch the news on TV Station 1, which emphasizes sports coverage. In an independent random sample of 400 females, 140 reported that they preferred to watch the news on TV Station 1. Test the null hypothesis that the proportions of males and females who prefer Station 1 are identical using a 1% level of significance.

4. A quality control manager in an electronics plant thinks that foreign-born employees (Population 1) do better work than employees born in the United States (Population 2). The manager takes a random sample of 400 products produced by foreign-born employees and finds that 20 contain a defect. In a random sample of 400 products produced by employees born in the United States, 25 are defective. Test H_0: $p_1 - p_2 = 0$ against H_1: $p_1 - p_2 < 0$ using a 5% level of significance.
5. Let p_1 denote the percentage of people who were unemployed in March, and let p_2 denote the percentage of people who were unemployed in April. Suppose that during late March, the government instituted policies designed to lower the unemployment rate. We want to test whether the policies were effective. That is, we want to test H_0: $p_1 - p_2 = 0$ against H_1: $p_1 - p_2 > 0$ using, say, a 5% level of significance. In March, in a random sample of 1000 people, 75 were unemployed. During April, in an independent random sample of 1000 people, 65 were unemployed. Do you reject H_0?
6. A researcher desires to test whether the proportion of children born with defects is the same for mothers over 30 years of age and for mothers under 30 years of age. In a random sample of 500 babies whose mothers were over 30, 60 had defects. In a random sample of 400 babies whose mothers were under 30, 40 had defects. Test H_0: $p_1 - p_2 = 0$ against H_1: $p_1 - p_2 \neq 0$ using a 5% level of significance.
7. The Russell Construction Company purchases bricks from two different suppliers. In a random sample of 400 bricks from the first supplier, 26 were defective. In a random sample of 400 bricks from the second supplier, 44 were defective. Test the hypothesis that the defect rates are the same against the alternative hypothesis H_1: $p_1 - p_2 < 0$. Use a 5% level of significance.

12.5 ▪ The F Distribution

Occasionally it is necessary to compare two population variances. To test for the equality of two population variances, we calculate the ratio of the observed sample variances s_1^2/s_2^2. If this ratio is approximately equal to 1, we have no reason to doubt the hypothesis that the population variances σ_1^2 and σ_2^2 are equal. On the other hand, a very large or very small value for s_1^2/s_2^2 would provide evidence that the population variances are different.

How large or small must the ratio S_1^2/S_2^2 be before we reject the null hypothesis that the population variances are equal? To answer this question, we need to study the sampling distribution of the random variable S_1^2/S_2^2. When independent random samples are drawn from two normal populations with equal variances, then S_1^2/S_2^2 possesses a sampling distribution that is called the ***F* distribution**. We need to be able to find critical values of the F distribution to test hypotheses about the equality of two population variances and to construct confidence intervals for the ratio σ_1^2/σ_2^2. In this section we discuss the F distribution, and in the next section we will show how to perform tests and construct confidence intervals for a pair of population variances.

The F distribution is named in honor of the British statistician Sir Ronald Fisher (1890–1962), who began studying the distribution in the 1920s. Like the normal, t, and chi-square distributions, the F distribution is actually a family of distributions. For the F distribution, two parameters ν_1 and ν_2, called the *numerator* and *denominator degrees of freedom*, determine each different distribution. The random variable F is a continuous variable that can take any nonnegative value (it can never be negative because variances can never be negative). The F distribution is not symmetric; rather it is skewed to the

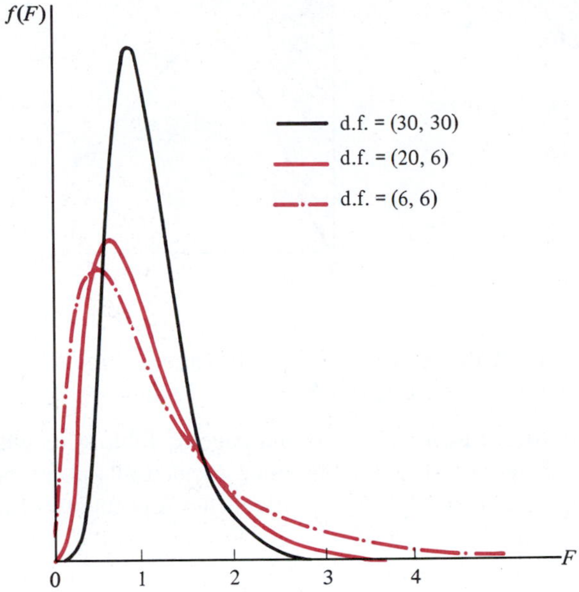

FIGURE 12.3
Three examples of the *F* distribution.

right for small values of ν_1 and ν_2. Some typical F distributions for various combinations of ν_1 and ν_2 are shown in Figure 12.3.

When using the F distribution to test hypotheses, we need to be able to find the critical values of F such that the area in the right and/or left tail of the distribution is some prespecified level of significance α. Suppose we want to find the critical value of F having ν_1 and ν_2 degrees of freedom such that the area in the right tail of the distribution is α. The critical values of the F statistic for different (ν_1, ν_2) combinations and various levels of significance α are provided in Table A.8 of the Appendix, which contains critical values for the levels of significance $\alpha = .05$ and $\alpha = .01$.

Critical Value of *F*

Let the random variable F follow the F distribution with ν_1 and ν_2 degrees of freedom. Let α denote the area in the right-hand tail of the F distribution. The critical value F_{α,ν_1,ν_2} is the value such that

$$P(F > F_{\alpha,\nu_1,\nu_2}) = \alpha$$

Example 12.7

Critical Value of the *F* Distribution I: Find the critical value of F such that the right tail of the distribution contains 5% of the area under the curve where F has numerator degrees of freedom $\nu_1 = 2$ and denominator degrees of freedom $\nu_2 = 9$.

Solution: Refer to Table A.8 in the Appendix. Find the value located at the intersection of the column representing $\nu_1 = 2$ degrees of freedom and the row representing $\nu_2 = 9$ degrees of freedom. We obtain $F_{.05,2,9} = 4.26$, which is shown in Figure 12.4.

FIGURE 12.4
The *F* distribution for Example 12.7.

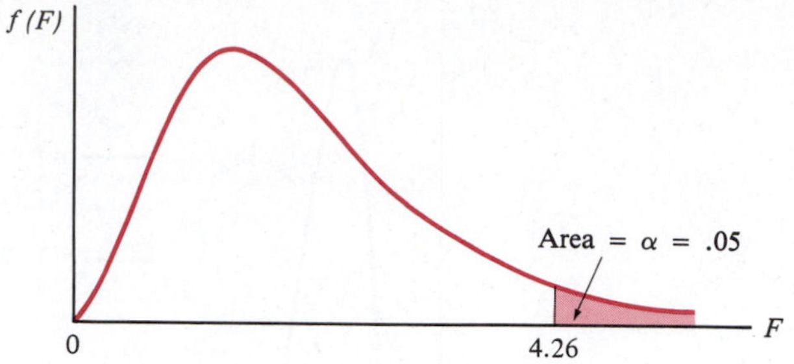

Example 12.8

Critical Value of the *F* Distribution II: Find the critical value of F such that the right-hand tail has area .01 where $\nu_1 = 2$ and $\nu_2 = 9$.

Solution: Refer to the second page of Table A.8, which shows critical values associated with $\alpha = .01$. Find the value located at the intersection of the column representing $\nu_1 = 2$ degrees of freedom and the row representing $\nu_2 = 9$ degrees of freedom. We obtain $F_{.01,2,9} = 8.02$.

Occasionally we may need critical values of F for values of ν_1 and ν_2 that are not given in Table A.8. For example, suppose we need the value $F_{.05,11,15}$. We can usually get a good estimate of the required F value by interpolation. From Table A.8, we obtain $F_{.05,10,15} = 2.54$ and $F_{.05,12,15} = 2.48$. By interpolation we obtain $F_{.05,11,15} = 2.51$. A more detailed table would show that $F_{.05,11,15} = 2.51$, so in this case interpolation works very well.

In most statistics books, including this one, the tables for the F distribution show only the critical values for the right-hand tail. Fortunately, we can determine the critical values for the left tail of the F distribution from the right-tail critical values. To find the value of F such that the area in the left tail is α, we use the fact that the lower-tail critical value, denoted by $F_{1-\alpha,\nu_1,\nu_2}$, can be determined from the upper-tail critical value F_{α,ν_2,ν_1} by using the relationship

$$F_{1-\alpha,\nu_1,\nu_2} = \frac{1}{F_{\alpha,\nu_2,\nu_1}}$$

Notice that in this formula, the degrees of freedom are reversed. Thus, $F_{1-\alpha,\nu_1,\nu_2}$ is the value of F having ν_1 and ν_2 degrees of freedom such that the area in the lower, or left, tail is α and the area in the right tail is $(1 - \alpha)$. On the other hand, F_{α,ν_2,ν_1} is the value of F having ν_2 and ν_1 degrees of freedom such that the area in the upper, or right, tail is α.

Example 12.9

Critical Values of the *F* Distribution III: Suppose the degrees of freedom of an F statistic are $\nu_1 = 8$ and $\nu_2 = 4$, respectively. Find the critical values of F such that each tail of the F distribution has area .05.

Solution: We seek the two critical values $F_{.95,8,4}$ and $F_{.05,8,4}$. From Table A.8, we obtain $F_{.05,8,4} = 6.04$, but we still need to find $F_{.95,8,4}$. First we obtain the value $F_{.05,4,8} = 3.84$; then we obtain

$$F_{.95,8,4} = \frac{1}{F_{.05,4,8}} = \frac{1}{3.84} = 0.26$$

If the F statistic has $\nu_1 = 8$ and $\nu_2 = 4$ degrees of freedom, then

$$P(0.26 \leq F \leq 6.04) = .90$$

This relationship is illustrated in Figure 12.5.

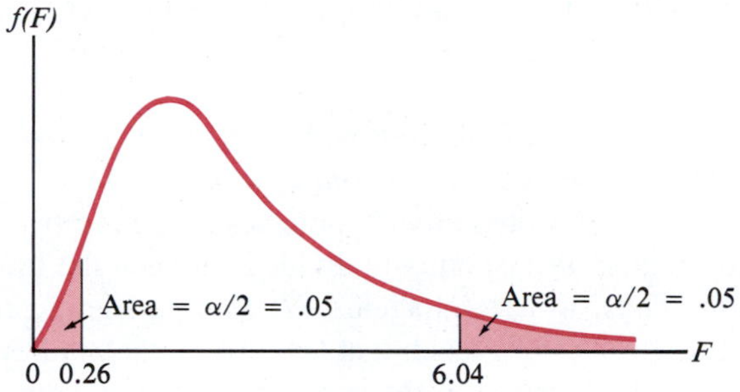

FIGURE 12.5
The F distribution for Example 12.9.

Exercises for Section 12.5

1. Using Table A.8 of the Appendix, find the following critical values:
   a. $F_{.05,9,15}$ b. $F_{.01,9,15}$ c. $F_{.05,15,9}$
2. Using Table A.8 of the Appendix, find the following critical values:
   a. $F_{.01,15,9}$ b. $F_{.05,5,4}$ c. $F_{.01,5,4}$
3. Find the critical value of F such that the left tail of the distribution has area .01 when the numerator and denominator degrees of freedom are the following:
   a. 5 and 4 b. 4 and 5 c. 5 and 5
4. Find the critical value of F such that the left tail of the distribution has area .05 when the numerator and denominator degrees of freedom are the following:
   a. 5 and 4 b. 4 and 5 c. 5 and 5

12.6 ▪ Testing Hypotheses and Constructing Confidence Intervals for Two Population Variances

Testing Hypotheses of Two Population Variances

Suppose we want to test the null hypothesis that the variances of two normal populations are equal. That is, we want to test the null hypothesis

$$H_0: \sigma_1^2 = \sigma_2^2$$

against one of the alternative hypotheses

$$H_1: \sigma_1^2 \neq \sigma_2^2, \quad H_1: \sigma_1^2 > \sigma_2^2, \quad \text{or} \quad H_1: \sigma_1^2 < \sigma_2^2$$

The null hypothesis $H_0: \sigma_1^2 = \sigma_2^2$ is equivalent to the null hypothesis

$$H_0: \sigma_1^2/\sigma_2^2 = 1$$

To test H_0 against H_1, we take random samples of size n_1 and n_2 from the two populations and calculate the sample variances S_1^2 and S_2^2. If the two populations are normally distributed and if $\sigma_1^2 = \sigma_2^2$ (so that H_0 is true), then the random variable

$$F = S_1^2/S_2^2$$

follows the F distribution with numerator degrees of freedom $\nu_1 = (n_1 - 1)$ and denominator degrees of freedom $\nu_2 = (n_2 - 1)$.

When the alternative hypothesis requires a two-tailed test ($H_1: \sigma_1^2 \neq \sigma_2^2$), the rejection region will be equally divided between the lower and upper tails of the F distribution. Thus, to test H_0 against H_1 using a significance level α, we need to find the two critical values of F such that the area in each tail of the F distribution equals $\alpha/2$.

The discussion in the accompanying box shows how to test hypotheses concerning the equality of two variances.

Testing the Equality of Variances of Two Normal Populations

Let s_1^2 and s_2^2 be observed sample variances from independent random samples of n_1 and n_2 observations from normal populations with variances σ_1^2 and σ_2^2.

Case 1: To test the null hypothesis

$$H_0: \sigma_1^2 = \sigma_2^2 \quad \text{or} \quad H_0: \sigma_1^2 \leq \sigma_2^2$$

against the one-sided alternative hypothesis

$$H_1: \sigma_1^2 > \sigma_2^2$$

calculate the test statistic

$$F = s_1^2/s_2^2$$

and use the decision rule

$$\text{Reject } H_0 \text{ in favor of } H_1 \text{ if } F > F_{\alpha,\nu_1,\nu_2},$$

where $\nu_1 = (n_1 - 1)$ and $\nu_2 = (n_2 - 1)$. To perform the test when the alternative hypothesis is $H_1: \sigma_1^2 < \sigma_2^2$, just reverse the definitions of Populations 1 and 2 and proceed as described above.

Case 2: To test the null hypothesis

$$H_0: \sigma_1^2 = \sigma_2^2$$

against the two-sided alternative hypothesis

$$H_1: \sigma_1^2 \neq \sigma_2^2$$

use the decision rule

$$\text{Reject } H_0 \text{ in favor of } H_1 \text{ if } F < F_{1-\alpha/2,\nu_1,\nu_2} \text{ or if } F > F_{\alpha/2,\nu_1,\nu_2}$$

Example 12.9

Testing the Equality of Variances from Two Normal Populations: An employee for the Metropolitan Bank thinks that the starting weekly salaries of newly hired male and female MBA graduates follow normal distributions. The employee wants to test the null hypothesis that the variance among the men's starting salaries σ_1^2 is the same as the variance among the women's starting salaries σ_2^2. The employee obtains a random sample of 10 recently hired men and 7 recently hired women and obtains the sample variances $s_1^2 = 275$ and $s_2^2 = 225$, respectively. Test the null hypothesis H_0: $\sigma_1^2 = \sigma_2^2$ against the alternative hypothesis H_1: $\sigma_1^2 \neq \sigma_2^2$ using a 10% level of significance.

Solution: The degrees of freedom are $\nu_1 = (n_1 - 1) = 9$ and $\nu_2 = (n_2 - 1) = 6$. For a two-tailed test using $\alpha = .10$, we obtain the critical values

$$F_{.05,9,6} = 4.10$$

and

$$F_{.95,9,6} = \frac{1}{F_{.05,6,9}} = \frac{1}{3.37} = 0.30$$

The value of the test statistic is given by

$$F = s_1^2/s_2^2 = 275/225 = 1.22$$

We do not reject H_0, because $F = 1.22$ falls in the acceptance region. See Figure 12.6.

FIGURE 12.6
The F distribution for Example 12.9.

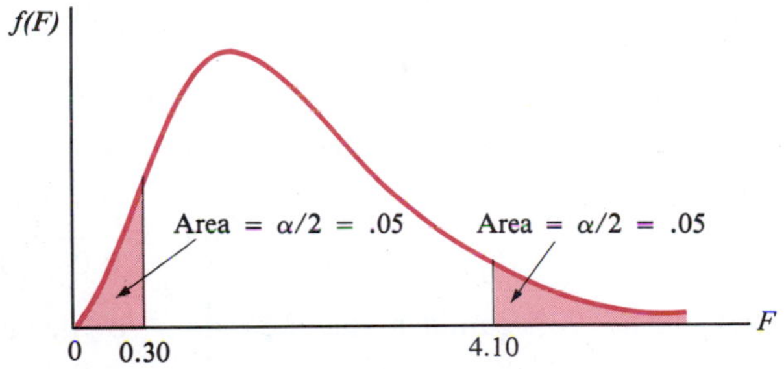

Confidence Intervals for σ_1^2/σ_2^2

Suppose we take independent samples of size n_1 and n_2 from normal populations having variances σ_1^2 and σ_2^2. To construct a confidence interval for the ratio σ_1^2/σ_2^2, we utilize the fact that the random variable

$$F = \frac{S_1^2/\sigma_1^2}{S_2^2/\sigma_2^2}$$

has the F distribution with numerator degrees of freedom $\nu_1 = (n_1 - 1)$ and denominator degrees of freedom $\nu_2 = (n_2 - 1)$, and we utilize the probability statement

$$P\left(F_{1-\alpha/2,\nu_1,\nu_2} \leq \frac{S_1^2/\sigma_1^2}{S_2^2/\sigma_2^2} \leq F_{\alpha/2,\nu_1,\nu_2}\right) = 1 - \alpha$$

Some algebraic manipulation yields the following equivalent probability statement:

$$P\left[\frac{S_1^2}{S_2^2}\left(\frac{1}{F_{1-\alpha/2,\nu_1,\nu_2}}\right) \leqslant \frac{\sigma_1^2}{\sigma_2^2} \leqslant \frac{S_1^2}{S_2^2}\left(\frac{1}{F_{\alpha/2,\nu_1,\nu_2}}\right)\right] = 1 - \alpha$$

Formula for a Confidence Interval for σ_1^2/σ_2^2

A confidence interval for σ_1^2/σ_2^2 having level of confidence $(1 - \alpha)$ is given by

$$\frac{s_1^2}{s_2^2}\left(\frac{1}{F_{\alpha/2,\nu_1,\nu_2}}\right),\quad \frac{s_1^2}{s_2^2}\left(\frac{1}{F_{1-\alpha/2,\nu_1,\nu_2}}\right)$$

Example 12.10 **Constructing a Confidence Interval for the Ratio of Two Variances:** Two machines fill containers with fluid. The populations are assumed to be normal. Independent random samples are obtained of 21 containers filled by Machine 1 and 16 containers filled by Machine 2. The observed sample variances are $s_1^2 = 0.25$ and $s_2^2 = 0.08$. Construct a 90% confidence interval for σ_1^2/σ_2^2.

Solution: The degrees of freedom are $\nu_1 = 20$ and $\nu_2 = 15$, and the critical values of F are

$$F_{.05,20,15} = 2.33$$

and

$$F_{.95,20,15} = \frac{1}{F_{.05,15,20}} = \frac{1}{2.20} = 0.45$$

The desired confidence interval is

$$\frac{0.25}{0.08}\left(\frac{1}{2.33}\right),\quad \frac{0.25}{0.08}\left(\frac{1}{0.45}\right)$$

Thus, we are 90% confident that the ratio σ_1^2/σ_2^2 lies in the interval (1.34, 6.94). ■

Exercises for Section 12.6

1. Two different brands of golf balls are being tested to determine if one brand is more variable than the other. A small variance is extremely important, because a golfer would like every golf ball to travel approximately the same distance when hit with the same force. If the balls are highly variable, then the distance that the ball travels depends not only on the golfer's swing but also on whether the ball is a "live" ball or a "dead" ball. A random sample of $n_1 = 21$ Maxi balls are hit by a mechanical device, and the distances are measured. The observed sample variance is $s_1^2 = 225$. A random sample of $n_2 = 11$ Pro Staff balls are hit by the same mechanical device, and a sample variance of $s_2^2 = 174$ is obtained.
   a. Use a 1% level of significance and test H_0: $\sigma_1^2/\sigma_2^2 = 1$ against H_1: $\sigma_1^2/\sigma_2^2 > 1$.
   b. Construct a 90% confidence interval for σ_1^2/σ_2^2.
2. Two methods of filling boxes of cereal produce the same package fill weight on the average. The second method is faster, but some people suspect that this method produces a greater variance

than the first method does. A random sample of 31 packages filled by Method 1 is obtained, and the observed sample variance is $s_1^2 = 0.4$. A random sample of 26 packages filled by Method 2 yields a sample variance of $s_2^2 = 0.6$.

a. Let $\alpha = .05$. Test H_0: $\sigma_1^2 = \sigma_2^2$. Use a one-tailed test.

b. Construct a 90% confidence interval for σ_1^2/σ_2^2.

3. Two different brands of milk are randomly sampled, and the fat content in each bottle of milk is determined. Twenty-six bottles of Brand A milk yielded an average fat content of $\bar{x}_1 = 26$ grams with $s_1^2 = 5$, and 31 bottles of Brand B yielded an average fat content of $\bar{x}_2 = 25.8$ grams with $s_2^2 = 7$.

a. Let $\alpha = .02$ and test H_0: $\sigma_1^2 = \sigma_2^2$. Use a two-tailed test.

b. Find a 90% confidence interval for σ_1^2/σ_2^2.

4. Suppose two machines produce 1-inch diameter pipes with different degrees of precision. A random sample of 20 pipes is taken from each machine, yielding observed sample standard deviations of $s_1 = 0.002$ and $s_2 = 0.005$.

a. Let $\alpha = .02$. Should we conclude that σ_1^2 is different from σ_2^2? Use a two-tailed test.

b. Determine a 90% confidence interval for σ_1^2/σ_2^2.

12.7 ▪ Computer Applications

Refer to the data in Table 2.2 of Chapter 2, showing selected characteristics of a sample of statistics students. Suppose it is desired to test the null hypothesis that in the population of students, the mean SAT score for the males is the same as the mean SAT score for the females. In Section 9.8, we showed how to use the BREAKDOWN command in an SPSSX program to request the sample mean and sample standard deviation for a variable, such as SAT, broken down according to the values of another variable, such as SEX. The appropriate command would be

```
BREAKDOWN TABLES = SAT BY SEX
```

When the sample size is large, we obtain the appropriate sample means and sample standard deviations and substitute them into the Z score

$$Z = \frac{(\bar{X}_1 - \bar{X}_2) - (\mu_1 - \mu_2)}{\sqrt{S_1^2/n_1 + S_2^2/n_2}}$$

This statistic is approximately a standard normal variable when the sample sizes are large.

Exercises for Section 12.7

1. Use the SPSSX program and the BREAKDOWN command to find the sample mean and sample standard deviation for the variable SALARY broken down according to the variable SEX using the data in Table 2.1 of Chapter 2. Let $\alpha = .05$ and test the null hypothesis that the mean salaries of males and females are equal. Use a two-tailed t test based on the assumption that the population variances are equal and the populations are normal.

2. Use the SPSSX program and the BREAKDOWN command to find the sample mean and sample standard deviation for the variable SALARY broken down according to the variable RACE using the data in Table 2.1 of Chapter 2. Let $\alpha = .05$ and test the null hypothesis that the mean salaries of whites and blacks are equal. Use a two-tailed t test based on the assumption that the population variances are equal and the populations are normal.

3. Use the SPSSX program and the BREAKDOWN command to find the sample mean and sample standard deviation for the variable SALARY broken down according to the variable DEGREE using the data in Table 2.1 of Chapter 2.
   a. Let $\alpha = .05$ and test the null hypothesis that the mean salaries of high school graduates and college graduates are equal. Use an appropriate one-tailed test.
   b. Let $\alpha = .05$ and test the null hypothesis that the mean salaries of college graduates and individuals with postgraduate degrees are equal. Use an appropriate one-tailed test.

4. Use the SPSSX program and the BREAKDOWN command on the data in Table 2.1 of Chapter 2 to find the sample mean and sample standard deviation for the variable SENIOR broken down according to the variable DIV. Let $\alpha = .05$ and test the null hypothesis that the mean seniorities of individuals in the office and of individuals in the sales division are equal. Use an appropriate one-tailed test.

5. Use the SPSSX program and the BREAKDOWN command on the data in Table 2.2 of Chapter 2 to find the sample mean and sample standard deviation for the variable SAT broken down according to the variable SEX. Let $\alpha = .05$ and test the null hypothesis that the mean SAT scores of males and females are equal. Use an appropriate two-tailed test.

6. Use the SPSSX program and the BREAKDOWN command on the data in Table 2.2 of Chapter 2 to find the sample mean and sample standard deviation for the variable GPA broken down according to the variable SEX. Let $\alpha = .05$ and test the null hypothesis that the mean GPA scores of males and of females are equal. Use an appropriate two-tailed test.

7. Use the SPSSX program and the BREAKDOWN command on the data in Table 2.2 of Chapter 2 to find the sample mean and sample standard deviation for the variable SAT broken down according to the variable CLASS. Let $\alpha = .05$ and test the null hypothesis that the mean SAT scores of juniors and of seniors are equal. Use an appropriate two-tailed test.

8. Use the SPSSX program and the BREAKDOWN command on the data in Table 2.2 of Chapter 2 to find the sample mean and sample standard deviation for the variable GPA broken down according to the variable RES. Let $\alpha = .05$ and test the null hypothesis that the mean GPA scores of in-state and of out-of-state students are equal. Use an appropriate two-tailed test.

9. Use the SPSSX program and the BREAKDOWN command on the data in Table 2.2 of Chapter 2 to find the sample mean and sample standard deviation for the variable GPA broken down according to the variable MAJOR. Let $\alpha = .05$ and test the null hypothesis that the mean GPA scores of business majors and of math majors are equal. Use an appropriate two-tailed test.

Chapter 12 Summary

Chapter 12 introduces tests of hypotheses concerning the parameters of two populations. To test the null hypothesis H_0: $(\mu_1 - \mu_2) = D_0$ when the populations are normal with known variances, calculate the test statistic

$$z = \frac{(\bar{x}_1 - \bar{x}_2) - D_0}{\sqrt{\sigma_1^2/n_1 + \sigma_2^2/n_2}}$$

and compare with the critical values obtained from the standard normal distribution. If the sample sizes are large, the observed sample variances can be substituted for the unknown population variances. For small independent samples, testing hypotheses concerning the difference $(\mu_1 - \mu_2)$ requires the assumption that the populations are both approximately normal. For this situation, we must also pay special attention to whether the population variances (σ_1^2 and σ_2^2) are equal. If we assume that the variances are equal, calculate the test statistic

$$t = \frac{(\bar{x}_1 - \bar{x}_2) - D_0}{\sqrt{s_p^2/n_1 + s_p^2/n_2}}$$

where the pooled estimate of the variance is

$$s_p^2 = \frac{(n_1 - 1)s_1^2 + (n_2 - 1)s_2^2}{n_1 + n_2 - 2}$$

and compare with the critical values obtained from the t distribution having $(n_1 + n_2 - 2)$ degrees of freedom.

When two samples are obtained such that corresponding observations are paired (matched), the resulting samples are dependent or paired. To test the null hypothesis H_0: $\mu_d = \mu_0$ when the population variance is unknown and the samples are paired or dependent, calculate the test statistic

$$t = \frac{\bar{d} - \mu_0}{s_d/\sqrt{n}}$$

and compare with the critical values obtained from the t distribution having $(n - 1)$ degrees of freedom.

A test of the hypothesis H_0: $(p_1 - p_2) = 0$ relies on the assumption that the samples are independent and that the sample estimates are approximately normally distributed. For this to hold, we require $n_1p_1 \geqslant 5$, $n_1q_1 \geqslant 5$, $n_2p_2 \geqslant 5$, and $n_2q_2 \geqslant 5$. If these conditions hold, calculate the test statistic

$$z = \frac{\hat{p}_1 - \hat{p}_2}{\sqrt{\hat{p}\hat{q}/n_1 + \hat{p}\hat{q}/n_2}} = \frac{\hat{p}_1 - \hat{p}_2}{\sqrt{\hat{p}\hat{q}\left(\dfrac{n_1 + n_2}{n_1n_2}\right)}}$$

where $\hat{p}$ is the pooled estimate of p given by

$$\hat{p} = \frac{n_1\hat{p}_1 + n_2\hat{p}_2}{n_1 + n_2} = \frac{x_1 + x_2}{n_1 + n_2}$$

and compare with the critical values obtained from the standard normal distribution.

To test for the equality of the variances of two normal populations, calculate the test statistic

$$F = \frac{s_1^2}{s_2^2}$$

and compare with critical values obtained from the F distribution having $\nu_1 = (n_1 - 1)$ and $\nu_2 = (n_2 - 1)$ degrees of freedom.

Chapter 11 showed how to test hypotheses concerning the parameters of a single population and Chapter 12 shows how to compare the means, proportions, or variances of two populations. In Chapter 13 we show how to test hypotheses concerning three or more population proportions. Chapter 14 completes the discussion of classical tests of hypotheses by showing how to test hypotheses concerning three or more population means or variances. Additional tests of hypotheses are discussed in Chapter 21 where some of the assumptions underlying the tests are relaxed.

Chapter 12 • Supplementary Exercises

1. We want to test the hypothesis that the average IQ of math majors, denoted μ_1, is the same as the average IQ of economics majors, denoted μ_2. In a sample of 36 math majors, the sample mean is $\bar{x}_1 = 120$ and the sample variance is $s_1^2 = 144$. In a sample of 36 economics majors, we obtain $\bar{x}_2 = 123$ and $s_2^2 = 112$. Test H_0: $(\mu_1 - \mu_2) = 0$ against H_1: $(\mu_1 - \mu_2) \neq 0$ using a 5% level of significance. Assume the population variances are equal, the populations are normal, and the samples are independent.
2. In a TV commercial, Company 1 claims that its golf balls are livelier than those made by Company 2. A mechanical device hits 200 balls made by Company 1 and 200 balls made by Company 2. We measure how far each ball travels. The sample results are $\bar{x}_1 = 212$ yards, $s_1^2 = 81$ yards; $\bar{x}_2 = 208$ yards, $s_2^2 = 81$ yards. Test H_0: $(\mu_1 - \mu_2) = 0$ against H_1: $(\mu_1 - \mu_2) \neq 0$ using a 5% level of significance.
3. A sports publication claims that the average income of people who attend hockey games (Population 1) is higher than the average income of people who attend pro football games. In a random sample of 200 hockey fans, we obtain $\bar{x}_1 = \$35,000$ with $s_1^2 = 9,000,000$. In a random sample of 200 football fans (Population 2), we obtain $\bar{x}_2 = \$32,500$ with $s_2^2 = 9,000,000$. Test H_0: $(\mu_1 - \mu_2) = 0$ against H_1: $(\mu_1 - \mu_2) > 0$ using a 5% level of significance.
4. The Environmental Protection Agency wants to test the null hypothesis that Denver and Los Angeles have the same amount of air pollution. The air quality in each city is measured on 20 randomly selected days. In Denver, the sample mean was $\bar{x}_1 = 85$ and the sample variance was $s_1^2 = 1000$. In Los Angeles the sample mean was $\bar{x}_2 = 92$ with $s_2^2 = 800$. Test H_0: $(\mu_1 - \mu_2) = 0$ against H_1: $(\mu_1 - \mu_2) \neq 0$ using a 5% level of significance. Assume the populations are normal with equal variances and use a t test.
5. An advertising firm wants to test the null hypothesis that men will have better retention of TV commercials in which a female appears. Two similar commercials are produced for use on a TV show that is shown in City 1 and City 2. A female appears in Commercial 1 but not in Commercial 2. Only Commercial 1 is seen in City 1, and only Commercial 2 is seen in City 2. On the following day, a poll is taken of 100 men from City 1 who saw the TV show; 43 could remember the name of the product. In City 2, 37 of 100 men could remember the name of the product. Test the hypothesis H_0: $(p_1 - p_2) = 0$ against H_1: $(p_1 - p_2) > 0$ using a 5% level of significance.
6. The army is interested in determining whether Method 1 or Method 2 is a better way to teach soldiers. In a random sample of 1000 soldiers taught using Method 1, 700 pass the marksmanship test after three days of training; in an independent random sample of 1000 soldiers taught by Method 2, 740 pass the test after three days of training. Test H_0: $(p_1 - p_2) = 0$ against H_1: $(p_1 - p_2) \neq 0$ using a 5% level of significance.
7. A woman is running for governor of a southern state. Pollsters argue that men are biased against female candidates and that women are biased in favor of female candidates. In a sample of 100 women, 54 say that they favor a particular female candidate. In an independent sample of 100 men, 46 say that they favor this candidate. Test H_0: $(p_1 - p_2) = 0$ against H_1: $(p_1 - p_2) \neq 0$ using a 1% level of significance.
8. On a sample of 50 plots of land, a farmer plants wheat and uses fertilizer made by Company 1; on another 50 plots, fertilizer by Company 2 is used. When the wheat is harvested, the farmer measures how many bushels of wheat are obtained on each plot. The average yield on the plots using Company 1 fertilizer was $\bar{x}_1 = 141$ with sample variance 400, and on the plots using

Company 2 fertilizer, the sample mean was $\bar{x}_2 = 127$ with sample variance 400. Test H_0: $(\mu_1 - \mu_2) = 0$ against H_1: $(\mu_1 - \mu_2) > 0$ using a 5% level of significance. Assume the population variances are equal, the populations are normal, and the samples are independent.

9. In an agricultural experiment to determine the effects of a particular insecticide, a field was planted with corn. Half of the plants were sprayed with the insecticide, and half were unsprayed. Several weeks later, independent random samples of 200 sprayed plants and 200 unsprayed plants were examined. The number of healthy plants in each sample was as follows:

	Sprayed	Unsprayed
Healthy	131	111
Not healthy	69	89

If the significance level is set at .05, does the evidence indicate that a higher proportion of sprayed than of unsprayed plants were healthy? Use a one-tailed test.

10. Suppose that on a certain nationwide exam, 64% of the students got the first question correct. This exam is given to 100 candidates for a certain civil service position. On the basis of their total scores, the 100 candidates are divided into two groups: Group 1 contains 20 individuals who passed, and Group 2 contains 80 individuals who failed the test. Of the 20 candidates who passed the exam, 15 answered the first question correctly. Of the 80 candidates who failed the test, 40 answered the first question correctly. At a 5% level of significance using a one-tailed test, determine whether the first question successfully discriminated between passing and failing students. That is, determine whether the percentage of passing students who answered the first question correctly was significantly higher than the percentage of failing students who answered the first question correctly.

11. The "fog index" is used to measure the reading difficulty of a written text. The fog index is the sum of the average number of words per sentence plus the percentage of words with three or more syllables. A random sample of six pages of material from *The Wall Street Journal* had the following fog indices:

61 45 59 38 42 55

An independent random sample of six pages from *Sports Illustrated* had the following fog indices:

40 36 29 28 35 42

Use a 5% level of significance and test the null hypothesis that the population mean fog indices are the same against the alternative that the population mean is higher for *The Wall Street Journal* than for *Sports Illustrated*.

12. A charity uses two procedures for soliciting funds from wealthy donors. In the first, a phone call is made, the charity's objectives for the coming year are discussed, and any questions are answered. In the second, an agent of the charity arranges to meet with donors in their homes. For a random sample of 100 donors contacted by telephone, the mean donation was \$125 and the sample standard deviation was \$71. For an independent random sample of 100 donors who were visited at home, the mean donation was \$140 and the sample standard deviation was \$83. Test the null hypothesis that the two population means are equal against the alternative that the mean is higher for donors contacted at home.

13. We want to determine if a new cover improves the distance that a golf ball will travel. Random samples of 200 new balls and 200 old balls are hit by a mechanical device. After measuring how far each ball travels, we obtain $\bar{x}_1 = 208$, $s_1^2 = 1000$; $\bar{x}_2 = 198$, $s_2^2 = 800$. Use a 5% level of significance and test the null hypothesis H_0: $(\mu_1 - \mu_2) = 0$ against H_1: $(\mu_1 - \mu_2) > 0$. Assume the population variances are equal and that the populations are normal.

14. In random samples of 200 males and 200 females, the proportions of individuals who attend church regularly were calculated. Suppose that 90 males and 110 females claimed that they attend church regularly. Test the null hypothesis that the population proportions are equal. Use $\alpha = .05$.

15. In a random sample of 400 people from Atlanta, 300 said Coca-Cola was their favorite soft drink. In an independent random sample of 300 people from Kansas City, 175 said Coca-Cola was their favorite soft drink. At the 1% level of significance, test the hypothesis that there is no difference in preference in the two cities.

16. The braking ability of two new compact cars was being studied. The cars were driven 50 miles per hour when the brakes were applied, and the distances required to stop were measured. Ten cars of each type were studied. The sample means and sample standard deviations were $\bar{x}_1 = 138$ feet, $s_1 = 11$ feet; $\bar{x}_2 = 144$ feet, $s_2 = 13$ feet. Test H_0: $(\mu_1 - \mu_2) = 0$ against H_1: $(\mu_1 - \mu_2) \neq 0$ using a 1% level of significance. Assume the population variances are equal, the populations are normal, and the samples are independent.

17. Two independent samples of 80 equally intelligent schoolchildren are taught to read by different methods: The first group memorizes words, and the second tries to learn words by pronouncing the sounds of the letters. After several months of instruction, a reading test is given to all of the children. The test results were $\bar{x}_1 = 70$, $s_1 = 8$; $\bar{x}_2 = 63$, $s_2 = 7$. Test H_0: $\mu_1 - \mu_2 = 0$ against H_2: $\mu_1 - \mu_2 \neq 0$ using a 1% level of significance. Assume the population variances are equal, the populations are normal, and the samples are independent.

18. In a random sample of 200 men, 120 favored the death penalty for certain crimes. In an independent random sample of 300 women, 250 favored the death penalty for the same crimes. Can we conclude that a greater proportion of women than men favor the death penalty? Use a 5% level of significance.

19. Last year in a random sample of 250 beer drinkers, 100 named Budweiser as their favorite. This year in an independent random sample of 350 beer drinkers, 130 named Budweiser as their favorite. Let $\alpha = .01$. Can we conclude that the proportion of beer drinkers who favor Budweiser has declined? That is, test H_0: $(p_1 - p_2) = 0$ against H_1: $(p_1 - p_2) > 0$.

20. A new energy conservation bill is being considered in the U.S. Senate. In a random sample of 200 West Virginia residents, 160 were against the bill. In a random sample of 300 Maine voters, 200 favored the bill and 100 were against it. Let $\alpha = .05$. Can it be concluded that the proportion of voters who are against the bill is the same in Maine and West Virginia?

21. A governmental agency hired a doctor to investigate the impact of a lead smelter on the level of lead in the blood of children living near the smelter. Ten of these children were chosen at random, and the following lead levels (micrograms per 100 milliliters of blood) were measured:

18	16	21	14	17
19	22	24	15	18

An independent sample of 7 children living in an area relatively free from possible lead pollution was also obtained, whose blood samples had the following lead levels:

9	13	8	15	17	12	11

a. State the null hypothesis and the alternative hypothesis.

b. With $\alpha = .05$, what do you conclude?

22. A study was made of 10,000 men who had vasectomies, and each was matched to a man of approximately the same age, race, and marital status who had not been vasectomized. Over the 15-year period covered by the study, 220 of the vasectomized men and 310 of the nonvasectomized men died.

a. Let $\alpha = .05$ and test the null hypothesis that the two population proportions are equal. Does it appear to you that vasectomized men have a lower death rate?

b. Do you think the vasectomy causes the lower death rate? Could it be that men who choose to have a vasectomy are healthier than men who do not? Can you think of any possible explanation for these results?

23. In 1954, a study of the effects of Salk polio vaccine on the incidence of paralytic polio in children yielded the following data:

	Number Inoculated	Number of Polio Cases
With Salk vaccine	200,745	28
With placebo	201,229	71

Is there a statistically significant difference in polio incidence between the two groups of children? Let $\alpha = .01$.

References

COCHRAN, WILLIAM G., and G. M. COX. *Experimental Designs*. 2d ed. New York: Wiley, 1957.

FISHER, RONALD A. *Statistical Methods for Research Workers*. 14th ed. New York: Hafner, 1970.

NIE, NORMAN E., C. HADLAI HULL, JEAN JENKINS, KARIN STEINBRENNER, and DALE H. BENT. *SPSS Statistical Package for the Social Sciences*. 2d ed. New York: McGraw-Hill, 1975.

NORUSIS, MARIJA J. *SPSSX Introductory Statistics Guide*. New York: McGraw-Hill, 1983.

________. *SPSSX Advanced Statistics Guide*. Chicago: SPSS, 1985.

________. *The SPSS Guide to Data Analysis*. Chicago: SPSS, 1986.

RYAN, THOMAS A., BRIAN L. JOINER, and BARBARA F. RYAN. *Minitab Handbook*. 2d ed. Boston: PWS-KENT, 1985.

________. *Minitab Reference Manual*. University Park, Pa.: Minitab Project, 1985.

SAS Introductory Guide. 3d ed. Cary, N.C.: SAS Institute, 1985.

SAS Procedures Guide for Personal Computers. Version 6 ed. Cary, N.C.: SAS Institute, 1986.

SAS Statistics Guide for Personal Computers. Version 6 ed. Cary, N.C.: SAS Institute, 1986.

SAS User's Guide: Basics. Version 5 ed. Cary, N.C.: SAS Institute, 1985.

SAS User's Guide: Statistics. Version 5 ed. Cary, N.C.: SAS Institute, 1985.

SPSSX User's Guide. Chicago: SPSS, 1983.

Chapter Thirteen
Chi-Square Tests

In Chapters 11 and 12, we showed how to test hypotheses about a single population mean, a single population proportion, the difference between two means, and the difference between two proportions. In this chapter we discuss methods for testing hypotheses about a whole set of proportions. In addition, we show how to test the null hypothesis that two qualitative random variables, such as the sex of an applicant and admittance to medical school, are independent of one another. Because all the tests discussed in this chapter use a test statistic that follows the chi-square distribution, they are called chi-square tests. To perform these tests, we need to find the critical values that separate the acceptance region and the critical region using the chi-square distribution.

13.1 ▪ The Chi-Square Goodness-of-Fit Test

In many situations in business and economics, we want to test the null hypothesis that a sample of data was selected from a population having certain characteristics. For example, we may wish to test the null hypothesis that the distribution of incomes or ages in a certain city is the same as it was in the last census. Usually the population is divided into several, say K, categories, and the null hypothesis states that the proportions of observations in categories $1, 2, \ldots, K$ are $p_1, p_2, \ldots, p_K$. To test the null hypothesis, we determine how many observations in a sample of size n would be expected to fall in each category if the null hypothesis were true, and we compare these expected frequencies to the frequencies actually observed in the sample. The comparison is done by performing a *chi-square goodness-of-fit test,* which was developed in 1900 by the British statistician Karl Pearson (1857–1936). The following example introduces the chi-square goodness-of-fit test.

Example 13.1 **Testing a Hypothesis About a Set of Population Proportions:** The Department of Commerce classifies households in the United States according to income. The publication *Current Population Reports* (Series P-23, No. 126 [Washington, D.C.: Bureau of the Census, August 1983]) states that in the 1980 census, 20% of the households in the United States had incomes from $0 to $7499, 30% had incomes from $7500 to $17,499, 40% had incomes from $17,500 to $39,999, and 10% had incomes of $40,000 or higher. The mayor of Joliet, Illinois, wants to test whether the distribution of income in Joliet is the same as that in the entire United States because if incomes in Joliet are lower than in the United States, Joliet will be eligible for additional federal revenue-sharing funds. The null hypothesis is that the distribution of income in Joliet, Illinois, is the same as in the United States. If the null hypothesis is true, then the proportions of households in Joliet that fall into each of the four income categories will be .20, .30, .40, and .10. Thus, the null hypothesis is

$$H_0: p_1 = .20,\ p_2 = .30,\ p_3 = .40,\ p_4 = .10$$

where p_i refers to the proportion of households falling into the ith income category. The alternative hypothesis is

$$H_1: \text{At least one of the four proportions in } H_0 \text{ is incorrect.}$$

To test H_0 against H_1, we obtain a random sample of $n = 200$ households in Joliet and count the number of observations that fall into each category. These four frequencies, called the *observed frequencies,* are denoted o_1, o_2, o_3, and o_4. If the null hypothesis is true, we expect to obtain approximately 40 households with incomes from $0 to $7499, approximately 60 households with incomes from $7500 to $17,499, approximately 80 households with incomes from $17,500 to $39,999, and approximately 20 households with incomes of $40,000 or higher. These four values, called the *expected frequencies,* are denoted e_1, e_2, e_3, and e_4. Large discrepancies between the observed frequencies and the expected frequencies cast doubt on the validity of the null hypothesis.

As a measure of the amount of discrepancy between the observed and expected frequencies, we calculate the chi-square statistic. In Example 13.1 there are four proportions in the null hypothesis, and the test statistic would be calculated as follows:

$$\chi^2 = \frac{(o_1 - e_1)^2}{e_1} + \frac{(o_2 - e_2)^2}{e_2} + \frac{(o_3 - e_3)^2}{e_3} + \frac{(o_4 - e_4)^2}{e_4}$$

If each observed frequency o_i is close to the corresponding expected frequency e_i, then the test statistic χ^2 is close to 0 and we do not reject H_0. In contrast, large differences between o_i and e_i lead to large values of χ^2 and cast doubt on the validity of the null hypothesis. As with any other test statistic, the problem at this point is to determine how large the test statistic χ^2 should be before we want to reject the null hypothesis. ■

Characteristics of the Goodness-of-Fit Test

The chi-square goodness-of-fit test is used when testing hypotheses in experiments involving the following characteristics:

1. Every unit in the population falls into exactly one of K categories or cells, denoted $C_1, C_2, \ldots, C_K$.

2. The hypothesized proportion of items in the population that are members of category i is p_i. Thus, if an item is selected randomly, the probability that the item belongs to category i is p_i.
3. The null hypothesis H_0 states that the K proportions equal the K specific values $p_1, p_2, \ldots, p_K$.
4. The alternative hypothesis states that at least one of the proportions specified in H_0 is incorrect.
5. Because every observation belongs to one and only one category, the K probabilities sum to 1; that is,

$$p_1 + p_2 + \cdots + p_K = 1$$

In order to test H_0, we take a random sample of n observations and determine how many observations belong to each of the K categories. These **observed frequencies**, denoted by $o_1, o_2, \ldots, o_K$, must sum to n:

$$o_1 + o_2 + \cdots + o_K = n$$

To test H_0, we compare the observed frequencies with what would be expected if the null hypothesis were true.

Definition: Expected Frequency

For the ith category, the **expected frequency** is denoted e_i. If the sample contains n observations, the expected frequency for category i is

$$e_i = np_i \qquad i = 1, 2, \ldots, K$$

The sum of the expected frequencies is n because

$$\begin{aligned} e_1 + e_2 + \cdots + e_K &= np_1 + np_2 + \cdots + np_K \\ &= n(p_1 + p_2 + \cdots + p_K) = n \end{aligned}$$

The Chi-Square Test Statistic

To test the null hypothesis, we examine how close the observed frequencies $o_1, o_2, \ldots, o_K$ are to the expected frequencies $e_1, e_2, \ldots, e_K$. When they are close, the null hypothesis is supported; that is, the data provide a *good fit* to the proposed model, hence the name "goodness-of-fit" test. If the observed frequencies are quite different from the expected frequencies, the null hypothesis becomes doubtful. The larger the differences between o_i and e_i, the more doubtful we are that the null hypothesis is true.

Definition: Chi-Square Test Statistic

Suppose each observation must fall in exactly one of K categories. The chi-square goodness-of-fit test is based on the following **chi-square test statistic**:

$$\chi^2 = \frac{(o_1 - e_1)^2}{e_1} + \frac{(o_2 - e_2)^2}{e_2} + \cdots + \frac{(o_K - e_K)^2}{e_K}$$

If the null hypothesis is true and the sample size is large so that each of the expected frequencies $e_1, e_2, \ldots, e_K$ is 5 or larger, the chi-square test statistic approximately follows a chi-square distribution with $(K - 1)$ degrees of freedom. If the expected frequency for any cell is less than 5, that particular cell should be combined with another cell or the sample size should be increased.

The degrees of freedom parameter $\nu = (K - 1)$ indicates the number of proportions p_i that can be chosen freely. Because the sum of the K proportions must be 1, only $(K - 1)$ of the proportions are free. Once any $(K - 1)$ proportions are specified, the last proportion is determined and thus no longer is free.

The chi-square goodness-of-fit test is summarized in the accompanying box.

The Chi-Square Goodness-of-Fit Test

We observe a random sample of n observations, where each observation falls into exactly one of K categories. In the population, the hypothesized proportion of observations in category i is denoted by p_i. Assume we want to test the null hypothesis

$$H_0\text{: } p_1, p_2, \ldots, p_K \text{ are equal to a set of prespecified values}$$

against the alternative hypothesis

$$H_1\text{: At least one of the proportions is not correct}$$

Assume the level of significance of the test is α. The observed frequencies are $o_1, o_2, \ldots, o_K$. The expected frequencies are obtained using the equation $e_i = np_i$, and each expected frequency should be at least 5.

The test statistic is

$$\chi^2 = \sum_{i=1}^{K} \frac{(o_i - e_i)^2}{e_i}$$

and is distributed as chi-square with $\nu = (K - 1)$ degrees of freedom. The decision rule is

$$\text{Reject } H_0 \text{ in favor of } H_1 \text{ if } \chi^2 > \chi^2_{\alpha,\nu}$$

where $\chi^2_{\alpha,\nu}$ is the critical value such that

$$P(\chi^2 > \chi^2_{\alpha,\nu}) = \alpha$$

Example 13.2

Using the Chi-square Goodness-of-Fit Test: In Example 13.1, a random sample of 200 households was obtained in Joliet, Illinois, in order to test the null hypothesis

$$H_0\text{: } p_1 = .20,\ p_2 = .30,\ p_3 = .40,\ p_4 = .10$$

where p_i refers to the proportion of households falling into the ith income category. The observed frequencies are shown in Table 13.1 along with the expected frequencies. Test the null hypothesis using a 1% level of significance.

Solution: There are $\nu = (K - 1) = 3$ degrees of freedom. For level of significance $\alpha = .01$, the critical value is $\chi^2_{.01,3} = 11.34$. The expected frequencies, shown in Table

TABLE 13.1 **Observed and expected frequencies for Example 13.2**

Income Category i	o_i	e_i	$o_i - e_i$	$(o_i - e_i)^2$	$(o_i - e_i)^2/e_i$
1	55	40	15	225	5.625
2	65	60	5	25	0.417
3	72	80	−8	64	0.800
4	8	20	−12	144	7.200
Total	200	200	0		14.042

$$X^2 = \Sigma[(o_i - e_i)^2/e_i]$$
$$= 5.625 + 0.417 + 0.800 + 7.200 = 14.042$$

13.1, are calculated as follows: $e_1 = np_1 = 200(.20) = 40$, $e_2 = np_2 = 200(.30) = 60$, and so forth. The chi-square test statistic is

$$\chi^2 = \frac{(55 - 40)^2}{40} + \frac{(65 - 60)^2}{60} + \frac{(72 - 80)^2}{80} + \frac{(8 - 20)^2}{20}$$
$$= 5.625 + 0.417 + 0.800 + 7.200 = 14.042$$

Note that this value is equal to the sum of the last column in Table 13.1. We reject H_0 because $\chi^2 = 14.042$ exceeds the critical value $\chi^2_{\alpha,\nu} = 11.34$, as illustrated in Figure 13.1. The data provide strong evidence that the income distribution in Joliet is different from the income distribution in the United States.

FIGURE 13.1
Chi-square distribution for Example 13.2

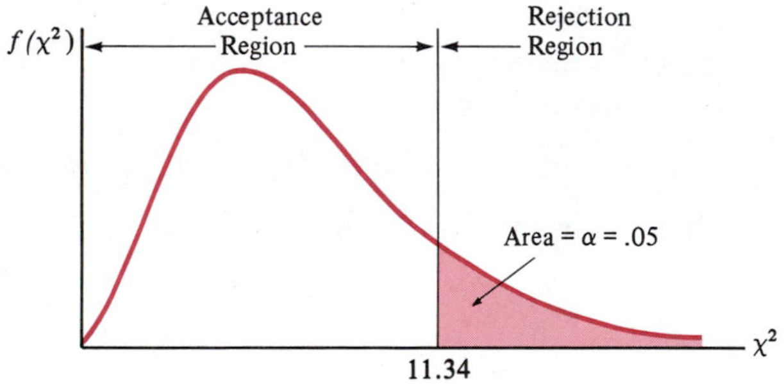

Testing Whether a Random Variable Has a Poisson Distribution

The chi-square goodness-of-fit test can be used to test whether there is a significant difference between an observed frequency distribution and any theoretical probability distribution. If the hypothesized distribution is a discrete distribution such as the Poisson distribution, the test can be carried out as described in Example 13.3.

Example 13.3 **Testing Whether a Random Variable Has a Poisson Distribution:** It is hypothesized that the number of breakdowns per month of a computer system at a major university follows a Poisson distribution with mean $\mu = 2$. The data in Table 13.2 show the observed number of breakdowns per month during a sample of 100 months. Use a 5% level of significance and test the null hypothesis

H_0: The population distribution of breakdowns is Poisson with mean $\mu = 2$

against the alternative hypothesis

H_1: The population does not follow a Poisson distribution with mean $\mu = 2$

TABLE 13.2 **Observed and expected frequencies for Example 13.3**

Breakdowns	o_i	e_i	$o_i - e_i$	$(o_i - e_i)^2$	$(o_i - e_i)^2/e_i$
0	14	13.5	0.5	0.25	0.019
1	20	27.1	−7.1	50.41	1.860
2	34	27.1	6.9	47.61	1.757
3	22	18.0	4.0	16.00	0.889
4	5	9.0	−4.0	16.00	1.778
5 and over	5	5.3	−0.3	0.09	0.017
Total	100	100.0			6.320

Solution: Before we can determine the expected frequencies using the formula $e_i = np_i$, we must find the probabilities p_i. For the Poisson distribution, we have

$$P(X = x) = \frac{e^{-\mu}\mu^x}{x!}$$

From this formula (or from Table A.4), using $\mu = 2.0$, we obtain the following probabilities:

x	0	1	2	3	4	5 or more
$P(X = x)$	.1353	.2707	.2707	.1804	.0902	.0527

The expected frequencies e_i are obtained by using the rule $e_i = np_i$ where $n = 100$. For example, the expected frequency of $X = 3$ is

$$np_i = 100(.1804) = 18.04$$

The expected frequencies e_i are also shown in Table 13.2 (the expected frequencies have been rounded off to simplify the calculations). Note that each expected frequency exceeds 5.

There are $K = 6$ categories, so there are $\nu = (K - 1) = 5$ degrees of freedom. For $\alpha = .05$, the critical value is $\chi^2_{.05,5} = 11.07$. The chi-square test statistic is

$$\chi^2 = \sum_{i=1}^{6} \frac{(o_i - e_i)^2}{e_i}$$

$$= \frac{(14 - 13.5)^2}{13.5} + \frac{(20 - 27.1)^2}{27.1} + \cdots + \frac{(5 - 5.3)^2}{5.3} = 6.32$$

The test statistic falls in the acceptance region because the value 6.32 is less than the critical value 11.07. Hence, the null hypothesis is not rejected. ■

Testing Whether a Population Has a Normal Distribution

When using the chi-square goodness-of-fit test to determine whether a hypothesized distribution is continuous, such as the normal distribution, we must first divide the range of the theoretical density function into a number of intervals, or cells, and we use the areas above these intervals to represent the theoretical cell probabilities p_i. The expected cell frequencies are determined from the equation $e_i = np_i$, where n is the sample size. We then test whether the observed frequencies o_i differ significantly from the expected frequencies e_i by calculating the chi-square test statistic.

The following example illustrates how to test the null hypothesis that a sample of observations was selected from a normal population having a specific mean and variance.

Example 13.4

Testing Whether a Population Has a Normal Distribution with Given Mean and Variance: The manufacturer of robots used in car assembly claims that the time required for the robots to perform a certain task follows a normal distribution with mean $\mu = 5$ seconds and variance $\sigma^2 = 0.04$. To test this hypothesis, we obtain a random sample of $n = 200$ observations. Use a 5% level of significance and test the null hypothesis that the times required to complete the task are distributed $N(5, 0.04)$ against the alternative hypothesis that the population is not $N(5, 0.04)$.

Solution: First we divide the range of the hypothesized distribution into K intervals. Suppose we choose $K = 10$ and select the 10 intervals so that each category has probability equal to .10, as shown in Figure 13.2. (The fact that each category has the same probability is unimportant.)

We want to determine the values $x_1, x_2, \ldots, x_9$ such that each shaded area and each unshaded area has probability .10. In Figure 13.2, the value x_5 is the mean of the distribution, so $x_5 = 5$ seconds.

FIGURE 13.2
Ten equal areas under the normal curve for $N(5, 0.04)$.

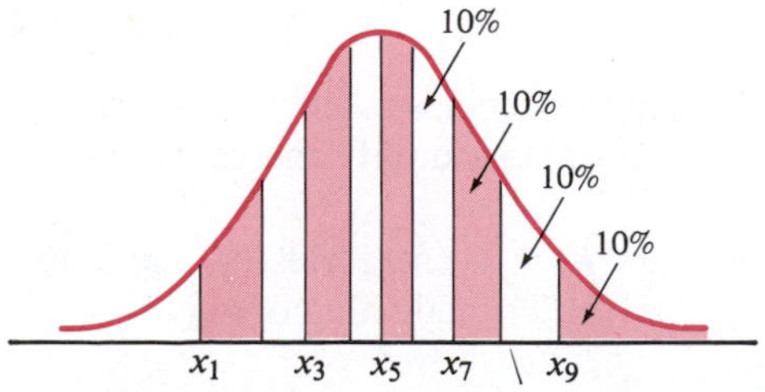

Now let us obtain the value of, say, x_7. In Figure 13.2, the area between x_5 and x_7 is .20. We obtain the value x_7 by first finding the standard normal variate such that the area between 0 and the variate is .20. From Table A.5, this standard normal variate is $z_7 \approx .52$ (see Figure 13.3). We then obtain x_7 by solving the equation

$$z_7 = .52 = \frac{x_7 - 5}{\sqrt{0.04}}$$

The solution is $x_7 = 5.104$.

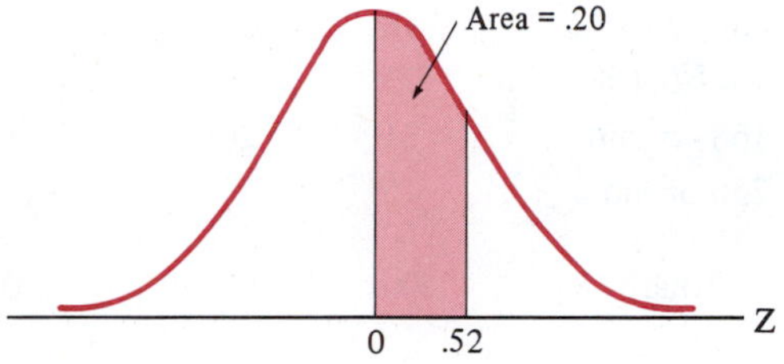

FIGURE 13.3
Area under the standard normal curve for Example 13.4.

Similarly, to find the value of, say, x_1, we observe that the area from x_1 to x_5 is .40. The standard normal variate associated with x_1 is $z_1 = -1.28$. Thus, we obtain

$$z_1 = -1.28 = \frac{x_1 - 5}{\sqrt{0.04}} \quad \text{and} \quad x_1 = 4.744$$

By proceeding in a similar manner, we can find the values of $x_1, x_2, \ldots, x_9$ as follows:

$$\begin{array}{lll} x_1 = 4.744 & x_2 = 4.832 & x_3 = 4.896 \\ x_4 = 4.950 & x_5 = 5.000 & x_6 = 5.050 \\ x_7 = 5.104 & x_8 = 5.168 & x_9 = 5.526 \end{array}$$

These results indicate that we expect 10% of the observations to be less than 4.744, 10% to be between 4.744 and 4.832, and so forth. The expected frequency for each cell is

$$e_i = np_i = 200(.10) = 20$$

The expected frequencies are shown in Table 13.3 along with the observed frequencies based on the sample of 200 observations.

Because there are $K = 10$ categories, there are $\nu = (K - 1) = 9$ degrees of freedom. For $\alpha = .05$, the critical value is $\chi^2_{.05,9} = 16.92$. The chi-square test statistic is

$$\chi^2 = \frac{(18 - 20)^2}{20} + \frac{(23 - 20)^2}{20} + \cdots + \frac{(15 - 20)^2}{20}$$
$$= 4.10$$

We do not reject H_0 because $\chi^2 = 4.10$ is less than 16.92 and thus falls in the acceptance region.

TABLE 13.3 **Observed and expected frequencies for Example 13.4**

Time (in seconds)	o_i	e_i	$o_i - e_i$	$(o_i - e_i)^2$	$(o_i - e_i)^2/e_i$
Less than 4.744	18	20	−2	4	0.20
4.744–4.832	23	20	3	9	0.45
4.832–4.896	19	20	−1	1	0.05
4.896–4.950	22	20	2	4	0.20
4.950–5.000	24	20	4	16	0.80
5.000–5.050	17	20	−3	9	0.45
5.050–5.104	18	20	−2	4	0.20
5.104–5.168	23	20	3	9	0.45
5.168–5.256	21	20	1	1	0.05
5.256 or more	15	20	−5	25	1.25
Total	200	200	0		4.10

In the goodness-of-fit tests discussed thus far, the appropriate number of degrees of freedom was $\nu = (K - 1)$, where K is the number of categories. This is because the only constraint placed on the expected frequencies was that they had to sum to n, the total number of observations. When either of the population parameters (the mean or variance) has been estimated from the sample of data, the number of degrees of freedom must be reduced by the number of parameters that have been estimated. This procedure is discussed in the next section.

Exercises for Section 13.1

1. Suppose we toss a fair die 240 times and count how many times each value (1 through 6) occurs. We obtain the following results:

Value	1	2	3	4	5	6
Observed frequency	36	47	35	42	44	36

a. Find the expected frequencies if the coin is fair.
b. Calculate the value of the chi-square statistic.
c. Find the critical value $\chi^2_{\alpha,\nu}$ in order to test the hypothesis that the die is fair using a 5% level of significance.
d. Test the hypothesis that the coin is fair using $\alpha = .05$.

2. At the last census, 20% of the people in a town were less than 16 years of age, 20% were aged 16 to 30, 25% were aged 31 to 45, 15% were aged 46 to 60, and 20% were over 60. The planning commission wants to determine if the age structure of the town has changed since the last census. A random sample of 200 residents of the town yields the following data:

Age (in years)	Less than 16	16–30	31–45	46–60	Over 60
Observed frequency	30	31	37	50	52

Test the hypothesis that the age structure of the town has not changed since the last census. Use a 1% level of significance.

a. Find the expected frequencies if the age structure has not changed.
b. Calculate the value of the chi-square statistic.
c. Find the critical value $\chi^2_{\alpha,\nu}$ in order to test the hypothesis that the age structure has not changed using a 1% level of significance.
d. Test the hypothesis using $\alpha = .01$.

3. A civil service exam is given to 200 job applicants. In recent years, grades have followed a normal distribution with mean 66.5 and variance 100. The grades of the job applicants are distributed as follows:

Grade	Under 49.5	49.5–59.5	59.5–69.5	69.5–79.5	79.5 and over
Observed frequency	22	38	56	50	34

a. Graph the observed frequencies on a histogram. Does the histogram appear to have the shape of a normal distribution with mean 66.5 and variance 100?
b. Test the hypothesis that the data came from a normal distribution with mean 66.5 and variance 100. Use a 5% level of significance.

4. *USA Today* reported that 40% of the population watched the last Super Bowl on TV. In a random sample of 500 people, 175 watched the game. Test H_0: $p = .40$ against H_1: $p \neq .40$ using a 5% level of significance.

a. Perform the test by using the normal distribution and the techniques described in Chapter 11.
b. Perform the test using the chi-square test. (The two categories are people who saw the game and people who did not.)

5. A gambler claims that horses having starting positions near the rail have an advantage in a race because they have a shorter distance to run. A sample of 120 races is examined, each of which involved 6 horses. If starting position is not a factor, then each starting position should have produced 20 winners on the average. The following data show the number of winners from each starting position:

Starting position	1	2	3	4	5	6
Number of winners	25	22	18	19	21	15

Use the chi-square test to determine whether starting position is a significant factor. Assume a 5% level of significance.

6. Over a long period of time, the grades at a university have been distributed as follows: 15% As, 20% Bs, 40% Cs, 20% Ds, and 5% Fs. Last semester a random sample of 1000 grades showed 190 As, 220 Bs, 370 Cs, 180 Ds, and 40Fs. Determine at a 5% level of significance whether the grading pattern has changed.

7. Over a long period of time at a suburban restaurant, 60% of the customers ordered coffee, 20% ordered tea, 15% ordered milk, and 5% ordered cola. The owners opened a new restaurant in the business section of town, where they think that the drinking preferences of the customers may be different. In a random sample of 1000 customers at the new restaurant, 550 ordered coffee, 240 ordered tea, 150 ordered milk, and 60 ordered cola. Determine at a 5% level of significance whether drinking patterns are different in town than at the suburban restaurant.

8. The city council of Greenville is writing a master plan for the city. The provision of certain services will depend on demographic characteristics. In a recent census, 20% of the Greenville population was under 22 years of age, 30% was between 22 and 40, 25% was between 40 and 60, and 25% was over 60. A random sample of 400 residents were questioned, whose ages are shown in the following table:

Age of resident	Under 22	22–40	41–60	Over 60
Number in sample	86	130	90	94

Use a 5% level of significance to determine if the age distribution has changed.

9. Psychologists claim that people who suffer from severe depression tend to get depressed on Sundays and Mondays and tend to be less depressed on other days. The psychologists conjecture that this pattern is caused by the fact that people dread the thought of going back to work on Monday. You test the psychologists' claim by studying police department records on suicides in Philadelphia. A random sample of 350 suicides were distributed as follows: Monday, 60; Tuesday, 30; Wednesday, 40; Thursday, 45; Friday, 50; Saturday, 45; and Sunday, 80. Test the hypothesis that suicides are uniformly distributed throughout the week. That is, test H_0: $p_i = \frac{1}{7}$ for $i = 1, 2, \ldots, 7$. Use a 5% level of significance.

10. An investor is planning to buy some property in the heart of town in order to build a parking garage. The profitability of the project depends on the parking patterns of the potential customers at the garage. The investor assumes that 40% of the customers will stay less than one hour, 20% will stay from one to two hours, 15% will stay from two to four hours, and 25% will stay more than four hours. At a nearby lot, a random sample of 200 customers produced the following distribution:

Time of parking (in hours)	0–1	1–2	2–4	4 or more
Observed frequency	100	35	25	40

Should we reject the owner's assumptions? Use a 1% level of significance.

11. The safety engineer at a manufacturing firm claims that most plant accidents occur near quitting time, when employees are getting tired and are anxious to go home. Plant management will introduce new safety measures, such as an additional afternoon coffee break, if the engineer can prove his claim. The engineer examines a random sample of 80 plant accidents. The times of occurrence of the accidents were as follows:

Time	Number of Accidents
8 A.M.–10 A.M.	16
10 A.M.–noon	16
Noon–1 P.M. (lunch)	—
1 P.M.–3 P.M.	21
3 P.M.–5 P.M.	27

Use a 5% level of significance and test whether the accidents are uniformly distributed throughout the day.

13.2 ▪ Goodness-of-Fit Tests When Population Parameters Are Estimated

Frequently we want to test the hypothesis that a sample of data is from a certain distribution having unknown parameters, such as the mean or variance. Before finding the probabilities for each category, the unknown population parameters must be estimated from the sample data. When r population parameters, such as the mean and variance, have been estimated from the sample of data, then the number of degrees of freedom must be reduced by r. If we classify the data into K categories, then the appropriate number of degrees of freedom will be $(K - r - 1)$.

Calculating the Degrees of Freedom

The appropriate number of degrees of freedom is

$$\nu = K - r - 1$$

where ν = degrees of freedom, K = number of categories, and r = number of estimated population parameters.

Example 13.5 **Testing Whether a Population Is Normal When Mean and Variance Are Estimated:** A loan officer is examining a bank's new car loans and randomly selects 80 files, recording the payments made last month by each of the 80 borrowers. The officer wants to test the null hypothesis

H_0: The sample of payments came from a normal population

against the alternative hypothesis

H_1: The sample of payments did not come from a normal population

Use a 5% level of significance.

Solution: First we estimate the sample mean and sample variance. Suppose we obtain $\bar{x} = 150$ and $s^2 = 400$. Based on these estimates, the officer would want to test the null hypothesis that the data came from a normal distribution with mean 150 and variance 400.

Suppose that, as in Example 13.4, we split this normal distribution into 10 intervals such that each interval had probability .10, as shown in Figure 13.4. The expected frequency for each cell would be

$$e_i = np_i = 80(.10) = 8$$

The expected frequencies and the observed frequencies from the 80 observations are shown in Table 13.4.

The chi-square test statistic is

$$\chi^2 = \frac{(10 - 8)^2}{8} + \frac{(7 - 8)^2}{8} + \cdots + \frac{(6 - 8)^2}{8} = 6.500$$

FIGURE 13.4
Ten equal areas under the normal curve $N(150, 400)$.

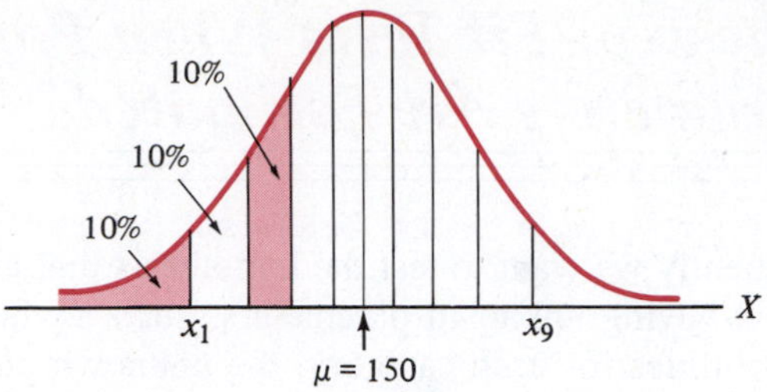

TABLE 13.4 **Observed and expected frequencies for Example 13.5**

Monthly Payment (in dollars)	o_i	e_i	$o_i - e_i$	$(o_i - e_i)^2$	$(o_i - e_i)^2/e_i$
Less than 124.40	10	8	2	4	0.500
124.40–133.20	7	8	−1	1	0.125
133.20–139.60	6	8	−2	4	0.500
139.60–145.00	8	8	0	0	0.000
145.00–150.00	11	8	3	9	1.125
150.00–155.00	9	8	1	1	0.125
155.00–160.40	12	8	4	16	2.000
160.40–166.80	6	8	−2	4	0.500
166.80–175.60	5	8	−3	9	1.125
175.60 or more	6	8	−2	4	0.500
Total	80	80	0		6.500

We must now calculate the appropriate number of degrees of freedom. There are $K = 10$ categories. The expected frequencies must sum to 80, which puts one constraint on the expected frequencies. In addition, we have estimated two population parameters from the sample data, thus giving us

$$\nu = K - r - 1 = 10 - 2 - 1 = 7$$

When $\alpha = .05$ and $\nu = 7$, the critical value of the chi-square statistic is $\chi^2_{.05,7} = 14.07$. We do not reject H_0 because $\chi^2 = 6.5$ falls in the acceptance region, as can be seen in Figure 13.5. ■

Exercises for Section 13.2

1. In a random sample of 100 one-minute intervals, a total of 180 cars arrived at an expressway tollbooth. The accompanying table shows the frequency of arrivals per minute over this period:

Number of arrivals	0	1	2	3	4 or more
Observed frequency	14	26	32	22	6

FIGURE 13.5
Chi-square distribution for Example 13.5.

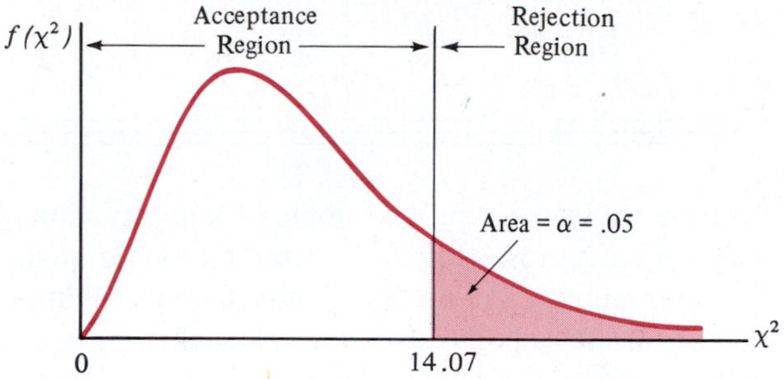

a. Test the null hypothesis that the number of arrivals per minute follows a Poisson distribution. Let $\alpha = .05$.
b. What is the sample mean?
c. What is the appropriate number of degrees of freedom?

2. The chief of police in a large city finds that over a 100-day period, there were 230 homicides. The following table shows the frequencies of homicides per day over that period:

Number of homicides	0	1	2	3	4	5 or more
Observed frequency	21	34	19	13	12	11

a. Find the sample mean number of homicides per day.
b. Test the hypothesis that the distribution is Poisson. Let $\alpha = .05$.
c. What is the appropriate number of degrees of freedom?

3. The number of cars entering the parking lot of a large shopping mall was recorded for 90 weeks (excluding busy seasons such as Christmas and Easter). The records show the following distribution:

Number of Shoppers per Week (in thousands)	Observed Frequency
0.00–10.99	2
11.00–13.99	10
14.00–16.99	10
17.00–19.99	15
20.00–22.99	19
23.00–25.99	12
26.00–28.99	14
29.00–31.99	4
32.00–34.99	4

a. Calculate the mean and standard deviation of the sample data.
b. Test the hypothesis that the distribution is normal. Use $\alpha = 0.05$.

13.3 ▪ Tests of Independence and Contingency Tables

Suppose we have a random sample of n observations from some population where each observation is cross-classified according to two qualitative characteristics, or variables. An important application of the chi-square distribution involves testing the null hypothesis that, in such a population, the value taken by one variable is independent of the value taken by the other variable. Such a test is called a *chi-square test of independence*. For example, a random sample of employees are classified according to education and occupation. The data show whether an individual has a grade school, high school, or college education and whether the individual's occupation is professional, blue collar, or other. It seems reasonable to conjecture that the two variables Education and Occupation are not independent. As another example, suppose that a sample of individuals are classified according to whether they live in Canada, the United States, or Mexico and according to whether they prefer to watch hockey, baseball, or soccer on television. Once again, it seems reasonable to conjecture that the two variables Nationality and Favorite Sport are not independent.

Example 13.6

Testing a Hypothesis About the Independence of Variables: A company planning a television advertising campaign wants to determine which TV shows its target audience watches. Suppose the company wants to test the null hypothesis

H_0: Choice of TV program that an individual watches is independent of the individual's income

against the alternative hypothesis

H_1: Income and choice of TV program are not independent

In a random sample of $n = 500$ people, each person is classified into one of three income categories ("low," "medium," or "high"). In addition, each individual is classified according to which TV program the person watched (a hockey game, a movie, or a documentary).

The sample data are presented in Table 13.5. This table, which is a two-way classification table containing three rows and three columns, is referred to as a 3×3 *contingency table*. In general, if one of the variables contains H categories and the other variable contains K categories, then we obtain an $H \times K$ contingency table. Each combination of two attributes represents a *cell* in the contingency table.

TABLE 13.5
Contingency Table for Example 13.6

	Type of TV Show			
Income	Hockey	Movie	News	Total
Low	143	70	37	250
Medium	90	67	43	200
High	17	13	20	50
Total	250	150	100	500

In a contingency table, the value in row i and column j is denoted o_{ij} and called an *observed frequency*. For example, the value in row 3, column 2 of Table 13.5 is $o_{32} = 13$. This observed frequency represents the number of people who watched the movie on TV and had a high income. This contingency table contains nine cells. ■

Calculating Expected Frequencies

If the contingency table contains H rows and K columns, then there are $H \times K$ observed frequencies. Corresponding to the $H \times K$ contingency table is another $H \times K$ table containing the expected frequency for each cell based on the assumption that the null hypothesis is true. To compute the expected frequencies under the null hypothesis of independence, we first need to determine the probability that an observation will fall into a particular cell if H_0 is true.

Let the K column categories be denoted $C_1, C_2, \ldots, C_K$, and let the column totals be denoted $c_1, c_2, \ldots, c_K$. Similarly, let the H row categories be denoted $R_1, R_2, \ldots, R_H$, and let the H row totals be denoted $r_1, r_2, \ldots, r_H$. We use the following rule: If events R_i and C_j are independent, then

$$P(R_i \cap C_j) = P(R_i)P(C_j)$$

Although we do not know the true population probabilities $P(R_i \cap C_j)$, $P(R_i)$, and $P(C_j)$, we can estimate them by using our sample of n observations to calculate relative frequencies. Because the number of observations that fall in row i is r_i, the relative frequency of row i is r_i/n. We use this value to estimate $P(R_i)$. Similarly, we use the relative frequency c_j/n to estimate the probability $P(C_j)$.

We want to test the null hypothesis

$$H_0\colon P(R_i \cap C_j) = P(R_i)P(C_j) \quad \text{for all } i \text{ and } j$$

against the alternative hypothesis

$$H_1\colon P(R_i \cap C_j) \neq P(R_i)P(C_j) \quad \text{for at least one } i \text{ and } j$$

Let e_{ij} denote the expected frequency in row i, column j. The expected frequency e_{ij} is

$$e_{ij} = nP(R_i \cap C_j)$$

If H_0 is true, this becomes

$$e_{ij} = nP(R_i)P(C_j)$$

If we use $(r_i/n)(c_j/n)$ to estimate the unknown probability $P(R_i \cap C_j) = P(R_i)P(C_j)$, the expected frequency becomes

$$e_{ij} = n(r_i/n)(c_j/n) = r_i c_j/n$$

Formula for Expected Frequencies

The estimated expected frequency for the cell in row i and column j is

$$e_{ij} = \frac{r_i c_j}{n}$$

where r_i is the number of observations in row i and c_j is the number of observations in column j.

The Chi-Square Test Statistic

A test of the null hypothesis that the variables are independent of one another is based on the magnitudes of the differences between the observed frequencies and the expected frequencies. Large differences between o_{ij} and e_{ij} provide evidence that the null hypothesis is false. The test is based on the following chi-square test statistic:

$$\chi^2 = \sum_{i=1}^{H} \sum_{j=1}^{K} \frac{(o_{ij} - e_{ij})^2}{e_{ij}}$$

We again impose the rule that each of the expected cell frequencies must be at least 5. If the null hypothesis is true, this chi-square test statistic approximately follows the chi-square distribution. The appropriate number of degrees of freedom represents the number of expected frequencies that can be chosen freely, provided the row and column totals of the expected frequency table are identical to the row and column totals of the observed frequency table. If we know the expected frequencies in the first $(H - 1)$ rows and $(K - 1)$ columns of the $H \times K$ table, then the remaining expected frequencies are uniquely determined. It follows that the appropriate degrees of freedom is

$$\nu = (H - 1)(K - 1)$$

Performing the Chi-Square Test of Independence

We take a random sample of n observations and classify each observation according to two variables. In the population, let $P(R_i)$ denote the probability that an observation possesses attribute R_i and let $P(C_j)$ denote the probability that an observation possesses attribute C_j. The null hypothesis states that the two classification schemes are independent of one another. We wish to test the null hypothesis

$$H_0\colon P(R_i \cap C_j) = P(R_i)P(C_j) \quad \text{for } i = 1, 2, \ldots, H; \quad j = 1, 2, \ldots, K$$

against the alternative hypothesis

$$H_1\colon P(R_i \cap C_j) \neq P(R_i)P(C_j) \quad \text{for some } i \text{ and } j$$

Let o_{ij} denote the number of observations in the cell in row i and column j of a contingency table. The expected frequency for this cell is e_{ij}, which is estimated using the formula

$$e_{ij} = r_i c_j / n$$

where r_i is the observed row total for row i and c_j is the observed column total for column j. Each expected frequency should be at least 5.

The chi-square test statistic is

$$\chi^2 = \sum_{i=1}^{H} \sum_{j=1}^{K} \frac{(o_{ij} - e_{ij})^2}{e_{ij}}$$

which has a chi-square distribution with $\nu = (H - 1)(K - 1)$ degrees of freedom. To test H_0 against H_1 using a level of significance α, use the decision rule

Reject H_0 in favor of H_1 if $\chi^2 > \chi^2_{\alpha,\nu}$.

Example 13.7

Using the Chi-Square Test of Independence I: Table 13.5 showed the observed frequencies relating to the incomes and choice of TV show for a random sample of $n = 500$ individuals described in Example 13.6. Let $\alpha = .05$ and test the null hypothesis that income and choice of TV program are independent of one another.

Solution: The observed row and column frequencies are $r_1 = 250$, $r_2 = 200$, $r_3 = 50$, $c_1 = 250$, $c_2 = 150$, and $c_3 = 100$.

Table 13.6 contains the estimated expected cell frequencies along with the observed frequencies. For example, the expected frequency in row 2, column 3 is $e_{23} = 40$. This expected frequency is calculated as follows:

$$e_{23} = \frac{r_2 c_3}{n} = \frac{(200)(100)}{500} = 40$$

The other estimated expected frequencies are calculated in a similar manner.

TABLE 13.6
Contingency Table for Example 13.7

	Type of TV Show			
Income	Hockey	Movie	News	Total
Low				
o_{ij}	143	70	37	250
e_{ij}	125	75	50	250
Medium				
o_{ij}	90	67	43	200
e_{ij}	100	60	40	200
High				
o_{ij}	17	13	20	50
e_{ij}	25	15	10	50
Total				
o_{ij}	250	150	100	500
e_{ij}	250	150	100	500

The chi-square test statistic is

$$\chi^2 = \frac{(143 - 125)^2}{125} + \frac{(70 - 75)^2}{75} + \frac{(37 - 50)^2}{50} + \frac{(90 - 100)^2}{100}$$
$$+ \frac{(67 - 60)^2}{60} + \frac{(43 - 40)^2}{40} + \frac{(17 - 25)^2}{25} + \frac{(13 - 15)^2}{15}$$
$$+ \frac{(20 - 10)^2}{10} = 21.174$$

The appropriate number of degrees of freedom is

$$\nu = (H - 1)(K - 1) = (3 - 1)(3 - 1) = 4$$

For $\alpha = .05$, the critical value is $\chi^2_{.05,4} = 9.49$. We reject the null hypothesis that program choice and income level are independent because $\chi^2 = 21.174$ falls in the rejection region. See Figure 13.6.

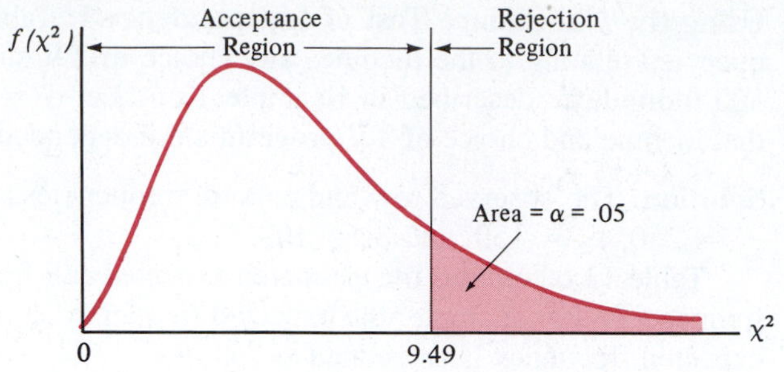

FIGURE 13.6
Chi-square distribution for Example 13.7.

Example 13.8 **Using the Chi-Square Test of Independence II:** The manager of a bank is examining the mortgage payments made by customers of the bank. A payment is classified as "good" if it arrives on time and as "delinquent" if it arrives late or is not paid. In addition, the customer's income is classified as "low," "medium," or "high." Table 13.7 shows the number of "good" and "delinquent" payments according to the person's income category. Use a 5% level of significance and test the null hypothesis

H_0: The probability of a payment being "good" or "delinquent" is independent of the person's income.

against the alternative hypothesis

H_1: The probability of a payment being "good" or "delinquent" is not independent of the person's income.

TABLE 13.7
Observed frequencies for Example 13.8

Payment	Income Level: Low	Medium	High	Total
Good	45	50	65	160
Delinquent	5	20	15	40
Total	50	70	80	200

Solution: Our first task is to estimate the expected frequencies. We use the rule $e_{ij} = r_i c_j / n$. For example, $e_{23} = (40)(80)/(200) = 16$. The expected frequencies are shown in Table 13.8.

TABLE 13.8
Expected frequencies for Example 13.8

Payment	Income Level: Low	Medium	High	Total
Good	40	56	64	160
Delinquent	10	14	16	40
Totai	50	70	80	200

The chi-square test statistic is

$$\chi^2 = \frac{(45 - 40)^2}{40} + \frac{(5 - 10)^2}{10} + \frac{(50 - 56)^2}{56} + \frac{(20 - 14)^2}{14} + \frac{(65 - 64)^2}{64} + \frac{(15 - 16)^2}{16} = 6.418$$

The appropriate number of degrees of freedom is

$$\nu = (H - 1)(K - 1) = (2 - 1)(3 - 1) = 2$$

For $\nu = 2$ degrees of freedom and $\alpha = .05$, the critical value is $\chi^2_{.05,2} = 5.99$. We reject H_0 because $\chi^2 = 6.418$ exceeds the critical value of 5.99, as shown in Figure 13.7.

FIGURE 13.7
Chi-square distribution for Example 13.8.

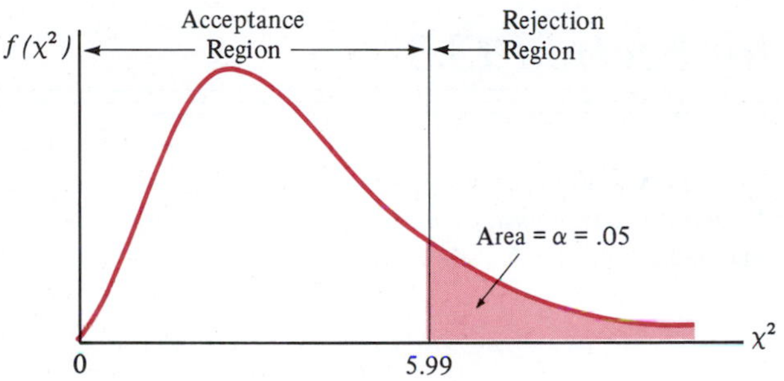

Does this result seem reasonable? That is, based on the observed frequencies in Table 13.7, does it appear that the payment of the loan depends on the level of income? In the entire sample of 200 mortgages, 40 (or 20%) were delinquent. In Table 13.7, observe that only 5 of 50 (or 10%) of the low-income individuals were delinquent, while 20 of 70 (or 28%) medium-income individuals were delinquent. Thus it appears that in our sample too many medium-income people and too few low-income people were delinquent to claim that the probability of being delinquent is independent of income. ■

Some Comments

The chi-square test for independence is useful in helping to determine whether a relationship exists between two variables, say, between choice of TV program and income or between expenditures on a certain type of product and income, but it does not enable us to estimate or predict the values of one variable based on the value of the other. If it is determined that a dependence does exist between two quantitative variables, then the techniques of regression analysis developed in Chapters 15, 16, and 17 are useful in helping to find a mathematical formula that expresses the nature of the mathematical relationship.

If we think two quantitative variables Y and X are related, we might want to estimate some functional relationship $Y = f(X)$ or test the hypothesis that the variables Y and X are related in a certain way.

Finally, when performing the chi-square test, the critical region of the test statistic is placed in the right-hand tail of the distribution; thus when the chi-square test statistic is large, the null hypothesis is rejected. Some statisticians have argued that part of the critical region should be placed in the left-hand tail of the distribution, so that the null hypothesis is rejected if the computed value of χ^2 is too close to 0. They argue that values of χ^2 close to 0 indicate that the observed and expected frequencies agree "too well," possibly because the data have been incorrectly gathered, miscalculated, or erroneously reported.

Actually, small values of χ^2 should not be interpreted as evidence that the null hypothesis is false. Instead, they should prompt the investigator to examine the data carefully to see whether the observed and expected frequencies have been reported correctly. If no sources of error or bias can be found, the null hypothesis should not be rejected.

Exercises for Section 13.3

1. We take a sample of 500 people, all of whom drive approximately 10,000 miles per year. The following data classify the individuals according to age and the number of auto accidents each has had during the last three years:

	Age (in years)		
Number of Accidents	Under 30	30–40	Over 40
0	61	109	180
1	27	25	48
More than 1	12	16	22

Test the hypothesis that the number of accidents is independent of the age of the driver using a 5% level of significance.

a. Find the expected frequencies based on the assumption that the number of accidents is independent of age.
b. Find the appropriate number of degrees of freedom to perform the test.
c. Calculate the chi-square test statistic.
d. What is the critical value $\chi^2_{\alpha,\nu}$ if $\alpha = .05$?
e. Perform the test.

2. Some professors at a university are trying to get the state legislature to approve a faculty union. Some faculty members favor the idea of union representation and some oppose it. To get information about faculty opinions, a random sample of faculty members was obtained. Faculty members were classified according to rank and according to whether they favored unionization. The results of the survey are as follows:

	Rank		
Support for Union	Assistant	Associate	Full
Yes	264	124	112
No	136	76	88

Test the hypothesis that the rank of the faculty member and the decision to join the union are independent. Use a 1% level of significance.

a. Find the expected frequencies based on the assumption that Rank and Support for Unionization are independent variables.
b. Find the appropriate number of degrees of freedom to perform the test.
c. Calculate the chi-square test statistic.
d. What is the critical value $\chi^2_{\alpha,\nu}$ if $\alpha = .01$?
e. Perform the test.

3. A recent Supreme Court decision dealt with the legality of abortion. A national women's organization has claimed that men and women tend to have different views concerning abortion. A random sample of men and women responded as follows:

	Response		
Sex	In Favor	Opposed	Undecided
Men	86	74	40
Women	119	65	22

Test the hypothesis that there is no difference between men's and women's opinions of abortion. Use a 5% level of significance.

4. A standard argument of students in all universities is that grades in certain departments tend to be higher or lower than grades in other departments. To test this claim, samples of grades from three departments were obtained. Students' grades were distributed as follows:

Department	A	B	C	D	F
Math	50	140	200	180	20
Economics	40	50	90	60	12
History	60	100	180	110	25

Test the hypothesis that there is no difference in the grading policies of the three departments. Use a 5% level of significance.

5. A survey was taken to determine which TV network's evening news people prefer. Responses were classified according to the viewer's age for advertising purposes. Use a 5% level of significance and determine if age and network preference are independent.

Age (in years)	ABC	NBC	CBS
Under 20	30	20	20
20–30	60	70	80
30–40	100	110	70
Over 40	110	100	80

6. A survey of 200 stockholders of a corporation was taken to determine if they favored distributing the profits as dividends or reinvesting the profits in the firm. Test whether the opinions are independent of the number of shares owned. Use a 5% level of significance.

Number of Shares Owned	Pay Dividends	Reinvest	Indifferent
0– 99	35	17	8
100–249	31	23	6
250 or more	34	30	16

7. The Department of Transportation wants to determine if the occurrence of fatal accidents is dependent upon the weight of the car. The following data show the outcomes of 300 accidents:

	Weight of Car (in pounds)		
Type of Accident	0–1599	1600–2299	2300 or more
Fatal	72	20	18
Nonfatal	128	40	22

Let $\alpha = .05$ and test whether the variables are independent of one another.

8. Suppose that a national trade association has proposed Miami and New York as sites for the next national convention. A random sample of 150 delegates is polled to determine which site is favored. Let $\alpha = .05$ and test whether their choice of site is independent of age.

	Age (in years)		
Site Favored	0–34	35–49	50 and over
New York	32	63	15
Miami	8	22	10

9. A congressman sent questionnaires to 600 voters seeking their opinions on certain critical issues. One of the congressman's aides has warned him not to attach too much importance to the results because they do not represent a random sample of all voters' opinions since more poor than rich people tend to return such questionnaires. Let $\alpha = .01$ and test whether the return of the questionnaire is independent of income.

	Income (in dollars)		
Questionnaire Returned	0–9999	10,000–29,999	30,000 and over
Yes	90	50	60
No	110	150	140

13.4 ▪ Computer Applications

By using a CROSSTABS command with the appropriate options, we can get the SPSSX program to perform a chi-square test of independence for us. As we showed in Chapter 4, a CROSSTABS command can be used to generate an $H \times K$ contingency table, which shows the observed frequencies for each cell. By using the OPTIONS subcommand with the CROSSTABS command, we can get the program to print out the expected cell frequencies, the value of the chi-square test statistic, and the prob-value associated with the chi-square test statistic. Thus, the problem of performing a chi-square test of independence can be reduced to entering the data into the SPSSX program and inserting the appropriate CROSSTABS and OPTIONS commands.

Refer to the data in Table 2.1 in Chapter 2, the characteristics of a random sample of 120 employees at the Computech Corporation. Suppose we want to test the null hypothesis that the division in which an individual is employed is independent of the individual's academic degree. To obtain the two-way contingency table containing the observed frequencies o_{ij}, issue the command

```
CROSSTABS TABLES = DEGREE BY DIV
```

To obtain the expected frequencies e_{ij} as well, issue the additional command

```
OPTIONS 14
```

Finally, to obtain the value of the chi-square test statistic and the associated prob-value, issue the command

```
STATISTICS 1
```

Figure 13.8 shows the SPSSX computer output obtained by issuing the three commands

```
CROSSTABS TABLES = DEGREE BY DIV
OPTIONS 14
STATISTICS 1
```

on the data in Table 2.1. In the figure, each cell in the contingency table contains two numbers. The top entry is the observed cell frequency o_{ij}, and the second entry is the

FIGURE 13.8 **SPSSX-generated contingency table cross-tabulating DEGREE and DIV from data in Table 2.1.**

```
                          DIV
               COUNT    |
             EXP VAL    |OFFICE    MANUFACT  SALES         ROW
                        |          URING                  TOTAL
                        |    1.00|    2.00|      3.00|
DEGREE          --------+--------+--------+----------+
                  1.00  |     35 |     53 |        1 |      89
   HIGH SCHOOL          |   28.2 |   43.0 |     17.8 |    74.2
                        +--------+--------+----------+
                  2.00  |      3 |      5 |       15 |      23
   COLLEGE              |    7.3 |   11.1 |      4.6 |    19.2
                        +--------+--------+----------+
                  3.00  |      0 |      0 |        8 |       8
   POST-GRAD            |    2.5 |    3.9 |      1.6 |     6.7
                        +--------+--------+----------+
                COLUMN        38       58         24      120
                 TOTAL      31.7     48.3       20.0    100.0

 CHI-SQUARE     D.F.      SIGNIFICANCE       MIN E.F.     CELLS WITH E.F.< 5
 ----------     ----      ------------       --------     ------------------

   81.21948       4          0.0000            1.600      4 OF     9 ( 44.4%)

NUMBER OF MISSING OBSERVATIONS =          0
```

expected cell frequency e_{ij} assuming that H_0 is true. For example, the observed frequency for the first row and second column is $o_{12} = 53$ and the expected frequency is $e_{12} = 43.0$. The observed frequency represents the number of individuals in the sample who have a high school degree and are employed in the manufacturing division.

The value of the chi-square test statistic, $\chi^2 = 81.21948$, is shown at the bottom of the computer output, along with the appropriate number of degrees of freedom 4. The number shown under the word SIGNIFICANCE, 0.0000, is the prob-value associated with $\chi^2 = 81.21948$. That is, if χ^2 follows the chi-square distribution with 4 degrees of freedom, then $P(\chi^2 > 81.21948) = 0.0000$. The chi-square statistic provides extremely strong evidence that academic degree and division of employment are not independent.

Figure 13.9 shows the corresponding computer output obtained from the SAS program. To obtain the frequency distribution, issue the SAS commands

```
PROC FREQ;
TABLES DEGREE * DIV;
```

Figure 13.10 shows the corresponding computer program and output obtained from the Minitab program. Note that the output is almost identical to the SAS output.

FIGURE 13.9
SAS-generated contingency table cross-tabulating DEGREE and DIV from data in Table 2.1.

```
                 TABLE OF DEGREE BY DIV

DEGREE      DIV

FREQUENCY|
 PERCENT |
 ROW PCT |
 COL PCT |       1|       2|       3|  TOTAL
---------+--------+--------+--------+
       1 |     35 |     53 |      1 |     89
         |  29.17 |  44.17 |   0.83 |  74.17
         |  39.33 |  59.55 |   1.12 |
         |  92.11 |  91.38 |   4.17 |
---------+--------+--------+--------+
       2 |      3 |      5 |     15 |     23
         |   2.50 |   4.17 |  12.50 |  19.17
         |  13.04 |  21.74 |  65.22 |
         |   7.89 |   8.62 |  62.50 |
---------+--------+--------+--------+
       3 |      0 |      0 |      8 |      8
         |   0.00 |   0.00 |   6.67 |   6.67
         |   0.00 |   0.00 | 100.00 |
         |   0.00 |   0.00 |  33.33 |
---------+--------+--------+--------+
TOTAL          38       58       24      120
            31.67    48.33    20.00   100.00
```

FIGURE 13.10 **Minitab-generated contingency table cross-tabulating DEGREE and DIV from data in Table 2.1.**

```
MTB >
READ 'COMPUTEC.DAT' INTO C1-C8
     120 ROWS READ
ROW   C1   C2   C3   C4   C5     C6   C7   C8
  1    0    1    1   35    1   1575   16    5
  2    1    1    1   31    2   1980   10    3
  3    1    1    1   51    2   2480   28    2
  4    0    1    1   57    1   1925   30    2
MTB >
NAME C1 = 'SEX', C2 = 'RACE', C3 = 'DEGREE', C4 = 'AGE'
MTB >
NAME C5 = 'DIV', C6 = 'SALARY', C7 = 'SENIOR', C8 = 'EXEMPT'
MTB >
TABLE C3,C5;
SUBC>
COUNTS;
SUBC>
ROWPERCENTS;
SUBC>
COLPERCENTS;
SUBC>
TOTPERCENTS.
ROWS: DEGREE        COLUMNS: DIV

              1         2         3       ALL

 1           35        53         1        89
          39.33     59.55      1.12    100.00
          92.11     91.38      4.17     74.17
          29.17     44.17      0.83     74.17

 2            3         5        15        23
          13.04     21.74     65.22    100.00
           7.89      8.62     62.50     19.17
           2.50      4.17     12.50     19.17

 3            0         0         8         8
            -         -      100.00    100.00
            -         -       33.33      6.67
            -         -        6.67      6.67

ALL          38        58        24       120
          31.67     48.33     20.00    100.00
         100.00    100.00    100.00    100.00
          31.67     48.33     20.00    100.00
```

continued

FIGURE 13.10 continued

```
CELL CONTENTS -
                    COUNT
                    % OF ROW
                    % OF COL
                    % OF TBL
MTB >
STOP
```

Exercises for Section 13.4

Use the SPSSX program and a CROSSTABS command on the data in Table 2.1 of Chapter 2 to complete Exercises 1–4.

1. Test the null hypothesis that the variables SEX and DEGREE are independent for the employees at the Computech Corporation.
a. What is the value of the chi-square test statistic?
b. What is the appropriate number of degrees of freedom?
c. What is the critical value of the test statistic if we use a 5% level of significance?
d. Do you reject the null hypothesis of independence?

2. Test the null hypothesis that the variables RACE and DEGREE are independent for the employees at the Computech Corporation.
a. What is the value of the chi-square test statistic?
b. What is the appropriate number of degrees of freedom?
c. What is the critical value of the test statistic if we use a 5% level of significance?
d. Do you reject the null hypothesis of independence?

3. Test the null hypothesis that the variables SEX and DIV are independent for the employees at the Computech Corporation.
a. What is the value of the chi-square test statistic?
b. What is the appropriate number of degrees of freedom?
c. What is the critical value of the test statistic if we use a 5% level of significance?
d. Do you reject the null hypothesis of independence?

4. Test the null hypothesis that the variables RACE and DIV are independent for the employees at the Computech Corporation.
a. What is the value of the chi-square test statistic?
b. What is the appropriate number of degrees of freedom?
c. What is the critical value of the test statistic if we use a 5% level of significance?
d. Do you reject the null hypothesis of independence?

Use the SPSSX program and a CROSSTABS command on the data in Table 2.2 of Chapter 2 to complete Exercises 5 and 6.

5. Test the null hypothesis that the variables SEX and MAJOR are independent for the students in the statistics class.
a. What is the value of the chi-square test statistic?
b. What is the appropriate number of degrees of freedom?

c. What is the critical value of the test statistic if we use a 5% level of significance?
d. Do you reject the null hypothesis of independence?

6. Test the null hypothesis that the variables CLASS and MAJOR are independent for the students in the statistics class.
a. What is the value of the chi-square test statistic?
b. What is the appropriate number of degrees of freedom?
c. What is the critical value of the test statistic if we use a 5% level of significance?
d. Do you reject the null hypothesis of independence?

Chapter 13 Summary

The *chi-square goodness-of-fit test* is used to test a null hypothesis concerning a set of population proportions or to test whether a sample of observations came from a certain specific probability distribution. Each observation must fall into exactly one of K categories or *cells* and the null hypothesis specifies the probability of each cell. The *expected frequency* of the ith cell is $e_i = np_i$, where p_i is the cell's hypothesized probability and o_i is the cell's *observed frequency*. To perform the test, we calculate the *chi-square test statistic*

$$\chi^2 = \sum_{i=1}^{K} \frac{(o_i - e_i)^2}{e_i}$$

and compare it with the critical value obtained from the chi-square distribution having $(K - 1)$ degrees of freedom. Because large differences between the observed and expected frequencies provide evidence against the null hypothesis, large values of the chi-square test statistic lead us to reject the null hypothesis. When r population parameters have been estimated before determining the expected frequencies, the appropriate number of degrees of freedom is $(K - r - 1)$. We showed how to test the null hypotheses that a sample of data came from a discrete distribution (the Poisson) and from a continuous distribution (the normal), but any theoretical distribution can be tested.

A chi-square test can also be used to test whether two qualitative variables, such as occupation and academic degree, are independent by using the *chi-square test of independence*. First we create a *contingency table* that shows the observed frequency o_{ij} for each combination of values of the two variables. Then the expected frequency e_{ij} of each cell is determined based on the assumption that the variables are independent of one another. The expected frequencies are calculated using the formula $e_{ij} = r_i c_j / n$ where r_i and c_j are the respective observed row and column totals in the contingency table. The test is performed by calculating the chi-square statistic

$$\chi^2 = \sum_{i=1}^{H} \sum_{j=1}^{K} \frac{(o_{ij} - e_{ij})^2}{e_{ij}}$$

and comparing it with the critical value obtained from the chi-square distribution having $(H - 1)(K - 1)$ degrees of freedom. Because large differences between o_{ij} and e_{ij} cast doubt on the validity of the null hypothesis, large values of the chi-square statistic lead us to reject the null hypothesis of independence.

Chapter 13 shows how to test hypotheses concerning sets of two or more population proportions. In Chapter 14 we continue the discussion of hypothesis testing by showing how to test hypotheses concerning sets of population means.

Chapter 13 ▪ Supplementary Exercises

1. In past years, 40% of students majored in humanities, 35% majored in social sciences, and 25% majored in natural sciences. In a recent survey of the student body, the following distribution of students was obtained: humanities, 341; social sciences, 382; and natural sciences, 277. Test the null hypothesis that there has been no change in the distribution of students' choice of major. Use a 5% level of significance.

2. An executive thinks that more employees tend to be absent on Mondays and Fridays than on other days. A sample was obtained of 1000 employees who were absent for just one day during a particular week. The results were as follows: Monday, 277; Tuesday, 162; Wednesday, 127; Thursday, 126; and Friday, 308. Test the hypothesis that an employee is equally likely to be absent on any weekday. Use a 5% level of significance.

3. A group of 500 children were asked to identify their favorite colors. A toy manufacturer wants to know if the color preferences of boys and girls differ. We obtain the following data:

	Favorite Color			
Sex	Yellow	Red	Blue	Brown
Boys	107	85	33	25
Girls	93	65	67	25

Test the hypothesis that Sex and Favorite Color are independent. Use a 1% level of significance.

4. In the sample of 500 children in Exercise 3, 200 children favored yellow, 150 favored red, 100 favored blue, and 50 favored brown. Test the hypothesis that, in the total population, these colors are favored according to the following proportions: 30% favor yellow, 30% favor red, 30% favor blue, and 10% favor brown. Use a 5% level of significance.

5. A magazine takes a survey of 100 of its subscribers and 100 subscribers of its major competitor to determine if the readers of the two magazines have similar incomes. The results are as follows:

	Income (in dollars)		
Magazine	0–10,000	10,001–20,000	Over 20,000
A	22	37	41
B	28	43	29

Test the hypothesis that magazine choice is independent of level of income using a 1% level of significance.

6. The manager of a supermarket would like to arrange the advertising displays so that the advertising is close to the checkout lane used by the most customers. During a given week, the number of shoppers choosing each of the five checkout lanes was as follows: lane 1, 420; lane 2, 380; lane 3, 520; lane 4, 470; and lane 5, 410. Do these figures indicate that some checkout lanes are preferred over others? Use a 5% level of significance.

7. In a random sample of 485 voters, each individual was asked whether he or she thought inflation or unemployment was a more serious problem. The individuals were also classified by party affiliation. The results were as follows:

Party	Inflation	Unemployment
Republican	162	58
Democrat	98	67
Other	70	30

Use a 5% level of significance and test whether political party affiliation and perceived problem are independent.

8. A sample of adult males was obtained to study the relationship between age and annual expenditures on magazines. The results follow:

	Age (in years)			
Expenditures (in dollars)	20–29	30–39	40–49	50 and over
0–24	20	30	25	15
25–49	30	35	50	40
50–99	55	40	35	25
100 and over	25	40	40	15

Use a 1% level of significance and test whether expenditures on magazines and age are independent of one another. (Observe that it might be better to use a regression model to analyze this problem. Regression models will be discussed in Chapter 15.)

9. A baseball player claims that he hits better during night games than during day games. Last season, the player's performance was as follows:

	Day Games	Night Games
Base hits	60	90
Outs	150	180

Do the data substantiate the player's claim? Use a 5% level of significance.

10. A pollster wants to test if political party affiliation is independent of religious affiliation. A sample of voters yielded the following results:

Religion	Democrat	Republican	Other
Catholic	250	175	75
Protestant	400	300	100
Jewish	100	50	50
Other	150	75	75

Use a 5% level of significance. What decision should the pollster make?

11. In a sample of students, the distribution of grades was as follows:

Department	A	B	C	F
Social sciences	140	160	100	75
Natural sciences	160	190	90	75
Humanities	300	350	110	50

Use a 5% level of significance and test if the grading scale is independent of the department.

12. What is the appropriate number of degrees of freedom when we wish to test that a sample of data was obtained from a normal distribution if the number of intervals is 12 and the mean and standard deviation are unknown?

13. A new franchise cafeteria proposes three main entrees. The data from other cities show that the proportions of each entree selected were as follows: steak, .4; hamburger, .5; and fish, .1. The first 1000 customers of the franchise in the new city ordered the following meals: steak, .3; hamburger, .55; and fish, .15. Test whether the tastes in the new city are significantly different from those of the other cities using a 1% level of significance.

14. The manager of a restaurant claims that dinner bills are approximately normally distributed with mean $\mu = \$50$ and standard deviation $\sigma = \$10$. Let $\alpha = .05$ and use the following data to test the manager's claim:

Dinner Bill (in dollars)	Frequency
20–29.99	28
30–49.99	52
50–59.99	58
60–69.99	36
70–79.99	20
80–89.99	16

15. A psychologist wants to test whether a relationship exists between mental ability and manual dexterity. An IQ test is given to a random sample of individuals. Then each person is timed while performing certain tasks. Let $\alpha = .05$. Test the null hypothesis that the two variables are independent of one another.

	IQ		
Time (in seconds)	89 or less	90–110	111 or more
0–29	18	92	78
30–59	27	145	80
60–90	16	78	50

16. An economist wants to test whether the starting salaries of college graduates are independent of a graduate's major. A random sample of 400 students at the state university is selected. To control for ability, all the students in the sample have IQs between 115 and 120. Let $\alpha = .05$. Do the accompanying data indicate that starting salary and undergraduate major are independent?

Starting Salary (in dollars)	Subject			
	Math	English	Economics	Business
0–12,999	26	40	25	20
13,000–15,999	44	40	50	60
16,000 or more	30	20	25	20

17. The chef at Antonelli's Restaurant claims that men and women tend to order different types of meals. Use the following data from a random sample of customers at Antonelli's to test whether choice of meal is independent of sex with $\alpha = .05$:

Sex	Meat	Fish	Fowl
Male	280	40	50
Female	86	42	42

18. In the banking industry, mortgage loans are classified as "current" if all payments are up to date, "late" if the mortgage payment is 1 to 45 days overdue, and "delinquent" if the payment is more than 45 days overdue. Nationwide, the proportions in each category are .80, .15, and .05, respectively. In a random sample of 1000 mortgages from the Ashton National Bank, 750 are current, 190 are late, and 60 are delinquent. Use a 5% level of significance and test whether this bank is significantly different from the industry norm.

19. In an April 22, 1987, decision (*McClesky* v. *Kemp,* 55 LW 4537), the U.S. Supreme Court upheld, by a 5 to 4 margin, Georgia's death penalty. The challenge had concerned a black man's conviction in the killing of a white policeman during a 1978 robbery. The Court was given evidence purporting to show a disparity in the imposition of the death penalty in Georgia depending on the race of the murder victim and, to a lesser extent, the race of the defendant. The Supreme Court upheld the death penalty despite statistical evidence of racial disparity in its application. The crucial evidence in the trial was the following contingency table:

Death Penalty	Race of Defendant/Race of Victim			
	Black/ Black	Black/ White	White/ Black	White/ White
Yes	18	50	2	58
No	1420	178	62	687

a. Find $P(\text{death penalty} \mid \text{victim black})$.
b. Find $P(\text{death penalty} \mid \text{victim white})$. Compare with part (a).
c. Find $P(\text{death penalty} \mid \text{defendant black})$.
d. Find $P(\text{death penalty} \mid \text{defendant white})$. Compare with part (c).
e. Find $P(\text{death penalty} \mid \text{defendant black and victim white})$.
f. Find $P(\text{death penalty} \mid \text{defendant white and victim white})$. Compare with part (e).
g. Perform a chi-square test of independence to determine if the variable Death Penalty is independent of the Race of Defendant and Race of Victim. Use a 5% level of significance.

20. A sales manager wants to determine at the 5% level of significance whether the proportion of people who own a VCR is the same in all parts of the country. A random sample of individuals shows that a VCR is owned by 15 of 80 Easterners, 12 of 48 Southerners, and 24 of 100 Westerners. Perform the test.

21. The computer center at a major university keeps records of the number of times per day the computer system is down. The following data show the number of breakdowns per day for a random sample of 100 days:

Breakdowns	0	1	2	3	4	5	6	7
Observed Frequency	34	25	18	12	6	2	2	1

a. Test the null hypothesis that the distribution of breakdowns is Poisson. Let $\alpha = .05$.
b. In part (a), what did you use as the mean?
c. What is the appropriate number of degrees of freedom to use?

22. An experiment was performed to determine the effects of an incentive on the response rate to mail questionnaires. A survey was sent to three groups of people. One group was offered no incentive to return the form, the second group was offered $0.25 and the third group was offered $1.00. The results obtained are as follows:

	Incentive		
Response	$0.25	$1.00	None
Yes	318	167	114
No	492	637	697

a. Test the null hypothesis of no association between response rate and incentive. Let $\alpha = .05$.
b. What is the appropriate number of degrees of freedom?

23. Respondents to a questionnaire were cross-classified according to the amounts of time spent reading newspapers and watching television daily. The sample results are shown in the following table:

	Hours Reading Newspaper		
Hours Watching TV	Less than 0.5	0.5 to 1.0	More than 1.0
Less than 2.5	10	16	9
2.5 or more	8	10	5

a. Let $\alpha = .05$. Test the null hypothesis that the number of hours spent watching TV and reading the newspaper are independent of one another.
b. What is the appropriate number of degrees of freedom?

24. The following data show the number of households that paid all or part of their credit card bills for the previous month according to the age of the head of the household:

	Charges Paid	
Age (in years)	All	Part
Under 31	200	200
31–40	210	190
41–50	240	160
51–60	300	100
Over 60	240	160

Let $\alpha = .05$. Test to see if paying all or part of the charges is independent of the age of the head of the household.

25. The annual income tax payments of 1000 randomly selected individuals are distributed as follows:

Payment	Frequency
Less than \$1000	50
\$1000 to under \$1500	70
\$1500 to under \$2000	160
\$2000 to under \$2500	240
\$2500 to under \$3000	250
\$3000 to under \$4000	150
\$4000 or more	80

Test the hypothesis that the distribution is normal with a mean of \$2500 and a standard deviation of \$1000. Use $\alpha = 0.05$.

26. In a study of social mobility, the occupations of a random sample of employees and of their fathers were recorded. These occupations were then ranked by status. The results are as follows:

Father's Status	Worker's Status		
	Upper	Middle	Lower
Upper	572	390	161
Middle	351	720	433
Lower	118	327	440

a. If there was no social mobility whatsoever, what would the data look like?
b. If there was completely free social mobility, what would you expect the data to look like?
c. Perform a chi-square test of the null hypothesis that status of the worker and status of the father are independent. Use $\alpha = .05$.

References

COCHRAN, WILLIAM G. "The χ^2 Test of Goodness of Fit." *Annals of Mathematical Statistics* 23 (1952): 315–345.

FREUND, JOHN E., and R. E. WALPOLE. *Mathematical Statistics*. 4th ed. Englewood Cliffs, N.J.: Prentice-Hall, 1987.

Handbook of Tables for Probability and Statistics. 2d ed. Cleveland: Chemical Rubber Co., 1968.

HOEL, PAUL G. *Elementary Statistics*. 4th ed. New York: Wiley, 1976.

NETER, JOHN, WILLIAM WASSERMAN, and G. A. WHITMORE. *Fundamental Statistics for Business and Economics*. 4th ed. Boston: Allyn and Bacon, 1973.

NORUSIS, MARIJA J. *SPSSX Introductory Statistics Guide*. New York: McGraw-Hill, 1983.

———. *SPSSX Advanced Statistics Guide*. Chicago: SPSS, 1985.

———. *The SPSS Guide to Data Analysis*. Chicago: SPSS, 1986.

PEARSON, KARL. "On the Criterion That a Given System of Deviations from the Probable in the Case of a Correlated System of Variables Is Such That It Can Be Reasonably Supposed to

Have Arisen from Random Sampling." *Philosophical Magazine*. 5th series (1900), pp. 157–175.

RYAN, THOMAS A., BRIAN L. JOINER, and BARBARA F. RYAN. *Minitab Handbook*. 2d ed. Boston: PWS-KENT, 1985.

———. *Minitab Reference Manual*. University Park, Penn.: Minitab Project, 1985.

SAS Introductory Guide. 3d ed. Cary, N.C.: SAS Institute, 1985.

SAS Procedures Guide for Personal Computers. Version 6 ed. Cary, N.C.: SAS Institute, 1986.

SAS Statistics Guide for Personal Computers. Version 6 ed. Cary, N.C.: SAS Institute, 1986.

SAS User's Guide: Basics. Version 5 ed. Cary, N.C.: SAS Institute, 1985.

SAS User's Guide: Statistics. Version 5th ed. Cary, N.C.: SAS Institute, 1985.

SPSSX User's Guide. Chicago: SPSS, 1983.

Chapter Fourteen
Analysis of Variance

In Chapter 12 we explained how to test the null hypothesis that the means of two different populations are equal to one another. Frequently we want to test the null hypothesis that three or more population means are equal. For example, we may want to examine the gasoline mileage of several different brands of automobiles, the incomes of workers in different occupations, or the costs of production using several different processes.

When testing for differences in the means of more than two populations, we usually do not proceed by considering all combinations of two populations at a time and testing for differences in each pair. First, such an approach would require several tests rather than just one. Second, if each individual test were conducted using a level of significance of, say, $\alpha = .05$, then the overall level of significance would be higher than .05. For example, if

$$H_0: \mu_1 = \mu_2 = \mu_3$$

were true, and if the three null hypotheses $\mu_1 = \mu_2$, $\mu_1 = \mu_3$, and $\mu_2 = \mu_3$ were each tested using a .05 level of significance, then the probability of accepting each single hypothesis would be .05, and the probability of accepting all three hypotheses would be at least $.95^3 = .857$. (If the three tests were independent, this probability would be exactly $.95^3$.) Consequently, the probability of rejecting the null hypothesis when it was true could be as large as .143, which is substantially greater than .05.

Thus, we want to test *simultaneously* for differences among the means of all the populations, and we want the joint level of significance of the test to be α. To perform this test, we make use of the F distribution and use a method called **analysis of variance**, or **ANOVA**.

14.1 ▪ The One-Factor ANOVA Model

Suppose we obtain samples of data from K populations and want to test the null hypothesis

$$H_0: \mu_1 = \mu_2 = \cdots = \mu_K$$

against the alternative hypothesis

$$H_1: \text{At least two of the means differ}$$

We might consider comparing sample means two at a time, repeatedly applying the t test described in Section 12.2. However, if $K = 5$, then there would be ${}_5C_2 = 10$ different pairs of means to test. Furthermore, if the null hypothesis were true and each test used α as the level of significance, the probability would be much greater than α that we would reject H_0 at least once. For a true null hypothesis, the more tests we perform, the greater the probability that we will reject H_0.

Example 14.1

Comparing Fuel Consumption of Three Makes of Automobile: There is a great deal of interest in comparing the mileage ratings of different makes of automobiles. Other things being equal, customers buy the car that gets the best mileage. Suppose we wish to compare the mean fuel consumption for $K = 3$ different makes of automobile, Car 1, Car 2, and Car 3. Suppose 5 cars of each make are selected randomly and the gasoline mileage (in miles per gallon) is recorded for each car. Table 14.1 shows the results.

TABLE 14.1
Gasoline mileage results for Example 14.1

	Car 1	Car 2	Car 3
	18.2	19.8	21.2
	19.4	21.0	21.8
	19.6	20.0	22.4
	19.0	20.8	22.0
	18.8	20.4	21.6
Sample mean	19.0	20.4	21.8
Sample standard deviation	0.547	0.510	0.447
Sample variance	0.300	0.260	0.200

From Table 14.1, we see that the three sample means are $\bar{x}_1 = 19.0$, $\bar{x}_2 = 20.4$, and $\bar{x}_3 = 21.8$. These sample means all differ, but this would be the case even if all three population means were identical. The appropriate question is: "Do the observed differences in the sample means provide evidence against the null hypothesis

$$H_0: \mu_1 = \mu_2 = \mu_3$$

or can the observed differences be attributed to chance?" That is, we want to determine if the differences between the sample means are large enough to convince us that the population means differ.

Before discussing how to perform an analysis of variance (or ANOVA) test, let us present an intuitive explanation of how analysis of variance works. In Table 14.1, examine the differences between the sample means:

$$\bar{x}_1 - \bar{x}_2 = 19.0 - 20.4 = -1.4$$
$$\bar{x}_1 - \bar{x}_3 = 19.0 - 21.8 = -2.8$$
$$\bar{x}_2 - \bar{x}_3 = 20.4 - 21.8 = -1.4$$

These differences (or their squares) provide a measure of the amount of variation *between* the three samples. We want to test if these differences are due to chance or are indicative of true differences in the population means.

For example, the absolute difference between the sample means for Cars 1 and 2 is 1.4 miles per gallon. Is this difference large enough to make us believe that μ_1 and μ_2 differ? The answer depends, at least in part, on whether $\bar{x}_1$ and $\bar{x}_2$ are good estimates of μ_1 and μ_2. If the sample variances s_1^2 and s_2^2 are small, then $\bar{x}_1$ and $\bar{x}_2$ should be fairly good estimates of μ_1 and μ_2, and a relatively small difference between the sample means could indicate that the population means differ. On the other hand, if s_1^2 and s_2^2 are relatively large, then the sample means $\bar{x}_1$ and $\bar{x}_2$ might not be very close to the population values μ_1 and μ_2, and even a sizable difference between the sample means would not necessarily indicate that μ_1 and μ_2 differ.

The sample variances (or standard deviations) measure the amount of variation present in each sample. If the amount of variation *within* each sample is small, then sizable differences between the sample means provide evidence of differences in the population means. If the sample variances are large, however, then observed differences in the sample means do not necessarily provide much evidence against the null hypothesis. Thus testing for the equality of means involves finding the amount of variation that exists *between* the samples and comparing this to the variation *within* samples. Hence the name "analysis of variance."

Figure 14.1 is a **dot diagram** showing the mileage data in Table 14.1. Each dot represents a sample observation. In Figure 14.1, observe how the observations for Car 1 are clustered together about the sample mean $\bar{x}_1 = 19.0$, the observations for Car 2 about the sample mean $\bar{x}_2 = 20.4$, and the observations for Car 3 about the sample mean $\bar{x}_3 = 21.8$. Figure 14.1 strongly suggests that the mileage data come from three populations having different means.

FIGURE 14.1
Dot diagram for data in Table 14.1.

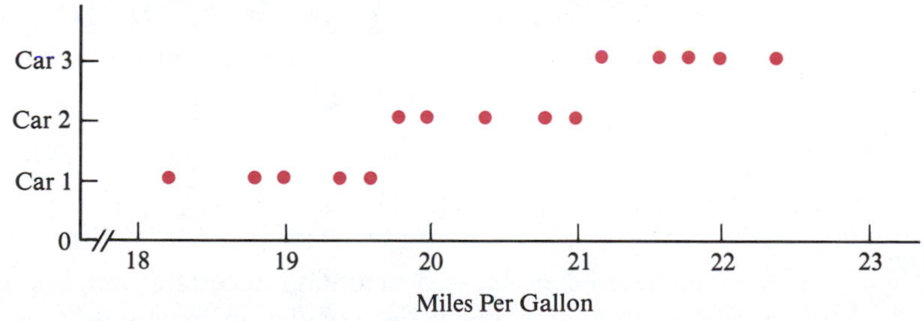

Now consider the data in Table 14.2, which show mileage figures for three different brands of cars. The sample means in Table 14.2 are identical to those in Table 14.1, and so the variation *between* the samples in Table 14.2 is identical to the variation between the samples in Table 14.1. In Table 14.2, however, all the sample standard deviations

TABLE 14.2
New gasoline mileage figures for Example 14.1

	Car 1	Car 2	Car 3
	17.0	24.2	26.0
	20.4	22.0	19.8
	24.0	17.8	24.4
	15.8	16.2	16.0
	17.8	21.8	22.8
Sample mean	19.0	20.4	21.8
Sample standard deviation	3.26	3.29	3.97
Sample variance	10.66	10.84	15.76

are much larger than the corresponding values in Table 14.1. Thus, the variation *within* each sample is much greater in Table 14.2. For example, in Table 14.1 the standard deviation of gasoline mileage for Car 1 is $s_1 = 0.547$, and in Table 14.2 the standard deviation for Car 1 is $s_1 = 3.26$.

Figure 14.2 shows the dot diagram for the mileage data in Table 14.2. In the figure, the observations for each car are less concentrated than in Figure 14.1. Thus it is not so obvious that the three populations are different, and we would not be greatly surprised if all three samples came from the same population.

FIGURE 14.2
Dot diagram for data in Table 14.2.

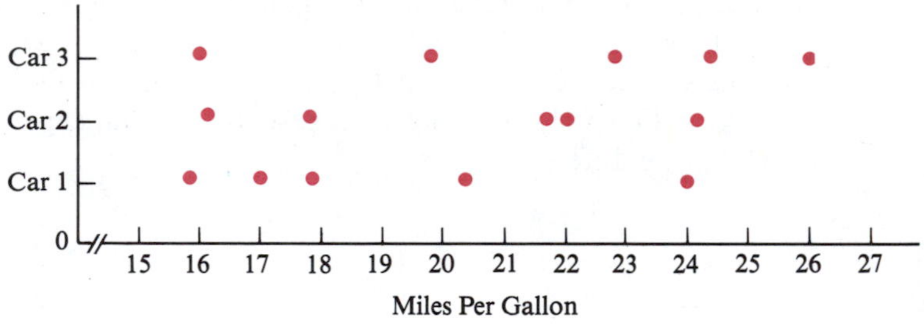

■

Terminology in Experimental Design

When data have been obtained according to certain sampling procedures, they may contain more information about the population means than could be obtained by using simple random sampling. The procedure used for obtaining sample data is called the design of the experiment. The development of experimental design originated with agricultural studies, where experiments have to be carefully designed, since it takes an entire growing season to get a single observation. Thus it is very important to get as much information as possible out of small samples.

Definition: Dependent Variable and Independent Variable

The variable being studied is called the **dependent variable** or **response variable**. A variable that influences the dependent variable is called an **independent variable** or a **factor**.

In Example 14.1, the *dependent variable* is gasoline mileage. In Example 14.1, it is conjectured that gasoline mileage might depend on the make of car. Thus the make of car is an *independent variable,* or *factor* which affects the values of the dependent variable. A factor may be either a quantitative or qualitative variable. In Example 14.1, Make of Car is a qualitative variable that takes three different values. Another study could be performed to test the fuel consumption of cars of different ages. In this case, the factor Age of Car would be a quantitative variable. In a study of crop yields using different brands of fertilizer, the factor would be qualitative, while in a study of crop yields using different quantities of fertilizer, the factor would be quantitative.

Definition: Factor Level and Treatment

A **factor level** is a particular value of a factor. If only a single factor is being considered, each factor level is called a **treatment**; if more than one factor is being considered, each combination of factor levels is called a **treatment**.

In Example 14.1, there is only one independent variable or factor, Make of Car, that influences mileage, so the analysis of the differences in the three population means is called *one-way ANOVA*. There are three factor levels or treatments being considered—Car 1, Car 2, and Car 3. Later, when we study two-way ANOVA, we will see that studies can be performed using two or more factors. In such cases, a combination of different factor levels is called a treatment. For example, suppose it is conjectured that gasoline mileage depends on Make of Car and Brand of Gasoline. Each combination of a specific brand of car and a specific brand of gasoline would represent a treatment.

Example 14.1 represents what is called a *completely randomized design*. In a completely randomized design, the means are compared for K different treatments based on independent random samples of $n_1, n_2, \ldots, n_K$ observations drawn from populations associated with treatments $1, 2, \ldots, K$, respectively.

Definition: Completely Randomized Design

A **completely randomized design** compares K population means by drawing independent random samples from each of the K populations.

The Logic Behind ANOVA

As stated earlier, the heart of the ANOVA technique is that variability in the sample data is divided into two components: the variation within each sample and the variation between the means of different samples. To perform the analysis of variance test, we compare the within-sample variation to the between-sample variation by computing an

F statistic. If the appropriate assumptions hold, the F statistic will follow the F distribution, which was discussed in Section 12.5.

Format for One-Way Analysis of Variance

We have K independent random samples of $n_1, n_2, \ldots, n_K$ observations from K populations. Each population is assumed to be normally distributed with a common variance σ^2. The K population means are denoted $\mu_1, \mu_2, \ldots, \mu_K$. One-way analysis of variance is used to test the null hypothesis

$$H_0: \mu_1 = \mu_2 = \cdots = \mu_K$$

against the alternative hypothesis

$$H_1: \text{At least two of the means differ}$$

The Sample Observations

There are K populations, and the sample size for the jth sample is denoted n_j. We denote the sample observations by

$$x_{ij} \quad \text{where } i = 1, 2, \ldots, n_j \text{ and } j = 1, 2, \ldots, K$$

The symbol x_{ij} denotes the ith observation from the jth sample. The sample observations can be displayed as in Table 14.3.

TABLE 14.3
Sample observations from independent random samples from K populations

Population			
1	2	$\cdots$	K
x_{11}	x_{12}	$\cdots$	x_{1K}
x_{21}	x_{22}	$\cdots$	x_{2K}
$\vdots$	$\vdots$	$\ddots$	$\vdots$
$x_{n_1 1}$	$x_{n_2 2}$	$\cdots$	$x_{n_K K}$

Thus, we have a random sample of n_1 observations from Population 1, a sample of n_2 observations from Population 2, and so on up to a sample of n_K observations from Population K. (The sample sizes do not have to be equal.) The total sample size is thus

$$n = n_1 + n_2 + \cdots + n_K$$

The Sample Means

Let $\bar{x}_1, \bar{x}_2, \ldots, \bar{x}_K$ denote the sample means of the K samples, and let $\bar{x}$ denote the average value of all n observations. The jth sample mean $\bar{x}_j$ is calculated as follows:

$$\bar{x}_j = \frac{\sum_{i=1}^{n} x_{ij}}{n_j} \quad \text{for } j = 1, 2, \ldots, K$$

In Table 14.1, the three sample means are $\bar{x}_1 = 19.0$, $\bar{x}_2 = 20.4$, and $\bar{x}_3 = 21.8$.

The null hypothesis states that the three population means are equal to some common value μ. To estimate this common value, we calculate the sample mean of all the sample observations. This overall sample mean, which is the sum of all the sample values divided by n, is denoted $\bar{x}$. Thus, the overall sample mean is calculated using the following formula:

$$\bar{x} = \sum_{j=1}^{K} \sum_{i=1}^{n_j} \frac{x_{ij}}{n} = \sum_{j=1}^{K} \frac{n_j \bar{x}_j}{n}$$

For the data in Table 14.1, the overall mean is

$$\bar{x} = \frac{(5)(19.0) + (5)(20.4) + (5)(21.8)}{15} = 20.4$$

Sums of Squares in ANOVA

As mentioned, the test of equality of means is based on comparing the variability within the samples to the variability between the samples. The *total sum of squares*, or the *sum of squares total*, measures the total variation in the entire sample of data and is denoted SST. SST is the sum of the squared deviations of all n observations x_{ij} about the overall mean $\bar{x}$.

Definition: Total Sum of Squares

The **total sum of squares**, denoted SST, is calculated as

$$\text{SST} = \sum_{j=1}^{K} \sum_{i=1}^{n_j} (x_{ij} - \bar{x})^2$$

ANOVA partitions this total sum of squares into two components, the variation between the K samples and the variation within each sample. First, consider the variation within the K samples. The variability within the first sample is measured as the sum of the squared deviations of the observations about their sample mean $\bar{x}_1$. Denote this sum of squares within sample 1 as SS_1, that is,

$$\text{SS}_1 = \sum_{i=1}^{n_1} (x_{i1} - \bar{x}_1)^2$$

From Table 14.1, we obtain

$$\begin{aligned}\text{SS}_1 &= (18.2 - 19.0)^2 + (19.4 - 19.0)^2 + (19.6 - 19.0)^2 \\ &\quad + (19.0 - 19.0)^2 + (18.8 - 19.0)^2 \\ &= 1.20\end{aligned}$$

Similarly, for the samples from the second population, we obtain

$$SS_2 = \sum_{i=1}^{n_2} (x_{i2} - \bar{x}_2)^2$$

From Table 14.1, we obtain

$$\begin{aligned} SS_2 &= (19.8 - 20.4)^2 + (21.0 - 20.4)^2 + (20.0 - 20.4)^2 \\ &\quad + (20.8 - 20.4)^2 + (20.4 - 20.4)^2 \\ &= 1.04 \end{aligned}$$

Finally, we obtain

$$\begin{aligned} SS_3 &= (21.2 - 21.8)^2 + (21.8 - 21.8)^2 + (22.4 - 21.8)^2 \\ &\quad + (22.0 - 21.8)^2 + (21.6 - 21.8)^2 \\ &= 0.80 \end{aligned}$$

Definition: Sum of Squares Within

The total variation within each of the K samples, denoted SSW, is called the **sum of squares within** and is calculated

$$\begin{aligned} SSW &= \sum_{i=1}^{n_1} (x_{i1} - \bar{x}_1)^2 + \sum_{i=1}^{n_2} (x_{i2} - \bar{x}_2)^2 + \cdots + \sum_{i=1}^{n_K} (x_{iK} - \bar{x}_K)^2 \\ &= \sum_{j=1}^{K} \sum_{i=1}^{n_1} (x_{ij} - \bar{x}_j)^2 \\ &= SS_1 + SS_2 + \cdots + SS_K \end{aligned}$$

Within the jth sample, the observations x_{ij} differ from the jth sample mean $\bar{x}_j$ due to unexplained random variation. Thus, the sum of squares within is also called the **sum of squares due to error** or the **error sum of squares**, and is frequently denoted SSE.

Thus, for the data in Table 14.1, the sum of squares within is

$$SSW = SS_1 + SS_2 + SS_3 = 1.20 + 1.04 + 0.80 = 3.04$$

Next we need to measure the variability between the samples. This is based on the squared differences

$$(\bar{x}_j - \bar{x})^2 \quad \text{for } j = 1, 2, \ldots, K$$

Each of these squared deviations is weighted by the number of observations in the corresponding sample so that samples with more observations are given greater weights. Then we calculate the *between-group sum of squares*.

Definition: Between-Group Sum of Squares

The total variation between the K samples is called the **between-group sum of squares** or the **sum of squares between**, denoted SSB, and is calculated as follows:

$$\begin{aligned} \text{SSB} &= n_1(\bar{x}_1 - \bar{x})^2 + n_2(\bar{x}_2 - \bar{x})^2 + \cdots + n_K(\bar{x}_K - \bar{x})^2 \\ &= \sum_{j=1}^{K} n_j(\bar{x}_j - \bar{x})^2 \end{aligned}$$

The between-group sum of squares is sometimes called the **treatment sum of squares**, denoted SSTR.

For the data in Table 14.1, the between-group sum of squares is

$$\begin{aligned} \text{SSB} &= (5)(19.0 - 20.4)^2 + (5)(20.4 - 20.4)^2 + (5)(21.8 - 20.4)^2 \\ &= 19.6 \end{aligned}$$

It can be shown algebraically that the total sum of squares always equals the sum of the between-group sum of squares plus the within-group sum of squares. Thus, we obtain the fundamental ANOVA identity in the accompanying box.

Sum-of-Squares Identity

$$\text{SST} = \text{SSB} + \text{SSW}$$

The sum-of-squares identity shows how the total variation in the sample data can be decomposed into variation within samples and variation between samples. For the data in Table 14.1, the total sum of squares is

$$\text{SST} = \text{SSB} + \text{SSW} = 19.6 + 3.04 = 22.64$$

Calculating the Mean Square Within

The test of the equality of the population means is based on three assumptions:

- *Assumption 1:* The observations X_{ij} are independent.
- *Assumption 2:* For each population, the variance of X_{ij} is σ^2.
- *Assumption 3:* For each population, X_{ij} has a normal distribution.

The ANOVA test is based on different ways of estimating the unknown variance σ^2. An unbiased estimate of σ^2 can be obtained using the sample data from Population 1 as follows:

$$s_1^2 = \frac{\sum_{i=1}^{n_1} (x_{i1} - \bar{x}_1)^2}{n_1 - 1}$$

Similarly, another unbiased estimate of σ^2 can be obtained using the sample data from the second population as follows:

$$s_2^2 = \frac{\sum_{i=1}^{n_2} (x_{i2} - \bar{x}_2)^2}{n_2 - 1}$$

This procedure can be repeated using any of the K samples. If H_0 is true, then $\bar{x}_1$, $\bar{x}_2, \ldots, \bar{x}_K$ are all unbiased estimates of the common mean μ, and $s_1^2, s_2^2, \ldots, s_K^2$ are all unbiased estimates of the variance σ^2. Each of these K estimates of σ^2 is inefficient, however, because none utilizes the entire sample of data. A better estimate of the common variance σ^2 of the K populations can be obtained by using the entire sample of $(n_1 + n_2 + \cdots + n_K)$ observations and calculating the pooled estimate

$$s_p^2 = \frac{(n_1 - 1)s_1^2 + (n_2 - 1)s_2^2 + \cdots + (n_K - 1)s_K^2}{(n_1 + n_2 + \cdots + n_K - K)}$$

where

$$s_j^2 = \frac{\sum_{i=1}^{n_j} (x_{ij} - \bar{x}_j)^2}{n_j - 1}$$

The pooled estimate s_p^2 is a weighted average of the sample variances s_j^2, where the weight given to the sample variance s_j^2 is

$$\frac{n_j - 1}{n_1 + n_2 + \cdots + n_K - K} \qquad i = 1, 2, \ldots, K$$

and the weights sum to 1. Observe that

$$(n_j - 1)s_j^2 = \sum_{i=1}^{n_j} (x_{ij} - \bar{x}_j)^2 = \text{SS}_j$$

Thus, the numerator of s_p^2 is the same as the sum of squares within (SSW), and we can write

$$s_p^2 = \frac{\text{SSW}}{n - K}$$

This pooled estimate s_p^2 is an unbiased estimate of σ^2 even when the population means differ. In one-way ANOVA, the estimate s_p^2 is called the *mean square within* and is denoted MSW.

Definition: Mean Square Within

The **mean square within**, denoted MSW, is

$$\text{MSW} = \frac{\text{SSW}}{n - K}$$

The denominator $(n - K)$ is the *degrees of freedom* for MSW. The mean square within is also called the **within-group mean square** and the **mean square error**, and is sometimes denoted MSE.

For the data in Table 14.1,

$$\text{MSW} = \text{SSW}/(n - K) = 3.04/(15 - 3) = 0.253$$

Calculating the Mean Square Between

Another way of estimating σ^2 utilizes the overall mean $\bar{x}$, the K sample means $\bar{x}_1$, $\bar{x}_2, \ldots, \bar{x}_K$, and the squared deviations $(\bar{x}_j - \bar{x})^2$. If the populations are all normal, then the sampling distribution of $\bar{X}_j$ is normal with mean μ and variance $\mathrm{Var}(\bar{X}_j) = \sigma^2/n_j$. That is, the sampling distribution of $\bar{X}_j$ is $N(\mu, \sigma^2/n_j)$. Assume for the moment that all the samples sizes are equal, so that $n_1 = n_2 = \cdots = n_K$. If H_0 is true, then the random variables $\bar{X}_1, \bar{X}_2, \ldots, \bar{X}_K$ all have the same probability distribution. Since these random variables are independent, they represent a random sample of K observations selected from a normal distribution with mean μ and variance σ^2/n_j. Thus, the sample variance of the $\bar{X}_j$'s can be used to estimate the population variance σ^2/n_j. To estimate $\mathrm{Var}(\bar{X}_j) = \sigma^2/n_j$, we use the formula

$$S^2_{\bar{X}_j} = \frac{\sum_{j=1}^{K} (\bar{X}_j - \bar{X})^2}{K - 1}$$

The observed sample variance $s^2_{\bar{X}_j}$ is an unbiased estimate of $\sigma^2_{\bar{X}_j} = \sigma^2/n_j$, where n_j is the common sample size, so $n_j s^2_{\bar{X}_j}$ is an unbiased estimate of σ^2. However, $n_j s^2_{\bar{X}_j}$ equals SSB/$(K - 1)$ in the special case when all sample sizes are equal, so we have

$$n_j s^2_{\bar{X}_j} = \frac{\sum_{j=1}^{K} n_j(\bar{x}_j - \bar{x})^2}{K - 1} = \frac{\mathrm{SSB}}{K - 1}$$

The estimator SSB/$(K - 1)$ is called the *mean square between* and is denoted MSB. For the data in Table 14.1,

$$\mathrm{MSB} = 19.6/(3 - 1) = 9.80$$

Thus, when the null hypothesis that all means are equal is true, SSB/$(K - 1)$ provides an unbiased estimate of σ^2. SSB depends on the sum

$$\sum_{j=1}^{K} n_j(\bar{x}_j - \bar{x})^2$$

If H_0 is false, this sum increases, and then $n_j s^2_{\bar{X}_j}$ tends to overestimate σ^2. When the means μ_j are not all equal, $n_j s^2_{\bar{X}_j}$ is not an unbiased estimator of σ^2. It can be shown that the expected value of $n_j s^2_{\bar{X}_j}$ is

$$E(n_j s^2_{\bar{X}_j}) = \sigma^2 + \frac{\sum_{j=1}^{K} n_j(\mu_j - \mu)^2}{K - 1}$$

where $\mu = \Sigma\mu_j/K$. Hence, if H_0 is false, then $n_j S^2_{\bar{X}_j}$ will be a biased estimator of σ^2, and the bias will be positive. Also, the bias increases as $(\mu_j - \mu)^2$ increases.

Definition: Mean Square Between

The **mean square between** is

$$\text{MSB} = \frac{\text{SSB}}{K - 1}$$

The denominator $(K - 1)$ is called the *degrees of freedom* for MSB. The mean square between is also called the **between-group mean square** and the **mean square due to treatments** and is sometimes denoted MSTR.

When the population means are *not* equal, MSB is *not* an unbiased estimator of σ^2. If the means differ, the expected value of MSB *exceeds* σ^2. Thus, the ratio of MSB to MSW provides information concerning whether the population means are equal.

The ANOVA Test Statistic *F*

In one-way ANOVA, the appropriate test statistic is

$$F = \frac{\text{MSB}}{\text{MSW}}$$

The ANOVA Test Statistic

If the null hypothesis is true, MSB and MSW both provide unbiased estimates of σ^2, and F should not be significantly different from 1. Thus, when F is close to 1, the data do not provide evidence against H_0. In contrast, if the population means differ, MSB tends to overestimate σ^2 while MSW remains an unbiased estimator of σ^2. Consequently, when H_0 is false, the F statistic tends to exceed 1. Thus, large values of F provide evidence against the null hypothesis.

If the three assumptions hold and if the null hypothesis of equality of means is true, the F statistic follows the F distribution with numerator degrees of freedom $(K - 1)$ and denominator degrees of freedom $(n - K)$.

Explanation of the Degrees of Freedom

The number of degrees of freedom for SSB is $(K - 1)$, or 1 less than the number of populations. The appropriate number of degrees of freedom for SST is $(n - 1)$, and the number of degrees of freedom for SSW is $(n - K)$.

Formula for Degrees of Freedom

$$\begin{aligned} &\text{Sums of Squares:} && \text{SST} = \text{SSB} + \text{SSW} \\ &\text{Degrees of Freedom:} && (n - 1) = (K - 1) + (n - K) \end{aligned}$$

These values for the degrees of freedom can be explained as follows: It is always the case that the sum of the deviations from the overall sample mean is 0. This puts one constraint on the deviations from the overall sample mean. For SST, only $(n - 1)$ of the n deviations from the overall mean are free. The last deviation can always be determined from the first $(n - 1)$ deviations. Thus, SST has $(n - 1)$ degrees of freedom.

SSB depends on the K squared deviations $(\bar{x}_j - \bar{x})^2$. But once $\bar{x}$ and the sample sizes are known, only $(K - 1)$ of the sample means $\bar{x}_j$ are free. Once the first $(K - 1)$ sample means and $\bar{x}$ are known, the last sample mean can be determined from the equation

$$\bar{x} = \frac{n_1\bar{x}_1 + n_2\bar{x}_2 + \cdots + n_K\bar{x}_K}{n}$$

Thus, SSB has $(K - 1)$ degrees of freedom.

SSW depends on the squared deviations of the x_{ij}'s from the appropriate sample means $\bar{x}_j$. In each sample, the deviations from the appropriate sample mean $\bar{x}_j$ sum to 0, so in each sample one of the deviations is not free. Thus, one observation in each sample can be determined from the other $(n_j - 1)$ observations and thus is not free. Since one deviation is not free in each of the K samples, only $(n - K)$ of the n deviations from the K sample means are free. Thus, the sum of squares within SSW has $(n - K)$ degrees of freedom.

Performing a One-Way ANOVA Test

The procedure for a one-way analysis of variance test for a completely randomized design is presented in the accompanying box.

One-Way ANOVA Test

Suppose we wish to test the null hypothesis

$$H_0: \mu_1 = \mu_2 = \cdots = \mu_K$$

against the alternative hypothesis

$$H_1: \text{At least two means are different}$$

It is assumed that the K populations are normally distributed with a common variance σ^2.

Step 1: Obtain K independent random samples of $n_1, n_2, \ldots, n_K$ observations from the K populations. Let n denote the total sample size; that is,

$$n = n_1 + n_2 + \cdots + n_K$$

Step 2: Calculate MSW and MSB as follows:

$$\text{MSW} = \frac{\text{SSW}}{n - K} \quad \text{and} \quad \text{MSB} = \frac{\text{SSB}}{K - 1}$$

Step 3: Calculate the F statistic

$$F = \frac{\text{MSB}}{\text{MSW}}$$

To test H_0 against H_1 using level of significance α, use the rule

$$\text{Reject } H_0 \text{ in favor of } H_1 \text{ if } F > F_{\alpha,K-1,n-K}$$

The critical value $F_{\alpha,K-1,n-K}$ is determined using the F distribution with numerator degrees of freedom $(K - 1)$ and denominator degrees of freedom $(n - K)$ such that

$$P(F > F_{\alpha,K-1,n-K}) = \alpha$$

Example 14.2 **A One-Way ANOVA Test:** Use the data in Table 14.1 and test

$$H_0\colon \mu_1 = \mu_2 = \mu_3$$

against the alternative hypothesis

$$H_1\colon \text{At least two means differ}$$

Let $\alpha = .05$.

Solution: For the data in Table 14.1, we have shown that the mean squares within and between are MSW = 0.253 and MSB = 9.80. The observed value of the test statistic is

$$F = \frac{\text{MSB}}{\text{MSW}} = \frac{9.80}{0.253} = 38.735$$

The critical value is obtained using the F distribution with numerator degrees of freedom $(K - 1) = 2$ and denominator degrees of freedom $(n - K) = 12$. The critical value is

$$F_{.05,2,12} = 3.89$$

The observed test statistic ($F = 38.735$) far exceeds the critical value (3.89) and thus falls in the critical region, so we reject H_0. (See Figure 14.3.) Now, refer back to the dot diagram in Figure 14.1, which shows the sample observations from the three populations. The ANOVA test confirms our suspicion that the data came from three populations having different means. The one-way ANOVA test says that there is too much variation between samples relative to the variation within each sample for us to believe that the population means are equal. Figure 14.1 supports this conclusion.

FIGURE 14.3
Critical region of the one-way ANOVA Test in Example 14.2.

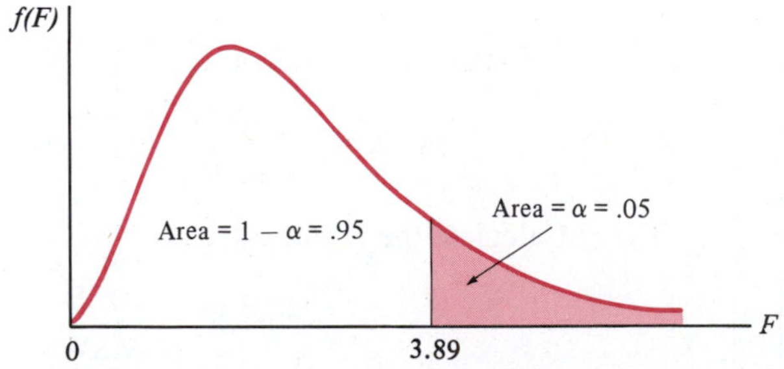

The One-Way ANOVA Table

The various computations needed for one-way ANOVA are usually presented in a standard format called an *analysis of variance table*. Such a format is shown in Table 14.4. The one-way ANOVA table shows the three sums of squares SST, SSB, and SSW; their respective degrees of freedom; the respective mean squares; and the appropriate value of the F statistic. Table 14.5 is the one-way ANOVA table for the data in Table 14.1.

TABLE 14.4 **Format of a one-way ANOVA table**

Source of Variation	Sum of Squares	Degrees of Freedom	Mean Square
Between-group	SSB	$K - 1$	$MSB = SSB/(K - 1)$
Within-group	SSW	$n - K$	$MSW = SSW/(n - K)$
Total	SST	$n - 1$	
			$F = MSB/MSW$

TABLE 14.5
ANOVA table for mileage data in Table 14.1 and Example 14.2

Source of Variation	Sum of Squares	Degrees of Freedom	Mean Square
Between-group (make of car)	19.60	2	9.800
Within-group (random error)	3.04	12	0.253
Total	22.64	14	
			$F = 38.735$

Example 14.3

Another One-Way ANOVA Test: Use the data in Table 14.2 and test

$$H_0: \mu_1 = \mu_2 = \mu_3$$

against the alternative hypothesis

$$H_1: \text{At least two means differ}$$

Let $\alpha = .05$.

Solution: For the data in Table 14.2, the sum of squares within is

$$\begin{aligned} SSW &= (n_1 - 1)s_1^2 + (n_2 - 1)s_2^2 + (n_3 - 1)s_3^2 \\ &= (4)(10.66) + (4)(10.84) + (4)(15.76) \\ &= 149.04 \end{aligned}$$

The mean square within is

$$MSW = SSW/(n - K) = 149.04/12 = 12.42$$

and the overall mean is $\bar{x} = 20.4$.

The sum of squares between is

$$\begin{aligned} SSB &= n_1(\bar{x}_1 - \bar{x})^2 + n_2(\bar{x}_2 - \bar{x})^2 + n_3(\bar{x}_3 - \bar{x})^2 \\ &= (5)(19.0 - 20.4)^2 + (5)(20.4 - 20.4)^2 + (5)(21.8 - 20.4)^2 \\ &= 19.6 \end{aligned}$$

The between-group mean square is

$$MSB = SSB/(K - 1) = 19.6/2 = 9.8$$

The observed F statistic is

$$F = \frac{MSB}{MSW} = \frac{9.80}{12.42} = 0.79$$

The critical value of the test statistic is obtained using the F distribution with numerator degrees of freedom $(K - 1) = 2$ and denominator degrees of freedom $(n - K) = 12$. The critical value is

$$F_{.05,2,12} = 3.89$$

Because the observed test statistic (0.79) is less than the critical value (3.89) and thus falls in the acceptance region, we do not reject H_0.

Now refer back to the dot diagram in Figure 14.2. Although the three sample means are the same as in Example 14.2, the conclusion is reversed because the within-sample variation is much greater for these data than for the data in Table 14.1. Table 14.6 shows the corresponding one-way ANOVA table.

TABLE 14.6
ANOVA table for mileage data in Table 14.2 and Example 14.3

Source of Variation	Sum of Squares	Degrees of Freedom	Mean Square
Between-group (make of car)	19.60	2	9.80
Within-group (random error)	149.04	12	12.42
Total	168.64	14	

$F = 0.79$ ■

Assumptions Underlying the ANOVA Test

The one-way ANOVA test requires that the populations have normal distributions, otherwise the distribution of the F statistic would not exactly follow the F distribution. The use of the F distribution will be approximately correct, however, if the distributions of the populations do not differ too much from normality; the accuracy of the approximation improves as the distributions approach normality.

The test also depends on the assumption that the variances of the different populations are equal. If the variances are not equal, the test is inappropriate. The idea underlying the F test is that if the means of the populations are equal, we can pool all the data together and treat the observations as if they had all been obtained from the same population. If the population variances differ, this argument does not hold. Thus, the assumption that each population has the same variance is important. Section 14.3 shows how to test whether the variances are all equal.

Exercises for Section 14.1

1. According to the *Statistical Abstract of the United States, 1988,* in 1985 the average weekly expenditure per household on poultry was \$3.25. The profits earned by farmers depend on the cost of producing the food. To determine the cheapest way to raise chickens, three brands of feed were given to samples of chicks to determine if the brands were equally good in inducing weight gain. The weight gains of the chicks in pounds are as follows:

Sample Observation	Brand of Feed 1	2	3
1	2	3	7
2	4	6	4
3	3	3	3
4	5	5	4
5	4	–	6

Calculate the following:

a. n, K, n_1, n_2, n_3. (Note that the sample sizes differ.)
b. $\overline{x}_1$, $\overline{x}_2$, $\overline{x}_3$
c. $\overline{x}$
d. SST, SSB, SSW
e. MSB, MSW
f. F
g. Degrees of freedom for SSB and SSW
h. Test the null hypothesis that the three population means are equal. Let α = .05.

2. An agronomist at the Department of Agriculture wants to test the effects of three different brands of fertilizer on the yields of tomato plants: 5 plants are fertilized with Brand 1, 4 plants with Brand 2, and 6 plants with Brand 3. The yields of the tomato plants in pounds are as follows:

Brand 1: 5.4, 4.8, 4.6, 5.2, 5.9
Brand 2: 4.7, 4.4, 3.7, 4.2
Brand 3: 6.1, 6.0, 6.2, 4.7, 5.2, 6.0

Calculate the following:

a. Sample means for the three brands of fertilizer
b. SST, SSB, SSW
c. MSB, MSW
d. F
e. Degrees of freedom for SSB and SSW

f. Present the relevant information in an ANOVA table.
g. Test the null hypothesis that the three population means are equal.

3. A study was undertaken to determine if the mean cost of a market basket of food is the same in four cities. Five stores were sampled in each city and the cost of the market basket of goods recorded as follows:

Store	New York 1	Boston 2	Chicago 3	Detroit 4
1	75	80	81	68
2	78	79	79	74
3	82	83	84	75
4	79	77	80	73
5	74	77	77	75

Calculate the following:
a. $\bar{x}_1$, $\bar{x}_2$, $\bar{x}_3$, $\bar{x}_4$
b. SST, SSB, SSW
c. MSB, MSW
d. F
e. Degrees of freedom for SSB and SSW
f. Test the null hypothesis that the four population means are equal. Let $\alpha = .05$.

4. During rush hour, policemen are assigned to various downtown intersections to speed up the flow of traffic and reduce congestion. To determine the intersections most in need of police supervision, the number of automobiles passing through four intersections was recorded for a 30-minute period on six days. The data are as follows:

Day	Exit 1	Exit 2	Exit 3	Exit 4
1	400	470	360	320
2	470	490	400	410
3	430	420	425	440
4	490	470	455	400
5	510	500	450	460
6	390	360	370	380

a. Calculate the mean number of cars passing through each intersection.
b. Calculate SST, SSB, and SSW.
c. Let $\alpha = .05$. Test whether the population mean is the same at each intersection.

5. The following data show the starting weekly salaries of random samples of secretaries at a university, an insurance company, and a book publishing firm:

Secretary	University	Insurance Company	Publisher
1	\$106	\$122	\$130
2	112	112	116
3	104	126	118
4	118	116	120
5	116	120	124

a. Let $\alpha = .05$. Test H_0: $\mu_1 = \mu_2 = \mu_3$.
b. Present the data in an ANOVA table.

6. The pollution index for five cities was taken on eight randomly selected days. The data were as follows:

City	$\bar{x}_i$	s_i^2
1	108	25
2	111	28
3	116	26
4	104	32
5	109	36

Use $\alpha = .05$ and test H_0: $\mu_1 = \mu_2 = \mu_3$.

7. A random sample of 25 civil engineers with two years' experience at a certain firm had an average salary of $\bar{x}_1 = \$22{,}500$ with sample standard deviation $s_1 = \$2000$. For a random sample of 25 mechanical engineers with two years' experience at the same firm, $\bar{x}_2$ was \$23,600 and s_2 was \$2400, and for a random sample of 25 electrical engineers having two years' experience at the firm, $\bar{x}_3$ was \$24,000 and s_3 was \$3200. Let $\alpha = .05$. Test H_0: $\mu_1 = \mu_2 = \mu_3$.

14.2 ▪ The Statistical Model for One-Way ANOVA

In this section, we describe the one-way ANOVA model and provide additional insight into how the one-way ANOVA test works.

One-Way ANOVA Model for a Completely Randomized Design

Let X_{ij} denote the ith observation selected from the jth population where $i = 1, 2, \ldots, n_j$ and $j = 1, 2, \ldots, K$. Let μ_j denote the jth population mean. Let e_{ij} denote the amount by which X_{ij} differs from μ_j, so that

$$e_{ij} = X_{ij} - \mu_j$$

The mathematical model for a one-way ANOVA model is

$$X_{ij} = \mu_j + e_{ij}$$

where e_{ij} represents a random effect associated with the ith observation from the jth population.

The random effects e_{ij} are assumed to be normally and independently distributed with mean 0 and homogeneous variance σ^2. That is,

1. $E(e_{ij}) = 0$ for all i and j.
2. $\text{Var}(e_{ij}) = \sigma^2$ for all i and j.
3. The e_{ij}'s are independently distributed.
4. The e_{ij}'s are normally distributed.

The equation

$$X_{ij} = \mu_j + e_{ij}$$

states that the random variable X_{ij} consists of two components: the jth population mean μ_j plus a random amount by which X_{ij} differs from μ_j.

The mean value of population j can be denoted

$$\mu_j = \mu + t_j \qquad j = 1, 2, 3, \ldots, K$$

where μ denotes the overall mean in all K populations, and

$$t_j = \mu_j - \mu$$

denotes the treatment effect associated with being in Population j. The null hypothesis states that all the population means are equal to a common value μ (with no subscript):

$$H_0: \mu_1 = \mu_2 = \cdots = \mu_K = \mu$$

This is equivalent to the null hypothesis that the treatment effects are all 0:

$$H_0: t_1 = t_2 = \cdots = t_K = 0$$

If the null hypothesis is true, there is no treatment effect, and each value X_{ij} consists of the common effect μ and a random error e_{ij}.

Derivation of the Sum of Squares Identity

We have the following relationships:

1. $X_{ij} = \mu_j + e_{ij} = \mu + t_j + e_{ij} \quad i = 1, 2, \ldots, n_j; j = 1, 2, \ldots, K$
2. $t_j = \mu_j - \mu$
3. $e_{ij} = X_{ij} - \mu_j$

Rearranging the first equation yields

$$X_{ij} - \mu = t_j + e_{ij}$$

Substituting for t_j and e_{ij} yields

$$X_{ij} - \mu = (\mu_j - \mu) + (X_{ij} - \mu_j)$$

If we replace μ by its estimate $\bar{x}$ and μ_j by its estimate $\bar{x}_j$, we obtain the sample identity

4. $x_{ij} - \bar{x} = (\bar{x}_j - \bar{x}) + (x_{ij} - \bar{x}_j)$

Squaring both sides of (4) yields

$$(x_{ij} - \bar{x})^2 = (\bar{x}_j - \bar{x})^2 + (x_{ij} - x_j)^2 + 2(\bar{x}_j - \bar{x})(x_{ij} - \bar{x}_j)$$

If this equation is summed over all i and j, the last term on the right sums to 0 and we obtain

$$\sum_{j=1}^{K} \sum_{i=1}^{n_j} (x_{ij} - \bar{x})^2 = \sum_{j=1}^{K} \sum_{i=1}^{n_j} (x_j - \bar{x})^2 + \sum_{j=1}^{K} \sum_{i=1}^{n_j} (x_{ij} - \bar{x}_j)^2$$

The first term to the right of the equals sign can be simplified to give the following formula, which shows the relationship between the three sums of squares SST, SSB, and SSW:

$$\sum_{j=1}^{K}\sum_{i=1}^{n_j}(x_{ij} - \bar{x})^2 = \sum_{j=1}^{K} n_j(\bar{x}_j - \bar{x})^2 + \sum_{j=1}^{K}\sum_{i=1}^{n_j}(x_{ij} - \bar{x}_j)^2$$

or

$$\text{SST} = \text{SSB} + \text{SSW}$$

A Graphical Explanation of ANOVA

In one-way ANOVA, the F test statistic is the ratio of the two mean squares MSB and MSW. When the null hypothesis that the population means are all equal is true, then MSB and MSW are both unbiased estimators of the variance σ^2. When the null hypothesis is false, then the mean square MSB tends to overestimate σ^2. This relationship can be shown graphically.

Examine Figure 14.4, which depicts $K = 3$ populations of data. Each population is assumed to have a normal distribution with the same variance σ^2. If H_0 is true, the three populations are identical, and we can treat all the observations as one sample of size $(n_1 + n_2 + n_3)$ from a single population having mean μ and variance σ^2.

FIGURE 14.4
Three normal distributions having equal means.

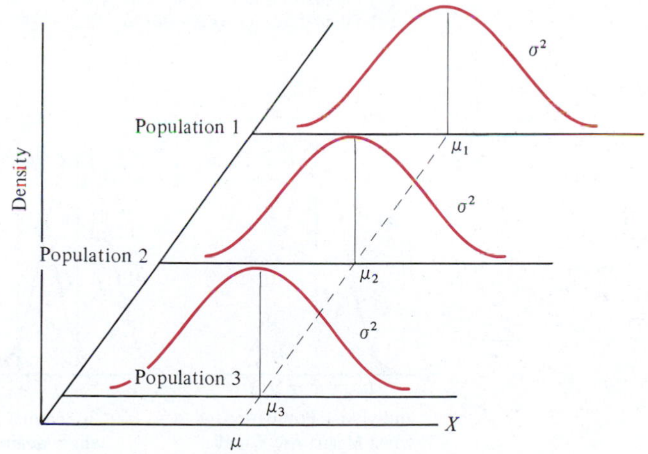

The null hypothesis is true:
(a) Populations are normal.
(b) Populations have the same variance σ^2.
(c) Populations have the *same* mean ($\mu_1 = \mu_2 = \mu_3 = \mu$).

To estimate the variance σ^2, we could pool all the sample data and obtain one pooled sample variance. Alternatively, we could obtain the sample variance for each of the three samples and estimate the pooled variance by taking a weighted average of the three sample variances. If H_0 is true, both of these methods should yield unbiased estimates of the population variance.

Now consider the case when H_0 is false, so that at least two of the population means are different. This situation is illustrated in Figure 14.5, which shows three normal distributions having equal variances but different means. A weighted average of the three sample variances will still yield an unbiased estimate of the variance σ^2.

FIGURE 14.5
Three normal distributions having different means.

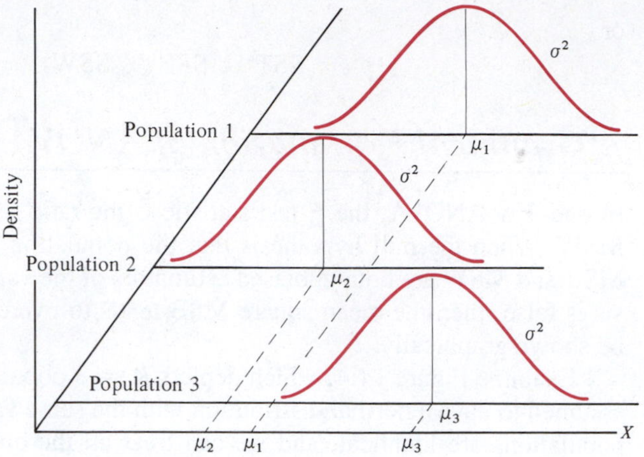

The null hypothesis is false:
(a) Populations are normal.
(b) Populations have the same variance σ^2.
(c) Populations have *different* means.

FIGURE 14.6
Pooling data from normal distributions with equal means and pooling data from normal distributions with different means.

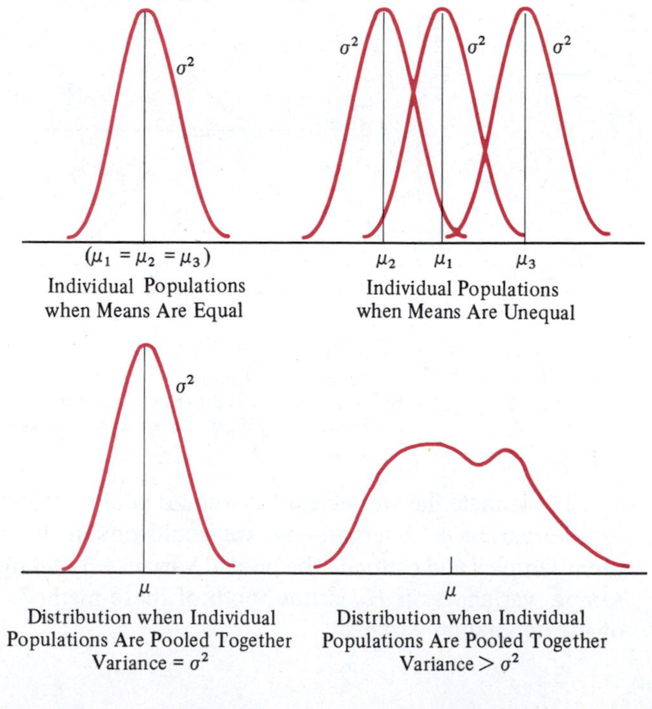

Now consider what happens if we pool the data from the three populations. Figure 14.6 shows how the total variation in the data remains constant if we pool populations having equal means and variances, whereas the total variation in the data increases if we pool populations having equal variances but different means. The term *analysis of variance* is derived from the fact that when testing H_0 against H_1, we are in a sense testing whether the variance of each individual population is the same as the variance of the pooled data after the populations have been pooled.

Equivalence of the t Test and One-Way ANOVA When Testing H_0: $\mu_1 = \mu_2$ Against H_1: $\mu_1 \neq \mu_2$

Suppose we have independent random samples of n_1 and n_2 observations from two populations and we wish to test the null hypothesis H_0: $\mu_1 = \mu_2$ against the alternative hypothesis H_1: $\mu_1 \neq \mu_2$. It is assumed that both populations are normal and have the same unknown variance σ^2. In Section 12.2 we showed how to test H_0 against H_1 by using the t statistic

$$t = \frac{\bar{x}_1 - \bar{x}_2}{\sqrt{s_p^2(1/n_1 + 1/n_2)}}$$

where s_p^2 is the pooled estimate of the variance

$$s_p^2 = \frac{\Sigma(x_{i1} - \bar{x}_1)^2 + \Sigma(x_{i2} - \bar{x}_2)^2}{n_1 + n_2 - 2}$$

It is also possible to perform the test using the one-way ANOVA test based on the test statistic

$$F = \text{MSB}/\text{MSW}$$

where the number of populations is $K = 2$. We will show that when $K = 2$, the one-way ANOVA test is equivalent to the t test discussed in Section 12.2 because the F statistic used in one-way ANOVA equals the square of the t statistic; that is, $F = t^2$. This can be shown as follows.

When there are only two populations, the F statistic is

$$F = \frac{\text{MSB}}{\text{MSW}} = \frac{\text{SSB}/(K - 1)}{\text{SSW}/(n - K)}$$

$$= \frac{[n_1(\bar{x}_1 - \bar{x})^2 + n_2(\bar{x}_2 - \bar{x})^2]/(2 - 1)}{[\Sigma(\bar{x}_{i1} - \bar{x}_1)^2 + \Sigma(x_{i2} - \bar{x}_2)^2]/(n_1 + n_2 - 2)}$$

If we square the t statistic we obtain

$$t^2 = \frac{(\bar{x}_1 - \bar{x}_2)^2}{s_p^2(1/n_1 + 1/n_2)} = \frac{n_1 n_2}{n_1 + n_2}\left[\frac{(\bar{x}_1 - \bar{x}_2)^2}{s_p^2}\right]$$

To show that $F = t^2$, we use the following identity:

$$\bar{x} = \frac{n_1\bar{x}_1 + n_2\bar{x}_2}{n_1 + n_2}$$

From this we obtain

$$\bar{x}_1 - \bar{x} = \frac{n_2(\bar{x}_1 - \bar{x}_2)}{n_1 + n_2}$$

and

$$(\bar{x}_2 - \bar{x}) = \frac{n_1(\bar{x}_2 - \bar{x}_1)}{n_1 + n_2}$$

Substituting these two equations into the formula for SSB yields

$$\begin{aligned} \text{SSB} &= n_1(\bar{x}_1 - \bar{x})^2 + n_2(\bar{x}_2 - \bar{x})^2 \\ &= \frac{n_1 n_2^2(\bar{x}_1 - \bar{x}_2)^2 + n_2 n_1^2(\bar{x}_2 - \bar{x}_1)^2}{(n_1 + n_2)^2} \\ &= \frac{n_1 n_2}{n_1 + n_2}(\bar{x}_1 - \bar{x}_2)^2 \end{aligned}$$

Next we obtain

$$\begin{aligned} \frac{\text{MSW}}{n_1 + n_2 - 2} &= \frac{\Sigma(\bar{x}_{i1} - \bar{x}_1)^2 + \Sigma(x_{i2} - \bar{x}_2)^2}{n_1 + n_2 - 2} \\ &= s_p^2 \end{aligned}$$

Substitution for SSB and MSW/$(n_1 + n_2 - 2)$ in the formula for F gives the desired result of $F = t^2$.

Furthermore, when the numerator degrees of freedom is $\nu_1 = 1$ and the denominator degrees of freedom is ν_2, then the critical value of the F distribution will always be the square of the critical value of t having ν_2 degrees of freedom. This last statement is easy to verify by checking some values from the t and F tables in the Appendix. For example, if the level of significance of a two-tailed t test is $\alpha = .05$ and the number of degrees of freedom is $\nu_2 = 10$, then the critical values of t are ± 2.228 (where 2.5% is the area in each tail of the distribution). For the F test, we would use the F value for $\alpha = .05$ using degrees of freedom $\nu_1 = 1$ and $\nu_2 = 10$. This critical value is $F = 4.96$, which is equal to $t^2 = (2.228)^2$. This relationship is illustrated in the next example.

Example 14.4 **Equivalence of One-Way ANOVA and the Two-Sample *t* Test:** Suppose we want to test H_0: $\mu_1 = \mu_2$ against H_1: $\mu_1 \neq \mu_2$ using a 5% level of significance. Two independent random samples of size $n_1 = 21$ and $n_2 = 21$ are obtained, which have the following sample means and sample variances: $\bar{x}_1 = 30$, $s_1^2 = 8$; $\bar{x}_2 = 33$, $s_2^2 = 10$. It is assumed that both populations are normal and have equal variances.

Solution: For the t test, we first calculate the pooled estimate of the variance. We obtain

$$\begin{aligned} s_p^2 &= \frac{\Sigma(x_{i1} - \bar{x}_1)^2 + \Sigma(\bar{x}_{i2} - \bar{x}_2)^2}{n_1 + n_2 - 2} \\ &= \frac{(n_1 - 1)s_1^2 + (n_2 - 1)s_2^2}{n_1 + n_2 - 2} \\ &= \frac{(20)(8) + (20)(10)}{40} \\ &= 9 \end{aligned}$$

Next we calculate the t statistic as follows:

$$t = \frac{\bar{x}_1 - \bar{x}_2}{\sqrt{s_p^2(1/n_1 + 1/n_2)}}$$

$$= \frac{30 - 33}{\sqrt{9/21 + 9/21}} = -3.240$$

The critical values of the t statistic are $t = \pm 2.021$. We reject H_0 because the t statistic is less than -2.021 and thus falls in the critical region.

For the ANOVA test, we use the F statistic

$$F = \frac{\text{MSB}}{\text{MSW}} = \frac{\text{SSB}/(K - 1)}{\text{SSW}/(n - K)}$$

$$= \frac{[n_1(\bar{x}_1 - \bar{x})^2 + n_2(\bar{x}_2 - \bar{x})^2]/(2 - 1)}{[\Sigma(x_{i1} - \bar{x}_1)^2 + \Sigma(x_{i2} - \bar{x}_2)^2]/(n_1 + n_2 - 2)}$$

To calculate F, we need to find the overall mean $\bar{x}$. We obtain

$$\bar{x} = \frac{n_1\bar{x}_1 + n_2\bar{x}_2}{n_1 + n_2}$$

$$= \frac{(21)(8) + (21)(10)}{42} = 31.5$$

We have already shown that $\text{MSW}/(n - K) = s_p^2$. Thus, the denominator of the F statistic is 9, and the F statistic becomes

$$F = \frac{[n_1(\bar{x}_1 - \bar{x})^2 + n_2(\bar{x}_2 - \bar{x})^2]/(2 - 1)}{[\Sigma(x_{i1} - \bar{x}_1)^2 + \Sigma(x_{i2} - \bar{x}_2)^2]/(n_1 + n_2 - 2)}$$

$$= \frac{[(21)(30 - 31.5)^2 + (21)(33 - 31.5)^2]/1}{9}$$

$$= 10.5$$

Note that $F = 10.5 = (-3.240)^2 = t^2$.

The critical value of F having degrees of freedom $\nu_1 = 1$ and $\nu_2 = 40$ is $F = 4.08$, which is the square of the critical value of t. We reject H_0 because $F = 10.5$ falls in the critical region. This example illustrates that when only two means are being tested, the one-way ANOVA test and the t test yield equivalent results. ■

Exercises for Section 14.2

1. Suppose we want to test the null hypothesis H_0: $\mu_1 = \mu_2$ against the alternative hypothesis H_1: $\mu_1 \neq \mu_2$ using $\alpha = .05$. It is assumed that the populations are normal with equal variances σ^2. Two independent random samples of $n_1 = 21$ and $n_2 = 21$ observations are obtained from the two populations. The sample means are $\bar{x}_1 = 30$ and $\bar{x}_2 = 33$, and the sample variances are $s_1^2 = 8$ and $s_2^2 = 10$.
   a. Calculate s_p^2, the pooled estimate of the variance.

b. Calculate the t statistic based on the sample data.
c. Find the critical value of t using $\alpha = .05$.
d. Do you accept or reject H_0?

2. Perform a one-way ANOVA test using $\alpha = .05$ on the data in Exercise 1.
a. Calculate the observed value of the F statistic.
b. Verify that this value is the square of the t statistic obtained in Exercise 1(b).
c. Calculate the critical value of F using $\alpha = .05$.
d. Verify that the critical value of F is the square of the critical value of t.
e. Do you accept or reject H_0?

3. A marketing representative wants to determine if the mean income of subscribers to *Sports Illustrated* is the same as that of *Newsweek* subscribers. A random sample of $n_1 = 15$ subscribers to *Sports Illustrated* and an independent random sample of $n_2 = 15$ subscribers to *Newsweek* are obtained. The incomes (in thousands of dollars) are as follows:

Sports Illustrated:	24, 34, 32, 45, 13, 17, 24, 27, 31, 19, 20, 42, 13, 41, 25
Newsweek:	41, 37, 65, 15, 26, 35, 52, 27, 28, 47, 36, 44, 68, 21, 33

a. Calculate the sample means and sample variances.
b. Calculate s_p^2, the pooled estimate of the variance.
c. Calculate the t statistic based on the sample data.
d. Find the critical value of t using $\alpha = .05$.
e. Do you accept or reject H_0?

4. Use the data in Exercise 3 and perform a one-way ANOVA test using $\alpha = .05$.
a. Calculate the observed value of the F statistic.
b. Verify that this value is the square of the t statistic obtained in Exercise 3(b).
c. Calculate the critical value of F using $\alpha = .05$.
d. Verify that the critical value of F is the square of the critical value of t.
e. Do you accept or reject H_0?

14.3 ▪ Computer Applications I

Statistical computer packages are readily available that perform all the arithmetic calculations necessary to perform a one-way analysis of variance test. The example below uses computer output generated by the SPSSX statistical program, but other computer packages, including Minitab and SAS, generate similar outputs.

Example 14.5

Using SPSSX for One-Way ANOVA: The cost of maintaining and repairing a car can be an important factor in determining what make of car a customer will buy. The annual maintenance and repair costs are recorded for each car in samples of 20 cars of each of three makes. Use the data in Table 14.7 and the SPSSX computer package to test the null hypothesis

$$H_0: \mu_1 = \mu_2 = \mu_3$$

against the alternative hypothesis

$$H_1: \text{The means are not all equal}$$

Use a 5% level of significance. The populations are assumed to be normal and the population variances to be equal.

TABLE 14.7
Annual automobile repair costs for Example 14.5

Car	Make 1	Make 2	Make 3
1	\$280	\$ 90	\$100
2	164	80	92
3	301	67	84
4	114	86	86
5	88	43	96
6	76	119	128
7	123	172	61
8	94	74	184
9	204	27	58
10	89	62	67
11	53	80	82
12	40	128	110
13	27	104	90
14	104	32	64
15	33	60	80
16	27	40	66
17	43	27	75
18	36	18	48
19	40	24	57
20	61	50	63

Solution: The following instructions perform a one-way ANOVA test using the SPSSX program:

```
TITLE 'ANNUAL MAINTENANCE COSTS'
DATA LIST FREE/CAR COST
BEGIN DATA
1 280
2  90
3 110
1 164
2  80
3  93
   .
   .
   .
END DATA
ONEWAY COST BY CAR(1,3)
STATISTICS ALL
FINISH
```

When inputting the data, each observation is coded as a 1, a 2, or a 3, depending on the make of car. Figure 14.7 shows the SPSSX computer output. The output shows the three sample means and standard deviations to be $\bar{x}_1 = 99.85$, $s_1 = 80.3782$; $\bar{x}_2 = 69.15$, $s_2 = 39.9648$; $\bar{x}_3 = 85.05$, $s_3 = 31.0339$. For the entire sample of 60 observations, the overall sample mean and standard deviation are $\bar{x} = 84.68$, $s = 55.3612$. The output also shows a 95% confidence interval for each of the means.

FIGURE 14.7 SPSSX-generated output for Example 14.5.

```
                                        O N E W A Y

        Variable  COST         ESTIMATED ANNUAL COST OF REPAIRS
     By Variable  CAR          TYPE OF CAR

                                      ANALYSIS OF VARIANCE

                                   SUM OF          MEAN              F       F
        SOURCE            D.F.     SQUARES        SQUARES          RATIO   PROB.

BETWEEN GROUPS               2    9428.9333      4714.4667        1.5678   .2174

WITHIN GROUPS               57  171398.0500      3006.9833

TOTAL                       59  180826.9833

                                   STANDARD     STANDARD
GROUP        COUNT        MEAN    DEVIATION        ERROR      MINIMUM      MAXIMUM     95 PCT CONF INT FOR MEAN

Grp 1           20     99.8500      80.3782      17.9731      27.0000     301.0000      62.2318 TO     137.4682
Grp 2           20     69.1500      39.9648       8.9364      18.0000     172.0000      50.4459 TO      87.8541
Grp 3           20     85.0500      31.0339       6.9394      48.0000     184.0000      70.5257 TO      99.5743

TOTAL           60     84.6833      55.3612       7.1471      18.0000     301.0000      70.3820 TO      98.9847

          FIXED EFFECTS MODEL       54.8360       7.0793                               70.5073  TO      98.8594

         RANDOM EFFECTS MODEL                     8.8642                               46.5432  TO     122.8234

RANDOM EFFECTS MODEL - ESTIMATE OF BETWEEN COMPONENT VARIANCE          85.3742

Tests for Homogeneity of Variances

      Cochrans C = Max. Variance/Sum(Variances) =   .7162, P =  .000 (Approx.)
      Bartlett-Box F =                             9.364 , P =  .000
      Maximum Variance / Minimum Variance          6.708
```

The sums of squares, mean squares, and F statistic are SSB = 9428.9333, MSB = 4714.4667, SSW = 171,398.0500, MSW = 3006.9833, and $F = 1.5678$.

The computer printout shows the value "F PROB." as .2174. "F PROB." is the prob-value, or observed significance level, associated with $F = 1.5678$. That is, if the random variable F follows the F distribution with 2 and 57 degrees of freedom, then $P(F > 1.5678) = .2174$. Because this prob-value exceeds the 5% level of significance of the test, the F statistic falls in the acceptance region and we would not reject the hypothesis that the population group means are equal. ■

Exercises for Section 14.3

Use the data in Table 2.2 of Chapter 2 to complete Exercises 1–4.

1. Test the null hypothesis that the mean SAT scores are equal for students having different majors.
   a. Find the sample mean and sample standard deviation for each major.
   b. Find SST, SSB, and SSW.
   c. Find MSB and MSW.
   d. Find the F statistic.
   e. Let $\alpha = .05$. Test the null hypothesis that the population means are equal.

2. Test the null hypothesis that the mean grade point averages are the same for students having different majors.
   a. Find the sample mean and sample standard deviation for each major.
   b. Find SST, SSB, and SSW.
   c. Find MSB and MSW
   d. Find the F statistic.
   e. Let $\alpha = .05$. Test the null hypothesis that the population means are equal.

3. Test the null hypothesis that the mean grade point averages are the same for freshmen, sophomores, juniors, and seniors.
   a. Find the sample mean and sample standard deviation for each class.
   b. Find SST, SSB, and SSW.
   c. Find MSB and MSW
   d. Find the F statistic.
   e. Let $\alpha = .05$. Test the null hypothesis that the population means are equal.

4. Test the null hypothesis that the mean SAT scores are the same for freshmen, sophomores, juniors, and seniors.
   a. Find the sample mean and sample standard deviation for each class.
   b. Find SST, SSB, and SSW.
   c. Find MSB and MSW
   d. Find the F statistic.
   e. Let $\alpha = .05$. Test the null hypothesis that the population means are equal.

Use the data in Table 2.1 of Chapter 2 to complete Exercises 5–9.

5. Test the null hypothesis that the mean seniority is the same for employees working in different divisions.
   a. Find the sample mean and sample standard deviation for each division.
   b. Find SST, SSB, and SSW.
   c. Find MSB and MSW

d. Find the F statistic.
e. Let $\alpha = .05$. Test the null hypothesis that the population means are equal.

6. Test the null hypothesis that the mean salary is the same for employees working in different divisions.
a. Find the sample mean and sample standard deviation for each division.
b. Find SST, SSB, and SSW.
c. Find MSB and MSW
d. Find the F statistic.
e. Let $\alpha = .05$. Test the null hypothesis that the population means are equal.

7. Test the null hypothesis that the mean age is the same for employees working in different divisions.
a. Find the sample mean and sample standard deviation for each division.
b. Find SST, SSB, and SSW.
c. Find MSB and MSW
d. Find the F statistic.
e. Let $\alpha = .05$. Test the null hypothesis that the population means are equal.

8. Test the null hypothesis that the mean age is the same for employees having different academic degrees.
a. Find the sample mean and sample standard deviation for each academic degree.
b. Find SST, SSB, and SSW.
c. Find MSB and MSW
d. Find the F statistic.
e. Let $\alpha = .05$. Test the null hypothesis that the population means are equal.

9. Test the null hypothesis that the mean salary is the same for employees having different academic degrees.
a. Find the sample mean and sample standard deviation for each academic degree.
b. Find SST, SSB, and SSW.
c. Find MSB and MSW
d. Find the F statistic.
e. Let $\alpha = .05$. Test the null hypothesis that the population means are equal.

14.4 ▪ *Testing the Equality of Several Variances: The Hartley Test*

Several assumptions underlie the analysis of variance test described in Section 14.1:

1. The populations have equal variances.
2. The populations are normal.
3. The observations are independent of one another.

The first assumption can be tested by using the Hartley test, which is discussed next. (The second assumption can be tested using the chi-square test discussed in Section 13.2 or by using the Kolmogorov–Smirnov test, which will be discussed in Section 21.7.)

The Hartley Test of Homogeneity of Variances

If the sample sizes for each of the K samples are equal, then the Hartley test can be used to test the null hypothesis

$$H_0: \sigma_1^2 = \sigma_2^2 = \cdots = \sigma_K^2$$

against the alternative hypothesis

$$H_1: \sigma_i^2 \neq \sigma_j^2 \quad \text{for some } i \text{ and } j$$

There are K underlying populations, and each population is assumed to be normally distributed. The Hartley test statistic is

$$H = \frac{\max(s_j^2)}{\min(s_j^2)}$$

where $\max(s_j^2)$ is the largest of the K sample variances and $\min(s_j^2)$ is the smallest. Values of H near 1 provide support for the null hypothesis, whereas large values of H lead us to reject it. The sampling distribution of H depends on the number of populations K and on the sample size n_j within each population. Table A.16 in the Appendix contains ritical values of H for a 5% level of significance.

Hartley Test of Homogeneity of Variances

Suppose we take a random sample of n_j observations from each of K normal populations having equal variances. To test the null hypothesis

$$H_0: \sigma_1^2 = \sigma_2^2 = \cdots = \sigma_K^2$$

against

$$H_1: \sigma_i^2 \neq \sigma_j^2 \quad \text{for some } i \text{ and } j$$

using a level of significance α, use the decision rule

$$\text{Reject } H_0 \text{ if } H > H_\alpha$$

where $H = \max(s_j^2)/\min(s_j^2)$ and H_α is the value such that

$$P(H > H_\alpha) = \alpha$$

Example 14.6

Testing Homogeneity of Variances: In Example 14.5, we have samples of $n_j = 20$ cars from each of $K = 3$ groups. From the computer output in Figure 14.7, we can calculate the three sample variances as follows:

$$s_1^2 = 80.3782^2 \approx 6460.66$$

$$s_2^2 = 39.9648^2 \approx 1597.19$$

$$s_3^2 = 31.0339^2 \approx 963.10$$

Test the null hypothesis that the three population variances are equal.

Solution: We obtain $\max(s_j^2) = 6460.66$ and $\min(s_j^2) = 963.10$. The H statistic is

$$H = 6460.66/963.10 \approx 6.71$$

Table A.16 does not show $H_{.05}$ for $n = 20$ and $K = 3$, so we use the critical value of H for the case when $K = 3$ and $n = 21$ as an approximation, which is $H_{.05} = 2.95$. Because the H statistic exceeds the critical value and falls in the rejection region, we would reject the hypothesis that all three group variances are equal. ■

When the sample sizes are not all equal, a more complicated test derived by M. S. Bartlett can be used, which is not described in this text. For details, see *Applied Linear Statistical Models* by J. Neter and W. Wasserman (Homewood, Ill.: Irwin, 1974).

The Normality and Independence Assumptions

The ANOVA test also requires that each population have a normal distribution. The effects of violating this assumption are usually not too serious unless the deviations are extreme. ANOVA is robust in the sense that if significant differences exist among the population means, analysis of variance will usually lead us to decide that differences exist even if the assumptions behind the test are only approximately satisfied. The analysis of variance test is especially robust with respect to the normality assumption, but nonindependence of the observations can have serious effects on the validity of the test.

Exercises for Section 14.4

1. Test the null hypothesis that the three population variances in the data in Table 14.1 are equal with $\alpha = .05$. Use the Hartley test.

2. Test the null hypothesis that the three population variances in the data in Table 14.2 are equal with $\alpha = .05$. Use the Hartley test.

14.5 ▪ Multiple-Comparison Methods

An alternative to one-way ANOVA for testing the equality of three or more means is to test means two at a time or to construct confidence intervals for all pairs $(\mu_i - \mu_j)$. This approach involves performing a series of tests sequentially or constructing a series of confidence intervals. Such an approach is called a *multiple-comparison method*.

Multiple-comparison methods deal with a dilemma that arises in statistical analysis: On the one hand, it is desirable to analyze all aspects of a set of data; on the other hand, performing several significance tests or constructing several confidence intervals for the same data compounds the error rates (significance levels); in addition, it is often difficult to compute the overall level of significance of multiple tests. Multiple-comparison and related methods are designed to give simple overall error probabilities for analyses that examine several aspects of data simultaneously.

Simultaneous Limits for Several Means

As a simple example of an application of a multiple-comparison method, suppose that independent random samples are drawn from $K = 3$ normal populations with unknown means μ_1, μ_2, and μ_3 but known variances σ_1^2, σ_2^2, and σ_3^2. If only the first sample were available, a 95% confidence interval could be constructed for μ_1 as follows:

$$\bar{x}_1 - 1.96(\sigma_1/\sqrt{n_1}), \quad \bar{x}_1 + 1.96(\sigma_1/\sqrt{n_1})$$

where $\bar{x}_1$ is the sample mean and n_1 is the size of the first sample.

In repeated sampling, this confidence interval will include the true value of μ_1 95% of the time. Confidence intervals like the one above can also be made for the means of the other two populations, but the probability that all three confidence intervals contain the mean is not .95, but

$$.95 \times .95 \times .95 = .8573$$

In a coordinate system with three axes marked $\bar{x}_1$, $\bar{x}_2$, and $\bar{x}_3$, the three intervals together define a 85.73% confidence box (Figure 14.8). To obtain a 95% confidence box (that is, to have all three statements hold simultaneously with probability .95), the confidence levels for the three individual statements must be increased. One method would be to make each individual confidence level equal to .983, the cube root of .95.

FIGURE 14.8
An 85.73% multiple-comparison box.

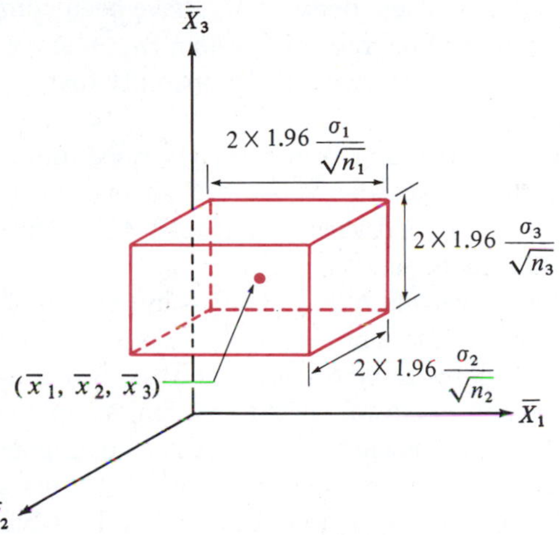

The simple two-tailed test of the null hypothesis H_0: $\mu_1 = 0$ rejects H_0 (at significance level .05) if the value 0 is not contained inside the confidence interval given in equation (1). To extend this test to the null hypothesis

$$H_0: \mu_1 = 0, \mu_2 = 0, \mu_3 = 0$$

we reject the composite hypothesis if the point (0, 0, 0) is outside the confidence box pictured in Figure 14.8. The significance level of this procedure, however, is not .05, but (1.0 − .8573) = .1417. To reduce the significance level to .05, the Z score 1.96 in the confidence interval must be replaced by a larger number. If this replacement is done symmetrically, the significance level for each of the three individual statements must be (1 − .983) = .017. In this argument, any hypothetical values of the means μ_1^*, μ_2^*, and μ_3^* may be used in place of (0, 0, 0) to specify the null hypothesis. The point $(\mu_1^*, \mu_2^*, \mu_3^*)$ then takes the place of (0, 0, 0).

The same principles can be applied to the case where the three variances are not known but are estimated from the respective samples, in which case critical values from the t distribution take the place of 1.96. Of course, the significance level may be different from 5%.

Pooled Estimate of Variance

The problem considered so far is atypically simple because the three intervals are statistically independent. Therefore, probabilities can simply be multiplied. This situation does not hold if the variances are unknown but are assumed to be equal and are estimated by a single pooled estimate of variance s_p^2, which is the sum of the three within-group sums of squares divided by $(n_1 + n_2 + n_3 - 3)$. This estimate is the within-group mean square MSW. The confidence intervals

$$\bar{x}_i - M\frac{s_p}{\sqrt{n_i}} < \mu_i < \bar{x}_i + M\frac{s_p}{\sqrt{n_i}} \qquad i = 1, 2, 3$$

(where M is a critical value to be chosen from the t distribution) use the same s_p and hence are not statistically independent. Thus, the probability that all three conditions hold simultaneously is not the product of the three separate probabilities.

Critical values, denoted M_α, have been computed for $\alpha = .05$ and $\alpha = .01$ and for any number of degrees of freedom $(n_1 + n_2 + n_3 - 3)$ of s_p^2. If M_α is substituted for M in the three intervals, the probability that all three conditions simultaneously hold is $(1 - \alpha)$.

Exactly the same principles described for the problem of estimating, or testing, three population means also apply to K means. A table providing critical values M_α for $K = 2, 3, \ldots, 10$ and various numbers of degrees of freedom has been computed by Pillai and Ranachandran.

Whenever multiple tests or comparisons of population means are made simultaneously, it is important to find the correct significance level for the series of tests. Also, the hypotheses to be tested should be chosen *before* examining the data. For example, it is inappropriate to calculate several sample means and then select the two most disparate sample means and test that the corresponding population means are unequal.

The standard methods for multiple comparisons of normal means were developed in the 1950s by J. W. Tukey, Henry Scheffe, Charles Dunnett, and David Duncan. A detailed discussion of multiple-comparison methods is beyond the scope of this book. For more information on this topic, see R. G. Miller, *Simultaneous Statistical Inference* (New York: McGraw-Hill, 1966). However, we will discuss the Bonferroni method because it is the easiest one to apply and utilizes techniques that have already been discussed. It yields results that are conservative in the sense that, if (1) k comparisons are made, (2) an overall level of significance is chosen to be α, and (3) all null hypotheses are true, the probability is *at least* $(1 - \alpha)$ that none of the null hypotheses will be wrongly rejected.

The Bonferroni method of multiple comparisons is a variation of the t test for the difference of two means, discussed in Section 12.2. There we assumed that the two population variances were unknown but equal, and we used the pooled sample variance s_p^2 as an estimate of σ^2. In the Bonferroni method of multiple comparisons, the common variance of all populations is estimated by the mean square within (MSW), where

$$\text{MSW} = \text{SSW}/(n - K)$$

To test each pair of means, the t test is performed using the critical value $t_{\nu,\alpha^*/2}$, where $\nu = (n - K)$ is the appropriate degrees of freedom and α^* is $\alpha^* = \alpha/c$, where α is the appropriate overall level of significance for the series of tests and c is the number of comparisons to be made. To use the Bonferroni method of multiple comparisons, follow the procedure described in the accompanying box.

Bonferroni Method of Multiple Comparisons

Suppose it is desired to test

$$H_0: \mu_i = \mu_j$$

against

$$H_1: \mu_i \neq \mu_j$$

for c different pairs of means.

Step 1: Choose an overall level of significance α.

Step 2: Determine the number of comparisons to be made. For example, if there are K different populations and all distinct pairs of population means are to be compared, then the number of comparisons will be $c = {}_KC_2 = K(K - 1)/2$.

Step 3: Find the critical value $t_{\alpha/2c,(n-K)}$ from the t table using degrees of freedom $\nu = (n - K)$. The two-tailed level of significance is α/c, so the area in one tail of the t distribution is $\alpha/2c$. If the exact critical value is not in the table, it might be necessary to use interpolation.

Step 4: To compare μ_i with μ_j, calculate the test statistic

$$t = \frac{\bar{x}_i - \bar{x}_j}{\sqrt{s_p^2(1/n_i + 1/n_j)}}$$

where s_p^2 is the pooled estimate of the variance

$$s_p^2 = \frac{\Sigma(n_j - 1)s_j^2}{n - K}$$

Step 5: Reject H_0 in favor of H_1 if $t > t_{\alpha/2c,n-K}$ or if $t < -t_{\alpha/2c,n-K}$. An equivalent procedure is to use the decision rule

$$\text{Reject } H_0 \text{ in favor of } H_1 \text{ if } |\bar{x}_i - \bar{x}_j| > t_{\alpha/2c,n-K}\sqrt{s_p^2(1/n_i + 1/n_j)}$$

Step 6: Repeat this procedure for each pair of means μ_i and μ_j.

Example 14.7

Multiple Comparisons Using the Bonferroni Method: In Example 14.2 the null hypothesis of no difference in the gasoline mileage of three makes of cars was rejected using one-way ANOVA. Use the data in Table 14.1 and Bonferroni's method to find which means appear to differ from the others.

Solution: First, we choose $\alpha = .05$ because this was the level of significance used for the one-way ANOVA test. If we make all possible comparisons of the three makes of cars, we will make $c = {}_3C_2 = 3$ comparisons. To find the critical value of t, we have $\alpha/2c = .05/6 = .008$, and the appropriate degrees of freedom is $(n - K) = (15 - 3) = 12$. The critical values of t will be (approximately)

$$t_{\alpha/2c,n-K} = t_{.008,12} \approx 2.91$$

We obtained this critical value by interpolating between $t_{.01,12} = 2.681$ and $t_{.005,12} = 3.055$.

The pooled estimate of the variance is

$$s_p^2 = \frac{\Sigma(n_j - 1)s_j^2}{n - K}$$
$$= \frac{(4)(.300) + (4)(.260) + (4)(.200)}{12} = 0.2533$$

Next we calculate

$$t_{\alpha/2c,n-K}\sqrt{s_p^2(1/n_i + 1/n_j)} = 2.91\sqrt{.2533(1/5 + 1/5)}$$
$$= 0.926$$

Now we compare the absolute differences $|\bar{x}_i - \bar{x}_j|$ with the value 0.926. The sample means are $x_1 = 19.0$, $\bar{x}_2 = 20.4$, and $\bar{x}_3 = 21.8$. The difference

$$|\bar{x}_1 - \bar{x}_2| = |19.0 - 20.4| = 1.4$$

exceeds 0.926, so we reject the hypothesis that $\mu_1 = \mu_2$. Similarly, the difference

$$|\bar{x}_1 - \bar{x}_3| = |19.0 - 21.8| = 2.8$$

exceeds 0.926, so we reject the hypothesis that $\mu_1 = \mu_3$. Finally, the difference

$$|\bar{x}_2 - \bar{x}_3| = |20.4 - 21.8| = 1.4$$

also exceeds 0.926, so we reject the hypothesis that $\mu_2 = \mu_3$. ■

Exercises for Section 14.5

1. Use the data in Table 14.2 and Bonferroni's method to test if any pair of means differ. Use $\alpha = .05$.
a. Find c, $\alpha/2c$, and $t_{\alpha/2c,(n-K)}$.
b. Find s_p^2.
c. Find $t_{\alpha/2c,n-K}\sqrt{s_p^2(1/n_i + 1/n_j)}$.
d. Perform the test.

2. Use the data in Example 14.5 and Bonferroni's method to test if any pair of means differ. Use $\alpha = .05$.
a. Find c, $\alpha/2c$, and $t_{\alpha/2c,n-K}$.
b. Find s_p^2.
c. Find $t_{\alpha/2c,n-K}\sqrt{s_p^2(1/n_i + 1/n_j)}$.
d. Perform the test.

14.6 ▪ Two-Way ANOVA Models: Introduction

In one-way ANOVA, the main interest is in determining if one particular independent variable, or factor, influences the values of the dependent variable. In many situations, we may suspect that a second independent variable also influences the dependent variable. In two-way ANOVA, the model relates the value of the dependent variable to two independent variables and to random effects. Because ANOVA models can be classified in many ways, we shall introduce some technical terminology before proceeding.

An ANOVA experiment is said to be *balanced* if for each factor or combination of factors, there are an equal number of observations. Otherwise, the experiment is said to be *unbalanced*. For instance, in Example 14.1, we had five cars of each make. This is a balanced design. If we had had seven cars of one make, the design would have been unbalanced. Most of the computational formulas simplify if we use a balanced experimental design.

In a one-way ANOVA problem, each observation belongs to one of K groups or populations based on the value of a single factor. For example, in Example 14.1, observations of car mileages were grouped according to the make of car. In a two-way ANOVA model, each observation is classified according to the values of two independent variables, or factors. In a two-way ANOVA problem, we have a different levels for factor A and b different levels for factor B. Thus, there are $(a \times b)$ different possible combinations of values for the two factors. In two-way ANOVA, each possible combination of values is called a *treatment*.

It is customary to record the observations in a rectangular table containing $a \times b$ *cells,* where a is the number of rows and b is the number of columns. Each row represents a different level of factor A, and each column represents a different level of factor B, and the intersection of a particular row and column represents a *cell*.

Definition: A Factorial Experiment

An experiment that utilizes every possible combination of factor levels is called a **factorial experiment**.

In many problems, there is only one observation per cell. For example, we might record the gasoline mileage obtained by each of $a = 3$ makes of automobiles (Factor A), each of which was driven using $b = 4$ different brands of gasoline (Factor B). That is, we drive one car of each make using each brand of gasoline. Although there are $(a \times b) = (3 \times 4) = 12$ observations of gasoline mileage, there is only one observation per cell. We would have exactly one observation for each combination of automobile and gasoline.

In other two-way models, we could have more than one observation per cell. For example, suppose we have 40 cars of Make 1, 40 of Make 2, and 40 of Make 3. Suppose 10 cars of each brand are driven using Gasoline A, 10 using Gasoline B, 10 using Gasoline C, and 10 using Gasoline D. Then the sample would contain 10 automobiles of each brand using each of the 4 different gasolines, so each of the 12 cells would contain 10 observations.

In an experiment containing many observations per cell, it is possible to estimate and test for the presence of *interaction effects* between the two factors. For example, does the mean gasoline mileage of automobiles of a particular make differ depending on which gasoline the automobile is running on? When we have only one observation per cell, we cannot test for the presence of interaction effects; all we can do is examine the separate additive effects attributed to Factor A and Factor B.

In some experiments, some cells of the table will contain no observations. If at least one cell is empty, the design is *incomplete;* otherwise, the design is *complete*. For example, suppose we are testing three makes of cars using four brands of gasoline. If Gasoline A is never used in a car of Make 1, then the design is incomplete.

Analysis of variance can be extended to cover situations where three or more factors influence a dependent variable. For example, when examining the fuel mileage for different makes of cars, we might want to take into account the make of car (factor 1), the type of gasoline used (factor 2), whether the car has a manual or automatic transmission (factor 3), and whether the car has air conditioning (factor 4).

Randomization and Blocking

Another important consideration is how the experimental units are allocated to the various row and column combinations of the explanatory variables. In a completely randomized design, the experimental units are assigned at random to the treatments, since any lack of homogeneity among the experimental units increases the error mean square and decreases our chances of detecting differences among treatments. When the experimental units are heterogeneous, we should first divide them into relatively homogeneous groups called **blocks**, a procedure called **blocking**.

As an example, suppose a teacher wants to compare three different methods for teaching a statistics course. In Course 1, the students use the computer extensively. In Course 2, the students work in small groups and work on group projects. In Course 3, the teacher lectures and assigns lots of homework problems. At the end of the semester, all the students in the three courses take the same final exam. The teacher can then test the null hypothesis that the mean exam score is identical for all the courses.

A potential problem is that even if students are randomly assigned to the three courses, the good students may tend to be allocated to one course, the average students to another, and the weak students to the third. Because of this possibility, one teaching method may appear to be better than the others when in fact it is not. If this happened, the abilities of the students would be confounded with the effect of the teaching method. To prevent this problem, we should block on the students' abilities; that is, we should sort the students into, say, $b = 3$ relatively homogeneous groups, or blocks, according to performance and intelligence tests. Thus, Block 1 might contain the good students, Block 2 the average students, and Block 3 the weak students. Then we should randomly assign one-third of the students in each block to each course.

In this example, the second independent variable, the ability of the student, is called a *blocking variable*, and the experiment is said to be arranged in blocks. In two-way ANOVA, we can test the null hypothesis that the mean exam score is the same for each course and also test the null hypothesis that the mean exam score is the same for each level of ability.

The experiment just described is called a *randomized block design*. The experimental units, the students, are arranged into homogeneous blocks, and students within each block are randomly assigned to the three courses. Within each block, any significant differences in the observations are due to the effect of the factor of interest—in this case, the teaching method.

Definition: Randomized Block Design

A **randomized block design** allocates treatments to experimental units that have first been sorted into homogeneous groups called **blocks**.

The main reason for using a randomized block design is to remove from the experiment a source of variation that is not of interest in order to improve our measurement of the effects that are of interest. Thus blocking reduces the probability of not detecting differences in effects when differences do exist.

The analysis of variance for a randomized block design is a two-way analysis because both the treatment (course) effects and the block (ability) effects can be estimated and tested. No special techniques are needed to study a randomized block model, because it is computationally equivalent to a completely randomized model.

14.7 ▪ Two-Way ANOVA Models with One Observation per Cell

This section treats two-way ANOVA models that contain exactly one observation per cell. In Section 14.8, we will consider two-way ANOVA when there are multiple observations per cell.

When we have only one observation per cell, we use the symbol x_{ij} to denote the sample observation corresponding to the ith level of Factor A and the jth level of Factor B. The sample data can be arranged as in Table 14.8, where the observation x_{ij} is in row i and column j.

TABLE 14.8
Arrangement of data for a two-way ANOVA with one observation per cell

		Level of Factor B				
		1	2	...	b	Sample Mean
Level of Factor A	1	x_{11}	x_{12}	...	x_{1b}	$\bar{x}_{1\cdot}$
	2	x_{21}	x_{22}	...	x_{2b}	$\bar{x}_{2\cdot}$
	⋮	⋮	⋮	⋱	⋮	⋮
	a	x_{a1}	x_{a2}	...	x_{ab}	$\bar{x}_{a\cdot}$
Sample Mean		$\bar{x}_{\cdot 1}$	$\bar{x}_{\cdot 2}$	...	$\bar{x}_{\cdot b}$	

The sample mean for the ith level of Factor A is denoted $\bar{x}_{i\cdot}$, $i = 1, 2, \ldots, a$, where

$$\bar{x}_{i\cdot} = \frac{\sum_{j=1}^{b} x_{ij}}{b} \qquad i = 1, 2, \ldots, a$$

The sample mean for the jth level of Factor B is denoted $\bar{x}_{\cdot j}$, $j = 1, 2, \ldots, b$, where

$$\bar{x}_{\cdot j} = \frac{\sum_{i=1}^{a} x_{ij}}{a} \qquad j = 1, 2, \ldots, b$$

Example 14.8 **Two-Way ANOVA Test:** Table 14.9 shows sample data for an experiment involving five makes of automobiles and four types of gasoline. The data show the mileages (in

TABLE 14.9 **Two-way ANOVA table for Example 14.8**

Type of Gasoline (Factor A)	Type of Car (Factor B) 1	2	3	4	5	Row Sum	Sample Mean $\bar{x}_{i\cdot}$
1	78	82	88	72	80	400	80
2	70	76	78	66	70	360	72
3	68	76	76	62	68	350	70
4	80	90	98	72	90	430	86
Column Sum	296	324	340	272	308	1540	
Sample Mean $\bar{x}_{\cdot j}$	74	81	85	68	77		$\bar{x} = 77$

miles per gallon) obtained by driving each make of car using each type of gasoline. We are interested in answering the following questions:

1. Are the mean mileages associated with various types of gasoline (Factor A) different?
2. Are the mean mileages traveled by the various makes of cars (Factor B) different?

Solution: The statistical model states that mileage depends on the type of gasoline (Factor A), the make of car (Factor B), and random factors. The data in Table 14.9 are arranged in $a = 4$ rows and $b = 5$ columns. The values in the margins of the table show the sum and the sample mean for each row and column.

Table 14.9 shows the sample mean for each row and column of data. The sample mean for column j (the jth level of Factor B) is denoted $\bar{x}_{\cdot j}$ (that is, a dot replaces the row subscript). From Table 14.9, the five column means are

$$\bar{x}_{\cdot 1} = 74, \quad \bar{x}_{\cdot 2} = 81, \quad \bar{x}_{\cdot 3} = 85, \quad \bar{x}_{\cdot 4} = 68, \quad \bar{x}_{\cdot 5} = 77$$

The sample mean for row i (the ith level of Factor A) is denoted $\bar{x}_{i\cdot}$ (that is, a dot replaces the column subscript). The four row means for the levels of Factor A are:

$$\bar{x}_{1\cdot} = 80, \quad \bar{x}_{2\cdot} = 72, \quad \bar{x}_{3\cdot} = 70, \quad \bar{x}_{4\cdot} = 86$$

The location of the dot in the subscript for a row or column mean indicates the subscript over which summation has taken place.

The mean for all ab observations is called the *sample grand mean,* or *overall mean,* and is denoted $\bar{x}$, where

$$\bar{x} = \frac{\sum_{i=1}^{a}\sum_{j=1}^{b} x_{ij}}{ab} = \frac{\sum_{i=1}^{a} \bar{x}_{i\cdot}}{a} = \frac{\sum_{j=1}^{b} \bar{x}_{\cdot j}}{b}$$

For the data in Table 14.9, the overall mean is

$$\bar{x} = \frac{1540}{20} = 77$$

■

The Theoretical Model: Two-Way ANOVA

Before actually testing any hypotheses, it is useful to study the underlying statistical model that is being used. The statistical model states that the random variable X_{ij} is the sum of the following four components:

1. the overall population mean for all possible values (denoted μ),
2. an effect due to the ith level of Factor A (denoted A_i),
3. an effect due to the jth level of Factor B (denoted B_j), and
4. a random effect (denoted e_{ij}), which represents that part of the observation that cannot be explained by the other components of the model; e_{ij} is called a *random error term.*

Theoretical Two-Way ANOVA Model

The random variable X_{ij} is determined by the equation

$$X_{ij} = \mu + A_i + B_j + e_{ij} \qquad i = 1, 2, \ldots, a; j = 1, 2, \ldots, b$$

The random factors e_{ij} are assumed to be mutually independent, normally distributed variables having 0 mean and variance σ^2. That is,

1. $E(e_{ij}) = 0$ for all i and j.
2. $\text{Var}(e_{ij}) = \sigma^2$ for all i and j.
3. The e_{ij}'s are mutually independent.
4. The e_{ij}'s are normally distributed.

Absence of Interaction Effects

It is important to note that this model assumes no interaction between Factor A and Factor B. That is, the effect of any level of Factor A is the same regardless of the level of Factor B. This means, for example, that the effect of Gasoline 3 does not vary with the make of car. The factors would interact, for example, if certain makes of cars are especially suited to get better mileage with certain types of gasoline. Thus, a certain type of gasoline might have a different effect on one car's mileage than on another car's mileage.

Explanation of the Null Hypothesis

In the two-way ANOVA model with no interaction effects, there are two different null hypotheses that we might be interested in testing. The first states that different levels of Factor A have no effect on the mean value of variable X_{ij}. This null hypothesis could be expressed as

$$H_0: A_1 = A_2 = \cdots = A_a = 0$$

where a represents the number of levels of Factor A. The alternative hypothesis is

$$H_1: \text{At least one } A_i \text{ differs from } 0$$

In Example 14.8, this null hypothesis states that the four brands of gasoline all yield the same mean mileage.

The second null hypothesis states that Factor B has no effect on mean mileage. This null hypothesis and the corresponding alternative hypothesis could be expressed as

$$H_0\colon B_1 = B_2 = \cdots = B_b = 0$$

$$H_1\colon \text{At least one } B_j \text{ differs from } 0$$

where b represents the number of levels of Factor B. In Example 14.8, this null hypothesis states that, in the population, the five different makes of cars have no effect on the mean gasoline mileage.

Let $\mu_{i\cdot}$ denote the population mean for level i of Factor A, and let $\mu_{\cdot j}$ denote the population mean for level j of Factor B. The mean $\mu_{i\cdot}$ can be expressed as

$$\mu_{i\cdot} = \mu + A_i \qquad i = 1, 2, \ldots, a$$

and the means $\mu_{\cdot j}$ can be expressed as

$$\mu_{\cdot j} = \mu + B_j \qquad j = 1, 2, \ldots, b$$

The effects A_i represent deviations of the population means $\mu_{i\cdot}$ from the population grand mean μ. (In Example 14.8, A_i measures the difference between the mean mileage using Gasoline i and the mean overall mileage for all types of gasoline.) The a deviations $A_1, A_2, \ldots, A_a$ always sum to 0; therefore,

$$\sum_{i=1}^{a} A_i = 0$$

This result implies that the effects A_i have only $(a - 1)$ degrees of freedom. (Note, however, that the null hypothesis of interest states that *each* A_i is 0, not that their sum is 0.)

Similarly, the effects B_j represent deviations of the population means $\mu_{\cdot j}$ from the population grand mean μ. (In Example 14.8, B_j represents the difference between the mean mileage for cars of Make j and the mean overall mileage for all cars.) These deviations must also sum to 0. The constraint

$$\sum_{j=1}^{b} B_j = 0$$

implies that the effects B_j have only $(b - 1)$ degrees of freedom.

Testing the null hypothesis

$$H_0\colon A_1 = A_2 = \cdots = A_a = 0$$

is equivalent to testing the null hypothesis about the means

$$H_0\colon \mu_{1\cdot} = \mu_{2\cdot} = \cdots = \mu_{a\cdot} = \mu$$

A similar argument for Factor B shows that testing the null hypothesis

$$H_0\colon B_1 = B_2 = \cdots = B_b = 0$$

is equivalent to testing the hypothesis about the means

$$H_0\colon \mu_{\cdot 1} = \mu_{\cdot 2} = \cdots = \mu_{\cdot b} = \mu$$

If Factor B (the column factor) has no effect, then the theoretical population means $\mu_{\cdot 1}, \mu_{\cdot 2}, \ldots, \mu_{\cdot b}$ are all equal to one another and to μ, and the sample means $\bar{x}_{\cdot 1}$,

$\bar{x}_{\cdot 2}, \ldots, \bar{x}_{\cdot b}$ should differ only because of random factors. Similarly, if Factor A (the row factor) has no effect, then the population means $\mu_{1\cdot}, \mu_{2\cdot}, \ldots, \mu_{a\cdot}$ are all equal to one another and to μ. Also the sample means $\bar{x}_{1\cdot}, \bar{x}_{2\cdot}, \ldots, \bar{x}_{a\cdot}$ should not be significantly different from one another or from $\bar{x}$ and should differ only because of random effects.

We can rewrite the basic equation of our model as

$$X_{ij} - \mu = A_i + B_j + e_{ij}$$

which shows that X_{ij} can differ from the overall mean for three reasons: the row effect A_i, the column effect B_j, and the random effect e_{ij}.

We have

$$B_j = \mu_{\cdot j} - \mu \quad \text{and} \quad A_i = \mu_{i\cdot} - \mu$$

The two-way analysis of variance model

$$X_{ij} - \mu = A_i + B_j + e_{ij}$$

can be rewritten as the algebraic identity

$$X_{ij} - \mu = (\mu_{i\cdot} - \mu) + (\mu_{\cdot j} - \mu) + (X_{ij} - \mu_{i\cdot} - \mu_{\cdot j} + \mu)$$

The term

$$A_i = \mu_{i\cdot} - \mu$$

measures the effect of the ith level of Factor A, the term

$$B_j = \mu_{\cdot j} - \mu$$

measures the effect of the jth level of Factor B, and the term

$$e_{ij} = X_{ij} - \mu_{i\cdot} - \mu_{\cdot j} + \mu$$

measures the random effect.

The sample model corresponding to the population model is

$$\bar{x}_{ij} - \bar{x} = (\bar{x}_{i\cdot} - \bar{x}) + (\bar{x}_{\cdot j} - \bar{x}) + (x_{ij} - \bar{x}_{i\cdot} - \bar{x}_{\cdot j} + \bar{x})$$

If both sides of this equation are squared and summed over i and j, we obtain the following formula:

Formula for Sums of Squares

$$\sum_{i=1}^{a}\sum_{j=1}^{b}(x_{ij} - \bar{x})^2 = \sum_{i=1}^{a}\sum_{j=1}^{b}(\bar{x}_{i\cdot} - \bar{x})^2 + \sum_{i=1}^{a}\sum_{j=1}^{b}(\bar{x}_{\cdot j} - \bar{x})^2 + \sum_{i=1}^{a}\sum_{j=1}^{b}(x_{ij} - \bar{x}_{i\cdot} - \bar{x}_{\cdot j} + \bar{x})^2$$

In the formula for the sum of squares, several sums involving cross product terms are missing because they are equal to 0. The four sums of squares shown are the total sum of squares, denoted SST; the sum of squares due to Factor A, denoted SSA; the sum of squares due to Factor B, denoted SSB; and the random, or unexplained, sum of squares, denoted SSE. We thus obtain the basic identity in the accompanying box.

Sum of Squares Identity for Two-Way ANOVA with One Observation per Cell

The sum of squares identity is

$$\text{SST} = \text{SSA} + \text{SSB} + \text{SSE}$$

where

$$\text{SST} = \sum_{i=1}^{a} \sum_{j=1}^{b} (x_{ij} - \bar{x})^2$$

$$= \sum_{i=1}^{a} \sum_{j=1}^{b} x_{ij}^2 - ab\bar{x}^2$$

$$\text{SSA} = \sum_{i=1}^{a} \sum_{j=1}^{b} (\bar{x}_{i\cdot} - \bar{x})^2 = b\sum_{i=1}^{a} (\bar{x}_{i\cdot} - \bar{x})^2$$

$$\text{SSB} = \sum_{i=1}^{a} \sum_{j=1}^{b} (\bar{x}_{\cdot j} - \bar{x})^2 = a\sum_{j=1}^{b} (\bar{x}_{\cdot j} - \bar{x})^2$$

$$\text{SSE} = \text{SST} - \text{SSA} - \text{SSB}$$

SSE represents the residual, or random, variation that is unexplained.

When the sample sizes are large, calculating the sums of squares in the identity can be quite tedious. In actual practice, a computer program is almost always used to perform a two-way analysis of variance.

From the data in Table 14.9, we obtain

$$\text{SST} = \sum_{i=1}^{4} \sum_{j=1}^{5} (x_{ij} - \bar{x})^2 = 1604$$

$$\text{SSA} = 5\sum_{i=1}^{4} (\bar{x}_{i\cdot} - \bar{x})^2 = 820$$

$$\text{SSB} = 4\sum_{j=1}^{5} (\bar{x}_{\cdot j} - \bar{x})^2 = 680$$

$$\text{SSE} = 1604 - 820 - 680 = 104$$

If, in the population, the different makes of cars have equal mean mileages, the sum SSB should be nonzero solely because of random variation. If the cars do have different mean mileages, SSB should be much larger. A similar argument applies to the different types of gasoline.

Degrees of Freedom and Mean Squares

As in one-way ANOVA, a specific number of degrees of freedom is associated with each sum of squares, and mean squares are calculated by dividing the various sums of squares by their respective degrees of freedom.

Sums of Squares and Mean Squares in Two-Way ANOVA

In two-way ANOVA, the various sums of squares, degrees of freedom, and mean squares are as follows:

	Sum of Squares	Degrees of Freedom	Mean Square
Factor A	SSA	$a - 1$	MSA = SSA/$(a - 1)$
Factor B	SSB	$b - 1$	MSB = SSB/$(b - 1)$
Error (random effect)	SSE	$(a - 1)(b - 1)$	MSE = SSE/$[(a - 1)(b - 1)]$
Total	SST	$(n - 1)$	MST = SST/$(n - 1)$

In two-way ANOVA, the error mean square SSE corresponds to the within-group mean square (SSW) of one-way ANOVA. That is, it measures the variance of the random effects based on the assumption that all population means are equal.

If the column effects B_j are all 0, then the mean squares MSB and MSE are both unbiased estimates of σ^2, and the ratio

$$F = \text{MSB}/\text{MSE}$$

should be approximately equal to 1. On the other hand, if the effects B_j are nonzero, then MSB tends to overestimate σ^2 and the F statistic is larger. Thus, large values of F provide evidence against the null hypothesis that all the effects B_j are 0. In a similar fashion, large values of the F statistic

$$F = \frac{\text{MSA}}{\text{MSE}}$$

provide evidence against the null hypothesis that all the effects A_i are 0.

To test either null hypothesis, we compare the appropriate F statistic with the critical value of F obtained from tables of the F distribution. The procedure described in the accompanying box shows how to perform a two-way ANOVA test.

Two-Way ANOVA Test for One Observation per Cell

Suppose we want to test the null hypothesis that the column effects B_j are all 0 using level of significance α. Calculate the F statistic

$$F = \text{MSB}/\text{MSE}$$

If H_0 is true, then this F statistic follows the F distribution having numerator degrees of freedom

$$\nu_1 = b - 1$$

and denominator degrees of freedom

$$\nu_2 = (a - 1)(b - 1)$$

Use the decision rule

$$\text{Reject } H_0 \text{ if } F > F_{\alpha,b-1,(a-1)(b-1)}$$

To test the null hypothesis that the row effects A_i are all 0, calculate the F statistic

$$F = \text{MSA/MSE}$$

If H_0 is true, then this F statistic follows the F distribution having numerator degrees of freedom

$$\nu_1 = a - 1$$

and denominator degrees of freedom

$$\nu_2 = (a - 1)(b - 1)$$

Use the decision rule

$$\text{Reject } H_0 \text{ if } F > F_{\alpha,a-1,(a-1)(b-1)}$$

Example 14.9 **Another Two-Way ANOVA Test:** Use the data in Table 14.9 and test the two null hypotheses that, in the populations, the different makes of cars have the same mean mileages and the different types of gasoline yield the same mean mileages. Use a 5% level of significance.

Solution: From the data in Table 14.9, we have

$$\text{MSB} = \frac{\text{SSB}}{b-1} = \frac{680}{4} = 170$$

$$\text{MSA} = \frac{\text{SSA}}{a-1} = \frac{820}{3} = 273.33$$

$$\text{MSE} = \frac{\text{SSE}}{(a-1)(b-1)} = \frac{104}{12} = 8.67$$

If the population column means are equal, then the F statistic

$$F = \frac{\text{MSB}}{\text{MSE}} = \frac{170}{8.67} = 19.61$$

follows the F distribution with numerator degrees of freedom $(b - 1) = 4$ and denominator degrees of freedom $(a - 1)(b - 1) = 12$. The critical value of F is $F_{.05,4,12} = 3.26$. We reject H_0 because the F statistic exceeds the critical value and falls in the rejection region. Thus, in the population, different makes of cars appear to have different mean mileages.

To test the hypothesis that the row effects A_i are all 0, we obtain the F statistic

$$F = \frac{\text{MSA}}{\text{MSE}} = \frac{273.33}{8.67} = 31.53$$

If we use a 5% level of significance, the critical value of F having degrees of freedom $(a - 1) = 3$ and $(a - 1)(b - 1) = 12$ is $F_{.05,3,12} = 3.48$. The observed F statistic $F = 31.53$ far exceeds the critical value 3.48. Thus, we reject the null hypothesis that the type of gasoline has no effect on mileage. ■

A Table for Two-Way ANOVA

The results of a two-way analysis of variance test are usually presented in tabular form. The data in Table 14.10 show the results from Example 14.9.

TABLE 14.10 **Two-way ANOVA table for Example 14.9**

Source of Variation	Degrees of Freedom	Sum of Squares	Mean Square
Factor A (Gasoline)	$a - 1 = 3$	SSA = 820	MSA = 273.33
Factor B (Car)	$b - 1 = 4$	SSB = 680	MSB = 170.00
Error	$(a - 1)(b - 1) = 12$	SSE = 104	MSE = 8.60
Total	$ab - 1 = 19$	SST = 1604	

$$F_B = \frac{\text{MSB}}{\text{MSE}} = 19.61 \qquad F_A = \frac{\text{MSA}}{\text{MSE}} = 31.53$$

Inappropriate Use of One-Way ANOVA

One-way analysis of variance can be an inappropriate tool when the response variable depends on two factors rather than just one. Suppose we had used the data in Table 14.9 and performed a one-way ANOVA test to see if the make of car influences the mean mileage. We would then have ignored the effects of Factor A, the gasoline. We would have obtained the same total sum of squares (SST) reported in Table 14.10, SST = 1604 with 19 degrees of freedom. For a one-way test, the between-group sum of squares SSB would have been the same as SSB in Table 14.10. Thus, we would have obtained SSB = 680 with $(K - 1) = 4$ degrees of freedom. In one-way ANOVA, the remaining variation would have been attributed to random error (although, in fact, much of the variation was due to the gasoline effect). We would have obtained the within-group sum of squares

$$\text{SSW} = \text{SST} - \text{SSB} = 1604 - 680 = 924$$

where SSW would have had $(n - K) = 15$ degrees of freedom.

We would then have obtained the mean squares

$$\text{MSB} = \frac{\text{SSB}}{K - 1} = \frac{680}{4} = 170$$

$$\text{MSW} = \frac{\text{SSW}}{n - K} = \frac{924}{15} = 61.6$$

For one-way ANOVA, the F statistic would have been

$$F = \frac{\text{MSB}}{\text{MSW}} = \frac{170.0}{61.6} = 2.76$$

For $\alpha = .05$, the critical value of F would have been $F_{.05,4,15} = 3.06$. The observed F statistic would have been $F = 2.76$ and fallen in the acceptance region, so we would not have rejected H_0.

In Example 14.9, by using a two-way analysis of variance test, we rejected the hypothesis that the mean mileages of the cars are equal. Here we see that by using an inappropriate one-way analysis of variance test, we would have accepted the null hypothesis. The reason for this is that, in this problem, one-way ANOVA exaggerates the random effects. By ignoring the effects of different brands of gasoline, one-way ANOVA attributes all the variation in each column of data to the random effects. This causes MSW in the one-way ANOVA model to overestimate σ^2, thus reducing the F statistic and causing it to fall in the acceptance region.

Refer to the data in Table 14.9. Given the large differences in the five column sample means $\bar{x}_{.j}$ (74, 81, 85, 68, and 77), the question arises as to why one-way ANOVA does not reject the null hypothesis that the population column means are equal. To answer this question, examine, for example, the data in column 5. The four sample values (80, 70, 68, and 90) exhibit a great deal of variation, which one-way ANOVA attributes to random effects. This large amount of variation in column 5 indicates that the sample mean $\bar{x}_{.5}$ is not a very precise estimator of $\mu_{.5}$. The same argument holds for each of the other treatment sample means $\bar{x}_{.j}$. One-way ANOVA attributes all of the variation within any specific column to random effects. Because the within-column variations are large, it is difficult to reject the null hypothesis that the population column means are equal, even though the sample means seem to differ by large amounts.

Using one-way ANOVA in this problem attributes the large amount of variation within each column to a random effect, making it appear as though our sample means could be subject to substantial sampling error. In two-way ANOVA much of the within-column variation is attributed to the effect of Factor A (the gasoline), and the variation attributed to random effects is much smaller than in one-way ANOVA. In two-way ANOVA, the five column sample means are judged to be significantly different from one another because, after Factor A is taken into account, we seem to get relatively precise estimates of the population column means. In the two-way ANOVA problem, the random effect is very small, and even small differences in the sample column means are sufficient to make us reject the null hypothesis.

An examination of all the formulas in this section shows that it makes no difference which variable is called Factor A and which is called Factor B when performing a two-way analysis of variance.

Exercises for Section 14.7

1. The Krimbill Corporation owns three machines, A_1, A_2, and A_3, which are used to produce items on an assembly line. The plant manager wishes to test for a difference in the number of items that the machines produce per hour. Three operators, O_1, O_2, and O_3, work the machines, and three working periods are set up for each operator. During each period, the operators are assigned to the three machines by a random procedure so that each operator works once with each machine. The results in items produced per hour are shown in the following table:

	Machine		
Operator	A_1	A_2	A_3
O_1	116	98	114
O_2	102	104	108
O_3	126	118	128

Use a 5% level of significance and test whether the mean yields of the machines are different.

2. The Folino Carton Company manufactures cereal boxes for major food companies. After the designs are printed on large cardboard sheets, the sheets are passed through machines that cut the sheets into the appropriate forms. Mr. Folino thinks that the speed of the cutting machines may depend on the type of cardboard used. He wishes to examine cardboard having three different weights W_1, W_2, and W_3. He owns four cutting machines, M_1, M_2, M_3, and M_4. He uses each type of cardboard on each machine and determines the time in seconds required to cut 1000 boxes. The data are as follows:

	Machine			
Cardboard	M_1	M_2	M_3	M_4
W_1	900	930	860	870
W_2	840	880	890	860
W_3	820	850	830	840

Let $\alpha = .05$. Test the null hypothesis that the weight of the cardboard does not affect cutting time.

3. An insurance company has three employees who provide estimates of the cost of repairing wrecked vehicles. Because estimates that are too high reduce the profits of the insurance company, the company wants to compare the mean of each employee's estimates. To study this, each employee estimated the repair cost of the same four vehicles. The estimates of the three employees are as follows:

	Employee		
Vehicle	1	2	3
1	\$480	\$440	\$520
2	520	500	440
3	640	600	640
4	380	420	460

a. What is the blocking variable and what is the treatment variable?
b. Find the treatment sum of squares and the treatment mean square.
c. Find the blocking sum of squares and the blocking mean square.
d. Find the error sum of squares and the mean square error.
e. Find the F statistic to test the null hypothesis that the employees have the same mean estimates in the population.
f. Find the critical value of the F statistic with $\alpha = .05$.
g. Do you accept the null hypothesis?

4. The Internal Revenue Service employs four different individuals who audit randomly selected income tax returns. The IRS wants to compare the mean of each employee's estimates. Each employee audits the same five income tax returns and estimates the amount of tax due. The estimates of the four employees are as follows:

Tax Return	Employee 1	2	3	4
1	$140	$120	$220	$180
2	110	230	240	240
3	220	320	240	190
4	180	120	260	160
5	100	80	140	150

a. What is the blocking variable and what is the treatment variable?
b. Find the treatment sum of squares and the treatment mean square.
c. Find the blocking sum of squares and the blocking mean square.
d. Find the error sum of squares and the mean square error.
e. Find the F statistic to test the null hypothesis that the employees have the same mean estimates in the population.
f. Find the critical value of the F statistic with $\alpha = .05$.
g. Do you accept the null hypothesis?

5. The analysis of variance for a randomized block design produced the following results:

Source of Variation	Degrees of Freedom	Sum of Squares	Mean Square
Treatment	3	45.6	?
Block	6	?	15.00
Error	?	30.4	?
Total	?	?	?

a. Complete the ANOVA table.
b. Find the F statistic to test whether the treatment means are equal.
c. Let $\alpha = .05$. Find the critical value of the F statistic.
d. Do the data provide sufficient evidence to indicate a difference in the population treatment means? Test using $\alpha = .05$.

6. An agricultural experiment was conducted to examine potential differences in crop yields using four different varieties of wheat and three different fertilizers. The output of the experiment in bushels is as follows:

Type of Fertilizer	Variety of Wheat 1	2	3	4
1	88	92	90	84
2	94	86	80	82
3	90	82	82	76

a. Complete the ANOVA table.
b. Find the F statistic to test whether the mean yields are equal for the four varieties of wheat.
c. Let $\alpha = .05$. Find the critical value of the F statistic.
d. Test the null hypothesis that the population mean yields are the same for the three brands of fertilizer. Test using $\alpha = .05$.

14.8 ▪ *Two-Way ANOVA with Interaction Effects*

As in Section 14.7, suppose we hypothesize that a dependent variable X_{ij} is related to two explanatory factors and to random effects. As before, let Factor A have a levels and Factor B have b levels, so that the two factors together have ab combinations. If we have only one observation for each combination, we can perform a two-way analysis of variance to test for the effects due to Factor A or to Factor B, as was shown in Section 14.7.

In this section, we examine the more common case where the entire experiment is replicated c times so that we have c observations in each of the ab cells. That is, for each factor combination, we have c observations. There are two advantages to multiple observations per cell. First, we can make more accurate estimates of the population means. Second, we can extend the two-way analysis of variance model to analyze *interaction effects*. Interaction effects occur when treatment effects are not the same for different blocks. For example, Gasoline A might affect the mileage of cars of Make 1 differently than it affects cars of Make 2. Thus, the effect of Gasoline A would not be the same for all makes of cars. Such car–gasoline interactions can be detected in an analysis of variance experiment that contains more than one observation per cell. As another example, consider the statistics teacher who has three different methods of teaching. Emphasizing the use of the computer in a statistics course may have a different effect on good students than on weak ones. Once again there could be an interaction effect.

When there are multiple observations per cell, the total sum of squares SST can be partitioned into four components: a component due to the different levels of Factor A, a component due to the different levels of Factor B, a component due to the interaction between both factors, and the error component.

Example 14.10 **A Two-Way ANOVA Test with Multiple Observations per Cell:** Suppose that doctors are studying the length of stay in a hospital for patients who have been admitted for a certain illness. As part of their treatment, each patient is given a certain type of medicine and a certain type of vitamin supplement. We wish to test whether there are differences in the average length of hospital stay that can be attributed to the type of vitamin supplement given or to the type of medicine given. Suppose there are $a = 3$ types of vitamin supplements, V_1, V_2, and V_3, and $b = 3$ types of medicine, M_1, M_2, and M_3. (The fact that $a = b$ is not important.)

In this experiment, we may be interested not only in the separate effects of M_i and V_j but also in the combined effects of M_i and V_j. For example, medicine M_1 could have a different effect on length of stay when combined with vitamin V_1 than with V_2 or V_3.

In this case, an interaction effect exists between type of medicine and type of vitamin. To include the possibility of interaction, we introduce a new term into the two-way analysis of variance model. ■

The General Model

The general two-way ANOVA model with interaction can be expressed as

$$X_{ijk} = \mu + A_i + B_j + I_{ij} + e_{ijk}$$
$$i = 1, 2, \ldots, a; j = 1, 2, \ldots, b; k = 1, 2, \ldots, c$$

In this notation, the random variable X_{ijk} is the kth observation associated with level i of the row factor (Factor A) and level j of the column factor (Factor B). There are ab combinations of levels of Factor A and Factor B, and there are c observations for each combination. The value X_{ijk} is the kth observation in cell (i, j). As usual, x_{ijk} denotes the observed value of the random variable X_{ijk}.

Once again, A_i represents the effect of the ith level of Factor A, and B_j represents the effect of level j of Factor B. I_{ij} represents an interaction effect between level i of Factor A and level j of Factor B. To estimate and test for the presence of interaction effects, we need multiple observations per cell. We consider here only the case with an equal number of observations per cell and let c denote the number of observations in each cell. The sample data can be arranged in a table containing a rows and b columns and ab cells. Each of these cells contains c observations, so the total number of observations is $n = abc$. This notation is illustrated in Table 14.11.

There are three null hypotheses that can be tested: no difference in the population means associated with different levels of Factor A, no difference in the population means associated with different levels of Factor B, and no Factor A–Factor B interaction. To perform the tests, we again need to calculate various sample means and sums of squares.

Let $\mu_{ij\cdot}$ denote the population mean of all observations at the ith level of Factor A and the jth level of Factor B, let $\mu_{i\cdot\cdot}$ denote the population mean of all observations at the ith level of Factor A, and let $\mu_{\cdot j\cdot}$ denote the population mean of all observations at the jth level of Factor B. Let $\bar{x}_{ij\cdot}$, $\bar{x}_{i\cdot\cdot}$, and $\bar{x}_{\cdot j\cdot}$ denote the corresponding sample means. The location of the dot in the subscript indicates the index over which the sum is taken.

The effect A_i is

$$A_i = \mu_{i\cdot\cdot} - \mu$$

and the effect B_j is

$$B_j = \mu_{\cdot j\cdot} - \mu$$

The interaction effect is

$$I_{ij} = \mu_{ij\cdot} - \mu_{i\cdot\cdot} - \mu_{\cdot j\cdot} - \mu$$

Finally, the random effect is

$$e_{ijk} = X_{ijk} - \mu_{ij\cdot}$$

TABLE 14.11
Arrangement of data for a two-way ANOVA with c observations per cell

Level of Factor A	Level of Factor B: 1	2	$\cdots$	b
1	x_{111}	x_{121}	$\cdots$	x_{1b1}
	x_{112}	x_{122}	$\cdots$	x_{1b2}
	$\vdots$	$\vdots$	$\cdots$	$\vdots$
	x_{11c}	x_{12c}	$\cdots$	x_{1bc}
2	x_{211}	x_{221}	$\cdots$	x_{2b1}
	x_{212}	x_{222}	$\cdots$	x_{2b2}
	$\vdots$	$\vdots$	$\cdots$	$\vdots$
	x_{21c}	x_{22c}	$\cdots$	x_{2bc}
$\vdots$	$\vdots$	$\vdots$	$\ddots$	$\vdots$
a	x_{a11}	x_{a21}	$\cdots$	x_{ab1}
	x_{a12}	x_{a22}	$\cdots$	x_{ab2}
	$\vdots$	$\vdots$	$\cdots$	$\vdots$
	x_{a1c}	x_{a2c}	$\cdots$	x_{abc}

If we substitute these definitions into the model

$$X_{ijk} = \mu + A_i + B_j + I_{ij} + e_{ijk}$$

we obtain

$$X_{ijk} = \mu + (\mu_{i\cdot\cdot} - \mu) + (\mu_{\cdot j\cdot} - \mu) + (\mu_{ij\cdot} - \mu_{i\cdot\cdot} - \mu_{\cdot j\cdot} + \mu) + (X_{ijk} - \mu_{ij\cdot})$$

or

$$X_{ijk} - \mu = (\mu_{i\cdot\cdot} - \mu) + (\mu_{\cdot j\cdot} - \mu) + (\mu_{ij\cdot} - \mu_{i\cdot\cdot} - \mu_{\cdot j\cdot} + \mu) + (X_{ijk} - \mu_{ij\cdot})$$

The corresponding sample identity is

$$(x_{ijk} - \bar{x}) = (\bar{x}_{\cdot j\cdot} - \bar{x}) + (\bar{x}_{i\cdot\cdot} - \bar{x}) + (\bar{x}_{ij\cdot} - \bar{x}_{i\cdot\cdot} - \bar{x}_{\cdot j\cdot} + \bar{x}) + (x_{ijk} - \bar{x}_{ij\cdot})$$

If both sides of this equation are squared and summed over i, j, and k, we obtain

$$\sum_{i=1}^{a}\sum_{j=1}^{b}\sum_{k=1}^{c}(x_{ijk} - \bar{x})^2 = \sum_{i=1}^{a}\sum_{j=1}^{b}\sum_{k=1}^{c}(\bar{x}_{i\cdot\cdot} - \bar{x})^2 + \sum_{i=1}^{a}\sum_{j=1}^{b}\sum_{k=1}^{c}(\bar{x}_{\cdot j\cdot} - \bar{x})^2$$
$$+ \sum_{i=1}^{a}\sum_{j=1}^{b}\sum_{k=1}^{c}(\bar{x}_{ij\cdot} - \bar{x}_{i\cdot\cdot} - \bar{x}_{\cdot j\cdot} + \bar{x})^2 + \sum_{i=1}^{a}\sum_{j=1}^{b}\sum_{k=1}^{c}(x_{ijk} - \bar{x}_{ij\cdot})^2$$

In this equation, several cross product terms are missing because they sum to 0. This equation is the sum of squares identity that forms the basis for the two-way analysis of variance test with interaction.

Sum of Squares Identity with Multiple Observations per Cell

For the two-way analysis of variance problem with multiple observations per cell, the sum of squares identity is

$$\text{SST} = \text{SSA} + \text{SSB} + \text{SSI} + \text{SSE}$$

The corresponding degrees of freedom are

$$(abc - 1) = (a - 1) + (b - 1) + (a - 1)(b - 1) + ab(c - 1)$$

where the sums of squares and associated degrees of freedom are as follows:

Source of Variation	Sums of Squares	Degrees of Freedom
Factor A	$\text{SSA} = bc \sum_{i=1}^{a} (\bar{x}_{i\cdot\cdot} - \bar{x})^2$	$a - 1$
Factor B	$\text{SSB} = ac \sum_{j=1}^{b} (\bar{x}_{\cdot j\cdot} - \bar{x})^2$	$b - 1$
Interaction	$\text{SSI} = \sum_{i=1}^{a} \sum_{j=1}^{b} (\bar{x}_{ij\cdot} - \bar{x}_{i\cdot\cdot} - \bar{x}_{\cdot j\cdot} + \bar{x})^2$	$(a - 1)(b - 1)$
Error	$\text{SSE} = \sum_{i=1}^{a} \sum_{j=1}^{b} \sum_{k=1}^{c} (x_{ijk} - \bar{x}_{ij\cdot})^2$	$ab(c - 1)$
Total	$\text{SST} = \sum_{i=1}^{a} \sum_{j=1}^{b} \sum_{k=1}^{c} (x_{ijk} - \bar{x})^2$	$abc - 1$

Dividing each sum of squares by its corresponding degrees of freedom yields the corresponding mean square, giving us the following:

$$\text{MSA} = \text{SSA}/(a - 1)$$
$$\text{MSB} = \text{SSB}/(b - 1)$$
$$\text{MSI} = \text{SSI}/(a - 1)(b - 1)$$
$$\text{MSE} = \text{SSE}/ab(c - 1)$$

The procedure for performing a two-way ANOVA test with interaction effects is described in the accompanying box.

Two-Way ANOVA Test with Multiple Observations per Cell

Suppose we wish to test the null hypothesis that Factor A has no effect,

$$H_0\colon \mu_{1\cdot\cdot} = \mu_{2\cdot\cdot} = \cdots = \mu_{a\cdot\cdot}$$

against the alternative hypothesis

H_1: The means are not all equal

using a level of significance α. The appropriate decision rule is

$$\text{Reject } H_0 \text{ in favor of } H_1 \text{ if } F > F_{\alpha,\nu_1,\nu_2}$$

where

$$F = \text{MSA/MSE}$$

and where $\nu_1 = (a - 1)$ and $\nu_2 = ab(c - 1)$.

To test the null hypothesis that Factor B has no effect, or

$$H_0\colon \mu_{\cdot 1 \cdot} = \mu_{\cdot 2 \cdot} = \cdots = \mu_{\cdot b \cdot}$$

against the alternative hypothesis

$$H_1\text{: The means are not all equal}$$

use the decision rule

$$\text{Reject } H_0 \text{ in favor of } H_1 \text{ if } F > F_{\alpha,\nu_1,\nu_2}$$

where

$$F = \text{MSB/MSE}$$

and where $\nu_1 = (b - 1)$ and $\nu_2 = ab(c - 1)$.

To test the null hypothesis

$$H_0\colon I_{ij} = 0 \qquad \text{for all } i \text{ and } j$$

against the alternative hypothesis

$$H_1\text{: The interaction effects are not all zero}$$

use the decision rule

$$\text{Reject } H_0 \text{ in favor of } H_1 \text{ if } F > F_{\alpha,\nu_1,\nu_2}$$

where

$$F = \text{MSI/MSE}$$

and where $\nu_1 = (a - 1)(b - 1)$ and $\nu_2 = ab(c - 1)$.

Table 14.12 shows the general format of the two-way analysis of variance table with c observations per cell.

Example 14.11 **A Two-Way ANOVA Test with Interaction Effects:** A doctor wishes to determine if the mean length of stay in the hospital for patients is related to the type of medicine and type of vitamin supplement that are administered. Suppose three types of medicine M_1, M_2, and M_3 and three types of vitamin supplements V_1, V_2, and V_3 are used. Each of the 9 combinations M_iV_j was given to a random sample of $c = 4$ patients. Thus, there are 9 cells with 4 observations per cell for a total of 36 observations. Four patients were given the combination (M_1, V_1), four were given the combination (M_1, V_2), and so forth. The data are shown in Table 14.13. Use a 5% level of significance and test the three null hypotheses that the medicine effects, the vitamin effects, and the interaction effects are 0.

TABLE 14.12 **Two-way ANOVA table with multiple observations per cell**

Source of Variation	Sum of Squares	Degrees of Freedom	Mean Square	F Ratio
Factor A	SSA	$a - 1$	MSA = SSA/$(a - 1)$	MSA/MSE
Factor B	SSB	$b - 1$	MSB = SSB/$(b - 1)$	MSB/MSE
Interaction	SSI	$(a - 1)(b - 1)$	MSI = SSI/$(a - 1)(b - 1)$	MSI/MSE
Error	SSE	$ab(c - 1)$	MSE = SSE/$ab(c - 1)$	
Total	SST	$abc - 1$		

TABLE 14.13 **Data on length of stay in hospital for Example 14.11**

Vitamin Supplement (Factor A)	Type of Medicine (Factor B) M_1	M_2	M_3	$\bar{x}_{i\cdot\cdot}$
V_1	10	9	12	
	6	3	10	
	8	5	12	
	4	7	10	
	$\bar{x}_{11\cdot} = 7$	$\bar{x}_{12\cdot} = 6$	$\bar{x}_{13\cdot} = 11$	$\bar{x}_{1\cdot\cdot} = 8$
V_2	9	8	6	
	9	6	8	
	6	14	10	
	12	12	8	
	$\bar{x}_{21\cdot} = 9$	$\bar{x}_{22\cdot} = 10$	$\bar{x}_{23\cdot} = 8$	$\bar{x}_{2\cdot\cdot} = 9$
V_3	6	12	8	
	4	13	12	
	4	15	11	
	6	16	13	
	$\bar{x}_{31\cdot} = 5$	$\bar{x}_{32\cdot} = 14$	$\bar{x}_{33\cdot} = 11$	$\bar{x}_{3\cdot\cdot} = 10$
$\bar{x}_{\cdot j\cdot}$	$\bar{x}_{\cdot 1\cdot} = 7$	$\bar{x}_{\cdot 2\cdot} = 10$	$\bar{x}_{\cdot 3\cdot} = 10$	$\bar{x} = 9$

Solution: First, we need to calculate the sample means that are used in ANOVA. For the (i, j) cell, the sample mean is

$$\bar{x}_{ij\cdot} = \frac{\sum_{k=1}^{c} x_{ijk}}{c}$$

For example, using the data in Table 14.13, we obtain

$$\bar{x}_{11\cdot} = \frac{10 + 6 + 8 + 4}{4} = 7$$

$$\bar{x}_{12\cdot} = \frac{9 + 3 + 5 + 7}{4} = 6$$

and so forth. For Table 14.13, the nine cell means are

$$\bar{x}_{11\cdot} = 7, \quad \bar{x}_{12\cdot} = 6, \quad \bar{x}_{13\cdot} = 11$$
$$\bar{x}_{21\cdot} = 9, \quad \bar{x}_{22\cdot} = 10, \quad \bar{x}_{23\cdot} = 8$$
$$\bar{x}_{31\cdot} = 5, \quad \bar{x}_{32\cdot} = 14, \quad \bar{x}_{33\cdot} = 11$$

The sample mean for the observations at the ith level of Factor A is

$$\bar{x}_{i\cdot\cdot} = \frac{\sum_{j=1}^{b}\sum_{k=1}^{c} x_{ijk}}{bc}$$

From Table 14.13, we obtain

$$\bar{x}_{1\cdot\cdot} = \frac{10 + 6 + 8 + 4 + 9 + 3 + 5 + 7 + 12 + 10 + 12 + 10}{12} = 8$$
$$\bar{x}_{2\cdot\cdot} = \frac{9 + 9 + 6 + 12 + 8 + 6 + 14 + 12 + 6 + 8 + 10 + 8}{12} = 9$$
$$\bar{x}_{3\cdot\cdot} = \frac{6 + 4 + 4 + 6 + 12 + 13 + 15 + 16 + 8 + 12 + 11 + 13}{12} = 10$$

The sample mean for the observations at the jth level of Factor B is

$$\bar{x}_{\cdot j\cdot} = \frac{\sum_{i=1}^{a}\sum_{k=1}^{c} x_{ijk}}{ac}$$

From Table 14.13, we obtain

$$\bar{x}_{\cdot 1\cdot} = \frac{10 + 6 + 8 + 4 + 9 + 9 + 6 + 12 + 6 + 4 + 4 + 6}{12} = 7$$
$$\bar{x}_{\cdot 2\cdot} = \frac{9 + 3 + 5 + 7 + 8 + 6 + 14 + 12 + 12 + 13 + 15 + 16}{12} = 10$$
$$\bar{x}_{\cdot 3\cdot} = \frac{12 + 10 + 12 + 10 + 6 + 8 + 10 + 8 + 8 + 12 + 11 + 13}{12} = 10$$

The overall mean $\bar{x}$ is the mean of all the sample observations

$$\bar{x} = \frac{\sum_{i=1}^{a}\sum_{j=1}^{b}\sum_{k=1}^{c} x_{ijk}}{abc}$$

For the data in Table 14.13, the overall mean is $\bar{x} = 9$.

Table 14.14 shows the ANOVA table derived from the data in Table 14.13. To test the null hypothesis that the interaction effects are 0, we obtain the F statistic $F = 7.83$. Because the appropriate degrees of freedom are $\nu_1 = (a - 1)(b - 1) = 4$ and $\nu_2 = ab(c - 1) = 27$, the critical value $F_{.05,4,27} = 2.73$. Since the F statistic exceeds the critical value, we reject the null hypothesis that there are no interaction effects.

TABLE 14.14 ANOVA table for Example 14.11

Source of Variation	Degrees of Freedom	Sum of Squares	Mean Square	F
Vitamin	$a - 1 = 2$	SSA = 24	MSA = 12	MSA/MSE = 2.35
Medicine	$b - 1 = 2$	SSB = 72	MSB = 36	MSB/MSE = 7.05
Interaction	$(a - 1)(b - 1) = 4$	SSI = 160	MSI = 40	MSI/MSE = 7.83
Error	$ab(c - 1) = 27$	SSE = 138	MSE = 5.11	
Total	$abc - 1 = 35$	SST = 394		

To test the null hypothesis that the medicine effects are 0, we find the critical value of F having $\nu_1 = (b - 1) = 2$ and $\nu_2 = 27$ degrees of freedom, which is $F_{.05,2,27} = 3.35$. The appropriate F statistic is $F = 7.05$, which exceeds the critical value, so we reject the null hypothesis.

To test the null hypothesis that the vitamin effects are 0, we find the critical value of F having $\nu_1 = (a - 1) = 2$ and 27 degrees of freedom. The critical value is $F_{.05,2,27} = 3.35$ and the appropriate F statistic is $F = 2.35$. Because this value does not exceed the critical value, we do not reject the null hypothesis that the vitamin effects are 0. ■

Explanation of Results for Example 14.11

Do the results in Example 14.11 seem reasonable? Examine the data in Table 14.13. The sample mean for M_1 is 7, whereas the sample means for M_2 and M_3 are both 10. Based on the F statistic, we reject the hypothesis that the corresponding population means are equal. This result seems reasonable.

Can we explain why the analysis of variance test rejects the hypothesis that there are no interaction effects? Refer to Table 14.13 and observe how the mean length of stay varies when medicine M_1 is used with the three types of vitamin. The sample mean for combination M_1V_1 is 7; for the combination M_1V_2, 9; and for M_1V_3, 5. Thus, it appears that when used with medicine M_1, vitamin supplement V_3 reduces a patient's length of stay in the hospital relative to V_2 or V_1. Next, observe how the mean length of stay changes when the vitamin supplements are used with medicine M_2 rather than medicine M_1. Combination M_2V_1 has a sample mean of 6 days, M_2V_2 has a sample mean of 10 days, and M_2V_3 has a sample mean of 14 days. Thus, when used with medicine M_2, supplement V_1 reduces the patient's length of stay relative to V_2 and V_3. We see that the vitamins have a different effect when used with medicine M_1 than when used with medicine M_2. The apparent interaction effect shows that it is reasonable to reject the hypothesis of no interaction effects.

It is possible to show interaction effects graphically. Consider Figure 14.9, which is a plot of the cell means in Table 14.13 corresponding to each vitamin–medicine combination. For example, patients have a much shorter average length of stay when given the combination (M_2, V_1) than when given the combination (M_3, V_1). Thus, when vitamin V_1 is administered, medicine M_2 is more effective than medicine M_3. On the other hand, patients have a much shorter average length of stay when given the combination (M_3, V_3) than (M_2, V_3). Thus, when used with vitamin V_3, medicine M_3 is more effective than medicine M_2. The lines in Figure 14.9 connect the sample means associated

FIGURE 14.9
Plot showing interaction effects in Example 14.11.

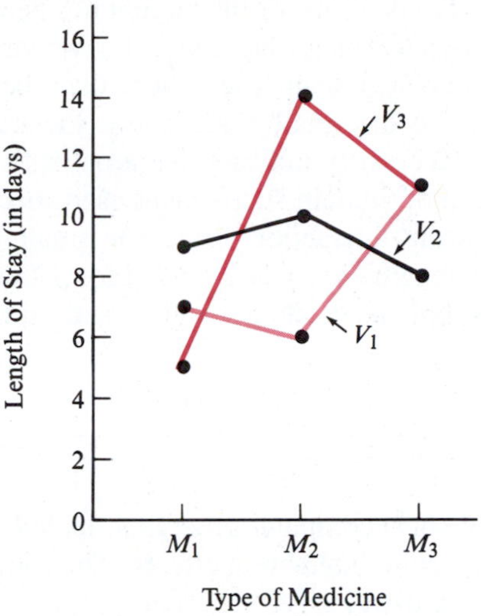

with different factor combinations. These lines may not be parallel because of random chance or because of interaction effects. Based on the two-way ANOVA test, we concluded that interaction effects are present.

If there had been no interaction between the two factors in Example 14.11, then a plot of the cell population means would have yielded a figure similar to that shown in Figure 14.10, where the three lines are parallel to one another. In Figure 14.10, the difference between using, say, Vitamin 1 and Vitamin 2 is shown to be the same for all three medicines; that is, one vitamin is always better than the other vitamin and by the same amount, regardless of which medicine is used. Similarly, the difference between using Vitamin 1 and Vitamin 3 is shown to be the same for all three medicines. The fact that the lines in Figure 14.9 are not parallel indicates that there is potential interaction between the independent variables.

FIGURE 14.10
Plot showing no interaction effects.

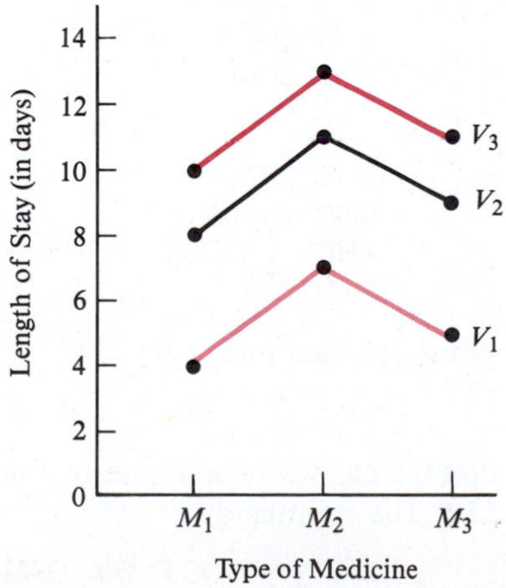

Once the presence of interaction has been established, it is not particularly useful to continue hypothesis testing, since the two variables *jointly* affect the dependent variable. If there is no significant interaction, then the two factors can be tested individually.

Note that the small F statistic associated with the vitamin supplement (Factor A) does not necessarily indicate that a patient's length of stay in the hospital is unaffected by the type of vitamin supplement used, because the vitamin supplement *is* included in the significant interaction term. The small F statistic associated with Factor A shows that when length of stay is averaged for patients given all types of medicine, the different vitamin supplements are not significantly different.

14.9 ▪ Computer Applications II

Many statistical computer programs, including SPSSX, can perform a two-way analysis of variance with interaction effects. The following example illustrates the use of SPSSX to solve a two-way ANOVA problem.

Example 14.12 **Two-Way ANOVA Using the SPSSX Program:** An accountant for a car rental agency is examining the cost per mile of operating three makes of cars, Car 1, Car 2, and Car 3, that are leased by the agency. Random samples of each brand of car are tested in the Northeast (Region 1), South (Region 2), Midwest (Region 3), and Far West (Region 4). The accountant wants to test the null hypothesis that the mean cost of operation is the same for the three makes of cars. In addition, the accountant wants to test that the mean cost of operation is the same in different regions of the country. Finally, the accountant wants to test that there are no interaction effects, which would indicate that the geographical region affects different cars in different ways. Use the data in Table 14.15 and a 5% level of significance and perform each of the tests.

Solution: The following instructions were used to obtain the appropriate SPSSX output:

```
TITLE 'TWO-WAY ANOVA'
DATA LIST FREE/CAR REGION COST
BEGIN DATA
1 1 33
1 2 34
1 3 32
1 4 25
1 1 28
   .
   .
   .
3 4 36
END DATA
ANOVA COST BY CAR(1,3) REGION(1,4)
FINISH
```

In the program, the data line

```
1 4 25
```

indicates that the car was Car 1, the region was Region 4 (Far West), and the cost per mile was 25¢. The command

```
ANOVA COST BY CAR(1,3) REGION(1,4)
```

TABLE 14.15
Cost of operating cars (in cents per mile) for Example 14.12

Car (Factor A)	Geographical Region (Factor B) 1	2	3	4
1	33	34	32	25
	28	36	31	23
	25	41	34	26
	30	36	28	27
	35	35	26	22
	33	29	29	30
	26	30	24	26
	28	32	24	29
	31	43	27	32
	24	43	29	31
2	31	33	32	35
	27	32	31	33
	27	31	37	36
	32	34	38	37
	32	31	36	32
	33	29	39	30
	36	30	34	36
	29	34	34	39
	32	33	37	34
	26	32	39	36
3	29	30	33	34
	25	32	34	33
	24	30	37	32
	35	34	34	37
	32	32	36	35
	31	29	35	30
	33	36	34	32
	29	34	33	39
	36	35	31	31
	36	32	39	36

requests a two-way analysis of variance. The dependent variable is COST, and there are two factors, CAR and REGION. CAR has 3 levels, REGION has 4 levels, and each combination of levels has 10 observations. Thus, we have $a = 3$, $b = 4$, and $c = 10$. The computer output is shown in Figure 14.11. In Figure 14.11, the *residual mean square* is another term for the *mean square error,* MSE.

The test for comparing the operating costs for each brand of car is

H_0: Mean operating costs are the same for all three cars

H_1: Mean operating costs differ for at least two cars

The appropriate test statistic is

$$F = \frac{\text{MS(Car)}}{\text{MS(Residual)}} = \frac{114.114}{10.376} = 10.99792$$

FIGURE 14.11 **SPSSX-generated output for Example 14.12.**

```
           * * *  A N A L Y S I S   O F   V A R I A N C E  * * *

                COST
          BY    CAR
                REGION

                                   SUM OF                 MEAN                      SIGNIF
SOURCE OF VARIATION                SQUARES      DF       SQUARE         F            OF F

MAIN EFFECTS                       399.719       5       79.944      7.704737       0.000
   CAR                             228.227       2      114.114      10.99792       0.000
   REGION                          171.088       3       57.029      5.496316       0.001

2-WAY INTERACTIONS                 558.806       6       93.134      8.976004       0.000
   CAR       REGION                558.806       6       93.134      8.976004       0.000

EXPLAINED                          958.525      11       87.139      8.398155       0.000

RESIDUAL                          1120.600     108       10.376

TOTAL                             2079.125     119       17.472

     120 CASES WERE PROCESSED.
       0 CASES (   0.0 PCT) WERE MISSING.
```

These values are shown in Figure 14.11. The numerator degrees of freedom is $(a - 1) = 2$, and the denominator degrees of freedom is $ab(c - 1) = 108$. Using $\alpha = .05$, the critical value of the test statistic is $F_{.05,2,108} = 19.49$. Since the observed F statistic does not exceed the critical value, we do not reject the null hypothesis that the three cars have equal mean operating costs.

The test for comparing the operating costs for each geographical region is

H_0: Mean operating costs are the same for all four geographical regions

H_1: Mean operating costs differ for at least two regions

The appropriate test statistic is

$$F = \frac{\text{MS(Region)}}{\text{MS(Residual)}} = \frac{57.029}{10.376} = 5.496316$$

These values are shown in Figure 14.11. The numerator degrees of freedom is $(b - 1) = 3$, and the denominator degrees of freedom is $ab(c - 1) = 108$. Using $\alpha = .05$, the critical value of the test statistic is $F_{.05,3,108} = 8.56$. Since the observed F statistic does not exceed the critical value, we do not reject the null hypothesis that the mean operating costs are the same in each geographical region.

The test for the presence of interaction effects is

H_0: All interaction effects between make of car and geographical region are 0

H_1: Not all interaction effects are 0

The appropriate test statistic is

$$F = \frac{\text{MS(Interaction)}}{\text{MS(Residual)}} = \frac{93.134}{10.376} = 8.976004$$

These values are shown in Figure 14.11. The numerator degrees of freedom is $(a - 1)(b - 1) = 6$, and the denominator degrees of freedom is $ab(c - 1) = 108$. Using

$\alpha = .05$, the critical value of the test statistic is $F_{.05,6,108} = 3.72$. Since the observed F statistic exceeds the critical value, we reject the null hypothesis that all interaction effects are 0. ■

Exercises for Section 14.9

1. The Wright Meatpacking Company is interested in how quickly livestock fatten when given various feeds. The company uses two types of feed F_1 and F_2 and two types of vitamin supplement V_1 and V_2. Twenty heifers similar in age and weight are chosen for an experiment to test the effectiveness of the feeds and vitamin supplements. Each combination F_iV_j is given to 5 heifers. The weight in pounds gained during the experiment are as follows:

F_1V_1	F_1V_2	F_2V_1	F_2V_2
240	200	310	300
280	210	280	250
210	260	260	260
310	240	270	240
250	230	290	250

Use a 5% level of significance and a model containing interaction effects.

a. Test the null hypothesis that the feeds are equally effective.

b. Test the null hypothesis that the vitamin supplements are equally effective.

c. Test the null hypothesis that there are no interaction effects.

2. A study was conducted to compare automobile gasoline mileage for three brands of gasoline and four makes of automobile. Five different cars of each make were driven using each brand of gasoline. The following data show the miles per gallon for the various gasoline-automobile combinations.

	Automobile			
Gasoline	1	2	3	4
1	22.1	24.3	25.2	24.0
	23.6	23.8	25.0	27.2
	21.2	23.3	26.7	28.2
	20.0	24.6	23.5	27.7
	21.1	25.2	24.0	29.1
2	24.2	25.1	25.2	26.8
	23.5	25.2	25.4	24.8
	25.0	25.7	24.3	26.9
	25.6	24.9	27.7	27.2
	24.6	26.3	26.5	27.5
3	24.3	25.0	25.3	27.2
	23.8	23.2	24.6	23.4
	25.6	24.8	23.2	24.2
	24.1	26.6	27.6	24.7
	25.7	26.1	25.3	26.0

a. Calculate the sample mean for each cell.
b. Calculate the sample mean for each brand of gasoline.
c. Calculate the sample mean for each make of automobile.
d. Denote brand of gasoline as Factor A and make of automobile as Factor B. Calculate SST, SSA, SSB, SSI, and SSE.
e. Calculate the mean squares MSA, MSB, and MSE.
f. Calculate the F statistic F = MSI/MSE and test that the interaction effects are 0 using $\alpha = .05$.

Chapter 14 Summary

One-way analysis of variance (ANOVA) is a method of testing the null hypothesis that the means of two or more normal populations are all equal. Alternatively, one-way ANOVA is used to test the null hypothesis that the mean of a *dependent variable* is unaffected by the value (or *level*) of an independent variable (or *factor*). The populations are assumed to have equal variances and independent random samples are obtained from each population.

The *total sum of squares* SST is calculated as

$$\text{SST} = \sum_{j=1}^{K} \sum_{i=1}^{n_j} (x_{ij} - \bar{x})^2$$

and measures the total amount of variation in the data. The *between group sum of squares* SSB measures the variation between different sample means and is calculated as

$$\text{SSB} = \sum_{j=1}^{K} n_j(\bar{x}_j - \bar{x})^2$$

The *sum of squares within* SSW, also called the *error sum of squares* SSE, measures the variation within the samples and is calculated as

$$\text{SSW} = \sum_{j=1}^{K} \sum_{i=1}^{n_j} (x_{ij} - \bar{x}_j)^2$$

$$= \sum_{j=1}^{K} (n_j - 1)s_j^2$$

Dividing each sum of squares by its corresponding degrees of freedom yields a corresponding *mean square:* MSB = SSB/$(K - 1)$ and MSW = SSW/$(n - K)$, or MSE = SSE/$(n - K)$.

To perform a one-way ANOVA test of the equality of the means of K normal populations, calculate the F *statistic*

$$F = \text{MSB/MSW}$$

and compare it with the critical value obtained from the F distribution having $\nu_1 = (K - 1)$ and $\nu_2 = (n - K)$ degrees of freedom. Large values of the F statistic lead to rejection of the null hypothesis.

The *Hartley test* is used to test the null hypothesis that the variances of K normal populations are equal. To perform the test, calculate the *H statistic*

$$H = \frac{\max(s_j^2)}{\min(s_j^2)}$$

and compare H with the critical value obtained from Table A.16 in the Appendix. Large values of the H statistic lead to rejection of the null hypothesis.

Multiple-comparison methods provide an alternative method of testing the equality of a set of three or more population means by testing the means two at a time. To perform the *Bonferroni test,* calculate the test statistic

$$t = \frac{\bar{x}_i - \bar{x}_j}{\sqrt{s_p^2(1/n_i + 1/n_j)}}$$

where s_p^2 is the pooled estimate of the variance

$$s_p^2 = \frac{\sum_{j=1}^{K}(n_j - 1)s_j^2}{(n - K)}$$

We reject H_0 if $t > t_{\alpha/2c,(n-K)}$ or if $t < -t_{\alpha/2c,(n-K)}$ where c denotes the number of comparisons being made.

In *two-way ANOVA,* we test the null hypothesis that the mean of a dependent variable is unaffected by the values of two explanatory variables or factors. The method of analysis differs depending on whether there is *one observation* per cell or *multiple observations* per cell. As in one-way ANOVA, the variation present in the sample data is measured by computing various sums of squares. When there is one observation per cell, the sums of squares are

$$\text{SST} = \sum_{i=1}^{a}\sum_{j=1}^{b}(x_{ij} - \bar{x})^2$$

$$\text{SSA} = b\sum_{i=1}^{a}(\bar{x}_{i\cdot} - \bar{x})^2$$

$$\text{SSB} = a\sum_{j=1}^{b}(\bar{x}_{\cdot j} - \bar{x})^2$$

$$\text{SSE} = \text{SST} - \text{SSA} - \text{SSB}$$

Dividing each sum of squares by its corresponding degrees of freedom yields a corresponding *mean square*

$$\text{MSA} = \text{SSA}/(a - 1)$$
$$\text{MSB} = \text{SSB}/(b - 1)$$
$$\text{MSE} = \text{SSE}/(n - 1)$$

To test that Factor A has no effect on the mean of the dependent variable, calculate the F statistic

$$F = \text{MSA}/\text{MSE}$$

and compare it with the critical value obtained from the F distribution having $\nu_1 = (a - 1)$ and $\nu_2 = (a - 1)(b - 1)$ degrees of freedom. To test that Factor B has no effect on the mean of the dependent variable, calculate the F statistic

$$F = \text{MSB}/\text{MSE}$$

and compare it with the critical value obtained from the F distribution having $\nu_1 = (b - 1)$ and $\nu_2 = (a - 1)(b - 1)$ degrees of freedom. Large values of the F statistic lead to rejection of the null hypothesis.

When there are multiple observations per cell, we can also test for the presence of *interaction effects* associated with particular combinations of values of the two independent variables. When there are multiple observations per cell, the total sum of squares SST can be partitioned into four components: a component due to the different levels of Factor A, a component due to the different levels of Factor B, a component due to the interaction between Factors A and B, and the error component.

There are three null hypotheses that can be tested: Factor A does not affect the dependent variable; Factor B does not affect the dependent variable; there is no Factor A–Factor B interaction effect. To perform the tests, we calculate the following sums of squares:

Source of Variation	Sums of Squares	Degrees of Freedom
Factor A	$\text{SSA} = bc \sum_{i=1}^{a} (\bar{x}_{i\cdot\cdot} - \bar{x})^2$	$a - 1$
Factor B	$\text{SSB} = ac \sum_{j=1}^{b} (\bar{x}_{\cdot j\cdot} - \bar{x})^2$	$b - 1$
Interaction	$\text{SSI} = \sum_{i=1}^{a} \sum_{j=1}^{b} (\bar{x}_{ij\cdot} - \bar{x}_{i\cdot\cdot} - \bar{x}_{\cdot j\cdot} + \bar{x})^2$	$(a - 1)(b - 1)$
Error	$\text{SSE} = \sum_{i=1}^{a} \sum_{j=1}^{b} \sum_{k=1}^{c} (x_{ijk} - \bar{x}_{ij\cdot})^2$	$ab(c - 1)$
Total	$\text{SST} = \sum_{i=1}^{a} \sum_{j=1}^{b} \sum_{k=1}^{c} (x_{ijk} - \bar{x})^2$	$abc - 1$

Dividing each sum of squares by its corresponding degrees of freedom yields the following mean squares:

$$\text{MSA} = \text{SSA}/(a - 1)$$
$$\text{MSB} = \text{SSB}/(b - 1)$$
$$\text{MSI} = \text{SSI}/(a - 1)(b - 1)$$
$$\text{MSE} = \text{SSE}/ab(c - 1)$$

To test the null hypothesis that Factor A has no effect, calculate the test statistic $F = \text{MSA}/\text{MSE}$ and reject H_0 if F exceeds the critical value obtained from the F distribution having $\nu_1 = (a - 1)$ and $\nu_2 = ab(c - 1)$ degrees of freedom. To test the null hypothesis that Factor B has no effect, use the test statistic $F = \text{MSB}/\text{MSE}$ and reject H_0 if F exceeds the critical value obtained from the F distribution having $\nu_1 =$

$(b - 1)$ and $\nu_2 = ab(c - 1)$ degrees of freedom. To test the null hypothesis that there are no interaction effects, use the test statistic $F = \text{MSI/MSE}$ and reject H_0 if F exceeds the critical value obtained from the F distribution having $\nu_1 = (a - 1)(b - 1)$ and $\nu_2 = ab(c - 1)$ degrees of freedom.

In this chapter we show how to perform one-way and two-way ANOVA, but more advanced analysis of variance techniques can be used with any number of explanatory variables or factors. Thus, we could examine how a dependent variable is affected by three or more different factors, rather than just two factors. In addition, ANOVA techniques exist for the case when there are unequal numbers of observations per cell.

Chapter 14 completes our discussion of classical hypothesis testing. ANOVA enables us to determine if the mean value of a dependent variable is affected by the values of one or more independent variables. In Chapter 15 we turn to the problem of testing and estimating functional relationships that may exist between two quantitative variables. This field of study is known as *regression and correlation analysis*.

Chapter 14 ▪ Supplementary Exercises

1. Suppose we measure the gasoline mileage in miles per gallon of three different makes of compact automobiles. Five cars of each make are sampled. All cars are driven over the same route using the same driver, fuel, and so forth. Thus all possible influences on mileage except for make of car are controlled as much as possible. Use a 5% level of significance to test if the three makes of cars get equal mileage on the average.

	Make of Car		
Observation	1	2	3
1	28	25	30
2	26	24	26
3	27	27	28
4	29	26	27
5	25	25	27

2. Suppose there are four classes in a statistics course. All use the same text and have the same exams, but each has a different teacher. Use a 1% level of significance to test whether the test scores of the students in the following table indicate that the teacher has an effect on a student's score:

	Teacher ($K = 4$)			
Student	1	2	3	4
1	8	9	8	9
2	6	4	10	8
3	4	7	8	9
4	5	8	6	7
5	7		6	10
6			5	7

3. Two different brands of golf balls are hit by a mechanical device, and the distance each ball travels is recorded. The experiment is performed 100 times and yields the following information: $\bar{x}_1 = 200$ yards, $\bar{x}_2 = 204$ yards, and SSE = 20,000.

a. Calculate SSB and SST.

b. Calculate MSB, MSE, and F.

c. Use a 5% level of significance and test whether the average distances of the balls are equal. Use the F test.

d. Perform the test in part (c) using the t test.

4. Over the years a controversy has developed over whether the resilience of baseballs used in the major leagues has changed over the years. Five balls that were made for use in each of the years 1960, 1965, 1970, and 1975 are randomly selected. Each ball is dropped onto a cement floor from a height of 30 feet, and the height of the ball's bounce in feet is recorded in the following table:

	Year			
Observation	1960	1965	1970	1975
1	9.2	9.3	8.8	9.0
2	9.0	9.1	8.9	8.8
3	9.3	9.3	8.7	9.3
4	8.9	9.0	9.2	8.8
5	8.8	9.1	9.0	8.9

Use a 5% level of significance to test if the resiliencies of the balls are equal.

5. Twenty babies are randomly selected for an experiment to determine if different brands of baby food affect a child's weight. The babies are separated into 5 groups, and each group is fed a different diet. The weight gained in pounds by each baby after being on the diet for four months is recorded in the following table:

	Type of Diet				
Baby	1	2	3	4	5
1	10	9	12	6	11
2	11	6	11	8	9
3	7	8	8	9	10
4	8	7	10	8	7

Use a 1% level of significance to test if the type of diet affects weight gain.

6. A plastics manufacturer tests the tensile strength of 3 different types of polyethylene material. A random sample of 5 products is taken for each material type. The data in pounds per square inch are as follows:

Product	Type 1	Type 2	Type 3
1	380	385	365
2	400	435	415
3	410	375	380
4	390	410	400
5	420	430	410

a. Present the relevant information in an ANOVA table.
b. Let $\alpha = .05$. Determine if the mean tensile strengths of the types of materials differ significantly.

7. Four packaging materials were tested for moisture retention by storing the same food product in each for three days and then determining the moisture loss. Each type of package was used to wrap 6 food samples. The moisture losses are given in the accompanying table.
a. Construct the ANOVA table.
b. Let $\alpha = .01$. Determine if the mean moisture losses differ significantly.

Material 1	Material 2	Material 3	Material 4
27	18	18	22
29	22	17	25
21	19	23	29
24	23	20	27
25	25	25	26
20	20	17	25

8. Individuals having Ph.D. degrees in economics tend to be employed by the government, universities, or large corporations. The following data show the annual incomes (in thousands of dollars) of a random sample of Ph.D. economists according to occupation:

Salary		
Government	University	Corporation
22	18	30
32	16	26
38	20	40
46	26	34
26	20	48
50		46
32		

a. Construct the ANOVA table.
b. Let $\alpha = .05$ and test whether mean salaries differ significantly.

9. In order to compare 3 brands of gasoline, 7 identical cars were driven under identical conditions using each brand of gasoline. The average miles per gallon achieved by each car for each gasoline brand is listed in the accompanying table. At the 1% level of significance, can we conclude that the brands are equally good?

Gasoline Mileage		
Gasoline A	Gasoline B	Gasoline C
16	19	23
18	22	24
17	23	22
20	20	23
19	22	25
20	21	20
18	23	22

10. The accompanying data show the ratio of gross profits to total sales for a random sample of firms classified by asset size. At the 5% level of significance, can we conclude that mean profit ratios are the same for different-sized firms?

Profit-to-Sales Ratio

Small Firms	Medium Firms	Large Firms
.10	.17	.22
.06	.16	.02
.22	.22	.08
.15	.06	.12
.19	.04	.14
.13	.08	.10

11. A police department wanted to compare 3 makes of cars before ordering an entire fleet. Each car was driven for 20,000 miles, and the cost of operation per mile was noted. Because purchase prices were equal, they were ignored. The accompanying data show the costs of operation per mile (in cents).

a. Construct an ANOVA table.

b. Let $\alpha = .01$. Can we conclude that mean operating costs differ?

Operating Costs

Make A	Make B	Make C
9.2	9.0	8.6
9.0	10.2	8.4
9.6	9.6	9.6
8.6	9.8	9.0
8.2	8.6	9.2
	11.2	
	10.4	

12. The manager of a Burger World store suspects that the average number of noontime customers may depend on the day of the week. The manager wants to know if the daily averages differ in order to determine the number of employees to use on any given day. The accompanying data show the number of customers at noon on randomly selected days. Let $\alpha = .05$ and test H_0: $\mu_1 = \mu_2 = \mu_3 = \mu_4 = \mu_5$.

Monday	Tuesday	Wednesday	Thursday	Friday
116	97	89	98	114
126	122	111	107	118
146	84	116	109	124
108	128	104	114	142
96	106	112	102	106
130	114	98	104	132

13. In a figure skating competition, there are 6 contestants, each of whom receives a score from 4 judges, who are from Russia, France, England, and Holland. The scores are shown in the accompanying table.

a. Let $\alpha = .05$ and test whether $\mu_1 = \mu_2 = \mu_3 = \mu_4$. (In this situation we assume that the 6 skaters represent a sample from a larger population of skaters.)

b. Let $\alpha = .10$ and test whether the variance for the Russian judge is the same as the variance for the French judge.

	Judge			
Skater	Russian	French	English	Dutch
1	5.2	5.1	5.4	5.2
2	5.4	5.3	5.4	5.4
3	5.9	5.7	5.8	5.8
4	4.8	5.1	5.0	5.2
5	5.1	5.0	4.9	4.9
6	5.3	5.5	5.6	5.2

14. Three different automatic printing machines are used to print the designs on cereal boxes. Observations were taken randomly to determine how many boxes were being printed per minute by each machine. Each machine was checked during 5 randomly selected minutes. Test the hypothesis that the mean outputs per minute for the machines are equal. Use $\alpha = .05$. The following data show the number of boxes printed by each machine during the randomly selected minutes:

	Machine		
Sample	1	2	3
1	64	68	70
2	62	66	72
3	65	67	66
4	67	69	72
5	66	67	68

15. The Carpenters Union has gathered data on the weekly wages earned by random samples of carpenters in 5 large cities. The relevant data are as follows:

	City				
	1	2	3	4	5
$\bar{x}_i$	\$227	\$240	\$236	\$225	\$232
n_i	26	26	30	35	28
s_i	23	28	21	25	26

Test the hypothesis that average weekly wages of carpenters are equal in the 5 cities. Use $\alpha = .01$.

a. Find the overall mean $\bar{x}$.

b. Find MSE.

c. Find MSB.
d. Find the F statistic.
e. Find the critical value of F from Table A.8 for $\alpha = .01$.
f. Test H_0: $\mu_1 = \mu_2 = \cdots = \mu_5$.

16. The Midwest Rent-a-Car Company owns 4 maintenance and repair facilities. All of Midwest's cars are sent to these shops when they need repairs. The director of maintenance thinks that the 4 facilities do not do an equally good job of repairing the cars, so he takes 20 identical cars and has his mechanics create identical mechanical problems in them all. Five different cars are sent to each of the 4 repair shops, and the repair times (in hours) are as follows:

	Repair Shop			
Sample	1	2	3	4
1	4.2	5.2	6.2	5.4
2	5.4	5.8	5.4	5.8
3	4.8	6.2	6.0	6.6
4	3.8	6.0	6.0	4.8
5	4.4	5.6	5.8	4.8

a. Calculate the sample means.
b. Calculate the overall mean.
c. Calculate the F statistic.
d. Test H_0: $\mu_1 = \mu_2 = \mu_3 = \mu_4$. Use $\alpha = .05$.

17. Mr. Donnelly owns an automobile franchise and employs 5 car salespersons. He wants to test whether the average profits per car sold are the same for all his salespeople. The data in the accompanying table show the gross profit (that is, the car's selling price minus its cost) obtained on each car sold last month. Each salesperson sold 15 cars.

	Salesperson				
i	A	B	C	D	E
1	160	140	220	180	250
2	220	200	300	170	260
3	190	150	280	200	250
4	230	170	260	190	200
5	280	180	220	220	150
6	310	210	210	240	180
7	180	100	200	180	240
8	270	220	190	170	170
9	160	170	180	160	180
10	190	170	200	150	200
11	220	160	230	180	170
12	240	150	250	180	200
13	200	150	240	190	250
14	190	140	220	170	230
15	200	160	200	200	250

a. Calculate $\bar{x}$ and s^2 for each salesperson.
b. Test for equality of variances using the Hartley test. Let $\alpha = .05$.
c. Use ANOVA and test for equality of means. Let $\alpha = .05$.

18. The daily outputs (in thousands) produced by 3 machines A, B, and C on 20 randomly selected days are as follows:

i	1	2	3	4	5	6	7	8	9	10	11	12	13	14	15	16	17	18	19	20
A	20	22	26	19	17	24	18	23	21	23	17	24	25	18	22	21	23	20	19	20
B	24	27	25	20	27	16	28	26	25	24	23	24	22	23	25	26	25	22	24	21
C	19	18	18	22	21	19	24	23	22	21	20	19	21	19	17	22	22	23	20	18

a. For each machine, calculate $\bar{x}_i$ and s_i^2.
b. Test the null hypothesis that the three population variances are equal using the Hartley test. Let $\alpha = .05$.

19. An advertising agency wants to examine the effects of three different methods of advertising a certain brand of detergent. The three advertising methods are as follows:

$$A_1 = \{\text{increased advertising on television}\}$$
$$A_2 = \{\text{increased advertising on radio and in the newspaper}\}$$
$$A_3 = \{\text{increased use of coupon discounts}\}$$

Each of these methods was used for one month in each of 4 cities. In each city the method used during any particular month was chosen randomly. Do the sales data in the following table (expressed in thousands of dollars) provide sufficient evidence to indicate a difference in the average effect of the 3 advertising techniques using a 5% level of significance?

	City			
	1	2	3	4
A_1	27	33	57	17
A_2	24	35	60	16
A_3	21	29	50	16

20. A trucking company wants to compare the costs of operation of 3 makes of trucks using 4 types of gasoline. The company purchased one truck of each type and tested each truck using 100 gallons of each brand of gasoline. The variable cost in cents per mile for operating each truck with each brand of gasoline is given in the following table:

	Truck		
Gasoline	1	2	3
1	33.2	35.2	34.8
2	35.7	37.1	35.2
3	31.6	33.3	32.8
4	30.8	30.9	32.4

a. Do the data provide sufficient evidence to indicate a difference in the average variable cost per mile of operation for the 3 trucks? Use a 5% level of significance.

b. Do the data provide sufficient evidence to indicate a difference in the average variable cost per mile of operation for the 4 types of gasoline? Use a 5% level of significance.

21. Theresa owns a clothing outlet store that sells jeans at discount prices. She buys large quantities of plain jeans and has her 3 employees, who operate 3 different brands of sewing machines, stitch a fancy design on the rear pockets of the jeans, which greatly increases their value. She wants to determine, on the average, whether the 3 operators turn out equal amounts of work per day and whether the 3 sewing machines are equally fast. Theresa has each operator use each machine for two hours on 5 randomly selected days and records the number of designs completed on each day (shown in the accompanying table).

a. Construct an ANOVA table that includes an interaction effect.
b. Let $\alpha = .05$. Can we reject the null hypothesis that the operators are equally good?
c. Let $\alpha = .05$. Can we reject the null hypothesis that the sewing machines are equally efficient?
d. Let $\alpha = .05$. Can we reject the null hypothesis that no interaction is present?

	Machine		
Operator	1	2	3
1	40	50	52
	42	56	58
	48	48	54
	40	44	50
	44	50	54
2	38	46	39
	36	40	43
	40	38	47
	34	44	41
	38	40	40
3	48	52	52
	47	54	54
	41	48	55
	45	47	49
	50	49	50

22. A college professor wants to determine the best way to present an important topic to his class. He has the following three choices: He can lecture (condition 1), he can lecture plus assign supplementary reading (condition 2), or he can show a film and assign the same supplementary reading as in condition 2 (condition 3). He decides to do an experiment to evaluate the three options. He solicits 27 volunteers from his class and randomly assigns 9 to each of the 3 conditions. The following scores (percentage correct) on an exam were obtained from these 27 students:

Condition 1	92	86	87	76	80	87	92	83	84
Condition 2	86	93	97	81	94	89	98	90	91
Condition 3	81	80	72	82	83	89	76	88	83

a. What is the overall null hypothesis?
b. What is the conclusion? Use $\alpha = .05$.

23. To test whether memory changes with age, a researcher conducts an experiment on 4 groups differing in age containing 6 subjects in each. Assume all individuals are in good health and the groups do not differ by IQ, education, or any other possible contaminating variable. Each subject is shown a series of nonsense syllables (like DUT or FAM) at a rate of one syllable every four seconds. The series are shown twice, and the subjects are asked to write down as many syllables as they can remember. The number of syllables remembered by each subject grouped by age is as follows:

Age (in years)			
30	40	50	60
14	12	17	13
13	15	14	10
15	16	14	7
17	11	9	8
12	12	13	6
10	18	15	9

Does age have an effect on memory? Use $\alpha = .05$.

References

FISHER, RONALD A. *The Design of Experiments.* 9th ed. New York: Hafner Press, 1971.

FISHER, RONALD A., and W. A. MACKENZIE. "Studies in Crop Variation." *Journal of Agricultural Science,* 1923, pp. 311–320.

NETER, JOHN, and WILLIAM WASSERMAN. *Applied Linear Statistical Models.* Homewood, Ill.: Irwin, 1974.

NIE, NORMAN E., C. HADLAI HULL, JEAN G. JENKINS, KARIN STEINBRENNER, and DALE H. BENT. *SPSS Statistical Package for the Social Sciences.* 2d ed. New York: McGraw-Hill, 1975.

NORUSIS, MARIJA J. *SPSSX Introductory Statistics Guide.* New York: McGraw-Hill, 1983.

———. *SPSSX Advanced Statistics Guide.* Chicago: SPSS, 1985.

———. *The SPSS Guide to Data Analysis.* Chicago: SPSS, 1986.

RYAN, THOMAS A., BRIAN L. JOINER, and BARBARA F. RYAN. *Minitab Reference Manual.* University Park, Penn.: Minitab Project, 1985.

———. *Minitab Handbook.* 2d ed. Boston: PWS-KENT, 1985.

SAS Introductory Guide. 3d ed. Cary, N.C.: SAS Institute, 1985.

SAS Procedures Guide for Personal Computers. Version 6 ed. Cary, N.C.: SAS Institute, 1986.

SAS Statistics Guide for Personal Computers. Version 6 ed. Cary, N.C.: SAS Institute, 1986.

SAS User's Guide: Basics. Version 5 ed. Cary, N.C.: SAS Institute, 1985.

SAS User's Guide: Statistics. Version 5 ed. Cary, N.C.: SAS Institute, 1985.

SCHEFFE, HENRY. *The Analysis of Variance.* New York: Wiley, 1959. A classic and fairly advanced book on the subject.

SPSSX User's Guide. Chicago: SPSS, 1983.

Chapter Fifteen
Regression and Correlation

15.1 ▪ Stochastic Relationships and Scatter Diagrams

In many instances the values taken by one variable Y are influenced by or related to the values taken by some other variable X, and we are interested in exploring the relationship between these two variables. If a relationship exists, we may be able to use values of X to estimate or predict values of Y.

For example, we may be interested in determining what relationship (if any) exists between a person's consumption expenditures (Y) and the person's annual income (X), the annual sales of a corporation (Y) and annual advertising expenditures (X), or the rate of inflation (Y) and the change in the money supply (X).

In each of the preceding examples, the variable Y represents the *dependent variable* and the variable X the *independent variable,* and we construct a mathematical model to describe the hypothesized relationship between Y and X. For example, we may think that there is an approximately linear relationship between a person's consumption (Y) and the person's income (X). To see if this hypothesis is true, it would be natural to obtain a sample of data and examine whether the observed data points lie close to a straight line.

Scatter Diagrams

When the hypothesized model contains only one independent variable (X), the appropriateness of some hypothesized mathematical model can be examined by plotting the observed data on a graph called a *scatter diagram.*

Definition: Scatter Diagram

Suppose we have a sample of n pairs of values (x_i, y_i). A **scatter diagram** is a graph showing the n sample observations $(x_1, y_1), (x_2, y_2), \ldots, (x_n, y_n)$.

On a scatter diagram, the dependent variable is always plotted on the vertical axis and the independent variable on the horizontal. A scatter diagram is useful for *revealing the form of the relationship* (if any) that exists between two variables. Various scatter diagrams are shown in Figure 15.1. The data in plots (b) and (d) can be described quite well by linear equations because the observed points cluster more or less around straight lines. The data in plot (a) are better described by an exponential, or quadratic, equation. No type of equation appears to describe the data in plot (c) well, and there does not appear to be any discernible relationship between the two variables. A scatter diagram can also be useful for *revealing the strength of the relationship* between two variables. A linear equation fits the data much better in plots (b) and (d) than in plot (c), for example.

FIGURE 15.1
Scatter diagrams.

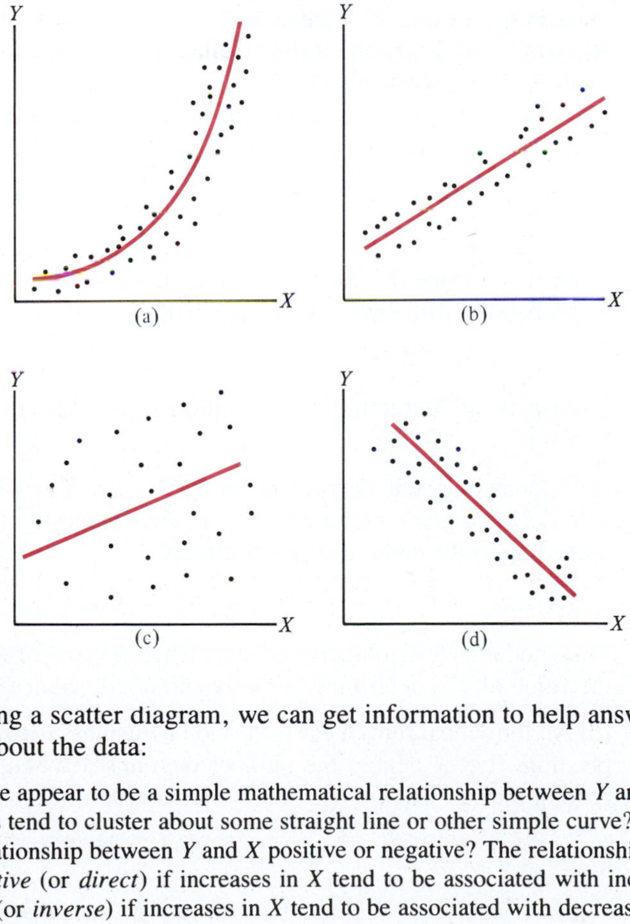

By inspecting a scatter diagram, we can get information to help answer four important questions about the data:

1. Does there appear to be a simple mathematical relationship between Y and X? That is, do the points tend to cluster about some straight line or other simple curve?
2. Is the relationship between Y and X positive or negative? The relationship between Y and X is *positive* (or *direct*) if increases in X tend to be associated with increases in Y, and *negative* (or *inverse*) if increases in X tend to be associated with decreases in Y.

3. Is the relationship between Y and X approximately linear or nonlinear? A relationship between Y and X is approximately linear if the plotted points tend to lie close to some straight line. The relationship is approximately nonlinear if the plotted points tend to lie close to some nonlinear function.
4. How strong is the relationship between Y and X? The relationship between Y and X is relatively strong if the plotted points tend to lie close to some line or simple curve. In general, the closer the points lie to the line or curve, the stronger the relationship between Y and X.

Besides linear relationships, various other functions are useful in fitting models to data, including polynomial functions and logarithmic functions. If the scatter diagram indicates that a straight line describes the relationship between Y and X well, we assume that Y and X are approximately related to one another according to the equation

$$Y = \beta_0 + \beta_1 X$$

where the coefficients β_0 and β_1 are unknown numbers. This is the equation of a straight line where β_0 is the *Y-intercept* of the line and β_1 is the *slope* of the line. The coefficient β_1 measures the change in Y associated with a 1 unit increase in X. The coefficient β_0 measures the value of Y when $X = 0$. Our task is to estimate the unknown coefficients β_0 and β_1 and determine if the resultant straight line provides a good explanation of the relationship between Y and X.

In a *deterministic relationship,* for any given value of X, the value of the variable Y is a constant whose value depends on X and can be determined with certainty.

Definition: Deterministic Relationships and Stochastic Relationships

A relation $Y = f(X)$ is **deterministic** if each value of X is paired with one and only one value of Y, and **stochastic** if each value of X is associated with a whole probability distribution of values of Y.

Example 15.1

Examples of Deterministic Relationships: The following relationships are deterministic:

(a) A company sells computers for \$960 each. Let X denote the number of computers sold during a given month, and Y the total monthly revenue. Then Y and X are related according to the deterministic relationship

$$Y = 960X$$

This model is deterministic because, when a value of X is substituted into the equation, the value of Y is determined exactly and no allowance need be made for error.

(b) An individual rents a car for use on a business trip. The rental fee is \$100 plus \$0.20 per mile. Let X denote the number of miles driven and let Y denote the total cost of renting the car. Then Y and X are related according to the deterministic relationship

$$Y = 100 + 0.20X$$

■

In a *stochastic relationship,* for any given value of X, the variable Y is a random variable whose value depends on X but cannot be predicted with certainty. Nevertheless, knowledge of X helps predict the value of Y. A stochastic model contains a probabilistic, or random, component that is added to the deterministic portion of the model to account for the random or unexplained error of prediction.

Example 15.2

Examples of Stochastic Relationships: The following relationships are stochastic:

(a) Let X denote annual income for a household, and let Y denote the household's annual expenditures on recreation and entertainment. For a given value $X = x$, the value of Y cannot be predicted exactly, since other factors influence a family's expenditures on recreation. In general, however, as X increases, Y also increases; thus, knowledge of X is helpful in predicting Y. A probabilistic model relating expenditures for the ith household Y_i to income of the ith household $X = x_i$ is given by the equation

$$Y_i = \beta_0 + \beta_1 x_i + e_i$$

where e_i is assumed to be a random error variable with expected value equal to 0 and variance equal to σ_e^2. As an example, we might have the hypothesis that expenditures on recreation and entertainment are related to household income according to the equation

$$Y_i = 250 + 0.1x_i + e_i$$

where e_i is the random factor that makes expenditures greater or less than $(250 + 0.1x_i)$. Thus, for a given value $X = x_i$, there is an entire probability distribution of possible values of Y.

(b) Let the random variable Y_i denote the income that will be received by the main performer at the ith rock concert, and let $X = x_i$ denote the observed number of spectators at the ith concert. Suppose the performer will receive \$50,000 plus 20% of all concession sales. Assume the typical spectator spends about \$3.00 on concessions, plus or minus some random amount. Thus, the performer would receive approximately \$0.60 per spectator in income from concessions. Thus, total income from the ith concert is a random variable (Y_i) that is related to the number of spectators (x_i) according to the stochastic relation

$$Y_i = 50{,}000 + 0.60x_i + e_i$$

For a given value of $X = x_i$, total revenue cannot be predicted exactly, and there is an entire distribution of possible values of Y associated with each value of X. ■

There are numerous situations in economics and business where a dependent variable Y is stochastically related to some independent variable X. Our goal is to express Y as some function of X and possibly a random error variable. Some possibilities are

$$Y_i = \beta_0 + \beta_1 x_i + e_i \quad \text{and} \quad Y_i = \beta_0 + \beta_1 x_i + \beta_2 x_i^2 + e_i$$

There are numerous other possibilities, including models that contain other explanatory variables besides the variable X. These models will be discussed in Chapters 16, 17, and 18.

In this chapter, we will restrict ourselves to the model

$$Y_i = \beta_0 + \beta_1 x_i + e_i$$

where β_0 and β_1 are unknown coefficients that have to be estimated.

Goals of Regression Analysis

The technique of estimating stochastic relationships and analyzing the estimators is called **regression analysis**. In regression analysis, we estimate a *mathematical model* that explains the relationship between a dependent variable Y and one or more independent variables. The mathematical model consists of a hypothesized equation and some assumptions that together provide a simplified or idealized representation of behavior observed in the real world. In constructing the model two problems must be addressed: (1) In many applications in business and economics, the precise mathematical form of any underlying relationship will not be known, and (2) in many cases no deterministic relationship holds *exactly* in the real world. Thus, in general, our mathematical models will only be approximations of real-world behavior.

In this chapter, we discuss the *simple linear regression model,* where we explain the value of the dependent variable Y based on the known value of an explanatory variable X. When there are two or more explanatory variables in the equation to explain Y, the mathematical model is called a *multiple regression model.*

Reasons for Using Regression Analysis

There are at least four reasons for using regression analysis:

1. Regression analysis enables us to *quantify* a theory about how the variables Y and X are related.
2. Regression analysis enables us to *test* a theory about the relationship of a variable Y to a variable X.
3. Regression analysis enables us to *measure the strength of the relationship* between Y and X.
4. Regression analysis enables us to *predict,* or forecast, the value of Y, given the value of some independent variable X.

The following discussion provides some examples of how regression analysis can be used to quantify theories, test theories, measure the strength of relationships, and forecast values of Y.

1. *Quantifying a theory:* According to economic theory, expenditures on entertainment and recreation tend to increase as income increases. An economist would want to know *by how much* expenditures would increase if income increased by, say, $10,000. If we estimate a stochastic relationship between expenditures and income, we have quantified the theory.

2. *Testing theories:* It is hypothesized that annual sales of a corporation are positively related to advertising expenditures. Is this theory true? By gathering data and constructing a model showing how sales and advertising expenditures are related, we can eventually test the hypothesis that advertising expenditures influence sales.

3. *Measuring the strength of relationships:* The annual incomes earned by adult males tend to increase with years of education, but many other variables also influence an individual's income. How important is education as a determinant of income? Is income closely related to years of education? Regression analysis enables us to estimate the relationship between income and education and also to measure the strength of the relationship.

4. *Forecasting:* An executive thinks that annual sales are influenced by the dollar amount of advertising expenditures. Regression analysis can be used to estimate an equation explaining the relationship between annual sales and advertising expenditures. Once the relationship between advertising expenditures and sales has been estimated, the equation can be used to forecast annual sales for any given level of advertising expenditures.

Example 15.3

A Simple Linear Regression Model: A large corporation is planning to open a nationwide chain of sporting goods stores. The corporation hires a marketing agency to perform a market analysis to help determine optimal locations for the stores. One of the factors that the marketing agency is asked to study is the relationship between the explanatory variable family income (X) and the dependent variable household expenditure on recreation (Y).

Suppose the marketing agency contacted a random sample of 20 families and obtained the data in Table 15.1 on weekly expenditures on recreation and on weekly income. (In actual practice, hundreds of families might be contacted.) The observations $(x_1, y_1), (x_2, y_2), \ldots, (x_{20}, y_{20})$ are plotted in the scatter diagram in Figure 15.2. (On the scatter diagram, a straight line has been drawn that is the *estimated* line that best describes the sample data. This idea will be described in more detail in Section 15.2.)

We would expect expenditures on recreation to depend on income and perhaps on other factors as well. Specifically, we would expect families with relatively high incomes to have relatively high expenditures on recreation, and families with relatively low incomes to have relatively low expenditures on recreation. The scatter diagram shows that this pattern seems to hold for the sample of 20 data points.

TABLE 15.1
Data for Example 15.3

Family	Weekly Expenditure on Recreation Y	Weekly Income X
1	$90	$900
2	60	800
3	45	600
4	70	650
5	30	300
6	40	350
7	50	400
8	55	700
9	85	950
10	75	700
11	90	800
12	70	750
13	60	500
14	40	300
15	25	250
16	65	700
17	60	600
18	50	450
19	35	250
20	35	200

FIGURE 15.2
Scatter diagram for Example 15.3.

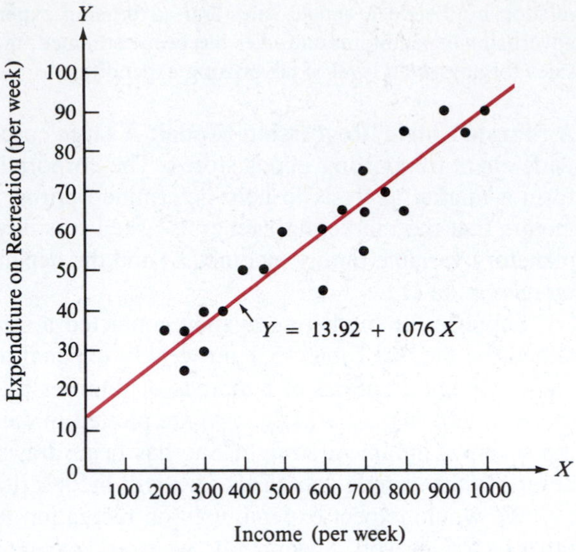

The relationship between expenditures on recreation and family income in Example 15.3 is stochastic rather than deterministic. Thus, it is not reasonable to associate just a single level of expenditure on recreation with a particular level of family income. Rather, it is more realistic to think of a whole distribution of possible levels of expenditures on recreation for each possible level of family income.

Exercises for Section 15.1

1. Let X denote the number of steaks sold at a restaurant, and let Y denote the total cost (in dollars) of buying and preparing those steaks. Suppose that total cost is a linear function of X and is given by the equation

$$Y = 2 + 4X$$

a. If $x_1 = 2$, find y_1.
b. If $x_2 = 4$, find y_2.
c. Plot the two points (x_1, y_1) and (x_2, y_2).
d. Graph the line $Y = 2 + 4X$.

2. Let $Y = 12 - 3X$.
a. If $x_1 = 1$, find y_1.
b. If $x_2 = 3$, find y_2.

c. Plot the points (x_1, y_1) and (x_2, y_2).
d. Graph the line $Y = 12 - 3X$.

3. Graph each of the following equations:
a. $Y = 4 + 2X$ b. $Y = 4 - 2X$ c. $Y = 2 + 2X$ d. $Y = 2 + 3X$

4. Suppose that a company installs and repairs copying machines. The company studied the relationship between repair costs for a sample of six machines and the number of pages copied by each machine. The goal is to identify machines whose costs are too high relative to their copying volumes. The repair costs in dollars and the pages copied in thousands for the six machines are as follows:

Machine	1	2	3	4	5	6
Repair cost	85	120	70	165	125	90
Pages copied	900	1350	550	850	1500	800

a. Which variable is the dependent variable and which is the independent variable? Why?
b. Make a scatter diagram of these observations.
c. Does the maintenance cost of any machine seem out of line?

15.2 ▪ The Simple Linear Regression Model

In the simple linear regression model, it is assumed that for every value of X, there is an entire distribution of values of Y. We use the symbol $E(Y_i|X = x_i)$, or more simply $E(Y_i|x_i)$, to denote the conditional expected value of the random variable Y_i when the variable X takes the specific value x_i.

In the simple linear regression model, the null hypothesis states that the relationship between the expected value of Y_i and the value x_i can be expressed as

$$E(Y_i|x_i) = \beta_0 + \beta_1 x_i$$

where β_0 and β_1 are unknown parameters that have to be estimated. This means that the mean value of Y_i for a given value x_i lies on a straight line whose intercept is β_0 and whose slope is β_1. See Figure 15.3.

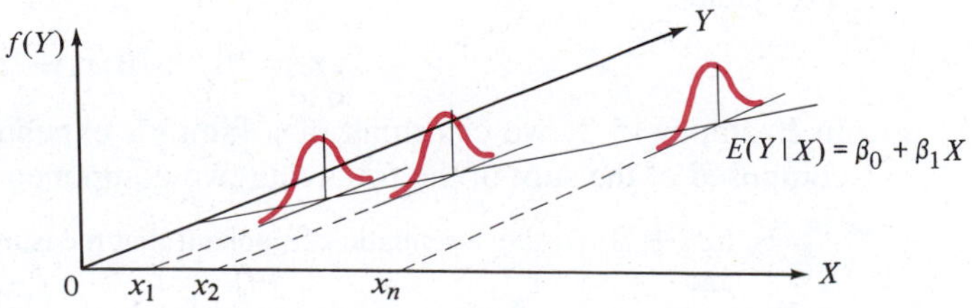

FIGURE 15.3
The population regression line

Definition: Population Regression Line

The equation

$$E(Y_i|X = x_i) = \beta_0 + \beta_1 x_i$$

is called the **population regression line**. The equation states that for a given value $X = x_i$, the expected value of Y_i is $(\beta_0 + \beta_1 x_i)$.

The model states that the *mean values of the subpopulations of Y* associated with different values of X lie on a straight line. In Figure 15.3, there is a whole population of values of Y associated with each value of X, and the mean of each distribution falls on the population regression line. Although the distributions have different means, it is assumed that the distributions have the same variance σ^2.

Because the population parameters β_0 and β_1 are unknown, the equation of the population regression line is unknown and has to be estimated using a sample of observations (x_i, y_i). Once we have estimated the parameters β_0 and β_1, we obtain an estimated regression line, which is called the *sample regression line*.

Because the observed sample points (x_i, y_i) do not lie exactly on the population regression line, the observed value y_i will differ from the expected value $E(Y_i|x_i)$. The quantity

$$e_i = Y_i - E(Y_i|X = x_i) = Y_i - (\beta_0 + \beta_1 x_i)$$

measures the amount by which the random value Y_i differs from the expected value of Y_i, given that $X = x_i$. The quantity e_i is called a *random error term*.

Definition: Random Error Term e_i

In the population regression model, the **random error term**, denoted e_i, is the difference between the random variable Y_i and the mean value of Y_i given that $X = x_i$. That is,

$$\begin{aligned} e_i &= Y_i - E(Y_i|X = x_i) \\ &= Y_i - (\beta_0 + \beta_1 x_i) \end{aligned}$$

The random error e_i is also called a **random disturbance term**.

Rearranging the equation defining the random error term (see the accompanying box) yields

$$Y_i = \beta_0 + \beta_1 x_i + e_i$$

In Example 15.3, we can think of a family's expenditures on recreation (Y_i) as being composed of the sum of the following two components:

1. $(\beta_0 + \beta_1 x_i)$, the systematic component that measures the mean value of Y_i given $X = x_i$, and
2. e_i, which represents a deviation from the systematic component.

The component e_i reflects the multitude of factors other than income that influence expenditures on recreation, such as the size of the family, the ages of the family members, and so forth.

Given the sample of observations (x_i, y_i) for $i = 1, 2, \ldots, n$, we want to estimate the parameters β_0 and β_1.

Definition: Sample Regression Line

The estimated equation

$$\hat{y}_i = b_0 + b_1 x_i$$

is called the **sample regression line**. The value b_0 is the sample estimate of the population parameter β_0, and the value b_1 is the sample estimate of the population parameter β_1. The value $\hat{y}_i$ is called the *fitted value* of Y_i or the *predicted value* of Y_i when $X = x_i$.

In Section 15.3, we show the formulas that are used to determine the sample estimates b_0 and b_1 for a given sample of data. Using the data in Table 15.1, we obtained the sample regression line

$$\hat{y}_i = 13.92 + 0.076x_i$$

This line is plotted on the scatter diagram in Figure 15.2. Note that although the observations (x_i, y_i) do not lie exactly on the line, they do lie relatively close to it. This leads us to believe that the regression model describes fairly accurately the relationship between expenditures on recreation and family income.

Definition: Residuals

For the given value $X = x_i$, the difference between the actual value y_i and the fitted value $\hat{y}_i$ is denoted $\hat{e}_i$. The values $\hat{e}_1, \hat{e}_2, \ldots, \hat{e}_n$ are called the **residuals** and are obtained using the equation

$$\begin{aligned}\hat{e}_i &= y_i - \hat{y}_i \\ &= y_i - (b_0 + b_1 x_i)\end{aligned}$$

In Figure 15.2, the distances between the sample points and the estimated line are the residuals. Figure 15.4 shows the relationship between y_i, $\hat{y}_i$, and $\hat{e}_i$. As can be seen, the residual will be positive if the sample observation (x_i, y_i) lies above the sample regression line and negative if it lies below. If (x_i, y_i) lies exactly on the line, the residual will be 0 and the predicted value $\hat{y}_i$ and the actual value y_i will be exactly the same. That is, the residual $\hat{e}_i$ will be 0 if $y_i = \hat{y}_i$. If each of the residuals is close to 0, then each predicted value $\hat{y}_i$ will be close to the actual value y_i, and each of the observed points (x_i, y_i) will lie close to the estimated line $\hat{y}_i = b_0 + b_1 x_i$.

An analysis of the residuals can tell us a lot about whether the estimated model is satisfactory. A good model will have small residuals with no regular patterns evident in a graph of the residuals versus the dependent or independent variable. Residual analysis is discussed in detail in Chapter 18.

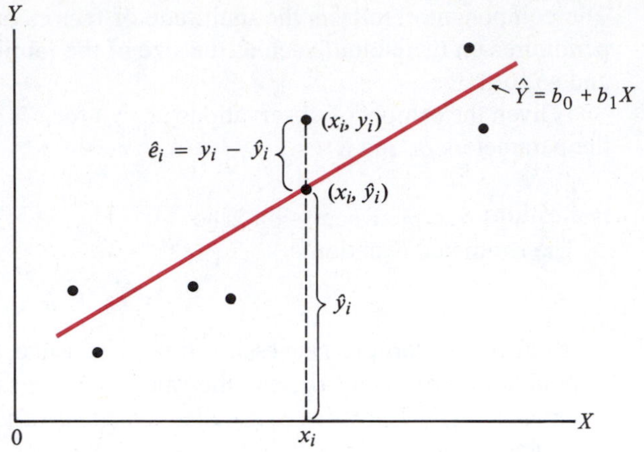

FIGURE 15.4
Scatter diagram showing the relationship between y_i, $\hat{y}_i$, and the residual $\hat{e}_i$.

Basic Assumptions of the Simple Linear Regression Model

The basic assumptions of the simple linear regression model are summarized in the accompanying box.

Basic Assumptions of the Simple Linear Regression Model

In the simple linear regression model, it is assumed that the dependent variable Y_i is related to the observed value of the independent variable $X = x_i$ according to the equation

$$Y_i = \beta_0 + \beta_1 x_i + e_i \qquad i = 1, 2, \ldots, n$$

where the random error terms e_i are assumed to have the following properties, which are called the *basic assumptions of the simple linear regression model*:

1. *Normality*: For any value x_i, the error term has a normal distribution.
2. *Zero mean*: For any value x_i, $E(e_i) = 0$.
3. *Homoscedasticity*: The variance of e_i, denoted σ_e^2, is the same for all values of X.
4. *No serial correlation*: The error terms are independent of one another.
5. *Independence of e_i and x_i*: The error terms e_i are independent of the values of the independent variable X.

The first three assumptions state that for each value x_i, the error term e_i is a normally distributed random variable with 0 mean and variance σ_e^2.

The assumption concerning homoscedasticity means that every disturbance has the same variance. This assumption rules out, for example, the possibility that the dispersion of the disturbances is greater for high values of X than for low values. This means that the variance for each subpopulation of values of Y is the same regardless of the value of X. When the assumption of equal variances is violated, some of the optimal properties of our estimators will no longer hold. For example, our estimates of variances become biased and our tests of hypotheses lose their validity. This will be discussed in more detail in Chapter 18.

The assumption of independence of the error terms means that a disturbance in one time period is unrelated to disturbances at other time periods. A violation of this assumption indicates that something systematic has been omitted from the model, in which case estimates of variances will be biased and tests of hypotheses invalid.

The assumptions underlying the regression model are used in making inferences about the values of the three unknown regression parameters β_0, β_1, and the disturbance variance σ_e^2.

Figure 15.5 shows a population regression line and an estimated sample regression line. The lines differ because, in general, b_0 and b_1 will differ from the true values of β_0 and β_1.

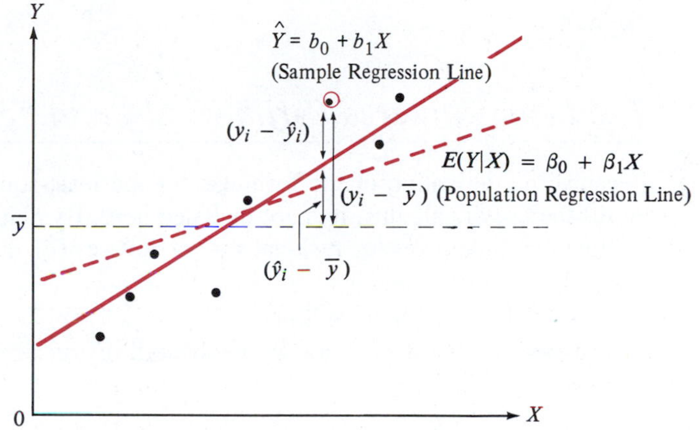

FIGURE 15.5
A population and sample regression line.

Exercises for Section 15.2

1. Explain the meaning of the population regression equation.
2. Explain the meaning of the sample regression equation.
3. Explain why the population and sample regression equations differ.
4. Explain why the magnitude of the residuals can be used as an indicator of whether the model is satisfactory.
5. Suppose a sample regression equation is

$$\hat{y}_i = 10 + 3.5x_i$$

a. The first observation is ($x_1 = 10$, $y_1 = 50$). Find the first residual.
b. The second observation is ($x_2 = 14$, $y_2 = 58$). Find the second residual.

15.3 ▪ Method of Least Squares

In this section, we show how to use the sample observations (x_i, y_i) to estimate the population parameters β_0 and β_1. Because the sample observations do not fall exactly on a straight line, many different lines can be drawn through the plotted data points. The problem is to select the line that, in some sense, best describes the data.

To avoid individual judgment in constructing the sample regression line, we need a definition of what is the best-fitting line. It might seem reasonable to define the best line as the line that produces the smallest residuals $\hat{e}_i$ on the average. The problem with this method is that some of the residuals are positive and some are negative. As a result, the sum of the residuals can be 0 even though none of the individual residuals are close to 0. To avoid this problem, we define the best line as the line for which the sum of the squared residuals is the smallest. This procedure is called the **method of least squares**.

The method of least squares produces a line that minimizes the sum of the squared vertical distances from the observed data points to the line. Any other line has a larger sum. In Figure 15.2, the least-squares line has been superimposed on the scatter diagram.

The Least-Squares Estimates b_0 and b_1

Because the derivation of the formulas for the least-squares coefficients b_0 and b_1 requires the use of calculus, it is not included here. By definition, the least-squares line is the line that minimizes the residual sum of squares ($\hat{e}_1^2 + \hat{e}_2^2 + \cdots + \hat{e}_n^2$).

Definition: Residual Sum of Squares

The **residual sum of squares**, denoted SSE (an acronym for "sum of squared errors"), is given by

$$\text{SSE} = \sum_{i=1}^{n} \hat{e}_i^2 = \sum_{i=1}^{n} (y_i - \hat{y}_i)^2 = \sum_{i=1}^{n} (y_i - b_0 - b_1 x_i)^2$$

This is algebraically equal to

$$\text{SSE} = \sum_{i=1}^{n} y_i^2 - b_0 \sum_{i=1}^{n} y_i - b_1 \sum_{i=1}^{n} x_i y_i$$

Given the sample points (x_i, y_i), the least-squares estimates of the population coefficients β_0 and β_1 are the values b_0 and b_1 that minimize SSE, which are given in the accompanying box.

Formula for the Slope of the Sample Regression Line

Either of the following two formulas can be used to obtain the value of b_1, the **slope** of the sample regression line:

$$b_1 = \frac{\sum_{i=1}^{n} x_i y_i - n\overline{xy}}{\sum_{i=1}^{n} x_i^2 - n\overline{x}^2}$$

or

$$b_1 = \frac{n \sum_{i=1}^{n} x_i y_i - \left(\sum_{i=1}^{n} x_i\right)\left(\sum_{i=1}^{n} y_i\right)}{n \sum_{i=1}^{n} x_i^2 - \left(\sum_{i=1}^{n} x_i\right)^2}$$

The advantage of the second formula is that it avoids the potential round-off error that might result from calculating $\bar{x}$ and $\bar{y}$.

When calculating and reporting the estimated coefficients, it is important to maintain as many significant digits as possible. Rounding off the coefficient early on in an analysis can lead to substantial errors later on.

Formula for the Intercept of the Sample Regression Line

The value of b_0, the **intercept** of the sample regression line, is

$$b_0 = \bar{y} - b_1\bar{x}$$

where b_1 is the slope of the sample regression line.

Residuals Sum to Zero

For the sample regression line, the residuals will sum to 0. That is,

$$\Sigma\, \hat{e}_i = 0$$

The proof is as follows. The sum of the residuals is

$$\begin{aligned}\Sigma\, \hat{e}_i &= \Sigma\, y_i - \Sigma\, \hat{y}_i \\ &= \Sigma\, y_i - \Sigma(b_0 + b_1 x_i) \\ &= \Sigma\, y_i - nb_0 - b_1\, \Sigma\, x_i\end{aligned}$$

If we divide both sides of this equation by n, we obtain

$$(\Sigma\, \hat{e}_i)/n = \bar{y} - b_0 - b_1\bar{x}$$

Replacing b_0 by its value $(\bar{y} - b_1\bar{x})$, we obtain

$$(\Sigma\, \hat{e}_i)/n = 0$$

which proves that $\Sigma\, \hat{e}_i = 0$.

Because the residuals sum to 0, we can check our estimation results. If the residuals do not sum to 0, then we know that we have made an error in calculating our estimates. Many computer packages print out the sum of the residuals. Occasionally the sum will be slightly different from 0 in the fourth or fifth decimal place. This small discrepancy can usually be attributed to round-off error.

The arithmetic calculations involved in obtaining all the appropriate estimates and test statistics associated with the simple linear regression model become very tedious as the number of observations increases. In addition, when there is more than one independent variable in the model, the computational burden increases tremendously. Fortunately, many computer programs exist that make it very easy to obtain the appropriate estimates and test statistics without doing any arithmetic computations.

In this book, whenever any arithmetic computations are required to illustrate some point, the number of observations will be kept small in order to keep the number of computations to a minimum. The reader should note, however, that it is not unusual to estimate actual regression models in which there are hundreds or even thousands of sample observations.

Example 15.4

A Linear Regression Model: A stockbroker thinks that the selling prices of individual stocks are approximately linearly related to the annual dividends paid by the stocks. The data for a random sample of 10 stocks are shown in Table 15.2 and are plotted in Figure 15.6. Calculate the sample regression line and then find the predicted value of Y given that $X = 10$.

TABLE 15.2 **Data for Example 15.4**

Stock i	Annual Dividend (in dollars) x_i	Price (in dollars) y_i	x_iy_i	x_i^2	y_i^2
1	13	115	1,495	169	13,225
2	4	45	180	16	2,025
3	12	100	1,200	144	10,000
4	5	50	250	25	2,500
5	6	55	330	36	3,025
6	8	85	680	64	7,225
7	3	40	120	9	1,600
8	4	50	200	16	2,500
9	5	45	225	25	2,025
10	7	70	490	49	4,900
	67	655	5,170	553	49,025

Solution: To find the estimates b_0 and b_1, we need the sums $\Sigma\, x_i$, $\Sigma\, y_i$, $\Sigma\, x_iy_i$, and $\Sigma\, x_i^2$, which are calculated in Table 15.2. The sum $\Sigma\, y_i^2$ is calculated for later use. From the table, the sums are $\Sigma\, x_i = 67$, $\Sigma\, y_i = 655$, $\Sigma\, x_iy_i = 5170$, $\Sigma\, x_i^2 = 533$, and $\Sigma\, y_i^2 = 49{,}025$.

The sample means are $\bar{x} = 6.7$ and $\bar{y} = 65.5$. The slope estimate is

$$b_1 = \frac{\Sigma\, x_iy_i - n\bar{x}\bar{y}}{\Sigma\, x_i^2 - n\bar{x}^2}$$

$$= \frac{5170 - 10(6.7)(65.5)}{553 - 10(6.7)(6.7)}$$

$$= 7.5072$$

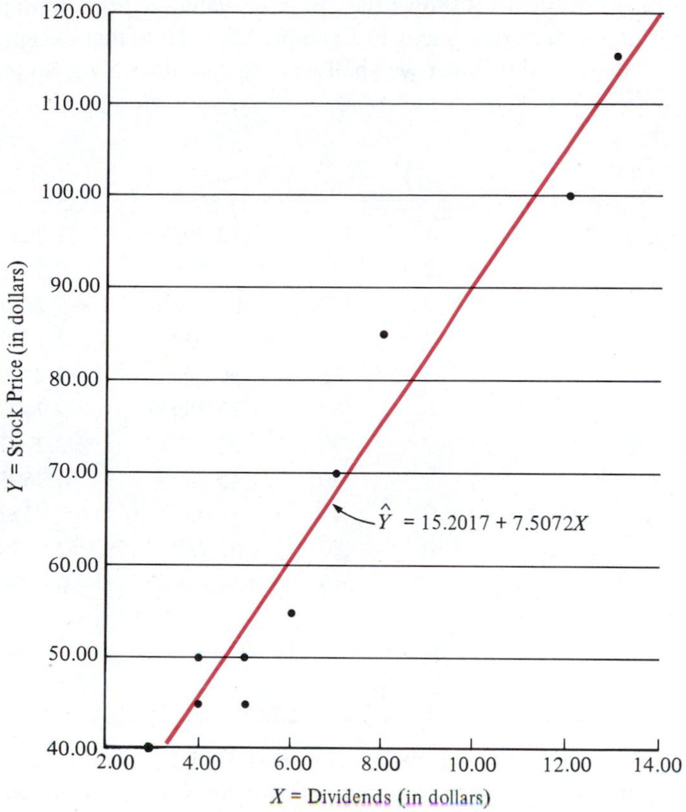

FIGURE 15.6
Scatter diagram of data in Table 15.2.

and the intercept is

$$\begin{aligned} b_0 &= \bar{y} - b_1\bar{x} \\ &= 65.5 - (7.5072)(6.7) \\ &= 15.2017 \end{aligned}$$

The sample regression equation is thus

$$\hat{y}_i = 15.2017 + 7.5072x_i$$

This equation can be used to predict the price of a stock based on its annual dividend. For example, suppose a stock's dividend is \$13. The predicted selling price of this stock would be

$$\hat{y} = 15.2017 + 7.5072(13) = 112.80$$

To show how to calculate a residual, let us calculate the first residual $\hat{e}_1$. The first stock paid a dividend of $x_1 = \$13$, and the actual selling price was $y_1 = \$115$. Since the predicted price of a stock that pays a \$13 dividend is \$112.80, the first residual is

$$\hat{e}_1 = y_1 - \hat{y}_1 = 115.00 - 112.80 = 2.20$$

The sample data and the sample regression line are shown in Figure 15.6. ■

Table 15.3 shows the observed values y_i, the predicted values $\hat{y}_i$, and the residuals $\hat{e}_i$ for the stock prices in Example 15.4. Note that except for round-off error, the residuals sum to 0. Later we shall want to calculate $\Sigma\, \hat{e}_i^2$, so the values $\hat{e}_i^2$ are also shown.

TABLE 15.3
Observed values, predicted values, and residuals for Example 15.4

i	y_i	$\hat{y}_i$	$\hat{e}_i$	$\hat{e}_i^2$
1	115	112.7953	2.2047	4.8607
2	45	45.2305	−0.2305	.0531
3	100	105.2881	−5.2881	27.9640
4	50	52.7377	−2.7377	7.4950
5	55	60.2449	−5.2449	27.5090
6	85	75.2593	9.7407	94.8812
7	40	37.7233	2.2767	5.1834
8	50	45.2305	4.7695	22.7481
9	45	52.7377	−7.7377	59.8720
10	70	67.7521	2.2479	5.0531
	655	654.9994	0.0006	255.6196

Estimation of σ_e^2

The simple linear regression model contains three unknown parameters, β_0, β_1, and σ_e^2. We still need to obtain an estimate for σ_e^2. To do so, we utilize the sum of squared errors SSE. The following formula shows how to calculate an unbiased estimate of the population variance σ_e^2, which is denoted s_e^2:

Formula for Unbiased Estimate of σ_e^2 in the Simple Linear Regression Model

$$s_e^2 = \text{SSE}/(n - 2)$$

In this formula, the denominator $(n - 2)$ is the degrees of freedom of SSE, where n is the sample size and 2 represents the number of coefficients to be estimated in the regression line, namely β_0 and β_1.

Degrees of Freedom for Multiple Regression Model

In the multiple regression model, which includes several explanatory variables, the degrees of freedom of SSE is n minus the number of coefficients to be estimated in the regression line.

For example, in the regression model

$$E(Y_i|x_i) = \beta_0 + \beta_1 x_i$$

SSE has $(n - 2)$ degrees of freedom because there are two coefficients to be estimated. In the regression model

$$Y_i = \beta_0 + \beta_1 x_{i1} + \beta_2 x_{i2} + e_i$$

SSE has $(n - 3)$ degrees of freedom because there are 3 coefficients to be estimated, β_0, β_1, and β_2. In the *multiple regression model*

$$Y_i = \beta_0 + \beta_1 x_{i1} + \beta_2 x_{i2} + \cdots + \beta_K x_{iK} + e_i$$

SSE has $[n - (K + 1)]$ degrees of freedom because there are $(K + 1)$ coefficients to be estimated, $\beta_0, \beta_1, \ldots, \beta_K$.

Standard Error of the Regression

The square root of σ_e^2 is the standard deviation σ_e and represents the standard deviation of the subpopulation of Y's associated with a given value $X = x$. This standard deviation measures the amount of variation, or scatter, about the population regression line. The smaller the value of σ_e, the more concentrated are the values of Y about the population regression line and the closer the points (x_i, y_i) lie to it. The sample statistic used to estimate σ_e is denoted s_e and is called the *estimated standard error of the regression*.

Definition: Estimated Standard Error of the Regression

For the simple linear regression model, the **estimated standard error of the regression** is defined as

$$s_e = \sqrt{\frac{\Sigma(y_i - \hat{y}_i)^2}{n - 2}} = \sqrt{\frac{\Sigma\, \hat{e}_i^2}{n - 2}} = \sqrt{\frac{\text{SSE}}{n - 2}}$$

When performing calculations by hand, the following expression can be used to calculate s_e:

Formula for s_e

$$s_e = \sqrt{\frac{\Sigma\, y_i^2 - b_0\, \Sigma\, y_i - b_1\, \Sigma\, x_i y_i}{n - 2}}$$

Example 15.5

Calculation of s_e: Calculate the estimated standard error of the regression s_e for Example 15.4.

Solution: From Table 15.3 we obtain

$$\text{SSE} = \Sigma\, \hat{e}_i^2 = 255.6196$$

Alternatively, we can obtain SSE from the formula

$$\begin{aligned} \text{SSE} &= \Sigma\, y_i^2 - b_0 \,\Sigma\, y_i - b_1 \,\Sigma\, x_i y_i \\ &= 49025 - (15.2017)(655) - (7.5072)(5170) \\ &= 255.663 \end{aligned}$$

(The slight difference in the two values of SSE is due to round-off error.)

An unbiased estimate of σ_e^2 is given by

$$s_e^2 = \frac{\text{SSE}}{n-2} = \frac{255.6196}{8} = 31.952$$

and the estimated standard error of the regression is

$$s_e = 5.653$$

This means that the subpopulation of stock prices associated with a given dividend $X = x_i$ has an estimated standard deviation of \$5.65. ■

Rounding Inaccuracies

Whenever you use a hand calculator to estimate a regression equation, you should carry as many significant digits as possible. For example, the estimate b_0 depends on $\bar{y}$, $\bar{x}$, and b_1. If any of these three quantities have been rounded off, then the estimate b_0 will be affected. Similarly, because all the residuals $\hat{e}_i$ depend on b_0 and b_1, rounding b_0 or b_1 will affect all the residuals. This, in turn, will affect the calculation of SSE and s_e.

Exercises for Section 15.3

1. Let x_i denote the percentage change in advertising expenditures for a firm during the ith sales period, and let y_i denote the eventual percentage change in sales revenue during the next period. The data are as follows:

x_i	8	10	7	6	9	5	6	7	5	6
y_i	6	9	5	5	10	8	7	9	7	8

a. Plot the data on a scatter diagram.
b. Find $\Sigma\, x_i$, $\Sigma\, y_i$, $\Sigma\, x_i y_i$, and $\Sigma\, x_i^2$.
c. Find $\bar{x}$ and $\bar{y}$.
d. Find b_1.
e. Find b_0.
f. Graph the sample regression line $\hat{y}_i = b_0 + b_1 x_i$.
g. If $X = 11$, predict Y.
h. Find the residuals $\hat{e}_i$.

2. Determine if the unemployment rate for nonwhites is linearly related to the unemployment rate for whites. Use the following data for the years 1977 to 1987 from the *Economic Report of the President*:

Year	Nonwhite Unemployment Rate	White Unemployment Rate
1977	14.0	6.2
1978	12.8	5.2
1979	12.3	5.1
1980	14.3	6.3
1981	15.6	6.7
1982	18.9	8.6
1983	19.5	8.4
1984	15.9	6.5
1985	15.1	6.2
1986	14.5	6.0
1987	13.0	5.3

a. Plot the data on a scatter diagram.
b. Find Σx_i, Σy_i, $\Sigma x_i y_i$, and Σx_i^2.
c. Find $\bar{x}$ and $\bar{y}$.
d. Find b_1.
e. Find b_0.
f. Graph the sample regression line $\hat{y}_i = b_0 + b_1 x_i$.
g. If $X = 11$, predict Y.
h. Find the residuals $\hat{e}_i$.

3. For a certain type of automobile, yearly repair costs in dollars (Y) are approximately linearly related to the age in years (X) of the car. The following data show these data for 10 cars:

Repair Costs Y	Age X
80	2
99	3
79	1
138	7
170	10
140	8
114	4
83	1
94	2
110	5

a. Plot the data on a scatter diagram.
b. Determine the linear regression of Y on X and graph it.
c. Estimate the repair costs of a 6-year-old car and a 3-year-old car.

4. The selling price of a used car is inversely (or negatively) related to the age of the car. That is, as the age increases, the selling price tends to decrease. The following data show data for 10 cars of a certain make and model:

Selling Price (in dollars) Y	Age (in years) X
980	5
1760	3
1100	5
600	8
2100	2
1600	3
1400	4
710	7
800	6
1800	3

a. Plot the data.
b. Find the equation of the sample regression line and graph it.
c. Estimate the selling price of a 4-year-old car.

5. A utility company believes that (except for July and August, when air conditioners are used) the per customer usage of electricity in kilowatt-hours per month is inversely (or negatively) related to the average monthly temperature. The following data show the average monthly temperature in degrees Fahrenheit (computed as the average temperature at noon during the month) and the per customer usage of electricity for a northeastern city for a sample of 10 months:

Electricity Usage Y	Average Monthly Temperature X
1000	18
420	50
400	55
705	30
550	45
850	25
1020	17
670	35
610	38
560	42

a. Plot the data.
b. Find the equation of the regression line and graph it.
c. Estimate per customer usage of electricity during a month when the average temperature is 40 degrees.

15.4 ▪ Explanatory Power of a Linear Regression Equation

After we have estimated the sample regression line, we want to determine if the line provides a good fit and we want to measure the goodness of fit. The underlying population regression model states that the random variable Y_i is related to x_i by the equation

$$Y_i = \beta_0 + \beta_1 x_i + e_i$$

According to this model, Y varies for two reasons. One source of variability in Y values is due to variation in the X values. This variability can be explained by the regression model. The other source of variability in Y values is due to the random error e. This variability is unexplained by the regression model.

The ith residual $\hat{e}_i$ is defined by the equation

$$\hat{e}_i = y_i - \hat{y}_i$$

We can rearrange this equation to obtain

$$y_i = \hat{y}_i + \hat{e}_i$$

After subtracting the sample mean $\bar{y}$ from both sides of this equation, we obtain

$$(y_i - \bar{y}) = (\hat{y}_i - \bar{y}_i) + \hat{e}_i$$

Squaring all these deviations and summing them over the index i, we obtain

$$\Sigma(y_i - \bar{y})^2 = \Sigma(\hat{y}_i - \bar{y}_i)^2 + \Sigma\, \hat{e}_i^2 + 2\, \Sigma(\hat{y}_i - \bar{y})\hat{e}_i$$

It can be shown that the last sum on the right is 0, provided the regression line contains the constant b_0. Thus, we obtain

$$\Sigma(y_i - \bar{y})^2 = \Sigma(\hat{y}_i - \bar{y})^2 + \Sigma\, \hat{e}_i^2$$

These three sums of squares are denoted SST, SSR, and SSE, respectively. Thus, we obtain

$$\text{SST} = \text{SSR} + \text{SSE}$$

where SST is a measure of the total variation in the dependent variable Y, SSR is a measure of the total variation in the fitted values $\hat{y}_i$, and SSE measures the variation in Y that is unexplained by the model.

Sum of Squares Decomposition

The equation

$$\sum_{i=1}^{n} (y_i - \bar{y})^2 = \sum_{i=1}^{n} (\hat{y}_i - \bar{y})^2 + \sum_{i=1}^{n} \hat{e}_i^2$$

can be expressed as

Total variation = Explained variation + Unexplained variation

or

$$\text{SST} = \text{SSR} + \text{SSE}$$

where

Total sum of squares: $\text{SST} = \sum_{i=1}^{n} (y_i - \bar{y})^2$

Regression sum of squares: $\text{SSR} = \sum_{i=1}^{n} (\hat{y}_i - \bar{y})^2$

Sum of squared errors: $\text{SSE} = \sum_{i=1}^{n} \hat{e}_i^2$

Because SST, SSR, and SSE are all sums of squares, each sum must be nonnegative. It follows that SST $\geqslant$ SSR and SST $\geqslant$ SSE.

The equation

$$\text{SST} = \text{SSR} + \text{SSE}$$

has an important interpretation. For a given value of SST, the smaller the value of SSE, the smaller the deviations of the observed values of Y from the sample regression line. Thus, the smaller the value of SSE, the better the sample regression line fits the data.

To measure how well a sample regression line fits the data, we divide the total variation in the dependent variable (SST) into two components: (1) the variation in Y that can be explained by the sample regression line (SSR), and (2) the variation in Y that cannot be explained by the sample regression line (SSE).

Coefficient of Determination R^2

The equation

$$\text{SST} = \text{SSR} + \text{SSE}$$

can be expressed as

$$\text{SSR} = \text{SST} - \text{SSE}$$

If we divide both sides of this equation by SST, we obtain

$$\frac{\text{SSR}}{\text{SST}} = 1 - \frac{\text{SSE}}{\text{SST}}$$

This gives us the coefficient of determination R^2, described in the accompanying box.

Definition: Coefficient of Determination R^2

The ratio SSR/SST, denoted by the symbol R^2, is called the **coefficient of determination** and is equal to the following:

$$R^2 = \frac{\text{SSR}}{\text{SST}} = 1 - \frac{\text{SSE}}{\text{SST}}$$

SSR measures the variation in Y that is explained by the regression equation, while SST measures the total variation of Y in the sample. Thus, the ratio SSR/SST measures the *proportion* of the variation in Y that is explained by the regression equation. Because SST $\geqslant$ SSR, it follows that

$$0 \leqslant R^2 \leqslant 1$$

The coefficient of determination R^2 provides a measure of the relative amount of variation in Y explained by the regression line. The higher the value of R^2, the greater the explanatory power of the regression equation. If SSE is small relative to SST, then R^2 will be close to 1, and the regression equation explains most of the variation in Y. If every observation falls exactly on the sample regression line, then each residual will be 0. In this case, SSE = 0 and $R^2 = 1$, and we have a perfect fit.

On the other hand, if SSE/SST is close to 1, then the residuals account for a large part of the variation in Y and R^2 will be close to 0. When R^2 is close to 0, the regression line does not explain the dependent variable Y well. In the extreme case, SSE = SST and SSR = 0. When SSR = 0, every predicted value $\hat{y}_i$ is equal to $\bar{y}$ and there is no variation in the predicted values. That is, when SSR = 0, the predicted values do not change as X changes. Thus, $R^2 = 0$ (or $R^2 \approx 0$) indicates that the independent variable X does not influence the dependent variable.

The use of the symbol R^2 is based on the fact that in the simple linear regression model, R^2 equals the square of the sample correlation coefficient between Y and X, which is denoted by the symbol R. The correlation coefficient R is discussed in Section 15.9.

An alternative formula for R^2 is shown in the accompanying box.

Alternative Formula for R^2

The sample variances of X and Y are

$$s_X^2 = \frac{\Sigma(x_i - \bar{x})^2}{n - 1} = \frac{\Sigma\, x_i^2 - n\bar{x}^2}{n - 1}$$

and

$$s_Y^2 = \frac{\Sigma(y_i - \bar{y})^2}{n - 1} = \frac{\Sigma\, y_i^2 - n\bar{y}^2}{n - 1}$$

Then

$$R^2 = b_1^2 \frac{s_X^2}{s_Y^2}$$

The sample variances are positive values, so $R^2 = 0$ if and only if $b_1 = 0$. If $b_1 = 0$, then the regression line is a horizontal line and the predicted values of Y do not change for different values of X.

Example 15.6 **Calculating the Coefficient of Determination:** In Example 15.4, we obtained the following sample regression equation relating fitted stock prices ($\hat{y}_i$) to cash dividends (x_i):

$$\hat{y}_i = 15.2017 + 7.5072x_i$$

In Example 15.5, we obtained all the residuals and SSE. Calculate R^2 for this model.

Solution: Using the data from Tables 15.2 and 15.3, we obtain

$$\begin{aligned} SST &= \Sigma(y_i - \bar{y})^2 = \Sigma y_i^2 - n\bar{y}^2 \\ &= 49{,}025 - 10(65.5)^2 \\ &= 6122.5 \end{aligned}$$

From Table 15.3 we obtain SSE = 255.6196. Finally, we obtain

$$\begin{aligned} R^2 &= 1 - \frac{SSE}{SST} \\ &= 1 - \frac{255.6196}{6122.5} \\ &= .9582 \end{aligned}$$

Alternatively, we could calculate

$$\begin{aligned} s_X^2 &= \frac{\Sigma x_i^2 - n\bar{x}^2}{n - 1} \\ &= \frac{533 - 10(6.7)^2}{9} = 11.567 \end{aligned}$$

and

$$s_Y^2 = \frac{\Sigma y_i^2 - n\bar{y}^2}{n - 1} = \frac{49{,}025 - 10(65.5)^2}{9} = 680.278$$

We can then calculate R^2 using the formula

$$\begin{aligned} R^2 &= b_1^2\left(\frac{s_X^2}{s_Y^2}\right) \\ &= (7.5072)^2\left(\frac{11.567}{680.278}\right) \\ &= .9582 \end{aligned}$$

The R^2 value indicates that, in the sample, dividends explain more than 95% of the total variation in stock prices. Figure 15.6 shows that most of the sample observations lie very close to the sample regression line. ■

Exercises for Section 15.4

1. Use the following data:

X	8	10	7	6	9	8	4	5	2	2
Y	6	9	5	5	10	9	5	6	1	2

a. Estimate the sample regression line.

c. Find SSE.
d. Find R^2 using $R^2 = 1 - (\text{SSE/SST})$.
e. Find R^2 using $R^2 = b_1^2 s_X^2 / s_Y^2$.

2. In a certain industry, costs are believed to be approximately linearly related to output. The following data show the cost of production (in thousands of dollars) and the number of units produced for several firms in the industry:

Cost Y	Units Produced X
140	40
158	50
150	45
195	80
215	100
212	90
180	75
165	60

a. Plot the data.
b. Estimate the regression line of Y on X.
c. Find R^2 and s_e.
d. Predict Y if $X = 85$.

3. The following data were obtained from a random-number table:

Y	66	9	5	35	21	28	36	71	51
X	39	42	54	66	18	25	72	85	57

Since the numbers are random, there is no reason to believe that Y is linearly related to X. Thus, b_1 should be close to 0, and R^2 should be small.
a. Plot the data and estimate the regression line.
b. Find R^2 and s_e.

4. Does a high value of R^2 imply that two variables are causally related? Explain.

15.5 ▪ *Estimating Variances in the Regression Model*

The estimators b_0 and b_1 are random variables whose values change from sample to sample. Thus, b_0 and b_1 have sampling distributions. Their variances are denoted $\sigma_{b_0}^2$ and $\sigma_{b_1}^2$. In general, these variances are unknown and must be estimated. Our estimates of the true variances are denoted $s_{b_0}^2$ and $s_{b_1}^2$. Similarly, the symbols σ_{b_0} and σ_{b_1} denote the true standard deviations of b_0 and b_1, and s_{b_0} and s_{b_1} represent the estimated standard deviations of b_0 and b_1.

If the basic assumptions of the simple linear regression model hold, then the variances of b_0 and b_1 are given by the following formulas:

Formulas for the True Variances of b_0 and b_1

$$\sigma_{b_0}^2 = \frac{\sigma_e^2 \sum_{i=1}^{n} x_i^2}{n\left(\sum_{i=1}^{n} x_i^2 - n\bar{x}^2\right)}$$

and

$$\sigma_{b_1}^2 = \frac{\sigma_e^2}{\sum_{i=1}^{n} x_i^2 - n\bar{x}^2} = \frac{\sigma_e^2}{\sum_{i=1}^{n}(x_i - \bar{x})^2}$$

The variances of b_0 and b_1 depend on σ_e^2, the variance of the random terms. The value σ_e^2 will generally be unknown and will have to be estimated. This implies that the variances of b_0 and b_1 also have to be estimated. To estimate them, we replace σ_e^2 in the preceding equations by its unbiased estimate s_e^2. To obtain an unbiased estimate of the variance of b_1, we use the following formula:

Unbiased Estimate of the Variance of b_1

$$s_{b_1}^2 = \frac{s_e^2}{\sum_{i=1}^{n} x_i^2 - n\bar{x}^2} = \frac{s_e^2}{\sum_{i=1}^{n}(x_i - \bar{x})^2}$$

Definition: Estimated Standard Error of b_1

The estimated standard deviation of b_1, called the **estimated standard error of b_1**, is denoted s_{b_1} and is calculated as follows:

$$s_{b_1} = \frac{s_e}{\sqrt{\sum x_i^2 - n\bar{x}^2}} = \frac{s_e}{\sqrt{\sum(x_i - \bar{x})^2}}$$

The estimated standard error of b_1 is used in testing hypotheses about the value of the population parameter β_1 and in constructing confidence intervals for the value of β_1. Observe that s_{b_1} decreases as the sum $\Sigma(x_i - \bar{x})^2$ increases. That is, as the amount of variation in the X's increases, our estimate of the slope of the regression line becomes more precise.

In a similar fashion, s_{b_0} is called the *estimated standard error of* b_0 and is defined in the accompanying box.

Definition: Estimated Standard Error of b_0

The estimated standard deviation of b_0, called the **estimated standard error of b_0**, is denoted s_{b_0} and calculated as follows:

$$s_{b_0} = \frac{s_e\sqrt{\Sigma\, x_i^2}}{\sqrt{n(\Sigma\, x_i^2 - n\bar{x}^2)}} = \frac{s_e\sqrt{\Sigma\, x_i^2}}{\sqrt{n\,\Sigma(x_i - \bar{x})^2}}$$

Example 15.7

Estimating the Standard Errors of the Estimated Coefficients: Using the data in Table 15.4 on average weekly expenditures (in dollars) and average weekly after-tax income (in dollars), estimate the coefficients β_0 and β_1 in the model

$$E(Y_i|x_i) = \beta_0 + \beta_1 x_i$$

Also calculate R^2 and the estimated standard errors of the estimated coefficients. The data are graphed in Figure 15.7.

TABLE 15.4 Data for Example 15.7

Income (in dollars) x_i	Expenditures (in dollars) y_i	$x_i y_i$	x_i^2	y_i^2
400	350	140,000	160,000	122,500
300	250	75,000	90,000	62,500
350	325	113,750	122,500	105,625
400	370	148,000	160,000	136,900
200	180	36,000	40,000	32,400
300	270	81,000	90,000	72,900
375	330	123,750	140,625	108,900
380	350	133,000	144,400	122,500
325	300	97,000	105,625	90,000
400	360	144,000	160,000	129,600
3,430	3,085	1,092,000	1,213,150	983,825

Solution: From the data in Table 15.4, we obtain $\bar{x} = 3430/10 = 343$; $\bar{y} = 3085/10 = 308.5$. Therefore,

$$b_1 = \frac{\sum_{i=1}^{10} x_i y_i - 10\bar{x}\bar{y}}{\sum_{i=1}^{10} x_i^2 - 10\bar{x}^2}$$

$$= \frac{33,845}{36,660} = 0.923213$$

$$b_0 = \bar{y} - b_1\bar{x} = -8.16217$$

FIGURE 15.7
Scatter diagram of data in Table 15.4.

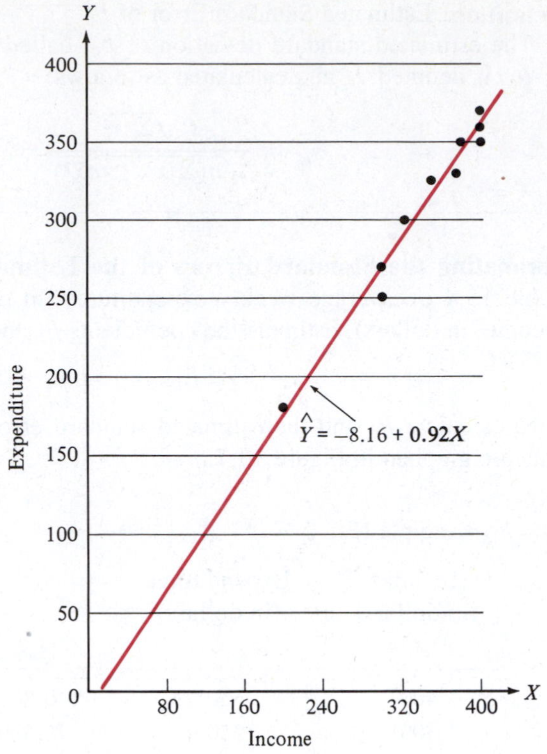

Thus, we obtain the sample regression equation

$$\hat{y}_i = -8.16217 + 0.923213x_i$$

Next, we obtain

$$\text{SST} = \sum_{i=1}^{10}(y_i - \bar{y})^2 = \sum_{i=1}^{10} y_i^2 - 10\bar{y}^2 = 32{,}102.50$$

$$\text{SSE} = \Sigma\, y_i^2 - b_0\, \Sigma\, y_i - b_1\, \Sigma\, x_i y_i = 856.367$$

$$s_e^2 = \frac{\text{SSE}}{n-2} = 107.046, \quad s_e = 10.346$$

$$R^2 = 1 - \frac{\text{SSE}}{\text{SST}} = 0.9733$$

$$s_{b_0}^2 = 354.236, \quad s_{b_0} = 18.8211$$

$$s_{b_1}^2 = 0.0029, \quad s_{b_1} = 0.054$$

To evaluate the results, it is useful to note the following facts:

1. R^2 is close to 1. This indicates that, in the sample, the variable income explains almost all the variation in expenditures. Thus, the linear equation provides a very good fit to the data.

2. The estimated standard error of the regression is $s_e = 10.346$. This means that the estimated standard deviation of the subpopulation of Y's associated with a given value of X is 10.346.

For a variable with a normal distribution, we should expect approximately 68% of the observations to lie within 1 standard deviation of the mean and about 95% of the observations to lie within 2 standard deviations of the mean. Thus we would expect Y to lie within 10.346 units of the regression line about 68% of the time and within 20.693 units of the line 95% of the time.

3. The coefficient $b_1 = 0.923213$ indicates that every \$1.00 increase in income tends to be associated with about a \$0.92 increase in expenditure. The estimated standard error of b_1 is $s_{b_1} = \$0.054$. ■

Exercises for Section 15.5

1. A government agency is involved in an urban renewal project designed to make the poor and middle-class families intermingle in many areas of the city. A study was undertaken to determine what relationship, if any, exists between housing values and family income. Let y_i denote the value of the ith individual's home in thousands of dollars, and let x_i denote the annual income of the ith individual in thousands of dollars. The data are as follows:

Y	22	32	28	40	30	60	55
X	10	14	12	15	14	23	20

Our model is

$$E(Y_i|x_i) = \beta_0 + \beta_1 x_i$$

a. Estimate β_0, β_1, and σ_e^2.
b. Calculate SST, SSE, and SSR.
c. Estimate the population variances $\sigma_{b_0}^2$ and $\sigma_{b_1}^2$.
d. Calculate R^2 and s_e.

2. The managers of the Ajax Corporation want to determine if profits are linearly related to sales revenue. Let y_i denote profits (in millions of dollars) at the Ajax Corporation in year i, and let x_i denote sales (in millions) in year i. The data are as follows:

Y	1	4	7	2	5	4	9	8
X	8	12	33	10	22	16	45	38

Use the model

$$E(Y_i|x_i) = \beta_0 + \beta_1 x_i$$

a. Estimate β_0, β_1, and σ_e^2.
b. Calculate SST, SSE, and SSR.
c. Calculate R^2 and s_e.
d. Estimate the variances of b_0 and b_1.
e. Discuss possible violations of the classical assumptions.

3. Several economists are helping to prepare the annual state budget. Because they know that the press will sharply criticize the amount of money budgeted for state employees' wages, the economists have designed a study to show the relationship between wages and the number of state employees. Let x_i denote the number in thousands of state government employees in year i, and y_i denote their total wages in millions of dollars for year i. The data are as follows:

Year	Total Wages Y	Number of Employees X
1950	20	2.0
1955	27	2.5
1960	33	3.0
1965	42	3.7
1970	50	4.3
1975	70	5.5
1980	78	5.8
1985	83	6.3

a. Estimate the population regression equation.
b. Find R^2 and s_e.
c. Estimate the variances of b_0 and b_1.

4. It is hypothesized that states with high unemployment rates tend to decrease in population and states with low unemployment rates tend to gain population. Let x_i denote the percent unemployment rate of state i, and let y_i denote the net influx in thousands of migrants into state i. (If y_i is negative, the state suffered a net loss.) The data are as follows:

Influx Y	Unemployment Rate X
270	4
50	6
−400	12
−30	9
−5	7
45	5
73	6
−10	9
−80	10

a. Estimate the population regression equation.
b. Find R^2 and s_e.
c. Estimate the variances of b_0 and b_1.

5. Sam's Pizza has several stores in the suburbs around a city. Sam wants to know how the demand for his pizzas depends on the prices he charges. Occasionally he raises or lowers his prices to see how the demand increases or decreases. The following data show the prices in dollars Sam charged during certain months and the number of large pepperoni pizzas sold during those months:

Pizzas sold	(Y)	490	480	480	400	410	440
Price	(X)	4.75	5.00	5.25	5.50	5.20	5.30

a. Estimate the population regression equation.
b. Calculate R^2.
c. Estimate the variances of b_0 and b_1.

6. A market analyst for the Weber Refrigerator Company has visited various appliance stores in a city in order to get data on the selling prices of different brands of refrigerators. Use the following data to help determine if the selling price in dollars is linearly related to the volume in cubic feet of the refrigerator:

Price Y	Volume X
320	15.8
580	21.3
669	24.4
480	18.2
525	19.5
420	17.5
400	16.3
550	21.0

a. Estimate the population regression equation.
b. Estimate the variances of b_0 and b_1.
c. Calculate R^2.

15.6 ▪ Hypothesis Testing in the Linear Regression Model

We frequently are interested in testing whether knowledge of an independent variable X is useful in explaining the values of Y. For example, we may want to test whether a linear relationship exists between X and Y. If X and Y are not linearly related, then in the population regression line

$$E(Y_i|x_i) = \beta_0 + \beta_1 x_i$$

we should have $\beta_1 = 0$. If $\beta_1 = 0$, the values of X are of no use in predicting Y. In Chapters 16, 17, and 18, we will examine more complex potential relationships between dependent and independent variables. If Y is linearly related to X, then $\beta_1 \neq 0$. Thus, we are usually interested in testing the null hypothesis

$$H_0: \beta_1 = 0$$

against the alternative hypothesis

$$H_1: \beta_1 \neq 0$$

At times, we may use a one-sided null hypothesis such as

$$H_0: \beta_1 \geqslant 0 \quad \text{or} \quad H_0: \beta_1 \leqslant 0$$

or a one-sided alternative hypothesis such as

$$H_1\colon \beta_1 > 0 \quad \text{or} \quad H_1\colon \beta_1 < 0$$

For example, if we reject $H_0\colon \beta_1 = 0$ in favor of the hypothesis $H_1\colon \beta_1 > 0$, then we are saying that the sample data support the hypothesis that the slope of the population regression line is positive. The following examples show some of the different hypotheses that we might want to test.

Example 15.8

A One-Sided Test: Let y_i be the annual income of individual i, and x_i be the years of formal education of individual i. The relationship between Y and X is assumed to have the form

$$E(Y_i|x_i) = \beta_0 + \beta_1 x_i$$

It is reasonable to assume that either education has no effect on income or its effect is positive. Thus, we would test the null hypothesis

$$H_0\colon \beta_1 = 0$$

against the one-sided alternative hypothesis

$$H_1\colon \beta_1 > 0$$

■

Example 15.9

Another One-Sided Test: Let x_i be the annual tuition charged at a state university during year i, and let y_i be the number of students who enroll during year i. Again we assume that

$$E(Y_i|x_i) = \beta_0 + \beta_1 x_i$$

It is reasonable to assume either tuition cost has no effect on the number of students who enroll or that tuition cost and the number of students who enroll are negatively related. Thus, we would test the null hypothesis

$$H_0\colon \beta_1 = 0$$

against the one-sided alternative hypothesis

$$H_1\colon \beta_1 < 0$$

■

Example 15.10

A Two-Sided Test: Suppose we want to test if the grade point average (GPA) of a college student is linearly related to the income of the student's parents. Let y_i be the GPA of student i, and let x_i be the income of the parents of student i. We assume

$$E(Y_i|x_i) = \beta_0 + \beta_1 x_i$$

Because we have no reason a priori to think that β_1 is positive rather than negative, we would test the null hypothesis

$$H_0\colon \beta_1 = 0$$

against the two-sided alternative hypothesis

$$H_1\colon \beta_1 \neq 0$$

■

The parameter β_1 represents the slope of the population regression line and measures the change in the expected value of Y associated with a 1-unit change in X. If $\beta_1 = 0$, then the expected value of Y does not change as X changes, and the population regression line will be a horizontal line (see Figure 15.8). We can also test hypotheses about β_0, but usually there is much more interest in testing hypotheses about β_1. If we reject the hypothesis that $\beta_1 = 0$, then we are saying that the values of X are helpful in predicting Y.

FIGURE 15.8
A horizontal regression line.

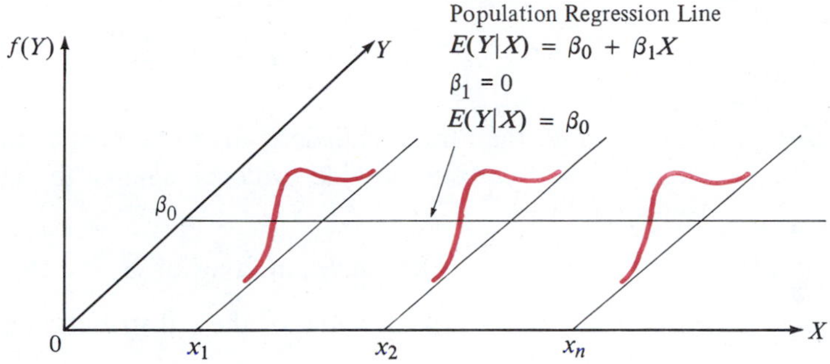

Example 15.11 **Another Two-Sided Test:** The null hypothesis does not always have the form

$$H_0: \beta_1 = 0$$

although this is by far the most frequent case. Suppose an economist claims that, in the United States, annual income is linearly related to years of education and the slope of the population regression line is approximately $\beta_1 = \$2000$. That is, the economist claims that, in the United States, an increase of one year in education tends to be associated with an increase of approximately \$2000 in annual income. Suppose we want to test the null hypothesis that the slope of the population regression line is $\beta_1 = \$2000$. Then we would test the null hypothesis

$$H_0: \beta_1 = \$2000$$

against the two-sided alternative hypothesis

$$H_1: \beta_1 \neq \$2000$$

Tests of hypotheses concerning the value of β_1 are based on the fact that if the basic assumptions of the simple linear regression model hold, then the random variable

$$t = \frac{b_1 - \beta_1}{S_{b_1}}$$

follows the Student t distribution with $(n - 2)$ degrees of freedom. The procedure in the accompanying box shows how to test a hypothesis about the slope of the population regression line.

Tests Concerning the Slope of the Population Regression Line

Case 1: Suppose we want to test the null hypothesis

$$H_0: \beta_1 = \beta_1^* \quad \text{or} \quad H_0: \beta_1 \leq \beta_1^*$$

against the one-sided alternative hypothesis

$$H_1: \beta_1 > \beta_1^*$$

where β_1^* is some hypothesized value of β_1. Suppose the level of significance of the test is α. The test is based on the t statistic

$$t = \frac{b_1 - \beta_1^*}{s_{b_1}}$$

If H_0 is false, then the t statistic tends to be greater than 0. Thus, large positive values of the t statistic provide evidence against the null hypothesis. We use the decision rule

$$\text{Reject } H_0 \text{ in favor of } H_1 \text{ if } t > t_{\alpha,n-2}$$

where $t_{\alpha,n-2}$ is the critical value of the t distribution having $(n - 2)$ degrees of freedom such that

$$P(t > t_{\alpha,n-2}) = \alpha$$

Case 2: Suppose we want to test the null hypothesis

$$H_0: \beta_1 = \beta_1^* \quad \text{or} \quad H_0: \beta_1 \geq \beta_1^*$$

against the one-sided alternative hypothesis

$$H_1: \beta_1 < \beta_1^*$$

Use the decision rule

$$\text{Reject } H_0 \text{ in favor of } H_1 \text{ if } t < -t_{\alpha,n-2}$$

Case 3: To test the null hypothesis

$$H_0: \beta_1 = \beta_1^*$$

against the two-sided alternative hypothesis

$$H_1: \beta_1 \neq \beta_1^*$$

use the decision rule

$$\text{Reject } H_0 \text{ in favor of } H_1 \text{ if } t < -t_{\alpha/2,n-2} \text{ or if } t > t_{\alpha/2,n-2}$$

The most frequently performed test involves testing the null hypothesis $H_0: \beta_1 = 0$ against one of the alternative hypotheses

$$H_1: \beta_1 \neq 0, \quad H_1: \beta_1 > 0, \quad \text{or} \quad H_1: \beta_1 < 0$$

To perform the test, the test statistic is simply the t statistic $t = b_1/s_{b_1}$.

Example 15.12 **Testing the Null Hypothesis: H_0: $\beta_1 = 0$:** Refer to Example 15.7 where we used data concerning Y_i = average weekly expenditures of the ith individual and X_i = average weekly after-tax income of the ith individual to obtain the sample regression line

$$\hat{y}_i = -8.16217 + .923213x_i \qquad R^2 = .9733$$
$$(18.82) \qquad (.054) \qquad n = 10$$

The values in parentheses are estimated standard deviations. It is quite obvious that expenditures depend on income. Thus, if we formally tested the null hypothesis that $\beta_1 = 0$, the results should overwhelmingly reject H_0. To show this, let us test the null hypothesis

$$H_0: \beta_1 = 0$$

against the one-sided alternative hypothesis

$$H_1: \beta_1 > 0$$

using a 1% level of significance.

Solution: We have $n = 10$ observations so the degrees of freedom is $(n - 2) = 8$. For $\alpha = .01$, we obtain the critical value $t_{.01,8} = 2.90$. We have $b_1 = 0.923213$ and $s_{b_1} = 0.054$. We calculate the t statistic

$$t = \frac{b_1 - 0}{s_{b_1}} = \frac{0.923213}{0.054} = 17.10$$

We reject the null hypothesis that $\beta_1 = 0$ because the t statistic falls in the critical region. In regression analysis, it is quite common to get results like this where the absolute value of the t statistic is very large. This provides very strong evidence that the population regression coefficient is nonzero. ■

Example 15.13 **Testing the Null Hypothesis H_0: $\beta_1 = 0.9$:** Suppose an economist analyzing the data in Example 15.7 argues that the marginal propensity to consume is 0.90 when using net income. That is, the economist claims that if after-tax income increases by $1.00, the average increase in consumption is $0.90. Let us use a 5% level of significance, and test the null hypothesis

$$H_0: \beta_1 = .90$$

against the two-sided alternative hypothesis

$$H_1: \beta_1 \neq .90$$

Solution: We have $\alpha = .05$ and $(n - 2) = 8$ degrees of freedom. Thus, we have $\alpha/2 = .025$. The critical values of t are $t_{.025,8} = 2.31$ and $-t_{.025,8} = -2.31$. Thus, we will reject H_0 in favor of H_1 if $t < -2.31$ or if $t > 2.31$. We calculate the t statistic

$$t = \frac{b_1 - \beta_1^*}{s_{b_1}} = \frac{0.923213 - 0.90}{0.054} = 0.4298$$

We do not reject H_0 because $t = 0.4298$ falls in the acceptance region. ■

Testing Hypotheses About the Intercept

Let β_0^* be some hypothesized value of β_0. To test hypotheses about the intercept of the population regression line, calculate the t statistic

$$t = \frac{b_0 - \beta_0^*}{s_{b_0}}$$

and proceed exactly as when testing hypotheses about the slope of the population regression line. When H_0 is true, this t statistic follows the t distribution with $(n - 2)$ degrees of freedom. To perform the test, we compare this t statistic with the critical values of the t distribution using α as the level of significance.

In most cases, there is little or no interest in testing hypotheses about the intercept of the regression equation. Occasionally we may be interested in testing that the intercept is 0, which would indicate that the regression line passes through the origin. The following example shows how to perform the test.

Example 15.14 **Testing a Null Hypothesis About the Intercept:** For the data in Example 15.7, use a 5% level of significance and test the null hypothesis

$$H_0: \beta_0 = 0$$

against the two-sided alternative hypothesis

$$H_1: \beta_0 \neq 0.$$

Solution: We have $\alpha = .05$ and $(n - 2) = 8$ degrees of freedom. We obtain $\alpha/2 = .025$, which we use to calculate the critical values $t_{.025,8} = 2.31$ and $-t_{.025,8} = -2.31$. The acceptance region for H_0 is $-2.31 \leq t \leq 2.31$. We have $b_0 = -8.16217$ and $s_{b_0} = 18.82$, and so we obtain the t statistic

$$t = \frac{b_0 - 0}{s_{b_0}} = \frac{-8.16217}{18.82} = -0.4337$$

We do not reject H_0 because $t = -0.4337$ falls in the acceptance region. ■

Exercises for Section 15.6

1. Refer to Exercise 1 at the end of Section 15.5.
a. Test H_0: $\beta_1 = 0$ against H_1: $\beta_1 > 0$ using a 5% level of significance.
b. Test H_0: $\beta_0 = 0$ against H_1: $\beta_0 \neq 0$ using a 1% level of significance.
c. Test H_0: $\beta_1 = 2$ against H_1: $\beta_1 \neq 2$ using a 5% level of significance.
d. Test H_0: $\beta_1 = 2.5$ against H_1: $\beta_1 \neq 2.5$ using a 5% level of significance.
e. Interpret the results of parts (a) through (d).

2. Refer to Exercise 2 at the end of Section 15.5.
a. Test H_0: $\beta_1 = 0$ against H_1: $\beta_1 > 0$ using a 1% level of significance.
b. Test H_0: $\beta_0 = 0$ against H_1: $\beta_0 \neq 0$ using a 1% level of significance.
c. Test H_0: $\beta_1 = 0.2$ against H_1: $\beta_1 \neq 0.2$ using a 1% level of significance.
d. Test H_0: $\beta_1 = 0.25$ against H_1: $\beta_1 \neq 0.25$ using a 10% level of significance.

3. An employee claims that drinking beer has no effect on the amount of time it takes for him to perform a task. The following data show how many minutes he took to perform the task after consuming various quantities of beer, measured in ounces:

Time Y	Beer Consumption X
10.0	16
10.2	32
10.3	48
12.0	64
11.8	80
12.0	96
14.0	112

a. Estimate the linear regression equation.
b. Test H_0: $\beta_1 = 0$ against H_1: $\beta_1 > 0$ using a 5% level of significance.

4. It is claimed that a judge tends to give shorter sentences to wealthy people than to poor people for the same crime. The following data show the length of jail sentences in days given to 8 individuals who committed similar crimes and their respective incomes in thousands of dollars:

Jail Sentence Y	Income X
10	45
30	6
25	12
20	20
15	30
20	22
25	25
15	25

a. Estimate the linear regression equation.
b. Test H_0: $\beta_1 = 0$ against H_1: $\beta_1 < 0$ using a 5% level of significance.

5. The manager of Discount Distributing Company claims that sales of soda pop at her store are not very responsive to changes in price. The price of the best-selling brand has changed six times during the last six months. The following data show the prices charged in dollars and the number of cases of soda pop sold during the 20 days following each price change:

Cases sold (Y)	600	550	560	500	520	540
Price per case (X)	4.25	5.25	4.75	5.50	5.00	4.50

a. Estimate the linear regression equation.
b. Let $\alpha = .05$. Test H_0: $\beta_1 = 0$ against H_1: $\beta_1 < 0$.
Do you agree with the manager's claim?

6. A teaching tennis pro claims that a player can increase the speed of his or her serve by stringing the racket tighter. To prove this point, the pro takes 10 identical rackets and has them strung at different tensions from 56 to 65 pounds. A playing pro then serves five times with each racquet, and the average speed of the serve is recorded in miles per hour. The data are as follows:

Average Speed	Tension
98	56
102	57
100	58
101	59
104	60
107	61
104	62
108	63
109	64
110	65

a. Estimate the population regression equation.
b. Let $\alpha = .05$. Test the pro's conjecture.

15.7 ▪ Confidence Intervals for the Regression Coefficients

A confidence interval for the population parameter β_1 is based on the fact that, if the basic assumptions of the simple linear regression model hold, the t statistic

$$t = \frac{b_1 - \beta_1}{S_{b_1}}$$

follows the Student t distribution with $(n - 2)$ degrees of freedom. A confidence interval having level of confidence $(1 - \alpha)$ is based on the probability statement

$$P(-t_{\alpha/2,\nu} < t < t_{\alpha/2,\nu}) = 1 - \alpha$$

or equivalently

$$P\left(-t_{\alpha/2,\nu} \leqslant \frac{b_1 - \beta_1}{S_{b_1}} \leqslant t_{\alpha/2,\nu}\right) = 1 - \alpha$$

where the degrees of freedom is $\nu = (n - 2)$. By rearranging terms, we can obtain the equation

$$P(b_1 - t_{\alpha/2,\nu}S_{b_1} < \beta_1 < b_1 + t_{\alpha/2,\nu}S_{b_1}) = 1 - \alpha$$

This probability statement means that, in repeated sampling, the random interval

$$(b_1 - t_{\alpha/2,\nu}S_{b_1},\ b_1 + t_{\alpha/2,\nu}S_{b_1})$$

will contain the true value β_1 approximately $100(1 - \alpha)\%$ of the time, where the value $t_{\alpha/2,\nu}$ is obtained from the t distribution having $\nu = (n - 2)$ degrees of freedom. For our specific values of b_1 and s_{b_1}, we cannot be sure that β_1 lies in that interval. If we were to repeat the estimation procedure many times with many samples of data, the confidence interval would contain the true value of β_1 approximately $100(1 - \alpha)\%$ of the time.

Confidence Interval for the Slope

The interval

$$(b_1 - t_{\alpha/2,\nu}\, s_{b_1},\ b_1 + t_{\alpha/2,\nu}\, s_{b_1})$$

is called a $100(1 - \alpha)\%$ confidence interval for β_1.

By proceeding in a similar fashion, it is possible to obtain the formula for a confidence interval for the intercept of the population regression line, which is shown in the accompanying box.

Confidence Interval for the Intercept

A confidence interval for the regression intercept β_0 having level of confidence $(1 - \alpha)$ is given by

$$(b_0 - t_{\alpha/2,\nu}\, s_{b_0},\ b_0 + t_{\alpha/2,\nu}\, s_{b_0})$$

Example 15.15

A Confidence Interval for the Slope: Refer to the data in Example 15.7. We obtained the results

$$\hat{y}_i = -8.16217 + .923213x_i \qquad R^2 = .9733$$
$$(18.82) \qquad (.054) \qquad n = 10$$

where the values in parentheses are estimated standard errors of the corresponding estimated coefficients. Construct a 90% confidence interval for the slope β_1.

Solution: We have $\alpha/2 = .05$ and the degrees of freedom is $(n - 2) = 8$. We obtain $t_{\alpha/2,\nu} = t_{.05,8} = 2.31$. The desired confidence interval is

$$(b_1 - t_{\alpha/2,\nu}\, s_{b_1},\ b_1 + t_{\alpha/2,\nu}\, s_{b_1})$$

or

$$[0.923213 - 2.31(0.054),\ 0.923213 + 2.31(0.054)]$$

Thus, the confidence interval is (0.79847, 1.04797). In this example, the coefficient β_1 measures the marginal propensity to consume (MPC) out of disposable income. The confidence interval indicates that it is not unreasonable to suspect that the MPC could be as low as 0.79. On the other hand, a value as large as 1.04 is unreasonable, because this would indicate that a \$1.00 increase in disposable income leads to a \$1.04 increase in expenditures. It is unreasonable to suspect that the MPC exceeds 1.00. ■

Example 15.16

Effect of Cigarette Smoking by Expectant Mothers on the IQ of the Child: On March 15, 1987, the newspaper *USA Today* reported the results of a study in which researchers in Baltimore determined that 3-year-old children whose mothers smoked during pregnancy scored an average of 5 points lower on an IQ test than children of women who did not smoke while pregnant. Suppose that after reading this report, you decide to examine the relationship between the number of cigarettes smoked per day by an expectant mother and the IQ of her child at age 3. Let x_i denote the average number of cigarettes smoked per day by the ith expectant mother, and let y_i denote the IQ of the ith child at age 3. Suppose all of the women in your study have approximately the same IQ, and suppose that all of the fathers also have approximately the same IQ so that differences in the IQs of the children cannot be attributed to differences in the IQs of the parents. It is hypothesized that differences in the IQs of the children can be attributed to the number of cigarettes smoked per day by the expectant mother and other random factors.

The hypothesized model is

$$E(Y_i|x_i) = \beta_0 + \beta_1 x_i$$

We obtain a random sample of $n = 20$ observations showing the IQs of children at age 3 and the number of cigarettes smoked per day by the child's mother during pregnancy. The estimated results are as follows:

$$\hat{y}_i = \underset{(1.2)}{104} - \underset{(0.15)}{0.60}x_i \qquad R^2 = .17 \qquad s_e = 7.8$$

The values in parentheses are the estimated standard errors of the estimated coefficients. Analyze the regression results.

Solution: The slope of the sample regression line is $b_1 = -0.60$. This indicates that an increase of 1 cigarette per day is associated with a decrease of 0.6 point in IQ. The coefficient $b_0 = 104$ indicates that the predicted IQ for children whose mothers do not smoke ($x_i = 0$) is 104.

It is natural to test the null hypothesis that the number of cigarettes smoked by the expectant mother does not influence the IQ of the child. The alternative hypothesis is that increased smoking causes the child's IQ to decrease. Test the null hypothesis

$$H_0: \beta_1 = 0$$

against the one-sided alternative hypothesis

$$H_1: \beta_1 < 0$$

Suppose the level of significance is chosen to be $\alpha = .05$. If the null hypothesis is true, then the t statistic follows the t distribution with $(n - 2) = 18$ degrees of freedom. The critical value of the test statistic is $t_{.05,18} = -1.734$. The observed value of the test statistic is

$$t = b_1/s_{b_1} = -0.60/0.15 = -4.00$$

This value exceeds the critical value and thus falls in the rejection region, so we reject the null hypothesis that $\beta_1 = 0$. The sample regression line provides very strong evidence that the number of cigarettes smoked by the expectant mother does affect the IQ of the child.

Once we have rejected H_0, we would want to construct a confidence interval for the population coefficient β_1. Suppose we decide to construct a confidence interval for β_1 having level of confidence $(1 - \alpha) = .95$. The critical value of t is $t_{.025,18} = 2.101$.

The confidence interval utilizes the estimated coefficient $b_1 = -0.60$ and the estimated standard error $s_{b_1} = 0.15$. The 95% confidence interval for β_1 is

$$(b_1 - t_{\alpha/2,\nu}s_{b_1},\ b_1 + t_{\alpha/2,\nu}s_{b_1})$$

or

$$[-0.60 - 2.101(0.15),\ -0.60 + 2.101(0.15)]$$

The desired confidence interval extends from -0.9152 to -0.2849. This means that we can be 95% confident that the true value of β_1 falls within this interval. If the population regression coefficient is as low as -0.9152, then an increase of $X = 10$ cigarettes per day would lead to a decrease in IQ of 9.152 points. If the population regression slope is -0.2849, then an increase of $X = 10$ cigarettes per day would lead to a decrease in IQ of 2.849 points.

A researcher would also be interested in observing whether the number of cigarettes smoked by the expectant mother explained most of the variation in the IQs of the children at age 3. (Recall that the IQs of all the mothers were approximately equal and the IQs of all the fathers were approximately equal, so that parents' IQs do not explain variations in the children's IQs.) The coefficient of determination is $R^2 = .17$, indicating that the number of cigarettes smoked by the expectant mother explains 17% of the observed variation in the IQs of the children. Alternatively, we could say that the model does not explain 83% of the variation in the IQs of the children.

A researcher would also examine the estimated standard error of the regression $s_e = 7.8$. This indicates that the standard deviation of the error term is estimated to be 7.8. From the Empirical Rule, which was discussed in Chapter 4, we know that about 95% of the observations for a bell-shaped distribution should lie within 2 standard deviations of the mean. Using $s_e = 7.8$, about 95% of the IQs should lie within 15.6 units of the population regression line for a given value of X. Because an error of 15.6 units in an estimate of a child's IQ is relatively large, the unexplained random factors that influence a child's IQ are relatively sizable. This reinforces the information obtained by examining the value of R^2.

After examining these data, the general conclusion should be that cigarette smoking by the expectant mother apparently does affect the child's IQ. An increase of 1 cigarette per day smoked by the expectant mother is associated with roughly a 0.6-unit decrease in the child's IQ, but the decrease could be as small as a 0.2849-unit decrease in IQ or as large as a 0.9152 unit decrease in IQ. The data are not highly concentrated about a straight line because the value of R^2 is only .17. This means that 83% of the variability in the IQs of the children is unexplained. It should be kept in mind, however, that if the number of cigarettes smoked by the expectant mother explains 17% of the variation in IQs of the children, then this can be a sizable and important influence on IQ. ■

Exercises for Section 15.7

1. Refer to Exercise 1 in Sections 15.5 and 15.6.
   a. Calculate 90%, 95%, and 99% confidence intervals for β_1.
   b. Calculate 90%, 95%, and 99% confidence intervals for β_0.

2. Refer to Exercise 2 in Sections 15.5 and 15.6. Construct 90%, 95%, and 99% confidence intervals for β_0 and β_1.
3. The mileage per gallon of a race car depends on the speed of the car. The following data show the mileage per gallon achieved at different speeds measured in miles per hour:

Mileage (Y)	7.0	5.1	5.8	3.2	8.0	4.0
Speed (X)	100	120	110	150	80	130

a. Estimate the linear regression equation.
b. Calculate a 95% confidence interval for β_1.
c. Test the null hypothesis H_0: $\beta_1 = 0$ against H_1: $\beta_1 \neq 0$ using a 5% level of significance.

4. The unemployment rate in a midwestern city tends to depend on the number of employees working at a large steel mill located in the city, as shown in the following table:

Unemployment Rate (in percent) Y	Employees (in thousands) X
4	14
6	11
12	8
8	10
5	12
9	9
11	7
10	8
14	7
9	8

a. Plot the data.
b. Estimate the population regression equation and plot the sample regression line on the scatter diagram.
c. Calculate a 95% confidence interval for β_1.

5. The Acme Corporation manufactures color televisions. It is felt that the number of color televisions sold per month is linearly related to the amount of money spent on advertising. The following data show the number of color TVs sold in thousands and total advertising expenditures in thousands of dollars during 8 months:

Number Sold (Y)	Advertising Expenditure (X)
62	22
50	15
58	17
64	20
68	22
64	23
70	25
72	26

a. Plot the data.
b. Estimate the population regression equation and plot the sample regression line.
c. Construct a 95% confidence interval for β_1.
d. Test H_0: $\beta_1 = 0$ against H_1: $\beta_1 > 0$. Let $\alpha = .05$.

6. The Quick-In-Quick-Out Food Store specializes in giving fast service to customers who are in a hurry and only want to buy a few items. The manager thinks that the daily sales revenue during the spring is related to temperature. He thinks that the higher the temperature, the more customers the store has and the higher the revenue. Use the following data on daily revenue (in thousands of dollars) and noon temperature (in degrees Fahrenheit) to test this hypothesis:

Daily Revenue (Y)	2.6	3.4	2.5	3.2	3.3	2.7
Temperature (X)	58	66	63	40	52	60

a. Estimate the population regression equation.
b. Construct a 99% confidence interval for β_1.
c. Let $\alpha = .01$. Test H_0: $\beta_1 = 0$ against H_1: $\beta_1 > 0$.

15.8 ▪ *Prediction Using the Regression Model*

One of the goals of regression analysis is to obtain an equation that will enable us to predict Y for a given value of X. There are two different prediction problems of interest:

1. We may want to estimate or predict the *actual value* of the random variable Y_i from the equation $Y_i = \beta_0 + \beta_1 x_i + e_i$ when the independent variable takes the value x_i.
2. We may want to estimate the *conditional mean* $E(Y_i|x_i)$ that results when the independent variable takes the value x_i. This conditional mean represents the *average value* of the random variable Y_i when the independent variable is fixed at x_i.

To predict Y for a given value of X, we use the equation

$$\hat{y}_i = b_0 + b_1 x_i$$

We use this equation whether we are predicting an individual Y value or predicting the mean value of Y associated with a given value of X.

Formula to Predict Y_i and $E(Y_i|x_i)$

The best point estimate of Y_i and $E(Y_i|x_i)$ is given by

$$\hat{y}_i = b_0 + b_1 x_i$$

Although the prediction of an individual value Y_i and the estimate of the mean value $E(Y_i|x_i)$ are the same for a given value x_i, the sampling errors associated with the two predictions are different. This is reasonable because the estimate of the mean value of Y_i does not require an estimate of the random error e_i.

Effects of Sampling Error

In general, the estimated value $\hat{y}_i$ will differ from the mean value $E(Y_i|x_i) = (\beta_0 + \beta_1 x_i)$ because b_0 and b_1 are only estimates of the unknown coefficients β_0 and

β_1. Thus, the sampling error involved in predicting the mean value of Y for a given X is due to the sampling error involved in estimating β_0 and β_1.

The prediction of an individual value Y_i is subject to sampling error because we use $(b_0 + b_1x_i)$ as our prediction of the actual value y_i, which is actually $(\beta_0 + \beta_1x_i + e_i)$. We have sampling error because b_0 and b_1 are estimates of β_0 and β_1 and because we have used 0 as our estimate of the random error e.

Confidence Intervals for Predictions

Just as we constructed confidence intervals for the mean of a population based on a sample of values, it is natural to construct confidence intervals for the mean value of Y_i and for an individual value of Y_i based on our estimated value $\hat{y}_i = b_0 + b_1x_i$.

To construct confidence intervals for the mean value of Y associated with a given value of X, say, $X = x_p$, we use the sampling distribution of $\hat{Y}_p$. If the basic assumptions of the simple linear regression model hold, then $\hat{Y}_p$ is normally distributed with mean

$$E(\hat{Y}_p|x_p) = \beta_0 + \beta_1x_p$$

and variance

$$\mathrm{Var}(\hat{Y}_p) = \sigma_e^2\left(\frac{1}{n} + \frac{(x_p - \bar{x})^2}{\sum x_i^2 - n\bar{x}^2}\right)$$

Figure 15.9 shows the characteristics of the sampling distribution of $\hat{Y}_p$. The formulas in the following boxes show how to construct confidence intervals for $E(Y_p|x_p)$ and for an individual value of Y_p.

FIGURE 15.9
Sampling distribution of $\hat{Y}_p$.

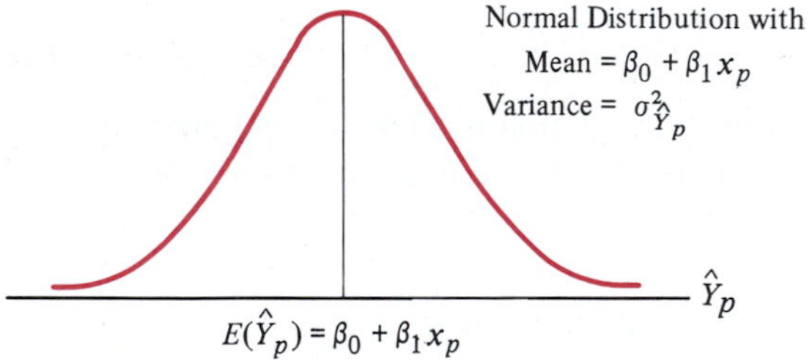

To estimate $\mathrm{Var}(\hat{Y}_p)$, we replace σ_e^2 by its estimate $s_e^2 = \mathrm{SSE}/(n - 2)$. We obtain the estimated variance of $\hat{Y}_p$.

Formula to Estimate the Variance of $\hat{Y}_p$

$$s_{\hat{Y}_p}^2 = s_e^2\left(\frac{1}{n} + \frac{(x_p - \bar{x})^2}{\sum x_i^2 - n\bar{x}^2}\right)$$

Formula for a Confidence Interval for $E(Y_p|x_p)$

Given a specific value x_p, a confidence interval for the mean value of Y_p having level of confidence $(1 - \alpha)$ is given by

$$\hat{Y}_p \pm t_{\alpha/2,\nu} s_e \sqrt{\frac{1}{n} + \frac{(x_p - \bar{x})^2}{\Sigma x^2 - n\bar{x}^2}}$$

where the degrees of freedom is $\nu = (n - 2)$.

Formula for a Confidence Interval for Y_p

Given a specific value x_p, a confidence interval for the actual value of Y_p having level of confidence $(1 - \alpha)$ is given by

$$\hat{Y}_p \pm t_{\alpha/2,\nu} s_e \sqrt{1 + \frac{1}{n} + \frac{(x_p - \bar{x})^2}{\Sigma x^2 - n\bar{x}^2}}$$

The confidence interval for an individual Y is always wider than the confidence interval for the mean value of Y. This is reasonable because the mean value of Y does not involve the random error e. For a given level of confidence, the wider the confidence interval, the greater the uncertainty surrounding our prediction. We make the following observations concerning the width of a confidence interval for a prediction of Y_i or $E(Y_i|x_i)$:

1. Other things being equal, the larger the sample size n, the smaller the width of the confidence interval. This reflects the fact that we become more certain about a prediction as we obtain more sample information.

2. Other things being equal, the larger the value s_e, the greater the width of the confidence interval. Recall that s_e^2 is an estimate of σ_e^2, the variance of the error terms. The error terms represent the discrepancy between the observed values of the dependent variables and their expected values. The standard deviation of the error s_e is an estimate of the standard deviation of the population of Y_i values associated with the value x_i. A large value s_e indicates that the distribution of Y values is not highly concentrated about the population regression line, thus making a precise estimate of the population regression line difficult to obtain.

3. The quantity $(\Sigma x_i^2 - n\bar{x}^2) = \Sigma(x_i - \bar{x})^2 = (n - 1)s_x^2$, where s_x^2 is the sample variance of the X values. Thus, $(\Sigma x_i^2 - n\bar{x}^2)$ is a multiple of the sample variance of X and can be used as a measure of the amount of variation in the sample of observations on the independent variable. A large variance implies that we have information for a wide variety of values of X. This fact makes it easier to determine how the variable Y depends on the variable X. Consequently, our estimates of the slope and intercept of the population regression line improve and our predictions become more precise. As a result, the larger the value of $(\Sigma x_i^2 - n\bar{x}^2)$, the narrower the confidence intervals for our predictions.

4. The larger the value of $(x_p - \bar{x})^2$, the wider the confidence intervals for the predictions. This means that our predictions become less precise the farther x_p is from the sample mean of the independent variable. This result reflects the fact that, if our sample data are centered at $\bar{x}$, we would have more confidence in a prediction of Y_p when x_p is close to $\bar{x}$ than when it is far from $\bar{x}$.

Example 15.17 **Confidence Interval for a Prediction:** Suppose the annual repair cost of an automobile Y_i, is approximately linearly related to the age of the car x_i. A sample of 15 cars was used to estimate the equation

$$\hat{y}_i = 50 + 25x_i$$

Assume that $s_e = 30$, $\bar{x} = 5$, and $(\Sigma x^2 - n\bar{x}^2) = 50$. Let us find 95% confidence intervals for the mean value of Y_p for cars aged $x_p = 1, 2, 3, 4, 5, 6, 7, 8$, and 9 years.

Solution: We have $\alpha = .05$ and $(n - 2) = 13$ degrees of freedom. The critical value of the t distribution is $t_{.025,13} = 2.160$. We obtain the predicted values and confidence intervals shown in Table 15.5. The sample regression line with the confidence intervals are shown in Figure 15.10. Note that the width of the confidence interval increases as x_p gets farther away from $\bar{x} = 5$.

TABLE 15.5 **Confidence intervals for $E(Y_p|x_p)$ in Example 15.17**

x_p	$\hat{y}_p$	$\sqrt{\frac{1}{n} + \frac{(x_p - \bar{x})^2}{\Sigma x^2 - n\bar{x}^2}}$	$\hat{y}_p \pm t_{.025}s_e \sqrt{\frac{1}{n} + \frac{(x_p - \bar{x})^2}{\Sigma x^2 - n\bar{x}^2}}$
1	75	.62	(34.82, 115.18)
2	100	.50	(67.59, 132.41)
3	125	.38	(100.37, 149.63)
4	150	.29	(131.20, 168.80)
5	175	.26	(158.15, 191.85)
6	200	.29	(181.20, 218.80)
7	225	.38	(200.37, 249.63)
8	250	.50	(217.59, 282.41)
9	275	.62	(234.82, 315.18)

Some Cautionary Comments

Be careful when forecasting the value of a dependent variable if the value of the independent variable lies beyond the sample range. For example, suppose that the sample regression line indicates that annual repair costs for cars aged 1 to 5 years are related to the age of the car according to the equation $\hat{y}_i = 50 + 25x_i$, where y_i denotes the predicted annual repair costs of car i and x_i denotes the age of car i. We should hesitate to use this equation to forecast annual repair costs for a car that is, say, 10 years old. The relationship between Y and X might shift or become nonlinear outside the sample range 0 to 5 years. The process of forecasting the dependent variable when the independent variable falls outside the sample range is called *extrapolation*. Extrapolation is risky because the sample data provide no evidence that the relationship between Y and X is linear beyond the range of the data.

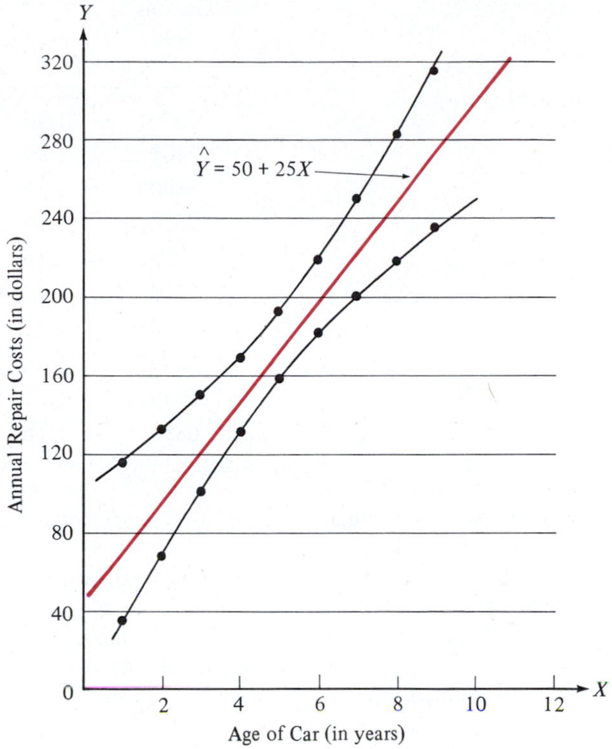

FIGURE 15.10
Regression line with confidence intervals for $E(Y_i|x_i)$ for Example 15.17.

Another potential pitfall is a prediction based on a sample regression line that has been estimated using outdated data. The less recent the data used in estimating a sample regression line, the more likely it is that there will have been a change in the population regression line.

Finally, after estimating a regression line, examine the residuals to see whether any of the basic assumptions have been violated. It also is useful to examine the scatter diagram. Such an examination is probably the easiest way to find evidence of a nonlinear relationship between Y and X.

Exercises for Section 15.8

1. The manager of a gas station has changed the price of a gallon of gas numerous times and noted how sales changed in response. Let y_i denote the gallons sold on the ith day, and let x_i denote price charged in dollars on the ith day. The data are as follows:

Gallons Sold Y	Price X
7500	1.12
7200	1.14
6800	1.16
7350	1.14
6750	1.18
5700	1.24
6250	1.22
6200	1.20
5950	1.22
6850	1.16

a. Plot the data and estimate the population regression equation.
b. Predict Y if $x = \$1.20$.
c. Find 95% confidence intervals for Y and for the mean value of Y if $x = \$1.20$.
d. Predict Y if $x = \$1.26$.
e. Find 95% confidence intervals for Y and for the mean value of Y if $x = \$1.26$.

2. The following data show the number of pairs of shoes produced and the costs of production in thousands of dollars during several weeks at a shoe factory:

Weekly Cost Y	Number of Pairs X
9.6	1860
8.7	1760
8.6	1720
7.9	1640
8.2	1700
10.0	1900
9.7	1850

a. Plot the data and estimate the population regression equation.
b. Find a 95% confidence interval for Y and the mean value of Y if $x = 1700$.

3. Suppose you obtained the sample regression line $\hat{y} = 3 + 2x$. Suppose the number of observations is 10 and you obtained $\bar{x} = 6$, $s_e = 1$, and $(\Sigma x^2 - n\bar{x}^2) = 20$.
a. Plot the regression line.
b. Find 95% confidence intervals for the mean values of Y_p if $x_p = 2, 3, 4, 5, 6, 7, 8, 9$, and 10.
c. Plot the endpoints of these confidence intervals on the graph with the regression line, and draw a smooth curve through these points.

4. Explain the difference between an interval estimate of the mean value of Y for a given X and an interval estimate for an individual value of Y for a given X.

15.9 ▪ The Correlation Coefficient

Often we are not as interested in a mathematical equation relating two variables as we are in the strength of the linear relationship between the variables Y and X. In such cases, the statistical technique known as **correlation analysis** can be used. In correlation analysis, it is assumed that both Y and X are random variables.

The Population Correlation Coefficient, ρ

Suppose we want to find a suitable way of measuring the strength of the relationship between Y and X. One way of doing this is by measuring how well a regression line fits a sample of data and using the coefficient of determination R^2. Using the correlation coefficient provides a second way.

Suppose we are studying two random variables Y and X that vary together in a joint distribution. In the population of (X, Y) values, there is a mean value of X, denoted μ_X, and a mean value of Y, denoted μ_Y. The population variances of X and Y are denoted σ_X^2 and σ_Y^2. Recall that σ_X^2 measures the average value of $(X - \mu_X)^2$ in the population, and similarly for σ_Y^2. That is,

$$\sigma_X^2 = E[(X - \mu_X)^2] \quad \text{and} \quad \sigma_Y^2 = E[(Y - \mu_Y)^2]$$

Given a sample of data, we estimate σ_X^2 by calculating the sample variance s_X^2, where

$$s_X^2 = \frac{\Sigma(x_i - \bar{x})^2}{n - 1}$$

We use a corresponding approach to calculate the sample variance for Y.

One way of measuring whether two quantitative variables are related is to calculate a covariance between the variables. If we have a population of observations, we calculate a *population covariance;* otherwise, we calculate a *sample covariance*. The population and sample covariances are defined in the accompanying boxes.

Definition: Population Covariance

The **population covariance**, denoted by the symbol σ_{XY}, measures the average value of $(X - \mu_X)(Y - \mu_Y)$ in the population of (X, Y) values. The population covariance is given by

$$\sigma_{XY} = \text{Cov}(X, Y) = E[(X - \mu_X)(Y - \mu_Y)]$$

Definition: Sample Covariance

Given a sample of (X, Y) values, we use the **sample covariance** to estimate σ_{XY}. The sample covariance, denoted s_{XY}, is calculated using the formula

$$s_{XY} = \frac{\Sigma(x_i - \bar{x})(y_i - \bar{y})}{n - 1}$$

A problem with using the covariance to measure the strength of the relationship between X and Y is that the magnitudes of σ_{XY} and s_{XY} (but not the signs) depend on the units used to measure X and Y. For example, if we are studying the relationship between the circumference of a tree X and the height of the tree Y, then $\text{Cov}(X, Y)$ will be much larger if X and Y are measured in inches than if they are measured in feet. This scaling problem is especially common in economics and business, where dollar values are frequently expressed in thousands, millions, or billions.

Note that the standardized score $(X - \mu_X)/\sigma_X$ does not depend on the dimensions used to measure X, and similarly for $(Y - \mu_Y)/\sigma_Y$. It follows that the *standardized covariance*

$$E\left[\frac{(X - \mu_X)(Y - \mu_Y)}{\sigma_X \sigma_Y}\right]$$

does not depend on the units used to measure X and Y.

Definition: Population Correlation Coefficient

The standardized covariance, called the **population correlation coefficient** and denoted by the Greek letter ρ (rho), is defined by the formula

$$\rho = \frac{\sigma_{XY}}{\sigma_X \sigma_Y}$$

It can be shown that for any population of (X, Y) values, it is always the case that

$$-1 \leqslant \rho \leqslant 1$$

That is, ρ cannot exceed $+1$ or be less than -1.

The sign of ρ is the same as the sign of σ_{XY} and depends on the average of the cross products $(X - \mu_X)(Y - \mu_Y)$. The amounts $(X - \mu_X)$ and $(Y - \mu_Y)$ measure the amounts by which X and Y are above or below average. If X and Y are both above average or both below average, then the cross product $(X - \mu_X)(Y - \mu_Y)$ will be positive. If the average cross product is positive, then the covariance σ_{XY} is positive and ρ is positive; in such a case, we say that X and Y are positively correlated. If X is above average when Y is below average or vice versa, then the cross product $(X - \mu_X) \times (Y - \mu_Y)$ will be negative and ρ will be negative. Then we say that X and Y are negatively correlated.

Three values of ρ are of special interest. When $\rho = 0$, then X and Y are not linearly related, and we say that X and Y are uncorrelated. When all the values of X and Y lie exactly on a straight line having a positive slope, then $\rho = 1$. If all values of X and Y lie exactly on a straight line having a negative slope, then $\rho = -1$. If the values of X and Y lie close to a straight line having a positive (or negative) slope, then ρ will be close to $+1$ (or -1). This shows that ρ measures the strength, or closeness, of the linear relation between two variables.

We thus have the following results:

1. A correlation of -1 implies perfect negative linear association.
2. A correlation of 1 implies perfect positive linear association.

3. The larger the absolute value of the population correlation coefficient, the stronger the linear association between the random variables.
4. A correlation of 0 implies no *linear* association. In particular, if X and Y are independent random variables, then $\rho = 0$. On the other hand, $\rho = 0$ does not necessarily imply that X and Y are independent of one another, because they may be related in a nonlinear way.

Figures 15.11, 15.12, and 15.13 show that (X, Y) populations can be quite different but still have the same correlation coefficient. The correlation coefficient indicates

FIGURE 15.11
Examples of positive correlation.

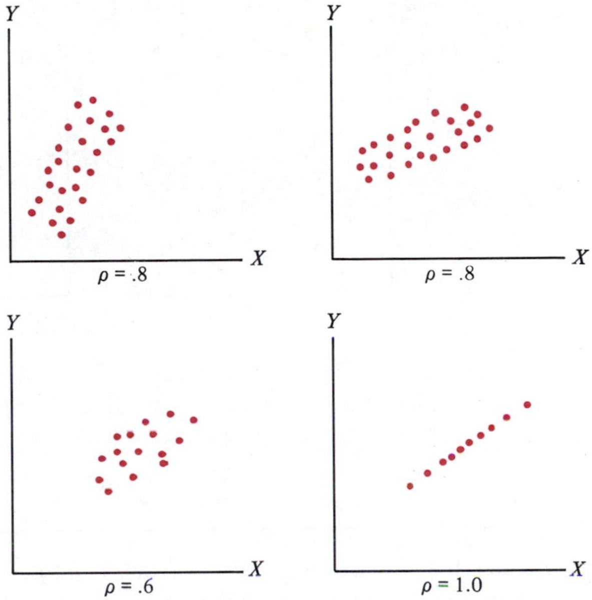

FIGURE 15.12
Examples of zero correlation.

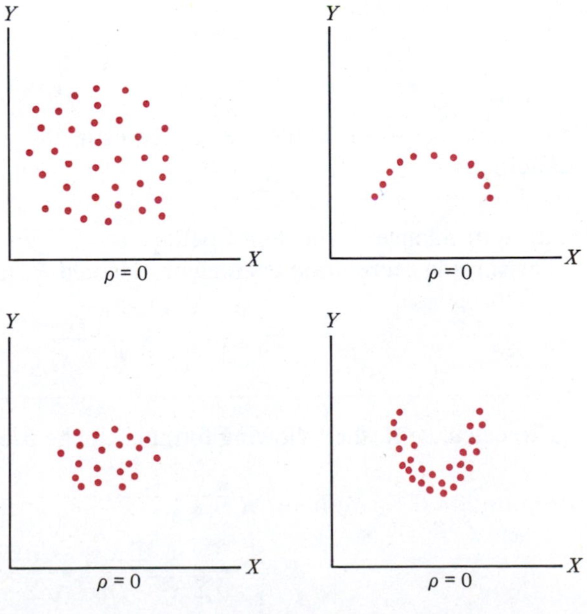

FIGURE 15.13
Examples of negative correlation.

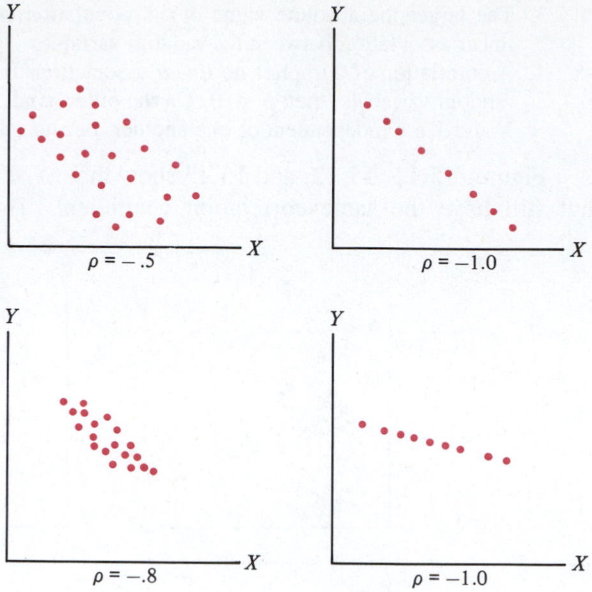

whether the data lie close to a straight line. Two different sets of data might be scattered about two population regression lines, one line having slope $\beta_1 = 0.1$ and the other line having slope $\beta_1 = 100$, and in each case the correlation coefficient could be, say, .7.

The Sample Correlation Coefficient

To estimate the population correlation coefficient ρ, we calculate the sample correlation coefficient, denoted by the symbol R. The sample correlation coefficient R measures the strength of the linear relationship of the sample data (x_i, y_i). Recall that the population correlation coefficient is

$$\rho = \frac{\sigma_{XY}}{\sigma_X \sigma_Y}$$

To estimate ρ, we substitute the sample estimates s_{XY}, s_X, and s_Y for their population counterparts.

Definition: Sample Correlation Coefficient

The **sample correlation coefficient**, denoted R, is obtained by the formula

$$R = \frac{s_{XY}}{s_X s_Y}$$

To calculate R, the following formula can be used:

Computational Formula for *R*

$$R = \frac{\sum x_i y_i - n\bar{x}\bar{y}}{\sqrt{\sum x_i^2 - n\bar{x}^2}\sqrt{\sum y_i^2 - n\bar{y}^2}}$$

Independence of Unit of Measurement

For the population correlation coefficient and the sample correlation coefficient, interchanging the definitions of the two variables X and Y in the formulas does not change the results. Thus, when calculating the correlation coefficient, it does not matter which variable is denoted as X and which as Y.

The correlation coefficient is not expressed in any unit of measure and does not change when a different unit of measure is used for either of the variables. For example, we will get the same correlation coefficient if some variable X that measures distance is recorded in yards or centimeters or if some variable Y that measures time is recorded in seconds or hours.

Relationship Between Sample Correlation Coefficient and Slope of Sample Regression Line

The sample correlation coefficient is related to the slope of the sample regression line. The slope of the sample regression line can be calculated as

$$b_1 = \frac{\Sigma(x_i - \bar{x})(y_i - \bar{y})}{\Sigma(x_i - \bar{x})^2}$$

If we divide both numerator and denominator by $(n - 1)$, we obtain

$$b_1 = \frac{s_{XY}}{s_X^2}$$

Recall that the sample correlation coefficient can be expressed as

$$R = \frac{s_{XY}}{s_X s_Y}$$

Thus we obtain the following equations:

Relationship Between R and b_1

$$b_1 = R\frac{s_Y}{s_X} \quad \text{and} \quad R = b_1\frac{s_X}{s_Y}$$

where s_Y and s_X are the sample standard deviations of X and Y.

Because s_Y and s_X are both positive, it follows that $R = 0$ if and only if $b_1 = 0$. That is, the sample correlation coefficient is 0 if and only if the sample regression line is a horizontal line having 0 slope. When the sample regression line is horizontal, this indicates that knowledge of X does not help in predicting Y. When $R = 0$ this implies that, for the sample data, X is uncorrelated with Y. Thus, saying X and Y are uncorrelated is basically the same as saying that X and Y are not linearly related.

Also, because both s_Y and s_X are positive, the sign of R is the same as the sign of b_1. R will be positive when the sample regression line has a positive slope and negative when the sample regression line has a negative slope.

As with the population correlation coefficient ρ, it is possible that $R = 0$ and that X and Y are related in a nonlinear fashion. Thus, $R = 0$ indicates only the absence of a linear relationship between X and Y and does not imply anything about nonlinear relationships.

Recall that the coefficient of determination R^2 measures the goodness of fit of the sample regression line. In the simple linear regression model, the coefficient of determination R^2 is the square of the sample correlation coefficient R. Since $0 \leq R^2 \leq 1$ and since R is the square root of R^2, it follows that

$$-1 \leq R \leq 1$$

Example 15.18 **Calculation of a Sample Correlation Coefficient:** The data in Table 15.6 show the depth X in thousands of feet and the cost of drilling Y in thousands of dollars for a sample of oil wells. Calculate the correlation coefficient between the depth of the well and the cost of drilling.

TABLE 15.6
Depth of oil wells

Well i	Depth x_i	Cost y_i	x_iy_i	x_i^2	y_i^2
1	3	6	18	9	36
2	5	12	60	25	144
3	1	3	3	1	9
4	6	13	78	36	169
5	8	14	112	64	196
6	7	12	84	49	144
	30	60	355	184	698

Solution: We obtain $\bar{x} = 5$ and $\bar{y} = 10$. We then calculate R as follows:

$$\begin{aligned} R &= \frac{\sum x_iy_i - n\bar{x}\bar{y}}{\sqrt{\sum x_i^2 - n\bar{x}^2}\sqrt{\sum y_i^2 - n\bar{y}^2}} \\ &= \frac{355 - 6(5)(10)}{\sqrt{184 - 6(5)(5)}\sqrt{698 - 6(10)(10)}} \\ &= .953 \end{aligned}$$

This sample correlation coefficient is quite close to 1 and indicates that the data lie close to a straight line having a positive slope. The graph of the data in Figure 15.14 indicates that the drilling cost and the depth of the well are positively correlated.

By using the data in Table 15.6, we can obtain the sample regression line

$$\hat{y}_i = 1.912 + 1.6176x_i$$

and the value of the coefficient of determination is $R^2 = .91$, which is the square of the sample correlation coefficient. ■

Testing Hypotheses About the Population Correlation Coefficient

The sample correlation coefficient R can be interpreted as an estimate of the population correlation coefficient ρ, where X and Y are both random variables having a joint prob-

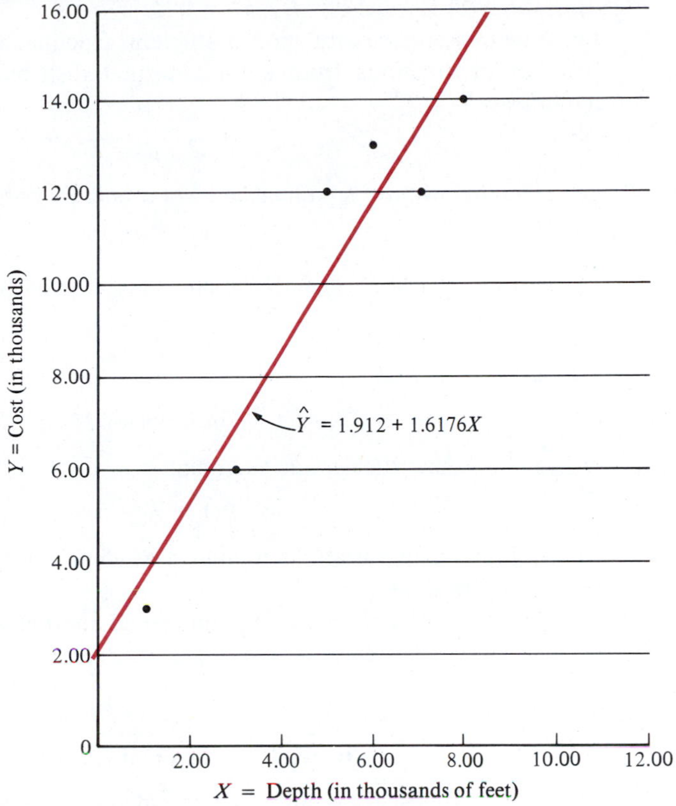

FIGURE 15.14
Scatter diagram of data in Example 15.18.

ability distribution. If we use this interpretation, then it is natural to develop hypotheses about the value of ρ in the population and to test these hypotheses by making use of the estimate R. By far the most frequently performed test is of the null hypothesis that the population correlation coefficient is 0. Note that since $b_1 = R(s_Y/s_X)$, testing $\rho = 0$ is equivalent to testing that $\beta_1 = 0$ where β_1 is the slope of the population regression line.

Tests of the null hypothesis H_0: $\rho = 0$ are based on the assumption that X and Y follow a bivariate normal distribution. Suppose we have a random sample (x_1, y_1), $(x_2, y_2), \ldots, (x_n, y_n)$ of observations from the bivariate normal distribution. When $\rho = 0$, the t statistic

$$t = R/s_R$$

follows the Student t distribution with $(n - 2)$ degrees of freedom, where s_R is the estimated standard deviation of R. We calculate s_R by the formula

$$s_R = \sqrt{\frac{1 - R^2}{n - 2}}$$

The appropriate tests are then derived as indicated in the accompanying box.

Testing the Null Hypothesis H_0: $\rho = 0$

Let R be the sample correlation coefficient, calculated from a random sample of n pairs of observations from a joint normal distribution. The tests of the null hypothesis

$$H_0: \rho = 0$$

described below have significance level α and are based on the test statistic

$$t = R/s_R$$

Case 1: To test H_0 against the one-sided alternative hypothesis

$$H_1: \rho > 0$$

use the decision rule

$$\text{Reject } H_0 \text{ in favor of } H_1 \text{ if } t > t_{\alpha,\nu}$$

where $t_{\alpha,\nu}$ is the critical value such that

$$P(t > t_{\alpha,\nu}) = \alpha$$

where the random variable t follows a Student t distribution with $\nu = (n - 2)$ degrees of freedom.

Case 2: To test H_0 against the one-sided alternative hypothesis

$$H_1: \rho < 0$$

use the decision rule

$$\text{Reject } H_0 \text{ in favor of } H_1 \text{ if } t < -t_{\alpha,\nu}$$

Case 3: To test H_0 against the two-sided alternative

$$H_1: \rho \neq 0$$

use the decision rule

$$\text{Reject } H_0 \text{ in favor of } H_1 \text{ if } t < -t_{\alpha/2,\nu} \text{ or if } t > t_{\alpha/2,\nu}$$

Example 15.19

Testing the Null Hypothesis H_0: $\rho = 0$: For the data in Example 15.18, the sample correlation between the depth of an oil well and the cost of drilling was $R = .953$. It is reasonable to suspect that there is a positive relationship between these two variables. Thus we would want to test the null hypothesis

$$H_0: \rho = 0$$

against the one-sided alternative hypothesis

$$H_1: \rho > 0$$

Solution: Because we have $n = 6$ observations and $\alpha = .05$, we obtain the t statistic

$$t = \frac{.953}{\sqrt{(1 - .953^2)/(6 - 2)}} = 6.29$$

We use a one-sided test. For $\alpha = .05$, the critical value of t having $(n - 2) = 4$ degrees of freedom is $t_{.05,4} = 2.132$. We reject H_0 in favor of H_1 because the t statistic exceeds the critical value and falls in the rejection region of the test. ■

Inappropriate Use of Correlation Analysis

If correlation analysis is used indiscriminately, conclusions can be misleading or even false. A common mistake is to assume that correlation implies causation. However, the fact that X and Y are correlated does not imply that X causes Y or vice versa. It may be that X causes Y, that Y causes X, that both X and Y are influenced by some other variable, or that the correlation between X and Y is *spurious*.

Definition: Spurious Correlation

Two variables are said to be **spuriously correlated** when their correlation is nonzero and there is no reason to believe that the variables are related to one another.

An example of spurious correlation can be illustrated by calculating the sample correlation coefficient between the annual number of crimes committed in New York City and the average salary of full professors at Harvard University during the years 1950 to 1970. These variables are highly positively correlated, but there is no apparent reason to believe that one variable is connected to the other. In this case, the correlation coefficient does not measure causality.

Another problem occurs when X and Y are, say, negatively related, but correlation analysis indicates that the effect of X on Y is positive. The next example illustrates this.

Example 15.20 **An Inappropriate Use of Correlation Analysis:** An important theory in economics states that, other things being equal, the higher the price of a commodity, the less the demand for it. Thus, if other things were equal, we would expect to find that the prices of tickets to professional football games and the number of tickets sold were negatively correlated. However, the data show that since 1960 both prices of tickets and the number of tickets sold per year have steadily increased. Thus, the data reveal a positive correlation between the price of tickets and the quantity sold. Does this evidence support the hypothesis that the law of demand is false? Does the sample evidence support the hypothesis that, in order to sell more tickets, professional football teams should increase prices? Did the increase in prices cause the increase in quantity sold?

Using correlation analysis on sales of tickets and the price of tickets is inappropriate because we are neglecting other important variables that affect the number of tickets sold. Since 1960 sales have increased for several reasons: the total population of the United States has increased, so there are more potential ticket buyers; people's incomes have increased, so they have more money to spend on football tickets; the number of professional teams has increased; the popularity of professional football has increased; and so forth. Once these things are taken into account, the law of demand still holds true. That is, once population, income, number of teams, and other pertinent factors are considered, we still find that the higher the price of tickets, the lower the quantity sold.

The following argument shows that the law of demand holds (as prices increase, the quantity demanded decreases) and that the sample correlation coefficient is giving misleading results. Assume that, at the present time, 50,000 people are willing to pay, say, \$10 each to see a certain game. Consider what would happen if tomorrow the home team announced that the price of each ticket had been increased to, say, \$15. Immediately after the announcement, the number of individuals who would want to buy a ticket would decrease and fewer than 50,000 tickets would be sold. This shows that, *other things being kept constant*, the quantity of football tickets demanded and the price of football tickets are negatively related. ■

The problem with correlation analysis is that it ignores all the variables that may influence Y other than the single variable X. In economics and business, there are many cases where it is unreasonable to assume that a variable Y is a function of just a single variable X. A more appropriate way to determine the true relationship between Y and X may be to construct a multiple regression model that includes all the important variables influencing Y. Such models are discussed in Chapter 16.

Nevertheless, the correlation coefficient can be useful in finding potential variables to insert into a multiple regression model. There might be a relatively high correlation between Y and some variable X_1 and between Y and some other variable X_2. If this is the case, it might be that a regression model should contain both variables X_1 and X_2 as independent variables.

Multiple regression is a statistical technique that enables the investigator to discover how Y is influenced by a whole set of other variables, and thus it overcomes many of the problems inherent in simple correlation analysis.

Correlation and Statistical Significance

Suppose we use a 5% level of significance and reject the null hypothesis $H_0: \rho = 0$ in favor of the alternative hypothesis $H_1: \rho > 0$. Frequently the statistician will say that the sample correlation coefficient R is "significantly different from 0 at the 5% level of significance." This does not mean that variable X explains a "significant" amount of the variation in Y. The word *significant* is being used with two different meanings here.

For example, if we use a 5% level of significance and the sample is large enough ($n > 28$), then a sample correlation coefficient of $R = .1$ will be significantly different from 0 if we perform a formal statistical test using the t statistic. Although a sample correlation coefficient of $R = .1$ may be "statistically significant" (i.e. it is significantly different from 0), it may be of no practical significance. When $R = .1$, this means that $R^2 = .01$ and thus X explains only 1% of the variation in Y, leaving 99% of the variation in Y still unexplained.

Finally, it should be noted that if a variable Y is correlated with each of two other variables, say X_1 and X_2, this does not imply that those two variables together in a regression equation will explain significantly more of the variation in Y than just one of them alone. It might be that X_1 and X_2 are highly correlated with one another and contribute virtually the same information for explaining or predicting Y.

Exercises for Section 15.9

1. Calculate the sample correlation coefficient for the following data concerning grades of 8 students on math and economics tests:

Math (X)	89	86	74	90	46	82	68	94
Physics (Y)	82	72	80	96	68	89	74	90

Plot the data on a scatter diagram.

2. Calculate the sample correlation coefficient for the following data concerning annual wages (in thousands of dollars) and years of employment at a certain company:

Years of employment (X)	10	2	8	21	6	7	12	8	1
Annual wages (Y)	35	16	24	44	26	32	33	27	18

Plot the data (x_i, y_i) on a scatter diagram.

3. Calculate the sample correlation coefficient using the following data concerning the unemployment rate and the inflation rate (measured as the percent change in the Consumer Price Index) for the years 1978 to 1987 (data from *Economic Report of the President*):

Year	CPI Y	Unemployment Rate X
1978	7.7	6.1
1979	11.3	5.8
1980	13.5	7.1
1981	10.4	7.6
1982	6.1	9.7
1983	3.2	9.6
1984	4.3	7.5
1985	3.6	7.2
1986	1.9	7.0
1987	3.7	6.2

Plot the data on a scatter diagram.

4. The following data show the total number of priests and ministers in a certain town and the total expenditures on alcohol in thousands of dollars in that town between 1960 and 1985:

Year	Expenditure on Alcohol Y	Number of Clergy X
1960	480	64
1965	500	69
1970	535	74
1975	565	85
1980	610	106
1985	640	114

a. Calculate the sample correlation coefficient between X and Y.

b. Do you think that increases in X cause increases in Y, increases in Y cause increases in X, or neither? How do you explain the high value of R?

5. The accompanying data show the size of various houses (in square feet) and the annual heating expenditures in dollars in those houses during the last year:

Heating Expenditures (Y)	260	345	420	235	400	280
Size of House (X)	800	1000	1600	750	1700	850

Calculate the sample correlation coefficient.

6. A sample of 18 values of X and Y yielded a correlation coefficient of $R = .5$. Test H_0: $\rho = 0$ against H_1: $\rho \neq 0$ using a 5% level of significance.

7. A correlation coefficient based on a sample of size 27 was computed to be .4. Can we conclude that ρ differs from 0 at a significance level of 5%? Of 1%?

8. The data below show the prices of six houses in dollars and their distances from town in miles:

Price of House (Y)	10,000	12,000	17,000	32,000	62,000	45,000
Distance (X)	1	2	2	4	8	7

a. Calculate the correlation coefficient.
b. Test H_0: $\rho = 0$ against H_1: $\rho \neq 0$ using a 5% level of significance.
c. Do you think increases in X cause increases in Y? Can you explain why $R > 0$?

9. The following data show the prices of several houses in dollars and their distances from town in miles (each house in the sample is the same age and contains 3000 square feet of floor space):

Price of House (Y)	60,000	40,000	45,000	38,000	30,000	32,000
Distance (X)	1	2	2	4	8	7

a. Calculate R.
b. Test H_0: $\rho = 0$ against H_1: $\rho \neq 0$ using a 5% level of significance.
c. Why do the results in this problem differ from the results in Exercise 8?

10. Suppose that the Goodyear Tire Company collects data on the relationship between a car's speed and the distance it travels before stopping (after the brakes are applied). Would you expect the correlation coefficient to be positive or negative? Is there a causal relationship in this case?

11. If a regression line can explain 36% of the variation in the dependent variable, what is the correlation coefficient?

15.10 ▪ Computer Applications

In actual practice, statisticians almost always use computers for regression and correlation analysis. Many different computer programs are available that will generate all of the information we have discussed in this chapter. The following example illustrates how to obtain and interpret computer output using the SPSSX computer program.

Example 15.21 **Using SPSSX for Regression Analysis:** We will use the SPSSX computer program to obtain the sample regression line and various other useful statistical information for the data presented in Table 15.1 on the weekly expenditures on recreation and weekly incomes for a sample of 20 families, described in Example 15.3. The data and the sample regression line were plotted in Figure 15.4.

Following is the complete SPSSX set of instructions for reading the data, generating a scatter diagram showing the pairs of values of the variables EXPEND and INCOME, and printing out the sample regression equation that explains EXPEND as a linear function of INCOME:

```
TITLE 'EXPENDITURE STUDY'
DATA LIST FREE/EXPEND INCOME
BEGIN DATA

   90   900
   60   800
    .     .
    .     .
    .     .
   35   200
```

```
END DATA
SCATTERGRAM EXPEND WITH INCOME
REGRESSION VARIABLES = EXPEND INCOME/
   DEPENDENT = EXPEND/
   ENTER INCOME
FINISH
```

FIGURE 15.15 SPSSX-generated output for Example 15.21.

```
                          * * * *   M U L T I P L E   R E G R E S S I O N   * * * *

Listwise Deletion of Missing Data

Equation Number 1    Dependent Variable..   EXPEND   EXPENDITURES ON RECREATION

Beginning Block Number  1.  Method:  Enter      INCOME

Variable(s) Entered on Step Number  1..     INCOME    WEEKLY INCOME

Multiple R            .91067      Analysis of Variance
R Square              .82932                       DF      Sum of Squares      Mean Square
Adjusted R Square     .81984      Regression        1          6016.72585       6016.72585
Standard Error       8.29416      Residual         18          1238.27415         68.79301

                                  F =       87.46130      Signif F =  .0000

------------------ Variables in the Equation ------------------

Variable              B          SE B        Beta          T  Sig T

INCOME          .076379       .008167     .910671      9.352  .0000
(Constant)    13.918919      4.916352                  2.831  .0111

End Block Number   1   All requested variables entered.
```

The computer output from this set of instructions, shown in Figure 15.15 above, is explained as follows:

Estimated coefficients: The estimated slope b_1 and the estimated intercept b_0 are found in the column labeled "B." We have $b_1 = 0.076379$ and $b_0 = 13.918919$.

Estimated standard deviations: The estimated standard deviations of b_1 and b_0 are found in the column labeled "SE B." We obtain $s_{b_1} = 0.008167$ and $s_{b_0} = 4.916352$.

t statistics: The t statistics used to test the null hypotheses H_0: $\beta_0 = 0$ and H_0: $\beta_1 = 0$ are printed in the column labeled "T." The t statistic used to test H_0: $\beta_1 = 0$ is $t = 9.352$. Note that this is $t = b_1/s_{b_1} = 0.076379/0.008167$. The t statistic used to test H_0: $\beta_0 = 0$ is $t = 2.831$. Note that this is $t = b_0/s_{b_0} = 13.918919/4.916352$.

Prob-values: In the table, the values found in the column labeled "Sig T" refer to observed significance levels, or prob-values, for the t statistics. For the slope coefficient, the observed significance level is Sig $T = .0000$. This means that for the t distribution having $(n - 2) = 18$ degrees of freedom, the combined area to the right of $t = 9.352$ and to the left of $t = -9.352$ is .0000. For the intercept (constant) coefficient, the observed significance level is Sig $T = .0111$. This means that, for the t distribution having $(n - 2) = 18$ degrees of freedom, the combined area to the right of $t = 2.831$ and to the left of $t = -2.831$ is .0111. Having these prob-values printed out is especially convenient, because we don't have to refer to tables of the t distribution to test the null hypothesis that a population regression coefficient is 0.

The SPSSX program also prints out what is called an Analysis of Variance Table. This table contains information concerning the sample correlation coefficient R, the value of R^2, the regression sum of squares (SSR), the residual sum of squares (SSE), and the estimated standard error of the regression (s_e). The following values and their interpretations are printed in the table.

Sample correlation coefficient: The sample correlation coefficient, which equals the square root of R^2, is shown in the row labeled "Multiple R" as $R = .91067$.

Coefficient of determination: The coefficient of determination is shown in the row labeled "R Square" as $R^2 = .82932$.

Standard error: The estimated standard deviation of the error terms s_e is shown in the row labeled "Standard Error" as 8.29416.

Regression sum of squares: The regression sum of squares SSR is shown to be 6016.72585.

Residual sum of squares: The residual sum of squares SSE is shown to be 1238.27415 and has $(n - 2) = 18$ degrees of freedom. Recall that an unbiased estimate of the variance of the error terms is given by $s_e^2 = \text{SSE}/(n - 2) = 1238.27415/18 = 68.79301$. After taking the square root, we obtain $s_e = 8.29416$, which agrees with the value given above.

F statistic: The statistic F is used to test the null hypothesis that all of the independent variables considered together do not help explain the value of the dependent variable. In the simple linear regression model, the value of the F statistic is the square of the t statistic used to test the null hypothesis H_0: $\beta_1 = 0$. Note that $F = 87.46130 = (9.352)^2 = t^2$.

At the present time, we are not interested in the remaining numbers in the Analysis of Variance Table. ■

Figure 15.16 shows the SAS computer output for Example 15.21. Compare the regression coefficients, t statistics, s_e, R^2, SSE, and other statistics with the corresponding output from the SPSSX program.

FIGURE 15.16 **SAS-generated output for Example 15.21.**

SAS

GENERAL LINEAR MODELS PROCEDURE

DEPENDENT VARIABLE: EXPEND

SOURCE	DF	SUM OF SQUARES	MEAN SQUARE	F VALUE	PR > F	R-SQUARE	C.V.
MODEL	1	6016.72585141	6016.72585141	87.46	0.0001	0.829321	14.6799
ERROR	18	1238.27414859	68.79300825		ROOT MSE		EXPEND MEAN
CORRECTED TOTAL	19	7255.00000000			8.29415507		56.50000000

SOURCE	DF	TYPE I SS	F VALUE	PR > F	DF	TYPE III SS	F VALUE	PR > F
INCOME	1	6016.72585141	87.46	0.0001	1	6016.72585141	87.46	0.0001

PARAMETER	ESTIMATE	T FOR H0: PARAMETER=0	PR > |T|	STD ERROR OF ESTIMATE
INTERCEPT	13.91891892	2.83	0.0111	4.91635194
INCOME	0.07637862	9.35	0.0001	0.00816702

Exercises for Section 15.10

1. Using the data in Table 2.2 of Chapter 2, determine if the college grade point averages (GPA) of students in the statistics class are related to their SAT scores.

a. Estimate the simple linear regression model that explains GPA as a function of SAT score.

b. Does this equation seem to do a good job of explaining GPA? Generate a scatter diagram of the data.

c. Find the value of R^2 and s_e.

d. Test the null hypothesis that the slope of the population regression line is 0 against the alternative hypothesis that it is positive. Let $\alpha = .05$.

Use the data in Table 2.3 of Chapter 2 to complete Exercises 2–5.

2. Test the hypothesis that the average teachers' salary in a state (X_2) is linearly related to per capita income in the state (X_5).

a. Estimate the simple linear regression model that explains SALARY as a function of INCOME.

b. Does this equation seem to do a good job of explaining the variable SALARY? Generate a scatter diagram of the data.

c. Find the value of R^2 and s_e.

d. Test the null hypothesis that the slope of the population regression line is 0 against the alternative hypothesis that it is positive. Let $\alpha = .05$.

3. Test the hypothesis that the average teachers' salary in a state (X_2) is linearly related to tax revenue per capita in the state (X_3).

a. Estimate the simple linear regression model that explains SALARY as a function of REVENUE.

b. Does this equation seem to do a good job of explaining the variable SALARY? Generate a scatter diagram of the data.

c. Find the value of R^2 and s_e.

d. Test the null hypothesis that the slope of the population regression line is 0 against the alternative hypothesis that it is positive. Let $\alpha = .05$.

4. Test the hypothesis that tax revenue per capita in a state (X_3) is linearly related to per capita income in the state (X_5).

a. Estimate the simple linear regression model that explains REVENUE as a function of INCOME.

b. Does this equation seem to do a good job of explaining the variable REVENUE? Generate a scatter diagram of the data.

c. Find the value of R^2 and s_e.

d. Test the null hypothesis that the slope of the population regression line is 0 against the alternative hypothesis that it is positive. Let $\alpha = .05$.

5. Test the hypothesis that the average hourly earnings in manufacturing in a state (X_6) is linearly related to the percentage of employees in the state who are unionized (X_1).

a. Estimate the simple linear regression model that explains PCTUNION as a function of WAGE.

b. Does this equation seem to do a good job of explaining the variable PCTUNION? Generate a scatter diagram of the data.

c. Find the value of R^2 and s_e.

d. Test the null hypothesis that the slope of the population regression line is 0 against the alternative hypothesis that it is positive. Let $\alpha = .05$.

Chapter 15 Summary

Chapter 15 discusses methods of examining sample data collected on two quantitative variables where the data occur in pairs. A useful first step is to represent the data graphically in a scatter diagram, where each pair of data values is represented as a single point. Often the scatter diagram will reveal whether the relationship between the two variables is *positive* (as one increases, the other increases), *negative* (as one increases, the other decreases), or *uncorrelated* (the scatter diagram does not exhibit a linear pattern).

When dealing with a pair of quantitative variables (say, X and Y), we are generally interested in determining whether the variables are related in some manner. If a relationship does exist, perhaps the independent variable can be used to predict values of the dependent variable. If a significant linear relationship exists within the sample data, both the direction (positive or negative) and the strength of this linear relationship can be measured using the *sample correlation coefficient* R. Another commonly used measure of association between two variables is the *sample covariance* s_{XY}. If R is near 1.0, then the variables are strongly positively related; if R is near -1.0, the variables are strongly negatively related. If R is near 0, the sample data support the hypothesis that the variables are uncorrelated and not linearly related.

The *sample regression line* is the line that best fits the sample of data. It is obtained by minimizing the squared residuals using the *method of least squares*. The sample regression equation can be used to predict values of the dependent variable. To describe the assumptions behind this procedure, we introduced the *population regression model*. When we perform any test of an hypothesis using the regression model, we should check that the underlying assumptions of the model are satisfied. These assumptions will be examined more closely in Chapter 18. The assumptions include that the random errors have a mean of 0, have a common variance σ^2, and are independent of one another. An estimate of the variance is $\text{SSE}/(n - 2)$, where SSE is the *residual sum of squares*.

Methods for determining the strength of the model as a predictor of the dependent variable include the following: (1) a t test to test the null hypothesis that the slope of the population regression line is 0, which would indicate that X has no predictive ability; (2) a t test to test whether the population correlation coefficient ρ is 0, which would indicate that there is no linear relationship between the two variables; and (3) a confidence interval for the slope β_1. Because the two t tests and their computed values and degrees of freedom are identical, there is no point in performing both.

Another measure of how well the model fits the sample data is given by the *coefficient of determination* R^2 where $R^2 = 1 - \text{SSE}/\text{SST}$. For the simple linear regression model containing one explanatory variable, R^2 is the square of the sample correlation coefficient between Y and X. SSE is the *sum of squared errors* and SST represents the *total variation in the sample* Y *values*. R^2 measures the proportion of variation in the Y values explained by the regression model, and its value is always between 0 and 1. Values of R^2 close to 1 indicate that the model fits the data well.

To evaluate the predictive ability of the model for a specific value of X, a confidence interval for the average value of Y given this value of X can be obtained. Similarly, we can derive a prediction interval for a particular value of the dependent variable given this specific value of X.

In this chapter we have analyzed relationships between two quantitative variables. In Chapter 16 we analyze relationships between more than two quantitative variables.

Summary of Important Formulas

Formula	Comments
$b_1 = \dfrac{\sum x_i y_i - n\bar{x}\bar{y}}{\sum x_i^2 - n\bar{x}^2} = \dfrac{n \sum x_i y_i - (\sum x_i)(\sum y_i)}{n \sum x_i^2 - (\sum x_i)^2}$	b_1 is the point estimate of the slope of the regression line.
$b_0 = \bar{y} - b_1\bar{x} = \left(\dfrac{\sum y_i}{n}\right) - b_1\left(\dfrac{\sum x_i}{n}\right)$	b_0 is the point estimate of the intercept of the regression line.
$\text{SSE} = \sum y_i^2 - b_0 \sum y_i - b_1 \sum x_i y_i$ $s_e^2 = \dfrac{\text{SSE}}{n-2} = \dfrac{\sum (y_i - \hat{y}_i)^2}{n2}$	(a) s_e^2 is the point estimate of the variance of the probability distribution of Y for a given value of X. (b) σ_e^2 represents the variance of the random error terms.
$R = b_1 \dfrac{s_X}{s_Y} = \dfrac{s_{XY}}{s_X y_X}$ $R = \dfrac{\sum x_i y_i - n\bar{x}\bar{y}}{\sqrt{\sum x_i^2 - n\bar{x}^2}\sqrt{\sum y_i^2 - n\bar{y}^2}}$	(a) R is the sample correlation coefficient. (b) $-1 \leq R \leq 1$. (c) s_X and s_Y are the sample standard deviations for X and Y. (d) R measures the strength of the linear relationship between X and Y.
$R^2 = b_1^2 \dfrac{s_X^2}{s_Y^2}$ $R^2 = \dfrac{\text{SST} - \text{SSE}}{\text{SST}} = 1 - \dfrac{\text{SSE}}{\text{SST}}$	(a) R^2 is called the coefficient of determination. (b) $0 \leq R^2 \leq 1$. (c) R^2 measures the relative strength of the relationship between Y and X. (d) SSE is the residual sum of squares. (e) SST is the total sum of squares.
$s_{b_1}^2 = \dfrac{s_e^2}{[\sum x_i^2 - n\bar{x}^2]}$	$s_{b_1}^2$ is the estimated variance of b_1.
$s_{b_0}^2 = \dfrac{s_e^2 \sum x_i^2}{n[\sum x_i^2 - n\bar{x}^2]}$	$s_{b_0}^2$ is the estimated variance of b_0.
$t = \dfrac{b_1 - \beta_1^*}{s_{b_1}}$	This t statistic is used to test H_0: $\beta_1 = \beta_1^*$. The t value has $(n - 2)$ degrees of freedom.
$t = \dfrac{b_0 - \beta_0^*}{s_{b_0}}$	This t statistic is used to test H_0: $\beta_0 = \beta_0^*$. The t value has $(n - 2)$ degrees of freedom.
$b_1 \pm t_{\alpha/2} s_{b_1}$ $b_0 \pm t_{\alpha/2} s_{b_0}$	These are confidence intervals for β_1 and β_0 having level of confidence $(1 - \alpha)$.
$s_{\hat{Y}_p}^2 = s_e^2\left(\dfrac{1}{n} + \dfrac{(x_p - \bar{x})^2}{\sum x_i^2 - n\bar{x}^2}\right)$	$s_{\hat{Y}_p}^2$ is the estimated variance for the mean value of Y associated with $X = x_p$.
$\hat{y}_p \pm t_{\alpha/2} s_{\hat{Y}_p}$	This is the confidence interval for the mean value of Y associated with $X = x_p$.

Chapter 15 ▪ Supplementary Exercises

1. Graph the following straight lines:
a. $Y = 2 + 2X$ b. $Y = 3 + 2X$ c. $Y = 3 - 2X$ d. $Y = 3 - 0.5X$

2. The accompanying data from the *Economic Report of the President* show the interest rates paid on three-month Treasury bills and three- to five-year government securities from 1978 to 1987.
a. Plot the data (x_i, y_i) on a scatter diagram.
b. Obtain the least-squares estimates b_0 and b_1.
c. Graph the line $\hat{y}_i = b_0 + b_1x_i$.

Year	3-Month Treasury Bills X	3- to 5-Year Government Securities Y
1978	7.2	8.3
1979	10.0	9.7
1980	11.5	11.6
1981	14.0	14.4
1982	10.7	12.9
1983	8.6	10.5
1984	9.6	11.9
1985	7.5	9.6
1986	6.0	7.1
1987	5.8	7.7

d. Calculate R, the correlation coefficient. Using a 5% level of significance, test H_0: $\rho = 0$ against H_1: $\rho \neq 0$.
e. Calculate R^2.

3. We are interested in determining if the selling price of a used car of a specific model is related to the age of the car. We take a sample of 8 cars of the same model and obtain the following data:
a. Plot the data (x_i, y_i) on a scatter diagram.
b. Obtain the least-squares estimates b_0 and b_1.
c. Graph the line $\hat{y}_i = b_0 + b_1x_i$.

Age (in years) (X)	2	4	5	3	1	3	5	1
Selling Price (in dollars) (Y)	1600	800	800	1300	2000	1100	600	1800

d. Calculate R, the correlation coefficient. Using a 5% level of significance, test H_0: $\rho = 0$ against H_1: $\rho \neq 0$.
e. Calculate R^2.

4. The accompanying data show the annual incomes (X) of 10 families and their annual expenditures on entertainment and recreation (Y), all expressed in thousands of dollars. It is hypothesized that expenditures on entertainment and recreation are linearly related to incomes.

Recreation Expenditures (Y)	2.0	4.2	3.4	4.9	6.6	5.9	4.8	2.8	5.1	8.6
Income (X)	11	16	14	26	45	32	24	18	25	50

a. Plot the data.
b. Estimate and graph the linear regression line.
c. Calculate R^2.
d. Calculate the correlation coefficient between X and Y.
e. Using a 5% level of significance, test whether the population correlation coefficient is 0.

5. An analyst claims that the quantity of ice sold (in dollars) per week by a beer distributor depends on the average temperature (in degrees Fahrenheit) at noon during the week. The analyst obtains the following data:

Weekly Sales (Y)	350	245	260	110	150	290	185
Temperature (X)	91	82	85	75	76	83	74

a. Plot the data.
b. Calculate the correlation coefficient.
c. Test H_0: $\rho = 0$ versus H_1: $\rho > 0$. Let $\alpha = .05$.

6. The U.S. Government publishes numerous documents and sells them to the public. The following data show the selling prices in dollars of various documents and their lengths in pages:

Price (Y)	8	19	14	16	10	12	16
Number of Pages (X)	240	890	430	620	330	425	535

a. Plot the data.
b. Estimate the regression equation $\hat{y}_i = b_0 + b_1 x_i$.
c. Calculate the coefficient of determination R^2.
d. Predict the selling price for a 700-page book.

7. A pro football analyst had a theory that teams that threw many passes during a game tended to win fewer games than teams that seldom passed. The following data show the number of games won by various teams and the average number of passes they threw per game throughout the season:

Games Won (Y)	13	10	6	4	7	9	5	8
Passes per game (X)	18	26	34	32	27	29	32	28

a. Plot the data.
b. Calculate the correlation coefficient.
c. Test H_0: $\rho = 0$ against H_1: $\rho < 0$. Let $\alpha = .05$.
d. Can you think of any reason that X and Y would be negatively correlated?

8. What is the correlation coefficient between Y and X in the following situations:
a. The variable X is a constant.
b. X always exceeds Y by 10 units.
c. X is always twice as large as Y.
d. X and Y are related by the equation $Y = 1 + 3X$.

9. A company owns a large fleet of taxicabs. The cost per mile of operating a cab is believed to be influenced by its age. Ten cabs were selected, and a careful study was made to determine the operating costs per mile of each cab. The data are as follows:

Cost per mile (in cents) (Y)	10.1	11.4	13.8	13.7	14.0	11.7	15.2	12.0	13.2	12.0
Age (in months) (X)	3	7	19	16	27	8	36	10	14	9

a. Plot the data.
b. Calculate the correlation coefficient. Test H_0: $\rho = 0$ against H_1: $\rho > 0$. Let $\alpha = .05$.
c. Estimate and graph the linear regression equation.
d. Estimate the cost per mile of operating taxicab that is 20 months of age.

10. Whether intelligence is inherited or determined mainly by environmental factors has long been debated. A random sample of 8-year-old children is selected, and the children and their parents are given IQ tests. The results of the test follow:

Child's IQ (Y)	101	111	122	103	95	99	89	103
Average of parents' IQs (X)	105	122	116	98	88	108	102	105

a. Plot the data.
b. Calculate the correlation coefficient and test H_0: $\rho = 0$ against H_1: $\rho > 0$. Let $\alpha = .05$.
c. Estimate and graph the linear regression equation.
d. Predict a child's IQ if the average IQ of the parents is 112.

11. A baseball player and the team's general manager are discussing the player's contract for the next season. The player wants a raise because he claims that people come to watch him play. The manager claims that people do not pay to watch stars play but to see the team win. To support his theory, the manager offers the following data concerning percentage of games won and average per game attendance in thousands during recent years:

Year	Average Attendance (Y)	Percent Games Won (X)
1980	22	64
1981	20	60
1982	14	48
1983	18	56
1984	10	42
1985	11	46
1986	17	55
1987	23	65
1988	25	68

a. Plot the data.
b. Calculate the correlation coefficient. Test H_0: $\rho = 0$ against H_1: $\rho > 0$. Let $\alpha = .05$.
c. Estimate the sample regression line and graph it.

12. The transit authority for a major city wants to determine if there is any relationship between the age of a bus in years and the annual maintenance cost in dollars. A sample of 10 buses resulted in the following data:

Age of Bus (X)	1	2	2	2	2	3	4	4	5	5
Maintenance Cost (Y)	310	375	465	520	590	520	650	800	740	950

a. Compute the sample correlation coefficient for the above data.
b. Using the sample correlation coefficient, test if the two variables are correlated. Use a one-tailed test and $\alpha = .05$.

c. Find the sample regression equation.
d. Test the null hypothesis that the population slope is 0. Use a one-tailed test and $\alpha = .05$. Compare this answer with the answer obtained in part (b).
e. Did the least-squares line provide a good fit to the observed data? Calculate the coefficient of determination.
f. Find a 90% confidence interval estimate of the expected maintenance cost for a bus that is 4 years old.

13. Suppose that we calculate the sample regression equation for a given set of sample data and obtain $b_0 = 2.0$ and $b_1 = 0$. Explain which of the following will be true and which false:
a. SSE = 0 b. $R^2 = 0$ c. $R = 0$ d. SSR = SST
e. SSR = SSE f. SSR = 0 g. SSE = SST

14. Let Y represent the resale price of the ith used motorcycle and X represent the mileage the motorcycle has traveled. Suppose we have the following data showing the selling prices in dollars and mileages in thousands of a sample of 6 motorcycles:

Y	100	400	600	500	300	300
X	30	8	5	7	9	12

a. Estimate β_0, β_1, and σ_e^2 for the linear regression model.
b. Calculate R^2 and s_e.
c. Estimate the variances of b_0 and b_1.
d. Test H_0: $\beta_1 = 0$ against H_1: $\beta_1 < 0$ using a 5% level of significance.
e. Test H_0: $\beta_0 = 0$ against H_1: $\beta_0 \neq 0$ using a 5% level of significance.
f. Calculate a 95% confidence interval for β_1.

15. A teacher thinks that the absentee rate is closely related to the temperature: Students cut classes on warm days. The following data on temperature in degrees Fahrenheit and number of absentees were obtained:

Temperature (X)	50	70	66	80	65	72	85	72
Number absent (Y)	3	6	7	8	5	6	9	4

a. Estimate β_0, β_1, and σ_e^2 for the linear regression model.
b. Calculate R^2 and s_e.
c. Estimate the variances of b_0 and b_1.
d. Test H_0: $\beta_1 = 0$ against H_1: $\beta_1 > 0$ using a 5% level of significance.
e. Test H_0: $\beta_0 = 0$ against H_1: $\beta_0 \neq 0$ using a 5% level of significance.
f. Calculate a 95% confidence interval for β_1.

16. A company believes that its sales are linearly related to its advertising expenditures and obtained the following data expressed in millions of dollars:

Sales (Y)	500	200	400	900	860	940	770
Advertising Expenditures (X)	60	35	45	80	75	85	70

a. Estimate the population regression equation.
b. Calculate R^2.
c. Calculate a 95% confidence interval for β_1.
d. Predict sales if advertising expenditures equal 100.
e. Calculate a 95% confidence interval for the mean value of Y if $X = 100$.

17. A firm wants to study the relationship between the age of the machines (in years) in its factory and the annual repair expenditures (in dollars) for the machines. It obtained the following data:

Age (X)	2	4	5	7	9	8	3	5	6	10
Repair costs (Y)	50	60	80	90	105	110	60	85	95	110

a. Plot the data on a scatter diagram.
b. Estimate and graph the population regression equation.
c. Calculate R^2 and a 95% confidence interval for β_1.
d. Estimate the repair cost of a 10-year-old machine and calculate a 95% confidence interval for the mean value of Y when $X = 10$.

18. The owner of a large firm that manufactures furniture believes that annual national expenditures on furniture are linearly related to national personal disposable income. Use the accompanying data, expressed in billions of dollars, from the *Economic Report of the President* and perform the following tasks:
a. Plot the data on a scatter diagram.
b. Estimate and graph the population regression line.
c. Calculate R^2 and s_e.
d. Estimate the variances of b_0 and b_1.
e. Test H_0: $\beta_1 = 0$ against H_1: $\beta_1 > 0$ using a 5% level of significance.
f. Construct a 95% confidence interval for β_1.
g. Estimate expenditures on furniture if disposable income is $900 billion.
h. Construct a 95% confidence interval for the mean value of Y if $X = 900$.

Expenditures on Furniture (Y)	20	18	22	24	26	30	30	30	38	40
Personal Disposable Income (X)	350	364	385	404	438	473	511	546	591	634

19. A professor thinks that a student's score Y in a statistics course is linearly related to the student's IQ X. A sample of 8 students yields the following data:

Y	72	83	65	70	86	90	95	79
X	107	112	98	100	120	124	127	108

a. Estimate the population regression equation.
b. Estimate the variances of b_0 and b_1.
c. Find 95% confidence intervals for β_0 and β_1.
d. Use a 5% level of significance and test the null hypothesis H_0: $\beta_1 = 0$ against H_1: $\beta_1 > 0$.
e. Predict Y for a student whose IQ is 100.
f. Calculate a 95% confidence interval for the mean value of Y for students whose IQs are 110.

20. You are given the following data on sales (in tens of thousands of dollars) and advertising expenditures (in thousands of dollars):

Sales (Y)	31	40	25	30	20	26
Advertising expenditures (X)	5	11	3	4	3	5

a. Calculate the regression equation of sales on advertising expenditures.
b. Find 95% confidence intervals for β_0 and β_1.
c. Use a 5% level of significance and test H_0: $\beta_1 = 0$ against H_1: $\beta_1 > 0$.

d. Predict sales if \$6000 is spent on advertising.
e. Calculate a 95% confidence interval for the mean value of Y if $X = 6$.

21. The following data show monthly expenditures on food and housing and monthly income for families containing two children, all expressed in dollars:

Expenditures (Y)	250	600	350	400	500	400
Income (X)	1000	2000	1500	1600	1800	1200

a. Estimate the regression line of Y on X.
b. Test H_0: $\beta_1 = 0$ against H_1: $\beta_1 > 0$ using a 5% level of significance.
c. Construct a 95% confidence interval for the mean value of Y given $X = \$2000$.

22. The following data show the number of minutes required to type reports of varying lengths:

Typing time (Y)	60	130	100	290	175
Number of pages (X)	10	20	15	50	30

a. Estimate the linear regression line of Y on X.
b. Find a 95% confidence interval for β_1.
c. Predict how long it will take to type a 40-page report.
d. Find a 95% confidence interval for the actual value of Y given that $X = 40$.

23. The following figures show the weekly hours worked by production workers in manufacturing industries in the United States (Y) and the annual unemployment rate (X) for selected years:

Year	Average Hours Y	Percent Unemployment X
1981	39.8	7.6
1982	38.9	9.7
1983	40.1	9.6
1984	40.7	7.5
1985	40.5	7.2
1986	40.7	7.0
1987	41.0	6.2

a. Estimate the regression line of Y on X.
b. Test H_0: $\beta_1 = 0$ against H_1: $\beta_1 < 0$ using 5% level of significance.
c. Construct a 95% confidence interval for β_1.

24. The Metropolitan Fuel Company has collected data to study the relationship between the temperature at noon in degrees Fahrenheit and the gallons of fuel oil consumed in single-family dwellings on that day. The company needs to estimate the relationship between temperature and consumption of fue! oil in order to predict the supplies of fuel oil that will be needed on cold days. The following table shows a sample of the data collected by Metro executives:

Fuel Oil Consumption (Y)	7.2	6.7	6.3	5.1	4.7	3.5	2.8	1.2
Temperature at Noon (X)	12	18	21	33	38	46	52	70

a. Plot the data and estimate the linear regression line. Draw this line on the scatter diagram.
b. Construct a 95% confidence interval for the coefficient β_1.
c. Predict average consumption if the daily temperature at noon is 60° F.
d. Calculate R^2. Does this value indicate that the linear model is appropriate for explaining the values of Y?
e. Construct a 95% confidence interval for the mean value of Y given that $X = 70°$ F.

25. The Jones Rustproofing Company operates a chain of outlets in Chicago. The company rustproofs automobiles. Management believes that the number of customers in a quarter of the year can be predicted relatively accurately by using a linear regression model in which the explanatory variable is the number of new automobile registrations in Chicago in the previous quarter. The following data show the number of customers in hundreds during the last 8 quarters and the number of new car registrations in thousands for each previous quarter.

Customers per Quarter (Y)	7.1	8.2	6.3	9.1	8.7	6.4	5.2	8.1
New Cars Registered (X)	14.4	17.1	11.9	20.2	17.0	14.0	11.1	15.2

a. Plot the data on a scatter diagram.
b. Calculate the correlation coefficient between Y and X.
c. Test H_0: $\rho = 0$ against H_1: $\rho > 0$ using a 5% level of significance.
d. Based on your answer to part (c), does it appear that using X will be helpful in predicting Y?
e. Estimate the linear regression equation.
f. If $X = 12$ in some quarter, what would you predict for Y in the following quarter?
g. Construct 95% confidence intervals for b_0 and b_1.
h. Let $\alpha = .05$. Test H_0: $\beta_1 = 0$ against H_1: $\beta_1 > 0$.
i. Assume that $X = 15$ in some quarter. Predict Y for the following quarter.
j. Construct a 95% confidence interval for $E(Y|X = 15)$.
k. Construct a 95% confidence interval for Y given that $X = 15$.
l. Note that in the sample the values of X vary between 11.1 and 20.2. Would you be more confident in a forecast of Y for a period when $X = 15$ than for a period when $X = 25$? Why or why not?

26. Economists have long debated whether changes in government spending (ΔG) or changes in the money supply (ΔM) cause changes in gross national product (ΔGNP). Suppose we want to examine this issue. The accompanying data from the *Economic Report of the President* show the level of GNP, the level of government spending, and the money supply (measured as the sum of currency, demand deposits, travelers checks, other checkable deposits, money market mutual funds, savings, and small time deposits).
a. Calculate the year-to-year change in each variable. Denote these annual changes as ΔGNP_t, ΔG_t, and ΔM_t.
b. Plot ΔGNP_t versus ΔG_t on a scatter diagram.
c. Estimate the linear regression equation $\Delta \text{GNP}_t = \beta_0 + \beta_1 \Delta G_t + e_t$.
d. Plot the sample regression equation on the scatter diagram.
e. Find R^2. Is this value large enough to make you believe that changes in GNP are caused (or explained by) changes in G?
f. Plot ΔGNP_t versus ΔM_t on a scatter diagram.
g. Estimate the linear regression equation $\Delta \text{GNP}_t = \beta_0 + \beta_1 \Delta M_t + e_t$.
h. Plot the sample regression equation on the scatter diagram.
i. Find R^2. Is this value large enough to make you believe that changes in GNP are caused (or explained by) changes in M?

Year	GNP	G	M
1970	2416	573	628
1971	2484	567	713
1972	2608	571	805
1973	2744	565	861
1974	2729	573	908
1975	2695	581	1023
1976	2827	580	1163
1977	2959	589	1286
1978	3115	604	1389
1979	3192	609	1498
1980	3187	621	1630
1981	3249	630	1792
1982	3166	642	1952
1983	3279	649	2186
1984	3490	675	2374
1985	3585	721	2567
1986	3677	748	2805

Note: All data measured in billions of 1982 dollars.

27. The manager of a life insurance company wants to determine if there is a relationship between people's life insurance coverage (Y) and their annual income (X). Given the accompanying data, expressed in thousands of dollars, do the following:

a. Plot the data on a scatter diagram.
b. Determine the equation of the sample regression line.
c. Plot the sample regression line on the scatter diagram.
d. Find R^2.

Life Insurance Coverage (Y)	62	83	100	125	150	160	200	250	260	300	350	400
Annual Income (X)	14	20	26	30	30	28	40	45	50	70	65	80

28. Plutonium has been produced in the Pacific Northwest since the 1940s, and some radioactive wastes have leaked into the Columbia River. A study of cancer incidence in 9 communities bordering the river compared an exposure index (X) and the cancer mortality rate per 100,000 residents (Y). The results are as follows:

Exposure Index (X)	8.34	6.41	3.41	3.83	2.57	11.64	1.25	2.49	1.62
Cancer Mortality (Y)	210.3	177.9	129.9	162.3	130.1	207.5	113.5	147.1	137.5

a. Calculate the sample correlation coefficient and test whether the population correlation coefficient is 0. Use $\alpha = .05$.
b. Estimate the simple linear regression model.
c. Calculate R^2 and plot the data.

29. In a study involving a large sample of U.S. males aged 21 to 54, there was a positive correlation between income and blood pressure, a positive correlation between income and age, and a positive correlation between blood pressure and age. Do you think any of these variables is causing the other to change? Can you explain the results?

References

AMES, EDWARD, and STANLEY REITER. "Distributions of Correlation Coefficients in Economic Time Series." *Journal of the American Statistical Association* 56 (1961): 637–656.

DRAPER, NORMAN R., and HARRY SMITH. *Applied Regression Analysis*. 2d ed. New York: Wiley, 1981.

JOHNSTON, JOHN. *Econometric Methods*. New York: McGraw-Hill, 1972.

KMENTA, JAN. *Elements of Econometrics*. 2d ed. New York: Macmillan, 1986.

NETER, JOHN, and WILLIAM WASSERMAN. *Applied Linear Statistical Models*. 2d ed. Homewood, Ill.: Irwin, 1985.

NETER, JOHN, WILLIAM WASSERMAN, and G. A. WHITMORE. *Applied Statistics*. 3d ed. Boston: Allyn and Bacon, 1988.

NIE, NORMAN E., C. HADLAI HULL, JEAN G. JENKINS, KARIN STEINBRENNER, and DALE H. BENT. *SPSS Statistical Package for the Social Sciences*. 2d ed. New York: McGraw-Hill, 1975.

NORUSIS, MARIJA J. *SPSSX Introductory Statistics Guide*. New York: McGraw-Hill, 1983.

———. *SPSSX Advanced Statistics Guide*. Chicago: SPSS, 1985.

———. *The SPSS Guide to Data Analysis*. Chicago: SPSS, 1986.

RYAN, THOMAS A., BRIAN L. JOINER, and BARBARA F. RYAN. *Minitab Handbook*. 2d ed. Boston: PWS-KENT, 1985.

———. *Minitab Reference Manual*. University Park, Penn.: Minitab Project, 1985.

SAS Introductory Guide. 3d ed. Cary, N.C.: SAS Institute, 1985.

SAS Procedures Guide for Personal Computers. Version 6 ed. Cary, N.C.: SAS Institute, 1986.

SAS Statistics Guide for Personal Computers. Version 6 ed. Cary, N.C.: SAS Institute, 1986.

SAS User's Guide: Basics. Version 5 ed. Cary, N.C.: SAS Institute, 1985.

SAS User's Guide: Statistics. Version 5 ed. Cary, N.C.: SAS Institute, 1985.

SPSSX User's Guide. Chicago: SPSS, 1983.

Chapter Sixteen
Multiple Regression Models

In Chapter 15 we discussed the simple linear regression model, where the values taken by a dependent variable are related to the values taken by one independent variable. In this chapter we discuss multiple regression models, where the values taken by a dependent variable are related to the values taken by several independent variables. In the first section, we discuss how to estimate and analyze multiple regression models. In later sections we study several specialized topics involving multiple regression analysis.

Some of the exercises in this chapter will involve small samples of data so that the computations will not be too burdensome and can be solved by hand. Some problems have large data sets, however, and require the use of a computer. Although it is not necessary to use a computer to understand the material presented in this chapter, you should learn how to use a computer regression package in order to duplicate the results of some examples in this chapter.

16.1 ▪ Models with Two Explanatory Variables

Multiple regression is a generalization of the simple linear regression analysis, discussed in Chapter 15. Simple regression analysis enables us to analyze a relationship between a dependent variable and a single explanatory variable. The same ideas can be extended to analyze relationships between a dependent variable and two or more explanatory variables. If knowledge of one variable X helps us predict the value of Y, then it is natural to consider whether knowledge of several variables $X_1, X_2, \ldots, X_K$ enables us to provide an even better prediction of the value of Y. The symbol x_{i1} denotes the ith observation on the variable X_1; similarly, x_{i2} denotes the ith observation on the variable X_2, and in general x_{ij} denotes the ith observation on the jth independent variable X_j.

In multiple regression analysis, the dependent variable Y is related to two or more explanatory variables according to some hypothesized model. Usually it is assumed that the dependent variable is linearly related to the explanatory variables, but this does not have to be the case.

Regression Model with Two Explanatory Variables

The regression model with two explanatory variables is given by

$$Y_i = \beta_0 + \beta_1 x_{i1} + \beta_2 x_{i2} + e_i \qquad i = 1, 2, \ldots, n$$

where x_{i1} represents the ith observation on the explanatory variable X_1 and x_{i2} denotes the ith observation on the second explanatory variable X_2. As for the simple linear regression model, the following assumptions are made:

1. e_i $(i = 1, 2, \ldots, n)$ is normally distributed.
2. $E(e_i) = 0,\ i = 1, 2, \ldots, n$
3. $\text{Var}(e_i) = \sigma_e^2,\ i = 1, 2, \ldots, n$
4. e_i and e_j are independent of one another for all i and j.
5. The errors e_i and the x_{ij} values are independent.

In the multiple regression model, we need the following additional assumption:

6. The variables X_1 and X_2 are not perfectly linearly related. That is, it is not possible to find a set of numbers c_0, c_1, and c_2 such that

$$c_0 + c_1 x_{i1} + c_2 x_{i2} = 0$$

for every $i = 1, 2, \ldots, n$.

For given values of x_{i1} and x_{i2}, the mean value of the random variable Y_i lies on the *population regression plane* given by

$$E(Y_i|x_{i1}, x_{i2}) = \beta_0 + \beta_1 x_{i1} + \beta_2 x_{i2}$$

Assumption 6 rules out a condition called *perfect multicollinearity,* in which one of the explanatory variables can be expressed exactly as a linear function of the other explanatory variables and a constant term. If this occurs in the two-variable model, then it is not possible to determine if changes in Y are related to changes in X_1 or changes in X_2 because the latter two variables are perfectly linearly related. Whenever one changes, the other changes in a perfectly predictable way.

There are four unknown parameters in the population regression model, β_0, β_1, β_2, and σ_e^2. The coefficient β_0 is the constant term. The coefficient of the first explanatory variable x_{i1} is β_1 and measures the increase in the mean value of Y_i associated with a 1-unit increase in x_{i1} for a fixed value of the second variable x_{i2}. The coefficient of the second explanatory variable x_{i2} is β_2 and measures the increase in the mean value of Y_i associated with a 1-unit increase in x_{i2} for a fixed value of the first variable x_{i1}.

Sample Regression Equation

For the model containing two explanatory variables, the sample regression equation is

$$\hat{y}_i = b_0 + b_1 x_{i1} + b_2 x_{i2}$$

where $\hat{y}_i$ is the fitted, or predicted, value of the random variable Y_i, and b_0, b_1, and b_2 are the estimated values of the parameters β_0, β_1', and β_2.

The ith residual $\hat{e}_i$ is given by

$$\hat{e}_i = y_i - \hat{y}_i$$
$$= y_i - b_0 - b_1 x_{i1} - b_2 x_{i2} \qquad i = 1, 2, \ldots, n$$

The least-squares method says we should choose the estimates b_0, b_1, and b_2 so as to minimize the residual sum of squares SSE where

$$\text{SSE} = \sum_{i=1}^{n} \hat{e}_i^2 = \sum_{i=1}^{n} (y_i - \hat{y}_i)^2$$
$$= \sum_{i=1}^{n} (y_i - b_0 - b_1 x_{i1} - b_2 x_{i2})^2$$

To find the estimates b_0; b_1, and b_2, we apply some calculus to obtain the following equations:

$$\sum y_i = nb_0 + b_1 \sum x_{i1} + b_2 \sum x_{i2} \tag{1}$$
$$\sum x_{i1} y_i = b_0 \sum x_{i1} + b_1 \sum x_{i1}^2 + b_2 \sum x_{i1} x_{i2} \tag{2}$$
$$\sum x_{i2} y_i = b_0 \sum x_{i2} + b_1 \sum x_{i1} x_{i2} + b_2 \sum x_{i2}^2 \tag{3}$$

If we divide equation (1) by n, we obtain

$$b_0 = \bar{y} - b_1 \bar{x}_1 - b_2 \bar{x}_2 \tag{4}$$

For convenience, we define the following totals:

$$T_{11} = \sum x_{i1}^2 - n\bar{x}_1^2 \qquad T_{1Y} = \sum x_{i1} y_i - n\bar{x}_1 \bar{y}$$
$$T_{12} = \sum x_{i1} x_{i2} - n\bar{x}_1 \bar{x}_2 \qquad T_{2Y} = \sum x_{i2} y_i - n\bar{x}_2 \bar{y}$$
$$T_{22} = \sum x_{i2}^2 - n\bar{x}_2^2 \qquad T_{YY} = \sum y_i^2 - n\bar{y}^2$$

(The value T_{YY} will be needed later but is not needed to find the estimated coefficients.)
Substituting equation (4) into equations (2) and (3) and simplifying yields

$$T_{1Y} = b_1 T_{11} + b_2 T_{12} \tag{5}$$
$$T_{2Y} = b_1 T_{12} + b_2 T_{22} \tag{6}$$

Then solving equations (5) and (6) yields

$$b_1 = \frac{T_{22} T_{1Y} - T_{12} T_{2Y}}{\Delta} \tag{7}$$

$$b_2 = \frac{T_{11} T_{2Y} - T_{12} T_{1Y}}{\Delta} \tag{8}$$

where $\Delta = T_{11} T_{22} - T_{12}^2$. Once we obtain b_1 and b_2, we get b_0 from equation (4). We have

$$b_0 = \bar{y} - b_1 \bar{x}_1 - b_2 \bar{x}_2 \tag{9}$$

Thus, the computational procedure is as follows:

1. Obtain all the means, $\bar{y}$, $\bar{x}_1$, and $\bar{x}_2$.
2. Obtain all the sums of squares and sums of cross products, $\Sigma\, x_{i1}^2$, $\Sigma\, x_{i2}^2$, $\Sigma\, x_{i1}x_{i2}$, $\Sigma\, x_{i1}y_i$, and $\Sigma\, x_{i2}y_i$.
3. Obtain T_{11}, T_{12}, T_{22}, T_{1Y}, T_{2Y}, and T_{YY}.
4. Find b_1 and b_2 from equations (7) and (8).
5. Substitute these into equation (9) to obtain b_0.

It is much easier to express the formulas for computing the regression coefficients using matrices, but we will not pursue the matrix approach here, since a knowledge of matrix algebra is not assumed for this book. (The interested reader should consult an econometrics textbook such as John Johnston, *Econometric Methods,* 2d ed. [New York: McGraw-Hill, 1972].)

Figure 16.1 shows a hypothetical regression plane fitted to a hypothetical sample of observations. The sample regression plane is the plane that minimizes the squared deviations from the plane in the vertical direction.

FIGURE 16.1
A hypothetical regression plane.

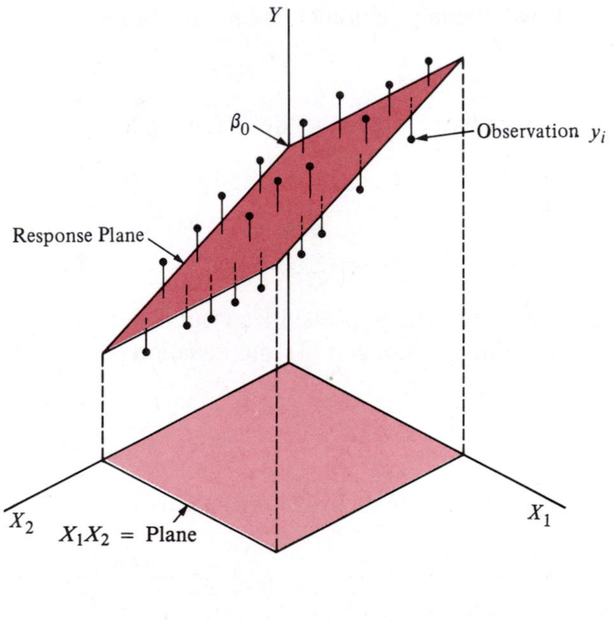

Example 16.1

Estimating a Multiple Regression Model: It is reasonable to suspect that gasoline mileage for a car is determined mainly by the car's weight and engine size. An automotive engineer gathered information for a sample of $n = 10$ different cars. The data in Table 16.1 show y_i, the gasoline mileage (in miles per gallon) of the ith car; x_{i1}, the engine size of the ith car (in hundreds of cubic inches); and x_{i2}, the weight of the ith car (in tons). Estimate the regression plane and predict the mileage for a car that has a 240-cubic-inch engine (i.e., a 2.4-hundred-cubic-inch engine) and weighs 0.9 ton.

TABLE 16.1 **Data for Example 16.1**

Miles per Gallon Y	Engine Size X_1	Weight X_2	X_1Y	X_2Y	X_1^2	X_2^2	X_1X_2	Y^2
32	1.0	1.0	32.0	32.0	1.00	1.00	1.00	1024
27	1.4	1.3	37.8	35.1	1.96	1.69	1.82	729
22	2.1	1.5	46.2	33.0	4.41	2.25	3.15	484
14	3.2	1.7	44.8	23.8	10.24	2.89	5.44	196
21	2.2	1.4	46.2	29.4	4.84	1.96	3.08	441
19	2.4	1.7	45.6	32.3	5.76	2.89	4.08	361
32	1.4	1.2	44.8	38.4	1.96	1.44	1.68	1024
18	2.3	1.7	41.4	30.6	5.29	2.89	3.91	324
38	1.2	0.8	45.6	30.4	1.44	0.64	0.96	1444
35	1.3	0.9	45.5	31.5	1.69	0.81	1.17	1225
258	18.5	13.2	429.9	316.5	38.59	18.46	26.29	7252

Solution: Typically, we would use a computer to solve this problem. For purposes of illustration, we used a hand calculator to calculate the sums shown in Table 16.1. We have

$$\sum y_i = 258 \qquad \sum x_{i1} = 18.5 \qquad \sum x_{i2} = 13.2 \qquad \sum x_{i1}x_{i2} = 26.29$$

$$\sum x_{i1}^2 = 38.59 \qquad \sum x_{i2}^2 = 18.46 \qquad \sum x_{i1}y_i = 429.9 \qquad \sum x_{i2}y_i = 316.5$$

and the means $\bar{y} = 25.8$, $\bar{x}_1 = 1.85$, and $\bar{x}_2 = 1.32$. The sums of squares of deviations from the respective means are as follows:

$$T_{11} = 4.365 \qquad T_{12} = 1.87 \qquad T_{22} = 1.036$$

$$T_{1Y} = -47.4 \qquad T_{2Y} = -24.06 \qquad T_{YY} = 595.6 \qquad \Delta = 1.02524$$

Finally, we compute the estimated coefficients:

$$b_1 = \frac{(1.036)(-47.4) - (1.87)(-24.06)}{1.02524} = -4.01291$$

$$b_2 = \frac{(4.365)(-24.06) - (1.87)(-47.4)}{1.02524} = -15.98055$$

$$b_0 = 25.8 - (-4.0129)(1.85) - (-15.98055)(1.32) = 54.3182$$

We obtain the estimated equation (after rounding) of

$$\hat{y}_i = 54.3182 - 4.0129x_{i1} - 15.9806x_{i2}$$

The predicted mileage for a car that has a 2.4-hundred-cubic-inch engine and weighs 0.9 ton is obtained by substituting the values $x_{i1} = 2.4$ and $x_{i2} = 0.9$ into the estimated equation. The predicted value is then

$$\hat{y} = 54.3182 - 4.0129(2.4) - 15.9806(0.9) = 30.3047$$

or about 30.3 miles per gallon.

The computer output for this problem as it appears from the SPSSX program is shown in Figure 16.2. The regression coefficients computed by the program are shown in the bottom half of the figure in the column labeled "B." The printout indicates that the estimated coefficients are as follows:

$$b_0 = \text{constant} = 54.318218$$
$$b_1 = \text{coefficient of Size of Engine} = -4.012914$$
$$b_2 = \text{coefficient of Weight of Car} = -15.980551$$

All these values agree with the values just calculated. The rest of the information shown in the computer output will be explained later in this chapter. ■

FIGURE 16.2 SPSSX-generated output for Example 16.1.

```
                              * * * *   M U L T I P L E   R E G R E S S I O N   * * * *

Equation Number 1    Dependent Variable..   MILEAGE   MILES PER GALLON

  Descriptive Statistics are printed on Page    5

Beginning Block Number  1.  Method:  Enter     SIZE     WEIGHT

Variable(s) Entered on Step Number  1..    WEIGHT    WEIGHT IN TONS
                                    2..    SIZE      SIZE OF ENGINE IN HUNDREDS OF CUBIC INCH

Multiple R            .98230            Analysis of Variance
R Square              .96492                               DF      Sum of Squares      Mean Square
Adjusted R Square     .95489            Regression          2           574.70418        287.35209
Standard Error       1.72775            Residual            7            20.89582          2.98512

                                        F =      96.26158       Signif F =  .0000

------------------ Variables in the Equation ------------------

Variable               B          SE B        Beta          T   Sig T

WEIGHT        -15.980551    3.565004   -0.666491     -4.483   .0029
SIZE           -4.012914    1.736792   -0.343538     -2.311   .0541
(Constant)     54.318218    2.484910                 21.859   .0000

End Block Number   1   All requested variables entered.
```

Exercises for Section 16.1

1. It is hypothesized that a student's grade point average in college is related to the student's college entrance scores on math and English tests. Estimate the model

$$Y_i = \beta_0 + \beta_1 x_i + \beta_2 z_i + e_i$$

where Y = grade point average, X = math score, and Z = English score. The data are shown in the accompanying table.

Y	X	Z
2.5	320	470
3.1	545	530
3.8	690	570
3.5	570	570
2.7	460	490
3.0	540	550
3.7	710	680
3.2	600	590
2.4	490	520

2. A department store has eight retail outlets. It is hypothesized that annual revenue (Y_i) at the ith outlet depends on the percentage of residents with incomes over \$20,000 who live within three miles of the store (X_i) and the total population living within three miles of the store (Z_i). Estimate the model

$$Y_i = \beta_0 + \beta_1 x_i + \beta_2 z_i + e_i$$

Y (in millions of dollars)	X	Z (in thousands)
1.2	77	88
1.6	78	94
0.8	77	85
1.0	75	85
1.4	79	90
0.7	77	64
0.8	75	68
1.1	78	76

3. The number of tennis racquets sold per year by a nationwide distributor depends on the price of the racquet and on the number of tennis players. Estimate the multiple regression equation using the data in the accompanying table.

Quantity Sold (in thousands) Y	Price (in dollars) X	Number of Players (in millions) Z
40	20	2.0
60	20	3.0
50	40	3.2
60	30	4.0
80	25	4.0
64	44	4.5
72	30	5.1
53	34	4.4

4. Suppose the price of a house in thousands of dollars (Y) depends on the size of the house in thousands of square feet (X) and the area of the yard in thousands of square feet (Z). The data are shown in the accompanying table.

Price Y	Size of House X	Area of Yard Z
48	2.2	4.3
54	2.1	5.2
35	1.3	2.4
89	3.3	7.8
59	3.2	3.8
67	2.8	4.0
76	2.9	5.0
51	2.5	4.8

a. Calculate the correlation coefficient between price and the size of the house.
b. Estimate the multiple regression equation relating price to the size of the house and the area of the yard.
c. Calculate the correlation between the size of the house and the area of the yard.

5. A researcher is trying to evaluate the potential benefits of a proposed irrigation project on crop yields in a developing country. The only variables affecting output in bushels per acre (Y) are total rainfall in inches during the growing season (R) and average temperature in degrees Fahrenheit during the growing season (T). Use the accompanying data and estimate the model

$$Y_i = \beta_0 + \beta_1 r_i + \beta_2 t_i + e_i$$

Year	Yield Y	Total Rainfall R	Average Temperature T
1981	55	19	69
1982	65	17	78
1983	80	21	67
1984	75	17	80
1985	70	19	75
1986	50	18	70
1987	60	20	73
1988	65	21	71

16.2 ▪ The General Multiple Regression Model

The theory of least squares can be extended to cases in which the regression equation contains more than two explanatory variables.

Multiple Regression Model

The multiple regression model is

$$Y_i = \beta_0 + \beta_1 x_{i1} + \beta_2 x_{i2} + \cdots + \beta_K x_{iK} + e_i$$

where

Y_i is a random variable representing the ith value of the dependent variable Y

$\beta_0, \beta_1, \ldots, \beta_K$ are unknown population coefficients

x_{i1} is the ith observed value of the first independent variable X_1

x_{i2} is the ith observed value of the second independent variable X_2

⋮

x_{iK} is the ith observed value of the Kth independent variable X_K

e_i is the ith value of the unobservable random disturbance term

The same basic assumptions are made for the multiple regression model as for the two-explanatory-variable regression model discussed in Section 16.1. These basic assumptions are repeated in the accompanying box.

Basic Assumptions of the Multiple Regression Model

The following basic assumptions are made about the error terms e_i and the values of the independent variables $X_1, X_2, \ldots, X_K$:

1. *Normality*: For any set of values of the independent variables, the error term e_i is a normally distributed random variable.
2. *Zero mean*: For any set of values of the independent variables, $E(e_i) = 0$.
3. *Homoscedasticity*: The variance of e_i, denoted σ_e^2, is the same for all values of the independent variables.
4. *No serial correlation*: The error terms are independent of one another for $i \neq j$.
5. *Independence of e_i and x_{ij}*: The error terms e_i are independent of the values of the independent variables. The independent variables are either fixed numbers or random variables that are independent of the error terms. If the x_{ij}'s are random variables, then all inferences are carried out conditionally on the observed values of the x_{ij}'s.
6. *No perfect multicollinearity*: It isn't possible to find a set of numbers $c_0, c_1, \ldots, c_K$ such that

$$c_0 + c_1 x_{i1} + c_2 x_{i2} + \cdots + c_K x_{iK} = 0$$

for every $i = 1, 2, \ldots, n$.

The purpose of the assumption of no perfect multicollinearity is to exclude independent variables that can be determined exactly as a linear function of other independent variables. For example, if our model contains the variables X_1, X_2, and X_3, then the last assumption rules out a case such as

$$x_{i3} = d_0 + d_1 x_{i1} + d_2 x_{i2}$$

for $i = 1, 2, \ldots, n$. Note that if X_3 could be perfectly explained in terms of X_1 and X_2, then the variable X_3 would provide no information that was not already included in the variables X_1 and X_2. In such a case, we would not be able to determine the separate effect that X_3 has on the dependent variable. As a practical matter, it is safe to assume that the last assumption is not violated.

Population Regression Equation

The population regression equation is

$$E(Y_i|x_{i1}, x_{i2}, \ldots, x_{iK}) = \beta_0 + \beta_1 x_{i1} + \beta_2 x_{i2} + \cdots + \beta_K x_{iK}$$

and shows the mean value of Y_i associated with the given values $x_{i1}, x_{i2}, \ldots, x_{iK}$ of the explanatory variables.

The parameter β_0 is the constant term, or Y-intercept, and measures the mean value of Y_i when all the independent variables are set to 0. The parameter β_1 measures the change in the mean value of Y_i corresponding to a 1-unit increase in the value of x_{i1}, when all the other independent variables are held constant; the parameter β_2 measures the change in the mean value of Y_i corresponding to a 1-unit increase in the value of x_{i2}, when all other independent variables are held constant, and so forth. For example, if we increase x_{i2} by 1 unit, we obtain

$$E(Y_i|x_{i1}, x_{i2} + 1, \ldots, x_{iK}) = \beta_0 + \beta_1 x_{i1} + \beta_2(x_{i2} + 1) + \cdots + \beta_K x_{iK}$$

After subtracting, we obtain

$$E(Y_i|x_{i1}, x_{i2} + 1, \ldots, x_{iK}) - E(Y_i|x_{i1}, x_{i2}, \ldots, x_{iK}) = \beta_2$$

Definition: Random Error Term e_i

In the population regression model, the **random error term**, denoted e_i, is the difference between the value of the random variable Y_i and the expected value $E(Y_i|x_{i1}, x_{i2}, \ldots, x_{iK})$. We obtain

$$\begin{aligned} e_i &= Y_i - E(Y_i|x_{i1}, x_{i2}, \ldots, x_{iK}) \\ &= Y_i - (\beta_0 + \beta_1 x_{i1} + \beta_2 x_{i2} + \cdots + \beta_K x_{iK}) \end{aligned}$$

After rearranging terms in the equation for the random error term e_i, we obtain the equivalent expression

$$Y_i = \beta_0 + \beta_1 x_{i1} + \beta_2 x_{i2} + \cdots + \beta_K x_{iK} + e_i$$

where, for any values of the independent variables, the mean value of e_i is 0.

The population parameters $\beta_0, \beta_1, \ldots, \beta_K$ are unknown and are estimated using a sample of n observations on the dependent variable Y and the K independent variables $X_{i1}, X_{i2}, \ldots, X_{iK}$. Once we have estimated the parameters $\beta_0, \beta_1, \ldots, \beta_K$, we obtain an estimated regression equation, which is called the *sample regression equation*.

Definition: Least-Squares Estimates

The **least-squares estimates** of the population parameters $\beta_0, \beta_1, \ldots, \beta_K$ are the values $b_0, b_1, \ldots, b_K$ that minimize the residual sum of squares SSE, where

$$\text{SSE} = \Sigma(y_i - \hat{y}_i)^2 = \Sigma(y_i - b_0 - b_1x_{i1} - b_2x_{i2} - \cdots - b_Kx_{iK})^2$$

An alternative formula for SSE is

$$\text{SSE} = \Sigma\, y_i^2 - b_0 \Sigma\, y_i - b_1 \Sigma\, x_{i1}y_i - b_2 \Sigma\, x_{i2}y_i - \cdots - b_K \Sigma\, x_{iK}y_i$$

Definition: Sample Regression Equation

The estimated equation

$$\hat{y}_i = b_0 + b_1x_{i1} + b_2x_{i2} + \cdots + b_Kx_{iK}$$

is called the **sample regression equation**. The value b_0 is the sample estimate of the population parameter β_0, the value b_1 is the sample estimate of the population parameter β_1, and so forth. The value $\hat{y}_i$ is called the *fitted value of* Y_i or the *predicted value of* Y_i.

If we estimate the multiple regression model by the method of least squares and if the model contains a constant term, then we obtain

$$\Sigma\, \hat{e}_i = 0$$

that is, the sum of the residuals is always 0 provided the sample regression model contains a constant term b_0.

The Gauss–Markov Theorem

The estimated coefficients $b_0, b_1, \ldots, b_K$ are random variables whose values change from sample to sample. If the basic assumptions hold, the least-squares estimates have several important properties described by the Gauss–Markov Theorem, which is summarized in the following box. By virtue of the Gauss–Markov Theorem, the least-squares estimators are said to be *best linear unbiased estimators*.

The Gauss–Markov Theorem

If basic assumptions 2 through 6 (p. 683) hold, the method of least squares provides estimates $b_0, b_1, \ldots, b_K$, which have the following properties:

1. The estimated coefficients are *unbiased* estimates of the true population parameters $\beta_0, \beta_1, \ldots, \beta_K$.
2. The estimators $b_0, b_1, \ldots, b_K$ have the *minimum variances* among the class of linear unbiased estimators.

If, in addition to assumptions 2 through 6, we add basic assumption 1 (normality of the errors) to our model, then the sampling distributions of the least-squares estimators are normal. The assumption of normality is required if we want to determine the sampling distributions of our estimators for testing hypotheses and constructing confidence intervals.

To test hypotheses and to construct confidence intervals, we need an estimate of σ_e^2. From Chapter 15, recall that in the simple linear regression model an unbiased estimator of σ_e^2 is $s_e^2 = \text{SSE}/(n - 2)$, where $(n - 2)$ is the degrees of freedom of the model. An unbiased estimator of σ_e^2 is defined in an analogous manner in the multiple regression model. In the formula for s_e^2, the denominator is n minus the number of coefficients that have to be estimated. In the multiple regression model, there are $(K + 1)$ coefficients $\beta_0, \beta_1, \ldots, \beta_K$ to be estimated, and so the denominator in the formula for s_e^2 is

$$n - (K + 1) = n - K - 1$$

Thus the formula for s_e^2 is

$$s_e^2 = \text{SSE}/(n - K - 1)$$

which is an unbiased estimator of σ_e^2. The value

$$\nu = n - K - 1$$

is the degrees of freedom of the regression equation. In a sense we use up $(K + 1)$ degrees of freedom before calculating SSE because we first estimate the $(K + 1)$ coefficients $\beta_0, \beta_1, \ldots, \beta_K$.

Estimated Standard Error of the Regression

The estimated standard error of the regression, denoted s_e, is an estimate of σ_e, the standard deviation of the error terms, and is simply the square root of s_e^2:

Definition: The Standard Error of the Regression

The **estimated standard error of the regression** is

$$s_e = \sqrt{\frac{\text{SSE}}{n - K - 1}}$$

Example 16.2

Calculation of s_e: Use the data in Table 16.1 along with the estimated coefficients b_0, b_1, and b_2 from Example 16.1 to determine SSE and s_e for the model estimated in Example 16.1 for predicting gasoline mileage.

Solution: We obtain

$$\begin{aligned} \text{SSE} &= \Sigma\, y_i^2 - b_0 \Sigma\, y_i - b_1 \Sigma\, x_{i1} y_i - b_2 \Sigma\, x_{i2} y_i \\ &= 7252 - 54.3182(258) - (-4.0129)(429.9) - (-15.9806)(316.5) \\ &= 20.8958 \end{aligned}$$

An unbiased estimate of the variance of the errors is

$$s_e^2 = \text{SSE}/(n - K - 1)$$
$$= 20.8958/(10 - 3) = 2.9851$$

and the estimated standard error of the regression is

$$s_e = \sqrt{2.9851} = 1.7277$$

Based on the Empirical Rule, for a normal population, approximately 95% of the error terms should be less than $2s_e$ (or 3.4554) units from the estimated plane and approximately 95% of the sample observations should lie within $2s_e = 3.46$ units of the estimated plane. ■

Reading SPSSX Computer Output

Refer again to the SPSSX computer output shown in Figure 16.2. At the top of the output is the Analysis of Variance Table, or ANOVA table. In the ANOVA table, the residual sum of squares (SSE) is one of the entries in the column labeled "Sum of Squares." From the SPSSX computer output, we see that the residual sum of squares is SSE = 20.8958. The estimated standard error of the regression (s_e) is reported next to the label "Standard Error." From the SPSSX output, we obtain the standard error s_e = 1.7277, which agrees with the value calculated previously. The value s_e^2 is reported under the column "Mean Square" in the row labeled "Residual." From the ANOVA table, we obtain $s_e^2 = 2.9851$. Note that the computer-generated values for SSE and s_e agree with the values we calculated by hand.

Exercises for Section 16.2

1. State the assumptions of the classical normal linear regression model.
2. Give an example of how each of these assumptions can be violated.
3. Explain what is meant by the statement that b_0 and b_1 are unbiased estimators of β_0 and β_1. What assumptions are needed if b_0 and b_1 are to be unbiased estimators of β_0 and β_1?
4. State the Gauss–Markov Theorem and explain its significance.
5. The Gauss–Markov theorem holds even though the error terms are normally distributed. Of what value, then, is the assumption that the errors are not normally distributed?
6. The following model was fitted to a sample of supermarkets in order to explain profit levels:

$$Y_i = \beta_0 + \beta_1 x_{i1} + \beta_2 x_{i2} + \beta_3 x_{i3} + e_i$$

where

$$Y_i = \text{profits in thousands of dollars}$$
$$X_{i1} = \text{food sales in tens of thousands of dollars}$$
$$X_{i2} = \text{nonfood sales in tens of thousands of dollars}$$
$$X_{i3} = \text{store size in thousands of square feet}$$

The estimated regression coefficients were $b_1 = 0.031$, $b_2 = 0.089$, and $b_3 = 0.487$. Interpret these estimates.

7. The accompanying data show product sales (Y), expenditure on advertising (X_1), and expenditure on salespeople (X_2), all measured in thousands of dollars for a sample of 12 sales districts. Compute the multiple regression of Y on X_1 and X_2.

Y	X_1	X_2
132	18	10
148	25	11
112	19	6
160	24	16
100	15	7
178	26	17
161	25	14
128	16	12
139	17	12
144	23	12
159	22	14
138	15	15

16.3 ▪ Measuring Goodness-of-Fit

Just as in the simple linear regression model, we can decompose the total variation in the dependent variable (SST) into two components: (1) the variation in Y that can be explained by the sample regression equation, denoted SSR, and (2) the variation in Y that cannot be explained by the sample regression equation, denoted SSE.

Decomposition of Sum of Squares

The total variation SST is decomposed into the explained variation SSR and the unexplained variation SSE,

$$\Sigma(y_i - \bar{y})^2 = \Sigma(\hat{y}_i - \bar{y})^2 + \Sigma\, \hat{e}_i^2$$

or

$$\text{SST} = \text{SSR} + \text{SSE}$$

where

Total Sum of Squares: $\text{SST} = \Sigma(y_i - \bar{y})^2 = \Sigma\, y_i^2 - n\bar{y}^2$

Regression Sum of Squares: $\text{SSR} = \Sigma(\hat{y}_i - \bar{y})^2$

Residual Sum of Squares: $\text{SSE} = \Sigma\, \hat{e}_i$

As in the simple linear regression model, the *coefficient of multiple determination* is denoted R^2 and is calculated using the following formula:

$$R^2 = \frac{\text{SSR}}{\text{SST}}$$
$$= 1 - \frac{\text{SSE}}{\text{SST}}$$

As in simple linear regression, the coefficient of multiple determination R^2 measures the proportion of the variation in the dependent variable that is explained by the independent variables, and it must be that

$$0 \leq R^2 \leq 1$$

Values of R^2 close to 1 indicate that the independent variables explain most of the variation in Y and that the sample data tend to lie near the estimated regression equation. Values of R^2 close to 0 indicate that a large proportion of the variation in Y is unexplained. If $R^2 = 1$, then SSE $= 0$ and every observation exactly satisfies the estimated regression equation. In this case, we have a perfect fit.

Example 16.3 **Calculation of R^2:** Calculate R^2 for the data in Table 16.1, referring also to Examples 16.1 and 16.2.

Solution: From the sums in Table 16.1, we obtain

$$\text{SST} = T_{YY} = \Sigma\, y_i^2 - n\bar{y}^2 = 7252 - 10(25.8)^2 = 595.6$$

In Example 16.2, we found that the sum of squared residuals SSE is 20.8958. We obtain

$$R^2 = 1 - \frac{\text{SSE}}{\text{SST}} = 1 - \frac{20.8958}{595.6}$$
$$= .9649$$

This value indicates that our multiple regression equation explains approximately 96% of the variation in gasoline mileage.

Refer again to the SPSSX computer output shown in Figure 16.2. In the ANOVA table, the regression sum of squares (SSR) is given as one of the entries in the column labeled "Sum of Squares" next to the label "Regression" and has a value of 574.70418. Also, from the ANOVA table, the residual sum of squares (SSE) is given as 20.89582, and the value of R^2, reported next to the label "R Square," is listed as .96492. This agrees with the value we computed by hand. ■

Adjusted Coefficient of Determination $\overline{R}^2$

Recall that

$$R^2 = 1 - \frac{\text{SSE}}{\text{SST}}$$

where

$$\text{SST} = \sum_{i=1}^{n} (y_i - \bar{y})^2 \quad \text{and} \quad \text{SSE} = \sum_{i=1}^{n} \hat{e}_i^2$$

The SST remains constant when another explanatory variable is added to a model because such an addition has no effect on the sum $\Sigma(y_i - \bar{y})^2$. On the other hand, adding an additional explanatory variable to the model causes SSE to decline provided the estimated coefficient of the new variable is not exactly 0 and thus causes the value of R^2 to increase. To this extent, then, the value of R^2 depends on the number of explanatory variables included in the model. This causes a problem when we try to compare the goodness of fit of two models that have the same dependent variable but different numbers of explanatory variables.

Another measure of goodness-of-fit takes into account the number of explanatory variables included in an equation. The measure, called the **adjusted *R* square** and denoted $\bar{R}^2$, is calculated as shown in the accompanying box.

Formula for the Adjusted *R* Square

The formula for the **adjusted *R* square** is

$$\bar{R}^2 = 1 - \frac{\text{SSE}/(n - K - 1)}{\text{SST}/(n - 1)}$$

$$= 1 - \frac{n - 1}{n - K - 1}(1 - R^2)$$

The term

$$s_Y^2 = \text{SST}/(n - 1)$$

measures the sample variance of the *Y*'s, which is the total variance to be explained. The term

$$s_e^2 = \text{SSE}/(n - K - 1)$$

is an unbiased estimate of σ_e^2, the variance of the error terms, which is the unexplained variance. By substituting we obtain

$$\bar{R}^2 = 1 - (s_e^2/s_Y^2)$$

Thus, $\bar{R}^2$ measures the proportion of the variation in the *Y*'s that is explained by the *X*'s. If $\bar{R}^2$ is close to 1, the model explains a large proportion of the total variation in the *Y*'s.

Unlike R^2, $\bar{R}^2$ can decrease when an additional explanatory variable is added to a model. Although SSE will decrease when an extra explanatory variable is included, so will the term $(n - K - 1)$. Thus the term $s_e^2 = \text{SSE}/(n - K - 1)$ can increase or decrease.

Some statisticians object to using the statistic $\bar{R}^2$ as a measure of goodness-of-fit because it can take negative values whenever the term

$$\frac{n - 1}{(n - K - 1)}(1 - R^2)$$

exceeds 1. This can occur if R^2 is close to 0 and *K* is large.

Example 16.4 **Calculation of the Adjusted *R* Square:** Refer to Example 16.3 and Figure 16.2, which shows the SPSSX computer output for Example 16.1. Calculate $\bar{R}^2$.

Solution: We have SST = 595.6, SSE = 20.8958, $n = 10$, and $K = 2$. We obtain

$$\bar{R}^2 = 1 - \frac{20.8958/7}{595.6/19} = .95489$$

In the ANOVA table of Figure 16.2, the value of $\bar{R}^2$ is reported next to the label "Adjusted R Square" as .95489. ■

Exercises for Section 16.3

1. Must R^2 always be greater than the adjusted R^2? Prove your answer.

2. Calculate $\bar{R}^2$ under the following conditions:
a. $R^2 = .60$, $n = 25$, $K = 3$
b. $R^2 = .10$, $n = 25$, $K = 3$
c. $R^2 = .10$, $n = 15$, $K = 5$
d. $R^2 = .05$, $n = 15$, $K = 5$

3. I estimate a multiple regression model and calculate the value of R^2. Then I decide to reestimate the model using an additional explanatory variable that has an estimated coefficient that is nonzero.
a. Explain why it must be the case that R^2 will be larger for the model with the additional variable.
b. Discuss what happens to the value of $\bar{R}^2$. Does it necessarily increase? Decrease?

4. In Exercise 1 of Section 16.1, a model was estimated that explained a student's grade point average as a function of entrance scores on a math test (X) and on an English test (Z).
a. Calculate R^2 and $\bar{R}^2$ for the estimated multiple regression equation.
b. Omit the variable Z from the equation and reestimate the model.
c. Calculate R^2 and $\bar{R}^2$ for the reestimated model and compare the results with the results in part (a). Do the changes in R^2 agree with the conclusions from Exercise 3?
d. Reestimate the model but omit the variable X and keep Z as an explanatory variable.
e. Calculate R^2 and $\bar{R}^2$ for the reestimated model and compare the results with the results in part (a). Do the changes in R^2 agree with the conclusions from Exercise 3?
f. Compare these results with the results in part (c). Can you make any prediction about what will happen to R^2 if we simultaneously add a new variable to a model and delete a variable from a model?

5. In Exercise 4 of Section 16.1, a model was estimated that explained the selling price of a house as a function of the size of the house (X) and the area of the yard (Z).
a. Calculate R^2 and $\bar{R}^2$ for this model. Does it appear that the model provides a good fit to the data?
b. Reestimate the original model but exclude the variable Z. Observe how the coefficient of the variable X changes.
c. Calculate R^2 and $\bar{R}^2$ for the reestimated model. Compare these results with the results in part (a).

6. In Exercise 5 of Section 16.1, a model was estimated that explained crop yield as a function of rainfall (R) and temperature (T).
a. Calculate R^2 and $\bar{R}^2$ for the estimated multiple regression equation.
b. Omit the variable T from the equation and reestimate the model.
c. Calculate R^2 and $\bar{R}^2$ for the reestimated model and compare the results with the results in part (a). Do the changes in R^2 agree with the conclusions from Exercise 3?
d. Reestimate the model but omit the variable R and keep T as an explanatory variable.
e. Calculate R^2 and $\bar{R}^2$ for the reestimated model and compare the results with the results in part (a). Do the changes in R^2 agree with the conclusions from Exercise 3?
f. Compare these results with the results in part (c).

7. Consider the following information from a multiple regression equation:

$$\Sigma \hat{e}_i^2 = 90$$

$$\text{Values of } Y = 11, 13, 15, 18, 23, 26, 28, 38, 45$$

a. Find SST, SSE, and SSR.
b. Find R^2.
c. Find s_e.

16.4 ▪ Confidence Intervals and Tests of Hypotheses Concerning the Regression Coefficients

To construct confidence intervals for the true population parameters $\beta_0, \beta_1, \ldots, \beta_K$, it is necessary to estimate the standard deviations of the estimated coefficients $b_0, b_1, \ldots, b_K$ and to make use of the t distribution. These estimated standard deviations are called the estimated standard errors of the estimated coefficients.

Definition: Estimated Standard Error of b_i

The estimated standard deviation of b_i is called the **estimated standard error of b_i** and is denoted by the symbol s_{b_i}.

The estimated standard error of each regression coefficient has the same interpretation as the estimated standard error for a regression coefficient in the simple linear regression model, which was discussed in Section 15.5. The symbol s_{b_i} denotes a specific value of the random variable S_{b_i}.

The construction of confidence intervals and the testing of hypotheses is based on the fact that if the basic assumptions hold, then the random variable

$$t = \frac{b_i - \beta_i}{S_{b_i}}$$

is distributed as the Student t with $(n - K - 1)$ degrees of freedom.

The formulas for calculating s_{b_i} are quite complicated and will not be given here. Fortunately, every computer regression package reports the values for s_{b_i} along with the estimated coefficients b_i.

Formula for Confidence Interval for β_i

A $100(1 - \alpha)\%$ confidence interval for a coefficient β_i takes the form

$$(b_i - t_{\alpha/2,\nu} s_{b_i},\; b_i + t_{\alpha/2,\nu} s_{b_i})$$

where s_{b_i} is the estimated standard deviation of b_i and $t_{\alpha/2,\nu}$ is the critical value of the t distribution that has $\nu = (n - K - 1)$ degrees of freedom such that

$$P(t > t_{\alpha/2,\nu}) = \alpha/2$$

Example 16.5 **Construction of Confidence Intervals for Regression Coefficients:** In Example 16.1, we obtained the sample regression equation

$$\hat{y}_i = 54.3182 - 4.0129x_{i1} - 15.9806x_{i2}$$

where Y is the gasoline mileage, X_1 is the engine size in hundreds of cubic inches, and X_2 is the weight of the car in tons. Let us construct 95% confidence intervals for each of the regression coefficients.

Solution: We have $n = 10$ observations and $K = 2$ explanatory variables in the model, so the appropriate degrees of freedom is $\nu = n - K - 1 = 7$. To construct a 95% confidence interval, we need the critical values from the t distribution having 7 degrees of freedom. We obtain $t_{.025,7} = 2.365$.

From the computer printout in Figure 16.2, we obtain the estimated standard deviations

$$s_{b_0} = 2.485, \quad s_{b_1} = 1.737, \quad \text{and} \quad s_{b_2} = 3.565$$

The desired confidence intervals are

$$\beta_0: 54.318 \pm 2.365(2.485) \quad \text{or} \quad (48.441, 60.195)$$

$$\beta_1: -4.013 \pm 2.365(1.737) \quad \text{or} \quad (-8.121, 0.095)$$

$$\beta_2: -15.981 \pm 2.365(3.565) \quad \text{or} \quad (-24.412, -7.550)$$

Recall that the variable X_1 is engine size, so the coefficient b_1 measures the estimated influence of engine size on gasoline mileage. We would expect this influence to be negative; that is, the larger the engine, the lower the gasoline mileage. However, observe that the 95% confidence interval for β_1 contains the value 0. This implies that if we performed a two-sided test using $\alpha = .05$, we would not reject H_0: $\beta_1 = 0$.

The confidence interval for β_2 is fairly wide, which indicates that our sample of data has not provided a very precise estimate of the effect of car weight on gas mileage. Nevertheless, the confidence interval for β_2 does not contain the value 0, so we can feel quite confident that increasing a car's weight does have a negative effect on gas mileage. ■

Hypothesis Testing

The procedure in the accompanying box describes how to test the null hypothesis that the parameter β_i is equal to some specific value β_i^*.

Tests of Hypotheses Concerning the Regression Coefficients

Let β_i^* denote some hypothesized value of the regression coefficient β_i. If the basic assumptions hold, then the appropriate test statistic is

$$t = \frac{b_i - \beta_i^*}{s_{b_i}}$$

Case 1: Suppose we wish to test the null hypothesis

$$H_0: \beta_i = \beta_i^* \quad \text{or} \quad H_0: \beta_i \leq \beta_i^*$$

against the one-sided alternative hypothesis

$$H_1: \beta_i > \beta_i^*$$

using a level of significance α. Use the decision rule

$$\text{Reject } H_0 \text{ in favor of } H_1 \text{ if } t > t_{\alpha,\nu}$$

where the degrees of freedom of the Student t distribution is $\nu = (n - K - 1)$.

Case 2: To test the null hypothesis

$$H_0: \beta_i = \beta_i^* \quad \text{or} \quad H_0: \beta_i \geqslant \beta_i^*$$

against the one-sided alternative hypothesis

$$H_1: \beta_i < \beta_i^*$$

use the decision rule

$$\text{Reject } H_0 \text{ in favor of } H_1 \text{ if } t < -t_{\alpha,\nu}$$

Case 3: To test the null hypothesis

$$H_0: \beta_i = \beta_i^*$$

against the two-sided alternative hypothesis

$$H_1: \beta_i \neq \beta_i^*$$

use the decision rule

$$\text{Reject } H_0 \text{ in favor of } H_1 \text{ if } t < -t_{\alpha/2,\nu} \text{ or if } t > t_{\alpha/2,\nu}$$

An important special case arises when the hypothesized value of an individual parameter is 0. If $\beta_j = 0$, then a change in the value of the independent variable (X_j) will not affect $E(Y_i)$, the expected value of the dependent variable. For example, in the regression model

$$E(Y_i|x_{i1}, x_{i2}, \ldots, x_{iK}) = \beta_0 + \beta_1 x_{i1} + \beta_2 x_{i2} + \cdots + \beta_K x_{iK}$$

suppose the true value of the parameter β_1 is 0. Then, given that the variables X_2, $X_3, \ldots, X_K$ are also to be used, information on the variable X_1 contributes nothing further toward explaining the behavior of the dependent variable and the mean value of Y_i is the same for all values of X_1.

Example 16.6

Testing Hypotheses About a Regression Coefficient: In Example 16.1, it is reasonable to conjecture either that engine size has no effect on gasoline mileage or that the larger the engine, the lower the mileage. Thus, it is natural to test the null hypothesis

$$H_0: \beta_1 = 0$$

against the one-sided alternative hypothesis

$$H_1: \beta_1 < 0$$

Test this hypothesis using a 5% level of significance.

Solution: We have $\alpha = .05$, $n = 10$, and $K = 2$. The appropriate degrees of freedom is $\nu = (10 - 2 - 1) = 7$. The critical value of t having 7 degrees of freedom is

$-t_{.05,7} = -1.895$. The hypothesized value is $\beta_1^* = 0$. To test H_0, we calculate the t statistic

$$t = \frac{b_1 - 0}{s_{b_1}} = \frac{-4.0129}{1.737} = -2.31$$

In Figure 16.2, the observed t statistic for the variable SIZE (X_{i1} in Example 16.1), shown in the column labeled "T," is $t = -2.311$, which corresponds to the value just calculated. Because this observed t statistic is less than the critical value, it falls in the rejection region. Thus, if we use $\alpha = .05$, we reject H_0 in favor of H_1. However, if we had used the slightly different level of significance $\alpha = .025$, then the critical value of the test would have been $-t_{.025} = -2.365$. In this case, the observed t statistic would have fallen in the acceptance region and we would not have rejected H_0.

Under the column "Sig T" and in the row for "SIZE" is the value .0541. This is the two-tailed prob-value associated with $t = -2.311$, indicating that the combined areas in the tails of the t distribution to the left of -2.311 and to the right of 2.311 is .0541.

In the model, the variable X_2 measures the weight of the car. We would expect heavy cars to get lower gasoline mileage than light cars, so it is natural to test H_0: $\beta_2 = 0$ against H_1: $\beta_2 < 0$. The appropriate t statistic is

$$t = \frac{b_2}{s_{b_2}} = \frac{-15.9806}{3.565} = -4.48$$

This t statistic falls in the critical region if we use a 5% level of significance, so we reject the null hypothesis. The computer printout in Figure 16.2 shows that the two-tailed prob-value associated with $t = -4.48$ is .0029, so this t statistic provides extremely strong evidence that the population correlation coefficient β_2 is negative. ■

In Example 16.6, we showed that if we performed a one-tailed test using a 2.5% level of significance, we would accept the null hypothesis that $\beta_1 = 0$, but if we used a 5% level of significance we would reject the null hypothesis that $\beta_1 = 0$. The question becomes "Should we keep the variable X_1 in the model or remove it and express gasoline mileage solely as a function of car weight?" This is a difficult question to answer, and the decision depends partly on the opinions of the investigator. Remember that statistical evidence is a guide to decision making, but it is not a replacement for common sense and sound judgment. Most people would probably keep X_1 in the model because its prob-value is fairly low and because there are strong theoretical reasons for believing that engine size affects gasoline mileage. On the other hand, we should not lose sight of the fact that a major reason for carrying out a statistical analysis is to determine if the facts support these intuitive feelings. In Section 16.5, when we discuss what is called the *multicollinearity problem,* we shall get more insight into why it is difficult to determine whether $\beta_1 = 0$.

Using the F *Test to Test* H_0: $\beta_1 = \beta_2 = \cdots = \beta_K = 0$

The t test can be used to test a hypothesis about any single coefficient in the regression model, but testing a hypothesis about β_1 and then testing a hypothesis about β_2 is not the same as performing a *joint test* about β_1 and β_2 simultaneously. To test whether our model explains a significant portion of the variation in Y, we need to perform a joint test of the regression coefficients. In the general regression model, we may want to test the null hypothesis

$$H_0: \beta_1 = \beta_2 = \cdots = \beta_K = 0$$

against the alternative hypothesis

$$H_1: \text{At least one of the coefficients } \beta_1, \beta_2, \ldots, \beta_K \text{ is nonzero.}$$

Sequentially performing a series of t tests, each at the 5% level of significance, on each of the coefficients $\beta_1, \beta_2, \ldots, \beta_K$ is not the same as jointly testing the null hypothesis that all K coefficients are 0. For example, when we perform two separate t tests on the coefficients β_1 and β_2, each at the 5% level of significance, the joint level of significance will not be .05. If the probability of rejecting $\beta_1 = 0$ is .05 and the probability of rejecting $\beta_2 = 0$ is also .05, the joint probability of rejecting *both* $\beta_1 = 0$ and $\beta_2 = 0$ is less than .05 and depends on the correlation between the sample estimators b_1 and b_2. (If the estimators were independent, the joint probability of rejecting both hypotheses would be $.05 \times .05 = .0025$.) The correct method for testing all the coefficients jointly is based on an F statistic, which follows the F distribution. The procedure is described in the accompanying box.

Testing the Null Hypothesis $H_0: \beta_1 = \beta_2 = \cdots = \beta_K = 0$

Consider the multiple regression model

$$E(Y_i|x_{i1}, x_{i2}, \ldots, x_{iK}) = \beta_0 + \beta_1 x_{i1} + \beta_2 x_{i2} + \cdots + \beta_K x_{iK}$$

Suppose the basic assumptions hold and we wish to test the joint null hypothesis

$$H_0: \beta_1 = \beta_2 = \cdots = \beta_K = 0$$

against the alternative hypothesis

$$H_1: \beta_1, \beta_2, \ldots, \beta_K \text{ are not all } 0$$

using a level of significance α. To perform the test, calculate the F statistic

$$F = \frac{\text{SSR}/K}{\text{SSE}/(n - K - 1)}$$

The validity of the null hypothesis would be in doubt if the regression sum of squares was large compared with the error sum of squares. Hence, the null hypothesis would be rejected for large values of the test statistic F.

To test H_0 against H_1, use the decision rule

$$\text{Reject } H_0 \text{ in favor of } H_1 \text{ if } F > F_{\alpha,K,(n-K-1)}$$

where $F_{\alpha,K,(n-K-1)}$ is the value such that

$$P(F > F_{\alpha,K,(n-K-1)}) = \alpha$$

and where the test statistic F follows the F distribution with degrees of freedom K and $(n - K - 1)$.

Example 16.7 **Testing the Joint Hypothesis H_0: $\beta_1 = \beta_2 = 0$:** From the computer output in Figure 16.2 we see that the estimated equation for Example 16.1 is

$$\hat{y}_i = 54.3182 - 4.0129x_{i1} - 15.9806x_{i2}$$

where Y is the gas mileage, X_1 is the engine size, and X_2 is the weight of the car. Use a 5% level of significance and test the joint null hypothesis

$$H_0: \beta_1 = \beta_2 = 0$$

against the alternative hypothesis

$$H_1: \beta_1 \text{ and } \beta_2 \text{ are not both } 0$$

Solution: From the ANOVA table in Figure 16.2, we see that SSE (the residual sum of squares) is 20.8958. Thus, we obtain

$$\text{SSE}/(n - K - 1) = 20.8958/(10 - 3) = 2.985$$

In the ANOVA table, the quantity $\text{SSE}/(n - K - 1)$ is called the *residual mean square*.
The regression sum of squares is SSR = 574.7042 and we obtain

$$\text{SSR}/K = 574.7042/2 = 287.3521$$

In the ANOVA table, the quantity SSR/K is called the *regression mean square*. We calculate the F statistic by finding the ratio of the regression mean square (MSR) and the residual mean square (MSE). We obtain

$$F = \text{MSR}/\text{MSE} = 287.3521/2.985 = 96.26$$

This F statistic can be obtained directly from the ANOVA table. In the table, we see that the F statistic is

$$F = 96.26158$$

Large values of F indicate that the null hypothesis is false. For $\alpha = .05$, the critical value of F having $K = 2$ and $(n - K - 1) = (10 - 2 - 1) = 7$ degrees of freedom is $F_{.05,2,7} = 4.74$. We reject H_0 in favor of H_1 because the F statistic of 96.26 far exceeds the critical value.

In Figure 16.2, the value "Signif F" represents the prob-value associated with $F = 96.26$ and is shown to be .0000. This provides extremely strong evidence that H_0 is false. ■

Comments on the F *Test*

Example 16.7 represents a typical regression model using economic or business data. When we build a model to explain some economic or business variable, it is almost always the case that we will reject

$$H_0: \beta_1 = \beta_2 = \cdots = \beta_K = 0$$

in favor of H_1. Rejection of H_0 means that, *as a group,* the explanatory variables do help explain the values of the dependent variable Y, but this result alone does not imply that we have a good model or that the estimated equation will yield good predictions of Y. Nor does it mean that the estimated equation provides a good fit to the data. In general, a good model explains most of the variation in Y and satisfies the statistical assumptions. In practice, most statisticians rely more on R^2, s_e, and the individual t tests than on the overall F test when assessing the quality of some regression model.

The F statistic is related to the value of R^2 according to the following equation:

$$F = \frac{\text{SSR}/K}{\text{SSE}/(n - K - 1)} = \frac{(n - K - 1)R^2}{K(1 - R^2)}$$

A small value of F strongly indicates that our model is inadequate, but, in general, a small value of F will be accompanied by a small value of R^2; consequently, the F statistic does not provide much additional information about the quality of a model that cannot be learned from inspection of R^2 alone.

Exercises for Section 16.4

1. You have obtained the following sample regression equation:

$$\hat{y}_i = \underset{(0.87)}{2.304} + \underset{(1.23)}{3.412}\, x_{i1} - \underset{(3.78)}{4.657}\, x_{i2}$$

The values in parentheses are estimated standard deviations. The sample size was $n = 25$.

a. Let $\alpha = .05$ and test H_0: $\beta_1 = 0$ against H_1: $\beta_1 > 0$.
b. In part (a), what is the appropriate number of degrees of freedom?
c. Let $\alpha = .05$ and test H_0: $\beta_2 = 0$ against H_1: $\beta_2 < 0$.

2. In Exercise 1, construct the following:

a. A 99% confidence interval for β_1
b. A 95% confidence interval for β_2

3. In Exercise 1, suppose $R^2 = .86$. Let $\alpha = .05$.

a. Calculate the F statistic used to test the joint null hypothesis H_0: $\beta_1 = \beta_2 = 0$ against the alternative hypothesis that at least one of these two population regression coefficients is nonzero.
b. What are the appropriate numbers of degrees of freedom for the F statistic?
c. What is the critical value for the F statistic?
d. Do you reject the null hypothesis?

4. Refer to Exercise 4 in Section 16.3. Let $\alpha = .05$.

a. Calculate the F statistic used to test the joint null hypothesis H_0: $\beta_1 = \beta_2 = 0$ against the alternative hypothesis that at least one of the two population regression coefficients is nonzero.
b. What are the appropriate numbers of degrees of freedom for the F statistic?
c. What is the critical value for the F statistic?
d. Do you reject the null hypothesis?

5. Consider the following sample regression results:

$$\hat{y}_i = \underset{(6.14)}{15.4} + \underset{(0.42)}{2.20}\, x_{i1} + \underset{(5.21)}{48.14}\, x_{i2} \qquad R^2 = .355, \quad n = 27$$

The numbers in parentheses are the estimated standard errors of the sample regression coefficients.

a. Construct a 95% confidence interval for β_1.
b. Would you reject H_0: $\beta_2 = 0$ at the 5% level of significance?
c. Construct a 99% confidence interval for β_2.

d. Would you reject H_0: $\beta_2 = 0$ at the 1% level of significance? Explain how this answer could be obtained from the results in part (c).

16.5 ▪ The Multicollinearity Problem

Determining the final form of a multiple regression equation is not an easy task. In most situations, numerous variables are likely candidates for inclusion in any regression model. The **multicollinearity problem** occurs when two or more explanatory variables are highly correlated. If two explanatory variables X_j and X_k are highly correlated, then Y will be explained about equally as well by an equation containing only X_j or only X_k as by an equation containing both X_j and X_k. The reason is that most of the information about Y learned by examining X_k can be learned about Y by examining X_j, because X_j and X_k tend to move together. Furthermore, if X_j and X_k tend to move together, it is difficult to separate their effects on Y, and it will not be possible to obtain very reliable estimates of the coefficients β_j and β_k (i.e., estimates having small variances). A high degree of multicollinearity between X_j and X_k is undesirable because the estimates of the regression coefficients β_j and β_k will tend to have large standard errors and the confidence intervals for the true values of β_j and β_k will tend to be very wide; thus we cannot be very sure about the correct values of these coefficients.

The main purpose of multiple regression analysis is to separate and estimate these effects, but the researcher should realize that if both X_j and X_k influence Y and if X_j and X_k tend to move together, then determining how variations in Y are related to variations in X_j or in X_k alone will always be difficult.

When trying to predict values of Y, the multicollinearity problem may not be so important. Example 16.1 presented a multiple regression model in which gasoline mileage was related to the two explanatory variables Size of Engine and Weight of Car. Usually, Size of Engine and Weight of Car tend to be highly positively correlated, making it difficult to determine what the separate effects are that engine size and car weight have on mileage and whether changes in mileage are due to changes in engine size or in car weight. When predicting Mileage (Y), however, it should make little difference whether our model contains just Size of Engine, just Weight of Car, or both, provided these variables move together. If only Size of Engine is included in the model, then the variations in Y caused by the variable Weight of Car will be attributed to the variable Size of Engine.

This example shows the heart of the multicollinearity problem. If Size of Engine and Weight of Car are highly correlated, determining how each affects Mileage will be extremely difficult. On the other hand, our predictions of Mileage will be approximately the same if we use as explanatory variables only Size of Engine, only Weight of Car, or both. A serious problem arises, however, if we want to predict Mileage for cars where Size of Engine and Weight of Car are not correlated. In this case we can get very different estimates depending on what we use as explanatory variables.

Multicollinearity in Macroeconomic Models

The multicollinearity problem is especially troublesome when estimating macroeconomic models, because most aggregate economic variables tend to move relatively closely together. For example, some economists argue that changes in gross national product (GNP) are caused primarily by changes in the money supply (M). Estimating a regression equation using GNP as the dependent variable and M as the explanatory variable, they obtain high values of R^2, regression coefficients with the correct signs, and large t statistics. Therefore, they argue that the data tend to support their hypothesis. On the other hand, many other economists argue that changes in GNP are caused primarily by changes in government spending (G). With a regression equation using GNP as the dependent variable and G as an explanatory variable, these economists also obtain a high value for R^2, coefficients having the correct signs, and large t statistics. They, too, argue that the data support their hypothesis.

Suppose an arbitrator is asked to decide who is correct. The arbitrator suggests estimating a third equation that includes both G and M as explanatory variables. This equation will also have a high value of R^2, coefficients with the expected signs, and large t statistics. However, the estimated coefficients in the third equation will differ from those in the first two equations, and the standard errors of the estimated coefficients will be much larger than in either of the models containing a single explanatory variable. This indicates that we have a multicollinearity problem. Because the explanatory variables M and G tend to move together over time, separating their effects on GNP is difficult.

The available data are not adequate enough to enable us to determine which model (if any) is correct. If we had additional data from periods when G and M moved in opposite directions, it would be easier to choose the correct model and to determine precisely the effects of G and M on GNP. In most economic and business problems, however, we are not so fortunate to find data that enable us to choose between competing models easily.

Multicollinearity is a problem because explanatory variables in economics and business tend to be correlated. A regression coefficient is usually interpreted as a measure of the change in the mean value of Y when the value of the particular explanatory variable is increased by 1 unit while the values of all other explanatory variables remain unchanged. This idea is nice theoretically, but in practice it may not be possible to change certain economic variables while holding the other variables fixed. Usually we do not obtain data from a controlled experiment where the investigator is free to select the desired values for the explanatory variables.

Multicollinearity is not an error in a regression model. Instead, multicollinearity is a data problem. The purpose of regression analysis is to determine the separate effects of the independent variables $X_1, X_2, \ldots, X_K$ on Y, but when the independent variables tend to move together, it is extremely difficult to get good estimates of these effects.

We do not test for the presence or absence of multicollinearity, since in economic models some degree of multicollinearity is always present. What we want to do is examine the *degree* of multicollinearity so that we can better interpret the various regression coefficients.

The Correlation Matrix

A good way to examine the degree of multicollinearity is to calculate the sample correlation coefficients between each possible pair of explanatory variables X_j and X_k. The sample correlation coefficient between, say, X_3 and X_4 is denoted R_{34}. When some correlation coefficient such as R_{34} is close to $+1$ or -1, then we know that X_3 and X_4 tend to move together, and it will be difficult to estimate their separate effects on Y.

Example 16.8 **The Multicollinearity Problem:** In Example 16.1, gasoline mileage (Y) was related to the engine size of a car and the weight of a car. This hypothesized relationship seems reasonable, but the estimated coefficient for Size of Engine was of questionable statistical significance. One possible explanation for this lack of statistical significance is that the sample correlation between Size of Engine (X_1) and Weight of Car (X_2) is $R_{12} = .879$. Thus, it is possible that some of the effect of X_1 on Mileage has been shifted to X_2. The high correlation between X_1 and X_2 explains why the estimated coefficient b_1 is barely statistically significant. ■

Exercises for Section 16.5

1. Refer to Exercise 1 in Section 16.1 where a model was estimated which explained a student's grade point average (Y) as a function of the student's entrance exam scores on a math test (X) and an English test (Z).
   a. Calculate the sample correlation coefficient between Y and X. What will be the sign of the estimated regression coefficient of X if we estimate a simple linear regression model having Y as a function of X? Verify this result by actually estimating the equation.
   b. Calculate the sample correlation coefficient between Y and Z. What will be the sign of the estimated regression coefficient of Z if we estimate a simple linear regression model having Y as a function of Z? Verify this result by actually estimating the equation.
   c. Calculate the sample correlation coefficient between Z and X. Can you predict what will happen to the estimated regression coefficients in parts (a) and (b) if we estimate the multiple regression model having Y as a function of both X and Z? Verify this result by actually estimating the equation.
2. Refer to Exercise 2 in Section 16.1.
   a. Calculate the sample correlation coefficient between Y and X. What will be the sign of the estimated regression coefficient of X if we estimate a simple linear regression model having Y as a function of X? Verify this result by actually estimating the equation.
   b. Calculate the sample correlation coefficient between Y and Z. What will be the sign of the estimated regression coefficient of Z if we estimate a simple linear regression model having Y as a function of Z? Verify this result by actually estimating the equation.
   c. Calculate the sample correlation coefficient between Z and X. Is there any reason to believe that the relationship between Z and X is causal?
   d. Can you predict what will happen to the estimated regression coefficients in parts (a) and (b) if we estimate the multiple regression model having Y as a function of both X and Z? Verify this result by actually estimating the equation.
3. You have estimated a model containing three explanatory variables. You then add a fourth explanatory variable to the model. The value of R^2 increases by only a small amount, and the estimated coefficient of the new explanatory variable is not statistically significant. Could multicollinearity be a problem?
4. You have estimated a model containing three explanatory variables. You then add a fourth explanatory variable to the model. The value of R^2 increases by only a small amount and the estimated coefficient of the new explanatory variable is statistically significant. The coefficients of the other variables change substantially, and all of their standard deviations increase substantially. Could multicollinearity be a problem?

5. You have estimated a model containing three explanatory variables. You then add a fourth explanatory variable to the model. The value of R^2 increases by a substantial amount and the estimated coefficient of the new explanatory variable is statistically significant. Could multicollinearity be a problem?
6. You have estimated a model containing three explanatory variables. You then add a fourth explanatory variable to the model. The correlation coefficient between the fourth explanatory variable and the third explanatory variable is .98, but the sample correlation is .02 between X_4 and X_2 and .04 between X_4 and X_1. Could multicollinearity be a problem?
7. You have estimated a model containing three explanatory variables. You then add a fourth explanatory variable to the model. The correlation coefficient between the fourth explanatory variable and the third explanatory variable is .98, and the sample correlation is .92 between X_4 and X_2 and .94 between X_4 and X_1. Could multicollinearity be a problem?
8. Refer to Exercise 5 in Section 16.1 and Exercise 6 in Section 16.3.
   a. Find the sample correlation coefficient between rainfall (R) and temperature (T).
   b. Predict what you think would happen to the estimated coefficient of T if the variable R was omitted from the model.
   c. Compare your prediction in (b) with the actual result obtained in Exercise 6 in Section 16.3.
9. Are the following statements true or false? If false, why?
   a. Multicollinearity between independent variables means that the least-squares estimated regression coefficients will be biased.
   b. Multicollinearity makes it easier to get estimated regression coefficients that are statistically significant.
   c. If no sample correlation coefficient between any pair of explanatory variables is large, then multicollinearity is not a problem.
10. A researcher has obtained the following sample regression equation:

$$\hat{y}_i = 23.45 + 32.74x_{i1} + 62.09x_{i2}$$

The sample correlation between X_1 and X_2 is .95. What will happen to the estimated coefficient of X_1 if the variable X_2 is removed from the model and the equation is reestimated?

11. An economist wants to estimate the following production function relating to output for a given firm during period t:

$$Q_t = \beta_0 + \beta_1 L_t + \beta_2 K_t + e_t$$

where

$$L_t = \text{dollars of labor employed in period } t$$

$$K_t = \text{dollars of capital expenditure in period } t$$

The firm's budget is such that the firm always spends \$80,000 per year for capital and labor.
   a. Is there a multicollinearity problem?
   b. Can the equation be estimated using annual data?

16.6 ▪ Testing a Subset of Coefficients (Optional)

So far we have shown how to test a hypothesis about any individual regression coefficient β_i and to test the joint hypothesis H_0: $\beta_1 = \beta_2 = \cdots = \beta_K = 0$. It also is possible to test hypotheses about some *subset* of coefficients in the regression model. For example, in the regression model

$$E(Y_i|x_{i1}, x_{i2}, \ldots, x_{iK}) = \beta_0 + \beta_1 x_{i1} + \beta_2 x_{i2} + \cdots + \beta_5 x_{i5}$$

we might want to test the joint hypothesis

$$H_0\text{: } \beta_4 = \beta_5 = 0$$

Let us denote the set of potential explanatory variables in a model as $X_1, X_2, \ldots, X_K, X_{K+1}, \ldots, X_{K+Q}$. An important test concerns testing the joint influence of the set of Q explanatory variables $X_{K+1}, X_{K+2}, \ldots, X_{K+Q}$ on the mean of Y. Consider two regression models, one of which states that the regression equation is

$$E(Y_i|x_{i1}, x_{i2}, \ldots, x_{iK}) = \beta_0 + \beta_1 x_{i1} + \beta_2 x_{i2} + \cdots + \beta_K x_{iK} \qquad (1)$$

while the other model states that Y depends not only on $X_1, X_2, \ldots, X_K$, but also on the additional explanatory variables $X_{K+1}, X_{K+2}, \ldots, X_{K+Q}$. That is, the competing model is

$$E(Y_i|x_{i1}, x_{i2}, \ldots, x_{iK+Q}) = \beta_0 + \beta_1 x_{i1} + \beta_2 x_{i2} + \cdots + \beta_K x_{iK} + \beta_{K+1} x_{iK+1} + \cdots + \beta_{K+Q} x_{iK+Q} + e_i \qquad (2)$$

Model (1) is the *restricted* model, because the coefficients $\beta_{K+1}, \beta_{K+2}, \ldots, \beta_{K+Q}$ are all restricted, or constrained, to be 0. Model (2) is the *unrestricted* model because there are no restrictions or constraints on any of the regression coefficients.

We are interested in testing the joint hypothesis

$$H_0\text{: } \beta_{K+1} = \beta_{K+2} = \cdots = \beta_{K+Q} = 0$$

against the alternative that H_0 is not true. This is a joint test that the Q population regression coefficients are all zero. If H_0 is true, then the variables $X_{K+1}, X_{K+2}, \ldots, X_{K+Q}$ do not help explain variations in the dependent variable. We will denote the residual sum of squares from the restricted model (1) as SSE_R and the residual sum of squares from the unrestricted model (2) as SSE_U.

If H_0 is true, then the residual sum of squares SSE_R obtained from estimating the restricted model (1) should be approximately the same as the residual sum of squares SSE_U obtained from estimating the unrestricted model (2). If the null hypothesis is false and the variables $X_{K+1}, X_{K+2}, \ldots, X_{K+Q}$ do help explain the value of Y, then SSE_U should be less than SSE_R.

The procedure for testing that a subset of coefficients are all 0 is described in the accompanying box.

Testing the Null Hypothesis H_0: $\beta_{K+1} = \beta_{K+2} = \cdots = \beta_{K+Q} = 0$

Suppose we want to test the joint null hypothesis

$$H_0\text{: } \beta_{K+1} = \beta_{K+2} = \cdots = \beta_{K+Q} = 0$$

against the alternative hypothesis

$$H_1\text{: The } Q \text{ coefficients } \beta_{K+1}, \beta_{K+2}, \ldots, \beta_{K+Q} \text{ are not all } 0$$

First we estimate the restricted model and the unrestricted model. Then we calculate the residual sum of squares from each model and calculate the F statistic

$$F = \frac{(\text{SSE}_R - \text{SSE}_U)/Q}{\text{SSE}_U/(n - K - Q - 1)}$$

where SSE_R is the residual sum of squares from the restricted model and SSE_U is the residual sum of squares from the unrestricted model. If H_0 is true, the F statistic follows the F distribution with numerator degrees of freedom Q and denominator degrees of freedom $(n - K - Q - 1)$. To test H_0 using a level of significance α, use the decision rule

$$\text{Reject } H_0 \text{ in favor of } H_1 \text{ if } F > F_{\alpha,Q,(n-K-Q-1)}$$

Example 16.9

A Joint Test of Several Coefficients: There are substantial differences between the states in the average salary paid to teachers in the public elementary and secondary schools. It is natural to hypothesize that the average salary of elementary and secondary school teachers in state i Y_i is influenced by the state and local tax revenue per capita in state i x_{i1}. Suppose you think that it is possible that the percentage of the labor force that is unionized in state i x_{i2}, and the income per capita in state i x_{i3} also influence Y_i.

Since salaries are paid out of tax revenue, it is reasonable to conjecture that the coefficient of x_{i1} should be positive. In addition, it might be expected that highly unionized states tend to pay higher salaries than other states and that states with high average incomes might tend to pay higher salaries. Thus it might be conjectured that both β_2 and β_3 are positive.

The conjectured model is thus

$$E(Y_i|x_{i1}, x_{i2}, x_{i3}) = \beta_0 + \beta_1 x_{i1} + \beta_2 x_{i2} + \beta_3 x_{i3}$$

and we wish to test whether the two variables X_2 and X_3 jointly help explain Y. That is, we wish to test the joint null hypothesis

$$H_0: \beta_2 = \beta_3 = 0$$

against the alternative hypothesis

$$H_1: \beta_2 \text{ and } \beta_3 \text{ are not both } 0$$

Let us use a 5% level of significance. Use the data in Table 2.3 in Chapter 2, which are taken from the *Statistical Abstract of the United States 1987* and refer to the year 1985.

Solution: The unconstrained regression model is

$$E(Y_i|x_{i1}, x_{i2}, x_{i3}) = \beta_0 + \beta_1 x_{i1} + \beta_2 x_{i2} + \beta_3 x_{i3}$$

and the constrained model is

$$E(Y_i|x_{i1}) = \beta_0 + \beta_1 x_{i1}$$

To perform the test, we estimate the constrained model and then estimate the unconstrained model. The SPSSX computer output for the constrained model is shown in Figure 16.3 and for the unconstrained model in Figure 16.4. The SPSSX program that generated the output for the unconstrained model is discussed in Section 16.7.

There are $n = 51$ observations, representing the 50 states and the District of Columbia. The constrained model contains one explanatory variable (tax revenue per capita), so $K = 1$. There are $Q = 2$ additional variables in the unconstrained model, represent-

FIGURE 16.3 **SPSSX-generated output for constrained model in Example 16.9.**

```
                                         * * * *   M U L T I P L E   R E G R E S S I O N   * * * *
Listwise Deletion of Missing Data

Equation Number 1    Dependent Variable..   SALARY   AVERAGE TEACHER SALARY IN 1

Beginning Block Number  1.  Method:  Enter     REVENUE

Variable(s) Entered on Step Number  1..   REVENUE   STATE AND LOCAL REVENUE PER CAPITA IN 19

Multiple R           .83963          Analysis of Variance
R Square             .70497                              DF     Sum of Squares        Mean Square
Adjusted R Square    .69895          Regression           1    615889001.80986    615889001.80986
Standard Error   2293.48457          Residual            49    257743502.81760      5260071.48607

                                     F =      117.08757       Signif F =  .0000

------------------ Variables in the Equation ------------------

Variable                 B        SE B       Beta          T  Sig T

REVENUE           3.325321     .307311    .839628     10.821  .0000
(Constant) 12105.539794 1176.959875                   10.285  .0000

End Block Number    1   All requested variables entered.
```

FIGURE 16.4 **SPSSX-generated output for unconstrained model in Example 16.9.**

```
                                         * * * *   M U L T I P L E   R E G R E S S I O N   * * * *
Listwise Deletion of Missing Data

Equation Number 1    Dependent Variable..   SALARY   AVERAGE TEACHER SALARY IN 1

Beginning Block Number  1.  Method:  Enter     REVENUE  PCTUNION INCOME

Variable(s) Entered on Step Number  1..   INCOME     PERSONAL INCOME PER CAPITA IN 1985
                                    2..   PCTUNION   % UNION MEMBERSHIP IN 1982
                                    3..   REVENUE    STATE AND LOCAL REVENUE PER CAPITA IN 19

Multiple R           .89492          Analysis of Variance
R Square             .80088                              DF     Sum of Squares        Mean Square
Adjusted R Square    .78817          Regression           3    699673630.26439    233224543.42146
Standard Error   1923.86399          Residual            47    173958874.36306      3701252.64602

                                     F =       63.01233       Signif F =  .0000

------------------ Variables in the Equation ------------------

Variable                 B        SE B       Beta          T  Sig T

INCOME             .445013     .197333    .229615      2.255  .0288
PCTUNION        149.303607   41.585449    .266464      3.590  .0008
REVENUE           2.176366     .398163    .549522      5.466  .0000
(Constant)     7501.498262 1757.305539                 4.269  .0001

End Block Number    1   All requested variables entered.
```

ing the two variables X_2 and X_3. The computer output in Figure 16.3 yields the estimated constrained model

$$\hat{y}_i = 12{,}105.54 + 3.325x_{i1}$$

In the SPSSX ANOVA table, the constrained residual sum of squares is

$$\text{SSE}_R = 257{,}743{,}502.82$$

From Figure 16.4, the estimated equation for the unconstrained model is

$$\hat{y}_i = 7501.50 + 2.176x_{i1} + 149.304x_{i2} + 0.445x_{i3}$$

and the residual sum of squares is

$$\text{SSE}_U = 173{,}958{,}874.36$$

The F statistic is

$$\begin{aligned} F &= \frac{(\text{SSE}_R - \text{SSE}_U)/Q}{\text{SSE}_U/(n - K - Q - 1)} \\ &= \frac{(257{,}743{,}502.82 - 173{,}958{,}874.36)/2}{173{,}958{,}874.26/(51 - 1 - 2 - 1)} \\ &= 10.84 \end{aligned}$$

The level of significance is $\alpha = .05$. The critical value of F having numerator degrees of freedom $Q = 2$ and denominator degrees of freedom $(n - K - Q - 1) = 47$ is approximately

$$F_{.05,2,47} = 3.23$$

(This is the critical value when the denominator degrees of freedom is 40, since the table does not list degrees of freedom of 47.) Because the observed F statistic $F = 10.84$ exceeds the critical value and falls in the critical region, H_0 is rejected in favor of H_1. The sample evidence supports the hypothesis that the variables X_2 and X_3 jointly help explain variations in Y. ■

Exercises for Section 16.6

1. Suppose we have estimated the population regression model

$$Y_i = \beta_0 + \beta_1 x_{i1} + \beta_2 x_{i2} + \beta_3 x_{i3} + e_i$$

   a. Explain how testing the null hypothesis H_0: $\beta_1 = \beta_2 = \beta_3 = 0$ differs from performing three individual tests of the hypotheses H_0: $\beta_i = 0$ for $i = 1, 2, 3$.
   b. Explain what it means if we cannot reject the joint null hypothesis

$$H_0\colon \beta_1 = \beta_2 = \beta_3 = 0$$

2. An economist claims that a dependent variable Y is linearly related to an explanatory variable X_1. Another economist claims that Y is a function of the three variables X_1, X_2, and X_3. The economists decide to test the joint hypothesis H_0: $\beta_2 = \beta_3 = 0$, where β_2 is the coefficient of X_2 and β_3 is the coefficient of X_3. The economists have 24 observations. The estimated regression equation obtained with one explanatory variable is

$$\hat{y}_i = 152.519 + 11.567x_{i1}$$

with SSE = 801.33. The regression equation with three explanatory variables is

$$\hat{y}_i = 23.451 + 4.582x_{i1} + 2.435x_{i2} + 21.356x_{i3}$$

with SSE = 686.35.

a. Calculate the F statistic that is used to test the joint null hypothesis H_0: $\beta_2 = \beta_3 = 0$.
b. What are the appropriate numbers of degrees of freedom?
c. Let $\alpha = .05$. What is the critical value of the F statistic?
d. Do you reject H_0?

3. An individual claims that a dependent variable Y is linearly related to two explanatory variables X_1 and X_2. Another individual suggests that Y is a function of the five variables X_1 to X_5. The individuals decide to test the joint hypothesis H_0: $\beta_3 = \beta_4 = \beta_5 = 0$ where β_1 is the coefficient of X_1, and so forth. The individuals have 35 observations. The regression equation estimated for five explanatory variables is

$$\hat{y}_i = 1.109 + 1.982x_{i1} + 4.657x_{i2} + 4.223x_{i3} + 1.218x_{i4} + 0.223x_{i5}$$

For this equation, we obtain SSE = 36.62. A regression equation for the two explanatory variables X_1 and X_2 is

$$\hat{y} = 45.730 + 9.803x_{i1} + 7.451x_{i2}$$

For this equation, we obtain SSE = 45.21.

a. Calculate the F statistic used to test the joint null hypothesis H_0: $\beta_3 = \beta_4 = \beta_5 = 0$.
b. What are the appropriate numbers of degrees of freedom?
c. Let $\alpha = .05$. What is the critical value of the F statistic?
d. Do you reject H_0?

16.7 ▪ Computer Applications

It is almost a necessity to use a statistical computer package when performing multiple regression analysis. As the numbers of explanatory variables and observations increase, it becomes extremely time consuming to calculate the sample regression coefficients, the standard deviations, and other associated test statistics. The next example shows how to use the SPSSX program to estimate a multiple regression model.

Example 16.10 **Estimating a Multiple Regression Model Using SPSSX:** In Example 16.9 we regressed the dependent variable Y_i (average salary of elementary and secondary school teachers in state i) against the three explanatory variables

x_{i1} = state and local tax revenue per capita in state i

x_{i2} = percentage of the labor force that is unionized in state i

x_{i3} = income per capita in state i

The conjectured model was

$$E(Y_i|x_{i1}, x_{i2}, x_{i3}) = \beta_0 + \beta_1 x_{i1} + \beta_2 x_{i2} + \beta_3 x_{i3}$$

The following SPSSX instructions were used to generate the regression output for this regression equation, shown in Figure 16.4:

```
TITLE    'SALARY STUDY'
DATA LIST FREE/SALARY REVENUE PCTUNION INCOME
BEGIN DATA

22934    2729    18.2    10673
41480    8349    30.4    18187
  .
  .
  .
27244    5440    15.6    13223

END DATA
REGRESSION VARIABLES = SALARY REVENUE PCTUNION INCOME/
    DEPENDENT = SALARY/
      ENTER REVENUE, PCTUNION, INCOME
FINISH
```

The command

```
REGRESSION VARIABLES = SALARY REVENUE PCTUNION INCOME/
```

tells the computer that you want to perform regression analysis and names the variables that you will be working with. The command

```
DEPENDENT = SALARY/
```

tells the computer to estimate a regression equation whose dependent variable is SALARY, and the command

```
ENTER REVENUE, PCTUNION, INCOME
```

tells the computer to use the three variables REVENUE, PCTUNION, and INCOME as explanatory variables.

Exercises for Section 16.7

1. Refer to the data in Table 2.3 of Chapter 2.

a. Estimate the multiple regression equation that explains per capita income as a function of the percentage of employees who are unionized and average hourly earnings in manufacturing.

b. Find the value of R^2. Does this model seem to do a reasonably good job of explaining per capita income?

c. Find s_e.

d. Test the null hypothesis that the coefficient of the variable Hourly Earnings is 0. Use a 5% level of significance. What is the prob-value of the test?

2. Refer to the data in Table 2.3 of Chapter 2.

a. Estimate the multiple regression equation that explains tax revenue per capita as a function of per capita income, percentage of employees who are unionized, and average hourly earnings in manufacturing.

b. Find the value of R^2. Does this model seem to do a reasonably good job of explaining tax revenues per capita?

c. Find s_e.

d. Test the null hypothesis that the coefficient of the variable Hourly Earnings is 0. Use a 5% level of significance. What is the prob-value of the test?
e. Construct a 95% confidence interval for the coefficient of the variable Hourly Earnings.

3. Refer to the data in Table 2.3 of Chapter 2.
a. Estimate the multiple regression equation that explains tax revenue per capita as a function of per capita income and average hourly earnings in manufacturing.
b. Find the value of R^2. Does this model seem to do a reasonably good job of explaining tax revenues per capita?
c. Find s_e.
d. Test the null hypothesis that the coefficient of the variable Hourly Earnings is 0. Use a 5% level of significance. What is the prob-value of the test?
e. Compare the values of R^2 here and in Exercise 2. Observe that R^2 is larger for the model that contains an additional explanatory variable.
f. Compare the estimated regression coefficients in Exercise 2 with the corresponding estimates here. Observe how all the values change when a variable is added or deleted from the model.
g. Compare the estimated standard deviations for the regression coefficients in Exercise 2 with the corresponding standard deviations here. Once again observe how all the standard deviations change when a variable is added or deleted from the model.

4. Refer to the data in Table 2.3 of Chapter 2.
a. Estimate the multiple regression equation that explains per capita tax revenue as a function of per capita income and average hourly earnings in manufacturing.
b. Find the value of R^2. Does this model seem to do a reasonably good job of explaining per capita income?
c. Find s_e.
d. Test the null hypothesis that the coefficient of the variable Hourly Earnings is 0. Use a 5% level of significance. What is the prob-value of the test?
e. Construct a 95% confidence interval for the coefficient of the variable Hourly Earnings.

Chapter 16 Summary

Multiple linear regression provides a method of predicting (or modeling) the behavior of a particular dependent variable (Y) using two or more independent (explanatory) variables. As in the case of simple linear regression, which uses one explanatory variable, the estimated least squares regression coefficients are those that minimize the residual sum of squares SSE.

To measure the goodness of fit of the model, we rely on the *coefficient of determination* R^2 and the *standard error of the regression* s_e. The coefficient of determination measures the proportion of the total variation in the sample of Y values explained by the set of explanatory variables.

To test hypotheses about a specific population regression coefficient, we rely on an observed t score and test using the t distribution having $(n - K - 1)$ degrees of freedom. To test the null hypothesis that a regression coefficient equals a specific value, say, β_i^*, we use the test statistic $t = (b_i - \beta_i^*)/s_{b_i}$ where s_{b_i} represents the estimated standard deviation of b_i, β_i^* is the hypothesized value of the coefficient, and b_i is the least-squares estimate of the population parameter. To determine the contribution of a particular subset of the explanatory variables—say, X_2 and X_4—SSE is computed with X_2 and X_4

included and then with X_2 and X_4 excluded from the regression equation. A partial F test is then used to determine whether the resulting increase in SSE is significant.

The problem of *multicollinearity* arises in multiple linear regression when two or more independent variables are highly correlated. Because all data sets used in applied economic research are afflicted with some degree of multicollinearity, it is difficult to get precise estimates of the individual population regression coefficients. Multicollinearity among the explanatory variables typically leads to an estimated regression equation whose estimated coefficients have large variances. Thus confidence intervals for the population coefficients will be wide, and it may be difficult to reject many hypotheses concerning the values of the population coefficients. One potential signal of a multicollinearity problem is the presence of high values for the estimated standard errors of the estimated regression coefficients. Another signal is a high sample correlation coefficient between two explanatory variables.

There is no special critical level signifying the presence of severe multicollinearity. One possible way to cope with multicollinearity is to eliminate one or more of the explanatory variables from the model. However, such action might introduce other problems, such as introducing bias into the estimates of the regression coefficients retained in the equation.

In this chapter we have discussed multiple regression models that show how the value of a dependent variable is related to two or more independent variables. Special cases of multiple regression models include polynomial models containing squares, cubes, and higher powers of an independent variable and models that contain indicators of qualitative variables. These indicator variables are called dummy variables. Polynomial models and dummy variable models are discussed in Chapter 17.

Chapter 16 ▪ Supplementary Exercises

1. An economist wants to determine the relationship between the annual amount spent on clothing and the number of family members and family income. The data in the accompanying table refer to 10 randomly selected families.

Amount Spent on Clothing (in thousands of dollars)	Number of Family Members	Family Income (in thousands of dollars)
0.7	1	21
1.4	2	25
0.4	1	12
2.3	2	39
3.9	2	48
2.1	3	27
3.3	4	36
2.8	3	35
3.0	5	25
4.1	3	53

a. Calculate the sample multiple regression equation where clothing expenditure depends on the number of family members and family income.
b. What is the estimated effect of an additional family member on annual clothing expenditure?
c. What is the estimated effect of an additional thousand dollars of income on annual clothing expenditure?
d. Would you expect this relationship to be linear for all values of the independent variables?
e. Predict annual clothing expenditure for a family with 2 members and income of $25,000.
f. Predict annual clothing expenditure for a family with 4 members and income of $35,000.

2. A marketing research company has been hired by the American Meat Packers Association to analyze family expenditures on beef. The research company gets data from a large number of families and estimates the following regression equation:

$$\hat{y}_i = 108.7 + 50.5x_{i1} + 162.4x_{i2}$$

where

$$Y = \text{annual dollar expenditures on beef for a family}$$
$$X_1 = \text{total family income in thousands of dollars}$$
$$X_2 = \text{number of people in the family}$$

a. A 4-person family has a total income of $20,000. Predict expenditures on beef for this family.
b. A 6-person family has a total income of $20,000. Predict expenditures on beef for this family.
c. What does the coefficient 162.4 indicate?
d. What does the coefficient 50.5 indicate?
e. If you estimated a regression equation to explain expenditures on beef, would you expect to get a large or a small value for R^2? Is it reasonable to expect $R^2 \geqslant .95$ in the given model?

3. Suppose the following results are obtained from a computer printout for Exercise 2:

Variable	Coefficient	Standard Deviation	t
Constant	108.7	11.2	9.7
Income (in thousands of dollars)	50.5	38.3	1.3
Number of people	162.4	9.5	17.1

a. How were the t statistics obtained?
b. Test the hypothesis that the coefficient of income is 0. Use a one-tailed test and let $\alpha = .05$.
c. Construct 95% confidence intervals for β_0, β_1, and β_2. Assume the sample size was 90, so the appropriate degrees of freedom is 87.

4. As the age of an automobile increases, its resale value decreases. The resale value also decreases as the mileage of the car increases. An auto insurance appraiser has obtained data from the sales of numerous used cars. The appraiser has estimated the following regression equation from data on a certain car model:

$$\hat{y}_i = 5.462.1 - 412.9x_{i1} - 52.3x_{i2}$$

where

$$Y = \text{resale price of car}$$
$$X_1 = \text{age of car (in years)}$$
$$X_2 = \text{mileage of car (in thousands)}$$

In the sample, cars varied from 1 to 6 years in age and from 5000 to 50,000 in mileage.

a. Predict the selling price of a 3-year-old car driven 30,000 miles.
b. Predict the selling price of a 10-year-old car driven 90,000 miles.
c. Does this problem show the danger of extrapolating far outside the range of the observed data?

5. The accompanying data show the output of sugar beets in tons, the mean July temperature in degrees Fahrenheit, and the rainfall in July in inches at a certain farm during a 10-year period.

Production of Sugar Beets Y	Mean July Temperature X_1	July Rainfall X_2
470	62	3.3
520	64	4.2
560	63	3.2
510	60	3.8
500	64	3.1
550	61	4.0
630	62	4.3
640	64	3.7
650	61	3.0
620	58	4.3

a. Estimate the regression equation $E(Y_i|x_{i1}, x_{i2}) = \beta_0 + \beta_1 x_1 + \beta_2 x_{i2}$.
b. Calculate R^2. Is this value large enough to make you think that X_1 and X_2 can be used to make good predictions of Y?
c. Let $\alpha = .05$. Test H_0: $\beta_1 = 0$ and H_0: $\beta_2 = 0$.

6. In a study of production costs at 62 coal mines, data were obtained on costs per ton (Y). Costs were related to degrees of mechanization (X_1), measure of geological difficulty (X_2), and percentage of absenteeism (X_3). The following estimates were obtained from a computer printout:

Variable	Coefficient	Standard Deviation
Constant	8.1	2.0
X_1	3.2	0.8
X_2	4.1	0.4
X_3	2.2	1.3

a. Test H_0: $\beta_1 = 0$ against H_1: $\beta_1 > 0$. Use $\alpha = .05$.
b. Test H_0: $\beta_3 = 0$ against H_1: $\beta_3 > 0$. Use $\alpha = .05$.
c. Construct a 95% confidence interval for β_3.
d. Construct a 95% confidence interval for β_2.

7. Consider the following estimated sample regression equation:

$$\hat{y}_i = 12 + 6x_{i1} - 3x_{i2}$$

Determine which of the following statements are true, which are false, and which are indeterminate. Explain your answer.

a. When x_{i2} increases by 1 unit, $\hat{y}_i$ increases by 3 units.
b. For a given x_{i2}, when x_{i1} increases by 1 unit, $\hat{y}_i$ increases by 6 units.

c. Y is more correlated with X_1 than with X_2 because the coefficient of X_1 is larger.

d. It is possible that the coefficient 6 might not be significantly different from 0 and that the coefficient -3 could be significantly different from 0 if we tested each coefficient using $\alpha = .05$.

8. The executive vice-president of a large corporation has been studying the annual salaries of the corporation's salespeople. A regression equation is estimated having the following variables:

$$Y = \text{annual salary of employee (in thousands of dollars)}$$
$$X_1 = \text{employee's number of years of education}$$
$$X_2 = \text{employee's number of years seniority}$$
$$X_3 = \text{value of equipment sold by employee (in thousands of dollars)}$$

The estimated equation is

$$\hat{y}_i = 16 + 0.5x_{i1} + 1.2x_{i2} + .06x_{i3}$$

a. Interpret each of the four regression coefficients.

b. Suppose a salesperson has 16 years of education and 5 years of seniority, and sold \$100,000 worth of equipment. Predict this person's salary.

c. Should X_3 be dropped from the model because its coefficient is so small?

d. Is X_2 the most important explanatory variable because its coefficient is the largest?

9. The sales manager of Norbert's Cracker Company thinks that the company's yearly sales revenues are related to annual advertising expenditures and to the number of sales representatives employed by the company. Using data for the last 10 years, the following regression results are obtained for the dependent variable of sales revenues (in thousands of dollars):

Variable	Coefficient	Standard Deviation	t
Constant	147.6	10.2	14.5
Advertising (in thousands of dollars)	65.4	4.1	16.0
Number of salespeople	32.3	9.6	3.4

a. Suppose the company has 20 sales reps and spends \$10,000 on advertising. Predict the sales revenue.

b. Construct a 95% confidence interval for β_0, β_1, and β_2.

c. Let $\alpha = .05$. Test H_0: $\beta_2 = 0$ against H_1: $\beta_2 > 0$.

References

DRAPER, NORMAN R., and HARRY SMITH. *Applied Regression Analysis*. 2d ed. New York: Wiley, 1981.

INTRILIGATOR, MICHAEL. *Econometric Models, Techniques and Applications*. Englewood Cliffs, N.J.: Prentice-Hall, 1978.

JOHNSTON, JOHN. *Econometric Methods*. New York: McGraw-Hill, 1972.

KMENTA, JAN. *Elements of Econometrics*. 2d ed. New York: Macmillan, 1986.

NIE, NORMAN E., C. HADLAI HULL, JEAN G. JENKINS, KARIN STEINBRENNER, and DALE H. BENT. *SPSS Statistical Package for the Social Sciences*. 2d ed. New York: McGraw-Hill, 1975.

Norusis, Marija J. *SPSSX Introductory Statistics Guide*. New York: McGraw-Hill, 1983.

———. *SPSSX Advanced Statistics Guide*. Chicago: SPSS, 1985.

———. *The SPSS Guide to Data Analysis*. Chicago: SPSS, 1986.

Pindyck, Robert S., and Daniel L. Rubinfeld. *Econometric Models and Economic Forecasts*. 2d ed. New York: McGraw-Hill, 1981.

Ryan, Thomas A., Brian L. Joiner, and Barbara F. Ryan. *Minitab Reference Manual*. University Park, Penn.: Minitab Project, 1985.

———. *Minitab Handbook*. 2d ed. Boston: PWS-KENT, 1985.

SAS Introductory Guide. 3d ed. Cary, N.C.: SAS Institute, 1985.

SAS Procedures Guide for Personal Computers. Version 6 ed. Cary, N.C.: SAS Institute, 1986.

SAS Statistics Guide for Personal Computers. Version 6 ed. Cary, N.C.: SAS Institute, 1986.

SAS User's Guide: Basics. Version 5 ed. Cary, N.C.: SAS Institute, 1985.

SAS User's Guide: Statistics. Version 5 ed. Cary, N.C.: SAS Institute, 1985.

SPSSX User's Guide. Chicago: SPSS, 1983.

Theil, Henri. *Principles of Econometrics*. New York: Wiley, 1971.

Wonnacott, Thomas H., and Ronald J. Wonnacott. *Regression: A Second Course in Statistics*. New York: Wiley, 1981.

Chapter Seventeen
Special Topics in Multiple Regression Analysis

17.1 ▪ Models Involving Polynomials

Many different mathematical functions can be used to describe relationships between economic variables. Only a few are used in practice, however, and generally the formulas used are not too complicated.

The linear relationship discussed in Chapter 15 is a special case of a larger class of functions called the *class of polynomial functions*. The general equation for the class of polynomial functions is

$$Y = \beta_0 + \beta_1 X + \beta_2 X^2 + \beta_3 X^3 + \cdots$$

If the highest exponent is 2, we have a *second-degree polynomial,* called a *parabola.* If the highest exponent is 3, we have a *third-degree polynomial,* or *cubic polynomial.* Higher-degree polynomials are seldom used. Figure 17.1 shows three representative polynomial curves.

FIGURE 17.1
Examples of various polynomials.

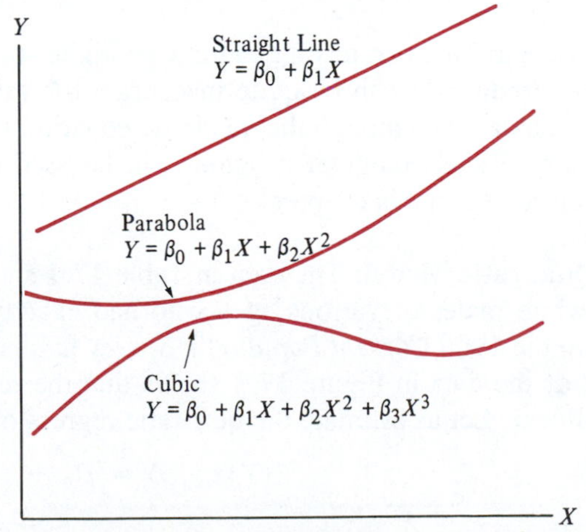

Definition: Second-Degree Polynomial Regression Model

The **second-degree polynomial regression model** (also called the *quadratic regression model*) is based on the equation

$$Y_i = \beta_0 + \beta_1 x_i + \beta_2 x_i^2 + e_i$$

where e_i is a random variable that satisfies all the basic assumptions. For a given value x_i, the mean value of Y_i is given by

$$E(Y_i|x_i) = \beta_0 + \beta_1 x_i + \beta_2 x_i^2$$

Figure 17.2 shows a situation in which the values of Y are scattered about a second-degree polynomial, or quadratic, regression curve. The sample quadratic regression equation is

$$\hat{y}_i = b_0 + b_1 x_i + b_2 x_i^2$$

where the coefficients b_0, b_1, and b_2 are the estimated values of the population parameters β_0, β_1, and β_2, respectively. To obtain the estimates b_0, b_1, and b_2, we proceed exactly as when estimating the regression model with two explanatory variables, where we use X as the first explanatory variable and X^2 as the second.

FIGURE 17.2
A quadratic regression model.

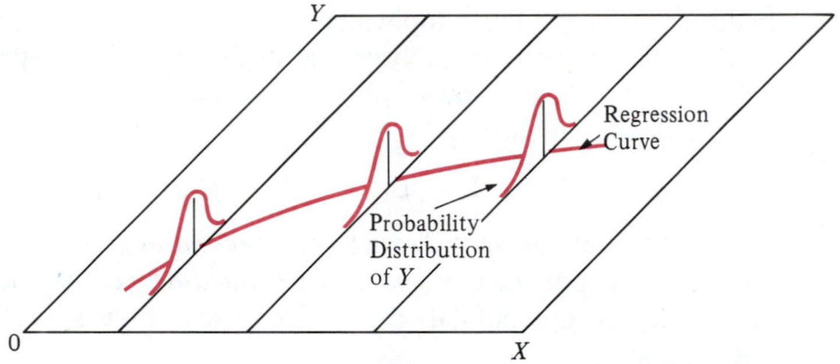

Be careful when using quadratic or higher-order regression models to make predictions. Predictions can be quite inaccurate for values of X outside the range of the observed data, even though the quadratic equation fits the sample data well. As in Chapter 16, the SPSSX computer program will be used to estimate the regression models that are discussed in this chapter.

Example 17.1

A Quadratic Model: The data in Table 17.1 show the average income in 1985 earned by white males of various ages who had exactly four years of high school education (from the 1986 *Current Population Survey* published by the Bureau of the Census). The plot of the data in Figure 17.3 shows that the relationship between income and age is nonlinear. Let us estimate the quadratic regression model

$$E(Y_i|x_i, x_i^2) = \beta_0 + \beta_1 x_i + \beta_2 x_i^2$$

TABLE 17.1
Data for Example 17.1 on average 1985 income of white male high school graduates

Group	Age Group	Average Age X	Income Y
1	18–24	21	\$14,108
2	25–29	27	20,523
3	30–34	32	22,471
4	35–39	37	26,017
5	40–44	42	27,314
6	45–49	47	28,093
7	50–54	52	27,288
8	55–59	57	26,706
9	60–64	62	25,951

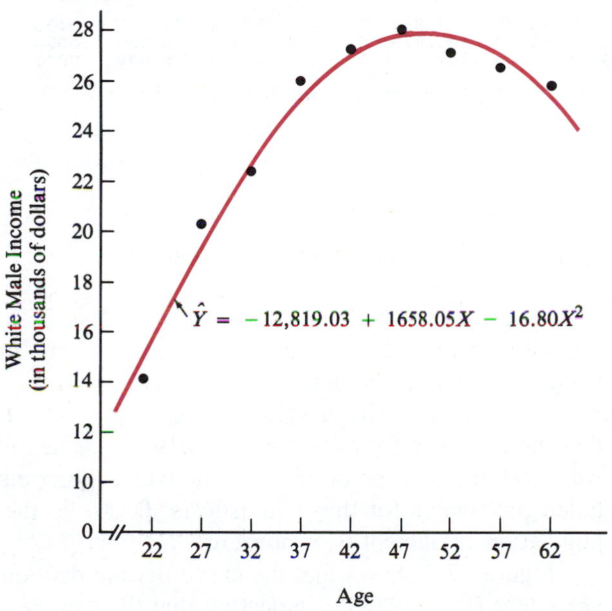

FIGURE 17.3
Income versus age in 1985 for white male high school graduates (Example 17.1).

Solution: The SPSSX computer output is shown in Figure 17.4. The sample regression equation, which is graphed on the scatter diagram in Figure 17.3, is

$$\hat{y}_i = -12{,}819.03 + 1658.05x_i - 16.80x_i^2 \qquad R^2 = .98535$$

$$t \text{ statistics:} \quad (-5.65) \qquad (14.30) \qquad (-12.19)$$

The values in parentheses are the t statistics used to test the null hypothesis that the corresponding coefficient is 0. Let us test the null hypothesis

$$H_0: \beta_2 = 0$$

FIGURE 17.4 SPSSX-generated output for Example 17.1, explaining income as a function of age.

```
                              * * * *   M U L T I P L E   R E G R E S S I O N   * * * *
Listwise Deletion of Missing Data

Equation Number 1    Dependent Variable..   INCOME

Beginning Block Number  1.  Method:  Enter      AGE      AGESQ

Variable(s) Entered on Step Number  1..    AGESQ
                                    2..    AGE

Multiple R            .99265        Analysis of Variance
R Square              .98535                          DF     Sum of Squares       Mean Square
Adjusted R Square     .98047        Regression         2    162921784.80527    81460892.40263
Standard Error     635.36570        Residual           6      2422137.41695      403689.56949

                                    F =      201.79093       Signif F =  .0000

------------------ Variables in the Equation ------------------

Variable                B          SE B        Beta         T  Sig T

AGESQ           -16.802749     1.378766   -4.314698   -12.187  .0000
AGE            1658.048471   115.976280    5.061611    14.296  .0000
(Constant) -12819.02566 2269.258525                    -5.649  .0013

End Block Number   1   All requested variables entered.
```

against the one-sided alternative hypothesis

$$H_1\colon \beta_2 < 0$$

Suppose we use a 5% level of significance. There are $n = 9$ observations and $K = 2$ explanatory variables. The t statistic has $\nu = (n - K - 1) = 6$ degrees of freedom. For $\alpha = .05$, the critical value of t is $-t_{.05,6} = -1.943$. The computer output shows that the t statistic for b_2 is $t = -12.19$. Because this value falls in the critical region, we reject H_0 in favor of H_1. Alternatively, the computer printout shows that the two-tailed prob-value for this t statistic is .0000, so the evidence is quite strong that the population coefficient β_2 is nonzero.

Figure 17.3 shows that the curve fits the data quite well. The computer output reveals that $R^2 = .98535$, indicating that the sample regression equation explains more than 98% of the variation in income. We can be confident that predictions made with this model should be very good as long as the X value is in the range of the observed data. That is, the model should predict income accurately if the age variable is, say, 30, but not if it is 75.

Suppose we want to predict the average income of white males who are age 30. We substitute $x = 30$ into the sample regression equation and obtain the predicted income

$$\begin{aligned}\hat{y} &= -12{,}819.03 + 1658.05(30) - 16.80(30)^2 \\ &= \$21{,}802.47\end{aligned}$$

Figure 17.4 shows that the estimated standard error of the regression is $s_e =$ \$635.36570 which is relatively small when one considers that we are predicting the average income of white males based on age; i.e. an error of \$635 would be considered a relatively small error.

Finally, note that the F statistic used to test the joint hypothesis H_0: $\beta_1 = \beta_2 = 0$ is $F = 201.79093$. Because the prob-value for this value of F is .0000, we can certainly reject the null hypothesis. ■

Exercises for Section 17.1

1. When publishing a daily newspaper, the number of errors made by a typesetter tends to be related to the speed at which the typesetter is working. The following data show the number of errors made in an hour (Y) and the speed of the typesetter (X) in lines set per minute:

Y	9	34	15	50	28	5	66	44	23	17
X	25	40	30	50	40	20	60	45	35	30

a. Plot the data on a scatter diagram. Does a linear or quadratic relationship seem to describe the relationship between Y and X better?
b. Estimate the linear regression model

$$E(Y_i|x_i) = \beta_0 + \beta_1 x_i$$

c. Estimate the quadratic regression model

$$E(Y_i|x_i, x_i^2) = \beta_0 + \beta_1 x_i + \beta_2 x_i^2$$

d. Let $\alpha = .05$. Test H_0: $\beta_2 = 0$ against H_1: $\beta_2 \neq 0$.
e. Plot the estimated equations on the scatter diagram.

2. An economist is interested in examining the relationship between an individual's annual income in thousands of dollars X and the individual's annual income tax payments in thousands of dollars Y. The data are as follows:

Y	3.1	6.0	3.3	4.2	7.7	11.0	8.1	6.0	1.0	5.0
X	20	40	27	36	54	90	74	60	18	45

a. Plot the data on a scatter diagram. Does a linear or quadratic relationship seem to describe the relationship between Y and X better?
b. Estimate the linear regression model.
c. Estimate the quadratic regression model.
d. Plot the estimated equations on the scatter diagram.
e. The income tax system is supposedly a progressive system: As income increases, people pay a higher proportion of their income in taxes. Do these data support the hypothesis that the tax system is progressive? Let $\alpha = .05$. Test H_0: $\beta_2 = 0$ against H_1: $\beta_2 > 0$.

3. An architect claims that the cost of constructing an office building is related to the area of the floor space in the building according to the quadratic regression model

$$E(Y_i|x_i, x_i^2) = \beta_0 + \beta_1 x_i + \beta_2 x_i^2 + e_i$$

where Y is the cost per square foot in dollars and X is the floor space in 100,000s of square feet. The data are as follows:

Y	16	19	22	26	28	29	30	33	36	40
X	2.6	3.4	4.3	4.5	5.0	6.2	6.8	7.2	8.4	9.7

a. Plot the data on a scatter diagram. Does a linear or quadratic relationship seem to describe the relationship between Y and X better?
b. Estimate the linear regression model and find the adjusted R^2.
c. Estimate the quadratic regression model and find the adjusted R^2.
d. Plot the estimated equations on a scatter diagram.
e. Let $\alpha = .05$. Test H_0: $\beta_2 = 0$ against H_1: $\beta_2 > 0$.
f. Predict the cost of constructing a building that is 200 feet by 200 feet and has 6 floors. Use the equation estimated in part (b) and then the estimated equation in part (c). Which prediction do you think is better?

17.2 ▪ *Dummy Variables in Regression Models*

Some observed phenomena are qualitative rather than quantitative and thus cannot be measured on a continuous scale. The presence or absence of some particular quality may be important in explaining the value of some dependent variable Y, however, and we may want to take this into account when constructing regression models. For example, an individual's income might depend on whether the person possesses a college degree, an individual's expected expenditure on recreation might depend on whether the person is male or female, and the value of a car might depend on whether it has air conditioning.

Up to now, in the multiple regression model

$$E(Y_i|x_{i1}, x_{i2}, \ldots, x_{iK}) = \beta_0 + \beta_1 x_{i1} + \beta_2 x_{i2} + \cdots + \beta_K x_{iK}$$

we have implicitly assumed that the X variables were all measured on some continuous scale. We can greatly increase the scope of the regression model by incorporating qualitative variables into it in the form of *dummy variables*.

Definition: Dummy Variables

Dummy variables are specially constructed variables that indicate the presence or absence of some characteristic. They assume a value of 1 or 0, depending upon whether a certain characteristic is present.

In this section, we incorporate dummy variables into the multiple regression model and explain how to interpret the estimated coefficients of the dummy variables.

Some Uses of Dummy Variables

Dummy variables may be used to represent and compare factors such as the following:

1. *Temporal effects*: Examples include wartime versus peacetime, Christmas season versus non-Christmas season, summer versus nonsummer, strike period versus nonstrike period, and different quarters of the year.

2. *Spatial effects*: Examples include north versus south, urban versus rural, City A versus City B, developed versus underdeveloped countries, and farm versus nonfarm communities.

3. *Qualitative variables*: Examples include male versus female, college graduate versus non-college graduate, skilled versus unskilled employee, married versus single, renter versus home-owner, employed versus unemployed, and white versus nonwhite.

4. *Broad groupings of quantitative variables*: Income over $50,000 versus income under $50,000, age over 25 versus age under 25, 3 or more children versus fewer than 3 children, and sales less than $1 million per year versus sales greater than $1 million per year.

Base Case and the Coefficient of a Dummy Variable

The **base case** refers to any observation for which the dummy variable is equal to 0. The coefficient of a dummy variable measures the difference between being in the base case and not being in the base case.

The following example shows a model that contains a dummy variable and explains how to interpret the estimated coefficients.

Example 17.2

Dummy Variables—The Ph.D. Effect: Suppose the salaries of employees at a particular research institute depend on seniority (or number of years employed at the institute), whether the employee has a Ph.D. degree, and other random factors.

Suppose we express the relationship between the variables in terms of the following multiple regression model:

$$E(Y_i|x_i, z_i) = \beta_0 + \beta_1 x_i + \beta_2 z_i$$

where

$$Y = \text{salary in dollars}$$
$$X = \text{years of seniority}$$
$$Z = \begin{cases} 1 & \text{if individual has a Ph.D.} \\ 0 & \text{if individual does not have a Ph.D.} \end{cases}$$

We assume that all the basic assumptions of the multiple regression model hold.

Suppose the ith individual has seniority of x_i years and does not have a Ph.D. Thus, the variable Z assumes the value 0. The expected salary would be

$$\begin{aligned} E(Y_i|x_i, z_i = 0) &= \beta_0 + \beta_1 x_i + \beta_2(0) \\ &= \beta_0 + \beta_1 x_i \end{aligned}$$

A person who has a Ph.D. and the same seniority of x_i years would have an expected salary of

$$\begin{aligned} E(Y_i|x_i, z_i = 1) &= \beta_0 + \beta_1 x_i + \beta_2(1) \\ &= \beta_0 + \beta_1 X_i + \beta_2 \end{aligned}$$

Thus, for a non-Ph.D. with x_i years of seniority, we obtain

$$E(Y_i|x_i, \text{non-Ph.D.}) = E(Y_i|x_i, z_i = 0) = \beta_0 + \beta_1 x_i$$

For a Ph.D. with x_i years of seniority, we obtain

$$E(Y_i|x_i, \text{Ph.D.}) = E(Y_i|x_i, z_i = 0) = \beta_0 + \beta_1 x_i + \beta_2$$

Suppose β_0 is \$15,000, β_1 is \$1000, and β_2 is \$2500. The expected salary of a non-Ph.D. with x_i years of seniority would be

$$E(Y_i|x_i, z_i = 0) = 15{,}000 + 1000x_i$$

The constant $\beta_0 = 15{,}000$ represents the starting salary, and the coefficient $\beta_1 = 1000$ represents the annual salary increment.

The expected salary of a Ph.D. with x_i years of seniority would be

$$E(Y_i|x_i, z_i = 1) = 15{,}000 + 1000x_i + 2500$$

The coefficient $\beta_2 = 2500$ represents the effect of having the Ph.D. ($z_i = 1$) as opposed to not having the Ph.D. ($z_i = 0$) and indicates that a person who has a Ph.D. earns, on the average, \$2500 more per year than a person with the same seniority who does not have a Ph.D. Thus testing the hypothesis that $\beta_2 = 0$ is equivalent to testing the hypothesis that there is no difference between the salaries of Ph.D.'s and the salaries of non-Ph.D.'s.

Figure 17.5 illustrates the relationship between salary, years of seniority, and educational level. The regression model is

$$E(Y_i|x_i, z_i) = 15{,}000 + 1000x_i + 2500z_i$$

where

$$Z = \begin{cases} 1 & \text{if individual has a Ph.D.} \\ 0 & \text{otherwise} \end{cases}$$

FIGURE 17.5
Illustrating the Ph.D. effect using a dummy variable.

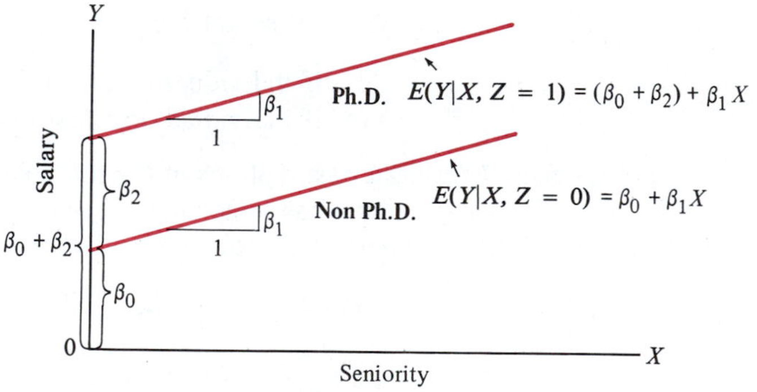

The expected salary of a non-Ph.D. is determined by

$$E(Y_i|x_i, z_i = 0) = 15{,}000 + 1000x_i$$

This is the base case, represented by the lower line on Figure 17.5. The expected salary of a Ph.D. is determined by the equation

$$E(Y_i|x_i, z_i = 1) = 15{,}000 + 1000x_i + 2500$$

This is the upper line on Figure 17.5. Having a Ph.D. shifts the intercept of the line from \$15,000 to \$17,500, although the slope of the line remains 1000. ■

Example 17.3 **Effect of Air Conditioning on a Car's Resale Price:** Suppose we want to estimate the coefficients in a multiple regression model in which the resale value of a certain model car depends on the age of the car and on whether the car has air conditioning. Let Y be the resale price in dollars, and X_1 be the age of the car in years; let X_2 be 1 if air conditioning is present and 0 if it is not.

The data in Table 17.2 refer to a sample of 20 used cars of a certain make and model. Estimate the multiple regression model.

TABLE 17.2
Data for Example 17.3 on used cars

Car	Price Y	Age X_1	Dummy X_2
1	4000	1	0
2	3050	2	0
3	4350	1	1
4	3900	1	0
5	1950	3	0
6	3000	2	0
7	1400	4	1
8	4500	1	1
9	2950	2	0
10	900	4	0
11	3600	2	1
12	4100	1	0
13	2100	3	0
14	1000	4	0
15	2400	3	1
16	4000	1	0
17	4400	1	1
18	2900	2	0
19	4450	1	1
20	2050	3	0

Solution: There are 7 cars that have air conditioning and 13 that do not. The relevant computer output is shown in Figure 17.6.

We obtain the estimated regression equation

$$\hat{y}_i = 5005.22 - 1005.79x_{i1} + 448.39x_{i2} \qquad R^2 = .996222$$

$$t \text{ statistics:} \quad (120.46) \quad (-62.93) \quad (12.27)$$

FIGURE 17.6 **Computer output for predicting used car prices in Example 17.3.**

```
DEPENDENT VARIABLE: PRICE
SUM OF SQUARED RESIDUALS = 100,598
STANDARD ERROR OF THE REGRESSION = 76.9254
R-SQUARED = .996222
ADJUSTED R-SQUARED = .995777
F STATISTIC (2, 17) = 2241.18
```

VARIABLE	ESTIMATED COEFFICIENT	STANDARD DEVIATION	t STATISTIC
CONSTANT	b_0 = 5005.22	41.5501	120.462
AGE	b_1 = -1005.79	15.9829	-62.929
DUMMY	b_2 = 448.387	36.5542	12.266

The coefficient $b_1 = -1005.79$ indicates that an increase of 1 year in the car's age tends to be associated with a decrease of \$1005.79 in the car's value. The coefficient $b_2 =$ 448.39 measures the effect of an air conditioner. A car with air conditioning ($x_{i2} = 1$) tends to be worth \$448.39 more than a car of the same age that does not have air conditioning ($x_{i2} = 0$).

The price of a car without air conditioning would be predicted using the equation

$$\begin{aligned}\hat{y}_i &= 5005.22 - 1005.79x_{i1} + 448.39(0) \\ &= 5005.22 - 1005.79x_{i1}\end{aligned}$$

and the price of a car with air conditioning would be predicted using the equation

$$\begin{aligned}\hat{y}_i &= 5005.22 - 1005.79x_{i1} + 448.39(1) \\ &= 5453.61 - 1005.79x_{i1}\end{aligned}$$

The t statistics are all significant at the 5% level of significance, which supports the hypotheses that β_0, β_1, and β_2 are all nonzero. The value $R^2 = .996222$ indicates that the regression model fits the data very well. Since the estimated standard error of the regression is $s_e = 76.9254$, the Empirical Rule indicates that about 95% of the observations should lie within $2s_e = \$153.85$ of the regression equation. The large value of the F statistic indicates that we would reject the null hypothesis H_0: $\beta_1 = \beta_2 = 0$.

The data and the two regression equations are plotted in Figure 17.7. The lower line refers to cars without air conditioning, and the upper line to cars with air conditioning. The vertical distance between the two lines is 448.397. ■

Example 17.4 **Effect of Sex on Income of an Employee:** The data in Table 17.3 (from the *Current Population Survey,* 1986, by the Bureau of the Census) show the average annual incomes earned in 1985 by white males and white females of various ages who had exactly four years of high school education. The data are plotted in Figure 17.8 (page 726). In Example 17.1 we used the data for the males to estimate a quadratic equation that explained

FIGURE 17.7
Resale prices of used cars versus age of the car for Example 17.3.

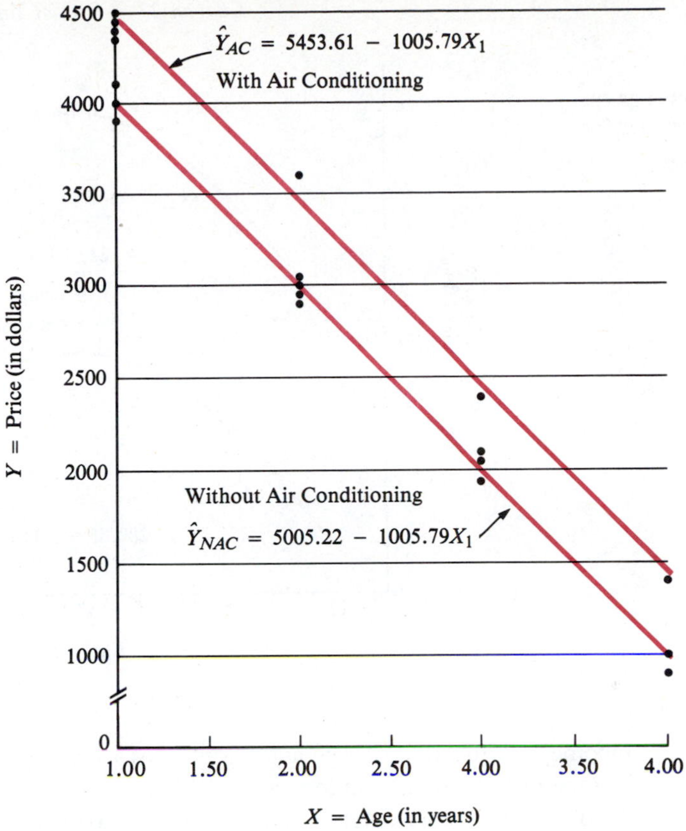

TABLE 17.3
Data on income, age, and sex for Example 17.4

Group	Age Group	Average Age	S^a	Income
1	18–24	21	1	$14,108
2	25–29	27	1	20,523
3	30–34	32	1	22,471
4	35–39	37	1	26,017
5	40–44	42	1	27,314
6	45–49	47	1	28,093
7	50–54	52	1	27,288
8	55–59	57	1	26,706
9	60–64	62	1	25,951
10	18–24	21	0	11,154
11	25–29	27	0	14,517
12	30–34	32	0	16,215
13	35–39	37	0	16,199
14	40–44	42	0	15,777
15	45–49	47	0	15,906
16	50–54	52	0	16,217
17	55–59	57	0	15,755
18	60–64	62	0	15,240

[a] S is 1 if individuals are male and 0 if individuals are female.

FIGURE 17.8
Income versus age for males and females for Example 17.4.

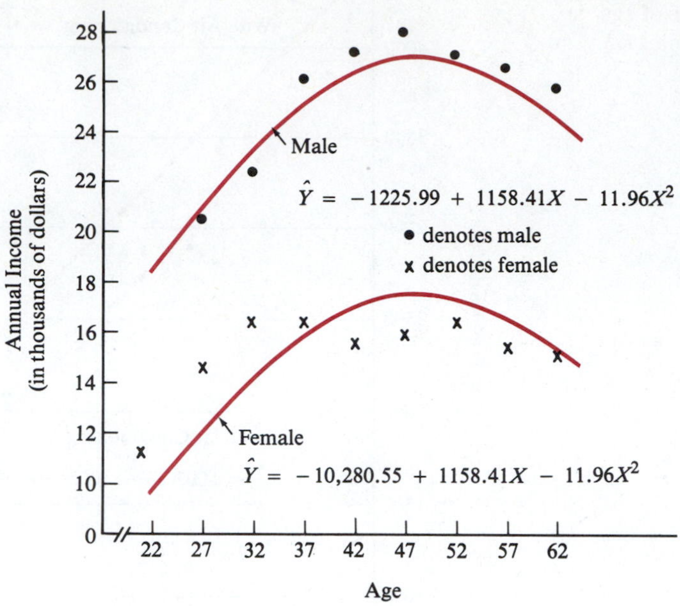

Income as a function of Age and $(\text{Age})^2$. Now let us estimate a model that explains the income of both males and females.

From the scatter diagram, income appears to depend on age and on sex. In addition, it appears that the relationship between income and age is nonlinear. Let us estimate the multiple regression model

$$E(Y_i | x_i, x_i^2, s_i) = \beta_0 + \beta_1 x_i + \beta_2 x_i^2 + \beta_3 s_i + e_i$$

where

$$Y = \text{income}$$
$$X = \text{age}$$
$$S = \begin{cases} 1 & \text{if individual is male} \\ 0 & \text{if individual is female} \end{cases}$$

Solution: The SPSSX computer output is shown in Figure 17.9. The estimated regression equation is

$$\hat{y}_i = -10{,}280.55 + 1158.41x_i - 11.96x_i^2 + 9054.56s_i \qquad R^2 = .92048$$
$$t \text{ statistics:} \quad (-2.82) \qquad (5.05) \qquad (-4.39) \qquad (10.81)$$

The value $R^2 = .92048$ indicates that the model explains more than 92% of the variation in average income. The base case is $S = 0$, where the individual is a white female. Thus the population regression coefficient β_3 indicates the difference in income between a

FIGURE 17.9 **SPSSX-generated output for Example 17.4, explaining income as a function of age and sex.**

```
                                   * * * *   M U L T I P L E   R E G R E S S I O N   * * * *

Listwise Deletion of Missing Data

Equation Number 1     Dependent Variable..     INCOME

Beginning Block Number   1.   Method:   Enter      AGE       AGESQ     SEX

Variable(s) Entered on Step Number   1..     SEX
                                     2..     AGESQ
                                     3..     AGE

Multiple R              .95942      Analysis of Variance
R Square                .92048                        DF      Sum of Squares       Mean Square
Adjusted R Square       .90344      Regression         3   511156373.90450   170385457.96817
Standard Error      1775.95953      Residual          14    44156451.70661     3154032.26476

                                    F =       54.02147       Signif F =   .0000

----------------- Variables in the Equation -----------------

Variable              B         SE B        Beta          T  Sig T

SEX         9054.555556   837.195353     .815088     10.815  .0000
AGESQ        -11.955059     2.725116   -2.368984     -4.387  .0006
AGE         1158.413808   229.225790    2.728950      5.054  .0002
(Constant) -10280.55246  4504.654889                 -2.282  .0386

End Block Number    1    All requested variables entered.
```

white male of a certain age and a white female of the same age. The estimated coefficient of variable S is $b_3 = 9054.56$, which indicates that, on the average, a white male earns approximately \$9054.56 more than a white female of the same age.

The plotted data show quite clearly that white males earn more than white females of the same age. Suppose we wanted to put this statement to a formal test. To test the null hypothesis that white males and white females of the same age earn the same annual income, let us test the null hypothesis

$$H_0\colon \beta_3 = 0$$

against the one-sided alternative hypothesis

$$H_1\colon \beta_3 > 0$$

Let us use a 1% level of significance. To perform the test, the appropriate number of degrees of freedom is $(n - K - 1) = (18 - 3 - 1) = 14$. The critical value of the test statistic is $t_{.01,14} = 2.624$. Because the SPSSX output shows that the t statistic for b_3 is $t = 10.815$, we reject the null hypothesis. Alternatively, the computer output shows that the prob-value associated with $t = 10.815$ is .0000.

To predict the average income for white males of a given age, we substitute $s_i = 1$ into the sample regression equation. We obtain

$$\hat{y}_i = -10{,}280.55 + 1158.41x_i - 11.96x_i^2 + 9054.56(1)$$

or

$$\hat{y}_i = -1225.99 + 1158.41x_i - 11.96x_i^2$$

To predict the average income for white females of a given age, we substitute $s_i = 0$ into the sample regression equation and obtain

$$\hat{y}_i = -10{,}280.55 + 1158.41x_i - 11.96x_i^2$$

These two curves are plotted in Figure 17.8.

For females, the intercept is $-10{,}280.55$. For males, the intercept is $-1225.99 = (-10{,}280.55 + 9054.56)$. The difference between these two intercepts of 9054.56 estimates that a white male of a given age earns, on the average, \$9054.56 more than a white female of the same age. ■

Could it be argued that the data in Example 17.4 provide evidence of sex discrimination in the United States labor market, or are there other reasons that might explain why men get paid more than women? Recall that in Chapter 15 we showed that if we omit important explanatory variables from a model, then it is possible to obtain misleading results. The data in Example 17.4 might indicate that there is sex discrimination in the job market, but other factors should also be considered.

As an extreme example, suppose that there are only two types of jobs for male and female high school graduates, office clerk and truck driver. Suppose that truck drivers earn about \$10,000 per year more than clerks. Furthermore, suppose that 90% of the males are truck drivers and 10% are clerks, while 10% of the females are truck drivers and 90% are clerks. Finally, assume that male and female truck drivers are paid identical salaries and that male and female clerks are paid identical salaries. A regression model that ignores the individual's occupation would indicate that the average male earns much more than the average female, but this result would be misleading because males and females who do identical work are paid identical salaries.

Regression Models with More Than One Dummy Variable

Frequently it is necessary to include more than one dummy variable in a regression model. In the following example, we attempt to explain the level of income based on the age, sex, and race of the individual. Because the variables Sex and Race are both qualitative variables, we need to construct two dummy variables in our model.

Example 17.5

A Regression Model with Two Dummy Variables: In Example 17.4, we estimated a regression model to explain the average incomes of white males and females who have four years of high school education. The *Current Population Survey* also reports data concerning the incomes earned by black high school graduates. Let us introduce a second dummy variable R into the model to take into account the race of the individual. The population regression model becomes

$$E(Y_i|x_i, x_i^2, s_i, r_i) = \beta_0 + \beta_1 x_i + \beta_2 x_i^2 + \beta_3 s_i + \beta_4 r_i$$

where

$$Y = \text{income}$$

$$X = \text{age}$$

$$S = \begin{cases} 1 & \text{if individual is male} \\ 0 & \text{if individual is female} \end{cases}$$

$$R = \begin{cases} 1 & \text{if individual is white} \\ 0 & \text{if individual is black} \end{cases}$$

Note that according to our definitions of the dummy variables S and R, the base case is $S = 0$ and $R = 0$, which refers to a black female. The data are in Table 17.4 (page 730).

Solution: The computer output is shown in Figure 17.10. The estimated regression equation is

$$\hat{y}_i = -6719.12 + 870.71x_i - 8.28x_i^2 + 6703.49s_i + 2578.36r_i$$

t statistics: (−1.58) (4.02) (−3.21) (8.14) (3.27)

The value $R^2 = .80583$ indicates that this expanded model fits the data fairly well.

The coefficient of interest in this problem is the coefficient of the dummy variable R. The computer output shows that $b_4 = 2578.36$, which indicates that, in our sample data, whites of a given sex and age earn \$2578.36 more than blacks of the same age and sex.

FIGURE 17.10 **SPSSX-generated output for Example 17.5, explaining income as a function of age, sex, and race.**

```
                       * * * *   M U L T I P L E   R E G R E S S I O N   * * * *
Listwise Deletion of Missing Data

Equation Number 1    Dependent Variable..   INCOME

Beginning Block Number  1.  Method:  Enter      AGE       AGESQ      SEX       RACE

Variable(s) Entered on Step Number   1..     RACE
                                     2..     AGESQ
                                     3..     SEX
                                     4..     AGE

Multiple R              .89768        Analysis of Variance
R Square                .80583                              DF      Sum of Squares        Mean Square
Adjusted R Square       .78078        Regression             4     719444071.37365    179861017.84341
Standard Error      2364.76175        Residual              31     173355042.18190      5592098.13490

                                      F =        32.16342        Signif F =   .0000

------------------ Variables in the Equation ------------------

Variable                 B          SE B         Beta            T    Sig T

RACE           2578.361900    789.495712      .258874        3.266    .0027
AGESQ            -8.275096      2.575913    -1.828902       -3.212    .0031
SEX            6703.485802    796.739820      .672007        8.414    .0000
AGE             870.713232    216.446597     2.287778        4.023    .0003
(Constant)    -6719.120776   4242.660540                    -1.584    .1234

End Block Number   1   All requested variables entered.
```

TABLE 17.4 **Data on income, age, sex, and race for Example 15.4**

Group	Age Group	Average Age	S^a	R^b	Income
1	18–24	21	1	1	$14,108
2	25–29	27	1	1	20,523
3	30–34	32	1	1	22,471
4	35–39	37	1	1	26,017
5	40–44	42	1	1	27,314
6	45–49	47	1	1	28,093
7	50–54	52	1	1	27,288
8	55–59	57	1	1	26,706
9	60–64	62	1	1	25,951
10	18–24	21	0	1	11,154
11	25–29	27	0	1	14,517
12	30–34	32	0	1	16,215
13	35–39	37	0	1	16,199
14	40–44	42	0	1	15,777
15	45–49	47	0	1	15,906
16	50–54	52	0	1	16,217
17	55–59	57	0	1	15,755
18	60–64	62	0	1	15,240
19	18–24	21	1	0	11,698
20	25–29	27	1	0	16,809
21	30–34	32	1	0	17,420
22	35–39	37	1	0	19,657
23	40–44	42	1	0	21,393
24	45–49	47	1	0	21,772
25	50–54	52	1	0	20,423
26	55–59	57	1	0	22,775
27	60–64	62	1	0	22,775
28	18–24	21	0	0	9,573
29	25–29	27	0	0	12,696
30	30–34	32	0	0	14,180
31	35–39	37	0	0	16,548
32	40–44	42	0	0	15,763
33	45–49	47	0	0	14,471
34	50–54	52	0	0	15,379
35	55–59	57	0	0	14,366
36	60–64	62	0	0	14,366

[a] S is 1 if individuals are male and 0 if individuals are female.
[b] R is 1 if individuals are white and 0 if individuals are black.

To test the null hypothesis that whites of a certain age and sex earn the same annual income as blacks of the same age and sex, let us test the null hypothesis

$$H_0: \beta_4 = 0$$

against the one-sided alternative hypothesis

$$H_1: \beta_4 > 0$$

using a 1% level of significance. The appropriate degrees of freedom is $(n - K - 1) = (36 - 4 - 1) = 31$, and so the critical value of the test statistic is $t_{.01,31} = 2.457$. The computer output shows that the t statistic for b_4 is $t = 3.266$. We reject the null hypothesis because the t statistic falls in the critical region. In addition, the computer output shows that the prob-value for $t = 3.266$ is .0027. We thus reject the null hypothesis and conclude that the variable R does help explain income. ■

Qualitative Variables with More Than Two Classes

In Examples 17.2, 17.3, 17.4, and 17.5, the dummy variables classified an observation into one of two categories. Now suppose we want to classify observations according to a characteristic that takes more than two possible values. For example, when using quarterly data, it is customary to include dummy variables in the multiple regression model to represent the different quarters or seasons of the year.

Because there are $m = 4$ quarters, we need to create $(m - 1) = 3$ dummy variables. Suppose we select the fourth quarter to be the base case. We could define the three dummy variables as follows:

$$Q_1 = \begin{cases} 1 & \text{if observation refers to the first quarter} \\ 0 & \text{otherwise} \end{cases}$$

$$Q_2 = \begin{cases} 1 & \text{if observation refers to the second quarter} \\ 0 & \text{otherwise} \end{cases}$$

$$Q_3 = \begin{cases} 1 & \text{if observation refers to the third quarter} \\ 0 & \text{otherwise} \end{cases}$$

For an observation from the fourth quarter, we have $q_{i1} = 0$, $q_{i2} = 0$, and $q_{i3} = 0$. For an observation from the first quarter, we have $q_{i1} = 1$, $q_{i2} = 0$, $q_{i3} = 0$. For an observation from the second quarter, the values of the dummy variables are $q_{i1} = 0$, $q_{i2} = 1$, $q_{i3} = 0$. If the observation is from the third quarter, the values are $q_{i1} = 0$, $q_{i2} = 0$, and $q_{i3} = 1$. The coefficient of variable Q_1 measures the difference in the dependent variable as a result of its being in quarter 1 rather than in quarter 4, the base case, and similarly for Q_2 and Q_3.

A dummy variable takes on only the values 0 and 1. We *do not* create a dummy variable that takes on the values, say, 0, 1, and 2, or 1, 2, and 3. The two values 0 and 1 work like a light switch which is either "on" or "off." A value of 0 means that a certain condition is false and a value of 1 means that the condition is true.

Number of Dummy Variables

If a qualitative variable falls into one of m classes, then $(m - 1)$ dummy variables are required to represent the variable in the multiple regression model.

Suppose that every observation falls into exactly one of $m = 3$ categories. In the regression model, we must create $(m - 1) = 2$ dummy variables, which we will call D_1 and D_2. Let's label the three categories 0, 1, and 2, and call category 0 the base category. If an observation falls in Category 0, then set $d_{i1} = 0$ and $d_{i2} = 0$. If an observation falls in Category 1, we set $d_{i1} = 1$ and $d_{i2} = 0$. If an observation falls in Category 2, we set $d_{i1} = 0$ and $d_{i2} = 1$. If we use this framework, then each observation is classified as follows:

$$d_{i1} = \begin{cases} 1 & \text{if and only if the } i\text{th observation falls in Category 1} \\ 0 & \text{otherwise} \end{cases}$$

$$d_{i2} = \begin{cases} 1 & \text{if and only if the } i\text{th observation falls in Category 2} \\ 0 & \text{otherwise} \end{cases}$$

This idea can easily be extended to cover observations that fall into exactly one of m categories where m is any value greater than or equal to 2.

Example 17.6

Using Dummy Variables to Represent Three Categories: A research economist for a large bank has been examining the selling prices of corporate and municipal bonds and thinks that the selling prices of bonds depend on four criteria: the interest rate paid by the bond, the interest rate paid on Treasury bills on the day that the bond is sold, the bond's Moody's rating, and whether the income from the bond is tax exempt. The economist obtains data on 15 different bonds at various times. We define the following variables:

P_i = price of the ith bond in dollars

I_i = interest rate of the ith bond in percentage points

T_i = interest rate on Treasury bills in percentage points on day bond was sold

$$E_i = \begin{cases} 1 & \text{if income from the } i\text{th bond is tax exempt} \\ 0 & \text{if income from the } i\text{th bond is not tax exempt} \end{cases}$$

Suppose that each bond is rated AAA, AA, or A. There are $m = 3$ categories, so it is necessary to construct $(m - 1) = 2$ dummy variables. Suppose we call these two dummy variables R_1 and R_2. We define the values taken by these dummy variables as follows:

$$R_{i1} = \begin{cases} 1 & \text{if the } i\text{th bond is rated AAA} \\ 0 & \text{otherwise} \end{cases}$$

$$R_{i2} = \begin{cases} 1 & \text{if the } i\text{th bond is rated AA} \\ 0 & \text{otherwise} \end{cases}$$

It follows that for a bond with an A rating, we have $R_{i1} = 0$ and $R_{i2} = 0$, which represents the base case.

The multiple regression model is

$$P_i = \beta_0 + \beta_1 I_i + \beta_2 T_i + \beta_3 E_i + \beta_4 R_{i1} + \beta_5 R_{i2} + e_i$$

The economist hypothesizes the following: β_1 should be positive because bonds paying high interest rates should be worth more than bonds paying low interest rates, other things being equal; β_2 should be negative because the demand for corporate bonds will decline when the interest rate on government bonds increases; β_3 should be positive, because when the income from the bond is tax exempt, the bond is more valuable than when the income is taxable, other things being equal; and β_4 and β_5 should both be positive because AAA and AA bonds should be more valuable than A bonds, other things being equal.

Each bond has a stated value of $100, but its actual selling price varies as the other variables change. The actual selling prices and the other data are shown in Table 17.5. Figure 17.11 shows the relevant computer output.

TABLE 17.5 **Data for bonds in Example 17.6**

Bond	Price P_i	Interest Rate I_i	Treasury Bill Rate T_i	Tax Status E_i^a	AAA Status R_{i1}^b	AA Status R_{i2}^c
1	89	6	8	0	0	0
2	98	8	8	0	0	1
3	100	8	6	0	1	0
4	100	10	7	1	0	1
5	97	5	6	0	1	0
6	105	9	7	1	1	0
7	108	10	8	1	1	0
8	97	6	4	1	0	0
9	89	5	5	0	0	0
10	87	9	9	0	1	0
11	100	9	6	0	0	1
12	86	6	10	0	0	0
13	90	7	7	0	0	0
14	106	9	7	1	0	1
15	103	11	6	0	1	0

[a] E_i is 1 if bond is tax exempt and 0 if it is not.
[b] R_{i1} is 1 if bond has AAA rating and 0 otherwise.
[c] R_{i2} is 1 if bond has AA rating and 0 otherwise.

The estimated regression equation is

$$\hat{P}_i = 93.615 + 0.764 I_i - 1.357 T_i + 6.166 E_i + 7.213 R_{i1} + 6.931 R_{i2}$$

t statistics: (14.706) (.904) (−1.885) (2.564) (2.252) (1.954)

FIGURE 17.11 SPSSX-generated output for Example 17.6, explaining bond prices as a function of other interest rates and bond rating.

```
                              * * * *   M U L T I P L E   R E G R E S S I O N   * * * *
Listwise Deletion of Missing Data
Equation Number 1     Dependent Variable..    PRICE
Beginning Block Number  1.  Method:  Enter      I         T         E         R1        R2

Variable(s) Entered on Step Number  1..   R2        aa dummy
                                    2..   T         treasury bill rate
                                    3..   E         tax exempt dummy
                                    4..   I         interest rate
                                    5..   R1        aaa dummy

Multiple R            .89903        Analysis of Variance
R Square              .80825                      DF      Sum of Squares      Mean Square
Adjusted R Square     .70172        Regression     5          588.40532        117.68106
Standard Error       3.93834        Residual       9          139.59468         15.51052

                                    F =        7.58718       Signif F =  .0047

----------------- Variables in the Equation -----------------

Variable               B          SE B        Beta          T   Sig T

R2              6.930957      3.546328     .439955      1.954   .0824
T              -1.357273       .720047   -0.288682     -1.885   .0921
E               6.166209      2.404593     .417246      2.564   .0305
I                .763545       .845038     .203542       .904   .3898
R1              7.213173      3.203508     .507238      2.252   .0509
(Constant)     93.614943      6.365676                 14.706   .0000

End Block Number   1   All requested variables entered.
```

All of the estimated coefficients have the appropriate sign, and all of the t statistics are statistically significant at a 5% level of significance. The value $R^2 = .80825$ indicates that the regression equation explains approximately 81% of the variation in bond prices.

The coefficient of E_i, 6.166, indicates that the price of a tax-exempt bond ($E_i = 1$) is approximately \$6.17 more than the price of a non-tax-exempt bond, other things being equal. The coefficient of R_{i1}, 7.213, indicates that the price of an AAA bond is approximately \$7.21 more than the price of an A-rated bond. Similarly, the coefficient of R_{i2} indicates that the price of an AA-rated bond is approximately \$6.93 more than the price of an A-rated bond. The difference between these coefficients, (\$7.21 − \$6.93) = \$0.28, measures the difference in price between an AAA-rated bond and an AA-rated bond.

Let us predict the selling price of a tax-exempt, AA-rated bond where the interest rate is $I_i = 6\%$ and the Treasury bill rate is $T_i = 8\%$. Because the bond is tax exempt, we use $E_i = 1$. Because the bond is AA-rated, we set R_{i1} equal to 0 and R_{i2} equal to 1. We obtain

$$\begin{aligned}\hat{P}_i &= 93.615 + 0.764(6) - 1.357(8) + 6.166(1) + 7.213(0) + 6.931(1) \\ &= \$100.44\end{aligned}$$

■

The Dummy Variable Trap: Creating Too Many Variables

Suppose we want to estimate a regression model where each observation falls into exactly one of m categories. For example, if we think that income depends on age and on sex, each observation can be classified according to whether the individual is male or female. Thus there are $m = 2$ categories. A common error is to construct a multiple regression model that contains a constant term, some explanatory variables, and m rather than $(m - 1)$ dummy variables. This mistake of creating one too many dummy variables is called the **dummy variable trap**.

To classify observations into m categories we need $(m - 1)$, not m, dummy variables. When the observation falls into the base case, each dummy variable takes the value 0. The coefficient of the jth dummy variable measures the effect of being in category j as opposed to being in the base category. If we do not specify a base case, the coefficients will lose this interpretation.

If we create m rather than $(m - 1)$ dummy variables for a qualitative variable that contains m categories, the least-squares estimation procedure breaks down and will not yield unique estimates of the regression coefficients if the equation contains a constant term.

Exercises for Section 17.2

1. Suppose data from a large corporation are used to estimate a regression model that explains the corporation's salary structure. The estimated equation is

$$\hat{y}_i = 10{,}000 + 1000x_{i1} + 1000x_{i2} + 3000x_{i3} - 2000x_{i4}$$

where

$$y_i = \text{salary of individual i}$$

$$x_{i1} = \text{years of service of individual i}$$

$$x_{i2} = \begin{cases} 1 & \text{if highest degree is B.A. for individual i} \\ 0 & \text{otherwise} \end{cases}$$

$$x_{i3} = \begin{cases} 1 & \text{if individual i has master's or Ph.D.} \\ 0 & \text{otherwise} \end{cases}$$

$$x_{i4} = \begin{cases} 1 & \text{if individual i is a female} \\ 0 & \text{male} \end{cases}$$

a. Suppose a female Ph.D. has been employed for 4 years. Predict her salary.
b. Suppose a male with no college degree has been employed 5 years. Predict his salary.
c. Suppose a new male recruit who has a B.A. is hired. Predict his salary.
d. What is the difference in starting salaries between a B.A. and a Ph.D. recruit of the same sex?
e. Interpret the coefficient of x_{i4}. How would the coefficient change if we let x_{i4} be 1 for a male and 0 otherwise?

2. Suppose a regression equation has been estimated to explain housing values in a city. The estimated equation is

$$\hat{y}_i = 20{,}000 - 200(\text{age of house}) + 2000(\text{number of rooms}) - 500(\text{miles from city hall}) + 4000x_{i1} - 1000x_{i2} + 2000x_{i3}$$

where

$$x_{i1} = \begin{cases} 1 & \text{if house is in eastern part of city} \\ 0 & \text{otherwise} \end{cases}$$

$$x_{i2} = \begin{cases} 1 & \text{if house is in western part of city} \\ 0 & \text{otherwise} \end{cases}$$

$$x_{i3} = \begin{cases} 1 & \text{if house is in northern part of city} \\ 0 & \text{otherwise} \end{cases}$$

a. A 7-room, 5-year-old house is 4 miles from the city hall and in the eastern part of town. Estimate its value in dollars.
b. Which part of town is most desirable?
c. Which part of town is least desirable?
d. Which part of town is the base case?
e. Rank the four sections of town in terms of desirability.
f. A 5-room house is 6 miles from the city hall, 8 years old, and in the southern part of town. Estimate its value.

3. Suppose that the values of a dummy variable are recorded as 0 and 2 rather than 0 and 1. What will happen?

4. Explain how three dummy variables whose values are denoted q_{i1}, q_{i2}, and q_{i3} can be used in a regression model designed to forecast quarterly sales of a firm. The dummy variables should represent the quarterly effect or quarterly deviation from the base quarter.

5. At a certain university, faculty salaries depend on the number of years of service and on whether the individual has received tenure. Let $z_i = 1$ if the ith faculty member has tenure and $z_i = 0$ otherwise. Use the accompanying data and perform the indicated tasks.

Salary Y	Years of Service X	Tenure Status Z[a]
\$26,000	1	0
28,000	3	0
32,500	5	1
33,500	6	1
34,500	7	1
30,000	5	0
33,000	8	0
35,000	10	0
29,500	2	1

[a] Z is 1 if faculty member has tenure and 0 if he or she does not.

a. Plot Y versus X on a scatter diagram.
b. Estimate the following population regression equation:

$$Y_i = \beta_0 + \beta_1 x_i + \beta_2 z_i + e_i$$

c. Predict Y if an individual has tenure and 8 years of service.
d. Predict Y if an individual has no tenure and 5 years of service.

6. The following regression model was obtained to explain weekly sales in thousands of dollars at a fast-food outlet:

$$\hat{y}_i = 10.1 - 4.4x_{i1} + 6.9x_{i2} + 14.3x_{i3}$$

where

$$y_i = \text{weekly sales at the } i\text{th outlet}$$
$$x_{i1} = \text{number of competitors within one mile of the } i\text{th outlet}$$
$$x_{i2} = \text{population in thousands within one mile of the } i\text{th outlet}$$
$$x_{i3} = \begin{cases} 1 & \text{if drive-up window is present at the } i\text{th outlet} \\ 0 & \text{otherwise} \end{cases}$$

a. What is the expected amount of sales attributable to the drive-up window?
b. Predict sales for a store with two competitors, a population of 8000 within one mile, and no drive-up window.
c. Predict sales for a store with one competitor, a population within one mile of 3000 people, and a drive-up window.

7. Each of the following variables is proposed as an explanatory variable in a regression model. For which of the variables would it be necessary to create one or more dummy variables? If one or more dummy variables should be created, explain how to do it.
a. Age of consumer
b. Income of household
c. Sex of employee
d. Price of a product
e. Season of the year
f. Country of birth
g. Highest academic degree of an employee
h. Years of seniority of an employee
i. Marital status of an employee

8. Consider the following sample regression results:

$$\begin{aligned} \hat{y}_i &= 17{,}000 + 1000s_i + 3000x_{i1} + 5000x_{i2} \qquad R^2 = .78 \\ &\quad\ (2121.7) \quad (167.1) \quad (365.7) \quad (562.3) \qquad n = 45 \end{aligned}$$

where

$$y_i = \text{annual salary of the } i\text{th employee}$$
$$s_i = \text{years of seniority of the } i\text{th employee}$$
$$x_{i1} = \begin{cases} 1 & \text{if B.A. is highest degree of the } i\text{th employee} \\ 0 & \text{otherwise} \end{cases}$$
$$x_{i2} = \begin{cases} 1 & \text{if M.S. or higher is highest degree of the } i\text{th employee} \\ 0 & \text{otherwise} \end{cases}$$
$$x_{i3} = \begin{cases} 1 & \text{if high school or lower is highest degree} \\ 0 & \text{otherwise} \end{cases}$$

The values in parentheses are estimated standard errors.
a. Explain why the variable X_3 is not included in the equation.
b. Are the signs of the coefficients plausible? Explain.
c. Predict the salary of an employee with a B.A. degree and 10 years of seniority.

d. Predict the salary of an employee with a Ph.D. degree and 10 years of seniority.
e. Predict the salary of an employee with a high school degree and 10 years of seniority.
f. At the 5% level of significance, would you conclude that salaries for employees with a B.A. degree are higher than salaries for employees with a high school degree, assuming the same amount of seniority?
g. Suppose you reestimate the model and replace the variable X_1 by the variable X_3. What would the new estimated equation be?
h. Suppose you reestimate the model and replace the variable X_2 with the variable X_3. What would the new estimated equation be?

9. Consider the following sample regression results:

$$\hat{y}_i = 17{,}000 + 1000s_i - 3000x_{i1} + 5000x_{i2} + 600x_{i3}$$

where

$$y_i = \text{annual salary of the } i\text{th employee}$$

$$s_i = \text{years of seniority of the } i\text{th employee}$$

$$x_{i1} = \begin{cases} 1 & \text{if individual is female} \\ 0 & \text{otherwise} \end{cases}$$

$$x_{i2} = \begin{cases} 1 & \text{if individual has a Ph.D. degree} \\ 0 & \text{otherwise} \end{cases}$$

$$x_{i3} = x_{i1}x_{i2}$$

a. Explain the meaning of the coefficient of the variable X_3.
b. Are the signs of the coefficients plausible? Explain.
c. Predict the salary of a female employee with a B.A. degree and 10 years of seniority.
d. Predict the salary of a female employee with a Ph.D. degree and 10 years of seniority.
e. Predict the salary of a male employee with a B.A. degree and 10 years of seniority.
f. Predict the salary of a male employee with a Ph.D. degree and 10 years of seniority.
g. According to these results, is a Ph.D. worth more or less to a woman than to a man? How much more or less? Explain.

17.3 ▪ *Estimating Equations in Logarithmic Form*

Frequently economic variables are related by some nonlinear functional relationship. One such relationship, the polynomial relationship, was discussed in Section 17.1. Another important functional relationship is the *logarithmic* relationship.

Suppose we have n sample observations on the variables X and Y, and it is hypothesized that values of Y are approximately related to values of X according to the equation

$$Y = AB^X$$

where A and B are unknown population parameters. If we take the natural logarithm of both sides of the equation, we obtain

$$\ln Y = \ln A + (\ln B)X$$

If we let

$$Y' = \ln Y, \quad \beta_0 = \ln A, \quad \text{and} \quad \beta_1 = \ln B$$

we obtain the equivalent expression

$$Y' = \beta_0 + \beta_1 X$$

If we add an error term to the equation to indicate that the values of Y' are not perfectly explained by the values of X, we obtain the population regression model

$$Y'_i = \beta_0 + \beta_1 x_i + e_i$$

The coefficients β_0 and β_1 can be estimated by the method of least squares, provided we use $Y' = \ln Y$ in all the formulas in place of Y. If we apply the method of least squares to the transformed model, we obtain the estimated coefficients b_0 and b_1. We obtain estimates for A and B in the equation $Y = AB^X$ by taking antilogarithms of b_0 and b_1.

The transformation of the equation

$$Y = AB^X$$

into the equation

$$Y' = \beta_0 + \beta_1 X$$

is called the *semilogarithmic transformation*. In this model the variable Y is transformed, but the variable X retains its original values.

Another exponential function that is sometimes used to describe the relationship between X and Y is the equation

$$Y = AX^B$$

If we take the natural logarithm of both sides of this equation, we obtain

$$\ln Y = \ln A + B(\ln X)$$

By redefining the variables, we obtain the linear equation

$$Y' = \beta_0 + \beta_1 X'$$

where

$$Y' = \ln Y, \quad \beta_0 = \ln A, \quad \beta_1 = B, \quad \text{and} \quad X' = \ln X$$

Once again we add an error term to the model to indicate that the values of Y' are not perfectly explained by the values of X', and we obtain the population regression model

$$Y'_i = \beta_0 + \beta_1 X'_i + e_i$$

Once again the parameters β_0 and β_1 can be estimated by using the least-squares method, provided we use the logs of the original values of Y and X as data. The transformation of the equation

$$Y = AX^B$$

into the equivalent equation

$$Y' = \beta_0 + \beta_1 X'$$

is called the *double logarithmic transformation*.

Example 17.7

Using the Double Logarithmic Transformation: Suppose an analyst for the Environmental Protection Agency is studying the relationship between the speed at which a car travels (S) and the amount of gasoline consumed per mile (G). It is believed that the variables are approximately related in a nonlinear way according to the equation

$$G = AS^B$$

where G represents gasoline consumption measured in miles per gallon and S represents the average speed of the car in miles per hour. A car is driven around a track at different speeds under carefully controlled conditions; the results are found in Table 17.6 and plotted in Figure 17.12. We want to obtain the least-squares estimates of the population coefficients.

TABLE 17.6 **Data on gasoline mileage and car speed for Example 17.7**

Miles per Gallon G	Average Speed S	$\ln G$ Y	$\ln S$ X	XY	X^2
36	30	3.584	3.401	12.188	11.568
30	35	3.401	3.555	12.092	12.641
25	40	3.219	3.689	11.874	13.608
23	45	3.135	3.807	11.936	14.491
20	50	2.996	3.912	11.719	15.304
19	55	2.944	4.007	11.799	16.059
17	60	2.833	4.094	11.600	16.764
16	65	2.773	4.174	11.574	17.426
14	70	2.639	4.249	11.212	18.050
13	75	2.565	4.317	11.074	18.641
		30.089	39.206	117.069	154.549

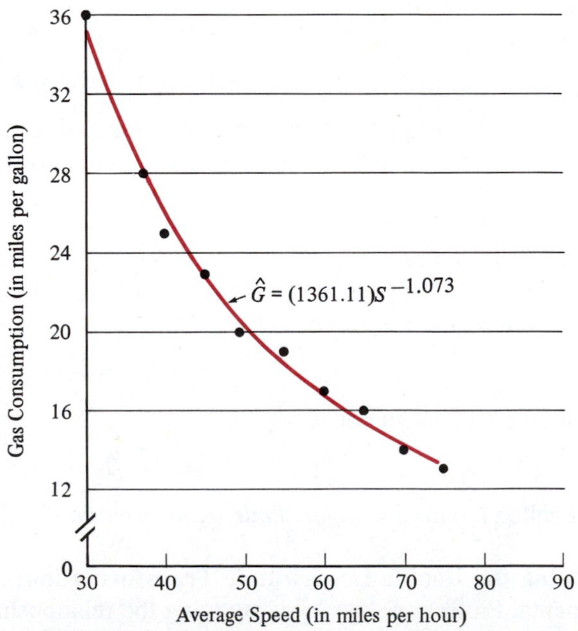

FIGURE 17.12
Gas consumption versus average speed for Example 17.7.

We transform the equation $G = AS^B$ by taking natural logarithms and obtain

$$\ln G = \ln A + \beta_1 \ln S$$

We define $Y = \ln G$, $X = \ln S$, $\beta_0 = \ln A$, and $\beta_1 = B$. After adding an error term, we obtain the population regression equation

$$Y_i = \beta_0 + \beta_1 x_i + e_i$$

Solution: To show the types of calculations that are involved, we have solved the problem using a hand calculator. The necessary calculations are shown in Table 17.6. First, we obtain the values $y_i = \ln G_i$ and $x_i = \ln S_i$. Next, we obtain $\bar{x} = 39.206/10 = 3.9206$ and $\bar{y} = 30.089/10 = 3.0089$. We obtain b_1 and b_0 from the equations

$$b_1 = \frac{\Sigma x_i y_i - n\bar{x}\bar{y}}{\Sigma x_i^2 - n\bar{x}^2} = -1.073$$

$$b_0 = \bar{y} - b_1\bar{x} = 7.216$$

The sample regression equation is

$$\hat{y}_i = 7.216 - 1.073x_i$$

or

$$\ln \hat{G}_i = 7.216 - 1.073 \ln S_i$$

After taking antilogarithms, we obtain the estimated coefficient

$$\hat{A} = e^{7.216} = 1361.11$$

Also we have

$$\hat{B} = b_1 = -1.073$$

In estimated form, the original model can be written as

$$\hat{G} = 1361.11S^{-1.073}$$

Thus, if a car was driven at a speed of 68 miles per hour, the predicted gas mileage would be

$$\hat{G} = 1361.11(68)^{-1.073} = 14.71 \text{ miles per gallon}$$ ■

Exercises for Section 17.3

1. A tire manufacturer is testing a new tire that is supposed to have superior road-handling qualities. In testing the tires, it became necessary to determine how the distance required to stop a car depended on the speed at which the car was being driven. Assume that the speed of a car and the distance required to come to a complete stop are related by the equation

$$D = AS^{\beta_1}$$

where D is stopping distance (in feet) and S is speed (in miles per hour). Use the following data:

S	20	30	40	50	60
D	56	94	140	210	300

a. Plot the data on a scatter diagram. Does the relationship between D and S appear to be linear or nonlinear?
b. Estimate the population regression equation

$$\ln D_i = \beta_0 + \beta_1 \ln S_i + e_i$$

c. Estimate D when S is 45.
d. Plot ln D versus ln S.
e. Graph the sample regression equation obtained in Part b.

2. Assume that sales of a firm are related to advertising expenditures according to the equation

$$S = AB^X$$

where S is sales in thousands of dollars and X is advertising expenditures in thousands of dollars. The data are as follows:

S	70	90	140	200	152
X	10	12	16	20	17

a. Plot the data on a scatter diagram.
b. Plot ln S versus X.
c. Estimate the equation

$$\ln S_i = \beta_0 + \beta_1 x_i + e_i$$

d. Plot the estimated equation on the scatter diagram.

3. A theory states that the yield in pounds Y of a certain agricultural product is related to the amount of fertilizer in pounds X used according to the model

$$\ln Y_i = \beta_0 + \beta_1 \ln x_i + e_i$$

The data are as follows:

Y	6	8	16	19	26	47	63
X	2	3	4	5	6	8	10

a. Plot ln Y versus ln X on a scatter diagram.
b. Estimate the population regression model.
c. Plot the estimated equation on the scatter diagram.
d. Predict the yield if 7 pounds of fertilizer are used.

4. A chemist studied the concentration of a solution (Y) at various time intervals (X). Fifteen identical solutions were prepared and then examined after various time delays. The results follow:

Solution	1	2	3	4	5	6	7	8
X	9	9	9	7	7	7	5	5
Y	0.07	0.09	0.08	0.16	0.17	0.21	0.49	0.58

Solution	9	10	11	12	13	14	15
X	5	3	3	3	1	1	1
Y	0.53	1.22	1.15	1.07	2.84	2.57	3.10

a. Plot the data.
b. Estimate the simple linear regression model and plot the sample regression line.
c. Calculate R^2 and s_e.

d. Test the null hypothesis that β_1 is 0. Let $\alpha = .05$.
e. What transformations might you try to achieve linearity?

5. Refer to Exercise 4.
a. Let the dependent variable be $Y' = \ln Y$ and obtain the estimated regression function for the transformed data.
c. Plot the estimated regression line and the transformed data. Does the regression line appear to provide a good fit to the transformed data?
d. Obtain the residuals and plot them against the fitted values. What do your plots show?

17.4 ▪ Stepwise Regression

When constructing a multiple regression model, it is frequently difficult to determine which explanatory variables to include. Researchers often estimate various models using different sets of explanatory variables, examine the t statistics of the estimated coefficients, and then delete those variables with insignificant t statistics. This is a questionable procedure because a variable can have a coefficient whose t statistic is statistically significant in one formulation of the model but not in another formulation.

Because most economic variables are highly correlated with one another, it is difficult to determine which variables belong in a model. To use an extreme example, suppose that a researcher has data on a dependent variable Y and on six potential explanatory variables X_1, X_2, X_3, X_4, X_5, and X_6. Because the researcher does not know which variables to include in the model, he or she decides to estimate all possible regression models. That is, Y is regressed on each combination of the X_j variables taken one at a time, two at a time, three at a time, and so on. There are a total of 63 different such combinations of the explanatory variables. Suppose that in each equation the researcher examines the signs of the estimated coefficients and their t statistics and rejects equations containing estimated coefficients whose signs do not agree with some underlying theory or whose t statistics are insignificant. At this stage the researcher probably still has several nonrejected equations. Estimating all possible regressions is an example of a practice called "data mining," whereby a researcher performs numerous statistical procedures on a given set of data and reports only the most favorable results.

To obtain a suitable model, some researchers use a technique known as **stepwise regression**. Suppose that we have data on a dependent variable Y and six proposed explanatory variables X_1, X_2, X_3, X_4, X_5, and X_6. A stepwise regression computer program works in the following way. First, the computer estimates each of the simple linear regression models

$$Y_i = \beta_0 + \beta_j x_{ij} + e_i \qquad j = 1, 2, \ldots, 6$$

The computer selects and prints the results for the equation having the highest R^2. Suppose this equation is

$$\hat{y}_i = b_0 + b_3 x_{i3}$$

Next, the program estimates each of the equations

$$Y_i = \beta_0 + \beta_3 x_3 + \beta_j x_{ij} + e_i \qquad j = 1, 2, 4, 5, 6$$

and prints the results for the equation having the highest R^2. Note that in this second step, variable X_3 remains in the model; the computer includes as the second explanatory variable the one that increases R^2 the most. Suppose that after the second step the estimated model is

$$\hat{y}_i = b_0 + b_3 x_{i3} + b_5 x_{i5}$$

In the next step, each of the equations

$$Y_i = \beta_0 + \beta_3 x_{i3} + \beta_5 x_{i5} + \beta_j x_{ij} + e_i \qquad j = 1, 2, 4, 6$$

is estimated. Again the equation having the highest R^2 is selected. Suppose this equation is

$$\hat{y}_i = b_0 + b_3 x_{i3} + b_5 x_{i5} + b_6 x_{i6}$$

Now the stepwise regression routine examines whether any of the X_j variables already in the model should be dropped. For example, it is possible that X_5 and X_6 together explain Y perfectly but by themselves neither explains Y as well as does X_3. After X_5 and X_6 have been included in the equation, X_3 would no longer be needed, and it would drop out in the next round.

At each step, the stepwise regression routine examines each variable not in the equation and selects the variable that increases R^2 the most. Then the routine reexamines each variable that has been included in the equation and determines if any of them should be dropped. At each stage, the criterion used for adding or dropping a variable is the resultant effect on R^2. The procedure stops when no variable can be added that causes R^2 to increase by more than a prespecified amount R_1^2 and no variable can be deleted that causes R^2 to decrease by less than some other prespecified amount R_2^2, where $R_1^2 > R_2^2$. The stepwise regression routine is available in many standard regression packages, including the SPSSX program and the SAS program.

A problem with stepwise regression is that at each step, all the estimated coefficients, standard deviations, and t statistics change. As a result, in one step an estimated coefficient b_j could be significantly different from 0 according to the t test, whereas at the next step the new estimated coefficient b_j may not be significantly different from 0.

Some researchers use stepwise regression because it removes the biases and opinions of the model builder from the task of selecting what variables to include in the model. Other researchers condemn stepwise regression for exactly the same reasons, claiming that the form of the model should be based on theoretical considerations.

The following example shows in detail how a stepwise regression program works.

Example 17.8

Using Stepwise Regression to Build a Model Explaining the Dow Jones Industrial Average: Suppose we wish to estimate a model that explains the value of the dependent variable Y = DOWJONES, which is the Dow Jones industrial average at the end of a particular year. This variable could depend on many potential explanatory variables. For example, it might be thought that DOWJONES depends on the level of the Gross National Product (GNP) during the year: When GNP increases, it might be expected that DOWJONES also increases. It might also be conjectured that DOWJONES depends on the level of the Consumer Price Index because when the general price level increases, the prices of stocks should also increase. Other potential explanatory variables that will be considered here are the level of federal government spending, the level of national defense spending, the national unemployment rate, and the level of interest rates in the national economy.

It might be that one, some, or all of these variables might help explain the value of the Dow Jones industrial average. Thus it might be wise to let the data help us decide which variables to include in the final model. This is exactly the type of problem that stepwise regression is helpful in solving.

The data in Table 2.4 in Chapter 2 show annual values from 1960 through 1986 for the following variables:

$$Y = \text{Dow Jones industrial average (DOWJONES)}$$
$$X_1 = \text{Gross National Product (GNP)}$$
$$X_2 = \text{federal government spending (TOTALGOV)}$$
$$X_3 = \text{federal government defense spending (DEFENSE)}$$
$$X_4 = \text{national unemployment rate (URATE)}$$
$$X_5 = \text{Consumer Price Index (CPI)}$$
$$X_6 = \text{6-month Treasury bill rate (TBILL)}$$

All data were taken from the 1987 *Economic Report of the President*. To request stepwise regression in the SPSSX program, the following three commands were issued:

```
REGRESSION VARIABLES = DOWJONES GNP TOTALGOV DEFENSE
   URATE CPI TBILL/
   DEPENDENT = DOWJONES/
   STEPWISE
```

Solution: Figure 17.13 shows the first step of the SPSSX stepwise regression output. A brief explanation of the steps follows.

Step 1: The variable DEFENSE is the first to be included in the model. That is, it is

FIGURE 17.13 **SPSSX-generated output for step 1 of stepwise regression for Example 17.8, explaining the Dow Jones industrial average as a function of defense spending.**

```
                         * * * *   M U L T I P L E   R E G R E S S I O N   * * * *

Equation Number 1    Dependent Variable..   DOWJONES   DOW JONES INDUSTRIAL AVER

  Descriptive Statistics are printed on Page   25

Beginning Block Number  1.  Method:  Stepwise

Variable(s) Entered on Step Number  1..    DEFENSE   TOTAL GOV. EXPENDITURE ON DEFENSE

Multiple R             .83418      Analysis of Variance
R Square               .69586                        DF      Sum of Squares      Mean Square
Adjusted R Square      .68369      Regression         1        999643.51633     999643.51633
Standard Error      132.19909      Residual          25        436914.97450      17476.59898

                                   F =        57.19897       Signif F =  .0000

------------------ Variables in the Equation ------------------       ------------ Variables not in the Equation ------------

Variable              B          SE B        Beta          T  Sig T   Variable      Beta In   Partial   Min Toler          T  Sig T

DEFENSE        2.860302       .378197     .834182      7.563  .0000   GNP        -0.903639 -.379705    .053700      -2.011  .0557
(Constant)   600.408660     48.954657                 12.265  .0000   TOTALGOV   -2.570624 -.411574    .007796      -2.212  .0367
                                                                      URATE      -0.343628 -.482634    .599975      -2.700  .0125
                                                                      CPI        -1.299957 -.589886    .062626      -3.579  .0015
                                                                      TBILL      -0.420853 -.595200    .608330      -3.629  .0013
```

the single best predictor of DOWJONES (the Dow Jones industrial average). The sample regression equation is

$$\text{DOWJONES} = 600.41 + 2.86\ \text{DEFENSE} \qquad R^2 = .69586$$
$$t \text{ statistics:} \quad (12.27) \quad (7.56)$$

When just DEFENSE is used to explain DOWJONES, we have $R^2 = .69586$. That is, by itself DEFENSE explains almost 70% of the total variation in DOWJONES; no other variable explains DOWJONES as well. The coefficient of DEFENSE is positive, which is reasonable because we would expect the Dow Jones industrial average to increase as defense spending increases. The computer output shows a t statistic of 7.563 for the coefficient of DEFENSE, which has a prob-value of .0000.

Step 2: The SPSSX output for the second step is given in Figure 17.14. The variable TBILL is included in the second step, because it creates the greatest marginal improvement in explaining DOWJONES. The model relating DOWJONES to DEFENSE and TBILL is

$$\text{DOWJONES} = 720.00 + 3.76\ \text{DEFENSE} - 33.75\ \text{TBILL} \qquad R^2 = .80361$$
$$t \text{ statistics:} \quad (13.9) \quad (9.46) \quad (-3.63)$$

For this model R^2 is .80361 and the adjusted R^2 is .78724, which means that the two variables DEFENSE and TBILL explain approximately 80% of the variation in DOWJONES. Thus, the inclusion of the variable TBILL causes R^2 to increase from .70 to .80.

FIGURE 17.14 **SPSSX-generated output for step 2 of stepwise regression for Example 17.8, explaining the Dow Jones industrial average as a function of defense spending and the Treasury bill rate.**

```
                          * * * *   M U L T I P L E   R E G R E S S I O N   * * * *

Variable(s) Entered on Step Number  2..    TBILL     INTERST YIELDED ON 6 MONTH T-BILLS

Multiple R              .89644          Analysis of Variance
R Square                .80361                                DF       Sum of Squares       Mean Square
Adjusted R Square       .78724          Regression             2       1154426.34782       577213.17391
Standard Error       108.42281          Residual              24        282132.14301        11755.50596

                                        F =       49.10152        Signif F =  .0000

                          * * * * * * * * * * * * * * * * * * * * * * * * * * * * *

Equation Number 1    Dependent Variable..   DOWJONES   DOW JONES INDUSTRIAL AVER

----------------- Variables in the Equation -----------------        ------------ Variables not in the Equation ------------

Variable               B          SE B        Beta         T  Sig T        Variable      Beta In   Partial  Min Toler        T  Sig T

DEFENSE         3.763413       .397686    1.097566     9.463  .0000        GNP        -0.008880 -.003590    .032102   -0.017  .9864
TBILL         -33.749187      9.300849   -0.420853    -3.629  .0013        TOTALGOV   -0.287633 -.043724    .004538   -0.210  .8356
(Constant)    719.998142     51.944337                13.861  .0000        URATE      -0.283143 -.488529    .469473   -2.685  .0132
                                                                           CPI        -0.740329 -.291832    .030517   -1.463  .1569
```

In this model the t statistics for the coefficients of DEFENSE and TBILL are 9.463 and -3.629. Because the prob-values for these t statistics are each less than .002, we can feel very confident that both of the population regression coefficients are nonzero. Also note that both coefficients have the correct sign. That is, we would expect increases in defense spending to have a positive effect on the Dow Jones industrial average and increases in interest rates to have a negative effect. Also observe that the coefficient of the variable DEFENSE changes from 2.86 in the first step to 3.76 in the second step.

Step 3: The SPSSX computer output for the third step is shown in Figure 17.15. The variable URATE (the national unemployment rate) is included in the model on the third step because it creates the next greatest marginal improvement in explaining DOWJONES. The model relating DOWJONES to DEFENSE, TBILL, and URATE is

$$\begin{array}{lllll} \text{DOWJONES} = 879.53 & + 4.28\ \text{DEFENSE} & - 30.15\ \text{TBILL} & - 39.94\ \text{URATE} & R^2 = .85048 \\ t \text{ statistics:} \quad (11.7) & (10.6) & (-3.59) & (-2.69) & \end{array}$$

Including URATE causes R^2 to increase from .80361 to .85048. In this model, the t statistics for the coefficients of DEFENSE, TBILL, and URATE are 10.610, −3.590, and −2.685, respectively. Since the prob-values for these t statistics are all less than .02, we can feel confident that all three of the population regression coefficients are nonzero. Also note that all three coefficients have the correct sign. We would expect increases in the unemployment rate (URATE) to have a negative effect on the Dow Jones industrial average.

FIGURE 17.15 **SPSSX-generated output for step 3 of stepwise regression for Example 17.8, explaining the Dow Jones industrial average as a function of defense spending, the Treasury bill rate, and the national unemployment rate.**

```
Variable(s) Entered on Step Number  3..   URATE    THE RATE OF UNEMPLOYMENT

Multiple R            .92221        Analysis of Variance
R Square              .85048                                  Sum of Squares      Mean Square
Adjusted R Square     .83097        Regression                1221760.24652     407253.41551
Standard Error      96.63878        Residual                   214798.24431       9339.05410

                                    F =        43.6          Signif F =  .0000

------------------ Variables in the Equation ------------------      ------------- Variables not in the Equation -------------

Variable                B          SE B        Beta          T  Sig T    Variable      Beta In   Partial  Min Toler        T  Sig T

DEFENSE          4.281039       .403493    1.248528     10.610  .0000    GNP           .718034   .293629    .025004    1.441  .1637
TBILL          -30.146025      8.397881   -0.375921     -3.590  .0015    TOTALGOV     1.468848   .228159    .003608    1.099  .2836
URATE          -39.935204     14.872723   -0.283143     -2.685  .0132    CPI           .546984   .156410    .012226     .743  .4655
(Constant)     879.526760     75.321584                 11.677  .0000
```

When the SPSSX computer program was used on the data in Table 2.4, the stepwise regression procedure stopped at this stage when the default value was $\alpha = .05$. The program stopped because no remaining explanatory variable when inserted into the equation had a coefficient whose prob-value was less than .05. In order to increase the number of steps in this example and to show a few other interesting features of stepwise regression, the default prob-value was increased to .65. Thus the program continued to insert values into the equation as long as the prob-value of the test was less than .65. This is a very lenient criterion; an estimated regression coefficient could be less than 1 standard deviation from 0 and still be included in the model.

Step 4: The SPSSX computer output for the fourth step is shown in Figure 17.16. The variable GNP (Gross National Product) is included at this step. The model relating DOWJONES to DEFENSE, TBILL, URATE, and GNP is

FIGURE 17.16 **SPSSX-generated output for step 4 of stepwise regression for Example 17.8, explaining the Dow Jones industrial average as a function of defense spending, the Treasury bill rate, the national unemployment rate, and Gross National Product.**

```
                           * * * *   M U L T I P L E   R E G R E S S I O N   * * * *
Equation Number 1    Dependent Variable..  DOWJONES   DOW JONES INDUSTRIAL AVER

Variable(s) Entered on Step Number  4..    GNP        GROSS NATIONAL PRODUCT

Multiple R            .92918        Analysis of Variance
R Square              .86337                          DF      Sum of Squares      Mean Square
Adjusted R Square     .83853        Regression         4       1240279.73501     310069.93375
Standard Error      94.45508        Residual          22        196278.75582       8921.76163

                                    F =       34.75434       Signif F =  .0000

------------------ Variables in the Equation ------------------      ------------- Variables not in the Equation -------------
Variable               B          SE B         Beta         T  Sig T    Variable      Beta In   Partial  Min Toler        T  Sig T

DEFENSE         2.320975      1.416454      .676892     1.639  .1155    TOTALGOV  -0.230646 -.021585    .001197   -0.099  .9221
TBILL         -39.989073     10.679317    -0.498664    -3.745  .0011    CPI       -4.208678 -.400755    .001239   -2.004  .0581
URATE         -51.093365     16.471012    -0.362254    -3.102  .0052
GNP              .143127      .099342      .718034      1.441  .1637
(Constant)    974.915445     99.011538                  9.846  .0000
```

$$
\begin{aligned}
\text{DOWJONES} &= \underset{(9.85)}{974.92} + \underset{(1.64)}{2.32\ \text{DEFENSE}} - \underset{(-3.74)}{39.99\ \text{TBILL}} \qquad t \text{ statistics} \\
&\quad - \underset{(-3.10)}{51.09\ \text{URATE}} + \underset{(1.44)}{0.14\ \text{GNP}} \qquad R^2 = .86337
\end{aligned}
$$

For this model R^2 is .86337 and the adjusted R^2 is .83853. Thus the inclusion of GNP increased R^2 from .85048 to .86337. The t statistic for the coefficient of GNP, 1.441, has a prob-value of .1637, so there is some doubt as to whether the population coefficient for GNP is nonzero. However, the signs for the estimated coefficients of the four explanatory variables all agree with theoretical considerations.

Step 5: The SPSSX computer output for the fifth step is shown in Figure 17.17. The variable CPI (Consumer Price Index) is included here, resulting in the model

FIGURE 17.17 **SPSSX-generated output for step 5 of stepwise regression for Example 17.8, explaining the Dow Jones industrial average as a function of defense spending, the Treasury bill rate, the national unemployment rate, Gross National Product, and the Consumer Price Index.**

```
Variable(s) Entered on Step Number  5..    CPI        CONSUMER PRICE INDEX

Multiple R            .94091        Analysis of Variance
R Square              .88531                          DF      Sum of Squares      Mean Square
Adjusted R Square     .85801        Regression         5       1271803.02769     254360.60554
Standard Error      88.57482        Residual          21        164755.46314       7845.49824

                                    F =       32.42122       Signif F =  .0000

------------------ Variables in the Equation ------------------      ------------- Variables not in the Equation -------------
Variable               B          SE B         Beta         T  Sig T    Variable      Beta In   Partial  Min Toler        T  Sig T

DEFENSE         5.241340      1.971519     1.528591     2.659  .0147    TOTALGOV    .096860  .009865    .001190     .044  .9652
TBILL         -10.168219     17.933604    -0.126798    -0.567  .5767
URATE          10.547305     34.412241      .074781      .306  .7622
GNP              .699234      .292653     3.507898     2.389  .0263
CPI           -11.797944      5.885736    -4.208678    -2.004  .0581
(Constant)   1115.205912    116.271144                  9.591  .0000
```

$$\begin{aligned}\text{DOWJONES} &= 1115.21 + 5.24\ \text{DEFENSE} - 10.17\ \text{TBILL} \\ t \text{ statistics:} &\quad (9.59) \quad (2.66) \qquad\qquad (-.57) \\ &\quad + 10.55\ \text{URATE} + 0.70\ \text{GNP} - 11.80\ \text{CPI} \qquad R^2 = .88531 \\ &\qquad (.31) \qquad\qquad (2.39) \qquad (-2.00)\end{aligned}$$

The t statistic for the coefficient of CPI, -2.004, has a prob-value of .0581, so there is some doubt about whether the population coefficient for CPI is nonzero. In addition, the coefficients of all the other explanatory variables have changed from the previous step, and the coefficient of the unemployment rate (URATE) has changed in sign from negative to positive. Also note that the prob-values for the coefficients of TBILL and URATE have increased to .5767 and .7622, respectively. Now it appears that neither of these estimated coefficients is significantly different from 0. Thus we have an example of estimated coefficients that were statistically significant at one step of the analysis but not at a later step.

Step 6: The SPSSX computer output for the sixth step is shown in Figure 17.18. Here the variable URATE (unemployment rate) is *removed* from the model, leaving the model

$$\begin{aligned}\text{DOWJONES} &= 1106.66 + 4.78\ \text{DEFENSE} - 14.51\ \text{TBILL} \\ t \text{ statistics:} &\quad (10.01) \quad (3.82) \qquad\qquad (-1.35) \\ &\quad + 0.63\ \text{GNP} - 10.19\ \text{CPI} \qquad R^2 = .88480 \\ &\qquad (3.51) \qquad (-3.93)\end{aligned}$$

The stepwise regression program stops at this stage because no additional explanatory variable has a regression coefficient whose t statistic satisfies the .65 prob-value criterion.

FIGURE 17.18 **SPSSX-generated output for step 6 of stepwise regression for Example 17.8, explaining the Dow Jones industrial average as a function of defense spending, the Treasury bill rate, Gross National Product, and the Consumer Price Index.**

```
                        * * * *   M U L T I P L E   R E G R E S S I O N   * * * *

Equation Number 1    Dependent Variable..   DOWJONES   DOW JONES INDUSTRIAL AVER

Variable(s) Removed on Step Number  6..    URATE     THE RATE OF UNEMPLOYMENT

Multiple R           .94064     Analysis of Variance
R Square             .88480                      DF      Sum of Squares       Mean Square
Adjusted R Square    .86385     Regression        4      1271066.01054      317766.50263
Standard Error     86.73169     Residual         22       165492.48029        7522.38547

                                F =      42.24278       Signif F =   .0000

----------------- Variables in the Equation -----------------      ------------ Variables not in the Equation ------------

Variable               B          SE B        Beta          T  Sig T      Variable     Beta In  Partial  Min Toler        T  Sig T

DEFENSE         4.781237      1.251455    1.394406      3.821  .0009      TOTALGOV     .084672  .008606    .001190     .039  .9689
TBILL         -14.507965     10.777061   -0.180914     -1.346  .1919      URATE        .074781  .066734    .001239     .306  .7622
GNP              .629274       .179343    3.156926      3.509  .0020
CPI           -10.185895      2.586787   -3.633612     -3.938  .0007
(Constant)   1106.664365    110.533066                 10.012  .0000

End Block Number   1   PIN =     .200 Limits reached.
```

This stepwise regression problem illustrates the problems that can occur when data are highly collinear. Variables that are important at one step of the analysis can be insignificant at a later step. Because GNP, total government spending, and federal defense spending are all highly correlated with one another, it is difficult to separate their individual effects on DOWJONES.

By examining the correlations between potential explanatory variables in a stepwise regression model, it is sometimes possible to anticipate some of the estimation problems. This idea is discussed in the next section.

17.5 ▪ The Correlation Matrix

In addition to stepwise regression, there is another useful computer tool called the **correlation matrix** that helps us select explanatory variables for a regression model.

Suppose we wish to build a regression model to explain some dependent variable Y using a set of K potential explanatory variables $X_1, X_2, \ldots, X_K$. Before estimating any regression equations, it is useful to know the sample correlation coefficients between Y and each explanatory variable X_i. In addition, it is useful to know the sample correlation coefficient between each potential explanatory variable X_i and every other potential explanatory variable X_j. Many computer programs, including SPSSX and SAS, routinely calculate all these correlation coefficients. The resulting set of sample correlation coefficients is presented in a rectangular array called a sample correlation matrix.

Definition: Sample Correlation Matrix

Suppose we have a sample of observations on K variables $X_1, X_2, \ldots, X_K$. The **sample correlation matrix** shows the sample correlation between each pair of variables X_i and X_j. We denote the sample correlation between X_i and X_j as R_{ij}.

Example 17.9

A Sample Correlation Matrix: Let us generate a sample correlation matrix for the data in Table 2.3 of Chapter 2, which show the values in 1985 for the 50 states and the District of Columbia for the following variables:

PCTUNION_i = percentage of employees who are unionized in State i

SALARY_i = average annual salary of secondary school teachers in State i

REVENUE_i = state and local tax revenue per capita in State i

EXPEND_i = expenditures per elementary and secondary school pupil in State i

INCOME_i = income per capita in State i

WAGE_i = average hourly wage in manufacturing employment in State i

The following commands generated the sample correlation matrix shown in Figure 17.19 using the SPSSX program:

```
REGRESSION DESCRIPTIVES = CORR/
   VARIABLES = PCTUNION, SALARY, REVENUE, EXPEND, INCOME,
   WAGE/
```

Figure 17.19 also shows the mean and standard deviation for each variable.

FIGURE 17.19 SPSSX-generated sample correlation matrix for Example 17.9.

```
                              * * * *   M U L T I P L E   R E G R E S S I O N   * * * *
Listwise Deletion of Missing Data

               Mean   Std Devi  Label

PCTUNION     19.731     7.460   % UNION MEMBERSHIP IN 1982
SALARY    24357.784  4180.030   AVERAGE TEACHER SALARY IN 1986
REVENUE    3684.529  1055.438   STATE AND LOCAL REVENUE PER CAPITA IN 19
EXPEND     2509.275  1479.569   EXPENDITURES PER PUPIL IN 1986
INCOME    13238.804  2156.789   PERSONAL INCOME PER CAPITA IN 1985
WAGE          9.407     1.245   AVERAGE HOURLY EARNINGS IN MANUFACTURING

N of Cases =     51

Correlation:

           PCTUNION     SALARY    REVENUE     EXPEND     INCOME       WAGE

PCTUNION      1.000       .613       .438       .326       .460       .706
SALARY         .613      1.000       .840       .747       .767       .562
REVENUE        .438       .840      1.000       .797       .755       .425
EXPEND         .326       .747       .797      1.000       .474       .413
INCOME         .460       .767       .755       .474      1.000       .373
WAGE           .706       .562       .425       .413       .373      1.000
```

Several interesting observations can be made about the values in the sample correlation matrix.

The largest correlation coefficient in the table is .840, which represents the sample correlation between SALARY and REVENUE. This means that the single variable that best explains variations in teachers' salaries is the variable REVENUE. Also observe that SALARY is highly correlated with EXPEND and INCOME. The sample correlation between SALARY and PCTUNION is .613, which indicates that teachers tend to earn more in heavily unionized states.

The sample correlation between PCTUNION and INCOME is .460. This means that average annual income tends to be higher in heavily unionized states. The square of this correlation coefficient is .2116, which means that in a linear regression model the variable PCTUNION explains 21.16% of the state-by-state variation in annual income. Although unionization is positively correlated with income per capita, the correlation is relatively low. This implies that the single variable PCTUNION does not account for income in states very well.

The positive sample correlation between INCOME and WAGE of .373 indicates that states that pay high wages to manufacturing employees tend to have high per capita incomes. Although the sample correlation between INCOME and WAGE is positive, it is not very high, and the single variable WAGE does not explain well why some states have high average incomes and others have low average incomes.

The sample correlation between PCTUNION and WAGE is .706. Most people probably think that states that are heavily unionized pay higher manufacturing wages than states that are not; the data tend to support this belief.

Also, note that the sample correlation between EXPEND and REVENUE is .797. This tells us that states which tend to spend the most money per pupil on elementary and secondary school students also tend to be the states which have the highest tax revenue per capita.

Finally, every variable is perfectly correlated with itself. Thus, in the correlation matrix, every value on the main diagonal of the correlation matrix is 1.00. In addition, the correlation between X_i and X_j is the same as the correlation between X_j and X_i, so the correlation matrix is symmetric. That is, the value in row i and column j is the same as the value in row j and column i. ■

The correlation matrix can be useful in helping to select variables to include in a regression model. Variables that are highly correlated with a dependent variable are obvious candidates for inclusion in a regression equation. In addition, the correlation matrix can be helpful in detecting multicollinearity. If the sample correlation between X_i and X_j is relatively large, it may be difficult to determine the separate effects of X_i and X_j on a dependent variable Y.

Example 17.10

Examining the Sample Correlation Matrix: Let us examine the sample correlation matrix in Figure 17.18 and see how this information can help us build a regression model. The variables are as defined in Example 17.9. We are interested in finding variables that help explain why different states have different expenditures on education per pupil; in other words, EXPEND is our dependent variable. Although we could use stepwise regression to help build a suitable model, first let us examine the sample correlation matrix and see if we can predict in advance what will happen when we apply the stepwise regression procedure.

Solution: In Figure 17.19, examine the sample correlation coefficient between the dependent variable EXPEND and each of the potential explanatory variables. The largest of these sample correlation coefficients is .797, so REVENUE will be the first variable to enter the regression equation in the stepwise regression procedure. The next variable to enter the regression in the stepwise procedure is the one that adds most to explaining EXPEND after taking into account the presence of REVENUE. We cannot determine this with complete accuracy from the sample correlation matrix, but we can get some clues. After REVENUE, EXPEND is most highly correlated with the variable INCOME. Thus it is reasonable to conjecture that INCOME would enter the regression model on the second step. INCOME is also highly correlated with REVENUE (R = .755), however, so INCOME might not explain much of the variation in EXPEND that has not already been explained by REVENUE.

Now examine some of the other potential candidates for entry into the regression model. The sample correlation between PCTUNION and WAGE is .706. Because this value is relatively high, these two variables together might not explain much more of the variation in EXPEND than either of the variables individually. In addition, neither WAGE nor PCTUNION is highly correlated with EXPEND, so it is likely that the stepwise regression procedure will not insert either variable. ■

Now let us see if the correlation matrix helped us predict which variables would enter the regression model by using the stepwise regression procedure.

Example 17.11

Using Stepwise Regression to Explain a State's Expenditures per Pupil: We will use the SPSSX stepwise regression procedure to build a model to explain EXPEND as a function of the variables PCTUNION, REVENUE, INCOME, and WAGE.

Step 1: The computer output for the first step is shown in Figure 17.20. The variable REVENUE is the first to be included in the model. That is, it is the single best predictor

FIGURE 17.20 **SPSSX-generated output for step 1 of stepwise regression for Example 17.11, explaining expenditures per pupil as a function of tax revenue per capita.**

```
                   * * * *   M U L T I P L E   R E G R E S S I O N   * * * *
Equation Number 1    Dependent Variable..   EXPEND   EXPENDITURES PER PUPIL IN 1

  Descriptive Statistics are printed on Page   29

Beginning Block Number  1.  Method:  Stepwise

Variable(s) Entered on Step Number  1..    REVENUE   STATE AND LOCAL REVENUE PER CAPITA IN 19

Multiple R             .79684        Analysis of Variance
R Square               .63495                            DF      Sum of Squares      Mean Square
Adjusted R Square      .62750        Regression           1      69499117.52665   69499117.52665
Standard Error      903.02386        Residual            49      39957152.63022     815452.09449

                                     F =      85.22771       Signif F =  .0000

------------------ Variables in the Equation ------------------          ------------ Variables not in the Equation ------------

Variable                B          SE B        Beta          T  Sig T    Variable     Beta In   Partial  Min Toler       T   Sig T

REVENUE          1.117049       .120999     .796837      9.232  .0000    PCTUNION   -0.027704  -.041224    .808294  -0.286  .7762
(Constant)   -1606.523721    463.409636                 -3.467  .0011    SALARY       .264852   .238098    .295025   1.698  .0959
                                                                         INCOME     -0.297863  -.323076    .429468  -2.365  .0221
                                                                         WAGE         .090117   .134977    .818957    .944  .3500
```

of EXPEND. (By examining the correlation matrix, we already knew this.) The model representing this relationship is

$$\text{EXPEND} = -1606.52 + 1.117\ \text{REVENUE} \qquad R^2 = .63495$$
$$t \text{ statistics:} \quad (-3.47) \qquad (9.23)$$

When just REVENUE is used to explain EXPEND, the value of R^2 is .63495. That is, by itself, REVENUE explains about 63% of the total variation in EXPEND. The sign of the coefficient of REVENUE is positive, which agrees with economic theory. The computer output shows a t statistic of 9.232 for the estimated coefficient of REVENUE, which has a prob-value of .0000.

Step 2: The SPSSX computer output for the second step is shown in Figure 17.21. Here the variable INCOME enters the model, because it offers the greatest marginal improvement in explaining EXPEND. The model relating EXPEND to REVENUE and INCOME is

$$\text{EXPEND} = -63.457 + 1.432\ \text{REVENUE} - 0.204\ \text{INCOME} \qquad R^2 = .67305$$
$$t \text{ statistics:} \quad (-.08) \qquad (8.14) \qquad (-2.37)$$

FIGURE 17.21 **SPSSX-generated output for step 2 of stepwise regression for Example 17.11, explaining expenditures per pupil as a function of tax revenue per capita and income per capita.**

```
Variable(s) Entered on Step Number  2..    INCOME    PERSONAL INCOME PER CAPITA IN 1985

Multiple R             .82040        Analysis of Variance
R Square               .67305                            DF      Sum of Squares      Mean Square
Adjusted R Square      .65943        Regression           2      73669782.12424   36834891.06212
Standard Error      863.45343        Residual            48      35786488.03262     745551.83401

                                     F =      49.40621       Signif F =  .0000

------------------ Variables in the Equation ------------------          ------------ Variables not in the Equation ------------

Variable                B          SE B        Beta          T  Sig 1    Variable     Beta In   Partial  Min Toler       T   Sig T

REVENUE          1.432447       .176545    1.021823      8.114  .0000    PCTUNION     .021110   .032377    .408661    .222  .8252
INCOME          -0.204336       .086393   -0.297863     -2.365  .0221    SALARY       .464285   .409010    .253732   3.073  .0035
(Constant)     -63.456882    788.657058                 -0.080  .9362    WAGE         .109785   .173090    .405502   1.205  .2343
```

Including INCOME increases R^2 from .63495 to .67305, but the coefficient of INCOME has the wrong sign. Based on economic theory, we would expect increases in income per capita to have a positive effect on expenditures per pupil. The fact that the estimated coefficient of INCOME is negative shows that we have a multicollinearity problem. From the correlation matrix, we see that INCOME is positively correlated with EXPEND (R = .474), but INCOME is much more highly correlated with REVENUE (R = .755) than with EXPEND. After taking into account the effect of REVENUE on EXPEND, the effect of the variable INCOME on EXPEND is not clear. On theoretical grounds, we would reject the model resulting from the second step of the stepwise regression procedure, since it is highly implausible that increases in income per capita would lead to decreases in expenditures per pupil.

This example should be studied carefully. Quite frequently in applied research, estimated coefficients will have the wrong sign. In this example, the wrong sign can be explained by the fact that the effect of INCOME on EXPEND has already been accounted for by the inclusion of the variable REVENUE.

At this stage, the stepwise regression procedure stops because none of the remaining explanatory variables has a prob-value less than .05 when entered into the model. ■

Exercises for Section 17.5

1. Refer to the data in Table 2.4 in Chapter 2, which were used in Example 17.8 to predict the Dow Jones industrial average (DOWJONES).

a. Generate a correlation matrix using the SPSSX commands

```
REGRESSION DESCRIPTIVES = CORR/
    VARIABLES = GNP, TOTALGOV, DEFENSE, URATE, CPI, TBILL,
    DOWJONES/
```

b. Examine these sample correlation coefficients. Which variable has the highest correlation with the Dow Jones industrial average?

c. Which variable has the highest correlation with the Gross National Product?

d. Which variable has the highest correlation with the Consumer Price Index?

e. Find the correlation between the Consumer Price Index and the Treasury bill rate.

f. Find the correlation between the Dow Jones industrial average and the Consumer Price Index.

2. Refer to the data in Table 2.3 in Chapter 2, which were used in Examples 17.9 and 17.10.

a. Generate a correlation matrix using the SPSSX commands

```
REGRESSION DESCRIPTIVES = CORR/
    VARIABLES = PCTUNION, SALARY, REVENUE, EXPEND, INCOME,
    WAGE/
```

b. Examine these sample correlation coefficients. Which variable has the highest correlation with the variable SALARY?

c. Which variable has the highest correlation with REVENUE?

d. Which variable has the highest correlation with INCOME?

e. Find the correlation between SALARY and REVENUE and between SALARY and INCOME.

f. Find the correlation between WAGE and PCTUNION.

17.6 ▪ Computer Applications

To perform the types of statistical analyses described in this chapter, using a computer is almost mandatory. In this chapter, we discussed five different statistical procedures:

1. polynomial regression,
2. regression with dummy variables,
3. logarithmic regression,
4. stepwise regression, and
5. the correlation matrix.

All of these procedures are relatively easy to carry out using SPSSX or SAS. For example, polynomial regression is nothing more than multiple regression where one of the explanatory variables is the square (or cube or higher power) of another explanatory variable. To estimate a polynomial regression equation, we first instruct the computer to create a new variable that equals the original variable raised to the appropriate power. In SPSSX, this is done via a COMPUTE command. For example, suppose we wish to create a new variable (named SPEEDSQ) that is the square of the variable SPEED. Issue the command

```
COMPUTE SPEEDSQ = SPEED * SPEED
```

In SPSSX, an asterisk represents a multiplication sign. To create a variable (named SPEEDCUB) that is SPEED raised to the third power, issue the command

```
COMPUTE SPEEDCUB = SPEED * SPEED * SPEED
```

To estimate the polynomial regression model, proceed exactly as in any other multiple regression model and treat the newly created variables as any other explanatory variable.

To estimate a model that includes dummy variables, we can use an IF command to create the appropriate dummy variables. If the variable is dichotomous, such as SEX, then the values of the variable should be coded as 0 and 1 and the dummy variable is ready for use. If the variable is multinomial, such as academic class, then the appropriate dummy variables have to be created. For example, examine the data in Table 2.2 in Chapter 2, where the variable CLASS is coded as 1, 2, 3, or 4 to indicate whether a student is a freshman, sophomore, junior, or senior. Suppose we use freshman as the base case. Then we need to create three dummy variables to represent the sophomores, the juniors, and the seniors. To create a variable (named JUNIOR) that takes the value 1 if a student is a junior and 0 otherwise, issue the command

```
IF (CLASS EQ 3) JUNIOR = 1
```

The two additional commands

```
IF (CLASS EQ 2) SOPH = 1
IF (CLASS EQ 4) SENIOR = 1
```

will create the other two required dummy variables. At this stage, we have created three new variables whose values consist of 0's and 1's in the appropriate places.

To estimate a model that includes the logarithm of some variable, we again need to use a COMPUTE command to create the appropriate variable. For example, to create a variable (named LOGSPEED) which is the natural logarithm of the variable SPEED, issue the command

```
COMPUTE LOGSPEED = LN(SPEED)
```

In Section 17.4, we discussed how to obtain computer output for stepwise regression by adding the statement

```
STEPWISE
```

at the end of the regression commands.

In Section 17.5, we showed how to obtain a correlation matrix by issuing the command

```
DESCRIPTIVES = CORR/
```

along with the other regression commands.

Chapter 17 Summary

A nonlinear relationship between two variables X and Y often can be modeled by including an X^2 term in the regression equation. The resulting *quadratic regression model* is

$$Y_i = \beta_0 + \beta_1 x_i + \beta_2 x_i^2 + e_i$$

An alternative model for variables that seem to have a nonlinear relationship is the *logarithmic model*. We can choose between the models

$$\ln Y_i = \beta_0 + \beta_1 x_i + e_i$$

and

$$\ln Y_i = \beta_0 + \beta_1 \ln x_i + e_i$$

The use of *dummy variables* is widespread and extremely important in applied research. Dummy variables can be used in a regression application to represent the categories of a qualitative variable, such as sex, academic degree, or occupation. If a multinomial variable can take m different values, then $(m - 1)$ dummy variables are needed in the regression equation. The coefficient of each dummy variable measures the effect of being in that specific category compared with being in the base category. Dummy variables enable the researcher to incorporate a wide variety of qualitative variables in a regression equation and to test a wide range of hypotheses.

Stepwise regression is a technique by which explanatory variables can be inserted one at a time into the regression equation. At each step, the computer selects the remaining explanatory variable that most increases the explanatory power of the equation.

A sample *correlation matrix* can be helpful in detecting multicollinearity and in determining variables that are likely candidates to be included in a regression model. A correlation matrix is nothing more than a rectangular array of simple correlation coefficients showing the correlation between each pair of variables.

This chapter contains a discussion of special multiple regression models including polynomial models, logarithmic models, and dummy variable models. Chapter 18 provides a detailed discussion of each of the assumptions underlying the multiple regression model and shows how each of these assumptions can be tested.

Chapter 17 ▪ Supplementary Exercises

1. College students were studied to determine the relationship between annual expenditure on clothing and total annual family income. The following equation was obtained:

$$\text{Expenditure}_i = 85 + 0.02(\text{family income})_i + 175s_i + 45x_{i1} + 22x_{i2}$$

where

$$s_i = \begin{cases} 1 & \text{if female} \\ 0 & \text{if male} \end{cases}$$

$$x_{i1} = \begin{cases} 1 & \text{if student lives in Northeast} \\ 0 & \text{otherwise} \end{cases}$$

$$x_{i2} = \begin{cases} 1 & \text{if student lives in Midwest} \\ 0 & \text{otherwise} \end{cases}$$

a. Explain the meaning of the term $175s_i$ in the equation. Is it reasonable that the coefficient of s_i is positive?
b. A male student from Maine has a family income of \$40,000. Estimate his annual expenditure on clothing.
c. For male residents of the Midwest, graph the relationship between expenditures on clothing and family income. Do the same for female residents of the Midwest.

2. At a midwestern university, a study was undertaken to explain the school's salary structure. The following regression equation was estimated to explain salaries:

$$\text{Salary}_i = 24{,}000 + 1500(\text{years of service})_i + 900x_{i1} - 600x_{i2} + 5000t_i$$

where

$$x_{i1} = \begin{cases} 1 & \text{if individual teaches social sciences} \\ 0 & \text{otherwise} \end{cases}$$

$$x_{i2} = \begin{cases} 1 & \text{if individual teaches humanities} \\ 0 & \text{otherwise} \end{cases}$$

$$t_i = \begin{cases} 1 & \text{if individual has tenure} \\ 0 & \text{otherwise} \end{cases}$$

a. A tenured professor has taught for 10 years and teaches biology (a natural science). Estimate the professor's salary.
b. On a graph, plot the line relating salary to years of service for a tenured biology teacher.
c. On the same graph as in part (b), plot the line relating salary to years of service for a nontenured biology teacher.
d. On the same graph as in parts (b) and (c), plot the line relating salary to years of service for a tenured social science teacher.
e. Explain how and why the lines in parts (b), (c), and (d) differ.

3. The cost accountant for TLG Industries has estimated a quadratic regression equation to explain the number of refrigerators produced annually by the firm in terms of the total number of workers employed. The estimated equation is

$$\hat{y}_i = 372.6 + 984.3x_i - 4.7x_i^2$$

where

$\hat{y}_t$ = predicted number of washing machines produced in year t

x_t = number of full-time employees in year t at TLG Industries.

a. Plot the sample regression equation.
b. Predict output if the firm has 40 full-time employees.
c. Can you show that at some point $\hat{y}_t$ will level off and then decrease when x_t increases?
d. What is $\hat{y}_t$ if $x_t = 0$? Is this reasonable?
e. Do the answers to parts (c) and (d) imply that the equation is useless in predicting Y? Is it possible for the equation to be useful over a limited range of values of X?

4. A government study of eating habits contained the following regression results:

Variable	Coefficient	Standard Deviation
Constant	78.4	3.9
Log food price index	−17.3	4.2
Log income per capita	0.07	0.003

The dependent variable is the logarithm of food expenditures per capita. There were 200 observations in the study. Construct a 95% confidence interval for the following:
a. β_1 b. β_2

5. This problem requires the use of a computer. The Bardol Health Club has franchises in 15 different cities. The marketing manager believes that the profit Y_i that the ith franchise earned last year depended on four factors: x_{i1}, the average income (in thousands of dollars) in the community where the ith franchise is located; x_{i2}, the total population (in 100,000s) within 15 miles of the ith franchise; x_{i3}, annual advertising expenditures (in thousands of dollars) of the ith franchise; and x_{i4}, which equals 1 if there is a swimming pool and 0 if there is not. The data are shown in the accompanying table.

Franchise	Profits Y	Income X_1	Population X_2	Advertising X_3	Status X_4
1	94	34	4.3	21	1
2	22	17	1.0	4	0
3	44	23	2.5	8	0
4	81	33	4.0	15	1
5	74	26	3.1	14	1
6	54	26	2.0	9	0
7	112	40	4.2	20	1
8	28	19	1.1	7	0
9	56	25	2.1	8	0
10	77	29	3.8	16	1
11	62	25	2.9	14	0
12	80	31	3.7	19	1
13	48	24	2.2	10	0
14	50	24	2.4	9	0
15	40	22	3.1	7	0

a. Estimate the population regression model

$$Y_i = \beta_0 + \beta_1 x_{i1} + \beta_2 x_{i2} + \beta_3 x_{i3} + \beta_4 x_{i4} + e_i$$

b. Let $\alpha = .05$. Test H_0: $\beta_1 = 0$ against H_1: $\beta_1 > 0$.
c. Let $\alpha = .05$. Test H_0: $\beta_2 = 0$ against H_1: $\beta_2 > 0$.
d. Let $\alpha = .05$. Test H_0: $\beta_3 = 0$ against H_1: $\beta_3 > 0$.
e. Calculate s_e.
f. Calculate R^2. Given the value of R^2, would you have much faith in forecasts generated by this model?
g. A certain franchise plans to spend x_{i3} = \$12,000 on advertising next year. Assume that for this franchise x_{i1} = \$22,000, x_{i2} = 216,000, and $x_{i4} = 1$. Forecast profits for this franchise.
h. Calculate the correlation coefficient between X_1 and X_3. If this correlation coefficient is large, then multicollinearity could make it difficult to get good estimates of the coefficients of X_1 and X_3.

6. A tax consultant studied the relationship between selling price and assessed valuation of one-family residential dwellings in a large tax district. The accompanying data represent a random sample of nine recent sales transactions of one-family dwellings located on corner lots and another random sample of 14 recent sales of one-family dwellings not located on corner lots. In the data, both selling price (Y) and assessed valuation (X) are expressed in thousands of dollars. Assume that the error term variances in the two populations are equal. Estimate the regression model

$$Y_i = \beta_0 + \beta_1 x_{i1} + \beta_2 x_{i2} + e_i$$

where x_{i2} is 1 if the house is on a corner lot and 0 otherwise.

Corner Lots				Noncorner Lots			
Lot	Y	X_1	X_2	Lot	Y	X_1	X_2
1	56.2	17.5	1.0	10	31.2	10.0	0.0
2	42.5	12.5	1.0	11	36.9	13.8	0.0
3	68.6	20.0	1.0	12	41.0	15.0	0.0
4	54.8	16.0	1.0	13	51.8	19.5	0.0
5	50.0	15.0	1.0	14	48.0	17.0	0.0
6	47.5	14.7	1.0	15	33.3	12.5	0.0
7	56.9	17.5	1.0	16	38.0	14.5	0.0
8	34.0	12.3	1.0	17	35.9	12.8	0.0
9	39.0	11.5	1.0	18	32.0	12.0	0.0
				19	44.3	16.0	0.0
				20	29.0	10.0	0.0
				21	46.1	17.0	0.0
				22	30.0	10.8	0.0
				23	42.0	15.0	0.0

a. Plot the sample data for the two groups on one graph, using different symbols for the two samples. Does the regression relation appear to be the same for the two populations?
b. Let $\alpha = .05$. Use a two-tailed test and test whether β_2 is 0.
c. Plot the estimated regression functions for the two groups and describe the differences between them.
d. Prepare a residual plot for each sample. Does the assumption of equal error term variances appear to be reasonable here?

7. The accompanying data show Gross National Product per capita in U.S. dollars (Y), the population in millions (X_1), land in thousands of square kilometers (X_2), percentage of literate adults in the population (X_3), and the percentage of the economy attributed to agriculture (X_4) for a sample of 34 countries.

a. Compute the multiple regression of Y on X_1, X_2, X_3, and X_4.
b. Find the sample correlation matrix for the five variables.
c. Examine the sample correlation matrix and predict which variables will enter first, second, and third using stepwise regression.
d. Estimate Y as a function of the other four variables using stepwise regression.

Y	X_1	X_2	X_3	X_4
90	1.2	144	22	55
130	4.4	26	23	25
160	4.9	1267	8	47
190	16.4	945	66	45
240	1.3	30	40	30
270	1.5	1031	17	26
300	133.5	2027	62	31
140	5.6	118	25	47
240	8.1	587	58	40
320	7.9	1001	44	32
420	43.8	541	82	27
450	5.1	753	39	14
550	18.3	447	28	21
730	2.8	407	80	20
840	5.0	49	60	20
1110	17.0	2382	35	8
1160	10.6	757	88	10
1360	116.1	8512	76	12
1960	21.7	256	85	16
2850	3.6	21	88	7
1240	2.1	51	88	21
860	5.9	164	38	17
690	7.5	322	20	25
430	5.2	196	10	28
2880	3.2	70	98	22
6130	7.5	84	99	5
7590	9.8	31	99	2
8550	4.0	324	99	6
8520	220.0	9363	99	3
7340	14.1	7687	100	5
6680	2.8	1760	45	3
910	9.6	115	96	21
1580	21.6	238	98	31
3150	34.7	313	98	16

8. An economist wants to estimate a regression equation relating demand for a product (Y) to its price (X_1) and community income (X_2). The economist has 12 years of quarterly data. It is known that demand for this product is seasonal.

a. One possibility for accounting for seasonality is to estimate the model

$$Y_t = \beta_0 + \beta_1 x_{t1} + \beta_2 x_{t2} + \beta_3 x_{t3} + \beta_4 x_{t4} + \beta_5 x_{t5} + \beta_6 x_{t6} + e_t$$

where

$$x_{t3} = \begin{cases} 1 & \text{in first quarter of each year} \\ 0 & \text{otherwise} \end{cases}$$

$$x_{t4} = \begin{cases} 1 & \text{in second quarter of each year} \\ 0 & \text{otherwise} \end{cases}$$

$$x_{t5} = \begin{cases} 1 & \text{in third quarter of each year} \\ 0 & \text{otherwise} \end{cases}$$

$$x_{t6} = \begin{cases} 1 & \text{in fourth quarter of each year} \\ 0 & \text{otherwise} \end{cases}$$

Explain why this model cannot be estimated by least squares.

b. A model that can be estimated is

$$Y_t = \beta_0 + \beta_1 x_{t1} + \beta_2 x_{t2} + \beta_3 x_{t3} + \beta_4 x_{t4} + \beta_5 x_{t5} + e_t$$

Interpret the coefficients on the dummy variables in this model.

References

DRAPER, NORMAN R., and HARRY SMITH. *Applied Regression Analysis*. 2d ed. New York: Wiley, 1981.

JOHNSTON, JOHN. *Econometric Methods*. New York: McGraw-Hill, 1972.

KMENTA, JAN. *Elements of Econometrics*. 2d ed. New York: Macmillan, 1986.

LOVELL, MICHAEL C. "Data Mining." *Review of Economics and Statistics* 65 (1983): 1–12.

NIE, NORMAN E., C. HADLAI HULL, JEAN G. JENKINS, KARIN STEINBRENNER, and DALE H. BENT. *SPSS Statistical Package for the Social Sciences*. 2d ed. New York: McGraw-Hill, 1975.

NORUSIS, MARIJA J. *SPSSX Introductory Statistics Guide*. New York: McGraw-Hill, 1983.

———. *SPSSX Advanced Statistics Guide*. Chicago: SPSS, 1985.

———. *The SPSS Guide to Data Analysis*. Chicago: SPSS, 1986.

PINDYCK, ROBERT S., and DANIEL L. RUBINFELD. *Econometric Models and Economic Forecasts*. 2d ed. New York: McGraw-Hill, 1981.

RYAN, THOMAS A., BRIAN L. JOINER, and BARBARA F. RYAN. *Minitab Reference Manual*. University Park, Penn.: Minitab Project, 1985.

———. *Minitab Handbook*. 2d ed. Boston: PWS-KENT, 1985.

SAS Introductory Guide. 3d ed. Cary, N.C.: SAS Institute, 1985.

SAS Procedures Guide for Personal Computers. Version 6 ed. Cary, N.C.: SAS Institute, 1986.

SAS Statistics Guide for Personal Computers. Version 6 ed. Cary, N.C.: SAS Institute, 1986.

SAS User's Guide: Basics. Version 5 ed. Cary, N.C.: SAS Institute, 1985.

SAS User's Guide: Statistics. Version 5 ed. Cary, N.C.: SAS Institute, 1985.

SPSSX User's Guide. Chicago: SPSS, 1983.
SUITS, DANIEL. "Dummy Variables: Mechanics vs. Interpretation." *Review of Economics and Statistics* 66(1984): 177–180.
THEIL, HENRI. *Principles of Econometrics*. New York: Wiley, 1971.
WONNACOTT, THOMAS H., and RONALD J. WONNACOTT. *Regression: A Second Course in Statistics*. New York: Wiley, 1981.

Chapter Eighteen Residual Analysis and Violations of the Basic Assumptions

In the previous chapters, we showed how to estimate and interpret the parameters β_0, $\beta_1, \ldots, \beta_K$ and σ_e^2 in the population regression equation

$$E(y_i|x_{i1}, x_{i2}, \ldots, x_{iK}) = \beta_0 + \beta_1 x_{i1} + \beta_2 x_{i2} + \cdots + \beta_K x_{iK}$$

In addition, we showed that the coefficient of determination R^2 and the estimated standard error of the regression s_e can be used to measure the goodness of fit of the estimated model. Finally, we showed how to use the correlation matrix and stepwise regression to help select an appropriate model.

In deriving our results we made use of the basic assumptions concerning the error terms and the explanatory variables. When the basic assumptions hold, the least-squares estimators of the regression coefficients are normally distributed and unbiased and have minimum variance among the class of linear unbiased estimators. In addition, the estimated variances are unbiased estimators of the corresponding population parameters.

In this chapter, we discuss methods of testing to determine whether the basic assumptions hold, and we describe how the properties of the least-squares estimators are affected when any of the basic assumptions is violated. In addition, we develop alternative methods of estimation when the consequences of such a violation are serious.

There are many reasons that a specific model can be inadequate and many ways to check or test for the inadequacies. This chapter covers many of these reasons, shows how to test for violations of the basic assumptions, and gives procedures for improving inadequate models.

18.1 ▪ Searching for Model Inadequacies

The process of checking the adequacy of a proposed model involves many steps. Some of the things that should be examined are the following:

1. *Signs of coefficients*: Examine each estimated coefficient and determine whether the sign of the estimated coefficient agrees with theoretical expectations. When an estimated coefficient has the wrong sign, there is strong evidence that the model is inadequate and should be changed.

2. *Standard deviations of coefficients*: Examine the estimated standard deviation of each estimated coefficient. Coefficients with large standard deviations have not been estimated with much precision.

3. *t statistics and prob-values*: The t statistic $t = b_i/s_{b_i}$ is used to test the null hypothesis that the population regression coefficient is 0. When the t statistic is close to 0 or when the prob-value is large, we do not have strong evidence that the true population regression coefficient is nonzero. This raises the question of whether the variable should be included in the model.

4. *R^2 and adjusted R^2*: Examine the values of R^2 and the adjusted R^2 to get an idea of how well the explanatory variables explain variation in the dependent variable. Values of R^2 close to 0 indicate that the explanatory variables explain only a small proportion of the variation in the dependent variable.

5. *Estimated standard error of the regression*: Examine s_e to get an idea of the absolute size of the typical residual. If s_e is small, the sample data tend to lie close to the estimated equation. Approximately 95% of the observations should lie within 2 standard errors of the regression line. Large standard errors indicate that predictions typically will not be very accurate.

6. *Residual Analysis*: Examine the residuals to discover whether any of the basic assumptions have been violated. Plot the residuals against the sample values of the independent variables, against the fitted values of the dependent variable ($\hat{y}_i$), or against time if applicable. In addition, a histogram of the residuals may reveal a violation of the normality assumption. If there are no violations of the basic assumptions, the residual plots should show no distinct patterns of variation.

A problem with examining scatter plots to detect violations of the basic assumptions is that interpreting the plots is based on subjective judgment rather than well-defined statistical tests. In addition, unless the violation is quite obvious, interpreting the plots usually requires considerable skill and experience. In the remainder of this chapter, we discuss potential violations of the basic assumptions and we describe graphical techniques and formal statistical tests for detecting such violations.

Once we determine that some basic assumption fails to hold, we have to decide whether to adjust the least-squares model in some way or to use a different estimation technique. When an assumption fails to hold, it is sometimes possible to transform the model so that the basic assumptions will hold in the transformed model.

When a test indicates a violation, a common practice is to transform the model and reestimate the regression coefficients using an estimation method other than ordinary least squares that takes the violation into account. However, there is a statistical problem involved with estimating a model, testing it, revising it, and reestimating. If we construct confidence intervals and test for the significance of individual regression coefficients after we have performed tests and revised the model, the results are conditional on the outcome of the original tests. In statistical literature, this is known as "*pretest bias*." When this is done, the usual significance levels or confidence intervals are not the same as when no preliminary testing has been done.

If the regression model adequately describes real-world behavior, the residuals should possess properties that tend to confirm the assumptions we have made; at the very least, they should not lead us to reject the assumptions. When we examine the residuals, we should ask ourselves, "Do the residuals make it appear that the regression model is inadequate or that the assumptions are wrong?"

Searching for Outliers

Before performing any formal statistical tests, it is useful to examine scatter diagrams of the original data and the residuals to see if there are any obvious errors. Occasionally data are reported incorrectly or typing errors are made when feeding the data into the computer. Frequently such errors can be spotted by examining a scatter diagram or by searching for residuals that are much larger or much smaller than most of the others.

Definition: Outliers and Outlier Residuals

An **outlier** is any observation that is quite different in magnitude from other observations. An **outlier residual** is a residual that is much larger in absolute value than most of the other residuals.

For practical purposes, an outlier can be considered to be any observation that lies more than $3s_e$ units from the estimated regression equation.

Example 18.1

Using a Scatter Diagram to Detect an Outlier: Consider the data plotted in Figure 18.1. This is a scatter diagram showing the average salary of elementary and secondary school teachers (Y) against the average tax revenue per capita (X) for each of the 50 states and the District of Columbia. The data were presented in Chapter 2 in Table 2.3. The scatter diagram reveals one very obvious outlier—the point in the upper right-hand corner of the graph, which represents the data for the state of Alaska.

In Alaska, the average salary of teachers is approximately 25% higher than in any other state. In addition, Alaska has much higher tax revenue per capita than any other state. Including the data point for Alaska will have a strong effect on the estimated regression coefficients, because the estimated regression line is found by minimizing the squared residuals. To minimize SSE, the sample regression line will have to pass close to the Alaska data point. ■

Standardized Residuals

Another way of detecting outliers is by calculating what are called *standardized residuals*. Because the standardized residuals have a mean of 0 and a standard deviation of 1, the relative magnitudes of the residuals are easier to judge when they are divided by s_e. For example, the fact that a particular residual is, say, 6253.21 provides little information. However, if you know that its standardized value is 4.2, you know that this residual is much larger than most residuals in absolute value.

Definition: Standardized Residuals

The ith **standardized residual** is denoted by the symbol SR_i and is defined as

$$SR_i = \hat{e}_i / s_e$$

where $\hat{e}_i$ is the ith residual and s_e is the estimated standard error of the regression.

FIGURE 18.1 **Teachers' salaries versus tax revenue per capita in the 50 States and District of Columbia; Alaska is an outlier.**

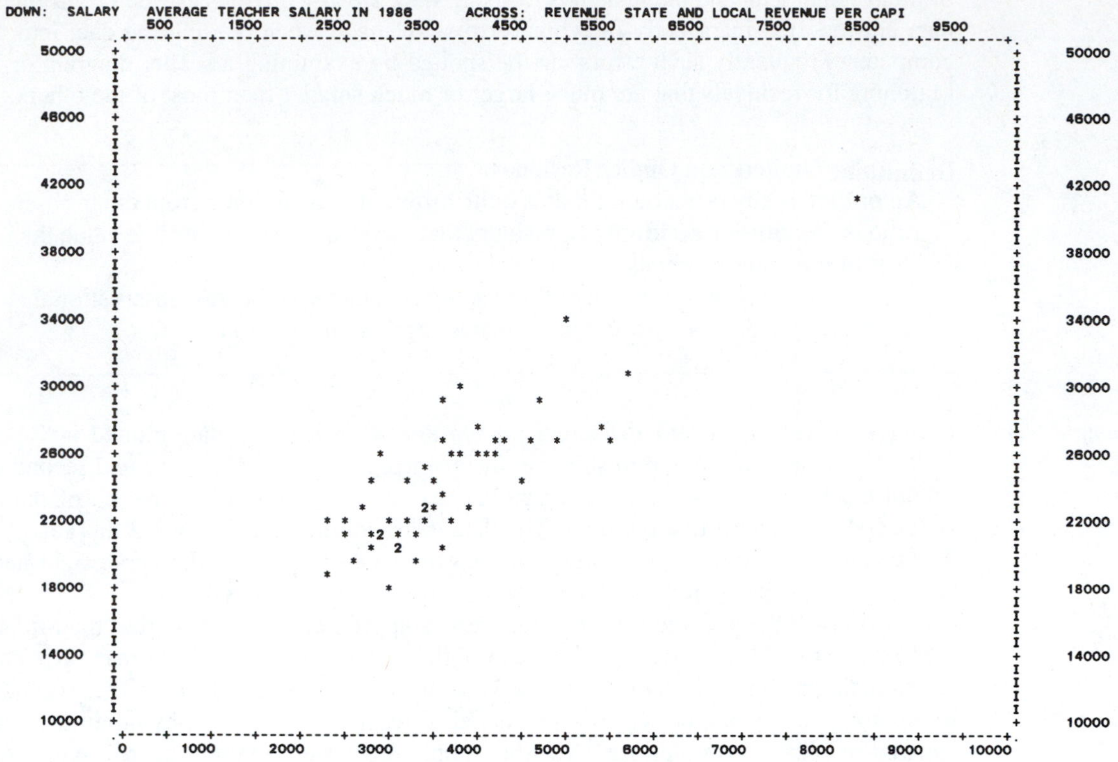

Many computer programs, including the SPSSX program, plot both the residuals and the standardized residuals along with their calculated values. If the standardized residuals are approximately normally distributed, the Empirical Rule tells us that approximately 95% of the standardized residuals should be between -2.00 and $+2.00$ and more than 99% of the standardized residuals should be between -3.00 and $+3.00$. Thus standardized residuals less than -3 or greater than $+3$ should not occur with great frequency.

One of the easiest ways to detect a violation of the basic assumptions is to plot the observations (x_i, y_i) on a scatter diagram or to plot each residual $\hat{e}_i$ versus the observation y_i, versus $\hat{y}_i$, versus x_{ij}, and so forth. There are many different residual plots that can be generated. Throughout this chapter, these plots are used to detect violations of the basic assumptions.

Exercises for Section 18.1

1. "In a regression model, the variable with the largest estimated coefficient is the most important." True or false? Explain.
2. "In a regression model, if the largest estimated coefficient is not statistically significant, then none of the estimated coefficients will be significant." True or false? Explain.
3. "In a regression model, the variable with the largest observed t statistic is the most important variable." True or false? Explain.
4. A student was told to discuss the population regression model. The student wrote the following:

$$E(Y_i|x_i) = \beta_0 + \beta_1 x_i + e_i$$

Is this correct? Explain.

5. A realtor studied the relation between household electricity consumption (Y) and the number of rooms in the house (X). The realtor estimated a linear regression model and obtained the following residuals:

House	1	2	3	4	5	6	7	8	9	10
X	2	3	4	5	5	5	6	7	7	8
$\hat{e}$	3.2	2.9	−1.7	−2.0	−2.3	−1.2	−0.9	0.5	0.7	0.8

a. Plot the residuals $\hat{e}_i$ against x_i.
b. What problem appears to be present here? Might a transformation alleviate this problem?

6. A sociologist estimated a linear regression model to relate per capita earnings (Y) to the average number of years of education (X) in 12 different cities. The fitted values $\hat{Y}$ and the standardized residuals (SR) follow:

City	1	2	3	4	5	6	7	8	9	10	11	12
$\hat{Y}$	9.9	9.3	10.2	9.6	10.2	12.4	14.3	9.6	9.2	15.6	11.2	13.1
SR	−1.12	0.81	−0.76	0.43	0.65	−0.17	1.62	1.79	−0.53	−3.78	0.74	0.32

a. Plot the standardized residuals against the fitted values. What does the plot suggest?
b. Do you detect an outlier?

18.2 ▪ Violations of Basic Assumption 1: Nonnormal Errors

The first basic assumption states that the error terms follow a normal distribution. In this section, we discuss potential problems when this basic assumption fails to hold.

Basic Assumption 1

Each of the random error terms e_i is selected from a normal distribution with mean 0 and variance σ_e^2.

Consequences of Nonnormality of the Error Terms

If the normality assumption does not hold, the least-squares estimators of the regression coefficients are still the best linear unbiased estimators. In other words, even with nonnormal errors, the least-squares estimators are unbiased and have the smallest variance among all linear unbiased estimators of the respective parameters. However, all confidence intervals and tests of hypotheses concerning the regression coefficients do depend on the assumption of normality.

Without the assumption of normality, the sampling distributions of the least-squares estimators $b_0, b_1, \ldots, b_K$ are not normal and the t statistics used for testing hypotheses about the population regression coefficients do not follow the t distribution. Strictly speaking, therefore, the confidence intervals and hypothesis tests that we have developed would not apply. Fortunately, however, if the distribution of the error terms does not differ too radically from normality, the use of the t distribution to construct confidence intervals and to test hypotheses is still approximately correct.

In many cases, as the sample size increases, the sampling distributions of the least-squares estimators approach normality even when the error terms are not normal. This implies that when the sample sizes are relatively large, our confidence intervals will be approximately correct and tests of hypotheses will have approximately the correct level of significance.

Detecting Nonnormality of Error Terms

The SPSSX computer program can print out a histogram of the residuals and the standardized residuals. If the errors are normally distributed and the sample size is fairly large, the histogram of the standardized residuals should appear like a standard normal distribution.

FIGURE 18.2
SPSSX-generated histogram of residuals.

```
HISTOGRAM
STUDENTIZED RESIDUAL
 N EXP N       ( * = 2 CASES,     . : = NORMAL CURVE)
 3  0.37   OUT **
 1  0.73  3.00 *
 3  1.85  2.66 :*
 4  4.23  2.33 *:
10  8.65  2.00 ***:*
14 15.85  1.66 *******.
21 26.01  1.33 ***********  .
31 38.23  1.00 ****************  .
48 50.34  0.66 ************************.
55 59.38  0.33 ****************************  .
63 62.74  0.00 ******************************:*
64 59.38 -0.33 *****************************:**
62 50.34 -0.66 ************************:******
44 38.23 -1.00 ******************:***
28 26.01 -1.33 ************:*
14 15.85 -1.66 *******.
 7  8.65 -2.00 ***:
 1  4.23 -2.33 *.
 1  1.85 -2.66 :
 0  0.73 -3.00
 0  0.37   OUT
```

Figure 18.2 shows a histogram of standardized residuals printed out by the SPSSX computer program.

18.3 ▪ Violations of Basic Assumption 2: Nonzero Mean

The second basic assumption states that each error term is a random variable selected from a distribution having a mean of 0.

Basic Assumption 2

Each of the random error terms e_i is a random variable selected from a distribution having a mean of 0.

The assumption that the mean of each of the error terms is 0 implies that the specification of the population regression equation is

$$E(Y_i|x_{i1}, x_{i2}, \ldots, x_{iK}) = \beta_0 + \beta_1 x_{i1} + \beta_2 x_{i2} + \cdots + \beta_K x_{iK}$$

If the mean of the error term is not 0, but, say, μ_i, we have

$$E(Y_i|x_{i1}, x_{i2}, \ldots, x_{iK}) = \beta_0 + \beta_1 x_{i1} + \beta_2 x_{i2} + \cdots + \beta_K x_{iK} + \mu_i$$

The consequences of violating this basic assumption depend on the nature of the mean μ_i. If μ_i differs for each observation, the intercept of the equation becomes $(\beta_0 + \mu_i)$ and differs for each observation. Thus, the mean value of Y_i changes not only because of changes in the values of the independent variables $x_{i1}, x_{i2}, \ldots, x_{iK}$ but also for other reasons. In other words, the relationship between Y_i and $x_{i1}, x_{i2}, \ldots, x_{iK}$ has not been correctly specified. For example, if we have omitted the important explanatory variable Z, it might be that the mean μ_i is

$$\mu_i = \beta_{K+1} z_i$$

Consequences of a Nonzero Mean of the Error Terms

If the errors do not have zero means, we have either omitted some important independent variables or used an incorrect functional expression. In either case, we have estimated the wrong model. As a result, the least-squares estimates of the regression coefficients will be biased. Omitting an important variable and estimating an incorrect functional form are examples of what are called *specification errors*.

Detecting a Nonzero Mean of the Error Terms

Omitted Variables. The omission of an important variable can frequently be detected by estimating different regression models using different sets of independent variables. It is customary to use the t statistic to examine the statistical significance of each estimated coefficient in order to determine which variables should be included in a model.

The discussion of stepwise regression in Section 17.4 showed that adding or deleting an explanatory variable causes the t statistics to change for all of the other estimated regression coefficients. An estimated coefficient that appears to be statistically significant in one formulation of a model may not be statistically significant in another formulation. Unless there are strong theoretical reasons for keeping a variable in a model, it is customary to remove any variable whose t statistic is not significant at some prespecified level of significance.

Detecting whether an important variable has been omitted from a model is frequently a trial-and-error process. Various models are estimated and the results are examined to determine if the coefficients have the appropriate signs and magnitudes. Tests are performed to determine if the estimated coefficients are statistically significant, and the values of R^2 and s_e are examined to see if the model provides a good fit. If the model seems to be lacking in some way, it is customary to include additional independent variables or to estimate some alternative functional form. There is no easy way to determine if an important explanatory variable has been omitted from the model except to include the variable in a model and examine the estimated coefficient of the variable.

Sometimes the estimated coefficients of a regression model do not seem to make sense. For example, sometimes economic theory tells us that a particular coefficient should be positive but the estimated coefficient is negative. Because such a result violates the economic theory, we would reject this model and search for a better one. Generally an estimated coefficient with the wrong sign indicates that the model has not been specified properly. Perhaps some other important explanatory variables have been omitted or perhaps the wrong functional form has been estimated.

Occasionally incorrect signs or unusual values for estimated coefficients can be attributed to *multicollinearity*. If two explanatory variables X_1 and X_2 are highly correlated, then it is difficult to determine their separate influences on the dependent variable Y. Because this is a data problem rather than a specification error, there is little that can be done about it. When two explanatory variables X_1 and X_2 are highly correlated, it is difficult to get precise estimates of their coefficients β_1 and β_2.

For example, consider what happens when variables X_1 and X_2 are highly positively correlated with each other and are both positively correlated to the dependent variable Y. In advance, we do not know if Y is a function of just X_1, just X_2, or both X_1 and X_2. There are three different models that we could estimate. Suppose we estimate all three different models and obtain the following three sample regression equations:

$$\hat{y}_i = b_0 + b_1 x_{i1} + b_2 x_{i2} \tag{1}$$

$$\hat{y}_i = c_0 + c_1 x_{i1} \tag{2}$$

$$\hat{y}_i = d_0 + d_1 x_{i2} \tag{3}$$

What would we expect to find, given that X_1 and X_2 are highly positively correlated? The estimated coefficient c_1 in equation 2 would be larger than the estimated coefficient b_1 in equation 1, because in the second equation some of the influence that X_2 has on Y has been attributed to the lone explanatory variable X_1. If the correct regression model contains both X_1 and X_2, that is, if the correct model is

$$Y_i = \beta_0 + \beta_1 x_{i1} + \beta_2 x_{i2} + e_i$$

then c_1 will tend to overestimate the true effect of X_1 on Y. For the same reason, the estimated coefficient d_1 will exceed the estimated coefficient b_2 and d_1 will tend to overestimate the true effect of X_2 on Y. Consequently, the estimates c_1 and d_1 will be biased estimates that tend to overestimate the true coefficients β_1 and β_2, respectively.

Thus, because of the high correlation between X_1 and X_2, it is difficult to get precise estimates of β_1 and β_2. The standard errors of the regression coefficients b_1 and b_2 will be large, causing the confidence intervals for the true values of β_1 and β_2 to be fairly wide. Although we have obtained the best estimates that we can, these estimates may not be very good.

When the explanatory variables are highly correlated, the precision of the estimates is affected. The standard errors of the estimated coefficients will tend to be large, indicating that the estimates are not very reliable.

One way to check for multicollinearity is to find the sample correlation coefficients between all pairs of potential explanatory variables in the model. When the sample correlation coefficient between X_i and X_j is large in absolute value, it may be difficult to separate the effects of these two variables on the dependent variable Y.

Incorrect Functional Form. The classical regression model states that the variables are related according to the equation

$$E(Y_i|x_{i1}, x_{i2}, \ldots, x_{iK}) = \beta_0 + \beta_1 x_{i1} + \beta_2 x_{i2} + \cdots + \beta_K x_{iK}$$

If the expected value of Y_i is related to the explanatory variables according to some other form of equation, we have made a specification error. For example, perhaps the logarithm of Y is related to the explanatory variables according to some equation, or perhaps $E(Y_i)$ is related to X^2 as well as X, or perhaps $E(\ln Y_i)$ is related to $\ln X$. If we estimate the model

$$Y_i = \beta_0 + \beta_1 x_{i1} + \beta_2 x_{i2} + e_i$$

when the variables are related according to some other equation, we have estimated an incorrect functional form. (Strictly speaking, when we omit an important explanatory variable, we estimate an incorrect functional form; however, we have already discussed this case.) One way to detect an incorrect functional form is to plot the observations (x_i, y_i) on a scatter diagram. This procedure works fine when there is only one independent variable, but other procedures have to be used when there are many explanatory variables.

Another way of discovering an incorrect functional form is to plot the residuals $\hat{e}_i$ versus the observations of the explanatory variables x_{ij}; that is, construct a scatter diagram showing the points $(x_{ij}, \hat{e}_i)$. Suppose that we plot the points $(x_{ij}, \hat{e}_i)$ and obtain a scatter diagram where the points lie in a shaded area as in Figure 18.3. This pattern occurs quite frequently when analyzing economic and business data. In the scatter diagram, small and large values of X tend to be associated with positive residuals, whereas middle values of X tend to be associated with negative residuals. Because the residuals should be randomly scattered, such patterns in a residual plot usually indicate that one of the assumptions has been violated. The pattern in Figure 18.3 indicates that we tend to overestimate Y for middle values of X and to underestimate Y when X is very small or very large. This is an indication that we have fitted a straight line to data better described by a curvilinear relationship, such as that illustrated in Figure 18.4.

When a model has several explanatory variables, each one should be plotted against Y and against the residuals. If the residual plot indicates that the relationship between Y

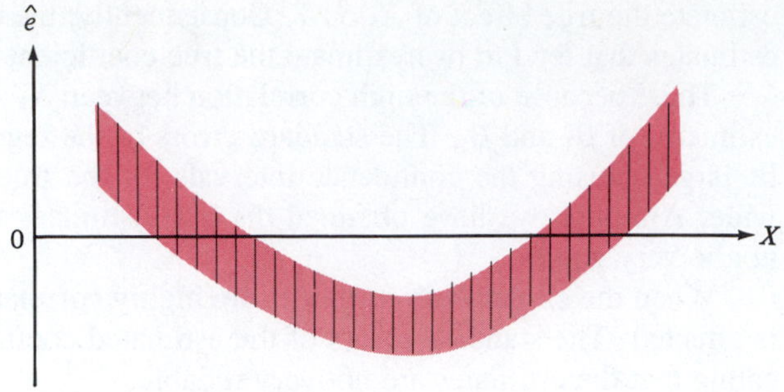

FIGURE 18.3
Plot of residuals versus an explanatory variable *X*.

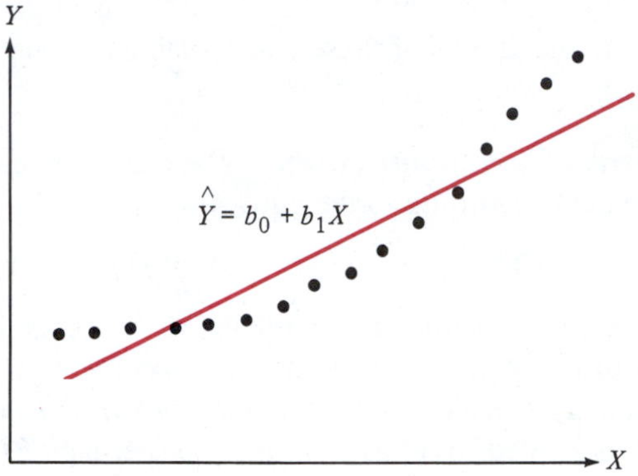

FIGURE 18.4
Fitting a straight line to curvilinear data.

and an explanatory variable X_j is curvilinear, we should try a different functional form such as a polynomial. These types of models were discussed in Section 17.1.

Example 18.2

Detecting a Nonlinear Relationship: The data in Table 18.1 show before-tax income in 1980 (X) and federal income taxes paid in 1980 (Y) for families covered in the 1980 census. Let us construct a model to explain taxes as a function of a family's income.

Solution: Suppose we estimate the linear model

$$Y_i = \beta_0 + \beta_1 x_i + e_i$$

The SPSSX computer output for this model is shown in Figure 18.5. The sample regression equation is

$$\hat{y}_i = -2189.33 + 0.234768x_i \qquad R^2 = .9609$$
$$t \text{ statistics:} \quad (-5.85) \qquad (20.43)$$

Income explains approximately 96% of the variation in Y ($R^2 = .9609$) so the data fall close to a straight line. The t statistics for both coefficients are very large in absolute value and both have a prob-value of .0000, so the evidence is very strong that both population regression coefficients are nonzero. At this stage, the computer output might lead us to believe that we have a fairly good model explaining tax expenditures as a linear function of income.

TABLE 18.1
Data for Example 18.2

Taxes Paid Y	Before-Tax Income X
$ 128	$ 3,750
329	6,250
519	8,750
801	11,250
1,085	13,750
1,464	16,250
1,903	18,750
2,389	21,250
2,847	23,750
3,369	26,250
3,830	28,750
4,454	31,250
5,048	33,750
5,650	36,250
6,294	38,750
7,259	42,500
8,829	47,500
11,158	55,000
15,767	67,500

Source: Current Population Reports, Series P-23, No. 126, 1983.

FIGURE 18.5 **SPSSX-generated output for Example 18.2, explaining tax expenditures as a linear function of before-tax income.**

```
                              * * * *   M U L T I P L E   R E G R E S S I O N   * * * *
Listwise Deletion of Missing Data

Equation Number 1    Dependent Variable..   TAX   FEDERAL INCOME TAX

Beginning Block Number  1.  Method:  Enter      INCOME

Variable(s) Entered on Step Number  1..    INCOME    BEFORE TAX INCOME

Multiple R             .98025        Analysis of Variance
R Square               .96090                             DF      Sum of Squares      Mean Square
Adjusted R Square      .95860        Regression            1     292839012.69294   292839012.69294
Standard Error      837.25220        Residual             17      11916851.09654      700991.24097

                                     F =      417.74989       Signif F =   .0000

------------------ Variables in the Equation ------------------

Variable                B         SE B         Beta          T  Sig T

INCOME             .234768      .011486      .980254     20.439  .0000
(Constant) -2189.330098   374.218973                     -5.850  .0000

End Block Number   1   All requested variables entered.
```

Now let us examine some scatter diagrams and computer-generated plots of the residuals to search for clues on how to improve the model. The data are plotted in Figure 18.6. From the scatter diagram, it is quite obvious that the relationship between Y and X is nonlinear.

Figure 18.7 shows the standardized residuals SR_i plotted against the observed standardized x_i values. This scatter diagram reveals that the residuals associated with low values of X are positive, the residuals associated with middle values of X are negative, and the residuals associated with large values of X are positive.

Figure 18.8 shows the standardized residuals SR_i plotted against the standardized values of $\hat{y}_i$. This scatter diagram reveals basically the same information as the scatter diagram of $\hat{e}_i$ plotted against x_i. The residuals are positive for small values $\hat{y}_i$, negative for middle values, and positive for very large predicted values $\hat{y}_i$.

From the scatter diagrams and plots of the residuals, the relationship between tax expenditures and income is better explained by a nonlinear equation. Let us estimate the nonlinear model

$$Y_i = \beta_0 + \beta_1 x_i + \beta_2 x_i^2 + e_i$$

FIGURE 18.6 SPSSX-generated scatter diagram showing tax expenditures versus before-tax income.

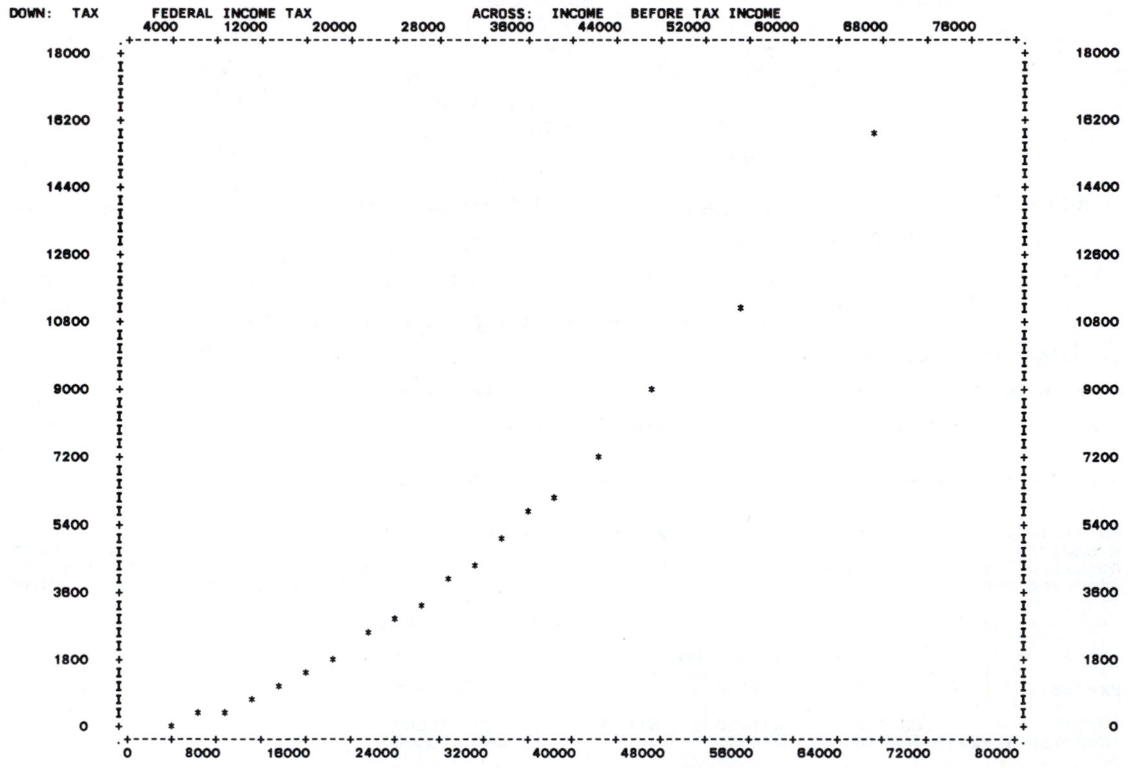

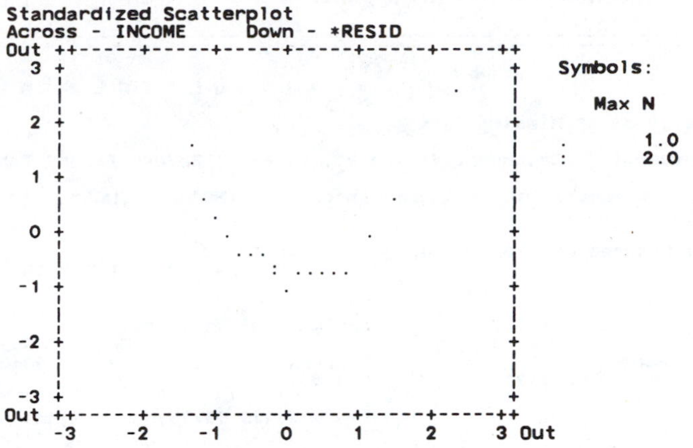

FIGURE 18.7
SPSSX-generated scatter diagram showing standardized values of $(x_i, \hat{e}_i)$ for Example 18.2.

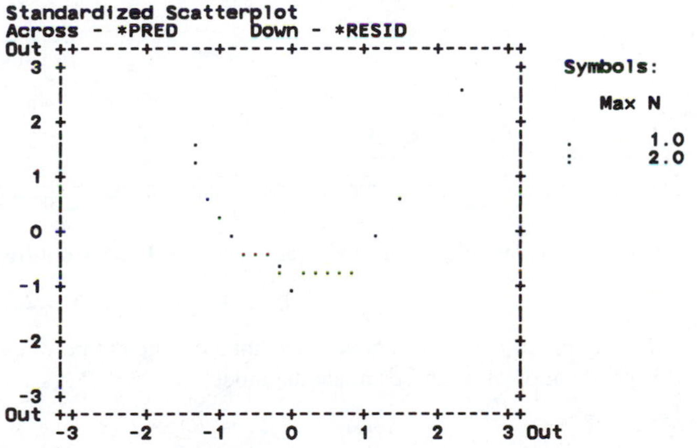

FIGURE 18.8
SPSSX-generated scatter diagram showing standardized values of $(\hat{y}_i, \hat{e}_i)$ for Example 18.2.

The computer output for this model is shown in Figure 18.9. The estimated model is

$$\hat{y}_i = -312.97 + 0.076x_i + 0.0000024x_i^2 \qquad R^2 = .99979$$
$$t \text{ statistics:} \quad (-7.02) \quad (25.02) \quad (54.46)$$

In the computer output, the coefficient of the variable x_i^2 is written as "2.41280E−06." The symbol "E−06" tells us to move the decimal point six places to the left. Thus, the coefficient of x_i^2 is $b_2 = .0000024128$. The quadratic equation explains more than 99.9% of the variation in taxes paid ($R^2 = .99979$). Each estimated regression coefficient has a t statistic whose prob-value is .0000, which supports the hypothesis that each population regression coefficient is nonzero.

FIGURE 18.9 **SPSSX-generated output for Example 18.2, explaining tax expenditures as a quadratic function of before-tax income.**

```
                                   * * * *   M U L T I P L E   R E G R E S S I O N   * * * *

Listwise Deletion of Missing Data

Equation Number 1    Dependent Variable..   TAX   FEDERAL INCOME TAX

Beginning Block Number  1.  Method:  Enter      INCOME   INCSQ

Variable(s) Entered on Step Number  1..    INCSQ
                                    2..    INCOME     BEFORE TAX INCOME

Multiple R             .99990           Analysis of Variance
R Square               .99979                           DF     Sum of Squares        Mean Square
Adjusted R Square      .99976           Regression       2    304691929.36914    152345964.68457
Standard Error       63.21314           Residual        16        63934.42033         3995.90127

                                        F =    38125.55775       Signif F =   .0000

------------------ Variables in the Equation ------------------

Variable                B          SE B        Beta          T   Sig T

INCSQ         2.41280E-06   4.4301E-08     .691370     54.463   .0000
INCOME            .076066      .003040     .317608     25.020   .0000
(Constant)    -312.971650    44.555543                 -7.024   .0000

End Block Number   1   All requested variables entered.
```

Exercises for Section 18.3

1. Suppose the variables Y, X, and Z are exactly related according to the equation

$$Y = 4.0 + 2.2X + 4.2Z$$

In a sample of data, the sample correlation coefficient between X and Z is .94. Suppose we make a specification error and estimate the model

$$Y_i = \beta_0 + \beta_1 x_i + e_i$$

a. Will we obtain an unbiased estimate of β_1? Explain.
b. Can we determine if the bias in part (a) will be positive or negative? Will we tend to overestimate or underestimate the true coefficient of X?
c. Suppose the sample mean of the variable Z is 10. What is the mean of the set of random error terms?

2. "In a multiple regression model, if the t statistic for an estimated coefficient is not significantly different from 0, the variable should be deleted from the model because we know that the population regression coefficient is 0." True or false? Explain.
3. "In a multiple regression model, if the t statistic for an estimated coefficient is significantly different from 0, we know that the population regression coefficient is nonzero." True or false? Explain.
4. "We can never be certain that our regression model correctly explains why the dependent variable changes." True or false? Explain.
5. Explain what happens to the properties of estimated regression coefficients if we omit an important explanatory variable.

6. Suppose the variables Y, X, and X^2 are exactly related according to the equation

$$Y = 2.0 + 1.2X + 2.5X^2$$

a. Plot this relationship.

b. Suppose we obtain a sample of data, and all the values of X are positive. We make a specification error and estimate the model

$$Y_i = \beta_0 + \beta_1 x_i + e_i$$

Discuss what the sample regression line will look like compared with the correct quadratic model.

c. What will happen if we use the estimated model to forecast values of Y?

18.4 ▪ Violations of Basic Assumption 3: Heteroscedasticity

The third basic assumption states that each of the error terms is a random variable selected from a distribution having the same variance σ_e^2. If the error terms all have the same variance, the errors are said to be *homoscedastic*. The word *homoscedastic* is derived from two Greek words that mean "having the same spread." If the error terms do not have equal variances, they are said to be *heteroscedastic*, from two Greek words meaning "having different spreads." In this section, we discuss the potential problems when this assumption fails to hold.

Basic Assumption 3

Each of the random variables $e_1, e_2, \ldots, e_n$ is a random variable selected from a distribution with finite variance σ_e^2. The variance σ_e^2 is the same for all values of the explanatory variables.

This assumption is violated if the dispersion of points about the true regression line varies with the magnitude of the explanatory variables. Figure 18.10 shows a situation where the errors are homoscedastic; that is, each of the probability distributions shown has the same variance, σ_e^2, regardless of the value of X.

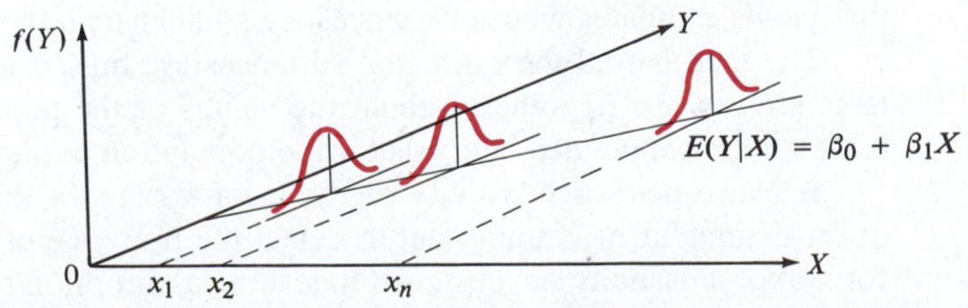

FIGURE 18.10
Population regression line with homoscedastic errors.

Figure 18.11 shows a population regression model in which the errors are heteroscedastic. In the figure, the mean of each distribution falls on the regression line, but the variance of the distributions increases as X increases. If the errors are heteroscedastic, each subpopulation of Y values associated with a different value of X will have a different variance. In economic and business data, variances frequently increase as the explanatory variables increase in magnitude, as illustrated in Figure 18.11.

FIGURE 18.11
Population regression line with heteroscedastic errors.

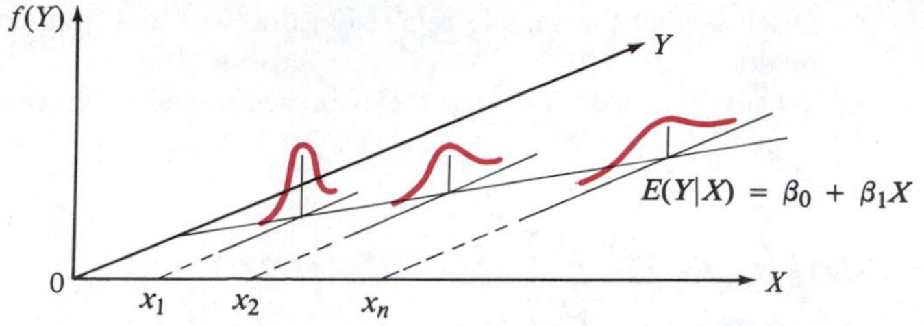

For example, suppose we have data on the annual income and annual consumption expenditures of individual families, and we formulate a model in which consumption expenditures are explained as a function of income. In this case, the assumption of homoscedasticity may not be very plausible because we would expect less variation in consumption for low-income families than for high-income families. At low incomes, the typical level of consumption is low and the variation about this level is relatively small. Consumption cannot fall too far below the average level, because this would mean near starvation for the family. In addition, consumption cannot rise too far above the average, because the family's assets and credit position would not allow it. These constraints are generally less binding for families with higher incomes. This argument implies that the consumption expenditures of families whose annual incomes are, say, \$10,000 per year are likely to be more highly concentrated than the consumption expenditures of families whose annual incomes are, say, \$80,000 per year. The appropriate model in this case would contain heteroscedastic error terms.

Consequences of Heteroscedasticity of Error Variances

If the errors do not have equal variances, the least-squares estimates $b_0, b_1, \ldots, b_K$ will still be unbiased estimates of the population parameters $\beta_0, \beta_1, \ldots, \beta_K$, but the estimates will not be efficient. In addition, the least-squares estimate of σ_e^2 and the estimates of the variances of the estimated coefficients b_i will be biased. If we know the nature of the heteroscedasticity, there exists an alternative linear unbiased estimator that yields estimates whose variances are smaller than the least-squares variances.

The fact that all the estimated variances are biased invalidates all the t tests and F tests used to test hypotheses about the values of the population parameters and invalidates all the confidence intervals for the population parameters.

Because heteroscedasticity of the error variances makes our tests and confidence intervals invalid, it is important to detect the presence of heteroscedasticity. Most tests for homoscedasticity are designed to test the assumption of equal error variances against some relatively simple alternative, such as the variance σ_i^2 of the ith error term e_i is related to the value of one of the independent variables, say, x_{ij}. For example, when trying to explain family consumption as a function of family income, it is reasonable to believe that the variance of the error terms increases as the independent variable of family income increases.

Detecting Heteroscedasticity of the Error Terms

Graphical Techniques. In some cases, plotting the residuals $\hat{e}_i$ against the values of the individual independent variables x_{ij} or against the predicted values $\hat{y}_i$ can be useful in detecting the presence of heteroscedasticity. For example, examine Figure 18.12, which shows a set of residuals $\hat{e}_i$ plotted against the values of an independent variable X. In the figure there does not appear to be any systematic relationship between the magnitudes of the residuals and the values of X. Thus the scatter diagram provides no evidence that the variances of the error terms are not constant. If the variances are all equal, the residuals should fall approximately within a rectangle, as illustrated in Figure 18.12.

FIGURE 18.12
Scatter diagram of (x_i, $\hat{e}_i$) showing homoscedastic residuals.

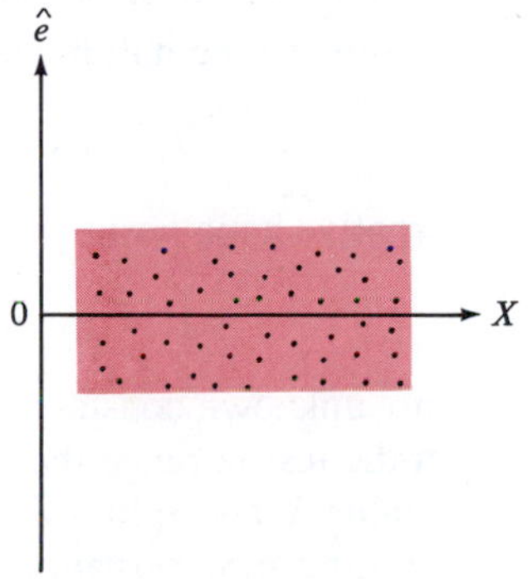

In Figure 18.13, the amount of variation in the residuals tends to increase with the values of X. This suggests that the variance of the error terms is related to the magnitude of the variable X. If the error variance is not constant for all values of X and if the variance increases as X increases, the residuals will tend to lie in a funnel, as illustrated in Figure 18.13.

FIGURE 18.13
Scatter diagrams of (x_i, $\hat{e}_i$) showing heteroscedastic residuals.

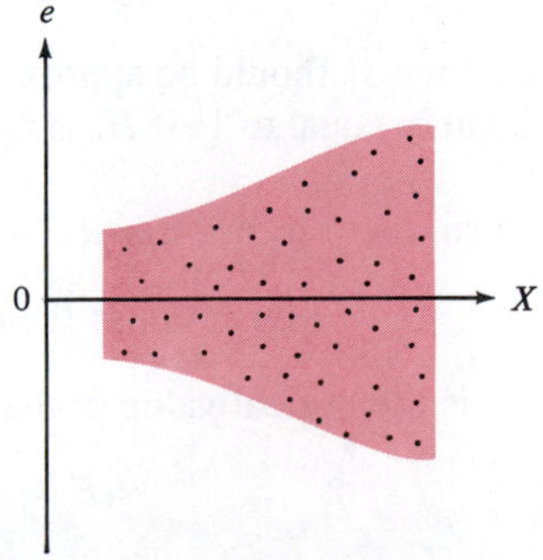

Except in relatively obvious situations, interpreting a scatter plot of residuals depends on subjective judgment. Next we consider a formal procedure for testing the null hypothesis that the errors are homoscedastic against the alternative hypothesis that the variance of the error term is related to the magnitude of one of the independent variables.

The Goldfeld–Quandt Test. The Goldfeld–Quandt test is designed to test the null hypothesis that errors are homoscedastic against the alternative hypothesis that the errors are not homoscedastic. It is used when the observations can be arranged in order of supposed increasing variance of the error terms. This can be done, for example, when we think that the variance is related to the values of some explanatory variable, say, x_{ij}. The null hypothesis is

$$H_0: \sigma_1^2 = \sigma_2^2 = \cdots = \sigma_n^2$$

where σ_i^2 is the variance of the ith error term. The test is described in the accompanying box.

Goldfeld–Quandt Test for Homoscedastic Errors

Suppose we wish to test the null hypothesis

$$H_0: \sigma_1^2 = \sigma_2^2 = \cdots = \sigma_n^2$$

against the alternative hypothesis

$$H_1: \text{Var}(e_i) = \sigma^2 x_{ij}^2$$

where σ^2 is some unknown constant. Let the level of significance of the test be α.

To perform the test, arrange the sample observations according to the magnitudes of the variable X_j and split the sample of observations into three subsamples containing n_1, p, and n_2 observations. Let n_1 denote the number of observations in the first subsample, p the number of observations in the second subsample, and n_2 the number of observations in the third subsample. Typically $n_1 = n_2$ and p is much smaller. The middle set of p observations is omitted from the analysis.

Estimate the proposed regression model twice. In one equation, use only the first n_1 observations; in the other equation, use only the last n_2 observations. Denote the estimated variance from the first regression equation as s_1^2 and that from the second regression equation as s_2^2. Calculate the F statistic

$$F = s_2^2/s_1^2$$

If H_0 is true, then s_2^2 should be approximately equal to s_1^2 and the ratio s_2^2/s_1^2 should be approximately equal to 1. If H_0 is false, the F should be large because s_2^2 should exceed s_1^2.

To perform the test, use the decision rule

$$\text{Reject } H_0 \text{ in favor of } H_1 \text{ if } F > F_{\alpha,\nu_1,\nu_2}$$

where F_{α,ν_1,ν_2} is the critical value of the F distribution such that

$$P(F > F_{\alpha,\nu_1,\nu_2}) = \alpha$$

When H_0 is true, the F statistic follows the F distribution with numerator degrees of freedom $\nu_1 = (n_1 - K - 1)$ and denominator degrees of freedom $\nu_2 = (n_2 - K - 1)$, where K denotes the number of explanatory variables in the model not counting the constant term.

The reason for omitting a set of observations from the middle of the sample is to make the variances in the two remaining subsamples more disparate. The best number of observations to omit is not clear. The power of the test is increased by increasing the difference between the "small" variances and the "large" variances, but at the same time the power is reduced because fewer observations are used in performing the test. Based on experiments, Goldfeld and Quandt recommend dropping about one-sixth of the observations. The arbitrariness in choosing p, the number of observations to be omitted, represents a rather unsatisfactory aspect to the test, because it might be possible for a statistician to tailor the results of the test to agree with his or her wishes by a clever choice of p.

Example 18.3

Testing for Heteroscedasticity of the Error Variances: The data in Table 18.2 show the annual incomes and the years of education for a sample of 28 adult males who work for a certain company and have the same number of years of seniority. Figure 18.14 shows a scatter diagram of the data. The scatter diagram shows that the dispersion of annual income tends to increase as the years of education increase. Thus, it is reasonable to suspect that the errors are heteroscedastic.

TABLE 18.2
Data on annual income and years of education for Example 18.3

Years of Education	Number of Individuals	Annual Income (in thousands of dollars)
8	6	14, 16, 18, 20, 22, 24
12	6	20, 24, 28, 32, 36, 40
14	4	22, 28, 38, 50
16	6	24, 30, 38, 42, 50, 56
18	6	26, 34, 44, 52, 56, 64

The hypothesized relationship between income (Y) and years of education (X) is

$$Y_i = \beta_0 + \beta_1 x_i + e_i$$

Let us estimate the population regression equation and perform the Goldfeld–Quandt test for heteroscedasticity.

Solution: The SPSSX computer output from estimating this model is given in Figure 18.15. The sample regression equation using all 28 observations is

$$\hat{y}_i = -2.333 + 2.667x_i \qquad R^2 = .499$$
$$t \text{ statistics:} \quad (-.32) \qquad (5.09)$$

If the errors are heteroscedastic, the estimated standard errors, the t statistics, and the prob-values shown in the computer output are all invalid.

FIGURE 18.14 **SPSSX-generated scatter diagram showing income versus years of education.**

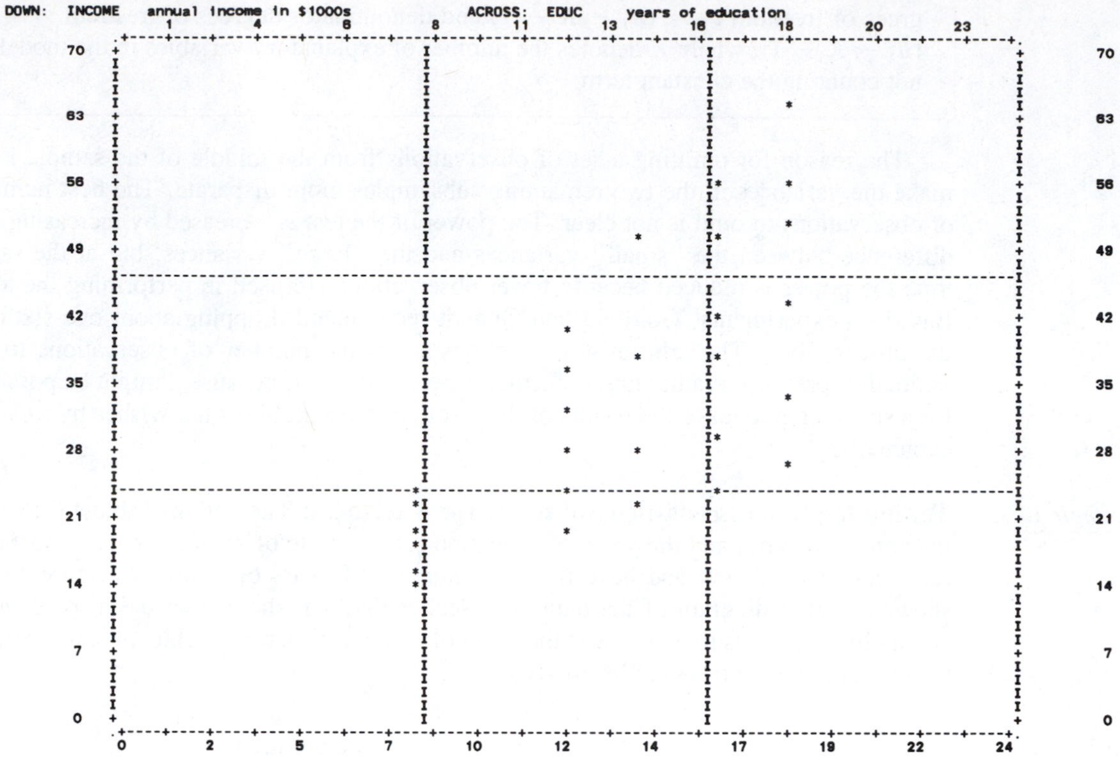

FIGURE 18.15 **SPSSX-generated output for Example 18.3, explaining income as a function of years of education.**

```
                          * * * *   M U L T I P L E   R E G R E S S I O N   * * * *

Listwise Deletion of Missing Data

Equation Number 1    Dependent Variable..   INCOME   annual income in $1000s

Beginning Block Number  1.  Method:  Enter      EDUC

Variable(s) Entered on Step Number  1..    EDUC      years of education

Multiple R             .70651         Analysis of Variance
R Square               .49915                           DF       Sum of Squares      Mean Square
Adjusted R Square      .47989         Regression         1           2523.42857       2523.42857
Standard Error        9.86836         Residual          26           2532.00000         97.38462

                                      F =       25.91198       Signif F =  .0000

------------------ Variables in the Equation ------------------

Variable                B          SE B        Beta          T  Sig T

EDUC             2.666667      .523864     .706507      5.090  .0000
(Constant)      -2.333333     7.350113                 -0.317  .7534

End Block Number   1   All requested variables entered.
```

Figure 18.16 shows a computer-generated scatter diagram of the residuals $\hat{e}_i$ plotted against the values of the explanatory variable X. (In the graph, the residuals and the values of X have all been standardized by subtracting the mean and dividing by the standard deviation.) Note how the residuals tend to have more dispersion for large values of X than for small values of X. This provides evidence supporting the hypothesis that the errors are heteroscedastic.

FIGURE 18.16 **SPSSX-generated scatter diagram showing $(x_i, \hat{e}_i)$ for Example 18.3.**

```
                                        * * * *   M U L T I P L E   R E G R E S S I O N   * * * *

Equation Number 1    Dependent Variable..   INCOME   annual income in $1000s

Residuals Statistics:

                  Min           Max      Mean   Std Dev    N

*PRED         19.0000       45.6667   33.8571    9.6675   28
*RESID       -19.6667       18.3333     .0000    9.6839   28
*ZPRED        -1.5368        1.2216     .0000    1.0000   28
*ZRESID       -1.9929        1.8578     .0000     .9813   28

Total Cases =      28

                                        * * * * * * * * * * * * * * * * * * * * * * * * * * * * *
```

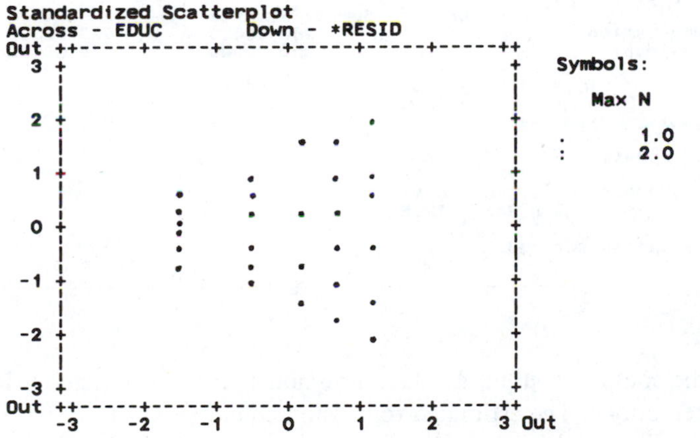

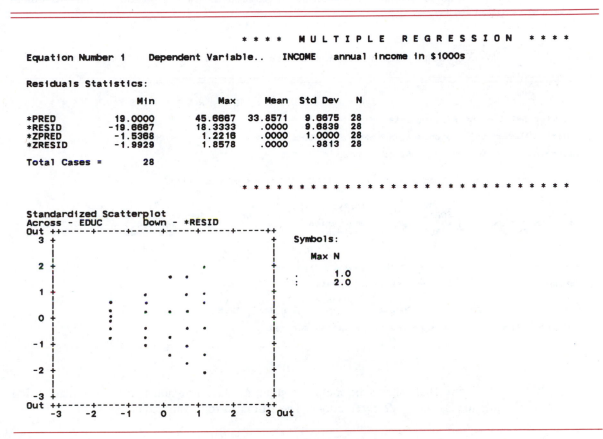

Let us use the Goldfeld–Quandt test to test the null hypothesis

$$H_0\colon \sigma_1^2 = \sigma_2^2 = \cdots = \sigma_n^2$$

against the alternative hypothesis that the variances increase as X increases. As suggested by the Goldfeld–Quandt test, the data have been placed in ascending order according to the magnitude of X. Suppose we let $p = 4$ and discard the middle 4 observations, corresponding to individuals with 14 years of education. We use the first $n_1 = 12$ observations to estimate the regression equation and then repeat the process using the last $n_2 = 12$ observations.

Figure 18.17 shows the SPSSX computer output for the regression equation estimated by using the first $n_1 = 12$ observations. The estimated regression equation is

$$\hat{y}_i = -3.000 + 2.750x_i \qquad R^2 = .509$$
$$t \text{ statistics:} \quad (-.35) \qquad (3.22)$$

To perform the Goldfeld–Quandt test, we need the value s_1^2 (s_e^2). This value, listed in the computer output as the residual mean square, is 35.00. Alternatively, recall that s_1^2 is the square of the estimated standard error of the regression. The computer output lists the estimated standard error of the regression as $s_1 = 5.91608$. Thus, we obtain $s_1^2 = 35.00$.

FIGURE 18.17 **SPSSX-generated regression output using first $n_1 = 12$ observations from Example 18.3.**

```
                          * * * *   M U L T I P L E   R E G R E S S I O N   * * * *

Listwise Deletion of Missing Data

Equation Number 1    Dependent Variable..   INCOME    annual income in $1000s

Beginning Block Number  1.  Method:  Enter      EDUC

Variable(s) Entered on Step Number  1..    EDUC        years of education

Multiple R              .71352          Analysis of Variance
R Square                .50912                             DF       Sum of Squares       Mean Square
Adjusted R Square       .46003          Regression          1           363.00000         363.00000
Standard Error         5.91608          Residual           10           350.00000          35.00000

                                        F =        10.37143       Signif F =  .0092

------------------ Variables in the Equation ------------------

Variable                  B          SE B         Beta          T  Sig T

EDUC               2.750000       .853913      .713524      3.220  .0092
(Constant)        -3.000000      8.708234                  -0.345  .7376

End Block Number   1   All requested variables entered.
```

Figure 18.18 shows the computer output for the regression equation estimated using only the last $n_2 = 12$ observations. The estimated regression equation is:

$$\hat{y}_i = -8.000 + 3.000x_i \qquad R^2 = .059$$
$$t \text{ statistics:} \quad (-.12) \qquad (.79)$$

and s_2^2 has the value 172.80.

To apply the Goldfeld–Quandt test, calculate the ratio

$$F = s_2^2/s_1^2 = 172.80/35.00 = 4.937$$

If the null hypothesis of homoscedasticity is true, this F value follows the F distribution with numerator degrees of freedom $\nu_1 = (n_1 - K - 1) = 10$ and denominator degrees of freedom $\nu_2 = (n_2 - K - 1) = 10$. Suppose we wish to test the null hypothesis that the errors are homoscedastic using level of significance $\alpha = .01$. The critical value of

FIGURE 18.18 **SPSSX-generated regression output using last $n_2 = 12$ observations from Example 18.3.**

```
                                  * * * *   M U L T I P L E   R E G R E S S I O N   * * * *

Listwise Deletion of Missing Data

Equation Number 1    Dependent Variable..   INCOME   annual income in $1000s

Beginning Block Number  1.  Method:  Enter      EDUC

Variable(s) Entered on Step Number  1..    EDUC      years of education

Multiple R            .24254          Analysis of Variance
R Square              .05882                                 DF      Sum of Squares      Mean Square
Adjusted R Square   -0.03529          Regression              1           108.00000        108.00000
Standard Error      13.14534          Residual               10          1728.00000        172.80000

                                      F =          .62500        Signif F =   .4475

------------------ Variables in the Equation ------------------

Variable                B          SE B        Beta          T  Sig T

EDUC             3.000000      3.794733     .242536       .791  .4475
(Constant)      -8.000000     64.621978                 -0.124  .9039

End Block Number   1   All requested variables entered.
```

the F statistic is $F_{.01,10,10} = 4.85$. Because the actual F statistic, 4.937, exceeds the critical value, we would reject the null hypothesis that the errors are homoscedastic.

Because we have multiple observations of Y for each given value of X, there is yet another way to show that the errors are homoscedastic. There are six individuals who have $X = 8$ years of education. For these six individuals, the sample variance of Y associated with $X = 8$ is $s^2 = 14$. Similarly, for the individuals with 12 years of education, the sample variance is $s^2 = 56$. The sample variance for the six values of Y associated with $X = 16$ is $s^2 = 144$, and the sample variance for the six values of Y associated with $X = 18$ is $s^2 = 201.6$. Observe that the sample variance of incomes for individuals with 18 years of education is more than 10 times greater than the sample variance of incomes for individuals who have only 8 years. Thus we see that income depends on years of education, and we also see that the amount of variation in income increases as the level of education increases. ■

Correcting for Heteroscedasticity of Error Terms Using Weighted Least Squares

When tests indicate that the error terms have unequal variances, estimating the regression coefficients by the method of least squares may not be the most appropriate procedure. In order to get (1) efficient estimates of the coefficients, (2) unbiased estimates of the variances of the estimated coefficients, and (3) valid t tests and confidence intervals, it is necessary to take into account the fact that the error terms have unequal variances. An alternative estimation procedure called *weighted least squares,* denoted WLS, can be used for this purpose.

The difficulty with the method of weighted least squares is that the values of σ_i^2 up to a factor of proportionality must be known. In most cases, these values will not be known and the weighted-least-squares method will not be feasible. Instead we must estimate the variances σ_i^2 from the sample and estimate the regression coefficients by using what is called *feasible weighted least squares.*

Weighted-Least-Squares Method of Regression

Suppose that the error terms are not homoscedastic and that, in fact, the variances of the error terms are directly proportional to the squared value of some variable Z; that is,

$$\sigma_i^2 \propto z_i^2 \quad \text{for } i = 1, 2, \ldots, n$$

where the values z_i are known. The variable Z may or may not be one of the independent variables in the regression equation. When the variances of the error terms follow this particular relationship, the weighted-least-squares estimation procedure will yield the best linear unbiased estimates of the population regression coefficients $\beta_0, \beta_1, \ldots, \beta_K$.

To obtain the weighted-least-squares estimates of the population regression coefficients, rather than estimating the equation

$$Y_i = \beta_0 + \beta_1 x_{i1} + \beta_2 x_{i2} + \cdots + \beta_K x_{iK} + e_i$$

we estimate the regression equation

$$Y_i/z_i = \beta_0(1/z_i) + \beta_1(x_{i1}/z_i) + \beta_2(x_{i2}/z_i) + \cdots + \beta_K(x_{iK}/z_i) + u_i$$

and the error term $u_i = e_i/z_i$ will have a constant variance.

In the weighted-least-squares regression model, the dependent variable is Y_i/z_i rather than Y_i. The values of the independent variables are $1/z_i, x_{i1}/z_i, x_{i2}/z_i, \ldots, x_{iK}/z_i$ rather than $1, x_{i1}, x_{i2}, \ldots, x_{iK}$. (Unless Z is one of the explanatory variables X_j, there is no intercept term in the weighted-least-squares model, while if $Z = X_K$, say, then the coefficient β_K will appear to be the constant term.) The coefficients in the weighted-least-squares model are estimated by applying the method of least squares to the transformed data. The resulting estimates $b_0, b_1, \ldots, b_K$ are the best linear unbiased estimates of the parameters $\beta_0, \beta_1, \ldots, \beta_K$, and the corresponding estimated variances are unbiased estimates of the true variances. In addition, the t tests, prob-values, and confidence intervals will be theoretically valid.

Example 18.4

Estimation by the Method of Weighted Least Squares: Example 18.3 contained data showing the years of education and annual incomes of 28 individuals. Based on the Goldfeld–Quandt test, we rejected the null hypothesis that the errors are homoscedastic.

Suppose the variances of the error terms follow the equation

$$\sigma_i^2 = \sigma^2 x_i^2 \quad \text{for } i = 1, 2, \ldots, n$$

To obtain efficient estimates of the regression coefficients, apply the method of weighted least squares. Transform the original model

$$Y_i = \beta_0 + \beta_1 x_i + e_i$$

to the weighted-least-squares model

$$Y_i/x_i = \beta_0(1/x_i) + \beta_1(x_i/x_i) + u_i$$

or

$$Y_i/x_i = \beta_0(1/x_i) + \beta_1 + u_i$$

where $u_i = e_i/x_i$. The SPSSX computer output is shown in Figure 18.19, where the dependent variable INVINC is Y_i/x_i and the explanatory variable INVEDUCT represents the inverse of the education variable (i.e., INVEDUCT $= 1/x_i$). The estimated equation is

$$\hat{y}_i/x_i = -2.263(1/x_i) + 2.661 \qquad R^2 = .008$$
$$t \text{ statistics:} \quad (-.46) \qquad\qquad (6.44)$$

FIGURE 18.19 **SPSSX-generated regression output for feasible weighted least squares.**

```
                                   * * * *   M U L T I P L E   R E G R E S S I O N   * * * *

Listwise Deletion of Missing Data

Equation Number 1    Dependent Variable..   INVINC

Beginning Block Number  1.  Method:  Enter      INVEDUC

Variable(s) Entered on Step Number  1..    INVEDUC

Multiple R            .08990      Analysis of Variance
R Square              .00808                           DF      Sum of Squares        Mean Square
Adjusted R Square   -0.03007      Regression            1              .09189             .09189
Standard Error        .65859      Residual             26            11.27713             .43374

                                  F =        .21185       Signif F =   .6491

------------------ Variables in the Equation ------------------

Variable                 B         SE B       Beta          T  Sig T

INVEDUC          -2.263625     4.918022  -0.089901     -0.460  .6491
(Constant)        2.661434      .413336                 6.439  .0000

End Block Number   1   All requested variables entered.
```

Multiply both sides of this equation by x_i to obtain the WLS model

$$\hat{y}_i = -2.263 + 2.661x_i$$

Now let us compare the estimated coefficients and the estimated standard deviations for the two models:

Model	b_0	s_{b_0}	b_1	s_{b_1}
Least squares	−2.333	7.350	2.667	0.524
Weighted least squares	−2.263	4.918	2.661	0.413

The WLS estimated coefficients are slightly different from the least-squares estimated coefficients, and the WLS standard deviations are smaller than the least-squares standard deviations. The WLS standard deviations are theoretically valid (assuming that the variance structure follows the assumptions made earlier) and lead to valid t tests and confidence intervals, while the least-squares standard deviations are not theoretically valid.

For the WLS model, the value $R^2 = .00808$ is quite small, but this does not necessarily mean that the model is of no use. Recall that we are trying to explain values of Y_i, not Y_i/x_i. To measure goodness of fit, it is not appropriate to examine the residuals from the model containing Y_i/x_i as the dependent variable. Instead, substitute the estimated coefficients from the WLS model back into the original (untransformed) model and calculate the residuals. Then calculate R^2 using the relationship $R^2 = (1 - \text{SSE/SST})$. ■

Heteroscedasticity of the Dependent Variable

Another form of heteroscedasticity has been proposed called *dependent-variable heteroscedasticity.* This involves the assumption that the variance of the error term is proportional to the squared mean of Y_i. That is, we assume

$$\sigma_i^2 = \sigma^2[E(Y_i)]^2 = \sigma^2(\beta_0 + \beta_1 x_i)^2$$

To obtain the feasible weighted-least-squares estimates, we follow a two-step procedure. First, we estimate the equation

$$Y_i = \beta_0 + \beta_1 x_i + e_i$$

by the method of least squares to obtain the fitted values $\hat{y}_i$. Then we transform the data to obtain the weighted-least-squares model

$$Y_i/\hat{y}_i = \beta_0(1/\hat{y}_i) + \beta_1(x_i/\hat{y}_i) + u_i$$

where $u_i = e_i/\hat{y}_i$. The estimated coefficients from this model are not the optimal weighted-least-squares estimates, because we have used the estimated weights $\hat{y}_i$ rather than the correct weights $(\beta_0 + \beta_1 x_i)$, which are unknown.

Exercises for Section 18.4

1. A doctor estimated a linear regression model to explain the relation between the concentration of a drug in plasma (Y) and the dosage of the drug in grams (X) given to the patient. The residuals and the dosages are as follows:

Dosage	1	2	3	4	5	6	7	8	9
X	0.15	0.64	0.81	0.23	0.77	0.98	0.48	0.83	0.99
$\hat{e}$	0.50	2.10	−3.40	0.30	−1.70	4.20	−0.60	2.60	−4.00

Plot the residuals $\hat{e}$ against X. What conclusions do you draw from the plot?

2. The following data show the number of students in 12 different sections of a computer class (X) and the weekly cost of computer time for the class in dollars (Y):

Section	1	2	3	4	5	6	7	8	9	10	11	12
X	16	14	22	10	14	17	10	13	19	12	18	11
Y	77	70	85	50	62	70	52	63	88	57	81	54

a. Fit a linear regression function by ordinary least squares.
b. Obtain the residuals and prepare a plot of the residuals against X. What does the residual plot suggest?
c. Assume that $\sigma_i^2 = kx_i^2$ and use weighted least squares to fit the linear regression function. Are the regression coefficients similar to those obtained in part (a) with ordinary least squares? How do the standard deviations of the regression coefficients compare?
d. What transformation of the variables was used?

18.5 ▪ Violations of Basic Assumption 4: Serial Correlation

The fourth basic assumption of the multiple regression model states that the error terms are independent of one another (or are uncorrelated with one another). If the error terms are not independent of one another, they are said to be *serially correlated* or *autocorrelated*. In this section, we discuss the problems that arise when this basic assumption fails to hold.

Basic Assumption 4

Let e_i and e_j be the random error terms associated with the random variables Y_i and Y_j. The error terms e_i and e_j are assumed to be independent of one another. We have $E(e_ie_j) = 0$ for $i \neq j$.

The problem of serially correlated error terms arises when we are studying *time series* data. For example, data concerning annual savings and annual income for one family for 10 consecutive years are time series data. Data from 15 different families concerning their savings and their income in one specific year are cross section data. A third possibility exists. Suppose we obtain data concerning savings and income for each of the 15 families for a period of 10 years. Then we have a study involving *pooled* time series and cross section data. Such a data set is called *panel data*.

Definition: Time Series and Cross Section Data

Time series data refer to observations that can be ordered chronologically. **Cross section** data refer to observations concerning many different individuals at one point in time.

With time series data, the order in which the observations are made is important. To emphasize that the data are time series data, it is customary to use the subscript t rather than i to denote different observations. Thus, y_t denotes the observed value of the random variable Y during time period t, y_{t-1} denotes the observed value of Y during period $(t - 1)$, and so forth. Serially correlated errors can occur in time series studies because random events that influence Y in period $(t - 1)$ can have lingering effects that influence Y in the following period t. If this is the case, we say that the random disturbances e_{t-1} and e_t are serially correlated.

With cross section data, the ordering of the observations is irrelevant and there is little reason to expect that the random errors associated with different observations are correlated. Thus, serially correlated errors is not a concern when the model involves cross section data.

With time series data, however, successive errors often tend to be positively correlated. That is, positive errors tend to be followed by positive errors, and negative errors tend to be followed by negative errors, because random events that cause positive errors in one period have lasting effects that also cause positive errors in the next period. In time series models, serially correlated errors can arise because an important explanatory variable has been omitted from the model.

The error term represents a summary of a large number of random factors that enter the relationship under study but are not measurable or have been omitted from the model for some reason. In a time series model, it would be reasonable to suspect that the effect of these factors in one period carries over somewhat to the following periods.

In general, the shorter the period between observations, the greater the likelihood of serially correlated error terms. Thus we would be more likely to find serial correlation in a model dealing with monthly or quarterly observations than in a model dealing with annual observations.

Consequences of Serially Correlated Data

The following are some of the problems caused by the presence of serially correlated errors:

1. The sample regression coefficients $b_0, b_1, \ldots, b_K$ are unbiased estimates of the population parameters $\beta_0, \beta_1, \ldots, \beta_K$, but the estimates are not efficient. That is, if the nature of the serial correlation is known, there is another estimation technique that results in unbiased estimators having smaller variances.

2. The least-squares estimate of σ_e^2 is biased. Typically, if the error terms are positively correlated, the true variance will be underestimated.

3. The estimated variances of the sample regression coefficients are biased. Typically, if the errors are positively correlated, the true variances will be underestimated.

4. Because the estimated variances are biased, the tests of hypotheses involving the t and F distributions and the confidence intervals for the population parameters are invalid. The t statistics do not follow the t distribution, and the associated prob-values will be incorrect.

When estimating any model using time series data, it is important to test whether the errors are serially correlated. The presence of serially correlated errors can indicate that something systematic has been omitted from the model, that an incorrect functional form has been estimated, or that an important explanatory variable has been omitted.

Generation of Serially Correlated Errors

When all the basic assumptions hold, each error term represents an independent random drawing from a normal distribution having 0 mean and variance σ_e^2. When the error terms are serially correlated, the drawings are no longer independent. In this case, it is necessary to postulate an alternative hypothesis concerning the generation of the error terms.

From basic assumption 2, we have

$$E(e_i) = 0 \quad i = 1, 2, \ldots, n$$

so we can write the covariance between e_i and e_j as

$$\begin{aligned} \text{Cov}(e_i, e_j) &= E\{[e_i - E(e_i)][e_j - E(e_j)]\} \\ &= E(e_i e_j) \end{aligned}$$

The null hypothesis that the errors are not serially correlated implies that

$$\text{Cov}(e_i, e_j) = E(e_i e_j) = 0 \quad \text{for } i \neq j$$

By far, the most frequently postulated alternative hypothesis states that the error terms follow what is known as a *first-order autoregressive scheme,* which is described in the accompanying box.

Definition: First-Order Autoregressive Scheme

Suppose the error term e_t is generated according to the equation

$$e_t = \rho e_{t-1} + u_t$$

where u_t is a random variable having a normal distribution with mean 0 and variance σ_u^2. It is assumed that all the random variables u_t and u_s are independent of one another for $t \neq s$. In addition, it is assumed that $-1 < \rho < 1$. Then the random variable e_t is said to follow a **first-order autoregressive scheme**.

If e_t follows a first-order autoregressive scheme, each error term e_t is equal to a proportion ρ of the preceding error term plus a new random effect represented by u_t. The amount ρe_{t-1} measures the amount of the previous error term that is carried over to the current period, while u_t represents new error effects created during the current period. The coefficient ρ is called the *population correlation coefficient* between e_t and e_{t-1}.

By a successive substitution for $e_{t-1}, e_{t-2}, \ldots, e_1$, we obtain

$$\begin{aligned} e_t &= \rho e_{t-1} + u_t \\ &= \rho(\rho e_{t-2} + u_{t-1}) + u_t \\ &= \rho^2 e_{t-2} + \rho u_{t-1} + u_t \\ &= \rho^2(\rho e_{t-3} + u_{t-2}) + \rho u_{t-1} + u_t \\ &= \rho^3 e_{t-3} + \rho^2 u_{t-2} + \rho u_{t-1} + u_t \\ &\;\;\vdots \\ &= \rho^{t-1} e_1 + \rho^{t-2} u_2 + \cdots + \rho^2 u_{t-2} + \rho u_{t-1} + u_t \end{aligned}$$

Thus, each error term e_t is generated as a function of the random effects $u_2, u_3, \ldots, u_t$ and the initial error term e_1. To make the description of the autoregressive process complete, it is assumed that

$$e_1 = \frac{u_1}{\sqrt{1 - \rho^2}}$$

Thus, e_1 is normally distributed with mean 0 and variance $\sigma_u^2/(1 - \rho^2)$. This form for e_1 greatly simplifies certain derivations in the regression model. The variance of e_t is described in the accompanying box.

Variance of e_t in a First-Order Autoregressive Scheme

If e_t follows the first-order autoregressive scheme, the variance of e_t is given by

$$\sigma_e^2 = \text{Var}(e_t) = \sigma_u^2/(1 - \rho^2)$$

for $t = 1, 2, \ldots$. (For a more detailed discussion, see John Johnston, *Econometric Methods* [New York: McGraw-Hill, 1972].)

In addition, it can be shown that the covariance between e_t and e_{t-1} is

$$E(e_t e_{t-1}) = \rho\sigma_e^2$$

In general, the covariance between e_t and e_{t-s} is

$$E(e_t e_{t-s}) = \rho^s\sigma_e^2$$

The correlation between e_t and e_{t-1} is ρ, while the correlation between e_t and e_{t-s} is ρ^s. The parameter ρ measures the degree of correlation between the two random variables e_t and e_{t-1}. If ρ is close to 1 in absolute value, there is a high degree of relationship between e_t and e_{t-1}, and the effect of the error term e_{t-1} will linger for many periods and take a long time to die out. When ρ is positive, there is a tendency for positive error terms to follow positive error terms and negative error terms to follow negative error terms. When ρ is negative, there is a tendency for the sign to change for successive error terms, so that positive error terms tend to follow negative error terms and vice versa.

When $\rho = 0$, we have

$$e_t = u_t$$
$$\text{Var}(e_t) = \sigma_e^2 = \sigma_u^2$$

If $\rho = 0$, all the basic assumptions about the error terms hold because the random variables u_t are normally and independently distributed with 0 mean and constant variance.

Detecting Serial Correlation of Error Terms

Graphical Techniques. The discussion of the first-order autoregressive scheme indicated that successive error terms tend to have the same sign when ρ is positive and opposite signs when ρ is negative. When $\rho = 0$, there is no pattern in the behavior of successive values of e_t, because successive values of e_t are independent of one another.

To get some information about the process that generated the error terms, we have to rely on the residuals $\hat{e}_t$ because the true error terms are unknown.

To detect serially correlated errors, it is useful to plot the residuals against time. If the errors are uncorrelated, the residuals should be randomly scattered about 0. If they are positively correlated (as is frequently the case), there should be a tendency for positive residuals to follow positive residuals, and negative residuals to follow negative residuals. Thus, a plot would tend to exhibit a wavelike pattern. If the errors are negatively correlated (a much less frequent occurrence), negative residuals should tend to follow positive residuals and vice versa, giving the plot a very choppy appearance.

Figure 18.20 shows two different plots of residuals versus time. In these two plots, the residuals are positively correlated, indicating the presence of positive serial correlation among the error terms. If the residuals look like those in plot 1, an appropriate equation to estimate would be $Y_t = \beta_0 + \beta_1 x_t + \beta_2 x_t^2 + e_t$, where $\beta_2 > 0$. If the residuals look like those in plot 2, the same quadratic equation should be estimated, and we would expect to find $\beta_2 < 0$.

FIGURE 18.20
Residual plots showing positive serial correlation.

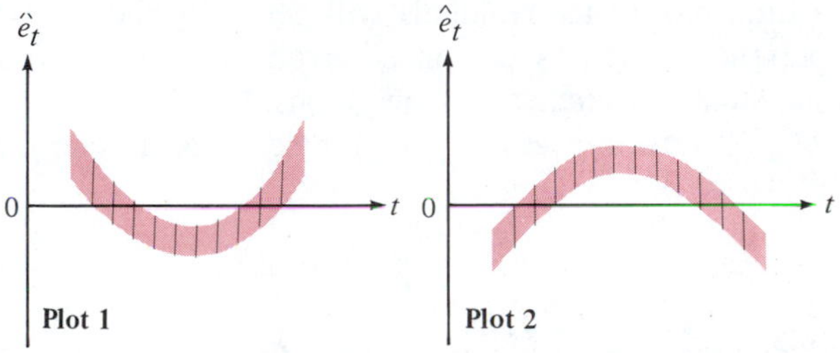

Figure 18.21 shows a typical series of noncorrelated residuals $\hat{e}_t$ plotted against time. There is no systematic pattern in this time series. In contrast, Figure 18.22 shows residuals with strong positive serial correlation. Positive residuals tend to be followed by positive residuals and negative residuals by negative residuals.

If there is strong negative serial correlation, positive residuals tend to be followed by negative residuals and negative residuals by positive residuals. If $\rho < 0$, there will be many more changes of sign between successive residuals than when the error terms are not autocorrelated.

FIGURE 18.21
Residual plot showing no serial correlation.

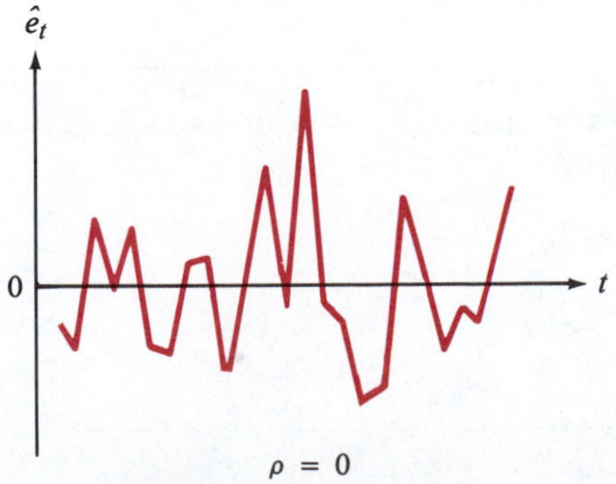

FIGURE 18.22 **Residual plots showing strong positive serial correlation.**

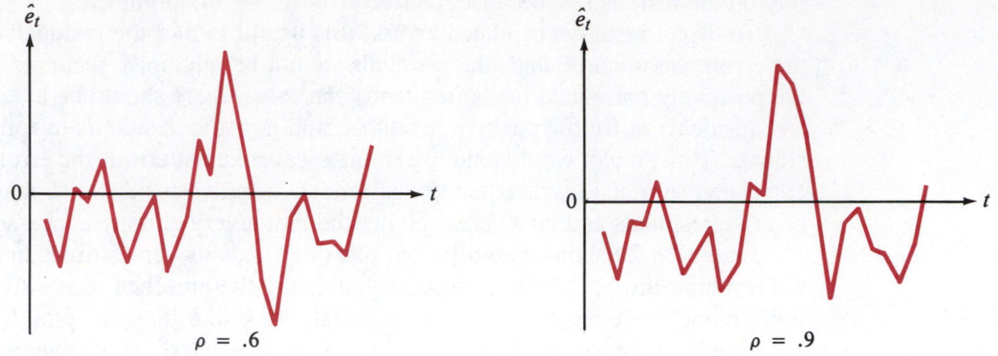

Graphing the residuals is a useful way to detect glaring errors in a model. For example, if we estimate a straight line when the data really follow a quadratic equation, a time plot of the residuals will generally indicate this. In many cases, however, the presence of serially correlated errors is not so obvious and we have to rely on various statistical tests rather than on graphs.

We now discuss how to estimate the parameter ρ and how to test the null hypothesis H_0: $\rho = 0$.

Estimation of ρ

Suppose we think that the error terms follow the first-order autoregressive scheme

$$e_t = \rho e_{t-1} + u_t$$

We want to test the null hypothesis

$$H_0: \rho = 0$$

against the one of possible alternative hypotheses

$$H_1: \rho \neq 0, \quad H_1: \rho > 0, \quad \text{or} \quad H_1: \rho < 0$$

There are several ways to estimate the parameter ρ and several tests to test H_0.

One estimator of ρ is defined in the accompanying box.

Estimator for ρ

The estimated value of ρ, denoted $\hat{\rho}$, is defined by the equation

$$\hat{\rho} = \frac{\sum_{t=2}^{n} \hat{e}_t \hat{e}_{t-1}}{\sum_{t=2}^{n} \hat{e}_{t-1}^2}$$

There are two popular tests for testing H_0 against H_1. For lack of a better name, we will call one test the *asymptotic test,* because the test is valid asymptotically, that is, when the sample size gets very large. The other test is called the *Durbin–Watson test* in honor of the two men, James Durbin and Geoffrey Watson, who developed it.

Testing for Serial Correlation

The Asymptotic Test. To test H_0: $\rho = 0$ against, say, H_1: $\rho > 0$, we use the fact that if H_0 is true and *the sample size is large,* $\hat{\rho}$ is approximately normally distributed with mean 0 and variance $1/n$, where n denotes the sample size. Thus, as the sample size increases, the sampling distribution of the standardized test statistic

$$Z = \hat{\rho}/\sqrt{1/n} = \sqrt{n}\hat{\rho}$$

approaches the standard normal distribution.

The Asymptotic Test

Suppose we wish to test the null hypothesis

$$H_0\text{: } \rho = 0$$

against the one-sided alternative hypothesis

$$H_1\text{: } \rho > 0$$

using a level of significance α. Calculate the test statistic

$$z = \hat{\rho}/\sqrt{1/n} = \sqrt{n}\hat{\rho}$$

and use the decision rule

$$\text{Reject } H_0 \text{ in favor of } H_1 \text{ if } z > z_\alpha$$

To test H_0 against H_1: $\rho < 0$, use the decision rule

$$\text{Reject } H_0 \text{ in favor of } H_1 \text{ if } z < -z_\alpha$$

To test H_0 against H_1: $\rho \neq 0$, use the decision rule

$$\text{Reject } H_0 \text{ in favor of } H_1 \text{ if } z < -z_{\alpha/2} \text{ or if } z > z_{\alpha/2}$$

The Durbin–Watson Test. The test that is used most often to test for the presence of serially correlated error terms is called the **Durbin–Watson test**. Most computer programs will compute the Durbin–Watson test statistic d, which is defined as follows:

$$d = \frac{\sum_{t=2}^{n}(\hat{e}_t - \hat{e}_{t-1})^2}{\sum_{t=1}^{n}\hat{e}_t^2}$$

If we expand the numerator, we obtain

$$d = \frac{\sum_{t=2}^{n} \hat{e}_t^2 - 2\sum_{t=2}^{n} \hat{e}_t\hat{e}_{t-1} + \sum_{t=2}^{n} \hat{e}_{t-1}^2}{\sum_{t=1}^{n} \hat{e}_t^2}$$

We then obtain the approximate relationship

$$d \approx 2 - 2\hat{\rho}$$

Thus, the following approximate relations hold:

- If $\hat{\rho} \approx 1$, then $d \approx 0$.
- If $\hat{\rho} \approx 0$, then $d \approx 2$.
- If $\hat{\rho} \approx -1$, then $d \approx 4$.

The value of d must lie between 0 and 4, with values of d near 2 supporting the null hypothesis of no serial correlation, values near 0 indicating positive serial correlation, and values near 4 indicating negative serial correlation.

The test statistic d is a random variable whose value varies from sample to sample. The sampling distribution of d is quite complicated and depends on the values assumed by the explanatory variables. As a result, the sampling distribution of d changes from one problem to another, and no single distribution can be tabulated to provide critical values. However, Durbin and Watson found bounds that hold for all data sets, and these bounds have been tabulated.

To test for positive serial correlation, the critical region falls in the left tail of the d distribution. Let d_α denote the critical value d_α such that the probability of obtaining a d statistic less than d_α is equal to the level of significance α. That is,

$$P(d < d_\alpha) = \alpha$$

Our decision rule is

$$\text{Reject } H_0\text{: } \rho = 0 \text{ in favor of } H_1\text{: } \rho > 0 \text{ if } d < d_\alpha$$

For a given value α, the critical value d_α is unknown, but Durbin and Watson found that this critical value must lie between two values called the *lower bound* $d_{\alpha,L}$ and the *upper bound* $d_{\alpha,U}$. Thus we have, for a given level of significance α,

$$d_{\alpha,L} \leqslant d_\alpha \leqslant d_{\alpha,U}$$

To perform the test, we compare the test statistic d to the two known values $d_{\alpha,L}$ and $d_{\alpha,U}$ rather than to the unknown value d_α. If $d < d_{\alpha,L}$, then $d < d_\alpha$ and we should reject H_0. Similarly, if $d > d_{\alpha,U}$, then $d > d_\alpha$ and d falls in the acceptance region. If d falls between $d_{\alpha,L}$ and $d_{\alpha,U}$, we cannot tell if d is less than or greater than the correct critical value d_α, and the test is inconclusive.

The procedure for performing the Durbin–Watson test is summarized in the accompanying box.

The Durbin–Watson Test

Consider the population regression model

$$Y_t = \beta_0 + \beta_1 x_{t1} + \beta_2 x_{t2} + \cdots + \beta_K x_{tK} + e_t$$

where

$$e_t = \rho e_{t-1} + u_t$$

where u_t follows the basic assumptions. Suppose we wish to test the null hypothesis

$$H_0: \rho = 0$$

against the one-sided alternative hypothesis

$$H_1: \rho > 0$$

using a level of significance α. Calculate the Durbin–Watson statistic:

$$d = \frac{\sum_{t=2}^{n} (\hat{e}_t - \hat{e}_{t-1})^2}{\sum_{t=1}^{n} \hat{e}_t^2}$$

Use the decision rule

Reject H_0 if $d < d_{\alpha,L}$

Accept H_0 if $d > d_{\alpha,U}$

Make no conclusion if $d_{\alpha,L} < d < d_{\alpha,U}$

The lower and upper bounds $d_{\alpha,L}$ and $d_{\alpha,U}$, respectively, depend on the sample size n, the number of explanatory variables included in the regression equation K, and the level of significance of the test α. (Tables for the Durbin–Watson test showing appropriate values of $d_{\alpha,L}$ and $d_{\alpha,U}$ can be found in Table A.13 in the Appendix for $\alpha = .05$.)

Occasionally, we want to test against the alternative of negative autocorrelation; that is,

$$H_1: \rho < 0$$

The appropriate test is precisely the same as for positive autocorrelation except that it is based on the statistic $(4 - d)$ rather than d. This quantity is then compared with tabulated values $d_{\alpha,L}$ and $d_{\alpha,U}$.

Example 18.5

Performing the Durbin–Watson Test: Suppose we wish to test $H_0: \rho = 0$ against $H_1: \rho > 0$ at the 5% level of significance using the Durbin–Watson test. Assume that there are 20 observations and $K = 1$ explanatory variable. Find the lower and upper bounds $d_{\alpha,L}$ and $d_{\alpha,U}$.

Solution: We have $\alpha = .05$, $n = 20$, and $K = 1$. From Table A.13 in the Appendix, the appropriate values are $d_{.05,L} = 1.20$ and $d_{.05,U} = 1.41$. Thus, we should reject H_0 if

$d < 1.20$, not reject H_0 if $d > 1.41$, and withhold judgment if $1.20 \leq d \leq 1.41$. Figure 18.23 illustrates the Durbin–Watson test.

FIGURE 18.23
Distribution of the Durbin Watson *d* statistic.

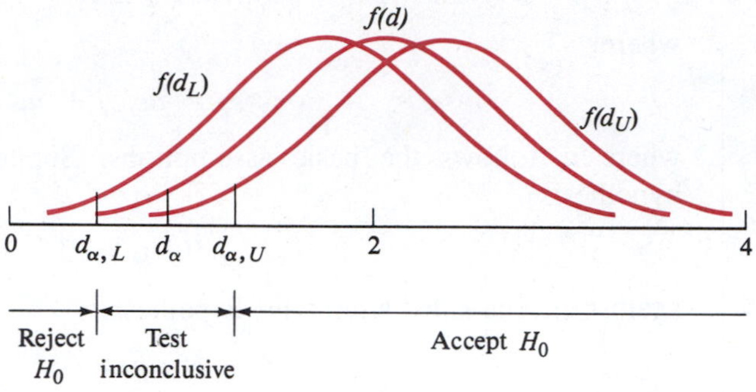

In most studies concerned with estimating regression equations from time series data, the value of the d statistic is presented along with the other estimates. If the tests indicate serially correlated errors, one response is to reestimate the equation using a more advanced estimation technique. Another approach is to reexamine the specification of the regression model, since serial correlation may indicate the presence of some unexplained systematic influence on the dependent variable.

Example 18.6

Testing for Serial Correlation Using the Durbin–Watson Test: The data in Table 2.4 of Chapter 2 show the values of the Dow Jones industrial average (Y) and the Gross National Product (X) for 1960 through 1986. Figure 18.24 provides a scatter diagram of the data.

Suppose it is hypothesized that the values of Y are related to the values of X according to the linear model

$$Y_t = \beta_0 + \beta_1 x_t + e_t$$

Estimate the linear regression model and test for the presence of positive serial correlation in the error terms.

Solution: The SPSSX computer output for this model is shown in Figure 18.25. The sample regression line is

$$\hat{y}_t = 648.438 + 0.152x_t \qquad R^2 = .582$$
$$t \text{ statistics:} \quad (11.93) \qquad (5.90) \qquad d = .72$$

Figure 18.26 shows a portion of the SPSSX computer output concerning the residuals. The graph shows a plot of the standardized residuals versus time. The printed values show the actual values of the Dow Jones industrial average, the predicted values $\hat{y}_t$, and the residuals $\hat{e}_t$. In the figure, negative residuals tend to follow negative residuals and positive residuals tend to follow positive residuals. For example, the first four residuals are negative, the next six residuals are positive, and so forth. The serpentine pattern of residuals leads us to suspect that the error terms are positively serially correlated.

Now use the Durbin–Watson test to test the null hypothesis

$$H_0\colon \rho = 0$$

FIGURE 18.24 **SPSSX-generated scatter diagram showing the Dow Jones industrial average versus Gross National Product.**

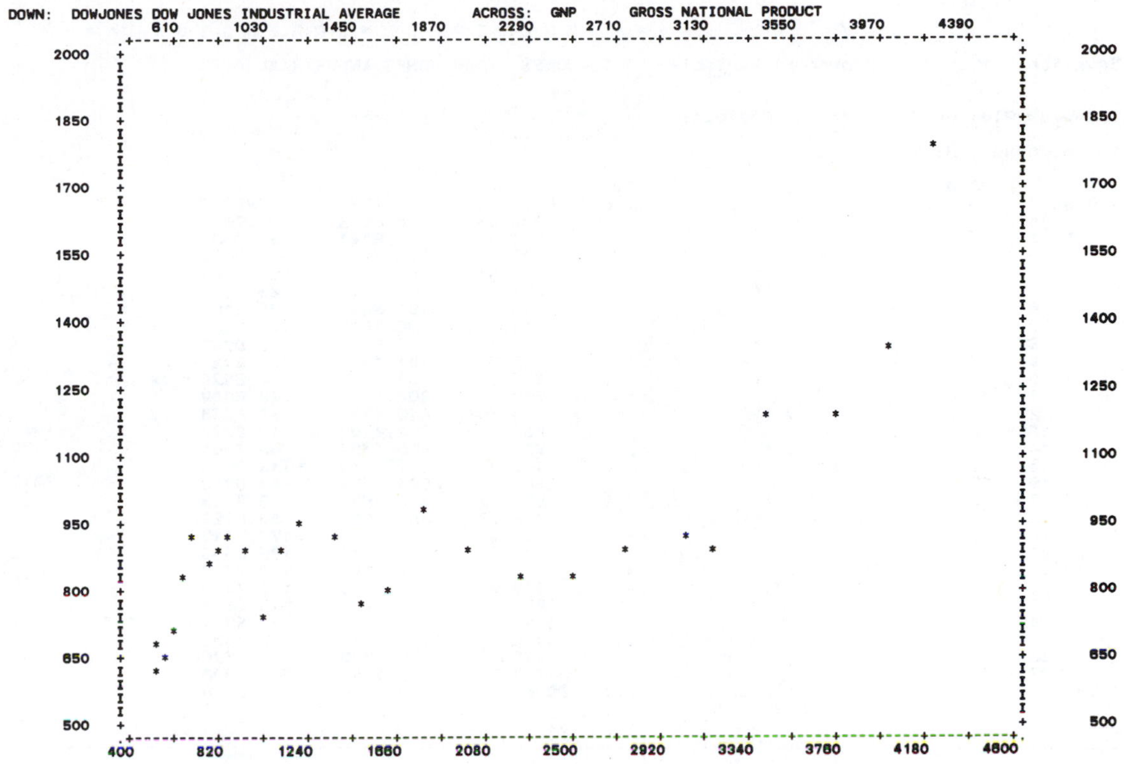

FIGURE 18.25 **SPSSX-generated regression output for Example 18.6, explaining the Dow Jones industrial average as a function of Gross National Product.**

```
                                   * * * *   M U L T I P L E   R E G R E S S I O N   * * * *

Listwise Deletion of Missing Data

Equation Number 1    Dependent Variable..   DOWJONES   DOW JONES INDUSTRIAL AVER

Beginning Block Number  1.  Method:  Enter      GNP

Variable(s) Entered on Step Number  1..    GNP       GROSS NATIONAL PRODUCT

Multiple R              .76295      Analysis of Variance
R Square                .58209                             DF      Sum of Squares       Mean Square
Adjusted R Square       .56538      Regression              1      836209.26588      836209.26588
Standard Error       154.96441      Residual               25      600349.22495       24013.96900

                                    F =      34.82179      Signif F =   .0000

------------------ Variables in the Equation ------------------

Variable               B          SE B        Beta          T  Sig T

GNP              .152080       .025772     .762950      5.901  .0000
(Constant)    648.437897     54.373382                 11.926  .0000

End Block Number   1   All requested variables entered.
```

FIGURE 18.26 **SPSSX-generated output showing the residuals from Example 18.6.**

```
                                   * * * *   M U L T I P L E   R E G R E S S I O N   * * * *

Equation Number 1    Dependent Variable..   DOWJONES   DOW JONES INDUSTRIAL AVER

Casewise Plot of Standardized Residual

*: Selected    M: Missing

          -3.0            0.0            3.0
Case #    O:...............:...............:O    DOWJONES      *PRED        *RESID
     1    .           *   .               .      618.04     726.8046    -108.7646
     2    .              *.               .      691.55     729.6181     -38.0681
     3    .            *  .               .      639.76     735.8229     -96.0629
     4    .              *.               .      714.81     740.7351     -25.9251
     5    .               .  *            .      834.05     747.2593      86.7907
     6    .               .    *          .      910.88     755.6693     155.2107
     7    .               .  *            .      873.60     765.8435     107.7565
     8    .               .  *            .      879.12     772.5958     106.5242
     9    .               .   *           .      906.00     781.1579     124.8421
    10    .               .  *            .      876.72     795.0276      81.6924
    11    .             * .               .      753.19     802.8749     -49.6849
    12    .               . *             .      884.76     816.1362      68.6238
    13    .               .   *           .      950.71     832.8802     117.8298
    14    .               . *             .      923.88     855.1599      68.7201
    15    .           *   .               .      759.37     872.4210    -113.0510
    16    .            *  .               .      802.49     891.5222     -89.0322
    17    .               . *             .      974.92     919.5657      55.3543
    18    .             * .               .      894.63     951.1526     -56.5226
    19    .          *    .               .      820.23     990.5717    -170.3417
    20    .         *     .               .      844.40    1029.8843    -185.4843
    21    .         *     .               .      891.41    1063.9198    -172.5098
    22    .         *     .               .      932.92    1112.6766    -179.7566
    23    .       *       .               .      884.36    1129.9224    -245.5624
    24    .               .*              .     1190.34    1166.3759      23.9641
    25    .              *.               .     1178.48    1221.0182     -42.5382
    26    .               . *             .     1328.23    1256.4680      71.7620
    27    .               .               *     1792.76    1288.5264     504.2336
Case #    O:...............:...............:O    DOWJONES      *PRED        *RESID
          -3.0            0.0            3.0
```

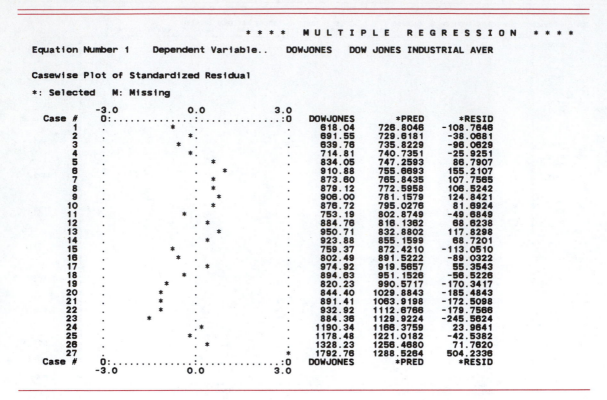

against the one-sided alternative hypothesis

$$H_1: \rho > 0$$

using a 5% level of significance.

The value of the Durbin–Watson test statistic is $d = 0.72139$. There are $n = 27$ observations and $K = 1$ explanatory variable, namely GNP. From Table A.13, for $\alpha = .05$, the two critical values for the Durbin–Watson test are $d_{.05,L} = 1.32$ and $d_{.05,U} = 1.47$. Since the calculated value $d = 0.72139$ is far below the lower critical value, we reject the null hypothesis of independence and conclude that the error terms are serially correlated. ■

Correcting for Serial Correlation of the Error Terms

When the error terms are serially correlated, we have several possible actions:

1. Search for additional explanatory variables in hopes that the error terms will then be serially uncorrelated.

2. Try other functional forms, such as a polynomial regression model or a logarithmic regression model.
3. Use the least-squares estimates even though we have evidence that the errors are serially correlated.
4. Use a different estimation technique that takes serial correlation into account.

The first two approaches are always recommended. Serially correlated errors indicate that there is something systematic in the error terms that the model is not explaining. The theory should be reexamined to try to find the source of these patterns. Sometimes use of a trend variable t can be helpful in reducing serial correlation. (The trend variable will be discussed in detail in Chapter 19.)

When the first two approaches fail, we still have the latter two options. We can continue to use the unbiased but inefficient least-squares estimates, or we can use another estimation technique that takes the serial correlation into account. The problem with using the least-squares estimates is that all of the variance estimates are biased, thus invalidating all confidence intervals and tests of hypotheses. In the remainder of this section, we discuss the Prais–Winsten estimation technique, which is designed to correct for serially correlated error terms.

The Prais–Winsten (PW) estimator is named after the two men, S. J. Prais and C. B. Winsten, who proposed it in 1954 (S. J. Prais and C. B. Winsten, "Trend Estimators and Serial Correlation," Cowles Commission Discussion Paper No. 383 [Chicago: 1954]). The idea behind the PW estimator is to transform the original model containing the serially correlated errors into a new model containing independent error terms that satisfy the basic assumptions.

The PW estimator works as follows. The original equation

$$Y_t = \beta_0 + \beta_1 x_t + e_t$$

can be multiplied by ρ and lagged by one period to obtain

$$\rho Y_{t-1} = \rho\beta_0 + \rho\beta_1 x_{t-1} + \rho e_{t-1}$$

If we subtract the second equation from the first, we obtain

$$Y_t - \rho Y_{t-1} = (1 - \rho)\beta_0 + \beta_1(x_t - \rho x_{t-1}) + e_t - \rho e_{t-1}$$

But since $e_t - \rho e_{t-1} = u_t$, we can write

$$Y_t - \rho Y_{t-1} = (1 - \rho)\beta_0 + \beta_1(x_t - \rho x_{t-1}) + u_t$$

for $t = 2, 3, \ldots, n$. In this way, we have replaced the serially correlated error terms e_t by the independent error terms u_t. However, we appear to have lost one observation in this process. To bring back u_1, we consider the first observation

$$Y_1 = \beta_0 + \beta_1 x_1 + e_1$$

Recall that

$$e_1 = \frac{u_1}{\sqrt{1 - \rho^2}}$$

After substituting for e_1, we obtain

$$Y_1 = \beta_0 + \beta_1 x_1 + \frac{u_1}{\sqrt{1 - \rho^2}}$$

We multiply both sides of this equation by $\sqrt{1 - \rho^2}$ to obtain

$$Y_1\sqrt{1 - \rho^2} = \beta_0\sqrt{1 - \rho^2} + \beta_1 x_1\sqrt{1 - \rho^2} + u_1$$

The Prais–Winsten estimator is obtained by estimating the model

$$Y_t^* = \beta_0 w_t^* + \beta_1 x_t^* + u_t$$

where, for $t = 1$,

$$Y_1^* = Y_1\sqrt{1 - \rho^2}, \quad w_1^* = \sqrt{1 - \rho^2}, \quad \text{and} \quad x_1^* = x_1\sqrt{1 - \rho^2}$$

and for $t = 2, 3, \ldots, n$,

$$Y_t^* = Y_t - \rho y_{t-1}, \quad w_t^* = 1 - \rho, \quad \text{and} \quad x_t^* = x_t - \rho x_{t-1}$$

In the transformed equation, there are two explanatory variables, w_t^* and x_t^*, and no constant term. Note that w_t^* has the same value for all observations except the first one. This transformation is known as the *Prais–Winsten transformation*.

By applying least squares to the transformed model, we obtain best linear unbiased estimates. That is, our estimates have all the nice properties possessed by the least-squares estimators when the basic assumptions hold. (These optimal properties are based on the assumption that the correct value of ρ is used when making the PW transformation.)

In general, the value of ρ will be unknown and must be estimated. There are various ways of estimating ρ, the most popular estimator being

$$\hat{\rho} = \frac{\sum_{t=2}^{n} \hat{e}_t \hat{e}_{t-1}}{\sum_{t=2}^{n} \hat{e}_{t-1}^2}$$

Another estimator of ρ can be obtained by making use of the Durbin–Watson statistic d and the approximate relationship

$$d \approx 2 - 2\hat{\rho}$$

which by rearranging yields

$$\hat{\rho} = 1 - d/2$$

When we replace the true value ρ by an estimate $\hat{\rho}$ in the PW transformation, the resulting estimates are called the *feasible PW estimates*.

Example 18.7

Using the Prais–Winsten Estimator: Use the results from Example 18.6 and obtain the feasible Prais–Winsten estimator for the model relating the value of the Dow Jones industrial average to the Gross National Product.

Solution: Using the result $d = 0.72139$ from Example 18.6, we obtain the estimated value of ρ,

$$\hat{\rho} = 1 - d/2 = .63905$$

After making the PW transformation, we obtain the PW estimated model

$$\hat{y}_t^* = 570.807w_t^* + 0.207x_t^*$$

The SPSSX computer results are shown in Figure 18.27.

FIGURE 18.27 **SPSSX-generated output for the feasible Prais–Winsten estimator in Example 18.7.**

```
                        * * * *  MULTIPLE REGRESSION THROUGH THE ORIGIN  * * * *

Listwise Deletion of Missing Data

Equation Number 1    Dependent Variable..   YSTAR

Beginning Block Number  1.  Method:  Enter      WSTAR    XSTAR

Variable(s) Entered on Step Number  1..    XSTAR
                                    2..    WSTAR

Multiple R              .95295          Analysis of Variance
R Square                .90812                           DF       Sum of Squares        Mean Square
Adjusted R Square       .90076          Regression        2        3888665.43485      1944332.71742
Standard Error       125.45325          Residual         25         393462.93751        15738.51750

                                        F =      123.53976       Signif F =  .0000

------------------ Variables in the Equation ------------------

Variable                  B         SE B         Beta          T   Sig T

XSTAR            570.807288   107.728273      .550235      5.299   .0000
WSTAR               .206925      .047705      .450444      4.338   .0002

End Block Number   1   All requested variables entered.
```

Table 18.3 shows the estimated coefficients and estimated standard deviations when the model is estimated by least squares and by the feasible Prais–Winsten technique. The feasible PW slope estimate is approximately 33% larger than the least-squares slope estimate, and the feasible PW estimated standard deviations are much larger than the (biased) least-squares estimates.

TABLE 18.3 **Least-squares estimates and feasible Praìs–Winsten estimates of regression model for Dow Jones industrial average problem**

Estimation Technique	b_0	s_{b_0}	b_1	s_{b_1}
Least squares	648.438	54.37	0.152	0.026
Feasible PW	570.807	107.73	0.207	0.048

Recall that the purpose of using the PW estimation technique is to correct for serially correlated errors in order to get unbiased variance estimates, correct t statistics, correct prob-values, correct confidence intervals, and efficient estimates. However, because we have used an estimated value of ρ rather than the true value, the feasible PW estimates do not necessarily possess the optimal properties of the PW estimator obtained from using the correct ρ. Nevertheless, economic research has indicated that, in general, the feasible PW estimates are preferable to the least-squares estimates, even though they do not necessarily possess the optimal properties of the true PW estimates. ■

Exercises for Section 18.5

1. The General Nutrient Corporation (GNC) sells various types of vitamin supplements in a regional market. GNC wants to predict its sales by using national sales figures for vitamin supplements. (To make future predictions, GNC relies on national predictions published by the industry's trade association.) The accompanying data show quarterly GNC sales in millions of dollars (Y) and national sales in millions of dollars (X) from 1984 through 1988.

Quarter	t	GNC Sales Y	Industry Sales X
1984			
1	1	20.96	127.3
2	2	21.40	130.0
3	3	21.96	132.7
4	4	21.52	129.4
1985			
1	5	22.39	135.0
2	6	22.76	137.1
3	7	23.48	141.2
4	8	23.66	142.8
1986			
1	9	24.10	145.5
2	10	24.01	145.3
3	11	24.54	148.3
4	12	24.30	146.4
1987			
1	13	25.00	150.2
2	14	25.64	153.1
3	15	26.36	157.3
4	16	26.98	160.7
1988			
1	17	27.52	164.2
2	18	27.78	165.6
3	19	28.24	168.7
4	20	28.78	171.7

a. Plot the data.
b. Find the sample regression line and plot it.
c. Calculate s_e.
d. Calculate the estimated variances for b_0 and b_1.
e. Find the residuals and plot them versus time.
f. Calculate the Durbin–Watson test statistic.
g. Let $\alpha = .05$. Test for the presence of positive serial correlation. What are the critical values $d_{\alpha,L}$ and $d_{\alpha,U}$?

2. Suppose it is believed that the errors in Exercise 1 follow the first-order autoregressive model

$$e_t = \rho e_{t-1} + u_t$$

a. Estimate ρ.
b. Calculate the transformed values $(y_t - \hat{\rho}y_{t-1})$ and $(x_t - \hat{\rho}x_{t-1})$.
c. Estimate β_0 and β_1 using the feasible Prais–Winsten estimator.
d. Calculate the estimated variances of b_0 and b_1. Compare these estimates with the estimates obtained in Exercise 1.

3. A researcher estimates a regression model that contains 3 explanatory variables and a constant, based on a random sample of 30 observations. The researcher wants to perform the Durbin–Watson test to test for positive serial correlation using a 5% level of significance. Find $d_{.05,L}$ and $d_{.05,U}$.

4. Repeat Exercise 3 if the model contains 2 explanatory variables and the sample size is $n = 25$.

18.6 ▪ Violations of Basic Assumption 5: Correlation Between Errors and Explanatory Variables

The fifth basic assumption of the multiple regression model states that the error terms are independent of the explanatory variables. In this section, we discuss potential problems when the fifth basic assumption fails to hold.

Basic Assumption 5

Each of the random variables $e_1, e_2, \ldots, e_n$ is assumed to be independent of the explanatory variables $X_1, X_2, \ldots, X_K$.

The fifth basic assumption means that when the explanatory variable takes the value x_{ij}, nothing can be inferred about the value of e_i. Violations of this assumption usually occur in one of two ways. The first case involves a simultaneous equation model, and the second involves a model containing the lagged value of the dependent variable.

For the first case, consider the following highly simplified model of income determination:

$$\text{Consumption function:} \quad C_t = \beta_0 + \beta_1 Y_t + e_t \tag{1}$$

$$\text{GNP or income identity:} \quad Y_t = C_t + I_t + G_t \tag{2}$$

where

C_t = aggregate consumption in time period t

Y_t = aggregate income in time period t

I_t = total investment in time period t

G_t = total government spending in time period t

e_t = random disturbance in time period t

I_t and G_t are assumed to be nonstochastic and are determined outside the model.

We want to estimate the parameters β_0 and β_1 based on a sample of data for C and Y. In this example the values of Y_t and e_t are not independent, so basic assumption 5 is violated. We can show that Y_t is not independent of e_t by substituting equation 1 into equation 2. We obtain

$$Y_t = \beta_0 + \beta_1 Y_t + e_t + I_t + G_t$$

or

$$Y_t = \frac{\beta_0}{1 - \beta_1} + \frac{1}{1 - \beta_1} I_t + \frac{1}{1 - \beta_1} G_t + \frac{1}{1 - \beta_1} e_t$$

which shows that Y_t depends on e_t.

The second way that basic assumption 5 can be violated is when the regression model contains a lagged dependent variable. For example, suppose that in a model the dependent variable Y_t depends on Y_{t-1}, the value of Y in the previous period (that is, at time $t - 1$) and on random effects. Suppose the value of Y at time t is determined by

$$Y_t = \beta_0 + \beta_1 Y_{t-1} + e_t \tag{3}$$

In this model the explanatory variable Y_{t-1} is the lagged value of the dependent variable. At time t, the value of Y_{t-1} is already determined. If e_t is independent of e_1, e_2, . . . , e_{t-1}, then e_t and Y_{t-1} will be independent. The problem is that Y_{t-1} is not independent of e_{t-1}, which means that the explanatory variable Y_{t-1} is not independent of *all* the error terms. It is assumed that equation 3 holds for past time periods, so if we lag the model one time period, we see that Y_{t-1} was determined by

$$Y_{t-1} = \beta_0 + \beta_1 Y_{t-2} + e_{t-1}$$

which shows that Y_{t-1} is dependent on e_{t-1}. In equation 3 we say that Y_{t-1} and e_t are *contemporaneously uncorrelated,* but the explanatory variable Y_{t-1} is not independent of e_{t-1}, e_{t-2}, and so forth. For basic assumption 5 to hold, the explanatory variable must be independent of *all* the error terms. Thus assumption 5 is violated whenever one or more lagged values of the dependent variable are used as explanatory variables.

Basic assumption 5 is needed to ensure that the least-squares estimators b_0 and b_1 are unbiased estimators of β_0 and β_1. When it is violated, the least-squares esimates are biased. Much of econometric theory concerns the problem of developing estimation techniques that produce estimators having good properties when basic assumption 5 is violated. Most econometrics texts treat these techniques in detail.

Consequences of Explanatory Variables Being Dependent on Error Terms

If basic assumption 5 fails to hold, the least-squares estimates b_0, b_1, . . . , b_K are not unbiased estimates of the population regression coefficients β_0, β_1, . . . , β_K. In addition, all the estimates of the variances of the estimated coefficients are biased. Thus, the confidence intervals and tests of hypotheses are invalid.

Models containing lagged dependent variables are called *autoregressive models* and are treated in more detail in Chapter 19.

18.7 ▪ Computer Applications

To test the assumptions of the multiple regression model, we usually resort to analyzing the residuals. In the SPSSX program, we can analyze the residuals by issuing one or both of the commands RESIDUALS and CASEWISE.

To illustrate how these commands are used, suppose we want to estimate the model

$$Y_i = \beta_0 + \beta_1 x_i + e_i$$

and analyze the residuals. Issue the REGRESSION command to generate the sample regression line. To obtain the Durbin–Watson statistic used to test for serial correlation, issue the command

```
RESIDUALS = DEFAULT, DURBIN/
```

To obtain a listing of all the actual values of the dependent variable along with the predicted values and the residuals, issue the command

```
CASEWISE = DEFAULT, ALL/
```

The following commands produce the estimated regression line, the Durbin–Watson statistic, a printout of the actual and predicted values of Y, and the residuals:

```
REGRESSION VARIABLES = Y, X/
    DEPENDENT = Y/
    ENTER X/
    RESIDUALS = DEFAULT, DURBIN/
    CASEWISE = DEFAULT, ALL/
```

Exercises for Section 18.7

1. Refer to the time series data in Table 2.4 in Chapter 2, which show data values for the variables GNP, TOTALGOV, DEFENSE, URATE, CPI, TBILL, and DOWJONES from 1960 through 1986.
   a. Generate a scatter diagram of DOWJONES versus GNP. Do these two variables appear to be linearly related?
   b. Estimate the linear model where DOWJONES is a function of GNP. Examine the value of R^2. Does GNP appear to do a good job of explaining the value of DOWJONES?
   c. Print out the residuals and obtain the Durbin–Watson statistic.
   d. Examine the residual plot and determine if GNP appears to explain DOWJONES adequately.
   e. Let $\alpha = .05$ and test the null hypothesis that the error terms are not serially correlated against the alternative hypothesis that the errors are positively correlated.
2. Refer to Exercise 1.
   a. Generate a scatter diagram of TBILL versus CPI. Do these two variables appear to be linearly related?
   b. Estimate the linear model where TBILL is a function of CPI. Examine the value of R^2. Does CPI appear to do a good job of explaining the value of TBILL?

c. Print out the residuals and obtain the Durbin–Watson statistic.
d. Examine the residual plot and determine if CPI appears to explain TBILL adequately.
e. Let $\alpha = .05$ and test the null hypothesis that the error terms are not serially correlated against the alternative hypothesis that the errors are positively correlated.

Chapter 18 Summary

In Chapter 18, we examined each of the assumptions underlying the multiple regression model. We determined which properties of the least-squares estimates depended on each assumption, what each assumption means and various ways in which each assumption can be violated, various ways of testing the validity of each assumption, and what steps should be taken when an assumption is violated.

A *specification error* exists if an important explanatory variable has been omitted or if an estimated equation has an incorrect functional form. Both cases will lead to biased estimated regression coefficients. To detect these types of errors, it is useful to plot the data, to plot the residuals in various ways, to estimate different models, or to examine correlation matrices. The fact that the estimated coefficients are biased invalidates all confidence intervals and tests of hypotheses and can even lead to estimates with the wrong sign. The solution to this problem is to include all relevant explanatory variables. Unfortunately, this solution will increase the degree of multicollinearity, making it more difficult to get precise estimates.

We examined the consequences of *heteroscedastic* and *serially correlated* error terms. In either situation, the estimated regression coefficients remain unbiased, but they do not have minimum variance. In addition, the estimated variance of the disturbance term is biased. This leads to biased estimates of the variances of the estimated regression coefficients, which invalidates our confidence intervals and tests of hypotheses.

Errors are heteroscedastic if they have different variances. This can be a common occurrence in models using *cross section data,* where the magnitudes of the variables differ greatly from one individual to another. The *Goldfeld–Quandt test* can be used to test for heteroscedastic error terms. If the errors are heteroscedastic and the form of the heteroscedasticity is known (or has been estimated), then a *weighted-least-squares* estimation procedure can be used to alleviate the problem.

In a *time series* model, the error terms are serially correlated if an error at one time is related to an error at another time. The Durbin–Watson test is the most popular method for detecting serially correlated errors. If the errors are serially correlated and the form of the serial correlation is known (or has been estimated), then the *Prais–Winsten estimation procedure* can be used to alleviate the problem.

The error terms and the explanatory variables will be correlated when one of the explanatory variables is the lagged dependent variable or when the dependent and explanatory variables are related according to a simultaneous equation model. Correlation between the error terms and the explanatory variables causes the least-squares estimates to be biased.

A common way of detecting violations of the basic assumptions is to plot the residuals against time, against the Y values, and against the X values. Residual plots can be used to detect the following departures from the classical model:

1. The regression function is not linear,
2. the error terms do not have constant variance,
3. the error terms are not independent,
4. the model fits all but one or a few outliers,
5. the error terms are not normally distributed, and
6. an important explanatory variable has been omitted.

This chapter concludes our discussion of the general multiple regression model. Special cases of regression models are models that contain time series variables or variables whose values are arranged chronologically. Chapters 19 and 20 provide an introduction to the analysis of time series models.

Chapter 18 ▪ Supplementary Exercises

1. At many universities, incoming freshmen are required to take a placement test in mathematics. The director of admissions selected 20 students randomly and recorded their placement scores (X_1) and their grade point averages at the end of the freshman year (Y). The data are as follows:

Student	Y	X_1	Student	Y	X_1
1	3.1	5.5	11	2.0	4.9
2	2.3	4.8	12	2.9	5.4
3	3.0	4.7	13	2.3	5.0
4	1.9	3.9	14	3.2	6.3
5	2.5	4.5	15	1.8	4.6
6	3.7	6.2	16	1.4	4.3
7	3.4	6.0	17	2.0	5.0
8	2.6	5.2	18	3.8	5.9
9	2.8	4.7	19	2.2	4.1
10	1.6	4.4	20	1.5	4.7

a. Estimate the simple linear regression model.
b. Plot the data and the estimated sample regression line.
c. Predict the grade point average for a student whose entrance test score is 4.0.
d. Find s_e and R^2.
e. Find the estimated standard deviations for each coefficient.
f. Obtain a 99% confidence interval for β_1. Does this confidence interval contain 0?
g. Let $\alpha = .01$. Test the null hypothesis H_0: $\beta_1 = 0$. Is it appropriate to perform a one-tailed test here?
h. Obtain a 95% confidence interval for the mean value of Y_i given that $x_{i1} = 4.0$.

2. Refer to Exercise 1. Find all the residuals.
a. Do the residuals sum to 0?
b. Plot the residuals against the fitted values $\hat{y}_i$. Does this plot indicate any shortcomings of the linear regression model?

3. Refer to Exercise 1. The following data show an IQ score (X_2) and a high school grade average (X_3) for each of the 20 students:

Student	X_2	X_3	Student	X_2	X_3
1	105	2.9	11	123	3.2
2	113	2.8	12	114	3.3
3	118	3.1	13	120	3.4
4	107	2.4	14	132	2.6
5	110	3.0	15	122	3.0
6	125	2.4	16	110	2.8
7	115	3.5	17	119	3.3
8	121	3.1	18	109	3.4
9	117	3.1	19	116	2.6
10	111	2.9	20	108	2.7

a. Plot the residuals versus each of these variables. Does it appear that the model could be improved by including either or both of these potential explanatory variables?

b. Estimate the model

$$Y_i = \beta_0 + \beta_1 x_{i1} + \beta_2 x_{i2} + e_i$$

c. Estimate the model

$$Y_i = \beta_0 + \beta_1 x_{i1} + \beta_2 x_{i3} + e_i$$

d. Estimate the model

$$Y_i = \beta_0 + \beta_1 x_{i1} + \beta_2 x_{i2} + \beta_3 x_{i3} + e_i$$

e. Compare the results from parts (b), (c), and (d). Note the changes in R^2, in the estimated coefficients, in their estimated standard deviations, and in the significance of the t statistics.

4. The data below show monthly data on the amount of assets in millions of constant dollars (Y) and on the number of clients in thousands (X) at a small bank for 20 months. A simple linear regression model is believed to be appropriate, but positively autocorrelated error terms may be present.

Month	Y	X	Month	Y	X
1	2.20	2.52	11	2.84	3.73
2	2.04	2.17	12	2.87	3.80
3	2.07	2.23	13	2.75	3.57
4	2.22	2.52	14	2.75	3.58
5	2.11	2.30	15	2.69	3.44
6	2.24	2.52	16	2.33	2.72
7	2.48	3.02	17	2.48	3.01
8	2.48	3.01	18	2.52	3.11
9	2.73	3.53	19	2.79	3.62
10	2.69	3.46	20	2.79	3.62

a. Fit a simple linear regression model by ordinary least squares and obtain the residuals. Also obtain the estimated variances of the regression coefficients.

b. Plot the residuals against time and explain whether you find any evidence of positive autocorrelation.

c. Conduct a formal test for positive autocorrelation using the Durbin–Watson test and a significance level of $\alpha = .01$. Is the residual analysis in part (b) in accord with the test result?

5. Refer to Exercise 4.

a. Obtain a point estimate of the autocorrelation parameter ρ using the formula

$$\hat{\rho} = \frac{\sum_{t=2}^{n} \hat{e}_t \hat{e}_{t-1}}{\sum_{t=2}^{n} \hat{e}_{t-1}^2}$$

b. Obtain an alternative estimate as $\hat{\rho} = 1 - d/2$, where d is the Durbin–Watson statistic.
c. Use the estimate in part (b) and obtain the feasible Prais–Winsten estimates for the population regression coefficients. Compare these estimates with the estimates obtained in Exercise 4.
d. Estimate the variances of the sample regression coefficients and compare with the estimates obtained in Exercise 4.

6. The accompanying data show seasonally adjusted quarterly sales for the Watson Company in millions of dollars (Y) and for the entire industry in millions of dollars (X) for 20 quarters.

Quarter	Y	X	Quarter	Y	X
1	20.9	127.3	11	24.5	148.3
2	21.4	130.0	12	24.8	146.4
3	21.9	132.7	13	25.0	150.2
4	21.5	129.4	14	25.6	153.1
5	22.4	135.0	15	27.4	157.3
6	22.8	137.1	16	27.0	160.7
7	23.5	140.3	17	27.5	164.2
8	23.7	142.8	18	27.8	165.6
9	24.1	145.5	19	28.2	168.7
10	24.0	145.3	20	28.8	171.9

a. Estimate the simple linear regression model.
b. Would you expect the autocorrelation parameter ρ to be positive, negative, or zero here?
c. Find the residuals and plot them against time. What do you find?
d. Conduct a formal test for positive autocorrelation using $\alpha = .05$.

7. Refer to Exercise 6.
a. Estimate the parameter ρ by using the Durbin–Watson statistic d and the equation $\hat{\rho} = 1 - d/2$.
b. Use the feasible Prais–Winsten technique and estimate the parameters β_0 and β_1.
c. Find the estimated standard deviations of these estimates.

8. Answer the following questions concerning the regression model:
a. What is the name for the problem associated with the assumption that $E(e_i^2) = \sigma^2$ is not true?
b. What is the name for the problem that results when the assumption that $E(e_i e_j) = 0$ for all $i \neq j$ is not true?
c. Do the problems named in parts (a) and (b) invalidate the best, the linear, or the unbiased part of the ordinary least-squares (OLS) estimators?
d. For which of the problems described in parts (a) and (b) are the OLS estimators of the variances unbiased?
e. Which type of misspecified disturbance term is more likely to occur in time series data? In cross section data?
f. With economic data, is the variance of the disturbance term more likely to be positively or negatively correlated with the independent variables?
g. With economic data, is autocorrelation more likely to be positive or negative?

9. The following regression model is heteroscedastic:

$$Y_i = \beta_0 + \beta_1 x_{i1} + \beta_2 x_{i2} + e_i$$

where

$$Y = \text{dollars spent by consumers on food in a city in a week}$$
$$X_1 = \text{dollars on income earned by consumers in a city during a week}$$
$$X_2 = \text{population of a city}$$

A researcher uses ordinary least-squares to estimate this model assuming that $E(e^2) = \sigma^2$.

a. Does $E(b_0) = \beta_0$? $E(b_1) = \beta_1$? $E(b_2) = \beta_2$? $E(S_e^2) = \sigma_e^2$?

b. Are the estimators b_0, b_1, b_2, and S_e^2 best estimators?

c. Assuming that b_0, b_1, and b_2 are unbiased estimators of the parameters in the regression model, can s_{b_i} be used to test hypotheses?

10. In Exercise 9, assume that the variance of the disturbance term increases proportionally with the square of population.

a. What is $E(e_i^2)$?

b. How would you transform the dependent and explanatory variables to get best linear unbiased estimates?

11. Suppose you want to estimate the following consumption function:

$$C_t = \beta_0 + \beta_1 I_t + \beta_2 W_t + e_t$$

where

$$C_t = \text{consumption in year } t$$
$$I_t = \text{income in year } t$$
$$W_t = \text{wealth in year } t$$

Assume that $E(e_t) = 0$ and $E(e_i^2) = (C_i^2)\sigma^2$. Transform the model into one in which the disturbance term is homoscedastic and describe the steps required to estimate it.

12. Apply the Goldfeld–Quandt test to the accompanying data and comment on the results. (Drop the middle six observations.)

Observation	Y	X	Observation	Y	X
1	29.5	49.6	11	115.1	140.2
2	31.8	55.7	12	121.5	150.7
3	38.4	63.3	13	137.4	167.3
4	49.8	75.4	14	154.3	181.3
5	54.7	78.3	15	172.0	207.9
6	73.2	96.7	16	196.5	235.0
7	80.4	109.3	17	216.6	258.9
8	87.2	115.8	18	224.7	227.7
9	89.1	118.8	19	252.0	297.6
10	106.3	133.0	20	268.6	309.4

13. Consider the following regression equation:

$$\hat{y}_t = \underset{(3)}{34} + \underset{(6)}{28}x_t \qquad n = 40, \quad d = 1.40$$

The numbers in parentheses are estimated standard errors of the coefficients.

a. Does positive autocorrelation exist at the 5% level of significance?

b. Is the coefficient of X significantly different from 0 at the 5% level of significance? Use a one-tailed test.

14. Suppose the following regression model has a serially correlated disturbance term:

$$Y_t = \beta_0 + \beta_1 x_t + e_t$$

where $e_t = \rho e_{t-1} + u_t$. The first three observations in the data set are as follows:

Y	140	204	310
X	12	15	20

a. If you estimate this model by ordinary least squares (OLS), would $E(b_1) = \beta_1$?
b. Using OLS to estimate, would $\text{Var}(b_1)$ be the minimum for linear and unbiased estimators of β_1?
c. Would the estimated variance of b_1 be unbiased?
d. Write the appropriate transformation for estimating this model using the Prais–Winsten technique.
e. Suppose $\rho = .5$. Write the Prais–Winsten transformation and calculate the values for the three observations above.

15. The population regression equation is

$$Y_t = \beta_0 + \beta_1 x_t + e_t$$

a. The researcher assumes that e_t is autoregressive with $\rho = 1$. Write the appropriate autoregressive transformation to estimate this model by ordinary least squares.
b. What is special about the transformed equation? Examine the constant term.

16. You are given the model

$$Y_t = \beta_0 + \beta_1 x_t + e_t$$

with the following data:

Observation	Y	X
1	2.4	1
2	2.5	2
3	2.5	3
4	1.6	4
5	3.7	5
6	5.8	6
7	6.9	7
8	7.0	8
9	11.1	9
10	11.2	10
11	11.3	11
12	13.4	12
13	16.5	13
14	11.5	14
15	12.6	15

a. Estimate the simple linear regression model.
b. Calculate the Durbin–Watson statistic and test for positive first-order autocorrelation at the .05 significance level.

17. Using a series of 25 annual observations, a student estimated the following regression model:

$$\hat{y}_t = -509 + \underset{(23.4)}{0.89x_{t1}} + \underset{(3.24)}{17.27x_{t2}} - \underset{(53.46)}{21.20x_{t3}} - \underset{(0.175)}{0.522x_{t4}} + \underset{(5.69)}{7.36x_{t5}}$$

$$R^2 = 0.885, \quad d = 1.046$$

where

Y = Dow Jones industrial yearly average
X_1 = ratio of annual corporate profit to annual corporate sales
X_2 = index of industrial production
X_3 = corporate bond yield
X_4 = disposable income per capita
X_5 = Consumer Price Index

The figures in parentheses below the estimated coefficients are the estimated standard errors.
a. Discuss the sign and statistical significance of each coefficient.
b. Do any of the coefficients appear to have the wrong sign?
c. Which coefficients appear to be statistically insignificant?
d. Examine the Durbin–Watson statistic. What does it indicate?

18. A study was performed to explore possible causes of motor vehicle deaths in the United States. The following regression model was obtained from 26 annual observations:

$$\hat{y}_t = -51{,}514 + \underset{(0.53)}{1.62x_{t1}} + \underset{(768)}{2111x_{t2}} - \underset{(0.0142)}{0.0221x_{t3}}$$

$$R^2 = .912, \quad d = 0.987$$

where

Y = total motor vehicle deaths in the United States in a year
X_1 = personal consumption of alcoholic beverages (in millions of dollars) in the United States in a year
X_2 = average highway speed (in miles per hour) of all motor vehicles in the United States in a year
X_3 = millions of miles traveled by motor vehicles in the United States annually

The figures in parentheses beneath the coefficient estimates are their estimated standard errors.
a. Do the coefficients have the correct signs?
b. Are the coefficients statistically significant?
c. What does the Durbin–Watson statistic tell you?

19. The following data show annual sales (Y) and annual advertising expenditures (X) for a period of 20 years:

Year	Y	X	Year	Y	X
1	102	61	11	133	75
2	92	45	12	198	61
3	93	53	13	222	86
4	98	54	14	220	86
5	93	53	15	251	102
6	105	55	16	273	136
7	118	52	17	318	148
8	109	58	18	335	161
9	109	61	19	344	180
10	115	54	20	292	185

a. Estimate the regression model

$$Y_t = \beta_0 + \beta_1 x_t + e_t$$

b. Find the residuals and plot them versus time.
c. Check for autocorrelated errors in this model.
d. If necessary, reestimate the model, allowing for autocorrelated errors.

20. The accompanying data show the number of ski tickets in thousands sold last season (Y) on a sample of 100 days at 10 different ski resorts. The data also show for each resort the number of miles of nonexpert trails (X_1) and the chair lift capacity in skiers per hour (X_2).

Resort	Tickets Sold Y	Miles of Trails X_1	Lift Capacity X_2
1	21,929	12.5	2300
2	5,729	4.5	1100
3	25,897	14.5	3200
4	9,786	5.2	1500
5	32,411	15.8	3900
6	7,331	4.7	1300
7	10,524	8.3	1900
8	46,572	23.6	5600
9	35,486	18.2	4300
10	13,165	7.7	1900

a. Find the correlation between Y and X_1.
b. Find the correlation between Y and X_2.
c. Find the correlation between X_1 and X_2.
d. Estimate the simple linear regression model where Y is a function of X_1.
e. Estimate the simple linear regression model where Y is a function of X_2.
f. Estimate the multiple regression model where Y is a function of X_1 and X_2.
g. Comment on the differences in the estimated coefficients in parts (d), (e), and (f). Can you explain these differences?
h. Comment on the differences in the estimated standard deviations in parts (d), (e), and (f). Can you explain these differences?

i. Comment on the differences in the values of R^2 in parts (d), (e), and (f). Can you explain these differences?

21. The accompanying data show total expenditures on education as a percentage of Gross National Product (Y), per capita income (X_1), median educational attainment in years of the population over 25 years of age (X_2), and the ratio of the population aged 0 to 14 to the total population (X_3).

Y	X_1	X_2	X_3
2.1	1160	5.71	0.30
4.5	2310	8.04	0.29
4.5	1570	3.18	0.24
8.5	2750	9.12	0.30
4.3	1360	5.71	0.24
6.2	2080	4.38	0.26
3.4	2360	4.39	0.25
4.4	1200	7.23	0.21
4.6	1100	5.36	0.31
5.6	1590	7.57	0.33
4.4	1410	3.62	0.24
4.2	1420	5.85	0.24
7.2	1760	4.42	0.27
5.9	2160	5.20	0.26
4.1	2700	5.38	0.23

a. Find the correlation matrix.
b. Estimate the multiple regression model

$$Y_i = \beta_0 + \beta_1 x_{i1} + \beta_2 x_{i2} + \beta_3 x_{i3} + e_i$$

c. Find the residuals. What can you learn by examining the residuals from the fitted model?
d. Do you find any evidence of heteroscedasticity? Do you see any outliers?
e. Do you observe any multicollinearity problems?
f. Is it reasonable to test for serially correlated error terms in this problem? Why or why not?

References

DURBIN, JAMES R. "Testing for Serial Correlation in Least Squares Regression When Some of the Regressors Are Lagged Dependent Variables." *Econometrica* 38 (1970):410–421.

DURBIN, JAMES R., and GEOFFREY S. WATSON. "Testing for Serial Correlation in Least Squares Regression." *Biometrika* (1950):409–428; (1951):159–178; (1971):1–20.

GOLDFELD, STEPHEN M., and RICHARD E. QUANDT. "Some Tests for Homoscedasticity." *Journal of the American Statistical Association* (1965):539–547.

INTRILIGATOR, MICHAEL. *Econometric Models, Techniques and Applications*. Englewood Cliffs, N.J.: Prentice-Hall, 1978.

JOHNSTON, JOHN. *Econometric Methods*. New York: McGraw-Hill, 1972.

JUDGE, GEORGE G., W. E. GRIFFITHS, R. CARTER HILL, HELMUT LUTKEPOHL, and TSOUNG-CHAO LEE. *The Theory and Practice of Econometrics*. 2d ed. New York: Wiley, 1985.

KADIYALA, KOTESWARA R. "A Transformation Used to Circumvent the Problem of Autocorrelation." *Econometrica* 36 (1968):93–96.

Kmenta, Jan. *Elements of Econometrics*. 2d ed. New York: Macmillan, 1986.

Nie, Norman E., C. Hadlai Hull, Jean G. Jenkins, Karin Steinbrenner, and Dale H. Bent. *SPSS Statistical Package for the Social Sciences*. 2d ed. New York: McGraw-Hill, 1975.

Norusis, Marija J. *SPSSX Introductory Statistics Guide*. New York: McGraw-Hill, 1983.

________. *SPSSX Advanced Statistics Guide*. Chicago: SPSS, 1985.

________. *The SPSS Guide to Data Analysis*. Chicago: SPSS, 1986.

Pindyck, Robert S., and Daniel L. Rubinfeld. *Econometric Models and Economic Forecasts*. 2d ed. New York: McGraw-Hill, 1981.

Ryan, Thomas A., Brian L. Joiner, and Barbara F. Ryan. *Minitab Handbook*. 2d ed. Boston: PWS-KENT, 1985.

________. *Minitab Reference Manual*. University Park, Penn.: Minitab Project, 1985.

SAS Introductory Guide. 3d ed. Cary, N.C.: SAS Institute, 1985.

SAS Procedures Guide for Personal Computers. Version 6 ed. Cary, N.C.: SAS Institute, 1986.

SAS Statistics Guide for Personal Computers. Version 6 ed. Cary, N.C.: SAS Institute, 1986.

SAS User's Guide: Basics. Version 5 ed. Cary, N.C.: SAS Institute, 1985.

SAS User's Guide: Statistics. Version 5 ed. Cary, N.C.: SAS Institute, 1985.

SPSSX User's Guide. Chicago: SPSS, 1983.

Theil, Henri. *Principles of Econometrics*. New York: Wiley, 1971.

Chapter Nineteen
Time Series Analysis I: Estimation of the Trend Component

The study of business and economic activity often requires the analysis of data that have been collected over a period of time. Any series of observations that can be arranged chronologically is called a **time series**, and the study of such series is called **time series analysis**. Business executives, economists, and government officials use time series analysis in forecasting sales, tax revenues, government expenditures, and so on.

Following are four major reasons for performing time series analysis:

1. *To forecast the value of a dependent variable*: For example, the seller of any product has to forecast demand for the product in order to know how many items to stock in inventory, investors in the bond market need to forecast interest rates, and investors in the stock market need to forecast stock prices and dividends.

2. *To describe or explain seasonal patterns*: For example, we might be interested in describing how department store sales fluctuate from season to season.

3. *To quantify theories*: Most economic theories can help us predict the signs of coefficients but not their magnitudes. For example, economic theory tells us that increases in interest rates have a negative effect on car sales, but it says nothing about the magnitude of this effect. We can use regression analysis and time series analysis to estimate the magnitude.

4. *To test theories*: Proposed economic theories often relate the value of a certain variable to the value of some other variable. We can use regression analysis and time series analysis to estimate the population regression coefficients in a model and to test hypotheses about the values of these coefficients.

19.1 ▪ Components of a Time Series

In general, the fluctuations in an economic time series result from four different components:

1. trend,
2. seasonal variation,
3. cyclical variation, and
4. irregular, or random, variation (sometimes called the random-error term).

In this chapter, we describe popular models used to determine the trend component of a time series and describe techniques used to determine the seasonal component.

All of these components need not be present in every time series, and some are more important in some series than in others. In fact, our goal is to verify the presence of these components and to determine and quantify their importance. In the remainder of this section, we describe each of these components and provide examples of variables possessing these components individually or in combination.

The Trend

Definition: Trend

The **trend** is the long-term movement in a time series.

Many economic variables, such as the Gross National Product, total government spending, and the sales of new cars, have generally increased over the years. This does not mean that each series has always moved upward from month to month or from year to year but that the long-term trend has been upward over a period of many years. Of course, not all trends are upward. For example, the total number of people employed on farms in the United States has steadily declined since 1947. Whether upward or downward, the trend of a time series is represented by a smooth curve.

Table 19.1 shows annual data for four variables containing a strong trend component, which are graphed in Figures 19.1 through 19.4. Examine the graphs and note the different trends. Figure 19.1 shows that U.S. Gross National Product follows a relatively smooth, nonlinear upward trend. In Figure 19.2, gross domestic investment also follows a nonlinear trend, but, unlike for the GNP, the growth has been irregular. Figure 19.3 shows that the U.S. population has followed a very smooth, approximately linear trend since 1961. Finally, Figure 19.4 shows that the farm population has followed an irregular negative trend since 1961. Each of the four variables has a different trend, illustrating the fact that trends may be positive or negative, approximately linear or nonlinear, regular or irregular.

Seasonal Variation

Definition: Seasonal Variation

Seasonal variation represents fluctuations in a time series that tend to repeat in a regular way year after year.

TABLE 19.1 **Trended Variables, 1961–1986**

Year	GNP (in billions)	Gross Investment (in billions)	Population (in millions)	Farm Population (in millions)
1961	$ 533.8	$ 77.1	183.7	14.8
1962	574.6	87.6	186.5	14.3
1963	606.9	93.1	189.2	13.4
1964	649.8	99.6	191.9	13.0
1965	705.1	116.2	194.3	12.4
1966	772.0	128.6	196.6	11.6
1967	816.4	125.7	198.7	10.9
1968	892.7	137.0	200.7	10.5
1969	963.9	153.2	202.7	10.3
1970	1015.1	148.8	205.1	9.7
1971	1102.7	172.5	207.7	9.4
1972	1212.8	202.0	209.9	9.6
1973	1359.3	238.8	212.0	9.5
1974	1472.8	240.8	213.9	9.3
1975	1598.4	219.6	216.0	8.7
1976	1782.8	277.7	218.0	8.3
1977	1990.5	344.1	220.2	6.2
1978	2249.7	416.8	222.6	6.5
1979	2508.2	454.8	225.1	6.2
1980	2732.0	437.0	227.8	6.1
1981	3052.0	515.5	230.1	5.8
1982	3166.0	447.3	232.5	5.6
1983	3405.7	502.3	234.8	5.8
1984	3765.0	662.1	237.0	5.8
1985	3998.1	661.1	239.3	5.4
1986	4208.5	686.4	241.5	N.A.

Source: Economic Report of the President, 1987 (Washington, D.C.: U.S. Government Printing Office, 1987).

Many variables measured monthly or quarterly show seasonal variation, which is often caused by the effects of the weather (hence the term *seasonal*). Energy consumption, travel and vacation expenditures, and farm output are all affected by changes in the weather. Holidays such as Christmas or Easter cause other seasonal effects. Still others are caused by schools being in session and income tax season.

For example, the demand for air conditioners is much higher in the summer than in the winter, and so one would expect data on factory shipments of air conditioners to show a pronounced, predictable seasonal pattern with most shipments just before the start of summer and only a few shipments during the winter. A seasonal index can be

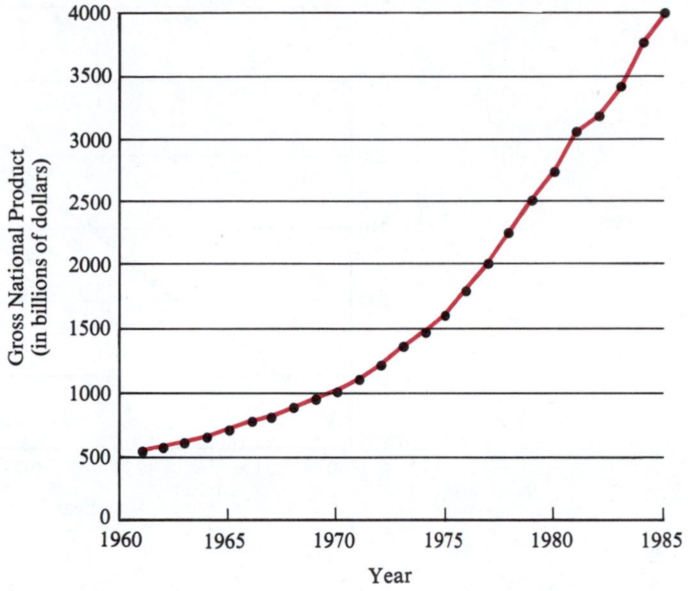

FIGURE 19.1
Gross National Product, 1961–1986.

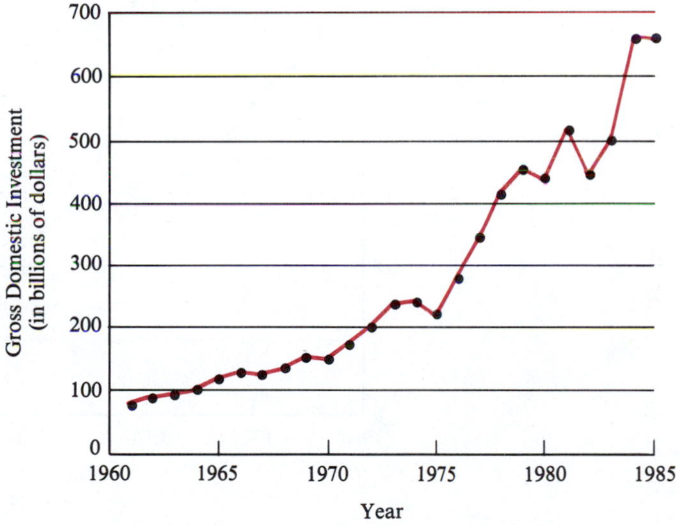

FIGURE 19.2
Gross domestic investment, 1961–1986.

calculated that indicates how each month departs from what would be expected on the basis of trend alone.

A knowledge of seasonal variation is often useful in interpreting data. For example, suppose that unemployment increased by 2% between May and July of 1987. Before taking any action, government officials would be likely to ask, "To what extent is this increase due to seasonal factors rather than to a downturn in economic conditions?" In other words, even if there were no change in the trend and cyclical factors had no effect, would one expect an increase of this magnitude because of seasonal factors alone?

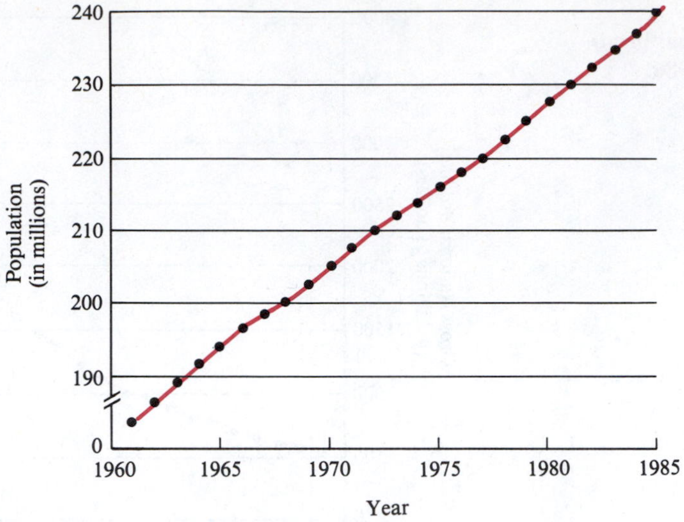

FIGURE 19.3 Population of the United States, 1961–1986.

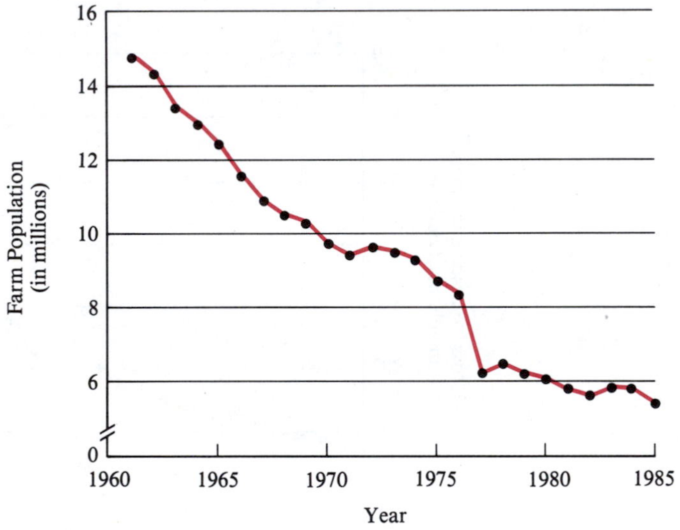

FIGURE 19.4 U.S. farm population, 1961–1985.

Usually it is much easier to make comparisons over time when data have been seasonally adjusted. For example, total unemployment always increases during the summer when schools let out and students begin to look for jobs. Similarly, unemployment always decreases during the Christmas season, when stores increase their sales staffs. To make valid comparisons over time, we should remove these seasonal effects. Otherwise, we might be inclined to take actions to effect a change in some variable when no such action is called for.

Table 19.2 shows data on three monthly variables containing seasonal components: monthly retail sales, monthly production of electric power, and monthly shipments of

TABLE 19.2 **Seasonal variables, 1983–1986**

	Retail Sales (in billions)	Electric Power (in millions of kilowatt-hours)	Shipments of Air Conditioners (in thousands)
1983			
January	$ 81.3	166.3	88
February	78.9	144.5	130
March	93.8	152.2	309
April	94.0	140.4	259
May	97.8	143.2	300
June	100.6	160.4	265
July	99.6	192.0	306
August	100.2	203.6	108
September	98.0	173.7	58
October	100.7	161.4	32
November	103.9	158.2	52
December	125.7	180.5	98
1984			
January	93.1	186.9	168
February	93.7	161.7	262
March	104.3	169.7	504
April	104.3	151.1	459
May	111.3	160.4	588
June	112.0	180.9	648
July	106.6	193.8	187
August	110.7	204.2	47
September	103.9	174.3	40
October	109.2	170.1	36
November	113.3	168.1	51
December	131.8	174.2	113
1985			
January	98.7	200.2	209
February	95.3	172.3	277
March	109.9	170.3	530
April	112.9	160.5	524
May	120.2	170.4	632
June	114.8	181.5	416
July	115.2	205.4	171
August	120.8	206.1	68
September	113.8	183.7	49
October	115.8	174.7	24
November	118.1	169.5	39
December	138.6	193.9	113

continued

TABLE 19.2 (continued)

	Retail Sales (in billions)	Electric Power (in millions of kilowatt-hours)	Shipments of Air Conditioners (in thousands)
1986			
January	105.6	195.9	131
February	99.7	169.1	175
March	114.2	168.4	422
April	115.7	159.6	456
May	125.4	171.1	451
June	120.4	188.8	427
July	120.7	218.6	361
August	124.1	204.0	89
September	124.6	185.5	89
October	123.1	176.3	53
November	120.8	173.3	56
December	151.5	—	92

Source: Survey of Current Business (Washington, D.C.: U.S. Department of Commerce, 1987).

air conditioners. These variables are graphed in Figures 19.5, 19.6, and 19.7, and each exhibits a different seasonal behavior and a different long-term behavior.

Figure 19.5 shows monthly retail sales from January 1983 through December 1986. Because the curve rises to the right, sales are positively trended over time. Since 1983 the trend has been approximately linear. However, note the seasonal peak each December and the seasonal trough each February.

Figure 19.6 shows the monthly production of electric power from fuel for the same time period. Once again the curve has a positive slope and thus a positive trend. Unlike

FIGURE 19.5
Monthly U.S. retail sales, 1983–1986.

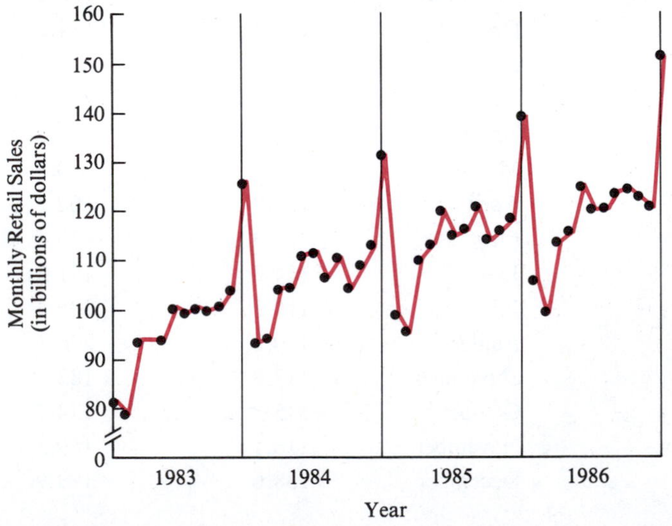

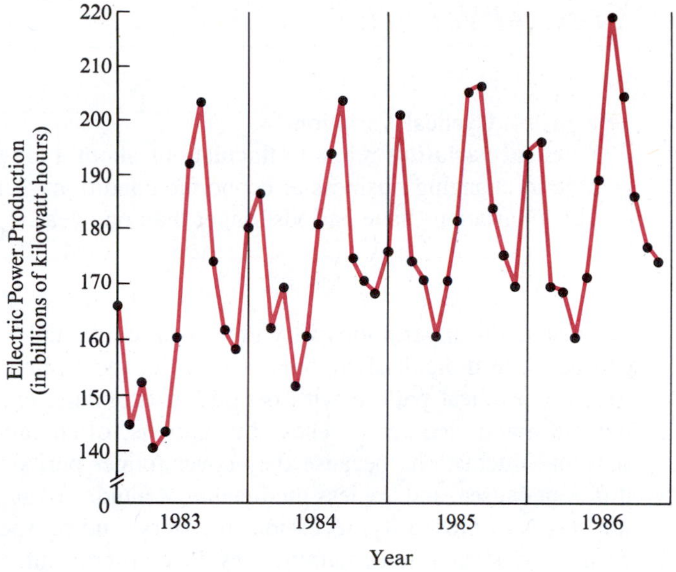

FIGURE 19.6
Monthly production of electric power, 1983–1986.

retail sales, however, the production of electric power tends to have two peaks each year, one during the middle of winter, when electric power is needed to produce heat, and the other during the middle of summer, when electric power is needed to produce air conditioning.

Figure 19.7 shows the monthly factory shipments of air conditioners, also for January 1983 through December 1986. This variable does not appear to have any positive or negative trend, but there is a seasonal pattern. Shipments peak prior to the warm-weather months and die out as the temperature drops. This seasonal pattern indicates that stores increase their inventories a few months before the peak demand period and do not replenish their inventories until the following spring.

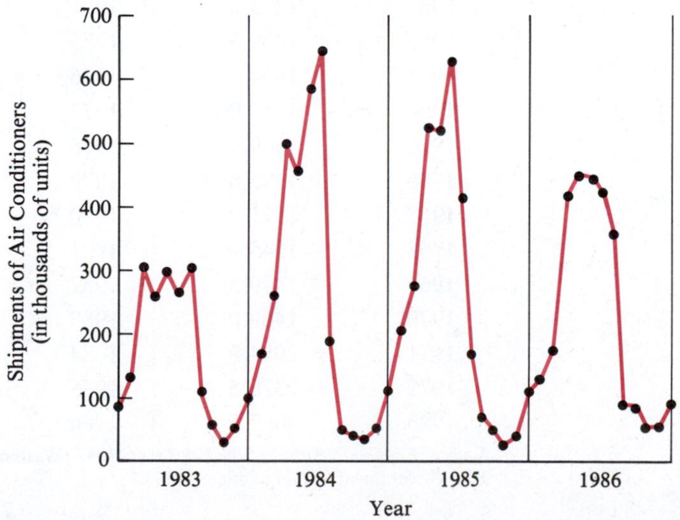

FIGURE 19.7
Monthly shipments of air conditioners, 1983–1986.

Cyclical Variation

Definition: Cyclical Variation

Cyclical variation refers to fluctuations about a long-term trend that are attributable to changing business or economic conditions. Unlike seasonal variations, cyclical variations have periods longer than one year.

Because cyclical variations vary greatly in length and magnitude, removing their effect can be quite difficult. Economic activity in the United States has always exhibited an irregular cyclical pattern with periods of economic expansion followed by periods of recession and vice versa. These fluctuations, often called *business cycles,* differ from seasonal fluctuations because they cover longer periods of time, are brought about by different causes, and are less predictable. An index of aggregate economic activity showing stages of prosperity, recession, recovery, and prosperity is an important example of a time series variable containing a cyclical component.

Table 19.3 shows the number of new public and private housing starts from 1961 through 1986; the data are plotted in Figure 19.8. The graph shows that a cyclical component is present. Since 1961 there has been no long-run trend, and annual variations have been quite irregular. Because there is no regular pattern in the graph of housing starts, it is difficult to produce a good forecast of housing starts by using a time series model.

TABLE 19.3
New Public and Private Housing Starts, 1961–1986

Year	Units (in thousands)	Year	Units (in thousands)
1961	1365.0	1974	1352.5
1962	1492.5	1975	1171.4
1963	1634.9	1976	1547.6
1964	1561.0	1977	2001.7
1965	1509.7	1978	2036.1
1966	1195.8	1979	1760.0
1967	1321.9	1980	1312.6
1968	1545.4	1981	1100.3
1969	1499.5	1982	1072.1
1970	1469.0	1983	1712.5
1971	2084.5	1984	1755.8
1972	2378.5	1985	1745.0
1973	2057.5	1986	1808.3

Source: Economic Report of the President, 1987 (Washington, D.C.: U.S. Government Printing Office, 1987).

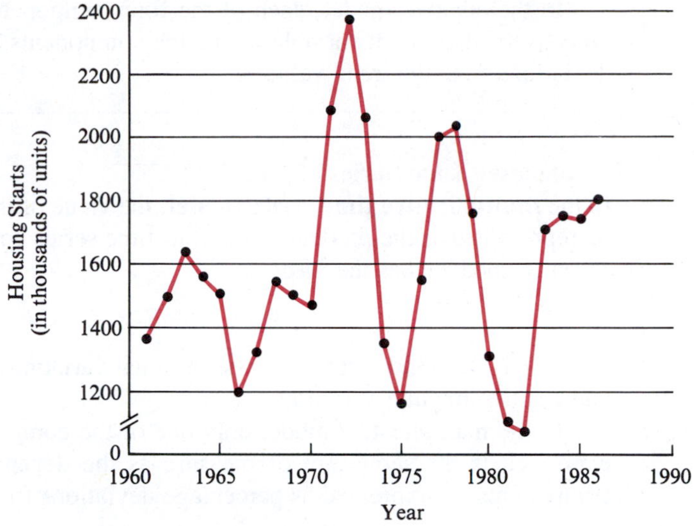

FIGURE 19.8
Public and private housing starts, 1961–1986.

Irregular (Random) Variation

Definition: Irregular Variation

Irregular variation, or **random variation**, is variation in a time series that is unpredictable, taking place randomly at various points of time. Such variation is not accounted for by trend, seasonal, or cyclical factors.

The irregular component of a time series is not systematic and is caused by unpredictable influences. Irregular variation is conceptually similar to the random-error term in regression analysis. The random-error term and irregular variation both represent movements that are unexplained by the model.

Relationships Between Time Series Components

It is of interest to identify the influence of the four components on a particular time series and to determine their relationships with one another. We do this by constructing a time series model, which usually takes one of two forms: additive or multiplicative. These two types of models are described in the accompanying boxes.

Additive Time Series Model

In the **additive time series model**, the value of the dependent variable Y can be represented as the sum of the four time series components. Thus, the additive model takes the form

$$Y = T + S + C + I$$

where T is the trend factor, S is the seasonal variation, C is the cyclical variation, and I is the irregular variation.

In the additive model, each of the four components is measured in the same units as the dependent variable Y, and the components S, C, and I are measured as deviations from the trend value T.

Multiplicative Time Series Model

In the **multiplicative time series model**, the value of the dependent variable Y can be represented as the product of the four time series components. Thus, the multiplicative model takes the form

$$Y = T \times S \times C \times I$$

where T is the trend factor, S is the seasonal variation, C is the cyclical variation, and I is the irregular variation.

In the multiplicative model only one of the components, usually the trend, is expressed in the same unit of measure as the dependent variable Y. The other components are expressed as percentage deviations from the trend.

In the additive model, the deviations from the trend are measured in absolute terms; in the multiplicative model, the deviations from the trend are measured in percentages. For example, suppose we have data showing monthly sales at a department store. If sales tend to increase year after year, there is a long-term upward trend. In general, sales will be highest during December (because of Christmas) and lowest during February. We would be estimating this seasonal effect in absolute terms if our model estimated that sales during December tended to be, say, \$1 million above the annual monthly average, and in percentage terms if our model estimated that sales during December tended to be, say, 40% above the annual monthly average.

The data in Tables 19.1, 19.2, and 19.3 show different patterns of behavior. The type of model used to explain the behavior of a time series variable depends on how frequently the data are gathered and on what pattern of behavior we are trying to describe. For instance, because annual data have no seasonal effects, we are concerned only with describing trend and cyclical effects. In contrast, monthly and quarterly data have not only trend and cyclical effects, but also seasonal effects. Daily data might also vary from day to day on a regular basis. For example, total sales at supermarkets tend to be high on Friday and Saturday and low on Monday and Tuesday. The same pattern holds for daily receipts at movie theaters and department stores and deposits into savings and checking accounts at banks.

In the remaining sections of this chapter, we discuss techniques for estimating the trend of a time series variable. In the next chapter, we discuss how to estimate the seasonal component.

Exercises for Section 19.1

1. Consider the following time-dependent variables:

   - Monthly department store sales
   - Monthly production of new automobiles

- Monthly average temperature in New York City
- Monthly sales of ski equipment
- Annual profits of ski manufacturers
- Annual housing starts
- Monthly sales of cigarettes
- Monthly sales of bread
- Daily receipts from newspaper sales
- Daily recordings of temperature at noon in New York City
- Hourly recordings of temperature in New York City
- Monthly, weekly, or daily number of births of children in the United States

a. State which time series contain a trend component and explain why.
b. State which time series contain a seasonal component and explain why.
c. State which time series contain a cyclical component.

2. Mention some time series that contain the following:
a. A trend component
b. A seasonal component
c. A cyclical component

3. Can you explain why most people prefer a multiplicative model to an additive model?

4. Are the following statements true or false? If false, why?
a. "Trends are always linear."
b. "Trends are always positive."
c. "A seasonal component is a regular fluctuation that occurs year after year."
d. "A cyclic component is a fluctuation that occurs over longer time periods and varies from year to year."

19.2 ▪ The Linear Trend Model

Usually the first step in analyzing a time series is to estimate the trend component T. If the amount of increase or decrease in a series from one time period to another is fairly constant, a straight line may describe the trend appropriately. At times, however, other types of curves may be needed to represent the trend component.

One of the most popular ways of forecasting values of a variable is to project a constant annual increase or decrease. A model for such a forecast is the *linear trend model*; the model is estimated by the *sample trend line*; both concepts are defined in the accompanying boxes.

Definition: Linear Trend Model

The **linear trend model** is represented by the equation

$$Y_t = \beta_0 + \beta_1 t + e_t$$

where

Y_t = value of the dependent variable Y during time period t

t = tth unit of time

e_t = random movement unexplained by the trend variable during time period t

Definition: Sample Trend Line

The estimated regression equation

$$\hat{y}_t = b_0 + b_1 t$$

is called the **sample trend line**, where b_0 and b_1 are the least-squares estimates of the population parameters β_0 and β_1.

Given the observations $y_1, y_2, \ldots, y_n$ and the values $t = 1, 2, \ldots, n$, we estimate β_0 and β_1 using the formulas

$$b_1 = \frac{\sum_{t=1}^{n} t y_t - n\bar{t}\bar{y}}{\sum_{t=1}^{n} t^2 - n\bar{t}^2} \quad \text{and} \quad b_0 = \bar{Y} - b_1\bar{t}$$

where $\bar{t} = \Sigma\, t/n$ and $\bar{y} = \Sigma\, y_t/n$. This estimation of the population parameters results in the *sample trend line*.

A linear trend model is exactly the same as the simple linear regression model discussed in Chapter 15, where the explanatory variable X is replaced by the variable t. Thus, every formula in Chapter 15 holds for the linear trend model if we replace X everywhere by the variable t.

Example 19.1

Estimating the Linear Trend Model: The data in Table 19.4 show annual sales of retail stores from 1981 through 1986 and are graphed in Figure 19.9. Let us estimate the coefficients in the linear trend model and forecast retail sales in 1987 and 1988. (Because the observations are annual data, there are no seasonal effects.)

TABLE 19.4
Computations to estimate the trend line

Year	Retail Sales (in trillions)	Period t	tY	t^2
1981	\$1.038	1	1.038	1
1982	1.075	2	2.150	4
1983	1.173	3	3.519	9
1984	1.293	4	5.172	16
1985	1.373	5	6.865	25
1986	1.445	6	8.670	36
Total	\$7.397	21	27.414	91

Source: Survey of Current Business (Washington, D.C.: U.S. Department of Commerce, 1987).

Solution: We use the explanatory variable Time (represented by t), where t equals 1 in 1981, 2 in 1982, and so on. To estimate the linear trend model, we need the sums $\Sigma\, y_t$,

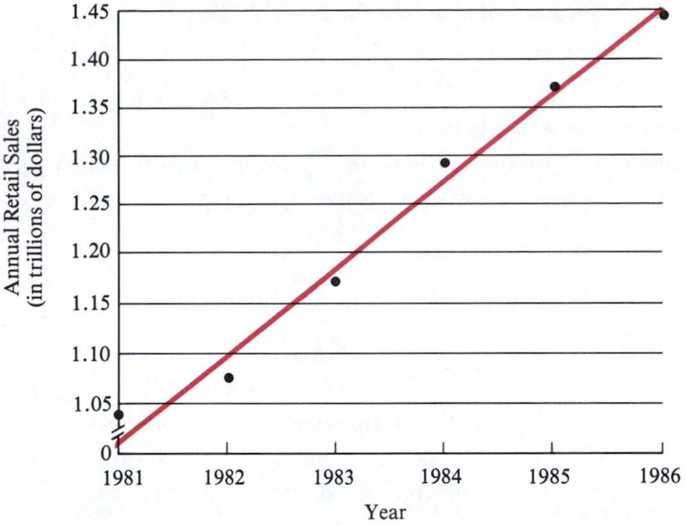

FIGURE 19.9
Annual retail sales, 1981–1986.

Σt, Σty_t, and Σt^2. These are calculated in Table 19.4. The least-squares estimates are then

$$b_1 = \frac{\Sigma ty_t - n\bar{t}\bar{y}}{\Sigma t^2 - n\bar{t}^2}$$

$$= \frac{27.414 - 6(21/6)(7.397/6)}{91 - 6(21/6)^2} = 0.0871$$

and

$$b_0 = (\Sigma y_t/n) - b_1(\Sigma t/n)$$

$$= (7.397/6) - 0.0871(21/6) = 0.9279$$

The estimated trend equation is

$$\hat{y}_t = 0.9279 + 0.0871t \qquad R^2 = .986$$

$$t \text{ statistics:} \quad (45.41) \qquad (16.6)$$

where $t = 1$ in 1981.

The sample trend line is plotted in Figure 19.9, and the SPSSX computer output for this model is shown in Figure 19.10. The trend variable t explains 98% of the annual variation in Y ($R^2 = .98570$). The estimated standard error of the regression is $s = .02195$, which indicates that the typical residual is quite small.

The slope of the sample trend line is $b_1 = 0.0871$, so we predict that retail sales will increase by \$0.0871 trillion, or \$87.1 billion, per year.

The value of the trend variable is $t = 1$ in 1981, so in 1987 the value of the explanatory variable is $t = 7$. The forecasted value for retail sales in 1987 would thus be

$$\hat{y}_7 = 0.9279 + 0.0871(7) = 1.5377$$

FIGURE 19.10 **SPSSX-generated output for Example 19.1.**

```
                                  * * * *   M U L T I P L E   R E G R E S S I O N   * * * *

Listwise Deletion of Missing Data

Equation Number 1    Dependent Variable..   SALES   ANNUAL RETAIL SALES

Beginning Block Number  1.  Method:  Enter     TIME


Variable(s) Entered on Step Number  1..    TIME

Multiple R           .99282        Analysis of Variance
R Square             .98570                          DF      Sum of Squares       Mean Square
Adjusted R Square    .98212        Regression         1              .13281            .13281
Standard Error       .02195        Residual           4              .00193            .00048

                                   F =     275.65856        Signif F =  .0001

----------------- Variables in the Equation ------------------

Variable              B         SE B         Beta         T   Sig T

TIME            .087114      .005247      .992823    16.603   .0001
(Constant)      .927933      .020434                 45.412   .0000

End Block Number   1   All requested variables entered.
```

and the forecasted value for retail sales in 1988 would be

$$\hat{y}_8 = 0.9279 + 0.0871(8) = 1.6248$$

The data are in trillions of dollars, so the forecasted values for 1987 and 1988 are \$1.5377 trillion and \$1.6248 trillion, respectively.

Figure 19.11 shows the actual and predicted values for annual retail sales along with the residuals, as computed by the SPSSX program. The residual plot does not show any striking patterns that would indicate that the model is inadequate. To test for the possible presence of serially correlated error terms, examine the Durbin–Watson statistic. In this problem, the Durbin–Watson statistic is $d = 2.0707$, which falls in the acceptance region if we are testing H_0: $\rho = 0$ against H_1: $\rho > 0$ using a 5% level of significance. ■

Example 19.2 **Forecasting Population Using a Linear Trend Model:** Let Y_t denote the population of the United States in millions in year t, where t equals 1 in 1961, 2 in 1962, and so on through 26 in 1986. The data are shown in Table 19.1 and plotted in Figure 19.3. From the graph, a linear trend model appears to be appropriate to describe the behavior of Y_t. Estimate the linear trend model.

Solution: The sample trend line is

$$\hat{y}_t = 182.3766 + 2.2678t \qquad R^2 = .999$$
$$t \text{ statistics: } (1053) \qquad (202.3)$$

where $t = 1$ in 1961.

The SPSSX computer output is shown in Figure 19.12. This trend model explains more than 99.9% of the variation in population. To forecast the population in 1990, we substitute $t = 30$ into the estimated equation and obtain

$$\hat{y}_{30} = 182.3766 + 2.2678(30) = 250.4106$$

FIGURE 19.11 **SPSSX-generated actual and predicted values and residuals for Example 19.1.**

```
                              * * * *   M U L T I P L E   R E G R E S S I O N   * * * *

Equation Number 1    Dependent Variable..   SALES   ANNUAL RETAIL SALES

Casewise Plot of Standardized Residual

*: Selected    M: Missing

            -3.0             0.0             3.0
   Case #    O:...............:...............:O          SALES       *PRED       *RESID
        1    .                :      *         .           1.04      1.0150        .0230
        2    .          *     .                .           1.08      1.1022     -0.0272
        3    .            *   .                .           1.17      1.1893     -0.0163
        4    .                .     *          .           1.29      1.2764       .0166
        5    .                . *              .           1.37      1.3635  9.4952E-03
        6    .               *.                .           1.45      1.4506 -5.6190E-03
   Case #    O:...............:...............:O          SALES       *PRED       *RESID
            -3.0             0.0             3.0

                              * * * * * * * * * * * * * * * * * * * * * * * * * * * * *

Residuals Statistics:

                    Min          Max      Mean   Std Dev    N

*PRED            1.0150       1.4506    1.2328     .1630    6
*RESID          -0.0272        .0230     .0000     .0196    6
*ZPRED          -1.3363       1.3363     .0000    1.0000    6
*ZRESID         -1.2375       1.0457     .0000      8944    6

Total Cases =         6

Durbin-Watson Test =     2.07070
```

FIGURE 19.12 **SPSSX-generated output for Example 19.2.**

```
                              * * * *   M U L T I P L E   R E G R E S S I O N   * * * *

Listwise Deletion of Missing Data

Equation Number 1    Dependent Variable..   POP   POPULATION

Beginning Block Number  1.  Method:  Enter     TIME


Variable(s) Entered on Step Number  1..    TIME


Multiple R              .99971       Analysis of Variance
R Square                .99941                        DF       Sum of Squares       Mean Square
Adjusted R Square       .99939       Regression        1           7521.70864        7521.70864
Standard Error          .42865       Residual         24              4.40982            .18374

                                     F =    40936.15077       Signif F =   .0000

------------------ Variables in the Equation ------------------

Variable               B         SE B        Beta          T   Sig T

TIME            2.267829      .011209     .999707    202.327   .0000
(Constant)    182.376615      .173102               1053.582   .0000

End Block Number    1    All requested variables entered.
```

Over a period of 5 to 10 years, the linear trend model should provide fairly accurate forecasts of the U.S. population, which has followed an essentially linear path during any one 20- to 30-year period. Over longer periods of time, however, the population of the United States has tended to follow a nonlinear path. ■

Table 19.5 shows the United States population from 1800 to 1980, and the data are plotted in Figure 19.13. In Figure 19.3, we saw that the time path of population appears to be linear from 1961 through 1986, but Figure 19.13 shows that the time path is definitely nonlinear over the longer period from 1800 through 1980. Figure 19.13 shows

TABLE 19.5
U.S. population 1800–1980

Year	Population (in millions)	Year	Population (in millions)
1800	5.3	1900	76.0
1810	7.2	1910	92.0
1820	9.6	1920	105.7
1830	12.9	1930	122.8
1840	17.1	1940	131.7
1850	23.2	1950	150.7
1860	31.4	1960	178.5
1870	39.8	1970	203.3
1880	50.2	1980	226.5
1890	62.9		

Source: Statistical Abstract of the United States, 1987 (Washington, D.C.: U.S. Department of Commerce, 1987).

FIGURE 19.13
U.S. population, 1800–1980.

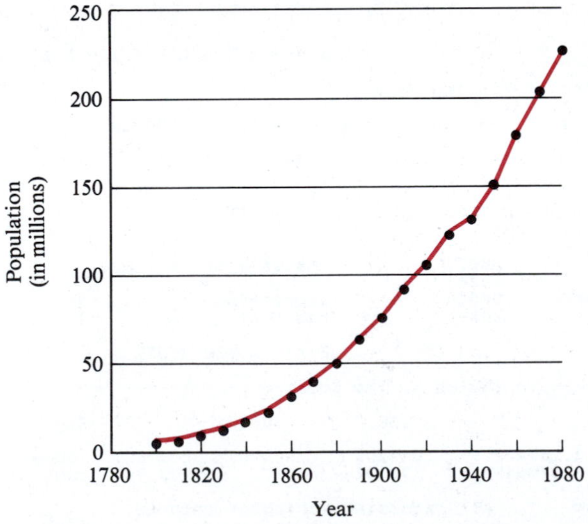

that a linear model might provide a reasonable representation of population growth during any particular 20- to 30-year period but not over longer periods. Thus, the use of the estimated linear trend equation to forecast population more than a few years in the future is not recommended. To describe the nonlinear trend in population, we could use a polynomial trend model, which is discussed in the next section.

When a trend variable is included as one of the explanatory variables in a multiple regression model, the model is a mixture of an explanatory model and a descriptive model. The pure trend model describes but does not explain broad movements in a variable over time. It is useful to consider why adding the trend variable to a multiple regression model seems to produce good results in many situations. For example, adding a trend variable to a regression model commonly increases the adjusted R^2 by a substantial amount. Why?

Refer to the omitted-variable problem discussed in Section 18.3. If one or more relevant explanatory variables are omitted from a model, the estimated coefficients will be biased. The nature and amount of the bias depend on how the included variables are correlated with the excluded variables and how the effects of the excluded variables can be shifted to the coefficients of the included variables. Because many of the variables omitted from a model may exhibit trends over time, a trend variable may pick up the effect of these omitted variables and thereby reduce the potential bias in the coefficients of the other variables included in the equation.

Exercises for Section 19.2

1. We are given the accompanying data on the money supply (currency plus demand deposits) for the years 1977 to 1986.

Year	Period t	Currency plus Demand Deposits (in billions) Y	Year	Period t	Currency plus Demand Deposits (in billions) Y
1977	1	$335.3	1983	7	$526.9
1978	2	363.0	1984	8	557.5
1979	3	391.7	1985	9	627.0
1980	4	416.6	1986	10	730.5
1981	5	443.2	1987	11	753.2
1982	6	481.3			

Source: Economic Report of the President, 1988 (Washington, D.C.: U.S. Government Printing Office, 1988).

a. Graph the data on a scatter diagram.
b. Estimate the trend line and graph it.
c. Calculate R^2.
d. Forecast Y for 1990.

2. The accompanying data show total employment in agriculture for the years 1978 to 1987.

Year	Period t	Farm Population (in millions) Y	Year	Period t	Farm Population (in millions) Y
1978	1	3.39	1983	6	3.38
1979	2	3.35	1984	7	3.32
1980	3	3.36	1985	8	3.18
1981	4	3.36	1986	9	3.16
1982	5	3.40	1987	10	3.21

Source: Economic Report of the President, 1988 (Washington, D.C.: U.S. Government Printing Office, 1988).

a. Graph the data on a scatter diagram.
b. Estimate the trend line and graph it.
c. Calculate R^2.
d. Forecast Y for 1990.

3. We have the accompanying data on the total population of the United States.

Year	Period t	Population (in millions) Y	Year	Period t	Population (in millions) Y
1860	1	31	1930	8	123
1870	2	40	1940	9	132
1880	3	50	1950	10	151
1890	4	63	1960	11	179
1900	5	76	1970	12	203
1910	6	92	1980	13	227
1920	7	106			

Source: Statistical Abstract of the United States, 1987 (Washington, D.C.: U.S. Government Printing Office, 1988).

a. Graph the data on a scatter diagram.
b. Estimate the trend line and graph it.
c. Calculate R^2.
d. Predict the population in 1990.

4. The accompanying data show personal disposable income in the United States for the years 1977 to 1986.

Year	Disposable Income (in billions)	Year	Disposable Income (in billions)
1977	\$1379	1983	\$2428
1978	1551	1984	2669
1979	1729	1985	2841
1980	1918	1986	3022
1981	2128	1987	3181
1982	2261		

Source: Economic Report of the President, 1988 (Washington, D.C.: U.S. Government Printing Office, 1988).

a. Estimate the trend line and graph it along with the data.
b. Forecast the disposable income for 1990 and 1991.

5. The accompanying data show personal expenditures on food and beverages.

Year	Expenditures on Food and Beverages (in billions)	Year	Expenditures on Food and Beverages (in billions)
1940	$ 20	1965	$101
1945	40	1970	142
1950	54	1975	219
1955	67	1980	349
1960	83	1985	469

Source: Economic Report of the President, 1987 (Washington, D.C.: U.S. Government Printing Office, 1987).

a. Plot the data; estimate the trend line and graph it.
b. Forecast personal expenditures on food and beverages for 1995.

6. The accompanying data show annual sales at Ostroski's World of Cycles. Revenues are expected to increase in future years because of the increasing popularity and rising prices of motorcycles.

Year	Revenue (in thousands)	Year	Revenue (in thousands)
1977	$100	1983	$144
1978	106	1984	148
1979	114	1985	160
1980	120	1986	163
1981	130	1987	170
1982	134		

a. Estimate the linear trend line using 1977 as $t = 1$.
b. Forecast revenue for the year 1993 using the trend line.

7. The following data show the populations in millions of two counties in recent years:

Year	County 1	County 2	Year	County 1	County 2
1981	14.2	11.8	1985	13.4	13.6
1982	13.8	12.2	1986	13.0	13.9
1983	13.9	12.3	1987	13.2	14.4
1984	13.7	12.9	1988	13.5	14.6

a. Estimate the trend line for County 1 using $t = 1$ in 1981.
b. Use the equation from part (a) to predict the population of County 1 in 1993.
c. Plot the data for County 1 and graph the trend line.
d. Note that since 1986, the population in County 1 has been increasing. Do you think that the population in County 1 is adequately explained by a linear trend line? Do you have a lot of faith in your answer to part (b)?
e. Estimate the trend line for County 2 using $t = 1$ in 1981.
f. Use the equation in part (e) to predict the population of County 2 in 1993.
g. Plot the data for County 2 and graph the trend line.

h. Do you have more faith in your prediction in part (f) than in part (b)? Calculate R^2 for each equation. Does this help explain your preference?

8. The following data show the price of a share of stock in the Molleran Manufacturing Corporation on the last day of the month for eight consecutive months:

Month	Price	Month	Price
January	$6.42	May	$10.14
February	7.27	June	11.61
March	8.42	July	12.50
April	9.10	August	13.42

a. Plot the data and estimate a linear trend line using $t = 1$ for January.
b. Predict the price of the stock on the last days of September, October, November, and December.
c. Calculate R^2. Is this value large enough to suggest that your predictions might be reliable?
d. Graph the trend line on the scatter diagram.

9. The regional sales manager has to set next quarter's sales quotas for the sales representatives in his region. During the last five quarters, sales have been growing approximately linearly. The sales data follow:

Quarter	Sales (in thousands)
1	$110
2	132
3	150
4	176
5	194

a. Plot the data and estimate the trend line using $t = 1$ for quarter 1.
b. What is a reasonable quota for quarter 6? For quarter 7?

10. The accompanying data show the number of new business incorporations for the years 1976 to 1985.

Year	Period t	Incorporations (in thousands)	Year	Period t	Incorporations (in thousands)
1976	1	376	1982	7	567
1977	2	436	1983	8	600
1978	3	478	1984	9	635
1979	4	525	1985	10	662
1980	5	534	1986	11	703
1981	6	581			

Source: Economic Report of the President, 1988 (Washington, D.C.: U.S. Government Printing Office, 1988).

a. Plot the data on a scatter diagram.
b. Estimate the linear trend equation.
c. Plot the estimated line on the scatter diagram.
d. Calculate R^2.
e. Predict Y for 1990.

11. The accompanying data show the number of business failures for the years 1976 to 1987.

Year	Period t	Business Failures (in thousands)	Year	Period t	Business Failures (in thousands)
1976	1	10	1982	7	25
1977	2	8	1983	8	31
1978	3	7	1984	9	52
1979	4	8	1985	10	57
1980	5	12	1986	11	62
1981	6	17	1987	12	61

Source: Economic Report of the President, 1988 (Washington, D.C.: U.S. Government Printing Office, 1988).

a. Plot the data on a scatter diagram.
b. Estimate the linear trend equation.
c. Plot the estimated line on the scatter diagram.
d. Calculate R^2.
e. Predict Y for 1990.

12. Are the following statements true or false? If false, explain why.

a. "A trend variable should be included in all regression equations that are estimated from time series data."
b. "One possible reason for including a trend variable in a multiple regression model is to pick up the effects of other variables that have been omitted."
c. "A possible reason for including a trend variable in a multiple regression model is that it picks up unobservable or hard-to-measure effects, such as changes in tastes, technology, or productivity that occur slowly but steadily over time."

19.3 ▪ *The Polynomial Trend Model*

When graphed over time, many economic variables approximately follow a quadratic curve rather than a straight line; in such cases it is appropriate to fit a quadratic trend curve. Occasionally a cubic or higher-order curve is appropriate to describe the path of an economic variable over time. The general polynomial trend model is described in the accompanying box.

Definition: Polynomial Trend Model

The **polynomial trend model** is

$$Y_t = \beta_0 + \beta_1 t + \beta_2 t^2 + \cdots + \beta_s t^s + e_t$$

where

Y_t = value of the dependent variable at time t

t = tth unit of time

s = degree of the polynomial

e_t = random-error term at time t

The linear trend model is a special case of the polynomial trend model in which $s = 1$. The *quadratic,* or *second-degree, trend model* is a special case of the polynomial trend model in which $s = 2$. For most variables studied in economics and business, s rarely exceeds 2 or 3.

Economic variables such as annual sales of a firm and annual profits often tend to follow a quadratic trend curve for a period of years. In addition, the time paths of many aggregate variables for the U.S. economy can be approximated by a quadratic trend curve. Naturally we have to be quite cautious in using these trend curves to predict future values because if the underlying forces that influence the dependent variable change in the future, the future path of the dependent variable will no longer follow the polynomial trend.

Example 19.3

Fitting a Second-Degree Polynomial: The data for the U.S. Gross National Product in Table 19.1 are plotted in Figure 19.1. From Figure 19.1, it is obvious that a linear trend model would be inadequate, and a second-degree polynomial might be appropriate to explain the values of the GNP. Let us estimate the coefficients in the second-degree polynomial model

$$Y_t = \beta_0 + \beta_1 t + \beta_2 t^2 + e_t$$

where t equals 1 in 1961, 2 in 1962, and so on.

Solution: Estimating this model is equivalent to estimating a multiple regression model in which the first explanatory variable is $t = 1, 2, 3, \ldots, 26$ and the second explanatory variable is $t^2 = 1, 4, 9, \ldots, 676$. Quadratic polynomial models were discussed in Section 17.1.

Figure 19.14 shows the SPSSX computer output for the second-degree polynomial model. The estimated GNP polynomial trend curve is

$$\begin{array}{lllll} \text{GNP}_t = & 625.148 & - 24.445t & + 6.364t^2 & R^2 = .998 \\ t \text{ statistics:} & (16.8) & (-3.86) & (27.9) & \end{array}$$

where t equals 1 in 1961, 2 in 1962, and so on.

The computer output shows that the t statistic for b_2 is 27.9 and the prob-value is .0000. Thus, the evidence is extremely strong that the population regression coefficient β_2 is nonzero. In addition, the R^2 value indicates that the model explains more than 99% of the annual variation in GNP. The data and the estimated second-degree polynomial are plotted in Figure 19.15; note that the data fall extremely close to the estimated trend curve.

Now let us use the estimated polynomial equation to predict GNP in 1990. Based on $t = 1$ in 1961, the value of t in 1990 is $t = 30$. After substituting $t = 30$ into the estimated equation, the predicted value of GNP (in billions of dollars) in 1990 is

$$\text{GNP}_{30} = 625.148 - 24.445(30) + 6.364(30)^2 = 5619.398$$

This forecast is based on the assumption that past trends will continue unchanged in the future. However, if economic conditions change, then another forecasting technique might be necessary. Also, the further into the future we forecast, the less confidence we have in our forecast.

FIGURE 19.14 **SPSSX-generated output for Example 19.3.**

```
                             * * * *   M U L T I P L E   R E G R E S S I O N   * * * *

Listwise Deletion of Missing Data

Equation Number 1    Dependent Variable..   GNP   GROSS NATIONAL PRODUCT

Beginning Block Number  1.  Method:  Enter      T       TSQ

Variable(s) Entered on Step Number  1..    TSQ
                                    2..    T

Multiple R            .99887        Analysis of Variance
R Square              .99773                            DF      Sum of Squares      Mean Square
Adjusted R Square     .99754        Regression           2      34417595.16481   17208797.58241
Standard Error      58.31070        Residual            23         78203.16134       3400.13745

                                    F =      5061.20645       Signif F =   .0000

------------------ Variables in the Equation ------------------

Variable             B          SE B        Beta         T  Sig T

TSQ           6.363675      .227804    1.152623    27.935  .0000
T           -24.445009     6.336883   -0.159168    -3.858  .0008
(Constant)  625.148000    37.126317                16.838  .0000

End Block Number   1   All requested variables entered.
```

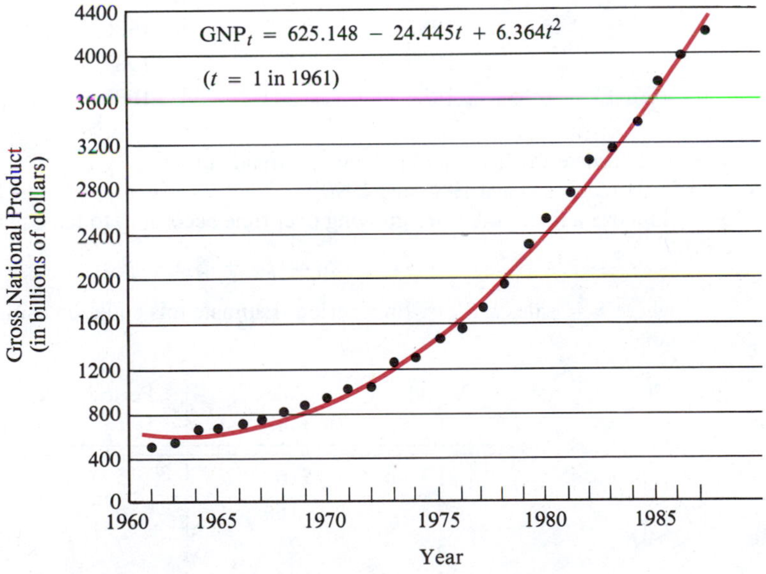

FIGURE 19.15 **Data and estimated polynomial model for Example 19.3.**

Exercises for Section 19.3

1. The accompanying table shows the index of production in the iron and steel industry for the years 1971 to 1985, where the index value for 1977 is 100. Plot the data.

Year	Index (1977 = 100)	Year	Index (1977 = 100)
1971	93.4	1979	108.0
1972	103.8	1980	86.3
1973	118.2	1981	92.5
1974	114.5	1982	57.5
1975	92.0	1983	66.1
1976	101.4	1984	73.4
1977	100.0	1985	70.4
1978	107.5	1986	63.4

Source: Economic Report of the President, 1988 (Washington, D.C.: U.S. Government Printing Office, 1988).

a. Estimate the linear trend line.
b. Estimate the second-degree polynomial trend curve.
c. Forecast the value of the index in 1988, 1989, and 1990 by using the linear trend line and the polynomial trend curve.

2. The accompanying data show annual sales of the TLG Corporation.

Year	Sales (in millions)	Year	Sales (in millions)
1981	\$576	1985	\$559
1982	546	1986	525
1983	524	1987	603
1984	541	1988	669

a. Estimate the linear and polynomial trend curves.
b. Forecast sales in 1989 and 1990.

3. Suppose a firm's sales are growing over time according to the equation

$$S_t = \beta_0 + \beta_1 t + \beta_2 t^2 + e_t$$

where S = sales and t = time period. Estimate this equation using the data in the accompanying table.

Period t	Sales (in millions)	Period t	Sales (in millions)
1	\$10	5	\$ 58
2	15	6	83
3	24	7	112
4	37	8	150

4. The following data show the annual sales in millions of dollars (Y) for the Bowen Candy Company during a ten-year period:

t	1	2	3	4	5	6	7	8	9	10
Y	1.2	1.6	1.9	2.5	3.1	3.8	4.7	5.7	7.0	8.0

a. Plot the data on a scatter diagram. Does a linear or quadratic relationship better describe the relationship between Y and t?
b. Estimate the linear trend model

$$Y_t = \beta_0 + \beta_1 t + e_t$$

c. Estimate the quadratic regression equation

$$Y_t = \beta_0 + \beta_1 t + \beta_2 t^2 + e_t$$

d. Calculate R^2 for each equation.
e. Test H_0: $\beta_2 = 0$ against H_1: $\beta_2 \neq 0$. Let $\alpha = .05$.
f. Plot the estimated equations on the scatter diagram.

5. An analyst for Ajax Records has estimated a quadratic regression equation to help forecast future revenues of the company. The estimated equation is

$$\hat{y}_t = 216.8 + 9.1t + 0.3t^2$$

where

$\hat{y}_t$ = predicted revenue in year t in thousands of dollars
t = 1 in 1976, 2 in 1977, and so forth

a. Plot the quadratic regression equation.
b. Predict revenue in 1991.
c. Predict revenue in 1992.

6. Another analyst for Ajax Records estimated the following cubic regression equation for forecasting revenues:

$$\hat{y}_t = 214.5 + 8.6t + 0.2t^2 + 0.1t^3$$

where

$\hat{y}_t$ = predicted revenue in year t in thousands of dollars
t = 1 in 1976, 2 in 1977, and so forth

a. Plot the cubic regression equation.
b. Predict revenue in 1991.
c. Predict revenue in 1992.

7. The following data show annual sales revenues (in thousands of dollars) during a 10-year period at a small manufacturing firm:

Week (t)	1	2	3	4	5	6	7	8	9	10
Sales (Y)	48	54	60	67	76	86	94	104	112	124

a. Estimate the quadratic equation $Y_t = \beta_0 + \beta_1 t + \beta_2 t^2 + e_t$.
b. Let $\alpha = .05$. Test H_0: $\beta_2 = 0$ against H_1: $\beta_2 > 0$.
c. Plot the data and the estimated equation.

19.4 ▪ The Exponential Trend Model

The exponential model is useful for finding the trend in a variable that tends to grow at a fairly constant percentage rate each time period.

Definition: The Exponential Trend Model

In the **exponential trend model**, it is assumed that Y_t can be explained by the equation

$$Y_t = c \exp(\beta_1 t + \beta_2 t^2 + \cdots + \beta_s t^s)$$

After taking the natural logarithm of both sides of this equation and adding a random-error term, we obtain

$$\ln Y_t = \ln c + \beta_1 t + \beta_2 t^2 + \cdots + \beta_s t^s + e_t$$

or

$$\ln Y_t = \beta_0 + \beta_1 t + \beta_2 t^2 + \cdots + \beta_s t^s + e_t$$

where $\beta_0 = \ln c$.

Like the polynomial trend model, the exponential trend model can be used to describe movements in a time series variable that follows a relatively smooth but nonlinear path over time. As an example, let us estimate the exponential trend model for the stock of currency in the United States since 1961.

Example 19.4

Estimating an Exponential Trend Model: Table 19.6 shows the stock of currency in the United States from 1961 through 1986, and the data are plotted in Figure 19.16. The data follow a smooth, nonlinear path, and an exponential model seems to be a good candidate for describing the behavior of Y_t, the stock of currency at time t. (A quadratic

TABLE 19.6 Stock of U.S. Currency, 1961–1986

Year	Currency (in billions) Y	$\ln Y$	Year	Currency (in billions) Y	$\ln Y$
1961	\$ 29.5	3.38	1974	\$ 67.9	4.22
1962	30.6	3.42	1975	73.8	4.30
1963	32.5	3.48	1976	80.6	4.39
1964	34.3	3.54	1977	88.6	4.48
1965	36.3	3.59	1978	97.6	4.58
1966	38.3	3.69	1979	106.4	4.67
1967	40.4	3.70	1980	116.7	4.76
1968	43.4	3.77	1981	124.1	4.82
1969	46.1	3.83	1982	134.3	4.90
1970	49.2	3.90	1983	148.3	5.00
1971	52.6	3.96	1984	158.5	5.07
1972	56.8	4.04	1985	170.6	5.14
1973	61.6	4.12	1986	183.5	5.21

Source: Economic Report of the President, 1987 (Washington, D.C.: U.S. Government Printing Office, 1987).

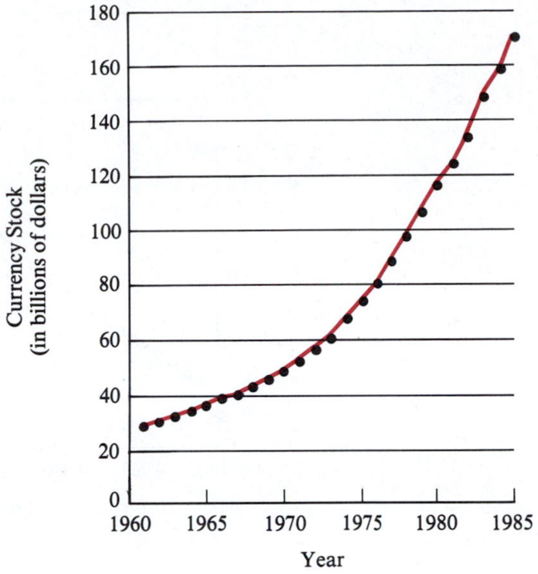

FIGURE 19.16
Scatter diagram of data in Table 19.6.

trend model would also do a good job of describing Y_t.) Let us estimate the exponential trend model

$$Y_t = ce^{\beta_1 t}$$

Solution: After transforming the model by taking logs and adding a random-error term, we obtain

$$\ln Y_t = \beta_0 + \beta_1 t + e_t$$

where $\beta_0 = \ln c$ and $\ln Y_t$ denotes the natural logarithm of the currency stock at time t. To estimate the coefficients, we use $\ln Y_t$ as the dependent variable and t as the explanatory variable where t equals 1 in 1961, 2 in 1962, and so forth. Table 19.6 also shows the values of $\ln Y_t$. From Figure 19.17, which shows the values of $\ln Y_t$ plotted against t, it appears that $\ln Y_t$ can be described as a linear function of time.

The estimated model is

$$\ln \hat{y}_t = 3.194981 + 0.076487t \qquad R^2 = .993$$
$$t \text{ statistics:} \quad (158.1) \qquad (58.5)$$

where t equals 1 in 1961, 2 in 1962, and so on. The SPSSX computer output for this model is shown in Figure 19.18. The computer output shows that the t statistic for b_1 is 58.478 and the prob-value is .0000, so we can feel very confident that the population regression coefficient β_1 is nonzero. From R^2, we see that the model explains more than 99% of the variation in $\ln Y_t$ (not Y_t). From the plot of the estimated logarithmic equation in Figure 19.17, we can see that the estimated logarithmic equation explains the data almost perfectly.

FIGURE 19.17
Scatter diagram showing the logarithm of stock of currency versus time from Table 19.6.

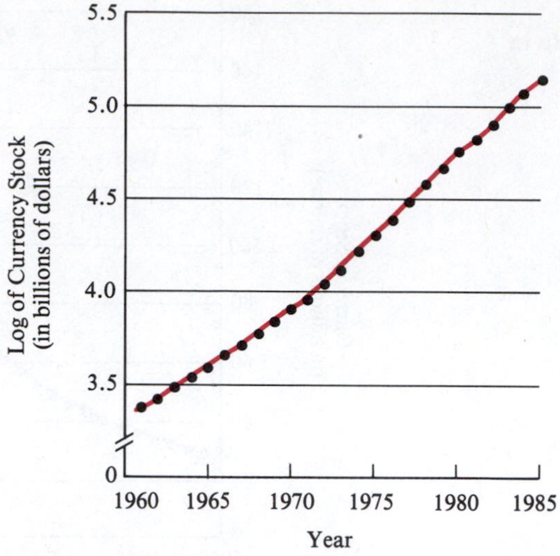

FIGURE 19.18 **SPSSX-generated output for Example 19.4.**

```
                                   * * * *   M U L T I P L E   R E G R E S S I O N   * * * *

Listwise Deletion of Missing Data

Equation Number 1    Dependent Variable..   LOGC

Beginning Block Number  1.  Method:  Enter      T

Variable(s) Entered on Step Number  1..    T

Multiple R           .99651          Analysis of Variance
R Square             .99303                              DF      Sum of Squares      Mean Square
Adjusted R Square    .99274          Regression           1             8.55596          8.55596
Standard Error       .05002          Residual            24              .06005           .00250

                                     F =     3419.71183       Signif F =  .0000

------------------ Variables in the Equation ------------------

Variable              B         SE B        Beta          T   Sig T

T                .076487     .001308     .996509     58.478   .0000
(Constant)      3.194981     .020199                158.173   .0000

End Block Number   1    All requested variables entered.
```

Recalling that $b_0 = \ln \hat{c} = 3.194981$, we obtain the estimate for c of

$$\hat{c} = e^{3.194981} = 24.4097$$

This yields the exponential trend curve

$$\hat{y}_t = 24.4097e^{0.076487t}$$

Now suppose we wanted to use this model to predict the value for the stock of currency in 1988. Based on $t = 1$ in 1961, the value of t in 1988 would be $t = 28$. The predicted value is then

$$\ln \hat{y}_{28} = 3.194981 + 0.076487(28) = 5.336617$$

After finding the antilogarithm, the predicted value is

$$\hat{y}_{28} = 207.8085$$

or approximately $207.8 billion.

In this example, we obtained an almost perfect fit ($R^2 = .993$) by using an exponential trend model. If a quadratic trend equation had been estimated instead, the estimated equation would have been

$$\hat{y}_t = 34.0434 - 1.2634t + 0.2678t^2$$

and the value of R^2 would have been .99893. This shows that if the exponential model provides a good description, then a quadratic trend model will probably provide a good description of the data also. ■

Exercises for Section 19.4

1. The accompanying data show the total interest paid by federal, state, and local governments in the United States from 1973 to 1987.

Year	Interest (in billions)	Year	Interest (in billions)
1973	$29.6	1981	$109.1
1974	33.6	1982	128.3
1975	37.7	1983	145.1
1976	43.6	1984	173.5
1977	47.9	1985	194.5
1978	56.5	1986	205.8
1979	68.2	1987	214.6
1980	83.2		

Source: Economic Report of the President, 1988 (Washington, D.C.: U.S. Government Printing Office, 1988).

a. Estimate the linear trend line using $t = 1$ for 1973. Calculate R^2.
b. Forecast interest payments in 1991 and 1992 using the linear trend line.
c. Estimate the model $\ln Y_t = \beta_0 + \beta_1 t + e_t$, where Y_t = interest payments in year t. Calculate R^2.
d. Forecast interest payments in 1991 and 1992 using the exponential trend line.

2. The accompanying data show the money supply (currency plus demand deposits) for the years 1970 to 1987.

Year	Money Supply (in billions)	Year	Money Supply (in billions)
1970	$216.6	1979	$391.1
1971	230.8	1980	416.6
1972	252.0	1981	443.2
1973	265.9	1982	481.3
1974	277.5	1983	526.9
1975	291.1	1984	557.5
1976	310.4	1985	627.0
1977	335.3	1986	730.5
1978	363.0	1987	753.2

Source: Economic Report of the President, 1988 (Washington, D.C.: U.S. Government Printing Office, 1988).

a. Estimate the linear trend line using $t = 1$ in 1970 and calculate R^2.
b. Estimate the money supply in 1990 and 1991 using the linear trend line.
c. Estimate the equation $\ln Y_t = \beta_0 + \beta_1 t + e_t$ and calculate R^2.
d. Estimate the money supply in 1990 and 1991 using the exponential trend line.

3. The accompanying data show federal government expenditures from 1970 to 1987.

Year	Expenditures (in millions)	Year	Expenditures (in millions)
1970	$207.8	1979	$ 521.1
1971	224.8	1980	615.1
1972	249.0	1981	703.3
1973	269.3	1982	781.2
1974	305.5	1983	835.9
1975	364.2	1984	895.6
1976	393.7	1985	984.6
1977	430.1	1986	1032.0
1978	470.7	1987	1069.1

Source: Economic Report of the President, 1988 (Washington, D.C.: U.S. Government Printing Office, 1988).

a. Estimate the equation $\ln Y_t = \beta_0 + \beta_1 t + e_t$.
b. Predict government expenditures for the years 1990 and 1991.
c. Plot the data against time.

4. Suppose it is hypothesized that the Gross National Product (GNP) can be explained by the model

$$\ln \text{GNP}_t = \beta_0 + \beta_1 t + e_t$$

where t represents time as measured in the accompanying data. The *Economic Report of the President* gives the following data, expressed in billions of 1982 dollars:

Year	t	GNP (in billions of 1982 dollars)	Year	t	GNP (in billions of 1982 dollars)
1945	1	$1354	1970	6	$2416
1950	2	1204	1975	7	2695
1955	3	1495	1980	8	3187
1960	4	1665	1985	9	3585
1965	5	2088			

a. Plot GNP versus time.
b. Plot ln GNP versus time.
c. Estimate and plot the equation $\ln \text{GNP}_t = \beta_0 + \beta_1 t + e_t$.
d. Forecast GNP for 1995.

5. The revenue of the Davidson Computer Company has been growing rapidly during the last six quarters. The manager thinks that revenue in future quarters can be predicted by using the logarithmic trend equation

$$\ln Y_t = 1 + 0.4t$$

where t equals 1 in quarter 1, 2 in quarter 2, and so forth, and where Y is expressed in thousands of dollars.

a. Predict Y for quarters 8, 9, and 10.
b. Does the coefficient 0.4 mean that Y increases $400 every quarter?

6. A marketing researcher studied annual sales of a product that had been introduced 10 years ago. The data were as follows, where t is the year (coded) and Y is sales in thousands of units:

t	1	2	3	4	5	6	7	8	9	10
y	98	135	162	178	221	232	283	300	374	395

a. Prepare a scatter plot of the data. Does a linear relation appear adequate here?
b. Use the transformation $Y'_t = \ln Y_t$ and obtain the estimated linear regression function for the transformed data.
c. Plot the estimated regression line and the transformed data. Does the regression line appear to be a good fit to the transformed data?
d. Obtain the residuals and plot them against the fitted values.
e. Express the estimated regression equation in the original units.

19.5 ▪ *Autoregressive Forecasting Models*

A frequently used time series model is the *autoregressive model*. This is a special case of the multiple regression model in which some or all the explanatory variables are lagged values of Y_t.

Definition: The Autoregressive Model

The **autoregressive model** takes the form

$$Y_t = \beta_0 + \beta_1 y_{t-1} + \beta_2 y_{t-2} + \cdots + \beta_s y_{t-s} + e_t$$

The value y_{t-s} is called the *lagged value* of Y at time $(t - s)$. The *order* of the autoregressive model is s.

In an autoregressive equation, the value of Y at time t is explained by the values of Y during the previous s periods. As usual, a random-error term e_t is included. This model might be criticized because it might be some set of variables $X_1, X_2, \ldots, X_K$ rather than $y_{t-1}, y_{t-2}, \ldots, y_{t-s}$ that causes Y to assume a specific value. On the other hand, if the true causal factors are $X_1, X_2, \ldots, X_K$ and they vary in a relatively systematic manner from one period to the next, then Y should also vary in a systematic manner from one period to the next. Thus, knowledge of the values $y_{t-1}, y_{t-2}, \ldots, y_{t-n}$ should provide us with information when forecasting y_t, y_{t+1}, and so on. In a sense, the lagged dependent variable Y_{t-1} can be thought of as being a proxy for the true causal variables $X_1, X_2, \ldots, X_K$.

If the time series we are trying to forecast follows a relatively smooth path over time, a low-order autoregressive model (i.e., an autoregressive model with a small value of s) can usually produce fairly accurate results. For example, since GNP follows a fairly smooth path over time (except for a few aberrations), a simple first-order or second-order autoregressive model produces a fairly accurate set of forecasts for most purposes.

A useful procedure for checking the forecasting ability of a model is to hold out the last few values of Y (e.g., y_n, y_{n-1}, and y_{n-2}) before estimating the model. After estimating the model, obtain the predicted values $\hat{y}_{n-2}$, $\hat{y}_{n-1}$, and $\hat{y}_n$ and compare them with the actual values. If the two sets of values are close to each other, then reestimate the model using all the data and use the reestimated model to forecast the future values y_{n+1}, y_{n+2}, and so forth.

One benefit of using an autoregression equation for forecasting is that it is not necessary to predict the future values of the explanatory variables first. If Y_t is expressed as a function of an explanatory variable X, then it is necessary to know or forecast x_{t+1} in order to forecast Y_{t+1}, but if Y_t is expressed as a function of y_{t-1}, we need only know or forecast Y_t in order to forecast Y_{t+1}. If a linear or quadratic trend model fits the data well, a low-order autoregressive equation will also provide a good fit.

Example 19.5

Estimating an Autoregressive Model: The data in Table 19.7 show gross business savings from 1960 to 1986 and are plotted in Figure 19.19. From the graph, it appears that knowing the gross business savings in period $(t - 1)$ is useful in predicting the value of gross business savings in period t. That is, it appears that Y_t can be explained as a function of y_{t-1}. Let us estimate the regression coefficients in the first-order autoregressive model

$$y_t = \beta_0 + \beta_1 Y_{t-1} + e_t$$

where Y_t = gross business savings in year t.

TABLE 19.7 **Autoregressive model for gross business savings Y_t**

Year	Y_t	Y_{t-1}	Y_tY_{t-1}	Y_{t-1}^2
1960	60.3	—	—	—
1961	62.0	60.3	3,738.60	3,636.09
1962	69.3	62.0	4,296.60	3,844.00
1963	73.3	69.3	5,079.69	4,802.49
1964	79.3	73.3	5,812.69	5,372.89
1965	88.7	79.3	7,033.91	6,288.49
1966	95.6	88.7	8,479.72	7,867.69
1967	98.6	95.6	9,426.16	9,139.36
1968	103.3	98.6	10,185.38	9,721.96
1969	106.7	103.3	11,022.11	10,670.89
1970	106.7	106.7	11,384.89	11,384.89
1971	124.3	106.7	13,262.81	11,384.89
1972	142.0	124.3	17,650.60	15,450.49
1973	155.0	142.0	22,010.00	20,164.00
1974	157.6	155.0	24,428.00	24,025.00
1975	198.9	157.6	31,346.64	24,837.76
1976	225.6	198.9	44,871.84	39,561.21
1977	263.8	225.6	59,513.28	50,895.36
1978	298.9	263.8	78,849.82	69,590.44
1979	327.7	298.9	97,949.53	89,341.21
1980	341.5	327.7	111,909.55	107,387.29
1981	391.1	341.5	133,560.65	116,622.25
1982	403.2	391.1	157,691.52	152,959.21
1983	461.6	403.2	186,117.12	162,570.24
1984	506.1	461.6	233,615.76	213,074.56
1985	544.5	506.1	275,571.45	256,137.21
1986	564.2	544.5	307,206.90	296,480.25
Total	5,989.5	5,845.6	1,872,015.22	1,723,210.12

Source: Survey of Current Business (Washington, D.C.: U.S. Department of Commerce, 1987).

Solution: This is the same problem as estimating the simple linear regression model

$$Y_t = \beta_0 + \beta_1 x_t + e_t$$

using $x_t = y_{t-1}$. In general, a computer would be used to estimate this model. To obtain the least-squares estimates using a hand calculator, we need the following sums: $\Sigma\, y_t = 5989.5$, $\Sigma\, y_{t-1} = 5845.6$, $\Sigma\, y_t y_{t-1} = 1{,}872{,}015.22$, and $\Sigma\, y_{t-1}^2 = 1{,}723{,}210.12$. The data and the appropriate calculations are shown in Table 19.7.

Note that in a sense we lose the first observation of Y_t because of the lagged variable y_{t-1}. That is, our first equation is

$$Y_{1961} = \beta_0 + \beta_1 y_{1960} + e_{1961}$$

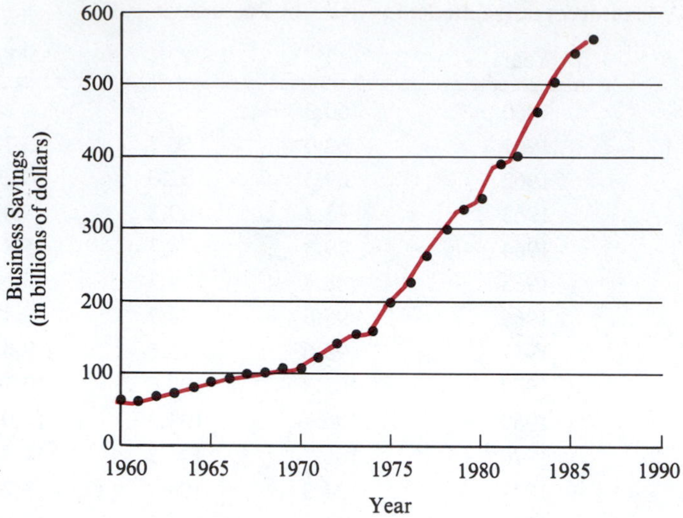

FIGURE 19.19 Scatter diagram of data for gross business savings in Table 19.7.

We have 27 observations on Y from 1960 through 1986, but the number of observations in the regression model is $n = 26$. The sum of the y_t's is calculated using the data for 1961 through 1986.

To obtain the least-squares estimates with a hand calculator, we substitute y_{t-1} for x_t in the equations for the least-squares coefficients.

The SPSSX computer output is shown in Figure 19.20.

FIGURE 19.20 SPSSX-generated output for Example 19.5.

```
                                   * * * *   M U L T I P L E   R E G R E S S I O N   * * * *
Listwise Deletion of Missing Data

Equation Number 1    Dependent Variable..   Y    GROSS BUSINESS SAVINGS

Beginning Block Number  1.  Method:  Enter       YLAG

Variable(s) Entered on Step Number  1..      YLAG

Multiple R             .99687          Analysis of Variance
R Square               .99374                                 DF       Sum of Squares      Mean Square
Adjusted R Square      .99348          Regression               1        654003.50604     654003.50604
Standard Error       13.10008          Residual                24          4118.69281        171.61220

                                       F =       3810.93829        Signif F =   .0000

------------------ Variables in the Equation ------------------

Variable                  B         SE B        Beta          T   Sig T

YLAG               1.075093      .017415     .996866     61.733   .0000
(Constant)         3.537353     4.483451                   .789   .4378

End Block Number   1   All requested variables entered.
```

The estimated model is

$$\hat{y}_t = 3.537 + 1.075 y_{t-1} \qquad R^2 = .994$$
$$t \text{ statistics:} \quad (0.789) \quad (61.73)$$

The estimated slope coefficient $b_1 = 1.075$ indicates that Y grows approximately 7.5% per year. The t statistic for b_1 is $t = 61.73$, and the prob-value for b_1 is .0000. The t statistic in an autoregressive model does not exactly follow the t distribution because one of the basic assumptions of the classical linear regression model has been violated: The error terms are not independent of the explanatory variables because of the presence of the lagged dependent variable. Nevertheless, this t statistic is so extreme that we can still feel quite confident that the population regression slope β_1 is nonzero.

The model explains more than 99% of the variation in Y, which is a common occurrence in autoregressive models. In an autoregressive model, the value of R^2 will be quite close to 1 whenever the trend of the dependent variable is relatively smooth, because it should be possible to get a good forecast of a value of Y when the previous value of Y is known.

Let us use the autoregressive equation to forecast gross business savings for 1987. From the autoregressive model, we obtain

$$\hat{y}_{1987} = 3.537 + 1.075 y_{1986}$$

We substitute $y_{1986} = 564.2$ and obtain

$$\hat{y}_{1987} = 3.537 + 1.075(564.2) = 610.052$$

Recall that the original data are in billions of dollars. Thus, the forecast for 1987 would be \$610.052 billion. ■

Exercises for Section 19.5

1. Refer to the data in Exercise 1 in Section 19.4.
a. Estimate the model $Y_t = \beta_0 + \beta_1 y_{t-1} + e_t$. Calculate R^2.
b. Forecast interest payments in 1991 and 1992.

2. Refer to the data in Exercise 2 in Section 19.4.
a. Estimate the model $Y_t = \beta_0 + \beta_1 y_{t-1} + e_t$. Calculate R^2.
b. Forecast Y_t in 1991 and 1992.

3. Refer to the data in Exercise 3 in Section 19.4.
a. Estimate the model $Y_t = \beta_0 + \beta_1 y_{t-1} + e_t$. Calculate R^2.
b. Forecast Y_t in 1991 and 1992.

4. Refer to the data in Exercise 4 in Section 19.4.
a. Estimate the model $Y_t = \beta_0 + \beta_1 y_{t-1} + e_t$. Calculate R^2.
b. Forecast Y_t in 1990 and 1995.

5. The accompanying data show quarterly observations on income (Y) and money supply (X). Estimate the model

$$Y_t = \beta_0 + \beta_1 x_t + \beta_2 y_{t-1} + e_t$$

t	Y	X	t	Y	X
1	116	42	11	168	63
2	120	43	12	173	66
3	124	44	13	182	68
4	132	47	14	190	72
5	139	50	15	191	74
6	145	52	16	195	77
7	150	54	17	201	80
8	153	56	18	204	83
9	157	59	19	210	85
10	161	60	20	214	87

19.6 ▪ Measuring Forecast Accuracy

The linear trend model is one of the most frequently used models for predicting or forecasting future values of some dependent variable *Y* and has certain advantages and disadvantages compared with other techniques for forecasting. Advantages include the following:

1. The trend line is very easy to estimate. Because we need only a set of observations on *Y*, we have none of the problems involved in collecting data for explanatory variables.
2. The trend line is easy to understand and interpret; nearly everyone intuitively understands how to forecast the value of some dependent variable *Y* by extrapolating into the future along a linear graph.

Disadvantages of the linear trend model include the following:

1. By using a trend line to forecast, we are not really identifying the underlying factors that cause *Y* to change over time.
2. If the behavior of the underlying factors changes in the future, then the trend line might produce very poor forecasts.

The basic problem with using an estimated trend line to forecast the future is that the trend line may oversimplify a relatively complicated situation. For example, it is easy to forecast future sales if we assume that sales will continue to grow in the future just as they have in the past, but sometimes this assumption may be naive and unfounded. In fact, sales depend on income, people's tastes, total population, the prices and availability of competing products, advertising expenditures, and so forth. If the behavior of any of these explanatory variables changes in the future, then sales can be expected to change accordingly. However, the linear trend line does not explicitly take into account the behavior of these independent variables. Using the trend line for forecasting becomes more and more suspect as the forecast period moves further and further into the future, because, as time passes, it becomes more likely that the behavior of the true explanatory variables will change.

On the other hand, there is also a major disadvantage in forecasting future values of *Y* by using a multiple regression model containing many different explanatory variables. Suppose we think a variable *Y* depends on the *K* explanatory variables X_1,

$X_2, \ldots, X_K$. To forecast future values of Y, we need to know the future values of X_1, $X_2, \ldots, X_K$. How do we get this information? In many cases we would have to forecast the future values of the X's (probably by using linear trend equations!).

Example 19.6

Difficulty of Forecasting the Future: The data in Table 19.8 show small-denomination time deposits from 1961 to 1981 and are plotted in Figure 19.21. It appears that a quadratic trend model describes the behavior of Y appropriately. Let us estimate the quadratic trend model

$$Y_t = \beta_0 + \beta_1 t + \beta_2 t^2 + e_t$$

and use this model to forecast the values of Y for 1982 to 1986.

TABLE 19.8
Small-denomination time deposits, 1961–1981

Year	Deposits (in billions) Y_t	Year	Deposits (in billions) Y_t
1961	\$ 14.8	1971	\$189.7
1962	20.1	1972	231.6
1963	25.5	1973	265.8
1964	29.2	1974	287.9
1965	34.5	1975	337.9
1966	55.0	1976	390.8
1967	77.8	1977	445.7
1968	100.5	1978	521.5
1969	120.4	1979	635.3
1970	151.1	1980	730.2
		1981	825.1

Source: Economic Report of the President, 1987 (Washington, D.C.: U.S. Government Printing Office, 1987).

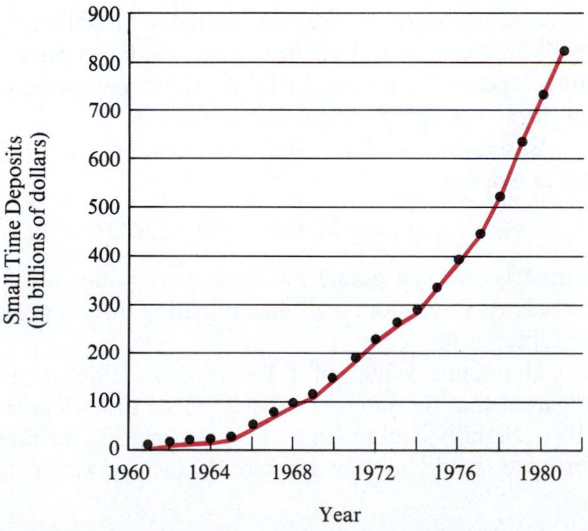

FIGURE 19.21
Scatter diagram for data in Example 19.6.

Solution: We obtain the estimated quadratic equation

$$\hat{y}_t = 48.159 - 14.622t + 2.373t^2 \qquad R^2 = .992$$
$$t \text{ statistics:} \quad (3.027) \quad (-4.38) \quad (16.1)$$

The SPSSX computer output for this model is shown in Figure 19.22.

FIGURE 19.22 SPSSX-generated output for Example 19.6.

```
                                **** M U L T I P L E   R E G R E S S I O N ****
Listwise Deletion of Missing Data

Equation Number 1    Dependent Variable..   Y   SMALL TIME DEPOSITS

Beginning Block Number  1.  Method:  Enter     T        TSQ

Variable(s) Entered on Step Number  1..   TSQ
                                    2..   T

Multiple R             .99642          Analysis of Variance
R Square               .99286                            DF     Sum of Squares      Mean Square
Adjusted R Square      .99206          Regression         2     1213896.32873     606948.16436
Standard Error       22.02769          Residual          18        8733.94365        485.21909

                                       F =      1250.87445     Signif F =  .0000

------------------ Variables in the Equation ------------------

Variable                B          SE B        Beta          T   Sig T

TSQ              2.372952       .147071    1.348968     16.135   .0000
T              -14.622469      3.331529   -0.366960     -4.389   .0004
(Constant)      48.159398     15.911930                  3.027   .0073

End Block Number   1   All requested variables entered.
```

Because R^2 is .99286, the estimated model explains more than 99% of the variation in Y. Suppose we wanted to use this model to predict the value for small-denomination time deposits from 1982 to 1986. Since these values are already known, we can check our forecasts against the actual values.

Based on $t = 1$ in 1961, the value of t in 1982 would be $t = 22$. We obtain the predicted value

$$\hat{y}_{22} = 48.159 - 14.622(22) + 2.373(22)^2 = 875.007$$

Similarly, we can obtain the forecasted values for 1983 through 1986. The actual and forecasted values for small-denomination time deposits for 1982 through 1986 are shown in Table 19.9.

The actual values of Y for 1961 to 1986 are plotted in Figure 19.23. It is quite apparent that the long-term behavior of time deposits changed in 1982. At the end of 1981, an individual making forecasts for 1982 through 1986 would have thought that the forecasts would be very accurate. In fact, however, the forecasts are very inaccurate.

TABLE 19.9
Actual and forecast values for small-denomination time deposits

Year	Actual Value (in billions) Y	Forecast Value (in billions) $\hat{Y}$
1982	$852.8	$ 875.007
1983	785.2	967.170
1984	887.5	1064.079
1985	880.3	1165.734
1986	852.4	1272.135

FIGURE 19.23
Actual small-denomination time deposits versus time, 1961–1986.

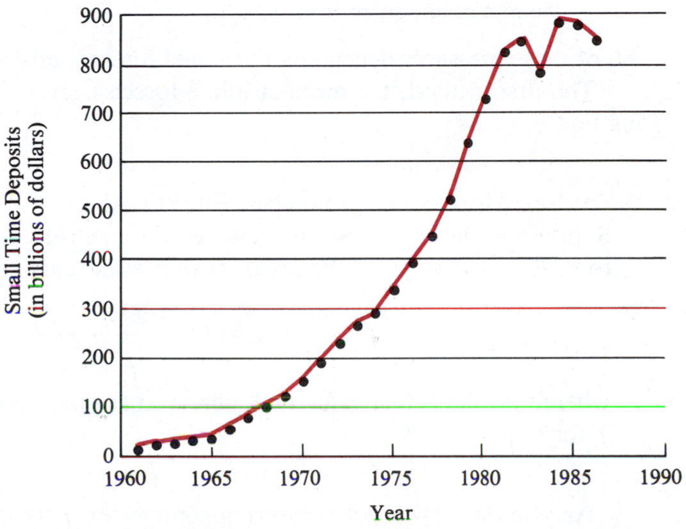

Prior to 1982, time deposits traced out an extremely smooth path on the scatter diagram, but afterwards the behavior of the variable became much more volatile and less predictable. Because of the recent change in the behavior of Y, any forecasts of future values of small-denomination time deposits based on data from 1961 to 1981 will be inaccurate. ■

The example above points out the problems in forecasting the value of any variable. Trend models rely on the assumption that past trends will continue unchanged in the future. In this example, such was not the case. An observer might wonder what caused the sudden change in the behavior of small-denomination time deposits in 1982. A likely explanation for the slowdown in their growth after 1981 is the rapid growth of a new investment vehicle, Money Market Deposit Accounts (MMDAs), which did not exist before 1982. MMDAs grew from $0 in 1981 to $43.2 billion in 1982, $379.2 billion in 1983, and $570.7 billion in 1986. This factor is not accounted for in the quadratic trend model used in Example 19.6.

Three Measures of Forecast Accuracy

When we make our forecast, there is no way of knowing with certainty whether it will be accurate. For example, given the data on small-denomination time deposits for 1961 through 1981, most people would think that they could produce very accurate forecasts for 1982 through 1986. We have shown, however, that the forecasts generated by the quadratic trend model in Example 19.6 are very inaccurate. Only after the actual values have been observed can we determine whether we have made a good forecast.

We want a model that minimizes the differences between the forecast values and the actual values. We discuss the following methods of measuring the quality of a forecast:

1. the mean absolute forecast error (MAFE),
2. the mean absolute percentage error (MAPE), and
3. the root mean square error (RMSE).

All of these measures depend on the actual forecast errors $(y_t - \hat{y}_t)$.

The first method, the mean absolute forecast error, is described in the accompanying box.

Definition: Mean Absolute Forecast Error (MAFE)

Suppose we have forecast the value of Y for m periods. The mean of the absolute forecast errors is called the **mean absolute forecast error** (MAFE). We obtain

$$\text{MAFE} = \frac{\Sigma|y_t - \hat{y}_t|}{m}$$

where y_t is the actual value of Y observed at time t and $\hat{y}_t$ is the forecast value of Y for time t.

An alternative way of measuring forecast error is in percentage terms. When the variable being forecast takes very large values, a forecast error that is quite large in absolute terms might be quite small in percentage terms. For example, Gross National Product currently exceeds \$4 trillion per year. A forecast error of \$1 billion is large in absolute terms, but quite small in percentage terms—less than 1%. The absolute percentage forecast error is defined as

$$\text{Absolute percentage forecast error} = \frac{|y_t - \hat{y}_t|}{y_t} \times 100$$

Definition: Mean Absolute Percentage Error (MAPE)

Suppose we have forecast the value of Y for m periods. The mean of the absolute percentage forecast errors is called the **mean absolute percentage error** (MAPE). We obtain

$$\text{MAPE} = \frac{\Sigma\left[|y_t - \hat{y}_t|/y_t\right]}{m} \times 100$$

A third measure of forecast accuracy is called the root mean square error, described in the accompanying box.

Definition: Root Mean Square Error (RMSE)

The **root mean square error** of a forecast is defined by the equation

$$\text{RMSE} = \sqrt{\frac{\Sigma(y_t - \hat{y}_t)^2}{m}}$$

where m is the number of time periods for which forecasts have been made.

The basic difference between MAFE and RMSE is that the latter penalizes extreme errors more heavily than does MAFE. For this reason RMSE is an appropriate measure of forecast error if the costs of making forecast errors increase more than proportionally to the size of the error. Regardless of which measure of forecast error is chosen, the model providing the smallest MAFE, MAPE, or RMSE is the most accurate.

Supposedly the statistics MAFE, MAPE, and RMSE are based on observed and forecast values at future points in time. When we are examining a model, however, it is usually impractical to fit the model to historical data and then wait for future actual values to become available in order to measure forecast accuracy. Thus the statistician will sometimes separate the historical data base into two sets, one for estimating the parameters in the model, which is then used to forecast the values of the remaining observations.

Example 19.7

Measuring Forecast Accuracy: In Example 19.6, we actually had 26 observations on small-denomination time deposits from 1961 through 1986. We used the first 21 observations to estimate the model and the last 5 observations to measure the model's forecast accuracy. Calculate MAFE, MAPE, and RMSE.

Solution: Refer to the actual and forecast values for the variable Small-Denomination Time Deposits, which are given in Table 19.9. For example, in 1982 the absolute forecast error is

$$|y_t - \hat{y}_t| = |852.8 - 875.007| = \$22.207 \text{ billion}$$

and the absolute percentage forecast error is

$$\frac{|y_t - \hat{y}_t|}{y_t} \times 100 = \frac{|852.8 - 875.007|}{852.8} \times 100 = 2.6\%$$

For 1983 the absolute forecast error is \$181.97 billion and the percentage forecast error is 23.2%. Thus, the forecast error is much larger in 1983 than in 1982.

The absolute forecast errors, the absolute percentage forecast errors, and the squared forecast errors for 1982 through 1986 are shown in Table 19.10. Observe that by 1986, the absolute forecast error has grown to \$419.735 billion and the absolute percentage forecast error to 49.2%. From 1982 through 1986, the MAFE is \$217.185 billion, the MAPE is 25.5%, and the RMSE is \$253.94 billion.

TABLE 19.10 Forecast errors for Example 19.7

Small Time Deposits (in billions)

Year	Actual Value Y	Forecast Value $\hat{Y}$	Absolute Forecast Error	Absolute Percentage Error	Squared Forecast Error
1982	\$852.8	\$ 875.007	\$ 22.207	2.6	\$ 493.15
1983	785.2	967.170	181.970	23.2	33,113.08
1984	887.5	1,064.079	176.579	19.9	31,180.14
1985	880.3	1,165.734	285.434	32.4	81,472.57
1986	852.4	1,272.135	419.735	49.2	176,177.47
			1,085.925	127.3	322,436.41

Note: MAFE = 1085.925/5 = 217.185; MAPE = 127.3/5 = 25.46%;
RMSE = $\sqrt{322{,}436.41/5}$ = 253.94.

■

19.7 ▪ Computer Applications

In this chapter we discussed four models for estimating the long-term trend in a time series:

1. the linear trend model,
2. the polynomial trend model,
3. the exponential trend model, and
4. the autoregressive model.

The SPSSX program can be used to estimate each of these models. To estimate the linear trend model, read in the n data values of the dependent variable along with the values 1 through n for the variable Time. Suppose we name the dependent variable Y and the explanatory variable TIME. To estimate the linear trend model

$$Y_t = \beta_0 + \beta_1 t + e_t$$

issue the following commands:

```
REGRESSION VARIABLES = Y, TIME/
   DEPENDENT = Y/
   ENTER TIME/
```

To estimate a quadratic trend model, we first have to create the squared term for Time. Thus to estimate the quadratic trend model

$$Y_t = \beta_0 + \beta_1 t + \beta_2 t^2 + e_t$$

issue the following commands:

```
COMPUTE TIMESQ = TIME * TIME
REGRESSION VARIABLES = Y, TIME, TIMESQ/
    DEPENDENT = Y/
    ENTER TIME, TIMESQ/
```

To estimate an exponential trend model, we first have to create the variable representing the natural logarithm of the dependent variable Y; let's call it LNY. If the model contains a squared term for the variable Time, we also have to create the appropriate variable. Then we estimate the model. To estimate the quadratic exponential trend model

$$\ln Y_t = \beta_0 + \beta_1 t + \beta_2 t^2 + e_t$$

issue the following commands:

```
COMPUTE LNY = LN(Y)
COMPUTE TIMESQ = TIME * TIME
REGRESSION VARIABLES = LNY, TIME, TIMESQ/
    DEPENDENT = LNY/
    ENTER TIME, TIMESQ/
```

To estimate an autoregressive trend model, we first have to create a new variable representing the lagged dependent variable. Suppose we name the new variable LAGY. To do this, we issue a LAG command and then we estimate the model. To estimate the single-period autoregressive model, issue the following commands:

```
COMPUTE LAGY = LAG(Y, 1)
REGRESSION VARIABLES = Y, LAGY/
    DEPENDENT = Y/
    ENTER LAGY/
```

Exercises for Section 19.7

1. Refer to the data in Table 2.4 in Chapter 2, which show data values for the time series variables TOTALGOV and DEFENSE indicated from 1960 through 1986.
   a. For each variable, generate a scatter diagram versus time.
   b. For each variable, estimate the linear trend model and examine the value of R^2 for each variable.
   c. For each variable, print out the residuals and obtain the Durbin–Watson statistic.
   d. Examine the residual plot and determine whether a quadratic model seems to be preferable to a linear model.
   e. For each model, let $\alpha = .05$ and test the null hypothesis that the error terms are not serially correlated against the alternative hypothesis that the errors are positively correlated.

2. Refer to Exercise 1.
   a. For each variable, estimate the quadratic trend model.
   b. For each variable, print out the residuals and obtain the Durbin–Watson statistic.
   c. Examine the residual plot and determine whether a quadratic model seems to be suitable.
   d. For each model, let $\alpha = .05$ and test the null hypothesis that the error terms are not serially correlated against the alternative hypothesis that the errors are positively correlated.

3. Refer to Exercise 1.
   a. For each variable, estimate the first-order autoregressive model.

b. For each variable, print out the residuals and obtain the Durbin–Watson statistic.
c. Examine the residual plot and determine whether an autoregressive model seems to be suitable.
d. For each model, let $\alpha = .05$ and test the null hypothesis that the error terms are not serially correlated against the alternative hypothesis that the errors are positively correlated. Is this test strictly valid? Discuss.

Chapter 19 Summary

A variable recorded chronologically is a *time series variable*. We describe the past behavior of a time-dependent random variable by deriving the components of the time series. Such a decomposition yields the components of (1) *trend* (a long-term growth or decline in the observations), (2) *seasonality* (within-year, recurrent fluctuations), (3) *cyclical activity* (upward and downward movements of differing lengths about the trend), and (4) *irregular activity* (what remains after the other three components have been removed). The first step in analyzing any time series is to plot the data versus time. In time series analysis, the objective is to describe time-related patterns in the path of a variable rather than to explain them. Estimated trend coefficients help describe period-to-period changes in the dependent variable, but they do not reveal the causes of these changes.

We discussed various methods of describing the long-term trend of a variable. The *linear trend model* assumes that Y increases (or decreases) by the same constant amount each period. The *polynomial trend model* assumes that the time path of Y can be described by a quadratic, cubic, or higher-order function of t. In the *exponential model,* it is assumed that the natural logarithm of Y is some polynomial function of t. In the *autoregressive model,* it is assumed that the value of Y_t is related to one or more lagged values Y_{t-1}, Y_{t-2}, and so forth.

One of the primary reasons for constructing time series models is to *forecast* future values of the dependent variable. In the pure time series model, no explanatory variables are considered; only past observations on the variable of interest are used to describe and predict the future values of the variable.

The *forecast error* is the difference between the actual value y_t and the forecast value $\hat{y}_t$. Forecast accuracy can be measured by calculating the *mean absolute forecast error,* the *mean absolute percentage error,* or the *root mean square error.* The mean square error is found by squaring each of the forecast errors obtained by applying this technique to the past observations and then deriving the average of the squared errors. This measure is very sensitive to one or two very large errors. The mean absolute deviation is calculated by averaging the absolute values of the errors and is less sensitive to a single large error.

The advantage of time series methods is that no external explanatory variables are needed to describe the behavior of the dependent variable. Multiple linear regression forecasting requires additional data. For each time period, data are recorded for each independent variable as well as for the dependent variable. The explanatory variables can include lagged dependent or independent variables or dummy variables to represent seasonality or the occurrence (or nonoccurrence) of a particular event (such as an election year).

The advantage of multiple linear regression on time series data is that it is very flexible because many different types of explanatory variables can be included in the model, including lagged values of the dependent variable. The disadvantage of the multiple regression technique for forecasting is that future values of the explanatory variables must be known or forecast before the model can be used.

In this chapter we have discussed various models that can be used to describe the trend component of a time series variable. In Chapter 20, we discuss models that can be used to describe the seasonal component of a time series variable.

Chapter 19 ▪ Supplementary Exercises

1. A physical fitness spa has been in existence for eight years. The number of customers using the spa each year are as follows:

Year	Customers (in thousands)	Year	Customers (in thousands)
1981	18	1985	48
1982	23	1986	59
1983	30	1987	74
1984	40	1988	88

a. Plot the data and estimate the linear trend line.
b. Graph the trend line.
c. Estimate the number of customers for 1989 and 1990.
d. Estimate the autoregressive equation $Y_t = \beta_0 + \beta_1 y_{t-1} + e_t$.
e. Use the autoregressive equation to predict the number of customers for 1989 and 1990.
f. Estimate the semilogarithmic equation $\ln Y_t = \beta_0 + \beta_1 t + e_t$.
g. Use the semilogarithmic equation to predict the number of customers for 1989 and 1990.

2. The following data show the number of college students in a state for selected years:

Year	Students (in thousands)	Year	Students (in thousands)
1978	103	1983	111
1979	105	1984	112
1980	106	1985	114
1981	108	1986	116
1982	109	1987	118

a. Plot the data.
b. Fit a linear trend line and calculate R^2.
c. Predict the number of students for 1988 and 1989.
d. Estimate the equation $Y_t = \beta_0 + \beta_1 Y_{t-1} + e_t$ and find R^2.
e. Use part (d) to predict the number of students for 1988.

3. The accompanying data show the annual earnings of a certain college professor for selected years.

Year	Income (in thousands)	Year	Income (in thousands)
1978	\$20.0	1984	\$25.1
1979	20.5	1985	26.4
1980	21.1	1986	27.8
1981	22.0	1987	29.2
1982	22.8	1988	30.7
1983	23.9	1989	32.2

a. Plot the data using Income (Y_t) and Time (X_t) as axis labels.
b. Plot the data using Y_t and Y_{t-1} as axis labels.
c. Fit the linear trend line, graph it, and predict Y_t for 1990 and 1995.
d. Fit the equation $Y_t = \beta_0 + \beta_1 Y_{t-1} + e_t$, graph it, and predict Y_t for 1990 and 1995.

4. A real estate agent has been studying the prices of new homes in Baldwin County. Let Y_t denote the average selling price (in thousands of dollars) of new homes sold in Baldwin County in year t. The agent has obtained the following regression equation:

$$\hat{y}_t = 1.02 + 1.06 y_{t-1}$$

Suppose the average price of homes sold in 1987 was \$40,000. Predict the average selling price in 1988, 1989, and 1990.

5. Many racquet clubs with indoor tennis facilities are experiencing financial difficulties because of the rapidly increasing costs of utilities. The manager of the Belleville Racquet Club has estimated the following regression equation:

$$\hat{y}_t = 1.14 + 1.04 y_{t-1} + 0.04 y_{t-2}$$

where y_t represents utility costs in thousands of dollars in year t at the club. Suppose that in 1987 and 1988 utility costs were \$22,000 and \$25,000, respectively. Predict utility costs in 1989, 1990, and 1991.

6. The following data show the annual sales of a corporation:

Year	Sales (in millions)	Year	Sales (in millions)
1978	\$320	1983	\$560
1979	366	1984	620
1980	390	1985	640
1981	422	1986	690
1982	456	1987	740

a. Estimate a linear trend line for the sales.
b. Predict sales in 1988, 1989, and 1990.
c. Plot the data and graph the estimated line.
d. Calculate R^2, the coefficient of determination.

7. The following data show the gross sales for a petroleum company from 1978 to 1987:

Year	Gross Sales (in billions)	Year	Gross Sales (in billions)
1978	$3.9	1983	$5.3
1979	3.9	1984	5.5
1980	3.6	1985	6.4
1981	4.8	1986	7.0
1982	4.5	1987	7.1

a. Estimate the linear trend line.
b. Plot the data and graph the line.
c. Predict sales for the year 1990.
d. Estimate a semilogarithmic trend line and predict sales for 1990.

8. The following data show the population of animals on a sheltered game preserve:

Year	Population	Year	Population
1981	40	1985	800
1982	90	1986	1900
1983	230	1987	4200
1984	440	1988	8800

a. Fit a quadratic curve to the data.
b. Plot the data and graph the estimated curve.
c. Predict the size of the population for 1988.

9. At a certain university, the average starting salaries in dollars for assistant professors hired during given years are as follows:

Year	Salary	Year	Salary
1979	$20,000	1983	$26,000
1980	21,300	1984	28,500
1981	22,800	1985	30,000
1982	24,400	1986	33,800

a. Fit a linear trend line to this data.
b. Plot the data and the trend line.
c. Predict the average starting salary for 1987 and 1988.

10. The accompanying data show the average gross weekly earnings of employees at a manufacturing firm for selected years.

Year	Average Weekly Earnings	Year	Average Weekly Earnings
1980	$331.71	1985	$390.96
1981	340.73	1986	410.11
1982	354.42	1987	428.49
1983	368.04	1988	452.11
1984	380.06		

a. Plot the data.
b. Fit a linear trend line.
c. Predict weekly earnings for 1989.
d. Fit the equation $\ln Y_t = \beta_0 + \beta_1 t + e_t$.
e. Predict weekly earnings for 1989 using part (d).

11. The following data show the number of mobile homes shipped by a national producer for selected years:

Year	Units Shipped	Year	Units Shipped
1980	90,200	1985	217,300
1981	118,000	1986	240,360
1982	150,840	1987	317,950
1983	191,320	1988	412,690
1984	216,470		

a. Plot the data.
b. Fit a linear trend line.
c. Predict shipments for 1990 using the linear trend line.
d. Fit a semilog trend line.
e. Predict shipments for 1990 using the semilog trend line.

12. The following data show daily hospital expenses in dollars per patient for selected years:

Year	Amount	Year	Amount
1950	$ 7.98	1970	$ 52.95
1955	11.24	1975	70.93
1960	16.46	1980	94.23
1965	25.29	1985	124.35

a. Plot the data.
b. Fit the equation $\ln Y_t = \beta_0 + \beta_1 t + e_t$.
c. Predict expenses for 1990 and 1995.

13. The following data show U.S. expenditures in billions of dollars on food for selected years:

Year	Amount (in billions)	Year	Amount (in billions)
1940	$20.2	1965	$101.0
1945	40.6	1970	142.1
1950	53.9	1975	218.7
1955	68.6	1980	349.1
1960	82.7	1985	469.3

Source: Economic Report of the President, 1987 (Washington, D.C.: U.S. Government Printing Office, 1987).

a. Plot the data.
b. Fit the linear trend line and predict expenditures for 1990 and 1995.
c. Estimate the quadratic trend curve.

14. The following data show the GNP for selected years:

Year	GNP (in billions)	Year	GNP (in billions)
1930	$ 90	1960	$ 515
1935	72	1965	705
1940	100	1970	1016
1945	213	1975	1598
1950	288	1980	2732
1955	406	1985	3998

Source: Economic Report of the President, 1987 (Washington, D.C.: U.S. Government Printing Office, 1987).

a. Plot the data on a scatter diagram.
b. Estimate the linear trend line and plot it.
c. Use the equation from part (b) to predict GNP in 1990.
d. Estimate the quadratic trend curve and plot it.
e. Use the equation from part (d) to predict GNP in 1990. Compare this prediction with the prediction in part (c).
f. Estimate a semilogarithmic trend line and predict GNP for 1990.

15. The accompanying data refer to local government revenues from property taxes for a county in Texas.

Year	Revenues (in millions)	Year	Revenues (in millions)
1977	$16	1983	$25
1978	18	1984	26
1979	19	1985	28
1980	20	1986	31
1981	21	1987	34
1982	23	1988	38

a. Plot the data and fit the linear trend line.
b. Predict tax revenues for 1990 using the linear trend line.
c. Plot and fit the semilogarithmic trend line.
d. Predict tax revenues for 1990 using the semilogarithmic trend line.

16. The Martin Jewelry Company has hired an advertising agency to promote its products. The advertising agency used data on the company's monthly sales revenues and monthly advertising expenditures in recent months to generate the sample regression equation

$$\hat{y}_t = 13.20 + 2.10x_{t1} + 1.24x_{t2} + 0.62x_{t3}$$

where

Y = monthly sales revenues (in thousands of dollars)

X_1 = monthly advertising expenditures (in hundreds of dollars)

$X_2 = X_1^2$

X_3 = time period (1 in month 1, 2 in month 2, etc.)

a. Suppose that in month 10 the Martin Jewelry Company intends to spend $500 on advertising. Predict sales revenues for that month.
b. Suppose that in month 11 the Martin Jewelry Company intends to spend $800 on advertising. Predict revenues for that month.
c. Suppose that in month 11 the Martin Jewelry Company intends to spend $900 on advertising. Predict revenues for that month.
d. What is the change in predicted revenue when advertising expenditures are increased from $800 to $900?
e. Suppose that in month 10 the Martin Jewelry Company intends to spend $600 on advertising. Predict revenues for that month.
f. What is the change in predicted revenue when advertising expenditures are increased from $500 to $600?
g. Why is the answer to part (f) different from the answer to part (d)?

17. A marketing analyst studied annual sales of a product that had been introduced 10 years ago. The data were as follows, where t is the year (coded) and Y is sales in thousands of units:

t	1	2	3	4	5	6	7	8	9	10
Y	98	135	162	178	221	232	283	300	374	395

a. Prepare a scatter plot of the data. Does a linear relation appear adequate here?
b. Use the transformation $Y' = \sqrt{Y}$ and obtain the estimated linear regression function for the transformed data.
c. Plot the estimated regression line and the transformed data. Does the regression line appear to be a good fit to the transformed data?
d. Obtain the residuals and plot them against the fitted values. What does your plot show?
e. Express the estimated regression equation in the original units.

References

Box, George E. P., and Gwilym M. Jenkins. *Time Series Analysis, Forecasting, and Control.* San Francisco: Holden-Day, 1970.

Granger, Clive, and Paul Newbold. *Forecasting Economic Time Series.* London: Academic Press, 1977.

Hoff, John C. *A Practical Guide to Box–Jenkins Forecasting.* Belmont, Calif.: Lifetime Learning, 1983.

Makridakis, Spyros G. "A Survey of Time Series Analysis." *International Statistical Review* 44 (1976): 29–70.

Makridakis, Spyros and Steven C. Wheelwright. *Forecasting: Methods and Applications.* New York: Wiley, 1978.

Morgenstern, Oskar. *On the Accuracy of Economic Observations.* 2d ed. Princeton, N.J.: Princeton University Press, 1963.

Nelson, Charles R. *Applied Time Series for Managerial Forecasting.* San Francisco: Holden-Day, 1973.

Nie, Norman, E., C. Hadlai Hull, Jean G. Jenkins, Karin Steinbrenner, and Dale H. Bent. *SPSS Statistical Package for the Social Sciences.* 2d ed. New York: McGraw-Hill, 1975.

Norusis, Marija J. *SPSSX Introductory Statistics Guide.* New York: McGraw-Hill, 1983.

———. *SPSSX Advanced Statistics Guide*. Chicago: SPSS, 1985.

———. *The SPSS Guide to Data Analysis*. Chicago: SPSS, 1986.

PANKRATZ, ALAN. *Forecasting with Univariate Box–Jenkins Models: Concepts and Cases*. New York: Wiley, 1983.

RYAN, THOMAS A., BRIAN L. JOINER, and BARBARA F. RYAN. *Minitab Reference Manual*. University Park, Penn.: Minitab Project, 1985.

———. *Minitab Handbook*. 2d ed. Boston: PWS-KENT, 1985.

SAS Introductory Guide. 3d ed. Cary, N.C.: SAS Institute, 1985.

SAS Procedures Guide for Personal Computers. Version 6 ed. Cary, N.C.: SAS Institute, 1986.

SAS Statistics Guide for Personal Computers. Version 6 ed. Cary, N.C.: SAS Institute, 1986.

SAS User's Guide: Basics. Version 5 ed. Cary, N.C.: SAS Institute, 1985.

SAS User's Guide: Statistics. Version 5 ed. Cary, N.C.: SAS Institute, 1985.

SPSSX User's Guide. Chicago: SPSS, 1983.

Chapter Twenty
Time Series Analysis II: Estimation of the Seasonal Component

Many time series in economics contain a *seasonal component,* a regular fluctuation about the trend that repeats year after year. In some applications, we want to estimate the size of the seasonal component either in absolute terms or as a percentage of the trend value. In other cases, the forecaster may want to determine the long-term trend of the time series and remove any seasonal influence. When we remove the seasonal component from the time series, we obtain a new time series that is said to be *seasonally adjusted*. In this chapter, we discuss different ways of estimating the seasonal component and of obtaining a seasonally adjusted series.

In Section 20.1, we show how to use the *method of moving averages* to obtain a seasonally adjusted series. This method smooths out the effect of any seasonal or irregular component by replacing each observation y_t by a smoothed value s_t, where s_t is an average of y_t and some of the adjacent values y_{t-2}, y_{t-1}, y_{t+1}, y_{t+2}, and so forth.

20.1 ▪ Seasonal Adjustment by Using Moving Averages

The simplest moving average is called a *simple centered (2m + 1)-point moving average,* where we replace y_t by the average of y_t, the previous m values $y_{t-m}, y_{t-m+1}, \ldots,$ y_{t-1}, and the succeeding m values $y_{t+1}, y_{t+2}, \ldots, y_{t+m}$. If the observations used in calculating the average are given different weights, we obtain a *weighted* $(2m + 1)$-point moving average as opposed to a simple moving average. The moving average is centered because y_t is the central value in the set of values used to calculate s_t.

Definition: A Simple Centered $(2m + 1)$-Point Moving Average

Let $y_1, y_2, \ldots, y_n$ be n observations on a time series, and let m be some non-negative integer. To calculate a **simple centered (2*m* + 1)-point moving average**, replace the value y_t by the smoothed value s_t where

$$s_t = \frac{y_{t-m} + y_{t-m+1} + \cdots + y_{t-1} + y_t + y_{t+1} + y_{t+2} + \cdots + y_{t+m}}{2m + 1}$$

for $t = m + 1, m + 2, \ldots, n - m$.

In calculating s_t, there are $(2m + 1)$ terms in the numerator and y_t is the central value. For example, suppose we want to compute a simple centered 5-point moving average. Let s_t denote the smoothed value of y_t. If the original data are denoted by y_1, $y_2, \ldots, y_n$, then a simple 5-point moving average would take the form

$$s_3 = \frac{y_1 + y_2 + y_3 + y_4 + y_5}{5}$$

$$s_4 = \frac{y_2 + y_3 + y_4 + y_5 + y_6}{5}$$

$$\vdots$$

$$s_{n-2} = \frac{y_{n-4} + y_{n-3} + y_{n-2} + y_{n-1} + y_n}{5}$$

The smoothed value s_3 is the average of five values, namely, y_3, the two previous values y_1 and y_2, and the two succeeding values y_4 and y_5. Note that the smoothed time series contains fewer observations than the original time series. In the 5-point moving average, the values s_1, s_2, s_{n-1}, and s_n cannot be calculated, and so we lose four observations, two at each end of the series. In general, when we compute a $(2m + 1)$-point moving average, we lose m observations at each end of the series. Thus, we lose a total of $2m$ observations.

Simple Versus Weighted Moving Averages

The simple centered $(2m + 1)$-point moving average gives an equal weight of $1/(2m + 1)$ to each original observation used to calculate the smoothed value. Thus, in a simple 5-point moving average, the smoothed value is obtained by giving a weight of $\frac{1}{5}$ to each of the five adjacent values.

By computing a **weighted moving average**, the relative importance of some of the original observations can be increased. For example, in a 5-point weighted moving average, the weights might be $\frac{1}{8}$, $\frac{1}{4}$, $\frac{1}{4}$, $\frac{1}{4}$, and $\frac{1}{8}$, based on the assumption that the middle values in a series of observations should have greater weight than the end observations. If we use some other weighting system, an entirely different moving average will be determined. The only requirement is that the weights sum to 1.

You may be wondering why we use $(2m + 1)$ observations to form the moving average rather than, say, $2m$ observations. Because the value $(2m + 1)$ is an odd number, the moving-average value for time t will be centered at that time. If we computed the moving average over an even number of observations, the moving-average values would lie *between* the time points rather than *at* the time points.

Constructing a Centered Four-Quarter Moving Average

Suppose we wish to smooth quarterly data by calculating a four-quarter moving average. Because the moving average consists of the average of an even number of observations, the moving average value will be centered in the middle of two observations. For example, the first value in the 4-quarter moving average would be calculated as

$$s_{2.5} = \frac{y_1 + y_2 + y_3 + y_4}{4}$$

where $s_{2.5}$ is centered between time $t = 2$ and $t = 3$. Similarly, we could calculate

$$s_{3.5} = \frac{y_2 + y_3 + y_4 + y_5}{4}$$

To center the moving-average values, we would calculate the moving-average value s_3 as the average of $s_{2.5}$ and $s_{3.5}$; thus we would obtain

$$\begin{aligned} s_3 &= \frac{s_{2.5} + s_{3.5}}{2} \\ &= \frac{\dfrac{y_1 + y_2 + y_3 + y_4}{4} + \dfrac{y_2 + y_3 + y_4 + y_5}{4}}{2} \\ &= \frac{y_1}{8} + \frac{y_2 + y_3 + y_4}{4} + \frac{y_5}{8} \end{aligned}$$

Definition: A Centered Four-Quarter Moving Average

Suppose we have the quarterly data $y_1, y_2, \ldots, y_n$. The **centered four-quarter moving average** at time t is denoted s_t, where

$$s_t = \frac{y_{t-2}}{8} + \frac{y_{t-1} + y_t + y_{t+1}}{4} + \frac{y_{t+2}}{8}$$

The values s_t can be calculated for $t = 3, 4, \ldots, (n - 2)$.

The formula shows that a centered four-quarter moving average is actually a weighted 5-point moving average with weights $\frac{1}{8}$, $\frac{1}{4}$, $\frac{1}{4}$, $\frac{1}{4}$, and $\frac{1}{8}$.

Constructing a Centered 12-Month Moving Average

In constructing a centered 12-month moving average, the first two noncentered values would be

$$s_{6.5} = \frac{y_1 + y_2 + \cdots + y_{12}}{12}$$

and

$$s_{7.5} = \frac{y_2 + y_3 + \cdots + y_{13}}{12}$$

We obtain the centered value

$$s_7 = \frac{s_{6.5} + s_{7.5}}{2} = \frac{y_1 + 2y_2 + \cdots + 2y_{12} + y_{13}}{24}$$

Thus, a centered 12-month moving average is actually a weighted 13-point moving average with weights $\frac{1}{24}, \frac{1}{12}, \ldots, \frac{1}{12}$, and $\frac{1}{24}$.

Definition: A Centered 12-Month Moving Average

Suppose we have the monthly data $y_1, y_2, \ldots, y_n$. The **centered 12-month moving average** at time t is denoted s_t, where

$$s_t = \frac{y_{t-6}}{24} + \frac{y_{t-5} + y_{t-4} + \cdots + y_t + \cdots + y_{t+4} + y_{t+5}}{12} + \frac{y_{t+6}}{24}$$

The values s_t can be calculated for $t = 7, 8, \ldots, (n - 6)$.

One objective in constructing a moving average is to eliminate seasonal, cyclical, and irregular fluctuations. Frequently a time plot of the smoothed values will give the analyst a good idea of the long-term behavior of the variable being studied because a moving average dampens fluctuations in a time series and thus reveals systematic movement. Graphs showing original data and smoothed values make it easy to recognize seasonal effects.

Estimating the Seasonal Component and Constructing a Seasonal Index

The centered moving-average values can be useful for gaining information about the structure of a time series. These values have been smoothed so that they are mainly free from seasonal and irregular components. The series of moving averages forms the basis for many seasonal adjustment procedures. An important application of moving averages is in estimating the seasonal component of a time series and constructing a seasonal index and a seasonally adjusted series.

The technique of seasonal adjustment called the *ratio-to-moving-average approach* is based on the assumption that the time series has a stable seasonal pattern year after year. For any given month or quarter in any year, the effect of seasonality is assumed to raise or lower the observation by some constant proportion from the moving-average value. The seasonal variations are estimated by a quantity called a *seasonal index,* which is defined in the accompanying box.

Definition: Seasonal Index

A **seasonal index** expresses the value of a time series variable in each month (or quarter) as a percentage of the trend or moving-average value for that month (or quarter).

For example, a seasonal index of 105 for some month (or quarter) means that, because of seasonal factors, the observation during the month (or quarter) in question is expected to be 5% above the trend, or moving-average, value. A seasonal index of 95 indicates that the monthly (or quarterly) value is expected to be 5% below the trend, or moving-average, value. The base value of a seasonal index is always 100, or 100%. The construction of a seasonal index is explained in the accompanying box.

Constructing a Seasonal Index from a Moving Average

Suppose we have a time series of monthly or quarterly observations $y_1, y_2, \ldots, y_n$. To construct a seasonal index, perform the following steps:

1. Calculate a centered 12-month moving average s_t for each time period when using monthly data or a centered four-quarter moving average s_t when using quarterly data.
2. For each time period, express y_t as a percentage of s_t. That is, calculate the percentage

$$100(y_t/s_t)$$

3. To find the average seasonal effect for each month or quarter, calculate the sample mean of all percentages for that month or quarter. These sample means are the unadjusted seasonal index values.
4. Scale the monthly or quarterly index values so that the mean of all the monthly or quarterly index values is 100%.

The example below shows how to calculate a seasonal index for monthly data.

Example 20.1

Constructing a Seasonal Index: The data in column 1 of Table 20.1 show the monthly shipments of air conditioners from 1983 through 1986; the data are plotted in Figure 20.1. The figure shows that shipments follow a seasonal pattern with a peak each year in May or June and a trough in October. Let us construct a seasonal index by using the ratio-to-moving-average method.

TABLE 20.1 **Shipments of air conditioners, in thousands of units**

Month	(1) y_t	(2) s_t	(3) $100(y_t/s_t)$	(4) Seasonal Index	(5) Adjusted Series
1983					
January	88	—	—	67.45	130.5
February	130	—	—	94.10	138.2
March	309	—	—	192.81	160.3
April	259	—	—	190.51	136.0
May	300	—	—	219.80	136.5
June	265	—	—	196.43	134.9
July	306	170.42	180	105.29	290.6
August	108	179.25	60	34.87	309.7
September	58	192.88	30	21.72	267.0
October	32	209.33	15	12.83	249.4
November	52	229.67	23	19.74	263.4
December	98	257.63	38	44.42	220.6
1984					
January	168	268.63	63	67.45	249.1
February	262	261.13	100	94.10	278.4
March	504	257.83	195	192.81	261.4
April	459	257.25	178	190.51	240.9
May	588	257.38	228	219.80	267.5
June	648	257.96	251	196.43	329.9
July	187	260.29	72	105.29	177.6
August	47	262.63	18	34.87	134.8
September	40	264.33	15	21.72	184.2
October	36	268.13	13	12.83	280.6
November	51	272.67	19	19.74	258.4
December	113	264.83	43	44.42	254.4
1985					
January	209	254.50	82	67.45	309.9
February	277	254.71	109	94.10	294.4
March	530	255.96	207	192.81	274.9
April	524	255.83	205	190.51	275.1
May	632	254.83	248	219.80	287.5
June	416	254.33	164	196.43	211.8
July	171	251.08	68	105.29	162.4
August	68	243.58	28	34.87	195.0
September	49	234.83	21	21.72	225.6
October	24	227.13	11	12.83	187.1
November	39	217.13	18	19.74	197.6
December	113	210.04	54	44.42	254.4
1986					
January	131	218.42	60	67.45	194.2
February	175	227.21	77	94.10	186.0

continued

TABLE 20.1 **(continued)**

Month	(1) y_t	(2) s_t	(3) $100(y_t/s_t)$	(4) Seasonal Index	(5) Adjusted Series
March	422	229.75	184	192.81	218.9
April	456	232.63	196	190.51	239.4
May	451	234.54	192	219.80	205.2
June	427	234.38	182	196.43	217.4
July	361	—	—	105.29	342.9
August	89	—	—	34.87	255.2
September	89	—	—	21.72	409.8
October	53	—	—	12.83	413.1
November	56	—	—	19.74	283.7
December	92	—	—	44.42	207.1

Source: Survey of Current Business (Washington, D.C.: U.S. Department of Commerce, 1987).

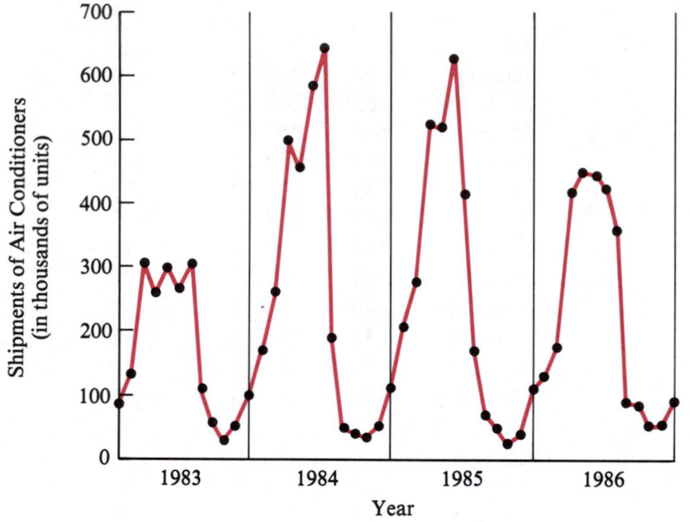

FIGURE 20.1 **Monthly shipments of air conditioners, 1983–1986.**

Solution:

Step 1: Calculate centered 12-month moving averages by using the equations

$$s_7 = \frac{y_1 + 2y_2 + \cdots + 2y_{12} + y_{13}}{24} = \frac{4090}{24} = 170.42$$

$$s_8 = \frac{y_2 + 2y_3 + \cdots + 2y_{13} + y_{14}}{24} = \frac{4302}{24} = 179.25$$

$$\vdots$$

$$s_{42} = \frac{y_{36} + 2y_{37} + \cdots + 2y_{47} + y_{48}}{24} = \frac{5625}{24} = 234.38$$

The centered moving averages s_t rounded off to two decimal places are shown in column 2 of Table 20.1. We lose 12 observations, 6 at each end of the series. This accounts for the blanks in Table 20.1.

Step 2: For each observation, express y_t as a percentage of the moving-average value s_t. That is, calculate $100(y_t/s_t)$ for $t = 7, 8, \ldots, 42$. For example, for July 1983 we have $t = 7$ and

$$100(y_7/s_7) = 100(306/170.42) \approx 180$$

Similarly, for August 1983 we have $t = 8$ and

$$100(y_8/s_8) = 100(108/179.25) \approx 60$$

After calculating $100(y_t/s_t)$ for the appropriate values of t, we have three percentages for each month, shown in column 3 in Table 20.1. For example, for January we have the three percentages 63, 82, and 60. Because these percentages differ, we still have some irregular variation in the data.

Step 3: Calculate the mean percentage for each individual month. By averaging the percentages for each month, we eliminate some of the irregular variation. The objective in averaging is to obtain a value that represents the typical seasonal effect for each month. For January we obtain the mean percentage

$$(63 + 82 + 60)/3 = 68.33$$

Similarly, for February we obtain

$$(100 + 109 + 77)/3 = 95.33$$

The twelve monthly averages are shown in Table 20.2.

Step 4: We want the average monthly percentage index to be 100 so that, on the average, we have not increased or decreased the series. Thus, it may be necessary to scale the monthly mean percentages. This is done by multiplying each monthly average

TABLE 20.2
Ratio-to-moving-average seasonal indexes for data in Table 20.1

Month	Monthly Average $100(y_t/s_t)$	Scaled Seasonal Index
January	68.33	67.45
February	95.33	94.10
March	195.33	192.81
April	193.00	190.51
May	222.67	219.80
June	199.00	196.43
July	106.67	105.29
August	35.33	34.87
September	22.00	21.72
October	13.00	12.83
November	20.00	19.74
December	45.00	44.42
Total	1215.66	1199.97

by the appropriate scale factor. For example, because the sum of our monthly means is 1215.66, their average is 101.305. Because we want the average to be 100, we should adjust the monthly means by multiplying each one by the appropriate scaling factor. In this case, the appropriate scaling factor is

$$100/101.305 = 1200/1215.66 = 0.9871$$

Multiplying each monthly average by this scale factor will yield a new set of monthly averages whose mean is 100. For example, the scaled average for January is $68.33 \times 0.9871 = 67.45$.

The scaled monthly averages, shown in Table 20.2, are the monthly seasonal indexes. Except for round-off error, these scaled averages have a mean of 100. If the sum of the original averages had been close to 1200 (instead of 1215.66) step 4 can be omitted without substantially altering the results.

The seasonal index for January of 67.45 indicates that shipments of air conditioners in January tend to be 67.45% of the centered moving-average value for January. Similarly, the seasonal index for May of 219.80 means that shipments in May tend to be 219.80% of the moving-average value for May. ■

Seasonal Adjustment

After we have obtained the seasonal index for each month (or quarter), we can *seasonally adjust* a time series by dividing each original observation y_t by the seasonal index and multiplying the quotient by 100. The seasonally adjusted data show the monthly or quarterly trend components after the seasonal influence has been removed.

For example, in Example 20.1 the total shipments of air conditioners in January 1984 were 168. Because the seasonal index for January is 67.45, the seasonally adjusted value for January 1984 is

$$(168/67.45) \times 100 = 249.07$$

The series of seasonally adjusted values is shown in column 5 of Table 20.1 and plotted in Figure 20.2. Compare the seasonally adjusted values in Figure 20.2 with the raw data

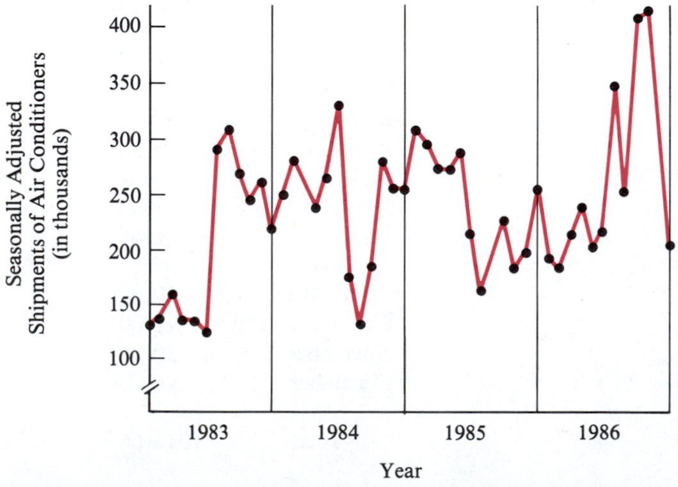

FIGURE 20.2
Seasonally adjusted values for data in Figure 20.1.

plotted in Figure 20.1. Note the marked seasonal pattern in the raw data, which has been removed in the seasonally adjusted data.

Definition: Seasonally Adjusted Value

Given a time series $y_1, y_2, \ldots, y_n$, a series of **seasonally adjusted values** y_t is obtained by using the formula

$$\text{Seasonally adjusted value} = \frac{y_t}{\text{seasonal index}} \times 100$$

Exercises for Section 20.1

1. Suppose a sequence repeats itself after K terms. Describe the unweighted moving average of order K. (See Exercise 2.)

2. For the following numbers:

8 6 5 1 7 8 6 5 1 7 8 6 5 1 7 8 6 5 1 7 8 6 5 1 7

compute an unweighted moving average of the following orders:

a. 2 b. 3 c. 4 d. 5 e. 6

3. Suppose a moving average of order 5 is calculated. How many numbers will be in the moving average if the original series contains the following numbers of observations:

a. 20 b. 25 c. 30

4. Suppose every number in a sequence is divided by 100. What happens to the moving average calculated from the same data?

5. Show that an unweighted centered moving average of order 4 is equivalent to a weighted moving average of order 5 with weights $\frac{1}{8}, \frac{2}{8}, \frac{2}{8}, \frac{2}{8}$, and $\frac{1}{8}$.

6. Let N be an even integer. Show that an unweighted centered moving average of order N is equivalent to a weighted moving average of order $(N + 1)$ with weights $1/2N, 1/N, \ldots, 1/N, 1/2N$.

7. Explain whether a 12-month moving average removes the following components:

a. Trend b. Seasonality

8. The following data show monthly sales in millions of dollars for a large corporation:

Month	1986	1987	1988
January	39	40	43
February	40	43	46
March	44	47	49
April	47	59	54
May	55	64	64
June	58	62	70
July	54	54	65
August	42	51	59
September	37	49	56
October	36	49	52
November	37	49	53
December	38	49	55

a. Smooth the data by using an unweighted five-month moving average.
b. Plot the original and smoothed data.
c. Construct a seasonal index.

9. The following data show monthly retail sales of a department store in millions of dollars for the years 1986 through 1988:

Month	1986	1987	1988
January	2.7	2.5	3.3
February	2.9	3.1	3.4
March	3.2	3.6	4.2
April	3.9	4.4	4.1
May	4.4	4.7	5.2
June	5.1	4.8	5.8
July	4.4	3.9	5.4
August	3.9	3.8	4.6
September	3.6	3.4	4.5
October	4.2	4.5	5.2
November	5.1	5.2	6.0
December	6.3	7.1	8.3

a. Compute a seasonal index based on a 12-month moving average.
b. Plot the actual and the deseasonalized data.

20.2 ▪ *Seasonal Adjustment by Using Dummy Variables*

The ratio-to-moving-average method of seasonal adjustment measures the seasonal component of a time series as a percentage deviation from the moving-average value. Dummy variables can be used to measure seasonal components as absolute (or additive) deviations from the trend value rather than as a proportional (or percentage) deviation.

As shown in Section 17.2, if an observation can be classified into one of m categories, we can measure the effect of falling in any specific category by constructing $(m - 1)$ dummy variables. The coefficients of the dummy variables measure the effect of being in a specific category rather than in the base category. In time series models, any particular month or quarter can be picked as the base category, although dummy variables are more commonly used for quarterly data. With quarterly data we need to construct only three dummy variables, to measure differences between the base quarter and the other three quarters, while monthly data require 11 dummy variables. The next example shows how to use dummy variables to determine seasonal effects in a model containing quarterly data.

Example 20.2 **Using Dummy Variables for Seasonal Adjustment:** The data in Table 20.3, showing the quarterly production of beer from 1983 through 1986, are plotted in Figure 20.3. There appears to be a slightly positive linear trend and definite quarterly seasonal com-

TABLE 20.3
Quarterly beer production, 1983–1986 (in millions of barrels)

Quarter	t	Y	Coefficient Q_1	Q_2	Q_3
1983:1	1	46.11	1	0	0
2	2	52.18	0	1	0
3	3	52.48	0	0	1
4	4	41.38	0	0	0
1984:1	5	46.62	1	0	0
2	6	53.71	0	1	0
3	7	50.81	0	0	1
4	8	41.09	0	0	0
1985:1	9	46.72	1	0	0
2	10	55.06	0	1	0
3	11	50.84	0	0	1
4	12	40.61	0	0	0
1986:1	13	47.42	1	0	0
2	14	55.31	0	1	0
3	15	50.65	0	0	1
4	16	43.12	0	0	0

Source: Survey of Current Business (Washington, D.C.: U.S. Department of Commerce, 1987).

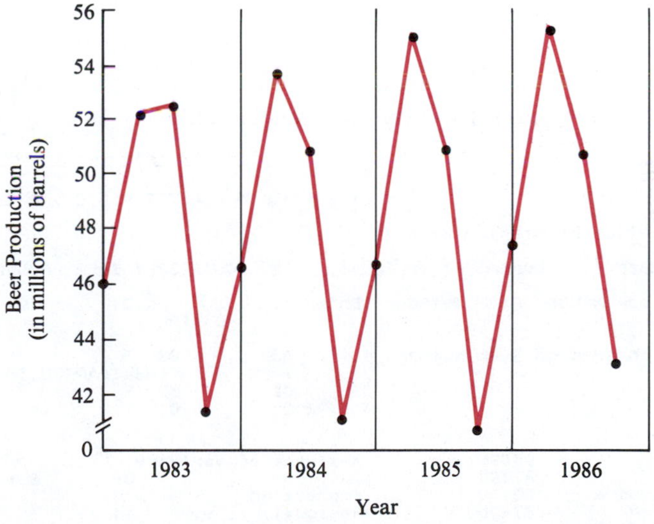

FIGURE 20.3
Quarterly beer production, 1983–1986.

ponents. For example, beer production is always higher in quarters 2 and 3 (the warm-weather quarters) than in quarters 1 and 4 (the cold-weather quarters).

Let us construct a multiple regression model to forecast quarterly production. As explanatory variables, we use a linear trend variable t to explain the trend component and quarterly dummy variables Q_1, Q_2, and Q_3 to measure the seasonal components. Quarter 4 is the base case.

Table 20.3 shows the values of the explanatory variable t, where t equals 1 in quarter 1 of 1983, 2 in quarter 2 of 1983, and so on up to 16 in quarter 4 of 1986. Table 20.3 also shows the values for the three dummy variables Q_1, Q_2, and Q_3, where

$$Q_1 = \begin{cases} 1 & \text{if observation of quarter 1} \\ 0 & \text{otherwise} \end{cases}$$

$$Q_2 = \begin{cases} 1 & \text{if observation of quarter 2} \\ 0 & \text{otherwise} \end{cases}$$

$$Q_3 = \begin{cases} 1 & \text{if observation of quarter 3} \\ 0 & \text{otherwise} \end{cases}$$

In this example, there are $m = 4$ categories (or quarters), so we have constructed $(m - 1) = 3$ dummy variables. We have arbitrarily chosen the fourth quarter to be the base category, so the estimated coefficient of the dummy variable Q_1 indicates the difference between projected production in quarter 1 and projected production in quarter 4, and similarly for dummy variables Q_2 and Q_3.

Solution: The SPSSX computer output is shown in Figure 20.4. The estimated regression model is

$$\hat{y}_t = 40.672 + 0.088t + 5.431Q_1 + 12.691Q_2 + 9.733Q_3 \quad R^2 = .97191$$

t statistics: (55.67) (1.61) (7.87) (18.2) (14.1)

FIGURE 20.4 SPSSX-generated output for Example 20.2.

```
                                * * * *   M U L T I P L E   R E G R E S S I O N   * * * *

Listwise Deletion of Missing Data

Equation Number 1     Dependent Variable..   Y    QUARTERLY BEER PRODUCTION

Beginning Block Number  1.  Method:  Enter      T        Q1       Q2       Q3


Variable(s) Entered on Step Number   1..    Q3       Q3
                                     2..    T        TIME ELAPSED IN QUARTERS
                                     3..    Q2       Q2
                                     4..    Q1       Q1


Multiple R            .98586          Analysis of Variance
R Square              .97191                         DF      Sum of Squares      Mean Square
Adjusted R Square     .96170          Regression      4           361.09250         90.27313
Standard Error        .97400          Residual       11            10.43534           .94867

                                      F =      95.15780       Signif F =  .0000

------------------ Variables in the Equation ------------------

Variable              B        SE B       Beta          T  Sig T

Q3             9.732813     .690868     .874588     14.088  .0000
T               .087812     .054448     .084004      1.613  .1351
Q2            12.690625     .697275    1.140376     18.200  .0000
Q1             5.430938     .707824     .488022      7.673  .0000
(Constant)    40.671875     .730497                 55.677  .0000

End Block Number   1   All requested variables entered.
```

The coefficient of determination is $R^2 = .97191$, and the adjusted R^2 is .96170. Thus, the model explains approximately 96% of the quarterly variation in beer production. The estimated coefficient of each dummy variable has a very large t statistic, and each of these three t statistics has a prob-value of .0000, indicating that there are definite quarterly seasonal effects. The t statistic for the coefficient of the trend variable t is 1.613, which is of questionable significance.

The graph shows that beer production tends to be lower in quarter 4 than in the other three quarters. Thus, we would expect the estimated coefficients of the three dummy variables to be positive, indicating that production in any of those quarters is higher than in the fourth quarter.

Does the time trend belong in the model? To answer this question, we could test the null hypothesis

$$H_0: \beta_1 = 0$$

against the one-sided alternative hypothesis

$$H_1: \beta_1 > 0$$

using, say, a 5% level of significance. We have $\nu = (n - K - 1) = (16 - 4 - 1) = 11$ degrees of freedom, and the critical value of t is $t_{.05,11} = 1.796$. This means that we would not reject the null hypothesis that the population regression coefficient of the trend variable t is 0. Although there might be a positive trend factor in beer production, the evidence is not extremely strong. Nevertheless, for purposes of illustration, we will retain the trend variable in the equation.

During the fourth quarter of any year we have $Q_1 = 0$, $Q_2 = 0$, and $Q_3 = 0$. For quarter 4, the estimated model becomes

$$\hat{y}_t = 40.672 + 0.088t$$

This represents a linear trend model having intercept 40.672 and slope 0.088.

During the first quarter of any year, we have $Q_1 = 1$, $Q_2 = 0$, and $Q_3 = 0$, and the estimated model becomes

$$\hat{y}_t = 40.672 + 0.088t + 5.431(1) = 46.103 + 0.088t$$

This represents a new trend line having intercept 46.103 and slope 0.088. For quarter 1, then, the trend line has the same slope as the trend line for quarter 4, but the intercept is 5.431 units higher than for the trend line of quarter 4. The coefficient of the dummy variable Q_1 measures the amount by which the trend line for the base case (quarter 4) should be shifted up or down to obtain the trend line for quarter 1. The coefficient 5.431 indicates that quarterly sales during quarter 1 tend to be 5.431 million barrels higher than during quarter 4 after we have taken the trend into account.

During the second quarter of any year, we have $Q_1 = 0$, $Q_2 = 1$, and $Q_3 = 0$, and the estimated model becomes

$$\hat{y}_t = 40.672 + 0.088t + 12.691 = 53.363 + 0.088t$$

The trend line for quarter 2 is 12.691 units above the trend line for quarter 4. As with the coefficient of Q_1, the coefficient of the dummy variable Q_2 measures the amount by which the trend line for the base case (quarter 4) should be shifted up or down to obtain the trend line for quarter 2. Similarly, the trend line for quarter 3 will be 9.733 units above the trend line for quarter 4.

In this example, all of the coefficients of the dummy variables are positive because the base case (quarter 4) was the quarter having the lowest production. Thus, the trend line for quarter 4 has to be raised in order to obtain the trend line for any other quarter. The raw data are plotted on Figure 20.3. ■

Example 20.3 **Forecasting with Dummy Variables:** Let us use the model developed in Example 20.2 to forecast beer production during each quarter of 1989.

Solution: For quarter 1 of 1989, the value of the trend variable is $t = 25$ and the values of the dummy variables are $Q_1 = 1$, $Q_2 = 0$, and $Q_3 = 0$. To forecast, we substitute these values into the estimated model and obtain

$$\begin{aligned}\hat{y}_{25} &= 40.672 + 0.088(25) + 5.431(1) + 12.691(0) + 9.733(0)\\ &= 48.303\end{aligned}$$

For quarter 2 of 1989, t equals 26, and the values of the dummy variables are $Q_1 = 0$, $Q_2 = 1$, and $Q_3 = 0$. Substitute these values into the estimated model and obtain the forecast

$$\begin{aligned}\hat{y}_{26} &= 40.672 + 0.088(26) + 5.431(0) + 12.691(1) + 9.733(0)\\ &= 55.651\end{aligned}$$

For quarter 3 of 1989, t equals 27, and the values of the dummy variables are $Q_1 = 0$, $Q_2 = 0$, $Q_3 = 1$. We obtain the forecast

$$\hat{y}_{27} = 40.672 + 0.088(27) + 5.431(0) + 12.691(0) + 9.733(1) = 55.651$$

Finally, for quarter 4 of 1989, t equals 28, and the values of the dummy variables are $Q_1 = 0$, $Q_2 = 0$, and $Q_3 = 0$. We obtain the forecast

$$\hat{y}_{28} = 40.672 + 0.088(28) + 5.431(0) + 12.691(0) + 9.733(0) = 43.136$$ ■

Exercises for Section 20.2

1. Consider the following regression results:

$$\hat{y}_t = 23.4 + 0.14t + 6.2Q_2 + 5.3Q_3 + 18.3Q_4$$

where $Q_i = 1$ in the ith quarter of each year and 0 otherwise, and y_t represents total sales in thousands of dollars in period t for a department store.

a. Explain the meaning of each of the regression coefficients.
b. Is it plausible that each of the coefficients is positive?
c. Explain why the coefficient of Q_4 is larger than the coefficients of Q_2 and Q_3.
d. Suppose the variable Q_4 had been omitted from the model and a dummy variable for Q_1 had been included. Would the coefficient of t change?
e. Suppose the variable Q_4 had been omitted from the model and a dummy variable for Q_1 had been included. Would the constant term change? If so, how?
f. Forecast sales in period 15.

2. The accompanying data refer to quarterly sales in hundreds of dollars of exterior house paint at a chain of hardware stores.

Quarter	t	Y	Q_1	Q_2	Q_3
1985:1	1	36.21	1	0	0
2	2	41.28	0	1	0
3	3	52.48	0	0	1
4	4	41.28	0	0	0
1986:1	5	38.62	1	0	0
2	6	46.57	0	1	0
3	7	58.81	0	0	1
4	8	42.09	0	0	0
1987:1	9	40.72	1	0	0
2	10	49.06	0	1	0
3	11	59.84	0	0	1
4	12	45.61	0	0	0
1988:1	13	42.42	1	0	0
2	14	53.31	0	1	0
3	15	62.65	0	0	1
4	16	47.12	0	0	0

a. Plot the data.
b. Estimate the model

$$Y_t = \beta_0 + \beta_1 t + \beta_2 Q_2 + \beta_3 Q_3 + \beta_4 Q_4 + e_t$$

c. Estimate the model

$$Y_t = \beta_0 + \beta_1 t + \beta_2 Q_2 + \beta_3 Q_3 + \beta_4 Q_1 + e_t$$

d. Compare the estimated constant terms in each equation. Can you explain why this change occurred?
e. Compare the coefficients of the trend variable in the two equations.
f. Compare the coefficients of Q_2 in the two equations. Can you explain why this change occurred?
g. Plot the relationship between sales and time separately for quarter 1, quarter 2, quarter 3, and quarter 4.
h. Forecast sales for each quarter of 1989.

20.3 ▪ Seasonal Adjustment by Using the Ratio-to-Trend Method

We estimated the seasonal component as a percentage deviation from the moving-average value in Section 20.1 and as an absolute deviation from a trend value in Section 20.2. A third method is called the *ratio-to-trend method,* which estimates the seasonal component as the percentage deviation from the trend.

Suppose that a given time series can be represented by the multiplicative model $Y_t = T_t \times S_t \times C_t \times I_t$. The ratio-to-trend method estimates the seasonal index (S) by removing the trend (T) from the series but not the cyclical (C) and irregular (I) variations. First, we obtain the monthly (or quarterly) trend values by fitting a least-squares trend line or some other curve. Let $\hat{y}_t$ denote the fitted trend value for time t. Trend can be eliminated from the original series by dividing each value y_t by the corresponding fitted value $\hat{y}_t$ ($= T$). Thus, we obtain

$$y_t/\hat{y}_t = y_t/T_t = S_t \times C_t \times I_t$$

The fluctuations in the product ($S \times C \times I$) are assumed to represent mainly seasonal fluctuations. We remove much of the random effect ($C \times I$) by averaging ($S \times C \times I$) for each month or quarter.

Calculating the Ratio-to-Trend Seasonal Index

The ratio-to-trend seasonal index for monthly data is calculated as follows:

1. Estimate the sample trend line for the original data $y_1, y_2, \ldots, y_n$.
2. Obtain the fitted, or trend, values $\hat{y}_1, \hat{y}_2, \ldots, \hat{y}_n$.
3. Obtain the detrended values $y_1/\hat{y}_1, y_2/\hat{y}_2, \ldots, y_n/\hat{y}_n$.
4. Obtain the average of all values $y_i/\hat{y}_i$ corresponding to January. Do the same for every other month.
5. Multiply each average by 100 to convert it to a percentage. These 12 averages are the seasonal indexes for each of the 12 months.

Example 20.4

Constructing a Seasonal Index with the Ratio-to-Trend Method: The data in Table 20.4 show the monthly sales of retail stores from 1983 through 1986 and are plotted in Figure 20.5. The data are highly seasonal with a peak each year in December and a trough each year in February. There appears to be a positive long-term trend. Let us obtain a seasonal index for these data using the ratio-to-trend method.

TABLE 20.4
Monthly retail sales, 1983–1986, (in billions of dollars)

Month	1983	1984	1985	1986
January	$ 81.3	$ 93.1	$ 98.8	$105.6
February	78.9	93.7	95.6	99.7
March	93.8	104.3	110.2	114.2
April	94.0	104.3	113.1	115.7
May	97.8	111.3	120.3	125.4
June	100.6	112.0	115.0	120.4
July	99.6	106.6	115.5	120.7
August	100.2	110.7	121.1	124.1
September	98.0	103.9	114.2	124.6
October	100.7	109.2	116.1	123.1
November	103.9	113.3	118.6	120.8
December	125.7	131.8	139.5	151.5

Source: Survey of Current Business (Washington, D.C.: U.S. Department of Commerce, 1987).

Solution:

Step 1: Estimate the linear trend model. The SPSSX computer program was used to obtain the estimated trend equation

$$\hat{y}_t = 92.055762 + 0.743047t \qquad R^2 = .55869$$
$$t \text{ statistics:} \qquad (33.6) \qquad (7.63)$$

where t equals 1 in January 1983, 2 in February 1983, and so on to 48 in December 1986.

The computer output is shown in Figure 20.6. The relatively low value of $R^2 = .55869$ shows that there is a great deal of unexplained seasonal variation about the trend line.

FIGURE 20.5
Monthly retail sales, 1983–1986.

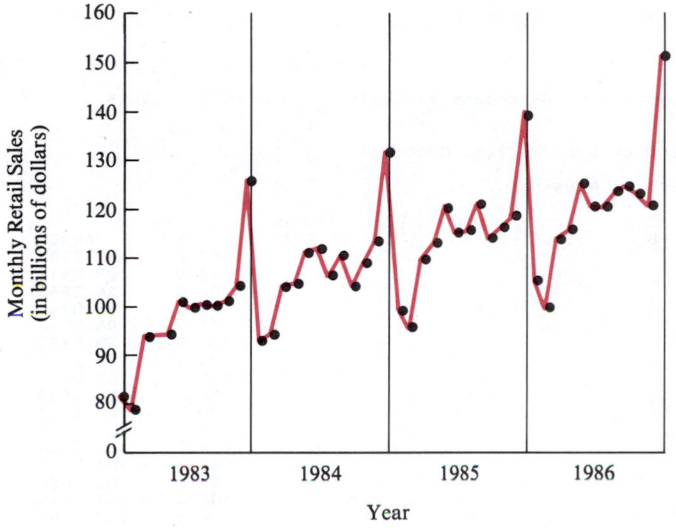

FIGURE 20.6 **SPSSX-generated output for Example 20.4.**

```
                         * * * *   M U L T I P L E   R E G R E S S I O N   * * * *

Listwise Deletion of Missing Data

Equation Number 1    Dependent Variable..   Y    RETAIL SALES

Beginning Block Number   1.  Method:   Enter       T


Variable(s) Entered on Step Number   1..    T          TIME ELAPSED IN MONTHS


Multiple R            .74746        Analysis of Variance
R Square              .55869                            DF       Sum of Squares        Mean Square
Adjusted R Square     .54910        Regression            1           5086.12033         5086.12033
Standard Error       9.34539        Residual             46           4017.47446           87.33640

                                    F =       58.23597       Signif F =  .0000

------------------ Variables in the Equation ------------------

Variable                 B          SE B         Beta          T  Sig T

T                  .743047       .097369      .747458      7.631  .0000
(Constant)       92.055762      2.740495                  33.591  .0000

End Block Number   1   All requested variables entered.
```

Step 2: Calculate the fitted, or estimated, trend value $\hat{y}_t$ for each month. For example, in December 1984 we have $t = 24$ and the fitted value is

$$\hat{y}_t = 92.055762 + 0.743047(24) = 109.8889$$

Figure 20.7 shows the actual values of y_t, the predicted values $\hat{y}_t$, and the residuals. For example, the predicted value for the 24th observation is $\hat{y}_{24} = 109.8889$ and the actual value is $y_{24} = 131.8$, giving a residual of 21.9111.

FIGURE 20.7 **SPSSX-generated actual values, predicted values, and residuals for Example 20.4.**

```
                                   * * * *   M U L T I P L E   R E G R E S S I O N   * * * *
Equation Number 1    Dependent Variable..   Y   RETAIL SALES

Casewise Plot of Standardized Residual
*: Selected   M: Missing
              -3.0            0.0             3.0
Case #        0:..............:..............:0         Y       *PRED      *RESID
     1        .         *     .               .      81.3     92.7988    -11.4988
     2        .       *       .               .      78.9     93.5419    -14.6419
     3        .               *               .      93.8     94.2849     -0.4849
     4        .              *.               .      94.0     95.0280     -1.0280
     5        .               .*              .      97.8     95.7710      2.0290
     6        .               . *             .     100.6     96.5140      4.0860
     7        .               .*              .      99.6     97.2571      2.3429
     8        .               .*              .     100.2     98.0001      2.1999
     9        .               *               .      98.0     98.7432     -0.7432
    10        .               .*              .     100.7     99.4862      1.2138
    11        .               . *             .     103.9    100.2293      3.6707
    12        .               .            *  .     125.7    100.9723     24.7277
    13        .          *    .               .      93.1    101.7154     -8.6154
    14        .          *    .               .      93.7    102.4584     -8.7584
    15        .               .*              .     104.3    103.2015      1.0985
    16        .               *               .     104.3    103.9445       .3555
    17        .               .   *           .     111.3    104.6876      6.6124
    18        .               .   *           .     112.0    105.4306      6.5694
    19        .               *               .     106.6    106.1737       .4263
    20        .               . *             .     110.7    106.9167      3.7833
    21        .             * .               .     103.9    107.6598     -3.7598
    22        .               *               .     109.2    108.4028       .7972
    23        .               . *             .     113.3    109.1458      4.1542
    24        .               .           *   .     131.8    109.8889     21.9111
    25        .         *     .               .      98.8    110.6319    -11.8319
    26        .       *       .               .      95.6    111.3750    -15.7750
    27        .              *.               .     110.2    112.1180     -1.9180
    28        .               *               .     113.1    112.8611       .2389
    29        .               .   *           .     120.3    113.6041      6.6959
    30        .               *               .     115.0    114.3472       .6528
    31        .               *               .     115.5    115.0902       .4098
    32        .               .  *            .     121.1    115.8333      5.2667
    33        .              *.               .     114.2    116.5763     -2.3763
    34        .              *.               .     116.1    117.3194     -1.2194
    35        .               *               .     118.6    118.0624       .5376
    36        .               .          *    .     139.5    118.8055     20.6945
    37        .        *      .               .     105.6    119.5485    -13.9485
    38        .    *          .               .      99.7    120.2916    -20.5916
    39        .           *   .               .     114.2    121.0346     -6.8346
    40        .            *  .               .     115.7    121.7776     -6.0776
    41        .               . *             .     125.4    122.5207      2.8793
    42        .             * .               .     120.4    123.2637     -2.8637
    43        .             * .               .     120.7    124.0068     -3.3068
    44        .               *               .     124.1    124.7498     -0.6498
    45        .               *               .     124.6    125.4929     -0.8929
    46        .             * .               .     123.1    126.2359     -3.1359
    47        .            *  .               .     120.8    126.9790     -6.1790
    48        .               .            *  .     151.5    127.7220     23.7780
Case #        0:..............:..............:0         Y       *PRED      *RESID
              -3.0            0.0             3.0
```

In the computer output, note that there are four very large positive residuals for observations 12, 24, 36, and 48, which are the residuals for the month of December.

Step 3: Divide each actual observation y_t by the corresponding fitted value $\hat{y}_t$ to obtain the ratio r_t, where r_t is defined by the equation

$$r_t = y_t/\hat{y}_t$$

for $t = 1, 2, \ldots, 48$. The ratios r_t yield a series of proportions showing each monthly observation as a proportion of the corresponding trend value. For example, in December 1984 the actual value is $y_{24} = 131.8$ and the fitted value is $\hat{y}_{24} = 109.8889$, yielding a ratio of

$$r_{24} = 131.8/109.9 = 1.20$$

All of the monthly ratios are shown in Table 20.5. All the ratios for January and February are less than 1, and all the ratios for December are greater than 1. Thus, observations for January and February are always below the trend line, and observations for December are always above the trend line.

TABLE 20.5 **Seasonal indexes for data in Table 20.4 obtained by ratio-to-trend method**

Month	(1) 1983 $y_t/\hat{y}_t$	(2) 1984 $y_t/\hat{y}_t$	(3) 1985 $y_t/\hat{y}_t$	(4) 1986 $y_t/\hat{y}_t$	(5) Average	(6) Seasonal Index
January	0.88	0.92	0.89	0.88	0.8925	89.25
February	0.84	0.92	0.86	0.83	0.8625	86.25
March	0.99	1.01	0.98	0.94	0.9800	98.00
April	0.99	1.00	1.00	0.95	0.9850	98.50
May	1.02	1.06	1.06	1.02	1.0400	104.00
June	1.04	1.06	1.01	0.98	1.0175	101.75
July	1.02	1.00	1.00	0.97	0.9975	99.75
August	1.02	1.04	1.05	0.99	1.0250	102.50
September	0.99	0.97	0.98	0.99	0.9825	98.25
October	1.01	1.01	0.99	0.98	0.9975	99.75
November	1.04	1.04	1.00	0.95	1.0075	100.75
December	1.24	1.20	1.17	1.19	1.2000	120.00

Step 4: Calculate the average (mean) ratio for each month. For example, for December the ratios are 1.25, 1.20, 1.17, and 1.19 for the four years studied. The average ratio for December is

$$\frac{1.24 + 1.20 + 1.17 + 1.19}{4} = 1.20$$

The mean ratio for each month is shown in Table 20.5 in column 5, labeled "Average." Months with mean ratios exceeding 1 tend to fall above the trend line, while months with mean ratios less than 1 tend to fall below it.

Step 5: Multiply each monthly mean ratio by 100 to obtain the monthly seasonal index. For example, the seasonal index for December is $1.20 \times 100 = 120.00$. The monthly seasonal indexes are shown in column 6 of Table 20.5.

The December seasonal index of 120.00 indicates that, on the average, sales during December are 20% above the trend line. Similarly, the seasonal index for February is 86.25, indicating that sales during February tend to be 13.75% below the trend line. ■

Forecasting with the Seasonal Index

Obtaining a Forecast with the Seasonal Index and Trend Value

Let $\hat{y}_t$ be the estimated trend value of a variable in period t, and let SI_t be the seasonal index for period t. The forecast value for period t is $(\hat{y}_t \times SI_t)/100$.

Example 20.5

Forecasting with the Ratio-to-Trend Model: Let us use the ratio-to-trend model to forecast retail sales in December 1988.

Solution: First, calculate the forecast trend value. For December 1988, t is 72. From the estimated trend equation, we obtain

$$\hat{y}_{72} = 92.063032 + 0.742835(72) = 145.547$$

This is the estimated trend value. Now we must adjust this value for seasonality. To do this, we multiply the estimated trend value by the seasonal index for that month and divide by 100 to obtain the monthly forecast. For December, the seasonal index is 120.00 and the trend value is 145.547. The forecast value for December 1988 is thus

$$(\hat{y}_{72} \times SI_{72})/100 = (145.547 \times 120.00)/100$$
$$= 174.656$$
■

Exercises for Section 20.3

1. Refer to the data in Exercise 8 of Section 20.1. Compute a seasonal index using the ratio-to-trend method and plot the actual and deseasonalized data.
2. Refer to the data in Exercise 9 of Section 20.1. Compute a seasonal index using the ratio-to-trend method and plot the actual and deseasonalized data.

20.4 • *Exponential Smoothing*

Another method of smoothing data is called **exponential smoothing**, a forecasting procedure used when the variable being predicted has no regular seasonal component and no regular upward or downward trend. When a time series has no trend or seasonal component, the usual objective is to forecast the *level* of the time series. Thus, given the values $y_1, y_2, \ldots, y_n$, we want to predict the value y_{n+1}.

One way of predicting a value y_{n+1} is to use the last observation y_n. However, this is impractical because each observation y_t contains a random component, and if the random component is large, then y_t is not a good predictor of the level of the time series.

If y_t contains a substantial irregular component, it is reasonable to use several previous values of the time series to predict a value in order to average out the random component. In the most extreme case, we would take the average of all n observations in order to predict y_{n+1}. The problem with this procedure is that the predicted value gives each previous value equal weight. In many cases, it is more reasonable to give recent observations greater weight than older observations. In general, we expect recent data to be more reliable indicators of the future than distant data.

Exponential smoothing generates a forecast as a weighted average of current and past values. In calculating the weighted average, more recent values of the time series get greater weights than distant observations, as described in the accompanying box. The smoothed value s_t that is obtained is an estimate of the level of the series at time t, whereas the actual value y_t measures the level of the series *plus* some random factor.

Definition: Exponential Smoothing

Suppose we have observations $y_1, y_2, \ldots, y_n$. Let s_t denote the smoothed value at time t. The method of **exponential smoothing** calculates the smoothed values in the following way: In period 1, set s_1 equal to y_1. For all succeeding periods, the smoothed value s_t is determined using the equation

$$s_t = cy_t + (1 - c)s_{t-1}$$

where c is some constant that satisfies the inequality $0 \leq c \leq 1$.

If we lag the model one period, we obtain

$$s_{t-1} = cy_{t-1} + (1 - c)s_{t-2}$$

Substituting s_{t-1} into the original equation yields

$$\begin{aligned} s_t &= cy_t + (1 - c)[cy_{t-1} + (1 - c)s_{t-2}] \\ &= cy_t + c(1 - c)y_{t-1} + (1 - c)^2 s_{t-2} \end{aligned}$$

Similarly, we can substitute for s_{t-2} and obtain

$$s_t = cy_t + c(1 - c)y_{t-1} + (1 - c)^2[cy_{t-2} + (1 - c)s_{t-3}]$$

If we continue substituting, we eventually obtain

$$s_t = c\sum_{j=0}^{t-2}(1 - c)^j y_{t-j} + (1 - c)^{t-1}y_1$$

This formula shows that the current smoothed value s_t depends on every past observation y_{t-j}. If the smoothing constant c is close to 1, the coefficients $(1 - c)^j$ die out quickly, and the smoothed value depends almost exclusively on recent values of y_t. When c is close to 0, the coefficients $(1 - c)^j$ die out much more slowly, and the smoothed value s_t is more heavily influenced by distant values of y_t than when c is near 1.

The choice of c depends on the characteristics of the series being smoothed. If the series is quite volatile, use a small value of c in order to give a large weight to the previous smoothed value s_{t-1} and only a small weight to the current value y_t. If the data are not too volatile, then the random component of the series is probably fairly small. In this case, y_t should get a large weight when calculating s_t.

Example 20.6 **Exponential Smoothing:** The data in Table 20.6 show the price of a share of stock on the first trading day of the month for a period of eight months. Construct a smoothed series using the exponential smoothing technique.

TABLE 20.6
Price of a share of stock

Time	Observation	Smoothed Value
1	16.4	16.400
2	17.6	16.880
3	16.1	16.568
4	15.5	16.141
5	17.2	16.565
6	16.8	16.659
7	18.1	17.235
8	17.0	17.141

Solution: Let us smooth the series using $c = .4$. We obtain

$$s_1 = y_1 = 16.4$$
$$s_t = cy_t + (1 - c)s_{t-1} \quad \text{for } t = 2, 3, \ldots, 8$$
$$s_2 = (.4)(17.6) + (.6)(16.4) = 16.88$$
$$s_3 = (.4)(16.1) + (.6)(16.88) = 16.568$$

and so forth. The smoothed data are also shown in Table 20.6. ■

Forecasting with the Exponential Smoothing Model

The exponential smoothing model is used to average out the effects of random variation so we can estimate the level of a time series not subject to trend or seasonal components. The model can be used to forecast the future level of a time series as described in the accompanying box.

Forecasting with Exponential Smoothing

Let $y_1, y_2, \ldots, y_n$ be a set of observations of a time series with no regular seasonal or trend component. Let $\hat{s}_{n+j}$ denote the forecast level of the series in period $(n + j)$. We use the forecast

$$\hat{s}_{n+j} = s_n = cy_n + (1 - c)s_{n-1}$$

where s_n is the smoothed value for period n and c is the smoothing constant. Thus, the forecast value of the level of the series for all future periods is the last estimate of the level of the series.

Example 20.7 **Forecasting with the Exponential Smoothing Model:** Use the data in Table 20.6 to forecast the stock price on the first trading day of months 9 and 10.

Solution: In Example 20.6, the smoothed value for period 8 is

$$s_8 = 17.141$$

At the end of period 8, the forecasts for periods 9 and 10 are

$$\hat{s}_9 = s_8 = 17.141$$
$$\hat{s}_{10} = s_8 = 17.141$$

At the end of period 9, we would get a new smoothed value s_9, from which we would obtain the estimate for period 10. Thus, at the end of period 9, the updated forecast for period 10 would be

$$\hat{s}_{10} = s_9$$

Forecasting by exponential smoothing is very easy to do, but whether this model will outperform a carefully designed regression model is questionable. Its major advantage is its simplicity, but this simplicity is also its major drawback. Unless the time series to be forecast moves very smoothly, the forecasts generated via exponential smoothing will be inaccurate, because the method does not take into account underlying factors that cause the behavior of y_t to change over time. A well-designed regression model can frequently identify these factors and take them into account.

Exercises for Section 20.4

1. The following data show the monthly unemployment rate in a midwestern city during 1988: Use the smoothing constant $c = .9$ in performing the following tasks:

Jan.	Feb.	Mar.	Apr.	May	June	July	Aug.	Sept.	Oct.	Nov.	Dec.
8.4	8.6	8.7	8.9	9.2	9.5	10.0	10.0	9.8	9.7	9.6	9.5

a. Forecast the unemployment rate one month ahead for February through December. Use the forecasting equation

$$\hat{y}_t = cy_{t-1} + (1 - c)\hat{y}_{t-1} \quad \text{where } \hat{y}_1 = y_1$$

b. Plot the original data and the corresponding forecasts.

c. Calculate the monthly forecast errors.

d. Plot the forecast errors.

2. The following data show monthly receipts in thousands of dollars of a new-car franchise during 1987 and 1988:

Year	Month											
	Jan.	Feb.	Mar.	Apr.	May	June	July	Aug.	Sep.	Oct.	Nov.	Dec.
1987	84	82	86	92	96	102	108	114	112	106	98	92
1988	90	90	94	100	110	110	114	120	122	116	112	106

a. Plot the data.
b. Let $c = .8$ and forecast receipts one month ahead from July 1987 to December 1988 using exponential smoothing.
c. Plot these forecasts and calculate the monthly errors in the forecast.

3. The accompanying data show the number of new cars sold in a southern county over 14 quarters.

Quarter	1985	1986	1987	1988
1	386	375	395	410
2	402	390	411	430
3	427	404	421	
4	398	390	416	

a. Plot the data.
b. Let $c = .7$ and forecast sales one quarter ahead using the exponential smoothing technique.
c. Plot the forecasts.
d. Calculate the forecast errors and plot them.

4. The following data show the number of gallons of gasoline sold per month (in hundreds of thousands) at a service station:

Year	Month											
	Jan.	Feb.	Mar.	Apr.	May	June	July	Aug.	Sep.	Oct.	Nov.	Dec.
1986	1.8	1.8	1.9	2.1	2.3	2.5	2.8	3.0	2.7	2.5	2.3	2.2
1987	2.2	2.3	2.4	2.5	2.7	2.7	3.1	3.2	2.8	2.8	2.4	2.4
1988	2.5	2.6	2.6	2.7	2.9	3.0	3.2	3.3	3.1	2.9	2.7	2.5

a. Plot the data.
b. Estimate the trend line $Y_t = \beta_0 + \beta_1 t + e_t$.
c. Use the estimated trend line and predict Y for each month.
d. Calculate the residuals and plot them.
e. Let $c = .8$ and calculate forecasts one month ahead by exponential smoothing.
f. Plot these forecasts and calculate the forecast errors.
g. Plot these errors.

20.5 ▪ *Leading Indicators*

Economists, business people, and government officials are interested in predicting *turning points* in the economy, where a rising economy begins to fall or a falling one begins to rise. Government officials want to forecast such turning points so they can adopt policies to reverse undesirable movements. When making investment decisions and planning inventory levels, business people need to forecast whether the economy will be expanding or contracting during the next few years and whether interest rates and prices will be rising or falling.

Definition: Turning Point

A **turning point** occurs when a time series that has been rising begins to fall, or vice versa.

Because so many decision makers consider turning points in the aggregate level of economic activity to be of special importance, considerable effort has been spent to forecast when these turns will occur. A reasonable way to forecast these turning points is to search for sectors of the economy that tend to lead the overall economy; observed turning points in these sectors would suggest that the overall economy will soon turn.

Since 1937, the National Bureau of Economic Research (NBER) has sought to identify groups of economic time series that typically lead, are coincident with, or lag behind aggregate economic activity. The original research was carried out under the leadership of Wesley C. Mitchell and Arthur F. Burns, and the NBER today continues to search for variables that can accurately predict when Gross National Product (GNP) will experience a turning point. Because GNP data are only available quarterly, the NBER has tried to forecast turning points in the index of industrial production, which is published monthly. Because studies show that the index of industrial production and GNP move together quite closely, forecasting a turning point in the index of industrial production is basically equivalent to forecasting a turning point in GNP. The index of industrial production ignores the agricultural and service sectors of the economy, however.

Not all sectors of the economy are behaving in the same way at any given time; some may be expanding while others are contracting. The NBER's index of leading indicators is designed to forecast turning points in the aggregate level of economic activity by calculating a weighted average of several important economic variables that tend to turn before the overall economy does. Before constructing the index, it is necessary to examine historical data to determine when turning points in the economy have actually occurred.

There are numerous problems in measuring the level of economic activity and determining exactly when a turning point has occurred. Economists sometimes disagree on when and even whether a turning point has occurred. Because most people have accepted the NBER's dating of past turning points, these reference dates are used to evaluate potential indicators.

The NBER has examined hundreds of economic time series and compiled a list of leading indicators. The variables included in this list have changed from time to time. In 1966, the NBER listed 36 variables as leading indicators, 25 as coincident indicators, and 11 as lagging indicators. In 1977, a revised list of 111 indicators was issued. No single series has always been able to forecast turning points in GNP, so it is natural to examine the entire list of potential indicators and form averages of the indicators chosen. These averages are thought to be the best indicators.

To decide which variables to use in forming this average, the economists at the NBER examine each variable and subjectively assign a score from 0 to 100 to every indicator in each of 6 categories: (1) economic significance, (2) statistical adequacy, (3) historical conformity to business cycles, (4) cyclical timing record, (5) smoothness, and (6) promptness of publication. The scores assigned are rather arbitrary and are based more on subjective opinion than on any sophisticated statistical analysis. The average scores are used to determine which variables should be included in the index and how those that are included should be weighted. The variables with the highest scores get the highest weights. All of the main U.S. indicators and the various leading, lagging, and coincident indexes are presented in numerical and diagrammatic form in the publication *Business Conditions Digest,* which is published monthly by the U.S. Department of Commerce.

Currently the NBER's index of leading indicators is a weighted average of the following 12 leading indicators:

1. average workweek of production workers in manufacturing,
2. index of net business formation,
3. index of stock prices for 500 common stocks,
4. index of new building permits for private housing units,
5. layoff rate in manufacturing (on an inverted scale),
6. new orders of consumer goods and materials (in 1972 dollars),
7. vendor performance (the percentage of companies receiving slower deliveries),
8. contracts and orders for plants and equipment (in 1972 dollars),
9. net change in inventories on hand and on order (in 1972 dollars, smoothed),
10. percent change in prices for sensitive crude materials (smoothed),
11. percent change in total liquid assets (smoothed), and
12. M2 money supply (in 1972 dollars).

The performance of the index of leading indicators from 1952 to 1987 is shown by the top curve in Figure 20.8. The remaining two curves on the figure show the *index of coincident indicators* and the *index of lagging indicators.* At the top of Figure 20.8 are a series of Ps and Ts indicating dates of turning points in aggregate economic activity. The Ps indicate the months when a *peak* occurred in economic activity and output began to decline. The Ts indicate the months when aggregate economic activity reached a *trough* and began to expand. The date above each P shows the month when output stopped increasing and a recession began. Similarly, the date above each T shows the month when output stopped falling and began to increase indicating the end of a recession and the beginning of an expansionary period. The shaded portions between the Ps and Ts indicate the seven periods of recession for the U.S. economy since 1952. The signed numbers on the figure next to the indexes of leading, coincident, and lagging indicators indicate the length of leads ($-$) and lags ($+$) in months from the reference turning dates. As indicated in Figure 20.8, the index of leading indicators is based on 12 economic variables, the index of coincident indicators on 4 variables, and the index of lagging indicators on 6 variables.

Figure 20.8 shows that the index of leading indicators turned down prior to each of the seven peaks and correctly predicted the onset of each recession. Now examine the behavior of the index during recessions. During every recession, the index turned up prior to the end of the recession, correctly signaling the future upturn in economic activity. This means that the onset of every recession and of every expansion was predicted in advance by the index of leading indicators. Note, however, that although the index

FIGURE 20.8 **Index of leading indicators, 1952–1987.**

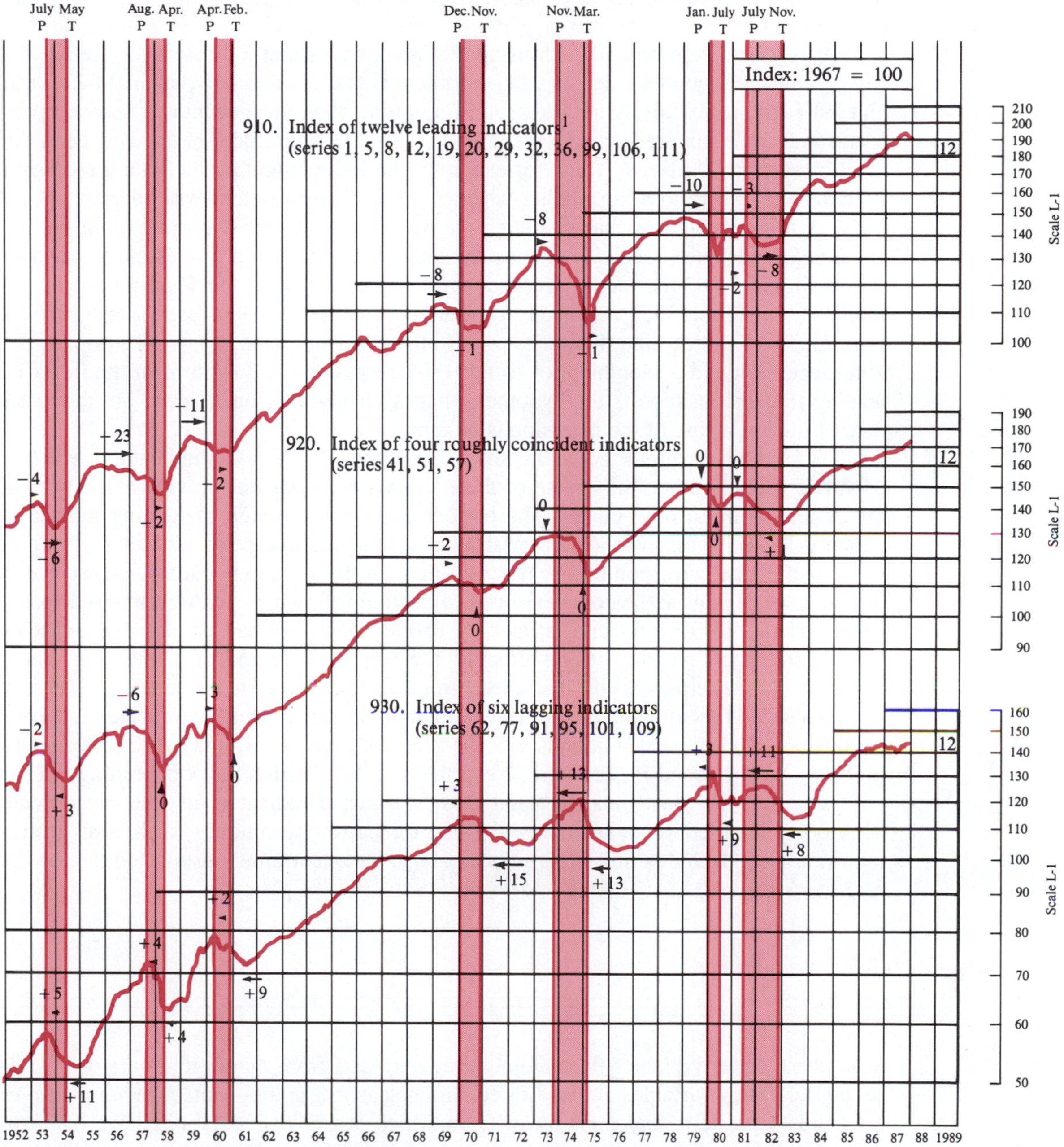

Note: Numbers entered on the chart indicate length of leads (–) and lags (+) in months from reference turning dates.
[1]Beginning with data for January 1984, series 12 has been suspended from this index.

Source: Business Conditions Digest, January 1988 (Washington, D.C.: U.S. Government Printing Office, 1988).

turned down in 1962, 1966, and 1984, no recessions followed. Thus, although the index did not miss predicting any recession, it incorrectly signaled three recessions that did not occur.

There are three problems with using the index of leading indicators to forecast the future course of economic activity. One problem is that occasionally, as in 1962, 1966, and 1984, the index falsely indicates a turning point when none occurs. A second problem is that the index predicts only the direction, not the magnitude, of any change in the level of economic activity. Thus, for example, the index might predict that a recession is imminent, but it does not predict whether the decline in output will be, say, 1% or 10%. A third problem is that, although the index typically leads turning points in the economy, the length of lead is not constant and is highly variable. For example, according to Figure 20.8, the index turned down 4 months prior to the 1953 recession, 23 months prior to the 1957 recession, 11 months prior to the 1960 recession, 8 months prior to the 1970 recession, 8 months prior to the 1973 recession, 10 months prior to the 1980 recession and 3 months prior to the 1981 recession. A downturn in the index of leading indicators supports the hypothesis that a recession is on its way, but the exact date of the beginning of the recession is unknown.

The middle curve in Figure 20.8 shows the index of coincident indicators, which is useful for helping track the course of the economy but does not provide much help in predicting future turning points. The bottom curve is the index of lagging indicators which is based on six economic variables that tend to have peaks or troughs several months after the corresponding peaks or troughs in the general economy. Observe that the index of lagging indicators continued to decline following each of the seven recessions and did not turn up until after each of the recessions had ended. The index of lagging indicators has no use in predicting the beginning or end of a recession, but it can be useful in helping verify that a recession has actually started or ended.

Evidence is accumulating that the leading indicator methodology as presently developed is not sophisticated enough to provide accurate predictions, and better indexes will probably be developed in the future. Nevertheless, the NBER's index of leading indicators is one of the most important and closely watched indicators of future economic activity. When used in conjunction with other forecasting techniques, such as an econometric model, the index of leading indicators can be an extremely useful tool.

Chapter 20 Summary

Many time series variables fluctuate on a regular basis from month to month or quarter to quarter. Such variables are said to contain a seasonal component. *Moving averages* are used to create a *smoothed series* from which seasonal fluctuations have been removed. There are many different techniques for creating a smoothed series based on moving averages. In general, a moving-average value is a weighted average of several adjacent observed values in a time series.

A popular technique for taking into account quarterly variations in a time series variable is to estimate a model using three *dummy variables* as explanatory variables.

The coefficients of the dummy variables measure how the values of the dependent variable in any particular quarter differ from the values of the variable in the base quarter.

Another method of seasonal adjustment is the *ratio-to-trend method*. With this method, we first estimate the trend by using one of the techniques described in Chapter 19. For each month (or quarter), we calculate the ratio of the actual value of the dependent variable to the trend value. For any month or quarter, the average of these ratios can be used to create a *seasonal index* that measures how the given month (or quarter) differs from the trend.

The NBER's *index of leading indicators* can be a useful tool for predicting that a turning point in aggregate economic activity will occur, but it is not so useful for predicting the exact date of the turning point.

This chapter concludes our discussion of time series analysis and model building. In the next chapter, we return to the topic of hypothesis testing that was initially introduced in Chapter 11.

Chapter 20 ▪ Supplementary Exercises

1. The accompanying data refer to monthly sales (in thousands of dollars) of a small clothing store.

Month	1986	1987	1988
January	13.4	14.4	14.5
February	14.6	15.9	14.6
March	17.4	16.8	16.4
April	16.3	15.3	15.8
May	17.6	17.9	18.2
June	16.4	16.4	17.0
July	14.9	15.1	16.4
August	16.8	17.0	17.4
September	16.6	16.0	16.6
October	22.3	20.8	21.5
November	23.8	22.1	21.3
December	25.2	24.4	25.8

a. Find the linear trend component.
b. Find the seasonal index using the ratio-to-trend method.
c. Seasonally adjust the data using the index from part (b).
d. Plot the original data, the seasonally adjusted data, and the linear trend line.
e. Remove the seasonal component by computing a centered 12-month moving average of the original data.
f. Plot the original data and the smoothed data.
g. Estimate the linear trend line using the smoothed data.
h. Use parts (a) and (b) to forecast sales for each month of 1989.

2. The accompanying data are monthly car sales at a small distributor in Chicago:

Month	1986	1987	1988
January	31	33	34
February	33	34	34
March	41	40	39
April	49	53	49
May	56	59	59
June	66	64	67
July	71	73	72
August	74	75	76
September	63	61	62
October	56	54	55
November	50	46	47
December	42	40	39

a. Calculate a seasonal index using the simple average method.
b. Deseasonalize the data using the index in part (a).
c. Deseasonalize the data by calculating a centered 12-month moving average.

3. The accompanying table shows quarterly sales data for a business firm in millions of dollars.

Quarter	1985	1986	1987	1988
1	2.6	3.6	4.9	7.2
2	2.9	4.1	5.8	7.5
3	3.5	4.8	6.4	8.2
4	5.7	6.9	8.8	10.7

a. Compute a centered four-quarter moving average.
b. Fit a logarithmic trend curve using the results from part (a).
c. Compute a quarterly index using the results from part (b) and the ratio-to-trend method.
d. Forecast the trend values for 1989.
e. Use parts (c) and (d) to forecast the actual values for 1989.

4. Usage of an indoor tennis facility has been increasing every year but fluctuating from month to month because of seasonal factors, as shown in the accompanying table showing the number of customers.

Month	1984	1985	1986	1987	1988
January	400	500	620	760	860
February	450	510	650	800	910
March	400	470	600	720	810
April	380	450	510	660	710
May	380	420	450	610	620
June	190	200	220	310	320
July	100	200	220	280	300
August	100	180	210	260	260
September	120	230	280	320	330
October	180	290	410	450	470
November	270	450	520	590	610
December	310	480	620	680	710

a. Plot the data.
b. Fit a linear trend line and graph it.
c. Construct a centered 12-month moving average and plot the smoothed values.
d. Construct a seasonal index using the method of simple averages.
e. Use the trend equation to predict the number of customers for January 1989 through December 1989. Adjust this value by using the seasonal index from part (d). Plot these predictions.
f. Construct a seasonal index using the ratio-to-trend method.
g. Predict the number of customers for January 1989 through December 1989 using the results of parts (b) and (f). Plot these predictions.
h. Construct a seasonal index using the ratio-to-moving-average method.
i. Predict the number of customers for January 1989 through December 1989 using the results of parts (b) and (h). Plot these predictions.

5. The accompanying data show retail sales in millions of dollars for a large corporation.

Month	1983	1984	1985	1986	1987	1988
January	347	361	371	399	427	466
February	315	312	321	365	367	428
March	457	418	421	487	433	544
April	401	496	474	449	536	604
May	434	463	452	492	496	563
June	405	407	413	454	456	532
July	358	368	383	418	440	492
August	399	414	438	451	443	524
September	438	455	439	482	496	571
October	462	468	463	530	553	596
November	483	513	499	522	602	614
December	770	801	817	895	992	979

a. Plot this time series.
b. Fit a linear trend line to the data and graph it.
c. Construct a centered 12-month moving average and plot these smoothed values.
d. Construct a seasonal index using the ratio-to-trend method.
e. Use parts (b) and (d) and predict sales for each month of 1989.
f. Construct a seasonal index using the ratio-to-moving-average method.
g. Use parts (b) and (f) and predict sales for each month of 1989.

References

BOX, GEORGE E. P., and GWILYM M. JENKINS. *Time Series Analysis, Forecasting, and Control.* San Francisco: Holden-Day, 1970.

GRANGER, CLIVE, and PAUL NEWBOLD. *Forecasting Economic Time Series.* London: Academic Press, 1977.

HOFF, J. C. *A Practical Guide to Box–Jenkins Forecasting.* Belmont, Calif.: Lifetime Learning, 1983.

MAKRIDAKIS, SPYROS G. "A Survey of Time Series Analysis." *International Statistical Review* 44 (1976): 29–70.

MAKRIDAKIS, SPYROS and STEVEN C. WHEELWRIGHT. *Forecasting: Methods and Applications.* New York: Wiley, 1978.

MOORE, GEOFFREY H., and JULIS SHISKIN. "Early Warning Signals for the Economy." In *Statistics: A Guide to the Unknown,* ed. by Judith M. Tanur *et al.* San Francisco: Holden-Day, 1972. A discussion of the history, nature, and reliability of leading, coincident, and lagging indicators of business cycles.

MORGENSTERN, OSKAR. *On the Accuracy of Economic Observations.* 2d ed. Princeton, N.J.: Princeton University Press, 1963. Mandatory reading for anyone working with business and economic statistics.

NELSON, CHARLES R. *Applied Time Series for Managerial Forecasting.* San Francisco: Holden-Day, 1973. An excellent introduction.

NIE, NORMAN E., C. HADLAI HULL, JEAN G. JENKINS, KARIN STEINBRENNER, and DALE H. BENT. *SPSS Statistical Package for the Social Sciences.* 2d ed. New York: McGraw-Hill, 1975.

NORUSIS, MARIJA J. *SPSSX Introductory Statistics Guide.* New York: McGraw-Hill, 1983.

———. *SPSSX Advanced Statistics Guide.* Chicago: SPSS, 1985.

———. *The SPSS Guide to Data Analysis.* Chicago: SPSS, 1986.

PANKRATZ, ALAN. *Forecasting with Univariate Box–Jenkins Models: Concepts and Cases.* New York: Wiley, 1983.

RYAN, THOMAS A., BRIAN L. JOINER, and BARBARA F. RYAN. *Minitab Handbook.* 2d ed. Boston: PWS-KENT, 1985.

———. *Minitab Reference Manual.* University Park, Penn.: Minitab Project, 1985.

SAS Introductory Guide. 3d ed. Cary, N.C.: SAS Institute, 1985.

SAS Procedures Guide for Personal Computers. Version 6 ed. Cary, N.C.: SAS Institute, 1986.

SAS Statistics Guide for Personal Computers. Version 6 ed. Cary, N.C.: SAS Institute, 1986.

SAS User's Guide: Basics. Version 5 ed. Cary, N.C.: SAS Institute, 1985.

SAS User's Guide: Statistics. Version 5 ed. Cary, N.C.: SAS Institute, 1985.

SPSSX User's Guide. Chicago: SPSS, 1983.

Chapter Twenty-One
Some Nonparametric Tests

The tests developed in the previous chapters depend on a rather strict set of assumptions concerning the distribution of the random variable being studied. For example, to use the t statistic for testing the hypothesis that the mean of a population is equal to a specified value, the underlying population must at least approximate a normal distribution. Sometimes, however, the distribution of the underlying population does not meet such requirements. In these situations it is desirable to base our inferences on tests that are valid over a wide range of distributions of the parent population. Such tests are called **nonparametric**, or **distribution-free**, tests. Besides requiring few assumptions, nonparametric statistics may be used to analyze data consisting of rankings or ratings as well as quantitative measurements.

In this chapter, we discuss the following seven nonparametric tests:

1. *Sign test*: This test is used to analyze samples of data (A_i, B_i) that occur in matched pairs. It tests the null hypothesis that, for a given pair, the probability that A_i exceeds B_i is $p = .5$ or that, in a certain population, half the individuals have a certain characteristic and half do not. The data may consist of numerical values, rankings, or preferences.

2. *The Mann–Whitney test*: This test is used to test the null hypothesis that two populations are identical, that their means are equal, or that their medians are equal. The data consist of numerical values or rankings from independent samples from two populations.

3. *The Wilcoxon signed rank test*: This test is used to test the null hypothesis that two populations are identical, that their means are equal, or that their medians are equal. The data consist of numerical values or rankings from matched pairs of data from two populations.

4. *The Kruskal–Wallis test*: This test is used as an alternative to analysis of variance for testing the null hypothesis that several populations are identical, that their means are equal, or that their medians are equal. The data may consist of numerical values or rankings from independent samples from several populations.

5. *Runs test*: This test is used to test the null hypothesis that the sequence of occurrence of observations in a sample is random. The data may consist of either numerical values or qualitative observations.

6. *Rank correlation coefficient test*: The rank correlation coefficient test is used to test the null hypothesis that there is no linear relationship between two variables when the variables X and

Y represent rankings of two variables. It is used as an alternative to the correlation coefficient discussed in Section 15.9.

7. *Kolmogorov–Smirnov test*: This test, an alternative to the chi-square goodness-of-fit test discussed in Sections 13.1 and 13.2, is used to test the null hypothesis that a sample of data came from a specific probability distribution. The Kolmogorov–Smirnov test also can be used to test the null hypothesis that two independent samples of data came from the same population.

21.1 ▪ The Sign Test

The easiest nonparametric test to perform is called the **sign test**, which is used to analyze data (A_i, B_i) which occur in matched pairs. The null hypothesis states that the probability is .5 that observation A_i exceeds observation B_i. The data may consist of numerical values, rankings, or preferences. The sign test can be used as an alternative to the paired t test discussed in Section 12.3, where we tested the null hypothesis that the mean difference is 0. The sign test can be used in any situation where the null hypothesis is that half the observations in a population have a certain characteristic and the other half do not.

For example, suppose we ask 15 different customers to rate each of two products on a scale of 1 to 10. For each individual, we have two ratings or scores. Let A_i denote the ith individual's rating for Product A and let B_i denote the ith individual's rating for Product B. The sign test can be used to test the null hypothesis that, for the entire population of ratings by all individuals, there is no overall tendency to prefer one product over the other.

For each individual in the sample, record a plus sign $(+)$ if $(A_i - B_i)$ is greater than 0 and a minus sign $(-)$ if $(A_i - B_i)$ is less than 0. If the difference equals 0, eliminate the observation from the sample and decrease the sample size accordingly. The sign test is used to test the hypothesis that positive differences are just as likely as negative differences.

For the entire population, let p denote the probability of obtaining a plus sign on any selection. The null hypothesis is

$$H_0\colon p = .5$$

and the alternative hypothesis takes one of the forms

$$H_1\colon p \neq .5, \quad H_1\colon p > .5, \quad \text{or} \quad H_1\colon p < .5$$

Let X denote the number of plus signs obtained in a random sample of n observations (after eliminating all ties). If H_0 is true, the random variable X follows the binomial distribution with $p = .5$. When the sample size is small (say 10 or less), the binomial distribution is used to find the critical region of the test, as described in the accompanying box. When the sample size is 10 or more, the normal distribution can be used to find the critical region, because the random variable X approximately follows the normal distribution.

Performing the Sign Test with Small Samples

Suppose we want to test the null hypothesis

$$H_0: p = .5$$

against the one-sided alternative hypothesis

$$H_1: p > .5$$

using the level of significance α where the sample size is 10 or less. Let x_0 denote the observed number of positive values (or successes) in a sample of size n where n is the sample size after eliminating all ties. Use the binomial distribution to calculate $P(X \geqslant x_0)$. Use the decision rule

$$\text{Reject } H_0 \text{ in favor of } H_1 \text{ if } P(X \geqslant x_0) < \alpha$$

When the alternative hypothesis is $H_1: p < .5$, use the decision rule

$$\text{Reject } H_0 \text{ in favor of } H_1 \text{ if } P(X \leqslant x_0) < \alpha$$

When the alternative hypothesis is $H_1: p \neq .5$, use the decision rule

$$\text{Reject } H_0 \text{ in favor of } H_1 \text{ if } P(X \leqslant x_0) < \alpha/2 \text{ or if } P(X \geqslant x_0) < \alpha/2$$

Example 21.1

Using the Sign Test with a Small Sample: Every summer the Coca-Cola and Pepsi-Cola companies conduct taste tests, where they ask random samples of people to taste the two drinks and select the one that tastes better. Suppose you blindfold a random sample of 12 people and have them taste and rate each drink from 1 to 10. Let A_i denote the rating given to Coca-Cola by the ith individual and B_i denote the rating given to Pepsi-Cola by the ith individual. Suppose you obtain the results given in Table 21.1. At a 5% level of significance, do the results indicate that one cola is preferred over the other?

TABLE 21.1
Ratings of colas for Example 21.1

Individual	Coca-Cola A_i	Pepsi-Cola B_i	Sign of $(A_i - B_i)$
1	10	8	+
2	7	5	+
3	5	7	−
4	6	6	0 delete
5	8	7	+
6	8	5	+
7	7	7	0 delete
8	6	3	+
9	6	7	−
10	5	3	+
11	7	5	+
12	8	6	+

Solution: After deleting the 2 ties from the sample, we are left with a sample of 10 observations, consisting of 8 plus values and 2 minus values. We want to test the null hypothesis

$$H_0: p = .5$$

against the two-sided alternative hypothesis

$$H_1: p \neq .5$$

We use a two-tailed test with each tail of the critical region having probability $\alpha/2 = .025$. For $x_0 = 8$, the binomial distribution yields

$$P(X = 8) = .0439, \quad P(X = 9) = .0098, \quad P(X = 10) = .0010$$

and

$$P(X \geq x_0) = P(X \geq 8) = .0439 + .0098 + .0010 = .0547$$

Thus, the probability of obtaining a result as extreme as we observed is .0547. Since .0547 exceeds .025, we do not reject the null hypothesis. ■

In Example 21.1, the effective sample size was $n = 10$. When the sample size is larger than 10, the normal distribution provides a good approximation to the sampling distribution of X; thus we can use the normal approximation to the binomial distribution when performing the sign test. When n exceeds 10, the sampling distribution of X is approximately normal with mean

$$\mu = np = .5n$$

and variance

$$\sigma^2 = npq = .25n$$

To perform the sign test when n exceeds 10, use the procedure described in the accompanying box.

Performing the Sign Test with Large Samples

Suppose we want to test the null hypothesis

$$H_0: p = .5$$

against the one-sided alternative hypothesis

$$H_1: p > .5$$

using level of significance α where the sample size exceeds 10. To perform the sign test, calculate the test statistic

$$z = \frac{x_0 - .5n}{\sqrt{.25n}}$$

where x_0 denotes the observed number of plus signs and n is the sample size after eliminating all ties. Use the decision rule

Reject H_0 in favor of H_1 if $z > z_\alpha$

where the critical value z_α is obtained from the standard normal distribution table.
When the alternative hypothesis is H_1: $p < .5$, use the decision rule

$$\text{Reject } H_0 \text{ in favor of } H_1 \text{ if } z < -z_\alpha$$

When the alternative hypothesis is H_1: $p \neq .5$, use the decision rule

$$\text{Reject } H_0 \text{ in favor of } H_1 \text{ if } z < -z_{\alpha/2} \text{ or if } z > z_{\alpha/2}$$

Example 21.2 **Using the Sign Test with a Large Sample:** A random sample of 110 customers were asked to test-drive two cars. Each customer was asked to rate the handling of each car. Suppose that 63 preferred Car A, 37 preferred Car B, and 10 were indifferent. Let p denote the probability that Car A is preferred in the population. Test the null hypothesis

$$H_0\text{: } p = .5$$

against the two-sided alternative hypothesis

$$H_1\text{: } p \neq .5$$

using a 5% level of significance.

Solution: Let the random variable X denote the number of individuals who prefer Car A. After omitting ties, we have a sample of $n = 100$ observations. The number who prefer Car A (a plus sign) is $x_0 = 63$. If H_0 is true, the random variable X is approximately normally distributed with mean $np = 50$ and variance $npq = 25$. For $\alpha = 5\%$, the critical values of the test statistic are $z_{.025} = 1.96$ and $-z_{.025} = -1.96$. The observed test statistic is

$$z = \frac{63 - 50}{\sqrt{25}} = 2.60$$

Because the observed Z score exceeds the critical value, we reject the null hypothesis in favor of $p \neq 5$. ■

Exercises for Section 21.1

1. A class is taught jointly by two professors. At the end of the semester, the class is asked to rate them both. Five students prefer Teacher A, 3 prefer Teacher B, and 2 are indifferent. Let $\alpha = .05$ and test the null hypothesis H_0: $p = .5$, where p is the probability that any student prefers Teacher A. Use a two-tailed test.
2. A random sample of 112 people examine two television sets. Sixty-two people prefer the picture on Television A, 38 prefer the picture on Television B, and 12 are indifferent. Use the two-tailed sign test and a 5% level of significance to test if the proportion of people in the population who prefer Television A is .5.
3. Seventy customers use two different brands of floor wax on their floors; 38 prefer Brand A, 26 prefer Brand B, and 6 are indifferent. Use the two-tailed sign test and a 5% level of significance to test if the proportion of people in the population who prefer Brand A is .5.
4. Two TV commercials for a certain brand of automobile are shown to a random sample of 100

people: 48 prefer Commercial 1, 42 prefer Commercial 2, and 10 are indifferent. Use the two-tailed sign test and a 5% level of significance to test if one commercial is preferred to the other.

5. An automobile manufacturer surveys a random sample of 120 dealers concerning what should be done to promote sales. Sixty favor increasing the amount of advertising, 40 favor reducing prices, and 20 are indifferent. Use the two-tailed sign test and a 5% level of significance to test if one proposal is favored over the other.

6. A congressman wants to know how the voters feel about a proposed tariff. In a random sample of 490 voters, 220 favor the tariff, 180 oppose it, and 90 are indifferent. Use the two-tailed sign test and a 5% level of significance to test if one proposal is favored over the other.

21.2 ▪ The Mann–Whitney Test

In Section 21.1 we discussed the sign test, which is designed to determine whether significant differences exist between two populations based on a random sample of matched pairs of observations. In this section, we introduce the Mann–Whitney test, which is designed to determine if significant differences exist when *independent random samples* are taken from two populations.

The test is named after Henry B. Mann and D. R. Whitney, who developed the test in 1947. It is used to test the null hypothesis that two population means or medians are identical when the data consist of ranks or when some of the assumptions underlying the *t* test do not apply. The Mann–Whitney test is thus an alternative to the *t* test for independent samples, which was discussed in Section 12.2.

The null hypothesis tested can take one of several forms:

1. The two samples have been selected from the same population.
2. The two samples have been selected from populations having identical means.
3. The two samples have been selected from populations having identical medians.

Assume we have two independent samples containing n_1 and n_2 observations from two populations. When applying the Mann–Whitney test, the first step is to pool the data from the two samples into one set of observations. Next, rank these observations from the lowest to the highest score.

If the null hypothesis is true, the observations from the two samples should be randomly scattered throughout the ranking of the pooled data. If the data do not come from populations having identical medians, the sample observations from the population having the smaller mean or median will tend to have lower rankings, whereas the sample observations from the population having the larger mean or median will tend to have higher rankings. The statistic used in the Mann–Whitney test, called U, is described in the accompanying box.

Formula for Calculating the Mann–Whitney U Statistic

Let R_1 denote the sum of the ranks of the observations from Population 1, and let R_2 denote the sum of the ranks of the observations from Population 2. The Mann–Whitney U statistic is

$$U = n_1 n_2 + \frac{n_1(n_1 + 1)}{2} - R_1$$

If the null hypothesis is true and the sample sizes are large, the random variable U is approximately normally distributed with mean

$$\mu_U = \frac{n_1 n_2}{2}$$

and variance

$$\sigma_U^2 = \frac{n_1 n_2 (n_1 + n_2 + 1)}{12}$$

The approximation to the normal distribution is adequate when n_1 and n_2 are both 10 or more.

In order to test the null hypothesis, we use the test statistic

$$z = \frac{u - \mu_U}{\sigma_U}$$

where u is the observed value of the random variable U. When the null hypothesis is true, the random variable Z approximately follows the standard normal distribution.

The procedure for performing the Mann–Whitney test with large samples is described in the accompanying box.

Performing the Mann–Whitney Test with Large Samples

Suppose we have independent random samples of n_1 and n_2 observations from two populations. Pool the observations together and rank them. Let R_1 denote the sum of the ranks of the observations from the first population. To test the null hypothesis that the populations have equal means or medians at a level of significance α, calculate the test statistic

$$z = \frac{u - \mu_U}{\sigma_U}$$

where u is the observed value of the Mann–Whitney U statistic.

Case 1: If the alternative hypothesis states that the mean or median of Population 1 exceeds the mean or median of Population 2, use the decision rule

Reject H_0 in favor of H_1 if $z < -z_\alpha$

Case 2: If the alternative hypothesis states that the mean or median of Population 1 is less than the mean or median of Population 2, use the decision rule

Reject H_0 in favor of H_1 if $z > z_\alpha$

Case 3: If the alternative hypothesis states that the mean or median of Population 1 differs from the mean or median of Population 2, use the decision rule

Reject H_0 in favor of H_1 if $z < -z_{\alpha/2}$ or if $z > z_{\alpha/2}$

Example 21.3 **Using the Mann–Whitney Test with a Large Sample:** In a sex discrimination suit against a large university, a female faculty member alleged that male assistant professors received larger pay raises than female assistant professors. Suppose you wish to test the null hypothesis that the average salary increases are the same for males and females. You obtain the following data on the pay increases (in thousands of dollars) received by a random sample of 20 males (Population 1) and 15 females (Population 2):

Population 1 (Males)

3.06	2.11	3.08	2.94	2.78	2.62	2.73	2.69	2.51	2.91
3.16	3.19	3.42	2.66	2.98	2.80	2.16	2.22	3.10	2.55

Population 2 (Females)

3.12	3.18	2.95	2.86	2.75	2.81	3.07	3.22	2.90	2.48
2.77	2.72	2.96	3.26	3.23					

The observations are ranked in Table 21.2. Use a one-tailed test and a 5% level of significance.

Solution: The sample sizes are $n_1 = 20$ and $n_2 = 15$. The sum of the ranks for males is $R_1 = 315$, and so the observed value of the U statistic is

$$U = 20(15) + \frac{20(20 + 1)}{2} - 315 = 195$$

If the null hypothesis is true, the random variable U is approximately normally distributed with mean

$$\mu_U = \frac{20(15)}{2} = 150$$

and variance

$$\sigma_U^2 = \frac{20(15)(20 + 15 + 1)}{12} = 900$$

The observed test statistic is

$$z = \frac{195 - 150}{\sqrt{900}} = 1.5$$

The critical value of the test statistic is $z_{.05} = 1.645$. Because the observed value of the test statistic falls in the acceptance region, we do not reject the null hypothesis that the means are equal. ■

If we thought that salary increases for males and females were normally distributed in Example 21.3, we could have used the t test to test the hypothesis that there was no difference in the mean increases. If increases are not approximately normally distrib-

TABLE 21.2
Rankings of pay raises for Example 21.2

Ordered Data	Sample	Rank for Sample 1	Rank for Sample 2
2.11	1	1	
2.16	1	2	
2.22	1	3	
2.48	2		4
2.51	1	5	
2.55	1	6	
2.62	1	7	
2.66	1	8	
2.69	1	9	
2.72	2		10
2.73	1	11	
2.75	2		12
2.77	2		13
2.78	1	14	
2.80	1	15	
2.81	2		16
2.86	2		17
2.90	2		18
2.91	1	19	
2.94	1	20	
2.95	2		21
2.96	2		22
2.98	1	23	
3.06	1	24	
3.07	2		25
3.08	1	26	
3.10	1	27	
3.12	2		28
3.16	1	29	
3.18	2		30
3.19	1	31	
3.22	2		32
3.23	2		33
3.26	2		34
3.42	1	35	
		$R_1 = 315$	$R_2 = 315$

uted, however, it is more appropriate to use a nonparametric test such as the U test. The t test is more powerful than the Mann–Whitney test and will detect true differences between two populations more often than will the Mann–Whitney test. The reason for this is that the t test uses more information from the data. The Mann–Whitney test substitutes ranks for the actual values of observations and loses useful information. In general, if the assumptions of the t test appear reasonable, it should be used. When the data are ranks or come from a markedly nonnormal distribution, the Mann–Whitney test is preferable.

If there are ties in observations, average the ranks of the tied observations and assign this averaged rank to each of the tied observations. For example, if the fourth, fifth, and sixth observations are all tied, assign the rank of 5 (the mean of 4, 5, and 6) to each of these observations. The next observation would receive a rank of 7. If the ninth and tenth observations are tied, assign the rank 9.5 to each; the next observation would receive a rank of 11.

The normal distribution does not necessarily give a good approximation to the probability distribution of U when n_1 or n_2 is less than 10. For such small values of n_1 or n_2, tables of probabilities for U are available such as Table A.9 in the Appendix. The procedure in the accompanying box shows how to perform the Mann–Whitney test when the sample size is small.

Performing the Mann–Whitney Test with Small Samples

Suppose we have independent random samples of n_1 and n_2 observations from two populations. Let Population 1 denote the population with the smaller sample size. Suppose we wish to test the null hypothesis that the populations have equal means or medians using a level of significance α. Pool the observations from the two samples and calculate the Mann–Whitney U statistic. Let u_0 denote the observed value of U. Refer to Table A.9. For given values of n_1 and n_2, Table A.9 shows $P(U \leqslant u_0)$. Use the decision rule

$$\text{Reject } H_0 \text{ in favor of } H_1 \text{ if } P(U \leqslant u_0) < \alpha$$

Example 21.4

Using the Mann–Whitney Test with a Small Sample: Suppose we have $n_1 = 4$ observations from Population 1 and $n_2 = 5$ observations from Population 2. Use the following data and a 5% level of significance to test the null hypothesis that the data came from populations having identical means or medians:

Population	2	2	1	2	1	1	2	1	2
Observation	18	21	22	25	29	30	31	34	36
Rank	1	2	3	4	5	6	7	8	9

Solution: Population 1 is designated as the population with the smaller sample size. The sum of ranks for the observations from Population 1 is

$$R_1 = 3 + 5 + 6 + 8 = 22$$

The observed value of the Mann–Whitney U statistic is

$$u_0 = 4(5) + \frac{4(4 + 1)}{2} - 22 = 8$$

From Table A.9, using $n_1 = 4$, $n_2 = 5$, and $u_0 = 8$, we obtain

$$P(U \leqslant 8) = .3651$$

Because this probability exceeds α, we do not reject the null hypothesis. ■

Exercises for Section 21.2

1. A national pizza distributor conducted taste tests to compare its pizza with the local neighborhood favorite. In a particular neighborhood, 7 individuals ate the national brand and 6 ate the local favorite, and each individual gave a rating from 1 to 20 for the pizza. Let $\alpha = .05$ and test the null hypothesis that there is no preference for one pizza over the other. The data follow:

Local pizza ratings:	18	10	12	15	9	16	
National pizza ratings:	16	5	7	11	19	11	13

2. A random sample is taken of 30 boys and 20 girls. The children's monthly expenditures on candy in cents are recorded and ranked from 1 to 50. The boys' ranks sum to 725 and the girls' ranks sum to 550. Use the U test and a 5% level of significance to determine if boys spend the same amount of money on candy as girls do.

3. An educator administers a reading test to a random sample of 13 boys and 12 girls. Their scores are as follows:

Boys' scores:	62	87	55	63	71	80	91	78	96	84	59	77	88
Girls' scores:	66	86	81	74	72	85	97	99	46	68	73	83	

Use the U test to determine if boys' scores are significantly different from girls' scores. Use a 5% level of significance.

21.3 ▪ The Wilcoxon Signed-Rank Test

The sign test is used to test whether two populations have equal means or medians based on a matched pair of observations. However, it utilizes only the signs of the differences between pairs of observations and ignores the magnitudes of the differences. The Wilcoxon signed-rank test, developed by Frank Wilcoxon (1892–1965) in 1945, is an alternative to the sign test. The test requires as data not only the signs of the differences between pairs of observations but also the ranks of the differences. Because it uses more information, the Wilcoxon signed-rank test is more powerful than the sign test. On the other hand, it is not as generally applicable as the sign test because at times the ranks of the differences of paired observations are not known. The Wilcoxon signed-rank test, like the sign test, utilizes data from two *related* samples. The samples may refer to before and after observations, husband–wife responses, an individual's scores on two tests, and so forth.

Suppose we obtain a sample of n observations from Population 1 and a sample of n observations from Population 2, where each observation in Sample 1 is related to an observation in Sample 2. The null hypothesis is that the two populations are identical. If the null hypothesis is true, we would expect half of the differences of paired observations to be negative and half to be positive. In addition, we would expect positive and negative differences of any given magnitude to occur with equal probability.

For each matched pair, calculate the absolute value of the difference. As in the sign test, differences of 0 are ignored. Rank the absolute values from lowest to highest and obtain the sum of the ranks for the differences that are positive. Denote this sum as T_p. Then sum the ranks of the differences that are negative and denote this number as T_n. If the two distributions are identical, we would expect these two rank sums to be approximately equal. The sum of all n rankings is

$$T_p + T_n = \frac{n(n+1)}{2}$$

and since we expect T_p to equal T_n, the mean value (or expected value) of T_p and of T_n is

$$\mu_{T_p} = \mu_{T_n} = \frac{n(n+1)}{4}$$

If T_p or T_n differs significantly from $n(n+1)/4$, the hypothesis that Populations 1 and 2 have different distributions is supported. Note that

$$\left| T_p - \frac{n(n+1)}{4} \right| = \left| T_n - \frac{n(n+1)}{4} \right|$$

That is, if T_p is, say, 5 units above the mean, then T_n is 5 units below the mean. Thus, T_p and T_n differ from the mean by exactly the same amount but in opposite directions. It makes no difference, therefore, whether we use T_p or T_n to test the hypothesis that the distributions are identical.

Define the random variable T to be the smaller of T_p and T_n. That is,

$$T = \min(T_p, T_n)$$

Small values of T support the alternative hypothesis H_1 that the population distributions are not identical.

When n is large (say, $n \geq 15$), then T is approximately normally distributed with mean

$$\mu_T = \frac{n(n+1)}{4}$$

and variance

$$\sigma_T^2 = \frac{n(n+1)(2n+1)}{24}$$

and the random variable

$$Z = \frac{T - \mu_T}{\sigma_T}$$

approximately follows the standard normal distribution. The procedure in the accompanying box shows how to perform the Wilcoxon signed-rank test when the sample size is large ($n > 15$).

Performing the Wilcoxon Signed-Rank Test with Large Samples

The Wilcoxon signed-rank test uses a random sample of matched pairs of observations. We wish to test the null hypothesis that the two population distributions are identical or the null hypothesis that the distribution of differences is centered at 0. Discard pairs for which the difference is 0 and rank the absolute differences in ascending order. Then calculate the sum of the ranks for positive differences and for negative differences. The observed Wilcoxon signed-rank test statistic t_0 is the smaller of these two sums. When the sample size exceeds 15, the observed test statistic

$$z = \frac{t_0 - \mu_T}{\sigma_T}$$

can be tested as an approximately standard normal variate.

Case 1: If the alternative hypothesis is one sided, reject the null hypothesis if $z < -z_{\alpha}$, where α is the level of significance of the test.

Case 2: If the alternative hypothesis is two sided, reject the null hypothesis if $z < -z_{\alpha/2}$, where α is the level of significance of the test.

Any tied values are given the same rank, which is the average rank of the tied values.

Example 21.5

Using the Wilcoxon Signed-Rank Test with a Large Sample: A soft drink bottler has produced a new drink using two different recipes, one of which is much sweeter. The bottler asks 20 individuals to taste both drinks and rate the drinks on a scale of 1 to 10, where 10 means the individual likes the drink very much. Use the Wilcoxon signed-rank test to test the null hypothesis that neither drink is preferred over the other. Use a two-tailed test and a 5% level of significance. The data are in Table 21.3.

Solution: The sum of the ranks for the positive differences is $T_p = 154$ and for negative differences, $T_n = 17$. The Wilcoxon signed-rank test statistic is the smaller of these two values. Thus, t_0 is 17. The mean is

$$\mu_T = \frac{n(n+1)}{4} = \frac{18(19)}{4} = 85.5$$

(Remember n is 18 because we deleted 2 pairs of observations.) The variance is

$$\sigma_T^2 = \frac{n(n+1)(2n+1)}{24} = \frac{18(19)(37)}{24} = 527.25$$

Finally, the observed test statistic is

$$z = \frac{t_0 - \mu_T}{\sigma_T} = \frac{17 - 85.5}{\sqrt{527.25}} = -2.98$$

Using a 5% level of significance, we have $\alpha/2 = .025$, and the critical value of the test statistic is $-z_{.025} = -1.96$. We reject the null hypothesis because the observed value $z = -2.98$ falls in the critical region.

TABLE 21.3 **Ratings of soft drinks for Exercise 21.5**

Individual	Drink A	Drink B	Difference	Sign of $(A - B)$	Rank of Positives	Rank of Negatives
1	10	6	4	+	13	
2	8	5	3	+	8.5	
3	6	2	4	+	13	
4	8	2	6	+	16	
5	7	4	3	+	8.5	
6	5	6	−1	−		2
7	1	4	−3	−		8.5
8	3	5	−2	−		4.5
9	9	9	0	Omit		
10	7	8	−1	−		2
11	4	2	2	+	4.5	
12	5	2	3	+	8.5	
13	8	1	7	+	18	
14	6	3	3	+	8.5	
15	8	2	6	+	16	
16	7	6	1	+	2	
17	4	1	3	+	8.5	
18	8	2	6	+	16	
19	9	5	4	+	13	
20	3	3	0	Omit		
					$T_p = 154$	$T_n = 17$

■

When n is 15 or less, the normal distribution does not necessarily provide a good approximation to the distribution of the random variable T. For small values of n, tables of probabilities for T are available, such as Table A.10 in the Appendix. The procedure in the accompanying box shows how to perform the Wilcoxon signed-rank test when the sample size is small.

Performing the Wilcoxon Signed-Rank Test with Small Samples

Suppose we have matched samples of n observations from two populations and wish to test the null hypothesis that the populations have identical distributions using a level of significance α. Let t_0 denote the observed value of T. For given values of n, Table A.10 in the Appendix shows the critical value T_α such that $P(T \leqslant T_\alpha) = \alpha$. Use the decision rule

$$\text{Reject } H_0 \text{ in favor of } H_1 \text{ if } t_0 < T_\alpha$$

Example 21.6 **Using the Wilcoxon Signed-Rank Test with a Small Sample:** Two makes of tires are tested on the rear wheels of 6 different cars. The number of miles traveled until a tire fails is recorded. Because one tire of each make is used on each car, the observations occur in matched pairs. Use the Wilcoxon signed-rank test and a 5% level of significance to test the null hypothesis

H_0: The population means are equal

against the two-sided alternative hypothesis

H_1: The population means are not equal

The data are in Table 21.4.

TABLE 21.4 Tire mileage for Example 21.6

Car	Tire A (in miles)	Tire B (in miles)	Difference ($A - B$)	Rank of Positives	Rank of Negatives
1	20,000	19,000	1,000	1	
2	24,600	23,000	1,600	2	
3	32,500	37,000	−4,500		3
4	36,000	30,100	6,500	4	
5	37,000	25,500	11,700	5	
6	23,000	39,500	−16,500		6
				$T_p = 12$	$T_n = 9$

Solution: The sum of ranks for positive differences is $T_p = 12$; the sum of ranks for negative differences is $T_n = 9$. Thus, we have $t_0 = \min(T_p, T_n) = 9$. In Table A.10 using $\alpha = .05$ and a two-tailed test, we see that for $n = 6$ observations the critical value of t_0 is $T_{.025} = 1$. Because the value $T = 9$ exceeds the critical value, we do not reject the hypothesis that the tires are equally good. ■

Exercises for Section 21.3

1. A certain magazine is shown to 20 randomly selected married couples. Each person is asked to rate the magazine on a scale of 1 to 10. Perform the Wilcoxon signed-rank test using the accompanying data to test whether the husbands' tastes are the same as the wives'. Use a 5% level of significance.

Wife	7	2	4	3	5	9	2	1	3	2
Husband	9	6	2	8	6	8	8	6	2	6
Wife	4	5	4	3	5	6	3	6	2	1
Husband	5	6	8	9	9	5	4	9	3	7

2. Fifteen high school students are randomly selected and asked to listen to two songs and rate each one from 0 to 100. Test whether one song is preferred over the other using a 5% level of significance and the Wilcoxon signed-rank test.

Song A	90	93	75	60	80	95	90	80	65	75	90	86	88	77	62
Song B	80	86	79	75	70	50	70	64	78	63	81	82	76	61	60

3. Ten randomly selected companies are examined in 1980 and again in 1985 to determine if a smaller percentage of income is being allocated to research and development (R&D). The following data show the percentage of income spent on R&D by the companies:

Company	1	2	3	4	5	6	7	8	9	10
1980	18	26	17	22	19	31	24	20	14	20
1985	11	24	19	20	22	25	17	23	13	16

Using $\alpha = .05$, test to see whether the percentages declined in 1985.

4. A physician is studying the relationship between alcohol consumption and reaction time. Eight randomly selected subjects were studied before and after ingesting alcohol. The following response times (in seconds) were recorded:

Subject	1	2	3	4	5	6	7	8
Before drinking	5.3	4.8	5.7	6.3	6.4	4.7	5.6	5.9
After drinking	6.1	4.2	6.4	7.3	5.9	6.3	5.8	6.5

Let $\alpha = .05$. Test whether there is a significant difference between the before and after data. Use the Wilcoxon signed-rank test.

5. An advertising agency wishes to compare the opinions of seven randomly selected viewers before and after watching a TV special sponsored by a foreign car manufacturer. A series of questions are asked to measure the viewers' opinions of the firm (0 = very poor, 100 = very good). The following results were obtained:

Viewer	1	2	3	4	5	6	7
Before TV show	45	80	68	47	26	75	30
After TV show	72	81	60	58	20	87	45

Let $\alpha = .05$. Test for a significant difference between the before and after data.

21.4 ▪ *The Kruskal–Wallis Test*

In Chapter 14, one-way analysis of variance (ANOVA) was used to test the null hypothesis that J population means were equal to one another. The ANOVA test requires independent random samples from normal populations. An alternative test, the **Krus-**

kal–Wallis test, can be used when the normality assumption is questionable. Just as ANOVA is a generalization of a two-sample t test, the Kruskal–Wallis test is a generalization of the two-sample Mann–Whitney test.

The Kruskal–Wallis test, developed in 1952 by William H. Kruskal and W. Allen Wallis, is used to compare more than two population means or medians. The test is based on the ranks of the sample observations.

The null and alternative hypotheses are as follows:

H_0: The J population means (or medians) are all equal.

H_1: The J population means (or medians) are not all equal.

Alternatively, the Kruskal–Wallis test can be used to test

H_0: The J populations are identical.

H_1: The J populations are not identical.

To perform the test, obtain independent random samples from each of the J populations. Let n_j denote the size of the sample selected from the jth population. The total sample size is $n = \Sigma\, n_j$. Pool *all* n observations together and rank them from lowest to highest; assign the mean rank for tied observations. Let T_j denote the sum of the ranks of the n_j observations from Population j. Let $\overline{T}_j = T_j/n_j$ denote the sample mean rank of the sample of observations from Population j. If the values $\overline{T}_1, \overline{T}_2, \ldots, \overline{T}_J$ are not close to one another, the alternative hypothesis that the populations are not identical is supported.

Performing the Kruskal–Wallis Test

The Kruskal–Wallis test is used to test the null hypothesis

H_0: The J population means are equal

against the alternative hypothesis

H_1: The J population means are not equal

To perform the test, calculate the test statistic

$$K = \frac{12}{n(n + 1)}\left(\sum_{j=1}^{J} \frac{T_j^2}{n_j}\right) - 3(n + 1)$$

If H_0 is true, the sampling distribution of K is approximately chi-square with $\nu = (J - 1)$ degrees of freedom provided each sample contains 5 or more observations. The greater the differences in the central location of the J population distributions, the larger will be the value of K. Thus, large values of K lead us to reject the null hypothesis. The critical region is placed in the right tail of the chi-square distribution. To perform the test using a level of significance α, use the decision rule

Reject H_0 in favor of H_1 if $K > \chi_{\alpha,\nu}$

Example 21.7 **Performing the Kruskal–Wallis Test:** A corporation deciding which of $J = 4$ makes of automobile to order for its fleet examines independent random samples of five cars of each type. The operating cost per mile for each car was determined after each car was driven 15,000 miles. The data in Table 21.5 show operating costs per mile in cents as well as the ranks of operating costs. Use the Kruskal–Wallis test to determine whether the four distributions have equal means. Let $\alpha = .05$.

TABLE 21.5 Operating costs and ranks of cars for Example 21.7

Car 1		Car 2		Car 3		Car 4	
Cost	Rank	Cost	Rank	Cost	Rank	Cost	Rank
18.8¢	10	17.2¢	5	20.2¢	15	17.7¢	6
16.3	3	16.0	1	20.6	16	19.9	14
16.5	4	19.4	12	16.2	2	19.3	11
17.8	7	18.5	9	19.7	13	20.8	17
18.2	8	20.9	18	21.3	19	21.6	20
	$T_1 = 32$		$T_2 = 45$		$T_3 = 65$		$T_4 = 68$

Solution: For each of the four samples, we sum the ranks and obtain $T_1 = 32$, $T_2 = 45$, $T_3 = 65$, and $T_4 = 68$. The test statistic is

$$K = \frac{12}{n(n+1)}\left(\sum_{j=1}^{J} \frac{T_j^2}{n_j}\right) - 3(n+1)$$

$$= \frac{12}{20(21)}\left(\frac{1024}{5} + \frac{2025}{5} + \frac{4225}{5} + \frac{4624}{5}\right) - 3(21)$$

$$= 4.99$$

When $\alpha = .05$, the critical value of the chi-square statistic having 3 degrees of freedom is $\chi^2_{.05,3} = 7.81$. Because K is smaller than 7.81, we do not reject the null hypothesis that the population distributions are identical. ■

Exercises for Section 21.4

1. Random samples of chickens were fed four different types of feed to observe the effects of the food on weight gain. A random sample of 32 chickens was obtained, and each type of feed was given to 8 chickens for an identical period of time. The weight gains of the chickens (in ounces) are shown in the accompanying table. Let $\alpha = .05$. Use the Kruskal–Wallis test to test the null hypothesis that the population mean weight gains are all equal.

Feed 1	Feed 2	Feed 3	Feed 4
13.0	14.2	16.3	19.2
15.1	13.1	18.4	17.1
17.2	11.0	20.2	16.8
11.3	10.8	19.3	18.3
14.7	8.9	17.2	19.4
18.1	14.2	14.8	21.2
16.2	12.3	15.1	15.3
15.3	11.7	14.2	17.4

2. An engineer at a manufacturing plant uses wire cord in a certain production process. He has access to five different kinds of wire cord, and he wants to determine if the mean breaking strengths of the cords are the same. The data in the accompanying table show the force required in pounds to break each wire cord. Let $\alpha = .05$ and test whether the population means are equal using the Kruskal–Wallis test.

Wire A	Wire B	Wire C	Wire D
228	210	261	220
237	217	282	225
251	204	251	215
214	230	248	222
246	209	263	221
256		290	

3. An automotive engineer wants to test whether the mean times required to install spark plugs in new cars on an assembly line are the same for four different types of cars. The data in the accompanying table show the times (in seconds) for installation. Let $\alpha = .05$ and test whether the population means are equal using the Kruskal–Wallis test.

Car A	Car B	Car C	Car D
21.1	19.6	19.8	21.4
27.8	21.7	21.3	22.4
28.3	21.9	23.4	20.8
33.4	22.2	25.2	23.2
35.2	25.1	20.7	24.0

21.5 ▪ The Runs Test

When working with time series data, we frequently wish to test whether the order or sequence of occurrence of the observations in a sample is random. For example, suppose that on a typical day 10% of the products manufactured at a certain plant are found to be defective. If we selected products randomly and tested them, we would not expect to find any definite pattern, but if the products were selected sequentially as they came off the assembly line, we might expect a pattern to appear where good products tended to be followed by good products and defectives by defectives.

Alternatively, suppose we recorded the weights of packages after they were filled by a machine. If the process was in control, weights above the median and below the median should occur randomly. One way to detect if the process is out of control is to observe the sequence of weights and determine if the series of observations appears to be nonrandom. For example, if the process is out of control, we might expect above-average weights to follow above-average weights and below-average weights to follow below-average weights.

The **runs test** is designed to test whether a sequence of observations has unusual or unlikely patterns. Suppose we label each observation as a "success" or "failure." A success might denote that a product is satisfactory, the weight of a package is above the median, the diameter of a pipe is greater than the median, the income of a sample respondent is above the median, and so forth. We are interested in detecting any unusual patterns in the sequence of sample observations.

Definition: Run

A **run** is a sequence of like observations.

For example, we might ask a sample of 20 voters if they prefer Candidate A or Candidate B. If the election is expected to be very close, it would not be unusual to find that exactly 10 favor Candidate A and 10 Candidate B. It would be unusual, however, if the preferences were obtained in the sequence

$$A \quad A \quad A \quad A \quad A \quad A \quad A \quad A \quad A \quad A \quad B \quad B \quad B \quad B \quad B \quad B \quad B \quad B \quad B \quad B$$

where the first 10 voters all favored A and the last 10 favored B. This sequence contains only two *runs,* a run of 10 *A*s and a run of 10 *B*s. Such an occurrence would lead us to suspect that the first observations were selected in a manner favorable to Candidate A and the last 10 in a manner favorable to Candidate B. In other words, we suspect non-randomness because the number of runs is too small.

As another example, suppose a mechanical device is used to fill cans with oil. A sample of 20 filled cans is selected and the weight of each can is carefully measured. Denote a weight above the median by an *A* and a weight below the median by a *B*. It would seem unusual if the 20 observations occurred in the sequence

$$A \quad B \quad A \quad B \quad A \quad B \quad A \quad B \quad A \quad B \quad A \quad B \quad A \quad B \quad A \quad B \quad A \quad B \quad A \quad B$$

where overfilled cans are followed by underfilled cans and vice versa. This sequence contains 20 runs. Here we suspect nonrandomness because the number of runs is too large.

To test for the existence of patterns, we use the runs test, which is based on the probability of obtaining the observed number of runs. The first step is to determine the number of runs in the data. The following example shows the number of runs in two sequences of observations.

Example 21.8 **Number of Runs in a Sequence:** The following sequence contains two runs:

$$\underbrace{A\ A\ A\ A\ A}_{1}\ \underbrace{B\ B\ B\ B\ B}_{2}$$

The following sequence contains five runs:

$$\underbrace{A\ A\ A}_{1}\ \underbrace{B\ B}_{2}\ \underbrace{A}_{3}\ \underbrace{B\ B\ B}_{4}\ \underbrace{A}_{5}$$

■

Let the random variable r denote the number of runs in the data. We reject the null hypothesis that the observations occur randomly if r is either very small or very large. To perform the test, we need n_A (the number of observations of Type A) and n_B (the number of observations of Type B). Usually the runs test for randomness is a two-tailed test. If n_A and n_B both exceed 10, the random variable r approximately follows the normal distribution with mean and variance

$$\mu_r = \frac{2n_A n_B}{n_A + n_B} + 1$$

$$\sigma_r^2 = \frac{2n_A n_B(2n_A n_B - n_A - n_B)}{(n_A + n_B)^2\,(n_A + n_B - 1)}$$

The procedure in the accompanying box describes how to perform the runs test when the sample size is large.

Performing the Runs Test with Large Samples

Suppose we obtain a random sample of n observations that are ordered sequentially. We wish to test the null hypothesis

H_0: The sequence of As and Bs is random

against the alternative hypothesis

H_1: The sequence of As and Bs is nonrandom

Let α be the level of significance. Let n_A and n_B denote the number of As and Bs, respectively. Let r_0 denote the observed number of runs. Calculate the test statistic

$$z = \frac{r_0 - \mu_r}{\sigma_r}$$

For large values of n_A and n_B, the sampling distribution of the random variable Z is approximately standard normal.

Case 1: To test H_0 against the one-sided alternative that there are too many runs, use the decision rule

Reject H_0 in favor of H_1 if $z > z_\alpha$

Case 2: To test H_0 against the one-sided alternative that there are too few runs, use the decision rule

Reject H_0 in favor of H_1 if $z < -z_\alpha$

Case 3: To test H_0 against the two-sided alternative that there are either too many or too few runs, use the decision rule

Reject H_0 in favor of H_1 if $z < -z_{\alpha/2}$ or if $z > z_{\alpha/2}$

We assume that the approximation to normality is good if $n_A > 10$ and $n_B > 10$.

Example 21.9 **Using the Runs Test with a Large Sample:** A filling machine is set to put 16 ounces of oil into cans. Because of the viscosity of the oil, the weights differ from can to can. The weights of 50 cans of oil were obtained as they came off a filling machine. When the machine is in control, weights above (A) and below (B) the 16-ounce average occur randomly. The following sequence was observed:

A A B B B A B A A A B A B B B A A A A
B B B B B B A A A B A B A B B B B A A
A A B B B A B A B B B B

Test the null hypothesis that the sequence of As and Bs is random. Use a 5% level of significance.

Solution: There are 22 As and 28 Bs, so $n_A = 22$ and $n_B = 28$. There are $r_0 = 22$ runs. If the process is random, the random variable r is approximately normally distributed with mean

$$\mu_r = \frac{2n_A n_B}{(n_A + n_B)} + 1 = \frac{2(22)(28)}{(22 + 28)} + 1 = 25.64$$

and variance

$$\sigma_r^2 = \frac{2n_A n_B(2n_A n_B - n_A - n_B)}{(n_A + n_B)^2(n_A + n_B - 1)} = \frac{2(22)(28)[2(22)(28) - 22 - 28]}{(22 + 28)^2(22 + 28 - 1)} = \frac{1{,}456{,}224}{122{,}500} = 11.89$$

Let us use a two-tailed test to test the null hypothesis that the sequence is random against the two-sided alternative hypothesis that there are too few or too many runs. The observed test statistic is

$$z = \frac{22 - 25.64}{\sqrt{11.89}} = -1.055$$

For $\alpha = .05$, the two critical values are $\pm z_{.025} = \pm 1.96$. Since z falls in the acceptance region, we do not reject the null hypothesis that the process is random. ■

When n_A and n_B are 10 or less, Table A.11 in the Appendix shows critical values for r. To perform the runs test when n_A and n_B are small, use the procedure described in the accompanying box.

Performing the Runs Test with Small Samples

We wish to test the null hypothesis

$$H_0\text{: The sequence of } A\text{s and } B\text{s is random}$$

against the alternative hypothesis

$$H_1\text{: The sequence of } A\text{s and } B\text{s is nonrandom}$$

Refer to Table A.11, which shows one-sided prob-values for various values of r_0. To test H_0 against the one-sided alternative that there are too few runs, use Table A.11 and obtain $P(r < r_0)$ where r_0 is the observed number of runs. Use the decision rule

$$\text{Reject } H_0 \text{ in favor of } H_1 \text{ if } P(r < r_0) > \alpha$$

To test H_0 against the one-sided alternative that there are too many runs, use the decision rule

$$\text{Reject } H_0 \text{ in favor of } H_1 \text{ if } P(r > r_0) < \alpha$$

To test H_0 against the two-sided alternative that there are too many or too few runs, use the decision rule

$$\text{Reject } H_0 \text{ in favor of } H_1 \text{ if } P(r > r_0) < \alpha/2 \text{ or if } P(r < r_0) > \alpha/2$$

Example 21.10 **Using the Runs Test with a Small Sample:** A ski resort has annual observations on total winter snowfall for 16 years. The median level of snowfall is obtained, and for each year we record whether the annual snowfall was above or below the median. The sequence of above- and below-average years was as follows:

A A | *B B* | *A A A* | *B B* | *A A A*

Test the null hypothesis that the sequence is random. Perform a two-tailed test with $\alpha = .05$.

Solution: The number of As and Bs are $n_A = 8$ and $n_B = 4$. There are $r_0 = 5$ runs. To perform the test, refer to Table A.11. In the table, the value n_1 is always the smaller of n_A and n_B. For $n_1 = 4$ and $n_2 = 8$, we have $P(r \leqslant 5) = .279$. Because this value exceeds $\alpha/2 = .025$, we do not reject the null hypothesis that the sequence is random. The probability .279 indicates that if H_0 is true, we should observe 5 or fewer runs in a sample of 12 observations with probability .279. This prob-value exceeds the level of significance of the test, so we do not reject H_0. ■

Exercises for Section 21.5

1. A gambler is playing roulette. A common system is to bet red after a black has occurred and vice versa. This system could produce a profit if the sequence of occurrence of black and red is nonrandom. You observe the following sequence of black (B) and red (R) outcomes:

B R B B B R R B R B R R R B B R B R R R B B R B B R

Let $\alpha = .05$ and test for randomness. Use a two-tailed test.
a. How many runs are there?
b. State the mean and variance of the random variable r.
c. State the observed value of the test statistic z.
d. Do you reject the null hypothesis that the sequence is random?

2. A computer is used to generate digits from 0 to 9. The data that follow show the sequence of 40 observations:

8 1 5 7 1 3 7 8 6 7 2 9 3 2 9 6 5 6 6 6
5 6 1 1 3 2 3 4 7 4 8 4 3 5 6 1 5 9 3 7

Use the runs test and a 5% level of significance to test the following hypotheses:
a. Values above 4.5 and values below 4.5 occur randomly.
b. Odd values and even values occur randomly.

3. A basketball coach wants to test the hypothesis that, for a skilled basketball player, making or missing free throws occurs randomly. The alternative hypothesis is that some sort of learning process is involved, so that the runs test should show evidence of an unusual number of runs. Use a 5% level of significance. An S denotes a successful shot; an F denotes a failure, or missed shot. The results after 60 shots are as follows:

S S S F S F F S S S S S F F S S S S S S
F S S F F S S S S S F S S S S F F S S F
S S F F F S S S F S S S S F S S S F S S

4. The runs test can be used instead of the Durbin–Watson test to determine if the error terms in a regression model are serially correlated. In a regression model, positive (P) and negative (N) residuals occurred in the following sequence:

P N P P P N N N P P P P N N P N N P N N P N P N N P P P

Let $\alpha = .05$ and test for randomness. Use a two-tailed test.
a. How many runs are there?
b. State the mean and variance of the random variable r.
c. State the observed value of the test statistic z.
d. Do you reject the null hypothesis that the sequence is random?

5. A sequence of 50 bags of potato chips is produced and examined to determine if there is a periodicity, or lack of randomness, in deviations from the average weight. The average weight of a bag is 16 ounces. Each bag is examined to determine if its weight is above (A) or below (B) average. Use a 5% level of significance and test whether the positive and negative deviations occur randomly for the following observations:

A B A A B A A B B A B A B B B A A B B B A A A A B
A A A B B B B A A A A B B B B A B A B A A B B B A

6. Suppose we compare the rate of return on a security to the average rate of return in the market. The random-walk hypothesis states that rates of return above and below the market average are completely random, following no pattern over time. The following data show the market adjusted rate of return for a security for 30 consecutive days (negative values indicate below-market returns):

.05	.07	−.03	−.02	.06	.02	.04	−.03	.02	.01	−.02	.03	.04	.02	−.02
.03	.01	−.02	−.03	−.02	.06	−.10	−.06	.02	.01	−.03	.01	−.02	−.02	.04

Let $\alpha = .05$ and test for randomness. Use a two-tailed test.
a. How many runs are there?

b. State the mean and variance of the random variable r.
c. State the observed value of the test statistic z.
d. Do you reject the null hypothesis that the sequence is random?

21.6 ▪ Rank Correlation

The population correlation coefficient ρ, discussed in Chapter 15, measures whether above (or below) average values of a variable Y tend to occur with above (or below) average values of another variable X. To calculate the sample correlation coefficient R, it is necessary to know the magnitudes of the Y and X variables. At times the values of these variables are ranks rather than numerical magnitudes. The **population rank correlation coefficient**, denoted by the symbol ρ_s, measures the correlation between the ranks of two variables X and Y. To estimate the population rank correlation coefficient, we calculate the **sample rank correlation coefficient**, denoted R_s. The rank correlation coefficient was introduced by Charles E. Spearman (1863–1945), a British psychology professor, and is frequently called *Spearman's rank correlation coefficient* (hence the subscript s).

Let x_i and y_i denote the ranks of the ith observation on variables X and Y in a sample of n observations. We would like to determine if high (or low) rankings of Y tend to be associated with high (or low) rankings of X. The sample rank correlation coefficient R_s can be calculated just like the sample correlation coefficient R, as described in the accompanying box.

Formula for Calculating the Sample Rank Correlation Coefficient

Suppose we have a sample of n pairs of ranks (x_i, y_i). Spearman's sample rank correlation coefficient can be calculated as follows:

$$R_s = \frac{\sum_{i=1}^{n}(x_i - \bar{x})(y_i - \bar{y})}{\sqrt{\sum_{i=1}^{n}(x_i - \bar{x})^2 \sum_{i=1}^{n}(y_i - \bar{y})^2}}$$

However, the sample rank correlation coefficient is usually calculated in another way that gives an equivalent value provided no two of the x_i's or y_i's are given the same rank. This alternative method is shown in the accompanying box.

Alternative Formula for Calculating the Sample Rank Correlation Coefficient

If there are no ties in ranks of the x_i's or y_i's, the sample rank correlation coefficient can be calculated as follows:

$$R_s = 1 - \frac{6\sum_{i=1}^{n} d_i^2}{n(n^2 - 1)}$$

where $d_i = (x_i - y_i)$ denotes the difference in ranks between observations x_i and y_i.

If $R_s = 1$, the ranks x_i and y_i are identical ($d_i = 0$ for all i). If $R_s = -1$, the ranks x_i are in exactly the opposite order of the ranks y_i. Large positive (or negative) values of R_s support the hypothesis that ρ_s is positive (or negative) in the population.

The sample rank correlation coefficient is a random variable whose value changes from sample to sample. If the population rank correlation coefficient ρ_s is 0 and the sample size is 30 or more, then the t statistic

$$t = \frac{R_s}{s_{R_s}}$$

approximately follows the Student t distribution with $\nu = (n - 2)$ degrees of freedom, where the observed sample standard deviation is

$$s_{R_s} = \sqrt{\frac{1 - R_s^2}{n - 2}}$$

The procedure described in the accompanying box shows how to test the null hypothesis that the population rank correlation coefficient is 0 when the sample size is large ($n \geq 30$).

Spearman's Rank Correlation Test with Large Samples

Case 1: Suppose we wish to test the null hypothesis

$$H_0: \rho_s = 0$$

against the one-sided alternative hypothesis

$$H_1: \rho_s > 0$$

using level of significance α. Calculate the test statistic

$$t = \frac{R_s}{s_{R_s}}$$

If H_0 is true and n is 30 or larger, this t statistic is approximately distributed as Student's t with $\nu = (n - 2)$ degrees of freedom. To test H_0 against H_1, calculate the test statistic t and use the decision rule

$$\text{Reject } H_0 \text{ in favor of } H_1 \text{ if } t > t_{\alpha,\nu}$$

Case 2: To test the null hypothesis

$$H_0: \rho_s = 0$$

against the one-sided alternative hypothesis

$$H_1: \rho_s < 0$$

use the decision rule

$$\text{Reject } H_0 \text{ in favor of } H_1 \text{ if } t < -t_{\alpha,\nu}$$

Case 3: To test the null hypothesis

$$H_0: \rho_s = 0$$

against the two-sided alternative hypothesis

$$H_1: \rho_s \neq 0$$

use the decision rule

$$\text{Reject } H_0 \text{ in favor of } H_1 \text{ if } t < -t_{\alpha/2,\nu} \text{ or if } t > t_{\alpha/2,\nu}$$

Example 21.11 **Testing for Rank Correlation with a Large Sample:** A corporation uses private interviews and written tests to determine which job candidates to hire. Because interviews are much more expensive than written tests, the corporation would like to discontinue interviewing if the rankings of job candidates based on the written test are highly correlated with rankings based on personal interviews.

A random sample of 62 job candidates were ranked on an interview and again on a written test. The sample rank correlation between the two rankings is $R_s = .20$. Using $\alpha = .05$, test the null hypothesis

$$H_0: \rho_s = 0$$

against the one-sided alternative hypothesis

$$H_1: \rho_s > 0$$

Solution: The t statistic has $\nu = (n - 2) = 60$ degrees of freedom. The critical value of t is $t_{.05,60} = 1.67$, and the observed test statistic is

$$t = \frac{.20}{\sqrt{\dfrac{1 - .20^2}{(62 - 2)}}} = 1.58$$

Because the observed test statistic $t = 1.58$ does not exceed the critical value $t_{.05,60} = 1.67$, we do not reject H_0. ■

If the sample size is smaller than 30, the t distribution does not generally serve as a useful approximation to the distribution of the statistic t. Instead, to test the null hypothesis that the population rank correlation coefficient is 0, refer to Table A.12, which shows the critical values of R_s for a one-tailed test where α has the values .05, .025, .01, and .005. The table shows the critical values $R_{s,\alpha}$ such that $P(R_s \geq R_{s,\alpha}) = \alpha$.

Spearman's Rank Correlation Test with Small Samples

Case 1: Suppose we wish to test the null hypothesis

$$H_0: \rho_s = 0$$

against the one-sided alternative hypothesis

$$H_1: \rho_s > 0$$

using level of significance α. If $n \leq 30$, use the decision rule

$$\text{Reject } H_0 \text{ in favor of } H_1 \text{ if } R_s > R_{s,\alpha}$$

Case 2: To test the null hypothesis

$$H_0: \rho_s = 0$$

against the one-sided alternative hypothesis

$$H_1: \rho_s < 0$$

use the decision rule

$$\text{Reject } H_0 \text{ in favor of } H_1 \text{ if } R_s < -R_{s,\alpha}$$

Case 3: To test the null hypothesis

$$H_0: \rho_s = 0$$

against the two-sided alternative hypothesis

$$H_1: \rho_s \neq 0$$

use the decision rule

$$\text{Reject } H_0 \text{ in favor of } H_1 \text{ if } R_s < -R_{s,\alpha/2} \text{ or if } R_s > R_{s,\alpha/2}$$

Example 21.12 **Testing for Rank Correlation with a Small Sample:** Suppose we want to test the null hypothesis that the rankings given to 15 colleges by the general public are uncorrelated with the rankings given by college professors. Test $H_0: \rho_s = 0$ against $H_1: \rho_s > 0$ using $\alpha = .05$. The data are in Table 21.6.

TABLE 21.6
Ratings of colleges for Example 21.12

College	Ranking by Public	Ranking by Professors	d_i	d_i^2
1	4	5	−1	1
2	12	10	2	4
3	14	3	11	121
4	2	13	−11	121
5	1	2	−1	1
6	11	9	2	4
7	3	1	2	4
8	10	8	2	4
9	5	4	1	1
10	13	11	2	4
11	9	6	3	9
12	6	7	−1	1
13	15	15	0	0
14	7	12	−5	25
15	8	14	−6	36
				336

Solution: Refer to Table A.12 to obtain the critical value of the test statistic. For $n = 15$ and $\alpha = .05$, we obtain the critical value $R_{s,.05} = .441$. Because the calculated value $R_s = .40$ does not exceed the critical value, we do not reject the null hypothesis that $\rho_s = 0$. ■

Exercises for Section 21.6

1. The following data show the annual salaries in thousands of dollars Y for a sample of company presidents and the gross sales in millions of dollars X of their companies.

Company:	1	2	3	4	5	6	7	8	9	10	11	12
Y (in thousands)	\$120	132	98	86	145	210	450	104	80	80	180	150
X (in millions)	\$103	420	312	798	203	154	210	306	161	410	120	556

a. Obtain the ranks of the two variables.
b. Calculate the sample rank correlation coefficient R_s.
c. Let $\alpha = .05$. Test H_0: $\rho_s = 0$ against H_1: $\rho_s > 0$.
d. Calculate the sample correlation coefficient R. Is there much difference between R and R_s?

2. Ten different brands of beverage are ranked according to price. They are also ranked from 1 to 10 by a customer according to taste. Use a 5% level of significance to test if taste and price are related.

Brand:	1	2	3	4	5	6	7	8	9	10
Rank by Price	4	1	9	2	6	3	7	5	10	8
Rank by Taste	5	7	6	1	2	9	3	4	10	8

3. A political scientist wanted to examine the relationship between the rate of economic growth of a country and the stability of its government. Each of 10 countries was ranked on these two variables. Calculate R_s and test H_0: $\rho_s = 0$ using a 5% level of significance.

Country:	A	B	C	D	E	F	G	H	I	J
Rank by Growth	2	6	1	8	3	5	10	4	9	7
Rank by Stability	1	4	3	6	2	10	8	5	9	7

4. An executive determines which college graduates to hire based on the students' grades on an achievement test and an interview. Because interviewing the students is very expensive, the executive wonders if she could eliminate the interview and still choose the best candidates. The data for 12 candidates follow:

Candidate:	1	2	3	4	5	6	7	8	9	10	11	12
Test Score	88	64	95	86	80	70	66	70	75	60	65	84
Interview Rank	3	10	1	2	6	7	8	9	4	12	11	5

a. Use the accompanying data and calculate the rank correlation coefficient R_s.
b. Test H_0: $\rho_s = 0$ using a 5% level of significance.

5. A poll was taken to rank 10 cities according to where people would prefer to live and according to crime rate. Use the following data to calculate the rank correlation between a city's crime rate and people's desire to live in that city.

City:	A	B	C	D	E	F	G	H	I	J
Desirability of City	3	7	2	9	1	5	8	4	10	6
Crime Rate of City	1	9	2	8	4	3	7	5	6	10

21.7 ▪ The Kolmogorov–Smirnov Test

In Chapter 13 we showed how the chi-square goodness-of-fit test can be used to test whether a sample of observations was obtained from a population having a particular probability distribution. An alternative goodness-of-fit test is the Kolmogorov–Smirnov test, named after the two Russian mathematicians A. N. Kolmogorov (who proposed the test in 1933) and N. V. Smirnov (who later tabulated critical values and extended the test to the two sample case). The test is based on a comparison of the observed sample cumulative relative frequency distribution with the hypothetical population cumulative distribution function specified by the null hypothesis.

Before describing the test, recall the definitions of the population cumulative distribution function (CDF) and the sample cumulative relative frequency distribution function (SCDF). The SCDF is a step function that increases in value by $1/n$ at each observed value $X = x_i$. If k sample observations take the same value x_0, then the SCDF increases at x_0 by k/n.

Definition: Population Cumulative Distribution Function

Let x_0 be a specific value assumed by a random variable X. The population cumulative distribution function (CDF) of X is the function

$$F(x_0) = P(X \leq x_0)$$

Definition: Sample Cumulative Relative Frequency Distribution Function

The sample cumulative relative frequency distribution function (SCDF) is denoted by $S(x_0)$, where x_0 is a specific value of the random variable X. The value $S(x_0)$ represents the proportion of the sample observations that are less than or equal to x_0. Let n denote the sample size and let j denote the number of sample observations that are less than or equal to the value x_0; then

$$S(x_0) = j/n$$

The Kolmogorov–Smirnov test is based on the assumption that the random sample of n observations comes from a population whose cumulative probability distribution is

$F_0(x)$, where $F_0(x)$ is completely known. (Thus, all parameters are specified.) The null hypothesis is

H_0: The sample of data was selected from a population whose cumulative distribution function is $F_0(x)$

The alternative hypothesis is

H_1: The population cumulative distribution is not $F_0(x)$

The Kolmogorov–Smirnov test works as follows. Suppose it is claimed that a set of data was selected from a population having a specific distribution. For example, based on this claim, we might expect, say, 40% of the observations in the population to be less than or equal to some value x_0, which is thus the 40th percentile. If the claim is correct, we would expect approximately 40% of the sample observations to be less than or equal to x_0. If the difference between the theoretical proportion and the observed sample proportion is small, the null hypothesis is supported. If the difference between the theoretical proportion and the observed sample proportion is large, the alternative hypothesis is supported.

For every value x_0, calculate the theoretical proportion $F_0(x_0)$ and the observed sample proportion $S(x_0)$. The Kolmogorov–Smirnov test is based on the largest difference between the theoretical proportion and the observed sample proportion.

Formula for Kolmogorov–Smirnov Test Statistic

The Kolmogorov–Smirnov test statistic is

$$D = \sup|F_0(x) - S(x)|$$

where

$$F_0(x) = P(X \leqslant x)$$

and $S(x)$ denotes the proportion of sample observations less than or equal to the value x.

The symbol "sup" means the supremum (or maximum) of all possible values. Thus the test statistic D measures the greatest absolute difference between the hypothesized CDF, $F_0(x)$, and the observed SCDF, $S(x)$.

If H_0 is true, the value of D should get smaller as the sample size increases because the SCDF should approach $F_0(x)$. Values of D close to 0 support the null hypothesis, whereas large values of D support the alternative hypothesis.

Performing the Kolmogorov–Smirnov Test

Suppose we have a sample of n observations and wish to test the null hypothesis

H_0: The sample of data was selected from a population whose cumulative distribution function is $F_0(x)$

against the alternative hypothesis

H_1: The population cumulative distribution is not $F_0(x)$

Let the level of significance be α. To perform the test, calculate the Kolmogorov–Smirnov test statistic D and find the critical value D_α from Table A.14 in the Appendix. Use the decision rule

Reject H_0 in favor of H_1 if $D > D_\alpha$

Example 21.13 **Performing the Kolmogorov–Smirnov Test:** A scientist has used a computer to generate $n = 20$ random numbers. The values were supposed to be selected from a uniform distribution that varies from 0 to 10. The 20 sample values x_i were placed in ascending order as shown in Table 21.7. The scientist is worried that the computer program might have an error and wants to test the null hypothesis that the sample of data was selected from a uniform distribution varying from 0 to 10. Let $\alpha = .05$ and perform the Kolmogorov–Smirnov test.

TABLE 21.7
Random values for Example 21.13

Observation i	Value x_i	$F_0(x_i)$	$S(x_i)$
1	0.8	.08	.05
2	1.6	.16	.10
3	1.7	.17	.15
4	1.9	.19	.20
5	2.3	.23	.25
6	4.0	.40	.30
7	4.5	.45	.35
8	4.7	.47	.40
9	5.3	.53	.45
10	5.4	.54	.50
11	6.2	.62	.55
12	6.4	.64	.60
13	6.7	.67	.65
14	6.8	.68	.70
15	7.9	.79	.75
16	8.4	.84	.80
17	9.0	.90	.85
18	9.1	.91	.90
19	9.7	.97	.95
20	9.8	.98	1.00

Solution: To test H_0, calculate $S(x)$ and $F_0(x)$ for each observed value of the random variable X. If X is uniformly distributed between 0 and 10, then $F_0(x)$ represents the area under the uniform density function between 0 and x. The hypothesized uniform density function is illustrated in Figure 21.1. For example, in Figure 21.1, the shaded area between 0 and 4 is .4; this area represents $P(X \leqslant 4)$. The cumulative distribution

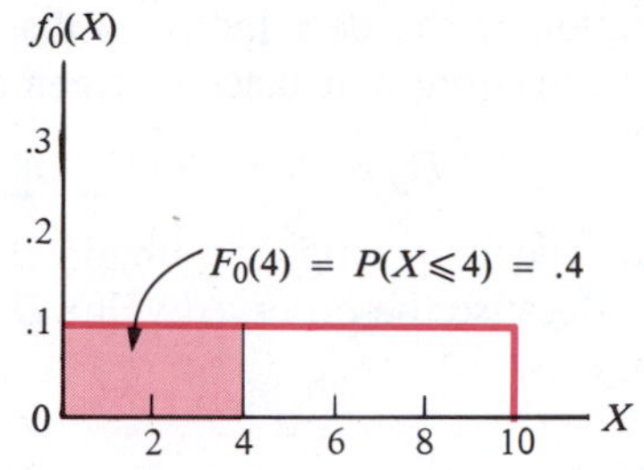

FIGURE 21.1
Uniform density function for Example 21.13.

function $F_0(x)$ represents the area under the density function between 0 and x. This area is $x/10$, so we obtain the null hypothesis

$$H_0\colon F_0(x) = x/10 \quad \text{for } 0 \leqslant x \leqslant 10$$

This test is illustrated in Figure 21.2.

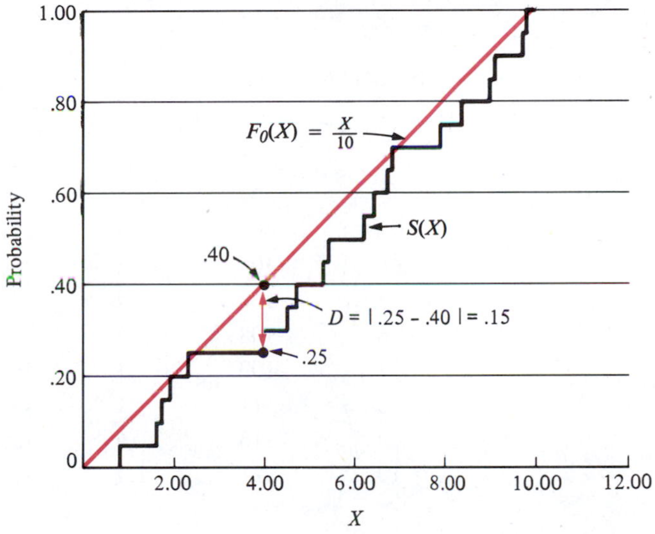

FIGURE 21.2
Kolmogorov–Smirnov test for Example 21.13.

Denote the 20 ordered sample values as $x_1, x_2, \ldots, x_{20}$. Then $S(x_1) = 1/20$, $S(x_2) = 2/20, \ldots, S(x_{20}) = 20/20 = 1$; in general, $S(x_i) = i/20$. Table 21.7 shows the 20 sample values x_i, $F_0(x_i)$, and $S(x_i)$.

In Figure 21.2 the cumulative distribution function $F_0(x)$ is shown as the straight line from (0, 0) to (10, 1). The sample cumulative distribution function $S(x)$ is the step function, which increases by $1/20 = .05$ at each observed value x_i. The Kolmogorov–Smirnov test is based on the single greatest difference between $S(x)$ and $F_0(x)$. For example, from Figure 21.2, for $X = 3.5$, we obtain $F_0(3.5) = .35$ and $S(3.5) = .25$. Thus, at $X = 3.5$, the distance between $S(x)$ and $F_0(x)$ is .10. When $X = 3.999$, we obtain $F_0(3.999) = .3999$ and $S(3.999) = .25$. At $X = 3.999$, the distance between $S(x)$ and $F_0(x)$ is .1499. As X increases and approaches 4.0, $F_0(x)$ approaches .40, while $S(x) = .25$.

Examination of the data indicates that the greatest difference occurs just prior to $X = 4.0$. The maximum distance between $S(x)$ and $F_0(x)$ here is

$$D = |S(x) - F_0(x)| = |.25 - .40| = .15$$

For $n = 20$ and $\alpha = .05$, we obtain the critical value of D from Table A.14 of $D_\alpha = .294$. Because the observed value $D = .15$ is less than the critical value D_α, we do not reject H_0. ■

Example 21.14 **Using the Kolmogorov–Smirnov Test:** The director of a job placement agency wants to test the null hypothesis that the IQs of students at a local high school are normally distributed with mean 110 and standard deviation 10. A random sample of $n = 10$ IQs was obtained. Let $\alpha = .05$ and test the null hypothesis using the Kolmogorov–Smirnov test.

Solution: The ten IQs are placed in ascending order and denoted x_i, $i = 1, 2, \ldots, 10$. These values along with the values $S(x_i)$ for the sample cumulative relative frequency distribution are shown in Table 21.8.

TABLE 21.8
IQ scores for Example 21.14

Student i	IQ x_i	z_i	$F_0(x_i)$	$S(x_i)$
1	93	−1.7	.0446	.10
2	99	−1.1	.1357	.20
3	102	− .8	.2119	.30
4	105	− .5	.3085	.40
5	106	− .4	.3446	.50
6	108	− .2	.4207	.60
7	109	− .1	.4602	.70
8	111	.1	.5398	.80
9	116	.6	.7258	.90
10	121	1.1	.8643	1.00

To calculate the values $F_0(x)$, we transform the IQ scores into standardized Z scores. For example, for $x_1 = 93$, we obtain

$$z_1 = \frac{x_1 - \mu}{\sigma} = \frac{93 - 110}{10} = -1.7$$

We have $P(X \leqslant 93) = P(Z \leqslant -1.7)$. We use Table A.5 for the standard normal distribution and obtain

$$P(Z \leqslant -1.7) = .5000 - .4554 = .0446$$

Similarly, for $x_6 = 108$, we obtain

$$z_6 = (108 - 110)/10 = -.2$$

and

$$P(X \leq 108) = P(Z \leq -.2)$$
$$= .5000 - .0793 = .4207$$

The values $P(X \leq x_i) = F_0(x_i) = P(Z \leq z_i)$ are shown in Table 21.8, and the SCDF and hypothesized CDF are shown in Figure 21.3.

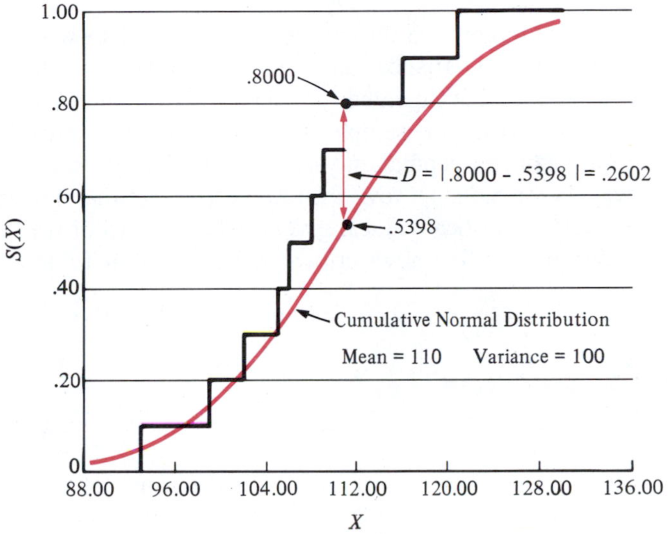

FIGURE 21.3
Kolmogorov–Smirnov test for Example 21.14.

The maximum difference between the two functions occurs at $X = 111^+$, where the symbol 111^+ indicates a value just larger than 111. We obtain

$$D = |S(111^+) - F_0(111^+)| = |.8000 - .5398| = .2602$$

For $n = 10$ and $\alpha = .05$, the critical value of D is $D_\alpha = .409$. Because the calculated value of D is less than the critical value, we cannot reject H_0. ■

Comparing the Kolmogorov–Smirnov and the Chi-square Tests

Both the Kolmogorov–Smirnov and chi-square tests can be used to test the null hypothesis that a sample was selected from a population with a specific distribution. The Kolmogorov–Smirnov test has been shown to be more powerful than the chi-square test for a given sample size and a given level of significance α; that is, the Kolmogorov–Smirnov test yields a higher probability of rejecting H_0 when H_0 is false than does the chi-square test. One disadvantage of the Kolmogorov–Smirnov test, however, is that it is based on the assumption that the population parameters are known a priori and are not estimated from the sample of data.

To use the Kolmogorov–Smirnov test, the population cumulative distribution function must be known. The most frequently performed test specifies that the population follows a normal distribution with a specific mean and variance, but any hypothesized continuous distribution can be used. The test also performs reasonably well as an approximate test when the hypothesized distribution is discrete.

Lilliefors Test

The Kolmogorov–Smirnov test is inappropriate when population parameters, such as the mean and variance, have been estimated from the sample of data. H. W. Lilliefors adjusted the critical values provided by Kolmogorov and Smirnov so that we can test for normality using the sample mean and sample variance instead of a hypothetical population mean and population variance. The *Lilliefors test* is performed in exactly the same way as the Kolmogorov–Smirnov test except that the critical value D_α is obtained from Lilliefors's critical values, given in Table A.15 of the Appendix, rather than from Kolmogorov and Smirnov's critical values given in Table A.14.

Exercises for Section 21.7

1. Mr. Plummer is an engineer for the state department of transportation. He argues that the number of cars crossing a certain bridge between 8 A.M. and 9 A.M. on weekday mornings is normally distributed with mean 1300 and standard deviation 200. On a random sample of 10 weekdays, the numbers of cars crossing the bridge between 8 A.M. and 9 A.M. were as follows:

1540 1700 1840 1642 1139 1227 1684 1782 1431 1302

Let $\alpha = .05$. Use the Kolmogorov–Smirnov test to test if the population is distributed as claimed.

2. A bank manager wants to test whether, during five-minute periods, the number of arrivals at a new branch bank on Friday afternoons follows a normal distribution with unknown mean and variance. The following data show the number of customers arriving during 15 random five-minute intervals:

10 12 18 13 7 23 8 10 19 7 15 9 21 6

a. Calculate the sample mean and sample variance.
b. Construct the sample cumulative relative frequency distribution.
c. Use the sample mean and sample variance to construct the normal cumulative frequency distribution.
d. Let $\alpha = .05$. Test for normality using the Lilliefors test.

3. Mr. Frost owns a fishery, where he grows fish for sale as feed for livestock in the Midwest. He weighs a random sample of 100 of his fish and constructs the cumulative relative frequency distribution. After calculating the sample mean and sample variance, he constructs a hypothetical normal cumulative distribution function. The maximum difference between the sample cumulative relative frequency distribution and the hypothetical normal cumulative frequency distribution is .08. Let $\alpha = .05$ and use the Lilliefors test to test for normality.

21.8 ▪ Computer Applications

Many statistical computer programs, including SPSSX, SAS, and Minitab, can perform the statistical tests described in this chapter. In this section, we show how to use the SPSSX program to perform these tests.

Mann–Whitney Test

The SPSSX computer program can be used to perform the Mann–Whitney test. The use of a computer is especially helpful when the sample sizes are large. The following example shows how to perform the Mann–Whitney test using the SPSSX computer program.

Example 21.15

Using SPSSX to Perform the Mann–Whitney Test: Nutrition is thought to be an important component in cancer development in humans. For example, there is evidence that the per capita consumption of dietary fats is positively correlated with the incidence of colon cancer. Medical studies have examined the relationship between diet and tumor development in rats. One hypothesis of interest is whether the length of time until a tumor develops in rats fed saturated diets differs from that in rats fed unsaturated diets. If it is reasonable to assume that the time for tumor development is normally distributed, the two-sample *t* test can be used to test the null hypothesis that the population means are equal. Otherwise, the Mann–Whitney test should be used.

Table 21.9 shows the number of days until tumor development for a random sample of 20 rats fed a saturated diet and an independent random sample of 20 rats fed an unsaturated diet. Let us test the null hypothesis that the population means are equal by using the Mann–Whitney test and the SPSSX computer program.

Solution: To perform the test using the SPSSX program, issue the command

```
NPAR TESTS M-W = TIME BY DIET(0,1)
```

TABLE 21.9
Number of days to tumor development in rats for Example 21.15

Saturated Diet		Unsaturated Diet	
84	102	121	107
116	112	80	93
90	77	60	65
74	83	81	74
83	90	78	85
124	94	54	107
161	104	62	67
114	109	73	91
85	83	91	84
100	117	111	87

This command tells the computer to perform a nonparametric Mann–Whitney test. The variable TIME measures the number of days until tumor development, and the variable DIET was recorded as 0 for rats on saturated diets and 1 for rats on unsaturated diets.

Figure 21.4 shows the output generated by the SPSSX program. The output shows that the mean rank is 24.98 for the rats fed a saturated diet and 16.02 for the rats fed an unsaturated diet. The U statistic has the value 110.5, and the value of the test statistic Z is $z = -2.4221$. This value of Z has a two-tailed prob-value of .0154. If we were using a 5% level of significance, we would reject the null hypothesis that the two population means are equal.

FIGURE 21.4 **SPSSX-generated output for the Mann–Whitney test for Example 21.15.**

```
- - - - - MANN-WHITNEY U - WILCOXON RANK SUM W TEST

     TIME       TIME ELAPSED IN DAYS
  BY DIET       TYPE OF FOOD

      MEAN RANK     CASES

          24.98        20  DIET = 0  SATURATED FATS
          16.02        20  DIET = 1  UNSATURATED FATS
                       --
                       40  TOTAL

                                   EXACT                 CORRECTED FOR TIES
          U               W      2-TAILED P                Z        2-TAILED P
        110.5           499.5      0.0143               -2.4221       0.0154
```

Wilcoxon Signed-Rank Test

The SPSSX computer program can be used to perform the Wilcoxon test, as shown in the following example.

Example 21.16 **Using SPSSX to Perform the Wilcoxon Signed-Rank Test:** Every Monday morning for 20 weeks two stockbrokers independently invested $1000 in mutual funds. Every Friday afternoon, each broker recorded the profit earned during the week measured as the difference between the price on Friday afternoon and the price on Monday morning, as shown in Table 21.10. Let us use the Wilcoxon signed-rank test to test the null hypothesis that the average returns earned by the two stockbrokers are the same.

Solution: To perform the test, issue the command

```
NPAR TESTS WILCOXON = S1 WITH S2
```

In the computer statement, the variable S1 measures the weekly profit earned by the first stockbroker; the variable S2, that by the second. The computer output in Figure 21.5 shows that the mean rank of weekly profits were 10.44 for the first stockbroker and 10.55 for the second. For the Wilcoxon test, the Z score is $z = -.4107$. The two-tailed prob-value associated with this value is .6813. If we tested the null hypothesis at a 5% level of significance, we would not reject the null hypothesis that the weekly profits earned by the two brokers have the same mean.

TABLE 21.10 **Weekly profits for Example 21.16**

Week	Broker 1	Broker 2	Week	Broker 1	Broker 2
1	5	7	11	8	4
2	4	7	12	6	5
3	6	5	13	10	11
4	11	8	14	14	12
5	2	4	15	12	10
6	8	4	16	7	8
7	3	7	17	9	12
8	6	7	18	6	8
9	9	12	19	8	6
10	5	4	20	5	7

FIGURE 21.5
SPSSX-generated output for Wilcoxon signed-rank test for Example 21.16.

```
- - - - - WILCOXON MATCHED-PAIRS SIGNED-RANKS TEST

       S1         STOCK 1
  WITH S2         STOCK 2

       MEAN RANK     CASES

           10.44         9   - RANKS (S2 LT S1)
           10.55        11   + RANKS (S2 GT S1)
                         0     TIES  (S2 EQ S1)
                        --
                        20     TOTAL

           Z =    -0.4107            2-TAILED P =   .6813
```

Kruskal–Wallis Test

The SPSSX computer program can be used to perform the Kruskal–Wallis test, as shown in the next example.

Example 21.17 **Using SPSSX to Perform the Kruskal–Wallis Test:** Tourism is the largest revenue producer in the state of Colorado. The state intends to begin an advertising campaign to recruit more tourists, and it wants to spend its advertising dollars in states whose residents are most likely to visit Colorado. Before deciding where to advertise, government officials commissioned a statistical study to determine where most of Colorado's tourists come from and how much they spend in Colorado. As part of the study, the officials want to determine if the average expenditures of tourists vary with their home state. The data in Table 21.11 show the total expenditures in Colorado by samples of tourists from four states. Let us use the Kruskal–Wallis test to test the null hypothesis that the population means are equal for the four states.

TABLE 21.11
Expenditures in Colorado by home state of tourists for Example 21.17

California	Texas	Illinois	Nevada
$564	$ 812	$550	$620
581	800	480	840
643	690	690	790
674	724	650	890
697	543	670	910
417	1060	820	940
806	840	740	860
392	680	760	880
	700		780
	1110		

Solution: The SPSSX output shown in Figure 21.6 was generated by executing the SPSSX computer statement

```
NPAR TESTS K-W = EXPENSE BY STATE(1,4)
```

In the printout, the variable EXPENSE measures the amount of tourist expenditures and the variable STATE was recorded as 1 for California, 2 for Texas, 3 for Illinois, and 4 for Nevada. The output shows the mean rank for each group, the number of observations in each group, the chi-square statistic uncorrected for ties, and the chi-square statistic and its significance level (or prob-value) corrected for ties. The corrected chi-square statistic is 13.1731, which has a prob-value of .0043. If we tested the null hypothesis that the population means are equal using a 1% level of significance, we would reject the null hypothesis that the four population means are equal. ■

FIGURE 21.6 SPSSX-generated output for Kruskal–Wallis test for Example 21.17.

```
- - - - - KRUSKAL-WALLIS 1-WAY ANOVA

     EXPENSE    AVERAGE AMOUNT SPENT
  BY STATE      TOURISTS STATE OF RESIDENCE

     MEAN RANK     CASES

         9.63          8    STATE = 1    CALIFORNIA
        21.10         10    STATE = 2    TEXAS
        13.56          8    STATE = 3    ILLINOIS
        25.94          9    STATE = 4    NEVADA
                      --
                      35    TOTAL

                                                   CORRECTED FOR TIES
        CASES     CHI-SQUARE   SIGNIFICANCE      CHI-SQUARE   SIGNIFICANCE
           35        13.1694         0.0043         13.1731         0.0043
```

Runs Test

The SPSSX computer program can be used to perform the runs test, as shown in the next example.

Example 21.18 **Using SPSSX to Perform the Runs Test:** The Huwalt Machine Tool Company produces pipes that are used in the engines of nuclear-powered submarines. Following are the diameters of a random sample of 50 pipes:

0.617	0.610	0.619	0.614	0.609	0.609	0.617	0.613
0.614	0.609	0.615	0.616	0.608	0.607	0.608	0.614
0.621	0.618	0.622	0.615	0.611	0.622	0.616	0.615
0.621	0.614	0.613	0.619	0.606	0.616	0.618	0.616
0.617	0.614	0.614	0.618	0.613	0.610	0.613	0.614
0.617	0.618	0.607	0.621	0.616	0.612	0.613	0.614
0.614	0.611						

When the production process is operating correctly, the diameters of successive pipes are independent of one another; when it is not, pipes with diameters above (below) average tend to follow other pipes with diameters that are above (below) average. That is, large pipes tend to follow large pipes, and small pipes tend to follow small pipes. When the production process is not operating correctly, costly adjustments have to be made. Use the runs test to test the null hypothesis that successive observations are independent of one another.

Solution: The SPSSX computer output shown in Figure 21.7 was generated by executing the SPSSX computer statement

```
NPAR TESTS RUNS (MEAN) = D
```

In the printout the variable D represents the diameter of the pipe. The code (MEAN) indicates that observations should be recorded as above or below average according to whether they do or do not exceed the sample mean. The figure shows that the mean diameter is $\overline{X} = .61436$. The Z score is $z = -.8169$, and the two-tailed prob-value associated with this score is .4140. If we were testing the null hypothesis at a 5% level of significance, we would not reject the null hypothesis that successive diameters are independent of one another.

FIGURE 21.7
SPSSX-generated output for the runs test for Example 21.18.

```
- - - - - RUNS TEST
     D          DIAMETER OF PIPE

          RUNS:   23                     TEST VALUE =  .61436 (MEAN)

          CASES:  27   LT MEAN
                  23   GE MEAN                    Z = -0.8169
                  --
                  50   TOTAL             2-TAILED P =   .4140
```

■

Kolmogorov–Smirnov Test

The next example shows how to use the SPSSX program to perform the Kolmogorov–Smirnov test.

Example 21.19 **Using SPSSX to Perform the Kolmogorov–Smirnov Test:** Refer to the data in Example 21.18. When the production process at the Huwalt Machine Tool Company is operating correctly, the diameters follow approximately a normal distribution. When the distribution is not normal, the production process is not operating correctly and costly adjustments have to be made. Use the Kolmogorov–Smirnov test to test the null hypothesis that the distribution of diameters of pipes is normal against the alternative hypothesis that the distribution is not normal.

Solution: The SPSSX computer output shown in Figure 21.8 was generated by executing the SPSSX computer statement

```
NPAR TESTS K-S (NORMAL) = D
```

The sample mean is $\overline{X} = .61436$ and the sample standard deviation is $S = .00406$. The maximum difference between the observed cumulative distribution and the theoretical normal distribution having mean $\mu = .61436$ and standard deviation $\sigma = .00406$ is $D = .10896$. The output shows that the two-tailed prob-value associated with $D = .10896$ is .593. If we were testing using a 5% level of significance, we would not reject the null hypothesis, because this prob-value exceeds the level of significance.

FIGURE 21.8 **SPSSX-generated output for the Kolmogorov–Smirnov test.**

```
- - - - - KOLMOGOROV - SMIRNOV GOODNESS OF FIT TEST

     D          DIAMETER OF PIPE

     TEST DISTRIBUTION   -   NORMAL                         MEAN:      .61436
                                            STANDARD DEVIATION:      .00406

               CASES:   50

               MOST EXTREME DIFFERENCES
        ABSOLUTE         POSITIVE         NEGATIVE             K-S Z        2-TAILED P
        0.10896          0.07529          -0.10896             0.770           0.593
```

■

Chapter 21 Summary

A key step in applying any statistical technique correctly is to make sure that the assumptions underlying the test hold at least approximately. When sample data consist of rankings or are obtained from populations that are not normally distributed, a *nonparametric test* is often preferable to the tests described earlier in this book. In this chapter, we introduced the following nonparametric tests:

1. Sign test
2. Mann–Whitney U test
3. Kruskal–Wallis test
4. Wilcoxon signed-rank test
5. Runs test

6. Spearman rank correlation test
7. Kolmogorov–Smirnov test

The *sign test* is used to analyze samples of data from two populations that occur in matched pairs. The goal is to determine if observations from one population tend to exceed the corresponding observations from the other population. The test is equivalent to testing the null hypothesis H_0: $p = .5$ where p is the proportion of items from Population 1 that exceed the corresponding observations from Population 2. The test statistic depends on the number of observations from Sample 1 that exceed the corresponding observations from Sample 2. We described tests for both small and large samples. The test for small samples utilizes the binomial distribution and the one for large samples utilizes the standard normal distribution.

The *Mann–Whitney* U *test* is a nonparametric procedure for testing the equality of the means (or medians) of two populations using two independent samples. Unlike the t test discussed in Chapter 12, the Mann–Whitney test does not require the assumption that the populations be at least approximately normally distributed. The data from the two samples are pooled and placed in ascending order. The test statistic depends on the sum of the ranks of the observations from one of the samples. We described tests for both small and large samples. The test for large samples utilizes the standard normal distribution.

The *Wilcoxon signed-rank test* is a nonparametric procedure used for testing the equality of the means (or medians) of two populations when dealing with two dependent (paired) samples. To perform the test, obtain the differences of the paired observations and place their absolute values in ascending order. The test statistic depends on the sum of the ranks of positive differences. We described tests for both small and large samples. The latter utilizes the standard normal distribution.

The *Kruskal–Wallis test* is an extension of the Mann–Whitney test and is used to test the equality of more than two population means (or medians) when using independent samples. As in the Mann–Whitney procedure, the samples are pooled and the values are ranked from smallest to largest. The test statistic depends on the sums of the ranks of the observations from each sample. The test utilizes the chi-square distribution.

The *runs test* examines a sequence containing two types of elements (such as success or failure, good or defective, yes or no) to determine whether the sequence was generated in a random manner. A *run* is a sequence of like elements, and the test statistic depends on the number of runs present in the sample. We described tests for both small and large samples. The latter utilizes the standard normal distribution.

The *Spearman rank correlation coefficient* is used to measure the strength of the relationship between sample values on two variables that consist of ranks. If the original data are quantitative measurements, they can be converted to ranks. The rank correlation coefficient can be used to test whether a linear relationship exists between the ranks of two variables. We described tests for both small and large samples. The latter utilizes the t distribution.

The *Kolmogorov–Smirnov test* is used to test the null hypothesis that a sample of data came from a specific probability distribution. It is a more powerful alternative to the chi-square goodness-of-fit test described in Chapter 13. The test statistic depends on the maximum difference between the hypothesized population cumulative distribution function and sample cumulative relative frequency distribution. The *Lilliefors test* is an extension of the Kolmogorov–Smirnov test to the case when some of the population parameters are estimated from the sample.

This concludes our discussion of hypothesis testing. In the next chapter, we discuss index numbers that are used to measure how variables have changed over time.

Chapter 21 ▪ Supplementary Exercises

1. A political scientist wishes to determine if the political preference of homeowners is independent of that of their next-door neighbors. A sequence of 30 adjacent homeowners were interviewed, and *R* was recorded for Republicans and *D* for Democrats. The results are as follows:

R D R R R D D D D D R R R R R D D D D D R D R D D D R R D D

a. Explain how the runs test can be used for this problem.
b. State the null and alternative hypotheses.
c. Complete the test using $\alpha = .05$.

2. A random sample of 28 pipes is selected from the output of a pipe-making machine, and the diameter of each pipe is recorded. Those with diameters smaller than the median are marked *S*, and those with diameters larger than the median are marked *L*. The data are as follows:

S L L L S S L L L S S L L L L L L S S S S L S L S S S S

a. Explain how the runs test can be used to test whether the sequence of large and small diameters is random.
b. State the null and alternative hypotheses.
c. Complete the test using $\alpha = .05$.

3. The general manager of a chain of 30 food stores is interested in determining whether containers used for storing food in home freezers will sell better when displayed next to frozen foods or paper goods. The containers are displayed with frozen foods for a week and then with paper products for a week. The data are shown in the accompanying table.

Store	Frozen Foods	Paper Goods	Store	Frozen Foods	Paper Goods
1	40	60	16	20	29
2	75	40	17	49	60
3	25	28	18	32	22
4	20	30	19	15	32
5	9	19	20	80	121
6	11	27	21	17	11
7	16	37	22	26	19
8	28	28	23	33	27
9	20	33	24	19	23
10	16	19	25	27	29
11	14	19	26	44	40
12	41	60	27	52	46
13	14	19	28	17	27
14	7	12	29	29	33
15	28	20	30	32	19

a. Let $\alpha = .05$ and use the sign test to determine if location affects sales.
b. Use the Wilcoxon test to determine if location affects sales.

4. Two mixes, A and B, are used to make concrete beams. A sample of 12 beams made from Mix A has an average strength of 5094 psi (pounds per square inch), and a sample of 10 beams made from Mix B has an average strength of 5745 psi. The following data show the strength of the concrete beams (in psi):

Mix A	Mix B	Mix A	Mix B
5050	4280	5120	4320
6120	5920	4900	7100
5000	5500	5210	6040
4650	4988	5020	6602
5100	6700	5041	
4800	6000	5117	

Let $\alpha = .05$ and test whether Mix B is better than Mix A.
a. Use the standard t test based on the assumption that the samples are independent and are obtained from normal populations.
b. Use the Mann–Whitney test.

5. A university owns or leases several hundred cars for use on official business. A random sample of 10 repair bills for Car 1 and 15 repair bills for Car 2 are shown in the accompanying data. Let $\alpha = .05$. Use the Mann–Whitney test to determine if one make is more expensive to repair than the other.

Car 1		Car 2		
$27.00	$106.81	$145.00	$25.00	$18.20
52.61	97.32	107.00	52.05	35.70
77.08	35.18	14.95	81.75	46.00
66.90	212.17	28.00	19.60	62.00
45.12	96.00	32.00	27.33	20.00

6. A tax consultant is studying the ratio of assessed value to sales value for properties in two sections of a city. A sample taken of 11 sales from Section 1 and 13 sales from Section 2 is shown in the accompanying data. Let $\alpha = .05$ and test whether the assessment ratios are the same in the two sections of town.

Section 1		Section 2	
.54	.62	.45	.57
.66	.60	.49	.62
.48	.61	.60	.64
.71	.68	.58	.56
.49	.70	.59	.61
.56		.66	.67
		.47	

7. A food processor undertook a study to compare consumer opinions of two brands of catsup. In a random sample of 30 consumers, each tasted both brands and gave a rating from 0 to 10 (a rating of 10 signifying the best catsup). Let $\alpha = .05$. Do the following data indicate that one brand is preferred to the other?

Consumer	Catsup A	Catsup B	Consumer	Catsup A	Catsup B
1	6	8	16	5	5
2	5	7	17	7	6
3	8	6	18	8	9
4	4	5	19	6	5
5	7	9	20	1	3
6	9	2	21	5	8
7	1	9	22	7	6
8	2	4	23	2	5
9	4	8	24	1	9
10	9	7	25	5	2
11	8	9	26	9	8
12	6	6	27	6	5
13	1	4	28	4	7
14	5	3	29	8	6
15	3	7	30	1	4

8. A psychologist wants to test her theory that people's impressions of how intelligent a person is depend on how well the person is dressed. She has male and female models walk past a random sample of viewers, who are then asked to rank the models from 1 to 10 on how well they are dressed and on how intelligent they appear to be (10 is the highest rating). She obtains the following results:

Model:	1	2	3	4	5	6	7	8	9	10
Rank on intelligence	6	4	3	1	2	8	9	5	10	7
Rank on dress	7	2	1	4	3	5	6	8	9	10

Calculate the rank correlation coefficient. Let $\alpha = .05$ and test the psychologist's theory.

9. Two brands of automobile tires were placed on the rear wheels of 10 cars. The number of miles in thousands before tire failure was recorded for each tire. The data are as follows:

Car:	1	2	3	4	5	6	7	8	9	10
Tire 1	22	33	30	41	36	29	35	40	37	32
Tire 2	33	20	19	27	31	26	36	22	27	33

Let $\alpha = .05$.

a. Use the t test to determine if the tires are equally good.
b. Use the sign test to test if the tires are equally good.
c. Use the Wilcoxon signed-rank test to test if the tires are equally good.

10. An administrator thinks that the academic reputation of many schools is positively correlated with the record of the school's football team. A panel of newscasters is asked to rank 10 colleges by academic quality and the quality of its football team. Calculate the rank correlation coefficient.

School:	1	2	3	4	5	6	7	8	9	10
Football rank	7	1	10	2	4	8	3	9	6	5
Academic rank	8	2	7	1	5	9	6	10	3	4

11. A corporation selects its executives from its sales force (S) or from its research department (R). During the past four years, 10 executives have been selected. The following sequence shows the order in which the 10 executives were selected:

$$R \quad R \quad S \quad R \quad S \quad S \quad S \quad S \quad R \quad R$$

Does this sequence imply that the order of selection was nonrandom?

12. Two different brands of shingles were used to cover houses in a certain neighborhood. The following data show the life in years of service before the shingles had to be replaced:

Brand A	20	23	27	24	29	26	30	20	18
Brand B	16	20	26	18	27	19	22	18	20

Let $\alpha = .05$. Determine if the shingles are equally good using the following tests:

a. t test

b. Mann–Whitney test

13. The advertising agent for a mail order company conducted an experiment to determine if multicolored advertisements were more effective than black-and-white advertisements containing bonus coupons. In each of 10 cities, 500 households received a color ad and 500 received a black-and-white ad. The number of orders placed by the recipients of these ads is shown in the accompanying data. Let $\alpha = .05$. Use the following tests to determine if the ads were equally effective:

a. Sign test

b. Wilcoxon signed-rank test

City	Color	Black and White
Cincinnati	106	97
Detroit	89	92
Boston	122	104
Chicago	144	112
Miami	85	94
Dallas	180	130
Houston	195	175
Atlanta	148	150
Denver	135	108
Pittsburgh	110	114

14. The typing speed (in words per minute) was determined for each of 20 secretaries using a standard typewriter and then using a new typewriter. The speed in words per minute was as follows:

Standard typewriter	37	48	43	31	46	47	49	51	44	43
New typewriter	38	46	42	34	36	42	48	42	37	35

Let $\alpha = .05$. Use the sign test to determine if one typewriter is better than the other.

15. The cost of land per acre in thousands of dollars for land in two neighboring towns follows:

Town 1	42	47	46	45	38	40	51	48	49
Town 2	37	42	39	44	38	43			

Let $\alpha = .05$. Use the following tests to test the null hypothesis that land prices are equal in the two towns:

a. Wilcoxon signed-rank test
b. t test

16. A securities analyst wants to investigate the association between the profitability of companies and their liquidity. He ranked 12 firms in an industry according to their profitability and liquidity as shown in the following data:

Firm:	1	2	3	4	5	6	7	8	9	10	11	12
Profitability	8	1	9	3	10	12	2	11	7	5	4	6
Liquidity	4	5	6	1	9	2	12	10	3	7	11	8

a. Calculate the rank correlation coefficient using the ranks in the given data.
b. Test whether the correlation is nonzero using $\alpha = .05$.

17. Two loan officers rank their bank's loan applications according to their desirability, as shown in the following data:

Loan:	1	2	3	4	5	6	7	8	9	10
Officer 1	2	3	10	4	5	9	1	6	8	7
Officer 2	1	2	6	3	5	10	4	7	9	8

a. Calculate the rank correlation coefficient.
b. Let $\alpha = .05$. Determine if the correlation is significantly different from 0.

18. A developmental psychologist was using a behavior modification program to help control the disruptive behavior of 40 children in a local school. After one month, 26 of these children improved, 10 were worse, and 4 showed no change in behavior. On the basis of these data, can the psychologist conclude that the program is working? Use the sign test.

19. Ten people are each driven blindfolded over a predetermined course twice, one time in each of two automobiles. In each case, the person rates the quality of the ride on a scale from 1 to 20. The results are as follows:

Person:	1	2	3	4	5	6	7	8	9	10
Automobile 1	14	20	15	9	16	12	10	13	14	13
Automobile 2	10	17	16	7	8	10	9	11	11	8

Do these data indicate any differences in the quality of the ride of the two automobiles? Use the sign test.

20. A leading toothpaste manufacturer advertises that in a recent medical study, 70% of the people tested had brighter teeth after using its Very Bright toothpaste than after using Brand X. The data upon which the above statements were based were collected from a random sample of 10 individuals in an experiment where each individual used both toothpastes. Half of the individuals used Brand X for three weeks and then Very Bright for the same time period; the other half used Very Bright first and then Brand X. A brightness test was given at the end of each three-week period. Thus, there were two scores for each individual, one from the brightness test following use of Brand X and one following the use of Very Bright. The following are the scores (the higher, the brighter):

Subject:	1	2	3	4	5	6	7	8	9	10
Very Bright	5	4	4	2	3	4	1	3	6	6
Brand X	4	3	2	3	1	1	3	4	5	4

a. Test the manufacturer's claim. What is the alternative hypothesis? What is the null hypothesis?
b. Using $\alpha = .05$, what do you conclude?
c. What error may you be making in your answer to part (b)?
d. Does the advertising seem misleading?

References

NIE, NORMAN E., C. HADLAI HULL, JEAN G. JENKINS, KARIN STEINBRENNER, and DALE H. BENT. *SPSS Statistical Package for the Social Sciences*. 2d ed. New York: McGraw-Hill, 1975.

NORUSIS, MARIJA J. *SPSSX Introductory Statistics Guide*. New York: McGraw-Hill, 1983.

________. *SPSSX Advanced Statistics Guide*. Chicago: SPSS, 1985.

________. *The SPSS Guide to Data Analysis*. Chicago: SPSS, 1986.

RYAN, THOMAS A., BRIAN L. JOINER, and BARBARA F. RYAN. *Minitab Handbook*. 2d ed. Boston: PWS-KENT, 1985.

________. *Minitab Reference Manual*. University Park, Penn.: Minitab Project, 1985.

SAS Introductory Guide. 3d ed. Cary, N.C.: SAS Institute, 1985.

SAS Procedures Guide for Personal Computers. Version 6 ed. Cary, N.C.: SAS Institute, 1986.

SAS Statistics Guide for Personal Computers. Version 6 ed. Cary, N.C.: SAS Institute, 1986.

SAS User's Guide: Basics. Version 5 ed. Cary, N.C.: SAS Institute, 1985.

SAS User's Guide: Statistics. Version 5 ed. Cary, N.C.: SAS Institute, 1985.

SPEARMAN, CHARLES E. "The Proof and Measurement of Association Between Two Things." *American Journal of Psychology* 15 (1904): 72–101.

SPSSX User's Guide. Chicago: SPSS, 1983.

WILCOXON, FRANK. "Individual Comparisons by Ranking Methods." *Biometrics Bulletin* 1, no. 6 (1945): 80–83.

Chapter Twenty-Two
Index Numbers

This chapter discusses how to construct and use index numbers to analyze time series data. An index number expresses the relationship between the value of some variable at one point in time, called the **base period**, and the value of that variable at some other point in time. The most frequently used index numbers are *price indexes,* which show percent price changes over time, and *quantity indexes,* which show changes over time in the quantity produced or sold of some item.

Consider, for example, how the price of a single product such as a Big Mac at McDonald's has changed since 1975. One way to describe the price changes is to construct a price index, which measures the price in any year as a percentage of the price in the base year 1975. Such a price index is called a *simple price index* because it measures the change in prices over time for a single commodity. Simple price indexes are discussed in Section 22.1.

Now consider a more complicated problem. Suppose we want to describe how the cost of feeding a family of four has changed since 1975. First we need to determine the contents of a typical market basket of food consumed by a family of four, and then we need to put a dollar value on the items. The prices of the items in the basket all vary from year to year. To measure the typical change in prices, we need to weight each price by the quantity purchased. This yields a *weighted aggregate price index.* Such indexes are discussed in Section 22.2.

The most important and widely used price index is the *Consumer Price Index* (CPI), also known as the *cost-of-living index,* which is prepared by the U.S. Department of Labor. The CPI is discussed in Section 22.3. Section 22.4 discusses another important index, the Dow Jones industrial average.

Every index number must have a base period, for which time the value of the index is 100. In constructing the index, all other values in the series are expressed as percentages of the value for this base period. The choice of the base period is arbitrary, but because all values of the index depend on the base period, a relatively recent period that is not particularly exceptional should be used.

Besides choosing a base period for the index, it is necessary to select the type of index to be used. For example, *price indexes* measure changes in prices paid by consumers or changes in prices received by producers at the wholesale level, *wage indexes* measure changes in wages earned by labor, *quantity indexes* measure changes in units produced, and *value indexes* measure changes in the total dollar value of various goods and services.

A *simple index* measures changes in a single time series, such as the price of a single commodity. An index showing the change in coal production over time is an example of a simple quantity index. The index measures the quantity of coal produced each year as a percentage of the quantity of coal produced during some base period. A **composite index** measures price, quantity, or value changes over time for several variables. The Consumer Price Index is a composite index because it takes into account the prices of hundreds of different commodities. The Producer Price Index, the Gross National Product deflator, the Federal Reserve Board's Index of Industrial Production, and the Dow Jones industrial average are other examples of composite indexes.

22.1 ▪ *Simple Price Indexes*

In this section, we consider how to measure price movements over time for a single item, such as the cost of tuition for a single semester at college. One way of describing such price movements is to plot the data on a scatter diagram. Another way is to construct a *simple price index* by choosing a base period and expressing the price in each period as a percentage of the base period price. An index value of 118 means that the price in year n is 18% higher than it was in year 0.

Definition: Simple Price Index

Suppose we have a time series of observations showing the price of a single item. To form a **simple price index**, choose one period as the base period and express the price in every period as a percentage of the base period price. Let P_0 denote the price in the base period and let P_n denote the price in period n. The price index for period n is denoted $I_{n,0}$ where

$$I_{n,0} = 100(P_n/P_0)$$

The index for the base year is always 100 because

$$I_{0,0} = 100(P_0/P_0) = 100$$

Example 22.1

Constructing a Simple Price Index: Suppose the cost of tuition for one semester at a certain university was \$500 in 1985, \$600 in 1986, and \$680 in 1987. Construct a simple price index using 1985 as the base period.

Solution: Using 1985 as base period, the price indexes are as follows:

$$I_{85,85} = \frac{P_{85}}{P_{85}} \times 100 = \frac{500}{500} \times 100 = 100$$

$$I_{86,85} = \frac{P_{86}}{P_{85}} \times 100 = \frac{600}{500} \times 100 = 120$$

$$I_{87,85} = \frac{P_{87}}{P_{85}} \times 100 = \frac{680}{500} \times 100 = 136$$

Thus, the cost of tuition was 20% higher in 1986 than in 1985 and 36% higher in 1987 than in 1985. ■

Exercises for Section 22.1

1. In 1986 a price index had a value of 150. In the following year the price index had a value of 160.

a. Did prices rise by 10% during the year?

b. By what percentage did prices rise during the year?

c. If we decided to use 1986 as the base period, what would be the value of the index in 1987?

2. The accompanying table shows the price of a share of stock for the first 12 weeks of 1988.

Week	Price	Week	Price
1	$\$33\frac{1}{8}$	7	$\$35\frac{3}{8}$
2	$33\frac{7}{8}$	8	$34\frac{3}{4}$
3	$34\frac{3}{4}$	9	$34\frac{3}{4}$
4	$34\frac{3}{8}$	10	$35\frac{1}{4}$
5	35	11	$38\frac{3}{4}$
6	$34\frac{7}{8}$	12	$37\frac{1}{8}$

a. Form a price index with week 1 as the base.

b. Form a price index with week 4 as the base.

3. The following data show the number of people (in millions) below the poverty level in the United States for selected years (from the *Statistical Abstract of the United States, 1988,* p. 434):

Year	1979	1983	1984	1985	1986
Number	26.1	35.5	33.7	33.1	32.4

Construct a simple index using 1979 as the base period.

4. The accompanying data show federal funding in millions of dollars for research and development in economics for various years (from the *Statistical Abstract of the United States, 1988,* p. 559):

Year	Funding	Year	Funding
1976	138	1983	166
1978	163	1984	147
1979	182	1985	160
1980	193	1986	147
1981	207	1987	163
1982	157		

Construct a simple index using 1976 as the base period.

5. The following data show the number of deaths in thousands from motor vehicle accidents in the United States for selected years (from the *Statistical Abstract of the United States, 1988,* p. 579):

Year	1970	1972	1975	1980	1984	1985
Deaths	54.8	56.5	46.0	53.5	46.5	46.2

Construct a simple index using 1970 as the base period.

6. The following data show the price per pound in cents for broiler chickens for various years (from the *Statistical Abstract of the United States, 1988,* p. 635):

Year	1978	1979	1980	1981	1982	1983	1984	1985	1986
Price	26.3	26.0	27.7	28.4	26.9	28.6	33.7	30.1	34.5

Construct a simple index using 1978 as the base period.

7. The following data show lumber production in billions of board feet in the United States for various years (from the *Statistical Abstract of the United States, 1988,* p. 642):

Year	1976	1977	1978	1979	1980	1981	1982	1983	1984	1985
Lumber Production	37.0	39.4	40.5	40.6	35.4	31.7	30.0	34.6	37.1	36.3

Construct a simple index using 1980 as the base period.

22.2 ▪ *Weighted Aggregate Price Indexes*

A simple price index is inadequate for tracing changes in price for a bundle of goods because it does not account for the relative quantities purchased of the various goods. If we merely sum the prices of items without taking into account the quantities in which they are purchased, we obtain an *unweighted aggregate price index.* For example, consider a family that consumes the three goods milk, bread, and cereal in various quantities. In 1967, the price of a quart of milk was \$0.20, a loaf of bread cost \$0.25, and a 12-ounce box of cereal cost \$0.50. A family that purchased one unit of each item in 1967 would have spent

$$0.20 + 0.25 + 0.50 = \$0.95$$

In 1988, suppose a quart of milk cost \$0.80, a loaf of bread cost \$1.00, and the cereal cost \$1.00. A family that purchased one unit of each item in 1988 would have spent

$$0.80 + 1.00 + 1.00 = \$2.80$$

Using 1967 as the base year, the unweighted aggregate price index for 1988 is

$$100(2.80/0.95) = 294.7$$

Did the cost of food increase 194.7% for the family? The unweighted index does not answer this question because it does not take into account the quantities purchased. For example, milk and bread both quadrupled in price while cereal doubled in price. A family that spent more of its budget on milk and bread would face a greater increase in costs than a family that spent more of its budget on cereal. When we take into account the quantities of each item consumed, we are calculating a **weighted aggregate price index**.

To measure the average change in price for a market basket of goods, we need to know the price of each item in the market basket and the quantity purchased of each item. There are three commonly used methods for forming a weighted aggregate price index.

The Laspeyres Index

The *Laspeyres price index* is a weighted aggregate price index that uses only the quantities purchased in the base period and compares their total cost in the base period with their total cost in other periods. The index was developed by the German statesman and economist Etienne Laspeyres (1834–1913).

The sum $\Sigma_{i=1}^{K} P_{0i}Q_{0i}$ represents the dollar cost of purchasing all K base period quantities at base period prices. The sum $\Sigma_{i=1}^{K} P_{ti}Q_{0i}$ represents the dollar cost of purchasing those same K quantities using the prices prevailing during period t. The ratio of these two values multiplied by 100 yields the Laspeyres price index.

Definition: Laspeyres Price Index

Let P_{0i} be the price and Q_{0i} the quantity purchased of the ith item in the base period (period 0) for $i = 1, 2, \ldots, K$. Let P_{ti} denote the price of the same item during period t. The **Laspeyres price index** for period t is

$$\frac{\sum_{i=1}^{K} P_{ti}Q_{0i}}{\sum_{i=1}^{K} P_{0i}Q_{0i}} \times 100$$

The Laspeyres price index is a comprehensive measure of the average change in prices between the base period and period t. A useful feature of this index is that only the base period quantities are used, because collecting quantity information in every period can be very expensive and time consuming. However, this feature is also a disadvantage. Because only base period quantities are used, the index does not reflect changes in consumption patterns. For two periods that are close together this fact does not pose a serious problem, but over longer periods of time, consumption patterns are likely to change and the index may lose some of its usefulness. Nevertheless, the Laspeyres price index is by far the most widely used price index.

Example 22.2

Constructing a Laspeyres Price Index: The data in Table 22.1 show some typical prices and quantities for daily food purchases by the athletic department for its basketball team. The quantities represent the average amounts purchased daily in 1985 and the prices are unit prices in 1985 and 1987. Construct the Laspeyres price index for 1987 with 1985 as the base period.

TABLE 22.1 **Prices and quantities of food purchased for Example 22.2**

Commodity	P_{85}	P_{87}	Q_{85}	$P_{85}Q_{85}$	$P_{87}Q_{85}$
Meat per pound	\$1.00	\$1.50	30	\$30.00	\$ 45.00
Milk per gallon	0.90	1.15	40	36.00	46.00
Bread per loaf	0.40	0.50	30	12.00	15.00
Fruit per pound	0.50	0.65	10	5.00	6.50
				\$83.00	\$112.50

Solution: The sums in Table 22.1 show that what cost \$83.00 in 1985 cost \$112.50 in 1987. The Laspeyres price index is thus

$$I_{87,85} = \frac{\Sigma\ P_{87}Q_{85}}{\Sigma\ P_{85}Q_{85}} \times 100$$

$$= \frac{\$112.50}{\$\ 83.00} \times 100 = 136$$

Thus, in 1987, it cost 36% more to purchase the commodities described in Table 22.1 than in 1985. If the basketball team ate the same meals in 1987 as in 1985, the cost of feeding the team increased 36%. ■

The Paasche Index

The Laspeyres price index uses base period weights Q_{0i} in both the numerator and denominator. The *Paasche index,* first proposed by the German economist Herman Paasche (1851–1925), uses quantity data for each time period. The sum $\Sigma_{i=1}^{K}\ P_{ti}Q_{ti}$ represents the total cost of purchasing the K quantities purchased in period t, while the sum $\Sigma_{i=1}^{K}\ P_{0i}Q_{ti}$ measures what the same K quantities of goods would have cost during the base period.

Definition: Paasche Price Index

Let P_{0i} be the price of commodity i in the base year, and let Q_{ti} be the quantity purchased in period t for $i = 1, 2, \ldots, K$. Let P_{ti} denote the corresponding price during period t. The **Paasche price index** is

$$\frac{\sum_{i=1}^{K} P_{ti}Q_{ti}}{\sum_{i=1}^{K} P_{0i}Q_{ti}} \times 100$$

Example 22.3 **Constructing a Paasche Price Index:** Suppose that, as in Example 22.2, we wish to construct a price index to measure changes in the daily expenditures for food by an athletic department. Assume the quantities listed in Table 22.2 represent the average daily quantities purchased in 1987.

TABLE 22.2 Prices and quantities of food purchased for Example 22.3

Commodity	P_{85}	P_{87}	Q_{87}	$P_{85}Q_{87}$	$P_{87}Q_{87}$
Meat per pound	$1.00	$1.50	40	$40.00	$ 60.00
Milk per gallon	0.90	1.15	40	36.00	46.00
Bread per loaf	0.40	0.50	20	8.00	10.00
Fruit per pound	0.50	0.65	20	10.00	13.00
				$94.00	$129.00

Solution: The sums in Table 22.2 show that what cost $129.00 in 1987 would have cost $94.00 in 1985. The Paasche price index is

$$I_{87,87} = \frac{\Sigma P_{87}Q_{87}}{\Sigma P_{85}Q_{87}} \times 100$$

$$= \frac{\$129.00}{\$94.00} \times 100 = 137$$

Thus, it cost 37% more to purchase the commodities described in Table 22.2 in 1987 than in 1985. ■

In Example 22.2, using the same prices but base period quantities, the Laspeyres index was 136. Using non-base-period quantities, the Paasche index is 137. These values are very similar, but this does not have to be the case. If the quantities consumed changed dramatically between the base period and the nonbase period, the two indexes could give substantially different values for the rate of inflation.

A serious disadvantage of the Paasche index is that year-to-year comparisons of price changes are not possible, because every year a new set of weights Q_{ti} is used. Since it is very expensive to obtain this quantity information, the Paasche index is not widely used.

The Fisher Price Index

The *Fisher price index* is the geometric mean of the Laspeyres and Paasche indexes and is designed as a compromise between the two measures.

Definition: Fisher Price Index

The **Fisher price index** is the geometric mean of the Laspeyres and Paasche indexes. It is calculated as

$$\sqrt{\left(\frac{\Sigma P_{ti}Q_{0i}}{\Sigma P_{0i}Q_{0i}}\right)\left(\frac{\Sigma P_{ti}Q_{ti}}{\Sigma P_{0i}Q_{ti}}\right)} \times 100$$

The Fisher index is named after Professor Irving Fisher, who first proposed it in 1922 in his book *The Making of Index Numbers*. Like the Paasche index, Fisher's index suffers from the disadvantage that new quantities must be calculated each year. Thus, it is expensive to calculate. Furthermore, year-to-year comparisons using the Fisher index are difficult because new quantities Q_{ti} are used each year.

Marshall–Edgeworth Price Index

Another proposed price index is the Marshall–Edgeworth price index. This index is constructed by using as quantity weights the arithmetic mean, or average, of the base year and given year quantities. That is, the weights are $\frac{1}{2}(Q_{0i} + Q_{ti})$. The formula for calculating the Marshall–Edgeworth price index is

$$\frac{\Sigma\, P_{ti}(Q_{0i} + Q_{ti})}{\Sigma\, P_{0i}(Q_{0i} + Q_{ti})} \times 100$$

The preceding discussion shows that a serious problem in constructing a price index is finding a suitable set of weights to use. Because prices of different items do not all change at the same rate, it is important to weight the price changes in some way. Simply adding the prices together is unsatisfactory because this procedure fails to take into account that some price changes are more important than others. A small price change in a commodity that is purchased many times in large quantities may be more important than a large price change in some commodity that is purchased only once or twice in a decade, such as a home appliance.

Some weighting scheme has to be used to construct a meaningful price index, but no weighting scheme has been found that is entirely satisfactory. The Laspeyres price index, which uses base period quantities as weights, is by far the most widely used price index.

Exercises for Section 22.2

1. The accompanying data show prices and quantities of food purchased by a family in 1986 and 1988. Use 1986 as the base period and assume that the prices are unit prices.

Commodity	P_{86}	Q_{86}	P_{88}	Q_{88}
Meat per pound	\$2.60	9	\$3.20	11
Vegetables per pound	1.18	8	1.28	7
Milk per gallon	0.90	5	1.05	5
Bread per loaf	0.45	3	0.65	4
Fruit per pound	1.15	3	1.50	6

Calculate the following price indexes:
a. Laspeyres   b. Paasche

2. Write answers to the following:
a. How do you construct the Fisher price index?
b. Why is the Fisher index seldom used?

c. What is a possible deficiency in the Laspeyres price index?
d. What are several deficiencies in the Paasche price index?

3. Use the data in Exercise 1 and calculate the following price indexes for 1986 using 1988 as the base period:
a. Laspeyres b. Paasche

4. The cost in cents per pound of meat products for several years is listed in the accompanying table.

Year	Beef	Steak	Ham	Chicken	Pork
1985	49¢	89¢	95¢	47¢	90¢
1986	53	94	99	52	97
1987	57	103	103	54	107
1988	61	110	107	60	112

a. Compute a simple price index for each type of meat.
b. Compute a Laspeyres price index using the following 1987 quantities: beef, 115 pounds; steak, 60 pounds; ham, 50 pounds; chicken, 95 pounds; and pork, 25 pounds.
c. Compute a Paasche price index for meat (base period = 1987) using 1988 quantities: beef, 120 pounds; steak, 85 pounds; ham, 30 pounds; chicken, 80 pounds; and pork, 20 pounds.
d. Use parts (b) and (c) to compute Fisher's price index.

5. Let the price of a box of cereal in 1986, 1987, and 1988 be \$0.77, \$0.85, and \$0.95, respectively. Use 1986 as the base period.
a. Calculate the price relatives.
b. Construct a simple price index.
c. Use 1987 as the base period. Construct a simple price index.
d. Convert the price index having base year 1986 into a price index having base year 1987.

6. Answer the following:
a. How do you calculate a simple aggregate price index?
b. Give two reasons that this index is an unsatisfactory way of measuring price changes.
c. Why is a Laspeyres index a potentially bad measure of price changes?

22.3 ▪ *The Consumer Price Index*

The *Consumer Price Index* (CPI) is the best-known price index. It is published monthly in the *Monthly Labor Review* by the Bureau of Labor Statistics of the U.S. Department of Labor. The CPI is designed to measure price changes in a typical market basket of goods and services purchased in a retail market by a typical urban clerical worker's family. Approximately 400 different items, such as food items, clothing, rent, luxuries, medical expenses, and recreational expenses are included in the CPI market basket. The CPI is computed using data obtained from a random sample of urban clerical workers' families. Besides the nationwide CPI, a CPI (or cost-of-living index) is also published for every major metropolitan area. With these metropolitan indexes, the cost of living for different cities in the United States can be compared. The CPI is essentially a Laspeyres price index.

Many union contracts contain cost-of-living escalation clauses, which tie increases in pay to increases in the CPI. In addition, the fiscal and monetary policies of the federal government are frequently influenced by movements in the CPI, as are the behavior and income of consumers and investors. Thus it is important to understand what the CPI measures and how it is calculated.

Actually, three consumer price indexes are published in the *Monthly Labor Review,* all designed to measure rates of inflation in the U.S. economy. The first index is called the "Consumer Price Index for Urban Wage Earners and Clerical Workers"; we will denote it as "CPI-O," to indicate that it is the old version of the CPI. The monthly price data for the CPI-O are obtained from personal visits, phone calls, and mail surveys in 56 urban areas. First published in 1919, the CPI-O has been revised several times to keep it up-to-date. The items in the typical market basket and the weights applied to these items were revised in 1940, 1946, 1953, 1964, and 1978. The CPI-O is limited because it measures changes in the prices of goods purchased by urban wage earners and clerical workers, a group representing only about 40% of the nation's population.

In 1978 the Bureau of Labor Statistics began publishing another consumer price index, the "Consumer Price Index for All Urban Consumers," which we will denote by "CPI-U." The CPI-U is based on data obtained in 85 urban areas and applies to all urban consumers; it represents expenses for approximately 80% of the nation's population.

The third consumer price index is called the "Revised Consumer Price Index for Urban Wage Earners and Clerical Workers," first published in 1978. Let us denote this index by "CPI-W." Like the CPI-O, the CPI-W represents only about 40% of the population, but it is calculated using weights based on data obtained in 85 urban areas rather than the 56 urban areas surveyed for the CPI-O weights.

As a general measure of inflation, the CPI-U is probably the best indicator because it uses relatively current weights and covers 80% of the population. Like the CPI-O, monthly price data for the CPI-U and CPI-W are obtained by personal visits, phone calls, and mail surveys. Each index is based on the prices of more than 400 goods and services.

Criticisms of the Consumer Price Index

There are several conceptual difficulties in measuring general trends in consumer prices using the Consumer Price Index.

First, the CPI is not really representative of all American families because the quantity weights are based on a sample taken mostly from middle-income, urban families. If consumption differs among lower- and middle- and upper-income families, so would the rate of inflation experienced by these groups.

Second, a family's personal rate of inflation may be quite different from that indicated by the CPI if it can purchase some goods at fixed prices. For example, housing costs have been one of the most rapidly rising components of the CPI. However, a family that owns a home and pays a fixed mortgage will not experience a rise in housing costs. The CPI would overestimate such a family's inflation rate.

Third, a major difficulty in computing the CPI concerns the measurement of quality changes over time. When a product's price has increased, part of the increase may be for improvements. In this case only part of the price increase represents pure inflation. Measuring quality improvements in such things as clothing, computers, and automobiles is extremely difficult. For example, although the price of a car has increased over time, cars today come equipped with many more options than those of yesteryear. These amenities include air conditioning, cruise control, and electric door locks—options that were unheard of 25 or 30 years ago. Thus, a car purchased in 1959 is not equivalent to a car purchased in 1988. In addition, many modern products did not exist years ago, and others are only remotely comparable to their counterparts of years ago.

The CPI uses constant quantity weights based on the base period (i.e., constant consumption patterns over time). Thus, it assumes that consumers do not substitute for those items whose relative prices are increasing. However, to keep the CPI up-to-date and meaningful, every few years the Bureau of Labor Statistics studies the consumer market basket to determine if any items should be added or deleted and if quantity weights should be changed to reflect changes in consumers' taste.

Because of the problems in comparing goods over time, one should be especially careful in interpreting price indexes and price changes that cover long periods of time. Table 22.3 shows the CPI for selected years. When interpreting the data, keep in mind that (1) the typical market basket of goods is different today than it was years ago, (2) many new products have been introduced, and (3) the quality of many goods has improved over time.

TABLE 22.3
Consumer Price Index (1967 = 100), 1929–1987

Year	CPI	Year	CPI
1929	51.3	1965	94.5
1933	38.8	1967	100.0
1939	41.6	1970	116.3
1940	42.0	1975	161.2
1945	53.9	1980	246.8
1950	72.1	1985	322.2
1955	80.2	1986	328.4
1960	88.7	1987	340.4

Source: Economic Report of the President, 1988 (Washington, D.C.: U.S. Government Printing Office, 1988), p. 313.

Because of the difficulties in constructing an aggregate price index like the Consumer Price Index, some economists treat such indexes with skepticism. Indeed, some argue that the CPI grossly overestimates the rate of inflation. To test their claim, they suggest that we give consumers $1000 and offer them the opportunity of purchasing $1000 worth of goods from either the 1955 Sears catalogue or the current Sears catalogue. The skeptics predict that most people would select goods from the current catalogue at current prices. If the skeptics are correct, this is strong evidence that the CPI has grossly overestimated the rate of inflation—at least with respect to the types of items included in the Sears catalogue.

Calculating Real Income Using a Price Index

The CPI is useful for determining changes in the standard of living over time. For example, if your annual income increases at approximately the same rate as prices, then your standard of living is unchanged because approximately the same goods can be purchased at the end of the period that could have been purchased at the start of the period. If your income increases faster than prices, your standard of living improves because you can purchase more goods at the end of the period than you could have at the start of the period. Similarly, if prices increase faster than your income, your standard of living declines.

To measure changes in income over time, we should compare the quantities of goods that incomes could buy at different periods. Thus, we should adjust the incomes to take into account changes in prices. When we compute the value of income in terms of prices prevailing in a base period, we are calculating *real income*.

Definition: Real Income

Choose a specific base period and let the Consumer Price Index in period t be CPI_t. Let Y_t denote nominal income in period t. To calculate **real income**, use the formula

$$\text{Real income}_t = \frac{\text{Nominal income}_t}{\text{CPI}_t} \times 100$$

$$= \frac{Y_t}{\text{CPI}_t} \times 100$$

Example 22.4

Calculating Real Income: A person's income in some base period is \$20,000. In period t, the person's income has increased to \$25,000. The CPI for period t is 120. Find the person's real income based on prices in the base year.

Solution: Real income is

$$\text{Real income}_t = 100(25{,}000/120) = 20{,}833.33$$

The person's standard of living increased, because in year t the person could buy everything that was purchased in year 0 and still have \$833.33 left over. Prices increased by 20%, while the person's income increased by 25%. ■

Calculating Real Gross National Product in Constant Prices

Table 22.4 shows the nominal Gross National Product (GNP) for various years. The term *nominal* means that no adjustment has been made for any price changes during this period. To determine if the production of goods and services has increased over time, the quantity of goods and services produced in different years should be valued at constant prices.

When GNP is measured in terms of prices prevailing at the time of measurement, it is said to be measured in *current dollars* and is called the *nominal GNP*. Measuring GNP year after year in terms of prices that prevailed in a base period yields a new series measured in *constant dollars*. This series is called the *real GNP*.

TABLE 22.4
Gross national product in current and constant dollars, 1950–1987

Year	Nominal GNP (in billions of current dollars)	Consumer Price Index (1967 = 100)	Real GNP (in billions of 1967 dollars)
1950	\$ 288.3	58.5	\$ 492.8
1960	515.3	88.7	580.9
1967	816.4	100.0	816.4
1970	1015.5	116.3	873.2
1980	2732.0	246.8	1107.0
1987	4486.2	340.4	1317.9

Source: Economic Report of the President, 1988 (Washington, D.C.: U.S. Government Printing Office, 1988), pp. 248, 313.

Calculating Real GNP in Constant Dollars

Suppose we have a series showing the Gross National Product in current dollars for various years. Denote nominal GNP in year t by GNP_t. Let CPI_t be the value of the Consumer Price Index in year t for a given base period. Real GNP measured in constant base period dollars is

$$\text{Real GNP}_t = 100(\text{GNP}_t/\text{CPI}_t)$$

Example 22.5

Calculating Real GNP in Constant Dollars: Refer to the data in Table 22.4. Calculate real GNP for each period and calculate the percent increase in output from 1980 to 1987.

Solution: The data show that what cost \$100 in 1967 could be purchased for \$246.80 in 1980 or \$340.40 in 1987. Based on 1967 prices, real GNP for 1980 is

$$\text{Real GNP}_{1980} = 100(2732.0/246.8) = \$1107.0 \text{ billion}$$

Similarly, based on 1967 prices, real GNP for 1987 is

$$\text{Real GNP}_{1987} = 100(4486.2/340.4) = \$1317.9 \text{ billion}$$

Now, let us determine the amount of growth in output from 1980 to 1987. Nominal GNP was \$2732.0 billion in 1980 and \$4486.2 billion in 1987. Thus, in dollar terms, GNP increased by

$$(4486.2 - 2732.0)/2732.0 = 64\%$$

Did output really increase 64% from 1980 to 1987? No. Much of this increase in dollar output was due to the large increase in prices and not to any increase in output.

From 1980 to 1987, real GNP increased by

$$(1317.9 - 1107.0)/1107.0 = 19\%$$

Thus, although nominal GNP increased by 64% between 1980 and 1987, real GNP (output) increased by only 19%. The rest of the increase was due to inflation. ■

Changing the Base Period

Series of index numbers are frequently updated by changing the base period to a more recent period. For example, suppose we have a price index that uses 1967 as the base period, and we want to create a new index whose base period is 1982. To do this, proceed as described in the accompanying box on changing a base period.

Changing the Base Period of an Index

Suppose we have an index that uses base period 0. Let $I_{t,0}$ denote the value of the index during period t, and let $I_{c,0}$ denote the value of the index in period c (using base period 0). To convert $I_{t,0}$ to a new index value having base period c, divide the value $I_{t,0}$ by $I_{c,0}$ and multiply by 100, as in the following formula:

$$I_{t,c} = \frac{I_{t,0}}{I_{c,0}} \times 100$$

Example 22.6

Changing the Base Period of an Index: The second column in Table 22.5 shows the Consumer Price Index for selected years using 1967 as the base period. Let us create a new index having 1982 as the base period.

Solution: Consider the new index value for 1987. Based on 1967 prices, the index for 1982 is 289.1 and the index for 1987 is 340.4. The new index value for 1987 based on 1982 as the base period is

$$I_{87,82} = (340.4/289.1) \times 100 = 117.7$$

Prices in 1987 were 17.7% higher than they were in 1982. Other values of the index based on 1982 as the base period are shown in the last column of Table 22.5.

TABLE 22.5
Consumer price index with different base periods

Year	1967 = Base Period	1982 = Base Period
1962	90.6	100(90.6/289.1) = 31.3
1967	100.0	100(100.0/289.1) = 34.6
1972	125.3	100(125.3/289.1) = 43.3
1977	181.5	100(181.5/289.1) = 62.8
1982	289.1	100(289.1/289.1) = 100.0
1987	340.4	100(340.4/289.1) = 117.7

Source: Economic Report of the President, 1988 (Washington, D.C.: U.S. Government Printing Office, 1988), p. 313.

■

Exercises for Section 22.3

1. State four problems in measuring changes in the Consumer Price Index.
2. Explain why the Consumer Price Index is not representative of all American families.

3. Average hourly (nominal) earnings in the United States for selected years were as follows: 1955, \$1.71; 1965, \$2.76; 1975, \$4.53; and 1985, \$8.57.

a. Use the Consumer Price Index values in Table 22.3 to calculate the real wage (in 1967 dollars) for each of these years.

b. Which decade had the greatest growth in nominal wages? In real wages?

4. The accompanying data show nominal Gross National Product (in billions of dollars) for the years 1981 to 1986. Also shown is the Consumer Price Index for those years (using 1967 = 100).

a. Find real GNP in terms of 1967 dollars.

b. Convert the price index into a new price index having 1982 as the base period.

c. Find real GNP in terms of 1982 dollars.

Year	Nominal Gross National Product	Consumer Price Index (1967 = 100)
1981	3052.6	272.4
1982	3166.0	289.1
1983	3405.7	298.4
1984	3777.2	311.1
1985	4010.3	322.2
1986	4235.0	328.4
1987	4486.2	340.4

Source: Economic Report of the President, 1988 (Washington, D.C.: U.S. Government Printing Office, 1988), pp. 248, 313.

5. Refer to the data in Exercise 4.

a. Find the percent increase in prices from 1981 to 1987.

b. Suppose an employee's annual income rose from \$20,200 in 1981 to \$23,000 in 1987. Did the employee's real income increase or decrease over this period?

6. An employee notices that the Consumer Price Index increased from 326.4 in 1986 to 340.4 in 1987. The employee observes that

$$340.4 - 326.4 = 14.0$$

and requests a 14% raise to maintain his standard of living. What would you say if you were the boss?

22.4 ▪ *The Dow Jones Industrial Average*

The Dow Jones industrial average is one of the best-known financial indexes. It is used to give a rough indication of what happened in the stock market on a given day. The first Dow Jones industrial average, published in 1896, was based on the movements of 12 common stocks. By 1928, the index had been expanded to include 30 stocks. Occasionally new stocks have been substituted into the index to be sure that the index remains representative of a substantial part of the industrial sector of the economy.

Because stock splits tend to cut a stock's price in half or even more, it is necessary to adjust the Dow Jones average every time one of the component stocks splits. Consequently, the Dow Jones average is not just a simple average of the prices of the stocks included in the index.

To show how the Dow Jones average is computed, assume that we want to construct a stock index showing the average price of the securities of three firms. Assume that the stocks of these firms sell at \$20, \$40, and \$60 per share, respectively. The initial average would be $(20 + 40 + 60)/3 = \$40$.

Now assume that the stock initially selling at \$60 per share has a 2-for-1 split, so that each share of the third stock is now worth \$30. If we did not take the stock split into account, we would obtain

$$\frac{20 + 40 + 30}{3} = \$30$$

In this case, the average price of the three stocks would have declined by \$10 per share, even though the value of the stocks after the split was the same as before the split. The method of calculating the Dow Jones average is designed to avoid this problem.

To compensate for the split, the Dow Jones average adjusts the divisor to keep the average at \$40, its value before the split. That is, the Dow Jones average uses as a divisor the number D such that

$$\frac{20 + 40 + 30}{D} = \$40$$

In this case, the divisor becomes $D = 2.25$.

Now if the first stock increases in price from \$20 to \$25, the new Dow Jones average is computed as

$$\frac{25 + 40 + 30}{2.25} = \$42.22$$

Initially the divisor D for the Dow Jones industrial average was 30, because the average was computed using the stock prices of 30 firms. Because of numerous stock splits, mergers, and so forth, the divisor has continually changed. As of January 1, 1988, the divisor was 0.754; the value of the divisor is published daily in the financial section of the *Wall Street Journal*.

The Dow Jones industrial average does not weight the prices of the stocks in the index by the sizes of the companies, the assets of the companies, the number of shares outstanding, or any other factor.

The data in Table 22.6 show the Dow Jones industrial average for selected years. At the end of 1987, the index was nearly 10 times as high as in 1950. From 1965 through 1980 the index actually declined; the 1980s, however, have been a period of rapid growth. Recently the behavior of the index has become much more volatile and less predictable. In August of 1987, the index reached a high of 2722.42. On "Black Monday," October 19, 1987, the index dropped 508 points, the largest single-day decline in history. Since then there have been many days when the index has fluctuated by more than 100 points.

As of January 1, 1988, the Dow Jones industrial average represented the average closing prices of the following 30 large companies:

Alcoa	Exxon	Philip Morris
Allied Signal	General Electric	Primerica
American Express	General Motors	Procter & Gamble
AT&T	Goodyear	Sears Roebuck
Bethlehem Steel	IBM	Texaco
Boeing Aircraft	International Paper	Union Carbide
Chevron	McDonald's	United Technologies
Coca-Cola	Merck	USX
DuPont	Minnesota Mining & Manufacturing	Westinghouse
Eastman Kodak	Navistar	Woolworth's

TABLE 22.6
Dow Jones industrial average, 1950–1987

Year	Average	Year	Average
1950	216.31	1975	802.49
1955	442.72	1980	891.41
1960	618.04	1985	1328.23
1965	910.88	1986	1895.95
1970	753.19	1987	1938.83

Source: Economic Report of the President, 1987 (Washington, D.C.: U.S. Government Printing Office and *The Wall Street Journal*).

Besides the Dow Jones industrial average, Dow Jones and Company prepares other stock market averages, which are published daily in the *Wall Street Journal.* The *Dow Jones transportation average* represents an average of the prices of 20 different transportation-related securities, including American Airlines, Chesapeake and Ohio, Eastern Airlines, Santa Fe Industries, Southern Pacific, Southern Railway, TWA, Union Pacific Corporation, and U.S. Freight Company.

The *Dow Jones utilities average* represents an average of the prices of 15 different utilities, including stocks such as Columbia Gas System, Commonwealth Edison, Consolidated Natural Gas, Detroit Edison, Houston Light and Power, Pacific Gas and Electric, and Southern California Edison.

The *Dow Jones composite average* is an index of the prices of the 65 stocks included in the Dow Jones industrial, transportation, and utilities indexes.

The Standard and Poor's Corporation also prepares a series of daily and weekly stock indexes. Because the price of each company's stock is multiplied by the company's number of outstanding shares of common stocks, the current market value of the entire issue is incorporated into the index. The total market values of all the stocks included in the index are added together. This composite current value is then expressed as an index relative to the base market value of 10 for the period 1941 to 1943. The basic indexes published by Standard and Poor's consist of 400 industrials, 20 transportation companies, 40 utilities, 40 financial firms, and 500 combined stocks. These common stocks represent more than 90% of the market value of all common stocks listed on the New York Stock Exchange. The Standard & Poor indexes are computed daily at the opening and closing as well as at each hour of the market day; they are published in the *Wall Street Journal* and in many other newspapers.

Chapter 22 Summary

An *index number* expresses a value at one point in time as a percentage of the value at another time, called the *base period*. The index for the base year always is 100. A *simple index* measures changes in just one variable, such as the price of a gallon of milk or a loaf of bread. An *aggregate price index* is used to compare the relative price of a set of items for any year with the price of those same items during the base year. The prices for the items can be averaged (simple aggregate price index) or weighted by the corresponding quantity purchased of each item (weighted aggregate price index). Different indexes can be constructed using different weighting schemes. Methods include using base year quantities (the *Laspeyres index*) or reference year quantities (the *Paasche index*).

The *Consumer Price Index* (CPI), which is a Laspeyres index, is the best-known price index. The CPI tries to measure changes in prices after taking into account changes in quality, the introduction of new products, and changes in consumers' tastes and buying habits.

The nominal Gross National Product (nominal GNP) is the dollar value of GNP in current dollars. To measure changes in output, it is necessary to compare GNP in constant dollars after changes in prices have been removed from the data. To calculate GNP in constant dollars, divide the nominal GNP in any period by the value of the CPI in the corresponding period.

The *Dow Jones industrial average* is an average of the prices of 30 popular stocks on the New York Stock Exchange. The index does not take into account the number of shares outstanding. The denominator of the index changes from time to time to take into account stock splits, which reduce the price of a share of stock but not the value of the total number of shares outstanding.

Chapter 22 ▪ Supplementary Exercises

1. The following data show the average prices in dollars for concrete used in road construction on highway contracts.

Year	1983	1984	1985	1986	1987	1988
Price per cubic yard	2.45	2.54	2.66	2.82	2.91	3.04

Calculate a price index for prices using the following years as base periods:
a. 1983 = 100 b. 1986 = 100 c. 1988 = 100

2. Suppose that the only data available on prices in a certain region of China come from two different sources. The price indexes from the two sources are shown in the accompanying table. Note that the sources used different base years.

Year	Source 1	Source 2
1982	100	
1983	107	
1984	111	
1985	116	
1986	122	100
1987		106
1988		112

a. Splice the two indexes to form a single series having base 1982. To do this, multiply all the values from source 2 by 1.22.
b. Splice the indexes using 1988 as base year.
c. Is the percent increase in prices from 1985 to 1987 independent of the base year? Check by using your answers to parts (a) and (b).

3. The following data show the Gross National Product in billions of dollars using current dollars and constant 1982 dollars:

Year	Current Dollars	1982 Dollars
1985	3998.1	3585.2
1986	4208.5	3676.5

a. Determine the price index for 1985 using 1982 = 100.
b. By how much did prices increase from 1985 to 1986?

4. The accompanying data show the annual sales revenues of Johnson's Restaurants, Inc., for the years 1980 to 1986. Also shown are the values of an aggregate price index using 1967 as the base year.
a. Restate the sales revenues for each year in terms of base year prices.
b. What type of information is disclosed by the time series of revenues at constant prices?

Year	Sales Revenue (in thousands)	Price Index (1967 = 100)
1980	$447	247
1981	510	272
1982	555	289
1983	588	298
1984	623	311
1985	660	322
1986	740	328

5. The following data appeared in a corporation's annual report:

Year	1985	1987	1988
Average hourly wage of employees	$4.92	$5.12	$5.37
Consumer Price Index (1985 = 100)	100.0	101.9	105.6

a. Compute the percent increase in wages from year to year.
b. Compute the real wage in each year using 1985 as the base period.
c. Compute the percent increase in real wages from year to year using the results from part (b).
d. Compare the answers from parts (a) and (c). What conclusion do you reach?

6. A firm uses three raw materials in manufacturing its product. The accompanying data show the prices and quantities consumed in 1978, 1983, and 1988.
a. Construct a Laspeyres price index using 1978 as the base year.
b. Construct a Laspeyres index using 1988 as the base year.
c. Construct a Paasche index using 1978 as the base year.

	Price per Unit			Quantity		
Material	1978	1983	1988	1978	1983	1988
A	$8	$10	$11	10	14	19
B	4	5	8	20	30	45
C	3	5	5	25	35	50

7. A construction firm has compiled data on the hourly wage rates of its employees and the number of hours worked, shown in the accompanying table:

	Hourly Wage Rate			Total Hours Worked (in thousands)		
Employees	1986	1987	1988	1986	1987	1988
Carpenters	$5	$6	$ 8	10	12	13
Plumbers	7	8	11	6	5	8
Electricians	6	9	10	3	5	7

a. Calculate a Laspeyres price index of hourly wage rates for the firm using 1986 as the base year.
b. Calculate a Laspeyres price index of hourly wage rates for the firm using 1988 as the base year.
c. Calculate a Paasche index of hourly wage rates using 1986 as the base year.
d. Calculate a total wage bill for the firm for each year.
e. Divide the yearly wage bill of the firm by the total number of hours worked that year in order to obtain an average hourly wage for each year.
f. Use the series in part (e) to construct an index for wages using 1986 as base year.
g. Compare the answer to part (f) with that to part (a) and explain the relative advantages of each series.

8. The following data show the annual generation of electric power in billions of kilowatt-hours in a region of the United States.

Year	1985	1986	1987	1988
Electricity generated	1329	1442	1532	1614

a. Calculate a simple index of output using 1985 as the base year.
b. Calculate a simple index of output using 1987 as the base year.

9. Suppose a stock market indicator contains five stocks, for which the prices per share in dollars are as follows:

Stock	1	2	3	4	5
Price	100	80	60	50	30

a. Find the average stock price.
b. Suppose that Stock 1 and Stock 3 each split 2-for-1. Find the new denominator D for your average. Use the same method as used for calculating the Dow Jones industrial average.
c. Shortly after the splits, the prices per share of the stocks in dollars settled at the following values:

Stock	1	2	3	4	5
Price	52	83	32	50	25

Find the new value of the stock price indicator.

10. Give examples of at least two commodities in which the quality in the past three decades has changed as follows:
a. Changed significantly b. Not changed much
c. Mention at least two products that are better buys today than two or three decades ago because quality has improved more than prices have increased.

11. In a metropolitan area, the Consumer Price Index had the following values using 1977 as base year:

Year	1983	1984	1985	1986	1987
CPI	120	126	135	142	148

a. In each year how much would $1 purchase relative to what could have been purchased in 1977? That is, for each year, find the purchasing power of the dollar relative to 1977.
b. Explain the meaning of these numbers.

12. In a given year, a teacher's salary was $11,600 and the Consumer Price Index was 120. In the following year, the salary was $12,300 and the CPI was 130.
a. Did the teacher's real income increase or decrease?
b. Calculate the percent change in nominal income.
c. Calculate the percent change in real income.

13. A firm produces four brands of computers. The prices of the computers and quantities sold are shown in the accompanying table. Calculate the Laspeyres price index for these computers using the following as base years:

	Price (in dollars)			Quantity Sold (in thousands)		
Computer	1982	1985	1988	1982	1985	1988
A	$2000	$2500	$2700	600	700	750
B	3100	3300	3700	300	320	330
C	5000	6000	7000	180	200	190
D	2500	2600	2800	400	600	800

a. 1982 b. 1988

14. In 1979 a university spent $3.8 million for a new classroom building. An index of construction costs is as follows:

Year	1977	1979	1983	1988
Index	100	120	140	175

How much would it cost to construct the building in the following years?
a. 1983 b. 1988 c. 1977

15. A company executive wishes to determine how the quantity of output produced by a firm has changed, but she does not have the annual prices of the product. The accompanying data show an index of price changes.

Year	Sales (in thousands)	Price Index
1973	$110	96
1978	125	100
1983	160	120
1988	220	145

a. Calculate an index for the quantity produced using 1978 as the base year.
b. Calculate an index for the quantity produced using 1973 as the base year.
c. What was the percent increase in output from 1983 to 1988?

16. By how much will the purchasing power of the dollar fall if prices rise by 25%?

17. Suppose that the Consumer Price Index in 1988 is 174 for both Kansas City and Cincinnati (1980 = 100).
a. Does this mean that in 1988 prices increased by the same amount in the two cities from 1980?
b. What does the statement mean?
c. Do products cost the same amount in the two cities?

18. The Consumer Price Index was 333.1 in January 1987 and 340.8 in July 1987 (1967 = 100).
a. Did prices increase 7.7% from January to July?
b. By what percentage did prices increase during the six-month period?
c. What is the annual inflation rate based on the increase during the first six months?

19. Suppose that the Consumer Price Index in 1988 was 115 (1985 = 100). Suppose that prices increase by 10% in 1989, increase by 5% in 1990, fall by 5% in 1991, and increase by 10% in 1992. Show the values of the CPI for each year using 1985 as the base year.

20. Suppose two employees each earn $200 per week in 1986. In 1987 employee 1 gets a 10% raise and employee 2 takes a 10% cut in pay. In 1988, employee 2 gets a 10% raise and employee 1 takes a 10% cut in pay.
a. Calculate the weekly earnings for each employee for each year.
b. Are the employees as well off in 1988 as they were in 1986?
c. Can you explain why a percent raise followed by a cut of an equal percentage always leaves you worse off than when you started? Can you prove it mathematically?
d. Does it make any difference to earnings in 1988 whether the raise follows or precedes the cut in pay?

21. The Laspeyres and Paasche price indexes use different weighting systems to compute a price index. Describe a situation when you would expect to get substantially different values for the two indexes.

References

CAGAN, PHILLIP and GEOFFREY H. MOORE. *The Consumer Price Index: Issues and Alternatives.* Washington, D.C.: American Enterprise Institute, 1981.

FISHER, IRVING. *The Making of Index Numbers: A Study of Their Varieties, Tests, and Reliability.* 3d rev. ed. Boston: Houghton Mifflin, 1927.

U.S. DEPARTMENT OF LABOR, BUREAU OF LABOR STATISTICS. *The Consumer Price Index: Concepts and Content over the Years.* Report 517. Washington, D.C.: U.S. Government Printing Office, May 1978.

———. *BLS Handbook of Methods.* 2 vols. Bulletins 2134-1 and 2134-2. Washington, D.C.: U.S. Government Printing Office, December 1982. Presents a detailed explanation of how the Bureau of Labor Statistics (BLS) obtains and prepares economic data. Volume 1 contains this information for all BLS programs except the Consumer Price Index (Chapter 7 deals with the Producer Price Index). Volume 2 explains the Consumer Price Index.

Chapter Twenty-Three
Introduction to Statistical Decision Theory

Chapter 11 covered the classical theory of hypothesis testing. We saw that, at the conclusion of a test, we must make a statistical decision either to reject or not to reject the null hypothesis. Classical hypothesis testing tells us how to make statistical decisions in problems in which the goodness of a test is determined by α and β, the probabilities of making Type I and Type II errors. The classical procedure discussed in Chapter 11, however, does not take into account the costs and benefits associated with different decisions and different actions.

Before taking any action, a decision maker should consider what the potential costs or benefits from any action might be. If incorrectly rejecting a true null hypothesis would be a very costly mistake, we might require a great deal of evidence supporting the alternative hypothesis before we would reject the null hypothesis. On the other hand, if a Type I error is relatively inexpensive, we might reject the null hypothesis on the basis of relatively weak contradictory evidence. In this chapter we show how to account for these economic consequences.

23.1 ▪ *Payoff Tables and Opportunity Loss Tables*

The process of decision making involves selecting a single action from a set of several possible actions. First, however, we have to specify what actions are available. Examples of types of actions (or choices) include the following:

1. which stocks, bonds, and mutual funds to invest in;
2. whether to build a manufacturing plant of small, medium, or large size;
3. whether to market a new product; and
4. which method to use for producing a product.

We will denote different actions as a_1, a_2, and so on. Associated with each action is a *payoff,* or consequence, resulting from that particular act.

Notation for Actions

Possible **actions** are labeled $a_1, a_2, \ldots, a_n$ and are assumed to form a mutually exclusive, collectively exhaustive set.

States of Nature

Generally, we do not know which action will be best unless we know with certainty the other factors that affect the payoff associated with each action. In decision making under uncertainty, the payoff from any action depends on factors beyond our control, which are called **states of nature**. These states of nature are denoted as s_1, s_2, and so on.

Notations for States of Nature

The **states of nature** in a decision problem are denoted $s_1, s_2, \ldots, s_k$. No two states of nature can be in effect at the same time, and all possible states of nature must be included in the analysis.

In decision making under certainty, we know which state will occur, and we evaluate the possible payoffs for each possible action. Then we select the best action given the possible payoffs. In decision making under uncertainty, we do not know which particular outcome will follow from an action because the state of nature is unknown at the time the action is taken. These ideas are illustrated in the following example.

Example 23.1

Decision Making Under Uncertainty I: A farmer must decide which of two crops to plant. The possible actions are:

$$a_1 = \{\text{plant crop A}\}$$
$$a_2 = \{\text{plant crop B}\}$$

The farmer's profits or losses depend not only on which crop is planted but also on the weather, the crop's selling price at harvest time, labor costs, and so forth. Thus, the states of nature include all the factors affecting the farmer's final profit. The farmer cannot predict profit with certainty, because the eventual states of nature are unknown at the time the decision is made about which crop to plant. ■

In many cases, the number of possible states of nature affecting the payoff can be so large that the analysis of the problem is almost impossible. Under such circumstances we have to reduce the number of possible states of nature to a workable number.

Payoffs and Payoff Tables

We assume that the payoff associated with taking a particular action when a particular state of nature occurs is known. In the real world, this assumption is often unrealistic. Usually many different states of nature are possible, each yielding a different set of payoffs for the various possible actions. In economics, it is customary to use the symbol Π to denote the payoff, or profit, from an action.

Notation for Payoffs

The symbol Π_{ij} denotes the **payoff** received when we take action a_i and state of nature s_j occurs. The payoffs may be positive, negative, or 0.

Definition: Payoff Table

A **payoff table** shows the payoff Π_{ij} associated with each possible action a_i and each possible state of nature s_j.

A general payoff table is shown in Table 23.1. The payoff Π_{ij} is in row i and column j of the table, where rows indicate the possible actions and columns indicate the different states of nature. For example, Π_{32} represents the payoff when action a_3 is taken and state of nature s_2 occurs and is found at the intersection of row 3 and column 2.

TABLE 23.1
A payoff table

	State of Nature			
Action	s_1	s_2	...	s_k
a_1	Π_{11}	Π_{12}	...	Π_{1k}
a_2	Π_{11}	Π_{22}	...	Π_{2k}
$\vdots$	$\vdots$	$\vdots$	$\ddots$	$\vdots$
a_n	Π_{n1}	Π_{n2}	...	Π_{nk}

Example 23.2

Decision Making Under Uncertainty II: You may buy 100 shares of one of four different stocks, each of which is currently selling for \$10 per share. None of the stocks will pay dividends next year. You want to buy the stock that will increase the most in price next year. Find the optimal action.

Solution: This problem involves decision making under uncertainty because you do not know the value of the stocks next year. Prices depend on the general state of the economy, interest rates, inflation rates, and so forth. There are many possible states of nature, each yielding a different set of payoffs.

You think stock prices in one year depend on whether the inflation rate increases, is constant, or decreases (states of nature s_1, s_2, and s_3, respectively). For s_1, you think that the respective prices of the four stocks a year from now will be \$5, \$10, \$15, and \$20; for s_2, \$9, \$13, \$7, and \$16; for s_3, \$12, \$14, \$16, and \$9.

There is a different potential payoff, or profit, associated with each particular action, depending on which state of nature actually occurs. For example, if the inflation rate increases (s_1), the price of Stock 4 will increase from \$10 to \$20, and action a_4 will yield a profit of \$1000. (At \$10 per share, 100 shares of Stock 4 would cost \$1000 today. If s_1 occurs, then the price of Stock 4 will increase to \$20 per share and the 100 shares will be worth \$2000, yielding a \$1000 profit.)

Table 23.2 shows the 12 potential payoffs associated with the four actions and the three states of nature described in this problem.

TABLE 23.2 Payoff table for Example 23.2

Action	State of Nature s_1 (inflation rate increases)	s_2 (inflation rate constant)	s_3 (inflation rate decreases)
a_1 (buy Stock 1)	−$500	−$100	$200
a_2 (buy Stock 2)	0	300	400
a_3 (buy Stock 3)	500	−300	600
a_4 (buy Stock 4)	1000	600	−100

In the payoff table, no single action is obviously the best one. If the inflation rate increases (s_1), the optimal action is a_4 because it yields the largest profit ($1000). Under s_2, action a_4 is again optimal, but if s_3 occurs, action a_3 is optimal.

Regardless of which state of nature occurs, a_2 always yields a larger payoff than a_1. This means that a_1 can never be the optimal action. Action a_1 is said to be *dominated* by action a_2. ■

Definition: Dominated Action

An action a_i is said to be a **dominated action** if another action a_j exists such that, for every possible state of nature, the payoff for a_j is at least as large as the payoff for a_i. A dominated action will never be the optimal action and can be eliminated from the analysis without affecting the solution. Action a_j dominates action a_i if $\Pi_{jk} \geq \Pi_{ik}$ for all values of k.

Example 23.3

Decision Making Under Uncertainty III: A grocer must decide each morning how many baskets of perishable fruit to purchase for sale during the day. He buys baskets of fruit for $3 each and sells them for $5 apiece, yielding a profit of $2 per unit. At the end of the day, all remaining units are sold to a senior citizens' group for $1 per unit (that is, at a loss of $2 each). The grocer can order either 5, 10, or 15 units, and the daily demand is 6, 11, or 14 units. Construct the payoff table for this problem.

Solution: There are the following possible actions

$$a_1 = \{\text{order 5 units}\}$$

$$a_2 = \{\text{order 10 units}\}$$

$$a_3 = \{\text{order 15 units}\}$$

and the following states of nature:

$$s_1 = \{\text{demand of 6 units}\}$$

$$s_2 = \{\text{demand of 11 units}\}$$

$$s_3 = \{\text{demand of 14 units}\}$$

To show how to calculate some potential payoffs, suppose action a_2 is taken (the grocer orders 10 units at a total cost of $30). If state s_1 prevails, the grocer sells 6 units at \$5 each and the remaining 4 units at \$1 each for a total revenue of \$34. Thus, the payoff associated with action a_2 and state of nature s_1 is \$4 (\$34 − \$30). As another example, suppose action a_3 is taken and state of nature s_1 occurs. Then the grocer orders 15 units at a total cost of \$45, sells 6 units at \$5 each, and sells the remaining 9 units at \$1 each, for a total revenue of \$39. Thus, the payoff is −\$6 (i.e., a loss of \$6). The other payoffs are shown in Table 23.3.

TABLE 23.3 **Payoff table for Example 23.3**

	State of Nature		
Action	s_1 (demand of 6)	s_2 (demand of 11)	s_3 (demand of 14)
a_1 (order 5)	\$10	\$10	\$10
a_2 (order 10)	4	20	20
a_3 (order 15)	−6	14	26

■

In Example 23.3, if the grocer knew the demand on a given day, it would be easy to choose the optimal action. Typically, however, we do not know what state of nature will occur, so we need some criteria for choosing which action to take. In the next section we discuss various criteria to use when choosing an optimal action.

Opportunity Loss

Another way of representing potential payoffs is by an opportunity loss table. Suppose we take action a_i and state of nature s_j occurs. Our payoff is Π_{ij}. First, we find the largest payoff associated with s_j. Suppose this payoff is Π_{mj}. If we had chosen action a_m, our payoff would have been Π_{mj} rather than Π_{ij}. The difference in payoffs is

$$L_{ij} = \Pi_{mj} - \Pi_{ij}$$

In a sense, by choosing the wrong action, we lost the opportunity to earn an additional L_{ij}.

Definition: Opportunity Loss

Let Π_{mj} be the highest payoff associated with state of nature s_j. Let Π_{ij} denote the payoff associated with taking action a_i when state s_j occurs. For state s_j, the **opportunity loss** from taking action a_i is

$$L_{ij} = \Pi_{mj} - \Pi_{ij}$$

For a given state of nature s_j, the opportunity loss L_{ij} is the difference between the highest possible payoff associated with state s_j and the payoff actually realized for the act selected. For a given state of nature, the opportunity loss associated with the optimal action is 0 and the opportunity loss for other actions is nonnegative. The opportunity loss L_{ij} can be obtained from the payoff table by subtracting the payoff Π_{ij} from the largest entry in the same column.

Formula for Opportunity Loss

$$L_{ij} = (\max_k \Pi_{kj}) - \Pi_{ij}$$

Example 23.4 **Constructing an Opportunity Loss Table:** Refer to Example 23.2 and Table 23.2. Construct the corresponding opportunity loss table.

Solution: We calculate the opportunity losses in the following way. Assume the state of nature is s_1. The maximum payoff is $\Pi_{41} = \$1000$ by choosing action a_4. That is, $\max_k \Pi_{k1} = \Pi_{41} = \$1000$ and the opportunity losses are

$$L_{11} = 1000 - \Pi_{11} = 1000 - (-500) = \$1500$$
$$L_{12} = 1000 - \Pi_{21} = 1000 - 0 = \$1000$$
$$L_{13} = 1000 - \Pi_{31} = 1000 - 500 = \$\ 500$$
$$L_{14} = 1000 - \Pi_{41} = 1000 - 1000 = \$\ 0$$

By following a similar procedure for states s_2 and s_3, we obtain the opportunity losses shown in Table 23.4.

TABLE 23.4
Opportunity loss table for Example 23.4

Action	State of Nature		
	s_1	s_2	s_3
a_1	\$1500	\$700	\$400
a_2	1000	300	200
a_3	500	900	0
a_4	0	0	700

Consider $L_{13} = \$500$. When s_1 occurs, we earn \$500 by taking action a_3, but by taking a_4 we could have earned \$1000. Consequently, by taking action a_3, we lose the opportunity of earning an additional \$500.

The opportunity loss table is sometimes called the *regret table.* ■

Exercises for Section 23.1

1. An investor has the opportunity to buy four different stocks. Each stock costs \$50 per share, and the investor will purchase 20 shares of one of the stocks and sell it one year later. If there is a recession (state s_1), the selling prices of the four stocks will be \$40, \$52, \$58, and \$45. If there is no recession (state s_2), the selling prices will be \$53, \$56, \$54, and \$60, respectively.
a. Determine the payoff table.

b. Are any of the actions dominated? If so, which one?
c. Determine the opportunity loss table.

2. The Bess Management Company (BMC) submits a proposal to the government to study the costs of repairing bridges in major eastern cities. BMC does not presently own a computer, but if it wins the contract, a large amount of computer work will be required. The company has the option of renting a computer for $45,000 today. If they wait a few months until the contract is awarded, the rent will be $72,000. If BMC does not win the contract, it will not rent a computer. If it does win the contract, the company's profits except for computer costs will be $160,000. The possible states of nature are s_1 (winning the contract) and s_2 (not winning the contract). The possible actions are a_1 (rent now) and a_2 (wait and possibly rent later). Determine the following:
a. The payoff table
b. The opportunity loss table
c. If any action is a dominated action

3. Terry Doherty owns a car franchise and sells new cars for $8000 each, which cost him $6000 each. Shipments of cars come in lots of 10, and Doherty can order either 30, 40, or 50 cars for an end-of-year sale. Doherty figures that, depending on the state of the economy, the agency will sell either 25, 40, or 45 cars. Cars not sold at the year-end sale will be sold to a rental agency for $5000 each. Determine the following:
a. The payoff table
b. The opportunity loss table

4. A common problem in business is deciding the quantity to order of perishable inventories—that is, items that lose the major portion of their economic value after a given date due to either obsolescence or spoilage. For example, if a newsstand orders too many papers and cannot sell them all, the excess papers have little value. These types of problems are common in retailing. Suppose a buyer for a large department store is trying to decide how many of a new style of bathing suit to order. Because of rapid changes in fashion, she does not want to order too many, but if she orders too few, she will lose profits for her department. The store pays $30 each for bathing suits and sells them for $50 each. Any bathing suits not sold at the end of the season will be sold for $15 each. The buyer believes that the department will sell 4, 5, 6, 7, or 8 dozen bathing suits. Bathing suits must be purchased by the department store in lots of 1 dozen.
a. Formulate the payoff table for this decision problem.
b. Convert the payoff table to an opportunity loss table.

23.2 ▪ Criteria for Making Decisions

Decision-making problems can be classified according to the degree of knowledge we have about the state of nature that will occur. In *decision making under certainty,* the state of nature that will occur is known in advance. In this case, the decision maker can determine which action to take to maximize profits. In decision making under uncertainty, the state of nature that will occur is unknown. However, there are two extreme cases for decision making under uncertainty. In one case, the probability that any state of nature will occur is known; in the other case, nothing is known about such probabilities. Probabilities that are known may be based on the relative frequency of occurrence of these states in the past or on theoretical grounds, or they may be nothing more than subjective estimates.

For most decision-making problems of interest, we have imperfect knowledge of the probability distribution of the various states of nature. In these problems we use all available information to get a subjective estimate of the pertinent probabilities. Problems in decision making where the probabilities for the states of nature are unknown can be further divided into categories based on how much information we have concerning the probability distribution of the states of nature.

In most situations of interest in business and everyday life, we have to make some assumptions concerning the probability of occurrence of each state of nature. After assigning a probability to each possible state, we can calculate the expected, or average, payoff that we would obtain by taking any action. We make this calculation by weighting each possible payoff by its probability of occurrence. In decision making under uncertainty, a commonly used rule is to select the action that yields the highest expected payoff. This idea is discussed in more detail later.

The Decision-Making Process

The following steps should be used to solve a statistical decision problem:

1. List all the alternative choices, or actions, a_i that are available.
2. List each possible event, or state of nature, s_j that has an influence on the potential payoff.
3. For each state of nature, list the payoff obtained from following each action.
4. If possible, assign a probability to the occurrence of each state of nature.
5. State a criterion for selecting an optimal action.
6. Select the optimal action based on the criterion in step 5.

Various criteria can be used to determine the optimal action. Some different criteria are as follows:

1. the maximax, or Hurwicz, criterion;
2. the maximin, or Wald, criterion;
3. the minimax, or Savage, criterion;
4. the Laplace, or strategy-of-insufficient-reason, criterion;
5. the expected monetary value (EMV) criterion;
6. the expected opportunity loss (EOL) criterion; and
7. the expected utility criterion.

These criteria are discussed next except for expected utility, which we discuss in Section 23.3.

Maximax Criterion

Definition: Maximax Criterion

Under the **maximax criterion**, we select the action with the largest possible payoff.

The maximax criterion is used by supreme optimists. Optimists assume that, of all the states of nature, the state that yields the maximum overall profit will occur. Then the optimist selects the action associated with this state of nature.

Example 23.5

Maximax Criterion: Find the optimal action in Example 23.2 based on the maximax criterion.

Solution: In Example 23.2 the maximax criterion would lead us to select action a_4 because \$1000 is the largest payoff in Table 23.2. ■

The maximax criterion is rarely used because it ignores the possibilities of large losses or small payoffs. Businesses on the brink of bankruptcy might adopt the maximax criterion if only a large payoff could save the company.

Maximin Criterion

Definition: Maximin Criterion

Under the **maximin criterion**, we find the worst possible payoff for each action and take the action yielding the largest (or maximum) of all these minimum payoffs (hence the name *maximin*).

Users of the maximin criterion are pessimists, assuming that no matter which action is taken, the worst possible state of nature will occur.

Example 23.6

Maximin Criterion: Find the optimal action in Example 23.2 according to the maximin criterion.

Solution: From the payoff table (Table 23.2), the worst payoff for a_1 is $-\$500$; for a_2, \$0; for a_3, $-\$300$; and for a_4, $-\$100$. The maximum of these four minimum payoffs is \$0, so the maximin criterion tells us to choose action a_2. By choosing a_2, the worst that could happen is a payoff of \$0; any other action could result in a loss. ■

The maximin criterion was developed by Abraham Wald and is sometimes called the Wald criterion. It is a conservative strategy that can be appropriate when a company is in financial difficulty and cannot afford a large loss. It selects actions that avoid large losses, but neglects large payoffs that are possible by choosing other actions.

This strategy is not as unrealistic as it may appear at first glance. In certain situations it may be necessary for an individual or a business to avoid a large possible loss or to guarantee a minimum profit.

Minimax Criterion

Definition: Minimax Criterion

Under the **minimax criterion**, we find the maximum opportunity loss possible for each action and take the action with the smallest such loss (hence the name *minimax*).

The minimax criterion was developed by L. J. Savage. The minimax criterion is concerned with opportunity loss rather than profits, and the criterion tells us to minimize the largest potential opportunity loss from each course of action.

Example 23.7

Minimax Criterion: Find the optimal action in Example 23.4 based on the minimax criterion.

Solution: The maximum opportunity loss for a_1 is \$1500; for a_2, \$1000; for a_3, \$900; and for a_4, \$700. The minimum of these maximum opportunity losses is \$700. Thus, under the minimax criterion, the optimal action is a_4. ■

The minimax criterion is a pessimistic strategy because it uses only the worst possible opportunity loss for each act.

Strategy of Insufficient Reason

If the decision maker has no information on the states of nature, a common assumption is that each state of nature is equally likely to occur. This idea was first developed by Pierre Laplace. Since each possible payoff is assumed to be equally likely, we find an expected payoff for each action by taking the arithmetic average of the possible payoffs associated with that action.

Definition: Laplace Criterion

Under the **Laplace criterion**, we take the action that has the largest expected payoff based on the assumption that every possible state of nature is equally likely.

Example 23.8

Laplace Criterion: Use the Laplace criterion to determine the optimal action in Example 23.3.

Solution: According to Table 23.3, the possible payoffs from action a_1 are \$10, \$10, and \$10; the average is \$10. The possible payoffs from action a_2 are \$4, \$20, and \$20; the average is \$44/3, or \$14.67. The possible payoffs from action a_3 are −\$6, \$14, and \$26; the average payoff is \$34/3 = \$11.33. The Laplace criterion tells us to select action a_2 because its expected payoff is the largest. ■

Unlike the other criteria discussed so far, the Laplace criterion uses all the data in the payoff matrix, not just the largest or smallest value in a row or column. Naturally, this criterion is inappropriate if the states of nature are not approximately equally likely. If we have no information whatsoever about the probabilities of the states of nature, it is debatable whether the assumption that all the states are equally likely is wise.

Each of the criteria discussed thus far ignores any information concerning the probabilities of occurrence of each state of nature. Because we usually want to weight the possible payoffs or losses by their probability of occurrence, the use of the maximax, maximin, minimax, and Laplace criteria is limited.

Expected Monetary Value Criterion

The expected monetary value (EMV) criterion is sometimes called the Bayes criterion after the Reverend Thomas Bayes, an eighteenth-century minister and mathematician. To use the EMV criterion, we must be able to assign a probability to each state of nature, and the sum of these probabilities must be 1. These probabilities represent our feelings about the likelihood of the various states of nature. Frequently, however, no data are available to help us determine such probabilities. Nevertheless, if we have had experience in similar situations, the probabilities in those circumstances may be useful. Since most people are influenced in their choice of actions by their subjective feelings about the likelihood of different events, it is reasonable to incorporate these probabilities into the decision-making process. However, because of this subjective procedure, some statisticians reject the EMV criterion.

Definition: Prior Probabilities

The probabilities assigned to the various states of nature are called **prior probabilities**. We let $p_j = P(s_j)$ denote the probability that state of nature s_j occurs.

Definition: Expected Monetary Value

The **expected monetary value** of action a_i, denoted $\text{EMV}(a_i)$, is defined as

$$\text{EMV}(a_i) = \sum_{j=1}^{k} \Pi_{ij} p_j$$

where

Π_{ij} = payoff of action a_i when state of nature s_j occurs

$p_j = P(s_j)$ = probability that state of nature s_j occurs $(j = 1, 2, \ldots, k)$

k = number of possible states of nature

Definition: Expected Monetary Value Criterion

Under the **expected monetary value criterion**, we take the action with the highest expected monetary value.

Example 23.9

Expected Monetary Value Criterion: Suppose that, based on previous experience, the investor in Example 23.2 believes that the prior probabilities for the possible states of nature are as shown in Table 23.5. Find the optimal action based on the EMV criterion.

Solution: From Table 23.2, the payoffs from action a_1 are $-\$500$ under s_1, $-\$100$ under s_2, and $\$200$ under s_3. To calculate the EMV from taking action a_1, these payoffs must be weighted by their probabilities. The expected monetary value of a_1 is

$$\text{EMV}(a_1) = (-500)(.5) + (-100)(.3) + (200)(.2) = -\$240$$

TABLE 23.5
Prior probabilities for Example 23.9

State of Nature s_j	Prior Probability $P(s_j)$
s_1 (inflation rate increases)	.5
s_2 (inflation rate constant)	.3
s_3 (inflation rate decreases)	.2

The payoffs under a_2 are \$0, \$300, and \$400, so the EMV is

$$\text{EMV}(a_2) = (0)(.5) + (300)(.3) + (400)(.2) = \$170$$

Similarly, for actions a_3 and a_4, we obtain

$$\text{EMV}(a_3) = (500)(.5) + (-300)(.3) + (600)(.2) = \$280$$
$$\text{EMV}(a_4) = (1000)(.5) + (600)(.3) + (-100)(.2) = \$660$$

By the EMV criterion, a_4 is the optimal action, because its expected payoff of \$660 is larger than the expected payoff from any other action. ■

Expected Opportunity Loss Criterion

Definition: Expected Opportunity Loss

The **expected opportunity loss** of action a_i, denoted $\text{EOL}(a_i)$, is defined as

$$\text{EOL}(a_i) = \sum_{j=1}^{k} L_{ij} p_j$$

where

L_{ij} = opportunity loss if action a_i is taken and state of nature s_j occurs
$p_j = P(s_j)$ = prior probability that s_j occurs $(j = 1, 2, \ldots, k)$
k = number of possible states of nature

Definition: Expected Opportunity Loss Criterion

Under the **expected opportunity loss criterion**, we take the action having the smallest expected opportunity loss.

Example 23.10 **Expected Opportunity Loss Criterion:** Using the prior probabilities in Table 23.5, find the optimal action for Example 23.4 based on the EOL criterion.

Solution: From Tables 23.4 and 23.5, the EOL for action a_1 is

$$\text{EOL}(a_1) = (1500)(.5) + (700)(.3) + (400)(.2) = \$1040$$

In a similar manner, we obtain

$$\text{EOL}(a_2) = (1000)(.5) + (300)(.3) + (200)(.2) = \$630$$
$$\text{EOL}(a_3) = (500)(.5) + (900)(.3) + (0)(.2) = \$520$$
$$\text{EOL}(a_4) = (0)(.5) + (0)(.3) + (700)(.2) = \$140$$

Action a_4 has the minimum EOL. Recall that a_4 also had the largest EMV. In fact, the EMV and EOL criteria always choose the same action. ■

The last decision criterion, the expected utility criterion, will be discussed in Section 23.3.

Expected Payoff Using Perfect Information

If we knew that state s_j was going to occur, it would be easy to select the action a_i having the largest payoff Π_{ij}. That is, for a given value of j, we would maximize Π_{ij} over $i = 1, 2, \ldots, n$. Suppose we knew that state s_j was going to occur. Let's denote the maximum payoff that we could obtain as $\max_i \Pi_{ij}$. For each state s_j, weight the maximum payoff by the probability that state s_j occurs. The sum of these weighted payoffs is called the *expected payoff using perfect information* (EPPI). EPPI represents the profit that would be realized under the following circumstances:

1. We could repeat the problem many times under identical conditions;
2. we knew with certainty on each trial which state s_j was going to occur; and
3. the states of nature occurred with the assumed prior probabilities.

Definition: Expected Payoff from Perfect Information

To calculate the **expected payoff from perfect information** (EPPI), multiply the highest payoff associated with each state by the state's probability of occurrence $P(s_j)$. EPPI is the sum of these products over all states of nature. Notationally we have

$$\text{EPPI} = \sum_{j=1}^{k} P(s_j)(\max_i \Pi_{ij})$$

Example 23.11 **Expected Payoff from Perfect Information:** Calculate the EPPI using the payoffs Π_{ij} given in Table 23.2 and the probabilities $P(s_j)$ given in Table 23.5.

Solution: If s_1 occurs, the maximum payoff is \$1000; this amount is $\max_i \Pi_{i1}$. If s_2 occurs, the maximum payoff is \$600; this is $\max_i \Pi_{i2}$. If s_3 occurs, the maximum payoff is \$600; this is $\max_i \Pi_{i3}$. Because the states s_1, s_2, and s_3 occur with probabilities .5, .3, and .2, respectively, we obtain

$$\text{EPPI} = .5(1000) + .3(600) + .2(600) = \$800$$

This result indicates that if we knew in advance which state was going to occur and each state occurred with the assumed probabilities, and if on each trial we took the optimal action, then in the long run our payoff would be \$800 per trial. ■

Expected Value of Perfect Information

Before actually selecting a course of action, there is another option available. We can postpone action until we obtain additional information about the state of nature. Before taking an action, we should determine the cost of obtaining additional information and the potential value of this information. The *maximum* value of additional information about the state of nature is the same as the value of *perfect information* on which state of nature will occur.

The *expected value of perfect information* (EVPI) is the maximum amount of money that should be spent to obtain perfect information on which state of nature will occur. The EVPI measures the difference between the maximum payoff with perfect information (that is, under conditions of certainty) and the expected payoff under uncertainty.

Definition: Expected Value of Perfect Information

The expected payoff using perfect information is EPPI. Without perfect information, the best we can do is to maximize EMV. Denote the maximum value of EMV as EMV*. The difference between EPPI and EMV* represents the expected additional profit we would obtain if we had perfect information about which state was going to occur. This additional profit represents an upper bound for the amount of money we should be willing to spend to obtain perfect information. This amount is called the **expected value of perfect information** (EVPI). Notationally we have

$$\begin{aligned} \text{EVPI} &= \text{EPPI} - \text{EMV}^* \\ &= \sum_{j=1}^{k} P(s_j)(\max_i \Pi_{ij}) - \max_i \left[\sum_{j=1}^{k} P(s_j)\Pi_{ij} \right] \end{aligned}$$

where EMV* is the maximum value of EMV.

Example 23.12 **Expected Value of Perfect Information:** Using the payoffs in Table 23.2 and the probabilities in Table 23.5, calculate the EVPI.

Solution: In Example 23.11, we found that the expected profit using perfect information was EPPI = \$800. In Example 23.9, we found that the maximum expected monetary value was EMV* = \$660 by using action a_4. We obtain

$$\text{EVPI} = \text{EPPI} - \text{EMV}^* = 800 - 660 = \$140$$ ■

Another way of calculating EVPI utilizes the data in an opportunity loss table. In such a table, the entries L_{ij} represent the potential cost of not knowing which state of nature will occur. EVPI measures the maximum amount we should spend to obtain information that would enable us to avoid these opportunity losses. EVPI equals the EOL associated with the optimal decision.

Example 23.13 **Calculating EVPI Using an Opportunity Loss Table:** Using Table 23.4, Example 23.4, and Example 23.10, calculate the EVPI.

Solution: In Example 23.4, the optimal action in stock purchasing was a_4, and from Example 23.10 we have EOL(a_4) = \$140. Thus, the investor should be willing to spend up to \$140 to obtain perfect information about next year's rate of inflation. This can be explained as follows. With no advance information concerning which state of nature is going to occur, a_4 is the optimal action. If we knew in advance that s_1 or s_2 was going to occur, the optimal action would still be a_4, so no opportunity is lost. On the other hand, if we knew in advance that s_3 was going to occur, the optimal action would be a_3, and the opportunity loss from choosing a_4 would be \$700. Recall that the states of nature were assumed to occur with probabilities $P(s_1) = .5$, $P(s_2) = .3$, and $P(s_3) = .2$. Thus, by choosing a_4, there is a 20% chance of suffering an opportunity loss of \$700. The EOL from choosing a_4 is 700(.2) = \$140. Thus, the investor should be willing to pay up to \$140 to determine if s_3 is going to occur. ■

Some Comments About the Expected Monetary Value Criterion

The EMV criterion is the most frequently used criterion for making decisions. If the same problem occurs repeatedly under approximately identical conditions, then in the long run we maximize profits by choosing the action with the highest EMV. In some situations, however, a decision maker may not want to take the action with the largest EMV. For example, if the action having the highest EMV has large negative and large positive payoffs, a conservative (or risk-averting) decision maker might take some other action to avoid the possibility of large losses.

The EMV criterion uses only the average, or expected, payoff. It does not take into account the variability, or variance, of the possible payoffs. A prudent decision maker will frequently accept a smaller expected payoff if the variability of the possible payoffs is also smaller.

Exercises for Section 23.2

1. Use the information in Exercise 1 of Section 23.1. As prior probabilities, use $P(\text{recession}) = .2$ and $P(\text{no recession}) = .8$. Find the optimal action using the following criteria:
a. Maximax b. Minimax c. Maximin
d. EMV e. EOL f. Calculate the EVPI.

2. Use the information presented in Exercise 2 of Section 23.1. Assume the company's prior probabilities are $P(s_1) = .4$ and $P(s_2) = .6$. Find the optimal action using the following criteria:
a. Maximax b. Minimax c. Maximin
d. EMV e. EOL f. Calculate the EVPI.

3. Use the information presented in Exercise 3 of Section 23.1. Assume the agency's prior probabilities are $P(\text{demand} = 25) = .3$, $P(\text{demand} = 40) = .5$, $P(\text{demand} = 45) = .2$. Find the optimal action using the following criteria:
a. Maximax b. Minimax c. Maximin
d. EMV e. EOL f. Calculate the EVPI.

4. The Bowen Hardware Store must decide how many cans of driveway sealer to order for the summer season. It takes a long time for an order to be delivered, so Mr. Bowen can place only one order early in the spring. The cost per can is \$12, and his selling price is \$18 per can. In October any unsold cans are sold to the local school district for \$9 per can. Mr. Bowen has to decide whether to buy 100, 200, 300, or 400 cans. He thinks the demand will be 100, 200, 300, or 400 cans with probabilities .2, .5, .2, and .1, respectively. These probabilities are based on Mr. Bowen's past business experience.

a. Determine the payoff table for this decision problem.
b. Find the optimal action if we use the EMV criterion.
c. Find the EPPI.
d. Find the EVPI.

5. Mr. Anderson is in charge of inventory control at a large department store. He has to decide how many lawn mowers to order for the summer season. Because the lawn mowers are widely available, Mr. Anderson loses the customer to another store if he is out of stock when a customer orders one. It takes one week for Mr. Anderson to receive new supplies, so each Monday he decides how many lawn mowers to order for the following week. Suppose Mr. Anderson makes \$70 profit on every sale, and every unsold lawn mower costs him \$15 in interest and storage costs. He has determined that the demand for lawn mowers approximately follows the Poisson distribution with mean $\mu = .9$. How many lawn mowers should Mr. Anderson order to maximize expected profits?

6. A woman is considering purchasing stock in one of the following three business lines: mining, oil refining, or computer software development. The expected profit in each line as a function of future inflation rates is given in the following payoff matrix:

	s_1 (inflation up)	s_2 (inflation down)	s_3 (inflation unchanged)
a_1 (mining)	140	510	290
a_2 (oil refining)	420	210	250
a_3 (software)	280	300	300

a. What is the maximin strategy?
b. What is the maximax strategy?
c. If the entrepreneur decides to invest in the mining industry, is she a pessimist or an optimist? Explain.

7. Refer to the payoff matrix in Exercise 6. Assume that the entrepreneur makes decisions according to the expected profit criterion.

a. Which activity will she choose if she believes that the following probabilities characterize the three states of nature: $P(s_1) = .3$, $P(s_2) = .3$, and $P(s_3) = .4$?
b. Which activity will she choose if it is given that $P(s_1) = .1$, $P(s_2) = .8$, and $P(s_3) = .1$?

8. Suppose the means and variances of the profits of six investment options are as follows:

Option:	A	B	C	D	E	F
Mean	5	8	8	9	10	5
Variance	14	10	8	3	12	8

Which of these options would you certainly reject if your goal was to maximize the mean return and minimize the variance of the return?

9. A car manufacturer is considering investing in an Asian country in order to manufacture cars for the local market. The manufacturer believes that it will earn a net profit of \$400 per car sold. The company will invest only if it believes that it can sell enough cars to earn \$4 million in net profits in the first year.

The population of the country consists of 10 million families, 5% of whom are wealthy and 95% of whom are poor. It is estimated that 70% of the wealthy and only 2% of the poor will buy cars from the company.

a. Should the firm invest in the country?

b. Suppose there is a 10% chance of a revolution in the country. If a revolution occurs, the company will continue to operate, but 50% of the wealthy citizens will emigrate. With this additional information, should the company invest?

10. Refer to Exercise 4 in Section 23.1. Use the payoff table drawn up in part (a) of that problem to do the following:

a. Find the action that would be prescribed by the maximax criterion.

b. Find the action that would be prescribed by the maximin criterion.

11. Refer to the payoff table for the decision problem in Exercise 4 of Section 23.1. The buyer has determined the following probability distribution for the number of bathing suits she can sell:

Dozens Sold	4	5	6	7	8
Probability	.25	.30	.20	.20	.05

How many dozen bathing suits should the buyer order according to the expected payoff criterion?

23.3 ▪ *Utility Theory and the Expected Utility Criterion*

Although people often use the expected monetary value criterion when deciding which action to take, there are situations where individuals clearly do not follow the EMV criterion. For example, almost all homeowners have some sort of insurance to protect themselves against fires, and drivers have insurance to protect themselves against traffic accidents. Historically, insurance companies have earned profits, which means that, on the average, they receive more money in premiums than they pay out in claims. Thus, on the average, people who buy insurance pay more in premiums than they receive in claims, so an individual who buys insurance can expect to lose money. Consequently, the expected monetary value from buying insurance is negative. If people followed the EMV criterion, no insurance would be purchased. The question, then, is "Why do people buy insurance?" or "Why do people pay more in premiums than they expect to receive in claims?" One possible explanation is that in many cases people do not maximize EMV. Rather, they maximize their expected utility.

The Concept of Utility

Definition: Utility

A person's **utility** for a quantity of money or for an object is the amount of happiness or satisfaction that the person obtains by possessing and using the money or object.

The *utility* of a given item varies from person to person. Thus, a loaf of bread could have an extremely high utility to a poor person and a very low utility to a rich person. In addition, the utility of a second loaf of bread is not necessarily the same as the utility of the first loaf of bread. According to the theory of diminishing marginal utility, each extra unit of a good tends to increase utility by less than the previous unit did. If this theory is correct, then winning N dollars (where $N > 1$) causes our utility to increase by less than N times the utility of winning \$1. Similarly, losing N dollars causes our utility to decrease by more than N times the utility lost by losing \$1. Rather than choose the action that maximizes the expected monetary value, people actually choose the action that maximizes the expected utility. This is the **expected utility criterion**.

Because utility is strictly a subjective concept, the decision maker's personal values must be taken into consideration when solving a problem by the expected utility criterion. To use the expected utility criterion, the payoffs in a payoff table should not be measured in monetary values but in values indicating the personal utility derived from that monetary payoff.

Assumptions of Utility Theory

A utility index for a rational person is assumed to satisfy the following requirements:

1. There is a complete ranking of preferences. For any pair of outcomes A and B, the decision maker can determine whether A is preferred to B, B is preferred to A, or there is no preference for either.

2. Preferences are transitive. If outcome A is preferred to outcome B and if outcome B is preferred to outcome C, then A is preferred to C. If we are indifferent between A and B and we are indifferent between B and C, then we are also indifferent between A and C.

3. Suppose that actions A and B have the same potential payoffs, but action A has a higher probability of success than action B. Then action A is preferred to action B.

4. It is assumed that if A is preferred to B and B is preferred to C, then there exists a gamble that offers A with probability p and C with probability $(1 - p)$ such that the decision maker will be indifferent between taking the gamble and receiving B with certainty.

To analyze a decision problem in terms of utilities rather than monetary payoffs, we need to transform the potential payoffs in a payoff table into utilities. To do this we need to know the decision maker's utility function. If the decision maker's utility function is unknown, we need to construct a utility index that will reveal the decision maker's preferences.

Constructing a Utility Index

The unit in which utility is measured is arbitrary, so we can scale the utility index in any way that is convenient. To construct a utility index, proceed as described in the accompanying box.

Constructing a Utility Index

1. Let L denote the lowest monetary payoff in the payoff table and let H denote the highest monetary payoff. Assign utility 0 to payoff L and 100 to payoff H. That is, $U(L) = 0$ and $U(H) = 100$, where $U(X)$ denotes the utility associated with payoff X.

2. Let Π be any payoff between L and H. Determine the probability p such that the decision maker is indifferent between receiving payoff Π with certainty and taking a gamble that pays H with probability p or L with probability $(1 - p)$.
3. Define the utility of payoff Π to be $100p$. That is,

$$U(\Pi) = 100p$$

The reason for defining utility as described in the box is that the expected utility from taking the gamble is

$$100p + 0(1 - p) = 100p$$

and the decision maker is indifferent between taking the gamble and receiving payoff Π for certain. Because the decision maker is indifferent, taking the gamble must have the same utility as receiving payoff Π for certain.

Example 23.14 **Constructing a Utility Index:** Suppose a decision maker is confronted with a problem that has two possible actions a_1 and a_2 and two possible states of nature s_1 and s_2. The payoff associated with action a_i and state s_j is Π_{ij}. The payoff table is shown in Table 23.6. Let us construct a utility index based on this payoff table.

TABLE 23.6
Payoff table for Example 23.14

	State of Nature	
Action	s_1	s_2
a_1	−\$400	\$800
a_2	\$400	\$200

Solution: The lowest payoff is $L = -\$400$ and the highest is $H = \$800$. The utilities assigned to these two payoffs are $U(L) = U(-400) = 0$ and $U(H) = U(800) = 100$. To find the utility associated with a payoff of \$200, we ask the decision maker which of the following situations he prefers:

1. receiving $\Pi_{22} = \$200$ with certainty or
2. receiving \$800 if a red card is drawn from a deck containing 1 red card and 99 black cards or losing \$400 if a black card is drawn.

Most people would choose option 1. Now ask the decision maker which of the following situations he would prefer:

1. receiving $\Pi_{22} = \$200$ with certainty or
2. receiving \$800 if a red card is drawn from a deck containing 2 red cards and 98 black cards or losing \$400 if a black card is drawn.

Suppose the decision maker again chooses option 1. We continue this process, increasing the number of red cards and decreasing the number of black cards until eventually we get the decision maker to switch from choosing option 1 to choosing option 2. Suppose the decision maker switches from option 1 to option 2 provided there are 65 red cards and 35 black cards. This means the point of indifference occurs when the probability of winning the maximum payoff is $p = .65$; thus the utility associated with payoff $\Pi_{22} = \$200$ is

$$U(\$200) = .65 \times U(\$800) + .35 \times U(-\$400)$$
$$= .65 \times 100 + .35 \times 0 = 65$$

Next we repeat this process for payoff $\Pi_{21} = \$400$. Suppose the decision maker is indifferent between receiving $400 with certainty and taking a gamble where he can gain $800 with probability $p = .85$ or lose $400 with probability .15. Then the utility associated with payoff $\Pi_{21} = \$400$ is

$$U(\$400) = .85 \times 100 + .15 \times 0 = 85$$

Now the utility index for payoffs of $800, $400, $200, and −$400 is known; it is plotted in Figure 23.1. By proceeding in a similar fashion, we can determine the value of the utility index for any payoff between $H = \$800$ and $L = -\$400$.

FIGURE 23.1
Utility curve for Example 23.14.

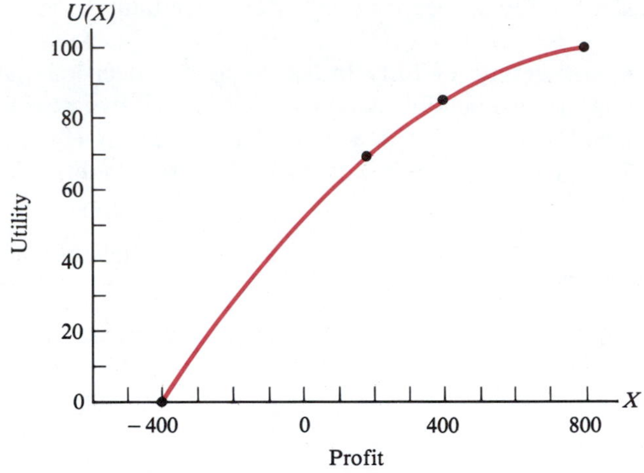

Attitudes Toward Risk and the Shape of the Utility Curve

The shape of the utility curve in Figure 23.1 is important because it characterizes the decision maker's attitude toward risk. Observe that, as required of all utility curves, total utility increases as the potential payoff increases, but in this figure utility increases at a decreasing rate as the payoff increases. This illustrates *declining marginal utility.*

The shape of Figure 23.1 is typical of decision makers who are said to be *risk averse*. In Example 23.14, consider the expected monetary value from taking the gamble in which the decision maker gains $800 with probability $p = .65$ or loses $400 with probability .35. The expected monetary value of this gamble is

$$\text{EMV} = .65 \times 600 + .35 \times -400 = \$380$$

Recall that in Example 23.14, the decision maker indicated that he was indifferent between taking the gamble or receiving $300 with certainty. The fact that the expected monetary value of the gamble is $380 and that the decision maker would be willing to accept $300 rather than take the gamble indicates an aversion to risk taking.

The decision maker has revealed that he is willing to take a smaller monetary payment ($300) with certainty rather than take a gamble with a higher expected monetary value ($380).

The shape of the utility function can be used to describe the person's attitude toward risk. Individuals are classified as being risk averse, risk neutral, or risk seeking. The utility functions for each basic attitude are shown in Figure 23.2.

FIGURE 23.2
Three types of utility curves showing attitudes toward risk.

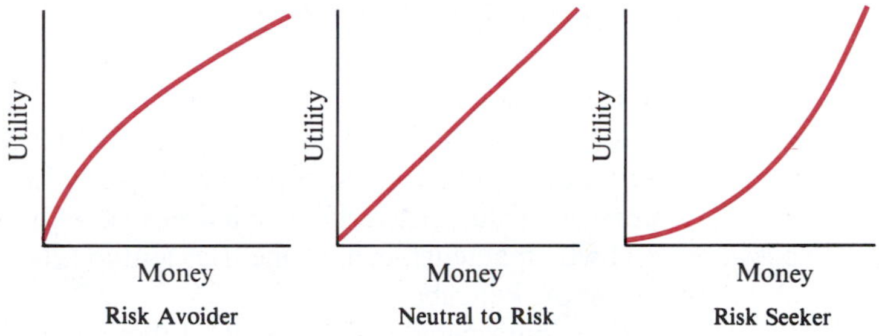

Risk Aversion Let X be a payoff that is less than Y. Whenever a decision maker prefers receiving the smaller payoff X with certainty to taking a gamble whose expected monetary value is Y, the person is said to be **risk averse**. This attitude is present when a person's marginal utility of money declines with larger amounts of money. The risk-averse individual tends to be conservative and will choose a certain fixed return over a gamble with a higher expected monetary value. Risk aversion is quite common, as shown by the fact that people buy insurance.

Risk Neutrality When a person considers the utility of receiving a given amount of money with certainty to be equal to the utility of taking a gamble whose expected monetary value is the same amount, the person is said to be **risk neutral**. The utility function for a risk-neutral individual is a straight line. For these people the marginal utility of money is constant; thus, every extra dollar of income increases utility by exactly the same amount as the previous dollar. Risk-neutral people behave as though they were maximizing expected monetary value. They would not buy insurance because the expected monetary payoff is negative; that is, the premium exceeds the expected claim.

When dealing with small sums of money, many people exhibit risk-neutral behavior. Thus, many people would be willing to take a gamble where they have an equal chance of winning or losing $1. For larger sums of money, however, their behavior becomes risk averse. Thus, few people would be willing to bet $10,000 on the toss of a coin. Risk neutrality is the implicit assumption made by those who use the expected monetary value criterion. For a person who is risk neutral, maximizing expected utility will yield the same optimal action as following the expected monetary value criterion.

Risk Seeking When a person considers the utility of receiving X dollars with certainty to be less than the utility of taking a gamble whose expected monetary value is X, the person is said to be **risk seeking**. The utility function for a risk seeker increases at an increasing rate. For these people, the marginal utility of money is increasing, so every extra dollar of income increases utility by more than the previous dollar. Risk seekers will accept huge riches-or-ruin gambles because they are motivated by the possibility of obtaining a large payoff.

When the stakes are large, most people tend to be risk averse. When the stakes are small, these same people often tend to be risk neutral. Therefore a given person's utility curve can have portions that are risk averse, portions that are risk neutral, and portions that are risk seeking.

The St. Petersburg Paradox

An indication that people frequently maximize expected utility rather than expected monetary value is apparent in a famous problem called the St. Petersburg paradox. This problem illustrates a situation where people refuse to take a fair gamble based on the expected monetary value criterion. A solution to the St. Petersburg paradox was proposed by the Swiss mathematician Daniel Bernoulli (1700–1782) who studied gamblers at the casinos of St. Petersburg.

The St. Petersburg paradox involves the following game between persons A and B: A fair coin is tossed repeatedly until a head appears. If a head appears on the first toss, A pays B \$1 and the game ends; if a head appears for the first time on the second toss, A pays B \$2 and the game ends; if a head appears first on the third toss, A pays B \$4 and the game ends. In general, the game ends when the first head appears and A pays B $\$2^{n-1}$ if the first head appears on the nth toss.

Bernoulli asked how much Player B should be willing to pay Player A for the privilege of playing this game in order to make the game an even gamble. To make the game fair, Player B should pay Player A the expected monetary value of the gamble. This value can be calculated as follows: The possible payments to B are \$1, \$2, \$4, \$8, and so forth depending on whether the first head appears on the first toss, the second toss, the third toss, the fourth toss, and so forth. The respective probabilities of these payments are $\frac{1}{2}$, $\frac{1}{4}$, $\frac{1}{8}$, and so forth. Thus the expected payment to B is the sum

$$1(1/2) + 2(1/4) + 4(1/8) + \cdots = 0.50 + 0.50 + 0.50 + \cdots = \infty$$

Even though the expected monetary value of the game is infinity, no person would be willing to pay an infinite sum of money for the privilege of playing this game (even though such a payment would make the gamble fair). Bernoulli argued that people making decisions under uncertainty do not attempt to maximize expected monetary value but try to maximize expected utility instead. He argued that the total utility of money (the overall welfare people derive from the possession of money) rises as people get more money, but the *marginal utility* of money (the increase in total utility associated with a one dollar increase in the quantity of money) decreases as people get more money. According to the theory of declining marginal utility, although each extra dollar of income increases our total utility, the amount of increase is less than that caused by the previous dollar of income. It follows that the decrease in total utility from losing \$1 exceeds the gain in total utility from winning \$1.

Thus, any game in which there is an equal probability of gaining or losing a given amount is a fair game in expected monetary terms. In expected utility terms, the same game would be considered unfair if the person's utility function exhibited decreasing marginal utility. As a result, if people maximize expected utility, they will refuse to take fair gambles because, although the expected monetary value of the gamble is \$0, the expected utility of the gamble is negative.

Expected Utility Criterion

Definition: Expected Utility Criterion

According to the **expected utility criterion**, a decision maker should choose the action for which the expected utility is the highest.

To employ the expected utility criterion, we first have to determine the utility associated with each possible payoff. This can be done by assuming that the decision maker has some specific utility function or by constructing a utility index. Next, it is necessary to determine the action that has the highest expected utility. For each action a_i, the k possible payoffs $\Pi_{i1}, \Pi_{i2}, \ldots, \Pi_{ik}$ occur with probabilities $P(s_1), P(s_2), \ldots, P(s_k)$. The utilities assigned to these payoffs are $U(\Pi_{i1}), U(\Pi_{i2}), \ldots, U(\Pi_{ik})$. For any given action a_i, we obtain the expected utility payoff by weighting each potential utility by its probability of occurrence. This yields the *expected utility* of action a_i. A decision maker using the expected utility criterion determines the expected utility of each possible action and then selects the action that maximizes expected utility.

Definition: Expected Utility

Suppose a decision maker has n possible actions $a_1, a_2, \ldots, a_n$ and there are k possible states of nature. Let Π_{ij} denote the payoff from action i if state j occurs. Let U_{ij} denote the utility corresponding to the ith action and jth state, and let p_j denote the probability of the jth state of nature occurring. The **expected utility** of action a_i, denoted $E[U(a_i)]$, is

$$E[U(a_i)] = \sum_{j=1}^{k} p_j U_{ij}$$

Example 23.15 **Expected Utility Criterion:** In Example 23.14, assume that state s_1 occurs with probability .3 and state s_2 with probability .7. Find the optimal action based on the expected utility criterion.

Solution: In terms of utility, the individual's payoff matrix is shown in Table 23.7. The expected utility of action a_1 is

$$E[U(a_1)] = (.3)(0) + (.7)(100) = 70$$

The expected utility of action a_2 is

$$E[U(a_2)] = (.3)(65) + (.7)(85) = 79$$

Under the expected utility criterion, the optimal action is a_2.

TABLE 23.7
Utility payoff table for Example 23.14

	State of Nature	
	s_1	s_2
Action	$P(s_1) = .3$	$P(s_2) = .7$
a_1	0	100
a_2	65	85

Under the EMV criterion, we would use the payoffs in Table 23.6. The expected payoffs from actions a_1 and a_2 are

$$\text{EMV}(a_1) = (.3)(-400) + (.7)(800) = \$440$$

$$\text{EMV}(a_2) = (.3)(400) + (.7)(200) = \$260$$

This example illustrates that, based on the expected utility criterion, the optimal action is a_2, but based on the expected monetary value criterion, the optimal action is a_1. ■

Exercises for Section 23.3

1. Suppose you have to choose one of the following two options:

Option A Probability	Profit	Option B Probability	Profit
.3	90	.3	80
.4	100	.4	100
.3	110	.3	120

a. Which option would you choose according to the expected monetary value rule?
b. Which option would you choose according to the expected utility rule, knowing that the marginal utility of money diminishes? Illustrate your answer graphically.

2. Refer to Exercise 11 in Section 23.2. Suppose the buyer's utility function for money is

$$U(X) = \frac{\sqrt{X + 4000}}{200}$$

How many bathing suits should the buyer order based on the expected utility criterion?

3. Suppose you are indifferent between receiving \$200 with certainty and participating in a gamble in which you have a probability of .2 of receiving \$2000 and a probability of .8 of receiving nothing. You are also indifferent between receiving \$1000 with certainty and participating in a gamble in which you have a probability of .7 of receiving \$2000 and a probability of .3 of receiving nothing. Finally, you are indifferent between receiving \$1600 with certainty and participating in a gamble in which you have a probability of .95 of receiving \$2000 and a probability of .05 of receiving nothing.
a. Let $U(\$2000) = 100$ and $U(\$0) = 0$. Find $U(\$200)$, $U(\$1000)$, and $U(\$1600)$.
b. Plot your utility function for money over the range from \$0 to \$2000.

4. Consider the utility function for money

$$U(X) = \sqrt{X}$$

and the following payoff table:

	State of Nature		
Action	s_1 $P(s_1) = .25$	s_2 $P(s_2) = .40$	s_3 $P(s_3) = .35$
a_1	\$120	\$25	\$ 0
a_2	30	60	40

a. Use the utility function to convert the outcomes in the payoff table from monetary values to utility values.
b. Which action is optimal based on the expected monetary value criterion?
c. Which action is optimal based on the expected utility criterion?

5. Consider the utility function for money

$$U(X) = \ln(X + 60)$$

and the following payoff table:

	State of Nature		
Action	s_1 $P(s_1) = .60$	s_2 $P(s_2) = .30$	s_3 $P(s_3) = .10$
a_1	−\$40	\$ 10	\$100
a_2	−10	20	20
a_3	10	45	40
a_4	−20	−50	200

a. Eliminate any dominated actions.
b. Use the utility function to convert the outcomes in the payoff table from monetary values to utility values.
c. Which action is optimal using the expected utility criterion?
d. Does this decision differ from the optimal action based on the expected monetary value criterion?

6. A doctor is involved in a malpractice suit. She can either settle out of court for \$300,000 or go to court. If she goes to court and loses, she must pay the plaintiff \$825,000 plus \$75,000 in court costs. If she wins in court, the plaintiff pays the court costs and the doctor pays \$0.
a. Construct a payoff table for this decision problem.
b. The doctor's lawyer estimates the probability of winning to be .2. Use the expected monetary value criterion to decide whether the doctor should settle or go to court.
c. Suppose the doctor's utility function for money is given by

$$U(X) = \sqrt{X + 900{,}000}$$

Convert the payoffs to utility values.
d. Use the expected utility criterion to decide whether the doctor should settle or go to court.

7. Graph each of the following utility functions and classify the decision maker's attitude toward risk:

a. $U(X) = \dfrac{200 + 1.5X}{250}$ b. $U(X) = \dfrac{\sqrt{X + 200}}{25}$ c. $U(X) = X^2 - X + 25$

23.4 ▪ Decision Tree Analysis

Decision problems can also be solved using decision tree analysis. When the number of acts and states is small, (say, fewer than 4 actions and fewer than 4 states), a decision tree is useful because it makes every possible action and every possible state of nature easy to see. When the number of actions or possible states of nature gets fairly large, a decision tree can become too large to be manageable. For example, a payoff table containing 10 actions and 10 possible states of nature would require a decision tree with 100 branches.

Definition: Decision Tree

A **decision tree** is a graph showing the possible actions that can be taken, the possible states of nature and their probabilities, and the possible payoffs associated with each action and each state of nature.

Decision trees can be especially useful when the problem involves a sequence of decisions to be made or a sequence of states of nature that can occur.

Decision trees use the following conventions:

1. Points in the tree where a decision must be made about an action are called *decision nodes* (represented by rectangles).
2. Points where a state of nature occurs are called *state nodes* or chance nodes (represented by circles).
3. Each path leading from a decision node represents a different action.
4. Each path leading from a state node represents a different state of nature.
5. Near each branch leading from a state node we record the prior probability of the occurrence of that specific state of nature. These probabilities must sum to unity.
6. At the end of each branch leading from a state node, we write the payoff that would occur at that point.
7. The branch probabilities are multiplied by the payoffs at the end of those branches. The sum of the products is then recorded in the circle from which these branches emanate. The value in the circle represents the EMV of an action.

We should examine all actions from a decision node and select the action resulting in the highest EMV. Other actions should be deleted (often denoted by drawing two small lines through the appropriate branches).

Example 23.16

Using a Tree Diagram: The Burns Chemical Corporation must decide whether to invest in the development of a new quick-acting glue. The corporation has three actions open to it: a_1 = {do not invest}, a_2 = {hire one chemist at a cost of \$40,000}, and a_3 = {hire two chemists at a cost of \$70,000}. If the product is developed successfully, Burns will be able to produce 80,000 units at a cost of \$1 each and sell them all for \$3 each. If development is unsuccessful, all the research costs will be lost. The probability that one chemist working alone can develop the product successfully is .3. If two chemists work together, the probability of successful development is .6. Let us construct a decision tree for this problem and determine the optimal action.

FIGURE 23.3 **Decision tree for Example 23.16.**

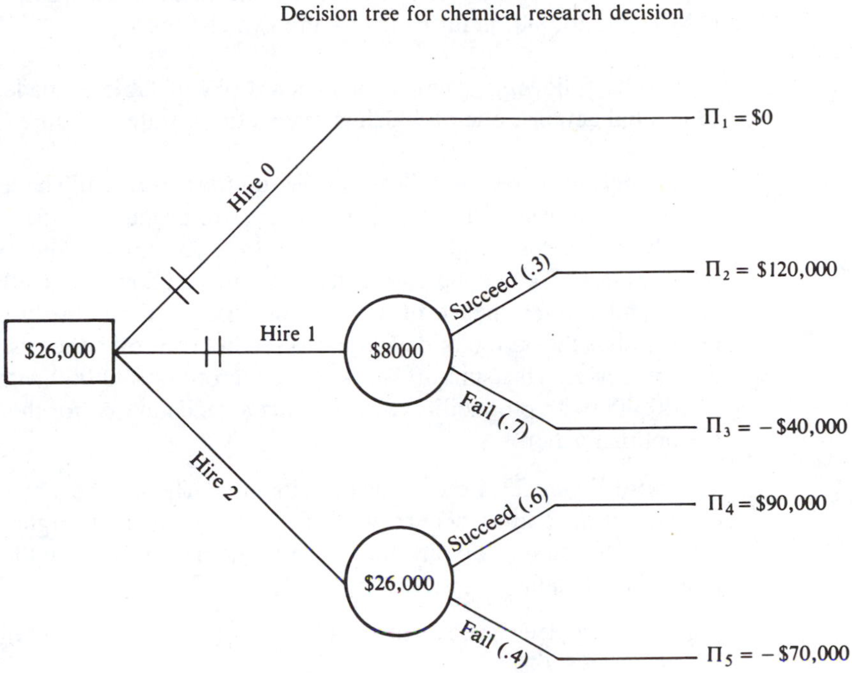

Solution: Figure 23.3 shows the decision tree. Although the sequence of actions and states of nature occur from left to right on the tree, the problem is solved by going from right to left on the tree.

Emanating from the first rectangle, or decision node, are the three possible actions: a_1 = {hire no one}, a_2 = {hire one chemist}, and a_3 = {hire two chemists}. The payoff from a_1 is $0. If we hire one chemist, we proceed across the tree to the first circle, or state node, where the project either succeeds (with probability .3) or fails (with probability .7). If it fails, the initial research costs are lost, so the payoff is − $40,000 (placed at the end of the branch). If it succeeds, there is a net payoff of $120,000 ($160,000 in gross profit from the sale of 80,000 units minus $40,000 in research costs). If two chemists are hired and the project fails, the loss is $70,000; if two chemists are hired and the project succeeds, the firm earns $160,000 in gross profits. Subtracting the $70,000 in research costs yields a payoff of $90,000. The relevant data is placed on the decision tree.

To solve the problem, we proceed from right to left. The number in the circle at the end of the "hire one chemist" branch is the EMV of hiring one chemist. We obtain

$$\text{EMV(hire one chemist)} = (120{,}000)(.3) + (-40{,}000)(.7) = \$8000$$

The expected payoff from hiring two chemists is

$$\text{EMV(hire two chemists)} = (90{,}000)(.6) + (-70{,}000)(.4) = \$26{,}000$$

The largest expected payoff, \$26,000, occurs when two chemists are hired. This value is placed in the rectangle, and the other two actions are eliminated. The optimal action (EMV = \$26,000) is for Burns to hire two chemists. ■

In the following example, a standard payoff table is inadequate because there are sequential actions, one of which is made after a state of nature is observed.

Example 23.17 **Constructing a Decision Tree for Sequential Actions:** The T. J. Television Network has to decide which of two television series to produce for next season. The first series is a detective show with a 30% chance of a \$300,000 profit and a 70% chance of an \$80,000 loss. The second possibility is a comedy show with a 40% chance of a \$200,000 profit and a 60% chance of a \$100,000 loss. If the comedy series is successful, the network has the option of developing a second spin-off series using one of the stars from the first series. This spin-off would yield a profit of \$80,000 with probability .2 or a loss of \$40,000 with probability .8. Construct a decision tree for this problem and determine the optimal action.

Solution: Figure 23.4 shows the decision tree. The numbers by the triangles show losses or gains at the point where they occur. The payoffs at the right end of the tree branches represent the sum of all payoffs shown in the triangles along the path leading to the end points. We obtain

$$\text{EMV(detective series)} = (300{,}000)(.3) + (-80{,}000)(.7) = \$34{,}000$$

FIGURE 23.4 Decision tree for Example 23.17.

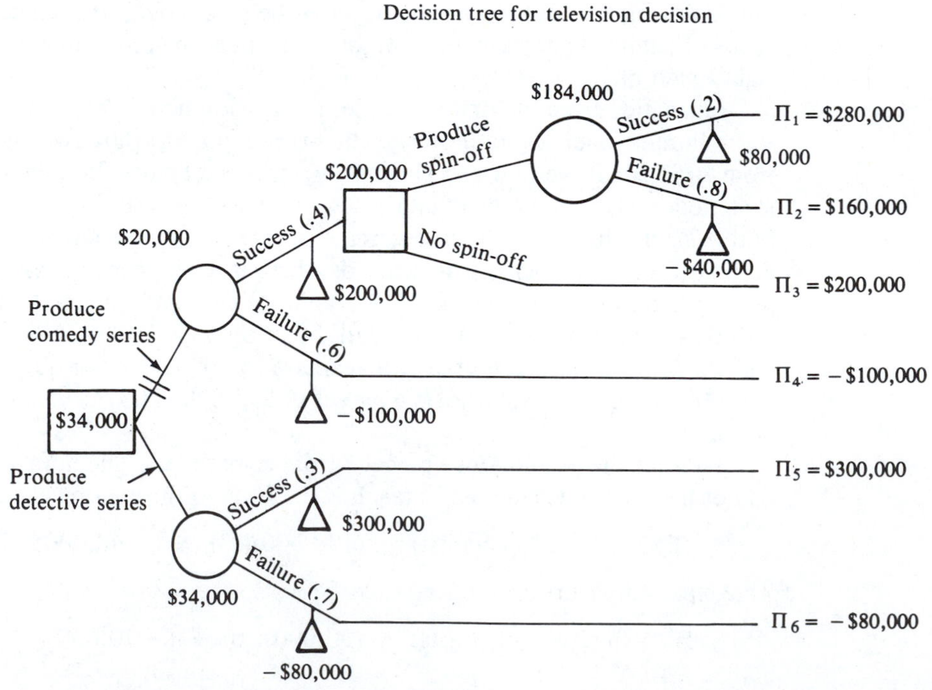

The upper path of branches shows that if the comedy series and its spin-off are both produced and are both successful, the total payoff is Π_1 = \$280,000, the sum of the payoffs by the triangles along the branches leading to Π_1 (\$200,000 + \$80,000). Similarly, if the comedy series succeeds and the spin-off fails, the total payoff is \$200,000 − \$40,000 = \$160,000.

The state node at the end of the branch labeled "Produce comedy series" shows the EMV for the comedy series

$$\text{EMV(comedy series)} = (200{,}000)(.4) + (-100{,}000)(.6) = \$20{,}000$$

where the number "200,000" is in the rectangle at the end of the branch labeled "success."

The action "No spin-off" yields a higher EMV than "Produce spin-off." Similarly, the action "Produce detective series" yields a higher EMV than "Produce comedy series." The optimal action is to produce the detective series, which has an expected payoff of \$34,000. ■

Sensitivity Analysis

We should use payoff tables and decision trees with caution, since the prior probabilities and possible payoffs are only approximately correct. Sometimes relatively small changes in the state-of-nature probabilities or in the potential payoffs can lead to a different optimal action.

For example, if in Example 23.17 we change the probability of a successful comedy series from .4 to .5, EMV(comedy series) changes from \$20,000 to \$50,000. The optimal action would then be to produce the comedy rather than the detective series.

In Example 23.17, the optimal decision is sensitive to the prior probabilities. Before taking an action based on the EMV criterion, it is advisable to perform a sensitivity analysis by making modest changes in payoffs and state-of-nature probabilities to see if the choice of optimal action is sensitive to any of these changes. If the choice is sensitive, it might be a good idea to invest some money in obtaining more reliable estimates.

Exercises for Section 23.4

1. Use the data in Exercise 1 in Sections 23.1 and 23.2.
a. Construct the decision tree.
b. Determine the optimal action based on the expected payoff.

2. Use the data in Exercise 2 in Sections 23.1 and 23.2.
a. Construct the decision tree.
b. Determine the optimal action based on the expected payoff.

3. Use the data in Exercise 3 in Sections 23.1 and 23.2.
a. Construct the decision tree.
b. Determine the optimal action based on the expected payoff.

4. Mr. Watkins owns a plot of land on the outskirts of Orlando, Florida, and has to decide whether to sell the land now or wait a year and sell it then. The land value will increase if a shopping center is built nearby and decrease if a factory is built instead. The probability is .6 that the shopping center will be built and .4 that the factory will be built. If Watkins sells today, he will get $400,000; if he sells next year and a shopping center is built, he thinks he will get $600,000. If the factory is built instead, he will get $250,000.

a. Construct the decision tree for this problem.
b. Determine the optimal action based on the expected payoff.

23.5 ▪ Revising Probabilities and Posterior Analysis

When prior probabilities are assigned to the states of nature, as in previous sections, the analyses discussed are called *prior analyses*. After undertaking a prior analysis, we must decide either to take the optimal action indicated or to obtain additional information through a marketing research study, a consumer survey, a product sampling study, or some other means. This additional information, called *sample information,* enables us to revise the prior probabilities of the states of nature. The sample information can be combined with the prior probabilities through a Bayesian procedure like that discussed in Chapter 5 to obtain the revised probabilities. These revised probabilities are called *posterior probabilities,* and we use them to recalculate the expected payoffs from the various actions.

Definition: Posterior Analysis

The calculation of EMV and EOL using posterior probabilities is called **posterior analysis**.

Suppose there are k possible outcomes or indicators of the sample study, denoted by the symbols $I_1, I_2, \ldots, I_k$. After we have obtained the sample information, we know which indicator I_j occurred, and we want to use this information to improve our estimates of the probabilities of the various states of nature. This process yields a set of posterior probabilities denoted $P(s_i|I_j)$, which represents the conditional probability that the state of nature s_i will occur given that the outcome of the sample study was the information I_j.

To calculate the conditional probability $P(s_i|I_j)$, we have to know something about the probability relationship between the indicators and the states of nature; that is, we need to know the conditional probabilities $P(I_j|s_i)$ for all values of j and i. These conditional probabilities can sometimes be obtained from historical data on relative frequencies; otherwise, some subjective probability estimates will have to be used. Note that $P(I_j|s_i)$ represents the conditional probability that our sample study will provide the information I_j given that the true state of nature is s_i.

Posterior Analysis

Definition: Preposterior Analysis

The process of determining if it is worthwhile to gather additional information before taking a final action is called **preposterior analysis**.

Example 23.18 **Preposterior Analysis:** The TJK Corporation owns a chain of fast-food outlets and plans to build a new suburban store. The outlet will be either 3000, 5000, or 9000 square feet, depending on whether the anticipated daily number of customers is low, medium, or high. TJK's advisers say that the probabilities of low demand (state s_1), medium demand (s_2), and high demand (s_3) are .2, .3, and .5, respectively. Using the payoff table in Table 23.8, let us analyze the actions that the corporation could take.

TABLE 23.8 **Payoff table for Example 23.18**

	State of Nature			
Action	s_1 (low) $P(s_1) = .2$	s_2 (medium) $P(s_2) = .3$	s_3 (high) $P(s_3) = .5$	EMV
a_1 (3000)	\$10,000	\$15,000	\$20,000	\$16,500
a_2 (5000)	− 5,000	25,000	30,000	21,500
a_3 (9000)	−15,000	−10,000	60,000	24,000

Solution: The expected monetary values are obtained as follows:

$$\text{EMV}(a_1) = (10{,}000)(.2) + (15{,}000)(.3) + (20{,}000)(.5) = \$16{,}500$$

Similarly, $\text{EMV}(a_2) = \$21{,}500$ and $\text{EMV}(a_3) = \$24{,}000$. This prior analysis indicates that the corporation should build the 9000-square-foot store because this action has the largest EMV.

When demand is low, s_1, the optimal action is to take action a_1 and earn \$10,000. When s_2 prevails, a_2 is best with earnings of \$25,000. When s_3 prevails, a_3 is the best action and earns \$60,000. Thus, in the long run, with perfect information, the corporation would earn \$10,000 with probability .2, \$25,000 with probability .3, and \$60,000 with probability .5.

The expected payoff from perfect information (EPPI) is

$$\text{EPPI} = (10{,}000)(.2) + (25{,}000)(.3) + (60{,}000)(.5) = \$39{,}500$$

Without any information the optimal action would be a_3 with expected monetary value $\text{EMV}(a_3) = \$24{,}000$. Thus, the expected value of perfect information (EVPI) is

$$\text{EVPI} = \text{EPPI} - \text{EMV}(a_3) = 39{,}500 - 24{,}000 = \$15{,}500$$

The value of EVPI tells us that the corporation should not spend more than \$15,500 to get perfect information about demand.

Suppose the corporation hires the Wilson Market Research Agency to conduct a survey to get more information about potential demand, and the agency's report indicates that the demand will be medium. If the corporation believes that this report is perfectly reliable, then getting the information I_2 is equivalent to knowing that state s_2 will occur. The revised probability of medium demand is $P(s_2) = 1$, and $P(s_1) = P(s_3) = 0$. In this case, the optimal action is a_2. ■

The situation described in Example 23.18 is unrealistic because it is rarely possible to obtain perfect information about what state of nature will occur. Assume instead that the Wilson Agency can report three types of sample information:

$$I_1 = \{\text{sample indicates low demand}\}$$
$$I_2 = \{\text{sample indicates medium demand}\}$$
$$I_3 = \{\text{sample indicates high demand}\}$$

Suppose that on the basis of similar previous surveys, Wilson can assess the reliability of its estimates. In the past when the actual demand was low (state s_1), the survey correctly predicted I_1 about 70% of the time. This relative frequency is a conditional probability that the sample evidence indicates low demand given that the actual state of nature is s_1. This relative frequency is symbolized as

$$P(I_1|s_1) = .7$$

Suppose that when state s_1 exists, the survey will predict I_2 about 20% of the time; that is,

$$P(I_2|s_1) = .2$$

All the conditional probabilities of observing the sample evidence (I_1, I_2, or I_3) given the states of nature (s_1, s_2, or s_3) are shown in Table 23.9.

TABLE 23.9 **Conditional probabilities $P(I_j|s_i)$ for fast-food problem**

Sample Information I_j	State of Nature s_1 (low)	s_2 (medium)	s_3 (high)
I_1 (predict low demand)	.7	.2	.1
I_2 (predict medium demand)	.2	.6	.4
I_3 (predict high demand)	.1	.2	.5

Calculating Posterior Probabilities

We want to use the sample information to revise our estimates of the probabilities that any particular state of nature will occur using Bayes' theorem (discussed in Section 5.7). These revised probabilities are called *posterior probabilities*. Thus, we want to find the conditional posterior probabilities $P(s_i|I_j)$ given the prior probabilities $P(s_i)$, $i = 1, 2, \ldots, k$, and given all the conditional probabilities $P(I_j|s_i)$.

From the definition of conditional probability, we have

$$P(s_i|I_j) = \frac{P(s_i \cap I_j)}{P(I_j)}$$

so we need to find expressions for $P(s_i \cap I_j)$ and $P(I_j)$ in terms of the known quantities $P(s_i)$ and $P(I_j|s_i)$.

To find $P(s_i \cap I_j)$, start with the following conditional probability formula:

$$P(I_j|s_i) = \frac{P(s_i \cap I_j)}{P(s_i)}$$

After rearranging terms, find the desired expression for $P(s_i \cap I_j)$, namely

$$P(s_i \cap I_j) = P(s_i)P(I_j|s_i)$$

To find $P(I_j)$, use the formula

$$P(I_j) = \sum_{i=1}^{k} P(I_j \cap s_i)$$

Formula for Calculating Posterior Probabilities $P(s_i|I_j)$

$$P(s_i|I_j) = \frac{P(s_i \cap I_j)}{P(I_j)}$$

where

$$P(s_i \cap I_j) = P(s_i)P(I_j|s_i)$$

and

$$P(I_j) = \sum_{i=1}^{k} P(I_j \cap s_i)$$

In the formulas, the conditional probability $P(s_i|I_j)$ represents the posterior probability of the state of nature s_i given the sample information I_j; k represents the number of possible states of nature.

The probabilities $P(I_j \cap s_i)$ are shown in Table 23.10. For example, the joint probability of I_1 and s_3 is

$$P(I_1 \cap s_3) = P(s_3)P(I_1|s_3) = (.5)(.1) = .05$$

TABLE 23.10 **Joint probabilities $P(I_j \cap s_i)$ for fast-food problem**

State of Nature	Prior Probability	$P(I_1 \cap s_j)$	$P(I_2 \cap s_j)$	$P(I_3 \cap s_j)$
s_1	.2	.14	.04	.02
s_2	.3	.06	.18	.06
s_3	.5	.05	.20	.25
	1.0	$P(I_1) = .25$	$P(I_2) = .42$	$P(I_3) = .33$

The values at the bottom of Table 23.10 represent the probabilities

$$P(I_j) = \sum_{i=1}^{k} P(I_j \cap s_i)$$

For example, we have

$$P(I_1) = \sum_{i=1}^{3} P(I_1 \cap s_i) = .14 + .06 + .05 = .25$$

Similarly, we have $P(I_2) = .42$ and $P(I_3) = .33$

Table 23.11 contains the posterior probabilities $P(s_i|I_j)$. Recall that three states of nature s_i and the three possible types of sample information I_j are in Example 23.18, so there are nine posterior probabilities to be calculated. For example, using the data in Table 23.10, we obtain

$$P(s_3|I_2) = \frac{P(s_3 \cap I_2)}{P(I_2)} = \frac{.20}{.42} = .476$$

This result is shown in Table 23.11 in row 3, column 2.

TABLE 23.11
Posterior probabilities $P(s_i|I_j)$ for fast-food problem

State of Nature	$P(s_i\|I_1)$	$P(s_i\|I_2)$	$P(s_i\|I_3)$
s_1 (low demand)	.560	.095	.061
s_2 (medium demand)	.240	.429	.182
s_3 (high demand)	.200	.476	.757
	1.000	1.000	1.000

Posterior Expected Payoffs

Once we know the posterior probabilities, we can use this added information to determine new expected payoffs. Calculating the *posterior expected payoff* is described in the accompanying box.

Formula for Posterior Expected Payoff

The **posterior expected payoff**, or expected monetary value from taking action a_i given sample information I_j, is denoted $\text{EMV}(a_i|I_j)$. We use the following formula:

$$\text{EMV}(a_i|I_j) = \sum_{r=1}^{k} \Pi_{ir} P(s_r|I_j)$$

where Π_{ir} is the payoff from taking action a_i when state of nature s_r occurs and $P(s_r|I_j)$ is the posterior probability that s_r occurs given I_j.

Let us use the formula to calculate the $\text{EMV}(a_1|I_1)$ for our fast-food problem in Example 23.18 using the posterior probabilities calculated in Table 23.11. We obtain $P(s_1|I_1) = .56$, $P(s_2|I_1) = .24$, and $P(s_3|I_1) = .20$. From Table 23.8, the payoffs are $\Pi_{11} = \$10{,}000$, $\Pi_{12} = \$15{,}000$, and $\Pi_{13} = \$20{,}000$. The posterior expected payoff from taking action a_1 given the sample information I_1 is thus

$$\begin{aligned} \text{EMV}(a_1|I_1) &= (10{,}000)(.56) + (15{,}000)(.24) + (20{,}000)(.20) \\ &= \$13{,}200 \end{aligned}$$

Similarly, we obtain

$$\begin{aligned} \text{EMV}(a_2|I_1) &= (-5000)(.560) + (25{,}000)(.240) + (30{,}000)(.20) \\ &= \$9200 \end{aligned}$$

and

$$\begin{aligned} \text{EMV}(a_3|I_2) &= (-15{,}000)(.095) + (-10{,}000)(.429) + (60{,}000)(.476) \\ &= \$22{,}845 \end{aligned}$$

All of the posterior expected payoffs $\text{EMV}(a_i|I_j)$ are shown in Table 23.12.

TABLE 23.12
Posterior expected payoffs for fast-food problem

Action	Sample Information		
	I_1	I_2	I_3
a_1 (3000 sq. ft.)	\$13,200	\$16,905	\$18,480
a_2 (5000 sq. ft.)	9,200	24,530	26,955
a_3 (9000 sq. ft.)	1,200	22,845	42,685

Suppose the agency estimates that demand will be low (I_1) and the corporation takes action a_1 (building the 3000-square-foot store). From the posterior probabilities in Table 23.11 and the payoffs in Table 23.8, we see that the probability is .56 of earning \$10,000, .24 of earning \$15,000, and .20 of earning \$15,000. The expected payoff from taking action a_1 given sample information I_1 is thus

$$(10{,}000)(.56) + (15{,}000)(.24) + (20{,}000)(.20) = \$13{,}200$$

Optimal Action Given Information I_j

If we follow the EMV criterion and are given the sample information I_j, we should take the action that yields the highest posterior expected payoff. That is, the optimal action given I_j is the action that maximizes $\text{EMV}(a_i|I_j)$. Let $\text{EMV}^*(I_j)$ denote the maximum expected payoff given the information I_j.

Once we have all the posterior expected payoffs, we would generally use the EMV criterion to choose our course of action. For example, from Table 23.12 we see that if the sample information is I_1, then the optimal action is a_1 and the maximum expected payoff is $\text{EMV}^*(I_1) = \$13{,}200$. If the sample information is I_2, then the optimal action is a_2 and $\text{EMV}^*(I_2) = \$24{,}530$. If the sample information is I_3, the optimal action is a_3 and $\text{EMV}^*(I_3) = \$42{,}685$.

The probability of obtaining the sample information I_j is $P(I_j)$, which is shown in Table 23.10. If we weight the maximum expected payoffs $\text{EMV}^*(I_j)$ by the probabilities $P(I_j)$, we obtain the *expected payoff with sample information* (EPSI).

Definition: Expected Payoff with Sample Information

The **expected payoff with sample information** (EPSI) is calculated as follows:

$$\text{EPSI} = \sum_{j=1}^{k} \text{EMV}^*(I_j)P(I_j)$$

where k represents the number of types of sample information and $\text{EMV}^*(I_j)$ is the maximum EMV given sample information I_j.

From Table 23.10 we have

$$P(I_1) = .25, \quad P(I_2) = .42, \quad \text{and} \quad P(I_3) = .33$$

We obtain

$$\text{EPSI} = (13{,}200)(.25) + (24{,}530)(.42) + (42{,}685)(.33) = \$27{,}688.65$$

Expected Value of Sample Information

Presumably we should be better off by deciding what action to take after obtaining sample information than by deciding what action to take before obtaining sample information. Since the additional information can only be obtained at a certain cost, however, it is natural to question whether the benefits of such information exceed the costs of the information. The value of the information is measured by calculating the *expected value of sample information* (EVSI), which is described in the accompanying box.

Definition: Expected Value of Sample Information

The **expected value of sample information** is the difference between the expected payoff with sample information and the expected payoff without sample information:

$$\text{EVSI} = \text{EPSI} - \text{EMV}^*$$

where EMV* is the expected monetary value of the optimal action using the prior probabilities and no sample information.

Without any sample information, the optimal action for Example 23.18 was a_3, which yielded EMV* = \$24,000. The expected value of sample information is

$$\text{EVSI} = \text{EPSI} - \text{EMV}^* = 27{,}688.65 - 24{,}000 = \$3688.65$$

It is reasonable to gather sample information provided the cost of the information is less than EVSI, or \$3688.65.

Expected Net Gain from Sampling

Definition: Expected Net Gain from Sampling

The **expected net gain from sampling** (ENGS) is the difference between EVSI and the cost of sampling.

Suppose that the Wilson Market Research Agency of Example 23.18 will perform a survey for \$8000. The expected net gain from sampling (ENGS) is \$3688.65 − \$8000 = −\$4311.35. The agency should not be hired because the cost of sampling exceeds the EVSI; the agency should be hired only if the fee is less than \$3688.65.

Suppose that the Wilson Agency agrees to provide the sample information for \$2000. Then the ENGS is \$3688.65 − \$2000 = \$1688.65. Because this value is positive, the expected benefits derived from getting sample information exceed the costs; thus the company should be hired to provide sample information.

Now suppose that the agency reports that the sample information is I_2. What action should be taken? We have seen that, given sample information I_2, the maximum expected payoff is $\text{EMV}^*(I_2)$ = \$24,530, and this payoff is associated with action a_2. Therefore the optimal action given I_2 is action a_2 (building a 5000-square-foot store).

A Word of Caution

The entire analysis should be subjected to a sensitivity analysis. The use of preposterior analysis and posterior analysis is quite logical and reasonable provided the background information is available, but keep in mind that the results obtained are derived from assumptions that may not be satisfied in the real world. To perform the type of posterior analysis described in this section, you need to know (or estimate) the payoffs Π_{ij}, the prior probabilities $P(s_j)$, and the conditional probabilities $P(I_j|s_i)$. In general, none of these numbers will be known with certainty, so the business person must estimate them as accurately as possible. This is why sensitivity analysis is so important. The decision maker should vary all of the numbers within reasonable ranges to see if the optimal decision is affected by relatively small changes in the assumptions made.

Example 23.19 **Posterior Analysis with Acceptance Sampling:** As an illustration of posterior analysis, consider a problem involving acceptance sampling of a manufactured product. Mr. Sweeney inspects incoming lots of items produced by a supplier in order to determine whether to accept or reject them. In the past, incoming lots from this supplier have contained 5% defective articles about 20% of the time, 10% defective articles about 60% of the time, and 20% defective articles about 20% of the time.

There are two possible actions: a_1 = {accept the incoming lot} and a_2 = {reject the incoming lot}. There are three possible states of nature referring to the possible proportions of defectives in the lot: s_1 = {5% defective}, s_2 = {10% defective}, and s_3 = {20% defective}. The payoffs are as given in Table 23.13. Let us analyze the data.

TABLE 23.13 **Payoff table for Example 23.19**

Action	State of Nature s_1 (5% defective) $P(s_1) = .2$	s_2 (10% defective) $P(s_2) = .6$	s_3 (20% defective) $P(s_3) = .2$	EMV
a_1 (accept lot)	\$300	\$100	−\$160	\$88
a_2 (reject lot)	0	0	0	0

Solution: First let us calculate the expected monetary value for each action. The EMVs for action 1 and action 2 are

$$\text{EMV}(a_1) = .2(300) + .6(100) + .2(-160) = \$88$$
$$\text{EMV}(a_2) = .2(0) + .6(0) + .2(0) = \$0$$

The optimal action is a_1 (accept the lot).

The expected payoff with perfect information is

$$\text{EPPI} = .2(300) + .6(100) + .2(0) = \$120$$

The expected value of perfect information is

$$\text{EVPI} = \text{EPPI} - \text{EMV}(a_1) = 120 - 88 = \$32$$

so it is worthwhile for Mr. Sweeney to pay up to \$32 to get perfect information about the true value of p, the proportion of defectives.

Because it is too time consuming and too expensive to inspect every item in the lot, Mr. Sweeney decides to inspect a random sample of n items to get additional information about p. This is a problem in acceptance sampling, which was discussed in Chapter 7.

Now let us turn to posterior analysis. Assume Mr. Sweeney selects a random sample of 12 items from the lot and finds that 3 of them are defective. If he takes this sample evidence into account, what is the optimal course of action? First, we revise the prior probabilities. We use the binomial distribution to find the probability of observing 3 defectives in 12 selections. If, in fact, the proportion of defectives is $p = .05$, then the probability of observing 3 defectives in 12 selections is

$$P(X = 3|n = 12, p = .05) = \frac{12!}{3!9!}(.05)^3(.95)^9 = .0173$$

If $p = .10$, we obtain

$$P(X = 3|n = 12, p = .10) = \frac{12!}{3!9!}(.10)^3(.90)^9 = .0852$$

If $p = .20$, we obtain

$$P(X = 3|n = 12, p = .20) = \frac{12!}{3!9!}(.20)^3(.80)^9 = .2362$$

Next we obtain the following joint probabilities:

$$P(p = .05 \text{ and } X = 3) = P(X = 3|n = 12, p = .05)P(p = .05) = (.0173)(.2) = .00346$$
$$P(p = .10 \text{ and } X = 3) = (.0852)(.6) = .05122$$
$$P(p = .20 \text{ and } X = 3) = (.2362)(.2) = .04724$$

Given these joint probabilities, we obtain

$$P(X = 3) = .00346 + .05112 + .04724 = .10182$$

Now we are ready to calculate the revised posterior probabilities $P(p|X = 3)$. We obtain

$$P(p = .05|n = 12, X = 3) = \frac{P(p = .05 \text{ and } X = 3)}{P(X = 3)}$$
$$= \frac{.00346}{.10182} = .0340$$
$$P(p = .10|n = 12, X = 3) = \frac{.05112}{.10182} = .5020$$
$$P(p = .20|n = 12, X = 3) = \frac{.04724}{.10182} = .4640$$

Based on the sample information, there is now a much higher probability that the lot contains 20% defectives than the prior probabilities indicated. Next, we calculate the EMV for each action using the payoffs in Table 23.13 and the posterior probabilities. We obtain

$$\text{EMV}(a_1) = .0340(300) + .0520(100) + .4640(-160) = -\$13.84$$
$$\text{EMV}(a_2) = 0$$

This indicates that, after observing the sample information, the optimal action is to reject the lot. ■

Effect of Sample Size on Posterior Probabilities

We can use the acceptance sampling problem to show the effect of sample size on the posterior probability distribution. In Example 23.19 Mr. Sweeney examined 12 items and found 3 defectives. Suppose, instead, he examined 36 items and found 9 defectives. In this latter sample, the proportion that is defective is .25, just as in the smaller sample. Using a more detailed table for the binomial distribution, we obtain the probabilities for the case when $n = 36$:

$$P(X = 3|n = 36, p = .05) = .0000460$$
$$P(X = 9|n = 36, p = .10) = .0054744$$
$$P(X = 9|n = 36, p = .20) = .1165437$$

Next we obtain the joint probabilities

$$P(X = 9 \text{ and } p = .05) = P(X = 9|n = 36, p = .05)P(p = .05)$$
$$= .000046(.2) = .0000092$$
$$P(X = 9 \text{ and } p = .10) = .0054744(.6) = .0032846$$
$$P(X = 9 \text{ and } p = .20) = .1165437(.2) = .0233087$$

Next we obtain

$$P(X = 9) = .0000092 + .0032846 + .0233087$$
$$= .0266025$$

Finally, we obtain the revised posterior probabilities:

$$P(p = .05 | n = 36, X = 9) = \frac{P(p = .05 \text{ and } X = 9)}{P(X = 9)}$$

$$= \frac{.0000092}{.0266025} = .0003458$$

$$P(p = .10 | n = 36, X = 9) = \frac{.032846}{.0266025} = .1234694$$

$$P(p = .20 | n = 36, X = 9) = \frac{.0233087}{.0266025} = .8761833$$

Compare these posterior probabilities with the posterior probabilities based on a sample size of 12. We see that the posterior probability that the proportion defective is $p = .20$ based on a sample size of 36 items is given by

$$P(p = .20 | n = 36, X = 9) = .8761833$$

This is much greater than

$$P(p = .20 | n = 12, X = 3) = .4640$$

That is, based on observing 9 defectives in a sample of 36 items, a much higher probability is assigned to the state of nature $p = .20$ than when we observed 3 defectives in 12 items.

This result shows that as the sample size increases, the posterior distribution of p is influenced more and more by the sample data and less by the prior probability distribution.

Exercises for Section 23.5

1. The Wiltman Chemical Company plans to build a new plant to manufacture a new brand of detergent. Three sizes of plant are under consideration:

$$a_1 = \{\text{small (50,000 square feet)}\}$$

$$a_2 = \{\text{medium (75,000 square feet)}\}$$

$$a_3 = \{\text{large (100,000 square feet)}\}$$

The potential net profits depend on light (s_1) or heavy (s_2) market demand. For light demand the payoffs from action a_1, a_2, and a_3 are \$20,000, \$30,000, and −\$40,000, respectively. For heavy demand the payoffs are −\$5000, \$10,000, and \$70,000, respectively. The executives feel that the probability is .2 that demand will be light and .8 that demand will be heavy.

a. Construct a payoff table for this problem.
b. Construct an opportunity loss table.
c. Determine the optimal action using the EMV criterion.
d. Calculate the EVPI.
e. Calculate the EPPI.

2. The Shapiro Corporation will undertake a market survey for the Wiltman Chemical Company in Exercise 1 for \$6000. Past data show that when demand is light (s_1), Shapiro predicts light demand (I_1) about 70% of the time; that is, $P(I_1|s_1) = .7$. When demand is heavy (s_2), Shapiro predicts heavy demand (I_2) about 90% of the time; that is, $P(I_2|s_2) = .9$. We also obtain

$$P(I_2|s_1) = .3 \quad \text{and} \quad P(I_1|s_2) = .1$$

a. Calculate the probabilities $P(I_1)$ and $P(I_2)$.
b. Calculate the posterior probabilities $P(s_i|I_j)$.
c. Calculate the posterior expected payoffs $\text{EMV}(a_i|I_j)$.
d. Find $\text{EMV}*(I_1)$ and $\text{EMV}*(I_2)$.
e. Calculate the expected payoff with sample information, EPSI.
f. Calculate the expected value of sample information, EVSI.
g. Calculate the expected net gain from sampling, ENGS.
h. Should Wiltman hire Shapiro?
i. Suppose Shapiro is hired for a minimal fee and predicts light demand. What size store should be built?

3. The Massey Corporation is considering whether to market a new breakfast cereal. The possible actions are $a_1 = \{\text{market the cereal}\}$, and $a_2 = \{\text{do not market the cereal}\}$. The states of nature are $s_1 = \{\text{high demand}\}$, and $s_2 = \{\text{low demand}\}$. Massey's prior probabilities, based on past experience, are $P(s_1) = .4$ and $P(s_2) = .6$. The net profits from action a_1 are $300,000 if s_1 occurs and −$100,000 if s_2 occurs. The net profits from action a_2 are always 0.
a. Construct the payoff table for this problem.
b. Determine the optimal action using the EMV criterion.
c. Construct the opportunity loss table for this problem.
d. Calculate the EVPI.
e. Construct a decision tree.

4. In Exercise 3 the Massey Corporation does a preposterior analysis to decide whether to hire the Foster Market Research Company to help determine demand. For $12,000 Foster will make one of two possible estimates: $I_1 = \{\text{high demand}\}$, and $I_2 = \{\text{low demand}\}$. From past experience, if the true state is s_1, they will estimate I_1 with probability .8 and I_2 with probability .2; if the true state is s_2, they will estimate I_1 with probability .3 and I_2 with probability .7.
a. Construct a joint probability and posterior probability table.
b. Calculate the EVSI.
c. Calculate the ENGS.
d. Should Massey hire Foster?

5. In Exercise 4 Massey hires Foster, and Foster's research estimates a high demand (I_1). Use the posterior probabilities and calculate the EMV of the optimal action.

6. Ms. McCown is a toy buyer for a nationwide chain of department stores. She has just received a shipment of several thousand electronic games from a large supplier. In the past, incoming lots from this supplier have contained the following percentage of defective items:

$$s_1 = \{5\% \text{ defective items}\} \text{ with } P(s_1) = .2$$
$$s_2 = \{10\% \text{ defective items}\} \text{ with } P(s_2) = .5$$
$$s_3 = \{25\% \text{ defective items}\} \text{ with } P(s_3) = .3$$

It is believed that the current lot also contains 5%, 10%, or 25% defective items with the same probabilities as in the past. Ms. McCown has two possible actions: $a_1 = \{\text{accept lot}\}$ or $a_2 = \{\text{reject lot}\}$. The payoff table for Ms. McCown is as follows:

	s_1	s_2	s_3
a_1	$80,000	$30,000	−$60,000
a_2	0	0	0

a. Calculate the EMV for each action and determine the optimal action.
b. Calculate the expected payoff with perfect information, EPPI.
c. Calculate the expected value of perfect information, EVPI.

7. In Exercise 6 suppose that Ms. McCown selects a random sample of 20 items from the lot and finds that 6 are defective.
a. Calculate the revised posterior probabilities given the sample information.
b. Calculate the EMV for each action using the posterior probabilities.
c. Determine the optimal action.

8. Mr. Wicks buys computer equipment for U.S. post offices. He has just received a shipment of several hundred new sorting machines, which could save the U.S. Postal Service substantial sums of money. Mr. Wicks has two possible actions: a_1 = {accept lot} or a_2 = {reject lot}. In the past the percentages of defective items received from the supplier have been as follows:

$$s_1 = \{5\% \text{ defective items}\} \text{ with } P(s_1) = .3$$

$$s_2 = \{10\% \text{ defective items}\} \text{ with } P(s_2) = .5$$

$$s_3 = \{40\% \text{ defective items}\} \text{ with } P(s_3) = .2$$

Mr. Wicks figures that his payoff table is as follows:

	s_1	s_2	s_3
a_1	\$300,000	\$200,000	−\$600,000
a_2	0	0	0

a. Calculate the EMV of each action and determine the optimal action.
b. Calculate EPPI.
c. Calculate EVPI.

9. Refer to Exercise 8. Mr. Wicks hired a computer expert to test a sample of 4 of the new sorting machines. The consultant determined that 2 of the devices were defective.
a. Calculate the revised posterior probabilities given the sample information.
b. Calculate the EMV of each action based on the posterior probabilities.
c. Determine the optimal action.

10. Refer to Exercises 8 and 9. Suppose the computer expert tested 20 of the devices and found that 10 were defective.
a. Calculate the posterior probabilities given the sample information.
b. Calculate the EMV of each action using the posterior probabilities.
c. Determine the optimal action.

23.6 ▪ Decision Making with Infinite Number of Alternative States of Nature

The decision-making processes discussed in this chapter are based on the assumption that the number of states of nature and the number of alternative actions are finite. In many cases, however, the states of nature and their probabilities can be expressed more realistically using a continuous distribution rather than a discrete distribution. In this section we discuss a problem where we can determine an optimal action when the states of nature follow a continuous distribution, that is, when there are an infinite number of possible states of nature.

Suppose we can buy an item for C dollars and sell it for S dollars. The difference $(S - C)$ is the marginal profit (MP) obtained by selling an additional unit of the item. When we stock an additional unit and do not sell it, a marginal loss (ML) of C dollars is incurred.

Let p denote the probability of selling one additional unit. Then $(1 - p)$ is the probability of not selling the unit. If one additional unit is sold, total profit increases by MP. If we stock an additional unit and it is not sold, total profit decreases by ML. An additional unit should be stocked as long as the expected marginal profit from stocking the item exceeds the expected marginal loss. The expected marginal profit from stocking an additional item is $p(\text{MP})$, and the expected marginal loss from stocking an additional item is $(1 - p)\text{ML}$. We should stock additional units as long as

$$p(\text{MP}) \geqslant (1 - p)\text{ML}$$

If we solve this inequality for p, we determine that we should stock additional units as long as

$$p \geqslant \frac{\text{ML}}{\text{MP} + \text{ML}}$$

Minimum Required Probability to Justify Stocking an Item

We should stock additional units as long as the probability of selling an additional unit is greater than p^*, where

$$p^* = \text{ML}/(\text{MP} + \text{ML})$$

Example 23.20 **Determining Whether to Stock an Additional Item I:** A grocer pays \$30 for each crate of mushrooms and sells each crate for \$50. Each unsold crate is a total loss. Find the minimum required probability of selling an additional unit to justify stocking an additional unit.

Solution: The marginal loss from stocking a crate of mushrooms and not selling it is ML = \$30. The marginal profit from stocking a crate of mushrooms and selling it is MP = \$50 − \$30 = \$20. The minimum required probability of selling an additional unit is $p = 30/(20 + 30) = .6$. That is, the grocer should stock an additional unit provided the probability of selling it is at least .6.

Let Q denote the quantity of crates of mushrooms that the grocer can sell at \$50 per crate. Suppose that Q is a random variable having a normal distribution with a mean of 18 and a standard deviation of 4 (see Figure 23.5). The area under the curve to the right

FIGURE 23.5
Optimal value of Q for Example 23.20.

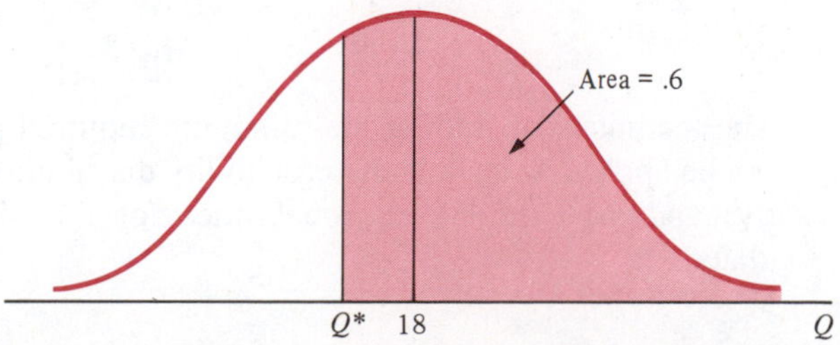

of Q^* represents the probability that the grocer can sell Q^* units or more. We need to find Q^* such that the area to the right of Q^* is .6.

From the standard normal distribution, the Z score having an area of .6 to its right is approximately $z = -.25$. From the standardizing transformation, we obtain $z = -.25 = (Q^* - 18)/4$. The solution is $Q^* = 17$; that is, the grocer should stock 17 crates of mushrooms. ■

Example 23.21

Determining Whether to Stock an Additional Item II: The Zielke Toy Store has to order items in October in order to receive them in time for sale during the Christmas season. A new toy robot modeled after a character in a science fiction movie is expected to be a big seller. The toy costs \$12 per unit and will be sold for \$28 per unit. Unsold toys will be sold to local discount stores for \$8 apiece. The demand for the robot is expected to be normally distributed with mean 140 and standard deviation 10. How many robots should Mr. Zielke order?

Solution: The marginal profit from selling a unit is MP = \$28 − \$12 = \$16. The marginal loss from not selling a unit is ML = \$12 − \$8 = \$4. The minimum required probability is

$$p^* = \frac{4}{4 + 16} = .2$$

Next, we use the standard normal table (Table A.5) and find the Z score such that the area to its right is .2. This Z score is approximately $z = .84$.

Now we find the optimal number of robots to order using the equation $z = .84 = (Q^* - 140)/10$. We obtain $Q^* = 148.4$. Mr. Zielke should order 148 toy robots (see Figure 23.6).

FIGURE 23.6
Optimal value of Q for Example 23.21.

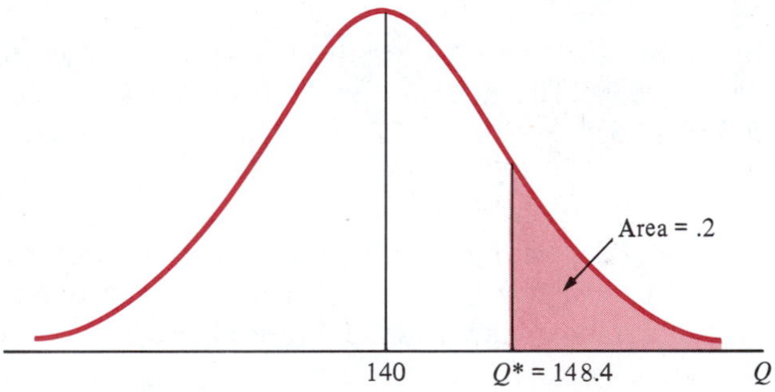

■

The technique of finding the minimum required probability and the optimal value Q^* can be applied as long as the probability distribution of Q is known (at least approximately) and the cumulative probabilities for the distribution are known or can be calculated.

Exercises for Section 23.6

1. Jo Ann's Clothing Store sells T-shirts each year to people attending the Rose Bowl football game. The shirts contain an appropriate decal showing the date and the nicknames of the teams participating in the game. Each shirt costs $2 to produce and is sold for $5. After the game any unsold shirts are sold to discount houses for $0.50 each. It is believed that demand is normally distributed with mean 20,000 and standard deviation 3000. How many shirts should be produced in order to maximize expected profits?
2. Every day a baker has to decide how many cookies to make. Cookies cost 7¢ apiece to make and sell for 10¢. Unsold cookies are given away to a local hospital. From past experience the baker thinks that daily demand is normally distributed with mean 600 and standard deviation 100. How many cookies should the baker make in order to maximize the expected profit?
3. Doherty's Fish Market sells fresh fish daily to the major restaurants and grocery stores in a large city. The fish cost Mr. Doherty $1.50 per pound and are sold for $2.29 per pound. Any unsold fish are sold on the following day for $1.00 per pound. Demand for fresh fish is normally distributed with mean 2500 pounds and standard deviation 200 pounds. How many pounds of fresh fish should Mr. Doherty stock to maximize his expected profits?
4. Millie is the proprietor of a florist shop. She has to decide how many dozen roses to order to be ready for the Valentine's Day crush. Roses cost Millie $9 per dozen, and she sells them for $15 per dozen. Unsold roses are given to the local hospitals. Millie thinks that the demand is approximately normally distributed with mean 190 dozen and standard deviation 30 dozen. How many dozen roses should Millie stock in order to maximize expected profits?

Chapter 23 Summary

Chapter 23 provides an introduction to statistical decision theory where we explicitly take into account the costs and benefits associated with different actions. It is assumed that there are k different possible states of nature s_j and n possible actions a_i. The decision maker must decide which action to take given information on the probability of occurrence $P(s_j)$ of each state of nature.

A *payoff table* shows the potential payoff Π_{ij} from taking action a_i when state s_j occurs. An action is *dominated* if there exists another action having a higher payoff associated with every possible state of nature. Dominated actions can be dropped from the analysis because they can never be the optimal action. We discussed seven criteria that are sometimes used when deciding which action to take:

1. The *maximax criterion* selects the action with the largest possible payoff. This criterion is used by extremely optimistic people.
2. The *maximin criterion* selects the action that maximizes the minimum possible payoff from taking any specific action. This criterion is used by extremely pessimistic people.
3. The *minimax criterion* selects the action that minimizes the maximum possible opportunity loss from taking any specific action.
4. The *Laplace criterion, or the strategy of insufficient reason,* selects the action that has the largest expected payoff based on the assumption that all states of nature are equally likely.

5. The *expected monetary value criterion* selects the action with the highest expected payoff given prior information concerning the probability of occurrence of each state of nature. The *expected monetary value* associated with action a_i is

$$\text{EMV}(a_i) = \sum_{j=1}^{k} \Pi_{ij} P(s_j)$$

6. The *expected opportunity loss criterion* selects the action that minimizes the expected opportunity loss.
7. The *expected utility criterion* selects the action that maximizes the expected utility given prior information concerning the probability of occurrence of each state of nature.

$$\text{Expected utility}(a_i) = \sum_{j=1}^{k} U_{ij} P(s_j)$$

The *expected value of perfect information* is the difference between the expected payoff with perfect information about which state will occur and the maximum expected monetary value for any action. To solve a decision problem, it is sometimes useful to construct a *decision tree* that shows all the states of nature and their probabilities along with all the possible actions and their potential payoffs.

The prior probabilities associated with each state of nature can be revised based on sample information concerning which state will occur. The calculation of expected monetary values based on the *posterior probabilities* is called a *posterior analysis*. Posterior probabilities $P(s_i|I_j)$ are revised estimates of the state probabilities conditional on sample information I_j. The process of determining if it is worthwhile to gather additional information before taking a final action is called *preposterior analysis*.

The *expected value of sample information* is the difference between the expected payoff with sample information and the maximum expected monetary value with no sample information. The *expected net gain from sampling* is the difference between the expected value of sample information and the cost of sampling. Any decision making problem should be subjected to a *sensitivity analysis* to determine if the optimal decision is sensitive to assumptions made about the state probabilities.

Usually problems involving an infinite number of possible actions or an infinite number of states of nature are much more difficult to solve than problems involving a finite number of actions and states. In Section 23.6, we showed how to solve a class of decision problems, called *inventory problems*, that are concerned with determining the optimal number of items to stock based on information concerning the potential demand for the item, the cost of the item and the selling price of the item.

Chapter 23 ▪ Supplementary Exercises

1. Mike Newman, just graduated from City College, has been offered a job in which the present value to Mike is \$200,000. If Mike declines the job offer and goes to graduate school, the probability is .2 that he will get a Ph.D. degree and a job in which the present value is \$350,000; the probability is .6 that he will get an M.A. degree and a job in which the present value is \$280,000; and the probability is .2 that he will quit graduate school without a degree and get a job in which the present value is \$140,000. Construct a decision tree and determine Mike's optimal action. Should he go to graduate school if he wants to maximize the expected present value of his income?

2. A grocer stocks a perishable product. Each item costs \$3 and is sold for \$5. Unsold items are a total loss. The grocer has to decide whether to stock 10, 20, or 30 units. The demand situation, in the grocer's opinion, is as follows: $P(\text{demand} = 8) = .4$, $P(\text{demand} = 17) = .5$, and $P(\text{demand} = 31) = .1$.

a. Construct payoff and opportunity loss tables.
b. Determine the optimal action using the EMV criterion.
c. Calculate EVPI using the opportunity loss table.
d. Construct a decision tree.

3. The National Oil Company has to decide whether to drill a well on a site in Alaska. Preliminary analysis indicates a 60% probability of striking oil on the site. A successful well will yield a net profit of \$400,000, but a dry well will cause a net loss of \$200,000.

a. Construct a payoff table and a decision tree.
b. Construct an opportunity loss table.
c. Determine the optimal action using the EMV criterion.
d. Calculate EVPI.

4. In Exercise 3 the oil company can perform some additional exploratory work at the site for \$20,000 prior to drilling. When oil is present (s_1), the exploratory study correctly predicts oil 90% of the time. When no oil is present (s_2), the study correctly predicts no oil about 80% of the time.

a. Determine the EVSI.
b. Calculate ENGS.
c. Should the exploratory study be performed?

5. Suppose that the exploratory study in Exercise 4 indicates that oil is present. Determine the optimal action and the expected payoff.

6. A farmer must decide which one of three crops (c_1, c_2, or c_3) to plant. The potential profits depend on the weather. If the weather is good, the farmer thinks the net profit from crop c_1 will be \$30,000; from c_2, \$40,000; and from c_3, \$50,000. If the weather is bad, each crop will yield a net loss of \$10,000 for c_1, \$15,000 for c_2, and \$20,000 for c_3. The farmer thinks the probability of good weather is .6.

a. Construct a payoff table and determine the optimal action.
b. Determine the optimal action by using the minimax criterion.

7. Mary Anderson has \$10,000 to invest for one year. She has three potential options: (a_1) she can buy a savings certificate that will yield \$900; (a_2) she can buy stock that she thinks will sell in one year for a profit of \$1100 if there is no recession or a profit of \$500 if there is a recession; (a_3) she can buy some real estate that she thinks will yield a profit of \$3000 if a new shopping center is built on the neighboring land, a profit of \$800 if a park is built there, or a loss of \$700 if the neighboring land is left undeveloped. Mary thinks the probability of a recession is .3; of a shopping center, .4; of a park, .3; and of no development, .3.

a. Construct a decision tree.
b. Determine the optimal action and find the expected payoff.

8. While preparing his income tax return, John Wilkinson has to decide whether to claim certain questionable entertainment costs as business expenses. If he claims the expenses as deductions and is not audited, he will save \$3000. If his return is audited, there is a 90% chance that the deductions will be denied, and he will have to pay the \$3000 in taxes plus a \$1000 penalty. John thinks that if he claims the deduction, the probability is .4 that his return will be audited.

a. Construct a payoff table and a decision tree.
b. Determine the optimal action and the expected payoff.
c. Calculate the EVPI.

9. The Petrol Company has drilling rights on a large tract of land in Alaska. A preliminary analysis indicates that $P(s_1) = .3$, where s_1 means that oil exists on the land. The prior probability that the land does not contain oil is $P(s_2) = .7$, where s_2 means that oil is not present. The company has two possible actions: a_1 = {drill} or a_2 = {do not drill}. The potential payoffs are as follows:

	s_1 = Oil	s_2 = No Oil
a_1 = drill	\$1,000,000	−\$500,000
a_2 = do not drill	0	0

a. Find the EMV of each action and determine the optimal action.
b. Determine the EPPI.
c. Determine the EVPI.

10. In the previous problem, suppose that Petrol can spend \$100,000 for an extensive geological study of the land to get more information about the probability of oil being present. Let I_1 = {information indicates that oil is present} and I_2 = {information indicates no oil is present}. From past explorations Petrol knows that the sample information is not always correct. The conditional probabilities I_j given s_i are

$$P(I_1|s_1) = .9 \quad P(I_1|s_2) = .2$$
$$P(I_2|s_1) = .1 \quad P(I_2|s_2) = .8$$

a. Calculate the joint probabilities $P(s_i|I_j)$.
b. Calculate the probabilities $P(I_j)$.
c. Calculate the conditional posterior probabilities $P(s_i|I_j)$.
d. Calculate the expected posterior payoffs $\text{EMV}(a_i|I_j)$.
e. Calculate the EPSI.
f. Calculate the EVSI.
g. Calculate the ENGS. Should Petrol commission the extensive geological study?
h. Suppose the study is performed and yields the sample information I_1. Determine the optimal action and the EMV from taking that action.

11. Refer to Exercises 9 and 10. Perform a sensitivity analysis by replacing the payoffs by the values $P(a_1|s_1) = \$3{,}000{,}000$ and $P(a_1|s_2) = -\$600{,}000$. Repeat all the calculations in Exercises 9 and 10.

12. The following data show the profits (in millions of dollars) associated with five actions and six states of nature. Determine the best action under the following criteria:
a. Maximin
b. Maximax
c. Expected monetary value assuming $P(s_1) = .10$, $P(s_2) = .20$, $P(s_3) = .30$, $P(s_4) = .10$, $P(s_5) = .05$, and $P(s_6) = .25$.

	State of Nature					
Action	s_1	s_2	s_3	s_4	s_5	s_6
a_1	0	−11	−32	−48	26	67
a_2	−15	−32	−47	33	67	102
a_3	−35	−50	21	65	102	139
a_4	−48	22	67	102	139	150
a_5	24	67	112	129	144	−110

13. The data below show profits (in millions of dollars) associated with four actions and five states of nature. Determine the best action under the following criteria:
a. Maximin
b. Maximax
c. Expected monetary value assuming $P(s_1) = .2$, $P(s_2) = .3$, $P(s_3) = .2$, $P(s_4) = .1$, and $P(s_5) = .3$.

	State of Nature				
Action	s_1	s_2	s_3	s_4	s_5
a_1	88	67	58	−14	0
a_2	0	14	62	105	2
a_3	5	6	9	70	−5
a_4	−53	89	0	−12	102

14. The following data show benefits associated with five actions and four states of nature. Determine the best action under the following criteria:
a. Maximin
b. Maximax
c. Expected monetary value assuming $P(s_1) = .1$, $P(s_2) = .3$, $P(s_3) = .2$, and $P(s_4) = .4$.

	State of Nature			
Action	s_1	s_2	s_3	s_4
a_1	20	37	51	−11
a_2	34	32	35	32
a_3	14	−53	−1	73
a_4	−63	17	18	74
a_5	0	0	12	66

15. An investor is thinking of buying a bankrupt resort, which would cost $500,000 in interest fees annually plus an additional expense of $200,000 per year for overhead. At a contemplated net profit of $200 per guest, the probabilities are .1, .5, and .4, respectively, that 3000 guests, 3500 guests, or 4000 guests per year will use the resort. Use a decision tree to determine the optimal action, given the desire to maximize expected monetary value and given the option of not making the investment at all.

References

LUCE, ROBERT D., and HOWARD RAIFFA. *Games and Decisions*. New York: Wiley, 1958.

NEUMANN, JOHN VON, and OSKAR MORGENSTERN. *The Theory of Games and Economic Behavior*. Rev. ed. Princeton: Princeton University Press, 1953.

RAIFFA, HOWARD. *Decision Analysis: Introductory Lectures on Choices Under Uncertainty.* Reading, Mass.: Addison-Wesley, 1968.

SAVAGE, LEONARD J. "The Theory of Statistical Decision." *Journal of the American Statistical Association,* March 1951, pp. 55–67.

SCHLAIFER, ROBERT. *Probability and Statistics for Business Decisions: An Introduction to Managerial Economics Under Uncertainty.* New York: McGraw-Hill, 1959.

———. *Analysis of Decisions Under Uncertainty.* New York: McGraw-Hill, 1969.

Appendix A
Tables

TABLE A.1 **Random numbers**

12651	61646	11769	75109	86996	97669	25757	32535	07122	76763
81769	74436	02630	72310	45049	18029	07469	42341	98173	79260
36737	98863	77240	76251	00654	64688	09343	70278	67331	98729
82861	54371	76610	94934	72748	44124	05610	53750	95938	01485
21325	15732	24127	37431	09723	63529	73977	95218	96074	42138
74146	47887	62463	23045	41490	07954	22597	60012	98866	90959
90759	64410	54179	66075	61051	75385	51378	08360	95946	95547
55683	98078	02238	91540	21219	17720	87817	41705	95785	12563
79686	17969	76061	83748	55920	83612	41540	86492	06447	60568
70333	00201	86201	69716	78185	62154	77930	67663	29529	75116
14042	53536	07779	04157	41172	36473	42123	43929	50533	33437
59911	08256	06596	48416	69770	68797	56080	14223	59199	30162
62368	62623	62742	14891	39247	52242	98832	69533	91174	57979
57529	97751	54976	48957	74599	08759	78494	52785	68526	64618
15469	90574	78033	66885	13936	42117	71831	22961	94225	31816
18625	23674	53850	32827	81647	80820	00420	63555	74489	80141
74626	68394	88562	70745	23701	45630	65891	58220	35442	60414
11119	16519	27384	90199	79210	76965	99546	30323	31664	22845
41101	17336	48951	53674	17880	45260	08575	49321	36191	17095
32123	91576	84221	78902	82010	30847	62329	63898	23268	74283
26091	68409	69704	82267	14751	13151	93115	01437	56945	89661
67680	79790	48462	59278	44185	29616	76531	19589	83139	28454
15184	19260	14073	07026	25264	08388	27182	22557	61501	67481
58010	45039	57181	10238	36874	28546	37444	80824	63981	39942
56425	53996	86245	32623	78858	08143	60377	42925	42815	11159
82630	84066	13592	60642	17904	99718	63432	88642	37858	25431
14927	40909	23900	48761	44860	92467	31742	87142	03607	32059
23740	22505	07489	85986	74420	21744	97711	36648	35620	97949
32990	97446	03711	63824	07953	85965	87089	11687	92414	67257
05310	24058	91946	78437	34365	82469	12430	84754	19354	72745
21839	39937	27534	88913	49055	19218	47712	67677	51889	70926
08833	42549	93981	94051	28382	83725	72643	64233	97252	17133
58336	11139	47479	00931	91560	95372	97642	33856	54825	55680
62032	91144	75478	47431	52726	30289	42411	91886	51818	78292
45171	30557	53116	04118	58301	24375	65609	85810	18620	49198
91611	62656	60128	35609	63698	78356	50682	22505	01692	36291
55472	63819	86314	49174	93582	73604	78614	78849	23096	72825
18573	09729	74091	53994	10970	86557	65661	41854	26037	53296
60866	02955	90288	82136	83644	94455	06560	78029	98768	71296
45043	55608	82767	60890	74646	79485	13619	98868	40857	19415
17831	09737	79473	75945	28394	79334	70577	38048	03607	06932
40137	03981	07585	18128	11178	32601	27994	05641	22600	86064
77776	31343	14576	97706	16039	47517	43300	59080	80392	63189
69605	44104	40103	95635	05635	81673	68657	09559	23510	95875
19916	52934	26499	09821	97331	80993	61299	36979	73599	35055
02606	58552	07678	56619	65325	30705	99582	53390	46357	13244
65183	73160	87131	35530	47946	09854	18080	02321	05809	04893
10740	98914	44916	11322	89717	88189	30143	52687	19420	60061
98642	89822	71691	51573	83666	61642	46683	33761	47542	23551
60139	25601	93663	25547	02654	94829	48672	28736	84994	13071

From *A Million Random Digits with 100,000 Normal Deviates*. N.Y.: The Free Press, 1955. Reprinted with permission of the Rand Corp.

TABLE A.2 **Binomial distribution**

The following table contains selected values of the binomial cumulative distribution function

$$P(X \leq c) = \sum_{x=0}^{c} \binom{n}{x} p^x (1-p)^{n-x}$$

		p												
n	*c*	.01	.05	.10	.20	.30	.40	.50	.60	.70	.80	.90	.95	.99
5	0	.951	.774	.590	.328	.168	.078	.031	.010	.002	.000	.000	.000	.000
	1	.999	.977	.919	.737	.528	.337	.188	.087	.031	.007	.000	.000	.000
	2	1.000	.999	.991	.942	.837	.683	.500	.317	.163	.058	.009	.001	.000
	3	1.000	1.000	1.000	.993	.969	.913	.812	.663	.472	.263	.081	.023	.001
	4	1.000	1.000	1.000	1.000	.998	.990	.969	.922	.832	.672	.410	.226	.049
6	0	.941	.735	.531	.262	.118	.047	.016	.004	.001	.000	.000	.000	.000
	1	.999	.967	.886	.655	.420	.233	.109	.041	.011	.002	.000	.000	.000
	2	1.000	.998	.984	.901	.744	.544	.344	.179	.070	.017	.001	.000	.000
	3	1.000	1.000	.999	.983	.930	.821	.656	.456	.256	.099	.016	.002	.000
	4	1.000	1.000	1.000	.998	.989	.959	.891	.767	.580	.345	.114	.033	.001
	5	1.000	1.000	1.000	1.000	.999	.996	.984	.953	.882	.738	.469	.265	.059
7	0	.932	.698	.478	.210	.082	.028	.008	.002	.000	.000	.000	.000	.000
	1	.998	.956	.850	.577	.329	.159	.063	.019	.004	.000	.000	.000	.000
	2	1.000	.996	.974	.852	.647	.420	.227	.096	.029	.005	.000	.000	.000
	3	1.000	1.000	.997	.967	.874	.710	.500	.290	.126	.033	.003	.000	.000
	4	1.000	1.000	1.000	.995	.971	.904	.773	.580	.353	.148	.026	.004	.000
	5	1.000	1.000	1.000	1.000	.996	.981	.937	.841	.671	.423	.150	.044	.002
	6	1.000	1.000	1.000	1.000	1.000	.998	.992	.972	.918	.790	.522	.302	.068
8	0	.923	.663	.430	.168	.058	.017	.004	.001	.000	.000	.000	.000	.000
	1	.997	.943	.813	.503	.255	.106	.035	.009	.001	.000	.000	.000	.000
	2	1.000	.994	.962	.797	.552	.315	.145	.050	.011	.001	.000	.000	.000
	3	1.000	1.000	.995	.944	.806	.594	.363	.174	.058	.010	.000	.000	.000
	4	1.000	1.000	1.000	.990	.942	.826	.637	.406	.194	.056	.005	.000	.000
	5	1.000	1.000	1.000	.999	.989	.950	.855	.685	.448	.203	.038	.006	.000
	6	1.000	1.000	1.000	1.000	.999	.991	.965	.894	.745	.497	.187	.057	.003
	7	1.000	1,000	1.000	1.000	1.000	.999	.996	.983	.942	.832	.570	.337	.077
9	0	.914	.630	.387	.134	.040	.010	.002	.000	.000	.000	.000	.000	.000
	1	.997	.929	.775	.436	.196	.071	.020	.004	.000	.000	.000	.000	.000
	2	1.000	.992	.947	.738	.463	.232	.090	.025	.004	.000	.000	.000	.000
	3	1.000	.999	.992	.914	.730	.483	.254	.099	.025	.003	.000	.000	.000
	4	1.000	1.000	.999	.980	.901	.733	.500	.267	.099	.020	.001	.000	.000
	5	1.000	1.000	1.000	.997	.975	.901	.746	.517	.270	.086	.008	.001	.000
	6	1.000	1.000	1.000	1.000	.996	.975	.910	.768	.537	.262	.053	.008	.000
	7	1.000	1.000	1.000	1.000	1.000	.996	.980	.929	.804	.564	.225	.071	.003
	8	1.000	1.000	1.000	1.000	1.000	1.000	.998	.990	.960	.866	.613	.370	.086

Example: If $p = .20$, $n = 7$, and $c = 2$, then $P(X \leq 2) = .852$.

continued

TABLE A.2 **Binomial distribution (*continued*)**

		p												
n	*c*	.01	.05	.10	.20	.30	.40	.50	.60	.70	.80	.90	.95	.99
10	0	.904	.599	.349	.107	.028	.006	.001	.000	.000	.000	.000	.000	.000
	1	.996	.914	.736	.376	.149	.046	.011	.002	.000	.000	.000	.000	.000
	2	1.000	.988	.930	.678	.383	.167	.055	.012	.002	.000	.000	.000	.000
	3	1.000	.999	.987	.879	.650	.382	.172	.055	.011	.001	.000	.000	000
	4	1.000	1.000	.998	.967	.850	.633	.377	.166	.047	.006	.000	.000	.000
	5	1.000	1.000	1.000	.994	.953	.834	.623	.367	.150	.033	.002	.000	.000
	6	1.000	1.000	1.000	.999	.989	.945	.828	.618	.350	.121	.013	.001	.000
	7	1.000	1.000	1.000	1.000	.998	.988	.945	.833	.617	.322	.070	.012	.000
	8	1.000	1.000	1.000	1.000	1.000	.998	.989	.954	.851	.624	.264	.086	.004
	9	1.000	1.000	1.000	1.000	1.000	1.000	.999	.994	.972	.893	.651	.401	.096
15	0	.860	.463	.206	.035	.005	.000	.000	.000	.000	.000	.000	.000	.000
	1	.990	.829	.549	.167	.035	.005	.000	.000	.000	.000	.000	.000	.000
	2	1.000	.964	.816	.398	.127	.027	.004	.000	.000	.000	.000	.000	.000
	3	1.000	.995	.944	.648	.297	.091	.018	.002	.000	.000	.000	.000	.000
	4	1.000	.999	.987	.836	.515	.217	.059	.009	.001	.000	.000	.000	.000
	5	1.000	1.000	.998	.939	.722	.403	.151	.034	.004	.000	.000	.000	.000
	6	1.000	1.000	1.000	.982	.869	.610	.304	.095	.015	.001	.000	.000	.000
	7	1.000	1.000	1.000	.996	.950	.787	.500	.213	.050	.004	.000	.000	.000
	8	1.000	1.000	1.000	.999	.985	.905	.696	.390	.131	.018	.000	.000	.000
	9	1.000	1.000	1.000	1.000	.996	.966	.849	.597	.278	.061	.002	.000	.000
	10	1.000	1.000	1.000	1.000	.999	.991	.941	.783	.485	.164	.013	.001	.000
	11	1.000	1.000	1.000	1.000	1.000	.998	.982	.909	.703	.352	.056	.005	.000
	12	1.000	1.000	1.000	1.000	1.000	1.000	.996	.973	.873	.602	.184	.036	.000
	13	1.000	1.000	1.000	1.000	1.000	1.000	1.000	.995	.965	.833	.451	.171	.010
	14	1.000	1.000	1.000	1.000	1.000	1.000	1.000	1.000	.995	.965	.794	.537	.140
20	0	.818	.358	.122	.012	.001	.000	.000	.000	.000	.000	.000	.000	.000
	1	.983	.736	.392	.069	.008	.001	.000	.000	.000	.000	.000	.000	.000
	2	.999	.925	.677	.206	.035	.004	.000	.000	.000	.000	.000	.000	.000
	3	1.000	.984	.867	.411	.107	.016	.001	.000	.000	.000	.000	.000	.000
	4	1.000	.997	.957	.630	.238	.051	.006	.000	.000	.000	.000	.000	.000
	5	1.000	1.000	.989	.804	.416	.126	.021	.002	.000	.000	.000	.000	.000
	6	1.000	1.000	.998	.913	.608	.250	.058	.006	.000	.000	.000	.000	.000
	7	1.000	1.000	1.000	.968	.772	.416	.132	.021	.001	.000	.000	.000	.000
	8	1.000	1.000	1.000	.990	.887	.596	.252	.057	.005	.000	.000	.000	.000
	9	1.000	1.000	1.000	.997	.952	.755	.412	.128	.017	.001	.000	.000	.000
	10	1.000	1.000	1.000	.999	.983	.872	.588	.245	.048	.003	.000	.000	.000
	11	1.000	1.000	1.000	1.000	.995	.943	.748	.404	.113	.010	.000	.000	.000
	12	1.000	1.000	1.000	1.000	.999	.979	.868	.584	.228	.032	.000	.000	.000
	13	1.000	1.000	1.000	1.000	1.000	.994	.942	.750	.392	.087	.002	.000	.000
	14	1.000	1.000	1.000	1.000	1.000	.998	.979	.874	.584	.196	.011	.000	.000
	15	1.000	1.000	1.000	1.000	1.000	1.000	.994	.949	.762	.370	.043	.003	.000
	16	1.000	1.000	1.000	1.000	1.000	1.000	.999	.984	.893	.589	.133	.016	.000
	17	1.000	1.000	1.000	1.000	1.000	1.000	1.000	.996	.965	.794	.323	.075	.001
	18	1.000	1.000	1.000	1.000	1.000	1.000	1.000	.999	.992	.931	.608	.264	.017
	19	1.000	1.000	1.000	1.000	1.000	1.000	1.000	1.000	.999	.988	.878	.642	.182

continued

TABLE A.2 **Binomial distribution (*continued*)**

		p												
n	*c*	.01	.05	.10	.20	.30	.40	.50	.60	.70	.80	.90	.95	.99
25	0	.778	.277	.072	.004	.000	.000	.000	.000	.000	.000	.000	.000	.000
	1	.974	.642	.271	.027	.002	.000	.000	.000	.000	.000	.000	.000	.000
	2	.998	.873	.537	.098	.009	.000	.000	.000	.000	.000	.000	.000	.000
	3	1.000	.966	.764	.234	.033	.002	.000	.000	.000	.000	.000	.000	.000
	4	1.000	.993	.902	.421	.090	.009	.000	.000	.000	.000	.000	.000	.000
	5	1.000	.999	.967	.617	.193	.029	.002	.000	.000	.000	.000	.000	.000
	6	1.000	1.000	.991	.780	.341	.074	.007	.000	.000	.000	.000	.000	.000
	7	1.000	1.000	.998	.891	.512	.154	.022	.001	.000	.000	.000	.000	.000
	8	1.000	1.000	1.000	.953	.677	.274	.054	.004	.000	.000	.000	.000	.000
	9	1.000	1.000	1.000	.983	.811	.425	.115	.013	.000	.000	.000	.000	.000
	10	1.000	1.000	1.000	.994	.902	.586	.212	.034	.002	.000	.000	.000	.000
	11	1.000	1.000	1.000	.998	.956	.732	.345	.078	.006	.000	.000	.000	.000
	12	1.000	1.000	1.000	1.000	.983	.846	.500	.154	.017	.000	.000	.000	.000
	13	1.000	1.000	1.000	1.000	.994	.922	.655	.268	.044	.002	.000	.000	.000
	14	1.000	1.000	1.000	1.000	.998	.966	.788	.414	.098	.006	.000	.000	.000
	15	1.000	1.000	1.000	1.000	1.000	.987	.885	.575	.189	.017	.000	.000	.000
	16	1.000	1.000	1.000	1.000	1.000	.996	.946	.726	.323	.047	.000	.000	.000
	17	1.000	1.000	1.000	1.000	1.000	.999	.978	.846	.488	.109	.002	.000	.000
	18	1.000	1.000	1.000	1.000	1.000	1.000	.993	.926	.659	.220	.009	.000	.000
	19	1.000	1.000	1.000	1.000	1.000	1.000	.998	.971	.807	.383	.033	.001	.000
	20	1.000	1.000	1.000	1.000	1.000	1.000	1.000	.991	.910	.579	.098	.007	.000
	21	1.000	1.000	1.000	1.000	1.000	1.000	1.000	.998	.967	.766	.236	.034	.000
	22	1.000	1.000	1.000	1.000	1.000	1.000	1.000	1.000	.991	.902	.463	.127	.002
	23	1.000	1.000	1.000	1.000	1.000	1.000	1.000	1.000	.998	.973	.729	.358	.026
	24	1.000	1.000	1.000	1.000	1.000	1.000	1.000	1.000	1.000	.996	.928	.723	.222

TABLE A.3 **Values of $e^{-\mu}$**

$0 < \mu < 1$

μ	0	1	2	3	4	5	6	7	8	9
0.0	1.0000	.9900	.9802	.9704	.9608	.9512	.9418	.9324	.9231	.9139
0.1	.9048	.8958	.8869	.8781	.8694	.8607	.8521	.8437	.8353	.8270
0.2	.8187	.8106	.8025	.7945	.7866	.7788	.7711	.7634	.7558	.7483
0.3	.7408	.7334	.7261	.7189	.7118	.7047	.6977	.6907	.6839	.6771
0.4	.6703	.6636	.6570	.6505	.6440	.6376	.6313	.6250	.6188	.6126
0.5	.6065	.6005	.5945	.5886	.5827	.5770	.5712	.5655	.5599	.5543
0.6	.5488	.5434	.5379	.5326	.5273	.5220	.5169	.5117	.5066	.5016
0.7	.4966	.4916	.4868	.4819	.4771	.4724	.4677	.4630	.4584	.4538
0.8	.4493	.4449	.4404	.4360	.4317	.4274	.4232	.4190	.4148	.4107
0.9	.4066	.4025	.3985	.3946	.3906	.3867	.3829	.3791	.3753	.3716

Example: $e^{-.48} = .6188$

$\mu = 1, 2, \ldots, 10$

μ	1	2	3	4	5	6	7	8	9	10
$e^{-\mu}$	.36788	.13534	.04979	.01832	.006738	.002479	.000912	.000335	.000123	.000045

Example: $e^{-3} = .04979$

Note: To obtain values of $e^{-\mu}$ for other values of μ, use the laws of exponents.

Example: $e^{-3.48} = (e^{-3.00})(e^{-.48}) = (.04979)(.6188) = .03081$

TABLE A.4 **Poisson distribution**

The following table gives the probability of exactly x occurrences for various values of μ, as defined by the Poisson mass function:

$$P(X = x) = \frac{e^{-\mu}\mu^x}{x!}$$

	μ									
x	0.1	0.2	0.3	0.4	0.5	0.6	0.7	0.8	0.9	1.0
0	.9048	.8187	.7408	.6703	.6065	.5488	.4966	.4493	.4066	.3679
1	.0905	.1637	.2222	.2681	.3033	.3293	.3476	.3595	.3659	.3679
2	.0045	.0164	.0333	.0536	.0758	.0988	.1217	.1438	.1647	.1839
3	.0002	.0011	.0033	.0072	.0126	.0198	.0284	.0383	.0494	.0613
4	.0000	.0001	.0002	.0007	.0016	.0030	.0050	.0077	.0111	.0153
5	.0000	.0000	.0000	.0001	.0002	.0004	.0007	.0012	.0020	.0031
6	.0000	.0000	.0000	.0000	.0000	.0000	.0001	.0002	.0003	.0005
7	.0000	.0000	.0000	.0000	.0000	.0000	.0000	.0000	.0000	.0001

	μ									
x	1.1	1.2	1.3	1.4	1.5	1.6	1.7	1.8	1.9	2.0
0	.3329	.3012	.2725	.2466	.2231	.2019	.1827	.1653	.1496	.1353
1	.3662	.3614	.3543	.3452	.3347	.3230	.3106	.2975	.2842	.2707
2	.2014	.2169	.2303	.2417	.2510	.2584	.2640	.2678	.2700	.2707
3	.0738	.0867	.0998	.1128	.1255	.1378	.1496	.1607	.1710	.1804
4	.0203	.0260	.0324	.0395	.0471	.0551	.0636	.0723	.0812	.0902
5	.0045	.0062	.0084	.0111	.0141	.0176	.0216	.0260	.0309	.0361
6	.0008	.0012	.0018	.0026	.0035	.0047	.0061	.0078	.0098	.0120
7	.0001	.0002	.0003	.0005	.0008	.0011	.0045	.0020	.0027	.0034
8	.0000	.0000	.0001	.0001	.0001	.0002	.0003	.0005	.0006	.0009
9	.0000	.0000	.0000	.0000	.0000	.0000	.0001	.0001	.0001	.0002

	μ									
x	2.1	2.2	2.3	2.4	2.5	2.6	2.7	2.8	2.9	3.0
0	.1225	.1108	.1003	.0907	.0821	.0743	.0672	.0608	.0550	.0498
1	.2572	.2438	.2306	.2177	.2052	.1931	.1815	.1703	.1596	.1494
2	.2700	.2681	.2652	.2613	.2565	.2510	.2450	.2384	.2314	.2240
3	.1890	.1966	.2033	.2090	.2138	.2176	.2205	.2225	.2237	.2240
4	.0992	.1082	.1169	.1254	.1336	.1414	.1488	.1557	.1622	.1680
5	.0417	.0476	.0538	.0602	.0668	.0735	.0804	.0872	.0940	.1008
6	.0146	.0174	.0206	.0241	.0278	.0319	.0362	.0407	.0455	.0504
7	.0044	.0055	.0068	.0083	.0099	.0118	.0139	.0163	.0188	.0216
8	.0011	.0015	.0019	.0025	.0031	.0038	.0047	.0057	.0068	.0081
9	.0003	.0004	.0005	.0007	.0009	.0011	.0014	.0018	.0022	.0027
10	.0001	.0001	.0001	.0002	.0002	.0003	.0004	.0005	.0006	.0008
11	.0000	.0000	.0000	.0000	.0000	.0001	.0001	.0001	.0002	.0002
12	.0000	.0000	.0000	.0000	.0000	.0000	.0000	.0000	.0000	.0001

	μ									
x	3.1	3.2	3.3	3.4	3.5	3.6	3.7	3.8	3.9	4.0
0	.0450	.0408	.0369	.0334	.0302	.0273	.0247	.0224	.0202	.0183
1	.1397	.1304	.1217	.1135	.1057	.0984	.0915	.0850	.0789	.0733
2	.2165	.2087	.2008	.1929	.1850	.1771	.1692	.1615	.1539	.1465
3	.2237	.2226	.2209	.2186	.2158	.2125	.2087	.2046	.2001	.1954
4	.1734	.1781	.1823	.1858	.1888	.1912	.1931	.1944	.1951	.1954
5	.1075	.1140	.1203	.1264	.1322	.1377	.1429	.1477	.1522	.1563
6	.0555	.0608	.0662	.0716	.0771	.0826	.0881	.0936	.0989	.1042
7	.0246	.0278	.0312	.0348	.0385	.0425	.0466	.0508	.0551	.0595
8	.0095	.0111	.0129	.0148	.0169	.0191	.0215	.0241	.0269	.0298
9	.0033	.0040	.0047	.0056	.0066	.0076	.0089	.0102	.0116	.0132
10	.0010	.0013	.0016	.0019	.0023	.0028	.0033	.0039	.0045	.0053
11	.0003	.0004	.0005	.0006	.0007	.0009	.0011	.0013	.0016	.0019
12	.0001	.0001	.0001	.0002	.0002	.0003	.0003	.0004	.0005	.0006
13	.0000	.0000	.0000	.0000	.0001	.0001	.0001	.0001	.0002	.0002
14	.0000	.0000	.0000	.0000	.0000	.0000	.0000	.0000	.0000	.0001

	μ									
x	4.1	4.2	4.3	4.4	4.5	4.6	4.7	4.8	4.9	5.0
0	.0166	.0150	.0136	.0123	.0111	.0101	.0091	.0082	.0074	.0067
1	.0679	.0630	.0583	.0540	.0500	.0462	.0427	.0395	.0365	.0337
2	.1393	.1323	.1254	.1188	.1125	.1063	.1005	.0948	.0894	.0842
3	.1904	.1852	.1798	.1743	.1687	.1634	.1574	.1517	.1460	.1404
4	.1951	.1944	.1933	.1917	.1898	.1875	.1849	.1820	.1789	.1755
5	.1600	.1633	.1662	.1687	.1708	.1725	.1738	.1747	.1753	.1755
6	.1093	.1143	.1191	.1237	.1281	.1323	.1362	.1398	.1432	.1462
7	.0640	.0686	.0732	.0778	.0824	.0869	.0914	.0959	.1002	.1044
8	.0328	.0360	.0393	.0428	.0463	.0500	.0537	.0575	.0614	.0653
9	.0150	.0168	.0188	.0209	.0232	.0255	.0280	.0307	.0334	.0363
10	.0061	.0071	.0081	.0092	.0104	.0118	.0132	.0147	.0164	.0181
11	.0023	.0027	.0032	.0037	.0043	.0049	.0056	.0064	.0073	.0082
12	.0008	.0009	.0011	.0014	.0016	.0019	.0022	.0026	.0030	.0034
13	.0002	.0003	.0004	.0005	.0006	.0007	.0008	.0009	.0011	.0013
14	.0001	.0001	.0001	.0001	.0002	.0002	.0003	.0003	.0004	.0005
15	.0000	.0000	.0000	.0000	.0001	.0001	.0001	.0001	.0001	.0002

continued

Example: If $\mu = 1.5$, then $P(X = 2) = .2510$; $P(X = 3) = .1255$.

TABLE A.4 **Poisson distribution (*continued*)**

	μ									
x	5.1	5.2	5.3	5.4	5.5	5.6	5.7	5.8	5.9	6.0
0	.0061	.0055	.0050	.0045	.0041	.0037	.0033	.0030	.0027	.0025
1	.0311	.0287	.0265	.0244	.0225	.0207	.0191	.0176	.0162	.0149
2	.0793	.0746	.0701	.0659	.0618	.0580	.0544	.0509	.0477	.0446
3	.1348	.1293	.1239	.1185	.1133	.1082	.1033	.0985	.0938	.0892
4	.1719	.1681	.1641	.1600	.1558	.1515	.1472	.1428	.1383	.1339
5	.1753	.1748	.1740	.1728	.1714	.1697	.1678	.1620	.1632	.1606
6	.1490	.1515	.1537	.1555	.1571	.1584	.1594	.1656	.1605	.1606
7	.1086	.1125	.1163	.1200	.1234	.1267	.1298	.1301	.1353	.1377
8	.0692	.0731	.0771	.0810	.0849	.0887	.0925	.0926	.0998	.1033
9	.0392	.0423	.0454	.0486	.0519	.0552	.0586	.0662	.0654	.0688
10	.0200	.0220	.0241	.0262	.0285	.0309	.0334	.0359	.0386	.0413
11	.0093	.0104	.0116	.0129	.0143	.0157	.0173	.0190	.0207	.0225
12	.0039	.0045	.0051	.0058	.0065	.0073	.0082	.0092	.0102	.0113
13	.0015	.0018	.0021	.0024	.0028	.0032	.0036	.0041	.0046	.0052
14	.0006	.0007	.0008	.0009	.0011	.0013	.0015	.0017	.0019	.0022
15	.0002	.0002	.0003	.0003	.0004	.0005	.0006	.0007	.0008	.0009
16	.0001	.0001	.0001	.0001	.0001	.0002	.0002	.0002	.0003	.0003
17	.0000	.0000	.0000	.0000	.0000	.0001	.0001	.0001	.0001	.0001

	μ									
x	6.1	6.2	6.3	6.4	6.5	6.6	6.7	6.8	6.9	7.0
0	.0022	.0020	.0018	.0017	.0015	.0014	.0012	.0011	.0010	.0009
1	.0137	.0126	.0116	.0106	.0098	.0090	.0082	.0076	.0070	.0064
2	.0417	.0390	.0364	.0340	.0318	.0296	.0276	.0258	.0240	.0223
3	.0848	.0806	.0765	.0726	.0688	.0652	.0617	.0584	.0552	.0521
4	.1294	.1249	.1205	.1162	.1118	.1076	.1034	.0992	.0952	.0912
5	.1579	.1549	.1519	.1487	.1454	.1420	.1385	.1349	.1314	.1277
6	.1605	.1601	.1595	.1586	.1575	.1562	.1546	.1529	.1511	.1490
7	.1399	.1418	.1435	.1450	.1462	.1472	.1480	.1486	.1489	.1490
8	.1066	.1099	.1130	.1160	.1188	.1215	.1240	.1263	.1284	.1304
9	.0723	.0757	.0791	.0825	.0858	.0891	.0923	.0954	.0985	.1014
10	.0441	.0469	.0498	.0528	.0558	.0588	.0618	.0649	.0679	.0710
11	.0245	.0265	.0285	.0307	.0330	.0353	.0377	.0401	.0426	.0452
12	.0124	.0137	.0150	.0164	.0179	.0194	.0210	.0227	.0245	.0264
13	.0058	.0065	.0073	.0081	.0089	.0098	.0108	.0119	.0130	.0142
14	.0025	.0029	.0033	.0037	.0041	.0046	.0052	.0058	.0064	.0071
15	.0010	.0012	.0014	.0016	.0018	.0020	.0023	.0026	.0029	.0033
16	.0004	.0005	.0005	.0006	.0007	.0008	.0010	.0011	.0013	.0014
17	.0001	.0002	.0002	.0002	.0003	.0003	.0004	.0004	.0005	.0006
18	.0000	.0001	.0001	.0001	.0001	.0001	.0001	.0002	.0002	.0002
19	.0000	.0000	.0000	.0000	.0000	.0000	.0000	.0001	.0001	.0001

	μ									
x	7.1	7.2	7.3	7.4	7.5	7.6	7.7	7.8	7.9	8.0
0	.0008	.0007	.0007	.0006	.0006	.0005	.0005	.0004	.0004	.0003
1	.0059	.0054	.0049	.0045	.0041	.0038	.0035	.0032	.0029	.0027
2	.0208	.0194	.0180	.0167	.0156	.0145	.0134	.0125	.0116	.0107
3	.0492	.0464	.0438	.0413	.0389	.0366	.0345	.0324	.0305	.0286
4	.0874	.0836	.0799	.0764	.0729	.0696	.0663	.0632	.0602	.0573
5	.1241	.1204	.1167	.1130	.1094	.1057	.1021	.0986	.0951	.0916
6	.1468	.1445	.1420	.1394	.1367	.1339	.1311	.1282	.1252	.1221
7	.1489	.1486	.1481	.1474	.1465	.1454	.1442	.1428	.1413	.1396
8	.1321	.1337	.1351	.1363	.1373	.1382	.1388	.1392	.1395	.1396
9	.1042	.1070	.1096	.1121	.1144	.1167	.1187	.1207	.1224	.1241
10	.0740	.0770	.0800	.0829	.0858	.0887	.0914	.0941	.0967	.0993
11	.0478	.0504	.0531	.0558	.0585	.0613	.0640	.0667	.0695	.0722
12	.0283	.0303	.0323	.0344	.0366	.0380	.0411	.0434	.0457	.0481
13	.0154	.0168	.0181	.0196	.0211	.0227	.0243	.0260	.0278	.0296
14	.0078	.0086	.0095	.0104	.0113	.0123	.0134	.0145	.0157	.0169
15	.0037	.0041	.0046	.0051	.0057	.0062	.0069	.0075	.0083	.0090
16	.0016	.0019	.0021	.0024	.0026	.0030	.0033	.0037	.0041	.0045
17	.0007	.0008	.0009	.0010	.0012	.0013	.0015	.0017	.0019	.0021
18	.0003	.0003	.0004	.0004	.0005	.0006	.0006	.0007	.0008	.0009
19	.0001	.0001	.0001	.0002	.0002	.0002	.0003	.0003	.0003	.0004
20	.0000	.0000	.0001	.0001	.0001	.0001	.0001	.0001	.0001	.0002
21	.0000	.0000	.0000	.0000	.0000	.0000	.0000	.0000	.0001	.0001

	μ									
x	8.1	8.2	8.3	8.4	8.5	8.6	8.7	8.8	8.9	9.0
0	.0003	.0003	.0002	.0002	.0002	.0002	.0002	.0002	.0001	.0001
1	.0025	.0023	.0021	.0019	.0017	.0016	.0014	.0013	.0012	.0011
2	.0100	.0092	.0086	.0079	.0074	.0068	.0063	.0058	.0054	.0050
3	.0269	.0252	.0237	.0222	.0208	.0195	.0183	.0171	.0160	.0150
4	.0544	.0517	.0491	.0466	.0443	.0420	.0398	.0377	.0357	.0337
5	.0082	.0849	.0816	.0784	.0752	.0722	.0692	.0663	.0635	.0607
6	.1191	.1160	.1128	.1097	.1066	.1034	.1003	.0972	.0941	.0911
7	.1378	.1358	.1338	.1317	.1294	.1271	.1247	.1222	.1197	.1171
8	.1395	.1392	.1388	.1382	.1375	.1366	.1356	.1344	.1332	.1318
9	.1256	.1269	.1280	.1290	.1299	.1306	.1311	.1315	.1317	.1318
10	.1017	.1040	.1063	.1084	.1104	.1123	.1140	.1157	.1172	.1186
11	.0749	.0776	.0802	.0828	.0853	.0878	.0902	.0925	.0948	.0970
12	.0505	.0530	.0555	.0579	.0604	.0629	.0654	.0679	.0703	.0728
13	.0315	.0334	.0354	.0374	.0395	.0416	.0438	.0459	.0481	.0504
14	.0182	.0196	.0210	.0225	.0240	.0256	.0272	.0289	.0306	.0324
15	.0098	.0107	.0116	.0126	.0136	.0147	.0158	.0169	.0182	.0194
16	.0050	.0055	.0060	.0066	.0072	.0079	.0086	.0093	.0101	.0109
17	.0024	.0026	.0029	.0033	.0036	.0040	.0044	.0048	.0053	.0058
18	.0011	.0012	.0014	.0015	.0017	.0019	.0021	.0024	.0026	.0029
19	.0005	.0005	.0006	.0007	.0008	.0009	.0010	.0011	.0012	.0014
20	.0002	.0002	.0002	.0003	.0003	.0004	.0004	.0005	.0005	.0006
21	.0001	.0001	.0001	.0001	.0001	.0002	.0002	.0002	.0002	.0003
22	.0000	.0000	.0000	.0000	.0001	.0001	.0001	.0001	.0001	.0001

TABLE A.5 **Areas under the standard normal distribution**

The following table gives the areas under the standard normal curve from 0 to z.

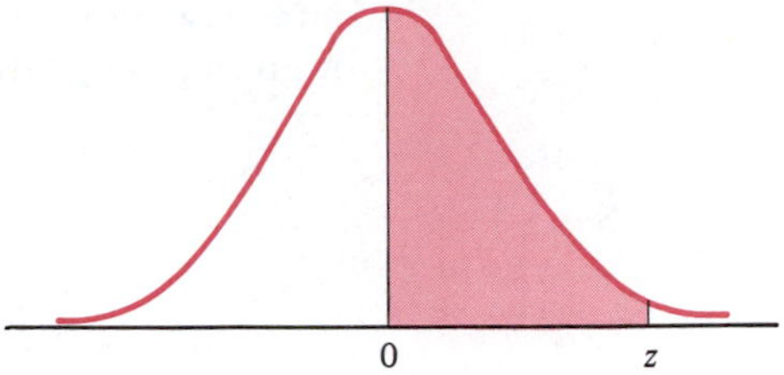

z	0	1	2	3	4	5	6	7	8	9
0.0	.0000	.0040	.0080	.0120	.0160	.0199	.0239	.0279	.0319	.0359
0.1	.0398	.0438	.0478	.0517	.0557	.0596	.0636	.0675	.0714	.0754
0.2	.0793	.0832	.0871	.0910	.0948	.0987	.1026	.1064	.1103	.1141
0.3	.1179	.1217	.1255	.1293	.1331	.1368	.1406	.1443	.1480	.1517
0.4	.1554	.1591	.1628	.1664	.1700	.1736	.1772	.1808	.1844	.1879
0.5	.1915	.1950	.1985	.2019	.2054	.2088	.2123	.2157	.2190	.2224
0.6	.2258	.2291	.2324	.2357	.2389	.2422	.2454	.2486	.2518	.2549
0.7	.2580	.2612	.2642	.2673	.2704	.2734	.2764	.2794	.2823	.2852
0.8	.2881	.2910	.2939	.2967	.2996	.3023	.3051	.3078	.3106	.3133
0.9	.3159	.3186	.3212	.3238	.3264	.3289	.3315	.3340	.3365	.3389
1.0	.3413	.3438	.3461	.3485	.3508	.3531	.3554	.3577	.3599	.3621
1.1	.3643	.3665	.3686	.3708	.3729	.3749	.3770	.3790	.3810	.3830
1.2	.3849	.3869	.3888	.3907	.3925	.3944	.3962	.3980	.3997	.4015
1.3	.4032	.4049	.4066	.4082	.4099	.4115	.4131	.4147	.4162	.4177
1.4	.4192	.4207	.4222	.4236	.4251	.4265	.4279	.4292	.4306	.4319
1.5	.4332	.4345	.4357	.4370	.4382	.4394	.4406	.4418	.4429	.4441
1.6	.4452	.4463	.4474	.4484	.4495	.4505	.4515	.4525	.4535	.4545
1.7	.4554	.4564	.4573	.4582	.4591	.4599	.4608	.4616	.4625	.4633
1.8	.4641	.4649	.4656	.4664	.4671	.4678	.4686	.4693	.4699	.4706
1.9	.4713	.4719	.4726	.4732	.4738	.4744	.4750	.4756	.4761	.4767
2.0	.4772	.4778	.4783	.4788	.4793	.4798	.4803	.4808	.4812	.4817
2.1	.4821	.4826	.4830	.4834	.4838	.4842	.4846	.4850	.4854	.4857
2.2	.4861	.4864	.4868	.4871	.4875	.4878	.4881	.4884	.4887	.4890
2.3	.4893	.4896	.4898	.4901	.4904	.4906	.4909	.4911	.4913	.4916
2.4	.4918	.4920	.4922	.4925	.4927	.4929	.4931	.4932	.4934	.4936
2.5	.4938	.4940	.4941	.4943	.4945	.4946	.4948	.4949	.4951	.4952
2.6	.4953	.4955	.4956	.4957	.4959	.4960	.4961	.4962	.4963	.4964
2.7	.4965	.4966	.4967	.4968	.4969	.4970	.4971	.4972	.4973	.4974
2.8	.4974	.4975	.4976	.4977	.4977	.4978	.4979	.4979	.4980	.4981
2.9	.4981	.4982	.4982	.4983	.4984	.4984	.4985	.4985	.4986	.4986
3.0	.4987	.4987	.4987	.4988	.4988	.4989	.4989	.4989	.4990	.4990
3.1	.4990	.4991	.4991	.4991	.4992	.4992	.4992	.4992	.4993	.4993
3.2	.4993	.4993	.4994	.4994	.4994	.4994	.4994	.4995	.4995	.4995
3.3	.4995	.4995	.4995	.4996	.4996	.4996	.4996	.4996	.4996	.4997
3.4	.4997	.4997	.4997	.4997	.4997	.4997	.4997	.4997	.4997	.4998
3.5	.4998	.4998	.4998	.4998	.4998	.4998	.4998	.4998	.4998	.4998
3.6	.4998	.4998	.4999	.4999	.4999	.4999	.4999	.4999	.4999	.4999
3.7	.4999	.4999	.4999	.4999	.4999	.4999	.4999	.4999	.4999	.4999
3.8	.4999	.4999	.4999	.4999	.4999	.4999	.4999	.4999	.4999	.4999
3.9	.5000	.5000	.5000	.5000	.5000	.5000	.5000	.5000	.5000	.5000

Example: The area between $z = 0$ and $z = 1.24$ is .3925.

TABLE A.6 Critical values of the t distribution

The following table contains critical values of t for given probability levels.

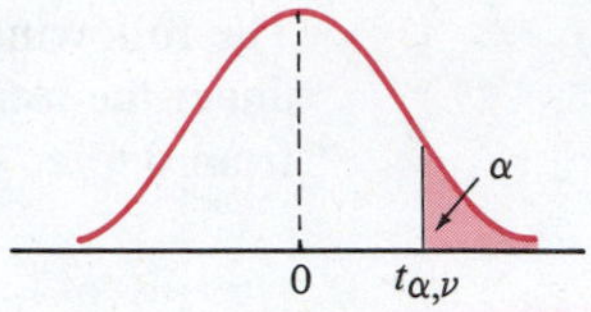

Degrees of Freedom, ν	Critical Values t_α $t_{.10}$	$t_{.05}$	$t_{.025}$	$t_{.01}$	$t_{.005}$
1	3.078	6.314	12.706	31.821	63.657
2	1.886	2.920	4.303	6.965	9.925
3	1.638	2.353	3.182	4.541	5.841
4	1.533	2.132	2.776	3.747	4.604
5	1.476	2.015	2.571	3.365	4.032
6	1.440	1.943	2.447	3.143	3.707
7	1.415	1.895	2.365	2.998	3.499
8	1.397	1.860	2.306	2.896	3.355
9	1.383	1.833	2.262	2.821	3.250
10	1.372	1.812	2.228	2.764	3.169
11	1.363	1.796	2.201	2.718	3.106
12	1.356	1.782	2.179	2.681	3.055
13	1.350	1.771	2.160	2.650	3.012
14	1.345	1.761	2.145	2.624	2.977
15	1.341	1.753	2.131	2.602	2.947
16	1.337	1.746	2.120	2.583	2.921
17	1.333	1.740	2.110	2.567	2.898
18	1.330	1.734	2.101	2.552	2.878
19	1.328	1.729	2.093	2.539	2.861
20	1.325	1.725	2.086	2.528	2.845
21	1.323	1.721	2.080	2.518	2.831
22	1.321	1.717	2.074	2.508	2.819
23	1.319	1.714	2.069	2.500	2.807
24	1.318	1.711	2.064	2.492	2.797
25	1.316	1.708	2.060	2.485	2.787
26	1.315	1.706	2.056	2.479	2.779
27	1.314	1.703	2.052	2.473	2.771
28	1.313	1.701	2.048	2.467	2.763
29	1.311	1.699	2.045	2.462	2.756
30	1.310	1.697	2.042	2.457	2.750
40	1.303	1.684	2.021	2.423	2.704
60	1.296	1.671	2.000	2.390	2.660
120	1.290	1.661	1.984	2.358	2.626
∞	1.282	1.645	1.960	2.326	2.576

From Merrington, Maxine. "Table of Percentage Points of the t-Distribution." *Biometrika*, vol. 32, 1941, p. 300.

Example: The value of t with 10 degrees of freedom for which 1% of the area is in the right-hand tail is 2.764; $t_{.01} = 2.764$ for $\nu = 10$.

TABLE A.7 **Chi-square distribution**

Entries in the table give χ^2_α values, where α is the area or probability in the upper tail of the chi-square distribution.

Example: With 10 degrees of freedom and a .01 area in the upper tail, $\chi^2_{.01} = 23.2093$.

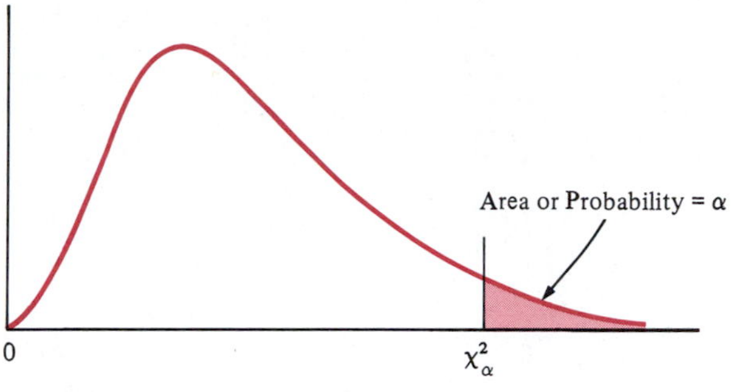

Degrees of Freedom	.995	.99	.975	.95	.90	.10	.05	.025	.01	.005
1	392704×10^{-10}	157088×10^{-9}	982069×10^{-9}	393214×10^{-8}	.0157908	2.70554	3.84146	5.02389	6.63490	7.87944
2	.0100251	.0201007	.0506356	.102587	.210720	4.60517	5.99147	7.37776	9.21034	10.5966
3	.0717212	.114832	.215795	.351846	.584375	6.25139	7.81473	9.34840	11.3449	12.8381
4	.206990	.297110	.484419	.710721	1.063623	7.77944	9.48773	11.1433	13.2767	14.8602
5	.411740	.554300	.831211	1.145476	1.61031	9.23635	11.0705	12.8325	15.0863	16.7496
6	.675727	.872085	1.237347	1.63539	2.20413	10.6446	12.5916	14.4494	16.8119	18.5476
7	.989265	1.239043	1.68987	2.16735	2.83311	12.0170	14.0671	16.0128	18.4753	20.2777
8	1.344419	1.646482	2.17973	2.73264	3.48954	13.3616	15.5073	17.5346	20.0902	21.9550
9	1.734926	2.087912	2.70039	3.32511	4.16816	14.6837	16.9190	19.0228	21.6660	23.5893
10	2.15585	2.55821	3.24697	3.94030	4.86518	15.9871	18.3070	20.4831	23.2093	25.1882
11	2.60321	3.05347	3.81575	4.57481	5.57779	17.2750	19.6751	21.9200	24.7250	26.7569
12	3.07382	3.57056	4.40379	5.22603	6.30380	18.5494	21.0261	23.3367	26.2170	28.2995
13	3.56503	4.10691	5.00874	5.89186	7.04150	19.8119	22.3621	24.7356	27.6883	29.8194
14	4.07468	4.66043	5.62872	6.57063	7.78953	21.0642	23.6848	26.1190	29.1413	31.3193
15	4.60094	5.22935	6.26214	7.26094	8.54675	22.3072	24.9958	27.4884	30.5779	32.8013
16	5.14224	5.81221	6.90766	7.96164	9.31223	23.5418	26.2962	28.8454	31.9999	34.2672
17	5.69724	6.40776	7.56418	8.67176	10.0852	24.7690	27.5871	30.1910	33.4087	35.7185
18	6.26481	7.01491	8.23075	9.39046	10.8649	25.9894	28.8693	31.5264	34.8053	37.1564
19	6.84398	7.63273	8.90655	10.1170	11.6509	27.2036	30.1435	32.8523	36.1908	38.5822
20	7.43386	8.26040	9.59083	10.8508	12.4426	28.4120	31.4104	34.1696	37.5662	39.9968
21	8.03366	8.89720	10.28293	11.5913	13.2396	29.6151	32.6705	35.4789	38.9321	41.4010
22	8.64272	9.54249	10.9823	12.3380	14.0415	30.8133	33.9244	36.7807	40.2894	42.7958
23	9.26042	10.19567	11.6885	13.0905	14.8479	32.0069	35.1725	38.0757	41.6384	44.1813
24	9.88623	10.8564	12.4011	13.8484	15.6587	33.1963	36.4151	39.3641	42.9798	45.5585
25	10.5197	11.5240	13.1197	14.6114	16.4734	34.3816	37.6525	40.6465	44.3141	46.9278
26	11.1603	12.1981	13.8439	15.3791	17.2919	35.5631	38.8852	41.9232	45.6417	48.2899
27	11.8076	12.8786	14.5733	16.1513	18.1138	36.7412	40.1133	43.1944	46.9630	49.6449
28	12.4613	13.5648	15.3079	16.9279	18.9392	37.9159	41.3372	44.4607	48.2782	50.9933
29	13.1211	14.2565	16.0471	17.7083	19.7677	39.0875	42.5569	45.7222	49.5879	52.3356
30	13.7867	14.9535	16.7908	18.4926	20.5992	40.2560	43.7729	46.9792	50.8922	53.6720
40	20.7065	22.1643	24.4331	26.5093	29.0505	51.8050	55.7585	59.3417	63.6907	66.7659
50	27.9907	29.7067	32.3574	34.7642	37.6886	63.1671	67.5048	71.4202	76.1539	79.4900
60	35.5346	37.4848	40.4817	43.1879	46.4589	74.3970	79.0819	83.2976	88.3794	91.9517
70	43.2752	45.4418	48.7576	51.7393	55.3290	85.5271	90.5312	95.0231	100.425	104.215
80	51.1720	53.5400	57.1532	60.3915	64.2778	96.5782	101.879	106.629	112.329	116.321
90	59.1963	61.7541	65.6466	69.1260	73.2912	107.565	113.145	118.136	124.116	128.299
100	67.3276	70.0648	74.2219	77.9295	82.3581	118.498	124.342	129.561	135.807	140.169

From Pearson, E. S. and H. O. Hartley. Table 8, "Percentage Points of the χ^2 Distribution," *Biometrika Tables for Statisticians,* Vol. 1. Reprinted by permisson of Biometrika Trustees.

TABLE A.8 ***F* distribution**

Entries in the following table give F_α values, where α is the area or probability in the upper tail of the F distribution.

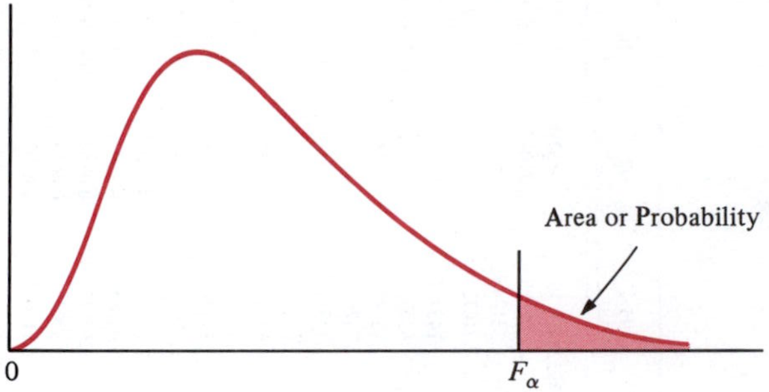

Table of $F_{.05}$ Values

Denominator Degrees of Freedom	Numerator Degrees of Freedom																		
	1	2	3	4	5	6	7	8	9	10	12	15	20	24	30	40	60	120	∞
1	161.4	199.5	215.7	224.6	230.2	234.0	236.8	238.9	240.5	241.9	243.9	245.9	248.0	249.1	250.1	251.1	252.2	253.3	254.3
2	18.51	19.00	19.16	19.25	19.30	19.33	19.35	19.37	19.38	19.40	19.41	19.43	19.45	19.45	19.46	19.47	19.48	19.49	19.50
3	10.13	9.55	9.28	9.12	9.01	8.94	8.89	8.85	8.81	8.79	8.74	8.70	8.66	8.64	8.62	8.59	8.57	8.55	8.53
4	7.71	6.94	6.59	6.39	6.26	6.16	6.09	6.04	6.00	5.96	5.91	5.86	5.80	5.77	5.75	5.72	5.69	5.66	5.63
5	6.61	5.79	5.41	5.19	5.05	4.95	4.88	4.82	4.77	4.74	4.68	4.62	4.56	4.53	4.50	4.46	4.43	4.40	4.36
6	5.99	5.14	4.76	4.53	4.39	4.28	4.21	4.15	4.10	4.06	4.00	3.94	3.87	3.84	3.81	3.77	3.74	3.70	3.67
7	5.59	4.74	4.35	4.12	3.97	3.87	3.79	3.73	3.68	3.64	3.57	3.51	3.44	3.41	3.38	3.34	3.30	3.27	3.23
8	5.32	4.46	4.07	3.84	3.69	3.58	3.50	3.44	3.39	3.35	3.28	3.22	3.15	3.12	3.08	3.04	3.01	2.97	2.93
9	5.12	4.26	3.86	3.63	3.48	3.37	3.29	3.23	3.18	3.14	3.07	3.01	2.94	2.90	2.86	2.83	2.79	2.75	2.71

10	4.96	4.10	3.71	3.48	3.33	3.22	3.14	3.07	3.02	2.98	2.91	2.85	2.77	2.74	2.70	2.66	2.62	2.58	2.54
11	4.84	3.98	3.59	3.36	3.20	3.09	3.01	2.95	2.90	2.85	2.79	2.72	2.65	2.61	2.57	2.53	2.49	2.45	2.40
12	4.75	3.89	3.49	3.26	3.11	3.00	2.91	2.85	2.80	2.75	2.69	2.62	2.54	2.51	2.47	2.43	2.38	2.34	2.30
13	4.67	3.81	3.41	3.18	3.03	2.92	2.83	2.77	2.71	2.67	2.60	2.53	2.46	2.42	2.38	2.34	2.30	2.25	2.21
14	4.60	3.74	3.34	3.11	2.96	2.85	2.76	2.70	2.65	2.60	2.53	2.46	2.39	2.35	2.31	2.27	2.22	2.18	2.13
15	4.54	3.68	3.29	3.06	2.90	2.79	2.71	2.64	2.59	2.54	2.48	2.40	2.33	2.29	2.25	2.20	2.16	2.11	2.07
16	4.49	3.63	3.24	3.01	2.85	2.74	2.66	2.59	2.54	2.49	2.42	2.35	2.28	2.24	2.19	2.15	2.11	2.06	2.01
17	4.45	3.59	3.20	2.96	2.81	2.70	2.61	2.55	2.49	2.45	2.38	2.31	2.23	2.19	2.15	2.10	2.06	2.01	1.96
18	4.41	3.55	3.16	2.93	2.77	2.66	2.58	2.51	2.46	2.41	2.34	2.27	2.19	2.15	2.11	2.06	2.02	1.97	1.92
19	4.38	3.52	3.13	2.90	2.74	2.63	2.54	2.48	2.42	2.38	2.31	2.23	2.16	2.11	2.07	2.03	1.98	1.93	1.88
20	4.35	3.49	3.10	2.87	2.71	2.60	2.51	2.45	2.39	2.35	2.28	2.20	2.12	2.08	2.04	1.99	1.95	1.90	1.84
21	4.32	3.47	3.07	2.84	2.68	2.57	2.49	2.42	2.37	2.32	2.25	2.18	2.10	2.05	2.01	1.96	1.92	1.87	1.81
22	4.30	3.44	3.05	2.82	2.66	2.55	2.46	2.40	2.34	2.30	2.23	2.15	2.07	2.03	1.98	1.94	1.89	1.84	1.78
23	4.28	3.42	3.03	2.80	2.64	2.53	2.44	2.37	2.32	2.27	2.20	2.13	2.05	2.01	1.96	1.91	1.86	1.81	1.76
24	4.26	3.40	3.01	2.78	2.62	2.51	2.42	2.36	2.30	2.25	2.18	2.11	2.03	1.98	1.94	1.89	1.84	1.79	1.73
25	4.24	3.39	2.99	2.76	2.60	2.49	2.40	2.34	2.28	2.24	2.16	2.09	2.01	1.96	1.92	1.87	1.82	1.77	1.71
26	4.23	3.37	2.98	2.74	2.59	2.47	2.39	2.32	2.27	2.22	2.15	2.07	1.99	1.95	1.90	1.85	1.80	1.75	1.69
27	4.21	3.35	2.96	2.73	2.57	2.46	2.37	2.31	2.25	2.20	2.13	2.06	1.97	1.93	1.88	1.84	1.79	1.73	1.67
28	4.20	3.34	2.95	2.71	2.56	2.45	2.36	2.29	2.24	2.19	2.12	2.04	1.96	1.91	1.87	1.82	1.77	1.71	1.65
29	4.18	3.33	2.93	2.70	2.55	2.43	2.35	2.28	2.22	2.18	2.10	2.03	1.94	1.90	1.85	1.81	1.75	1.70	1.64
30	4.17	3.32	2.92	2.69	2.53	2.42	2.33	2.27	2.21	2.16	2.09	2.01	1.93	1.89	1.84	1.79	1.74	1.68	1.62
40	4.08	3.23	2.84	2.61	2.45	2.34	2.25	2.18	2.12	2.08	2.00	1.92	1.84	1.79	1.74	1.69	1.64	1.58	1.51
60	4.00	3.15	2.76	2.53	2.37	2.25	2.17	2.10	2.04	1.99	1.92	1.84	1.75	1.70	1.65	1.59	1.53	1.47	1.39
120	3.92	3.07	2.68	2.45	2.29	2.17	2.09	2.02	1.96	1.91	1.83	1.75	1.66	1.61	1.55	1.50	1.43	1.35	1.25
∞	3.84	3.00	2.60	2.37	2.21	2.10	2.01	1.94	1.88	1.83	1.75	1.67	1.57	1.52	1.46	1.39	1.32	1.22	1.00

Example: With 7 numerator degrees of freedom, 9 denominator degrees of freedom, and a .05 area in the upper tail, $F_{.05} = 3.29$.

continued

TABLE A.8 **F distribution (*continued*)**

Table of $F_{.01}$ Values

Denominator Degrees of Freedom	Numerator Degrees of Freedom 1	2	3	4	5	6	7	8	9	10	12	15	20	24	30	40	60	120	∞
1	4052	4999.5	5403	5625	5764	5859	5928	5982	6022	6056	6106	6157	6209	6235	6261	6287	6313	6339	6366
2	98.50	99.00	99.17	99.25	99.30	99.33	99.36	99.37	99.39	99.40	99.42	99.43	99.45	99.46	99.47	99.47	99.48	99.49	99.50
3	34.12	30.82	29.46	28.71	28.24	27.91	27.67	27.49	27.35	27.23	27.05	26.87	26.69	26.60	26.50	26.41	26.32	26.22	26.13
4	21.20	18.00	16.69	15.98	15.52	15.21	14.98	14.80	14.66	14.55	14.37	14.20	14.02	13.93	13.84	13.75	13.65	13.56	13.46
5	16.26	13.27	12.06	11.39	10.97	10.67	10.46	10.29	10.16	10.05	9.89	9.72	9.05	9.47	9.38	9.29	9.20	9.11	9.06
6	13.75	10.92	9.78	9.15	8.75	8.47	8.26	8.10	7.98	7.87	7.72	7.56	7.40	7.31	7.23	7.14	7.06	6.97	6.88
7	12.25	9.55	8.45	7.85	7.46	7.19	6.99	6.84	6.72	6.62	6.47	6.31	6.16	6.07	5.99	5.91	5.82	5.74	5.65
8	11.26	8.65	7.59	7.01	6.63	6.37	6.18	6.03	5.91	5.81	5.67	5.52	5.36	5.28	5.20	5.12	5.03	4.95	4.86
9	10.56	8.02	6.99	6.42	6.06	5.80	5.61	5.47	5.35	5.26	5.11	4.96	4.81	4.73	4.65	4.57	4.48	4.40	4.31
10	10.04	7.56	6.55	5.99	5.64	5.39	5.20	5.06	4.94	4.85	4.71	4.56	4.41	4.33	4.25	4.17	4.08	4.00	3.91
11	9.65	7.21	6.22	5.67	5.32	5.07	4.89	4.74	4.63	4.54	4.40	4.25	4.10	4.02	3.94	3.86	3.78	3.69	3.60
12	9.33	6.93	5.95	5.41	5.06	4.82	4.64	4.50	4.39	4.30	4.16	4.01	3.86	3.78	3.70	3.62	3.54	3.45	3.36
13	9.07	6.70	5.74	5.21	4.86	4.62	4.44	4.30	4.19	4.10	3.96	3.82	3.66	3.59	3.51	3.43	3.34	3.25	3.17
14	8.86	6.51	5.56	5.04	4.69	4.46	4.28	4.14	4.03	3.94	3.80	3.66	3.51	3.43	3.35	3.27	3.18	3.09	3.00
15	8.68	6.36	5.42	4.89	4.56	4.32	4.14	4.00	3.89	3.80	3.67	3.52	3.37	3.29	3.21	3.13	3.05	2.96	2.87
16	8.53	6.23	5.29	4.77	4.44	4.20	4.03	3.89	3.78	3.69	3.55	3.41	3.26	3.18	3.10	3.02	2.93	2.84	2.75
17	8.40	6.11	5.18	4.67	4.34	4.10	3.93	3.79	3.68	3.59	3.46	3.31	3.16	3.08	3.00	2.92	2.83	2.75	2.65
18	8.29	6.01	5.09	4.58	4.25	4.01	3.84	3.71	3.60	3.51	3.37	3.23	3.08	3.00	2.92	2.84	2.75	2.66	2.57
19	8.18	5.93	5.01	4.50	4.17	3.94	3.77	3.63	3.52	3.43	3.30	3.15	3.00	2.92	2.84	2.76	2.67	2.58	2.49
20	8.10	5.85	4.94	4.43	4.10	3.87	3.70	3.56	3.46	3.37	3.23	3.09	2.94	2.86	2.78	2.69	2.61	2.52	2.42
21	8.02	5.78	4.87	4.37	4.04	3.81	3.64	3.51	3.40	3.31	3.17	3.03	2.88	2.80	2.72	2.64	2.55	2.46	2.36
22	7.95	5.72	4.82	4.31	3.99	3.76	3.59	3.45	3.35	3.26	3.12	2.98	2.83	2.75	2.67	2.58	2.50	2.40	2.31
23	7.88	5.66	4.76	4.26	3.94	3.71	3.54	3.41	3.30	3.21	3.07	2.93	2.78	2.70	2.62	2.54	2.45	2.35	2.26
24	7.82	5.61	4.72	4.22	3.90	3.67	3.50	3.36	3.26	3.17	3.03	2.89	2.74	2.66	2.58	2.49	2.40	2.31	2.21
25	7.77	5.57	4.68	4.18	3.85	3.63	3.46	3.32	3.22	3.13	2.99	2.85	2.70	2.62	2.54	2.45	2.36	2.27	2.17
26	7.72	5.53	4.64	4.14	3.82	3.59	3.42	3.29	3.18	3.09	2.96	2.81	2.66	2.58	2.50	2.42	2.33	2.23	2.13
27	7.68	5.49	4.60	4.11	3.78	3.56	3.39	3.26	3.15	3.06	2.93	2.78	2.63	2.55	2.47	2.38	2.29	2.20	2.10
28	7.64	5.45	4.57	4.07	3.75	3.53	3.36	3.23	3.12	3.03	2.90	2.75	2.60	2.52	2.44	2.35	2.26	2.17	2.06
29	7.60	5.42	4.54	4.04	3.73	3.50	3.33	3.20	3.09	3.00	2.87	2.73	2.57	2.49	2.41	2.33	2.23	2.14	2.03
30	7.56	5.39	4.51	4.02	3.70	3.47	3.30	3.17	3.07	2.98	2.84	2.70	2.55	2.47	2.39	2.30	2.21	2.11	2.01
40	7.31	5.18	4.31	3.83	3.51	3.29	3.12	2.99	2.89	2.80	2.66	2.52	2.37	2.29	2.20	2.11	2.02	1.92	1.80
60	7.08	4.98	4.13	3.65	3.34	3.12	2.95	2.82	2.72	2.63	2.50	2.35	2.20	2.12	2.03	1.94	1.84	1.73	1.60
120	6.85	4.79	3.95	3.48	3.17	2.96	2.79	2.66	2.56	2.47	2.34	2.19	2.03	1.95	1.86	1.76	1.66	1.53	1.38
∞	6.63	4.61	3.78	3.32	3.02	2.80	2.64	2.51	2.41	2.32	2.18	2.04	1.88	1.79	1.70	1.59	1.47	1.32	1.00

From Pearson, E. S. and H. O. Hartley. Table 18, "Percentage Points of the *F*-distribution." *Biometrika Tables for Statisticians,* Vol. I. Reprinted by permission of the Biometrika Trustees.

TABLE A.9
Mann–Whitney U Distribution

$P(U \leqslant U_0)$: $n_1 \leqslant n_2$; $3 \leqslant n_2 \leqslant 10$

$n_2 = 3$

	n_1	1	2	3
	0	.25	.10	.05
	1	.50	.20	.10
U_0	2		.40	.20
	3		.60	.35
	4			.50

$n_2 = 4$

	n_1	1	2	3	4
	0	.2000	.0667	.0286	.0143
	1	.4000	.1333	.0571	.0286
	2	.6000	.2667	.1143	.0571
	3		.4000	.2000	.1000
U_0	4		.6000	.3143	.1714
	5			.4286	.2429
	6			.5714	.3429
	7				.4429
	8				.5571

$n_2 = 5$

	n_1	1	2	3	4	5
	0	.1667	.0476	.0179	.0079	.0040
	1	.3333	.0952	.0357	.0159	.0079
	2	.5000	.1905	.0714	.0317	.0159
	3		.2857	.1250	.0556	.0278
	4		.4286	.1964	.0952	.0476
	5		.5714	.2857	.1429	.0754
U_0	6			.3929	.2063	.1111
	7			.5000	.2778	.1548
	8				.3651	.2103
	9				.4524	.2738
	10				.5476	.3452
	11					.4206
	12					.5000

Example: For $n_1 = 2$, $n_2 = 4$, and $U_0 = 2$, $P(U \leqslant 2) = .2667$.

continued

TABLE A.9
Mann–Whitney *U* Distribution (*continued*)

$n_2 = 6$

	n_1	1	2	3	4	5	6
	0	.1429	.0357	.0119	.0048	.0022	.0011
	1	.2857	.0714	.0238	.0095	.0043	.0022
	2	.4286	.1429	.0476	.0190	.0087	.0043
	3	.5714	.2143	.0833	.0333	.0152	.0076
	4		.3214	.1310	.0571	.0260	.0130
	5		.4286	.1905	.0857	.0411	.0206
	6		.5714	.2738	.1286	.0628	.0325
	7			.3571	.1762	.0887	.0465
	8			.4524	.2381	.1234	.0660
U_0	9			.5476	.3048	.1645	.0898
	10				.3810	.2143	.1201
	11				.4571	.2684	.1548
	12				.5429	.3312	.1970
	13					.3961	.2424
	14					.4654	.2944
	15					.5346	.3496
	16						.4091
	17						.4686
	18						.5314

$n_2 = 7$

	n_1	1	2	3	4	5	6	7
	0	.1250	.0278	.0083	.0030	.0013	.0006	.0003
	1	.2500	.0556	.0167	.0061	.0025	.0012	.0006
	2	.3750	.1111	.0333	.0121	.0051	.0023	.0012
	3	.5000	.1667	.0583	.0212	.0088	.0041	.0020
	4		.2500	.0917	.0364	.0152	.0070	.0035
	5		.3333	.1333	.0545	.0240	.0111	.0055
	6		.4444	.1917	.0818	.0366	.0175	.0087
	7		.5556	.2583	.1152	.0530	.0256	.0131
	8			.3333	.1576	.0745	.0367	.0189
	9			.4167	.2061	.1010	.0507	.0265
	10			.5000	.2636	.1338	.0688	.0364
	11				.3242	.1717	.0903	.0487
U_0	12				.3939	.2159	.1171	.0641
	13				.4636	.2652	.1474	.0825
	14				.5364	.3194	.1830	.1043
	15					.3775	.2226	.1297
	16					.4381	.2669	.1588
	17					.5000	.3141	.1914
	18						.3654	.2279
	19						.4178	.2675
	20						.4726	.3100
	21						.5274	.3552
	22							.4024
	23							.4508
	24							.5000

continued

TABLE A.9 **Mann–Whitney *U* Distribution (*continued*)**

$n_2 = 8$

U_0 \ n_1	1	2	3	4	5	6	7	8
0	.1111	.0222	.0061	.0020	.0008	.0003	.0002	.0001
1	.2222	.0444	.0121	.0040	.0016	.0007	.0003	.0002
2	.3333	.0889	.0242	.0081	.0031	.0013	.0006	.0003
3	.4444	.1333	.0424	.0141	.0054	.0023	.0011	.0005
4	.5556	.2000	.0667	.0242	.0093	.0040	.0019	.0009
5		.2667	.0970	.0364	.0148	.0063	.0030	.0015
6		.3556	.1394	.0545	.0225	.0100	.0047	.0023
7		.4444	.1879	.0768	.0326	.0147	.0070	.0035
8		.5556	.2485	.1071	.0466	.0213	.0103	.0052
9			.3152	.1414	.0637	.0296	.0145	.0074
10			.3879	.1838	.0855	.0406	.0200	.0103
11			.4606	.2303	.1111	.0539	.0270	.0141
12			.5394	.2848	.1422	.0709	.0361	.0190
13				.3414	.1772	.0906	.0469	.0249
14				.4040	.2176	.1142	.0603	.0325
15				.4667	.2618	.1412	.0760	.0415
16				.5333	.3108	.1725	.0946	.0524
17					.3621	.2068	.1159	.0652
18					.4165	.2454	.1405	.0803
19					.4716	.2864	.1678	.0974
20					.5284	.3310	.1984	.1172
21						.3773	.2317	.1393
22						.4259	.2679	.1641
23						.4749	.3063	.1911
24						.5251	.3472	.2209
25							.3894	.2527
26							.4333	.2869
27							.4775	.3227
28							.5225	.3605
29								.3992
30								.4392
31								.4796
32								.5204

continued

TABLE A.9 **Mann–Whitney *U* Distribution (*continued*)**

$n_2 = 9$

	n_1	1	2	3	4	5	6	7	8	9
	0	.1000	.0182	.0045	.0014	.0005	.0002	.0001	.0000	.0000
	1	.2000	.0364	.0091	.0028	.0010	.0004	.0002	.0001	.0000
	2	.3000	.0727	.0182	.0056	.0020	.0008	.0003	.0002	.0001
	3	.4000	.1091	.0318	.0098	.0035	.0014	.0006	.0003	.0001
	4	.5000	.1636	.0500	.0168	.0060	.0024	.0010	.0005	.0002
	5		.2182	.0727	.0252	.0095	.0038	.0017	.0008	.0004
	6		.2909	.1045	.0378	.0145	.0060	.0026	.0012	.0006
	7		.3636	.1409	.0531	.0210	.0088	.0039	.0019	.0009
	8		.4545	.1864	.0741	.0300	.0128	.0058	.0028	.0014
	9		.5455	.2409	.0993	.0415	.0180	.0082	.0039	.0020
	10			.3000	.1301	.0559	.0248	.0115	.0056	.0028
	11			.3636	.1650	.0734	.0332	.0156	.0076	.0039
	12			.4318	.2070	.0949	.0440	.0209	.0103	.0053
	13			.5000	.2517	.1199	.0567	.0274	.0137	.0071
	14				.3021	.1489	.0723	.0356	.0180	.0094
	15				.3552	.1818	.0905	.0454	.0232	.0122
	16				.4126	.2188	.1119	.0571	.0296	.0157
	17				.4699	.2592	.1361	.0708	.0372	.0200
	18				.5301	.3032	.1638	.0869	.0464	.0252
	19					.3497	.1942	.1052	.0570	.0313
U_0	20					.3986	.2280	.1261	.0694	.0385
	21					.4491	.2643	.1496	.0836	.0470
	22					.5000	.3035	.1755	.0998	.0567
	23						.3445	.2039	.1179	.0680
	24						.3878	.2349	.1383	.0807
	25						.4320	.2680	.1606	.0951
	26						.4773	.3032	.1852	.1112
	27						.5227	.3403	.2117	.1290
	28							.3788	.2404	.1487
	29							.4185	.2707	.1701
	30							.4591	.3029	.1933
	31							.5000	.3365	.2181
	32								.3715	.2447
	33								.4074	.2729
	34								.4442	.3024
	35								.4813	.3332
	36								.5187	.3652
	37									.3981
	38									.4317
	39									.4657
	40									.5000

continued

TABLE A.9 **Mann–Whitney *U* Distribution (*continued*)**

$n_2 = 10$

U_0 \ n_1	1	2	3	4	5	6	7	8	9	10
0	.0909	.0152	.0035	.0010	.0003	.0001	.0001	.0000	.0000	.0000
1	.1818	.0303	.0070	.0020	.0007	.0002	.0001	.0000	.0000	.0000
2	.2727	.0606	.0140	.0040	.0013	.0005	.0002	.0001	.0000	.0000
3	.3636	.0909	.0245	.0070	.0023	.0009	.0004	.0002	.0001	.0000
4	.4545	.1364	.0385	.0120	.0040	.0015	.0006	.0003	.0001	.0001
5	.5455	.1818	.0559	.0180	.0063	.0024	.0010	.0004	.0002	.0001
6		.2424	.0804	.0270	.0097	.0037	.0015	.0007	.0003	.0002
7		.3030	.1084	.0380	.0140	.0055	.0023	.0010	.0005	.0002
8		.3788	.1434	.0529	.0200	.0080	.0034	.0015	.0007	.0004
9		.4545	.1853	.0709	.0276	.0112	.0048	.0022	.0011	.0005
10		.5455	.2343	.0939	.0376	.0156	.0068	.0031	.0015	.0008
11			.2867	.1199	.0496	.0210	.0093	.0043	.0021	.0010
12			.3462	.1518	.0646	.0280	.0125	.0058	.0028	.0014
13			.4056	.1868	.0823	.0363	.0165	.0078	.0038	.0019
14			.4685	.2268	.1032	.0467	.0215	.0103	.0051	.0026
15			.5315	.2697	.1272	.0589	.0277	.0133	.0066	.0034
16				.3177	.1548	.0736	.0351	.0171	.0086	.0045
17				.3666	.1855	.0903	.0439	.0217	.0110	.0057
18				.4196	.2198	.1099	.0544	.0273	.0140	.0073
19				.4725	.2567	.1317	.0665	.0338	.0175	.0093
20				.5275	.2970	.1566	.0806	.0416	.0217	.0116
21					.3393	.1838	.0966	.0506	.0267	.0144
22					.3839	.2139	.1148	.0610	.0326	.0177
23					.4296	.2461	.1349	.0729	.0394	.0216
24					.4765	.2811	.1574	.0864	.0474	.0262
25					.5235	.3177	.1819	.1015	.0564	.0315
26						.3564	.2087	.1185	.0667	.0376
27						.3962	.2374	.1371	.0782	.0446
28						.4374	.2681	.1577	.0912	.0526
29						.4789	.3004	.1800	.1055	.0615
30						.5211	.3345	.2041	.1214	.0716
31							.3698	.2299	.1388	.0827
32							.4063	.2574	.1577	.0952
33							.4434	.2863	.1781	.1088
34							.4811	.3167	.2001	.1237
35							.5189	.3482	.2235	.1399
36								.3809	.2483	.1575
37								.4143	.2745	.1763
38								.4484	.3019	.1965
39								.4827	.3304	.2179
40								.5173	.3598	.2406
41									.3901	.2644
42									.4211	.2894
43									.4524	.3153
44									.4841	.3421
45									.5159	.3697
46										.3980
47										.4267
48										.4559
49										.4853
50										.5147

TABLE A.10 Critical values of the Wilcoxon test statistic

The following table gives critical values of T in the Wilcoxon matched-pair signed-rank test.

$n = 5, 6, 7, \ldots, 50$

1-sided	2-sided	$n = 5$	$n = 6$	$n = 7$	$n = 8$	$n = 9$	$n = 10$
$\alpha = .05$	$\alpha = .10$	1	2	4	6	8	11
$\alpha = .025$	$\alpha = .05$		1	2	4	6	8
$\alpha = .01$	$\alpha = .02$			0	2	3	5
$\alpha = .005$	$\alpha = .01$				0	2	3

1-sided	2-sided	$n = 11$	$n = 12$	$n = 13$	$n = 14$	$n = 15$	$n = 16$
$\alpha = .05$	$\alpha = .10$	14	17	21	26	30	36
$\alpha = .025$	$\alpha = .05$	11	14	17	21	25	30
$\alpha = .01$	$\alpha = .02$	7	10	13	16	20	24
$\alpha = .005$	$\alpha = .01$	5	7	10	13	16	19

1-sided	2-sided	$n = 17$	$n = 18$	$n = 19$	$n = 20$	$n = 21$	$n = 22$
$\alpha = .05$	$\alpha = .10$	41	47	54	60	68	75
$\alpha = .025$	$\alpha = .05$	35	40	46	52	59	66
$\alpha = .01$	$\alpha = .02$	28	33	38	43	49	56
$\alpha = .005$	$\alpha = .01$	23	28	32	37	43	49

1-sided	2-sided	$n = 23$	$n = 24$	$n = 25$	$n = 26$	$n = 27$	$n = 28$
$\alpha = .05$	$\alpha = .10$	83	92	101	110	120	130
$\alpha = .025$	$\alpha = .05$	73	81	90	98	107	117
$\alpha = .01$	$\alpha = .02$	62	69	77	85	93	102
$\alpha = .005$	$\alpha = .01$	55	61	68	76	84	92

1-sided	2-sided	$n = 29$	$n = 30$	$n = 31$	$n = 32$	$n = 33$	$n = 34$
$\alpha = .05$	$\alpha = .10$	141	152	163	175	199	201
$\alpha = .025$	$\alpha = .05$	127	137	148	159	171	183
$\alpha = .01$	$\alpha = .02$	111	120	130	141	151	162
$\alpha = .005$	$\alpha = .01$	100	109	118	128	138	149

1-sided	2-sided	$n = 35$	$n = 36$	$n = 37$	$n = 38$	$n = 39$	
$\alpha = .05$	$\alpha = .10$	214	228	242	256	271	
$\alpha = .025$	$\alpha = .05$	195	208	222	235	250	
$\alpha = .01$	$\alpha = .02$	174	186	198	211	224	
$\alpha = .005$	$\alpha = .01$	160	171	183	195	208	

Example: If $n = 30$, then $P(T \geqslant 120) = .01$ and $P(T \geqslant 109) = .005$.

continued

TABLE A.10 **Critical values of the Wilcoxon test statistic (*continued*)**

$n = 5, 6, 7, \ldots, 50$

1-sided	2-sided	$n = 40$	$n = 41$	$n = 42$	$n = 43$	$n = 44$	$n = 45$
$\alpha = .05$	$\alpha = .10$	287	303	319	336	353	371
$\alpha = .025$	$\alpha = .05$	264	279	295	311	327	344
$\alpha = .01$	$\alpha = .02$	238	252	267	281	297	313
$\alpha = .005$	$\alpha = .01$	221	234	248	262	277	292
1-sided	2-sided	$n = 46$	$n = 47$	$n = 48$	$n = 49$	$n = 50$	
$\alpha = .05$	$\alpha = .10$	389	408	427	446	466	
$\alpha = .025$	$\alpha = .05$	361	379	397	415	434	
$\alpha = .01$	$\alpha = .02$	329	345	362	380	398	
$\alpha = .005$	$\alpha = .01$	307	323	339	356	373	

TABLE A.11 **Distribution of number of runs**

The following table gives probabilities in the lower tail of the distribution of the number of runs r in samples of size (n_1, n_2): $P(r < r_0)$.

	r_0								
(n_1, n_2)	2	3	4	5	6	7	8	9	10
(2, 3)	.200	.500	.900	1.000					
(2, 4)	.133	.400	.800	1.000					
(2, 5)	.095	.333	.714	1.000					
(2, 6)	.071	.286	.643	1.000					
(2, 7)	.056	.250	.583	1.000					
(2, 8)	.044	.222	.533	1.000					
(2, 9)	.036	.200	.491	1.000					
(2, 10)	.030	.182	.455	1.000					
(3, 3)	.100	.300	.700	.900	1.000				
(3, 4)	.057	.200	.543	.800	.971	1.000			
(3, 5)	.036	.143	.429	.714	.929	1.000			
(3, 6)	.024	.107	.345	.643	.881	1.000			
(3, 7)	.017	.083	.283	583	.833	1.000			
(3, 8)	.012	.067	.236	.533	.788	1.000			
(3, 9)	.009	.055	.200	.491	.745	1.000			
(3, 10)	.007	.045	.171	.455	.706	1.000			
(4, 4)	.029	.114	.371	.629	.886	.971	1.000		
(4, 5)	.016	.071	.262	.500	.786	.929	.992	1.000	
(4, 6)	.010	.048	.190	.405	.690	.881	.976	1.000	
(4, 7)	.006	.033	.142	.333	.606	.833	.954	1.000	
(4, 8)	.004	.024	.109	.279	.533	.788	.929	1.000	
(4, 9)	.003	.018	.085	.236	.471	.745	.902	1.000	
(4, 10)	.002	.014	.068	.203	.419	.706	.874	1.000	
(5, 5)	.008	.040	.167	.357	.643	.833	.960	.992	1.000
(5, 6)	.004	.024	.110	.262	.522	.738	.911	.976	.998
(5, 7)	.003	.015	.076	.197	.424	.652	.854	.955	.992
(5, 8)	.002	.010	.054	.152	.347	.576	.793	.929	.984
(5, 9)	.001	.007	.039	.119	.287	.510	.734	.902	.972
(5, 10)	.001	.005	.029	.095	.239	.455	.678	.874	.958
(6, 6)	.002	.013	.067	.175	.392	.608	.825	.933	.987
(6, 7)	.001	.008	.043	.121	.296	.500	.733	.879	.966
(6, 8)	.001	.005	.028	.086	.226	.413	.646	.821	.937
(6, 9)	.000	.003	.019	.063	.175	.343	.566	.762	.902
(6, 10)	.000	.002	.013	.047	.137	.288	.497	.706	.864
(7, 7)	.001	.004	.025	.078	.209	.383	.617	.791	.922
(7, 8)	.000	.002	.015	.051	.149	.296	.514	.704	.867
(7, 9)	.000	.001	.010	.035	.108	.231	.427	.622	.806
(7, 10)	.000	.001	.006	.024	.080	.182	.355	.549	.743
(8, 8)	.000	.001	.009	.032	.100	.214	.405	.595	.786
(8, 9)	.000	.001	.005	.020	.069	.157	.319	.500	.702
(8, 10)	.000	.000	.003	.013	.048	.117	.251	.419	.621
(9, 9)	.000	.000	.003	.012	.044	.109	.238	.399	.601
(9, 10)	.000	.000	.002	.008	.029	.077	.179	.319	.510
(10, 10)	.000	.000	.001	.004	.019	.051	.128	.242	.414

Example: If $n_1 = 6$ and $n_2 = 10$, then $P(r < 5) = .047$.

continued

TABLE A.11 **Distribution of number of runs (*continued*)**

(n_1, n_2)	r_0: 11	12	13	14	15	16	17	18	19	20
(2, 3)										
(2, 4)										
(2, 5)										
(2, 6)										
(2, 7)										
(2, 8)										
(2, 9)										
(2, 10)										
(3, 3)										
(3, 4)										
(3, 5)										
(3, 6)										
(3, 7)										
(3, 8)										
(3, 9)										
(3, 10)										
(4, 4)										
(4, 5)										
(4, 6)										
(4, 7)										
(4, 8)										
(4, 9)										
(4, 10)										
(5, 5)										
(5, 6)	1.000									
(5, 7)	1.000									
(5, 8)	1.000									
(5, 9)	1.000									
(5, 10)	1.000									
(6, 6)	.998	1.000								
(6, 7)	.992	.999	1.000							
(6, 8)	.984	.998	1.000							
(6, 9)	.972	.994	1.000							
(6, 10)	.958	.990	1.000							
(7, 7)	.975	.996	.999	1.000						
(7, 8)	.949	.988	.998	1.000	1.000					
(7, 9)	.916	.975	.994	.999	1.000					
(7, 10)	.879	.957	.990	.998	1.000					
(8, 8)	.900	.968	.991	.999	1.000	1.000				
(8, 9)	.843	.939	.980	.996	.999	1.000	1.000			
(8, 10)	.782	.903	.964	.990	.998	1.000	1.000			
(9, 9)	.762	.891	.956	.988	.997	1.000	1.000	1.000		
(9, 10)	.681	.834	.923	.974	.992	.999	1.000	1.000	1.000	
(10, 10)	.586	.758	.872	.949	.981	.996	.999	1.000	1.000	1.000

From Swed, F., and C. Eisenhart. "Tables for Testing Randomness of Grouping in a Sequence of Alternatives." *Annals of Mathematical Statistics,* vol. 14, 1943.

TABLE A.12 **Critical values of Spearman's rank correlation coefficient**

n	$\alpha = .05$	$\alpha = .025$	$\alpha = .01$	$\alpha = .005$
5	.900	—	—	—
6	.829	.886	.943	—
7	.714	.786	.893	—
8	.643	.738	.833	.881
9	.600	.683	.783	.833
10	.564	.648	.745	.794
11	.523	.623	.736	.818
12	.497	.591	.703	.780
13	.475	.566	.673	.745
14	.457	.545	.646	.716
15	.441	.525	.623	.689
16	.425	.507	.601	.666
17	.412	.490	.582	.645
18	.399	.476	.564	.625
19	.388	.462	.549	.608
20	.377	.450	.534	.591
21	.368	.438	.521	.576
22	.359	.428	.508	.562
23	.351	.418	.496	.549
24	.343	.409	.485	.537
25	.336	.400	.475	.526
26	.329	.392	.465	.515
27	.323	.385	.456	.505
28	.317	.377	.448	.496
29	.311	.370	.440	.487
30	.305	.364	.432	.478

From Olds, E. G. "Distribution of Sums of Squares of Rank Differences for Small Numbers of Individuals." *Annals of Mathematical Statistics,* vol. 9, 1938.

Example: If $n = 20$, $P(R_s \geqslant .377) = .05$.

TABLE A.13 **Critical values of the Durbin–Watson statistic**

The letter k represents the number of explanatory variables in the regression equation *not* counting the constant term. The critical values in the table are for a 1-tailed test against positive serial correlation.

Significance Points of d_L and d_U: 5%

	$k = 1$		$k = 2$		$k = 3$		$k = 4$		$k = 5$	
n	d_L	d_U	d_L	d_U	d_L	d_U	d_L	d_U	d_L	d_U
15	1.08	1.36	0.95	1.54	0.82	1.75	0.69	1.97	0.56	2.21
16	1.10	1.37	0.98	1.54	0.86	1.73	0.74	1.93	0.62	2.15
17	1.13	1.38	1.02	1.54	0.90	1.71	0.78	1.90	0.67	2.10
18	1.16	1.39	1.05	1.53	0.93	1.69	0.82	1.87	0.71	2.06
19	1.18	1.40	1.08	1.53	0.97	1.68	0.86	1.85	0.75	2.02
20	1.20	1.41	1.10	1.54	1.00	1.68	0.90	1.83	0.79	1.99
21	1.22	1.42	1.13	1.54	1.03	1.67	0.93	1.81	0.83	1.96
22	1.24	1.43	1.15	1.54	1.05	1.66	0.96	1.80	0.86	1.94
23	1.26	1.44	1.17	1.54	1.08	1.66	0.99	1.79	0.90	1.92
24	1.27	1.45	1.19	1.55	1.10	1.66	1.01	1.78	0.93	1.90
25	1.29	1.45	1.21	1.55	1.12	1.66	1.04	1.77	0.95	1.89
26	1.30	1.46	1.22	1.55	1.14	1.65	1.06	1.76	0.98	1.88
27	1.32	1.47	1.24	1.56	1.16	1.65	1.08	1.76	1.01	1.86
28	1.33	1.48	1.26	1.56	1.18	1.65	1.10	1.75	1.03	1.85
29	1.34	1.48	1.27	1.56	1.20	1.65	1.12	1.74	1.05	1.84
30	1.35	1.49	1.28	1.57	1.21	1.65	1.14	1.74	1.07	1.83
31	1.36	1.50	1.30	1.57	1.23	1.65	1.16	1.74	1.09	1.83
32	1.37	1.50	1.31	1.57	1.24	1.65	1.18	1.73	1.11	1.82
33	1.38	1.51	1.32	1.58	1.26	1.65	1.19	1.73	1.13	1.81
34	1.39	1.51	1.33	1.58	1.27	1.65	1.21	1.73	1.15	1.81
35	1.40	1.52	1.34	1.58	1.28	1.65	1.22	1.73	1.16	1.80
36	1.41	1.52	1.35	1.59	1.29	1.65	1.24	1.73	1.18	1.80
37	1.42	1.53	1.36	1.59	1.31	1.66	1.25	1.72	1.19	1.80
38	1.43	1.54	1.37	1.59	1.32	1.66	1.26	1.72	1.21	1.79
39	1.43	1.54	1.38	1.60	1.33	1.66	1.27	1.72	1.22	1.79
40	1.44	1.54	1.39	1.60	1.34	1.66	1.29	1.72	1.23	1.79
45	1.48	1.57	1.43	1.62	1.38	1.67	1.34	1.72	1.29	1.78
50	1.50	1.59	1.46	1.63	1.42	1.67	1.38	1.72	1.34	1.77
55	1.53	1.60	1.49	1.64	1.45	1.68	1.41	1.72	1.38	1.77
60	1.55	1.62	1.51	1.65	1.48	1.69	1.44	1.73	1.41	1.77
65	1.57	1.63	1.54	1.66	1.50	1.70	1.47	1.73	1.44	1.77
70	1.58	1.64	1.55	1.67	1.52	1.70	1.49	1.74	1.46	1.77
75	1.60	1.65	1.57	1.68	1.54	1.71	1.51	1.74	1.49	1.77
80	1.61	1.66	1.59	1.69	1.56	1.72	1.53	1.74	1.51	1.77
85	1.62	1.67	1.60	1.70	1.57	1.72	1.55	1.75	1.52	1.77
90	1.63	1.68	1.61	1.70	1.59	1.73	1.57	1.75	1.54	1.78
95	1.64	1.69	1.62	1.71	1.60	1.73	1.58	1.75	1.56	1.78
100	1.65	1.69	1.63	1.72	1.61	1.74	1.59	1.76	1.57	1.78

TABLE A.14 Critical values of the Kolmogorov–Smirnov test statistic

Table entries are critical values D_α such that $P(D \geqslant D_\alpha) = \alpha$.

	α						α				
n	.20	.10	.05	.02	.01	n	.20	.10	.05	.02	.01
1	.900	.950	.975	.990	.995	21	.226	.259	.287	.321	.344
2	.684	.776	.842	.900	.929	22	.221	.253	.281	.314	.337
3	.565	.636	.708	.785	.829	23	.216	.247	.275	.307	.330
4	.493	.565	.624	.689	.734	24	.212	.242	.269	.301	.323
5	.447	.509	.563	.627	.669	25	.208	.238	.264	.295	.317
6	.410	.468	.519	.577	.617	26	.204	.233	.259	.290	.311
7	.381	.436	.483	.538	.576	27	.200	.229	.254	.284	.305
8	.358	.410	.454	.507	.542	28	.197	.225	.250	.279	.300
9	.339	.387	.430	.480	.513	29	.193	.221	.246	.275	.295
10	.323	.369	.409	.457	.489	30	.190	.218	.242	.270	.290
11	.308	.352	.391	.437	.468	31	.187	.214	.238	.266	.285
12	.296	.338	.375	.419	.449	32	.184	.211	.234	.262	.281
13	.285	.325	.361	.404	.432	33	.182	.208	.231	.258	.277
14	.275	.314	.349	.390	.418	34	.179	.205	.227	.254	.273
15	.266	.304	.338	.377	.404	35	.177	.202	.224	.251	.269
16	.258	.295	.327	.366	.392	36	.174	.199	.221	.247	.265
17	.250	.286	.318	.355	.381	37	.172	.196	.218	.244	.262
18	.244	.279	.309	.346	.371	38	.170	.194	.215	.241	.258
19	.237	.271	.301	.337	.361	39	.168	.191	.213	.238	.255
20	.232	.265	.294	.329	.352	40	.165	.189	.210	.235	.252
						Over 40	$\frac{1.07}{\sqrt{n}}$	$\frac{1.22}{\sqrt{n}}$	$\frac{1.36}{\sqrt{n}}$	$\frac{1.52}{\sqrt{n}}$	$\frac{1.63}{\sqrt{n}}$

Adapted from Miller, L. H. "Tables of Percentage Points of Kolmogorov Statistic." *Journal of the American Statistical Association*, vol. 51, 1956, pp. 111–21.

Example: For $n = 15$, $P(D \geqslant .338) = .05$.

TABLE A.15 **Critical values of the Lilliefors test statistic**

Table entries are critical values D_α such that $P(D \leqslant D_\alpha) = \alpha$.

	α				
n	.20	.15	.10	.05	.01
4	.300	.319	.352	.381	.417
5	.285	.299	.315	.337	.405
6	.265	.277	.294	.319	.364
7	.247	.258	.276	.300	.348
8	.233	.244	.261	.285	.331
9	.223	.233	.249	.271	.311
10	.215	.224	.239	.258	.294
11	.206	.217	.230	.249	.284
12	.199	.212	.223	.242	.275
13	.190	.202	.214	.234	.268
14	.183	.194	.207	.227	.261
15	.177	.187	.201	.220	.257
16	.173	.182	.195	.213	.250
17	.169	.177	.189	.206	.245
18	.166	.173	.184	.200	.239
19	.163	.169	.179	.195	.235
20	.160	.166	.174	.190	.231
25	.149	.153	.165	.180	.203
30	.131	.136	.144	.161	.187
Over 30	$\frac{.736}{\sqrt{n}}$	$\frac{.768}{\sqrt{n}}$	$\frac{.805}{\sqrt{n}}$	$\frac{.886}{\sqrt{n}}$	$\frac{1.031}{\sqrt{n}}$

Adapted from Lilliefors, H. W. "On the Kolmogorov–Smirnov Test for Normality with Mean and Variance Unknown." *Journal of the American Statistical Association,* vol. 62, 1967, pp. 399–402.

Example: If $n = 15$, $P(D \geqslant .220) = .05$.

TABLE A.16 **Critical values for Hartley's *H* statistic**

Table entries are critical values H_α such that $P(H \geq H_\alpha) \times \alpha$ for $\alpha = .05$.

$\alpha = .05$

K

n	2	3	4	5	6	7	8	9	10	11	12
3	39.0	87.5	142	202	266	333	403	475	550	626	704
4	15.4	27.8	39.2	50.7	62.0	72.9	83.5	93.9	104	114	124
5	9.60	15.5	20.6	25.2	29.5	33.6	37.5	41.1	44.6	48.0	51.4
6	7.15	10.8	13.7	16.3	18.7	20.8	22.9	24.7	26.5	28.2	29.9
7	5.82	8.38	10.4	12.1	13.7	15.0	16.3	17.5	18.6	19.7	20.7
8	4.99	6.94	8.44	9.70	10.8	11.8	12.7	13.5	14.3	15.1	15.8
9	4.43	6.00	7.18	8.12	9.03	9.78	10.5	11.1	11.7	12.2	12.7
10	4.03	5.34	6.31	7.11	7.80	8.41	8.95	9.45	9.91	10.3	10.7
11	3.72	4.85	5.67	6.34	6.92	7.42	7.87	8.28	8.66	9.01	9.34
13	3.28	4.16	4.79	5.30	5.72	6.09	6.42	6.72	7.00	7.25	7.48
16	2.86	3.54	4.01	4.37	4.68	4.95	5.19	5.40	5.59	5.77	5.93
21	2.46	2.95	3.29	3.54	3.76	3.94	4.10	4.24	4.37	4.49	4.59
31	2.07	2.40	2.61	2.78	2.91	3.02	3.12	3.21	3.29	3.36	3.39
61	1.67	1.85	1.96	2.04	2.11	2.17	2.22	2.26	2.30	2.33	2.36
∞	1.00	1.00	1.00	1.00	1.00	1.00	1.00	1.00	1.00	1.00	1.00

Example: If $n = 6$ and $K = 4$, then $P(H \geq 13.7) = .05$.

Appendix B
Answers to Selected Exercises

Chapter Two

Section 2.1

1. (a) A list containing the names of the 1000 bank customers.
(b) Each customer is an elementary unit.
(c) The population is the account balances of the 1000 customers.
(d) The sample observations are the account balances of the selected 50 customers.

3. Multinomial data are discrete.

9. (a) Continuous (b) Continuous (c) Discrete (d) Discrete

Section 2.3

1. Judgement or convenience samples are likely to contain biases. A random sample, on the other hand, has no tendency to favor elementary units possessing a certain characteristic.

3. One of the first five observations is selected randomly and then every fifth element after that is selected.

Section 2.4

1. (a) 42% are male; 48% are female
(b) Freshmen = 10%; Soph = 24%; Junior = 34%; Senior = 32%
(c) In-state = 44%; Out-of-state = 56%
(d) Economics = 22%; Math = 24%

3. (a)
```
TITLE 'NATIONAL DATA'
DATA LIST FREE/DATE,
     DOW JONES, GNP,
     TOTALGOV, DEFENSE,
     URATE, CPI, TBILL
BEGIN DATA
     insert data here
END DATA
LIST
FINISH
```

Chapter 2 ▪ Supplementary Exercises

1. Bias of self-selection

3. (a) Quantitative, discrete
(b) Qualitative, dichotomous
(c) Qualitative, multinomial
(d) Qualitative, multinomial
(e) Quantitative, continuous

5. (a) Quantitative, discrete
(b) Qualitative, multinomial
(c) Qualitative, multinomial
(d) Qualitative, multinomial
(e) Qualitative, multinomial
(f) Quantitative, continuous

7. (a) Convenience sample
(b) Judgement sample
(c) Systematic random sample
(d) Cluster sample with self-enumeration
(e) Systematic random sample
(f) Stratified random sample

9. Sample every tenth employee from an alphabetical listing.

23. Interviewer bias

25. Self-selection bias is present.

29. .16

Chapter Three

Section 3.1

1. Frequencies are: 5, 10, 19, 11, 5; Relative frequencies are: .10, .20, .38, .22, .10
3. Frequencies for 0, 1, 2, 3, 4 are: 4, 24, 16, 4, 2

Section 3.2

1. (a) Uniform (b) Uniform (c) Skewed to right (d) Symmetric, bell shaped

Section 3.4

1. (c) Sex = 0: 36; Sex = 1: 24 (d) Status = 0: 38; Status = 1: 22 (e) .4167 (f) .2917 (g) .6818
3. (a) .4; .6; 0 (b) .118; .647; .235 (c) 0; .230; .769

Section 3.6

1.
```
4 | 0 3 5 6 8 9
5 | 0 1 3 7 8 8 8 8 9
6 | 1 3 4 4 5 7 7 9
7 | 0 1 2 3 5 6
8 | 2
```
3.
```
0 | 1 2 2 3 3 4
  | 5 5 6 7 8 9
1 | 0 0 1 2 2 2 2 3 3 3 4 4
  | 5 6 6 6 7 7 8 8 9 9 9
2 | 0 2 2 3 4 4 4
  | 5 6 6
```

Section 3.7

5. (a) .52; .48 (b) .10; .24; .34; .32 (c) .44; .56 (d) .22; .24
7. (a) .625 (b) .80 (c) .317 (d) .200

Chapter 3 ▪ Supplementary Exercises

1. (b) Frequencies are: 2, 11, 9, 12, 3, 1, 1, 1
3. (b) Frequencies are: 11, 8, 12, 5, 3, 1 (c) Frequencies are: 6, 7, 6, 2, 10, 3, 2, 3, 1, 0
5. (b) Frequencies are: 3, 3, 6, 5, 6, 4, 1, 2
7. (b) Frequencies are: 6, 8, 7, 15, 4
9. (d) 12 years

Chapter Four

Section 4.1

1. (a) 71 (b) 142 (c) 615
3. (a) 2120 (b) 1620
5. (a) 7 (b) −2 (c) 6 (d) 49

Section 4.2

1. (a) $1.00 (b) $4.00 (c) 170 lbs. (d) 66 inches
3. $14,800; $14,000
5. 10.7; 11.5

Section 4.3

1. 1638.75; 1620; 1650
3. (a) 56.2158 (b) 56.0714; 57.5
5. (a) 6.925 (b) 7.2 (c) 6 to 8

Section 4.4

1. (a) $0.98 (b) $3.35 (c) 158 lbs (d) 62 inches
3. (a) 59.125 (b) 58 (c) 46.5, 71.5 (d) 47.5

Section 4.5

1. (a) $0.01 (b) 1000 (c) 12 lbs. (d) 2 inches
3. (a) 35 (b) $181 (c) $180 (d) 205 (e) 14.3178
5. 11.2
7. (a) 15,833.333; 15,500; 15,000 (b) 8,000; 6,966,666.6667; 2639.4444 (d) 1833.333
9. (a) 53 (b) 75.34 (c) 166.2244 (d) 12.8928 (e) 78 (f) 67; 84 (g) 17 (h) 10.472

Section 4.6

1. (a) mean = 12.8; median = 12.0571 (b) 28.8; 5.367
3. (a) 0.36 (b) 144 (d) 12.65 (e) 35.516; 5.96
5. (a) 1.44 (b) 1.088; 1.04 (c) .95
7. (a) 103.049; 89.0625 (b) 3795.649

Section 4.7

1. (a) 1 (b) −2 (c) 0 (d) .75 (e) .95
3. (a) 510; 60 (b) 1.5 (c) .1176
5. 50; 15; 342.857; 18.516; 0.54
7. (a) 98.033 (b) 112.864 (c) 2.068
11. The standardized score is higher in distribution B.

Section 4.8

1. (c) 12.85; 13.26 (d) Q_1 = 12.34; Q_3 = 13.57; IQR = 1.23 Lower inner fence = 10.495; Upper inner fence = 15.415; Lower outer fence = 8.65; Upper outer fence = 16.03

Section 4.9

1. 2.758
3. Mean GPA = 2.9212; s = .3875;
Mean SAT = 1122.40; s = 152.9247
5. (a) 24,357.784 (b) 3,684.529; s = 1055.438
(c) 2509.275 (d) 13,238.804 (e) 9.407
7. (a) 3 **9.** 12, 10, 6

Chapter 4 ▪ Supplementary Exercises

1. (b) 1.4833 (c) .778 (d) 1.125
3. (c) 3.5 (d) 3.935 **5.** (b) 14.5; 6.69
7. (b) Mean (Liked show) = 21.62;
Mean (Disliked show) = 31.85
(c) Median (Liked show) = 21.25;
Median (Disliked show) = 33.68
Mode (Liked show) = 10;
Mode (Disliked show) = 35
9. (b) Frequencies are: 2, 4, 9, 11, 12, 6, 4, 2
(f) 49.18; 290.926; 17.056
(g) Median = 49.09
11. $k\overline{x}$; k^2s^2 **15.** (a) 21 (b) 106.1224
17. 28,595.4998
19. 39.8169; 89.1918; 9.4444
23. (a) 482.5 (b) 403,604.8 (c) 300
(d) 125
25. (a) $54,800 (b) .5 **27.** 21.414508
29. (b) Relative frequencies are: .1354, .2604, .3542, .1667, .0833
(d) 920.833 (e) 451.878 (f) 800–1200
31. (a) .08 (b) Frequencies are: 24, 44, 96, 88, 68, 48, 32
(c) 29,875 (d) 11,489.207
35. The mean of the standardized scores should be 0.
39. (a) 1 (b) 1 (c) 1.416
43. (b) White: $32,850.00
Black: $20,212.50
45. (b) 29.5352; 24.73

Chapter Five

Section 5.1

1. $S = \{1, 2, 3, 4, 5, 6\}$

Section 5.2

1. Yes **3.** (a) No (b) 6 (c) 5/36
5. P(early) = 120/850; P(on time) = 340/850;
P(late) = 220/850; P(uncollectible) = 170/850
7. 2/7

Section 5.3

1. (b) 42 (c) Yes (d) 12 (e) .2857
3. .1429 **5.** 1/36
7. (a) .20 (b) .7333 (c) .1333
9. (a) False (b) Indeterminate (c) False
(d) False (e) False (f) Indeterminate
(g) True
11. .001

Section 5.4

1. (b) .6667; .1667; 0; 0; .8333
3. (a) .06 (b) .54 (c) .02 (d) .38
5. (a) .48; .52; .16; .26; .35; .23 (b) 1.00
(c) .05 (d) .05 (e) 0 (f) 0
7. (a) .35 (b) .65
9. (a) .62 (b) 620
11. (a) .04255 (b) .5106

Section 5.5

1. (a) .2 (b) .2 (c) .4
3. (a) .05 (b) .01 (c) .90 (d) .06
5. .333
7. (a) .100 (b) .30 (c) 550
9. (a) .40 (b) .60 (c) .50 (d) .25
(e) .222 (f) .125
11. (a) .25 (b) .65 (c) .35 (d) .875

Section 5.6

1. (a) $S = \{(S,J),(S,\overline{J}),(\overline{S},J),(\overline{S},\overline{J})\}$ (b) .25
(c) .75 (d) .25
3. .9606 **5.** (a) .0063
7. (a) .0003 (b) .9603 **9.** .69
11. (a) .343 (b) .027 (c) .973
13. (a) .000064 (b) .262144
15. (a) .88 (b) .18 (c) .42
17. (a) .4096 (b) .5904

Section 5.7

1. (a) .08 (b) .8696
3. (a) .2667 (b) .4000 (c) .1667 (d) .075
5. (a) .60 (b) .1385

Section 5.8

1. 720; 120; 42; 90 **3.** 120; 360; 1; 42; 1
5. 10; 10; 36; 36 **7.** 90 **9.** 120
11. 6720 **13.** 240

Section 5.9

1. (a) .0167; .4667; .1417
(b) .300; .0167; .0583

(c) .2267; .1556 (d) .0267; .8000
(e) .7467; .0444

3. (a) .0167 (b) .4667; .1417
(c) .0167; .0583 (d) .027; .747; .227
(e) .966; .034 (f) Yes

Chapter 5 ▪ Supplementary Exercises

1. (a) .0243 (b) .0111 (c) .9778
(d) .0568

5. (a) neither (b) neither (c) true
(d) neither

7. (a) no (b) .4095 **9.** .096

11. (a) .06 (b) .0528

13. (a) .4 (b) Dependent

15. (a) .2083 (b) .2083 exceeds .20, therefore recall the card.

17. (a) .10 (b) .333 (c) .1143
(d) Not independent

19. (a) .60; .40; .85; .10 (b) .9272; .0728

21. .9219 **23.** .2401 **25.** 11,520

27. 1680 **29.** .52

31. (a) .04725 (b) .105

33. (a) .27 (b) No (c) .50

35. (a) .245 (b) .918

37. (a) False (b) True (c) False

39. .64

41. (a) .030 (b) .533 (c) .967

43. .67232

45. (a) .69 (b) .913 **47.** 5

49. (a) .18 (b) .72

51. (a) .87 (b) .6585 (c) .3415

53. .85 **55.** .0039

57. For Pigeons: *P*(reward) = .58;
For Rats: *P*(reward) = .70; Thus, rats are more intelligent.

Chapter Six

Section 6.1

1. (a) Discrete (b) Continuous
(c) Continuous (d) Discrete (e) Discrete
(f) Discrete (g) Continuous (h) Discrete

5. $S = \{25, 35, 5, 15\}$

Section 6.2

1. $P(0) = .25$; $P(1) = .50$; $P(2) = .25$

3. (b) .35 (c) .65 (d) .50 (e) .35

5. (b) 1 (c) .8 (d) .5

7. (a) .60 (b) .55 (c) .85

9. (a) .2401 (b) .9919

11. (a) .65 (b) .35 (c) .75 (d) .85
(e) .60 (f) .65

Section 6.3

1. (a)

0	1	2	3	4
.30	.33	.18	.16	.03

3. (a)

1	2	3	4	5	6
.40	.36	.10	.11	.02	.01

(d) .14

Section 6.4

1. (a) .22

3. (a)

X	$P(X)$	$X \cdot P(X)$
−$5.60	.35	−1.96
−0.10	.40	−0.04
5.40	.25	1.35
		−0.65 = Expected profit if grocer stocks 2 units.

Y	$P(Y)$	$Y \cdot P(Y)$
−$2.80	.35	−0.980
2.70	.65	+1.755
		+0.775 = Expected profit if grocer stocks 1 unit.

(b) The grocer would be better off stocking one unit.

5. (a) $34,000 (b) $35,500 (c) Yes

7. (a) 1.3125 (b) 1.50

9. $140 **11.** (b) $495

Section 6.5

1. $0.639; 63.28 **3.** (b) 3.8 (c) 4.36

5. 10.6; 24.04

Section 6.6

1. (a) 0.47 (b) .7690 (c) $7.05
(d) 173.025 (e) .05

Section 6.7

1. (b) $P(X = 0) = .23$; $P(1) = .20$; $P(2) = .27$; $P(3) = .30$
(c) $P(Y = 1) = .32$; $P(2) = .33$; $P(3) = .35$
(d) .18 (e) .35 (f) No (g) .70
(h) 1.64

3. (b)

X	10	20	30	40	50
$P(X)$	.14	.27	.34	.14	.11

(c) $P(Y = 8) = .27$; $P(12) = .41$; $P(16) = .32$
(d) .333; .031 (e) .037; .250

5. (a) $P(X = 0) = .49$; $P(1) = .29$; $P(2) = .15$; $P(3) = .07$

(b) $P(Y = 0) = .23$; $P(1) = .26$; $P(2) = .29$; $P(3) = .22$
(c) .80 (d) 1.1723 (e) 1.50 (f) 1.07
(g) .655

Section 6.8

1. (a)

Class	Value	Freq.	Rel. Freq.
Fresh	1	5	.10
Soph	2	12	.24
Junior	3	17	.34
Senior	4	16	.32
		50	

(b) 2.88

Chapter 6 ▪ Supplementary Exercises

1. (b) $20,300
3. (a) $P(1) = .20$; $P(2) = .30$; $P(3) = .27$; $P(4) = .23$
(b) 2.53
(c) $P(1) = .29$; $P(2) = .27$; $P(3) = .21$; $P(4) = .23$
(d) 2.38
(e) $P(1) = .5217$; $P(2) = .3043$; $P(3) = .0870$; $P(4) = .0870$
(f) no
5. $60 **7.** (a) .8 (b) 1.7
9. $30,000 **11.** (a) 32.0; 162 (c) .97
13. (a) $P(9) = .0625$; $P(-1) = .9375$
(b) −$0.3750 (c) $15
15. (b) .55; 1.5475 (c) .20
17. (b) $13,000
19. (b) $6,431.50 **21.** $65
23. (a) $0.85 (b) $85.00 **25.** $16,500

Chapter Seven

Section 7.1

1. (a) $P(0) = .25$; $P(1) = .75$ (b) .75; .1875

Section 7.2

1. .3087 **3.** (a) .2005 (b) .2415
5. (a) .4096 (b) .6723 (d) 1
7. .5904 **9.** (b) .7443 (c) 4.2; 1.26
11. .0039 **13.** .0530
15. (a) .0005 (b) .5220 (c) .1095
17. (a) .6296 (b) .7939 (c) .2053
19. (a) False (b) True (c) False (d) True
(e) True
21. (a) .4 (b) $400,000
23. (a) 8,500 (b) $27,200

Section 7.3

1. .5987
3. (a) .8816 (b) .6590 (c) .2749

Section 7.4

1. (a) .5357 (b) .6429 (c) 1.25; .4018
3. (a) .0056 (b) .0783 (c) .3776
5. (a) .3991 (b) .4605 (c) .1316 (d) −$10
7. (a) .2917 (b) .0083 (c) .1750

Section 7.5

1. (a) .0498 (b) .1494 (c) .2241
(d) .5768
3. (a) .2019 (b) .3230 (c) .2584
(d) .1378
5. (a) .0758 (b) .0758 (d) .0126; .0016
7. (a) .2240 (b) .5768
9. $P(X \leq 4) = .9473$ and $P(X \leq 5) = .9834$; therefore, he should stock 5 mufflers to achieve 95%.
11. .0840 **13.** (a) .3679 (b) .2642
15. .4335

Section 7.6

1. (a) .9762 (b) .00392
3. .0600 **5.** .0384 **7.** .0518

Chapter 7 ▪ Supplementary Exercises

1. (a) .2344 (b) .8906
3. (a) .7599 (b) .2401 (c) .0081
5. (a) .8319 (b) .1029 **7.** .1536
9. (a) .8926 (b) .0655
11. (a) .1353 (b) .2707 (c) .5940
13. .30
15. (a) .3648 (b) .1609 (c) −$8.33
17. (a) 1 (b) .3487
19. (a) .2725 (b) .1052 (c) .8943
21. .7279 **23.** .0613
25. (a) .8507 (b) .8497
27. .0498 **29.** .0156
33. .0002 **35.** .5665
37. (a) .2240 (b) .1339 (c) .9380
(d) .9502
39. .5665 **41.** .3208 **43.** .8009
45. .0788 **47.** (a) .8171 (b) .3642
49. $P(X \leq 4) = .9473$; $P(X \leq 5) = .9834$; thus, $n = 5$
51. (b) ∞ **53.** .0313
55. (a) 9 (b) .9618
57. (a) .000977 (b) −$1.02

59. $P(X \leq 8) = .9786$; $P(X \leq 9) = .9919$; thus, $n \geq 9$
61. .1992 **63.** .1429

Chapter Eight

Section 8.1

3. (a) .5 (b) .5 **5.** no
7. (a) .3 (b) 15
9. (a) 1 (b) .5 (c) .375

Section 8.2

1. (a) .5 (b) .4 (c) .4 (d) .2
3. (a) .5 (b) .5 (c) 1.0 (d) .75 (e) .5 (f) 1
5. .667; 15 minutes
7. (b) .1429 (c) .2857 (d) .4286
9. (a) $f(X) = (1/40)$ for X in [100,140]; $f(X) = 0$ otherwise
(b) .625 (c) .375 (d) 120; 11.547 (e) 0

Section 8.3

1. .4332 **3.** .9495 **5.** .9367
7. 0 **9.** 0 **11.** .0967
13. .74 **15.** .9736

Section 8.4

1. .3777 **3.** .8849
5. (a) .3721 (b) .1498 (c) .1587 (d) .8944 (e) .0228
7. 110.8 **9.** .0062 **11.** .0808
13. (a) 11,280 (b) 9,326 **15.** 82.8
17. (a) .9772 (b) .8413 (c) .4045
19. (a) $P_A\left[Z > \dfrac{10 - 10.4}{1.2}\right] = .6306$

$P_B\left[Z > \dfrac{10 - 11}{4}\right] = .5987$

So, for a return of 10%, choose investment A.

(b) $P_A\left[Z > \dfrac{12 - 10.4}{1.2}\right] = .0912$

$P_B\left[Z > \dfrac{12 - 11}{4}\right] = .4013$

So, for a return of at least 12%, choose investment B.
21. .0013

Section 8.5

1. .7286 **3.** .0287
5. (a) .0846 (b) .0168
7. .0019 **9.** .0110 **11.** .0001
13. (a) .9452 (b) .2482 **15.** 1
17. (a) .0283 (b) 1 **19.** .00015

Section 8.6

1. (a) .7788 (b) .3935
3. (a) .2636 (b) .2835 **5.** .4512

Chapter 8 ▪ Supplementary Exercises

1. (a) .4370 (b) .4525 (c) .9628 (d) .0073 (e) .9949 (f) .0033 (g) .9713 (h) 1 (i) 0 (j) 1 (k) 0 (l) .0873 (m) .0704
3. (a) .5000 (b) .5000 (c) .6823 (d) .9544 (e) .9974 (f) .9500
5. .0013 **7.** .0002 **9.** 250.22
11. A: 82.8; B: 75.22; C: 64.78; D: 57.2
13. 0 **15.** .0252 **17.** .7769
19. (a) .0578 (b) .1545 (c) .4522 (d) .3413 (e) .1915
21. (a) $340,000 (b) $206,666.67
23. (a) .1657 (b) .0152 (c) .2935 (d) .9220
25. (a) .0179 (b) .0044 (c) .1481
27. .8413
29. (a) .0026 (b) .1151 (c) .0449
31. (a) .0004459 (b) .005837
33. (a) .0318 (b) .0029 (c) 84
35. (a) .0062 (b) 1.24 **37.** .3297
39. (a) .0001 **41.** 844 **43.** .7769
45. (b) 125 (c) 169 (d) .0708 (e) .9803
47. Normal **49.** (b) .7
51. (a) .2231 (b) .6321
53. 833 **55.** 1178

Chapter Nine

Section 9.1

1. 1.64; 1.64
3. Sample size $n = 50$, since it has the smaller variance.

Section 9.2

1. 125; 1.44; 1.2 **3.** 500; 8.1; 2.8460
5. 124; 237.7777; 15.4200
7. About 1.57 times as large

Section 9.3

1. .4938
3. (a) $N(50, 1.7778)$ (b) $N(50, 14.4)$
5. .6826 **7.** .9876
9. (a) 0 (b) 0 (c) 0 **11.** .0026

Section 9.4

1. .9998 **3.** .2112
5. .0000 **7.** .4840

Section 9.5

1. .7698 **3.** .9991 **5.** .0228
7. (a) .4854 (b) .1233 (c) 0
9. (a) .1251 (b) .1251 (c) .0104
11. .0708 **13.** (a) .0146 (b) 1

Section 9.6

1. .6730 **3.** .0749

Section 9.8

1.

	Seniority		*Age*	
	Mean	*Std. Dev.*	*Mean*	*Std. Dev.*
Female:	11.9333	8.861	38.6667	10.5701
Male:	17.4133	11.487	39.5867	12.8706

5. GPA: Mean = 2.9212 $s = .3875$;
SAT: Mean = 1122.4000 $s = 152.9247$

Chapter 9 ▪ Supplementary Exercises

1. .9876 **3.** .0028 **5.** .0228
7. .9998
9. (a) 2.8667 (b) .2050 (c) .02278
11. .9946 **13.** .9544 **15.** 625
17. .9974 **19.** .9050 **21.** .0001
23. 1.645 **25.** 1.645 **27.** .6892
29. (a) 0 (b) 0
31. (a) .05 (b) 200,000
33. (a) 0 (b) 0 **35.** (a) 0 (b) .0004
37. (a) .0110 (b) .1271
39. (a) .1586 (b) .4714 (c) .9544
41. (a) .5987 (b) .8944 (c) .9938

Chapter Ten

Section 10.1

1. 2.58; 2.33; 1.96; 1.645; 1.28
3. 1.28; 1.645; 1.96; 2.58

Section 10.2

1. 400 ± .98 **3.** 400 ± 1.29
5. (a) 300 ± 13.72 (b) 300 ± 4.5733
7. $n = 15$
9. (a) 325 ± 6.9791 (b) 325 ± 8.3156

Section 10.3

1. (a) $t_{.05,2} = 2.920$ (b) $t_{.05,5} = 2.015$
(c) $t_{.05,10} = 1.812$ (d) $t_{.05,20} = 1.725$
(e) $t_{.05,25} = 1.708$
3. (a) $\pm t_{.005,2} = \pm 9.925$ (b) $\pm t_{.005,5} = \pm 4.032$
(c) $\pm t_{.005,10} = \pm 3.169$
(d) $\pm t_{.005,25} = \pm 2.787$
5. (a) $t_{.05,\infty} = z_{.05} = 1.645$
(b) $t_{.025,\infty} = z_{.025} = 1.960$

Section 10.4

1. 240 ± 13.9587 **3.** 12.33 ± 2.3090
5. 7.2 ± .6983 **7.** 15.9157 ± 3.0466
9. (a) 20,000 ± 2476.8 (b) 20,000 ± 2053.2
11. (a) 147 ± 4.6801 (b) 147 ± 6.3974

Section 10.5

1. .4444 ± .02985 **3.** .1667 ± .02503
5. (a) .4 ± .06371 (b) .4 ± .0999
7. (a) .75 ± .07123 (b) .75 ± .1004
9. .22 ± .05741 **11.** .9708

Section 10.6

1. (a) 50 (b) 312
3. (a) 385 (b) 9604 (c) 6766
5. (a) 25 (b) 98 **7.** 2436
9. 1083 **11.** (a) 1554 (b) 1849
13. 217 **15.** (a) 1305 (b) 753

Section 10.7

1. (a) 4 ± 2.6139 (b) 4 ± 4.0996
3. 1.2 ± .5544 **5.** −.6 ± 1.2384

Section 10.8

1. .0675 ± .06429 **3.** .1875 ± .08185

Section 10.9

1. 2.9212 ± .1101 **3.** 2133 ± 124.5035

Chapter 10 ▪ Supplementary Exercises

1. 4 ± .7936 **3.** 1200 ± 65.8150
5. .6 ± .04029 **7.** 2401

9. (a) .6 ± .01960 (b) Yes
11. (a) .08 ± .01681 (b) 2828
13. (a) .2 ± .02081 (b) .2 ± .03264
15. (a) .2 ± .06464 (b) .2 ± .0851
17. (a) .8333 ± .02982 (b) No
19. (a) −.2 ± .09602
21. 385 23. 28
25. .1 ± .1315 27. .45 ± .04361
29. 666
31. (a) 1.812 (b) 1.725 (c) 1.697
(d) 1.684 (e) 1.645
33. For $\nu = 14$, $P(t > 1.761) = .05$
37. (a) 52 ± 3.7137 (b) 52 ± 2.3490
(c) $\nu = 199$
39. (a) 116 ± 17.6898 (b) 116 ± 10.8213
41. (a) 9.8; 4.1778 (b) 9.8 ± 1.1848
(c) 9.8 ± 1.4621
43. (a) 64 ± 4.2528 (b) 64 ± 5.1481
45. (a) 86 ± .5546 (b) 86 ± 1.0453
47. (a) 14.7 ± .8021 (b) 14.7 ± 1.2768
49. (a) 118.625 ± 3.7873
(b) 118.625 ± 5.1382
51. (a) .3 (b) 120,000 (c) .3 ± .0836
(d) If $p = .2164$, then $X = 400{,}000(.2164) = 86{,}560$. If $p = .3836$, then $X = 400{,}000(.3836) = 153{,}440$

Chapter Eleven

Section 11.1

5. H_0: $\mu = 2$ H_1: $\mu \neq 2$
11. (b) α should be very small.

Section 11.2

1. (a) No (b) No 3. (e) .0950
5. (e) .0174 7. $z = -2.6667$; reject
9. $z = 6$; reject

Section 11.3

1. (a) [955.0533; 1004.9467]; Accept H_0.
(b) $z = -1.5713$ (c) .1164
3. (a) $z = 6.6667$ (b) 0
5. (a) $z = -4.6188$ (b) 0

Section 11.4

1. (a) .1056 (b) .0668
3. (b) .1587 5. $z = 1.6482$

Section 11.5

1. $t = 1.5492$
3. (a) Approximately .0316
5. (a) 2943.375 (b) 478.9157
(c) $t = -.5648$; accept H_0 (d) .5754
7. (a) $t = -6.6667$

Section 11.6

1. (a) $z = -1.4697$ (b) [.1580; .2520]
3. $z = .5303$ 5. $z = 1.8642$
7. (a) $z = 4.2426$ 9. $z = -2.1667$

Section 11.7

1. (a) .2514 (b) .7123
3. (a) 26.8225 (b) Reject H_0 (c) .6406
5. (a) AR: [24.951; 25.049] (b) 1.00
(c) AR: [24.902; 25.098] (d) .9793
7. (a) Reject H_0 if $z < -1.645$, alternatively, reject H_0 if $\hat{p} < .0340$
(b) Accept H_0 (c) .4168

Section 11.8

1. (a) 15.5073 (b) 20.0902 (c) 13.3616
3. (a) 13.2767 (b) 14.0671

Section 11.9

1. (a) [125.2575; 446.2596]
(b) [107.0086; 575.7579]
3. (a) [.2864; .4687] (b) [.2743; .4936]
(c) $\chi^2 = 70.4348$

Section 11.10

1. $t = -1.4379$ 3. $t = 2.1194$

Chapter 11 ▪ Supplementary Exercises

1. $z = -5.5$; reject
3. (a) $z = -6.667$; reject (b) 0
5. .8051
7. (a) $z = -.8839$; do not reject
9. $z = -5$; reject 11. .9901
13. (a) .1094 (b) .4202
15. $z = 1.5309$; do not reject
17. $z = -4.3301$; reject
19. $t = -2.1082$; reject
21. (a) 93.6 (b) 8.5010
(c) $t = -2.3807$; reject
23. (a) .4417 (b) $z = -1.8074$; reject
25. (a) .225 (b) $z = -3.2733$; reject
27. $t = -8.2817$; reject
29. (a) 783.75 (b) 17.0608
(c) $t = -2.6940$; reject
31. Reject H_0 if $z > 1.645$ or if $\hat{p} > .2911$
33. .0764 35. 116.45, or 117

37. (a) .3897 (b) .5000 (c) .6103
(d) .7123 (e) .7967 (f) .8665
39. $z = 1.9799$; reject **41.** Agree
43. (a) Null (b) Small

Chapter Twelve

Section 12.1

1. $z = 5$; reject **3.** $z = 3.75$; reject
5. $z = 2$; reject **7.** $z = -10.62$; reject

Section 12.2

1. $t = -.8314$; do not reject
3. $t = 3$; reject

Section 12.3

1. $\bar{d} = .56$; $s_d = .5967$; $t = 2.97$; reject

Section 12.4

1. $z = .5893$; do not reject
3. $z = -1.2278$; do not reject
5. $z = .8764$; do not reject
7. $z = -2.2522$; reject

Section 12.5

1. (a) 2.59 (b) 3.89 (c) 3.01
3. (a) .0878 (b) .0644 (c) .0912

Section 12.6

1. (a) $F = 1.2931$; do not reject
(b) [.4668; 3.0388]
3. (a) $F = .7143$; do not reject
(b) [.3779; 1.3714]

Section 12.7

1. $t = -6.545$; reject
3. (a) $z = -3.0525$; reject
(b) $z = -1.6893$; reject
5. $z = 2.9665$; reject
7. $z = 4.6225$; reject
9. $t = -1.1077$; do not reject

Chapter 12 ▪ Supplementary Exercises

1. $t = -1.1250$; do not reject
3. $t = 8.3333$; reject
5. $z = .8660$; do not reject
7. $z = 1.1314$; do not reject
9. $z = 2.0456$; reject
11. $t = 3.2996$; reject
13. $t = 3.3333$; reject
15. $z = 4.6725$; reject
17. $t = 5.8898$; reject
19. $z = .7097$; do not reject
21. (b) $t = 3.999$; reject
23. $z = -4.3102$; reject

Chapter Thirteen

Section 13.1

1. (b) 3.15 (c) 11.0705 (d) Do not reject
3. $\chi^2 = 36.07$; reject H_0
5. $\chi^2 = 3.00$; do not reject
7. $\chi^2 = 14.167$; reject H_0
9. $\chi^2 = 31$; reject
11. $\chi^2 = 4.16$; do not reject

Section 13.2

1. $\chi^2 = 6.24$; do not reject
3. (a) 21.2444; $s = 6.1094$
(b) $\chi^2 = 6.9984$; do not reject

Section 13.3

1. (b) 4 (c) 5.6424 (d) 9.48773
(e) Do not reject
3. $\chi^2 = 11.0405$; reject
5. $\chi^2 = 14.4379$; reject
7. $\chi^2 = 1.5215$; do not reject
9. $\chi^2 = 19.5000$; reject

Section 13.4

1. (a) .73239 (b) 2 (c) 5.99147
(d) Accept H_0
3. (a) 82.52115 (b) 2 (c) 5.99147
(d) Reject H_0
5. (a) 8.41832 (b) 4 (c) 9.48773
(d) Accept H_0

Chapter 13 ▪ Supplementary Exercises

1. $\chi^2 = 14.54$; reject
3. $\chi^2 = 15.2067$; reject
5. $\chi^2 = 3.2271$; do not reject
7. $\chi^2 = 9.0198$; do not reject
9. $\chi^2 = 1.1794$; do not reject
11. $\chi^2 = 56.9461$; reject
13. $\chi^2 = 55$; reject
15. $\chi^2 = 4.6074$; do not reject
17. $\chi^2 = 34.1911$; reject
19. (a) .0133 (b) .1110 (c) .0408
(d) .0742 (e) .2193 (f) .0779
(g) $\chi^2 = 186.5395$; reject

21. (a) $\chi^2 = 18.73$; reject (b) 1.5 (c) 6
23. $\chi^2 = .2789$; do not reject
25. $\chi^2 = 77.6915$; reject

Chapter Fourteen

Section 14.1

1. (a) 14; 3; 5; 4; 5 (b) 3.6; 4.25; 4.8
(c) 4.21429
(d) SST $\approx$ 26.3571; SSB = 3.6071; SSW = 22.75
(e) MSB = 1.80355; MSW = 2.06818
(f) .872 (g) 2; 11
(h) Critical Region: $F > 3.98$; accept H_0

3. (a) 77.6; 79.2; 80.2; 73.0
(b) 279.00; 152.2; 126.8
(c) 50.7333; 7.9250 (d) 6.4017 (e) 3; 16
(f) Critical Region: $F > 3.24$; reject H_0

5. (a) $F = 4.571$; reject H_0

7. $F = 2.2625$; do not reject

Section 14.2

1. (a) 9 (b) 3.24037 (c) 2.021 (d) Reject

3. (b) 165.4667 (c) -2.3845 (d) ± 2.048
(e) Reject

Section 14.3

1. (b) SST = 1,145,912; SSB = 137,367.0505; SSW = 1,008,544.949
(c) MSB = 34,341.7626; MSW = 22,412.1100
(d) $F = 1.5323$ (e) CR: $F > 2.59$; accept H_0

3. (b) SST = 7.3565; SSB = 3.0638; SSW = 4.2928
(c) MSB = 1.0213; MSW = .0933
(d) $F = 10.9464$

5. (b) SST = 14,063.5917; SSB = 282.4552; SSW = 13,781.1364
(c) MSB = 141.2276; MSW = 117.7875
(d) $F = 1.1990$

7. (b) SST = 17,197.9917; SSB = 282.7194; SSW = 16,915.272376
(c) MSB = 141.3597; MSW = 144.5750
(d) $F = .9777$

9. (b) SST = 5,623,516.35; SSB = 15,494,653.65; SSW = 40,740,516.35
(c) MSB = 7,747,326.826; MSW = 348,209.5414
(d) $F = 22.2490$

Section 14.4

1. $H = 1.5$; CR: $H_{.05} = 15.5$; accept H_0

Section 14.5

1. (a) 3; .008333; $t_{.008333,12} \approx 3.2$ (b) 12.4208
(c) 6.3078
(d) $|95 - 102| = 7$, reject;
$|102 - 109| = 7$, reject;
$|109 - 95| = 14$, reject

Section 14.7

1. $F_1 = 84/25.333 = 3.316$; $F_{.05,2,4} = 6.94$, accept H_0.
$F_2 = 305.333/25.333 = 12.053$; $F_{.05,2,4} = 6.94$, accept H_0.

3. (a) The blocking variable is the vehicle.
$SSB_A = 1{,}266.667$; $MSB_A = 633.33$;
$SSB_V = 68{,}933.333$; $MSB_V = 22{,}977.778$;
SSE = 9,666.667; MSE = 1,611.111;
$F_A = .3931$; $F_{.05,2,6} = 5.14$, accept H_0;
$F_V = 14.262$; $F_{.05,3,6} = 4.76$, reject H_0

5. (b) 8.999 (c) 3.16 (d) Reject

Section 14.9

1. (a) $F = 5.297$; reject
(b) $F = 4.568$; do not reject
(c) $F = .1081$; do not reject

Chapter 14 ▪ Supplementary Exercises

1. $F = 3.18$; do not reject
3. (b) $F = 7.92$; reject
5. $F = 2.06$; do not reject
7. (b) $F = 4.75$; do not reject
9. $F = 15.31$; reject
11. (b) $F = 3.42$; do not reject
13. (a) $F = .071$; do not reject
(b) $F = 1.81$; do not reject
15. (d) $F = 1.85$
17. (b) $H = 3.629$; $H_{.05} \approx 4.37$, accept H_0
(c) $F = 8.22$; reject
19. $F_2 = 5.042$; do not reject
21. (b) $F_2 = 37.94$; reject
(c) $F_1 = 19.75$; reject
(d) $F_I = 1.32$; do not reject
23. $F = 5.4032$; reject

Chapter Fifteen

Section 15.1

1. (a) 10 (b) 18

Section 15.2

5. (a) 5 (b) -1

Section 15.3

1. (c) 6.9; 7.4 (d) .4177 (e) 4.5181 (g) 9.1
3. (b) $\hat{y}_i = 69.7548 + 9.5221x_i$
(c) 126.89; 98.32
5. (b) $\hat{y}_i = 1268.2769 - 16.6134x_i$
(c) 603.7395

Section 15.4

1. (a) $\hat{y}_i = .0183 + .9478x_i$ (b) 77.6
(c) 13.9148 (d) .8207
3. (a) $\hat{y}_i = 12.5852 + .4558x_i$
(b) .1850; 22.4485

Section 15.5

1. (a) $b_1 = 3.1085$; $b_0 = -9.8176$; $s_e^2 = 7.4799$
(b) SST = 1,232.8571; SSE = 37.3995; SSR = 1,195.4597
(c) 15.4608; .0605 (d) .9697; 2.7349
3. (a) $\hat{y}_i = -11.4369 + 14.9394x_i$
(b) .9942; 1.9749 (c) 4.1850; .2160
5. (a) $\hat{y}_i = 1{,}037.9310 - 113.7931x_i$ (b) .5764
(c) 63,628.0958; 2,378.5463

Section 15.6

1. (a) $t = 12.6418$; reject
(b) $t = -2.4968$; do not reject
(c) $t = 4.5081$; reject
(d) $t = 2.4747$; do not reject
3. (a) $\hat{y}_i = .90286 + .03817x_i$
(b) $t = 5.4298$; reject
5. (a) $\hat{y}_i = 829.1429 - 58.2857x_i$
(b) $t = -2.5792$; reject

Section 15.7

1. (a) [2.6130; 3.6040]; [2.4763; 3.7407]; [2.1170; 4.1000]
(b) [−18.0945; −1.5407]; [−19.9268; .2916]; [−25.6714; 6.0362]
3. (a) $\hat{y}_i = 13.9565 - .07339x_i$
(b) [−.08954; .05724]
5. (b) $\hat{y}_i = 26.1256 + 1.7588x_i$
(c) [1.1081; 2.4095] (d) $t = 6.6145$; reject

Section 15.8

1. (a) $\hat{y}_i = 24{,}045.7 - 14{,}762x_i$ (b) 6,330.2168
(c) [6225.0010; 6435.4326] (d) 5,444.4444
(e) [5229.2358; 5659.6531]
3. (b) 7 ± 2.1877; 9 ± 1.7102; 11 ± 1.2630; 13 ± .8931; 15 ± .7292; 17 ± .8931; 19 ± 1.2630; 21 ± 1.7102; 23 ± 2.1877

Section 15.9

1. .7258 **3.** −.2749 **5.** .9438
7. $t = 2.1822$; reject; if $\alpha = .01$, do not reject
9. (a) −.8521 (b) $t = -3.2560$; reject
11. ±.6

Section 15.10

1. (a) GPA = .3603 + .00228 SAT
(c) .81091; .17024
(d) $t = 14.347$; reject
3. (a) SALARY = 12105.54 + 3.325 REVENUE
(c) .70497; 2293.485 (d) $t = 10.821$; reject
5. (a) PCTUNION = −20.0498 + 4.2289 WAGE
(c) .49818; 5.338 (d) $t = 6.975$; reject

Chapter 15 ▪ Supplementary Exercises

3. (b) $b_1 = -311.1111$; $b_0 = 2183.3333$
(d) −.9731; $t = -10.3397$; reject
(e) .9469
5. (b) .9284 (c) $t = 5.5860$; reject
7. (b) −.9006 (c) $t = -5.0742$; reject
9. (b) .9337; $t = 7.3736$; reject
(c) $\hat{y}_i = 10.6178 + .1404x_i$ (d) 13.4261
11. (b) .9952; $t = 26.8478$; reject
(c) $\hat{y}_i = -14.5105 + .5766x_i$
13. (a) False (b) True (c) True (d) False
(e) False (f) True (g) True
15. (a) −5.0336; .1576; 1.4617
(b) .6868; 1.2090 (c) 9.4362; .001888
(d) $t = 3.6266$; reject
(e) $t = -1.6386$; do not reject
(f) [.0513; .2639]
17. (b) $\hat{y}_i = 37.5616 + 7.9557x_i$
(c) .9022; [5.8198; 10.0916]
(d) 117.1182; [106.8970 ; 127.3394]
19. (a) $\hat{y}_i = -25.5332 + .9423x_i$
(b) 96.5423; .007634
(c) [−49.5764; −1.4899]; [.7285; 1.1561]
(d) $t = 10.7841$; reject (e) 68.6968
(f) [75.9168; 80.3142]
21. (a) $\hat{y}_i = -31.3559 + .2954\, x_i$
(b) $t = 4.2552$; reject
(c) [518.4715; 600.4147]
23. (a) $\hat{y}_i = 43.6529 - .4356x_i$
(b) $t = -3.0441$; reject
(c) [−.8035; −.06770]

25. (b) .9401 (c) $t = 6.7546$; reject
(e) $\hat{y}_i = .8973 + .4295x_i$ (f) 6.0508
(g) [−1.4932; 3.2878]; [.2739; .5850]
(h) $t = 6.7546$; reject (i) 7.3392
(j) [6.9072; 7.7711] (k) [6.0442; 8.6341]

27. (b) $\hat{y}_i = -7.6229 + 5.0833x_i$ (d) .9550

Chapter Sixteen

Section 16.1

1. $\hat{y}_i = .9368 + .0036x_i + .00035z_i$
3. $\hat{y}_i = 34.971 - .6261x_i + 11.63z_i$
5. $\hat{y}_i = -150.61 + 4.68r_i + 1.738t_i$

Section 16.2

7. $\hat{y}_i = 38.34 + 2.4938x_{i1} + 4.3x_{i2}$

Section 16.3

5. (a) .85041; .79058 (b) $\hat{y}_i = 4.2615 + 21.92x_i$
(c) .72274; .67653

7. (a) 1064.89; 64.47; 1000.42 (b) .9395
(c) 3.278

Section 16.4

1. (a) $t = 2.77$; reject (b) 22
(c) $t = -1.23$; do not reject

3. (a) 67.57 (b) 2 and 22 (c) 3.44
(d) Reject

5. (a) [1.3331; 3.0669] (b) $t = 5.23$; reject
(c) [33.5676; 62.7124] (d) $t = 9.23$; reject

Section 16.5

1. (a) .8840; positive; $\hat{y}_i = 1.0423 + .0038x_i$
(b) .7890; positive; $\hat{y}_i = .4603 + .0064z_i$
(c) .8817; $\hat{y}_i = .9368 + .0036x_i + 3.502z_i$

3. Yes **5.** Probably not **7.** Yes

9. (a) False (b) False (c) Not necessarily

11. (a) Yes
(b) No; we have perfect multicollinearity.

Section 16.6

3. (a) 2.268 (b) 3 and 29 (c) 2.93
(d) Do not reject

Section 16.7

1. (a) INCOME = 9434.016 + 113.506 PCTUNION + 116.380 WAGE
(b) .2166 (c) 1948.3331
(d) $t = .533$; accept H_0

3. (a) REVENUE = −2136.065 + .339 INCOME + 141.44 WAGE
(b) .5945 (c) 685.951
(d) $t = 1.684$; do not reject

Chapter 16 ▪ Supplementary Exercises

1. (a) $\hat{y}_i = -1.246 + .4336x_i + .0785z_i$
(e) \$1,584.00 (f) \$3,236.00

3. (b) $t = 1.3$; do not reject
(c) [86.43; 130.97]; [−25.6; 126.6]; [143.52; 181.28]

5. (a) $\hat{y}_i = 855.056 - 5.778x_{i1} + 18.328x_{i2}$
(b) .066
(c) $t = -.450$; do not reject; $t = -.981$; do not reject

7. (a) False (b) True (c) False (d) True

9. (a) 1447.6
(b) [123.477; 171.723]; [55.7035; 75.0965]; [9.596; 55.004]
(c) $t = 3.4$; reject

Chapter Seventeen

Section 17.1

1. (b) $\hat{y}_i = -30.8286 + 1.598x_i$
(c) $\hat{y}_i = -18.7434 + .9307x_i + .0084x_i^2$
(d) $t = 1.515$; do not reject

3. (b) $\hat{y}_i = 8.994 + 3.254x_i$; $\bar{R}^2 = .95680$
(c) $\hat{y}_i = 4.4709 + 4.948x_i - .1388x_i^2$; $\bar{R}^2 = .9606$
(e) $t = -1.334$; do not reject
(f) 16.80; 15.55

Section 17.2

1. (a) 15,000 (b) 15,000 (c) 11,000
(d) 2,000
(e) The coefficient would change from −2000 to +2000. The intercept would decrease to 8000.

5. (b) $\hat{y}_i = 25{,}000 + 1{,}000x_i + 2{,}500z_i$
(c) \$35,500 (d) \$30,000

9. (c) 24,000 (d) 29,600 (e) 27,000
(f) 32,000

Section 17.3

1. (b) $\ln D = -.56334 + 1.513 \ln S$
(c) $\ln D = 5.196$; $D = 180.57$

3. (b) $\ln \hat{y}_i = .5842 + 1.528 \ln x_i$
(d) $\ln \hat{y}_i = 3.5576$; $\hat{y}_i = 35.077$

5. (a) $\ln \hat{y}_i = 1.6924 - .46217x_i$

Section 17.5

1. (a) The correlation matrix is shown at the top of the next page.

	GNP	TOTALGOV	DEFENSE	URATE	CPI	TBILL	DOW
GNP	1.000	.988	.973	.698	.996	.723	.763
TOTAL GOV	.988	1.000	.996	.660	.984	.668	.811
DEFENSE	.973	.996	1.000	.632	.968	.626	.834
URATE	.698	.660	.632	1.000	.738	.492	.321
CPI	.996	.984	.968	.738	1.000	.746	.726
TBILL	.723	.668	.626	.492	.746	1.000	.266
DOW JONES	.763	.811	.834	.321	.266	.266	1.000

(b) Defense (c) CPI (d) GNP (e) .746
(f) .726

Chapter 17 ▪ Supplementary Exercises

1. (b) \$930 **3.** (b) 32,224.6 (d) 372.6

5. (a) $\hat{y}_i = -27.154 + 2.634x_{i1} + .6859x_{i2} + 1.254x_{i3} + 4.196x_{i4}$
(b) $t = 5.125$; reject
(c) $t = .243$; do not reject
(d) $t = 1.844$; reject (e) 4.5775 (f) .97557
(g) 198.19 (h) .9023

7. (a) $\hat{y}_i = 2284.06 - 5.35x_{i1} + .2797x_{i2} + 25.04x_{i3} - 92.28x_{i4}$
(b) Correlation matrix:

	Y	X_1	X_2	X_3	X_4
Y	1.000	.263	.405	.582	−.702
X_1	.263	1.000	.736	.260	−.195
X_2	.405	.736	1.000	.216	−.133
X_3	.582	.260	.216	1.000	−.533
X_4	−.702	−.195	−.333	−.533	1.000

(c) X_4 should enter first, then X_3, then X_2.
(d) Step 1: $\hat{y}_i = 4998.21 - 135.34x_{i4}$; $R^2 = .492$
Step 2: $\hat{y}_i = 2827.25 + 24.51x_{i3} - 105.49x_{i4}$; $R^2 = .553$

Chapter Eighteen

Section 18.1

1. False **3.** False
5. (b) Use a quadratic model

Section 18.3

1. (a) No (b) Overestimate (c) 42
3. False

Section 18.4

1. Heteroscedastic errors

Section 18.5

1. (b) $\hat{y}_t = -1.455 + .176x_t$ (c) .08606
(d) .04586; .000002088
(f) $d = .73473$ (g) Reject
3. 1.21 and 1.65

Section 18.7

1. (b) DOW = 648.438 + .152 GNP; $R^2 = .582$
(c) $d = .721$ (e) Reject

Chapter 18 ▪ Supplementary Exercises

1. (a) $\hat{y}_i = -1.715 + .842x_i$ (c) 1.653
(d) .43877; .64783; (e) .739; .146
(f) [.422; 1.262]; no (g) $t = 5.754$; reject
(h) [1.2815; 2.0245]

3. (b) $y_i = -.360 + .903x_{i1} - .014x_{i2}$
St.Dev.: (1.7) (1.63) (.016)
t:(−.21) (5.55) (−.88)
$R^2 = .66327$; $s_e = .441$
(c) $\hat{y}_i = -1.831 + .8368x_{i1} - .0480x_{i3}$
St.Dev: (1.095) (.155) (.325)
t:(−1.67) (5.41) (.148)
$R^2 = .64828$; $s_e = .45120$
(d) $\hat{y}_i = -.413 + .901x_{i1} - .014x_{i2} + .018x_{i3}$
St.Dev: (2.01) (.173) (.017) (.329)
t:(−.21) (5.21) (−.85) (.05)
$R^2 = .66334$; $s_e = .45503$

5. (a) .42066 (b) .42074
(c) $b_0 = .941092$; $b_1 = .508123$; in Problem 4, the estimates were: $b_0 = .9395$; $b_1 = .5087$
(d) $s_{b_0} = .016243$; $s_{b_1} = .005177$; in Problem 4, the estimates were: $s_{b_0} = .011951$; $s_{b_1} = .003830$

7. (a) .010115

9. (a) b_0, b_1, and b_2 are unbiased; s_e^2 is biased.
(b) No (c) Tests are invalid

11. $C_t/W_t = b_0(1/W_t) + b_1(I_t/W_t) + b_2 + (e_t/W_t)$

13. (a) $d = 1.40$; reject H_0 (b) $t = 4.67$; reject

17. (b) b_4 (c) b_1, b_3, b_5
(d) $d = 1.046$; test is inconclusive

19. (a) $\hat{y}_i = 18.058 + 1.845x_i$
(c) $d = .88065$; reject H_0
(d) The PW model is: $\hat{y}_i = 33.322 + 1.6387x_i$

21. (a) Correlation matrix:

	Y	X_1	X_2	X_3
Y	1.000	.434	.310	.231
X_1	.434	1.000	.243	.002
X_2	.301	.243	1.000	.434
X_3	.231	.002	.434	1.000

(b) $y = .1407 + .0011x_1 + .1187x_2 + 7.930x_3$

Chapter Nineteen

Section 19.2

1. (b) $\hat{y}_t = 258.88 + 42.099t$ (c) .95517
(d) 848.266

3. (b) $\hat{y}_t = 1.23 + 16.01t$ (c) .97736
(d) 225.37

5. (a) $\hat{y}_t = -88.00 + 44.0727t$ (b) 440.8727

7. (a) $\hat{C}_{t1} = 12.3857 - .0107143t$ (b) 12.24
(e) $\hat{C}_{t2} = 11.27 + .4298t$ (f) 16.86
(h) R^2 for C_1 is .6617; R^2 for C_2 is .9808

9. (a) $\hat{y}_t = 88.8 + 21.2t$
(b) 216; 237.2

11. (b) $\hat{y}_t = -9.06 + 5.88t$ (d) .8823
(e) 79.157

Section 19.3

1. (a) $\hat{y}_t = 117.265 - 3.146t$
(b) $\hat{y}_t = 102.7 + 1.703t - .285t^2$

3. $\hat{S}_t = 12.304 - 4.36t + 2.685t^2$

5. (b) 439.2 (c) 458.2

7. (a) $\hat{y}_t = 41.55 + 5.616t + .2614t^2$
(b) $t = 6.209$; reject

Section 19.4

1. (a) $\hat{y}_t = -12.62 + 14.67t$; $R^2 = .94810$
(b) 266.11; 280.78
(c) $\ln \hat{y}_t = 3.1789 + .1568t$; $R^2 = .9869$
(d) 472.48; 552.8

3. (a) $\ln \hat{y}_t = 5.234 + .1035t$
(b) 1647.45; 1827.07

5. (a) 66.6863; 99.4843; 148.4132

Section 19.5

1. (a) $\hat{y}_t = 7.4469 + 1.0595y_{t-1}$; $R^2 = .98831$
(b) 302.9699; 328.4435

3. (a) $\hat{y}_t = 27.25 + 1.0428\hat{y}_{t-1}$; $R^2 = .99459$
(b) 1380.4189; 1466.7508

Section 19.7

1. (b) $\text{Totalgov}_t = -1.699715 + 10.897070t$; $R^2 = .84631$
$\text{Defense}_t = 2.805128 + 7.698840t$; $R^2 = .79459$
(c) For Totalgov, $d = .09905$; for Defense, $d = .08795$
(e) Reject H_0

3. (a) $\text{Totalgov}_t = -1.920745 + 1.097879\ \text{Totalgov}_{t-1}$; $R^2 = .99215$
$\text{Defense}_t = -3.724149 + 1.121857\ \text{Defense}_{t-1}$; $R^2 = .99333$
(b) For Totalgov, $d = 1.59093$; for Defense, $d = .71486$
(d) For Defense, reject H_0

Chapter 19 ▪ Supplementary Exercises

1. (a) $\hat{y}_t = 2.50 + 10t$ (c) 92.5; 102.5
(d) $\hat{y}_t = 3.143 + 1.164y_{t-1}$
(e) 105.61; 126.12
(f) $\ln \hat{y}_t = 2.704 + .228t$
(g) 116.408; 146.233

3. (c) $\hat{y}_t = 17.785 + 1.1318t$; 32.498; 38.157
(d) $\hat{y}_t = -1.1267 + 1.09y_{t-1}$; 33.97; 45.526

5. 28,020.00; 31,280.80; 34,792.83

7. (a) $\hat{y}_t = 2.953 + .4085t$; (c) 8.26
(d) $\ln \hat{y}_t = 1.898 + .0784t$; 9.11

9. (a) $\hat{y}_t = 17342.857 + 1890.476t$
(c) 34,357.141; 36,247.617

11. (b) $\hat{y}_t = 42667.5 + 34913.83t$
(c) 426,719.63
(d) $\ln \hat{y}_t = 11.35 + .16859t$
(e) 542,796.631

13. (b) $\hat{y}_t = -87.52 + 44.025t$; 396.755; 440.78
(c) $\hat{y}_t = 85.555 - 42.5t + 7.867t^2$

15. (a) $\hat{y}_t = 12.9394 + 1.843t$; (b) 38.7414
(c) $\ln \hat{y}_t = 2.7036 + .07368t$; (d) 41.89

17. (b) $\sqrt{\hat{y}_t} = 9.1846 + 1.07629t$
(e) $\hat{y}_t = (9.1846 + 1.07629t)^2 = 84.3576 + 2.15258t + 1.1584t^2$

Chapter Twenty

Section 20.1

3. (a) 16 (b) 21 (c) 26

7. (a) No (b) Yes

9. Index values are: .88, .90, .98, 1.07, 1.16, 1.21, 1.03, .94, .90, 1.12, 1.36, 1.92

Section 20.2

1. (d) No. (e) (23.4 + 18.3) = 41.7 (f) 30.8

Section 20.3

1. $\hat{y}_t = 42.095 + .441t$; the seasonal index values are: 85.67; 89.33; 96.00; 108.67; 123.33; 127.00; 114.67; 99.00; 91.33; 87.67; 88.33; 89.33

Section 20.4

1. (a) 8.4; 8.58; 8.688; 8.8788; 9.1679; 9.4668; 9.9467; 9.9947; 9.8195; 9.7119; 9.6112

Chapter 20 ▪ Supplementary Exercises

1. (a) $\hat{y}_t = 16.28 + .085t$
   (b) .81, .86, .96, .90, 1.01, .93, .86, .95, .91, 1.19, 1.23, 1.37.
   (g) $\hat{y}_t = 18.14 - .016t$ ($t = 1$ in January 1986)
   (h) Jan. = [16.28 + .085(37)](.81) = 15.7343
   Feb. = [16.28 + .085(38)](.86) = 16.7786, and so forth
3. (a)

Quarter	*1985*	*1986*	*1987*	*1988*
1	—	4.3875	5.8000	7.7000
2	—	4.7000	6.2375	8.1625
3	3.8000	5.0125	6.7625	—
4	4.0750	5.3875	7.2625	—

   (b) $\ln MA = 1.12303 + .0707t$ ($t = 1$ in Quarter 1 of 1985)
   (c) .87; .90; .94; 1.30.
   (d) 10.22; 10.97; 11.77; 12.64.
   (e) 8.89; 9.87; 11.06; 16.43.
5. (b) $\hat{y}_t = 394.614 + 2.594t$
   (d) .83, .73, .96, 1.01, 1.00, .91, .83, .90, .97, 1.03, 1.08, 1.75
   (e) 458.9, 405.5, 535.8, 566.2, 563.2, 514.9, 471.8, 513.9, 556.4, 593.5, 625.1, 1,014.4
   (f) .99, .84, 1.07, 1.08, 1.04, .92, .83, .92, 1.01, 1.11, 1.20, 2.03.
   (g) 547.3, 466.6, 597.1, 605.5, 585.8, 520.6, 471.8, 525.3, 579.3, 639.6, 694.5, 1,180.2

Chapter Twenty-One

Section 21.1

1. $P(X \geq 5) = .3633$; do not reject
3. $z = 1.625$; do not reject
5. $z = 2.1.$; reject

Section 21.2

1. $P(U \leq 18) = .3654$; do not reject
3. $z = -.2720$; do not reject

Section 21.3

1. $T = 23$; reject
3. $T = 14$; do not reject
5. $T = 5$; do not reject

Section 21.4

1. $K = 18.7095$; reject
3. $K = 5.5371$; reject

Section 21.5

1. (a) 16 (b) 14; 6.24 (c) .8006
   (d) Do not reject
3. $z = -.373$; do not reject
5. $z = -.2858$; do not reject

Section 21.6

1. (b) $-.3117$ (c) Do not reject (d) $-.2945$
3. .7333; do not reject
5. .6606

Section 21.7

1. $D = .8849 - .4 = .4849$; reject
3. $D = .08$; do not reject

Chapter 21 ▪ Supplementary Exercises

1. (c) $z = -1.4134$; do not reject
3. (a) $z = 2.04$; reject
   (b) $z = -1.8488$; do not reject
5. $z = -1.9969$; reject
7. $z = -1.1339$; do not reject
9. (a) $t = 2.3766$; reject
   (b) $z = -1.2649$; do not reject
   (c) $z = -1.83$; do not reject
11. $r = 5$; do not reject
13. (a) $z = -.6325$; do not reject
    (b) $z = -1.7328$; do not reject
15. (a) $U = 10$; reject (b) $t = 2.4821$; reject
17. (a) .8061 (b) Reject
19. $P(X \geq 9) = .0107$; reject

Chapter Twenty-Two

Section 22.1

1. (a) no (b) .067 (c) 106.7

Section 22.2

3. (a) 82 (b) 83
5. (a) 1.00; 1.10; 1.23 (b) 100; 110; 123
   (c) .91; 1.00; 1.12 (d) 91; 100; 112

Section 22.3

3. 2.13; 2.92; 2.81; 2.66
5. (a) 25% (b) Decrease

Chapter 22 ▪ Supplementary Exercises

1. (a) 100.0; 103.7; 108.6; 115.1; 118.8; 124.1
(b) 86.9; 90.1; 94.3; 100.0; 103.2; 107.8
(c) 80.6; 83.6; 87.5; 92.8; 95.7; 100.0
3. (a) 111.5 (b) 2.69%
7. (a) 100; 123; 160 (b) 62; 78; 100
(c) 100; 126; 161
(d) 110,000; 157,000; 262,000
(e) 5.79; 7.14; 9.36
(f) 100; 123; 162
9. (a) 64 (b) 3.75 (c) 64.5
11. (a) .83; .79; .74; .70; .68
13. (a) 100; 114; 127 (b) 80; 91; 100
15. (a) 92; 100; 107; 121 (b) 100; 109; 116; 132
(c) 13.79%
19. 126.5; 132.825; 126.184; 138.802

Chapter Twenty-Three

Section 23.1

1. (a) Payoffs if recession: −200; 40; 160; −100
Payoffs if no recession: 60; 120; 80; 200
(c) Opportunity losses if recession: 360; 120; 0; 260
Opportunity losses if no recession: 140; 80; 120; 0
3. (a) Payoffs if demand is 25: 45,000; 35,000; 25,000
Payoffs if demand is 40: 60,000; 80,000; 70,000
Payoffs if demand is 45: 60,000; 80,000; 85,000
(c) Opportunity losses if demand is 25: 0; 10,000; 20,000
Opportunity losses if demand is 40: 20,000; 0; 10,000
Opportunity losses if demand is 45: 25,000; 5,000; 0

Section 23.2

1. (a) a_4 (b) a_2 or a_3 (c) a_3
(d) a_4 (e) a_4 (f) 52
3. (d) EMV's are: 55,000; 66,500; 59,500
(f) 4,000
5. EMV's are: 0; 35.4390; 39.7765; 30.1145; 16.2535; 2.0930; −13.5255
7. (a) a_1 (b) a_1
11. 6

Section 23.3

1. (a) Both actions have the same EMV.
(b) Option A
3. (a) 20; 70; 95
5. (a) Ignore action a_2.
(c) $E[U(a_1)] = 3.58$; $E[U(a_3)] = 4.41$; $E[U(a_4)] = 3.46$
(d) EMV's are: −11; 23.5; −7

Section 23.4

1. (b) Optimal action is to buy Stock 4.
3. (b) Optimal action is to order 40 cars.

Section 23.5

1. (c) EMV's are: 0; 14,000; 48,000 (d) 14,000
(e) 62,000
3. (b) EMV's are: 60,000; 0 (d) 60,000
5. EMV(a_1) = \$156,000
7. (a) Revised probabilities are: .00109; .08078; .91813
(b) EMV's are: −52,577.20; 0
9. (a) Revised probabilities are: .04155; .24931; .70914
(c) EMV's are: −363,157; 0

Section 23.6

1. 18,710 **3.** 2,442

Chapter 23 ▪ Supplementary Exercises

1. Optimal action is to go to graduate school; EMV = 266,000
3. (c) Optimal action is to drill; EMV = \$160,000 (d) 80,000
5. Optimal action is to drill; expected payoff = \$322,000
7. Optimal action is to buy real estate; expected payoff is \$1,230
9. EMV's are: −50,000; 0; do not drill
11. EMV's are: \$480,000; 0; EPPI = 900,000; EVPI = 420,000; EPSI = 479,845.20; EVSI = −154.80; ENGS = −100,154.80. EMV with Information 1 is 1,770,600.
13. EMV's are: 47.9; 27.7; 10.1; 45.5
15. EMV's are: 0; 30,000

INDEX